DICTIONARY OF SCANDINAVIAN HISTORY

EDITED BY
BYRON J. NORDSTROM

Greenwood Press
Westport, Connecticut • London, England

Library of Congress Cataloging in Publication Data
Main entry under title:

Dictionary of Scandinavian history.

   Bibliography: p.
   Includes index.
   1. Scandinavia—History—Dictionaries.   2. Finland—
History—Dictionaries.   I. Nordstrom, Byron J.
DL43.D53   1986   948'.003'21   83–25204
ISBN 0–313–22887–6 (lib. bdg.)

Library of Congress Catalog Card Number: 83–25204
ISBN 0–313–22887–6

First published in 1986

Greenwood Press
A division of Congressional Information Service, Inc.
88 Post Road West
Westport, Connecticut 06881

Printed in the United States of America

The paper used in this book complies with the
Permanent Paper Standard issued by the National
Information Standards Organization (Z39.48-1984).

10   9   8   7   6   5   4   3   2   1

Contents

Preface

This dictionary deals with the histories of the five Nordic countries (Denmark, Finland, Iceland, Norway, and Sweden) since c. 1000 A.D.; that is, since the time when they were emerging from the shrouds of myth and legend and were becoming (with the exception of Finland) medieval monarchies or, in the case of Iceland, a "republic." Some attention has been given to earlier events or developments in the region, but it should be recognized that in a pure sense this is dealing with prehistory. There are very few written sources from before 1000 (virtually none from Scandinavia proper), and archeological evidence is generally the basis for discussion of the region before that time. The breadth and depth of coverage for the individual countries varies, but in general there are more entries on Danish, Norwegian, and Swedish history. An effort has been made, however, to include information on Finland, Iceland, the Faroe Islands, and Greenland.

The initial entry list was developed from surveys of a number of national histories, consideration of trends in recent scholarship and of topics which have not received attention in other available works, and a concern to give attention to questions which have arisen over the years in my own teaching of the field. The biases of the editor, the availability of entry authors, time, and other constraints have also shaped the contents of the volume.

In all, there are over 400 entries. These vary in length from a few hundred words to several thousand. Whenever possible scholars familiar with and/or active in the field being examined were secured to write entries. Every effort was made to have articles reflect the most recent scholarship on the topic being covered and to give users access to information not previously available in English.

Specifically, there are entries on most of the monarchs of Scandinavian history from the late Viking Age (c. late tenth century) to the present. There are also biographical entries on early modern and modern political figures, statesmen, and military and cultural leaders. Literary persons, with a few exceptions, have not been included, because they will be treated in Greenwood Press's *Dictionary of Scandinavian Literature*, edited by Virpi Zuck. There are entries on some of the major events or periods in Scandinavian history and on social groups, intellectual developments, political parties, and social movements. In some instances, topics are covered by a general introductory entry, followed by detailed consideration of the topic in all or several of the Nordic countries (see, for example, the entry on Languages). In instances where one or more of the countries have been omitted, readers should review the general and specific entries for information that may have relevance.

All topics covered, related references, and possible variant headings of the same topic are included in the index. In addition, entries in the text proper provide cross-references from variant headings to the heading where a topic is discussed. An asterisk within the text of an entry also indicates a cross-reference to a separate entry.

In most instances, each entry concludes with a reference paragraph, which contains citations in English (when available) and other languages. Users will be able to pursue a topic in depth through use of these references.

In addition to the entries, a bibliography, lists of monarchs, presidents, prime ministers, and governments, and a time line have been appended. The bibliography is brief and was developed chiefly to provide information about introductory materials for English-language users. It includes general works on each of the countries, basic reference works, periodicals, and some topic-focused monographs. The list of monarchs covers rulers since the Viking Age in Denmark, Norway, and Sweden. That of presidents covers Finland since 1918 and Iceland since 1944. The list of governments covers each of the Nordic countries from the mid-nineteenth or early twentieth century. The time line includes events in Scandinavian and Western or European history from the earliest settlement of Scandinavia about 14,000 years ago to the present.

The editor cannot claim that the dictionary is complete. The subject is far too vast to cover in a single volume, as anyone familiar with the field can attest or as a survey of the multi-volumed histories and encyclopedias developed in the Scandinavian countries will demonstrate. This dictionary was conceived as an entrance-level reference source to Nordic history, although it will also serve as a ready reference for the scholar. The varied contents provide users with information on specific topics and with information related to topics not covered directly. In instances where the latter is the case, users will find information in the body of entries and in the references which will enable them to pursue subjects not covered directly.

Acknowledgments

Einar Haugen includes in his Norwegian-English dictionary the word *ørken-vandring*, which he defines as a desert journey or wandering in the wilderness and, figuratively, as a "wearying task (e.g., the making of dictionaries)." The task of compiling this dictionary has consumed much of my time over the past five years and has been both wearisome and rewarding—but mainly the latter. And mainly the latter because of the many people who have so generously contributed their time, their knowledge, and their skills. My deepest thanks go to the entry contributors, without whose participation completion of this volume would have been impossible, to my colleagues and students and the members of the administration and staff at Gustavus Adolphus College who have helped me, and to my family.

Contributors

David D. Aldridge
Department of History
University of Newcastle upon Tyne
Newcastle upon Tyne, England

Eva M. Anderson
Historian and Freelance Writer
Westwood, Massachusetts

Carole Arwidson
Undergraduate Assistant
Gustavus Adolphus College
St. Peter, Minnesota

Michael P. Barnes
Department of Scandinavian Studies
University College London
London, England

H. Arnold Barton
Department of History
Southern Illinois University
Carbondale, Illinois

Brian Benson
Undergraduate Assistant
Gustavus Adolphus College
St. Peter, Minnesota

R. Michael Berry
University of Turku
Turku, Finland

Peter Berry
Area Specialist Librarian
New York Public Library
New York, New York

Ida Blom
Department of History
University of Bergen
Bergen, Norway

F. Herbert Capps
INR West Europe Specialist
United States Department of State
Washington, D.C.

John R. Christianson
Department of History
Luther College
Decorah, Iowa

Julie Dailey
Scandinavian Specialist and Freelance Writer
Seattle, Washington

Laura Deal
Graduate Student
Colorado State University
Fort Collins, Colorado

Martha Emelity
Department of German
University of Arizona
Tucson, Arizona

Tom Ericsson
History Department
University of Umeå
Umeå, Sweden

Norma Farquhar
Scandinavian Specialist and Freelance Writer
Los Angeles, California

Donald R. Floyd
Department of Social Sciences
California Polytechnic State University
San Luis Obispo, California

Erik Gøbel
Archivist
Rigsarkivet
Copenhagen, Denmark

Gerd S. Gordon
Scandinavian Specialist and Teacher
Pittsburgh, Pennsylvania

Kris Grey
Undergraduate Assistant
Gustavus Adolphus College
St. Peter, Minnesota

Frederick Hale
Historian and Freelance Writer
Oslo, Norway

Carolyn Storlie Halterman
Archives and Records Manager
North Dakota State Land Department
Bismarck, North Dakota

Pekka K. Hamalainen
Department of History
University of Wisconsin-Madison
Madison, Wisconsin

Bertil L. Hanson
Department of Political Science
Oklahoma State University
Stillwater, Oklahoma

Oddvar Hoidal
Department of History
San Diego State University
San Diego, California

Kai Hørby
Department of History
University of Copenhagen
Copenhagen, Denmark

Kristian Hvidt
Historian and Librarian
Folketing Library
Copenhagen, Denmark

Riitta Jallinoja
Department of Sociology
University of Helsinki
Helsinki, Finland

Louis Janus
Department of Norwegian
St. Olaf College
Northfield, Minnesota

Hans Christian Johansen
History Department
Odense University
Odense, Denmark

Owen V. Johnson
School of Journalism
Indiana University
Bloomington, Indiana

Walter Johnson, deceased
Department of Scandinavian Studies
University of Washington
Seattle, Washington

Yrjö Kaukiainen
Department of Economic and Social History
University of Helsinki
Helsinki, Finland

James E. Knirk
Nordisk Institutt
University of Oslo
Oslo, Norway

John I. Kolehmainen
Retired Historian
Tiffin, Ohio

Stein Kuhnle
Institute of Comparative Politics
University of Bergen
Bergen, Norway

Bruce L. Larson
Department of History
Mankato State University
Mankato, Minnesota

Karen Larson
Department of Sociology and Anthropology
Gustavus Adolphus College
St. Peter, Minnesota

Terje Leiren
Department of Scandinavian Studies
University of Washington
Seattle, Washington

Daniel Levine
Department of History
Bowdoin College
Brunswick, Maine

Joan D. Lind
Social Science Division
University of Kentucky
Louisville, Kentucky

Doris H. Linder
Department of History
College of San Mateo
San Mateo, California

George Maude
Department of History
Turku University
Turku, Finland

Michael F. Metcalf
Department of History
University of Minnesota
Minneapolis, Minnesota

Thomas Munck
Department of Modern History
The University
Glasgow, Scotland

Kim Nilsson
Department of Scandinavian
University of Wisconsin-Madison
Madison, Wisconsin

Byron J. Nordstrom
Department of History
Gustavus Adolphus College
St. Peter, Minnesota

Stewart P. Oakley
School of Modern European Languages and History
University of East Anglia
Norwich, England

Knud-Erik H. Pedersen, deceased
Graduate Student
Reykjavik, Iceland

Peter L. Petersen
Department of History
West Texas State University
Canyon, Texas

Paul Ries
Faculty of Modern and Medieval Languages
Cambridge University
Cambridge, England

Thomas Riis
Department of History
University of St. Andrews
St. Salvador College
St. Andrews, Scotland

Diane Sainsbury
Institute for English-speaking Students
University of Stockholm
Stockholm, Sweden

Lee Sather
School of Social Sciences
Weber State College
Ogden, Utah

R. Stephen Schwartz
Department of Sociology and Social Work
Winona State University
Winona, Minnesota

Franklin D. Scott
The Honnold Library
Claremont, California

Joseph M. Shaw
Department of Religion
St. Olaf College
Northfield, Minnesota

Melissa Lowe Shogren
Scandinavian Specialist
Pullman, Washington

Geir-Helge Sjøtrø
Norwegian School of Economics and Business
Administration
Bergen, Norway

Trygve R. Skarsten
Trinity Lutheran Seminary
Columbus, Ohio

Povl Skårup
Århus University
Århus, Denmark

George L. Small
Department of Geography
College of Staten Island
St. George Campus
Staten Island, New York

Håkon Stang
Centralinstitut for Nordisk Asienforskning
Copenhagen, Denmark

Nils Peter Stilling
Byhistorisk Arkiv for Søllerød Kommune
Holte, Denmark

Jan Sundberg
Department of Political Science
University of Helsinki
Helsinki, Finland

Lars Svåsand
Institute of Comparative Politics
University of Bergen
Bergen, Norway

Eric R. Terzuolo
Historian and Foreign Service Officer
United States Department of State
Washington, D.C.

David J. Thompson
Specialist and Freelance Writer
National Consumers Cooperative Bank
Oakland, California

Playford V. Thorson
Department of History
University of North Dakota
Grand Forks, North Dakota

Atle Thowsen
Bergens Sjøfartsmuseum
Bergen, Norway

Timothy Tilton
Department of Political Science
Indiana University
Bloomington, Indiana

Kåre Tønnesson
Historisk Institutt
University of Oslo
Oslo, Norway

Hal Vogel
Division of Business and Economics
Trenton State College
Trenton, New Jersey

Jerry L. Voorhis
Department of Political Science
California State Polytechnic University
Pomona, California

John F. West
Trent Polytechnic
Nottingham, England

Christer Winberg
History Department
Gothenburg University
Gothenburg, Sweden

Alan H. Winquist
Department of History
Taylor University
Upland, Indiana

Abbreviations of References

CMH	*Cambridge Modern History*
DBL	*Dansk biografisk leksikon*
DH	*Danmarks historie*
DSH	*Den svenska historien*
KLNM	*Kulturhistorisk Leksikon for Nordisk Middelalder*
NBL	*Norsk biografisk leksikon*
NCMH	*New Cambridge Modern History*
NH	*Norges historie*
SBL	*Svenskt biografiskt lexikon*
SMK	*Svenska män och kvinnor*
SU	*Svensk uppslagsbok*

DICTIONARY OF SCANDINAVIAN HISTORY

A

AALTO, ALVAR (3 February 1898–11 May 1976) Finnish architect

Aalto began his studies at the Technical Institute of Helsinki in Otaniemi, but left to participate in the Finnish War of Independence (see Civil War) in 1917. He graduated in 1921, toured Europe, and returned to Finland to live in Jyväskylä. In 1925 he married Aino Marsio, who was also an architecture student. She collaborated with him in his architecture business until her death in 1949. They had two children. In 1927 Aalto moved to Turku, where he worked with Erik Bryggman. In 1933 he moved to Helsinki. Aalto received commissions for three important buildings which established him as an architect. In 1929 he designed the Turun-Sanomat Building in Turku. From 1929 to 1933 he worked on the Tuberculosis Sanatorium in Paimio. In 1934 he completed the Municipal Library in Viipuri (now Vyborg). His work in Viipuri identified him with the "organic approach" or regional style of architecture. He used curved woods, irregular forms, and designs that would blend well with the surrounding area. In the late 1920s and early 1930s Aalto began to experiment with furniture design, using curved, laminated woods. In 1935 Artek Company was founded to manufacture his furniture. Three years after his wife's death he married another architect, Elissa Makiniemi, who also worked closely with him in his business. From 1945 to 1949 he was professor of architecture at Massachusetts Institute of Technology at Cambridge, where he designed Baker House dormitory. Aalto was a member of Soumen Aketmia (Academy of Finland) and its president from 1963 to 1968. He was also a member of Congrès Internationaux d'Architecture Moderne from 1928 to 1956.

REFERENCES: J. McAndrew, *Aalto* (New York: Museum of Modern Art, 1938); K. Fleig, *Alvar Aalto* (Zurich: Verlag für Architektur, 1963).

L. DEAL

ABEL (1218–29 June 1252) King of Denmark 1250–1252

Abel ruled for the shortest time of any monarch in Danish history. He was the second son of Valdemar II*. Before his succession he led almost constant

revolts against his brother, Erik IV*. He made no significant contributions to the country's history and died fighting the Frisians at the battle of Husumbro.
REFERENCES: *DBL*, vol. 1; *DH*, vol. 4.

B. NORDSTROM

ÅDALEN DISTURBANCES (Ådalenkravallerna) Labor demonstrations which led to the shooting of 10 persons by soldiers in May 1931 in Sweden

Ådalen (the valley of the Å river), located between Sollefteå and Härnösand in Ångermanland, was a center for forest product industries in the nineteenth and twentieth centuries. It was also a center of early labor organization and activism, largely because of the sensitivity of these industries to international market fluctuations.

In the late 1920s and early 1930s, this area became particularly volatile. World demand for timber and paper pulp declined during the international depression. In response, the operators of area plants sought to shorten the work week and reduce wages. The unions responded negatively to these demands. Strikes, lockouts, and blockades ensued. Class antagonisms were high in the area, and radical agitators fanned these emotions.

Most of the workers were members of unions affiliated with the Swedish Confederation of Trade Unions* (LO), particularly the Swedish Paper Industry Workers Union (Svensk Pappersindustriarbetareförbundet) and the Swedish Sawmill Industry Workers Union (Svensk Sågverksindustriarbetareförbundet). Other labor organizations were active in the area, however, including the syndicalists and Moscow-affiliated Communists (Sillén Communists). Representatives of these groups were more aggressive and less willing to compromise, and they tended to amplify the hostility between management and labor in the region.

In 1930 and 1931, area plant operators requested new labor agreements with workers, and they called for further reductions in the work week and wages and increased rents on plant-owned housing. The workers were unwilling and unable to accept these demands. In the fall of 1930 a blockade was initiated against a sulphate pulp plant in Marma owned by Långrörs AB. This action was the focus of labor unrest. In the spring of 1931, non-union strikebreakers were hired to load pulp at a Sandviken-owned plant at Lunde. The arrival of these workers triggered a series of demonstrations and marches which ended in tragedy on 14 May.

The strikebreakers arrived on 12 May. They were greeted by an angry crowd, and in a subsequent incident a number were beaten aboard the ship on which they were housed. Local authorities were frightened by the intensity of the situation and felt unable to control events. They requested that troops be sent in, and the county governor authorized this action. The soldiers arrived on 13 May and were greeted by an emotional crowd. Some rocks were thrown at the troops during this incident.

On 14 May a rally and meeting of local labor leaders was held at Fränö. The size of this meeting swelled far beyond expectations. While the leaders discussed possible actions, control of the crowd fell into the hands of radicals, primarily Communists. It was decided that the group should march to Lunde to protest the presence of the strikebreakers. While the union leaders stayed to discuss matters, the marchers departed. The crowd grew to between 4,- and 5,000.

The protestors arrived at Lunde in the late afternoon. They were confronted by the troops that had been stationed to stop them. A scuffle between the front marchers and several cavalry soldiers ensued. The marchers were asked three times to disperse, and when they did not the order was given to fire upon them. Four workers and a young woman were killed. Five others were wounded. For the first time in Swedish labor history, troops had fired upon and killed Swedish workers.

The response on both sides of the political spectrum was outrage. The Left attacked the system, the plant owners, the local and county authorities, the military, the central government of Carl Gustav Ekman*, and each other. The Communists were the most vehement in the press and the parliament. The Right attacked the workers, the unions, and the radical agitators. In many places in the country, sympathy actions were initiated. At noon on 21 May, when the victims of the incident were being buried, all work stopped in Stockholm* for five minutes.

In the wake of events, a number of workers, organizers, and journalists were fined and/or imprisoned for their actions or words. The government created a special commission to investigate the incident and issued a rather inconclusive report in July 1931. The local sheriff and two army officers were eventually given minimal punishments for their roles in the events. A general amnesty was subsequently issued by the government.

The consensus, once emotions had cooled, was that the tragedy could have been avoided. Although a number of similar incidents occurred over the next several months, labor leaders, politicians, and the military appear to have generally agreed that the army should not be called in to deal with civil disturbances, for which it had no particular training. Consequently, one of the tangible results of the events at Ådalen was the establishment of a state police force (*statspolis*) which would be trained to deal with future civil disorders. The army would be called in (henceforth only by the crown) in extraordinary instances. In addition, the events at Ådalen increased demands for legal control of the labor market, which was something neither organized labor nor the management sector desired. (From management's perspective, the fundamental issue at Ådalen was the right of the employer to hire and fire whomever he chose.) In 1936 the two parties in the labor market would sit down to negotiate a basic agreement to regulate the labor market (*see* Saltsjöbad Agreement). Finally, the incidents at Ådalen and the repercussions from them may have affected the outcome of the 1932 elections, which brought the Social Democrats to power.

REFERENCES: *Ådalskommissionens berättelse* (Stockholm, 1931); R. Casparsson, *LO under fem årtionden* (Stockholm: Tidens, 1948), vol. 2; *DSH*, vol. 14; I. Flink, *Strejk-*

bryteriet och arbetets frihet (Stockholm: Almqvist & Wiksell, 1978); B. Norman, *Ådalen 1931* (Stockholm: Raben & Sjögren, 1981); *SU*, vol. 32.

B. NORDSTROM

ADAM OF BREMEN (died c. 1081) Historian and geographer

Adam of Bremen wrote the *Gesta Hammaburgensis ecclesiae pontificum* (*GH*), a chronicle of the archbishops of the Hamburg-Bremen see from 900 to 1072. Adam came to Bremen from his home in central Germany in 1066. As head of the cathedral school, he began work on the chronicle, which he completed in 1076 but revised until his death in Bremen in 1081.

The *GH* is divided into four books. The third book, in which Adam describes the archiepiscopate of Adalbert of Bremen (1045–1072), is the focal point of the work. Book Four is especially valuable because it contains the earliest detailed information about the geography and customs of Scandinavia* (especially Denmark) and descriptions of Birka* and Old Uppsala*. Adam used a variety of sources. He was familiar with Gregory of Tours, Einhard, and Bede, and was influenced by written and oral genres such as histories, geographies, letters, and saints' legends. His viewpoint was Augustinian: he saw history as a continuous battle between the kingdoms of God and the devil. This translated itself in his work as the conflict between the leaders of the Church and their enemies.

Adam's chronicle is now recognized as a major source for the history of Scandinavia in the tenth and eleventh centuries. The standard edition is still the *Hamburgische Kirchengeschichte* edited by Bernhard Schmeidler in 1917.

REFERENCES: Adam of Bremen, *History of the Archbishops of Hamburg and Bremen*, trans. F. J. Tschan (New York: Columbia University Press, 1959); E. Johnson, "Adalbert of Hamburg-Bremen," *Speculum*, 9 (1934): 147–79; G. Kimble, *Geography in the Middle Ages* (London, 1938; New York: Russell and Russell, 1968).

M. EMELITY

ADOLF FREDRIK (14 May 1710–12 February 1771) King of Sweden 1751– 1771

Born the son of the prince-bishop of Lübeck, Kristian August, and his wife, Albertina Fredrika of Baden-Durlach, Adolf Fredrik became the prince-bishop of Lübeck at the age of 17. In addition, he became in 1739 the guardian of Duke Karl Peter Ulrik of Holstein-Gottorp and the administrator of the duke's territorial possessions, the duchies of Holstein and Gottorp. Through the influence of the Empress Elizabeth of Russia, whose armies had recently turned a Swedish invasion into a crushing Swedish defeat, Adolf Fredrik was elected heir apparent to the Swedish throne in 1743. He married Lovisa Ulrika*, a sister of Frederick II of Prussia, in 1744, and succeeded Fredrik I* as king of Sweden in 1751.

Politically unambitious and an intellectual light weight, Adolf Fredrik lived in the political, cultural, and intellectual shadow of Lovisa Ulrika, often content to work at his lathe or at other carpentry projects at his beloved Drottningholm*. Pressed by his wife into reluctantly pursuing an increase of his powers in the mid-1750s, Adolf Fredrik had to resign himself to the fact that his estates authorized the casting and use, at the discretion of the council of the realm, of a metal stamp bearing his signature. This came in the aftermath of the discovery in 1756 of plans for a coup d'etat in support of increased royal prerogatives, plans that led to a further weakening of his position.

Adolf Fredrik died of natural causes in 1771 and was succeeded by his eldest son, Gustav III*.

REFERENCES: L. Stavenow, "Adolf Fredrik," *SBL* 1 (1918): 200–209.

M. F. METCALF

AESIR (Norse Gods) The main family of gods in pagan Norse mythology

Norse mythology is known mostly through the *Poetic Edda**, the *Prose Edda*, and the *Heimskringla* of Snorri Sturluson* from the thirteenth century. Norse skaldic poetry and some Latin sources, including the works of Adam of Bremen* and Saxo Grammaticus*, are also useful sources.

The Aesir dwell in Ásgard (''god-residence'') in the supposed center of Midgard (''the middle dwelling,'' the land of mankind), which in turn is surrounded by the ocean and its giant Midgard serpent. Beyond the ocean is Utgard (''the outer dwelling''), with Jotenheim (home of the giants), where the enemies of the Aesir and of men (the *jotnir*) reside. The Aesir guard the world from the giants, but they will succumb, along with mankind, in the final onslaught of the *jotnir*, the Midgard serpent, and the Fenris wolf. Until then, the Aesir keep eternally young by eating the ''apples of Idun'' from the tree of life, and eternally fit through warriors' practice at Valhall in Ásgard.

The central god and keeper of Valhall is Odin. To Valhall all men killed in battle come. Two ravens inform Odin daily of all that happens on earth. Another ancient war-god is Tyr, whose name is related to Zeus, Indian Dyaus, and Indo-Germanic + dieus ''day, heaven.'' Thor is the one Aesir deity who is in regular combat with the *jotnir*, as he goes on one-man forays with his hammer, Mollnir.

Odin is associated with Frigg, by whom he has a son, Balder. Vidar is another son of Odin and is to kill the Fenris wolf. Vale, yet another son of Odin, will slay Balder's killer. Vile and Ve are Odin's brothers and are mentioned in connection with the creation of the world. Høner is Odin's ''companion'' or ''deputy.'' Other Aesir gods are Ull/Ullinn, who are associated with a fir tree and winter. Brage is a god of poetry. Idun is his wife. Kvaser is the wisest of all the Aesir and is killed to make the mead of poetry. Forsete is a god of peace and pacts. Heimdal, who dwells on the heaven-mountains, always is awake, all-seeing and -hearing. He stands erect, ready to blow his horn at the advent of the end of the world. A special role is played by Loki, a half-god/half-giant, who dwells among the Aesir and is ever-ready to stir up mischief. It is Loki who plots Balder's death and is the father of the Fenris wolf. Strictly speaking, Njord (a god of prosperity), Frey, and his sister Freya (god and goddess of fertility) are not Aesir, but Vanir, another family of gods who were anciently at war with the Aesir until a peace was concluded.

In addition to the Aesir and Vanir and the *jotnir*, Norse mythology knows of lesser classes of beings including the Diser, a group of unspecified goddesses or female spirits; Valkyrjer, female warrior-spirits who fetch the slain from the battlegrounds on earth and carry them to Valhall; Landvettir, local "guardian spirits" in nature; and Alfer, elves associated with Frey, who dwells in Alfheim.

The individual deities were of unequal and changing prominence. According to the *Edda,* Odin was the "all-father." Yet, Adam of Bremen says that in the pagan temple at Uppsala, Thor was flanked by Odin and Frey and was the mightiest of the three.

The origin of the term Aesir is the subject of a dispute which reflects the debates over the origins of Norse mythology itself. It has been suggested that the word derives from the Germanic *ansu* (pillar). Snorri, in *Heimskringla*, says that *Ass* means "Asia-man." This view fits with the argument of a number of scholars who see the roots of Norse mythology in cultures of the ancient Near East. The word Asia derives from the ethnonym *As*, which referred to the Ossetians, a north Iranian people in the Central Caucasus, who descended from the Scythians or neo-Scythians (Sarmatians). The latter dominated the south and central Russian plains between c. 700 B.C. and 400 A.D. Goths served with the neo-Scythians and may have transmitted neo-Scythian lore and art to Scandi-navia*. Thus, it has been suggested that *Ass* reflects the name of the Ossetians, and that Balder and Loki are refound in Ossetian folk poetry. More generally, it has been argued that major parts of Norse mythology derive from, or have parallels in, Iranian mythology.

REFERENCES: B. Branston, *Gods of the North* (New York: Thames and Hudson, 1955 and 1980); J. deVries, *Altnordische Religionsgeschichte*, vols. 1, 2 (Berlin, 1935 and 1956–1957); G. Dumézil, *Gods of the Ancient Northmen* (Berkeley: University of California Press, 1973); E. O. G. Turville-Petre, *Myth and Religion of the North* (New York: Holt, Rinehart and Winston, 1964).

H. STANG

AFTONBLADET The most widely-circulated Social Democratic paper in Sweden

The appearance of *Aftonbladet* marked the birth of the modern Swedish press, in the same way that the *New York Sun* (1833) did in the United States. It was established on 10 December 1830 by Lars Johan Hierta, a young government official with radical views, in support of Liberal ideals. Hierta, "father of the Swedish editorial," made the paper an organ of sharp, clear news and views addressed to a wide audience; it reflected democratic and humanitarian stand-points which were opposed to the prevailing aristocratic government. Throughout the 1830s, the government sought, but failed, to discourage the paper, especially by confiscation of printed issues. *Aftonbladet* played an important propaganda role in the abolition of the four estates (see Riksdag) in 1865. By then its circulation had reached about 10,000. Until the early twentieth century, it re-mained the most important and influential journal in the kingdom. Esaias Tegner once referred to it as the "bible of the Swedes." By the 1920s its circulation reached several hundred thousand. In the 1930s, the newspaper was reorganized into its present tabloid format, stressing sports, light entertainment, and features. It was pro-German during World War II*. In the 1950s and 1960s its circulation grew rapidly, but its competitive market position has declined since the 1970s. Today it is one of fourteen daily Swedish papers. An evening paper, it maintains a circulation of just under half a million and reaches just less than one-third of the households in Stockholm*. Using an efficient delivery system, it is one of only two newspapers with nationwide distribution.

O. V. JOHNSON

AGE OF LIBERTY (Frihetstiden) (1719–1772) Period of experimentation in parliamentary government in eighteenth-century Sweden

The Age of Liberty emerged with the new Form of Government drawn up by the Swedish estates (*see* Riksdag*) in January 1719, after the death of Karl XII* in November 1718; it lasted until Gustav III* overthrew this new "system" in his bloodless coup d'etat of 19 August 1772. The term derives from the fact that the estates of the realm adopted a form of government that stripped the monarch of the absolute role exercised by Karl XI* and Karl XII since 1680. The principal characteristic of the period lay in the political and constitutional arena, but the era also evokes images of development in manufacturing and agriculture, as well as of scientific and artistic achievements one normally associates with the Enlightenment. This was the age of Linnaeus and Celsius (both professors at Uppsala University), as well as of Carl Michael Bellman, Johan Helmich Roman, and Johan Tobias Sergel.

Meeting in Stockholm* in January 1719 to elect a successor to Karl XII, the four estates of the realm (nobles, clergy, burghers, and peasants) first adopted a carefully designed Form of Government that put sovereign power in their hands and then elected Karl's sister, Ulrika Eleonora (the Younger)*, as his successor. According to the new Form of Government (reinforced in 1720), the estates were to hold a Riksdag every three years, at which they were to review the custodianship of the council of state*, select new councilors as needed, discuss and act on the need for new laws, and grant such taxes as they found necessary for the well-being of the realm. Only the estates could declare war and make peace, and only they could levy taxes. The role of the council was that of a governing body, its actions subject to review by the estates, and the role of the monarch was essentially limited to that of having a seat on the council, having the tie-breaking vote in that body, and exercising some influence over appointments of civil and military officers.

As the role of the monarchs (Ulrika Eleonora, Fredrik I*, Adolf Fredrik*, and Gustav III) was kept within strict constitutional limits in reaction to the absolutism of Karl XI and Karl XII, the council of the realm became the central political actor in the interims between meetings of the estates. The council was chaired by the president of the chancery college, otherwise known as the chancery president, and during the first two decades of the period (1719 and then from

1720 to 1738) this position was held by the very able Count Arvid Horn*. In this period of its infancy and youth, the Age of Liberty saw Sweden adopt a very bureaucratic system of government in which no public servant, including councilors of the realm, could be removed from office without legal cause. While appropriate for lower offices, this standard of tenure was extremely cumbersome when politically important officers were to be turned out, and the impeachment process, in which political reasons for removal were hidden behind legalistic arguments and proceedings against the incumbent, was developed as a necessary but distasteful political tool.

By 1738 political opposition to Horn's government had led to the founding of the Hat Party* and the articulation of its views and strategy. Arvid Horn's government was forced to resign or face impeachment when the Hats captured control of the House of Nobility and of the key committees at the Riksdag. The very fact of parliamentary sovereignty had made it necessary for opposing political groups to mobilize voter and delegate support on a high level of planning and coordination, and with the formation of the Cap Party* by 1740, in essence a two-party system of politics emerged as a mechanism for amassing votes, articulating policy, and securing passage of legislation and the election of nominees for high office. From 1740 until 1772, these two parties competed for political ascendancy, and the end of the Age of Liberty came at a time when this party system had ceased to aggregate successfully the interests of the voters and political actors along meaningful political cleavages.

Successful in bringing a negotiated end to the Great Northern War* through the Treaty of Nystad (1721), the government of Arvid Horn pursued a policy of caution in foreign affairs that recognized Sweden's new second-rank status among the European powers. This realistic and cautious policy prompted much opposition from those who had held property in the lands lost to Russia, and foreign policy differences marked much of the political debate during Horn's regime. Indeed, the Hat Party was successful in attracting several young officers who joined these special landed interests in desiring a war of revenge against Russia. With Horn's fall to the Hats, such a war was not long in coming; the Russo-Swedish War of 1742–1743 proved once again that Sweden was no longer a first-rank power. Only once more during the Age of Liberty, that is, during the Seven Years' War, did Sweden enter into a military adventure, and this time her allies were strong enough to prevent her loss of any further territory.

With peace at home and abroad from 1719 to 1742, Sweden was able to pay off her war debts and bring about healthy economic growth. Under both Horn and the Hats, budding manufactories were given important subsidies in the form of premiums for their completed products, and the diversity of Swedish economic life increased. Equally important was the fact that peasants were allowed for the first time to purchase lands belonging to noblemen in the years after 1723. The resultant, if gradual, transformation of real estate into a commodity for capital investment went a long way toward moving Sweden into the capitalist stage of development.

Peace and economic expansion triggered an increased rate of population growth that in turn made necessary more productive agricultural methods and more control over the nation's economy. Moves were made by 1750 to consolidate strips of arable land in the farming villages, thus allowing peasants to experiment more freely with the new agricultural methods being discussed in the growing Enlightenment literature printed in Sweden. On the national level, the new appreciation of empirical methods led to the establishment of the first national bureau of statistics (1749) in the world.

These breakthroughs in the economic and governmental spheres were accompanied by a level of cultural activity affecting a much broader segment of the population than ever before. Part of the reason for this was the blooming of inquiry in the natural and physical sciences, through which the works of men like Linnaeus (Carl von Linné) and Anders Celsius enabled people better to understand their natural environment. Perhaps even more important was the popularization of Enlightenment ideas through the publication in Swedish (for the first time) of several journals, newspapers*, and books that exposed ''everyman'' to new and liberating questions about the nature of knowledge and authority and that made ''everyman''—especially son and daughter—reassess the structure of the society in which they lived and the place they occupied within that structure. For many this was an experience that led to demands for equal treatment or at least access to the favored avenues to wealth, independence, and privilege.

Growing demands from commoners for more equal and even-handed treatment began to be voiced in the years after 1762, when the long-ensconced Hat government was bogged down in its unpopular and unsuccesful participation in the coalition against Frederick the Great of Prussia. The vulnerability of the Hats in this situation also unleashed a spate of anti-officialdom, all of which fueled the defeat of the Hats and the victory of the Caps in 1764 and 1765. The new government—brought into office by these new categories of political activists, as well as by general discontent with the Hats' conduct of foreign and economic policy—soon moved to make important changes that addressed some of the economic and social needs of segments of the population long ignored by the Hats. Among other things, the Caps did away with political censorship, reduced the power of the guilds, deregulated domestic shipping, granted the peasantry freedom to sell their produce wherever they liked, and reformed the laws requiring unmarried workers to be under contract to an employer at all times.

This taste of political power seemed to fuel the newly active groups' appetites for change that would further their interests. In the years after 1768, in particular, the pace of public debate in the press moved ever more quickly, with individuals challenging almost every political and economic orthodoxy. Proposals were made to abolish the distinction before the law between commoner and noble, to transfer some tax revenues and legislative authority over local society to the local level, and to establish a set of privileges for the common person. With the death of King Adolf Fredrik in 1771 and the negotiations for an accession charter for his son, Gustav III, the representatives of the clergy, burghers, and peasants pressed the case of their constituents even harder. Gustav was forced, for example, to accept language that pledged him to make appointments to civil and military posts solely on the basis of merit, with no consideration given to the candidate's social origins.

The capacity of the nobility and of Gustav III to accept socioeconomic change, however, had been exhausted. Many Hats in the House of Nobility—and many Caps with them—realized that they had lost control of the course of events. In their minds, many of them now feared the "mob," that is, the commoners with their growing lists of demands, as a greater threat than the monarchy, against which the Form of Government of 1720 had originally been devised. Thus, either through their neutrality or their cooperation, many of these noblemen in effect aided Gustav III in his coup d'etat of August 1772 and in his consolidation of power immediately afterward. With that the Age of Liberty and its parliamentary sovereignty came to an end; political conformity now fell over the kingdom like a suffocating blanket. Yet, the irony of history was to play the ultimate trick on those noblemen who had abandoned "liberty" to preserve their privileges. It was Gustav III who eventually implemented many of the anti-bureaucratic and socioeconomic reforms that the three lower estates had advocated and that they had initiated in the Riksdag of 1771–1772.

REFERENCES: E. F. Heckscher, *An Economic History of Sweden* (Cambridge, Mass.: Harvard University Press, 1954); C. G. Malmström, *Sveriges politiska historia från konung Karl XII:s död till statshvälfningen 1772*, 6 vols. (Stockholm, 1893–1901); M. Metcalf, "Challenges to Economic Orthodoxy and Parliamentary Sovereignty in Eighteenth Century Sweden," *Legislative Studies Quarterly* 7 (1982): 251–61; M. Roberts, *Swedish and English Parliamentarism in the Eighteenth Century* (Belfast, 1973).

M. F. METCALF

AGRARIAN PARTY *See* Center Party: Finland; Center Party: Norway; Center Party: Sweden

AGRICULTURAL PRODUCER COOPERATIVES Denmark

Producer cooperatives are at the very core of agricultural organization in modern Denmark. They first appeared in the 1880s during the time Danish farmers were shifting from cereal grains to the production of animal products for export, especially butter and bacon. The first cooperative dairy was formed in 1882 at Hjedding on the west coast of Jutland. Under the rules of the cooperative, farmers agreed to sell their raw milk to a centrally located dairy where it could be processed. The money needed to purchase equipment, such as the newly invented cream separator, and to erect a building to house it came from a loan secured by the real property of the members. Each member, regardless of the size of his herd, had one vote at the general meeting, but any surplus profit was to be distributed according to the amount of milk delivered. The Hjedding experiment in combining individual farming with large-scale production methods proved to be a success and was quickly copied by other Danish dairymen. By 1890 nearly 700 cooperative dairies (*andelsmejerier*) had been formed throughout the nation. Today about 90 percent of all the milk produced in Denmark passes through cooperative dairies.

The first cooperative slaughterhouse for Danish hogs was established at Horsens in 1887. Despite considerable opposition from private firms, four more cooperatives were created the following year. By 1900 there were 26 cooperative "bacon factories" (*andelssvineslag*) scattered throughout the land which took about 80 percent of all market hogs. Eventually, they formed their own national organization, the Federation of Danish Cooperative Bacon Factories, to advise members on government policies, improve the quality of Danish bacon, and assist in overseas marketing. Cooperative export societies were also created by egg and cattle producers, but these never matched the market dominance of their counterparts in the dairy and pork industries.

Why did Danes more than any other people adopt cooperative methods? In part, economic conditions forced them to do so. As Danish agriculture became increasingly dependent upon the export of animal products, individual farmers were confronted with the necessity of selling to large commercial firms or developing their own cooperatives. The latter was the more attractive alternative, because it had the economic advantage of eliminating the middleman in the process. Moreover, the Folk School movement had taught many farmers to understand their problems and to seek solutions through joint economic undertakings.

REFERENCES: Chris L. Christensen, "Linking the Farm and the Market: What an American Can Learn from Danish Cooperative Agriculture," *American Scandinavian Review* 15 (1927): 350–56; Aage Axelsen Drejer, "The Danish Co-operative Movement," in J. Bukdahl et al., eds., *Scandinavia Past and Present* (Odense: Edvard Henriksen, 1959), III, pp. 776–86; Frederic C. Howe, *Denmark: The Cooperative Way* (New York: Coward-McCann, Inc., 1936); Peter Manniche, *Living Democracy in Denmark* (Copenhagen: G. E. C. Gad, 1952); Jens P. Warming, "Danish Agriculture with Special Reference to Cooperation," *Quarterly Journal of Economics* 37 (1923): 491–509.

P. L. PETERSEN

AGRICULTURAL REVOLUTION

Changes which occurred in European agriculture from the seventeenth century into the twentieth century are often referred to under the general (and perhaps increasingly meaningless) term, the "agricultural revolution." These changes included the consolidation of small holdings; the elimination of villages; the spread of freehold farms; the adoption of new crop rotations, new crops, extended use of fertilizers, and increasingly selective animal breeding; the adoption of new implements and mechanization; the extension of education; increased specialization; the development of banking facilities; and an increased emphasis on market agriculture. Scandinavia* experienced these transitions, although there were wide regional and chronological differences among the countries. At the same time, a demographic revolution occurred that involved rapid population growth, increased social and spatial mobility, and significant shifts in class distributions. Also, in parts of Scandinavia these changes were concurrent with industrialization*.

Denmark

Agriculture has long been of great importance in the Danish economy. Although the nation's soil is not particularly fertile, it is the basic natural resource of a country that processes little oil, coal, or iron. Danish farmers have a tradition of being uniquely skillful in adjusting to changing circumstances. Following the repeal of the English Corn Laws in 1846, a rapidly industrializing England became a lucrative market for Danish agricultural exports, especially cereal grains such as wheat and rye. For a time (c. 1840–1875) Danish agriculture boomed with prosperity.

Beginning in the 1870s, however, improvements in sea and land transportation brought cheaper grains from the United States, Russia, and Argentina into European markets. Danish farmers found it difficult to meet this new competition, and many faced financial ruin as grain prices dropped sharply. At this point, Danish agriculture underwent a remarkable revolution.

In a span of less than two decades, farmers shifted from raising grain for export to raising hogs, poultry, and milk cows for the production of bacon, eggs, and butter. So profound was this transformation that Denmark soon became a grain importing country. Not only did the number of animals on Danish farms increase dramatically, but there were significant improvements in the various breeds.

Students of Danish agricultural history identify at least three factors which help explain this successful change in direction. First, reforms in the late eighteenth century permitted the development of a class of independent farmers who were efficient in animal husbandry. Second, the Folk School movement created a high level of education among farmers, and thus many were receptive to the newest developments in scientific agriculture. Third, in order to market their products more effectively, Danish farmers adopted the cooperative method (*see* Agricultural Producer Cooperatives).

As before, England remained the primary export market for Danish farmers. In fact, as late as 1938 that country took 71 percent of Denmark's entire agricultural export. So great was the dependence upon English markets that the deep water port of Esbjerg, built by the Danish government on the west coast of Jutland following the loss of Slesvig and Holstein in 1864, became the nation's fifth largest city. The agricultural revolution of the late nineteenth century established patterns that to a large extent still guide Danish farmers: the importation and domestic production of livestock feed and the exportation of quality finished products in the form of butter, cheese, eggs, and pork via the cooperative method.

P. L. PETERSEN

Finland

In Finland the transitions came later and took longer to effect. The country was more extensively agricultural than its Nordic neighbors in the nineteenth century and remains so in the last quarter of the twentieth century (75 percent rural in 1880 and 12.6 percent rural in 1980). Problems with effecting consolidation of land holdings, elimination of small freehold farms, and general inefficiency have been chronic in Finnish agriculture outside the fairly fertile areas of the west and southwest. The small farms carved from the forest frontiers were and remain obstacles to rationalization of agriculture. As in the other Nordic countries, there was a shift away from grain-growing in the last quarter of the nineteenth century, accompanied by an increase in the cultivation of potatoes and concentration upon dairy products.

B. NORDSTROM

Norway

The agricultural revolution also came relatively late and slowly to Norway and was less far-reaching there than in Denmark or Sweden. The relative poorness of Norwegian soil and the scarcity of arable land made many of the usual changes connected with the revolution difficult or undesirable. The traditional pattern of communal (or semi-communal) farming based on the *tun* (literally, the yard around which the farm buildings were situated) was much more difficult to abandon than in the more fertile regions of southern Sweden or Denmark. Consolidation efforts were not initiated until the 1850s. At the same time, the practice of dividing farms through sale within a family continued through most of the nineteenth century, and the resulting problem of diminution of farm size was exacerbated by rapid population growth. In many areas, holdings became too small to support their owners. Extension of land under cultivation took place in the nineteenth century but did not offset these problems. The development of banking and credit facilities for agriculture came relatively late. Still, production did increase during the nineteenth century, and there was a shift from grain-growing to dairy products and the raising of potatoes. The adoption of new implements and mechanization was slow and came mostly after World War I. The agricultural proportion of the population was sixty-nine percent in 1870 and 7.2 percent in 1980.

B. NORDSTROM

Sweden

In Sweden, the consolidation of small holdings began in the eighteenth century and had been virtually completed by the mid-nineteenth century—except in Dalarna and Norrland, where it was considered less practicable. To some degree the consolidation process was offset by the practice of dividing farms among heirs, which continued until the middle of the nineteenth century. Credit banking facilities developed after 1850. As in Denmark, grain crops were central to the commercial side of Swedish agriculture until the last quarter of the century, when foreign competition forced a reorientation toward dairy products and new crops like the sugar beet and the potato. The trends toward specialization and mechanization have continued in the twentieth century. Of all the Scandinavian countries, Sweden has seen the most extensive exodus from rural areas. In 1870, 72 percent of the population was engaged in agriculture; in 1980, 5.5 percent. (*See also* Cooperatives; Emigration, 1825–1930; Enclosure; Inheritance Practices; Landownership; Population: Scandinavia.)

REFERENCES: S. Carlsson, *Bonden i svensk historia*, vol. 3 (Stockholm: Landbruks-förbundets tidskrift AB, 1956); E. Heckscher, *An Economic History of Sweden*, trans. G. Ohlen (Cambridge, Mass.: Harvard University Press, 1954); F. Hodne, *An Economic History of Norway 1815–1970* (a preliminary edition) (Bergen: Tapir, 1975), and *The Norwegian Economy 1920–1980* (New York: St. Martin's, 1983); F. C. Howe, "The Most Complete Agricultural Recovery in History," *The Annals of the American Academy of Political and Social Science* 172 (March 1934): 123–29; E. Jensen, *Danish Agriculture: Its Economic Development* (Copenhagen: J. H. Schultz, 1937); L. Jörberg, "The Nordic Countries 1850–1914," in *The Fontana Economic History of Europe: Emergence of Industrial Societies—2*, M. C.. ed. Cipolla (London: Collins/Fontana, 1973); J. Lieberman, *The Industrialization of Norway 1800–1920* (Oslo: Universitetsforlaget, 1970); H. Lund, "Danish Agriculture," in J. Bukdahl et al., eds., *Scandinavia Past and Present*, vol. 3 (Odense: Edvard Henriksen, 1959); P. Manniche, *Living Democracy in Denmark* (Copenhagen: G. E. C. Gad, 1952); D. S. Thomas, *Social and Economic Aspects of Swedish Population Movements 1750–1933* (New York: Macmillan, 1941); H. Westergaard, *Economic Development in Denmark Before and During the World War* (Oxford: Clarendon Press, 1922); C. Winberg, *Folkökning och proletarisering*(Gothenburg: Department of History, University of Gothenburg, 1975).

B. NORDSTROM

AIRLINES

The emergence of commercial aviation in Scandinavia* in general coincides with worldwide trends in twentieth-century transportation history. Regular airlines were established in the five Nordic countries between 1918 and 1927, with the earliest firms at times operating with only one or two seaplanes. Routes and services increased substantially during the late 1920s and 1930s but were curtailed by the onset of World War II*. Major expansion, including extensive international routes, occurred in the postwar era, and the major Scandinavian airlines, with one exception, shared in the technological transition to the jet age in the late 1950s and 1960s. The three principal Scandinavian air carriers are SAS, Finnair, and Icelandair.

Scandinavian Airlines System (SAS)

Originally formed in 1946 to offer intercontinental service between Europe and North America, SAS is a consortium of the three leading pre-war airlines of Denmark, Norway, and Sweden, namely, Det Danske Luftfartselskab (DDL), Det Norske Luftfartselskab (DNL), and Aktiebolaget Aerotransport (ABA) of Sweden. A fourth airline, Svensk Interkontinental Luftrafik (SILA), continued to operate transatlantic service under its own name for a time, but in 1948 it merged with ABA, the Swedish domestic carrier. By 1951 SAS was responsible for all international and domestic routes under one centralized management. Under the SAS arrangement capital investment, with the original airlines changed to nonoperating holding companies, was structured in the following manner: DDL two-sevenths, DNL two-sevenths, ABA-SILA three-sevenths. State ownership was 50 percent or more in each case.

Prior to the SAS merger, the earlier airlines provided service primarily in the

Scandinavian and European markets. Founded in 1918, DDL began international service to European cities in 1920. DNL, the Norwegian line formed in 1927, offered service to Denmark and Germany beginning in 1928, while ABA began operations in 1924. SILA, by contrast, was formed in 1943 as part of the anticipated transatlantic consortium for which negotiations date back to 1938 and which ultimately resulted in SAS.

SAS is by far the largest of the Scandinavian air carriers, and it is competitive with other major European airlines. The joint Scandinavian airline, for example, currently maintains regular operations to Europe, North and South America, the Far East, Africa, and the Middle East. Moreover, SAS pioneered commercial use of the "Great Circle" route over the Arctic area and North Pole in the 1950s—a route which Charles Lindbergh proved possible with his experimental flights in the early 1930s. By 1980 the SAS fleet consisted of almost 80 aircraft, primarily its main workhorse, the DC-9, as well as nine jumbo jets (747's and DC-10's).

Finnair

Finnair, the national airline of Finland, was established as *Aero O/Y* by private interests in 1923. It began operations to Estonia in 1924 and shortly thereafter initiated service to Sweden. Later, domestic routes in Finland and flights to Germany were developed. Until 1936, *Aero O/Y* routes were flown entirely by seaplanes. After World War II, domestic and international service was reopened, with the Finnish government acquiring over 70 percent control of the airline. It began to operate under the name Finnair in 1951, and this name was formally adopted in 1968. Finnair is small and cautious compared to other major European airlines, but it has slowly met increased demands. Finnair remained outside the SAS cooperative venture, probably, at least in part, because of the country's diplomatic situation vis-a-vis the Soviet Union. It was the first non-Communist airline to introduce service to Moscow (in 1956). It introduced jets in 1960, expanded its European routes, and added service to New York. By 1980 Finnair had a fleet of over 30 aircraft, principally DC-9's and Super Caravelles, with five DC-8's and DC-10's for long-range flights.

Icelandair

Icelandair (Flugleiðer H.F.) is the single airline of Iceland following a 1973–1979 merger of the original Icelandair (Flugfelag Íslands), a domestic and regional carrier, and Icelandic Airlines (Loftleiðer), the international carrier. While there had been limited charter and flight service within Iceland by two earlier firms, both known as Flugfelag Íslands, in 1919–1920 and 1928–1931, they failed due to financial difficulties and storm mishaps with their seaplanes. In 1937 Flugfelag Akureyar was formed in northern Iceland and later reorganized as Flugfelag Íslands H.F. (Icelandair) in 1940. There were no airfields in Iceland until World War II, when British and American air bases were established, including a major facility at Keflavik. These airports allowed expansion of commercial air transportation, and Icelandair developed additional routes in Iceland and to the British Isles and northern Europe.

Loftleiðer, the second airline, was established in 1944 and initially offered domestic and northern European services. In 1952 Loftleiðer began to concentrate on transatlantic service from Europe to New York, offering lower fares by not joining the International Air Transport Association. This competitive move proved successful, despite the utilization of slower aircraft. For example, Loftleiðer did not purchase jet aircraft until 1970, fully a decade behind most transatlantic carriers.

The new Icelandair, a consolidated 20 percent government-owned firm comprised of the two earlier carriers, had a fleet of eleven aircraft in 1980, including three long-range DC-8's and one DC-10.

In addition to the three main Scandinavian airlines, several regional and charter carriers currently maintain operations in Scandinavia, including Cimber A/S and Maersk A/S in Denmark; Braathen's South American and Far East Airtransport and Wideroe's Flyveselskab in Norway; Kar-Air O/Y in Finland; and Linjeflag in Sweden.

REFERENCES: R.E.G. Davies, *A History of the World's Airlines* (London: Oxford University Press, 1964); W. Green, *Observer's World Airlines and Airlines Directory* (New York: Warne, 1975); H. J. Hamar, "Iceland Air: Reorganizing for Future Challenges," in *Atlantica and Iceland Review* 17 (1979): 51–53; *World Airline Record* (Chicago: Roadcap and Associates, 1965); *World Aviation Directory* (New York: Ziff-Davis Publishing Company, 1980).

B. L. LARSON

ALTHING Iceland's parliament

The medieval assembly attended by Iceland's leaders was called the Althing (*alðing*). Each leader was invariably a *goði**, a priest and a chief for a particular group of families. The earliest meetings were held at Kjalarnes, but the first Althing called by that name met at the call of Ulfljot in 930 A.D. by the river Öxara near the mountain Armannsfell. A session of the Althing lasted a fortnight around midsummer. Those attending had to give up their weapons, but they took them back on the session's last day, which therefore was called *vapnatak*.

Refinement of the law and application of it in cases took place not in the Althing, but in an exclusive body of 48 *goðar* called the *lögretta*. The *lögretta* was presided over by the lawspeaker (*lögsögumaðr*), who was the most eminent personage in the commonwealth. He held office for three years, during which time part of his responsibility was to recite the entire law from memory. Among distinguished *lögsögumenn* was Snorri Sturluson*, who was twice elected to that office.

The Althing and its *lögretta* could make rulings on the law, but enforcement depended on the relative power of the *goðar*. Strife among them made the doing of justice uncertain. In hopes of rectifying the situation, allegiance was extended to the king of Norway in 1262.

The king reorganized the Althing in 1271 and 1281, giving himself the power to appoint 84 lifetime members, of which 36 would be picked each year to sit in the *lögretta*. His attempt to restrict membership in the Althing failed, as all Icelandic leaders felt drawn to assemble at midsummer as before.

The Althing in its thirteenth-century form survived for five centuries. During that time Iceland and Norway came under the rule of kings of Denmark, who, especially after 1660, governed by administrative fiat. The Althing was allowed to atrophy. In 1800 it was abolished by decree.

Christian VIII*, shortly after granting assemblies to his Danish domains, bestowed an assembly on Iceland in 1843. It was given the venerable name "Althing," though it was meant to be a purely consultative body. No sooner had it convened than its members began to ask for real powers. In 1874 the king promulgated a constitution giving the Althing authority to legislate on Iceland's internal affairs, though not without the safeguard of a royal veto.

The Althing was made an assembly of 36 members, 30 of whom were to be elected by voters who were heads of households and 6 of whom were to be the king's appointees. The Althing's members, once assembled, were to divide themselves (in the manner of the Norwegian Storting*) into two chambers: the "upper part" (Efri Dield) of 12 members, 6 of whom were the royal appointees, and the "nether part" (Neðri Dield) of 24 members. It was thought that this arrangement would assure the Althing the benefits of bicameralism.

Calls for more home rule and more democracy followed. Substantial reform took place in 1903, when Christian IX's* chief minister for Iceland was posted in Reykjavik and the Althing was conceded the power to approve or disapprove of the continuance in office of the ministers responsible for their internal affairs. The parliamentary principle was thus accepted.

The right to vote in Althing elections was extended in 1915 to all adults at age 25. Iceland was among the first to adopt women's suffrage.* The voting age later was reduced to 21 (in 1944), 20 (1967), and 18 (1983). Through all the years the electoral system featured a combination of single-member districts and proportional representation, multi-member districts.

With parliamentarism and popular elections firmly established, the modern version of the Althing became the object of contention among political parties. Until 1916 liberal and conservative parties were the main rivals. Then the Progressive Party (Framsóknarflokkurinn), which was essentially agrarian, took form, and the two older parties united to form the Independence Party (Sjálfstaeðisflokkurinn). The Social Democratic Party (Alþýðuflokkurinn) also took form, as did the Communist Party, which eventually was absorbed by the People's Alliance* (Alþýðubandalagið). Other parties appeared from time to time, including the Women's Group in 1983. The multitude of parties made one-party majorities in the Althing virtually unattainable and made coalition governments routine.

After Iceland became a republic in 1944 a popularly elected president rather than the king became responsible for convening the Althing and, in the event of a vote of no confidence in the government (i.e., the prime minister and the cabinet), for dissolving the Althing. The president was given a qualified veto of Althing enactments. His veto could be overruled when the enactment was approved again by the Althing and upheld in a popular referendum.

The term of the Althing as set by the constitution is four years, but it tends in practice to be shorter as governments fall, necessitating new elections. When a new Althing convenes, the dominant party coalition determines who becomes prime minister. An Althing selects three sets of presiding officers, one each for the upper house, the lower house, and the Althing as a whole.

An enduring source of controversy has been the mode of election to the Althing. Some Icelandic leaders have preferred more use of single-member districts, while others have sought more use of proportional representation. Single-member and two-member districts, which were to the advantage of regional and rural interests, used to predominate. The reform law of 1959, which emerged as a compromise, increased the size of the Althing to 60 seats (20 upper house and 40 lower house) and divided the country into eight multi-member districts, of which five elected 5 representatives each, two elected 6 each, and one elected 12. Eleven continued to be elected at large, as before. A similar constitutional reform in 1983 raised the membership to 63.

REFERENCES: E. Arnórsson, *Rettarsaga Alþingis* (Reykjavik: Alþingissögunefnd, 1945); K. Gunnar, *Fra endurskoðun til valtysku* (Reykjavik: Menningarsjoð, 1972); I. Johannesson, *Alþingi og atvinnumalin* (Reykjavik: Alþingissögunefnd, 1948); J. Johannesson, *A History of the Old Icelandic Commonwealth* (Winnipeg: University of Manitoba Press, 1974); D. E. Neuchterlein, *Iceland: Reluctant Ally* (Ithaca, N.Y.: Cornell University Press, 1961).

B. L. HANSON

ÄLVSBORG Swedish fortress at the mouth of the Göta River

Located within the present city of Gothenburg*, Älvsborg dates from the fourteenth century as an important fortification guarding Sweden's "window" on the Sound. (Until the mid-seventeenth century, Sweden controlled only a small finger of territory which was sandwiched between Danish-controlled Bohuslän and Halland.) The fortress and the area it protected changed hands frequently in the struggles between Denmark and Sweden until the mid-seventeenth century, and it was twice (following the Northern Seven Years' War and the Kalmar War) ransomed back to Sweden. For much of the seventeenth century it was the key to the protection of Gothenburg, which was founded by Karl IX* between 1600 and 1606. During the 1630s and 1640s the fortress was strengthened. It was razed and a new fort (Nya Älvsborg/Nya Elfsborg) was completed in 1670.

REFERENCES: *DSH*, vols. 3–5; *SU*, vol. 32.

B. NORDSTROM

ANDRÉE, SALOMON AUGUST (18 October 1854–? October 1897) Swedish engineer and balloonist

Salomon August Andrée, Nils Strindberg, and Knut Fraenkel made a dramatic but unsuccessful attempt to reach the North Pole by gas balloon in 1897. In the ill-fated mission all three men lost their lives. Andrée, leader of the expedition, was born at Grenna in Småland, the son of a chemist and apothecary. He received an engineering degree from the Royal Institute of Technology in 1873. Thereafter, he worked briefly in industry; visited the United States during the 1876 Centennial Exhibition in Philadelphia, where he met American balloonist John Wise; and then became assistant professor at a technical school in Sweden. During 1882–1883, Andrée joined a Swedish meteorological expedition at Spitsbergen as observer of atmospheric electricity; thereafter, in 1884, he was appointed chief engineer of the Swedish Patent Office and also held a professor's chair in Stockholm*.

Andrée's ballooning began in 1893, and subsequently his plans for the North Pole flight took shape. Aided by the Swedish Academy of Sciences, Andrée made preparations for an 1896 launch from Spitsbergen. The party's hydrogen balloon, named "Eagle" (Ornen) and made by Lachambre in Paris, had a capacity of over 160,000 cubic feet and was constructed of silk. Unfavorable winds delayed the departure of the expedition until the following year. Meanwhile, Andrée met Norwegian explorer Fridtjof Nansen*, who had just completed the first polar sea crossing aboard his vessel *Fram* (*see*Arctic Exploration).

On 11 July 1897, Andrée, Strindberg, and Fraenkel began their ascent from Danes Island in the Spitsbergen archipelago toward the Pole, but they were forced down within three days. Icing conditions on the balloon and the loss of guide ropes negated any chance of success. Using sledges and other equipment, but poorly clothed, the three explorers journeyed for three months over the Arctic ice, working their way to White Island, at the eastern end of the Spitsbergen chain. There they died, of trichinosis according to the Danish doctor E. A. Tryde, contracted by eating diseased polar bear meat, according to others of asphixiation. Except for early carrier pigeon messages and buoys, no signs from the Andrée party were found until 1930, when a Norwegian ship came upon the remains of their camp on White Island. Andrée's dairy, which ended in October 1897, and Fraenkel's meteorological observations, as well as film and other equipment from the expedition, were recovered and provide a remarkable record of the flight and the struggle to survive on the ice. The explorers' bodies were returned to Sweden for burial and posthumous honors as national heroes. Despite its failure, the Andrée expedition initiated an age of aerial discovery in the Arctic.

In addition to being a topic of scholarly studies, the expedition has been the subject of both documentary fiction and film, namely, in Per Olof Sudman's *Flight of the Eagle* and the film of the same title directed by Jan Troell.

REFERENCES: J. Grierson, *Challenge to the Poles: Highlights of Arctic and Antarctic Aviation* (Hamden, Conn.: Archon Books, 1964); R. T. Kahn, "A Swedish Film Re-Creates a Daring Flight That Failed," *Smithsonian* 14:2 (May 1983): 122–36; P. O. Sudman, *The Flight of the Eagle* (New York: Pantheon Books, 1967); Swedish Society for Anthropology and Geography, *Andrée's Story: The Complete Record of His Polar Flight, 1897* (Stockholm and New York, 1930).

B. L. LARSON

ANSGAR (801–865 A.D.) Archbishop of Hamburg-Bremen and ninth-century missionary to Sweden

Ansgar was a Benedictine monk from Corbie (northern France) who was sent as the first missionary to Scandinavia*. He was at the newly Christianized court of the Danish king Harald in 826, and three years later he made his way to Birka*, Sweden. His mission was successful, and Ansgar was appointed archbishop of Hamburg-Bremen, a center for the Christianization of northern Europe.

After Ansgar left Sweden, the pagan king Olof came to the throne and hostility toward missionaries grew. In spite of a second visit by Ansgar in 852, the new faith was resisted until the end of the tenth century.

Our major source of information about Ansgar is the *Vita Anskarii*, which was written by Rimbert in the 870s (most recent edition: G. Waitz, 1884). Rimbert accompanied Ansgar on his second mission to Birka and later succeeded him as archbishop of Hamburg-Bremen.

REFERENCES: Rimbert, *Anskar, the Apostle of the North 801–865*, trans. C. H. Robinson (London: Society for the Propagation of the Gospel in Foreign Parts, 1921).

M. EMELITY

ANTARCTIC EXPLORATION

The Antarctic is the earth's coldest, most southerly geographical region. The continent was not discovered until 1819–1820. Inland exploration did not begin for another 80 years, and the continent's limits were not fully defined until the mid-twentieth century. Most of Antarctica still has been seen only from the air. Geographic and scientific discovery motivated some of the early explorers, but economic interests led most to Antarctica in the nineteenth century as they probed more southerly hunting areas for whales and seals.

A Norwegian pioneering Antarctic whaling reconnaissance of 1892–1893 was led by C. A. Larsen. He collected fossils on Seymour Island, off the Antarctic Peninsula, and discovered Foyn Coast and penetrated Weddell Sea. The following season he returned to make more discoveries. At the same time, Norwegians Morten Pedersen and C. J. Evensen, aboard the *Castor* and *Hertha*, sighted Adelaide Island as they cruised near the peninsula. On 24 January 1895, a Norwegian reconnaissance for Svend Foyn's whaling company, led by Henrik Bull and Leonard Kristensen, aboard *Antarctic*, made the first landing on the continent at Cape Adare, Victoria Land. Norwegian Antarctic whaling and sealing activity continued for over 40 years, and as a result a number of geographic discoveries were made, coastlines charted, and anchorages identified. At times the whaling operations even supported purely scientific expeditions (e.g., Captain Nilsen's logistical assistance in 1928–1929 of the first Byrd expedition from the *C. A. Larsen*). The years 1930–1931 were particularly significant for the numerous Antarctic geographic finds by Norwegian whalers. These, combined with sightings by other Scandinavians, were later used to substantiate Norwegian sovereignty claims over Bouvet and Peter I Islands and Queen Maud Land.

A Norwegian established the precedent for onshore expeditions. C. E. Borchgrevinck, after sailing with Bull, returned to Cape Adare aboard the *Southern Cross* and with British support led the first expedition that planned to winter on the continent (1899–1900). A broad range of scientific exploration was conducted. He proved man could exist there in a semi-permanent base camp. The Sixth International Geographical Congress (1895) provided the impetus for Borchgrevinck's Antarctic expedition, as well as one from Sweden (1901). Otto Nordenskjöld, with C. A. Larsen commanding the *Antarctic*, established a shore base on Snow Hill Island from which extensive mapping and scientific research was done. Another party from this expedition was stranded at Hope Bay in 1901, and a third faced a forced wintering in another part of Antarctica after its ship sank in 1903. All three parties were rescued by an Argentine vessel in 1904, after a trying but fruitful three years. The Swedish Magellan Expedition, led by Carl Skottsberg, visited Antarctica during this period (1907–1909) and spent some time at South Georgia.

A Norwegian, Roald Amundsen, who had been with the first expedition to winter (unintentionally) in the Antarctic, when the Gerlache Belgian expedition vessel *Belgica* was beset in the pack ice (1897–1899), led his own expedition in 1910–1912. His group achieved one of the premier exploits of polar traverse. In an apparent contest with Robert Falcon Scott's British Antarctic Expedition, he left his Framheim station at the Bay of Whales and, with four others in the party, became the first to reach the South Pole (14 December 1911). Scott's party arrived at the Pole a month later, but the entire group died of starvation and exposure on the route back. An enormous sympathetic reaction to Scott's death in Britain and elsewhere overshadowed Amundsen's triumph.

Norwegian Lars Christensen promoted six Antarctic explorations between 1927 and 1937, during which extensive scientific studies and charting were accomplished. With leaders such as Ola Olstad, Hjalmar Riiser-Larsen, Gunnar Isachsen, and Christensen, they were among the first to use the airplane for Antarctic exploration and mapping.

In the period immediately after World War II*, three Antarctic expeditions were mounted under Scandinavian leadership. Holger Halgersen, abroad *Brategg*, made landings on Peter I Island and Deception Island (1947–1948) to conduct geological and zoological studies. At the same time, Norwegian-born and educated Finn Ronne, then a U.S. military officer, directed the last non-governmental expedition to Antarctica and established Oleana Base on Stonington Island. A Norwegian-British-Swedish Antarctic expedition, headed by John Gaiever (1949–1952), worked with aircraft from Maudheim in Queen Maud Land. This was the first international Antarctic expedition, and it helped to inaugurate a pattern of multi-national cooperation in polar research that became the hallmark of the International Geophysical Year (IGY) (1957–1958).

Norway (1960) and Denmark (1965) are signers of the Antarctic Treaty, the international agreement governing activities below 65°S latitude. Norway maintained a research station in Antarctica from 1957 to 1960 and since then has sponsored several more expeditions.

Scandinavians also were valuable members of the pre-IGY Antarctic expeditions from other nations. Most notable was pioneer aviator Bernt Balchen. He was a pilot in the first plane to overfly the South Pole on 28–29 November 1929 (First Byrd Antarctic Expedition).

Scandinavians continue to participate with other national research expeditions to the Antarctic, and the Norsk Polarinstitutt is one of the leading centers for polar research.

REFERENCES: L. P. Kirwan, *A History of Polar Expeditions* (New York: W. W. Norton, 1960); H. R. Mill, *The Siege of the South Pole* (London: Alston Rivers, 1905); Paul-Emile Victor, *Man and the Conquest of the Poles* (London: Hamish Hamilton, Ltd., 1964).

H. VOGEL

ARCTIC EXPLORATIONS

Arctic expeditions have been motivated by interest in geographic discovery, economic rewards, the opening of better trade routes (Northwest and Northeast Passages), intentions to establish sovereignty, adventure (e.g., reaching the North Pole), and scientific investigation.

As early as the late ninth century, Scandinavians were exploring the Arctic. By the eighteenth century, Danes and Norwegians already had colonized (or recolonized) Arctic territories and thereafter gained reputations, along with Swedish explorers, as dedicated, courageous, and inventive discoverers and scientists in the harsh Arctic environment. Explorers from Scandinavia* penetrated all the Arctic's sectors, including northern Russia, upper Canada, Alaska, and northern Europe. They had their greatest impact in and around Greenland*. Their involvement has continued down to the present.

Vikings* penetrated the high Arctic in the ninth century. Ingólfr Arnarson* established a permanent settlement on Iceland in 874, and in 930 Iceland became the first New World republic. Eirik the Red, banished from Iceland, discovered (or rediscovered) Greenland*, where a permanent colony had been established by 990. In the early eleventh century Leif Eiriksson and others, sailing from Greenland, may have sighted and landed on Baffin Island, Labrador, and Newfoundland. A seasonal settlement may have been briefly established in North America. Also, the settlers on Greenland clearly conducted regular expeditions into the Arctic regions north of their settlements. The Greenland colony mysteriously vanished sometime in the fourteenth century, but Scandinavian presence there was re-established by Denmark in 1721 as the result of an expedition headed by Hans Paulsen Egede.

Lt. W. A. Graah initiated the nineteenth-century Scandinavian exploration of Greenland with an expedition in 1828–1831. This exploration of Greenland would intensify in the latter part of the century with a number of other Danish, Norwegian, and Swedish explorers and scientists. Norwegians Fridtjof Nansen* and Otto Sverdrup became the first to cross the Greenland ice cap (1888–1889).

Nansen's greatest contribution to Arctic exploration was his drift in 1893–1896 aboard *Fram* in an attempt to cross the North Pole. Though he covered much of the Arctic Ocean above Russia and Europe, he never reached the Pole. He left the vessel and its crew under Sverdrup and attempted, with Hjalmar Johansen, to sledge to the top of the world. This attempt also failed, but the two did set a record for the time by reaching 86° 04'N. Nansen and Johansen then wintered on Franz Josef Land, met the British expedition under Frederick Jackson and Alfred Harmsworth (Lord Northcliff), and were taken back to Norway to arrive at almost the same time as the *Fram*. Sverdrup commanded the *Fram* on its second Arctic expedition (1898–1902). He focused on scientific research and made major land discoveries in the vicinity of Ellesmere, Canada.

After an unsuccessful attempt in 1896, Swedish scientist and airman Salomon August Andrée*, using a specially made balloon, the *Eagle*, made history's first serious attempt to fly to the North Pole. The expedition left from Danes Island, Spitsbergen but came down three days later on ice east of the island. Andrée's remains, along with those of his colleagues, were found in 1930. Some accounts argue they had all been asphixiated by fumes from a defective primus stove; others claim they died of trichinosis while attempting to trek back to civilization.

The twentieth century has seen more geographic discoveries, the solidification of territorial claims (e.g., Denmark was awarded Greenland in 1933), more sophisticated natural, physical, and social science investigations, and continued efforts to penetrate these hostile regions. Mylius-Ericksen's *Danmark* expedition to Greenland (1906–1908) was one of the most tragic scientific expeditions in this century, though it nevertheless was productive. Among the expedition's more prominent members were Alfred Wegener, J. P. Koch, and Peter Freuchen. Three of its members, including the leader, did not survive. Knud Rasmussen joined with Mylius-Ericksen in 1902–1904 to study Cape York Eskimo culture. Rasmussen returned on seven more expeditions to expand his wealth of ethnographic knowledge. His sixth ''Thule Expedition,'' as his series of ventures was called, covered the entire length of Arctic North America in a phenomenal traverse that took three and a half years. Einar Mikkelsen, J. P. and Lauge Koch, and Thakel Mathiassen were other Danes who made extensive efforts in the investigation of the Arctic region and its peoples.

The most important twentieth-century Arctic explorer from Scandinavia was the Norwegian Roald Amundsen. He became the first to conquer the Northwest Passage (1903–1906), when he transited a route from Europe to Alaska in the small ship, the *Gjøa*. From 1918 to 1925 he tried another drift expedition to the North Pole. Using a successor ship to the *Fram*, the *Maud*, he conducted commendable scientific work, but also failed to float over the Pole. He later attempted the first flight over the North Pole in a fixed-wing aircraft. Convinced that this could be done, he launched a two-plane expedition from Spitsbergen in 1925.

Although he was forced down in the Arctic Ocean, he came closer than anyone at that time to reaching the Pole by air. The following year he and American Richard E. Byrd separately tried again from Kings Bay. Byrd was successful and was followed a few days later by Amundsen, with Umberto Nobile and others, in an airship (*Norge*). Their airship continued on from the Pole and landed at Teller, Alaska (14 May 1926). Though second over the Pole, Amundsen was the first to cross the Arctic Ocean completely by air. In 1928 he perished in the Arctic while searching for the downed airship *Italia*, which crashed during a North Pole flight.

Today, Arctic scientific expeditions from Scandinavia continue. Primary emphasis is upon Greenland and Spitsbergen.

REFERENCES: *DSH*, vol. 13; J. G. Hayes, *The Conquest of the North Pole* (New York: Macmillan Co., 1934); J. Mirsky, *To the Arctic* (New York: A. A. Knopf, 1948); *NH*, vol. 12.

H. VOGEL

ARI ÞORGILSSON (1068–1148) Icelandic historian

Ari Þorgilsson (the Wise) is known as the father of Icelandic history; he was the first to write vernacular narrative prose in Iceland. Ari was raised in southwest Iceland and was ordained a priest.

The only surviving work by Ari is *Íslendingabók* (*Book of the Icelanders*). The book, written 1122–1132, is a somewhat arbitrary collection of facts about Icelandic history from 870 to 1120, which Ari acquired mainly from oral sources. His description of the Conversion* (1000) is especially detailed and dramatic.

Ari had great influence on later Icelandic authors of sagas and histories, such as Snorri Sturluson*. Modern scholars think this influence must be due in part to other works by Ari which have since been lost, but they have no certain proof. We have references to an earlier Icelandic history, and Ari may have assisted in compiling *Landnámabók* (*Book of Settlements*), the history of the settlement of Iceland.

REFERENCES: Ari Thorgilsson, *The Book of the Icelanders*, ed. and trans. H. Hermannsson, in *Islandica* 20 (1930; repr. New York: Kraus, 1979); G. Turville-Petre, *Origins of Icelandic Literature* (Oxford: Clarendon Press, 1953).

M. EMELITY

AUGSBURG CONFESSION (Latin: *Augustana*)

The *Augsburg Confession* was intended as a confession of Christian faith and a defense of historic Christian doctrine. Drawn up by Philip Melanchthon, it was signed by nine evangelical princes and city councils of the Holy Roman Empire at the Diet of Worms on 25 June 1530. When it was rejected by the emperor, Charles V, and his Roman Catholic advisors, it became the primary confessional document in the theological structure of Lutheranism*.

In Scandinavia*, a royal edict by Christian III* in 1536 proclaimed Denmark-Norway-Iceland to be a Lutheran realm. The next year, the king requested John

Bugenhagen to come from Wittenberg to draw up an evangelical Church Ordinance. This was accomplished in 1539 and stipulated that every pastor own
several books, among them being a copy of the Apology to the *Augustana*. The
latter presupposed familiarity with the *Augsburg Confession*, though actual ownership of the *Confession* was not specifically mentioned.

When the revised edition of the *Augustana* was published by Melanchthon in
1540, the *Variata* was ardently championed by the leading Danish theologian,
Niels Hemmingsen*. Accused of being a Crypto-Calvinist, Hemmingsen was
dismissed from the Theological Faculty of Copenhagen in 1579 by Frederik II*.
This marked the triumph of the *Unaltered Augsburg Confession* throughout the
Danish realm.

In Sweden-Finland, Gustav I Vasa* led a successful rebellion against the
Kalmar Union* in 1523 and guided his kingdom into the evangelical camp. No
formal subscription to the *Augsburg Confession* was called for until after the
death of Johan III*, when the Church Assembly of Uppsala hastily convened in
1593 to forestall the ascendancy of a Roman Catholic monarch in the person of
Sigismund*. Though Sigismund subscribed to the *Augustana* upon the counsel
of his Jesuit* advisors, the subterfuge was obvious to all and his position in
Sweden became untenable after 1598.

REFERENCES: Trygve R. Skarsten, "The Reception of the Augsburg Confession in
Scandinavia," *The Sixteenth Century Journal* 11:3 (1980): 87–98; Theodore G. Tappert,
ed., *The Book of Concord* (Philadelphia: Fortress Press, 1959).

T. R. SKARSTEN

B

BAPTISTS

Owing primarily to legal barriers, most of the Christian denominations familiar in Scandinavia* today did not arrive there until well into the nineteenth century. The Reformation* reached Sweden in the 1520s and Denmark-Norway during the following decade, but it hardly brought religious toleration. Throughout Scandinavia Lutheranism* was established as the state religion, and no other faiths were tolerated. Royal decrees issued in the seventeenth and eighteenth centuries forbade, in most instances, preaching other than by government-appointed pastors and religious meetings at which none of them was present. Other laws mandated infant baptism, confirmation, and related measures that in effect guaranteed the absolutist Scandinavian governments a firm grasp on national religious life. Stability, it was thought, could be preserved through unity in the spiritual life of the people.

Despite this inhospitable environment, some non-Lutheran denominations began to make tiny inroads in Scandinavia before religious freedom started to unfold. Baptists were among the first nonconformists. In Denmark, the first was a Jewish convert to Christianity, Julius Købner (1806–1884), who had been baptized in Lübeck. He came under the influence of the German Baptist evangelist Johann Gerhard Oncken of Hamburg, who rebaptized him in 1836. Oncken visited Denmark illegally in 1839 and immersed nine additional converts. They formed a congregation in Copenhagen* with an engineer, Peder Christian Mønster, as their minister. The Danish constitution of 1849, which guaranteed religious toleration while preserving the state church, legitimized the hitherto illegal congregation and allowed the denomination to evangelize and proliferate without legal interference. By 1887 it had 2,299 members, a figure which climbed to 3,310 in 1894, and 4,212 in 1914.

In Sweden, a Danish Baptist preacher named E. M. Forster baptized the members of the first congregation in 1848. But the state church and government there resisted free church incursions more firmly than in Denmark. The first

Swede who sought to evangelize as a Baptist in his native land, Fredrik Olaus Nilsson, had been converted while a sailor in the United States. His efforts to bring his new faith back to Sweden led to his deportation in 1850. During the early 1850s, at least several hundred people were arrested and fined for proclaiming Baptist views. Nevertheless, the infant denomination persevered, and by 1860 it numbered approximately 4,500 members in Sweden. A "dissenter law" enacted that year permitted Swedes to transfer their membership from the state church to any legally recognized free church. The Baptists thereupon began to grow rapidly, reaching 37,601 in 552 congregations by 1894.

In Norway, a "dissenter law" of 1845 allowed Norwegians to withdraw from the state church and to organize other Christian denominations. A Danish sailor, Frederik Rymker (1819–1894), came to Norway in 1857 and sought, with limited success, to convert people to the Baptist faith. In the meantime, part of the state church parish at Skien, including its pastor, Gustav Lammers (1802–1878), had seceded in 1856, and one wing, led by Lammers, became baptistic. Some of its members eventually joined a Baptist church there. The first explicitly Baptist congregation, in nearby Porsgrunn, dates from 1860. The denomination initially grew slowly in Norway, probably owing in part to a provision of the dissenter law which forbade anyone under age 19 to leave the state church. Baptist revivalists willingly violated it, however, by immersing younger converts, and as late as the 1880s they were occasionally jailed briefly for doing so. In 1875 there were still only 818 Baptists in Norway, but a liberalization of the dissenter law led to an increase to 4,228 in 1890.

In all three Scandinavian kingdoms, growth slowed markedly after the turn of the century. In 1980 there were slightly over 6,000 Norwegian Baptists and approximately the same number in Denmark. The Pentecostal movement (*see* Pentacostalism) in the twentieth century took a very heavy toll on the Swedish Baptist churches, contributing to a decline from a peak of over 60,000 members to about 20,000 in 1980.

Like most of the other non-Lutheran denominations in Scandinavia, the Baptists initially recruited their members from the working class, especially in growing coastal towns. Since World War II*, however, they have shared unprecedented prosperity, and today the Baptists are socially indistinguishable from most of their countrymen in the state churches.

Seminaries for training pastors were opened in Stockholm*, Christiania (Oslo), and Tølløse, Denmark. All of the Baptist denominations in Scandinavia have active mission fields in central Africa.

REFERENCES: F. Janson, *The Background of Swedish Immigration 1840–1930* (Chicago: University of Chicago Press, 1931), and *Nordisk teologisk uppslagsbok för kyrka och skola* (Lund: Gleerup, 1952–1957).

F. HALE

BERLINGSKE TIDENDE The oldest continuously published newspaper in Denmark

Berlingske Tidende's place in the history of newspapers* in Denmark may be compared to that of *The Times* of London. Its founder, Ernst Heinrich Berling (1708–1750), learned the printing trade in Germany and then established himself in Copenhagen* as printer and publisher. In 1747 he petitioned the crown for the royal privilege to publish a newspaper. The first issue appeared 3 January 1749 in sixteen octavo-sized pages (4 1/4 by 7 1/4 inches). It opened with a three-page poetic homage to King Frederik V*, followed by three pages of foreign news and ten pages of advertisements. It had about 800 subscribers. Foreign news was based largely on translations from German. Berling sought to emphasize Danish affairs. He established a network of provincial correspondents whose material he mixed with reports on court and diplomatic news and business affairs. First called the *Københavnske Danske Post Tidender*, it was published twice a week, on Tuesday and Saturday. By 1800 it had a circulation of 4,000, some of the copies going to the Danish provinces and to Danish-ruled Norway. The end of the Napoleonic Wars, the loss of Norway, and economic crisis reduced the paper's circulation to around 1,000 by the early 1830s. Then, the development of communications, especially the steamship, combined with economic and industrial growth, gradually helped to increase both the frequency of publication and circulation. By 1831 it was published every weekday, and by 1845 it appeared twice a day, the morning edition consisting of advertisements and a little news, and the evening edition emphasizing news rather than ads. (The morning edition became independent in 1881.) Mendel I. Nathanson (1780–1868), an economist and philanthropist, became editor in 1838 and for 21 years put his stamp on the paper's character and outlook. Under his leadership, the paper introduced the feuilleton to Danish journalism, and he promoted the discussion of economic issues. Although he aimed at an elite audience, Nathanson's guidance helped lift the paper's circulation from 1,400 to 9,000 copies, nearly double its nearest competitor. For 150 years, *Berlingske* maintained a close association with the government, both as the place of publication of official announcements, and occasionally as official organ of changing governments. The victory of popular representative government in the 1901 elections helped bring this to an end. Three years later, the government began issuing an official gazette, the *Statstidende*. By this time, the morning *Berlingske* had a daily circulation of 15,000, while the evening paper remained at 9,000. A technical and editorial revival, including the first use of photographs, began in 1913 under editor Christian Gulmann. It contributed to a dramatic increase in circulation (84,000 in 1925, 158,000 in 1939, and 171,000 in 1963). In the late 1970s, mounting wage costs, decreased advertising, and a bitter five-month strike (1977) eroded the capital base of the Berlingske publishing house. In 1982 only the threat of closing the *Berlingske Tidende* could raise $20 million in capital to continue publication of the flagship newspaper.   O. V. JOHNSON

BERNSTORFF, ANDREAS PETER (28 August 1735–21 June 1797) Danish statesman

The son of a substantial land owner and Hanoverian court official, Bernstorff was given a strict religious upbringing before studying in a number of German universities and traveling on a grand tour to Rome, Vienna, Paris, and London. In England he acquired a keen interest in the agricultural reforms being carried out there at the time. Through the influence of his uncle Johan Hartvig Ernst Bernstorff*, Bernstorff entered Danish service in 1758. He served for a time in the German Chancery under his uncle but during the 1760s was mainly concerned with financial administration. He exercised little influence on economic policy; however, during this period he supervised reforms on his uncle's estates in north Zealand, where tenants' holdings were enclosed and their labor services commuted for money rents. The dismissal of J.H.E. Bernstorff in 1770 also led to that of his nephew, who retired to Hamburg and his Mecklenburg estate. After the fall of Johann Friedrich Struensee* in 1772, Bernstorff was recalled to a post in the financial directorate, but in April 1773 he was placed at the head of foreign affairs with a seat on the royal council. He concluded the negotiations with Russia which led to the latter's recognition of Danish sovereignty over the whole of the duchies of Slesvig and Holstein and signed a new Russian alliance in August 1773. This formed the cornerstone of his foreign policy in subsequent years. In September 1778 he proposed to Catherine the Great the formation of a league of armed neutrality to protect neutral shipping from interference by the belligerents during the War of American Independence. Catherine rejected the proposal at this stage but in 1780 invited Denmark to join an alliance of a very similar kind. Bernstorff agreed to do so in July. At the same time, however, he concluded a convention with Britain which, by defining contraband more precisely, was designed to avoid conflict with that country. Bernstorff's relations with the ruling junta led by Ove Høegh-Guldberg had long been strained because of his opposition to the kind of cabinet government favored by the latter, and his enemies used the agreement with Britain to bring about his dismissal in November. He retired to Holstein and Mecklenburg.

Bernstorff played no part in the coup d'etat which toppled Guldberg in 1784 and established a government of reformers under the young crown prince (later King Frederik VI*), but he had been in close contact with those who led it and was recalled to Copenhagen to resume control of foreign policy. Until his death, during a period when the status of the Danish peasant was transformed and many other important social and economic changes took place, Bernstorff was in all essential respects first minister of the realm. While others were responsible for the character of the reforms that were carried out, his support was essential for their successful implementation in the face of strong conservative opposition. In 1788, when Gustav III* of Sweden attacked Russia, Bernstorff fulfilled Denmark's treaty obligations to the latter by sending an army into western Sweden from Norway, but he limited participation in the war as much as possible and readily agreed to an armistice arranged by the British envoy, which lasted until peace came in 1790. The outbreak of the French Revolutionary Wars in 1793 revived the problem of interference with neutral trade, and in March 1794 Bernstorff overcame his deep-seated antagonism to Sweden by concluding an armed neutrality alliance with her, while at the same time, as in 1780, trying to avoid giving offense to Britain. He was created a Danish count in 1767 and married twice, to two sisters, the countesses Stolberg.

REFERENCES: *DBL*, vol. 2; *DH*, vols. 9, 10; W. F. Reddaway, "Denmark under the Bernstorffs and Struensee," in *CMH*, vol. 6.

S. P. OAKLEY

BERNSTORFF, JOHAN HARTVIG ERNST (13 May 1712–18 February 1772) Danish statesman

Johan Hartvig Ernst Bernstorff was born in Hanover, where his maternal grandfather Andreas Gottlieb Bernstorff was leading minister of the elector (from 1714 King George I of England). After studying with his elder brother in Tübingen, the two set off on an extended grand tour through western and southern Europe, in the course of which Bernstorff made many valuable contacts. After his return in 1731, he entered Danish state service and as early as 1733 undertook his first diplomatic mission, to Saxony. After a number of other embassies to German courts, his talents were rewarded in 1743 with the embassy to France, with which Denmark had just concluded the first of a series of alliances. Bernstorff remained there for six years, during which he led a full (and expensive) social life, without, however, losing the serious moral purpose and religious piety with which he had grown up. In 1751 he was recalled to Copenhagen* to become head of the German Chancery, a position which gave him control of Danish foreign policy for the next nineteen years.

Denmark had been at peace since the end of the Great Northern War* in 1720, but while Bernstorff undoubtedly appreciated the benefits which neutrality could bring to Danish commerce, the avoidance of conflict was not the leading principle of his policy, as has been claimed in the past. He was quite willing to risk war in defense of what he regarded as the country's legitimate interests. In 1756 he concluded an agreement with Sweden to protect their trade against interference by the belligerents in the Seven Years' War, which had just broken out, and the following year he helped to mediate the Convention of Klosterzeven by which his native Hanover was temporarily neutralized. But in May 1758 he concluded a new alliance with France in order to protect Denmark against Russia. The threat from the latter became a reality in 1762, when the new tsar, Peter III, prepared to launch an attack in pursuance of his claims to the parts of the duchy of Slesvig belonging to the house of Gottorp that had been occupied by the Danes since 1721. Peter was murdered before fighting broke out, but the crisis had revealed to Bernstorff the limits to the protection afforded by the French alliance, and in 1765 he concluded an alliance with Peter's successor, Catherine (the Great). By this a peaceful settlement of the Gottorp dispute was promised and both countries committed themselves to act against any attempt to increase royal power in Sweden. The accession of King Christian VII* the following year weakened Bernstorff's position. Critics, jealous of his power, accused him of tying Denmark too closely to Russia, with which, however, he concluded a fresh alliance in 1769. In September 1770, after an unsuccessful naval expedition against the pirate base of Algiers, he was dismissed. He retired to his wife's estates in Holstein and died in Hamburg.

Bernstorff was from 1752 to 1767 a leading member of the College of Commerce and as such exercised a powerful influence on Denmark's economic policy; this followed an orthodox mercantilist line, attempting to encourage the development of industry through subsidies and controls. Of more lasting benefit was the support he gave to the reforms carried out by his nephew Andreas Peter Bernstorff* on his estates in north Zealand. He was a great admirer of French culture, but while he never learned Danish, he gave encouragement to a number of young Danish writers and was responsible for attracting foreigners such as the German poet Klopstock to Copenhagen. He was created a Danish count in 1767.

REFERENCES: *DBL*, vol. 2; *DH*, vol. 9; W. F. Reddaway, "Denmark under the Bernstorffs and Struensee," in *CMH*, vol. 6, and "Struensee and the Fall of Bernstorff," *English Historical Review* 27 (1912): 274–86.

S. P. OAKLEY

BIBLE SOCIETIES

The Scandinavian Bible societies all date from the early years of the nineteenth century and must be seen in the context of the revivalism and rising rates of literacy and lay leadership in the Scandinavian state churches at that time. Moreover, in each case they owe their inception and early growth to an international movement of great proportions to distribute the Bible to the masses.

Various organizations had distributed Christian literature on both sides of the Atlantic during the seventeenth and eighteenth centuries. A watershed was the formation of the British and Foreign Bible Society (BFBS) in 1804. More or less analogous societies came into being in Switzerland in 1804, Ireland in 1806, Scotland in 1809, Russia in 1812, the United States (the American Bible Society) in 1816, France in 1818, and several other countries. Many of these owed their existence partly to financial support from the groundbreaking British body.

Denmark provides a case of direct British influence. In 1804 a Scotsman, Ebenezer Henderson, and an Englishman, John Paterson, visited the country seeking passage to missionary posts in India. Both were members of the BFBS and arranged for support of an updated Icelandic translation of the New Testament. Conflicts between the United Kingdom and Denmark during the Napoleonic Wars forced them to leave the country, but Henderson returned to Copenhagen* in 1812 and worked for the founding of what became the Danish Bible Society two years later. Though personally inspired by low-church British revivalism, Henderson cooperated with the Lutheran state church, then the only legally recognized religious body in Denmark.

Paterson, meanwhile, had begun to work in Sweden, where his chief contacts were pastors and laymen of the Lutheran state church who had been influenced by Pietism. Owing largely to Paterson's efforts, they organized in 1808 the

Evangeliska Sällskapet, or Evangelical Society. It received support from the BFBS and vigorously distributed tracts and Bibles as well as segments of the latter. It published an edition of the New Testament in 1810 and the entire Bible two years later. Local Bible societies formed around this time coalesced as the Swedish Bible Society in 1815.

The first chairman of the Swedish Bible Society, Mathias Rosenblad (1758–1847), visited Norway in 1814, shortly after Denmark ceded the country to Sweden. He convinced the Swedish crown prince to subsidize the founding of the Norwegian Bible Society, which was constituted in 1816. The BFBS also contributed to it. Its first publication was Martin Luther's *Small Catechism*. In 1820 the society began to distribute its edition of the New Testament.

The Scandinavian Bible societies had considerable success in distributing free or inexpensive religious literature during the nineteenth century, nearly meeting the demand heightened by the population explosion and rising literacy rates. The availability of the Scriptures in many homes probably contributed to the religious revivals seen in all of the Scandinavian lands during the early and middle years of the century. The societies have continued to coordinate translation and distribution of the Scriptures, and all remain active today. They are members of the international United Bible Societies, formed in England in 1946. Through it they help to distribute the Bible in countries where it is less accessible than in lands where Christianity has long been a widespread religion.

REFERENCES: *Nordisk teologisk uppslagsbok för kyrka och skola* (Lund: Gleerup, 1952–1957).

F. HALE

BIRGITTA (Birgitta Birgersdatter) (1302/3?–23 July 1373) Swedish saint

Birgitta was in many respects the most important woman of fourteenth-century Sweden and the only Swede to earn an international reputation in the Middle Ages. During her long life, she made a mark on political events, religious and monastic development, literature, and language. Through her direct involvement with the royal family in Sweden, her revelations and the letters they produced—in which she advised and admonished her contemporaries—she attempted to influence events and left a permanent body of literature that tells us much about her and the world in which she lived.

Birgitta was the daughter of Birger and Ingeborg Persson. Her father was the *lagman* (chief judge) of Uppland. Through her mother she was related to the royal Yngling line. She had her first religious vision when she was only a child and was determined to devote her life to God, but when she was 13 she was married to Ulf Gudmarsson, son of the *lagman* of Östergötland. Just over two years later, she had the first of her eight children. Until the late 1330s she led a life typical of a wealthy and important woman of her age. Her husband became *lagman* of Närke and an advisor to King Magnus Eriksson*. Birgitta became a lady-in-waiting to the queen, Blanche of Namur. From this position she sought to turn the royal couple away from their worldliness and to affect the king's policies and actions.

In 1339 she and her husband made a pilgrimage to the shrine of St. Olaf at Nidaros/Trondheim, shortly thereafter the couple visited Compostella in Spain. These events marked a turning point for them, as they resolved to commit their lives to the Church. Ulf, however, died in 1343. Birgitta then turned away from her previous life. She lived for several years at the monastery at Alvastra. She had more and more visions, which led to increased admonitions of the king and an attempt to persuade the kings of France and England to end the Hundred Years' War. In her visions she saw Christ, Mary, or one of the saints. She regarded these revelations as direct communications of the Word of God, and she believed she was to be God's spokesperson. Her most vehement attacks fell on the king, whom she accused of laxness, ingenuousness, and homosexuality. She urged him to repent and to change his ways, but her efforts brought few results. She may have been influential in persuading Magnus to undertake a crusade in the eastern Baltic; but this crusade, which Birgitta hoped would focus on conversion, came to focus more on conflict with Russia and turned into a defeat for the Swedes. Also, in 1346 Birgitta won from the royal couple the donation of the estate at Vadstena on the shores of Lake Vättern for the founding of a new convent-monastery. The order that eventually took root there, the Birgittines, was a double house in which monks and nuns worked together. Birgitta wrote the rule for the order, and it was approved by Pope Urban V in 1370. The Birgittines spread through Scandinavia* and reached Germany, France, Spain, Italy, and Britain.

In 1349, perhaps for political reasons, Birgitta left Sweden. She never returned. She spent most of the remaining 34 years of her life in Italy, where she continued to experience her revelations and to dictate these to her confessor and secretary, who translated them into Latin. Often her revelations told her to go to or to write someone about specific religious or political problems. Her contacts were extensive. She worked to end the Babylonian Captivity, attacked the worldliness of the secular and monastic clergy, and meddled in the politics of Sweden (where she encouraged the revolt against Magnus in 1361–1362), Rome, the Empire, and Sicily. At the same time, she ministered to the sick and poor, and a number of miracles were attributed to her. Her reputation and popularity, along with her unpopularity, grew.

In 1372 she made her final pilgrimage, this time to the Holy Land. Shortly after her return to Rome in 1373 she became ill and died. Her remains were taken back to Sweden and buried at Vadstena in 1374. She was canonized, largely as a result of the efforts of her daughter (Saint) Catherine, in 1391.

Her lasting importance lies largely in her revelations. Nearly 700 in number (seven volumes), they form a body of literature that serves as a basis for our understanding of the religious mystic in the medieval world.

REFERENCES: *Bonniers Lexikon*, vol. 2; J. Jorgensen, *Saint Bridget of Sweden*, 2 vols., trans. I. Lund (London: Longmans, 1954); *KLNM*, vol. 1.

B. NORDSTROM

BIRKA Viking* trade center in Sweden, active c. 800–975

The town of Birka was situated on the island of Björkö in Lake Mälar in east-central Sweden. From approximately 800 to 975, Birka was an important link between Old Uppsala* and the sea. The merchants traded with Frisians to the west (Dorestad) and Russians to the east (Kiev), as well as with the other Scandinavian countries.

Two contemporary records attest to the importance of Birka: the biography of Ansgar* and Adam of Bremen's* history of the bishops of Hamburg. The thousands of rich grave finds and remains of a town on Björkö support the literary evidence. Birka appears to have been abandoned around 975, perhaps as a result of Danish attacks or a change in trade route. Baltic trade was then assumed by Gotland, while Sigtuna handled Scandinavian trade, and Hedeby* (Slesvig) controlled trade with northern Europe.

REFERENCES: J. Brøndsted, *The Vikings*, trans. Kalle Skov (Harmondsworth, Middlesex: Penguin Books, 1965); P. Foote and D. Wilson, *The Viking Achievement* (London: Sidgwick and Jackson, 1970).

M. EMELITY

BOSTRÖM, ERIK GUSTAF (11 February 1842–21 February 1907) Swedish landed proprietor, politician, and prime minister

Erik G. Boström was born in Stockholm*. His uncle was C. J. Boström (1797–1866), a renowned philosopher. From his mother Boström inherited an aristocratic estate. He studied at Uppsala University from 1861 to 1863. From 1870 to 1890 he was a leader of the Stockholmläns *landsting* and served as vice chairperson from 1884 to 1887 and subsequently as chair from 1888 to 1890 and again in 1901.

Boström was a representative in the Second Chamber of the Riksdag* from 1876 to 1893 and was head of the Riksbank Committee in 1878–1879. In 1894 he entered the First Chamber of the parliament and was chosen chair of the Riksbank Committee of that chamber in 1902.

In 1888 the Lantmannapartiet split, mainly over the question of protectionism, and Boström, along with A. P. Danielson, co-founded the New Ruralist Party. From 1891 to 1900 Boström was prime minister and advocated protectionist policies. When he took over the cabinet, protectionists held a majority in the Upper Chamber, but the Lower Chamber was split equally among the New Ruralists (largely rural and urban protectionists) and Old Ruralists (rural free traders), and the Centrists (urban free traders). An admirer of Bismarck, Boström viewed himself as an "honest broker" maintaining independence from all political groups in order to play one off against another. As a result, he frequently shuffled his ministers.

During his first ministry in the 1890s, Boström cemented an alliance between the upper class and agrarian interests by increasing the level of import duties on industrial products, by supporting an amendment in order to place a ceiling on the relative strength of urban representation in the Lower House, and, in 1892, by obtaining a defense agreement. In this agreement, a compromise was worked out by Boström whereby the training time for army recruits would be increased to 90 days, but the cost of recruiting and maintaining the soldiers would be transferred from the farmers to the government. There would also be a gradual abolition of the land tax. In the 1890s increased tensions with Russia as a result of Alexander III's infringements on Finnish autonomy prompted the Swedes to look at military preparedness more seriously. Boström was particularly concerned about protecting and developing Norrland. As a result, Boström spearheaded the construction of a railway from Boden near the Gulf of Bothnia to the Norwegian border. In the 1890s he also was able to improve rather significantly the government's general financial position. He proposed an old age and sickness insurance law, but *laissez faire* liberals and farmers opposed this. A government bill in 1896 to extend the franchise was also defeated.

By far the most difficult problem facing Boström was the Swedish-Norwegian union crisis. In 1893 he conceded Norwegian equality in the joint council and promised to appoint a common foreign minister who could be either Swedish or Norwegian. Boström also had to face the flag issue in 1898. In 1900 he agreed to equality of Swedes and Norwegians for posts in the foreign service. In June 1900, presumably from fatigue, Boström resigned as prime minister, but he found himself back in office two years later and again had to confront a union crisis. Attempts to negotiate with Norway failed, and Boström again resigned in 1905. The break-up of the union ultimately occurred late in 1905 under Boström's successor, Christian Lundeberg. Boström died two years later in Stockholm.

REFERENCES: H. Haralds, *E. G. Boström* (Stockholm: Bonnier, 1907); R. E. Lindgren, *Norway-Sweden Union, Disunion and Scandinavian Integration* (Princeton: Princeton University Press, 1959).

A. H. WINQUIST

BRAHE, TYCHO (1546–1601) Danish scientist and astronomer

Tycho Brahe was the greatest European scientist of the late sixteenth century and a founder of modern scientific methods. Born into the high nobility of Denmark on 14 December 1546, at Knutstorp manor in Skåne, he was educated at the universities of Copenhagen, Leipzig, Rostock, Wittenberg, and Basel. Science and mathematics were part of the general curriculum of Lutheran universities in those days, and Tycho became interested in astronomy as early as 1560.

Ten years later, his formal studies completed, Tycho established an observatory and alchemical laboratory at his uncle's seat, Herrevad Abbey in Skåne. Here his observations of the supernova of 1572 led him to disprove a key element of the Aristotelean world view, celestial immutability.

In the years 1576–1597, Tycho founded and directed the royal Danish observatory at Uraniborg on the isle of Ven (Hven) in the Sound. Patterned after the secularized Cistercian abbey of Herrevad, Tycho's observatory attracted young researchers from throughout Europe and became the prototype of the modern advanced research institute. Here Tycho worked out many of the fundamental theories and methods of modern science. His approach combined quantification, experimentation, observation, team research, and verification of results. With apparatus of his own design and construction, assisted by the many disciples and assistants he trained at Uraniborg, Tycho applied his methods to compile the most accurate body of astronomical data the world had ever seen. Tycho proved that the heavens changed, disproved the existence of celestial spheres, and made the first original contributions to lunar theory since classical antiquity.

In 1597 Tycho left Uraniborg. Two years later he became imperial mathematician at the court of the Holy Roman Emperor in Prague. Here young Johann Kepler joined his staff. After Tycho's sudden death in Prague on 24 October 1601, Kepler used Tycho's methods and data as the basis for his own epochal contributions to astronomy.

REFERENCES: J.L.E. Dreyer, *Tycho Brahe: A Picture of Scientific Life and Work in the Sixteenth Century* (Edinburgh: Adam and Charles Black, 1890; repr. New York: Dover, 1963); C. D. Hellman, "Tycho Brahe," *Dictionary of Scientific Biography*, ed. C. C. Gillispie (New York: C. Scribner's Sons, 1970), vol. 2; W. Norlind, *Tycho Brahe: En levnadsteckning med nya bidrag belysande hans liv och verk* (Lund: C.W.K. Gleerup, 1970).

J. R. CHRISTIANSON

BRANTING, K. HJALMAR (23 November 1860–24 February 1925) Swedish Social Democrat and prime minister

Few, if any, Socialist leaders contributed so greatly to the construction of a national party and working-class movement as Hjalmar Branting. From 1884, when he became the first member of Stockholms Socialdemokratiska Arbetarklubb, to his prime ministership in three Social Democratic governments in 1920, 1921–1923, and 1924–1925, Branting shaped a party that was pragmatic, moderate, liberal, closely attached to the union movement, and unusually coherent. He helped construct a social democratic theory stressing the capacity of working-class organizations and popular movements to resist capitalist development and to reshape capitalist society. He became a prominent figure in the international Socialist movement and in the League of Nations, but his outstanding accomplishments came as leader and spokesman for the movement that rose from a negligible extraparliamentary grouping to achieve universal suffrage, the eight-hour day, and political dominance of Swedish society.

Branting terminated his studies at Uppsala University and abandoned a promising career as an astronomer to devote himself to journalism and Social Democratic politics. In 1886 he became editor of *Socialdemokraten*.In its columns he not only propounded party theory, strategy, and policy, but contributed theater reviews as well. When the Social Democratic Party* constituted itself in 1889, Branting acted as secretary. He became the party's first Riksdag* deputy in 1896, having been elected from Stockholm* on the Liberal list. As the party's only deputy until 1902 and as the only surviving member of the original triumvirate (with Axel Danielsson and Fredrik Sterky), he became its natural leader, and in 1907 he was named party chairman.

Branting's immediate political strategy focused on the attainment of universal suffrage through an alliance with the Liberal Party; later, he believed, this alliance would have to yield to a more definitive class politics for Socialist aims. Branting early pursued the path of parliamentary socialism. He envisioned the Socialist revolution as an extended process of reform, education, and acquisition of power, and rejected violent political upheaval unless the enemies of democratic socialism provoked it. By welding together the party and the union movement and by minimizing conflicts over religious differences and the proper pace of Socialist advance, Branting fashioned a party capable of steadily augmenting its power.

Branting's pursuit of unity and power did not proceed without difficulty. In 1906 the party ousted anarchist spokesmen Hinke Bergegren and Carl Gustaf Schröder, in 1915 pro-German activists, and in 1917 a leftist group which later became Sweden's Communist Party*. The general strike* of 1909 and the Borggård coup of 1914 stemmed the party's progress. Finally, however, in 1918, under near-revolutionary conditions, universal suffrage and the eight-hour day were achieved. Branting acted as a moderating influence during the November 1918 crisis, preferring the secure establishment of voting rights and the eight-hour day to the more precarious objective of a democratic republic.

As a government minister, Branting was less successful. His brief stint as finance minister in 1917 and 1918 was not a happy one. The three Branting governments suffered from the lack of a working majority and an effective program, although they did demonstrate the Social Democrats' capacity to govern. Branting, as an advocate of international solidarity, naturally devoted much attention to defense and foreign affairs. In the heated pre-war controversies over defense, Branting rejected the defense nihilists' position. Following Jaurès he argued for a people's militia. His particular brand of anti-militarism led not to Swedish disarmament but to the democratization of the Swedish armed forces. Throughout the union crisis with Norway, Branting was a strong exponent of a peaceful solution, a major factor in the Nobel committee's selection of Branting to share the peace prize in 1921. Branting regularly led Sweden's representatives to the Socialist International; he presided at the 1910 Copenhagen meeting and at the 1919 Berne conference. During the war Branting worked steadily to preserve Sweden's neutrality and sought to encourage a peaceful settlement. He represented Sweden at the Paris Peace conference and at the League of Nations, where his reputation as a champion of the rights of small nations helped him gain election to a council seat in 1922. By his death in 1925, he was revered not only in Sweden as its preeminent democratic Socialist, but internationally as a spokesman of peace and solidarity.

REFERENCES: H. Branting, *Tal och skrifter i urval*, 11 vols. (Stockholm: Tidens, 1926–1929); Z. Höglund, *Hjalmar Branting och hans livsgärning*,2 vols. (Stockholm: Tidens, 1928–1929); *SU*, vol. 4.

T. TILTON

BREMER, FREDRIKA (17 August 1801–31 December 1865) Swedish feminist author

The fifth of seven children of the well-to-do land and foundry owner Karl Fredrik Bremer (died 23 July 1830) and Birgitta Charlotta Hollström, Fredrika was born on their estate near Åbo in Finland. When she was three years old the family moved to Stockholm*. She had an unhappy childhood because of the stiff and formal relations between parents and children and the strict regulation of the children's activities. However, the girls had a capable French governess whom they adored.

Her writing career began with *Teckningar utur hvardagslifvet* (*Sketches from Everyday Life*; 3 vols., 1828–1831), a collection of stories about home life among the educated classes. This was followed by *Presidentens döttrar* (*The President's Daughters*; 1834), *Nina* (1835), *Grannarne* (translated as *The Neighbors*; 1837), and *Hemmet* (*The Home*; 1839). From 1833 to 1840 she spent most of her time in Norway as the guest of Countess Sommerhielm, although she traveled to bathing spas and other places during the summers. In 1840 she moved back to Stockholm, wintering at the family's country estate, Årsta. She was now well known in Sweden and, through translations of her later works, in the English-speaking world as well.

An exponent of Christian liberalism, she published *Morgon-Väkter*(*Morning Watchman*), her confession of faith, in 1842. This was followed by another series of novels, none of which was outstanding.

In August 1848 Bremer set out alone to see the New World. Stopping first in Skåne, then in Denmark and England, she arrived in New York in October 1849. For two years she traveled widely in the United States, visiting and meeting all kinds of people, from literary celebrities to Indians in Minnesota Territory, and from slaves on southern plantations to President Fillmore in Washington, D.C. She was particularly interested in studying American institutions and customs. She also took a side trip to Cuba. She deplored slavery, but, on the positive side, she found that education and opportunities for non-slave females were better in the United States than in Europe. She was also impressed with the youthful vigor of life in the new land. She departed from New York in September 1851 and returned home via England. In 1853 her book *Hemmen i nya verlden* (*The Homes of the New World*) appeared and was soon translated into Danish, German, English, French, and Dutch. Her book *England in 1851 or Sketches of a Tour in England* appeared in English the same year.

Following a cholera outbreak in 1853 Bremer organized a committee of women in Stockholm to raise funds to care for orphaned children. In 1855 she formed a women's group which worked to improve prison conditions. After seeing America, she also wanted to do something for Swedish women. At that time an unmarried woman in Sweden was legally a minor all her life, under the guardianship of her father or some other male. Bremer wrote her deliberately propagandistic novel *Hertha* (1856) to focus attention on women's unequal status in society and especially on the plight of unmarried women of the educated class. The book was harshly criticized for its feminist ideas and alleged immorality, but it also gave rise to widespread discussion of women's rights. In 1858 a law was passed making unmarried women legally independent at age 25.

Because of the public storm over *Hertha*, Bremer decided to go abroad again. She left Sweden in May 1856 and stayed away for over five years. Again pursuing her interests in institutions and people, she visited Switzerland, Belgium, France, Italy, Sicily, Malta, the Holy Land, Turkey, and Greece. She described her experiences in *Lifvet i gamla verlden* (*Life in the Old World*; 1860–1862, 6 vols.).

Back in Stockholm again, she continued to take an interest in women's education and welfare as well as other social causes. She contributed articles to the women's magazine *Tidsskrift för hemmet* (*Journal for the Home*), which had supported women's rights since its inception in 1858. She died of pneumonia at age 64, having remained active until the last few days of her life. She had revealed since her childhood a strong, independent personality, a lively curiosity, and great perseverance in pursuing her goals. She had supported many worthy causes, especially women's rights, and had injected into Swedish literature a greater realism. The Fredrika Bremer Förbund (Fredrika Bremer Association*) was named after her.

REFERENCES: A. B. Benson, "A Meeting in Havana," *American-Scandinavian Review* 5:6 (Nov.–Dec. 1917): 351–56; C. Bremer, ed., *Life, Letters, and Posthumous Works of Fredrika Bremer* (New York: Hurd and Houghton, 1868); F. Bremer, *Hertha* (Askild & Kärnekull, 1971), *The Homes of the New World* (New York: Harper, 1853), and *The President's Daughters; including Nina*, trans. Mary Howitt (London: Bell, 1883); A. Gustafson, *A History of Swedish Literature* (Minneapolis: University of Minnesota Press, 1961).

N. FARQUHAR

BRIDGET, SAINT *See* Birgitta

BRONZE AGE (Scandinavian) c. 2000–500 B.C. Prehistoric period

Manifestations of this period's cultures are very unevenly distributed through Scandinavia* but are preeminent in Denmark. While there is a comparative paucity in the other countries, the evidence of an opulent society in Denmark, above all in Jutland, suggests that this part of Scandinavia enjoyed a level of prosperity unsurpassed elsewhere in Europe. The coming of a warmer climate before the period began encouraged early agriculture and the establishment of more settled communities. These developments meant a greater receptivity to external influences and trade, especially important for Denmark since it needed to import every ounce of copper and tin, the components of bronze, once the time had passed when home-produced flint weaponry could no longer compete with imported bronze exemplars from the west and south.

About 1500 B.C. Danish-made bronze weapons and ornaments began to enter Norway, where a native metal technology only advanced once its iron deposits were exploited during the first centuries A.D. Bronze Age cultures in Sweden appear to have been located on Gotland, in the Lake Mälar region, and in the southern provinces. Ship burials, characterized by settings of vertical stones, date from this period in Sweden. In the area of Lake Mälar there was a vigorous weapon industry, the products of which found their way to Finland and the Åland Islands. Bronze objects may also have been imported to Finland from Russia, and there is some evidence of abortive attempts to begin a home industry in the west and north of the country.

In Denmark, copper and tin were received in exchange for amber, available in bulk and much prized south of the Alps, and for live cattle. These exports were even sufficient to bring substantial quantities of gold objects into Denmark, as revealed in the excavations of the turf and stone burial mounds of Jutland. This archeology, expertly begun by Christian J. Thomsen in the early nineteenth century, disclosed the high-quality textiles worn by an agricultural aristocracy, which were fortunately preserved by the tannic acid present in their well-hewed oak coffins. Despite this obvious ability to work in hard wood, it is not known whether this society was maritime-oriented. Its most renowned artifacts in bronze are the several sun-discs which have been found. These were apparently votive offerings. Each was about one foot in diameter and gilded on one side only. Other notable finds include the nearly 30 lurs, some of them six feet in length, which have been recovered in different parts of Denmark. The lurs are curved horns which have a trombone-like sound. Some have been found in pairs and were evidently tuned together. Remarkable examples of early Danish craftsmanship, these are the oldest wind instruments in the world.

Another remarkable archeological treasure from the Scandinavian Bronze Age are the rock scribings (*hällristningar*). These are located primarily in southern Scandinavia and particularly in Bohuslän (Sweden) and Østfold (Norway). The most remarkable concentration of them is near Tanum in Bohuslän. (There are over 2,000 such scribings in Sweden.) The scribings depict, in a highly stylized manner, men, ships, animals, wagons, implements, and so on. They also include symbols such as crossed circles, footprints, spirals, and cup marks. It has been surmised that the scribings are the work of agrarian people and that they demonstrate the importance of boats in their culture and the central place of the sun in the religion of the period.

REFERENCES: H. C. Broholm and M. Hald, *Costumes of the Bronze Age in Denmark* (Copenhagen, 1940); J. Brøndsted, *Danmarks Oldtid*, vol. 2 (Copenhagen, 1958); *DH*, vol. 1; *DSH*, vol. 1; P. V. Glob, *The Mound People* (London: Faber & Faber/Paladin, 1974); E. Kivikoski, *Finland* (London: Thames & Hudson, 1967); *NH*, vol. 1; A. Spekke, *The Ancient Amber Routes* (Stockholm, 1957); M. Stenberger, *Sweden* (London: Thames & Hudson, 1964).

D. D. ALDRIDGE

BULL, OLE BORNEMANN (5 February 1810–17 August 1880) Norwegian violinist

Ole Bornemann Bull was born in Bergen, Norway. He was the eldest of 10 children born to Johan Storm Bull, a chemist, and his Dutch wife, Anna Dorothea Geelmuyden. His youth was spent in Bergen and at Valestrand, the family's summer home on Osterøy. He married Félicie Alexandrine Villeminot, a Frenchwoman, in Paris in 1836. They had five children—Alexander, Thorvald, Lucie, and Ole and Félicie, who both died as infants. Mrs. Bull died February 1862. In September 1870 Ole married 20–year-old American Sara Thorp. They had a daughter, Sara Olea. Bull died of cancer at Lysøen, his own "island of light," in 1880.

Bull began to play the violin at age 5 and was primarily self-taught. He devised a method for playing all four strings at once (*quartetto*) by lowering and flattening the bridge of his violin. Though he lacked classical training as a violinist, Bull was nevertheless widely recognized as a technical master of his instrument, an internationally acclaimed virtuoso. He concertized for more than 50 years and appeared in America for the first time on 25 November 1843 at New York's Park Theatre.

In addition to a lifetime of public and private concerts, Bull for a time conducted the Christiania Orchestra (1828), worked with Henrik Wergeland to establish the Norwegian Theatre (1849), established an emigrant colony in Potter County, Pennsylvania (Oleana, 1852), managed the Italian Opera at the New York Academy of Music (1854), supported the organization of a National Academy of Music in Norway, and chaired the Leif Eirickson Monument Committee (1876).

Bull's compositions include: Concerto in A major, Quartetto a violino solo, Polacca Guerriera, Adagio Religioso (during an Italian tour, 1833); Homage to Scotland, Farewell to Ireland (British Isles, 1836); Norges Fjelde (The Mountains of Norway; at Valestrand after his father's death, 1838); Concerto in E minor, Siciliano e Tarantella (Europe, 1838–1842); Agiaco Cubano, Recuerdos de la Habana (on Cuban themes; America, 1844); Niagara, To the Memory of Washington (on American themes; America, 1845); La Verbena de San Juan (composed for and dedicated to Queen Isabella during his first trip to Spain in 1846; Et Sæterbesøg (A Visit to the Sæter; principal melody is Sæterjentens Søndag, 1848); and The Nightingale (composed during his third Russian tour, 1866–1867).

REFERENCES: S. C. Bull, *Ole Bull: A Memoir* (Boston: Houghton Mifflin Company, 1883); S. Sadie, ed., *The New Grove Dictionary of Music and Musicians*, vol. 3 (London: Macmillan Publishers Limited, 1980); M. Smith, *The Life of Ole Bull* (Princeton, N.J.: Princeton University Press for the American Scandinavian Foundation, 1943).

C. S. HALTERMAN

C

CABO CORSO (1650–1663) Swedish fort in West Africa

This fort was located near the present city of Accra, Ghana. Originally a Portuguese factory, it became Swedish when Henrich Carloff, a German from Rostock, negotiated on behalf of the Swedish African Company with the local chieftain for land. In 1650 the Swedish African (Guinean) Company, founded by Louis De Geer, established a fort at Cabo Corso. The citadel was called Carlsborg, in honor of King Karl X*.

The Swedes held this fort on and off until 1663, and it was used as a trading base for gold, slaves, and ivory. Carloff complained when a new governor was named. When he was not paid by the Swedes, this German agent then decided to transfer his loyalty to the Danish king, Frederik III*. Thus, the intense seventeenth-century Dano-Swedish rivalry in the Baltic spilled over to the West African coast. In the war of 1656–1657 the Swedish fort came under Danish control, thanks to the traitorous behavior of Carloff. At the conclusion of the war, it was returned to Sweden, only to fall shortly thereafter to the Dutch. One of Carloff's subordinates was involved with this transfer. The indigenous people of the area attacked the Dutch and restored the fort to the Swedes. However, in 1663 the Dutch retook it and held it until 1664, when the English took over.

After this brief encounter, the Swedes ceased to organize colonial ventures in Africa. Thereafter Swedish interests in Africa generally moved in scientific, economic, or religious directions.

REFERENCES: V. Granlund, *En svensk koloni i Afrika eller Svensk Afrikansk Kompaniets Historia* (Stockholm: Norstedt & Söner, 1879); M. Mörner, "Cabo Corso på Guldkusten," *Allsvensk Samling* 37 (June 1950): 4–7; M. Lowenkopf, "Sweden and Africa," *Africa Report* (October 1968), pp. 59–65.

A. H. WINQUIST

CANUTE *See* Knud

CAP PARTY (c. 1740–1772) Political party in Sweden during the Age of Liberty*

Emerging as a response to the successes of the Hat Party* at the Riksdag* of 1738–1739, the Cap Party first made itself felt at the next meeting of the estates in 1740. While the Hats were to rule for more than a quarter of a century, the Caps succeeded in defeating them in the 1764 elections and then at the Riksdag of 1765–1766. Subsequent changes of government took place in 1769 and 1771, with new parliamentary elections leading first to the Hats defeating the Caps, and then to the latter defeating the former once again. The Cap Party was disbanded after the 19 August 1772 coup d'etat carried out by Gustav III* that brought the Age of Liberty to a close.

Basically, the Cap and Hat parties were non-antagonistic in nature, with neither at first questioning the social and economic basis of eighteenth-century Swedish society. The differences between the two were ones of degree and personality much more than ones of philosophy and ideology. The Caps gained much of their strength among the older landed families and from the officers of the navy (quartered at Karlskrona*) and of the provincial regiments. In geographic terms, Finland and Skåne provided much of the Caps' support. There were also party differences concerning foreign policy, with the Caps generally accepting—as had Arvid Horn*, with whom they tended to identify—Sweden's loss of her trans-Baltic territories and her military predominance in the North to Russia. While the Hats allied themselves with France, the Caps sought friendly relations with Great Britain and Russia.

In the 1760s, having been out of power since forming their party, the Caps proved very receptive to the newly politicized members of the craft guilds, the petty bourgeoisie, the rural clergy, and the landowning peasantry, all of whom rejected the politics of deference in favor of a more participatory type of political activity. The general disenchantment with the Hats' foreign and economic policies was given concrete expression in the demands and wishes of these newly politicized groups, and the Caps rolled to victory in 1764–1765. One of their most notable reforms was the introduction of freedom of the press in 1766, a reform all the more remarkable in view of the fact that it eliminated one of the tools—censorship—used successfully by the Hats to stay in office for 30 years.

The new political forces among the commoners, however, could not be restrained by the old-guard Cap Party leadership, and their demands for equal access to office and for a positive statement of their rights and liberties threatened to destroy the party and the party system. By 1772 the social cleavages between privileged and unprivileged subjects had replaced the old cleavage between Caps and Hats as the predominant fact of political life. With support from the army and from much of the nobility, Gustav III took advantage of this situation to carry out his coup d'etat, which put an end to this popular challenge to the old order and, with it, an end to parliamentary sovereignty in Sweden.

REFERENCES: Per-Erik Brolin, *Hattar och mössor i borgarståndet 1760–1766* (Uppsala, 1953); M. Metcalf, "The First 'Modern' Party System? Political Parties, Sweden's

Age of Liberty and the Historians," *Scandinavian Journal of History* 2 (1977): 265–87;
G. Nilzen, *Studier i 1730–talets partiväsen* (Stockholm, 1971); G. Olsson, *Hattar och mössor. Studier i partiväsendet i Sverige 1751–1762* (Gothenburg, 1963).

M. F. METCALF

CARL *See* Karl

CASTBERG, JOHAN (1862–1926) Twentieth-century Norwegian politician and social reformer

Johan Castberg was the greatest Norwegian social reformer of the early twentieth century. His political philosophy of eliminating social injustice through parliamentary reform rather than revolution laid the foundation for the contemporary social democratic welfare state*. He viewed social reform from an international as well as a national perspective, and admired in particular the British Liberal tradition of social change. But his strong personal commitment to reform was fueled by an intense feeling of compassion.

He rose to prominence in Oppland province, which would always be his political base. He first established himself as a leader within the United Workers Associations (De forenede norske Arbeidersamfund). He hoped to use the Workers Associations to join the growing labor movement with the more radical wing of the Liberal Party (Venstre) in a democratic reform party that would unite all forces of the left in Norwegian politics. In 1900 the Workers Associations formed their own party, the Labor Democrats (Arbeiderdemokratene). Castberg thereupon began his parliamentary career, which lasted from 1900 to 1910 and from 1913 to 1926. His effort to unite the Left failed, however, with both the Socialist Norwegian Labor Party* and the Liberals rejecting his bid. He therefore was unable to extend his political base to a national level. The non-Socialist Workers Associations were later outcompeted by the National Federation of Labor (LO) (see Swedish Confederation of Trade Unions), while the Labor Democrats were largely restricted to the two provinces of Oppland and Hedmark.

Within the Storting*, Castberg generally cooperated with the Liberals, and throughout most of his career he was associated with the Liberal Storting group. He was always a strong nationalist, as evidenced by his uncompromising attitude during the Union crisis with Sweden in 1905. After 1905 Castberg was in the forefront of the opposition to the government of Christian Michelsen*. The main issue of contention concerned waterfall concessions for industrial use, with Castberg insisting that the government closely regulate such concessions. During this period Castberg took the initiative which led to the consolidation of the Liberals into a cohesive reform party under Gunnar Knudsen*.

When Knudsen formed his minority government in 1908, Castberg became minister of justice. He was responsible for the enactment of concessions restrictions and also for the social reforms that were passed. The government fell in 1910, but Knudsen returned to power in 1913. Castberg joined the cabinet as trade minister, but soon thereafter he moved to head the newly created Social

Ministry. However, relations between Castberg and Knudsen became strained, and he resigned in April 1914 in protest against the government's protectionist tariff policy.

As a member of the Storting, Castberg continued to be the foremost exponent of social reforms, a number of which were passed during Knudsen's second ministry. Castberg's name in particular is identified with the Children's Laws (1915) protecting the interests of children born out of wedlock. Such children gained inheritance rights, the right to use their father's surname, and the right to receive paternal financial support. Castberg continued to serve in the Storting until the year of his death.

REFERENCE: T. K. Derry, *A History of Modern Norway, 1814–1972* (London: Oxford University Press, 1973).

O. HOIDAL

CELTIC IRON AGE c. 400 B.C.–0 A.D. Prehistoric period characterized by Celtic influences in Scandinavia*

This period remains archeologically impoverished in artifacts of native provenance, and hence it is tempting to accord the Celts a role in Scandinavia's development which may be disproportionately large, important though Celtic influences must have been in launching the Iron Age. Even in a broad European context, the Celts' artistic and technical nuances are sufficiently elusive, because they were nomadic and did not establish lasting states. Apart from occasional assaults on the Italian peninsula down to the late third century B.C., there is no clear evidence of a Celtic invasion in any military sense elsewhere in the West. But their supplanting of Persian power in Thrace some two centuries earlier meant that their exceptional skills as metal workers were exposed not only to interlace patterns, but also to Scythian zoomorphic motifs; and in this fusion of Celtic with Asian steppe art may lie the origins of the art which characterized the Migration and Viking* periods' art of Scandinavia. In addition, it may be assumed that the craft of metal inlay, so much favored during these epochs and transmitted northwards chiefly by the Goths in the early centuries A.D., was first revealed by Celtic craftsmen devoted to the production of what Stuart Piggott has described as "small, intense and exquisite pieces of gold, silver or bronze which capture and concentrate preciousness," (*Early Celtic Art*, introduction).

While it is difficult to assess the immediate and long-term effects of Celtic civilization in Scandinavia, it is important to note a number of archeological finds that clearly point to contacts between the various peoples of Scandinavia and the Celts. These finds include a number of metal objects from Närke (Sweden), a group of wooden shields modeled after Celtic patterns from the Hjortspring site in south Jutland, and a great, three-foot diameter Celtic cauldron from Brå, which has been dated to the third century B.C. Evidence from Norway indicates that Celtic-inspired metal workers were not active in southwest Norway before the first or second centuries A.D., though they may have held to their trade through the culmination of Norway's own Iron Age in the Viking era.

Certain finds from Jutland may be singled out as representative of Scandinavia's accessibility to Celtic culture. These include the silver cauldron from Gundestrup (early first century B.C.?), with its masterly embossings illustrative of a very complex iconography, and the expertly crafted carts found at Dejbjerg, Kraghede, and Langå. All were found in peat bogs, where they had been deposited as votive offerings. The famous Gundestrup piece brought to north Jutland an aesthetic rooted in the Aegean, the Black Sea, and further east, though it may itself have been made in northern France. The carts were highly sophisticated vehicles of a type upon which the Romans were unable to improve. All may have entered Denmark as war booty in the hands of the returning Cimbri, who raided the Celtic regions of the Rhine and Upper Marne in the second century B.C. But they remain outward signs, and it could be argued that Celtic skills in stone-masonry, road-building, and the making of iron tools were what percolated into Scandinavia when they were most needed, during the climatic deterioration of the last centuries B.C.

REFERENCES: P. M. Duval and C.F.C. Hawkes, eds., *Celtic Art in Ancient Europe* (London: Seminar Press, 1976); P. V. Glob, *The Bog People* (London: Faber and Faber/Paladin, 1969); P. Jacobsthal, *The Early Celtic Style*, 2 vols. (Oxford: Clarendon Press, 1944); O. Klindt-Jensen, "The Gundestrup Bowl: A Reassessment," *Antiquity* 33 (1959): 161–169; J. Moreau, *Die Welt der Kelten* (Stuttgart: J. G. Cotta, 1957); S. Piggott, *Early Celtic Art* (Edinburgh: Edinburgh University Press, 1970); N. K. Sanders, "Orient and Orientalizing in Early Celtic Art," *Antiquity* 45:178 (1971): 103–112.

D. D. ALDRIDGE

CENTER PARTY: FINLAND (formerly the Agrarian League)

The Agrarian League (or Agrarian Union) emerged out of the Finnish nationalist movement, the socioeconomic conditions of Ostrobothnia and eastern Finland, and the political upheavals of 1905–1906, which peaked with the Finnish General Strike of 1905 and led to the replacement of the four-estate Diet with a unicameral parliament elected by universal suffrage in 1907.

Two separate agrarian political organizations were founded in 1906: a political party in northern Ostrobothnia in which Kyösti Kallio, a future president of Finland, was an active member, and an Agrarian Youth Association in southern Ostrobothnia led by Santeri Alkio, the leading ideologist of agrarianism in Finland. By 1908 the two groups had joined forces and gained a strong foothold in eastern Finland. Working in rural regions, where small farmers, albeit often poor, constituted the vast majority of the population, and where agrarian associations, cooperatives, and local government had deep roots, the Agrarian Party appealed to those who had been ignored by the established parties of the Diet and to those who did not identify with the recently founded Social Democratic Party*. The party was in many respects typically populist, counterposing the Finnish culture to the Swedish, the rural culture to that of the towns, and the peasant ethic of hard work to the lazy lifestyle of central bureaucrats.

The party thus fused a nationalist, democratic, and agrarian ideology to defend the traditional values of the small farmer and his economic and political basis in a society which was undergoing gradual industrialization* and urbanization*. It advocated a "Third Alternative" to socialism's emphasis on class struggle and antipathy to private property and to conservatism's defense of the old social order and the monopolistic tendencies in capitalism. The party was an interest group, and its philosophy reflected an understanding of the principles of ecology.

After Finland gained its independence, the Agrarian Party became the largest non-Socialist party and gradually strengthened its position in rural areas, mainly at the expense of the Progressive Party (*see* Progressive/Liberal Party). The bulk of the party's support came from the independent peasantry in the peripheral areas of the north and east. In the 1919 election the party won 19 percent of the seats in the parliament, compared with 4 percent in 1907. This electoral increase was caused by the new political situation that emerged in the aftermath of the achievement of independence. The party was further aided by the passage of agrarian reform legislation in 1918. This legislation resulted in the addition of 177,000 independent land holdings between 1919 and 1935 owned by former leaseholders, many of whom were Social Democrats who became potential Agrarian supporters as a result of the reform.

In 1925 the Agrarian Lauri Relander was elected president, and in 1930 the party held 59 of the 200 seats in the parliament. It actively identified with the anti-Communist objectives of the Lapua movement, but when the Lapuans broadened their attacks to include the Social Democratic Party and the institutions of political democracy, the Agrarian Party gradually moved toward strengthening the political Center and cooperated with the Social Democrats against extremism on the Right and on the Left. After Kallio was elected president in 1937, an Agrarian-Social Democratic coalition government was formed, with a Progressive as prime minister. This was as far to the Left as a "popular front" government in Finland went, since the Communist Party* was outlawed. This Agrarian policy of cooperation with the moderate Left stood in contrast to agrarian politics in eastern Europe, however, and reflected a general trend in Finland after the mid-1930s away from politics of confrontation on the domestic front and toward identification with Scandinavia* in foreign affairs. In both domestic and foreign policy, Finnish politics, with the support of the previously anti-Swedish Agrarian Party, were moving toward identification with Swedish social democracy and neutrality.

After World War II* the party underwent two fundamental changes: the first in order to meet the twofold challenge of solving immediate postwar political and economic problems in cooperation with the now legal Communist Party and developing a new foreign policy vis-a-vis the Soviet Union; the second of adjusting to long-term population shifts to urban areas in the south. Under the leadership of Urho Kekkonen*, a new generation of leaders eventually emerged to support actively the Paasikivi-Kekkonin Line* and to cooperate with the People's Democratic League (the Communists). The party was in opposition from 1948 until the early 1950s, when they again cooperated with the Social

Democrats. The Agrarians dominated national politics from the late 1950s until the mid-1960s. Since 1966 Center-Left cabinets, with the SDP as a leading partner, have, with few exceptions, governed Finland.

In 1965 the agrarian image was dropped and a Center Party was formed to compete in urban areas for the votes of recent in-migrants, especially those who had entered white-collar positions and those who had not identified with the Socialist or Conservative parties. These changes came in response to a decline in the party's electoral fortunes. The Center Party began to make inroads in urban centers in the 1970s, but its role as the leading non-Socialist party has recently been threatened by the Conservative Party*. Similarly, the election of the Social Democrat Mauno Koivisto* as president in 1982 demonstrated that the Center Party was not regarded as the only party which could manage Finland's sensitive foreign policy. Although it remains the swing party in national politics and managed to gain 19 percent of the seats in parliament in 1983, the future of the party's influence in government will rest largely with its electoral successes or failures.

REFERENCES: R. Alapuro, *Akateeminen Karjala-Seura* (Helsinki, 1973), and "Regional Variations in Political Mobilisation: On the Incorporation of the Agrarian Population into the State in Finland, 1907–1932," *Scandinavian Journal of History* 1 (1976): 215–42; E. Allardt and O. Pessonen, "Cleavages in Finnish Politics," in S. M. Lipset and S. Rokkan, *Party Systems and Voter Alignments: Cross-National Perspectives* (New York: The Free Press, 1967); D. Arter, "The Emergence, Nature and Growth of an Agrarian Party: A Finnish Case Study," Ph.D. dissertation, University of Hull, 1967; S. Berglund and U. Lindström, *The Scandinavian Party System(s)*(Lund: Studentlitteratur, 1978); J. Lylly, "The Emergence of the Finnish Multi-Party System: A Comparison with Developments in Scandinavia, 1870–1920," *Scandinavian Journal of History* 5 (1980); J. Nousiainen, *The Finnish Political System* (Cambridge, Mass.: Harvard University Press, 1973); K. Törnudd, "Composition of Cabinets in Finland 1917–1968," *Scandinavian Political Studies* 4 (1969).

R. M. BERRY AND J. SUNDBERG

CENTER PARTY: NORWAY Senterpartiet

Although it changed its name in 1959 from Bondepartiet (Farmers' Party) to Senterpartiet (Center Party), the Center Party still appeals mainly to persons with an agricultural background. It was founded on 19 June 1920, when the country's major agricultural producers' association, Landmandsforbundet, voted to establish a party which would support agrarian interests. Initially the party was backed predominantly by the larger farmers, and its traditional areas of strength have been in the interior of east Norway and Trøndelag, regions with large farms and forests. Its philosophy until the 1960s was generally conservative on economic, social, and religious issues, but it has not refrained from urging state intervention on behalf of agriculture.

From its beginning the party gained a significant share of the popular vote, increasing to 15.9 percent and 25 Storting* representatives in 1930. During the period of minority governments between the world wars, the Agrarian Party formed one government, which held office from May 1931 to March 1933. Headed by Peder Kolstad, and upon his death by Jens Hundseid, it enjoyed little success. It entered office at the height of the Depression, and its policy of reducing state expenditures to the utmost did little to alleviate the misery of the times. The government is remembered chiefly for the notoriety gained from disagreements among its members, in particular controversies involving the minister of defense, Vidkun Quisling.*

The Depression severely affected Norwegian farmers, largely because of reduced prices and foreclosures. The Agrarian Party increasingly insisted that the only solution to the agricultural crisis lay in state support to make production profitable. In its frustration it joined the Norwegian Labor Party* in ousting the Liberal government of J. L. Mowinckel in 1935, allowing Johan Nygaardsvold* to form the first permanent Labor government. Thereafter followed the "crisis compromise" between the Agrarians and Labor whereby a significant part of the government's emergency funds benefited agricultural producers. Rather ironically, because of its nationalistic and anti-Socialist sentiments, the Agrarian Party thereby paved the way for Labor's long-term control of government. But within a Scandinavian perspective this development was not unique, with similar agreements occurring in Denmark and Sweden during the thirties.

Following World War II* the Agrarian Party faced serious challenges. Increased mechanization in agriculture and the continued transition of the nation to an urban society resulted in a steady decline in the number of persons employed in the farm sector. Since 1945 the party has never gained as large a percentage of the vote as it had before the war. Recognition of the fact that the farmers no longer were the dominant segment in the country caused it, along with sister parties in Sweden and Finland, to change its name in an effort to gain a broader base of support. In the sixties and seventies it increasingly stressed protection of the environment in an effort to secure the votes of ecological sympathizers in the cities.

Along with other parties, the Agrarians by the sixties held the view that only a non-Socialist coalition could serve as a viable alternative to a Labor government. The successful outcome of the 1965 election permitted the Agrarian Party's Per Borten to head a government which held office from October 1965 to March 1971. The coalition eventually disintegrated over the issue of whether Norway should join the European Economic Community. The Agrarian Party opposed membership unless Norwegian farmers could receive special concessions which made the EEC's agricultural rules nonapplicable in Norway. With the government's fall, the party played a prominent role in the successful campaign against EEC membership, determined by popular plebiscite in September 1972.

The Agrarians took part in the coalition formed under Lars Korvald (Christian People's Party*) in 1972 by parties which had opposed EEC membership. In 1973 the party gained 21 representatives and 11 percent of the vote, its best result since World War II. Subsequently, however, a rift developed between its more traditional members and its populist wing over whether to cooperate with the Conservatives in seeking to resurrect a non-Socialist coalition. The traditionalists favoring cooperation won out, but the split remained, and the party's voter support declined considerably in the 1977 election, from 21 to 12 representatives. The decline continued in 1981, when the party's representation fell to 10, the lowest since 1945.

REFERENCES: H. Allen, *Norway and Europe in the 1970s* (Oslo: Universitetsforlaget, 1979); S. Rokkan, "The Growth and Structuring of Mass Politics," in E. Allardt et al., eds., *Scandinavian Democracy* (Copenhagen: Det Danske Selskab, 1981); S. Berglund and P. Pesonen, with G. P. Gislason, "Political Party Systems," in E. Allardt et al., eds., *Scandinavian Democracy* (Copenhagen: Det Danske Selskab, 1981); H. G. Greenhill, "The Norwegian Agrarian Party: A Case Study of a Single Interest Party," Ph.D. dissertation, University of Illinois, 1962; S. Groennings, "Cooperation among Norway's Non-Socialist Political Parties," Ph.D. dissertation, Stanford University, 1962; J. Storing, *Norwegian Democracy* (Boston: Houghton Mifflin, 1963).

O. HOIDAL

CENTER PARTY: SWEDEN Centerpartiet (formerly the Agrarian Party, Bondeförbundet)

As a response to their declining political influence, disenchanted farmers established party organizations during the 1910s, and eventually in 1921 these organizations merged into the Agrarian Party, literally the Farmers' Union. In the late 1950s the Agrarians changed their name to the Center Party and gradually broadened their electoral base. Through the years the party's electoral support has ranged from 10 to 25 percent of the vote, and the party has participated in several governments: the short-lived Agrarian "summer" government (1936); the first Social Democratic-Agrarian coalition (1936–1939); the national wartime coalition (1939–1945); the second Social Democratic-Agrarian coalition (1951–1957); the first non-Socialist coalition comprised of the Center Party, Liberals, and Conservatives (1976–1978); the second non-Socialist coalition (1979–1981); and the Center-Liberal coalition (1981–1982). In the coalition cabinets during 1976–1982 the Center Party leader, Torbjörn Fälldin, was prime minister.

After the consolidation of the party in 1921, the Agrarians received around 10 percent of the vote, and their share of the vote fluctuated very little during the rest of the decade. Their electoral fortunes, organizational strength, and political influence improved significantly during the 1930s. In the 1932 and 1936 elections the party won 14 percent of the vote. Following the 1932 election the Agrarians and Social Democrats concluded the famous "crisis agreement" which provided aid to farmers and gave the Social Democrats the necessary parliamentary support for their anti-Depression program. Cooperation between the two parties was further cemented when the first red-green coalition government was formed after the 1936 election.

Despite the successes of the 1930s and the party's position in the executive for long periods during the 1940s and 1950s, the Agrarians faced a major electoral quandary: the mainstay of the party consisted of farm owners and especially small holders, and the farming population had been in decline since the founding of the party. In contrast to the other agrarian-based parties in Scandinavia*, the Swedish party succeeded in enlarging its electoral base in the 1960s and 1970s by attracting the votes of small businessmen, white-collar employees, and workers. Moreover, the party accomplished this without diminishing its support among farmers. As the party sought to broaden its social base there was a reorientation from collaboration with the Social Democrats to cooperation in the middle of the political spectrum with the Liberal Party (*see* Liberal People's Party). In 1968, for the first time in its history, the Center Party became the largest non-Socialist party, and it maintained this position until the late 1970s.

The changing electoral base of the party has not been without impact on the party's central aspirations and views as expressed in its programs. Originally, the proclaimed aim of the party was to unite the farmers as a political force and to promote their interests. Other early demands of the party often reflected a conservative outlook. However, in contrast to the Conservatives, with their ties to the establishment, the Agrarian Party was hostile toward the official bureaucracy, big business, and urban influences, and the party championed the cause of the small people.

In the 1930s both conservative and reformist elements grew more prominent in the Agrarians' program. The peasant class was lauded as a moral force in the preservation of Swedish traditions; protection of the purity of the Swedish race was stressed; and foreign elements as well as the influences of urban culture, moral degeneration, and laxity in law enforcement were deplored. During these years the Agrarians also become increasingly critical of big business and financial interests. As the Depression deepened, the Agrarians accepted greater state intervention and social reforms—initially in forms which specifically benefited the party's constituency, but eventually even broader measures. Prior to the 1930s the Agrarians had argued for controls pertaining to agriculture, but now the party's advocacy of state intervention also included the major features of the Social Democrats' expansionary economic policy and planning in the economy.

During most of the postwar period the party, in comparison to the other non-Socialist parties, has often been closer to the Social Democrats on issues of state intervention, welfare policies, and taxation. By the mid-1940s the extreme conservative pronouncements of the 1933 program and references to the peasant class had been discarded. However, in its views on the family, as well as on religious and moral issues, the party remained fairly traditionalist. Several of the Center Party's demands in the 1970s, which contributed to sharpening its profile, also reflected continuity in safeguarding rural interests and those of the periphery. The earlier advocacy of justice for the countryside was replaced by emphasis on regional equality and decentralization. The party also adopted a vigorous stance against environmental degradation, including opposition to the expansion of nuclear energy, and thus rode the wave of back-to-nature sentiments in the 1970s. The ability of the Center Party to integrate the issues of the 1970s with its former purposes was also an important factor in enabling it to expand its electoral base while retaining the loyalties of its traditional backers.

REFERENCES: D. A. Rustow, *The Politics of Compromise* (Princeton: Princeton University Press, 1955); S. A. Söderpalm, "The Crisis Agreement and the Social Democratic Road to Power," in S. Koblik, ed., *Sweden's Development from Poverty to Affluence* (Minneapolis: University of Minnesota Press, 1975).

D. SAINSBURY

CHARLES *See* Karl

CHILD LABOR

As in most other rural societies, child labor in agriculture and other family enterprises was accepted and commonplace in pre-modern Scandinavia*. The coming of the Industrial Revolution, however, created a juvenile urban proletariat that suffered widespread exploitation. Children who had not yet reached their teens dug coal, cured tobacco, and otherwise toiled long hours for niggardly wages. The practice was defended within limits as a cheap source of labor that in theory lowered costs of production and thus kept goods affordable domestically and competitive in international markets. Its use abroad naturally cancelled out the latter advantage. Advocates of child labor also argued that it helped to integrate youth in society, taught them production methods at an early age, and supplemented their parents' meager incomes.

Critics began to analyze child labor by the 1870s. The Danish physician Emil Hornemann (1810–1890), best known for his advocacy of scientific hygiene, investigated 45 factories in Copenhagen* in 1872 and discovered that children comprised 76 percent of the labor force in those producing chicory, 60 percent in the match factories, and 31 percent in the tobacco mills. Moreover, many worked at night, especially at printing establishments. Such jobs generally supplemented mandatory if uneven attendance at school. Hornemann was particularly disturbed that children tended to be employed in the more dangerous factories.

Hornemann's findings stimulated a wave of protest culminating in a law of 1873 regulating juvenile work in Danish industries. Its provisions, though weak by modern standards, were an important step forward. Children under age 10 could no longer be employed. Those under 14 could not work more than six and a half hours a day and not before 6 A.M. or after 8 P.M. On the other hand, it did not protect the far more numerous Danish children who labored in shops or assisted artisans. Moreover, the statute of 1873 was not vigorously enforced for several decades. In 1901, however, the minimum age of employment was raised from 10 to 12 years. In 1908 an investigation revealed that 37 percent of the schoolboys and 27 percent of the schoolgirls in Denmark held jobs. The figures for urban and rural areas did not vary markedly.

In Sweden, stronger legislation of 1881 regulated child labor in factories and trades. The minimum working age was fixed at 12 years, and nobody under 14 could be legally employed for more than six hours daily. Those from 14 to 18 could work a 10—hour day. Night shifts were forbidden for all under 18.

In Norway, it was reported that in 1875 3,370 children under 15—many of them under 12—worked in sawmills, factories, and other industrial facilities. Protests during the 1870s came to naught. In 1883 appeared a critical posthumous study by the statistician and economist Jacob Neumann Mohn (1838–1882). Two years later a special commission published corroborative findings which led to a law of 1892 forbidding work by children at night or by anyone under 12. Those between 12 and 14 required a medical certificate.

Throughout Scandinavia, twentieth-century legislation has gradually raised the minimum age of employment while lowering the maximum hours of legal work for all, regardless of age. Child labor as generally understood is for all practical purposes non-existent in Scandinavia today.

REFERENCE: I. Hammerström et al., *Ideologi och socialpolitik i 1800–talets Sverige* (Uppsala: Uppsala universitet, 1978).

F. HALE

CHRISTIAN I (1426–May 1481) King of Denmark 1448–21 May 1481, king of Norway 1450–1481, king of Sweden 1457–1464

Christian I, son of Dietrich of Oldenburg, was elected to succeed Kristopher of Bavaria (Christoffer III*) in 1448. He established the Oldenburg line that would rule Denmark until 1863. He has been described as tall, engaging and brave. He was also apparently very fond of ceremony and pageantry and spent a good deal of money on the trappings of his office. Furthermore, he appears to have been very much a monarch of his age, as he sought to create a strong and effective dynastic state and opposed the centrifugal forces represented in the nobility, the Church, the Hanseatic League* and even the commons, which preferred the looseness of the federative structure so characteristic of the medieval state. His 33–year reign was marked by almost perpetual conflict with these forces. In spite of these struggles, Christian has been treated as a relatively successful ruler in Denmark-Norway. He added Slesvig, Holstein, Delmenhorst, Oldenburg, and Stormarn to the kingdom. He worked to increase the efficiency of the administration by employing capable, non-noble officials. He established good relations with many of his German neighbors, especially with the emperor, Frederick III. He limited the independence of the Hanse merchants in Danish towns. He negotiated an alliance with James III of Scotland against England, which indirectly cost the Danes, or, more accurately, the Norwegians, the Orkney and Shetland islands. He established good working relations with the Church and negotiated an agreement with the papacy which allowed him to install his own candidates to high church offices—after the papal candidates were bought off—and to establish the University of Copenhagen in 1479. He also secured the recognition of his son, Hans (I*), as his successor.

His greatest disappointments came in relations with Sweden. He dreamed of preserving the Kalmar Union*. When the Swedish council elected Karl (VIII)

Knutsson* king in 1448, Christian was bitterly disappointed and carried on a small-scale war with Sweden for the next nine years. When the Swedes rose against Karl in 1457 and forced him into exile, Christian's dreams came true momentarily when he was chosen to succeed Karl. His relations with the Swedes soon soured. He antagonized many Swedish nobles when he followed the practice employed by his predecessors of appointing non-Swedes to administrative posts and their accompanying fiefs in Sweden. At the same time, he imposed extra taxes which alienated the commoners. New revolts in 1464 led to Christian's deposition and the return of Karl. When Karl died in 1470, Christian sought once again to secure his election. He sailed to Stockholm* with an army and fleet. The supporters of the Axelsson family and Sten Sture (the Elder)* united against him, however, and at the famous Battle of Brunkeberg (October 1471) Christian's forces were defeated. Sten Sture was chosen protector of the realm— a title he preferred over king—and Christian returned to Denmark.

Christian spent the last 10 years of his life consolidating his position in Denmark and the duchies (Slesvig and Holstein), improving his relations with some of his German neighbors, concocting marriage alliance schemes, and bettering his relations with the papacy. When he died Denmark appeared to be a reasonably well-governed and stable early modern dynastic state. The forces of discord, however, lay just below the surface.

Christian married Dorothea of Brandenburg in 1449. She was a capable and intelligent person, and she appears to have acted as a check upon some of her husband's grander schemes. Four children came from the union. Olav died in infancy. Hans succeeded his father. Frederik (I*) lived to succeed his nephew, Christian II*. Margrethe was married to James III of Scotland.

REFERENCES: *Bonniers Lexikon*; *DBL*, vol. 3; *DH*, vol. 5; *Gyldendals Lexikon*; *NH*, vol. 4.

B. NORDSTROM

CHRISTIAN II (1 July 1481–25 January 1559) King of Denmark and Norway 1513–1523, king of Sweden 1520–1521

Christian II has an almost singularly bad reputation in both Swedish and Danish history, where he often is referred to as Christian the Tyrant. From certain perspectives Christian deserves this title. From the viewpoint of Danish social history, especially the history of Danish peasant and middle-class interests, the title is undeserved. He is slightly less unpopular in Norwegian history.

The son of Hans I* and Christina of Saxony, Christian was given a fairly broad education, founded in the humanism of his period. He also lived for a time in Holland. His father began to include him in the affairs of state in the early sixteenth century, and from 1506 to 1512 he was the resident governor (*statholder*) in Norway. He inherited his father's desire to make Denmark a dynastic state, and his reign is in many respects similar to those of a number of his contemporaries, including Henry VIII and Gustav I Vasa*. His efforts, however, caused considerable friction between the crown and his subjects, especially the nobility. Following his father's death and in keeping with the traditional succession pattern in Denmark (which was in principle an elective monarchy), Christian was obliged to agree to an accession charter (*håndfæstning*) drafted by the council. This bound him to honor the traditional rights and privileges of the nobility, the Church, and the commons. According to this charter, Christian was to rule only with the advice of his council.

Christian's domestic and foreign policies stood in stark contrast to the promises he made at his accession. He by-passed the council at every opportunity. Instead, he ruled largely with the advice of Sigbrit Willums (Villoms) and Hans Mikkelsen. Sigbrit was the more extraordinary of the two. She was the mother of Dyveke, who was Christian's mistress until her mysterious death in 1517. (Both were Dutch-born. Christian had met Dyveke while in Norway and had brought them both back to court when he returned to Denmark in 1512.) Following Dyveke's death, Sigbrit remained at court and played a dominant role in the affairs of state until Christian's deposition in 1523. Sigbrit was hated by most Danes and earned the nickname "the troll woman," along with the less derogatory title Mother Sigbrit. While she was a person of remarkable abilities, especially in financial matters, she was also suspicious and vindictive, and her influence on Christian was not positive, as he had similar personality traits. Her importance at court increased after 1517, and she came to control the treasury, manage the Sound Tolls, compose official correspondence, and make policy in the name of the king. Mikkelsen, the mayor of Malmö, was less influential but stood very close to the king, much to the disgust of the traditional holders of power in the country.

The policies the crown pursued were designed to curtail the independent powers of the Church and the nobility. The administration of the country, based in Christian's chancery, was packed with foreign and/or non-noble appointees loyal to the king. Church appointments went increasingly to the king's supporters. Appointments to royal positions and to the lands that often accompanied them were made to royal favorites. The towns were given special attention, as Christian sought to build a native merchant class loyal to him, and as he sought to develop a viable national economy free of Hanse influence (*see* Hanseatic League). New law codes (Landsloven and Byloven) were assembled, which reflected Christian's centralizing tendencies. While these and other steps were appropriate to the desired ends, Christian alienated nearly every segment of the population by them. He moved too far, too fast. He has subsequently been accused of not understanding politics, people, or the Danes. By the summer of 1522 the country was in revolt. The nobility, the Church, the burghers, and the commons were opposed to Christian. The king was at war with Lübeck and Sweden. Taxes were burdensome and finances were in chaos. International commerce was disrupted.

Christian's actions in Sweden were the final precipitators of his downfall. Following the policy of his predecessors, Christian sought to rebuild the Kalmar Union* under Danish leadership. He had been promised the Swedish crown but had not secured it by 1517. He launched campaigns against Sweden in 1517,

1518, and 1520. The first two were costly and unsuccessful. In the third, how-ever, Christian overcame the Swedish forces. Sten Sture the Younger (*see* Sten Svantesson ''Sture''), the protector of the realm, died of wounds suffered at the battle of Åsunden (20 January 1520). Stockholm* fell into the king's hands. In March 1520 the Swedish council recognized him as hereditary ruler. He was crowned in Stockholm on 4 November 1520. But then Christian blundered. Either on his own account or under the influence of Sigbrit and/or the deposed archbishop of Uppsala, Gustav Trolle, he allowed the execution of 82 Swedes in the main square of the city. In what has come to be called the Stockholm Bloodbath, nobles, burghers, and commoners fell under the axe. Ostensibly, Christian's opposition was eliminated. To compound this outrage, Christian returned to Copenhagen* via central Sweden, and along the way a number of his opponents were similarly executed. The Swedes, under the leadership of Gustav Eriksson Vasa, rose in revolt. Christian was deposed in 1521. His forces in Sweden were defeated the following year.

Christian was surrounded by enemies in 1522. His uncle, Frederik of Holstein (*see* Frederik I), was designated by the council to replace him in early 1523. Confronted by what appeared to be insurmountable odds, Christian chose to flee Denmark with his family and closest advisors. He spent the next eight years living in Lier near Antwerp and wandering Germany in search of support for his restoration. Christian lived as a king-in-exile. He negotiated with foreign powers, and he carried on a running propaganda war with Frederik which took the form of countless pamphlets circulated in Europe and Denmark. He converted to the Lutheran faith sometime around 1523 but returned to Catholicism around 1530 in order to be assured Charles V's support in his attempts to regain the throne. With the assistance of Charles, who was his brother-in-law, he launched a counterattack in 1531. He sailed from northern Holland with 5,000 mercenary troops. His fleet was caught in a storm, however, and only one-quarter of his army managed to land in Norway. There he was quickly recognized king, prob-ably because of the Danish-centered policies of Frederik and the Reformation* tendencies of the Danish king. But Christian failed to capture the most important forts in the country, including Akershus in Oslo. Danish forces landed in Norway in the spring of 1532 and secured Christian's agreement to an armistice. He also agreed to come to Denmark, on the promise of safe conduct, to negotiate with his uncle. Frederik, however, did not want to risk civil war by having his nephew running loose. Christian was imprisoned in Sonderborg castle. (Civil war erupted in spite of Frederik's actions. *See* the Count's War.) He spent the next seventeen years in captivity and died in Kalundborg castle in 1559.

In 1515 Christian married Elizabeth of Habsburg, a granddaughter of the Emperor Maximilian and a sister of the future emperor, Charles V. She apparently loved Christian intensely and remained loyal and supportive throughout their marriage, in spite of his affair with Dyveke and his exile. She died in 1526. The marriage produced six children. Four sons (Hans, Maximilian, Filip, and one that went unnamed) died soon after birth or during childhood. Two daughters, Dorothea and Christine, survived.

REFERENCES: E. Arup, "Kong Christiern 2. Et Porträt," *Scandia* 18:1 (1947): 73–80; R. Bergström, *Studier till den stora krisen i Nordens historia 1517–1525* (Uppsala: Almqvist & Wiksell, 1943); *DBL*, vol. 3; *DH*, vol. 5; *DSH*, vols. 2, 3; *NH*, vol. 5; A. Pasternak, "Omkring Christiern IIs Landlov," *Scandia* 30:1 (1964): 191–216; M. Venge, ed., *Bondekær eller tyran* (Odense: Odense Universitetsforlag, 1975).

B. NORDSTROM

CHRISTIAN III (12 August 1503–1 January 1559) Duke of Schleswig and Holstein and King of Denmark 1534/1536–1559

Christian was the eldest son of Frederik I* of Denmark and his first wife, Anna of Brandenburg. He was educated in the tradition of humanism, studied in Germany, and took an extended grand tour. He became a Lutheran early in his life. As a young man he spent most of his time in Gottorp; he was, for most of his life, more German than Danish.

When Frederik I died in 1533, the Danish council met and decided to delay for a year the election of a new king. (The two strongest candidates were Frederik's sons Christian [III*] and Hans. Following this decision a civil-international war, called the Count's War*, ensued. Christian played only a small part in the first stages of this complicated struggle. In 1534, however, he was designated king by a segment of the council and entered the war in Denmark actively. His forces defeated the mercenaries of Lübeck and Christoffer of Oldenburg, crushed the civil disorders, and forced the capitulation of Copenhagen* by siege. In August 1536 Christian could rightfully claim that the throne was firmly in his hands. He was then a victorious king who had driven the foreigners from his country and restored internal order. He was supported in his position by most of the nobility.

Christian consolidated and defined his hold on power during the fall of 1536. In August he staged a coup in which the bishops of the Catholic Church in Denmark were arrested and detained. The council, then composed solely of lay nobles, gave approval to Christian's actions. In October a *herredage* (literally, a meeting of the full council) was held in Copenhagen. Representatives of the nobility, the towns, and the peasantry took part. This was not a "democratic" gathering, however, called to sanction the king's decisions. Rather, it was called so that representatives of the various social groups could hear the king chastise all who had taken part in the Count's War and to be informed of royal actions. The accession charter which Christian agreed to was the mildest in a century. The council saw its role in government significantly reduced, although the privileges of the nobility were actually extended. Council constitutionalism received a severe blow. Hereafter, the council was to assist the king in governing the country, but it was not to consider itself a body above or apart from the crown. At the same time, Christian's infant son (the future Frederik II*) was designated heir to the throne, and Norway was incorporated into the realm as simply another province or territory, thereby losing its status as an autonomous kingdom. Within a year, the Catholic Church had been swept away, its property confiscated by the crown, and replaced by a state-controlled Lutheran Church (*see* Reformation).

Following the chaos and horrors of the Count's War, Christian wanted nothing more than to maintain peace and develop stability at home. Whereas he had been somewhat brash and impulsive as a youth, he now became much more moderate, measured, and politically astute. Consequently, he pursued a foreign policy aimed at avoiding war and moved ahead with domestic and administrative reforms slowly. In both areas he was largely successful. His peace policy was broken only by a brief involvement in a war against the Habsburgs in 1542–1544, which was the result of Christian's alliance with Francis I of France and the continued support which the emperor, Charles V, gave to the aspirations of Christian II*. This war ended with the Peace of Speyer, by which Charles recognized Christian III's claim to the throne in Denmark and agreed to abandon his support of Christian II. In return, Christian III promised to adopt a policy of neutrality in any subsequent wars between the emperor and the Schmalkaldic League. A second element of his foreign policy was to maintain peace with Sweden. In 1541 he concluded a fifteen-year defensive pact at Brömsebro with Gustav I Vasa*. Although neither country actually extended assistance to the other in their subsequent conflicts, the two remained at peace throughout the reigns of the two kings. To bolster these policies, Christian developed the Danish navy and the country's internal fortifications. He also maintained a standing army of mercenaries.

The costs of the Count's War, coupled with those of his military and court, put tremendous burdens on the financial resources of the state. The traditional income of the crown, based on taxes on the peasantry, rents on estates, and the Sound Tolls, was insufficient. The confiscation of the property of the Catholic Church helped to alleviate some of these problems. The policy of allotting estates to nobles, ostensibly only on temporary terms, did much to wipe out the gains made by the confiscations. Repeatedly, the state was forced to pawn allotted estates in order to secure funds. Still, reforms and able administration during Christian's reign, plus the preservation of peace after 1544, resulted in a gradual improvement of the financial situation. There was even a surplus in the crown's coffers when Christian died. (One of the most significant reforms, directed by the king's chancellor, Johan Friis*, involved changing the rent system on estates allotted to nobles. Previously, the crown had demanded a fixed annual payment. The holder of the estate would then keep the balance of the income. Under the new system, this situation was reversed. A fixed sum was kept by the noble, while the balance was turned over to the state.)

In order to make government more effective, Christian was instrumental in developing a more ''modern'' administrative system in Denmark. Increasingly, Copenhagen became the center of government, although the king continued to move about the country until the close of his reign. Of the great officers of the realm (chancellor, court master, marshal, and master of rents), the chancellor became increasingly important in running the day-to-day affairs of the country. Christian operated with a dual administrative arrangement based on the German Chancery and the Danish Chancery. The former, which grew out of Slesvig and Holstein, was staffed largely with Germans and was responsible primarily for foreign policy. The latter, staffed largely with Danish nobles who had been educated in law or administration at continental universities, was responsible for domestic Danish affairs and relations with Sweden. This body was controlled by Johan Friis for nearly 40 years. At the same time, the Rentekammer (literally, the Rent Chamber) developed to coordinate the complex systems of rent collection from royal properties. (This chamber was also under Friis's guidance.) The Rentekammer was staffed with nobles and, increasingly, by middle-class persons with experience in finance and accounting. Christian III took an active part in all facets of administration, although he was most interested in defense and fortification construction.

When Christian died on New Year's Day 1559, Denmark was in a fairly sound financial postition, had been at peace since 1544, had a well-organized and ably staffed administration, and seemed to be blessed with social and religious peace. The constitutional quarrel between the council and the crown was quiet. The steps had been taken by Christian III to bring Denmark into the ''modern'' era, and he must be seen as an important figure in the transformation of the country from a medieval corporate state to a dynastic state very similar to those developing elsewhere in Europe at the same time.

Christian married Dorothea of Saxony-Lauenberg (1511–1571) in 1525. Five children came from this marriage, including Christian's successor, Frederik II.

REFERENCES: *CMH*, vol. 2; *DBL*, vol. 3; *DH*, vol. 6; *NCMH*, vol. 2; *NH*, vols. 5, 6.

B. NORDSTROM

CHRISTIAN IV (12 April 1577–28 February 1648) King of Denmark-Norway 1588/1596–1648

Christian is one of the best-known, if not the best-loved, of Denmark's monarchs. He was an extraordinarily energetic, cultured, and well-educated ruler, and he dominated the life of his country in virtually every respect for over 50 years. He took an active part in all aspects of governing his realm and is remembered for his work with legal and court reform, the continuation of a balanced relationship between the crown and his council for most of his reign, the building of a number of Denmark's best-known castles, an aggressive and initially successful foreign policy aimed at checking Sweden's expansion and preserving Denmark's influence in northern Europe, a splendid court life, and a remarkable succession of lovers and offspring. On the negative side, however, Christian was vain, self-assured, and possessed with an excessively uncritical view of his own abilities; and he is consequently remembered for having taken Denmark into the Thirty Years' War, for having precipitated an attack by Sweden, for having spent far beyond the means of the state, and for having upset the traditional constitutional balance between crown and council during the later years of his reign.

Christian's rule may be divided into two periods. The first extended from his coronation in 1596 to his entrance into the Thirty Years' War in 1625. During this time all seemed to work in the king's favor. The revenues of the state appeared adequate to support all of Christian's policies and projects. Although he lost his queen, Anna Katarina of Brandenburg (1575–1612), he filled the void with a succession of mistress-wives, including Kirsten Madsdatter, Karen Andersdatter, and Kirsten Munk (whom he married in 1615), who brought real happiness and a great many children to his life. Life at court was splendid, and Christian initiated a series of building projects which included the Blue Tower in Copenhagen*, Frederiksborg, Ibstrup/Jaegersborg, and Rosenborg. He directed the undertaking of legal and court reforms (1603–1623 and the early 1640s) which were aimed at but did not achieve legal uniformity (*see* Danish Law). He increased the size of the fleet, established a standing army, and strengthened internal fortifications. Towns, economic life, and mercantile development flourished. Christian also established himself as a popular figure in Norway. He personally visited the country no fewer than 26 times, and he encouraged economic development, legal reform, and administrative efficiency. (He founded Christiansand and rekindled Oslo, which he renamed Christiania.) In education, Christian instituted a new set of regulations for the University of Copenhagen, founded Søro Academy, and encouraged the growth of gymnasia. He enjoyed a peaceful working relationship with his council and was assisted by a succession of able advisors. In foreign affairs, his greatest success, though hardly a brilliant military performance, was the Kalmar War* (1611–1613) with Sweden, by which he appeared to have checked successfully Swedish expansion into the Sound and the eastern Baltic.

The second period of his reign, 1625–1648, stands in stark contrast. State revenues consistently fell short of expenses. Income from the Sound Tolls declined through the period, while taxes increased and had to be levied ever more frequently. The latter aroused constant complaints from the commons and nobles. His private life came under increasing criticism, as did the excesses of the court life. His building projects, including the reconstruction at Kronborg, had to be compromised or curtailed. The fleet, one of his greatest prides, was nearly destroyed. Internal reform languished, and his relations with his council and advisors and the aristocracy disintegrated. Most disastrous were Christian's international exploits. Using his connections in Germany and his election as commander of the Lower Saxon Circle, he brought an unwilling Denmark into the Thirty Years' War. Entering as a champion of the Protestant cause, Christian gained some initial successes but soon found himself badly outmatched by the forces of Tilly and Wallenstein. At Lutter am Barenberg (17 August 1626) his armies were nearly annihilated. Jutland was subsequently invaded and occupied and paid an enormous price in pillage and billeting. In June 1629 Christian concluded the Peace of Lübeck with the Habsburgs. The defeat was costly for

Denmark and a bitter one for Christian. It showed that Denmark was gradually becoming a second-rate power. This realization was a difficult one for the king, who was steeped in the history of Denmark's former greatness. As onerous as the defeat in the Emperor's War (Kejserkrigen), as the Danes called this involvement, was, the Swedish attack in 1643, known as Torstensson's War, was more costly in terms of Denmark's standing in the North. During this Jutland was again occupied and the fleet was nearly destroyed. By the Treaty of Brömsebro (August 1645) Denmark lost Gotland, Ösel, Jämtland, Härjedalen, and Halland. Some of these losses were supposed to be temporary, but they all proved permanent. Denmark's declining status in the region was painfully clear.

In the last years of his reign, Christian became increasingly sullen and mistrustful. Alienated from and increasingly dependent on his council, he withdrew from public view. The power of the crown declined, and the council sought to obstruct the king's independence. A process of decentralization was initiated under the guise of administrative reform. Perhaps most painful for Christian was the death of his eldest son and heir, Prince Christian, in 1647. The council demanded and secured the summons of the estates in order to guarantee the succession of the king's younger son, Frederik (III*). Christian died before the estates met and was spared the ordeal of seeing the powers of the crown severely diminished in the accession charter which Frederik was compelled to accept.

REFERENCES: *DBL*, vol. 3; *DH*, vols. 6, 7; J. Gade, *Christian IV* (London, 1927).

B. NORDSTROM

CHRISTIAN V (15 April 1646–25 August 1699), King of Denmark-Norway 1670–1699

The oldest son of Frederik III* and his queen Sophie Amalie of Braunschweig-Lüneburg, Christian succeeded to the throne of the dual kingdom, not after signing a coronation charter like his father and so many monarchs before him, but immediately on his father's death on 9 February 1670, being the first hereditary and absolutist monarch to accede to power under the new terms determined by the coup d'etat of 1660. His anointment ceremony, which replaced the former coronation act and which was a religious celebration between king and God, with his people as passive obedient observers, was deliberately delayed for some eighteen months to underline the difference between the old and the new, and its contents and purpose were a public demonstration and expression of the central dogma of Danish absolutism, namely, that the royal power was of divine origin and that the king was answerable to no man on earth.

In practice this meant that though Christian was dependent on the clergy for the Biblical justification for his powers, which they gladly gave, and dependent on his politicians for the pursuance of domestic and foreign policies, he was entirely free to choose his advisors; he continued his father's policy of subduing the Danish nobles by appointing to the highest offices in the land such Holstein nobles or rich and influential burghers as would serve best. And in order to underline that devotion to the regime and not birth was the hallmark of true nobility, Christian had his chief advisor, the non-noble Peder Schumacher (ennobled as Count of Griffenfeld), devise two new orders of nobility, which ranked above the ancient noble families but into which all loyal subjects could of course be elevated by royal proclamation and by no other means, as a result of which, for example, Schumacher himself became Count Griffenfeld. Griffenfeld further strengthened the king's hand by the concentration of most power in his own hands, overruling or outmaneuvering the chief secretaries in the central administration and alone digesting for and presenting to the king the issues on which his decision was required, until his fall in March 1676. The devolution of power which then followed only affected the office of prime minister, not the king's own power.

From an early age the idea of a war of revenge against Sweden, which would return to Denmark the provinces lost in 1645, 1658, and 1660, had been inculcated into the budding ruler, and when in 1675 the Brandenburg victory against Karl XI* of Sweden at Fehrbellin suggested that the archenemy was in a weak position, Christian disregarded the advice of the peace and alliance party at court, led by Griffenfeld, and instead followed his generals' advice and attacked Swedish positions in Mecklenburg and Pomerania. After the capture of the important city of Wismar in December 1675, Christian transferred his troops to Scania, which now became the main theater of war, and it was here that he suffered the decisive defeat at Lund exactly one year later. The peace at Lund (1679) confirmed the status quo and initiated a period of peace between the two countries which lasted 20 years and which was inaugurated by the marriage between Christian's sister Ulrikke Eleonora and Karl XI, a union which had already been part of her grandfather's dynastic strategy and which had only been delayed by the war it was originally intended to prevent.

Due to the leadership of Count Ahlefeldt, who succeeded Griffenfeld in 1676, the economic and political decline occasioned by the lost war was halted and reversed. A reduction in the expenses of the crown gave Christian a sounder financial base, and after many years of work lawyers and officials collated and brought up to date the much respected medieval regional laws in a form which created the basis for uniform justice throughout the kingdoms and which are usually known as Christian V's *Danske Lov* (1683) (*see* Danish Law) and Christian V's *Norske Lov* (1687). At the end of his reign Christian was presiding over one of the best-organized, or as some contemporaries saw it, one of the most intolerant and oppressive states, politically and in terms of religion, anywhere in the world.

In 1667 Christian married Charlotte Amalie of Hesse-Kassel, by whom he fathered Frederik IV* in 1671. Throughout his reign Christian cultivated the image of the king as the father of his people, and contemporary evidence confirms that both Christian and Frederik were able to understand and speak Danish. In addition, Christian brought royal hunting to a new peak, especially the art of hunting animals to death by hounds and horses, and it was while in pursuit of this pastime that he was killed on 25 August 1699.

REFERENCES: *DBL*, vol. 3; *DH*, vols. 7, 8.

P. RIES

CHRISTIAN VI (30 November 1699–6 August 1746) King of Denmark 1730–1746

Christian was born in Copenhagen*, the second son of King Frederik IV* (1671–1730), who had ascended the throne three months before Christian's birth, and Queen Louise of Mecklenburg-Güstrow (1667–1721). An older brother, also named Christian in accord with the tradition, kept since 1513, of Danish monarchs alternately bearing that name and Frederik, died in infancy.

Christian was taught at the Danish court by Pietistic German tutors who instilled in the crown prince a deep personal religiosity, made him bilingual, and gave him an education superior to that of most previous Danish monarchs. His childhood does not seem to have been a happy one, however. There is a consensus among Danish historians of the period that Christian reacted strongly against the private behavior of his father who, though outwardly religious, became a bigamist in 1703 by marrying Elisabeth Helena Vieregg (1679–1743), daughter of the Prussian ambassador in Copenhagen, and again in 1712 by marrying Anna Sofie Reventlow (1693–1743), daughter of the Danish chancellor Conrad Reventlow. Christian rejected his father's third wife, particularly because of the emotional burden Frederik's affairs placed on his mother, and in reaction to the chronic public scandal retreated further into an intense Pietism that later marked both his personality and his reign.

In 1721 Christian married Sofie Magdalene of Brandenburg-Kulmback (1700–1770), who mirrored his Pietistic personality. Their only son, Frederik (1723–1766), became King Frederik V* upon his father's death. Sofie Magdalene added to the German retinue at the Danish court and, critical of Frederik IV's bigamy, heightened the tension between him and her husband.

Christian reigned to some degree in the spirit of absolutism that his great-grandfather, Frederik III*, had introduced in 1660. Regarding the absolute monarchy as a necessity for preserving the kingdom's unity and stability, he began, while crown prince, an ambitious program to enhance the trappings of royalty. A series of new palaces formed its backbone. Hirschholm, erected in the 1720s northwest of Copenhagen, was razed less than a century later. The baroque Eremitage, constructed in the mid-1730s, still stands in the Deer Park which Frederik III had opened as a royal hunting retreat north of Copenhagen. Christian built a residence for his son in that city in the 1740s. On a larger scale, he began his own chief residence, Christiansborg, in Copenhagen in 1732. These projects and countless costly gifts, loans, and pensions to friends and relatives belied the royal couple's relatively simple personal lifestyle.

Christian matched his royal expenditures with paternalistic programs intended to improve the lot of the Danish peasantry. In one of his first acts, he dissolved the national militia that his father had created. Christian also reduced farmers' taxes by 10 percent, an amount too small to have any perceptible effect. In 1739 he mandated compulsory education, free for the children of the poor, but popular resistance doomed this reform. On the other hand, in 1733 the king decreed that rural men between the ages of 14 and 36 could not leave their home towns. This bondage (*stavnsbånd**) which ensured estate owners an adequate supply of inexpensive labor, was extended in the early 1740s to apply to males aged 9 to 40. It was abrogated in steps beginning in 1788. Along with this system, Christian reintroduced the militia in 1733, although he was the first Danish king for two centuries not to wage war. A corn law of 1735 forbade the importation of foreign grain into Denmark and southern Norway. It ensured the kingdom's land owners a monopoly on production but deprived the poor of a source of less expensive food. Christian's rural policies, in short, failed to lighten the burden of the peasantry.

More successful were his industrial and commercial reforms, based on the mercantilism* then current. The General National Economic and Commercial Commission, established in 1735, oversaw in theory all aspects of the kingdom's economy. Christian also supported the founding of the East Asia Trading Company in 1732 and the nation's first credit and currency bank four years later.

Christian sought to impose Pietism on his subjects while preventing it from disturbing the stability of the state Lutheran Church. He abrogated his father's strict Sabbath laws in 1731 but replaced most of them in 1735 and added far more extensive decrees that stifled much of the nation's cultural life during his reign and left a lasting impression on Dano-Norwegian Christianity. Attendance at worship services became mandatory, and compulsory confirmation was introduced in 1736. Many forms of popular entertainment, such as masquerade balls and the theater, were banned on Sundays and holidays as well as on the days preceding them. To keep lay religious activity channeled within the traditional structures of the church, Christian issued in 1741 a Conventicle Edict that regulated the home gatherings common among Pietists and made preaching a prerogative of the clergy.

Christian was small of stature, physically unattractive, and spoke in an unusually high voice. His health and that of his wife was poor; both suffered from various illnesses and discomforts for which they frequently took medications and curative baths. Though regarded as intelligent, Christian lacked self-confidence and relied heavily on advisors. His personality and stringent religious decrees prevented him from being a popular monarch.

REFERENCES: *DBL*, vol. 3; L. Koch, *Kong Christian VIs historie* (1886).

F. HALE

CHRISTIAN VII (29 January 1749–13 March 1808) King of Denmark 1766–1808

Christian VII was the son of King Frederik V* and his first queen, the English princess Louise. The latter died when Christian was only three years old, and his education was supervised by Ditlev Reventlow, a man of honest intentions but limited intelligence. A healthier influence was the Swiss Reverdil, who became one of the prince's tutors in 1760. Reverdil found him intellectually able but already showing signs of the mental instability which had led his father to sink into a life of debauchery. Traits which included frequent retreats into fantasy and bouts of both extreme passivity and hyperactivity (now diagnosed as a form of schizophrenia) became more pronounced after Christian ascended the throne in 1766.

In November of that year the king was married to Caroline Matilda, the sister of George III of England, in the hope that this would help to calm his restless nerves. But in the winter of 1767–1768 he roamed the streets of Copenhagen* at night in the company of the ex-prostitute Støvlet-Katrine (Catherine Boots) and other disreputable companions to assault the watch and break up brothels. His ministers, who were largely those who had served his father, succeeded in bringing to an end such scandals, but Christian took pleasure in humiliating them in other ways and in favoring their critics, who sought the young ruler's ear. Between May 1768 and January 1769 he traveled through Germany, the Netherlands, England, and France. He was accompanied on the journey by the German doctor Johan Friedrich Struensee*, who appears to have kept the king's illness under control for a time. After his return, however, Christian became rapidly incapable of conducting any state business, and the opportunity was seized by a group of would-be reformers to secure the dismissal of the old ministers and to push Struensee into a position of supreme power. For some eighteen months in 1770–1772 Struensee was virtual dictator, while the king was watched over by his friend Enevold Brandt. Christian, who was never deprived of the absolute power of a Danish monarch as defined in the Royal Law of 1665, passively signed the documents which at the beginning of 1772 sanctioned the execution of Struensee and Brandt and the divorce from his queen, who had borne him a son (later Frederik VI*) in 1767 but who had undoubtedly been Struensee's mistress. With equal equanimity he gave approval to the coup d'etat in 1784 which brought to an end the succeeding regime under Ove Høegh-Guldberg and the installation of a new one under Crown Prince Frederik. It was at this time ordained that all official documents were in the future to be countersigned by the latter. Christian continued to appear at court functions but played no further part in public life. He was taken by his son to Holstein in August 1807 before the British attack on Copenhagen and died the following March in Rendsborg.

REFERENCES: P. Nors, *The Court of Christian VII of Denmark*, ed. E. Steen (London: Hurst and Blackett, 1928); W. A. Reddaway, "Denmark under the Bernstorffs and Struensee," in *CMH*, vol. 6, and "King Christian VII," *English Historical Review* 31 (1916): 59–84; A. Ribiero, "The King of Denmark's Masquerade," *History Today* 27 (1977): 385–89.

S. P. OAKLEY

CHRISTIAN VIII (Christian Frederik) (18 September 1786–20 January 1848) Statholder of Norway 1813–1814, king of Norway 1814, and king of Denmark 1839–1848

Christian appears a curiously contradictory figure in modern Scandinavian history. On the one hand, he was one of the main forces behind the development of a temporarily independent (and quite liberal) constitutional monarchy in Norway in 1814, of which he was elected the king. On the other hand, during his brief reign he opposed constitutional reform in Denmark and the duchies of Slesvig and Holstein, apparently fearing the same forces he had championed in Norway.

The son of Prince Frederik (brother of Christian VII*) and Sophia Frederika of Mecklenburg, Christian spent his early years cut off from the government, largely because of his criticism of government policies during the Napoleonic Wars. In 1813 he was sent to Norway as *statholder*, and early the following year he became the center of the independence movement there. He encouraged the drafting of a separate constitution for Norway (Eidsvoll Constitution of 17 May*), and on 17 May 1814 he was elected king of an independent Norway by the parliament (Storting*). His actual reign lasted three months. Following the breakdown of talks with Sweden in late July 1814, a two-week war was fought that brought both parties back to the conference table. Christian played a central role in negotiating the Convention of Moss*, which defined the relationship between Sweden and Norway. Christian then gave up his role in the government of Norway, and on 10 October 1814 he abdicated and left the country. (In some sources he is criticized for his actions in 1814, especially for his lack of leadership during the war with Sweden. He does not, however, deserve all the blame for the failure of Norway's independence efforts.)

In the years between 1814 and his succession in 1839, Christian traveled widely and played only a minimal role as heir in the governing of Denmark. (He served as governor of Fyn.) His travels and contacts contributed to the continuation of his reputation as a liberal, and Frederik VI* did not trust him.

Hopes were high in 1839 that Christian would support the liberal and nationalistic aspirations of his subjects, but these hopes were quickly dashed. Christian's reign was a conservative one. He refused to grant the country a constitution that would have reduced the absolutist powers of the monarchy, and he opposed any loosening of the crown's ties with the duchies of Slesvig and Holstein, where German national sentiments grew during the 1840s. Christian was Denmark's last absolutist monarch, and he clearly found it difficult to deal with the serious problems which faced his kingdom. Prior to his death, however, he advised his son (Frederik VII*) to grant the country a new constitution.

Christian was married twice. His first wife was Charlotte Frederikke of Mecklenburg-Schwerin. Following her death in 1840, he married Caroline Amalie of Slesvig-Holstein. He was succeeded by his son, Frederik VII.

REFERENCES: *DBL*, vol. 3; *DH*, vol. 11; R. Lindgren, *Norway-Sweden: Union, Disunion, and Scandinavian Integration* (Princeton: Princeton University Press, 1959); A. Linvald, *Kong Christian VIII*, 3 vols. (Copenhagen, 1943–1965); *NH*, vol. 9.

B. NORDSTROM

CHRISTIAN IX (8 April 1818–29 January 1906) King of Denmark 1863–1906

Christian, the sixth of ten children, belonged to the house of Glücksbourg, one of the minor lines of the Dukes of Slesvig-Holstein. His father, Duke

Vilhelm, came from the duchies but served in the Danish army from 1803. Christian also entered a career as a Danish officer and as a young boy felt and behaved like a Dane, unlike some of his younger brothers, who supported the insurgents in the duchies when the national clash between Danes and Germans in the monarchy began in the 1840s. Christian was noble and formal in bearing, not very intelligent, but conscientious in his duties and loyal as an officer. In character he was very much like his distant relative, King Frederik VI*. King Frederik liked the young prince and became his tutor and protector as long as he lived.

Prince Christian came into the center of dynastic events in Denmark when it became clear around 1840 that the Oldenburg family, which had ruled Denmark since 1448, would die out. Christian was a possible candidate for the throne. Through his marriage to Princess Louise, a niece of Christian VIII*, he came into a very favorable position. His wife was entitled to inherit the Danish throne, and he could claim Slesvig-Holstein. Thus, the two main parts of the Danish monarchy would remain together. The Russian tsar, through his relation to the Gottorp family, was a deciding factor. Nicholas I gave his support to the plan that Christian and his wife inherit the throne when the last Oldenburg, Frederik VII*, died.

Christian's relations with Frederik VII were not good, but the prince and his wife did not interfere in Danish politics. It was against Christian's will, however, that the governments held to the so-called Eider Policy (Ejderpolitik) during the early 1860s. Supporters of this policy wanted to separate Holstein from the monarchy and unite Slesvig with Denmark. Such an action would be in violation of the London Protocol (1852) and would only antagonize the German nationalists. Frederik VII died suddenly in November 1863, and Christian, now king, was compelled to sign a new constitution which embodied the Eider program. War with the German powers, especially Austria and Prussia, followed. The war was a disaster, and the duchies were lost in 1864.

During the first decades of his reign, Christian IX was not at all popular. His slight German accent and his shyness kept him at a distance from his people. His conservatism set him at odds with the liberal trends of the period. Agrarian liberalism, embodied in the Venstre Party, was antithetical to Christian's limited political thinking. In order to block the development of greater democracy in Denmark, Christian supported very conservative governments. These governments stood in opposition to liberal majorities in the lower house (Folketing*) of the parliament. A group of ultra-conservative owners of large estates, loyal to the king and monarchy, held the reins of power for more than 30 years (1870–1901), provoked a serious constitutional crisis, and prevented, in many respects, necessary social and economic reforms. The constitutional crisis was not met until the so-called System Change (Systemskifte) in 1901, when Christian appointed the first truly parliamentary government in modern Danish history.

In fact, Christian understood very little about the constitutional struggles which engulfed his country during much of his reign. His interests were concentrated on his family life at Fredensborg and other royal castles and on his three daughters and three sons, who were married into the most influential European dynasties. His eldest daughter married England's Edward VII. His next oldest daughter married Alexander III of Russia. The third became the wife of the duke of Cumberland. One son became king of Greece, and a grandson became king of Norway (*see* Haakon VII). In his later years his lack of popularity gave way to high popular esteem, as the king became the patriarch of the European monarchs.

Christian IX was born during the last years of absolutism, and he never learned or understood the ideas of democracy. His intellectual horizons were very narrow, but he was a noble character and no doubt was loyal to the country which had adopted him.

REFERENCES: B. Bramsen, *Huset Glücksborg*, vols. 1, 2 (Copenhagen: Politikens forlag, 1975); *DBL*, vol. 3, p. 325; A. Thorsøe, *Kong Christian IX* (Copenhagen: Gyldendal, 1906).

KRISTIAN HVIDT

CHRISTIAN X (26 September 1870–20 April 1947) King of Denmark 1912–1947

Often called the "War King" because his reign spanned two world wars, Christian X was born at Charlottenlund Castle, the eldest son of Crown Prince Frederik of Denmark (Frederik VIII*) and Louise, Princess of Sweden and Norway. Christian's younger brother, Prince Carl, ascended the throne of Norway in 1905 as Haakon VII*.

A student at Copenhagen's Metropolitanskole, Christian was the first Danish monarch to receive a university education. He then served an eight-month term as a private in the army, during which he stood sentry duty at the palace of his grandfather, Christian IX*. After Officers' School and service with a cavalry regiment in Jutland, Christian returned to Copenhagen* as an officer in the Life Guards. Conspicuous because of his height of six feet seven inches, Christian was a popular soldier and an avid sailor. On 24 April 1898 he married Alexandrine, Duchess of Mecklenburg. They had two sons, Frederik (IX*) and Knud. Upon the death of Christian IX in 1906, Christian became crown prince. He succeeded to the throne six years later following his father's unexpected death.

World War I led directly to one of Christian's greatest triumphs. The Treaty of Versailles gave the residents of Slesvig, which had been lost to Prussia in 1864, the right of self-determination (*see* Slesvig Question). Following a plebiscite in which 75 percent of the North Slesvigers voted for a return to Danish rule, Christian X, mounted on a white horse, rode triumphantly across the former border on 10 July 1920, to the cheers of his restored subjects.

Only a few months earlier, others among Christian's subjects had been angrily demonstrating against the king and calling for the establishment of a republican form of government. Christian had initiated the crisis by dismissing the Radical government headed by Carl Zahle. Confronted with the likelihood of a general strike and continued demonstrations, the king reluctantly agreed to accept a compromise caretaker government and to await reforms extending proportional representation to rural districts before new elections. The "Easter Crisis" of 1920 was the last attempt by a monarch to intervene directly in Danish politics.

It was Christian's role as a symbol of Danish nationalism during the World War II* occupation by Germany that won him such a high degree of loyalty and affection among his countrymen. Until ended by a fall in October 1942, his daily horseback rides through the streets of Copenhagen were widely interpreted as a reminder of Danish independence. His laconic reply to a 1942 birthday greeting from Adolf Hitler greatly angered the German leader and resulted in worsening relations between the two countries. Following the liberation of Denmark in May 1945, hundreds of thousands of Danes once again cheered their aged king as he drove through the streets of the capital on his way to open the parliament of a free Denmark. Christian X emerged from the difficult days of World War II as one of Denmark's greatest heroes.

REFERENCES: Svenn Poulsen, "King Christian's Sixtieth Birthday," *American Scandinavian Review* 18 (1930): 535–42; Roar Skovamand, "Denmark During the Occupation," in J. Bukdahl et al., eds., *Scandinavia Past and Present* (Odense: Edvard Henriksen, 1959), II, pp. 1229–36; T. Thaulow, "King Christian X of Denmark," *American Scandinavian Review* 35 (1947): 234–39; *Time* 29 (17 May 1937): 23–25; *New York Times*, 21 April 1947.

P. L. PETERSEN

CHRISTIAN AUGUST (9 July 1768–28 May 1810) Prince of Slesvig-Holstein-Sonderburg-Augustenburg, served briefly in 1810 as crown prince of Sweden

Christian August was the third son of Duke Frederik Christian I and Princess Charlotte Amalie of Plön. Like his older brother, Duke Frederik Christian II*, Christian August was educated at Augustenburg and then at the University of Leipzig (1782–1784). After military training in Copenhagen*, Christian August commanded the Jutland Infantry Regiment at the fortress at Fredericia from 1788 to 1799. He then served as a volunteer officer in the Austrian army during the War of the Second Coalition (1799–1801).

Although hoping for a more significant military role thereafter, Christian August returned to Fredericia in 1801, until he was appointed the military commander of southern Norway in 1803. When Denmark-Norway was forced into war with Great Britain and Sweden in 1807, Crown Prince Frederik (later Frederik VI*) appointed Christian August as the president of the Government Commission* (Regjeringskommission) created to administer Norway during the conflict. In the spring of 1808, Christian August's Norwegian army repelled an invasion attempted by a Swedish army commanded by General Baron G. M. von Armfelt. This conflict and a tight blockade of Norway by the British caused such severe hardships in Norway that Christian August, with Frederik's approval, concluded an armistice with the Swedish West Army on 7 December 1808.

Christian August played a key and complicated role in Scandinavian affairs after the revolution in Sweden of March 1809. Hoping to establish peace in

Scandinavia* through the re-creation of a union, Christian August advocated the election of Frederik as Sweden's king. His efforts were impeded by Frederik's refusal to grant a liberal constitution to Denmark-Norway and by the king's belligerent policy toward Sweden. Christian August's intentions were also jeopardized by George Adlersparre's plans to unite Norway with Sweden. Adlersparre recognized Christian August's importance and popularity in Norway and therefore wished to elect him as Sweden's crown prince, if Christian August would lead a rebellion in Norway for the proposed union. Adlersparre also attempted to alienate Christian August from the Danish government so that the prince would be more willing to direct a separatist movement. The Norwegian Count Johan Casper Herman Wedel Jarlsberg assisted Aldersparre in these plans.

In the months that followed, Christian August continued to work for Frederik's election in Sweden but was also angered by the presence in Norway during 1809 of the Danish chancellor, Frederik Julius Kaas, who advocated the seizure by Frederik of the Swedish throne. In July 1809 Aldersparre informed Christian August that his election as crown prince was certain. Christian August decided to accept the offer to keep his hopes for a Scandinavian union alive. At the same time, however, he also refused to carry out Frederik's order of 14 July to invade Sweden, because he was certain the attack would fail and that it would lead as well to a continuation of the war with Sweden rather than peace and union, as he desired. Christian August's position was strengthened by the fact that he possessed the discretionary power to act in this way. Given his position at the time, however, his motives and assumptions have been debated ever since.

Assuming that Christian August would carry out his command, Frederik promoted Christian August on 24 July to field marshal and governor (statholder) of Norway. Frederik was angered at first by Christian August's conduct but in August allowed Christian August to accept the Swedish succession when he too wished peace with Sweden.

Christian August had actually accepted the succession in Sweden upon a different basis than it had been offered to him. Christian August continued to view the position as a springboard toward Scandinavian union and opposed Norway's separation from Denmark and union with Sweden. He therefore calmed anti-Danish sentiments in Norway during the last months of 1809 by urging Frederik to institute reforms there and prevented Wedel Jarlsberg from establishing an effective separatist movement.

Christian August entered Sweden on 6 January 1810 to assume his duties as crown prince. He had earlier agreed to change his name to Karl August as Sweden's King Karl XIII* had requested. Christian August died soon thereafter of a stroke while reviewing troops at Kvidingehed, Skåne. Rumors that he had been poisoned by aristocratic supporters of the Gustavian dynasty exiled in 1809 precipitated a political and social crisis. This culminated in the murder of Count Axel von Fersen*, marshal of the realm, by a mob on 20 June 1810 in Stockholm* as Christian August's body was escorted toward Riddarholm Church for burial.

Christian August was particularly popular among the common people of the three Scandinavian countries in which he lived and was instrumental in resolving the crisis of 1809 in Scandinavia. His place in Norway and Sweden, however, was soon overshadowed by the activities of Christian VIII* and Karl XIV Johan*.

REFERENCES: *DBL*, vol. 5; J. Forchhammer, "Christian August, Prinds af Augustenborg," *Dansk Maanedsskrift*, vols. 1–4 (1868), pp. 1–52, 241–322, 321–87; E. Forsberg, *Karl August, gustavianerna och 1809–års män* (Hälsingborg, 1942); *NBL*, vol. 2; *SBL*, vol. 20.

L. SATHER

CHRISTIAN FREDERIK *See* Christian VIII

CHRISTIAN PEOPLE'S PARTY (Kristeligt Folkeparti) Danish political party

The origins and development of the Christian People's Party must be seen against the backdrop of post-World War II political and social transitions in Denmark. The Social Democrats have led the Danish government, either alone or in coalitions with other left-of-center parties, with few interruptions since the mid-1920s. Bourgeois parties have found it difficult to check from their minority position what they perceive as the gradual disintegration of traditional Danish society. The Christian press and many of the clergy have long been dissatisfied with much of the rapid change in national life and, especially in the 1960s, have expressed increasing alarm at the evident secularization of the country, a process whose roots can be traced back at least to the nineteenth century. Another common complaint was that unprecedented postwar prosperity had overemphasized materialistic values at the cost of traditional religious ones. Such critics called for a reassertion of Christian values in political and social life but were frustrated by their lack of an effective means of realizing their goals.

In the late 1960s three developments, sometimes perceived as closely related aspects of a liberalization of sexual morality, immediately preceded the formation of the Christian People's Party. In 1967 the Danish parliament abrogated the law banning the sale of pornographic materials, and "porno shops" soon sprang up in many communities to meet an initially strong consumer demand. Sex education was introduced into the curriculum of Danish elementary schools without segregation of the boys and girls. The parliament also relaxed the requirements for granting abortions, eventually legalizing termination of pregnancies on demand.

Many pastors and Christian lay people reacted sharply to these measures and revived the idea of a political party representing Christian values but independent of the state church and all other denominations. In 1970 politically conscious Danes took the initiative toward the formation of such a party by drafting a preliminary platform and recruiting members. By March 1971 the Christian People's Party numbered enough supporters to be legally recognized and enter candidates in parliamentary elections. It fared poorly in the September 1971 election, however, falling 625 votes short of the minimum for gaining parliamentary representation. In 1973, though, the Christian People's Party captured

7 of the 179 seats in parliament. Two years later the party reached its parliamentary zenith with nine representatives. Since that time its strength has dwindled, and in an election held in late 1981 it received only 2.3 percent of the popular vote, reducing its parliamentary fraction to four seats.

The Christian People's Party has consistently advocated firm ties between church and society, favoring retention of the Lutheran establishment. Religious education, it believes, should remain in the curricula of the public schools. The party also supports public policies which it believes reflect Christian humanitarian values, such as retention of the welfare state* and increased assistance to the elderly and the handicapped. During most of the 1970s and in the early 1980s, however, the severe economic recession in Denmark has limited the possibility of expanding social benefits. Moreover, the party has simply lacked the political clout to reverse the legislation of the 1960s that prompted its formation. Secularization has continued to restrict the church's influence in Danish society.

With regard to foreign policy, the Christian People's Party's position differs little from most other Danish parties. It supports Denmark's continued membership in NATO and the European Community, increased inter-Scandinavian cooperation, and augmenting aid to developing countries.

REFERENCES: S. Berglund and U. Lindström, *The Scandinavian Party System(s)* (Lund: Studentlitteratur, 1978); K. H. Cerny, *Scandinavia at the Polls: Recent Trends in Denmark, Norway, and Sweden* (Washington, D.C.: American Institute for Public Policy Research, 1977).

F. HALE

CHRISTIAN PEOPLE'S PARTY (Kristelig Folkeparti) Norwegian political party

The Norwegian Christian People's Party is politically the most successful of the Christian parties in Scandinavia*. It was founded during the election campaign of 1933, when the Liberal Party in Hordaland province refused to renominate Nils Lavik, a popular Christian leader. It gained an additional representative from Bergen in 1936, but prior to World War II* it remained a small sectarian party restricted to the west coast. However, in the first Storting* election following the war it emerged as a national party with 7.9 percent of the vote, almost identical with the Agrarian Party (*see* Center Party: Norway). It has consistently received voter support from throughout the country, but its main center of strength remains in the west-southwest, where it receives on a percentage basis twice as many votes as in other areas.

The Christian People's Party's chief goal has been to defend fundamentalist Christian values and beliefs. Issues such as the sale of alcoholic beverages, religious instruction in schools, family questions, and, later, abortion are ones on which it has taken strong stands. In foreign policy its chief interest lies in promoting aid to Third World countries, which ties in directly with the party's promotion of missionary activity.

Similar to other non-Socialist parties, the Christian People's Party adopted the view that only in union with additional parties could it establish an alternative to Norwegian Labor Party* control. In 1965 the party joined the non-Socialist coalition headed by the Center Party's Per Borten. It always strove to maintain unity within the coalition, recognizing the benefits it enjoyed from being able to implement policies through its influence, in particular through administration of the Department of Church and Education. When the Borten government fell in March 1971 because of disagreement over membership in the European Economic Community, the party's leadership gradually moved toward an anti-EEC position in conformity with the bulk of the party members' wishes. Party members, however, were allowed to campaign as individuals on either side of this question, and since it did not involve Christian values, the question did not have the divisive impact that it had on such parties as Labor and the Liberals.

Following the plebiscite of September 1972 that rejected EEC membership, the Labor government of Trygve Bratteli was succeeded by a minority coalition government of parties that were in accord with the plebiscite's outcome, headed by Lars Korvald, the Christian People's Party foreman and parliamentary leader. Although having the support of only 38 out of 150 Storting members, it remained in office until the election of 1973, successfully negotiating a difficult trade agreement with the EEC. The party enjoyed a pronounced gain in the election, advancing from 14 to 20 seats and gaining 12.3 percent of the vote, its largest ever. This can be attributed to the skillful manner in which it retained its pro-EEC members while gaining anti-EEC voters from other parties, to the abortion issue, and to the popularity of Prime Minister Korvald. Yet, ironically, the Korvald government was forced to resign because the election gave the Socialist parties a combined majority.

The party retained its gains in the 1977 election, but since that time it has been affected by the deterioration of the center position in Norwegian politics which it shares with the Center and the Liberals, although not to the extent of the latter two parties. To a considerable degree the party most recently has focused its attention on opposition to abortion. Due to the Conservative Party's* more liberal attitude on this question, the Christian People's Party refused to join a non-Socialist coalition in 1981, which compelled the Conservatives to form a minority government under Kaare Willoch. In the election preceding the formation of the Willoch government, the Christian People's representation in the Storting declined from 22 to 15.

REFERENCES: H. Allen, *Norway and Europe in the 1970s* (Oslo: Universitetsforlaget, 1979); S. Berglund and P. Pesonen, with G. P. Gislason, "Political Party Systems," in E. Allardt et al., eds., *Scandinavian Democracy* (Copenhagen: Det Danske Selskab, 1981); O. Garvik, ed., *Kristelig Folkeparti: mellom tro og makt* (Oslo: Cappelen, 1983); S. Groennings, "Cooperation among Norway's Non-Socialist Political Parties," Ph.D. dissertation, Stanford University, 1962; A. Lomeland, *Da Kristeleg Folkeparti bli til* (Oslo: Universitetsforlaget, 1973); J.T.S. Madeley, "Scandinavian Christian Democracy: Throwback or Portent?" *European Journal of Political Research* 5 (1977): 267–86; S. Rokkan, "The Growth and Structuring of Mass Politics," in Allardt et al., eds., *op. cit.*;

J. Storing, *Norwegian Democracy* (Boston: Houghton Mifflin, 1963); H. Valen and E. Katz, *Political Parties in Norway* (Oslo: Universitetsforlaget, 1967).

O. HOIDAL AND L. SVÅSAND

CHRISTIE, WILHELM F.K. (7 December 1778–10 October 1849) Norwegian official and politician

Wilhelm Christie served as president of the Storting* during the negotiations with Sweden over the establishment of the Norwegian-Swedish Union* in 1814. He was in large measure responsible for maintaining the integrity of the Norwegian constitution when the country was threatened with absorption by Sweden.

Christie spent the first 10 years of his life in Kristiansund, where his father was a government official. At age 10 he was sent to Bergen to attend school. Because Norway had no university, he went on to the University of Copenhagen and graduated in 1799 with a degree in law. He remained in Copenhagen* until 1808, where he held various posts within the bureaucracy. When he returned to Norway, he served as chief magistrate for the rural districts north of Bergen. He was well liked by the farmers in the district, where conflicts between farmers and government officials characterized local politics and social attitudes. In 1810 his scholarly interests led him to collect examples of Norwegian dialects, a pastime indicative of the stirring of interest in Norwegian nationalism. Through a quasi-literary organization called Quodlibet, he participated in salon discussions of contemporary political questions. In early 1814, when the Treaty of Kiel* transferred Norway to Sweden, a liberal constitution was the group's favorite topic.

When the Norwegians resisted the transfer to Sweden and elected a constituent assembly to meet at Eidsvoll, Christie was sent as a representative from Bergen. Because of his background in the law and the bureaucracy, he was elected as the assembly's secretary. As such he had little opportunity to participate in the debate. The position did, however, give him a comprehensive knowledge and understanding of the constitution drafted by the assembly.

In an attempt to gain British support for their claim to independence, Christian Frederik (see Christian VIII) sent a delegation which included Christie to England. The English refused to meet with the delegation, however, having already decided to throw their support behind Sweden. Returning to Norway in August 1814, Christie arrived in time to witness the signing of the Convention of Moss*, which confirmed Norway's acceptance of the transfer. The agreement stipulated, however, that the Norwegians could keep their constitution.

In the fall of 1814 Christie was elected by the citizens of Bergen to the Storting, the new Norwegian parliament. He was instructed by his constituents to oppose the union with Sweden. Although practical politics and military realities mitigated against such a stance, Christie, as the Storting's president, set the agenda and led the debate in a way which meant the best terms possible for Norway.

As Storting president, Christie also made certain that the constitution was treated separately from other questions about the union. Only those changes required by demands of the union would be made to the document, such as adding the word "Sweden" where reference was made to Norway. The constitution was kept separate from union matters, making Norway, in effect, sovereign in Norwegian matters. As a result of Christie's efforts, the constitution came to symbolize Norwegian independence, in spite of the political reality.

In 1820 Christie left active politics to return to his magistrate's position. Ill health forced him to retire in 1828, but he was appointed customs inspector, a post he held until his death.

Because of his long-standing interest in the cultural past of Norway, Christie founded the Bergen Museum in 1825 to preserve that past. As its leader for 24 years, he built up its collections and established it as a scholarly and scientific institution. Following Christie's death, a statue of him was dedicated at the market square in Bergen, the first to be raised in Norway. It stands today in front of his museum, as a tribute to its founder and the preserver of the Norwegian constitution.

REFERENCES: H. Koht, *1814: Norsk dagbok hundre aar etterpaa* (Christiania, 1914); K. Mykland, ed., *Omkring 1814: En antologi* (Oslo, 1967); S. Steen, *1814* (Oslo, 1951).

T. LEIREN

CHRISTINA (8 December 1626–9 April 1689) Queen of Sweden 1632–1654

Born in Stockholm*, Christina was the only child of Gustav II Adolf* and Maria Eleanora of Brandenburg. The death of the king in 1632 left her under the general tutelage of Chancellor Axel Oxenstierna* who headed the Regency. Taken from the care of her mother at the age of 10, she proved to be a gifted student in all subjects and male activities and was averse to female skills. At 17 she secretly became engaged to her cousin, Karl Gustav of Holstein-Gottorp (the future Karl X*).

Assuming the throne of Sweden when she came of age in 1644, Christina was determined to become master in her own house. The most serious issues she had to deal with were the domestic crisis and the Thirty Years' War, in which Sweden was a major participant, in alliance with France and opposed by the Habsburgs. She skillfully forced an early peace settlement (Westphalia, 1648) in which Sweden emerged as a principal victor, with substantial territorial holdings on the southern shores of the Baltic.

The domestic crisis was an outgrowth of Sweden's participation in the war. Gustav II and later the council of regents had rewarded the aristocracy for service in the war by granting them the right to collect and keep taxes from peasants living on crown lands. The nobility increasingly came to regard the land as theirs and the peasants as serfs. This threatened both the crown and the existence of the free peasants. Christina, after becoming queen, had continued the practice of alienating crown land in order to strengthen her own authority vis-a-vis the aristocracy. This was the background to the crisis facing the parliament in 1650.

Christina used the tension between the upper and lower estates in the Riksdag* in 1650 to force parliament's recognition of her cousin, Karl Gustaf, as crown prince. She steadfastly refused marriage after assuming the throne, lavished favors on eligible noblemen, spent significant sums on art objects and visiting scholars, and thus gained a reputation both at home and abroad of being a profligate, albeit a highly intelligent one. Christina secretly decided to convert to Roman Catholicism in the early 1650s. She abdicated in 1654, left Sweden, and was officially received into the Roman Catholic Church the following year.

Contrary to speculations during her lifetime and to the present day, she was not a man, a homosexual, or a hermaphrodite, but was thoroughly female; nor was she a psychopath or a near schizophrenic. In all likelihood a congenital defect caused a marked curvature of the spine by her late teens. Her portraits reveal a decidedly unattractive woman physically, she accentuated this impression by wearing mannish clothes and by lack of attention to her grooming. She possessed a strong and independent personality and refused to be dominated by anyone. While she was a most unpious Catholic, to the chagrin of the faithful and the popes, she may have found spiritual peace through friendship with the quietist divine Miguel Molinus. She is buried in St. Peter's Basilica in Rome.

Christina is also important for her lifelong patronage of the arts. In Rome she was a dominant private citizen and cultural personality for three decades. Giovanni Bernini, Alessandro Scarlatti, and Arcangelo Corelli are only the best known of the many she knew and assisted. She patronized the theater and opera, was one of the great book and manuscript collectors of the century, and founded academies in both Sweden and Rome.

REFERENCES: *Christina of Sweden: A Personality of European Civilization* (Stockholm: National Museum, 1966); E. Essen-Möller, *Drottning Christina. En människostudie ur läkaresynpunkt* (Lund: Gleerup, 1937) (translation and introduction forthcoming by P. V. Thorson with afterword by E. G. Olmstead: *Queen Christina: A Physician's Analysis*); H. C. Hjortsjö, *The Opening of Queen Christina's Sarcophagus in Rome* (Stockholm: Norstedts, 1966); G. Masson, *Queen Christina* (New York: Farrar, Straus and Giroux, 1968); *Queen Christina of Sweden: A Medical, Anthropological Investigation of Her Remains in Rome* (Lund: Gleerup, 1966); S. Stolpe, *Christina of Sweden* (New York: Macmillan, 1966); M. von Platen, *Christina of Sweden: Documents and Studies* (Stockholm: National Museum, 1966).

P. V. THORSON

CHRISTOFFER I (c. 1219–25 June 1259) King of Denmark 1252–1259

Christoffer was the last of the quarrelsome sons of Valdemar II* to rule in Denmark. His brief reign was marked by opposition from Abel's* widow, Mechtild of Holstein, who championed the right of her son Valdemar to the throne, and by conflicts with the magnates and the Church, both demanding privileges, and with Norway. He was at war almost constantly with these opponents, and general revolt broke out in 1256. His position was made worse by his trial and imprisonment of Archbishop Jakob Erlandsen in 1259. This action violated the long-claimed privilege of the clergy to trial by Church courts. Denmark was placed under interdict, and Christoffer was excommunicated. A number of north

German princes joined in the revolt against Christoffer. He died suddenly in 1259.

REFERENCES: *DBL*, vol. 4; *DH*, vol. 4.

B. NORDSTROM

CHRISTOFFER II (1276–2 August 1332) King of Denmark 1319–1326, 1330–1332

Christoffer was a son of Erik V* and brother of Erik VI*. Like his predecessors, he wished to restore the power of the crown, but found throughout his reign that the forces opposing him (the Danish and German magnates, the Church, the north German princes, and increasingly the Hanseatic League*) were overwhelming. An indicator of the crown's weakness may be seen in the royal charter (*håndfæstning*) which Christoffer had to agree to as the price of his election. Representatives of the four estates of the Danish people (clergy, nobility, burghers, and freehold farmers) assembled at his coronation at Viborg in January 1320. (This may have been the first meeting of such an assembly in Danish history.) There Christoffer promised to respect the right of the clergy to trial only by Church courts and their right to tax exemption. To the nobles he promised the continuation of their tax privileges and released them from any obligation to fight outside of Denmark. The burghers were guaranteed free trade, and the peasants were promised that their taxes would be no greater than those levied 100 years earlier. Christoffer further promised to call annual meetings of the parliament (*hof*) to deal with law, court cases, and questions of war and peace, and the king's council of advisors (*råd*) became the council of state (*rigsråd*), a body representing the interests of the nobles.

In the 1320s he attempted to renege on his promises and triggered an open revolt which was dominated by Count Gerhard of Holstein. Christoffer fled to Mecklenburg, and Valdemar III*, a twelve-year-old distant descendant of Abel*, was installed as a puppet king. For the next four years Denmark was run as a "great men's republic" dominated by Gerhard. The magnates, including Ludvig Albrektsen Eberstein, Lars Jonsen Panter, Knud Porse, and the Archbishop Karl, expanded their holdings and consolidated their independence from royal interference. Chaos and violence reigned. A counter-revolt was triggered by this situation, and Christoffer took advantage of it to attempt a return to power. He failed to defeat Gerhard and his cronies, but the count considered it politic to drop Valdemar and restore Christoffer to the throne. For the next two years Christoffer was little more than the puppet of the magnates. The king had virtually no power, and nearly every large fief in the country became the personal kingdom of a magnate. As a final blow, Christoffer had to accept transfer of the Skåne provinces to Sweden in 1332.

Denmark had reached a crisis point in the struggle between the crown and its opponents that had begun nearly 100 years earlier. In the process of creating a monarchy, the opponents of monarchy were called into being. During Christoffer's reign those forces triumphed. For eight years after his death Denmark had no king. Gerhard dominated as a kind of military dictator, there was no central government, and the magnates ruled as they wished on their own lands.

REFERENCES: *DBL*, vol. 3; *DH*, vol. 4.

B. NORDSTROM

CHRISTOFFER III (of Bavaria) (c. 26 February 1416–6 January 1448) King of Denmark 1440–1448, king of Norway 1442–1448, king of Sweden 1441–1448

Christoffer succeeded Erik of Pomerania* as monarch of the Kalmar Union* following the revolts of the 1430s. The son of a sister of Erik, he was raised at the court of Sigismund, the German emperor. His greatest interest was in military strategy, which he learned fighting the Hussites. He showed little interest in asserting the powers of the crown and had far less drive than his predecessors. (What might have happened had he lived beyond age 32 is a moot question.)

Throughout his reign, Christoffer was content to accept the demands of the magnates in his three kingdoms, to agree to rule with the councils, and to respect the privileges of the nobles and the Church. In Denmark the council was dominated by the archbishop, Hans Laxmand, until about 1443. Thereafter Christoffer showed greater authority and independence. His only significant problem in Denmark was a peasant revolt in Jyland in 1441, and this he crushed with great brutality. In Sweden and Norway the councils ruled largely unopposed. In the latter, however, the disintegration of any form of real government continued, and, after some initial resistance, Christoffer extended the privileges of the Hanse (*see* Hanseatic League) in Norway at the price of increased dependence on the Germans for Norway's economic survival. Christoffer also had to deal with the troublesome Erik and the diplomatic tangle in the Baltic. Erik continued to conspire and tried to use the Dutch and the English, who wished to develop their trade in the Baltic, against Christoffer. A campaign was launched against the deposed king in 1446, but it was abandoned without result. Christoffer's sudden death in 1448 created a succession crisis that resulted in the election of two kings, Christian I* of Oldenburg in Denmark and Norway and Karl VIII Knutsson* in Sweden.

REFERENCES: *DBL*, vol. 3; *DH*, vol. 4.

B. NORDSTROM

CIVIL WAR (War of Freedom) Finland

The period 1917–1918 was a turning point and formative national experience in Finnish history. During those critical and decisive years many earlier developments culminated, while new long-term divisions opened up and new trends began. Finland experienced a number of crises that shook its foundations. The Russian Revolution of March 1917 progressively polarized non-Socialist and Socialist Finns. There followed a parallel struggle for national independence from Russia and for internal political power, intertwined with aspirations for social reform. The whole experience proved so bitter and divisive that in many ways it has affected the social psychology of the Finnish society up to the present.

The period and its significance have caused a great deal of controversy. The many names that have been used to describe it suggest a wide range of emotions and interpretations. Besides civil war and a war of freedom or independence, it has been called revolution, internal war, fraternal war, racial war, rebellion, class war; recently it has received a neutral and colorless designation: the events of 1918.

In 1917 Finland was a society which had been under the domination of its neighbors for centuries. By the end of the thirteenth century it had become a part of the realm of Sweden, but in 1809 it passed under the suzerainty of the Russian tsars, where it enjoyed extensive autonomy till the end of the nineteenth century. Finland had a national identity and most trappings of a sovereign state short of independence, but it was not a particularly homogeneous unit. By the turn of the century it was divided by serious and far-reaching cleavages. There was a long-lasting ethnolinguistic rivalry between the Finnish-speaking majority and a Swedish-speaking minority. As the former had traditionally been unable to exercise influence proportionate to its numerical superiority, it felt slighted by the latter. The traditional Swedish-speaking ruling elite by and large retained its dominance till the beginning of the twentieth century. Starting in the 1890s and continuing at an accelerating pace during the first two decades of the twentieth century, the political mobilization of the working class under the impact of socialism caused another deep and widening fissure in Finnish society.

At the turn of the century outside pressure aggravated already existing social and political strains in Finland and was in part responsible for new cleavages. From the late 1890s on, the Russian authorities forcefully sought to integrate the Finnish state and its institutions into the Russian Empire. This threat, known as the policy of "Russification," produced severe disagreements in Finnish society concerning the best means and tactics to resist it. During World War I, existing problems became accentuated and new ones were brought about by wartime dislocations in the economy. Those prepared to resort to armed struggle to gain Finnish independence put their hope in German victory. Their preparations eventually were to help the non-Socialist Whites to defeat the Socialist Reds and to oust the Russians.

In March 1917 the Russian Revolution toppled the tsarist system in Finland, put an end to Russification policies, and restored the autonomy of the Finnish state. It also triggered a complicated series of events leading to an increasingly acute internal conflict.

The Social Democratic Party* had already gained an absolute majority in the Finnish parliament as a result of elections held in 1916. Consequently, it became the strongest party in the O. Tokoi coalition government, referred to as a senate, which was established in Finland after the March 1917 Revolution. The following months saw continuing restlessness and intensification of tensions between the Socialists and the non-Socialist parties. A system of voting in local elections which favored the property-owning and high-income groups; growing scarcity of food; widespread and increasingly massive unemployment which resulted from the end of Russian war orders and fortification works; wild inflation which left wages running far behind rising prices—all these circumstances became sources of dissatisfaction and agitation. In particular, they enabled the Socialist press, intent on sharpening the class struggle, to intensify working-class frustration and unhappiness with the existing social order. Dissatisfaction derived from such sources combined with rising expectations that the early phases of the revolution had inspired in the laboring masses; the workers' association with the radicalized Russian troops stationed in the country, who were subject to strong, active, and increasingly successful Bolshevik propaganda; the outbreak and success of the October Revolution in Petrograd—such developments helped to radicalize the Finnish workers and to push them toward a showdown with the non-Socialist elements of the country.

When the growing discontent of the working class combined with its increasing self-confidence and sense of power, it produced strikes and demonstrations which sometimes received support from the Russian soldiers. The disintegration of the discredited police and the gendarmerie of the old regime allowed riots, physical violence, and unauthorized seizures and destruction of private and public property to become frequent occurrences. This in turn led the non-Socialist and property-owning sections of the society to create local volunteer units, called either order or protective corps, which acquired arms and engaged in military drill. The Socialists promptly formed units, known as order guards and eventually as the armed Red Guards. The nation was dividing into two armed camps, a tension that strained Finnish society to the breaking point during 1917.

Finland's relationship with Russia and the presence of tens of thousands of undisciplined revolutionary Russian soldiers in its territory further complicated the situation. In July 1917 the Socialist-dominated Finnish parliament unilaterally declared itself the supreme authority in the country, claiming all powers except those dealing with foreign policy and military affairs, which were left to the Russian provisional government. The Russian provisional government, having survived the Bolshevik coup in July, rejected the action of the Finnish parliament and proceeded to dissolve it, over the protests of the Finnish Socialists.

In the parliamentary elections held in the fall of 1917, the non-Socialist parties won a clear majority. They formed a coalition government under the veteran political leader P. E. Svinhufvud, who as speaker of the parliament had become a symbol of resistance to Russification, leaving the Left in opposition. The outcome of the elections shocked the Socialists, already greatly embittered over the dissolution of the previous parliament, in which they had held a majority. The election results further radicalized the working class, for the conviction gained ground among them that the Socialists could not gain political power through peaceful means. Other measures and tactics seemed to be needed. In November 1917, in the wake of the successful Bolshevik Revolution, the Finnish Socialists proclaimed a general strike. It generated a good deal of violence and additional pressure for revolutionary action from the radicalized masses. The Bolsheviks also urged the Finnish Socialist leaders in the same direction, but the Socialists still hesitated to seize power.

On 6 December 1917, the Svinhufvud government, supported by the non-Socialist majority of the parliament, unilaterally declared Finnish independence. The Socialists, although also in favor of independence, voted against the government's declaration, arguing that independence should be achieved through negotiations with the Russian Bolshevik government. And despite the Finnish declaration of independence and its acceptance by the Bolshevik regime at the end of December, Russian troops remained in Finland in substantial numbers. They continued to collaborate closely with the Finnish Socialists, providing arms and ammunition to the Red Guards and displaying solidarity with striking Finnish workers; individual Russian soldiers also participated in local outbreaks of violence. Faced with these circumstances, the Finnish government was intent on building up an armed force of its own. It wanted to bolster its authority, to reestablish public order, and to reinforce the credibility of the country's independence and its standing in relation to Russia. The Socialists vehemently opposed the government's plans for an armed force, arguing that it would be used to intimidate the workers and their organizations. On 27 January 1918, soon after the Svinhufvud government adopted the non-Socialists' protective corps as its official armed force, the social revolution and civil war broke out.

The very first events of the war indicated its complexity. Though both camps resorted to armed action simultaneously, their main efforts took place in different parts of the country, and both were unaware of their opponents' moves. Red revolutionaries moved against the non-Socialist regime in Helsinki. At the same time the White protective corps attacked the Russian garrisons in the coastal province of Ostrobothnia in western Finland. Confrontations and clashes between the White and the Red units ensued in communities and localities across the land. After these initial contests were settled, the Reds found themselves in control of the most densely populated, industrialized, and urbanized southwestern and southern regions. The Whites, led by General Carl Gustav Mannerheim*, took over the rest of the country.

During the war both the Reds (the revolutionary Socialists) and the Whites (the non-Socialists) asked for and received foreign military aid. The Reds gained arms, ammunition, and other supplies and equipment as well as officers and men from the Russians. Swedish volunteers, German and Swedish arms, ammunition, and other supplies, and during the latter part of the war, regular German troops helped the Whites. The arrival of the German expeditionary corps in April 1918 shortened the war, but even before that the Whites had scored decisive victories and had gained the upper hand in the conflict, which ended with the capitulation of the last Red units at the beginning of May 1918.

The victors called the conflict the war of freedom; in their view only their success confirmed the country's independence from Russia. But the Finnish Reds were also in favor of independence. And in terms of the people who did the actual fighting, the Finnish Reds were the Whites' principal opponents. Outsiders furnished aid to both the Whites and Reds, but the overwhelming majority of fighting men on both sides were Finnish citizens. Neither the White nor the Red government was a creature of foreign powers, although each had to grant concessions to its helpers. In terms of its participants, then, the war was primarily a civil war. At the same time, it was also a social or even a class war. Working men provided the bulk of the Red Guards; landowning farmers and their sons formed the largest single occupational group among the White fighting men. The overwhelming majority of the middle class and the upper social strata—that is to say, teachers, shopkeepers, technicians, engineers, officials, civil servants, large land owners, independent professional men, clergy, the intelligentsia, and businessmen—also sided or sympathized with the Whites.

The presence of the Russians, who were willing to aid the revolutionary Reds, served as a convenient rallying point for the Whites. Anger and resentment against the Russian troops were easily bonded with the general patriotism which had traditionally held together the diverse socioeconomic, cultural, and ethnolinguistic groups that formed Finnish society. This general patriotism, together with other factors, such as resentment of the dramatic overturning of traditional power relationships and social values, fears for physical safety, and fears for loss of property, helped to construct a conduit through which White energies could be temporarily channeled. Thus the Swedish-speaking upperclass, the Finnish-speaking middle class, and the Finnish-speaking farmers uniting to fight the predominantly Finnish-speaking Reds becomes more understandable and comprehensible. Unwittingly or inadvertently, the Russian military in Finland helped construct a temporary common front between such traditionally divided or mutually antagonistic elements.

The Whites undertook their first major coordinated military actions not against the Finnish Reds but against the Russian garrisons. Such a beginning allowed the Whites to capitalize on latent nationalist anti-Russian sentiment. It gave credence to their claim that they were primarily interested in driving the Russians out of the country and safeguarding its newly won independence. The Reds, in contrast, had to fight under the psychological disadvantage of association with and support from the Russians, who had become the object of universal apprehension and often dislike, particularly during the preceding two decades of Russification policies. The defeated Reds paid a heavy price in suffering and lost lives in the tragic aftermath of the war, which left deep and long-lasting wounds.

REFERENCES: P. K. Hamalainen, *In Time of Storm: Revolution, Civil War, and the Ethnolinguistic Issue in Finland* (Albany: State University of New York Press, 1978); D. G. Kirby, ed., *Finland and Russia 1808–1920: From Autonomy to Independence: A Selection of Documents* (London: Macmillan, 1975); M. Menger, *Die Finnlandpolitik des deutschen Imperialismus: 1917–1918* (Berlin: Akademie Verlag, 1974); Y. Nurmio, *Suomen Itsenäistyminen Ja Saksa* (Helsinki: WSOY, 1957); J. Paasivirta, *Suomen Itsenäisyyskysymys 1917*, 2 vols. (Helsinki: WSOY, 1947–1949), and *Suomi Vuonna 1918*

(Helsinki: WSOY, 1957); J. Paavolainen, *Poltiittiset VäkivaltaisuudetSuomessa*, 2 vols. (Helsinki: Tammi, 1966–1967); T. Polvinen, *Venäjän Vallankumous Ja Suomi*, 2 vols. (Helsinki: WSOY, 1967 and 1971); V. Rasila, *Kansalaissodan Sosiaalinen Tausta* (Helsinki: Tammi, 1968); C. J. Smith, *Finland and the Russian Revolution, 1917–1922* (Athens, Ga.: University of Georgia Press, 1958); A. F. Upton, *The Finnish Revolution 1917–1918* (Minneapolis: University of Minnesota Press, 1980).

P. K. HAMALAINEN

CNUT *See* Knud

COAT OF ARMS, DENMARK

Denmark has a small coat of arms, which is a crowned escutcheon bearing three blue lions and nine red hearts (or water lilies) on a gold field. Used by most government authorities, this coat of arms derives from one used by Canute IV (*see* Knud VI) around 1190. Denmark also has a great coat of arms, which is reserved for use by the crown, the Royal House, the court, and the Royal Guard. The present form of this was adopted by Margrethe II* in 1972. It is composed of a central escutcheon held by two "savages." This escutcheon is quartered by a straight Dannebrog. In the first and fourth quarters are the three lions and nine hearts. The second quarter contains the two lions representing Slesvig. The third quarter contains the three-crown symbol from the Kalmar Union* period, the Faroese ram and the Greenland bear. At the center is the shield symbol of the Oldenborg line. The arms rest on a pediment, beneath which hang the chains of the Elephant and Dannebrog orders.

The present great coat of arms reflects the territorial changes that have occurred in Denmark since 1814. Earlier great coats of arms were considerably more complex because of the number of territories that fell under or were claimed to fall under the authority of the Danish crown. For example, the arms of Christian IV* contained a central escutcheon bearing the Danish lions surrounded by thirteen smaller escutcheons containing the Norwegian lions, the three-crown symbol, the Gotland insignia of a lion with nine hearts, the Wendish dragon, Gotland's Agnus Dei, Iceland's crowned *stokfisk*, Slesvig's two lions, Holstein's nettle leaf, Stormarn's swan, Ditmarksen's knight, the Oldenborg coat of arms, the Delmenhorst cross, and the Øsel eagle. A later coat of arms also contained the Lauenberg horse head.

REFERENCES: *Denmark: An Official Handbook* (Copenhagen: Press and Cultural Relations Department, Ministry of Foreign Affairs, 1974); *DH*.

B. NORDSTROM

COAT OF ARMS, SWEDEN

Modern Sweden has a great coat of arms and a small coat of arms. The latter is comparatively simple, composed of a crowned shield with three gold crowns on a blue field surrounded by the chain of the Order of the Seraphim. The great coat of arms is more complex and is composed of a pair of lions holding the main escutcheon, which is quartered by a gold cross. In the first and fourth quarters are three gold crowns on blue fields. In the second and third quarters are gold lions, also on blue fields. In the center is a smaller escutcheon bearing the insignia of the Vasa dynasty on the left and the Bernadotte dynasty on the right. The chain of the Order of the Seraphim surrounds the main escutcheon, and the entire shield stands on a gold pediment. The coat of arms is draped with a tent capped with a royal crown.

The origins of this coat of arms lie in the Middle Ages. By the close of the thirteenth century, the kings of Sweden were using a coat of arms dominated by lions, representing the Folkung dynasty. The election of Albrekt of Mecklenburg to the throne in 1364 necessitated a change in the royal insignia. In July 1364 a new coat of arms based on the symbol of the three crowns appeared on a royal document. After 1397 this royal coat of arms was incorporated into the insignia of the Kalmar Union* and the great coat of arms of Denmark (*see* Coat of Arms, Denmark). The latter use led to considerable friction between Denmark and Sweden after the dissolution of the union in 1523, and Sweden did not accede to the Danes' use of the symbol until 1613. During the turmoil of the union period, the royal council and several protectors of the realm in Sweden also used the three crowns.

In 1448 Karl VIII Knutsson* first employed a coat of arms based on the quartered shield bearing both the lions and the three crowns with the smaller escutcheon of the royal line in the center. The contemporary great coat of arms has descended from Knutsson's. The principal changes in this design came with the addition of the Vasa insignia in the 1520s and the Bernadotte insignia after 1818.

REFERENCES: *DSH*, vol. 2, pp. 172f.; *SU*, vol. 24.

B. NORDSTROM

COLLETT, JACOBINE CAMILLA (23 January 1813–March 1895) Norwegian feminist author

Born in Christiansand, the fourth of five children of Nikolai Wergeland and Alette Dorothea Thaulow, Camilla grew up in Eidsvoll, where her father served as parish minister. She was educated at home until the age of 13, when she was sent to a boarding school in Christiania (Oslo) for a year, and then to a Moravian school in Christiansfeld for two years.

Attractive and graceful, she had many admirers. In 1830, at age 17, she met the young poet Johan S. C. Welhaven (1807–1873), for whom she came to harbor a fervent passion from which she never entirely recovered. A bitter public feud between Welhaven (leader of the "Danophiles") on one side and Camilla's brother, the poet Henrik Wergeland (1808–1845, leader of the "patriots"), and her father on the other made Welhaven unwilling to marry her. His reluctance caused her to break with him in the winter of 1836. In 1839 she became engaged to Peter Jonas Collett (1813–1851), who had also written critically of her brother, and when she informed Welhaven of the engagement, he exploded in jealousy. She did not speak or write to him for two decades thereafter.

She married Collett in 1841. She had fully informed him of her years of anguish over Welhaven, and he treated her with the utmost consideration, helping her to attain a better state of mind by encouraging her to write. Her first published articles, written under his guidance, appeared in *Den Constitutionelle* (*The Constitutionalist*), the organ of the Welhaven faction, in the years 1841–1843. She and her husband also contributed to a volume by Peter C. Asbjørnsen, and she wrote several stories. In the 1840s she also began planning a novel which would focus on the problems of females growing up in a society that stifled their mental and emotional development. But nothing came of these plans until after her husband died in 1851.

Left a widow with four young sons, Camilla Collett sought solace in writing. She moved to Copenhagen* for a year in 1852 and worked on her long-planned novel, *Amtmandens døtre* (*The Governor's Daughters*), which was published in two parts in 1854 and 1855. This novel portrayed the tragedy for young women of loveless marriages of convenience. Its heroine, like Camilla herself, married someone other than her heart's choice. Critics complained about the novel's polemic message regarding the oppression of females, but the book struck a chord with many of its female readers. It was also a landmark in Norwegian literature: it was the first novel to give a realistic portrayal of a segment of Norwegian society; it was Norway's first psychological novel and first "real" novel. Later Norwegian writers who built on her work included Henrik Ibsen, Jonas Lie, Ellen Key*, and Alexander Kielland.

Camilla Collett tried writing verse for a while, but without much success. From 1862 on she traveled a great deal, to Denmark, Germany, France, and Italy, and wrote for various periodicals. Among her later major works was *I de lange naetter* (*Through the Long Nights*; 1862), an anonymous autobiographical work. In 1868 she published *Sidste blade* (*Last Pages*), a collection of articles which had appeared earlier, intending it to be her final book. However, in 1872 and 1873 she put out two more volumes of "last pages" (*Sidste blade* 2–3 and 4–5), in which she boldly set forth her views regarding women and the society in nonfiction form. Her sons asked her old friend Jørgen Moe to dissuade her from publishing these feminist missiles, but Camilla paid no heed.

She lived to see the establishment of the Norwegian Feminist Union* in 1884 and the Woman Suffrage Union (Kvinnestemmerettsforening) in 1885. Her novel *Amtmandens døtre* has been reprinted a number of times, and she is regarded as the pioneer of the feminist cause in Norway.

REFERENCES: S. Aa. Aarnes, *Søkelys på Amtmandens døtre* (Oslo: Universitetsforlaget, 1977); F. Bull, *Norges Litteratur fra Februarrevolusjonen til Forste Verdenskrig*, vol. 4 in *Norsk Litteratur Historie*, ed. F. Bull, F. Paasche, A. H. Winsnes, and P. Houm (Oslo: Aschehoug, 1960); C. Collett, *Amtmandens døtre* (Oslo: Gyldendal Norsk, 1968); H. A. Larsen, "Sentences from Camilla Collett," *American-Scandinavian Review*

5: 6 (Nov.–Dec. 1917): 357–59; *NBL*; C. Tschudi, *Tre Nutidskvinder* (Copenhagen: Schous, 1887).

N. FARQUHAR

COMMUNIST PARTY: FINLAND

The Finnish Communist Party was founded in 1918 in Moscow. The founders were members of Finland's Social Democratic Party* and participants in the Finnish Red army, which had been defeated in the Civil War* in the same year. After the Civil War it was common for the most radical Social Democrats to be dissatisfied with the Social Democratic Party, and many were prepared for a new revolutionary attempt. Most of the leading Socialists, however, had to escape to Soviet Russia during the Civil War or soon after. The program of the Finnish Communist Party was therefore much influenced by the Russian Communists.

The party took on the profile of Marxism-Leninism with a distinct intention to make violent revolution and to replace the prevailing political system with a proletarian dictatorship. In 1919 the party joined the Communist International, and in the same year the party was officially banned in Finland. From 1919 to 1944 the party was illegal, and party activities and leadership were mainly concentrated among Finnish refugees in the Soviet Union. In fact, the Finnish Communists became more influential in Moscow than in Finland. The best-known of these refugees was Otto Wille Kuusinen, who became an advisor to Stalin in the ideological struggle against Trotsky and later against Titoism. He also became secretary of the Comintern and vice-president of the Supreme Soviet.

Notwithstanding these restrictions, the party contested the parliamentary election of 1922 under the name Socialist Workers' Party. This new party had broken away from the Social Democratic Party but was controlled by the Finnish Communist Party in Moscow. The SWP won between 9 and 13 percent of the seats in the four parliamentary elections between 1922 and 1929. In the 1929 election the party was banned in Finland and lost its right to contest elections. From then until the end of the Finnish-Soviet war (*see* Continuation War) in 1944, the party was forced underground. Many Communists became electorally passive, while others voted for the Social Democrats in the absence of other alternatives.

The Finnish defeat in the war against the Soviet Union in 1944 resulted in a liberation for the Communist organizations. The Communists contested the first postwar election in 1945 with great success. The voters were mobilized to support the left-wing popular front organization called the Finnish People's Democratic League. In practice, however, this organization was and has been dominated by the Communists. In the aftermath of World War II*, the league was very successful at the polls. In 1958 the Communists won 25 percent of the seats in the parliament and became the party with the greatest electoral strength in Finland. In the late 1960s, however, electoral support declined, and in 1983 the party won only 13 percent of the seats in parliament.

The Communist Party's electoral decline has been at least partly caused by the internal conflict in the party between the Euro-Communist faction and the orthodox Moscow-oriented faction. The continuous conflict has deeply divided the party since the late 1960s. It seems that the Finnish Communist Party has faced a great problem in maintaining its ideology in the welfare state* that has developed in postwar Finland. The process of ideological shifting has, however, been delayed compared to other Western European Communist parties because of the close ties the party has with the Communist Party in the Soviet Union.

REFERENCES: I. Hakalehto, *SKP ja sen vaikutus poliittiseen ja ammatilliseen työ-vaenliikkeeseen 1918–1928* (Helsinki, 1966); J. Hodgson, *Communism in Finland: A History and Interpretation* (Princeton: Princeton University Press, 1967); D. K. Matheson, *Ideology, Political Action and the Finnish Working Class: A Survey Study of Political Behavior*, Commentationes Scientiarum Socialium 10 (Helsinki, 1979); J. Nousiainen, *Kommunismi Kuopion laanissa* (Joensuu, 1956); A. Upton, *Communism in Scandinavia and Finland: Politics of Opportunity* (New York: Anchor Press, 1973).

J. SUNDBERG

COMMUNIST PARTY: ICELAND *See* People's Alliance

COMMUNIST PARTY: NORWAY (Norges Kommunistiske Parti)

The Norwegian Communist Party (NKP) was founded by a minority of the Norwegian Labor Party* on 4 November 1923, following an extraordinary congress where a Comintern ultimatum that atheism be a Marxist tenet in the Labor Party's program was rejected by a vote of 169 to 110. Both factions regarded themselves as revolutionary. The first chairperson of the NKP was Sverre Støstad. Peder Furubotn* became party secretary, and Olaf Scheflo became editor of *Norges Kommunistblad*, the party's principal press organ. Of the seats the Labor Party held in the Storting*, thirteen went to members of the NKP. This strength was reduced to six after the 1924 election, and it dwindled to three in 1927. (Of these three, two returned to the Labor Party, including Støstad, who left the NKP with a number of intellectual left-wingers.) Between 1930 and 1945 the NKP held no seats in the parliament, and the membership of the party remained very small. In 1936, for example, the NKP polled only 4,376 votes or 0.3 percent of the electorate.

The Molotov-Ribbentrop Pact (23 August 1939) created a dilemma for the NKP and further weakened the party's position with the public. This position was even further hampered during the Winter War*, when Norwegian public opinion was generally on the side of the Finns. After the German invasion of Norway on 9 April 1940, the official NKP line, dictated from Moscow, advocated "an end to the imperialistic war, avoiding any resistance, and proposing peace with Germany." This policy line compromised its proponents in the NKP. Direct collaboration did not take place, however, and the party became involved actively in cross-party resistance against the Germans at the grass-roots level. The party was outlawed by the Germans in August 1940, and its leaders were rounded up by the Gestapo.

Active NKP resistance was led by Furubotn, who was elected head of the clandestine party on 31 December 1940. (Of the 22 party members present at the secret meeting which elected Furubotn, none objected and all accepted his policy of active resistance. No words of approval or disapproval came from the Comintern.) Furubotn's policy caused friction between the Communists and the non-violent Home Front resistance groups. The clandestine Communist press was widely read, and *Friheten* (*Freedom*) alone had a circulation of around 20,000.

The heroic Communist resistance participation and possibly admiration for the Soviet Union's war effort resulted in a great election victory for the NKP in 1945. The party received nearly 12 percent of the votes and secured eleven seats in the Storting and two places in the Labor cabinet. Changes in the Norwegian election laws caused the NKP to lose all its seats in the Storting in 1949, in spite of the second highest popular vote in the party's history. After this defeat a Stalinist minority within the NKP staged a dramatic coup against the so-called second center, that is, the Furubotn-led majority which had not joined the Cominform in 1947 but had repudiated both the Marshall Plan and NATO and favored a nativist Communist line. In Norway, as in Hungary and other European countries, "Titoists, Trotskyists, and imperialistic agents of the CIA" were accused of a variety of crimes. Furubotn, his wartime cohorts, and other "bourgeois" party members were expelled, and Emil Løvlien took over as party leader. When the party celebrated its fortieth anniversary in 1963, no mention was made of Furubotn or the 1949 coup.

The decline of electoral support continued through the 1950s and 1960s. In 1961 a new splinter party, Socialistiske Folkeparti/SF (the Socialist People's Party), was formed, and it attracted members from both the Labor Party and the NKP. In 1965 the Labor Party lost its majority in the Storting and, after 30 years in power, Labor was replaced by a non-Socialist coalition. The NKP lost all its Storting seats and captured only 1.4 percent of the votes. In the wake of this defeat, party leadership changed again. Reidar Larsen replaced Løvlien, but this did not halt the party's decline. In 1969 its share of the vote sank to 1 percent. After the 1981 election the NKP was lumped with all the other small parties in the country under the label "Other Parties," which together captured only 1.7 percent of the total votes cast.

The chairperson of the party in 1983 was Hans I. Kleven, and Odd F. Karlsen was party secretary.

REFERENCES: *Facts about Norway* (Oslo: *Aftonposten*, 1971); T. Halvorsen, *NKP i Krise, om Oppgjøret med det annet Sentrum 1949–1950* (Oslo: Gyldendal, 1981); Norges Kommunistiske Parti, *Norges Kommunistiske Parti, Femti Aar i Kamp, 1923–1973* (Oslo: 1973).

G. S. GORDON

COMMUNIST PARTY: SWEDEN (Sveriges kommunistiska parti) since 1967 Left Party Communists (Vänsterpartiet Kommunisterna)

The Communist Party grew out of a faction which left the Social Democratic

Party* in February 1917. Eventually, part of the faction joined the Comintern and in 1921 became the Communist Party of Sweden. As a section of the Communist International, the party adapted its program and strategy to the guidelines laid down by the Comintern. Affiliation to the International and the periodic shifts of its strategy resulted in several party splits during the 1920s and 1930s. With the dissolution of the Comintern in 1943, the party drafted a new program discarding the call for a "dictatorship of the proletariat" and envisioning the possibility of a peaceful transition to socialism. The Communists sought collaboration with the Social Democrats and proposed a merger of the two parties. The advent of the Cold War was accompanied by a reformulation of party tasks and tactics. Ideas of a peaceful transition to socialism following a distinctively national path did not reappear until the next major reorientation in Soviet policy in the mid-1950s under Krushchev. This, along with diminishing support, set the stage for three changes altering the character of the party. First, the party stated unambiguously its espousal of parliamentarism and democratic elections. Revolution was no longer defined as seizing power by violent means but as a process of change in the direction of socialism. Second, the Communists adopted an increasingly independent stance from the Soviet Union. Third, the party apparatus was overhauled, resulting in an open organization comparable to those of other Swedish parties. This metamorphosis of the party did not occur without internal disputes. From the late 1960s through the mid-1970s the party again experienced several splits.

Since its founding the party has been represented in the Riksdag*, but its representation has been quite small. Through the years the Communist share of the vote has averaged about 5 percent. Traditionally, the mainstay of the Communist electoral support has been the workers. During the 1970s the Communists attracted the support of students and middle-class voters, and at the end of the decade workers no longer constituted an absolute majority among party voters. The geographical strongholds of the party are Norrbotten (the northernmost province), Stockholm*, and Gothenburg*.

In terms of institutional power, the influence of the Communists has been minimal. Until the 1970 Parliamentary Reform, Communist representation in the Riksdag was even lower than the party's share of the vote. Only rarely have the Communists been included in the parliamentary committees and inquiry commissions. Although the Communists have at times held the parliamentary balance during the postwar period (1957–1960, 1970–1977), they have been unable to exploit this to their advantage. Their leverage was limited because if they failed to support the Social Democrats they would have been held responsible for bringing down a Labor cabinet and allowing the non-Socialists to form a government. Nor have the Communists been particularly successful in gaining influence in the trade union movement.

Much of the political importance of the party has derived from its complex relationship with the Social Democrats—and the Communists' potential to draw support from the Social Democrats. The cycles of radicalization within the Social

Democratic Party in 1920, the mid-1940s, and late 1960s coincided with periods when the Communists posed a special challenge. The transformation of the Communist Party in the 1960s increased its legitimacy and credibility, probably enhancing what has been termed its "cultural power"—its influence in defining problems and setting the political agenda.

REFERENCES: A. Sparring, "The Communist Party of Sweden," in A. F. Upton, *Communism in Scandinavia and Finland* (New York: Anchor/Doubleday, 1973), and "Sweden," in Wm. Griffith, ed., *Communism in Europe*, vol. 2 (Cambridge, Mass.: MIT Press, 1966); D. Tarschys, "The Unique Role of the Swedish CP," *Problems of Communism*, May-June 1974, pp. 36–44, and "The Changing Basis of Radical Socialism in Scandinavia," in K. H. Cerny, ed., *Scandinavia at the Polls* (Washington, D.C.: American Enterprise Institute, 1977).

D. SAINSBURY

CONSERVATIVE PARTY: FINLAND *See* National Coalition (Conservative) Party

CONSERVATIVE PARTY: NORWAY Høyre

Høyre emerged in the early 1880s and was formally organized in 1884 as one of the two parties arising from a constitutional political crisis, the other party being the Liberal Party (Venstre). The name *Høyre* means literally "the Right." The party differs in origin from many other conservative parties in that it was mainly a party of higher civil servants and to some extent of business interests, rather than being a party of land owners. Over time, however, it became more and more identified with the latter group and with middle-class interests in general.

The Conservative Party in Norway is now, and has been through most of the post-World War II period, in many ways different from the pre-1940 party. Its original rejection of state intervention and its preference for economic liberalism have given way to an acceptance of the "mixed economy" wherein the state not only regulates competition but is also an active participant in production and a provider of services. The party has also accepted the idea of the state as the main pillar in an extensive welfare state*. However, in government it has favored greater deregulation, tax cuts, and privatizing of some functions. In general, the party argues for greater individual freedom of action. It sees the state as having become too great a regulator, particularly in the economic field. In terms of foreign policy, it is both Atlantic- and European-oriented. The party is strongly in favor of Norwegian NATO membership and is anxious to preserve American presence in European defense. The party was strongly in favor of Norwegian membership in the European Community in the early 1970s, and even now argues the need for Norway to have closer cooperation with the EC in matters of foreign and security policy.

In the 1970s the party grew sharply from 17.1 percent of the vote in 1973 to 30 percent in 1981. During the same period, the party almost doubled its membership from about 90,000. In 1981 the Conservative Party formed a minority government. This was expanded in 1982 to a majority coalition government including the Christian Democratic Party* and the Agrarian Party (see Center Party: Norway).

REFERENCES: T. Bjørklund and B. Hagtvet, eds., Høyrebølgen. Epokeskifte i norsk etterkrigshistorie? (Oslo, 1982); R. Danielsen et al., Høyres Historie (forthcoming); A. Kaartvedt, Kampen mot parlamentarisme 1880–1884 (Oslo: Universitetsforlaget, 1956); B. Kristiansen and L. Svåsand, "The Conservative Party in Norway: From Opposition to Alternative Government," in Z. Layton-Henry, ed., Conservative Politics in Europe (London: Macmillan, 1982), pp. 103–30; R. Stein, "Geography, Religion and Social Class: Cross-Cutting Cleavages in Norwegian Politics," in S. M. Lipset and S. Rokkan, eds., Party Systems and Voter Alignments (New York: Free Press, 1976); H. Valen, Valg og politik. Et samfunn i endring (Oslo: NKS-forlaget, 1981).

L. SVÅSAND

CONSERVATIVE PARTY: SWEDEN Moderata Samlingspartiet

The Swedish Conservative Party can trace its origins back to caucus parties which emerged in the Riksdag* after the 1866 Parliamentary Reform—more specifically to the Ruralist Party (Lantmannapartiet) formed in the Lower Chamber in 1867 and the conservative caucus in the Upper Chamber which eventually became the Majority Party (Protectionists) in 1888. A constituency organization, the General Voters Alliance (Allmänna Valmansförbundet), was established in 1904 to coordinate the campaign activities of various conservative groups in parliament. The final consolidation of the parliamentary party did not occur until the mid-1930s, at which time it officially adopted the label of the Right (Högern). In 1969 the Conservatives changed their name to the Moderate Unity Party (Moderata Samlingspartiet).

Prior to the first elections based on manhood suffrage in 1911, conservative circles generally dominated parliament and the cabinet, and in the Upper Chamber the Conservatives' dominance continued until the introduction of universal and equal suffrage in 1921. During the years 1906–1930, the Conservatives formed four governments: Arvid Lindman*, 1906–1911, Carl Swartz, 1917; Ernst Trygger, 1923–1924; and Arvid Lindman, 1928–1930. The Hjalmar Hammarskjöld cabinet, although not a party government, was also pro-Conservative (1914–1917). During World War II*, party representatives were members of the national coalition cabinet (1939–1945). In the late 1970s the Conservatives participated in two non-Socialist coalition governments (1976–1978 and 1979–1981).

From 1920 until 1948 the Conservatives were the largest non-Socialist party. But the long-range electoral trend of the party during this period was generally one of decline. In the 1920s the Conservative share of the vote averaged around 27 percent. By 1948 it had fallen to 12 percent. In the late 1950s, for a brief period, and again in the late 1970s the Conservatives became the largest non-Socialist party.

Although the lineage of the Conservative Party goes back to the Ruralists, and land owners and rural voters provided substantial backing through the mid-1950s, industrial and urban interests grew steadily prominent and entrenched their position in the party from the turn of the century onwards. Eventually the metropolitan areas became the party's major strongholds, and in the 1970s the Conservatives increasingly became an urban party. In recent decades the party mainly attracted the votes of professionals, managers, high-salaried officials, the self-employed and white-collar workers. The Conservatives have made little headway in winning working-class voters. From 1956 to 1976 only 2 to 4 percent of the workers voted for the party.

The philosophy of the Conservatives during the early years of the party bore the stamp of etatist tendencies and a paternalistic reformism. At the same time, the ideas of Manchester liberalism also became influential within the party, especially in industrial circles. The 1919 Party Program reflected both influences. The Program placed the "fatherland" above individual and class interests and called for obedience to the laws. It also advocated reforms to strengthen the people's sense of responsibility and identity with the realm and the nation. Simultaneously, the Program stressed private ownership and a vigorous economy unmenaced by state coercion and the threat of socialization. Gradually, etatist tendencies gave way to tenets of individualism. In the 1970s the party described its philosophy as combining conservative and liberal ideas. Vestiges of conservativism from the 1919 Program included emphasis on the nation and national independence through a strong defense, praise of traditional institutions as the cornerstones of society—the family, the church and the monarchy—and the preservation of the Swedish cultural heritage from generation to generation. Several program planks have recurred as Conservative pledges in election campaigns during the postwar period. Perennial party pledges focused on a strong defense, a property-owning democracy, lower taxes, cutbacks in the public sector, and opposition to economic intervention and government bureaucracy.

REFERENCES: E. Anners, "Conservatism in Sweden," in M. D. Hancock and G. Sjoberg, eds., *Politics in the Post-Welfare State* (New York: Columbia University Press, 1972); D. Rustow, *The Politics of Compromise* (Princeton: Princeton University Press, 1955); R. Torstendahl, *Mellan nykonservatism och liberalism* (includes, English summary) (Uppsala: Almqvist & Wiksell, 1969); D. Verney, *Parliamentary Reform in Sweden 1866–1921* (Oxford: Clarendon, 1957).

D. SAINSBURY

CONSTITUTIONAL DEVELOPMENT

Denmark

The earliest political institutions in Denmark about which documentable evidence exists date from the Viking Age*. Then, free men met in assemblies (*thing*) to revere gods, judge disputes, affirm laws and social obligations, and acknowledge the preeminence of him who most successfully pressed his claim to be king. Continual war favored the rise of chieftains capable of raising armies (*hird*). This process culminated at least as early as 930 when Denmark was united under King Gorm*.

For centuries the monarchy remained elective, and the kings remained bound (in theory) to respect the provincial *things*. But strong kings assumed ever greater powers. Svend Estridsen (Sven II*, elected 1047) and his successors issued edicts, granted titles to favorites, and assumed judicial functions. Under King Niels* (1104) a central administration took form.

As the monarchy grew in power, so did the intensity of the struggle to possess it. Thirty years of fierce civil war ended in 1157 with the triumph of Valdemar Knudson (Valdemar I*), who consolidated his power by courting the Church. Valdemar had his son, Knud VI*, designated the rightful heir to the throne by the archbishop, thus making any later attempt to make war for the throne seem impious. His move also had the effect of making the monarchy hereditary, which was a departure from accepted practice.

In the thirteenth century churchmen and nobles regretted the unlimited authority the hereditary monarch assumed. They rose against King Erik V* in 1282 and required him to accept a charter (*håndfæstning*) in which he promised to abide by the laws of the realm's provinces, accept the principle of habeas corpus, exempt the nobles from certain taxes, and bring the nobles into a council (Danehof) in his court. The monarchy was again made elective. The charter resembled England's Magna Charta and amounted to Denmark's first written constitution.

The Danehof failed to exercise effective restraint on the king for want of unity among the nobles. Some nobles sought advancement by moving closer to the king. Institutionally, this meant the forming of a Council of the Realm (Rigsråd), a smaller body of the king's confidants which soon eclipsed the Danehof. For over three centuries thereafter, Denmark was governed by king and council, a combination which protected the privileges of the nobility.

In the shadow of king and council appeared other assemblies: a Danish Diet (Herredagen) which admitted nobles beyond those on the council, and an assembly of estates (Staendermøderne), which included representatives of the clergy, burghers, and (when invited) free peasants. These assemblies were convened when the king wished to extract from his subjects sacrifices to defend the realm. They were not convened often, however, because some burghers would raise disquieting questions about the nobility's privileges.

In 1660, at the conclusion of a ruinous war, King Frederik III* convened the estates and indicated that he was prepared to move against the nobility. The two lower estates passed a resolution making the monarchy hereditary and unfettered by any *håndfæstning*. The king got a citizens' militia in Copenhagen* to intimidate the council into accepting it. The council then became defunct. The estates in 1665 adopted the Royal Law (Kongeloven) declaring the monarch "henceforth to be regarded by all his subjects as here on earth superior to all human laws and knowing no other superior save God." This turn to absolute monarchy offended British envoy Robert Molesworth, whose book *An Account of Denmark* (1693) later became a classic for Whig thinkers in England and America.

During the period of absolutism (1660–1849) Denmark's government was generally orderly and predictable. A tradition of law was maintained, and power emanated from administrative offices, which were no longer monopolized by nobles. Authorities and the established church (Lutheran after 1536) promoted loyalty and obedience.

Absolutism might have endured indefinitely had not King Frederik VI* been obliged by the Treaty of Kiel* (1814) to grant his duchy, Holstein, the privilege of electing a consultative assembly. He did this at the behest of the German Confederation, of which Holstein was a member. Reluctantly, but logically, the king granted assemblies to his Danish lands as well. Convening them led in due course to the establishment of a true parliament, the Rigsdag, which was ordained by the Constitution of 5 June 1849 (Junigrundloven). Members of the Rigsdag's upper house (Landsting) were indirectly elected by electoral colleges and had to be at least 40 and possess a certain amount of property. The king was empowered to designate his own ministers and to share in the legislative power, but he was not to levy taxes without the Rigsdag's consent. Freedom of the press, assembly, and religion were guaranteed, and a form of habeas corpus was provided. The new constitution was, for its time, one of the most liberal in Europe.

The Constitution of 1849 applied to Denmark proper, but not to the duchies of Slesvig, Holstein, or Lauenburg, over which the Danish monarch was also sovereign. For their sake a separate constitution for "associates under the Danish monarchy" was instituted in 1855. It set up a separate parliament, the Rigsråd, which was the first legislature anywhere in the world to be elected entirely by proportional representation. The constitution was controversial because of its democratic features, and many Germans could not be reconciled to remaining under Danish rule. The controversy led to a war in 1864, the loss of the duchies to Prussia, and the demise of the Rigsråd.

After the war the constitution was changed again. In 1866 the members of the Rigsdag's upper house were made electable by a system of indirect election and proportional representation. This gave the propertied classes a great advantage in that chamber. The result was a perpetual constitutional crisis in the form of a deadlock between a conservative, unrepresentative upper chamber and a liberal, representative lower chamber. The king tipped the balance in favor of the conservative side, because he appointed the cabinet and with it ruled by decree as long as the Rigsdag remained deadlocked. The electorate regularly voted liberal majorities into the Folketing*, but the votes could not change the cabinet.

After the party of the Left won a large majority in 1901, King Christian IX* relented. He asked a university professor to form a liberal cabinet acceptable to the Folketing. Parliamentarism was thus instituted in Denmark. The event was thereafter remembered as the "change of system" (systemskifte).

The change of system necessarily heightened the importance of elections and the parties contesting them. The Liberal Party and its offshoot, the Radical Liberals, enjoyed success. In 1915 they brought about further changes making the constitution still more democratic. The right to vote in Landsting elections was given to all citizens over 35, and the right to vote in Folketing elections was given to all over 25. Proportional representation was instituted for some seats for the first time. Also instituted were basic judicial reforms: the judiciary was clearly separated from the executive, and juries were provided for to determine guilt in serious criminal cases.

Though the change of system occurred in 1901, explicit incorporation of it in the written constitution lagged. Disagreement among the political parties about what to do with the upper chamber was the principal cause of the delay. Finally, an almost unanimous Rigsdag backed up by a popular referendum adopted the Constitution of 1953, which abolished the Landsting and the name Rigsdag. The parliament became one chamber, the Folketing, which was expanded from 159 to 179 seats. Under rules plainly laid down, the prime minister had to be a person acceptable to the majority in the Folketing. Were a vote of censure against the prime minister to pass, that official and the cabinet would have to resign or submit to a new election. The Folketing was to order a popular referendum on every measure on which a third of its members so requested. The Folketing was to appoint one or two persons as *ombudsmand* to investigate citizens' complaints against government officials and agencies. The Folketing was authorized to delegate powers to international agencies where it served the cause of international cooperation; this clause supported the Folketing's vote in 1972 allowing Denmark's entry into the Common Market.

Constitutional changes establishing parliamentary government diminished the monarch's power, but not the position. Monarchy endured. A new Act of Succession (Arvfølgelov) was enacted in the same year the new constitution was adopted. It restored the right of females to succeed to the throne, although with precedence reserved for male heirs.

The general voting age, lowered to 25 in 1953, was further lowered by constitutional amendment to 21 in 1961 and to 20 in 1971.

REFERENCES: R. T. Anderson, *Denmark: Success of a Developing Nation* (Cambridge, Mass.: Schenkman, 1975); W. Glyn Jones, *Denmark* (New York: Praeger, 1970); Poul Møller, *Vor nye grundlov* (Hellerup: Olsens, 1953); Bengt Rying, ed., *Denmark: An Official Handbook* (Copenhagen: Danish Press and Information Service, 1974); Sven Skovmand, *Danmarks riges grundlov* (Copenhagen: Shultz, 1977); Max Sørenson, *Statsforfatningsret* (Copenhagen: Juristforbundet, 1973); F. W. Wendt, *Håndbog i Danmarks politiske historie fra freden i Kiel til vore dage* (Copenhagen: Gyldendal, 1934).

Iceland

The early settlers of Iceland, like other Germanic peoples, met in assemblies called *things* where they reaffirmed their understanding of the laws that prevailed among them. Each local *thing* met at a holy place overseen by a *goði**, who was both priest and chief. At midsummer leading men from all parts of the country met in an Althing* (*alþing*). The Althing instituted regional courts in 964 A.D. and formally accepted the country's division into sections called *goðorð*.

The *goðar* dominated Icelandic life. Other men put themselves under the protection of a *goði* and in return supported him at the *thing*. A family protected by a *goði* who was weak was in peril. *Things* and their courts might make rulings in disputes, but unless the judgments were backed by strong *goðar*, justice might not be served. Families had the right to transfer allegiance from one *goði* to another if they could find one who would accept them. The *goðar* achieved among themselves a rough balance of power, which was the main safeguard of law and order. The introduction of Christianity in the eleventh century brought in its wake disputes about the status the priests of the new religion should have as against those of the old. The disputes were sometimes violent. In 1262, in apparent hope for peace, Icelanders pledged allegiance to the king of Norway, some less willingly than others.

The Norwegian king in 1271 and 1281 reorganized the Althing, assigning to the crown the right to appoint 84 lifetime members, of which 36 were to be picked to constitute the *lögretta*, the subdivision which considered laws. The king wished the Althing to be an instrument of the crown, but the Althing continued as before to be attended by all Icelandic leaders, some of whom owed little to the king. On occasion the Althing insisted that royal decrees could not be valid in Iceland without the Althing's consent. The king sent to Iceland royal governors with various titles (earl, *hirdstjori*, *stipamtsmaðr*), who found it expedient to solicit Althing support.

In 1380 the crown of Norway passed by inheritance to Oluf III (see Kalmar Union and Margrethe I) of Denmark, beginning a dynastic union of Norway and Denmark that lasted 434 years. The Danish kings assumed ever increasing authority over Iceland. Lutheran church reform was imposed in Iceland in the sixteenth century over the opposition of the Catholic bishop, Jon Arason. Danish trading monopolies, which stifled Icelandic commerce, were imposed in the seventeenth century. The Althing was abolished by royal decree in 1800.

Iceland's status as a passive domain of the Danish king was all too evident in 1814, when Denmark ceded Norway to Sweden but kept Iceland. The inhabitants of Iceland began to ask for a role in their own affairs. Danes in Denmark also asked for self-government, but not with the intent of undoing ties with Iceland.

Political reforms favoring self-government in the king's domains nevertheless led inexorably to Icelandic independence. King Christian VIII*, following precedents he set in Denmark, revived the Althing as a consultative body in 1843. Then Frederik VII* in 1849 promised not to promulgate laws in Iceland without the Althing's consent. A national constituent assembly convened in Iceland in 1851 and secured several concessions: the Danish trade monopoly was abolished, freedom of the press was guaranteed, and equality of Icelandic and Danish languages in state administration was established. In 1871 the Danish Rigsdag granted Iceland home rule, and in 1874, when commemorating the 1,000th anniversary of Iceland's first settlement, King Christian IX* conferred on Iceland its own constitution separate from Denmark's. The constitution declared Iceland a constitutional monarchy with its own legislature, the Althing, and with the king governing through a vice-regent and retaining an absolute veto.

King Christian IX in 1901 granted the Danish Rigsdag appointment of a government acceptable to its majority, and having thus conceded parliamentary government to Denmark, he extended it in 1903 to Iceland's Althing as well.

In response to further entreaties, Denmark agreed to an Act of Federation in 1908 renouncing all Danish responsibilities for Iceland save that of patrolling the coasts and handling foreign affairs. In 1918 the Rigsdag and the Althing adopted a new Act of Federation which made submission to the same king the sole tie between the two countries. Even that was made revocable after 25 years. Shortly thereafter the Althing on its own initiative adopted a new constitution, which was approved by a popular referendum and went into effect on 1 January 1921. The royal veto was eliminated. For all practical purposes, Iceland's independence was realized.

Final separation from Denmark occurred during World War II*. The Althing, supported by a popular referendum, withdrew allegiance to the crown and proclaimed Iceland an independent republic with a new constitution which became effective on 17 June 1944.

For all their efforts to disassociate themselves from the Danes, the Icelanders retained for themselves a constitution much like Denmark's. They kept a parliamentary system centered on the Althing. They kept composition of the Althing subject to popular elections. They kept for themselves rights of free speech, free association, and free assembly, and they ordained an independent judiciary to secure their rights. The constitution's novel feature was the office of the president, which was to be filled by a person elected by popular vote to a four-year term. The constitution gave the president the powers to appoint the government and to dissolve the Althing, but, like a constitutional monarch, the president was not meant to actually use the powers except as directed by the leaders of the parties dominant in the Althing. The spirit if not the letter of the constitution required the president to be essentially a ceremonial figure.

Amendment of the constitution was made possible by two favorable votes in the Althing, with a popular election intervening. The prime subject for amendment since the constitution was adopted in 1944 has been legislative apportionment. An electoral system of largely single-member districts led to the overrepresentation of the rural population, so the system was changed by constitutional amendment in 1959 to rely more heavily on multi-member districts and proportional representation. Further reform along the same lines was accomplished in 1983. The voting age was set at 21 in 1944; it was reduced to 20 in 1967 and to 18 in 1983.

REFERENCES: J. C. Griffiths, *Modern Iceland* (New York: Praeger, 1969); O. Johannesson, *Stjórnskipun Islands* (Reykjavik: Iðunn, 1978); S. A. Magnusson, *Northern Sphinx* (London: Hurst, 1977); J. Sigurðsson, *Om Islands statsretlige forhold* (Copenhagen: Gyldendal, 1855); V. Stefansson, *Iceland: The First American Republic* (New York: Doubleday, 1939); H. Þorleifsson, *Fra einveldi til lyðveldis* (Reykjavik: Bokaverzlun S. Emundssonar, 1973).

Norway

Medieval Norway was ruled by kings who governed with some regard for deliberative assemblies, *lagting*. In the fourteenth century, however, the Norwegian royal line came to an end, and Norway became subject to Danish kings, who established a centralized system of administration and claimed absolute authority.

When Norway was eventually detached from Denmark and ceded to Sweden, Norwegians seized the opportunity to restore institutions of self-government. In May 1814 a constituent assembly met to write the Eidsvoll Constitution* (Grunnloven). Its members were much influenced by eighteenth-century precepts like the idea of popular sovereignty and the principle of separation of powers, each of which barred absolute monarchy. The executive power was entrusted to the king and his ministers, who were explicitly barred from the legislature. The legislative power was entrusted to the Storting*, which was to be made up of representatives chosen by voters meeting property and other qualifications.The Storting's members were chosen as if they were to be members of a unicameral legislature, but by a unique provision of the constitution they were obliged, once they convened, to divide themselves into two chambers.

The Norwegians of 1814 had hoped to be able to choose their own king, preferably someone who would swear to respect their constitution and their Storting. This choice was denied them by the great powers, who assigned Norway to the Swedish monarch. The new king accepted the new constitution in order to acquire Norway peacefully, but throughout the nineteenth century conflict between the king and the Storting was the mainspring of constitutional development. In 1884 the king was forced to accept as prime minister Johan Sverdrup*, who enjoyed the support of the Storting's majority. The king thereby conceded that without a ministry acceptable to the legislature he could not rule.

Acceptance of the parliamentary principle undid the separation of powers established by the written constitution. It made the Storting predominant. In the 1890s the Storting made demands which caused King Oskar II* much distress, with the ultimate result that in 1905 the joint monarchy was dissolved. So strong was the Storting that it then might have declared Norway a republic, as indeed many Stortingsmen like Johan Castberg* wished it would. But other considerations, among them cosmetic ones, favored enthroning a new king, who by popular consent was Prince Karl of Denmark. He assumed the new name and title King Haakon VII* of Norway. Thereafter Norway was a constitutional monarchy with parliamentary supremacy over the executive. The king (and hence the prime minister as well) was never given the power to dissolve the Storting. Ministers, while entitled since 1884 to attend Storting sessions, were forbidden themselves to be voting Stortingsmen and ministers at the same time.

Just as Norway adopted parliamentarism without formally amending its written constitution, so did it acquire a form of judicial review in its courts. This exercise of power by the courts had been neither ordained nor even intended by the constitution's framers, but in the course of actual adjudication judges assumed the duty of striking down laws and administrative decrees adopted short of prescribed constitutional procedures.

Formal amendment of the constitution has required that a proposal be adopted by the Storting, that there be an intervening election, and that the same proposal be approved by a three-quarters vote by the newly elected Storting. The constitution has been formally amended several times since its adoption, notably in regard to the extension of the franchise, which was made universal in 1913, but with this exception none of the formal amendments has been as momentous as the informal changes described above.

The constitution in broad outline has remained the same as it was in 1814. It declared Norway an independent, sovereign kingdom, pronounced the evangelical Lutheran faith the official religion, and entrusted appropriate duties and powers to king, Storting, and courts. No separate "bill of rights" was included, but assorted provisions inserted at the end of the document affirmed freedoms of speech and press and forbade laws and decrees which would be retroactive, grant titles of nobility, entail loss of a citizen's liberty without due process of law, or appropriate private property without just compensation. The constitution was in suspension during the German occupation of 1940–1945 but was restored after liberation.

REFERENCES: J. Andenaes, *The Constitution of Norway* (Oslo: Oslo University Press, 1960), and *Grunnloven Vår, 1814 till 1975* (Oslo: Universitetsforlaget, 1976); P. Berg, F. Castberg, and S. Steen, *Arven fra Eidsvoll* (Oslo: S. Dahl, 1945); H. L. Braekstad, *The Constitution of the Kingdom of Norway* (London: D. Nutt, 1905).

Sweden

A rudimentary form of constitutionalism existed in Sweden as early as the twelfth century in the form of codes which defined and limited official prerogatives. In the middle of the fourteenth century Magnus Eriksson* promulgated a national code which, because it pronounced on such matters as succession to the throne and the extent of royal authority, amounted to a proto-constitution. Later kings swore upon their accession to the throne to abide by law and respect their subjects' rights.

King Gustav II Adolf* in 1611 granted in writing that the estates of the realm, convened in the Riksdag*, had substantial authority. This was reaffirmed by the Riksdag Act of 1617. Foundations were thus laid for a constitutional separation of powers, though with the king paramount.

The Riksdag in 1634 adopted a fundamental law, the Instrument of Government (Regeringsform), to delimit responsibilities of the regency established for Gustav Adolf's only child and heir, Christina*. It was Sweden's first constitution in the modern sense. When Queen Christina came of age the Instrument of Government lost force, but it was soon reinstituted to cover the regency established for Karl XI* in 1660. Having to prescribe basic rules to apply to regencies was what gave Swedish statesmen the impetus to draft constitutions. Assertive kings like Karl XII* nevertheless overstepped the rules and consolidated power in their own hands.

After Karl XII died, leaving Swedes disillusioned with absolute monarchy, the Riksdag instituted a new Instrument of Government (1720) which divided powers between the king, a ministerial council, and the Riksdag. The king was limited in that he was required to conform to decisions of the Riksdag and to yield to the majority on the council when he (with two votes of his own to cast) was outvoted. This arrangement ushered Sweden into its Age of Liberty*. The Riksdag adopted the Riksdag Act of 1723, which gave it control over the selection of its own presiding officers and rules of procedure. The act was accorded constitutional status, as was the Freedom of the Press Act of 1766, which abolished censorship. For an act to have constitutional status meant that it could not be changed except by agreement of all four estates of the Riksdag granted twice in successive sessions.

Constitutional development was suspended in 1772, when King Gustav III* used the army to impose on the country a new Instrument of Government giving him primary power. In 1789 he made himself virtually an absolute monarch, the better to wage war. In the midst of these irregularities Gustav III was assassinated. His successor, Gustav IV Adolf*, suffered setbacks both at home and abroad and was formally deposed by the Riksdag in 1809.

The Riksdag thereupon revived the constitutional tradition by adopting four fundamental laws: the Instrument of Government of 1809; the Act of Succession of 1809; the Riksdag Act of 1810; and the Freedom of the Press Act of 1810. These four laws served as the basis of Swedish government for 165 years, though not without evolutionary change. The Instrument of Government reestablished a separation of powers. Power to tax and to control the state budget was reserved for the Riksdag. Executive power was given to the king and the council of ministers. Legislative power was to be shared by the Riksdag and the king. Judicial power was given to a court system at the apex of which was a Supreme Court made up of judges serving for life. Investigative power was given to an ombudsman for the judiciary and civil administration. The Act of Succession conferred the crown on Karl XIII's* heir (by adoption), Field Marshal Jean Karl XIV Johan Baptiste Bernadotte (Karl XIV Johan*), and his male descendants. The Riksdag Act continued the four estates and reestablished their authority to select their own leaders and frame their own rules. The Freedom of the Press Act of 1810, renewed in a revised form in 1812, granted private publishers access to government documents and the right to disseminate news and opinion without censorship.

Despite the constitution, real power in the early nineteenth century gravitated back to the king. Karl Johan and his successors took initiatives in issuing major economic and administrative decrees and in dealing with foreign countries. When Oskar II reigned over Norway as well as Sweden, tension developed because the Norwegians more than the Swedes pressed the king to accept as a constitutional principle that a king should govern only with ministers acceptable to parliament. The king resisted, and many Swedes upheld him. The result was that whereas in Norway the parliamentary principle became popular and triumphed by 1884, in Sweden its acceptance was delayed.

The Instrument of Government was formally amended in 1840 to establish seven government departments, each of which was put under a minister. The ministers and departments made policy, but routine administration was left to independent boards and agencies. The constitution was again formally amended in 1866 to reform the parliament. The ancient division by estates was ended, and the Riksdag was made bicameral.

Extension of the suffrage, which in 1909 was granted all adult males, contributed to the rise of modern political parties*. The Riksdag came to be dominated by party leaders, and the king found it increasingly difficult to disregard its political complexion. King Gustav V* in 1917 realized that despite his personal popularity it had become hopeless for him to insist on a prime minister other than one acceptable to the majority of the Riksdag, especially that of its popularly elected Second Chamber. Democracy and parliamentary government thus became the norm even though the written constitution said otherwise.

The discrepancy between the written constitution and actual political practice invited criticism and calls for constitutional amendment. After much delay study commissions were appointed in 1954 and 1966. Thanks to their recommendations the Riksdag was made unicameral by constitutional amendment adopted in 1968–1969. A new Instrument of Government incorporating this change as well as others was then adopted in 1974. Provisions on civil rights and the availability of remedies for encroachments on rights provoked by far the most controversy because they posed a challenge to parliamentary supremacy. A new Riksdag Act setting forth basic rules of procedure was enacted in 1974 but given a slightly lower status. It was made amendable by a three-fourths vote of one Riksdag, whereas fully constitutional documents are amendable only by vote of two Riksdags with an election intervening. The Act of Succession, which like the Freedom of Press Act retained full constitutional status, was amended in 1978–1980 to permit accession to the throne of a female heir.

REFERENCES: *Constitutional Documents of Sweden: The Instrument of Government. The Riksdag Act, The Act of Succession, The Freedom of Press Act* (Stockholm: The Swedish Riksdag, 1975); N. Elder, *Government in Sweden* (Oxford: Clarendon Press, 1970); N. Herlitz, *Grunddragen av det Svenska Statsskickets Historia* (Stockholm: Norstedt, 1957); E. Holmberg, *Grundlagarna* (Stockholm: Allmanna Forlag, 1974); E. Holmberg and N. Stjernquist, *Vår Nya Författning* (Stockholm: PAN Norstedt, 1974); R. Malmgren, H. Sundborg, and G. Petren, *Sveriges Grundlagar och Tillhörande Författningar* (Stockholm: Norstedt, 1967).

B. L. HANSON

CONTINUATION WAR (June 1941–September 1944) War between Finland and the Soviet Union

For the fourteen months following the conclusion of the Treaty of Moscow between Finland and the Soviet Union that ended the Winter War* in March 1940, Finland was not directly involved in the greater conflict in Europe. The country's neutrality was compromised in a number of areas, including the granting of transit rights to both the Russians and the Germans, but the Finns were effectively isolated in the Baltic and had little choice but to comply with the demands of the two great powers in the area. Many Finns did not forget the war of 1939–1940, nor did they forget their long-standing fear of the Russians. These factors made the Finns susceptible to German diplomacy aimed at drawing them into German plans for an attack on the Soviet Union. As early as August 1940, Finland began to edge into the German camp. In December 1940 German and Finnish military personnel began to discuss hypothetical operations in Russia. Although no formal alliance was concluded before Operation Barbarossa began on 22 June 1941, Finland's participation in the war against the Soviet Union was expected. The Germans provided the Finns with material assistance, and German troops were given transit rights across the northern part of the country. In the actual fighting, however, the Finns fought their own war against the Russians.

On 25 June 1941 the Finns attacked into Karelia. By the end of August they had retaken the areas lost in 1940. They continued their advance until December. For some, the war was one of revenge; but there were also those who hoped to expand Finland at the expense of the Russians. Both groups expected a quick, cheap victory. But the Russians were not crushed by Hitler's *blitzkrieg*, and the fighting dragged on. The Soviet-Finnish front stabilized along a line beyond the 1940 borders, and the Soviets refused to conclude a separate peace with the Finns. Following the victory of the Russians at Stalingrad in February 1943, the balance of the war shifted, and Finland's bargaining position changed radically. Now the Finns were on the defensive, hoping to preserve what they had gained against an increasingly awesome Soviet Union. The Russians made it clear from spring 1943 on that there would be no territorial concessions made to the Finns. The terms upon which Stalin would accept an armistice were unacceptable to Finland's leaders, and the state of war continued. In June 1944 the Soviets launched a counter-offensive in eastern Karelia, and the Finns retreated before overwhelming odds. Some Finnish leaders now wanted to make a separate peace with Russia, but others, including President Risto Ryti*, held fast to the war policy, perhaps unable to see any cheap way out of the conflict. The Germans put considerable pressure on the Finns to keep them involved in the war, and in July 1944 Ryti personally signed an agreement that committed Finland to continued fighting. A few weeks after this agreement was reached, however, Ryti resigned and was replaced by C.G.E. Mannerheim*. This move allowed a change in Finnish policy. Mannerheim agreed to accept Stalin's terms for an armistice, and fighting between the two countries stopped. A formal agreement was signed on 19 September 1944. It was a costly peace for Finland. The boundaries of 1940 were restored. Petsamo was ceded to the Soviet Union. The Russians obtained a 50–year lease on the Porkkala Peninsula. Finland's anti-

Communist laws were repealed. The army (after it had driven the Germans from Finland) was to be demobilized and cut in size. Finland agreed to pay $300 million in reparations; the bill ended up being almost twice that amount. (These terms were echoed in the Treaty of Paris reached in 1947.) The fighting with the Soviets ended, the Finns turned to driving the Germans from Finland. This was not an easy task and was one of the most costly aspects of Finland's involvement in World War II.

World War II cost Finland 86,000 combat deaths. Another 57,000 were permanently disabled. Thousands were left homeless by the destruction wrought by the retreating Germans. Some 420,000 refugees from the regions given over to the Soviet Union had to be resettled. The direct costs of the war and the reparations affected the economy for decades. The agreements reached at the end of the war resulted in the incorporation of the Communists as legal participants in the political life of the country and in a fundamental realignment of Finland's foreign policy. The anti-Soviet approach was abandoned, and Finland's postwar leaders (Juho Paasikivi*, Urho Kekkonen*, and Mauro Henrik Koivisto*) learned to live with their great neighbor. (*See also* Finlandization; Passikivi-Kekkonen Line; Treaty of Friendship.)

REFERENCES: W. M. Carlgren, *Swedish Foreign Policy During the Second World War*, trans. A. Spencer (New York: St. Martin's, 1977); D. G. Kirby, *Finland in the Twentieth Century* (Minneapolis: University of Minnesota Press, 1979); H. S. Nissen, *Scandinavia During the Second World War* (Minneapolis: University of Minnesota Press, 1983); V. Tanner, *Vägen till fred 1943–1944*, trans. H. Dahl (Helsinki: J. Simelii Arvingars, 1952).

B. NORDSTROM

CONVENTICLE ACTS

Devotional gatherings for Bible study and prayer in private homes is today considered a good and proper way of enriching congregational life and reaching the unchurched. In 1670 it was considered a radical idea when Philip Jacob Spener introduced *collegia pietatis* into his parish at Frankfort/Main. Five years later he set forth his "pious desires" for church renewal in his now famous *Pia Desideria*, in which he outlined Pietism's vision for spiritual awakening. Fear was immediately expressed that the conventicles would lead to schism and become little churches within the large state church parish (*ecclesiolae in ecclesia*). Many orthodox Lutherans looked upon lay leadership of the conventicle meetings as improper and a violation of Article 14 of the *Augsburg Confession**. The Pietist leadership countered by adamantly maintaining their loyalty to the Lutheran state churches and the Lutheran doctrine (*see* Lutheranism) while insisting that Luther had encouraged greater lay leadership through his doctrine of the priesthood of all believers.

As Pietism spread into Scandinavia* in the eighteenth century, opposition developed to the free and unregulated proliferation of conventicle meetings, often from surprising sources. In Sweden-Finland a Conventicle Act was passed in 1726 under Lutheran orthodox auspices in order to curtail lay activity which threatened to become schismatic. And in Denmark-Norway-Iceland a Conventicle Act was passed in 1741 by the Lutheran Pietist leadership of the time. This legislation had as its intent the prohibition of Moravian Pietist lay preachers wandering from town to town and holding devotional services. Danish Lutheran Pietist leaders like Erik Pontoppidan* considered the Moravian lay preachers non-Lutheran and schismatic. In reality the Conventicle Act did not prohibit *collegia pietatis* but stipulated that godly assemblies could only be conducted or held in the presence of the local parish pastor or a layman of the pastor's choosing.

Though never really successful, the Conventicle Acts were used by the clergy during the nineteenth century to counteract the new revivals and upsurgence of lay activity as witnessed by the tragic imprisonment of Hans Nielsen Hauge* from 1804 to 1814. With the advent of modernity and the concept of religious liberty, each of the Scandinavian countries passed legislation abolishing their Conventicle Acts—Norway (1842), Denmark (1849), Iceland (1849), Sweden (1858), and Finland (1869).

REFERENCES: *DH*, vols. 8, 9; *DSH*, vols. 8, 12, 15.

T. R. SKARSTEN

CONVENTION OF MOSS August 1814. Peace agreement between Norway and Sweden

The test of Norway's will to maintain independence in defiance of Europe's Great Powers and Sweden developed nearly as soon as the constitution was proclaimed (May 1814). A single British emissary in June and a four-man commission from Russia, Prussia, Austria, and Britain informed Christian Frederik (later Christian VIII*) in early July of their states' intent to enforce Sweden's claims upon Norway. All left the country, however, certain of Norway's determination to resist and the Great Power commission even suggested to Karl Johan's (later Karl XIV Johan*) representatives that Sweden consider Norway's constitution as the basis for peace.

Nevertheless, Karl Johan sought a military solution to his problem when the Norwegian government refused to permit Swedish troops to occupy border fortresses as the precondition for future negotiations. The Swedes opened their attack upon Norway on 26 July 1814. The Norwegian army was able to defeat the Swedes in skirmishes around Kongsvinger before falling back before the advancing Swedish army. Fredrikstad surrendered without a shot being fired, and estimates that the army could only be provisioned for one week led to a deterioration of the war effort.

Armistice negotiations had begun almost as soon as the fighting started. Karl Johan wished, despite his bellicose "gasconades," to end the hostilities, because he feared that the Great Powers might show sympathy for Norway's plight; and after discrediting Christian Frederik as a general, he had every reason to end the war as rapidly as possible. Christian Frederik was aware of Norway's difficulties and therefore took the first steps to bring about peace. Despite advice from his Council of State to continue the war, on 13 August he agreed to formal peace negotiations with Sweden.

One day later, Niels Aall and Jonas Collett, both members of the Norwegian Council of State, met at Moss with their Swedish counterparts, Colonel M. F. Björnstjerna and General A. F. Sköldebrand, to arrange the Convention of Moss. In addition to a cease-fire, this agreement also specified that Sweden would accept the Eidsvoll Constitution of 17 May* as the fundamental law of Norway with only such changes to be made in it as were necessary to facilitate the union of the two nations. Christian Frederik agreed through Aall and Collett to relinquish his power to the Norwegian parliament and leave the country.

REFERENCES: See references under Norwegian-Swedish Union. O. Alin, "Bidrag til Mosskonventionens historie," *Historisk tidskrift* (S) 17 (1897): 209–58; Y. Nielsen, *1814. Fra Kiel til Moss: en historisk undersøgelse af Moss konventionen, des forudsætninger og politiske Betydninger* (Christiania, 1894), "Om Konventionen i Moss," *HT* (N) 3:5 (1899): 1–144, and *Der Vertrag von Moss vom 14 August 1814* (Kiel, 1895); L. Tingsten, "Från konventionen i Moss till den svensk-norsk rikssakten," *Historisk tidskrift* (S) (1927): 217–87.

L. SATHER

CONVERSION

Between the tenth and the thirteenth centuries the people of the Scandinavian region were converted to Christianity. This was an extended process in which there were several stages, including an initial phase when a few missionaries entered the region proselytizing the new faith and were met with resistance and hostility; a later phase when missionary activities were combined with serious efforts by kings or aspiring kings to convert the people of Scandinavia* if necessary by force; and a final phase when the new faith gradually came to dominate and permeate the whole of the Nordic societies, and when the structures of the Church were transplanted. The conversion must be seen as part of larger processes including the integration of Scandinavia into the realm of Western Christendom and the state-building efforts of the monarchs of the late Viking and medieval periods. The great length of time the conversion took should not be allowed to obscure the impact that the change had upon Scandinavia. Economics, politics, social structure, education, the arts, and literature were among the aspects of Scandinavian life affected. The following sections deal with events in each of the Scandinavian countries.

Denmark

Willibrord, "the Apostle to the Frisians," is the first Christian known to have visited pagan Denmark (c. 710). Nothing came of this venture, and it was over a century before Ebo, archbishop of Reims, journeyed to Denmark in 823 as an ambassador of Louis the Pious. In 826 Harald Flak, a petty Danish king, submitted to Christian baptism at Mainz on the condition that the Carolingian emperor would help him regain his throne. A Frankish Benedictine monk by the name of Ansgar* (801–865) from the monastery of New Corbie accompanied Harald back to Denmark and preached in Hedeby* for two years. Shortly thereafter Harald Flak was overthrown and Ansgar proceeded on to Sweden. In 831, while on a trip to Rome, Gregory IV named Ansgar as the first bishop of Hamburg and the next year archbishop and papal legate to Scandinavia. Opposition to Christianity on the part of the pagan Scandinavian Vikings* was fierce at this time, and Ansgar could do little toward their conversion. In 845 the Vikings destroyed Hamburg, and Ansgar was fortunate to escape with his life. In 850 he was allowed by King Haarik to return to Denmark, where he founded a church in Slesvig, but little of significance was accomplished. Called "the Apostle to Scandinavia," Ansgar is remembered not for his accomplishments but for his courage in evangelizing the pagan Vikings when most others were cringing in fear and praying "Deliver us, O Lord, from the fury of the Northmen." After Ansgar's death in 865 the pagan Danish king Gorm* destroyed all trace of Christianity in Denmark. But in 934, after Henry the Fowler (919–936) had defeated Gorm in battle, Unni, the archbishop of Hamburg-Bremen, went to Gorm and demanded toleration for the Christian religion. Though repulsed by Gorm, Unni's courageous demeanor impressed Gorm's successor, Harald I* (Bluetooth, or Blaatand), who became a Christian prior to his reign in 960.

Under Harald Bluetooth (960–986) Christianity was vigorously promoted throughout Denmark. Around 980 a large runic stone was erected in Jelling* (Jutland) that stated, "Harald united Denmark and made the Danes Christian." On the face of the stone is the earliest Scandinavian depiction of Christ hanging on the cross. Though Sven I* (Forkbeard, or Tjukkesjegg) spent much of his time raiding England, toward the latter part of his reign (986–1014), after he had conquered England, he brought some English bishops to Denmark as missionaries. Under Knud I* (Canute the Great, 1014–1035), Christianity was firmly established. Because he was king of both Denmark and England (after 1016) a close tie between the two churches was established. In 1022 English bishops were installed at Odense, Roskilde, and Lund. Christian culture was energetically promoted, and the ideals of the Cluny reform movement were instilled in Danish ecclesiastical and monastic life. In 1026 Knut made a pilgrimage to Rome, solidifying the Danish church's connection with the Roman see. During Sven II Estridsen's* reign (1047–1076) Denmark was organized into eight bishoprics, and in 1104 the archbishopric of Lund was established.

The Christianization of Denmark can thus be said to have been accomplished in two stages. The first, largely unsuccessful, was carried out by missionary monastics like Ansgar. The second, successful stage saw converted Danish Viking leaders unite their countrymen politically and lead their people into the Christian faith. Fear of political domination from the Carolingian and Holy Roman empires not only delayed Danish conversion to Christianity but also helps to account for the close ties with England rather than Hamburg-Bremen.

REFERENCES: J. O. Andersen, *Survey of the History of the Church in Denmark* (Copenhagen, 1930); H. Koch and B. Kornerup, *Den Danske Kirkes Historie*, vol. 1 (Copenhagen: Gyldendal, 1950).

T. R. SKARSTEN

Finland

According to sources of very questionable reliability, "Finland" (which then meant only the southwest region of modern Finland) was converted by force in a crusade launched by King Erik of Sweden (St. Erik) and Bishop Henry of Uppsala c. 1155/1157. The Finns were beaten at a battle supposedly fought somewhere near Åbo/Turku. Bishop Henry was subsequently killed and was buried near there. He quickly came to be regarded as the patron saint of the area. The actual process of conversion was probably far more gradual and involved contacts between the Finns and the Swedes, Russians, Germans, and others. E. Jutikkala presents the conversion as part of the process of the establishment of Swedish authority over Finland in competition with Novgorod. In this process, southwest Finland came under Swedish control and was Christianized in the second half of the twelfth century. (Papal bulls from the late twelfth and early thirteenth centuries indicate that by then "Finland" was considered part of the Christian West.) Tavastia, to the east, underwent the same experience in the early thirteenth century. Karelia was the focus of Swedish-Russian competition in the late thirteenth century, and by the Treaty of Pähkinäsaari (1323) Karelia was divided between the two powers. This marked the completion of the conversion and the establishment of Swedish control over the coastal regions of southwest and south Finland. Over the following centuries, Swedish influence and Christianity spread into the far less populated interior and north.

The early Church in Finland was first tied to the archbishopric of Lund, but in 1216 it came under the control of Uppsala, which probably reflected political as much as religious realities. Even then, however, the Finnish Church appears to have functioned largely independently. The bishopric of Åbo/Turku was the administrative and educational center of the Church in Finland.

REFERENCES: E. Jutikkala, with K. Pirinen, *A History of Finland*, trans. P. Sjöblom (New York: Praeger, 1962); J. Wuorinen, *A History of Finland* (New York: Columbia University Press, 1965).

B. NORDSTROM

Iceland

The conversion of Iceland was in certain respects unique among the Nordic countries. According to the extant sources, including Ari Þorgilsson's* *Islendingabok* and the description in *Njal's Saga*, the Icelanders were converted in 1000 (or more probably 999) as the result of the decision by the lawspeaker Thorgeirr. Confronted with the choice between holding to the old pagan faith and adopting Christianity, Thorgeirr, though a pagan himself, chose the latter. Why he did so is subject to debate. Ari and the sagas tell us that it was to ensure that Iceland would remain united under one law and one faith. This may be a romanticized explanation imposed on the events by Christian writers. More credible, perhaps, are arguments that he was bribed by adherents of Christianity or that he succumbed to the threat that Olaf I Tryggvason* of Norway was prepared to Christianize the island by force. The truth of the matter will, of course, never be known. It is clear, however, that the process of conversion was, as in the other Scandinavian countries, far more complicated. The adoption of Christianity was certainly determined by the efforts of missionaries and Icelanders converted abroad (in the British Isles or Norway, for example), weaknesses within the old pagan religion, the threat of internal chaos, and external threats to the Commonwealth's autonomy.

Whatever the truth may be surrounding the 999/1000 account, over the span of the ensuing century Christianity became firmly rooted in Iceland. Churches were built, a native clergy developed, bishoprics with native-born bishops were established at Skalholt (c. 1056) and Halar (1106), schools connected with the bishoprics appeared, and the Church in Iceland developed close ties with Christian Europe.

REFERENCES: J. Johanesson, *A History of the Old Icelandic Commonwealth*, trans. H. Bessason (Winnipeg: University of Manitoba Press, 1974); *Njal's Saga*, trans. M. Magnusson and H. Pálsson (Baltimore: Penguin, 1960); D. Strömbäck, *The Conversion of Iceland: A Survey*, trans. and annotated by P. Foote (London: Viking Society for Northern Research, 1975).

B. NORDSTROM

Norway

In 793 Norwegian Vikings thrust themselves into the pages of the *Anglo-Saxon Chronicle* and European history with the sacking of the monastery of Lindesfarne off the coast of Northumbria. For the next two centuries Christians in the British Isles and France were to pray, "Deliver us, O Lord, from the fury of the Northmen." That these ferocious, pagan people could ever be converted seemed doubtful indeed. Yet the conquerors became the conquered as they learned to know about Christus Victor, not the meek, mild Christ who died passively on a cross but the victorious Christ who from the cross strode into Hell and vanquished death itself. Once they had their Christology straight, Christianity became an attractive religion to espouse, and newly converted Norwegian Vikings were to return to their homeland to claim their thrones and zealously impose their newfound faith upon their countrymen.

The kingdom of Norway was "unified" under the pagan Harald Fairhair (872–933) after the Battle of Havrsfjord (872). Upon his death, a war of succession ensued in which Haakon I* (the Good, (? 935–961) emerged victorious. Haakon became a Christian while living in England, and it was his intention to Christianize Norway. He and his English clergy met such stiff resistance, however, that the king was even forced to compromise his own Christian faith. Under

Haakon Sigurdsson* (970–995) a pagan reaction set in, being only partly ame-
liorated by the Danish Christian king Harald Bluetooth's control of the Vik
region of southeastern Norway. After Haakon Sigurdsson's devastating defeat
of the Danish king, Sven Forkbeard, at Hjørungavaag, Christianity was virtually
wiped out in Norway.

The effective introduction of Christianity to Norway was the work of Olaf I
Tryggvason (995–1000) and was consolidated by Olaf II Haraldsson* (1016–
1030). Both were direct descendants of Harald Fairhair and had left Norway in
their youth as pagans to embark on notable marauding careers during the revival
of Viking activities which came in the late tenth century under Haakon Sigurdsson. Both were converted to Christianity while overseas.

Olaf Tryggvason had embraced Christianity in the Scilly Islands from a Christian hermit who made a deep impression upon him. In 955 he returned to Norway
to reunite the country, reclaim his throne, and impose Christianity upon his
fellow Norwegians. He landed at Moster, a little south of Bergen, where he was
later to build the first church in Norway. He then proceeded to travel throughout
Norway, demanding recognition of himself as king and Christ as Lord. Those
who refused to recognize him or submit to Christian baptism were slain. Pagan
temples were destroyed, idols toppled, and shrines desecrated. Though Olaf
Tryggvason's work was not without results, he was unable to establish any deep
institutional roots for Christianity in Norway before he was killed in 1000 by
Danish, Swedish, and exiled Norwegian Vikings who had formed a coalition
against him.

The task of consolidating Christianity in Norway was left to Olaf II Haraldsson,
better known as Saint Olaf. He had been baptized in Rouen (Normandy) and
brought with him Bishop Grimkell and scores of missionaries from England.
Upon his arrival in Norway, Olaf met with astonishing success. During the years
of peace that followed he systematically established Christianity throughout the
land. At Moster in 1024 the first ecclesiastical laws for the Church of Norway
were adopted. When Olaf Haraldsson was killed in the Battle of Stiklestad outside
of Trondhiem on 29 July 1030, his death solidified Christianity in Norway and
unified the nation. A century later (1152), when the bishoprics of Oslo, Stavanger, Bergen, and Hamar had come into being, Trondhiem (Nidaros) was
elevated to metropolitan status largely because of the legends surrounding the
slain Saint Olaf.

REFERENCES: O. Kolsrud, *Noregs Kyrkjesoga* (Oslo: H. Aschehoug, 1958); Snorri
Sturluson, *Heimskringla: History of the Kings of Norway*, trans. and ed. L. M. Hollander
(Austin: University of Texas Press, 1964); T. B. Willson, *History of the Church and
State in Norway* (St. Clair Shores, Mich.: Scholarly Press, 1971); C. Fr. Wisløff, *Norsk
Kirkehistorie*, vol. 1 (Oslo: Lutherstiftelsen, 1966).

T. R. SKARSTEN

Sweden

The conversion of Sweden in the twelfth century was a long time in coming.
The first Christian mission had occurred in 830, when Ansgar came to Birka*
(outside Stockholm*) with a companion named Witmar upon the invitation of
the local king, Bjorn. At Birka Ansgar found a small group of Christians.

Historians have speculated as to their origin. Were they captives brought back from the raids of Swedish Vikings? Others believe they were Swedish merchants and traders influenced by Eastern Orthodoxy as they plied the rivers of Russia to trade with Constantinople, which the Swedish Vikings (Varangians*) called Munkegaard. In any case, it was at Birka that Ansgar built the first church in Sweden in 830. Shortly thereafter Ansgar traveled to Rome, where Gregory IV extended to him the pallium as archbishop of Hamburg in 831. Upon his return to Hamburg, Ansgar dispatched Gautbert to Birka, while he turned eastward and concentrated on the Christianization of the Wends. During the intervening years little seemed to happen in Sweden until Gautbert fled Sweden during a violent outbreak of hostile Viking activity in 845, when Ansgar's archbishopric in Hamburg was also destroyed. In 852 Ansgar returned to Birka with Ardgar. Only after the local chieftain had cast lots was Ansgar allowed to stay and preach. It was said that "it was always good to have an extra god around." Though he was called "the Apostle to Scandinavia," the permanent results of Ansgar's work were negligible. The Viking expeditions of the ninth and tenth centuries severely hampered Christian mission activity. Nor did it help any that Scandinavian paganism's most sacred temple was located in Sweden. During these two centuries only two other Christian missionaries, Rimbert and Unni, are known to have briefly penetrated Sweden.

As the eleventh century dawned, Denmark and Norway had just recently become Christian. At the same time there was also more openness in Sweden to the message of the Christian missionary. From England came a remarkable trio of missionary bishops, Sigfrid (d. 1068), Eskil (d. 1072), and David (d. 1082), the last two dying as Christian martyrs. It was Sigfrid who baptized Olof Skötkonung (? 994–1022) in 1008 and brought Christianity to Västergötland (West Gothland). Unlike his Norwegian colleague, the Swedish King Olof did not seek to force his men to be baptized, and they in turn let their king bring in all the missionaries from England that he wanted. By 1020 Skara had been founded as the oldest episcopal see in Sweden. Though the Swedish Goths had largely become Christian by the mid-eleventh century, the Svear of middle Sweden were still pagan, and Anund Jacob (1021–1050) was counseled not to destroy the Uppsala temple lest Christianity be destroyed in a pagan backlash. Edmund the Old (1050–1057) concentrated his efforts on freeing the young Swedish Church from the clutches of Archbishop Adalbert (1045–1072) and the Hamburg-Bremen archdiocese. Fear of German domination goes a long way in explaining the protracted resistance to Christianity not only in Sweden but in all of Scandinavia. When King Inge (Ingi I Haraldsson*, 1066–1111) began to use strong-arm tactics on the Svear to force them to accept Christianity, a violent pagan reaction developed under Blotsvein (Sven the Sacrificer). In 1084 Blotsvein led the last recorded pagan ritual at the Uppsala temple in which human sacrifices were offered. With the advent of Christianity the pagan Viking kings lost their sacerdotal duties. Paganism in Sweden continued strong into the twelfth century, and it was not until 1138 that King Sverker was able to destroy the pagan temple at Uppsala and use the stones for the foundation of the Old Uppsala

Cathedral. By the end of the twelfth century Linköping, Strängnäs, Västerås, and Växjö had been added as episcopal sees, with Uppsala having been made the metropolitan see for the Church of Sweden in 1164.

REFERENCES: S. Blondal, *The Varangians of Byzantium* (Cambridge, England: Cambridge University Press, 1979); J. Wordsworth, *The National Church of Sweden* (Geneva, Ala.: Allenson, 1911).

T. R. SKARSTEN

COOPERATIVES (Sweden)

From their origins as local, democratic, self-help groups, Sweden's consumer cooperatives have emerged as the most formidable and far-reaching economic force in the nation. Many of them began in the late nineteenth and early twentieth centuries as popular responses to industrialization* and urbanization*. Today, cooperatives are the largest enterprises in retailing, petroleum products, housing, insurance, farming, funerals, and travel. Moreover, they are equally well known for their historic price victories over European cartels and their strong support of consumer education, protection, and legislation.

To provide legal protection and definition to the growing cooperatives, Sweden enacted its first law covering cooperative societies in 1895. In 1899 a number of the small, struggling societies created the Cooperative Union (Kooperative Förbundet/KF). The formation of a single national wholesale and trade association heralded the rapid advancement of the Swedish cooperative movement. In 1915 several of the smaller societies in Stockholm* joined together to create Konsum Stockholm. By 1980 this organization had over 300,000 member families and was the largest independent cooperative society in KF. Many other small societies repeated the Stockholm model by merging to build strong city or regional cooperative societies.

During the post-World War II period, the practice and philosophy of cooperation attracted the loyalty of a formidable group of young people, who brought missionary zeal and business acumen to the expanding cooperative movement. Notable for their efforts and success as national leaders were Anders Orne, Ernst Pers(s)on, Axel Gjores, and Albin Johansson. The last named was president of KF from 1924 to 1957 and is regarded as the architect of KF's powerful economic and social position in modern Sweden.

In the 1980s over 2 million families regularly shop at KF's member cooperative societies to obtain lower prices, higher quality goods, and consumer ownership and control. KF does 18 percent of the total national retail trade through over 2,000 stores, supermarkets, and department stores owned by its 170 local member societies. KF employs 67,000 people and is the largest single business in Sweden. Folksam, a cooperative insurance company jointly administered by KF and the Swedish Confederation of Trade Unions* (LO), administers nearly 3 million individual policies and covers nearly 6 million people. OK, a petroleum cooperative with over half a million family members, commands 22 percent of the market through its 400 gas stations and is the largest fuel business in Sweden.

The two housing cooperative organizations, Svenska Riksbyggen, SR and HSB (National Association of Tenants' Savings and Building Societies), have produced nearly 600,000 units of cooperative housing. Through their savings banks, the savings of the members are pooled to develop the capital required to purchase or build cooperative housing. The housing cooperative organizations also work closely with the labor unions to develop union-built, non-speculative cooperative housing for union members. The National Federation of Burial Societies (Fonus) is a consumer cooperative which administers over 25 percent of the burial commissions in the nation.

Spectrum of Consumer Cooperation in Sweden

Branch	Food and non-food	Housing	Housing	Fuel	Insurance
Central organization	KF	HSB	SR	OK	Folksam
Local societies	Konsum	HSB	SR	OK	
Individual members	1,696,000 Households	345,000 Apartment and House Owners	92,000 Apartment and House Owners	550,000 Car and House Owners	10,000,000 Policies

Although consumer cooperatives are a very visible part of Swedish society, mention should also be made of farmer cooperatives. The first one was started in Orsundsbro, Uppland, in 1850. The pioneer development age of the farm cooperative was between 1880 and 1930, when many were formed and a national farm cooperative structure was built. The total membership in the 350 farm cooperatives that existed in 1980 was 850,000. More than 80 percent of all Swedish farm products pass through producers' cooperatives. The Federation of Swedish Farmers (LRF) is the governing body for the farm cooperatives and provides many other services for its members. By tradition there are close relations between LRF and KF to ensure good quality and a fair price to the consumer and maximum distribution and price for the farmer.

The consumer cooperatives of Sweden, because they are consumer-owned and -controlled, represent the consumer interest in the marketplace. Due to their share of the economy, they also represent a yardstick by which consumers can measure the services of traditional private enterprise. All of the Swedish cooperatives are known for their commitment to consumer education, research, quality products, and fair prices. By cutting out the middleman and operating on sound business principles, the cooperatives have proved of great value to their members. Not content with their national success, the cooperatives also have played an important role in exporting cooperative principles and practices around the world, especially to the lesser-developed countries.

REFERENCES: Marquis Childs, *Sweden, The Middle Way* (New Haven: Yale University Press, 1936); KF/Konsum, *An Introduction to the Swedish Coop Group* (Stockholm: KF, 1972); W. T. Lundberg, *Consumer Owned: Sweden's Cooperative Democracy* (Palo Alto: Consumers Cooperative Publishing Association, 1978).

D. J. THOMPSON

COPENHAGEN (København) Capital of Denmark

A settlement called Havn (harbor) with a protected harbor seems to have existed since the mid-eleventh century, but very little is known before Valdemar I* (1157–1182) granted it to Absalon, bishop of Roskilde around 1167. This should be compared with the similar grant a few years later of Kalundborg to Absalon's brother, who, like the bishop, was the king's trusted collaborator. The two brothers thus became the wardens of important sea routes linking different parts of the country to each other (from Kalundborg to Aarhus in Jutland and from Copenhagen to Scania). Absalon constructed a castle on an island facing the settlement, which by 1186 he bequeathed to the bishopric of Roskilde. It was also under Absalon that the construction of Our Lady's Church (the actual cathedral) was begun. A collegiate chapter in Copenhagen seems to have been established by 1220.

The settlement that soon was called Købmannehavn (the merchants' port) may be considered as Roskilde's port on the Sound. Its extensive hinterland made it an important regional center, and its position at the gateway to the Baltic gave it a share of international trade, because until the mid-sixteenth century, many ships preferred to stop at Elsinore*, Copenhagen, or some other town on the Sound to exchange western goods with those of the Baltic region, instead of continuing directly to the Baltic ports.

The community must have grown rapidly and must have been constituted as a town by 1254, from which year its earliest statutes, granted by the bishop of Roskilde, date. Erik (VII) of Pomerania* (1397–1438/9) acquired Copenhagen in 1416, but still it was only an important trading town protected by a castle. Although the records of the crown and the royal family were kept elsewhere, Christoffer III* (1439–1448) moved the central financial administration to Copenhagen, where it remained. Because Copenhagen was the residence preferred by Christoffer III and his successors, it may be considered the capital of Denmark from about 1450, despite the fact that other towns (for example, Malmö or Ribe) were neither less prosperous nor less populous.

In the sixteenth century King Christian II* sought to concentrate the grain trade in Copenhagen and other towns on the Sound, and it is no wonder that in the civil war of 1534–1536 (*see* Count's War) the two most important towns of that region, Copenhagen and Malmö, favored the deposed king. Consequently, both had to suffer long sieges.

Copenhagen recovered during the latter half of the sixteenth century and, as in the case of Elsinore, compensation for the change in the pattern of international trade and navigation was found, especially in the royal shipyard and in the demands of the expanding central administration. This tendency became evident c. 1600 and especially after the introduction of absolutism (c. 1660), when most mercantilist enterprises, the court, the navy, and part of the new standing army were based in Copenhagen. In the 1660s, 40 to 50 percent of Copenhagen's inhabitants earned their living in royal service. As the provincial towns of Denmark proper stagnated during the later seventeenth and eighteenth centuries (unlike those of Norway and the duchies of Slesvig and Holstein), the concentration in Copenhagen of enterprise, wealth, and cultural institutions was spectacular and could be seen from the population figures (by comparison, even in 1801 no provincial town of Denmark exceeded 6,000 inhabitants): 1500: c. 10,000; 1600: c. 20,000; 1660: 25,000–30,000; 1769: 83,000; 1801 (greater Copenhagen): 102,147; 1850 (greater Copenhagen): 132,569; 1901 (greater Copenhagen): 491,276; 1980 (greater Copenhagen): 1,387,735. Although provincial towns have grown considerably since the mid-nineteenth century, the establishment in Copenhagen of important industries, banks, shipping, and other companies helped Copenhagen to maintain her leading position. Compared with the situation in about 1800, the preeminence of Copenhagen related to the provincial towns is less marked today (1983), but because of migration from the countryside to the towns (including Copenhagen) the capital's central role in relation to the country as a whole has been strengthened. Today 27 percent of Denmark's population lives in greater Copenhagen.

Like other Danish towns, Copenhagen had a city government with councilors and mayors, but because of the capital's contribution to the war effort in 1658–1659, it was given a popular representative assembly with 32 members and a status equal to that of the nobility. Under the name *borgerrepræsentationen* (assembly of the burgesses), a similar institution was created in 1840 that still exists. The size of Copenhagen has rendered its constitution more complex than those of other towns. It has several mayors, each with a special field of work, and over them a lord mayor (*overborgmester*). Since 1978 there have been no councilors.

The rapid growth of Copenhagen rendered necessary the annexation of more land to facilitate the construction of new quarters. Among these the earliest example was Christianshavn (founded 1618), which until the late seventeenth century, was an independent community with its own town government. The largest extensions, however, took place after the mid-nineteenth century. When the fortifications were abandoned; consequently, the city could expand beyond the former ramparts and moats.

The great fires of 1728 and 1795, as well as the bombardment by the British in 1807, caused extensive damage in Copenhagen. Outside Christianshavn very few private buildings are older than the eighteenth century.

REFERENCES: S. Cedergreen Bech et al., eds. *Københavns Historie*, vols. 1– (Copenhagen: Gyldendal, 1980–); S. Jensen, T. Riis, and P. Strømstad, ''København,'' in

A. Ságvári, ed., *The Capitals of Europe—Les capitales de l'Europe: A Guide to the Sources for the History of Their Architecture and Construction* (Budapest: Corvina Kiado; Munich: K. G. Saur, 1980) (Danish revised edition of this work: "Kilder til Københavns bygningshistorie," in *Historiske Meddelser om København* [1982]).

T. RIIS

COUNCIL OF STATE: NORWAY (*Rikets raad*) Thirteenth century–1536, 1814–present

A royal council of advisors to the crown appears to have developed in Norway in the late thirteenth century, at the same time that similar bodies were developing in Denmark and Sweden and in other parts of Europe. Haakon V was particularly important in the growth of this institution. He built a group of about a dozen councilors, composed of church prelates and lay nobles, which served as a base of support for the crown and as an agent of continuity in the event there was no direct male heir to the throne or a regency was necessitated by the minority of the royal successor.

The council flourished as an autonomous entity during parts of the fourteenth century, but it did not develop into a constitutional alternative to monarchy, as was the case in Sweden in the same period (*see* Council of State: Sweden). During the reign of Magnus Eriksson* (1319–1355), the day-to-day administration of the country was left largely in the hands of the council, first, because the king was only three in 1519 and second, because he spent most of his time in Sweden, where he was also king. Consequently, the council became an administrative body and law court representing the crown. Although aristocratic in composition, it sought to serve the interests of Norway, and it is generally argued that the council did not work solely to foster the personal or class interests of its members.

During the Kalmar Union* period (1397–1536), the council's position fluctuated, but these years should generally be seen as years of decline for both the council and Norway. During the succession crises and the minority of Hans I*, the council did assert some of its traditional (fourteenth-century) authority, but it never functioned as a counter-force to the encroachment of Danish royal power. The high point of the council's position was reached at Halmstad in 1483, when Hans was forced to accept a very restricting accession charter, one which he honored only as long as necessary. Under the rules of Christian I*, Hans, and Christian II*, who were intent upon building strong monarchy in the union kingdoms, the council was relegated to an increasingly minor position. Administration was placed largely in the hands of royal appointees, and these were usually Danes. The fundamental weaknesses of Norway in this period made it clearly an inferior partner in the union, and it was difficult, if not impossible, for the country to resist the gradual establishment of Danish hegemony. The native royal line in Norway died out in 1387, the country's commerce fell increasingly under the domination of the Hanse (*see* Hanseatic League), and the native nobility gradually vanished, as families died out or were diluted through marriage with foreigners. These and other conditions contributed to the weakness of the country, and they made it difficult for Norway to maintain its independent status. The council, as a possible agent of Norwegian autonomy, was diluted with Danish members and was further weakened by a split which put half its members in Bergen and half in Oslo.

In 1536, Norway, without consultation or agreement, was absorbed into the Danish realm. The independent or autonomous status of the country was eliminated. The council of state vanished, and for the next 278 years the country was governed as a province of Denmark.

The council reappeared in 1814 (now the *statsråd*) to serve as an advisory body to the crown. Originally, it was to have at least five members. The number was increased to eight when the Norwegian-Swedish Union* was finalized. (During much of the union period, 1814–1905, part of this council resided in Stockholm*.) At present the council has about fifteen members. With the exception of the prime minister, all members of the council head government departments. Over the course of the years following 1814, the council gradually developed into a cabinet/ministry responsible to the parliament.

REFERENCES: K. Gjerset, *History of the Norwegian People*, 2 vols. (New York: Macmillan, 1915); *NH*, vols. 4, 5; Y. Nielsen, *Det norske Rigsraad* (Oslo, 1880).

B. NORDSTROM

COUNCIL OF STATE: SWEDEN (*Riksråd*) Thirteenth century to the present

The Swedish council of state (often referred to simply as the council or *råd*) developed in the thirteenth century. An early reference to a body of royal advisors appears during the reign of Erik Eriksson (1222–1229). Composed of wealthy and highly placed individuals, it appears to have been a body of councilors close to the king, in which the latter functioned as a first among equals. In addition to acting as an advisory body, this group may have served to assure the succession (Sweden's monarchy was elective until 1544) and to act as a governing body during a minority. There is little mention of the council through the rest of the thirteenth century.

During the fourteenth and fifteenth centuries, the council developed into a formally structured unit, and it became the focus of one pole of a constitutional struggle which characterized Swedish political history for nearly 400 years. In Magnus Eriksson's* Land Law of c. 1350, the council was given clear organizational and functional definition. Composed of the archbishop, the bishops, and twelve lay magnates, the body was to advise the crown, act as a check upon royal authority, and constitute a "permanent residuary of sovereign power." The Land Law gave form to an ideology of aristocratic power called council constitutionalism (*råds konstitutionalism*) and served as a focal point in the struggles in subsequent periods between the crown and the upper nobility.

The council exerted and expanded its authority during the chaos of the fourteenth and fifteenth centuries. On the occasion of Albrekt of Mecklenburg's election in 1371, it extracted the first accession charter in Swedish history, in which the new king was compelled to recognize and guarantee the powers of the council. The council was instrumental in deposing Erik of Pomerania* in 1439 and imposed on his successor, Kristofer of Bavaria (Christoffer III*) an accession charter in which he promised that the king would rule only with the council's consent (med råds råde). The apogee of the council's position in this period was reached in 1483 in the Kalmar Recess*. This document asserted the council's right to rebel, recognized the right of the members of the council to act as kings on their own lands, and asserted the council's right to act as sovereign in the king's absence.

Set against a trend which may have pointed toward aristocratic oligarchy and which certainly was part of an attempt to preserve an old order were individuals who espoused more "modern" ideas of government and advocated strong monarchy. Karl VIII Knutsson*, Sten Sture the Elder*, Sten Svantesson "Sture" the Younger*, and Gustav I Vasa* were such individuals. Only Vasa, however, was able to put into practice these more modern notions. He took advantage of the changes in the nature of warfare, the Reformation*, the changing commercial balance in Europe, the emergence of the Swedish parliament as a check upon the political aspirations of the magnates, and a number of other factors. The council was set aside, and Vasa ruled primarily with the advice of foreign advisors. His immediate successor, Erik XIV* (1560–1568), followed a similar course, but Johan III* (1568–1592) was compelled to make some use of the council following his brother's criminal excesses. The succession of Sigismund*, also king of Poland, created a situation which the advocates of council constitutionalism believed would work in their favor. Erik Sparre was the most outspoken advocate of the council's revival. He argued that the body ought to function as an administrative element within the government and as a check upon royal tyranny. (Sparre rejected the Riksdag* as the element in the system which ought to be responsible for the latter.) The council nobles were unable to establish their position, however. Karl IX* (1592/1599–1611) used the Riksdag against the high nobles and established a virtual absolutism. Council constitutionalism was rejected and Sparre was executed, in part for his advocacy of a strong council.

Significant changes in the importance and role of the council occurred in the seventeenth century. The minority of Gustav II Adolf* (1611–1632) gave the magnates an opportunity to reassert their importance that they did not pass up. In his accession charter, the young king promised to recognize the historic rights and duties of the council. This did not mean, however, a return to the politics of the fourteenth or fifteenth century. The complexities of government in the early seventeenth century and the absence of the king during war made an effective administration essential. The council came to occupy a place at the top of this administration. The principal officers on the council (chancellor, marshal, steward, admiral) came to head government departments or colleges. The council managed the day-to-day functions of the state. At the same time, the council lost its representative nature—as representative of the nobility and the commons. The estates took over this function, and the council nobles were excluded from the House of the Nobility when it was formally constituted in 1626. Set apart, the members of the council appeared increasingly to constitute a caste of upper nobles intent upon serving its own interests. The Form of Government (1634) gave constitutional bases to the changes effected during Gustav II's reign. The work of Axel Oxenstierna*, the Form of Government embodied many of E. Sparre's ideas, and it (along with the Additamentum of 1660) served as the basis for the council's position until the 1670s. It has been argued that these documents might have made the crown a superfluous entity, a "Venetian Doge," but this did not happen, except perhaps during the minority of Karl XI*.

The abuses which the council made of its powers when it functioned as the regency for Karl XI alienated it from the estates and the young king. Between 1672 and 1693 the aristocracy in Sweden, and especially the council aristocracy, was stripped of its powers and its financial bases. Karl became an absolute monarch with the approval of the estates. In 1680 the council became the king's council (*kungliga råd*) and lost all its powers. For the next 40 years power resided almost entirely with the crown.

Following the death of Karl XII* in 1718, the aristocracy and the council, along with the estates, reasserted their roles in the Swedish political system. A series of new constitutional documents from 1719 to 1723 redefined the nature of government in the country (*see* Age of Liberty). The council returned to a central position and exerted considerable authority for nearly 20 years. The king came entirely under the control of the council. He had no veto power in its decisions. He chose the members of the council, but only from a list of approved candidates prepared by a parliamentary committee. Following the emergence of political factions (*see* Cap Party; Hat Party), however, the council's position was weakened. These factions used the power of impeachment (*licentiering*) given to the estates to make the council their pawn.

Gustav III*'s coup in 1772 overturned the Age of Liberty system, and a new constitution restored the council to a position of some importance, at least in an advisory capacity. Gustav, however, relied heavily on favorites for advice and by-passed the council frequently. Through the Act of Union and Security (1789), its powers were further limited, but it continued in existence through the reign of Gustav IV Adolf* (1792–1809).

In 1809 Gustavian absolutism was overthrown, and a new constitution was drafted. The council became a ministry or cabinet. The Swedish term shifted from *riks/kungliga råd* to *statsråd*. Its members were principally the heads of government departments, and it served in an advisory capacity to the crown, which could accept or reject the council's advice. The members of the ministry were responsible to the parliament for the advice they gave the crown. Over the course of the next 150 years, this body evolved into a modern executive cabinet with about nineteen members, responsible to the parliament. The constitution of 1975 is the most recent document to define the council's formation, composition, and functions.

REFERENCES: *DSH*; M. Roberts, *Essays in Swedish History* (Minneapolis: University of Minnesota Press, 1967).

B. NORDSTROM

COUNT'S WAR (Grevefejden) 1534–1536

The Count's War was one of the more complicated struggles of the sixteenth century in Scandinavia*. It involved the sons of Frederik I* (Christian III* and Hans), the Hanseatic League* (and especially Lübeck and its mayor Jürgen Wullenweber), the Catholic prelates of Denmark, the lay nobles of Denmark, the burghers of Copenhagen* and Malmö, the peasants of Denmark, Count Christoffer of Oldenburg (after whom the war was named), Albrekt of Mecklenburg, Christian II* ("The Imprisoned"), the Habsburgs, the Dutch, and the Swedes. It was a conflict in which constitutional and dynastic issues, religion, economic questions, social conflicts, personal factors, and international relations were woven together.

Following the death of Frederik I, the Danish council met to decide the succession. Gathering in Copenhagen in June 1533, the council decided not to decide. The choice was between the dead king's elder son, Duke Christian of Schleswig and Holstein, a Lutheran, and his younger son, Hans, then only 12 and a Catholic. Because of the split within the council and the absence of the Norwegian representatives, the decision was postponed and a meeting was scheduled for the following year. At the same time, the Catholic prelates in the council won the restoration of the old Church's place in the society. Administration of the country during the interregnum was placed in the hands of the nobles. In effect, the council chose to make Denmark an "aristocratic republic."

These decisions created an impression of weakness to those outside, and antagonized the citizens of Copenhagen and Malmö, Lutherans throughout the country, the lesser nobility, and the peasants. Religious freedom seemed threatened. Peasants and townspeople saw their economic and legal rights threatened by an increasingly powerful nobility. These concerns drove the discontented into the arms of Lübeck and that city's aggressive-minded new mayor, Jürgen Wullenweber. This adventuresome character believed that the situation in Denmark presented an ideal case in which the decline of the Hanse could be reversed, control of the Baltic and the Øresund assured, and Denmark transformed into a vassal state of the League.

The war began in the spring of 1534, when Lübeck's forces, led by Christoffer of Oldenburg, attacked Holstein. This attack was repulsed by Johan Rantzau, Duke Christian's very able commander, and German attentions were turned to the Danish territories in south Sweden and the Danish islands. In these areas, Lübeck was aided by a social revolt. Duke Christian had rejected an offer of the throne made to him by the citizens of Copenhagen. (A strict legalist, Christian would only accept the crown if the offer came from the council.) This rejection led the townspeople (who were intent upon establishing free city status based on the German model for Copenhagen and Malmö), the peasants, and religious reformers to turn to Lübeck and Christoffer, who promised the restoration of Christian II. (Christoffer had a legitimate claim to the throne, which he was not above asserting if the circumstances presented themselves.) Within a short time all of east Denmark was under the count's control—in the name of Christian II. In these areas social tensions mounted, and this led to attacks on the nobles and their estates. The civil war spread to Jutland, where Ålborg fell under the control of "Skipper" Klement Andersen and a peasant army.

Gradually, however, Lübeck's advantageous situation evaporated. The Swedish king, Gustav I Vasa*, concluded an alliance with the Danish council in early 1534, and Sweden entered the war against Lübeck. The success of the count and the social war precipitated a reaction by the nobles of Jutland and Fyn. In August 1534 the council nobles from these areas met at Ry and elected Christian king. Soon thereafter the duke's forces moved into Jutland. Ålborg fell to Rantzau's mercenaries in late 1534, and the way was opened to the eastern islands. In June 1535, Rantzau's army defeated the combined forces of Lübeck, Christoffer, and Albrekt of Mecklenburg at Øksnebjerg. A few days later the king's fleet, commanded by Peder Skram, defeated a Lübeck force at Svendborg Sund. The foreign aspect of the war was nearly over. Wullenweber was removed in Lübeck. Negotiations began in Hamburg in January 1536 and were completed by 14 February. Christian was recognized king by Lübeck, foreign forces were withdrawn, and the Hanse was assured its old trade privileges. The civil side of the war dragged on for another six months. Malmö capitulated in the spring of 1536, but Copenhagen, which had been under siege since the previous August, held out until the end of July 1536.

The Count's War settled very little. Christian II remained in prison, but his hopes for a restoration and the plottings of his relatives continued. Lübeck was defeated, and its powers had clearly passed their zenith, but the city remained a factor in Nordic history for another 60 years. The cause of social tension, the rights of the cities, and the religious question remained. The question of council constitutionalism versus strong central monarchy was not decided by the struggle. Relations with Sweden following the conflict were peaceful but cool. Christian III emerged with the throne, but also with the legacies of the war, including enormous debts which could only be met through drastic measures.

REFERENCES: *CMH*, vol. 2; *DH*, vol. 6; *NCMH*, vol. 2.

B. NORDSTROM

D

DACKE, NILS (?–1543) Leader of revolt against Sweden's king, Gustav I Vasa*

Little is definitely known about Nils Dacke, the leader of the last rebellion against Gustav Vasa. He may have been born in the province of Blekinge, although his family and lifetime residence were in Småland. He was a courageous and imaginative natural leader of both outlaws and rebels; he could plan guerilla warfare and see it executed effectively. He was involved in the slaying of a royal bailiff; he may on occasion have been brutal and ruthless.

Dacke's and his followers' complaints against Gustav I and his government in the 1530s and 1540s centered on changes from relatively autonomous folklands (such as Dacke's own Värend) to an ever increasing centralization of control by Stockholm.* The changes were economic, social, and religious: royal bailiffs enforced new regulations about taxation, limitations on hunting, the export of cattle to neighboring Denmark, and the cutting of trees; the clan and the family lost power to both bailiffs and nobles; and Lutheran Christianity was arbitrarily substituted for Roman Catholicism.

In 1542 Nils Dacke led his followers to one victory after another; was able for quite some time to make his headquarters in the royal fortified castle of Kronoberg near Växjö; offered Svante Sture support in gaining the Swedish crown; was encouraged by such foreign rulers as Albrecht of Mecklenburg, Emperor Charles, and Palatine Count Fredrik (who "ennobled" Dacke); forced King Gustav to negotiate with him seriously; and returned the Småland churches to Catholicism. But the highly gifted defender of the old systems (political, social, and religious), after successful guerilla warfare, was finally defeated by the king's forces in 1543, and either he or a double was assassinated and his head exhibited in Kalmar.* (A man claiming to be Dacke did appear long after King Gustav died, was placed in an asylum, and died there in 1580).

REFERENCES: A. Åberg, *Nils Dacke och landsfadern* (Stockholm: LTs förlag, 1956); *DSH*, vol. 4; L. O. Larsson, *Dackeland* (Stockholm: Norstedt, 1979); *SU*, vol. 6.

W. JOHNSON

DANISH (Language) *See* Languages: Scandinavian.

DANISH CONFEDERATION OF TRADE UNIONS *See* Swedish Confederation of Trade Unions

DANISH EAST INDIA COMPANY (Ostindiske Kompagnier) Danish trading company in the Far East

Trade between Denmark and India began as early as 1616, with the founding of the Danish East India Company. One of Christian IV's* greatest interests was the sea, and in November 1618 he sent a fleet of six ships to India under the command of Ove Giedde (Gjedde). At Tranquebar (Trankebar), on the Coromandel coast in southeast India, Giedde built a fort in 1620, nineteen years before the English settled Madras, 150 miles to the north. Behind the fort the Danes planned a little European town. Tranquebar and other possessions later acquired were under Danish administration (with brief exceptions during the Napoleonic War) until they were sold to the English East India Company in 1845 (*see* Danish Posts in Asia). The Danes never showed any strong desire to build an empire in India.

Tranquebar was regarded by the Danes as their headquarters in India. There they sought British capital in competition with the private traders operating under the Danish flag. British capital played a large part in the operations of the company, as revealed by the names of those connected with it. Throughout the seventeenth century, however, Danish-Indian trade remained ill-organized. It was not until 1732, when the Danish Asiatic Company (Asiatisk Kompagni) was founded, that connections with India were carefully managed. Danish possessions in India were managed by the Asiatic Company between 1732 and 1777, and they reached their greatest extent in the 1770s. The Asiatic Company was a joint-stock company with a capital of 2.4 million *rigsdaler*, which was divided into 4,800 shares. Even as late as 1772, more than one-fourth of the capital was still in foreign, particularly Dutch, hands. The company was controlled by a group of Copenhagen merchants.

The goods sent to India consisted of metals, especially copper, naval stores, munitions, wines and spirits, and silver. The value of the company's return cargoes far exceeded that of the cargoes from Europe. In the period 1772–1801, the company's return cargoes consisted almost exclusively of cotton textiles, which accounted for over 80 percent of the total value.

At the renewal of the Asiatic Company's charter in 1772, the Danish trade was given an organization that was unique in the eighteenth century. The company's Indian monopoly was abolished, and from 1772 to the British occupation of Danish possessions in 1808, private merchants competed with the company.

In order to ensure the equality of these two branches of the trade, the crown took over the administration of the company and allowed private merchants to compete on equal terms. The years 1772–1808 marked the high point of the Danish Indian trade.

REFERENCES: O. Feldbaek, *India Trade under the Danish Flag, 1772–1808* (Lund: Scandinavian Institute of Asian Studies, Monograph Series no. 2, 1969); H. Furber, *John Company at Work: A Study of European Expansion in India in the Late Eighteenth Century*, ch. 4, "The Danes and the Clandestine Trade of India" (Cambridge, Mass.: Harvard University Press, 1948); K. Glamann, "The Danish Asiatic Company, 1732–1772," *Scandinavian Economic History Review* 8:2 (1960): 109–149; A. Rasch and P. Sveistrup, *Asiatisk Kompagni i den florissante periode, 1772–1792* (Copenhagen: Institutet for Historie og Samfundsøkonomi, 1948).

A. H. WINQUIST

DANISH EMPLOYERS' FEDERATION *See* Swedish Employers' Federation

DANISH LAW *Danske Lov* (1683), major Danish law book replacing all earlier law codes

With the establishment of absolutism in Denmark from 1660 onwards, it was natural that the crown should consider a substantial revision of the law of the kingdom. The first of several commissions was set up in January 1661, but progress was uneven and sporadic over the next decade, especially since there was disagreement over the extent to which codification, rather than mere compilation, should be the guiding principle. Drafts tending in either direction were discussed in the early 1670s, but it was only with the work of the fourth commission (1681–1682) that a final text was produced. It was printed (with certain additions) and promulgated on 23 June 1683 as *Danske Lov*.

The final text owed much to earlier Danish law books, including both the medieval provincial laws and the later compilations of 1558 and 1615, and especially Christian IV's* *Reces* of 1643. Roman and other foreign influences were not very significant. Shortage of time, as well as personal disagreements between certain commission members (notably between Rasmus Vinding and the more radical revisionist Peder Lassen), and the lack of native expertise in some areas, meant that *Danske Lov* in the end was less comprehensive than some had hoped. Much of it amounted to a reorganized compilation of existing legislation and legal practices in the kingdom, sometimes reinterpreted or clarified in the interest of accessibility for non-specialists. Some parts, however, were new, notably those dealing with the nature of royal majesty and prescribing punishments for anyone offending against it. The introduction emphasized the king's desire to eliminate any parts of the legal tradition incompatible with absolutism, and this was elaborated in the very first article, where a succinct definition of Danish absolutism was provided (at a time when the text of the Royal Law of 1665 was still not generally available). The rest of Book I of *Danske Lov* deals extensively with the civil legal machinery, together with certain aspects of criminal procedure and punishments. Book II covers religion and the church, as well as censorship and restrictions on publishing. Book III covers a few aspects of administrative law and a range of civil law aspects (including citizenship, trades and guilds, weights and measures in general terms, peasant life, servants, vagrants, guardianship, and marriage), but intentionally omits detailed regulations of "law and order," reserved for separate ordinances on "police." Book IV is on maritime law (some of it showing foreign influences), but areas such as defense, the military, taxation, and customs impositions are not covered. Book V deals mainly with property, debt, and inheritance, while the last book, Book VI, covers a wide range of criminal law ranging from violence, theft, and fraud to heresy and treason. The original edition also has a substantial index for ease of reference.

Danske Lov was a major landmark in Danish legal history and stands out even in a European context. Although it had certain gaps and was considered for revision as early as 1701, much of it remained definitive. Its text, in simple and concise Danish, was intended to be readily intelligible, and it completed the process of standardization of the law in the whole kingdom.

REFERENCES: *Danske Lov* (1683), also available in facsimile and in recent editions, for example, S. Iuul (Copenhagen: Gad, 1949); S. Iuul, *Kodifikation eller kompilation?* (Copenhagen: Copenhagen University/Bianeo Luno, 1954, repr. Gad, 1967); P. J. Jørgensen, *Dansk Retshistorie* (Copenhagen: Gad, 1940); V. A. Secher and C. Støchel, eds., *Forarbejderne til Kong Kristian Vs Danske Lov*, 1–2 (Copenhagen: Gad, 1891–1894; repr. Selskab for Udgivning af Kilder til Dansk Historie).

T. MUNCK

DANISH POSTS IN AFRICA

Beginning in the 1640s, Danes from the Elbe began to send a few ships on trading expeditions to Africa's Gold Coast (today's Ghana). Expecting to acquire cargoes of gold and elephant ivory, a Guinea Company was set up in 1659, which quickly established the fort of Frederiksborg* and a number of smaller factories along the coast. Dutch and Swedish rivalry made the operation of these posts difficult for the Danes. Profits were small. Soon they had to give up sole control of the fort. Instead the Danes bartered for an area near the native village of Orsu on the extreme eastern end of the Gold Coast, where they established a new post, Christiansborg.

The location, as the most distant European outpost on the coast, assured nearly unhindered expansion eastward, and in about 1750 control had been established of a strip of coast which extended a few hundred kilometers from the mouth of the Volta River. The centers of this area were the small forts of Fredensborg and Prinsensten, which were erected at the eastern extreme in the 1780s near Ada and Keta, respectively.

How far inland Danish influence extended varied considerably and depended on the power relationships among the various native tribes, including the Asante,

Accra, Akwamu, and Akim. These tribes fought amongst themselves constantly until the mid-eighteenth century, when the Asante established predominance.

The tribal wars were in themselves unpleasant for the Danes, but they also assured a supply of slaves, many of whom were prisoners of war or criminals who were sold to the Europeans by the victors in these struggles. All our information indicates that the profit for the Danes remained generally modest. After the Danish West Indies* were brought under cultivation in the course of the eighteenth century, however, the export of slaves there became more necessary. In reality, this supply of a work force became the African stations' only reason for existence. The Danish share of the total slave trade was only a few percent.

After the liquidation of the West Indies and Guinea Company in 1755, the Danish state assumed responsibility for the administration and supply of the forts on the Gold Coast, which was then delegated to a succession of chartered trading companies. In spite of attempts to establish plantations on the uplands, slaves continued to be the colonies' most important trading commodity until the slave trade was abolished in 1802.

Abolition of the slave trade made continued operation of the African posts questionable. Furthermore, the Asante Wars and the English challenge to the Danes' claim to the uplands during the 1820s and 1830s cooled Denmark's interest in the area. After a number of unrealistic attempts to obtain a high price for the Danish posts in Guinea, they were transferred to England in 1850 for a nominal amount.

REFERENCES: E. Gøbel, "Danish Trade to the West Indies and Guinea 1671–1754," *Scandinavian Economic History Review* 31 (1983): 21–49; S. E. Green-Pedersen, "The History of the Danish Negro Slave Trade 1733–1807," *Revue française d'histoire d'outre-mer* 62 (1975): 196–220; O. Justesen, "The Danish Settlements on the Gold Coast in the Nineteenth Century," *Scandinavian Journal of History* 4 (1979): 3–33; O. Justesen and O. Feldbaek, *Kolonierne i Asien og Afrika* (Copenhagen: Politiken, 1980); G. Nørregaard, *Danish Settlements in West Africa 1658–1850* (Boston: Boston University Press, 1966).

E. GØBEL

DANISH POSTS IN ASIA

After England and the Netherlands established East India trading companies in 1600 and 1602, respectively, Denmark-Norway quickly entered into the Asian trade, and in 1616 Christian IV* awarded a monopoly to the Danish East India Company* for all trade east of the Cape of Good Hope. Subsequently, after fruitless attempts to secure a toehold in Ceylon, the company bought in 1620 the little village of Trankebar (Tranquebar) on India's east coast, 250 kilometers south of present-day Madras.

For more than 200 years the Danish headquarters were located there. Though the village, with its fort (Dansborg), could accommodate only 100 to 200 Danes, the total population of 3,000 made Trankebar Denmark's sixth largest town. In addition, a surrounding area of about 50 square kilometers was controlled. Although only seven of the eighteen ships sent out returned to Denmark in the period down to 1639, a number of smaller stations were established in the 1620s, including ones at Balasore in Bengal, Masulipatam on India's east coast, and Bantam in Java. The Asian trade was, however, not a profit-making operation, and investments vastly exceeded the profits that were secured through the sale of imported cloves and pepper. For periods as long as 30 years no ships were sent out from Denmark. The officials in India, however, held out hope, and they kept Trankebar in Danish control in spite of great hardships, before economic conditions improved toward the end of the seventeenth century. In the 1690s the East Indian possessions showed profits, and new sites were opened. Unfortunately, it was not long before a new slump set in.

As a result of the experience in India, involvement in China was strongly promoted in the 1730s. Tea and porcelain were obtained there, which sold at a profit in Denmark. The earnings which the company showed in China, however, depended in large part on the fact that its expenses there were minimal. No forts or personnel were maintained there. Following the example of the other European powers, the company only rented a warehouse in Canton. Concurrently, the India trade was intensified when the Royal Chartered Danish Asiatic Company took over the monopoly of the whole of Asia in 1732. Important new commodities such as saltpeter and cotton, both of which were obtained in Bengal, came into the trade. In 1754 commercial rights were purchased at Serampore near Calcutta, where the Danish factory was called Frederiksnagore. The year before the site at Calicut had been opened, and over the next few years large amounts of pepper were shipped from the west coast of India. At this time, the Nicobar Islands, which lie northwest of Sumatra and encompass about 2,000 square kilometers, were annexed. The highly unhealthy climate assured, however, that the islands would never hold much importance for the company, which managed them and the other possessions in the East for the crown until 1777.

From its establishment, the monopoly company added to the number of commercial posts in India. But with the renewal of its charter in 1772 its monopoly was lost, and private commercial houses began to compete with it in the Asian market. The government took over the responsibility of administering the possessions, which were, first and foremost, Trankebar and Frederiksnagore. In addition there were small factories at Calicut and Colachel on the southwest coast, Porto Novo a little north of Trankebar, and Balasore and Patna in Bengal.

The purpose of the state's takeover was to assure that private companies involved in the Asian trade would be able to compete. The result was a blossoming of trade for both the private firms and the Danish Asiatic Company.

As during previous and subsequent "world wars," in the late eighteenth century Denmark-Norway remained neutral during the American War of Independence. This meant that international trade could be conducted by the Danes in highly favorable circumstances, especially because the expeditions the belligerents could send into the Far East diminished in number. The years from the 1770s to 1807 were boom years. During this period over 200 Danish ships went to India, and nearly as many went to other parts of Asia, including Isle de France and Batavia. The Asiatic Company's 63 cargoes from India between 1772 and 1807, in which cotton was the most important good, sold in Copenhagen* for 35 million *rigsdaler*. (Individual profits fluctuated widely.) On the other hand, the company had exceptional profits in the China trade, where it retained its monopoly.

The small Danish possessions in India, however, were largely dependent on the ever-encroaching English, who sought to control the entire gulf in this period. Trankebar became the only free port on the entire east coast, and this contributed to the boom in trade.

During the wars of the last decade of the eighteenth century considerable hardships were experienced by the small colonial outposts, and even Trankebar began to experience some decline. In 1801 and 1802 England occupied all the Danish possessions, though this occupation was mild. The occupation of 1808–1815 was more severe, and in the interim the level of trade began to diminish. The state's losses in these colonies amounted to about 30,000 *rigsdaler* per year. Following 1815, trade levels never recovered. In some years no ships came out from Denmark, and Trankebar's environs were too poor to support the settlement. Trade was opened to all Danish subjects, and the Asiatic Company was dissolved in 1843. In 1845 all the mainland possessions in India were sold to the English East India Company (Trankebar, Frederiksnagore, and Balasore).

Subsequently, only the Nicobar Islands (or the Frederik Islands, as they were called) remained. Repeated attempts to colonize these islands failed, largely because of the unhealthy climate in their dense jungles. They were evacuated in 1848 and later taken over by England (1868) gratis.

The story of the rise and decline of Denmark's presence in India must be seen in its international context. Neutrality or belligerency in European wars determined the success or failure of activities there to a great extent. Furthermore, it was fatal for the colonies when the English Company lost its monopoly. This meant that goods which had formerly been sent home in Danish vessels (chartered) could now be sent home in private English ships. Finally, the emergence of the textile industry in Europe in the early 1800s resulted in a decline in the demand for Indian fabrics. Economic considerations were central to Denmark so far as these colonies were concerned, and these considerations were vital when the decision was made to sell them.

REFERENCES: O. Feldbaek, "The Danish Asiatic Company," *Asiatisk Plads*, ed. A. Georg (Copenhagen: Ministry of Foreign Affairs, 1980), and *India Trade under the Danish Flag 1772–1808* (Copenhagen: Studentlitteratur, 1969), pp. 6–32; O. Feldbaek and O. Justesen, *Kolonierne i Asien og Afrika* (Copenhagen: Politiken, 1980); G. Olsen, *Dansk Ostindien 1616–1732* (Copenhagen: Fremad, 1967); A. Rasch, *Dansk Ostindien 1777–*

1845 (Copenhagen: Fremad, 1967); K. Struwe, *Dansk Ostindien 1732–1776* (Copenhagen: Fremad, 1967).

E. GØBEL

DANISH WEST INDIES

European powers have been involved in the Caribbean's Virgin Islands since their discovery by Columbus in 1493. The Danes became involved there in the 1640s and annexed the uninhabited island of St. Thomas 20 years later in the name of Frederik III*. Activities in the area became more effective in 1671, when the Royal Chartered Danish West Indies and Guinea Company was founded. The company secured a monopoly on trade with the West Indies and Africa.

For the rest of the decade, efforts centered on the founding of plantations and the establishment of trade links. The allotment of land attracted people of various nationalities. By 1680 there were 156 whites and 175 slaves occupying 47 small plantations on the island. The only real village on St. Thomas was the administrative center at Charlotte Amalie. The most important products, which were shipped to Denmark in an annual ship, were tobacco, raw sugar, and small amounts of cotton. Problems for the Danish West Indies developed in the 1680s as a result of the company's constant need for capital and its stubborn insistence that both imports and exports be carried on its own ships and handled by its own personnel. In 1708 the company was forced to grant a long list of concessions to the prosperous plantation owners, including the acceptance of the latter's right (under license) to ship and trade their produce with North America and Europe.

Because of their neutrality during the War of the Spanish Succession, Danish colonial trade flourished in the early eighteenth century. Virtually all the land on St. Thomas was brought under cultivation. Consequently, the neighboring island of St. Jan was annexed in 1718.

Economic considerations also led to the purchase of St. Croix from France in 1733. The Danes' holdings in the Caribbean were now at their peak—333 square kilometers. St. Croix was more fertile, and the timbered lowlands were quickly cleared and covered with sugar plantations. By 1751 all the fertile land had been claimed, and 64 sugar works were in operation. A hope that the necessary workers could be obtained from Denmark through emigration went unfulfilled, and St. Croix also developed as a slave economy. The fortified villages of Christianssted and Frederikssted were established on the island.

Trade with the islands was liberalized in 1733. But dissatisfaction with the company's right to first claim to the principal products of the three islands continued. It was only after the plantation owners appealed directly to the king, however, that the company was dissolved in 1754. By this time St. Thomas's plantation culture had passed its peak. Production and population continued to grow on St. Croix, however, which quickly became the main Danish island. The population there included at this time 2,000 whites and 14,000 slaves. After the dissolution of the company, the crown took over administration of the West

Indies and possessions in Guinea, and trade was opened to all Danish and Norwegian citizens in 1755.

About 1,000 slaves were brought to the islands annually from Danish Guinea, and nearly as many were sold on other islands in the area. In 1792, however, Denmark became the first country in the world to outlaw the slave trade— although the islands were given 10 years to develop a population base of slaves large enough to maintain the necessary work force.

When the state took over the islands in 1755, the system of government was reorganized and the administration made more effective. For the sake of St. Thomas's trade, the harbor at Charlotte Amalie was opened to ships of all nations a few years later. Because of Denmark's neutral status, the islands became a commercial center for goods from all over the region, which were sent on to Europe in Danish ships. Until 1807 the boom also depended on St. Croix's sugar production—and the valuable by-product, rum, which was also exported in considerable quantities.

Following the occupation of the islands by Britain in 1801–1802 and 1807–1815, St. Croix continued to turn a profit until the 1840s. St. Thomas remained profitable until the 1870s. Hence, during the Revolutionary and Napoleonic wars, the islands were important for Copenhagen's* and the state's treasuries. In good years they accounted for half of Denmark's export tonnage, and it was common that the state's part of the profits were over 100,000 *rigsdaler* annually, or about 3 percent of its income. Copenhagen was the center for West Indies' trade, and half of the harbor's exports were made up of West Indian goods, the most important being sugar. Refining it became the city's most important industry, and it accounted for 80–90 percent of the country's total industrial exports.

Sugar prices fell, however, with the introduction into Europe of the sugar beet and the industrialization of sugar production on larger islands in the Caribbean. In addition, St. Croix's small and old-fashioned plantations, with their exhausted land, were no longer profitable. At the same time, technical developments rendered St. Thomas superfluous as a transit harbor for the Caribbean. Through the rest of the nineteenth century the islands experienced stagnation and decline and had to deal with numerous social and economic problems. The most obvious problem centered on the conditions of the slaves, who were caught in the economic squeeze. Their wretched living conditions led to disturbances in 1848, and the governor of the islands felt compelled to abolish slavery. (Blacks outnumbered whites on the islands by nearly 10 to 1. As early as 1733 there were disturbances which had to be forcibly crushed.) This did not solve the survival problems of the lower classes, however, and in 1878 an insurrection broke out, during which Frederikssted was burned.

The social unrest could not be quieted by the small means the Danish state were willing to use. Twice, therefore, Denmark sought to transfer the islands to the United States, which were interested in them as a naval base. It was not until 1917, however, that their sale was arranged and approved in Denmark's first popular referendum. For the last half-century the islands had been a drain on the Danish treasury; now $25 million were received for them.

Since 1917 the islands have been a protectorate of the United States. They are administered by the U.S. Department of the Interior. The population of the islands is over 90,000, 70 percent of which is black.

REFERENCES: J. O. Bro-Jørgensen, *Dansk Vestindien indtil 1755* (Copenhagen: Fremad, 1966); I. Dookhan, *A History of the Virgin Islands of the United States* (St. Thomas: Caribbean Universities Press, 1974); E. Gøbel, "Danish Trade to the West Indies and Guinea 1671–1754," *Scandinavian Economic History Review* 31 (1983): 21–49; O. Hornby, *Kolonierne i Vestindien* (Copenhagen: Politiken, 1980); G. Nørregaard, *Dansk Vestindien 1880–1917* (Copenhagen: Fremad, 1967); F. Skrubbeltrang, *Dansk Vestindien 1848–1880* (Copenhagen: Fremad, 1967); J. Vibaek, *Dansk Vestindien 1755–1848* (Copenhagen: Fremad, 1966); W. Westergaard, *The Danish West Indies under Company Rule 1671–1754* (New York: Macmillan, 1917).

E. GØBEL

DANISH WOMEN'S SOCIETY (Dansk Kvindesamfund/DK) Denmark's first feminist organization

The Danish Women's Society (DK) was founded in 1871 by the husband and wife team Fredrik and Matilde Bajer, Pauline Worm*, and Caroline Testman. Its original aim was to further the intellectual, moral, and economic development of women by enlarging their opportunities for self-support. To that end it established or aided the establishment of vocational schools for women and in 1887 organized a registry office for female domestic workers. By 1889 it was campaigning for "equal pay for equal work," a principle it adopted by formal resolution in 1896. It also worked for better educational opportunities for women.

A "morality controversy" erupted in 1885, provoked by George Brandes, who called for women's sexual emancipation while announcing his nonsupport of their political emancipation. The DK responded through articles in its newly founded journal, *Kvinden og Samfundet* (*Women and Society*). Attacking the double standard, the DK spokeswoman retorted that rather than women becoming more dissolute like men, men should become more chaste like women. The controversy spread to Sweden and Norway, and in the latter country it was enjoined by the Norwegian Feminist Union*.

In the political sphere the DK was sometimes a bit cautious. It did not demand the vote for women during the conservative Provisional Government period (1885–1894), although it had declared in 1883 that it would work for women's full rights as citizens. In 1904 it advocated making women eligible for appointment to public office on equal terms with men except in the area of military appointments. (Women finally gained this right after World War I.) Not until 1906 did the DK formally endorse women's suffrage* in national elections. In 1908 Danish women and men over 25 were permitted to vote in local elections, but only with the issuance of a new constitution in 1915 did women gain full political rights on the national level.

A DK committee was organized in 1908 to work out a new marriage ritual which would not declare the wife subservient to the husband. Four years later a reformed ritual closely resembling that proposed by the DK was officially adopted by the state church. By 1920 the DK was pressing for the right of women to become ministers of the church, and in 1947 the first three female ministers were ordained.

Other efforts of the DK included opposing special protective labor legislation for women, seeking to improve the legal status of married women, supporting women's right to keep their own family name after marriage and bestow it on their children, and advocating separate taxation for married women. After World War II* the DK took up the problems of single mothers and child support and called for provision of more day nurseries, school doctors, and dental care for school children. In the political realm it sought to get more women elected to government office—still one of its major goals. In its earlier years it had avoided the issues of contraception and abortion, but by 1969 it favored abortion on demand.

The neofeminist movement, which began in the United States in the 1960s, burst forth in Copenhagen* in spring 1970, when the Rødstrømper (Redstockings) staged a lively demonstration against conventional notions of femininity. Inspired by their example, some DK members formed an activist subgroup called *Thildes børn* (Thilde's Children) after Mathilde Fibiger*. However, DK membership declined during the neofeminist period. From a peak of about 12,000 in the 1950s it dropped to around 10,000 in the 1960s and to 2–3,000 in the 1970s. The Thilde's Children separated from the DK in 1978.

The DK keeps a watch and comments on legislation affecting women and continues to publish *Kvinden og Samfundet*, a biweekly. It sponsors courses for women in Greenland* and promotes family planning there. It also assists women in developing countries, particularly through seminars, held usually in Denmark.

REFERENCES: I. Dahlsgård, *Women in Denmark* (Copenhagen: Det Danske Selskab, 1980); K. Grønager, "Work and Achievements of Danish Women's Society," *International Women's News* 74:1 (Feb. 1979): 2–3; Å. Lading, *Dansk kvindesamfunds arbejde gennem 25 aar* (Copenhagen: Gyldendal, 1939); *Salmonsens Konversations Leksikon*, 2nd ed., vol. 5 (Copenhagen: Schultz, 1916); J. Steenstrup, *Den danske kvindes historie* (Copenhagen: Hagerups, 1917).

N. FARQUHAR

DANSKE LOV See Danish Law

DEATH PENALTY

The death penalty appears to have been used fairly extensively in prehistoric and medieval Scandinavia*, often locally in settling personal and clan disputes. The thirteenth-century Nordic sagas chronicling Viking* life some 300 years before contain frequent references to various kinds of executions. Among the most usual were decapitation for the more privileged classes and hanging for offenders from the lower social ranks. Scandinavia thus shared a general European way of dealing with offenders before prisons*—a relatively modern phenomenon—came into widespread use and made feasible a greater variety of punitive and rehabilitative alternatives.

As a codified measure, however, the death penalty played only a modest role in medieval northern Germanic law. Its legal position expanded significantly during the seventeenth and eighteenth centuries, when the monarchies of Denmark-Norway and Sweden became absolutist and state regulation of many aspects of life became the norm. The Danish king Christian V* (1646–1699) decreed the death penalty for various offenses, while in Sweden a law of 1734 prescribed death for a number of crimes but forbade torture, although the ineffectiveness of the latter provision is suggested by the fact that another statute prohibiting it came in 1772.

Yet the death penalty began to disappear soon after it reached its legal zenith. Much of the impetus for its eventual abolition stemmed from the Italian jurist and philosopher Cesare Beccaria's work of 1764, *Crimes and Punishments*, which was soon translated into many other languages, including Swedish in 1770 and Danish in 1796–1798. His tenets that punishment should be proportionate to the crime and serve the sole purpose of societal protection left little room for the death penalty and won international acclaim. Capital punishment soon receded in Scandinavian criminal codes. In 1778–1779 the Swedish parliament abolished it for witchcraft, rape, bigamy, and several other offenses. The enlightened Swedish monarch, Gustav III*, hoped to carry the reform further but met stiff opposition from some of his advisors and part of the state church clergy.

The nineteenth century brought further reductions. The Norwegian criminal code of 1842, for instance, prescribed capital punishment only for treason, premeditated murder, and certain other forms of homicide. It was later altered to allow lesser penalties for these crimes, however, and the last executions took place in 1876. A law of 1902 abolished the death penalty for civilians during times of peace. In Sweden the last execution took place in 1910, and capital punishment was legally abolished in 1921. In Denmark the civilian death penalty was last imposed in 1892 and abolished in 1930.

The German occupation of Norway and Denmark from 1940 until 1945 and the collaboration of many Danes and Norwegians with it brought new life to the death penalty at the end of World War II*. In Norway, 24 Norwegians, 13 Germans, and 1 Dane were executed for war crimes, the last in 1948. Capital punishment was reintroduced in Denmark shortly after the war to deal with similar offenders. Seventy-eight were sentenced to death there, and 46 were actually executed.

F. HALE

DE GEER, LOUIS G. (18 July 1818–24 September 1896) Swedish baron, public official, prime minister, and writer

Louis G. De Geer, a member of the well-known family, was born in Finspång,

Östergötland. After attending school in Linköping and the Uppsala Cathedral School, he entered Uppsala University in 1836, where he studied law. During his Uppsala years, De Geer developed a strong interest in literature. He was to author a book of essays, a book on judicial style, a couple of novels, and later in life his *Minnen* (1892), an outstanding example of Swedish memoir literature. In 1848 he married Countess Caroline Wachtmeister.

De Geer held various judicial positions. He entered the Riksdag* as a member of the Estate of the Nobility in 1853–1854, and he represented his family in the 1856–1858 session. In 1858 Karl XV*, noting his abilities and energy, persuaded De Geer to accept the post of minister of state for justice (Justitiestatsminister), which made him leader of the council of state* or cabinet. During his long tenure (1858–1870) in that position, De Geer converted the justice post into a premiership with independence in political affairs, a change that was officially confirmed in an 1876 constitutional amendment.

De Geer may be described as a conservative reformer. It was his fear of radicalism that led him to insist on moderate changes. He played a leading role in the extension of religious freedom in 1860, when the Conventicle Act of 1726 was rescinded (*see* Conventicle Acts), in furthering the rights of unmarried women, in abolishing (1864) the employer's right to inflict corporal punishment on workers, and in establishing internal free trade (1864). De Geer was also instrumental in the introduction in 1862 of the *landsting* (provincial assemblies) system, which extended local self-government.

De Geer is most noted for being the architect of the 1866 parliamentary reform act. As early as the 1859–1860 session, when the peasant and burgher estates raised the question, De Geer decided to make this reform his cause. His subsequent letter to the king spelled out clearly his desire to advocate parliamentary reform, a course of action to which Karl XV reluctantly agreed. De Geer's proposal was presented to the estates in January 1863. It called for the elimination of the four estates and the creation of a two-chamber parliament that was to meet annually and to be elected by common vote. The bill was to be acted upon at the 1865 session. After a vigorous debate, the nobility passed the bill by a vote of 361 to 294, and the clergy quickly followed suit. (The burgher and peasant estates favored reform and had passed the measure earlier.)

One of the ironies of history is that De Geer hoped the Riksdag Act of 1866 would eliminate the necessity of political parties*. In fact, the new Riksdag structure created a more favorable soil for party growth than the old estates system, as witnessed by the formation of the Lantmannapartiet (Ruralist Party) in the lower chamber shortly thereafter. Although this new bicameral system served to open doors to wider democratization, this was not immediately apparent. In fact, there were greater franchise restrictions immediately after 1866 than before. Also, a conflict arose between the common people represented in the lower house and the rich in the upper chamber. This situation continued in Swedish politics well into the twentieth century. Paradoxically, it was this conflict that De Geer had hoped to avoid.

In foreign affairs, De Geer failed to integrate Sweden and Norway more closely. In the early 1860s he hesitated about Karl XV's pro-Scandinavianist policy. He had grave misgivings about the king's proposed military aid to Denmark against Germany and Austria in the Slesvig-Holstein crisis, unless aid would also be forthcoming from England and France. This did not occur.

In the early 1870s De Geer was out of power, but he returned as prime minister between 1876 and 1880. (It was then that the title ''prime minister'' was first officially used.) The main issue during this period was the old military system of *indelning*, opposed by the Agrarian Party, which now held a majority of seats in the lower house. De Geer's proposal to change the system was rejected by the Agrarians. De Geer resigned in 1880, thus ending his leadership role in Swedish politics. He died in Stockholm* sixteen years later.

REFERENCES: L. De Geer, *Minnen* (Stockholm: Norstedt, 1892); L. De Geer (the Younger), *Ur Louis De Geers brevsamling* (1929); D. A. Rustow, *The Politics of Compromise: A Study of Parties and Cabinet Government in Sweden* (Princeton: Princeton University Press, 1955); D. V. Verney, *Parliamentary Reform in Sweden, 1866–1921* (Oxford: Clarendon Press, 1957).

A. H. WINQUIST

DEN DANSKE MERCURIUS The first newspaper in Denmark

Den Danske Mercurius was founded in 1666 by Anders Bordning (1619–1677) under license from King Frederik III*. The paper, a diminutive monthly of four quarto pages, was filled with alexandrine verse praising the king, his regime, and its policies. Bordning, who along with his license received a pension, modeled the paper on similar French and German publications. He incorporated small news items on visiting diplomats and some foreign events. The paper died with Bordning in 1677.

O. V. JOHNSON

DIOCESE TOWNS Denmark

Christianity came late to Denmark. By the 860s only two churches were known: Ribe and Hedeby* (predecessor of Slesvig). In 948, however, the first bishops were nominated to Danish sees: Slesvig, Ribe, and Aarhus, the three of them situated in Jutland and belonging to the ecclesiastical province of Hamburg. Although a fourth bishopric, Odense in Funen, was mentioned in 988, it is doubtful that several bishops nominated to Danish sees actually resided there in the tenth century. Under Sven I* (''Forkbeard,'' c. 985–1014), who conquered England, and his son Knud I* (d. 1035) the Christianization of Denmark advanced further. A missionary bishop (with no fixed see) was sent to Scania, and by 1022 a bishop of Roskilde had been nominated. About 1060 the Danish church was reorganized: in Jutland, Slesvig and Ribe were maintained as episcopal sees, Aarhus was reactivated, and two new dioceses were created: Viborg and the ''island of Wendila,'' that is, Vendsyssel and the other regions north of the Limfjord. In central Denmark Odense and Roskilde were maintained. East of the Sound bishoprics were established at Dalby and Lund. These merged by 1066.

The evangelization of Denmark had proceeded from the south and the west, and it was no wonder that the region north of the Limfjord was the last to be definitely organized. The episcopal see was at first at Vestervig, but had by c. 1120 moved to Børglum. Its transfer to the town of Hjørring may have been intended but was never realized. This diocese was the only one in Denmark whose cathedral was situated in the countryside, as the chapter was constituted by the Premonstratensians of Børglum. Similarly, in Odense, whose diocese comprised Funen with adjacent islands, Als, Lolland, and (some time after 1200) Falster, the members of the chapter were monks (by 1117), in this case of the order of St. Benedict. The canons of Viborg adopted the rule of St. Augustine in the mid-twelfth century. Collegiate chapters existed in some towns, including Copenhagen* (by c. 1220), Haderslev (c. 1300; Benedictine monks), and in the former cathedral churches of Dalby and Vestervig, both situated in the country-side. There are indications that in the late eleventh century Roskilde was intended to be the residence of the future Danish archbishop, but when in 1103 or 1104 the Scandinavian church province was created, it was the bishop of Lund who became its first archbishop.

In 1152 and 1164, respectively, Norwegian and Swedish archbishoprics were carved out from the ecclesiastical province of Lund, which after the latter date corresponded to the political entity of Denmark proper including the overseas possessions of Rügen (under Roskilde), Femern (under Odense), and Danish Estonia with her own bishop of Reval (Tallinn).

The Lutheran Reformation* maintained the medieval dioceses with the only modification that in 1553–1554 the *superintendent* (bishop) of Vendsyssel was made to reside in Aalborg, which consequently was transferred from the diocese of Viborg to the latter's northern neighbor. The territory belonging to the diocese of Lund corresponded entirely to the provinces ceded to Sweden in 1658–1660, with the exception of Bornholm, which accordingly was transferred to the bishopric of Roskilde. In 1803 Lolland and Falster were made an individual diocese with Maribo as its center, and in 1819 the islands of Als and Ærø (which also belonged to the diocese of Odense) were detached from it as a separate bishopric. In addition, the bishop of Slesvig was made to reside in Flensburg in 1854. After the loss in 1864 of the duchy of Slesvig, the bishop moved back to the town of Slesvig; Als was ceded with the duchy to Prussia, whereas Ærø remained Danish and was once more incorporated into the diocese of Odense. When in 1920 North Slesvig* returned to Denmark, a new diocese was created for the region with Haderslev as its cathedral city. After World War I the populous diocese of Roskilde was divided twice (1922 and 1958), and the bishoprics of Copenhagen and Elsinore* were created.

Among the cathedral cities Viborg, Lund, and Odense were centers of secular higher jurisdiction as the provincial courts (*landsting*) of northern Jutland, Scania, and Funen, respectively, were held there. Other cities like Roskilde may have been the seats of district courts (*herredsting**) as well as of borough courts for the cities themselves. Although most bishops had a share in the revenues of the mints of their cities (twelfth century–c. 1400), none of the cathedral cities had episcopal *seigneurs*. (Copenhagen, however, belonged to the bishop of Roskilde until the early fifteenth century.)

It is difficult to assess the effects of the episcopal presence upon the cathedral cities; cathedral schools founded during the twelfth and thirteenth centuries, and the existence in town of a numerous clergy, must have given work to the city's craftsmen. The clergy were allowed to trade for the use of their proper households, which made them rivals of the burgesses.

The victory of the Reformation meant that the clergy lost most privileges and became civil servants. In some cities with many ecclesiastical institutions (Lund, Roskilde, Viborg, Ribe) the closure of many of them must have affected the city's social and economic life considerably, especially in Roskilde, which as a regional center was much less important than Viborg and Lund with their provincial courts. In Ribe the trade in oxen flourished throughout the sixteenth century, thus rendering the economic impact of the Reformation less grave. In cities with few churches and monasteries (Aarhus, Odense, Slesvig) these effects must have been less important.

The centers of the dioceses were mainly placed in major trading towns (Slesvig, Ribe, Aarhus, and, after the Reformation, Aalborg, Copenhagen, and Flensburg; in the latter case Danish national concerns may have been involved as well), in regional administrative centers (Lund, Viborg), or near royal residences (Dalby, Roskilde, Copenhagen). The choice of Maribo as cathedral city was apparently caused by the existence of a church suitable as a cathedral, whereas the choice of Haderslev and Elsinore had demographic reasons as well.

REFERENCES: J. O. Arhnung, *Roskilde Domkapitels Historie*, vol. 1 (Flensborg, 1937); A. E. Christensen, *Vikingetidens Danmark paa oldhistorisk baggrund* (Copenhagen: Gyldendal, 1969); T. Dahlerup, *Det danske Sysselprovsti i Middelalderen* (Copenhagen: Gad, 1968); O. Degn, *Rig og fattig i Ribe. Økonomiske og sociale forhold i Ribe-samfundet 1560–1660*, vols. 1, 2 in *Skrifter udgivet af Jysk Selskab for Historie 39* (Aarhus: Universitetsforlaget, 1981); H. M. Jansen, T. Nyberg, and T. Riis, "Danske byers fremvekst og udvikling i middelaldern," in G. Authén Blom, ed., *Urbaniseringsprosessen i Norden 1: Middelaldersteder* (Oslo, Bergen, Tromsø: Universitetsforlaget, 1977); P. King, "The Cathedral Priory of Odense in the Middle Ages," in *Kirkehistoriske Samlinger* 7 (1966–1968): 1–20; T. Riis, "The Typology of Danish Medieval Towns," in *Storia della Città*, No. 18 (Milan: Electa, 1981); *Scandinavian Atlas of Historic Towns* (Odense: Odense Universitetsforlaget, 1983).

T. RIIS

DISSOLUTION OF THE NORWEGIAN-SWEDISH UNION *See* Michelsen, Christian

DROTTNINGHOLM Royal palace near Stockholm*

Located on Lovön in Lake Mälar about 10 kilometers west of Stockholm is the palace of Drottningholm. The property, then known as Torvesund, was acquired by the crown in the sixteenth century. Johan III* (1568–1592) had a stone castle built there during his reign, and at that time the current name was acquired. The property passed through a number of hands thereafter, due to the practice of alienation of crown lands. In 1661 it was purchased by the widow of Karl X*, Hedvig Eleonora, mother of Karl XI*. In 1662 she commissioned Nicodemus Tessin the Elder to design a new palace. Tessin was responsible for the baroque masterpiece which survives to this day. He created the three-story structure with its small adjoining two-story pavilions in French-Dutch style. The building was striking in its flowing ornateness. The interior of the palace was largely the work of Tessin's son, Nicodemus Tessin d.y*, who continued his father's work after 1681. He was also responsible for the design of the terraces and the French park. Many of Sweden's finest artists, including David Klocker Ehrenstrahl, contributed to the interiors. In 1744 Lovisa Ulrika* received the palace as a wedding gift. She commissioned C. Hårleman and J. E. Rehn to add the present two-story wings, which are in the rococo style. Later, Gustav III* commissioned F. M. Piper to redesign the gardens in the less formal English park style. Few changes have been made in the palace since the end of the eighteenth century, but it has been restored and is maintained by the state.

Also located on the palace grounds are the China Palace and the Palace Theater. The China Palace, designed by C. F. Adelcrantz and Rehn, was completed in 1763 and was used as a summer residence by the royal family. The original theater was constructed in 1754 but burned eight years later. The present theater, designed by Adelcrantz, was completed in 1766. The foyer, commissioned by Gustav III, was added in 1791. The theater was used extensively during the reigns of Fredrik I* and Gustav III, but it stood idle for much of the nineteeth century. It has been used regularly in the present century.

REFERENCES: *DSH*; S. B. Hegardt, *Drottningholm under 400 år* (Borås: Centraltryckeriet, 1972/1983); *SU*; *Värt att se i Sverige* (Stockholm: Bonniers, 1978).

B. NORDSTROM

E

EDUCATION

The following sections deal with the development of education, principally public education, in Denmark, Finland, Norway, and Sweden. There are a number of common features that will be noted, including the dominance of the Catholic Church in education before the Reformation*; the continued dominance of the reformed churches in education for nearly 300 years after the Reformation; the increased concern over education that emerged in the late seventeenth century and developed during the eighteenth century (concern that was not manifested in the development of effective public education systems); the development of reasonably inclusive but multi-layered public education systems in the nineteenth century that reflected different class interests and importance; and the efforts in the twentieth century to create educational systems that are uniform and reasonably egalitarian. In addition, universities and programs in adult and continuing education have enjoyed considered growth, especially since the 1930s. Finally, beginning in the second half of the nineteenth century, the folk high school movement resulted in the development of unique and important institutions in the history of education in the Nordic countries.

REFERENCE: E. Allardt et al., *Nordic Democracy* (Copenhagen: Det Danske Selskab, 1981).

Denmark

Little is known about education in Denmark before the country's conversion* to Christianity in the tenth century. It is fairly clear, however, that prior to this time formal schools did not exist, and education per se was largely the responsibility of families. While this remained true for the overwhelming portion of the population after the Conversion, and, in fact, until the nineteenth century, schools of a formal nature did develop in Denmark in the Middle Ages. These were based in the diocese towns* and included schools at Viborg, Ribe, and Roskilde. Their primary function was the training of priests. Literacy remained a near monopoly of the clergy until well into the sixteenth century. Beyond those trained in these schools, a few received an education at the hands of tutors. There was no university in Denmark until 1479, and students wishing to study at university had to go abroad.

A significant shift of interest in education developed in the second half of the sixteenth century. This concerned chiefly the nobility, which was compelled to adjust to the changing demands of government for increasing numbers of trained bureaucrats. Its military functions diminished, the nobility of Denmark underwent a kind of "educational revolution" as it sought to acquire the expertise necessary to retain importance in the changing state of the late sixteenth century.

Attention to the question of education for a larger portion of the population came in the early eighteenth century. Christian VI* established schools on his own estates for his tenants, and a number of nobles followed suit. By 1721 there were 241 of the so-called *rytterskoler* in Denmark. In 1736, largely as a result of a new concern with religious piety, compulsory confirmation was introduced. This meant, in effect, that all confirmants would have to be able to read. As a companion to this, a 1739 law declared that rural elementary schools should be established. In fact, the law had little effect. It was not strictly enforced, and rural districts resisted because the financial burden for the schools was placed on them. The fiscal responsibility of the state for education was not established at this time.

In 1789 a national school commission recommended the establishment of a system of universal elementary education. This had little immediate impact, but it did form the basis for legislation in 1809 aimed at reforming the curriculum and in 1814 aimed at the development of a system of seven-year compulsory education. It was nearly 50 years before this measure was implemented, and the quality of the education was very mixed. Curriculum reform during the century sought to shift attention away from classical and religious focuses toward basic skills in reading, writing, mathematics, religion, gymnastics, singing, history, and geography. In 1903 a new education act established so-called middle schools. These were set between the elementary schools and the grammar schools (gymnasia). At the same time, girls were included in the basic education system.

The focus of educational efforts in the twentieth century has largely been on the effort to rationalize the confusing array of educational institutions—some of them very old and some of them dating from the nineteenth century—including the basic elementary schools, the so-called Latin schools, the gymnasia, the town schools designed principally for the children of the merchant class, and so on. During the 1930s a two-track system of basic education was introduced which provided for five years of basic schooling followed by either a four-year middle school ending with an examination upon which admission to the gymnasia was based, or by a four-year non-examination middle school. In 1958 the middle schools were eliminated. Students were to spend seven years in basic education, and provisions were made for continuation in either academic or practical studies. The seven-year compulsory system was extended to nine years in 1972.

Higher education in Denmark developed slowly until this century. The University of Copenhagen, founded in 1479, was the country's only university until 1928, when the University of Aarhus was established. Subsequently, universities were founded at Odense and Roskilde. In addition, there are special professional schools for agriculture, medicine, dentistry, the arts, and so on. Since World War II* there has been an explosion in the number of students pursuing university studies, a trend facilitated by the support given to students by the state.

One of the most interesting aspects of education history in the nineteenth century was the appearance of the folk high schools. These developed first in Denmark and were the result of the ideas and work of N.F.S. Grundtvig (1783–1872) and Kristen Kold (1816–1870). The first such school was founded at Rødding in 1844. Initially, these schools were rural. Their purpose was to foster practical knowledge, Christian ideals, and national values among the rural population. By the 1980s there were over 70 folk high schools in Denmark. Many continued to reflect their rural origins and emphases, but others were established by such organizations as the trade unions.

In addition, adult and continuing education programs, developed under the auspices of government bodies, the folk high schools, and organizations, have come to play an increasingly important role in the ongoing education of the Danish people.

REFERENCES: S. Ellehof, ed., *Kobenhavns Universitet 1479–1979*, 14 vols. (Copenhagen: G.E.C. Gads Forlag, 1980); H. C. Johansen, *En samfundsorganisation i opbrud 1700–1870: Dansk Social Historie*, vol. 4 (Copenhagen: Gyldendal, 1979); S. Oakley, *The Story of Denmark* (London: Faber and Faber, 1972); E. L. Petersen, *Fra standssamfund til rangssamfund. Dansk Social Historie*, vol. 6 (Copenhagen: Gyldendal, 1979); B. Rying, ed., *Denmark: An Official Handbook* (Copenhagen: Ministry of Foreign Affairs, 1973).

B. NORDSTROM

Finland

Education in Finland first appeared in the 1200s when the Swedish branch of the Roman Catholic Church introduced itself, taxation, and education to the Finns. Until the mid-fifteenth century, education in Finland was entirely religious in nature and was provided only to men aspiring to the priesthood. A number of priests were educated in European universities. Michael Agricola, a priest who was influenced by Martin Luther, during the period 1542–1552 devised an "ABC" book in Finnish, authored a Finnish grammar, and translated the New Testament into Finnish. (Prior to Agricola's work, there was no written Finnish.) Swedish and Latin dominated the education process.

During the 1600s a progressively graded school was developed in the cities by the clergy. Emphasis was on classical education, discussions were in Swedish and Latin, and only the sons of nobility enjoyed an education.

The Church Law of 1686 reaffirmed Lutheranism* as the religion of Sweden-Finland, and it also established compulsory school attendance in Finland. Virtually all people, but especially children, were required to be able to read a few tracts from the Bible in order to take their first Communion, and Communion and literacy were prerequisites to marriage. Latin schools served the Swedish and Finnish burghers through the 1700s. Swedish replaced Latin as the basic language of instruction late in the 1700s. Swedish became a requisite to higher education in the Latin schools and the University of Turku (Åbo).

Incessant wars in Finland hindered the development of education through the early 1800s. Finland became a Russian Grand Duchy in 1809, and over a century of peace followed. Finnish began to find adherents in all classes, although the language did not have parity with Swedish. Finnish language use became inextricably bound to the kindling of nationalism during the period 1808–1917. Education became a rallying point for the nationalistic Finns who wanted an independent Finland. Finnish was taught to all classes in all schools beginning in 1840. In 1863 the Language Ordinance was passed, making Finnish equal to Swedish in business and government.

Private schools began in 1812. The range included separate schools for boys and girls, co-educational schools, and military, academic, and college preparatory institutions. These primarily served wealthy Swedish and Finnish families.

Uno Cygnaeus is referred to as the "father" of the Finnish public school. Influenced by Johann Heinrich Pestalozzi, in 1857 he advocated a free public education for the poor and the release of schools from church supervision. Cygnaeus freely borrowed educational ideas from Switzerland, Sweden, Denmark, and Germany for the embryonic Finnish system of public education. Education at all levels, public and private (primarily Swedish), continued to develop through the 1800s and early 1900s. After Finland became independent in 1917, free and compulsory public education for children ages 7–13 became law with the School Attendance Act of 1921.

Day care and non-compulsory pre-school is provided at the option of local communities for children age 6 and under. Free public education is provided for all children ages 7–13. Contemporary educational goals formally emphasize the ideal of egalitarianism for all Finnish citizens and the creation of social conditions conducive to improving Finland's quality of life.

A 1928 school law established a two-part middle or "modern" school. The middle school and the classical gymnasium were included in the lyceum. The six-year middle school provided several tracks: vocational, college or university preparatory, or a combination thereof. The eight-year classical system included five years in the middle school and three years in the gymnasium; this program was purely preparatory for a university or higher technical college.

The Educational System Act of 1968 provided a free, standard nine-year comprehensive school which is attended by all children beginning at age 7. The school is divided into a six-year lower and three-year upper level. A goal is to provide students with preparation for virtually all types of higher secondary education. In accordance with the 1978 Act on the Development of Secondary Education, the curriculum will be reviewed in the 1980s.

Following completion of the comprehensive school, the student may enter a vocational school, an upper secondary school, or the labor market. Upper secondary school lasts three years, and it is the primary route to institutions of higher education. The comprehensive school thus provides the opportunity for a vocationally oriented line of study. A general education curriculum prepares the student for eligibility for continuing with some form of higher education, either academic or technical.

Finland's first university, the University of Turku (Åbo), was founded in 1640 and was governed in the same manner as Sweden's University of Uppsala. German influence was evident in instruction methods. Classical education was emphasized, and it reflected philosophical perspectives from the Reformation. Instruction was in Swedish and Latin.

After a fire destroyed the University of Turku in 1827, the University was moved to Helsinki, the new capital, in 1828. University entrance requirements were quite high, with commensurate academic standards. The first lectureship in Finnish was established in 1828, and the first professorship in the subject was established in 1851. In 1858 doctoral dissertations could be published in Finnish as well as in Swedish, French, or German.

Fervent Finnish nationalism flourished at the University of Helsinki, and by 1917 well over two-thirds of the university's enrollment was Finnish-speaking. Language and social issues continued to be important, although the intensity of debate diminished somewhat after the 1917–1918 War of Independence (*see* Civil War). The Swedish citizenry of Finland opened Åbo Academy of Turku in 1917; the academy was and is today entirely Swedish-speaking. Not to be eclipsed by the Swedish constituency, the Finns established Turku University in 1920; the language of instruction is Finnish. In 1923 a law made the University of Helsinki bilingual (Finnish and Swedish).

In order to further social research, the Civic High School (post-gymnasiumlevel) of Helsinki was established in 1925. The name was changed to the School of Social Sciences in 1930. In 1960 the school was moved to Tampere, and it became the University of Tampere in 1966.

Finland currently has 21 universities or equivalent institutions evenly distributed in various parts of the country. Universities include those of Helsinki, Turku, Oulu, and Tampere. There are several universities of technology such as those in Helsinki, Tampere, and Lapeenranta. Equivalent institutions at the university level include the Turku and Helsinki Schools of Economics and Business Administration, College of Veterinary Medicine, and Institutions in the Industrial Arts, Theatre, and the Sibelius Academic of Music. The purpose of this distribution is to provide more opportunities for students to participate in higher education. Consideration is also given to the compatibility of higher education with secondary education in a region, as well as unique regional factors.

Eligibility for admission to a university or equivalent institution is achieved by passing the comprehensive school matriculation examination of an institution. There is still a *numerus clausus* limiting admission to virtually all fields of study in each institution. Academic admission standards are quite high, and competition for admission is intense. Through a plan which the government refers to as dimensioning, a national goal is to provide secondary education graduates with an opportunity to enter an appropriate institution of higher education. At present, each year there are approximately 12,000 openings available for the approximately 30,000 students who pass the matriculation examination.

Institutions of higher education have increased their involvement in complementary (continuing) education and adult education. Complementary education is composed of various complementary courses, including employment-orientedcourses, administered by the institutions themselves and the summer universities. A broad range of course offerings is designed for the adult, with an emphasis on the open university concept. Promotion of complementary education for all adults is a key project for higher education in the 1980s. This is a logical extension of the egalitarian principle of providing diverse educational opportunities for the population throughout Finland.

In 1863 the first teacher training institute was established at Jyväskylä. Today, the University of Jyväskylä (Educational Research Institute) is the most important of the research and study project institutes in the field of pedagogy.

Teacher education is required for kindergarten, comprehensive and upper secondary, and most full-time teachers in vocational and adult education. Teaching posts in higher education, except teacher education, do not require pedagogical training. Several universities have teacher education programs.

Popular (folk) education, workers' schools, and study circles are part of the adult education concept. Nationalistic Finns organized the Saturday Society, which in 1831 became the Finnish Literature Society. It provided the first sustained impetus to adult education. The Adult Education Society was founded in 1874. Adult education, including folk high schools, reflects some Danish influence. Workers' institutes were developed through the Workmen's Association, founded in 1884. The first Workers' Institute, often called the Workers' College or Workers' Academy, was established in Tampere in 1899.

There are two types of adult education, general and vocational. Folk high schools and folk academies, civic and workers' institutes, and the secondary evening schools provide general education. Vocational training centers and continuing education programs arranged by vocational training centers provide employment training. Emphasis in adult education is on educational equality and opportunity, assisting those who have received the least education.

Administration of the Finnish education system begins at the national level with parliament. Educational and cultural affairs are the responsibility of the Ministry of Education. Several advisory boards (e.g., the National Board of General Education) are part of the Ministry of Education.

On the regional level each of the eleven provinces has a school department. The state and the municipalities are jointly responsible for the expenses and organization of education. Private organizations such as labor unions and study groups provide some financial support in vocational and adult education.

REFERENCES: S.-E. Åström, ''Literature on Social Mobility and Social Stratification in Finland,'' *Transactions of the Westermarck Society* 2 (1953); Finnish Ministry of Education, *Educational Development in Finland, 1978–1981*. Report by the Finnish Ministry of Education to the 38th Session of the International Conference on Education in Geneva, November 1981 (Helsinki: Government Printing Center, 1981); M. Gustafson, *Education in Finland* (Helsinki: Ministry of Foreign Affairs, 1967); R. Nyberg, ed., *Educational Reform in Finland in the 1970s* (Helsinki: Ministry of Education, 1970); R. Ojansuu, ed., *Comprehensive School in Finland—Goals and an Outline for a Curriculum* (Helsinki: Ministry of Education, 1971); J. Wuorinen, *A History of Finland* (New York: Columbia University Press, 1955).

R. S. SCHWARTZ

Norway

The initial stages of the history of education in Norway parallel those in the other Scandinavian countries: the central role of the Church, the bases of school education in the cathedral or diocese schools, and so on. From the late fourteenth century to 1814, the development of education in Norway paralleled events in Denmark. Latin schools appeared after the Reformation in Oslo, Bergen, Trondheim, and Kristiansand. The introduction of compulsory confirmation (1736) was followed by attempts to develop a parish school system based on the law of 1739. Progress was slow, however, as the population resisted because of the costs. The pattern of education in the rural districts came to be based largely upon ambulatory schools (*omgangsskoler*) in which itinerant teachers held school for short periods of time in homes within a parish. These teachers had virtually no preparation (they were often retired army officers), and their pay and prestige were both very low.

During the nineteenth century, Norway made significant progress toward the development of a general education system. An 1827 act was aimed at the training of qualified teachers. Through an 1848 act, so-called common schools were to be established in towns, and attendance of children between 7 and 14 was compulsory. In 1860 rural schools were given a broader curriculum. Middle schools were established in 1869, and in 1889 the Folkeskole became the basic rural school. In 1896 the basic system was standardized, resting on an elementary school, a four-year middle school, and (for a few students) a three-year gymnasia. Still, there were wide differences in the quality of the schools and in the curriculum offered.

In the 1930s reforms were introduced to ''democratize'' the system, based on a seven-year elementary system followed by a three-year middle school that combined two years of study with one year of practical experience, followed by a three-year gymnasium for those passing the entrance examination. The system was reformed again in 1969, when nine-year compulsory education, including six years at elementary schools and three years at middle schools, was adopted. Thereafter, students could continue their studies at a gymnasium or other post-secondary school.

Universities are a relatively recent development in Norway. While Sweden opened its first university at Uppsala in 1477 and Denmark its first at Copenhagen* two years later, higher education was not offered in Norway until the early nineteenth century. The hegemony of the Danish crown over Norway from the 1380s, the country's sparse population, and its lack of large towns prior to that time help to account for this late start.

As early as the 1660s, Norwegian leaders discussed the desirability of opening a university of some sort, but the campaign to do so did not accelerate until the last 30 years of the eighteenth century. The Danish bureaucracy initially resisted the idea on the grounds that an institution rivaling the University of Copenhagen might contribute to the disintegration of the united monarchy. Beginning in 1809, the Royal Society for the Welfare of Norway pressed the issue, however, and gathered private contributions. The Danish government relented, and in a decree of 2 September 1811 granted permission to found a university in Kongsberg, a once prosperous silver mining town whose population and economy had begun to decline. A revised charter the following year moved its venue to Christiania (Oslo), though, and in 1813 the Royal Frederik University began to function with five professors, one lecturer, and seventeen students. Instruction was given in scattered rented facilities before the completion during the early 1850s of the neoclassical campus that still stands at Karl Johans gate 47 in central Oslo. From the outset a fairly wide spectrum of subjects was taught by the university's theological, judicial, medical, and philosophical faculties, but most were oriented toward training students for placement in the civil service as bureaucrats, teachers, or clergymen. Initially, only men could matriculate, and the overwhelming majority came from the privileged social classes. A gradual democratizationof the student body occurred during the nineteenth and twentieth centuries, although the children of farmers, fishermen, and other laborers and artisans have always been underrepresented. Women were first admitted in the 1880s, but only in recent times have they constituted roughly half of the student body.

As the curriculum expanded, the administration became increasingly complex. The present university, since 1939 called the University of Oslo, is divided into faculties of theology, medicine, law, liberal arts, social sciences, natural sciences, and dentistry.

At the beginning of the twentieth century there were about 1,600 students, a figure that rose to over 3,000 in the 1920s. After World War II unprecedented rapid population growth and rising educational expectations swelled the number to over 20,000 by the early 1970s. The increase necessitated expansion of the satellite campus at Blindern, which now accommodates most of the instructional and administrative facilities, as well as much of the student housing.

The need for universities in western and northern Norway was long apparent. In 1946 the parliament approved the founding of a new university in Bergen, which began to function two years later. The University of Bergen offers instruction in most of the fields offered by its counterpart in Oslo, except theology. In 1980 there were approximately 7,500 students in Bergen.

A 1968 law established the University of Trondheim, which encompasses that city's technical institute (founded in 1910) and the teachers' college (founded in 1922). In 1980 there were 8,600 students, more than 5,000 of them in the technical division.

Primarily to serve the distant northern regions, the 1968 law also established the University of Tromsö. It emphasizes medicine and fishing in accord with regional needs. Still expanding, the student body numbered 1,545 in 1979.

In addition to these full-fledged universities, Norway has teachers' colleges (founded in the nineteenth century), engineering schools, nine regional junior colleges, seminaries to serve the state church and other denominations, colleges of business administration and library science, a physical education academy, and various other institutions of higher education.

Shortly after the defeat of Denmark in the Napoleonic Wars, the Danish Lutheran theologian, folklorist, educator, and psalmist Nicolai Frederik Severin Grundtvig (1783–1872) began to campaign for the establishment of residential folk high schools. Their purpose would be to educate especially rural young adults in a practical way, instilling in them an amalgam of Christian and national values. These schools would be a departure from the rigid curricula and rote pedagogy of traditional schools, emphasizing personal maturation and preparation for adult life through shared experiences, rather than Latin and other subjects, which Grundtvig believed were of little relevance to most Danes. The first of these schools opened at Rødding in Jutland in 1844. Others soon followed, and by the end of the nineteenth century these schools had become a standard feature of Danish education.

As early as 1837, Grundtvig wrote a tract titled *To Norwegians Concerning a Norwegian High School*, which stirred some of his followers in Norway but produced no immediate results. In 1864, however, Herman Anker (1839–1896) and Olaus Arvesen (1830–1917), both recent theology graduates and Grundtvigians, opened Sagatun Folk High School near Hamar. Three years later Christopher Bruun (1839–1920) founded a similar school at Sel (later moved to Gausdal). Neither institution survived, but Bruun's 1878 book, *Folk Premises*, and a related volume by his colleague Fritz Hansen, *The Folk High School and Peasant Education*, published the previous year, popularized the concept and stimulated a movement that led to the establishment of many similar institutions.

The idea of the folk high school soon found support among liberal reformers aware of the difficulties of educating rural youth adequately through the traditional means, particularly the use of itinerant teachers. On the other hand, some academicians feared a decline of standards if the examination-free schools became a normal part of Norwegian education. Moreover, orthodox Lutherans opposed the distinctly Grundtvigian coloring of the early schools.

The movement suffered a setback after 1876, when the government began to sponsor regional public schools. The folk high schools, unwilling to accept the administrative control that would have attended governmental subsidies, could not compete. By 1896 only six remained.

A new dimension was added in 1893, when Asbjørn Knutsen (1842–1917), an educational administrator, founded at Heibo in Heddal Norway's first distinctly Christian folk high school. Several others soon followed, some of them owned by the Domestic Missionary Society, an organization unofficially attached to the state church. In the meantime, secular folk high schools enjoyed a moderate recrudescence. The two groups, often at odds, began to receive regular governmental support in 1912. Since 1949 the Department of Ecclesiastical Affairs and Education has administered all such institutions jointly. The national government pays five-sixths of their expenses, while county administrations underwrite the remaining one-sixth.

The postwar period has also brought other changes. Baptists*, Methodists*, Pentecostals, and other religious groups have opened schools. Many now enroll small numbers of students from abroad and refugees from Third World countries. Many young Norwegians who are unsure of their futures spend a year in residence gaining diverse skills or developing musical or other interests before proceeding into the labor market or to some form of higher education.

In 1982 Norway had 88 folk high schools, compared to over 80 in Denmark and Finland each and over 100 in Sweden.

REFERENCES: T. K. Derry, *A History of Modern Norway, 1814–1972* (Oxford: Oxford University Press, 1973); E. Fain, "The Quest for National Identity and Community in Norway," in R. G. Paulston, *Other Dreams, Other Schools: Folk Colleges in Social and Ethnic Movements* (Pittsburgh: University Center for International Studies, 1980); R. Popperwell, *Norway* (London: W. Benn Ltd., 1972); F. S. Skrubbeltrang, *The Danish Folk High Schools*, trans. R. Spink (Copenhagen: Det Danske Selskab, 1947); "Utdanningssystemet i Norge," in *Norge Informasjon* series (Oslo: Ministry of Foreign Affairs, 1982).

F. HALE and B. NORDSTROM

Sweden

Sweden shares the same pattern of medieval educational institutions as her Scandinavian neighbors based largely on the cathedral or diocese schools. The first university in the Nordic countries was established at Uppsala in 1477. Primarily, however, those seeking an education beyond that provided for the clergy had to rely on tutors and studies on the continent.

Significant changes came in the seventeenth century. Gustav II Adolf*, realizing the scarcity of properly trained experts for government posts, encouraged the development of schools at all levels. A 1620 school law set out to base the system upon three types of institutions: parish elementary schools, the trivial or "Latin" schools which had succeeded the cathedral schools in the Reformation, and a new institution, the gymnasium, designed to prepare students for continuing practical education at universities. Gustav also provided the nearly defunct university at Uppsala with endowments and support. The actual results of the king's actions were small, but a number of gymnasia were established (at Västerås in 1623, at Strängnäs in 1626, at Linköping and Åbo/Turku, and Reval), schools in towns for the children of merchants increased in number, and many rural schools for the peasantry were founded by various nobles. Still, education remained largely limited to aristocrats, clergy, and the merchants.

As in Denmark and Norway, the appearance of compulsory Confirmation resulted, in the eighteenth century, in some progress toward increased literacy. A 1724 act that remained the basis of general education until 1807 stipulated that basic education was the responsibility of parents. However, in instances where parents could not fulfill that obligation, parish schools were to be established. These were of very mixed quality. There were no professionally trained teachers, and the responsibility of instruction generally fell to the parish clerk.

Significant reform of curriculum, schools, and teacher preparation came in the nineteenth century, although many measures tended to reflect the divergent interests of various social groups in education. Perhaps most basic to the reforms was the 1842 law (resulting from the report of a commission issued in 1826) that determined that within five years every parish should have a basic school operated by local boards and paid for from local funds. At the same time, provisions were made to increase teacher training programs. By 1859 65 percent of all children of school age were enrolled in these schools, and by 1881 the figure had reached 83 percent. Ambulatory schools, like those in Norway, continued to exist even into the twentieth century. In 1882 a law making seven years of education in the folk schools compulsory was passed. In 1892 the old "trivial" schools or Latin schools were merged with the gymnasia. In 1905 the so-called Realskolar or practical schools were established. These provided a six-year curriculum with links to four-year gymnasia.

Reforms in the twentieth century have generally been designed to provide maximum educational opportunities to students with differing abilities and interests. Legislation passed in 1927 provided for a basic six-year compulsory school system and included equal opportunities for girls. In 1936 the compulsory portion of the system was extended to seven years. Following World War II, new efforts were initiated under the dominance of the Social Democrats to democratize education in Sweden. On the basis of the recommendations of the 1957 Schools Commission, a nine-year compulsory system was tried on an experimental basis. This was adopted in principle in 1962. Subsequently, a system has evolved that includes pre-school opportunities and three levels of compulsory education at three-year lower, middle, and upper schools. In 1966 the older general, technical, and commercial gymnasia were combined. The new gymnasia were to offer five three-year tracks for students interested in post-secondary education and two-year tracks in technical and theoretical subjects for students who did not intend to pursue further studies. The old student exam necessary for admission to the universities was abolished in 1968.

Uppsala is Sweden's (and Scandinavia's) oldest university. A university was established at Dorpat in 1632 and at Åbo/Turku in 1640. The University of Lund was founded in 1668. Universities were established at Gothenburg* in 1954, Stockholm* in 1960, Umeå in 1963, and Linköping in 1965. In addition, a number of "high schools" with links to one of the older universities were established at Växjö, Karlstad, and Orebro, which later received independent university status. In addition to these institutions, there are teacher training colleges and a broad range of specialty or professional schools covering medicine, commerce, crafts, fine arts, and so on. In 1977 a new higher education law was passed designed to coordinate the various units and options in higher education in the country.

The folk high school movement reached Sweden in 1868, when schools were founded at Hvilan and Onnestad in Skåne. As in the rest of Scandinavia, this movement has flourished, and in the postwar period Sweden had over 120 folk high schools. Similarly, the adult and continuing education programs in Sweden have flourished, based on state and organizational involvement.

REFERENCES: I. Andersson, *A History of Sweden*, trans. C. Hannay (Stockholm: Natur och Kultur, 1955); *DSH*, vols. 6–10; *Higher Education: Proposals by the Swedish 1968 Educational Commission* (Stockholm, 1973); S. Lindroth, *A History of Uppsala University* (Uppsala and Stockholm: Almqvist & Wiksell distributor, 1976); F. Scott, *Sweden: The Nation's History* (Minneapolis: University of Minnesota Press, 1977); Swedish Institute, "Higher Education in Sweden" and "Primary and Secondary Education in Sweden," in *Fact Sheets on Sweden* series (Stockholm: Swedish Institute, 1981); M. Weibull, *Lunds Universitets Historia*, 2 vols. (Lund: Gleerups, 1918).

B. NORDSTROM

EDUSKUNTA Finland's parliament

Finland's modern parliament emerged out of the revolutionary turmoil of 1905 in Russia and intense political and national debate in Finland from the same time. The new assembly, which was exceptional for its unicameral structure and its electoral base on universal suffrage, replaced the old four-estate Diet, which had rested on Swedish constitutional traditions left in place after Finland became a grand duchy of Russia in 1809.

The Eduskunta is considered the sovereign representative assembly of the Finnish people. Its 200 members are elected every four years. It actually shares power, however, with the president and cabinet, and can be by-passed through popular referenda. (*See also* Political Parties.)

REFERENCE: J. Nousiainen, *The Finnish Political System*, trans. J. H. Hodgson (Cambridge, Mass.: Harvard University Press, 1971).

B. NORDSTROM

EHRENSVÄRD, CARL-AUGUST (1745–1800) Swedish artist and naval commander

C. A. Ehrensvärd was the son of Augustin Ehrensvärd (1710–1772), artilleryman, seaman, and gifted painter, who also designed fortresses and first initiated Arméns Flottan (*see* Navy) in 1747. The father's many-sided accomplishments were strikingly reflected in the son, except that in Carl-August's case a visit to Italy from 1780 to 1782 rendered him an aesthete of note and a fervent disciple of Johann J. Winckelman's teachings on the art of classical Greece. Though Carl-August served in the artillery from the age of 15 and ultimately became chief of Arméns Flottan (he was in command at the first battle of Svensksund in August 1789), it is as an artistic personality in the neoclassical epoch that he is now best known.

A natural draughtsman, Ehrensvärd's sensitivity to landscape was aroused during a visit to Holland and France in 1766. The fourteen years of postings to Stockholm* and Sveaborg which followed, though professionally important for him as a fortress designer, otherwise fettered his creative instincts, and it was thus that the Italian journey proved such a release for Ehrensvärd's nervous energy. He quickly made the acquaintance of his fellow countrymen Johan Tobias Sergel* and L.-A. Masreliez, who later introduced the Pompeian style into Swedish furnishings. Ehrensvärd, in turn, was inspired through what he had learned from the Hamilton collection of southern Italian antiquities to introduce his own neoclassical designs into Swedish silverware. While it is inappropriate here to summarize Ehrensvärd's aesthetic reasonings, even if this were possible, it is no less valid to stress his practical bent, which in any case was given full rein through his military training. No single experience was more formative for Ehrensvärd than his exploration of the great Doric temples at Paestum—the masculinity and simplicity of this manifestation of the Doric style excited his imagination for the rest of his life. It directly inspired his celebrated plans for new buildings in Karlskrona* dockyard, a project which, though it did not materialize, is reckoned to place Ehrensvärd in the same class as such masters as Boullée and Ledoux.

The years 1782–1785 in Karlskrona had some fulfillment for Ehrensvärd in that he could write up his Italian experiences, work in friendly partnership with the greatest naval architect of the age, F. H. af Chapman (1721–1808), and rise to command his father's creation, Arméns Flottan. After the campaign of 1789, he withdrew from active service and in his last years revived an early interest in chemistry. He enthusiastically farmed his estate in Halland and enjoyed the friendship of the reforming agriculturalist Rutger Maclean. Ehrensvärd's importance has yet to be completely assessed, but his influential responsiveness to many neoclassical nuances should not be underrated.

REFERENCES: H. Frykenstedt, *Carl August Ehrensvärd 1745–1800: An Original Aesthetician and an Early Functionalist* (Uppsala, 1965); R. Josephson, *Carl August Ehrensvärd* (Stockholm, 1963).

D. D. ALDRIDGE

EIDSVOLL CONSTITUTION OF 17 MAY (Syttende Mai) 1814, Norway's Constitution

Although both those who advocated independence and the unionists regarded a constitution as vital for Norway's self-government, they clashed frequently within the National Assembly* because of their differences regarding the degree of Norway's complete independence. While establishing basic principles to guide the constitutional committee in its work, the independence party was able to impose its contention that Norway was to be both a limited, inherited monarchy and an independent, indivisible kingdom despite the protests of the unionists.

Paradoxically, the independence party was later forced to secure a provision in the constitution that Norway's monarch might accept a second crown upon the approval of the Storting*, the parliamentary body established by the constitution. They were compelled to do so because their choice as king, Christian Frederik (*see* Christian VIII) still stood to inherit Denmark eventually as well. The distinctly anti-Swedish position of the independence party was shown in the constitutional clause which specified that the king should always have professed the Lutheran faith, a slap at Karl XIV Johan's* very obviously forced conversion in 1810.

The two sides also clashed when the independence party secured the assent of the National Assembly to form a finance committee to devise the financial basis for the new state and a law committee to prepare a legal code. The unionists supported these measures but also proposed the establishment of a foreign affairs committee to examine Norway's status with the European Great Powers. Their intention was to demonstrate Norway's inability to maintain her independence because Sweden's allies still demanded the enforcement of the Treaty of Kiel*. The independence party was able to beat back this measure on two occasions but only by the closest of margins and after acrimonious debate.

Work on the constitution itself proceeded rapidly. A fifteen-member committee, including Wedel Jarlsberg and chaired by C. M. Falsen, took only eight days to write the 110 short paragraphs that make up the document. The committee was influenced by a number of the other constitutions written during the "Age of Revolution," such as the American and Batavian constitutions and especially the French Constitution of 1791, while still retaining basic premises within it from their own past experiences. The National Assembly discussed the committee's work for only seven days and made only minor revisions before approving the constitution.

Only a few of the constitution's clauses were truly controversial. Those relating directly to independence or union with Sweden certainly fall into this category. Equally divisive was the provision extending the right to vote to virtually all landowning taxpayers, men of substance, and long-term leaseholders. It is estimated, as a result, that approximately 45 percent of all adult males (over 25) could vote in Norway thereafter, by far the most liberal suffrage provision in Europe during most of the nineteenth century. Other constitutional clauses which generated significant controversy prevented the further augmentation of the nobility and established in principle a military obligation for all classes.

Although individual exceptions can be found, the National Assembly tended to divide on the measures in the same way that members had taken sides upon the matter of independence. Unionist sympathizers generally were also socially conservative, therefore opposing the above measures. Government officials had led the independence party and now sided with peasant representatives to include these provisions in the constitution. Officials often had no love for Norway's large land owners and businessmen, who were more liberal in their political and social views, and very likely also saw their own political future tied to their continued leadership of the peasantry. Political and social equality were therefore in many ways principles as inherent in the Norwegian constitution as that of independence.

The constitution also established the basic form of Norway's government. The king received the right to appoint ministers to the Council of State*, command the armed forces, and direct foreign policy. In the establishment of parliament (Storting) the constitution provided an interesting resolution to a perplexing problem for all Founding Fathers: whether the legislative body ought to consist of one or two houses. Although parliamentary members were to be elected to a single body, they would divide themselves into two houses, the Lagting and the Odelsting, for deliberations and voting upon most matters. The body was empowered to make law and grant taxes. Other parts of the constitution created a supreme court and ensured basic rights to all.

After the National Assembly completed its discussion and minor revision of the constitution, it was unanimously approved on 17 May 1814. Since the mid-1800s, this date (Syttende Mai) has been celebrated as Constitution Day, the country's chief holiday. On the same day, Christian Frederik was chosen unanimously (if somewhat reluctantly by the unionists) as the first king to rule only Norway in almost 400 years.

REFERENCES: See references under Norwegian-Swedish Union. A. Bergsgård, "Spørsmaalet om folksuveræniteten i 1814," *Historisk tidsskrift* (N) 5:7 (1927–1929): 225–67, and "Striden om folksuveræniteten i 1814," *Kunglige norske Videnskabs Selskabs forhandlinger* 1 (1929): 18–21; H. Koht, "Grundspørsmaalet i 1814," *Historisk tidsskrift* (N) 5:3 (1916): 1–16, "Innleg i stridspursmaal II: Folksuvereniteten i 1814," *Historisk tidsskrift* (N) 5:7 (1927–1929): 425–447, and "Trongen til demokrati," *Historisk tidsskrift* (N) 34 (1946–1948): 133–51; S. Kuhnle, "Stemmeretten i 1814: Beregninger over antall stemmekvalifiserte etter Grunnloven," *Historisk tidsskrift* (N) (1972): 373–90.

L. SATHER

EKMAN, CARL GUSTAV (1872–1945) Swedish politician and prime minister

Ekman was the son of a soldier from Munkstorp, Västmanland. He went to work at a very young age to support himself and to put himself through school. From these humble origins, he rose to become a leader of Sweden's prohibition movement, a successful journalist and editor, a local and national politician, the leader of a political party, and twice prime minister.

His earliest professional activities were in the temperance movement. By 1888 he was head of the Närke-Västmanland branch of the Order of Good Templars, and he became national director of the order in 1899. Although he stepped down from that position in 1908, he remained active in the movement for the rest of his life. During these years he also worked as a journalist for a number of temperance newspapers and was, for a time, editor of the *Eskilstuna Kuriren*.

Ekman's political career began in 1897, when he ran unsuccessfully for the Riksdag*. He then turned his attention to local and provincial politics and served in a number of public offices and in the Södermanland provincial assembly. In 1911 he ran successfully for a seat in the First Chamber of the Riksdag, and he remained a member of parliament until 1932.

His party attachments were with the Liberal Electoral Association, which represented a broad coalition of interests on the left of the non-Socialist party spectrum. Ekman identified with the temperance segment of the association, and he became the leader of that group after 1915. In 1923, when the association broke apart over the prohibition question, he formed and became the leader of the Liberal People's Party*.

Ekman's—and his party's—importance in parliament during the 1920s exceeded the popular support or the number of seats the party held. During the decade, the Liberal People's Party never received more than 13 percent of the popular vote or held more than 67 seats in the Riksdag. Yet, through the skillful enlistment of support from parties on one side of the political spectrum or the other, Ekman and his followers were shapers of policies and makers of governments. Through these tactics, Ekman earned the nickname "the Weighmaster." He employed these methods in the powerful parliamentary committees he belonged to, including budget, defense, and foreign affairs, and as prime minister. In so doing, he was able to give Sweden a measure of political stability that was atypical in the period. (There were no fewer than nine governments in Sweden during the 1920s.) During his first ministry (June 1926–October 1928), he enlisted the support of the Social Democrats to secure passage of a school reform program and then obtained the backing of the Conservatives to effect the passage of a law establishing a labor court. He employed the same tactics during his second ministry (June 1930–August 1932) to deal with labor unrest, agricultural problems, and tax questions. However, the parties on both sides of Ekman tired of the balancing tactics, and the Social Democrats, especially, were intent upon securing something more closely approaching majority parliamentarism.

In 1932 Ekman was forced to resign. The crises brought on by the worldwide depression deepened in Sweden, and social tensions increased. The viability of his approach to governing became increasingly tenuous. As important in forcing his resignation, however, was the revelation of certain questionable financial links with Ivar Kreuger*. Following his resignation, he withdrew from the general election, was stripped of the leadership position in his party, and retired from politics.

Ekman's political tactics and skills are of particular interest because of the similarities between the period in which he worked and Sweden in the late 1970s and early 1980s.

REFERENCES: *DSH*; Kenne Fant, *Ångerstolen* (Stockholm: P. A. Norstedt & Söner, 1978); *SU*; W. Svensson, *C. G. Ekman: Frisinnad hövding, nykterhetsman, statsman* (Stockholm: Frisinnad Tidskrift, 1972).

B. NORDSTROM

ELSINORE (Helsingør) Danish port on the Sound

The town is situated in Northeast Sjaelland at the narrowest part of the Sound. A settlement was mentioned here in the first half of the thirteenth century. The earliest parts of the main church, St. Olai, date from about the same period. By the mid-fourteenth century the settlement had a council and must have been a town. Very little is known of Elsinore before the 1420s, when the town was refounded at its present site, as can still be seen from its regular chessboard plan. At the same time a castle (Krogen) was constructed on the point of Sjaelland in order to protect and control both the town and the crossing to Scania. King Erik VII (of Pomerania)* founded three convents at Elsinore (Blackfriars, Greyfriars, and Whitefriars) and had the collecting of customs transferred from the Scanian fair to Elsinore. Without doubt expectations for the prosperity of Elsinore were high, as the mendicant friars were to live off the alms given by the town's inhabitants.

The refounded town's first century was very favorable to its trade, which was all the more important as its economic hinterland in Sjaelland was of modest dimensions. Many ships passed through the Sound on their way into the Baltic region. Since ships had to call at Elsinore in order to pay the customs, it acquired an important share of this exchange. Despite the fact that after the mid-sixteenth century most Western skippers entered the Baltic, Elsinore seems to have suffered little from this change in the pattern of trade. Victualling of ships would still be most favorable at Elsinore, because of the compulsory call, and as the number of passages was rising, this may have meant an increase in Elsinore's business as well. Equally important may have been the construction between 1574 and 1583 of the new castle of Kronborg as a modern royal residence protected by bastions.

The loss to Sweden in 1658 of the Scanian provinces deprived Elsinore of its hinterland beyond the Sound. The frequent wars with Sweden until 1720 and the absolutist economic policy in favor of the capital caused a period of stagnation for Elsinore. From the mid-eighteenth century, however, navigation and trade increased again, some new industrial enterprises were founded, and prosperity returned. This was cut short by the wars with England from 1807 to 1814 (which meant that trade through the Sound diminished), the national bankruptcy of 1813, and the crisis of the 1820s, which caused protracted economic difficulties. In the mid-1830s Elsinore's economic life improved. The abolition in 1857 of the Sound Tolls was a serious blow to Elsinore, as ships no longer needed to call there. A period of difficulties followed, until in the 1880s the crisis was overcome through a restructuring of the economic basis of the town. Originally a trade and navigation center, Elsinore became an industrial town with strengths in brewing and shipbuilding. The hinterland was opened up by the improvement of roads and the construction of railways. Elsinore was made a cathedral city in 1958. In 1983 Elsinore, which is situated less than 30 miles from the capital, is both a regional center and in some respects an annex of Copenhagen*.

Elsinore was by Danish standards a rather large town (1610: c. 5,000; 1735: c. 4,000; 1763: c. 3,600; 1801: 5,282; 1850: 8,111; 1901: 13,902; 1980 [greater Elsinore]: 56,566). Its dependence upon international trade can be seen from the large number of inhabitants of foreign origin (30 percent of taxpayers in the late sixteenth century, 17 percent of burgesses in the eighteenth century), mainly

Dutchmen, Germans, Englishmen, and Scots. Also, the many fine buildings that have survived, representing various styles of construction since 1500, indicate the wealth accumulated through trade.

REFERENCES: *Historiske Huse i Helsingør* (Copenhagen: National Museum, 1973); E. Kroman, ed., *Helsingør stadsbog 1549–1556* (Copenhagen, 1971); E. Kroman and K. Hjorth, eds., *Helsingør stadsbog 1554–1555, 1559–1560 og 1561–1565* (Copenhagen: 1981); K. Pedersen, "Industrier i Helsingør før det 20 århundrede," *Frederiksborg Amt* (1973): 5–46; P. Pedersen, ed., *Helsingør i Sundtoldstiden, 1426–1857*, vols. 1, 2, and supplement (Copenhagen, 1926–1931); A. Tønnesen, *Helsingørs udenlandske borgere og andre indbyggere i sidste halvdel af det 16. århundrede med særligt henblik på deres sociale stilling* (Copenhagen: University of Copenhagen, 1967).

T. RIIS

EMIGRATION, 1825–1930 The mass migration of Scandinavians to North America and other areas of the world

Migration is an almost constant theme in the histories of the Nordic countries. In many respects the movement of people into and out of the region has been one of the principal dynamic forces in their history. Notable instances of migration occurred during the prehistoric period, the Celtic Iron Age*, the German Migration Period, the Viking Age*, and, to lesser degrees, the Early Modern and Modern periods. The most extensive emigration from Scandinavia* in the Modern Period occurred between 1825 and 1930, when approximately 1.25 million Swedes, 800,000 Norwegians, 300,000 Danes, 300,000 Finns, and several thousand Icelanders emigrated. Primarily, these migrants established new homes in North America, but some went to Latin America, Africa, Australia, New Zealand, and other parts of the world. At the same time, the number of Scandinavians who moved to other parts of Europe, especially Germany, increased, as did internal mobility. All these population movements had significant impact upon the Nordic countries and the regions where the emigrants settled.

Although the causes of this migration are many, a certain number of causal factors were common to all the Nordic countries. First among these was the tremendous growth in population, resulting in a near-doubling of the Scandinavian population during the nineteenth century. The growth was triggered largely by a decline in death rates, which was the result of improved nutrition, better health conditions, and peace. Coupled with this population growth was a state of economic backwardness. The Nordic countries were relatively late to industrialize and modernize their transportation systems, and their agricultural bases could not absorb the increased numbers of people. Thus, the people of the Nordic countries were caught in a squeeze between growing numbers and insufficient opportunities. In contrast, the development of North American industries and transportation systems, as well as the availability of land, offered seemingly limitless opportunities.

However, the decision to emigrate was almost always a personal one, and to cite only one cause is to oversimplify and to depersonalize the situation. Many other factors weighed upon the individual, including indebtedness, inheritance practices*, a variety of religious issues, political concerns, military service obligations, and a host of personal reasons. In addition, the development of transatlantic and North American transportation systems that could carry vast numbers, the steamship and railroad companies' promotional efforts, the promotional work of states, provinces, companies, and individuals, the flow of letters (and money or prepaid tickets), and the attraction of settlements in the United States and elsewhere served to facilitate and affect the emigration rates.

The difficulty of explaining this mass exodus in simple terms is further complicated because those who emigrated, and their reasons for doing so, varied with place and time. For example, many of the Scandinavians who emigrated in the 1850s came from relatively prosperous farming backgrounds and emigrated in groups, whereas those who emigrated in the 1880s tended to come from less prosperous backgrounds and to emigrate individually. Similarly, a Finn emigrating in 1902 may have done so in response to Tsar Nicholas II's policy of Russification, whereas a Dane emigrating in the same year may have been motivated by economic concerns or concern over the lack of real democracy in Denmark.

The traditional beginning of Scandinavian emigration in the nineteenth century was in 1825, when a handful of Norwegians left Stavanger aboard the sloop *Restauration*. The group spawned the first sizeable Norwegian settlement in New York State and subsequently in Illinois. Swedish emigration began about 20 years later. Its beginning was marked by the founding of a number of pioneer settlements in Wisconsin, Illinois, Minnesota and Iowa. The most notable of these was the Bishop Hill Colony. What began as a trickle became a flood after the American Civil War. Peaks in what was a fluctuating outpouring came in 1869, 1872, 1882, 1887, 1893, 1903, and 1923. Danish emigration in significant numbers began somewhat later than Norwegian or Swedish emigration, but it followed similar patterns once begun. The same can be said for Icelandic emigration. Emigration from Finland did not reach large proportions until the early 1890s, and about 80 percent of the Finns who emigrated to North America left between 1893 and 1914. Following World War I emigration from the Nordic countries declined, except for a brief period between 1919 and 1923. This decline was due largely to the restrictive policies adopted by the American government and the changing environments in the Nordic countries. Since 1930 these countries have actually witnessed a net gain in population through immigration, largely from other parts of Europe.

The exodus of 2.7 million people left its marks upon the Nordic countries. On the negative side, the sheer loss of human talent and resources was immeasurable. On balance, however, the draining off of excess population may have fostered development. Extreme social and economic pressures were relieved, and the emigration may have played a major part in sparing Scandinavia from the unrest that plagued other parts of Europe. Concurrently, the contributions of the emigrants to virtually every aspect of life in their new homelands were considerable.

REFERENCES: K.Hvidt, *Flight to America* (New York: Academic Press, 1975); R. Kero, *Migration from Finland to North America Between the United States Civil War and the First World War* (Turku: Institute for Migration, 1974); L. Ljungmark, *Swedish Exodus* (Carbondale, Ill.: Southern Illinois University Press, 1979); H. Norman, *Nordisk emigrationsatlas* (Gävle: Cikada, 1980); I. Semmingsen, *Norway to America* (Minneapolis: University of Minnesota Press, 1979).

B. NORDSTROM

ENCLOSURE (of land)

In most of Denmark, southern and central Sweden, southern and western Finland, and western Norway, the peasant farmer, before the middle of the eighteenth century, grew his crops on a number of strips in the open fields of the village. He grazed his animals on the village's common pasture and in wooded areas shared the forest with his neighbors. Individual initiative was consequently discouraged, and with the growth of population from the early eighteenth century, subdivision of strips on arable land caused increasing inconvenience. The enclosure movement, which gathered momentum at this time, aimed at consolidating the land belonging to each farm into a single plot or at least a smaller number of unified parcels. Often this also involved the moving of farm buildings and the break-up of the village—with far-reaching social consequences.

In Sweden the leading advocate of enclosure was Jakob Faggot, director of the National Land Survey. His attempts in the 1740s and 1750s depended on the consent of all land owners in a village and had little success. The first effective legislation came in 1757. This enabled a single landholder to demand the consolidation of his property into a maximum of four lots after a public survey. Even this *storskifte* (major reallocation), as it was called, rarely resulted in more than a reduction in the number of strips belonging to each farm, and by the beginning of the nineteenth century only parts of the central lowlands and the extreme southwest of Sweden, as well as some areas in Finland, had been touched. In 1783, however, Rutger Maclean began to enclose fully his tenants' land in the four villages he owned at Svaneholm in Skåne and to move the farmhouses onto individual plots. This more drastic *enskifte* (unitary reallocation) was the subject of legislation in 1803 (for Skåne) and 1807 (for the rest of Sweden excepting Dalarna and Norrland). It proved difficult, however, to apply this system outside tenanted lands on the open plains. A modified *laga skifte* (legal reallocation) was consequently introduced in 1827. This allowed each farmer to have separate plots of forest and pasture in addition to his principal arable holding. Most of southern and central Sweden had been covered by 1875.

Neither *enskifte* nor *laga skifte* was applied in Finland. (Note that Finland passed from Sweden's control to Russia's control in 1809.) There the so-called *nyskifte* (new reallocation), introduced in 1848, encouraged the total abolition of communal farming along the lines of *enskifte*, but it was introduced very slowly, partly because before 1881 it could not be implemented before *storskifte* had been carried out in a village and because before 1916 the agreement of the whole community had to be obtained.

In Denmark, where most peasants were tenants, it was possible to apply full enclosure more rapidly. The first legislation was issued in 1758, but for many years progress was largely confined to royal estates, especially those in northern Zealand. In 1792, however, it was decreed that a landlord could pass on a large part of the cost of enclosure to his tenants, and within 10 years over half the communal land in the country had disappeared. By 1835 only some 3 percent was left.

In Norway the first enclosure act was passed in 1821. It threatened farmers with an increase in the tax value of their land if they did not enclose it. But the old land tax was abolished in 1836, before the time limit for implementation had expired, and consequently little was achieved. Enclosure did not begin on an appreciable scale until after the passage of an act in 1857 which offered state aid toward the cost of enclosure and the help of government surveyors.

While in Denmark the last enclosure was carried out in 1883, in Finland, Norway, and northern Sweden the process still goes on. On the Faroes legislation for the enclosure of the infield was not introduced until 1926.

REFERENCES: O. Bjurling, "The Barons' Revolution," *Economy and History* 2 (1959): 19–37; Ø. Østerud, *Agrarian Structure and Peasant Politics in Scandinavia* (Oslo: Univ-ersitetsforlaget, 1978); K. Tønnesson, "Tenancy, Freehold and Enclosure in Scandinavia from the Seventeenth to the Nineteenth Century," *Scandinavian Journal of History* 6 (1981): 191–206.

S. P. OAKLEY

Denmark

Until the last quarter of the eighteenth century, the vast majority of the land in Denmark was owned by the nobility, the crown, and absentee bourgeois landlords. This land was worked by tenant peasants, who were tied to particular localities and bound by labor and military service obligations (*see Stavnsbånd*). Unlike the other Scandinavian countries, Denmark did not have an extensive freehold peasantry with an independent status dating back to the Viking Age* and before. It was only in the late eighteenth century that Denmark's peasantry began to acquire landownership* and freedoms that their counterparts in the other Nordic countries had enjoyed for centuries. These changes in the nature of the Danish peasantry came largely as a result of conscious governmental policies, developed by a minority of reform-minded land owners and non-agricultural, bourgeois groups, aimed at reform of the agricultural system in Denmark and at changing the social order in the process.

Beginning in the mid-eighteenth century, the Danish government became actively involved in agricultural reform. Enclosure, the consolidation of peasant holdings into single-unit farms and their fencing, was one of these reforms. In the late 1850s a royal commission was created to examine the rural situation and to consider reforms. Although comparatively little came of this effort, a number of land owners, including A. G. Moltke and J.H.E. Bernstorff*, began to implement their own reforms, including enclosure, on their estates. Similar steps were taken on a number of crown estates.

In 1781 a Royal Ordinance was issued which called for the enclosure of peasant landholdings, and following Crown Prince Frederik's coup in 1784, the efforts to carry through this process were intensified. The Great Agricultural Commission, established in 1786, addressed itself in its first report to labor contracts and enclosure. In 1788 the *stavnsbånd* was abolished. Subsequently, the government established a loan program to aid individual peasants in the purchase of the lands they held under contract. Together these measures wrought a revolution in the Danish countryside. By 1807 three-quarters of the agricultural land on the islands and one-half of the land on Jutland had been consolidated. In a span of about 20 years, nearly 60 percent of Denmark's peasants became freehold farmers. The last enclosure of farmland occurred in 1861.

The willingness of the land owners to sell also aided enclosure and the conversion of the leasehold peasantry into a class of freeholders. Their willingness was due to the economic difficulties many of Denmark's nobles found themselves in and to the desire of both the noble and bourgeois land owners to acquire capital for other economic activities—either to finance reforms on portions of their estates or to finance non-agricultural enterprises. In addition, a general rise in farm produce prices during the century aided the process. Also, the government encouraged these changes for a number of reasons. First, they were in keeping with the new ideas of the Enlightenment, including those of individualism and rationalism. Second, these changes fit within the economic ideas of the age, which placed high importance upon efficiency and state self-sufficiency. A freehold peasantry was considered more efficient, and increased efficiency would in turn increase agricultural production and tax revenues.

Enclosure in Denmark, accompanied by other reforms, changed not only the social structure of the country, but also altered the landscape. Reluctant to give up the old village organization pattern in rural areas, the peasants worked to have their lands consolidated in pie-shaped wedges radiating from the village. Thus, the familiar star-pattern was preserved in the countryside, although now there were considerably fewer individual parcels of land. At the same time, the reforms created the basis for the important changes in methods and crop emphases that came in the nineteenth century.

REFERENCES: Claes Bjørn, "The Peasantry and Agrarian Reform in Denmark," *Scandinavian Economic History Review* 25:2 (1977): 117–37; *DH*; F. Skrubbeltrang, *Den danske bonde 1788–1938* (Copenhagen, 1938), and *Det danske landbosamfund 1500–1800* (Odense, 1978); K. Tønnesson, "Tenancy, Freehold, Enclosure in Seventeenth–Nineteenth Century Scandinavia," *Scandinavian Journal of History* 6 (1981): 191–206.

B. NORDSTROM

Norway

The vast program of enclosure of open fields and commons launched by the government of Denmark-Norway in the 1780s was applied only to Denmark proper. In 1803, however, the government started an investigation into the need for enclosure in Norway. Conditions in the two countries were quite different.

The village was unknown in Norway. Because of the division and subdivision of farms through inheritance practices, however, fields had been partitioned into smaller and smaller strips, and open-field practices and hamlet-like clusters of farmhouses had developed. More widespread were common rights of property and usage in woodlands and pastures. Conditions that seemed to invite enclosure were most common in small, subsistence farm areas of the country. There was less need for enclosure in the more prosperous areas, which first saw the development of more modern, market-oriented agriculture. In general, then, enclosure started later and proceeded more slowly than in the neighboring countries.

There were cases of enclosure of both forests and fields by common agreement in the 18th and early nineteenth centuries. The first enclosure act (1821) introduced consolidation by decision of judge and jury and was largely ineffective. Enclosure as a movement began with the law of 1857, which created a specialized administrative unit (Utskiftsningsvesenet [now Jordskifteverket]). Between 1859 and 1956, 31,500 enclosures were carried through, affecting 208,000 farm units.

REFERENCES: T. Grendahl, *Jordskifteverket gjennom 100 år* (Oslo: Norwegian Ministry of Agriculture, 1959); O. Juvkvam, "Traek av utskiftningsvaesenets historie," *Tidsskrift for det norske utskiftningsvaesens*, 1917, pp. 41–161.

K. TØNNESSON

Sweden

Until well into the eighteenth century, the typical patterns of landholding for freehold farmers in Sweden were based upon very old practices of parcel distribution. Agricultural life centered around the village (*by*), and plots of land were allocated by a variety of systems, the most common of which (*solskifte*) was based on the clockwise allocation of strips (*tegar*) mirroring the location of the farmsteads in the village. Inclusions in a number of provincial law codes from the thirteenth century indicate the age of these practices. The basic ideas behind such systems of allocations were the allotment of equal amounts of land (with attention given to quality as well as quantity) and the communal nature of farming. As a result of these methods, the average Swedish farmer held 30 to 40 small parcels of land by the mid-eighteenth century.

From the vantage point of the "enlightened" minds of the eighteenth century, the agricultural land distribution systems were inefficient, wasteful, and outmoded, violated the rationalistic ideals of the age, inhibited the economic development of the state, and infringed upon the ideal of individualism so characteristic of the century. As a result, the old methods came under considerable attack. A leader in this assault was Jacob Faggot, who became director of the government land survey office in 1747. He published a number of critiques and outlines for reform, and he urged government action to effect changes. Consequently, a series of parliamentary acts and royal proclamations (1749, 1757, 1762, and 1783) embodying the program called *storskifte* were issued. These called for the consolidation of the farmers' parcels. They did not, however, attack the village. Although as many as one-third of the freehold farmers in Sweden did take advantage of the program, which was voluntary, the effects were not far-reaching, and *storskifte* is generally seen only as a forerunner of the more energetic and concerted efforts that followed.

The real attack on the village system came in the early nineteenth century, as part of Gustav IV Adolf's* efforts to rationalize and modernize Sweden's economy. The program was designed and directed by Erik af Wetterstedt (1756–1822), who succeeded Faggot as director of the land survey office. It was modeled on the work of the Skåne land owner Rutger Maclean, who carried through a complete reorganization of the landholdings on his estate in the 1780s. Called *enskifte*, the program was defined by a series of decrees dating from 1803, 1804, and 1807. The intent of the program was to break up the villages and to create an agricultural system based upon single family farms. Beginning in Skåne in 1803, the program came to encompass all of Sweden except Dalarna, Norrland, and Finland by 1807. The effort proceeded slowly over the next 20 years, as government agents encountered stubborn resistance from the farmers who were being asked to abandon a way of life that had served for centuries. In 1827 *enskifte* was modified through new legislation (*laga skifte*), which softened the absolutist approach of Gustav IV but did not retreat from the goal of reform.

Although government programs were in place by the early nineteenth century, all were largely voluntary, and actual consolidation proceeded slowly. By the mid-nineteenth century less than half of Sweden's freehold farmland had been consolidated. By 1870, however, the reform had been effected in those areas where it was practicable. Today there are some areas where consolidation has not been carried through, but where it has, the agricultural life of Sweden has been revolutionized. Villages have vanished and have been replaced by scattered individual farms. New architectural styles have appeared, and new crops and methods have been adopted.

Consolidation efforts did not solve all the problems in Swedish agriculture. Division of land holdings, considered such a serious problem by reformers, continued through the practice of *hemmanklyvning*, which involved the division of the farm among the heirs. Also, consolidation brought with it new financial burdens for the individual farmer. These burdens forced many freeholders to abandon their farms and to emigrate or accept a step down in the social hierarchy.

REFERENCES: S. Dahl, "Strip Fields and Enclosure in Sweden," *Scandinavian Economic History Review* (1961); *DSH*, vols. 9–11; E. Heckscher, *An Economic History of Sweden* (Cambridge, Mass.: Harvard University Press, 1954); I. Ingers, *Bonden i svensk historia* (Stockholm: Landbruksförbundets tidskrif AB, 1949); *SU*, vols. 8, 27; O. Thulin, *Historisk utvecking av den svenska skifteslagstiftningen* (1911); K. Tønnessen, "Tenancy, Freehold, and Enclosure in Scandinavia from the Seventeenth to the Nineteenth Century," *Scandinavian Journal of History* 6 (1981): 191–206.

B. NORDSTROM

ERIK I (Ejegod) (c. 1056–10 July 1103) King of Denmark 1095–1103

Erik was the fourth son of Sven I Estridsen* to rule Denmark. Following his half-brother Knud II's* murder in 1086, Erik went into exile in Sweden. He returned only after receiving news of Oluf I's* death. His election was a victory for the faction in Denmark which supported Knud and the idea of a strong, centralized monarchy built at the expense of older political ideas and legal traditions.

Erik's reign was a peaceful one. He ruled in close cooperation with the Church and revived the efforts of his predecessors to establish an independent archbishopric for the North. He and his supporters also worked for the canonization of Knud. They succeeded in both efforts. Knud was made a saint in 1101, and an independent archbishopric was created with its center at Lund in 1103/1104. Asser, a relative of Erik through his wife and an ally of the king, became the first archbishop.

Erik was very much a man of the eleventh century. His concerns and actions reflect the secular-temporal dualism of the period. He worked to strengthen the monarchy and the Church and sought to live a life which reflected his devotion to the Church (hence the epithet Ejegod, "Always Good"). He made a pilgrimage to Italy in 1098, during which he met the pope and may have had a hand in the securing of the archbishopric for Denmark. In 1103 he left on a pilgrimage to the Holy Land. He died en route in Cyprus.

Erik married Bodil, the daughter of a powerful Jutland family from which Archbishop Asser and the future Archbishop Eskil also came. They had one legitimate son, Knud (Lavard). Erik also had a number of illegitimate children including the future king, Erik II* (Emune).

REFERENCES: *DBL*, vol. 2; *DH*, vol. 3.

B. NORDSTROM

ERIK II (Emune) (1090–18 September 1137) King of Denmark 1134–1137

Erik was an illegitimate son of Erik I*. He was chosen king following the defeat of the forces of Niels* and his son Magnus at Fodevig in 1134. His reign was a short and apparently a rather unpleasant one for all who opposed him.

Following his election he set about eliminating all potential opposition. He defeated his half-brother, Harald Kesja, and had him imprisoned. Harald was later executed, and his sons were hunted down. Only one, the future Oluf II*, survived. The bishops who had supported Niels were replaced, and he worked to create a subservient Church. Erik aroused strong opposition, and he was murdered at a *ting* meeting in Ribe in 1137. He had one son, Sven III Grathe*, who was under age at the time of his father's death.

Assessments of him differ widely in the medieval sources. To some he was Erik the Unforgettable (Emune). Others thought of him simply as a man of ruthless and cruel violence.

REFERENCES: *DBL*, vol. 4; *DH*, vol. 3.

B. NORDSTROM

ERIK III (the Meek/Lam) (1110–27 August 1146) King of Denmark 1137–1146

Erik was the son of a daughter of Erik I*. He was elected to the Danish throne following the murder of Erik II*. His reign was comparatively uneventful and was dominated by Eskil, the archbishop of Lund. Erik did attempt an invasion of England, but failed. The development of strong monarchy stopped during his nine years on the throne. In 1146 he abdicated and retired to St. Knud's monastery in Odense, where he died.

REFERENCES: *DBL*, vol. 4; *DH*, vol. 3.

B. NORDSTROM

ERIK IV (Ploughpenny/Plovpenning) (1216–10 August 1250) King of Denmark 1241–1250

Erik succeeded to the throne as the eldest surviving son of Valdemar II*. The reign was marred by almost constant violence. Erik's brothers, Abel* and Christoffer (I*), lived in their duchies like independent sovereigns and cooperated against their brother's attempts to consolidate the power of the monarchy. Erik's problems were complicated by poor relations with the Church and his alienation of the peasantry. The taxes he had to impose to pay for his campaigns against his rebellious brothers triggered peasant revolts. His epithet, Ploughpenny, arises from the tax he imposed on ploughs in 1249. He was murdered by Abel's supporters in 1250.

REFERENCES: *DBL*, vol. 4; *DH*, vol. 4.

B. NORDSTROM

ERIK V (Klipping) (c. 1249–22 November 1286) King of Denmark 1259–1286

Erik was the son of Christoffer I* and Margrete of Pomerania. He was a minor at the time of his father's death, and his mother and Albert, the Margrave of Brandenburg, ran the country for a number of years. Throughout the reign the crown had to face opposition from the secular magnates of the kingdom, the ecclesiastical lords of the Church, especially the archbishop, Jakob Erlandsen, the descendants of Abel*, and foreigners (especially Germans) who sought to take advantage of Denmark's weaknesses. None of these were effectively dealt with by Erik.

His personal reign began c. 1270, and he quickly made himself very unpopular with his people through his use of German mercenaries and his efforts to impose stricter feudal controls on his independent-minded magnates. In 1282 he was compelled to agree to a royal charter (*håndfæstning*) in which he guaranteed the privileges of the magnates. He also agreed to call meetings of a kind of parliament (*hof*) to deal with important questions. This charter is an important document in the centuries-long power struggle between the crown and the nobility. In 1286 Erik was murdered. The question of who was responsible for his death remains unanswered. A group of magnates, including the marshal of the realm, Stig Andersen Hvide, was tried and sentenced to exile. This was a political trial, however, and did not settle the question of responsibility.

REFERENCES: *DBL*, vol. 4; *DH*, vol. 4; Cambridge Medieval History, vol. 8.

B. NORDSTROM

ERIK VI (Bird of Ill Omen/Menved) (1274–13 November 1319) King of Denmark 1286–1319

Erik was a son of Erik V* and Agnes of Brandenburg. Like his father he faced constant challenges from opponents to his position, and especially from the Danish magnates, Archbishop Jens Grand, and the great men who, exiled following the murder of Erik V, found refuge and support in Norway. The early years of his reign were dominated by his mother. During his own majority he sought to consolidate his position through his marriage to Ingeborg, a daughter of Sweden's king, Magnus Ladulås, reconciliation with the Church, and an aggressive foreign policy in northern Germany. The marriage gained him little. The reconciliation was achieved c. 1303 and assured him of some support at home. His foreign adventures yielded only minor successes, were far too costly, and strengthened the forces aligned against the monarchy. The taxes he had to impose to pay for his involvement in Germany triggered peasant revolts at home, and, worst of all for Denmark and the monarchy, he had to mortgage crown holdings to Danish and German nobles to pay his bills.

REFERENCES: *DBL*, vol. 4; *DH*, vol. 4.

B. NORDSTROM

ERIK (VII) OF POMERANIA (c. 1382–1459) King of Denmark 1396–1439, king of Norway 1388–1442, king of Sweden 1396–1438

Erik was the grandnephew of Margrethe I*. Following the death of Margrethe's only son, Oluf II*, in 1387, he became the candidate for the throne in all three Nordic countries favored by Margrethe, and she succeeded over the ensuing 10 years to secure his election. He was crowned the first king of the Kalmar Union* in 1397. Until her death in 1412, Margrethe was the actual ruler of the union. Erik was compelled to observe and learn. Once the great lady was gone, however, Erik set about converting the government of the union to his liking and purposes and initiated an aggressive foreign policy which quickly made him enemies in the Baltic region. Erik was intelligent, forceful, and charming, but he lacked the wisdom and restraint which had made Margrethe so successful. As a result, he ended his life in exile, and the union his great-aunt had done so much to construct was soon in ruins.

Erik's troubles came in two areas. First, he replaced many of the fiefholders Margrethe had installed with his own people. While not unwise on the surface, his appointments antagonized many. In Sweden and Norway he often installed Danes who abused their powers and held office in violation of the understandings upon which the union was founded. In Denmark his appointees became similarly unpopular. These problems may not have been fatal for Erik had he not embarked on a foreign policy that forced him to increase taxation (thereby compelling his sheriffs to become the local villains); he introduced the Sound Tolls (*see* Elsinore) (later 1429), which required all ships passing through the Sound to stop at Krogen (Kronborg) and pay a toll, and hurt many areas of the economy including the iron industry in Sweden and the merchants of Denmark.

In 1416 he went to war with Holstein over Slesvig, which was then governed by the duke of Holstein. This ended in Erik's favor but only after the intervention of the German emperor. The war was renewed in 1426, and this time Lübeck and other cities in the Hanse (*see* Hanseatic League) joined with Holstein. This phase of the struggle ended in 1432 in Holstein's favor. During this war the iron producers of Sweden's Bergslagen were severely affected, because Sweden was placed under blockade, and the miners lost their outlets to Europe through Stockholm*.

In 1434 open revolt broke out in Sweden's Bergslagen, led by Engelbrekt Engelbrektsson. Quickly, many of the local forts held by Danish sheriffs were captured or destroyed. The revolt grew, and the magnates joined, hoping to regain their old influence at Erik's expense. Engelbrekt was murdered, but the struggle continued. Erik was deposed by the council, and Karl Knutsson Bonde (later Karl VIII Knutsson*) was elected regent in 1438.

The revolt spread to Norway and Denmark. In 1436 the Danish council began to act in open defiance of the king. By the end of the decade only Norway still recognized him as its king. (The Norwegians deposed him in 1442.) The union did not collapse with the revolt against Erik, and the magnates in the separate countries soon agreed upon Christoffer of Bavaria (Christoffer III*) as Erik's successor. Erik took refuge in Visby, where he ruled as a pirate king. In 1449 he left his island stronghold for Pomerania; from there he continued to plot for his return to power until his death.

Erik was not a villain or even a bad king. His ambitions exceeded his means. The union he ruled was a fragile one. The effectiveness of central governments in the fifteenth century was minimal. The territories of the realm were far-flung and communications poor. The enemies of the union, as he envisioned it, were strong. The great men of all three kingdoms (to a lesser degree Norway, where the native nobility was very small) were interested in a weak union, a kind of federation which they could dominate. Erik and his predecessors were trying to build a new kind of state, and they were working against magnates who represented a tradition of power and took a very different constitutional position. Erik's deposition was part of the feudal reaction of the fifteenth century. The Hanse also wished for a weak union. So long as its members squabbled, the German traders could easily maintain dominance of trade in the North. While Erik may have been right (and he always believed that he was), the forces working against him were too strong.

REFERENCES: *DBL*, vol. 4; *DH*, vol. 4. See also references under Margrethe I.

B. NORDSTROM

ERIK XIV (1533–1577) King of Sweden 1560–1568

The son of Gustav I Vasa* and his first queen, Katarina of Sachsen-Lauenburg, Erik was trained for the kingship in Renaissance fashion. Highly intelligent, he received broad training in history, logic, mathematics, military science, and the arts. He learned several foreign languages. He developed skills in swimming, riding, dancing, painting, songwriting, and musical composition. But, unfortunately, he was extremely suspicious, easily irritated, and had a violent temper. His interest and faith in astrology, his suspicion of his half brothers Johan (III*) and Karl (IX*) his distrust of aristocrats, and his reliance on commoners, such as his favorite Göran Persson*, as advisors are factors that helped determine the course of his life and reign.

He served effectively as an assistant to his father in the 1550s and as his substitute while Gustav Vasa was away at war in 1555–1557. When he ascended the throne in 1560, Erik XIV demonstrated genuine skill as a ruler on the one hand, and bizarre behavior on the other. Among his admirable actions were his continuing support of the Church of Sweden, then in the process of becoming a thoroughly national church under the leadership of Archbishop Lars Petri, brother of the reformer Olaus Petri*; founding a supreme or high court (*konungens nämnd*), which was badly needed; supporting the arts and education; permitting a high degree of religious freedom; and developing both army and navy. A seven-year war with Denmark broke out in 1563; Erik showed his skill as a commander on occasion.

While he was undoubtedly justified in limiting his half brothers' power in their largely autonomous duchies, he did so by taking halfway measures. He imprisoned Johan and his Polish wife Katarina Jagellonica at Gripsholm Castle but did not have an easy conscience about doing so. To some degree justified in his suspicion of the intentions and acts of the lords, in 1567 he had a number of them, including four members of the Sture family (leading rivals of the Vasas), imprisoned, tried, condemned, and, in a fit of fury, murdered. His high court handed down well over 200 sentences of death; most of these cases had been presented by his prosecutor, Göran Persson.

Because of the many acts of violence, some of which he directly participated in, he became beside himself, suffered agony of remorse, and tried to set things right by acknowledging his guilt and providing material compensation. For some time in late 1568 he was anything but sane. When he recovered, he freed Johan and Katarina and became, he thought, reconciled with his half brothers and the families of the aristocrats whom he had executed. In July 1568 he married his commoner mistress Karin Månsdotter; the Riksdag* approved the marriage and recognized infant Prince Gustav as heir to the throne. (Through the late 1550s and early 1560s Erik had hopes of securing Elizabeth of England, Mary Queen of Scots, or any of several continental princesses as his consort.)

A few days after the wedding dukes Johan and Karl started a rebellion, which resulted in Erik's deposal in January 1569 and his imprisonment for the rest of his life. He may have been poisoned on orders from his successor, King Johan III (1568–1572).

Both King Erik and Queen Karin have been popular subjects in Swedish literature. August Strindberg's drama *Erik XIV* is the most readily available treatment of both.

REFERENCES: V. Moberg, *A History of the Swedish People: From Renaissance to Revolution* (New York: Pantheon, 1973); R. Murray, *The Church of Sweden: Past and Present* (Malmö: Allhem, 1960); M. Roberts, *The Early Vasas: A History of Sweden, 1523–1611* (Cambridge, England: Cambridge University Press, 1968); F. Scott, *Sweden: The Nation's History* (Minneapolis: University of Minnesota Press, 1977).

W. JOHNSON

ERLANDER, TAGE FRITIOF (13 June 1901–21 June 1985) prime minister of Sweden 1946–1969

The son of a public school teacher and organist, Erlander was born in Ransäter, in the western province of Värmland. Reared in an intellectual environment, he entered Lund University in 1920 and received a liberal arts degree in 1928. He became active in the Social Democratic Party* while a university student and was elected to the Lund City Council in 1930 and to the Riksdag* in 1933. Erlander maintained his academic interests in political science, economics, and statistics and from 1932 until 1938 was managing co-editor of the Swedish encyclopedia, *Svensk Upplagsbok*.

Erlander quickly came to the attention of the party leaders. At the request of Minister of Finance Ernst Wigforss*, the chief party theoretician, he served in the mid-1930s on commissions investigating the difficult economic situation, particularly the unemployment problem and local government taxes. In 1937 he joined the Ministry of Social Affairs under Gustaf Möller, who was the driving force behind the budding social welfare programs. From 1938 to 1944 Erlander served as undersecretary of social affairs. In 1944 Erlander joined the wartime government coalition as a minister without portfolio and in 1945, when a Social Democratic government succeeded the wartime coalition, became minister of ecclesiastical affairs (now education and ecclesiastical affairs). He concentrated on reform of the school system. At the end of World War II*, Norway and Denmark cited Erlander for his part in aiding their refugees and maintaining certain secret communications facilities.

When the longtime Social Democratic Party leader and prime minister Per Albin Hansson* died in 1946, Erlander was unexpectedly chosen to succeed him. While quite different in personality from the father figure Hansson, he was politically astute and developed a folksy touch through his informality, friendliness, and dry wit. Pragmatic, intelligent, and hard-working, he gained the support of all party members and the respect of nearly all Swedes. His ability to work constructively with strong and conflicting personalities played a large role in the establishment of the modern Swedish welfare state* and the "Swedish model" of cooperation among interest groups and political leaders. The term "Harpsund democracy" was coined to describe Erlander's practice of calling representatives of unions, industry, the cooperative movement, banking, and other political parties to the prime minister's estate to settle disputes and strike compromise over party or economic interest lines.

Under Erlander's leadership, the immediate postwar years saw a burst of legislation establishing Sweden's current basic social welfare programs, led by old-age pensions and medical insurance for all. The threat of Soviet aggression in the late 1940s temporarily halted implementation of costlier programs, such as medical insurance, while, in cooperation with the other non-Communist leaders, a strong defense force was created to command respect for Sweden's nonalignment. Also, a decline of the Social Democrats' electoral strength, caused mainly by a decrease in traditional blue-collar unionists in Sweden's modernized society, weakened the government's parliamentary majority after 1948. Erlander attracted the Agrarian Party (now the Center Party*) into a coalition in 1952, which gave him the majority necessary to resume social reform. When the coalition broke up in 1957 over Center Party opposition to Sweden's compulsory retirement pension program, the Social Democrats again ruled alone, despite the fact that they were in a minority except for the years 1969–1970. By compromising with other non-Communist parties to secure legislation, Erlander carried through far-reaching reforms, such as expansion of old-age pensions, enactment of the retirement pension program, adoption of a unicameral legislature, democratization of the educational system, and establishment of a generous foreign aid program. While he had to rely on Communist Party* support for some economic and social legislation, Erlander never bargained for it, and he intervened in parliamentary debates to identify Sweden with Western democracies and to speak out against Soviet policies.

Erlander did not oppose the attacks of his protégé, Sven Olof Palme*, on the United States' policies toward Vietnam in the latter part of the 1960s, but refrained from personal criticisms and made efforts, after he relinquished control of the party and government to Palme in 1969, to restore good relations between Sweden and the United States. In 1982 he was still active in Swedish political debates.

REFERENCES: *DSH*, vol. 15; T. Erlander, *Tage Erlander*, 4 vols. (Stockholm: Tidens, 1972); S. U. Palme, *Vår längsta statsminister: en bok om Tage Erlander* (Stockholm: Åhlen & Åkerlund, 1963).

H. F. CAPPS

ERLENDR Bishop of the Faroe Islands*, 1269–1300

Erlendr, the fourteenth bishop to occupy the see of Kirkjubøur* in the Faroe Islands, is the only one about whom very much is known, since the bishopric archives have not survived. Early in the fifteenth century there was a proposal to canonize Erlendr, evidence having been produced of miracles he had performed in person and by the agency of his relics. His bones were thus exumed, and in his grave, it is said, was found a leaden memorial tablet in Latin, inscribed in runes*. From this it was learned that Erlendr was a canon and doctor in the church of Bergen, and that he was consecrated in Nidaros Cathedral on 25 January 1269. He died in Bergen on 13 June 1308.

The tablet records that he was a man of great piety, modesty, eloquence, and simplicity, of great wisdom and full of all virtues. Far beyond all his predecessors he enriched the Faroese church with privileges, estates, and worldly goods. He laid the foundations of the stone cathedral at Kirkjuböur and brought the work so far that the walls, at least in the chancel, were almost complete.

That Erlendr was honored by the great is witnessed by the detail from the tablet that he baptized King Magnus's son Haakon, later to become King Haakon V. From Seyðabrævið (see Sheep Letter) we learn that in 1298 he was consulted over this important enactment regulating the use of Faroese sheep pastures, a law that has formed the basis of Faroese legislation on this subject down to the present day.

It is clear, however, even from the tablet, that he met strong opposition to his plans. It is recorded that in his time the episcopal church and palace were destroyed by an arsonist and that for the last three years of his life he was detained in Bergen by a lawsuit brought by "a man by the name of Hergeir, a son of Belial, an enemy of God and Christ's Church, a disturber of the peace."

Erlendr was credited with second sight. On the day when fire broke out in the church and episcopal palace at Kirkjuböur, he is said to have been in Bergen but knew at the very moment of the outrage that a great blow had been struck at the Faroese church. The story occurs in the lead tablet and also in a commentary accompanying the Faroese section of Peder Hansen Resen's Atlas Danicus, written in the late seventeenth century. The stories diverge considerably in detail.

Contemporary belief in the sanctity of Erlendr is confirmed in a note added to a church calendar appended to the beautiful manuscript Lund 15, which contains copies of a number of laws, including Seyðabrævið.Opposite 13 June appears: "obitus dominj Erlendj bonj memorie pharensis episcopj"—the death of master Erlendr of worthy memory, bishop of Faroe.

REFERENCES: Seðabrævið (Torshavn: Föroya Fróðskaparfelag, 1971); J. F. West, Faroese Folk-Tales and Legends (Lerwick: Shetland Publishing Company, 1980).

J. F. WEST

EXPLORERS IN AFRICA

Scandinavian explorers in Africa have been most significant in the southern and central parts of the continent. Throughout the second half of the seventeenth century as well as the eighteenth century, numerous Scandinavians were employed in Cape Town and its environs by the Dutch East India Company (see South Africa). Chief among these were Oloff Bergh (1643–1724) and Henrik Jacob Wikar (1752–?). Between 1682 and 1699 Bergh engaged in a series of expeditions along the Atlantic coast north of Cape Town, as well as east of the city. He was also a member of the Cape Town government and owned several estates in the Cape. In the 1770s Wikar became one of the first Europeans to see the Orange River and the Augrabies Falls. He mapped approximately 300 miles of the river.

Carl Linnaeus's students, Anders Sparrman (1748–1820) and C. P. Thunberg (1743–1828), visited the Cape region of South Africa in the 1770s to study its botany. In the course of their studies they journeyed extensively along the southern coast.

An extensive part of eastern and northern Namibia (South West Africa) was explored in the 1850s and 1860s by Charles John Andersson (1827–1867). It was Andersson who gave the country of the Hereros and Namaquas the name South West Africa. In 1853 he became the first European to reach Lake Ngami in Botswana from the west. He discovered the Okavango River, which today is the Angolan-Namibian border, and made several journeys into other regions of Namibia. He was also a first-rate ornithologist and collected a wide variety of birds. Other Swedish explorers of Namibia included Axel Wilhelm Eriksson (d. 1901) and Johan August Wahlberg (1810–1856), who also explored Natal and the Transvaal in the 1830s and early 1840s.

The Congo (Zaire) and Cameroon regions of central Africa were other areas explored by Scandinavians. As early as 1816 Christen Smith, a Norwegian botanist, was in the lower Congo basin. A number of Scandinavians were employed in the late nineteenth and early twentieth centuries by Belgium's King Leopold as officers in the Congo Free State army or as navigators on the Congo River. Others were employed as engineers, explorers, scientists, farmers, and missionaries. It has been estimated that there were over 800 Scandinavians (the majority being Swedes) serving in various capacities in the Congo, making them one of the largest groups of Europeans in the area at the turn of the century, surpassed in numbers only by the Belgians. Included among these Scandinavians was Capt. Anton Andersson, who was part of Stanley's expedition in 1880 and who was employed as a Congo River navigator by Leopold's Congo Association. Stanley eulogized this Swede for his help in his book on the Congo. Edvard Gleerup, in the service of the Congo government, was one of the first Europeans to cross the continent (1885–1886) from the Atlantic to the Indian Ocean via the Congo River and Lake Tanganyika. While traveling in eastern Zaire, Gleerup named the Wester Falls on the Congo River in honor of his Swedish colleague, Lt. Arvid Wester, who was also employed by the Congo Free State. Wester had originally come to the Congo under Stanley in the latter part of 1883 as a captain over a contingent of Hausa mercenaries. For a time, he was engaged in defending the eastern Congo from Arabs who were penetrating from the east.

REFERENCES: C. J. Andersson, *Lake Ngami; or Explorations and Discoveries During Four Years' Wanderings in the Wilds of South Western Africa* (London: Hurst & Blackett, 1856); and *The Okavango River: A Narrative of Travel and Exploration and Adventure* (London: Hurst & Blackett, 1861; repr. Cape Town: C. Struik, 1968); O. Bergh, *Journals of the Expeditions of the Honourable Ensign Olof Bergh and the Ensign Isaq Schrijver* (Cape Town; repr. in *The Van Riebeeck Society Publications*, 12, 1931); H. Jenssen-Tusch, *Skandinaver i Congo* (Copenhagen: Gyldendal, 1902–1905); A. Sparrman, *A Voyage to the Cape of Good Hope*, 2 vols. (London: Johnson Reprint Co., 1971); C. P. Thunberg, *Travels in Europe, Africa, and Asia Made between the Years 1770 and 1779*, 4 vols. (London: F. & C. Rivington, 1793–1796); H. J. Wikar, *The Journal of Hendrik*

Jacob Wikar (Cape Town; repr. in *The Van Riebeeck Society Publications*, 15, 1935); A. Winquist, *Scandinavians and South Africa* (Cape Town: A. A. Balkema, 1978).

A. H. WINQUIST

F

FAMILY PLANNING Norway

Between 1900 and 1930 Norwegian marital fertility fell, and the average number of children per family declined from 5 to 2.5. The reduction was stronger in towns than in rural districts and greater in the west-end area of Kristiania (Oslo) than in the east-end. However, all over the country some families reduced the number of births after 1900. From the end of the 1930s, but especially after World War II*, Norway witnessed a baby boom. This was followed by a sharp reduction of fertility, especially in the 1970s.

Three groups of motives for family planning seem important: family economy, considerations of the health of the mother and the children, and—in the beginning of the century only for a small number of women, but increasingly important in the 1970s—the desire to spend more time on activities other than childcare.

Within these categories, the content varies with the social standing of the family. For middle-class families, birth control until the 1930s was a defense against the loss of class advantage over the working classes in terms of living standards. It also gave women in this class more time to conform to the rising standards of childcare and paved the way for social and political activities outside the home. For the families of the working classes, birth control was part of the struggle for economic and physical survival. For a minority of working-class women, it also meant a way to improve women's possibilities of taking part in the fight against capitalism.

After World War II the same categories of motives have been found, though family economy was then expected to cover items unknown to pre-war families. Marital discord and divorce became more common as reasons to avoid pregnancy.

In general, couples seem to have agreed upon the need for birth control, but men have shown a tendency to worry over the family's financial position, women over their own health and that of their children. Few men saw birth control as a means for women to take up activities outside the home before World War II.

Until oral contraceptives (the pill) were introduced, contraceptive practices usually left the final decision on having a child to men. The means adopted were usually coitus interruptus and abortion. Contraceptive devices, among them the diaphragm, were known, but were probably not very effective. The propagation of knowledge about contraceptives was, from 1889, punishable by imprisonment or fines, and abortion—if discovered—by up to three years in prison.

Around World War I a radical woman, Katti Anker Møller, started the campaign for women's right to decide if an abortion was needed. She argued along lines later followed by proponents of women's right to make decisions concerning their own bodies. Her supporters were mainly Socialist women, along with some radical liberals. Her daughter and granddaughter were in the forefront of the growing opposition to the strict regulations on abortion. They saw the adoption of the 1978 law which permitted women to decide on abortion within the first three months of pregnancy.

The state church and most doctors, however, opposed abortion as well as contraception until well into the 1920s. In spite of strong opposition, Katti Anker Møller managed to open a "mother clinic" in Oslo in 1924. Here women were advised on contraception, and knowledge was spread throughout the country. Such clinics were opened in about a dozen other towns prior to World War II.

In spite of the gradual spread of information, it was not until the 1960s that knowledge about contraception was fully accepted or available to unmarried women. The introduction of the pill made it possible for women to limit further the number of children. Motives for the marked reduction of marital fertility after 1970 have not yet been fully explained, and there is ample discussion of the problems created by the aging of the population.

REFERENCES: E. Aanesen, *Ikke send meg til en "kone," doktor. Fra 3 års fengsel til selvbestemt abort* (Oslo: Oktober forlag, 1981); I. Blom, *Barnebegrensning—synd eller sunn fornuft?* (Bergen, Oslo, Tromsø: Universitetsforlaget, 1980); S. Dyrvik, "Ekteskap og barnetal—ei granskning av fertilitetsutviklinga i Norge 1920–1970," *Artikler fra Statistisk Sentralbyrå*, no. 89 (Oslo, 1976); L. Walløe, ed., *Seksualitet, familieplanlegging og prevensjon i Norge* (Oslo, Bergen, Tromsø: Universitetsforlaget, 1978).

I. BLOM

FARMERS' MARCH (Bondetåget) (6 February 1914) Pro-defense demonstration in Stockholm*

Thirty-one thousand farmers converged on the royal palace in Stockholm* in 1914 to inform King Gustav V* that they were willing to support whatever military experts deemed necessary to bolster Sweden's defenses without delay. This upsurge of rustic patriotism was triggered by the liberal-dominated parliamentary defense committee's delay in submitting a unified defense bill acceptable to the military and the conservatives. While the committee and Karl Staaff*, the prime minister, had yielded considerably as a result of the increases in international tensions during the previous two years, there was still sharp disagreement over the amount of training time to be required of infantry recruits. The king's reply to the assembled farmers created a national crisis and triggered the resignation of the Liberal ministry four days later. In a response to the farmers, Gustav openly repudiated the cabinet's position on defense and then refused its request of prior consultation on political statements in the future.

The Farmers' March was planned well in advance and was carefully executed. Its inception was in mid-November 1913, when a land owner in Uppland made the observation that farmers should unite to show their support for the king, who was under attack from the radical Left. Shortly afterwards, this sentiment was linked to the defense controversy and was given organizational form by Uppsala wholesaler J. E. Frykberg, who had directed one of the F-boat* collections in 1912. By the end of December 1913, 3,000 farmers in Uppland had joined the movement, and the motto "With God and Sweden's Common People for King and Fatherland" had been adopted. While the movement soon spread to other provinces, most of those who came to Stockholm were from central Sweden. Reduced railroad fares and free lodging made the trip more feasible for many. Two days after the march (and in response to it), K. Hjalmar Branting*, leader of the Social Democratic Party*, led 50,000 workers in a demonstration in support of the Liberal government.

REFERENCES: R. Frykberg, *Bondetåget 1914. Dess upprinnelse, inre historia och följder* (Stockholm: Horsta, 1959); B. Schiller, "Years of Crisis 1906–1914," in S. Koblik, *Sweden's Development from Poverty to Affluence* (Minneapolis: University of Minnesota Press, 1975); F. Scott, *Sweden: The Nation's History* (Minneapolis: University of Minnesota Press, 1977).

P. V. THORSON

FARMERS' PARTY *See* Center Party: Finland; Center Party: Norway; Center Party: Sweden

FARMERS' PROTEST (1935–1936) A challenge to Danish democracy

A widespread mood of protest and rebellion swept the Danish countryside during the mid-1930s which, among other things, resulted in the emergence of an independent Farmers' or Peasants' Party, composed largely of dissatisfied members of the older Liberal Left or Venstre. This new Farmers' Party, at times referring to itself as the Free People's Party, received five seats in the Folketing* or the Lower House of the Danish parliament in the elections of 1935, the very year of its founding. In 1939 it secured four seats in the Folketing and remained the largest splinter party in Denmark. The Danish Nazis and Communists each received only three seats in the Folketing during that year. After 1939 the Peasants' Party plummeted in popularity because of the pro-German and at times pro-Nazi orientation of its leadership. It received only two seats in the Folketing in the wartime election of 1943 and no seats in the postwar elections of 1945 and 1947.

In addition to the formation of an independent agrarian political party, the farmers' protest brought about the establishment of a farmers' militia to prevent forced sales of Danish farms and evictions of farm families, a march on Copenhagen* by angry agriculturalists in 1935, and strikes which resulted in the withholding of farm produce from the urban market. There were two major farmers' organizations that spearheaded much of the protest activity during this period. The first and larger of these was the Landbrugernes Sammenslutning or LS. This group had the character of a populist mass movement somewhat on the order of the National Grange or the National Farmers' Organization (NFO) in the United States. Its total membership was somewhere between 100,000 and 200,000, and it was composed of people from all three middle-class parties: the Conservatives Party, Venstre, and the Radical Left. The LS. organized annual "Farmers' Meetings" which took care of major business. Consequently, the LS. had a relatively democratic political structure, even though it often came into conflict with the parliamentary traditions of Denmark through its advocacy of direct action. The second major farmers' organization had a somewhat aristocratic and decidedly more right-wing orientation than the LS. This was the Majoratsjernes Forening or Estate-Owners Union. Its leaders included men like Knuth Von Knuthenborg, a close associate of Danish Nazi leader Fritz Clausen, and Jorgen Sehested, a man with strong pro-Nazi leanings and a bitter hatred for the Social Democratic government of Thorvald Stauning*. The Estate-Owners Union represented larger land owners, who owned about one-sixth of the arable land in Denmark.

These agrarian groups were in general agreement that the Social Democrat-Radical coalition government of Stauning and Peter Munch* was too liberal, internationalist, and urban-oriented to merit their political support. The farmers' protest probably constituted the single most dangerous or effective challenge to the Stauning-Munch government before the outbreak of World War II*. It affected the two major opposition parties, the Conservatives and the Liberal Left or Venstre. Elements within the Conservative Party sympathized with the activism of the agrarians and also shared in the general admiration for Nazi Germany and Fascist philosophy which affected a number of agrarian leaders like Sehested and Knuth Von Knuthenborg. This group in the Conservative Party was best represented by Victor Peurschell, one-time auditor general of Denmark and a rigorous anti-Communist, and Jack Westergaard, who with Peurschell took control of the Conservative Youth Group (Konservativ Ungdom) in the late 1930s and steered it in an activist and even quasi-fascist direction. Democratic, anti-fascist leaders like Christmas Moeller*, K.V.K. Fibiger, and Ole Bjorn Kraft effectively counteracted the influence of individuals like Peurschell and Westergaard in the Conservative Party, but a sizeable minority of Conservatives continued to share the views of Peurschell and Westergaard.

Finally, Fritz Clausen's Nazis and other extreme right-wing groups often made blatant appeals to the protesting farmers, particularly over the problem of farm debts and forced auctions. Consequently, the farmers' protest tended to be a right-wing and at times pro-German movement. This is what ultimately discredited it during and immediately after World War II. However, for a brief period of time, 1935–1942, it was a major force in Danish politics.

REFERENCES: B. A. Arneson, *The Democratic Monarchies of Scandinavia* (New York: D. Van Nostrand, 1939); J. Joesten, *Rats in the Larder: The Story of Nazi Influence in Denmark* (New York: G. P. Putnam, 1939); K. Secher, *Kampf Ohne Waffen, Daenemark Unter der Besatzung* (Zurich: Europa Verlag, 1945); J. Voorhis, "A Study of Official Relations between the German and Danish Governments in the Period between 1940–1943," Ph.D. dissertation, Northwestern University, 1968.

J. L. VOORHIS

FAROE ISLANDS A group of islands in the North Atlantic constituting a self-governing community within the Danish kingdom

The Faroe Islands consist of seventeen inhabited and several tiny uninhabited islands, halfway between Shetland and Iceland. The capital, Tórshavn*, lies at 62°N 6°45'W. The archipelago is shaped like an inverted triangle with a base 50 miles (80 km) long, aligned WSW-ENE, and an apex 70 miles (110 km) south of its northern extremity—a geographical spread comparable to the state of Delaware. The total land area is a little under 550 square miles (a little over 1,400 square km), of which perhaps 7 percent is arable.

The islands consist of layer upon layer of gray-blue basalt, laid down by volcanic action in Tertiary times, separated by layers of tuff, often resembling a red sandstone. A couple of thin seams of coal are present in Suðuroy. Erosion by Ice Age glaciation, and since by climate and ocean, has worn down an original plateau into a score or so of islands, separated by channels all aligned NNW-SSE. In the north the islands are close together, but toward the south the straits become wider.

The islands are mountainous but not lofty, the highest summit being 2,894 feet (882 m). Coasts exposed to the Atlantic are often dramatically precipitous, vertical cliffs of 1,500 feet (460 m) being not uncommon. The areas suitable for cultivation and settlement are valley bottoms, isthmuses, or tiny coastal plains. There are today about 100 villages and 2 small towns.

Despite the subarctic latitude, the climate is mild, never very cold in winter or very warm in summer. There is much mist and rain, and storms, especially in winter, can be tremendous and last for days. Natural vegetation consists principally of grasses where the land is well drained and marsh plants where it is not. Trees are found only in a few modern plantations. Rats, mice, and hares are the only wild land mammals.

The seas around the Faroes are very rich in fish, and the sea-cliffs are the homes of millions of seabirds, in particular the guillemot, puffin, fulmar, kittiwake, gannet, and Manx shearwater. Mineral resources in the islands are scanty, and hydroelectric potential is limited.

Pollen evidence suggests that the Faroe Islands were already settled by 600 A.D., and the Irish geographer Dicuil, writing about 825, speaks of Irish hermits in the islands from about 700. Little is known of the Irish from legendary, historical, or archeological records. From about 800, Norse settlers began to arrive, probably from western Norway, and some from the Norse settlements in the Hebrides, after which no more is heard of the Irish. According to the Icelandic sagas, the first Norse settler in the Faroe Islands was Grímr Kamban*.

The name Faroe (Old Norse *Fareyjar*, modern Faroese *Föroyar*) means Sheep Islands, the name arising from the small wild sheep the Norsemen found on the islands, no doubt introduced by the hermits.

Viking Age* settlements have been excavated in Kvívík, Fuglafjörður, and Syðragöta, and Viking* graves have been found in Tjörnuvík. A runic stone found in Kirkjuböur* has been dated to the period 950–1050.

Historical materials for the pre-Reformation period are very scanty. The islands are briefly mentioned in several Icelandic sagas, and it is clear that the islands were Christianized about the same time as Iceland, that is, 1000 A.D. The *Færeyinga Saga*, with its attractive narratives of feuding chieftains of the conversion period, must unfortunately be discounted as fiction, though there is no reason to doubt that, as stated in the saga, the Faroes became tributary to Norway about 1035.

About 1100 a bishopric was set up in Kirkjuböur, but its records have not survived. It is known, however, that during the succeeding four centuries the Church acquired ownership of about 40 percent of the land in the islands.

According to the *Færeyinga Saga*, during their period of independence the islands already possessed a legislative body and high court, the althing, which met in Tórshavn on the peninsula still called Tinganes. This assembly is still referred to by that name in the *Sheep Letter** of 1298, but an ordinance dated about 1400 refers to the assembly as the lögting (*see* Lagting, Faroese), the title given to the provincial courts of Norway.

Commerce during the medieval period was channeled through Bergen, but there is evidence of Hanseatic penetration in the thirteenth century, and in 1361, the Hanse (*see* Hanseatic League) were given equal rights with the Norwegians to trade in the islands. The first mention of a Faroese Monopoly* comes in 1524.

After Norway was united with Denmark in 1380, the Faroes were increasingly governed as a Danish rather than a Norwegian province. However, throughout history Norwegian, not Danish, law has applied in Faroe, and even today the Faroese legal code starts with the Norwegian Law of Christian V*.

The Reformation* came to the Faroes at the time it came to Norway, 1535–1540. A Lutheran, Jens Gregerson Riber, was appointed to the Kirkjuböur see in 1540, but the bishopric was abolished in 1557. The church estates fell to the crown, as did the bishopric's third share of the tithes. The church language changed from Latin to Danish—almost equally foreign to the islanders, whose native tongue was a form of Old Norse.

Henceforward the principal officials in the Faroe Islands were the *landfoged* (provincial bailiff) usually a Dane; the lagmand* (lawman) or chief judge, nearly always a Faroeman; and from 1591 the *sorenskriver* (judicial clerk and under-judge), usually also a Faroeman. Each of the six *sysler* (legal districts) had its *sysselmand* (district sheriff), always a Faroeman, usually a prosperous peasant.

The *landfoged* was taxgatherer, provincial treasurer, and public prosecutor, and represented the king's interests in the island in all other ways.

The seven priests were usually Danes, but occasionally Faroemen are also found. At their head was the provost, responsible to the bishop—until about 1620 the bishop of Bergen, thereafter the bishop of Sjaelland. Two institutions were under joint civil and ecclesiastical control: the Argir Leper Hospital and the Tórshavn Latin School, which was perhaps the successor of the Kirkjubóur bishopric school once attended by the Norwegian King Sverre, (*see* Sverrir Sigurdsson).

Each *syssel* had a spring court of first instance. Annually on St. Olaf's Day (29 July) the Lagting would assemble in Tórshavn. This assembly had the dual function of assize court and provincial parliament. The Lagting sent annual reports on the conduct of the Faroese Monopoly (which until 1709 was in the hands of a series of concessionaries) to the authorities in Copenhagen*.

The seventeenth century was a period of hardship and insecurity for the islands. Hostile attacks had occurred in the fifteenth and sixteenth centuries, and in 1580 Mogens Heinesen* built the first Tórshavn fort a little to the east of the town to command the sea approaches and defend the Monopoly warehouses. From 1630 this was supplemented by a second battery in Tórshavn itself. There was no hope of defending the country as a whole. The villagers thus constructed cunning refuges in the hills, to which they could escape in troubled times with their portable valuables.

Serious pirate raids took place in 1615 and 1616; and in 1629 Barbary corsairs made a descent on Hvalböur in Suðuroy and carried away 30 inhabitants to be sold as slaves. Foreign fishermen were also inclined at this period to remove sheep and cattle from outlying villages, and there was little the authorities could do about it.

The risk to the islands was greatest during the many wars Denmark fought during this century. From 1675 to 1679 Denmark and Holland were allied against Sweden and France in the Scanian War, and French naval forces hovered about the Faroes in the hope of capturing returning East Indiamen, as the Dutch made a habit of calling at the Faroes for news of the European political situation before sailing through potentially dangerous waters. In 1677 the French plundered Tórshavn and destroyed both forts.

At times the Faroes were granted as a fief, and the *landfoged* would then send the provincial income not to the king but to the concessionary, who in turn paid a fixed sum into the royal treasury. The convenience of this for the king was that he received a predictable sum in cash in place of the traditional rents and taxes rendered in kind—butter, tallow, wool, and knitted stockings. The rising Christoffer von Gabel was granted the fief in 1655, and, after he had helped to mastermind the transition of the Danish kingdom to absolute monarchy in 1660, was granted further Faroese privileges. In 1661 he was granted the Faroese revenues free of all payments for his lifetime and that of his son Frederik, and in 1662 he was granted the Monopoly on similar terms.

The Faroese regard the regime of Christoffer von Gabel as the blackest period of their history. He himself was grasping and had rapacious and sometimes corrupt subordinates. In 1672 Faroese affairs were subjected to an official investigation in Copenhagen. Frederik von Gabel was an easier master, a spendthrift who dispersed his father's ample fortune and who was less inclined to grasp every penny of his dues. He died in 1708, and the following year a commission came to the Faroe Islands to investigate the public revenue and to integrate the administration of the province with that of the kingdom as a whole.

The early part of the eighteenth century was stable and uneventful. From 1709 to 1723 the administration of the islands was tidied up, and after an unsuccessful attempt at farming out the Monopoly on the Icelandic pattern, the trade was placed in the hands of a Copenhagen merchant under close supervision of the Danish exchequer, the Rentekammer. In 1720 the *stiftamtmand* of Iceland, Admiral Peter Raben, was given authority over the Faroe Islands also, but he too was closely under Rentekammer control.

The Great Northern War* (1700–1721) did not directly affect the Faroe Islands, though it caused difficulties for the trade, especially since during the winter of 1716–1717 there was a disastrous mortality of sheep in the Faroes. However, the return of peacetime conditions and a revision in the trading tariffs brought prosperity once again, and from 1724 to 1776 there were only five years that did not show a profit.

From about 1760 there seems to have been a conscious effort in Copenhagen to promote economic development in the Faroes. In Denmark itself, a far-reaching reform of customs duties, on a protectionist pattern, was carried through from 1760 to 1762, and the government began to disburse great sums for the encouragement of industry.

There was a revived interest in Faroese minerals. In 1769 two Kongsberg miners were sent to investigate copper deposits in the islands, but these were found to be unprofitable. From 1778, coal-mining began in earnest in Suðuroy (there had been a brief attempt in 1733). This continued at considerable loss to the government until 1804.

The one successful enterprise of the many attempted at this period was the use of Tórshavn as a depot for British smugglers. This was the brainchild of Niels Ryberg, one of the most brilliant of the Copenhagen merchants of the golden age of Danish commerce. Ryberg began operations in 1766 after receiving a grant of privileges from the Danish government. Rybergs Handel, as it was known, flourished most during the American War of Independence (1775–1783), when British customs rates were high and British warships too busy to police the Scottish and Irish coasts or make any effective protest to Denmark. The depot closed in 1788, probably because of diplomatic pressure from Britain and reduced profitability.

From 1772, efforts were made to improve the methods of peasant farming* in the Faroe Islands, both by direct government action and through the work of Det kongelige Landhusholdningsselskab (the Royal Society for Agricultural Development). No lasting effect was produced on Faroese farming, but one result was the brilliant description of late eighteenth-century Faroese life produced by Jens Christian Svabo*.

Adam Smith's book *The Wealth of Nations* appeared in England in 1776 and was available in Danish by 1780. Danish government policy now moved toward free trade. The Iceland and Finmark trades were freed from 1787, and there was a move to free the Faroese trade also, especially as since 1777 it had been operating at a loss. But Faroese opinion feared that the controlled state monopoly might be succeeded by an uncontrolled private monopoly, and was thus against free trade. However, a new tariff was introduced in 1790, and from 1801 provision was made for annual tariff amendments following the trend of world prices for both exports and imports, making the Faroese more conscious of the course of world trade.

At the turn of the century, the Faroese were profoundly influenced by the career of the brilliant Poul Poulsen Nolsöe*, whose schooner was the first Faroese-owned seagoing vessel since the early Middle Ages. The growth of a native maritime tradition brought with it a desire for free trade in place of the centuries-old monopoly.

The outbreak of war between Denmark and Britain in 1807 brought hard times to the Faroes. The British naval blockade of Denmark brought a threat of starvation, as the islands, like Norway, were heavily dependent on imported Danish grain. Two hostile incursions were made on Tórshavn in 1808. The first was by a British naval brig which disarmed the fort. The second was by a privateer sailing under British letters of marque, owned by a certain Baron Charles von Hompesch. Hompesch removed all the public money and goods from the Monopoly warehouses, which he claimed as lawful prize. His claim was, however, rejected by the Admiralty Prize Court in London, and the value of the money and goods was sent back to Tórshavn.

The years 1808 to 1810 were ones of distress in Faroe, less than half the required grain imports arriving in the islands. Moreover, the 1808 Faroese barley harvest was a failure. Sir Joseph Banks and others secured an Order in Council, published 7 February 1810, giving inhabitants of the Danish North Atlantic dependencies neutral status and exempting vessels plying between the dependencies and Leith or London from seizure as prize.

By the Treaty of Kiel*, signed 14 January 1814, Denmark surrendered Norway to the Swedes, but retained the Faroes, Iceland, and Greenland*. About the same time, reforms were made in the administration of the islands. In 1816 the Lagting was abolished, together with the ancient office of *lagmand*, and a resident *amtmand* was appointed, with more autonomous powers than the *landfoged* had been able to wield.

The period from 1814 to 1830 was one of depression for the Danish kingdom, and there was little economic advancement or free trade agitation in Faroe during this time. A change began in the 1830s with the development of the boat fishery and a great increase in fish exports. At the same time landless fishermen were aided by an allotment movement encouraging the enclosure of uncultivated sheep-pasture to permit landless families to be self-sufficient in milk and potatoes.

Economic advance was aided by a series of three talented *amtmaend* who governed the Faroes from 1825 to 1848. The third of these, Christian Plöyen, made a journey through Shetland, Orkney, and Scotland in the summer of 1839, and his book, published the following year, stimulated Faroese interest in new tools and techniques.

In addition, from 1800 onwards, the population* began to rise rapidly. Before 1700 the Faroese population probably had never exceeded about 4,500. In 1801 it was 5,265, by 1850 it was 8,137, and by 1900 it had passed 15,000.

A Royal Commission sat in the winter of 1835–1836 with the object of improving the Monopoly and preparing the Faroese for free trade. As a result, Monopoly out-stations were set up in Tvöroyri (1836), Klaksvík (1838), and Vestmanna (1839).

By this time, constitutional reform was beginning in Denmark, with the establishment of the Provincial Assemblies in 1835. The Faroes were represented at Roskilde from 1836 to 1848 by crown nominees, all officials who had served in the islands. In the Danish Constituent Assembly of 1848–1849 the Faroes were represented by yet another crown nominee, Christian Plöyen, then freshly returned from eighteen years of government service in the islands. The Danish Constitution of 5 June 1849 gave the Faroes a seat in both the Folketing* and the Landsting.

Two of the earliest decisions of the new Danish parliament were to revive the Faroese Lagting and to abolish the Monopoly. The new Lagting, set up in 1852, was an advisory body to the *amtmand* and only slightly more powerful than an *amtsråd* (provincial council) in Denmark proper. Free trade came into force on 1 January 1856.

The first Faroese newspaper appeared at this time; written in Danish, it was called *Færingetidende* and was edited by Niels Winther (1822–1892). Nine issues appeared, from 13 May to 27 July 1852, but a heavy fine for an allegedly defamatory article caused Winther to cease publication, and the Faroes thereafter had no newspaper until 1877.

Fish exports, particularly of *klipfisk* (dried salted cod) were now rapidly increasing, while the traditional export of knitted woolens (now principally sweaters rather than stockings) was stagnant. Until 1872 the fishery was still exclusively from open boats, but then the first wooden smack was bought from England, and by 1900 there were 81 such vessels, forming the first Faroese fishing fleet. Farming now declined in importance as landless laborers took to the sea.

There was rapid educational advance. A few village schools were built even before free trade. From 1870, teacher training began in Tórshavn. A law of 1872 established local government, with each parish council (*kommuneråd*) responsible for primary education. By 1900 all but the smallest Faroese villages had schools. From 1893, Tórshavn possessed a school of navigation.

The nineteenth century was marked not only by economic advance, but also by a growing interest in the Faroese language and its oral literature. The pioneer Jens Christian Svabo had been at work as early as 1771 and during the 1780s made a collection of 52 traditional poems, mostly heroic ballads. During the 1800s many others followed, and the Faroese ballad became a key factor in the upsurge of national consciousness.

Venceslaus Ulricus Hammershaimb* (1819–1909) provided Faroese with the orthography now used. Faroese nationalism may be said to date from 1888. Its first expression was cultural. The first Faroese-language newspaper, *Föringatíðindi*, appeared from 1890 until 1901, and a modern Faroese literature took root—first poetry, later prose.

The national movement spilled over into politics from 1903, when the young peasant-patriot and romantic poet Jóannes Patursson* (1866–1946), who had gained the Faroese Folketing seat in the Venstre landslide of 1901, published a program for greater self-government for the Faroe Islands. Patursson's opponents feared the economic price, combined to defeat him in the 1906 elections, and then constituted themselves into the Sambandsflokkurin, or Unionist Party. His allies countered by forming the Sjálvstýrisflokkurin, or Home Rule Party.

The Unionists were the dominant Faroese party until 1938, with a policy of frugality, economic reform, and preservation of full political union with Denmark. Many of them wanted to see the development of Faroese literature, yet favored the retention of Danish as the official language for use in church, school, law courts, and administration. The Home Rulers wanted to introduce the vernacular into every possible field. The battle was fiercest in education, where the letter of the law forbade teachers to use the mother tongue of their pupils except as an aid to understanding Danish, the official medium of instruction.

The issue was ultimately settled by the growth of Faroese literature. There was a determined effort to produce Faroese schoolbooks; the provost Jacob Dahl (1878–1944) began translating the prayer book and the Bible, and Faroese journalism became the rule rather than the exception. The work of the novelist Heðin Brú (born 1901) finally showed the heights that Faroese prose could attain.

Politically, the turning point was the rise to influence of the Javnaðarflokkurin, or Social Democratic Party, which in the 1936 Lagting elections made great gains at the expense of the Unionists. The Social Democrats sided with the Unionists on the constitutional issue but favored the use of Faroese for all public purposes. Just before the outbreak of World War II*, Faroese had for all practical purposes attained an equal status with Danish.

German forces occupied Denmark in the early morning of Tuesday, 9 April 1940. By the following Saturday, the Faroes were firmly in British hands, and the large, safe harbor of Skálafjörður was used throughout the war as a naval base. In 1944 the British completed an airfield on Vágar, though by that time the Battle of the Atlantic had been won and it was of little use.

The war years were financially prosperous for the Faroese, who used their fishing vessels to ferry fish from Iceland to Britain. The cost was heavy. Twenty-five ships and 132 fishermen were lost, the latter representing 0.5 percent of the total population, a loss comparable to that of any of the Western allied nations. The sterling balances of the war years were an important factor in the postwar modernization of the fishing fleet.

After the liberation of Denmark, the issue of the constitutional link with Faroe came up again. The ability to survive unaided had been demonstrated during the war, so it was impossible to return to the position where Faroe had merely been Denmark's most northerly *amt*. The Danish government proposed a modest degree of home rule. Many in Faroe now favored outright secession. The matter was put to a referendum on 14 September 1946.

It was an ill-designed referendum, offering only two extremes, mild home rule or secession. The poll was low, because many fishermen were still at sea, and extreme unionists abstained. Many who favored an intermediate solution marked their ballots improperly, rendering them unacceptable. Voting was as follows:

For the government home-rule proposal	5,499	(47.2%)
For secession	5,660	(48.7%)
Disqualified ballots	481	(4.1%)

    Total poll 66.4%

This result could be interpreted by every faction as a narrow victory. After a few days' uncertainty, the king, on the advice of the Danish government, dissolved the Lagting and ordered fresh elections. The secessionists were now convincingly defeated. In March 1947 the Lagting voted unanimously in favor of a request to the Danish government to grant legislative power to the Lagting, but on the basis of the Faroes remaining within the Danish kingdom.

The final outcome was the Home Rule Ordinance of 23 March 1948, defining the Faroe Islands as "within the framework of the law, a self-governing community within the Danish kingdom." Internal administration passed to the Lagting, while defense and foreign affairs stayed in the hands of Denmark. The Ordinance contains two schedules: List A of unequivocally local issues, and List B of issues with a local and a joint aspect. List A responsibility may be transferred to the Faroese as soon as either the Lagting or the Danish government requires it. Responsibility for List B affairs may be transferred after consultation.

Since Home Rule, the Faroe Islands have settled down to a political life partly linked to, partly independent of, that of Denmark. Two members represent the islands in the Danish Folketing. There is no longer an *amtmand* in Tórshavn, but there is a *rigsombudsmand* (state commissioner) in charge of Danish government responsibilities within the islands. The Faroese have their own flag, passports designating them as Faroese citizens, and the unfettered use of Faroese for public purposes. Faroese banknotes circulate in the islands, issued against an equivalent number of Danish notes in a Faroese government account in the Bank of Denmark. In 1976 the Faroese took over the postal services and now issue their own postage stamps. The islands have been governed by a succession of stable coalition administrations.

The fishery has prospered, despite a severe crisis in the early 1950s because wartime earnings had often been unwisely invested in old and sometimes worn-out trawlers bought from Britain and Iceland. From 1950 the Korean War forced up operating costs and caused many bankruptcies, and one of the banks in the islands had a severe upset.

However, since 1955 the fishing fleet has been reconstructed and renewed with the help of a mortgage finance corporation, the working capital of which was originally Marshall Aid of 10 million kroner. The outcome has been the development of a fishing fleet as advanced as any in the North Atlantic.

When Denmark joined the EEC on 1 January 1973, the Faroes were specifically excluded. The dependence of the islands on the fishing industry made it impossible to adhere to the common policy on fishing limits. The Faroese have, however, made various trading agreements with EEC, permitting duty-free export of fish products to the EEC countries.

By virtue of defense affairs being in Danish government hands, the Faroe Islands are part of NATO. There is a small naval presence in the islands and a Danish radar station on the mountains above Tórshavn. Faroe Islanders are not liable to conscription for Danish military service, though a number of them serve in the Danish navy.

REFERENCES: N. Annandale, *The Faroes and Iceland* (Oxford: Clarendon, 1905); Dansk-Faerosk Samfund, *Færöerne I-II* (Copenhagen: Dansk-Færösk Samfund, 1958); L. Debes, *A Description of the Islands and Inhabitants of Feroe*, trans. J. Sterpin (London: William Iles, 1676); G. Landt, *A Description of the Feroe Islands* (London: Longman et al., 1810); J. Nicoll, *An Historical and Descriptive Account of Iceland, Greenland and the Faroe Islands* (Edinburgh: Oliver & Boyd, 1841); C. Plöyen, *Reminiscences of a Voyage to Shetland, Orkney and Scotland in the Summer of 1839*, trans. C. Spence (Lerwick: T. & J. Manson, 1894); A. Somme, ed., *The Geography of Norden* (London: Heinemann, 1961); E. Thomsen, ed., *Faroe Isles Review*, 5 issues (Tórshavn: Bóka-garður, 1976–1978); J. P. Trap, *Danmark*, 5th ed., vol. 13; Færöerne (Copenhagen: G.E.C. Gads Forlag, 1968); J. F. West, "Communal Land Tenure and Land Utilisation in the Faroe Islands," *Tijdschrift voor economische en sociale geografie* 66: 6 (1975): 337–48, and *Faroe, the Emergence of a Nation* (London: C. Hurst; New York: Paul S. Eriksson, 1972); K. Williamson, *The Atlantic Islands* (London: Collins, 1948; 2nd ed. London: Routledge & Kegan Paul, 1970).

J. F. WEST

FAROESE (Language) *See* Languages: Scandinavian

F-BOAT Swedish battleship *Sverige*

The F-boat was a small Swedish battleship of about 7,000 tons' displacement with heavy armor plating and armaments; it was built with voluntary nationwide donations and presented to the government in 1912. Its construction, approved by a Conservative ministry in 1911, was postponed by a Liberal ministry the same year, creating an intense national debate. The navy and the Conservatives claimed it could meet a Russian invasion fleet on the open sea while still being able to maneuver in coastal waters. The parties of the Left thought it too expensive (14 million crowns) and that it suggested a resurgent imperialism. It was christened *Sverige* ("Sweden").

REFERENCES: B. Steckzen, ed., *Klart skepp. En bok om Sverigeskeppen* (Stockholm, 1940); P. V. Thorson, "Free Enterprise Defense in Sweden: The Pansar Boat Collection of 1912," *North Dakota Quarterly* 36:1 (1968): 42–49.

P. V. THORSON

FERSEN, COUNT HANS AXEL VON (4 September 1755–20 June 1810) Swedish army officer and diplomat

Fersen was born in Stockholm*, the son of Count Frederik Axel von Fersen, leader of the Hat Party* during the later Age of Liberty*. From 1770 to 1774 he made a grand tour of Europe and thereafter served at the court of Gustav III* until 1778, when he returned to France. To gain military experience, Fersen volunteered for the French army in the War of American Independence. He served in America from 1780 to 1783 as an aide to General Rochambeau.

Returning to France, he became proprietary colonel of the Royal-Suédois Regiment, while retaining his Swedish appointments. In 1788 he served in Finland as an adjutant to Gustav III in the latter's attack on Russia. In the constitutional crisis this war created in Sweden-Finland, Fersen initially sympathized with the aristocratic opposition to Gustav III's growing autocracy, but his ideas were quickly changed by witnessing the outbreak of the revolution in France in 1789. He would ever after remain a staunch upholder of strong monarchy.

Following his return from America, Fersen became involved in a romantic relationship with Queen Marie Antoinette, the exact nature and extent of which has eluded inquiry, despite the inordinate attention it has attracted. Fersen was in any event devoted to the French royal family and organized its escape from Paris in the ill-fated flight to Varennes in June 1791. Thereafter under condemnation in France, he was the key figure in Gustav III's efforts to organize a counter-revolutionary crusade against France in 1791–1792, then in various schemes to rescue the French royal family, up to Marie Antoinette's execution in October 1793. He served in 1797 as Swedish envoy to the Congress of Rastadt, at which he had a personal encounter with General Bonaparte.

Returning permanently to Sweden in 1799, Fersen was appointed chancellor of Uppsala University, charged with suppressing student "Jacobinism." In 1801 he was made *riksmarskalk*, or grand marshal of the royal household. During the War of the Third Coalition, he accompanied Gustav IV Adolf* to Germany in 1806 as an advisor on foreign affairs, but after attempting to restrain the king's rash actions he returned to Sweden in ill-concealed disgrace.

Fersen had no part in the revolution of March 1809 which deposed Gustav IV Adolf. When the newly elected successor to the Swedish throne, Christian August* of Augustenburg, suddenly died in May 1810, Fersen was unjustly suspected of having poisoned him. While officiating as grand marshal in Christian August's funeral cortège in Stockholm on 20 June 1810, Fersen was set upon by an infuriated mob and assassinated. The riot was clearly incited by his political enemies, although many details remain obscure.

REFERENCES: H. A. Barton, *Count Hans Axel von Fersen* (Boston: Twayne, 1975); R. M. Klinckowström, ed., *Le comte de Fersen et la cour de France*, 2 vols. (Paris: Firmin-Didot, 1877–1878); A. Söderhjelm, ed., *Axel von Fersens dagbok*, 4 vols. (Stockholm: Bonnier, 1926–1936), and *Fersen et Marie-Antoinette* (Paris: Kra, 1930).

H. A. BARTON

FIBIGER, MATHILDE LUCIE (31 December 1830–14 June 1872) Danish feminist author

One of nine children of Major (later Lieutenant-Colonel) Johan Adolf Fibiger (1791–1851) and Margrethe Cecilia Nielsen Aasen (1794–1844), Mathilde was born in Copenhagen* into a family with strong literary proclivities. Following her parents' divorce in 1843, she and most of the other children lived with their mother. Upon the latter's death the following year, Mathilde moved back with her father, who remarried in 1845. Unhappy with her new stepmother, Mathilde took private instruction in order to become a teacher, and in October 1849 she took a position as governess in Lolland.

Here she wrote her first novel, *Clara Raphael: Tolv Breve (Clara Raphael: Twelve Letters)*, the first significant feminist literary work by a Danish woman. Written in the form of letters from Clara, a young governess, the novel decried the fact that women were shut out from intellectual activity and asserted their right to develop and realize themselves in freedom. It criticized the way females were brought up and educated but made no concrete proposals for change. Clara did not seek equal political or occupational rights for women. She believed that God had separate plans for men and women and that women should represent the ideal and inspire men to rise above material concerns. Resolving to devote her life to the cause of women's emancipation, Clara renounced sexual love but soon agreed to marry and live platonically with her aristocratic suitor.

Published shortly before Christmas in 1850 (with a foreword by J. L. Heiberg, then Denmark's leading literary critic), the novel immediately provoked a barrage of letters and comments in newspapers and journals arguing for or against its ideas and debating sex roles in general. The "Clara Raphael Controversy," as it was called, raged on until early summer 1851. Notable opponents included author Meir Aron Goldschmidt (1819–1897) and radical Socialist Frederik Dreier. More sympathetic comments came from feminist author Pauline Worm* and a young woman, Lodovica de Bretteville ("Sybilla"), who defended women's rights in an exchange with Goldschmidt. N.F.S. Grundtvig (1783–1872) was supportive but took exception to Clara's renunciation of real marriage. Mathilde herself joined in the debate with a small pamphlet written under the pseudonym Sophie A., *Hvad er Emancipation? (What Is Emancipation?)*.

Young and inexperienced, she was hurt by all the unfavorable comment, but not daunted. Her next three novels, *Et Besøg* (*A Visit*, 1851), *En Skizze efter det virkelige Liv* (*A Sketch from Real Life*, 1853), and *Minona* (1854), continued to plead the feminist cause but met with little success. She then worked at a succession of jobs, including teaching and sewing, and in the 1860s became Denmark's first female telegrapher. From 1870 on she worked in Århus, where she became manager of the telegraph office. She lived to see the *Dansk Kvindesamfund* (Danish Women's Society*) organized in 1871 and became a member, but was unable to participate in its activities. She died of a pulmonary infection in 1872.

The Clara Raphael Controversy brought on a stream of ''governess'' novels (so called because the authors and heroines tended to be governesses), which dealt with women's lives and problems and usually took a critical view of women's place in society. Thus Fibiger and her successors ''put problems under debate'' long before Georg Brandes issued his famous call to writers to do so. But Fibiger was ahead of her time. Only after an organized women's movement formed did she begin to be recognized as a courageous pioneer.

REFERENCES: F. Bajer, *Klara-Rafael-Fejden* (Copenhagen: Topps, 1879); M. Fibiger, *Clara Raphael: Tolv Breve* (Lindhardt og Ringhof, 1976); O. Friis, and U. Andreasen, *Dansk Litteratur Historie* (Copenhagen: Politikens, 1976), III, pp. 432–38; A. B. Repsdorph, ''Mathilde Fibiger,'' *Kritik*, No. 22 (1972): 5–14; E. B. Steen, ''Tre skandinaviske pionerer i kampen for kvinnens frigjøring,'' *Edda* 14 (1945): 184–203; J. Steenstrup, *Den danske kvindes historie* (Copenhagen: Hagerups, 1917), III, pp. 92–104; F. Thomsen, ''Mathilde Fibiger,'' *American-Scandinavian Review* 10 (1922): 487–91.

N. FARQUHAR

FINLANDIZATION Foreign policy term

Finlandization and the Paasikivi-Kekkonen Line*, the two terms most often used to describe post-World War II Finnish foreign policy, reflect different schools of thought on the nature and significance of Finland's relationship with the Soviet Union. These two interpretative frameworks are not mutually exclusive, since questions raised in one often spill over into the other. There are, however, three fundamental differences in the assumptions which underpin the logic of these opposing views of Finnish foreign policy.

Finlandization means ''that process or state of affairs in which, under the cloak of maintaining friendly relations with the Soviet Union, the sovereignty of a country becomes reduced'' (W. Laqueur, p. 37. *See* references). The primary focus of concern is thus not Finland, but the possible decline of the West vis-a-vis the Soviet Union within the context of detente. The Paasikivi-Kekkonen Line interpretation, in contrast, emphasizes the benefits Finland has derived from maintaining friendly relations with the Soviet Union and the importance of detente to remaining a neutral country. Given these two different points of departure, the literature in English on Finland's postwar foreign policy, especially on the Kekkonen era, is often value-laden, based on assumptions and involved in political and academic debates about which the uninitiated reader of Finnish history is often unaware.

These two schools also view Soviet foreign policy objectives differently. Adherents of the Finlandization school assume that Soviet foreign policy is motivated by an ideological drive to expand and dominate, which is only held in check by a strong Western alliance. Finland's position is thus dependent upon the Nordic balance—which in turn is backed by NATO—and/or on unexplicable Soviet tactics of deception. The Paasikivi-Kekkonen Line interpretation acknowledges that Finland had no choice in 1944 but to develop a policy of cooperation with the Soviet Union. This policy was based, however, on the assumption (or hope) that Soviet interest in Finland was prompted by defensive strategic considerations. The Paasikivi-Kekkonen Line school bases its interpretation on the record of postwar Soviet-Finnish relations. The Finlandization interpretation implies, however, that Soviet efforts to build and maintain the Yalta system along its western border have been prompted by aggressive objectives.

Reference to Finlandization dates back to the political debate in Austria in the 1950s over whether a policy of cooperation with the Soviet Union would enhance or undermine Austrian neutrality. In the 1960s the metaphor was revived in a more generalized debate over Willi Brandt's Ostpolitik and later within the context of developments leading up to the Conference on European Security and Cooperation in Helsinki in 1975. It is quite logical, given the assumptions sketched out above, that the specter of Finlandization should appear on the horizon at just this juncture in European politics, when the Yalta system, which has been considered in the West to be a symbol of Soviet aggressive intent, was ratified. Expressing the fears of those in the West who believed that the Soviet Union had not changed its goals, but only its tactics, Finlandization became a metaphor—a symbolic warning of what was in store for Western Europe if it pursued a policy of cooperation with the Soviet Union.

Finlandization literature is full of examples of how Finland is run by remote control and continues to legitimize Soviet interference in its domestic and foreign affairs. According to this interpretation the Treaty of Friendship, Cooperation, and Mutual Assistance* with the Soviet Union not only prevents Finland from being neutral, but it also undermines Finnish ability and will to defend its own interests. The Soviet veto in the late 1950s and early 1960s of certain political groups and individuals which it considered to be anti-Soviet led to the period of the "Night Frost" and the "Note Crisis" during which the Soviet Union and President Urho Kekkonen* overstepped the lines of legitimacy dictated by geopolitical proximity. There have been no crises in Soviet-Finnish relations since the early 1960s, but Finland's policy of keeping a low profile on international issues related to Soviet security or prestige, plus its advocacy of causes which would also benefit the Soviet Union, for example, a Nordic nuclear-free zone, are considered proof of a decline in Finnish independence, especially when coupled with the Finnish practice of self-censorship. In short, the Soviet Union is encroaching on Finnish independence. This interpretation differs from that of the Paasikivi-Kekkonen Line, which recognizes the existence of these problems but sees them as (1) part of the growing pains associated with the postwar strengthening of Finnish independence and neutrality, or as (2) issues which have deep roots in Finnish society and are thus primarily the outgrowth of domestic Finnish politics rather than of Soviet-Finnish relations.

REFERENCES: G. Kennan, "Europe's Problems, Europe's Choices," *Foreign Policy* 14 (1974); H. P. Krosby, "Finland and Detente: Self-Interest Politics and Western Reactions," *Yearbook of Finnish Foreign Policy* (Helsinki: Finnish Institute of International Affairs, 1980), and "Scandinavia and 'Finlandization,' " *Scandinavian Review* 63 (1975); W. Laqueur, "Europe: The Specter of Finlandization," *Commentary*(December 1977): 37–41; G. Maude, "The Further Shores of Finlandization," *Cooperation and Conflict* 1 (1982); C. L. Sulzberger, "Finlandization Takes Strength," *International Herald Tribune*, 19 November 1981; J. Vloyantes, *Silk Glove Hegemony: Finnish-Soviet Relations 1944–1974* (Kent: Kent State University Press, 1975); K. Wahlbäck, "Finnish Foreign Policy: Some Comparative Perspectives," *Cooperation and Conflict* 4 (1969).

R. M. BERRY

FINNISH (Language) *See* Languages: Scandinavian

FINNISH CONFEDERATION OF TRADE UNIONS *See* Swedish Confederation of Trade Unions

FINNISH EMPLOYERS' FEDERATION *See* Swedish Employers' Federation

FISHING INDUSTRY Faroese

The Faroe Islanders have conducted an open-boat fishery from the first settlement of the islands, and the autumn and spring fishing formed an important part of the subsistence economy of the Faroese peasantry (*see* Peasant Farming). When catches were plentiful, fish were exported through the Faroese Monopoly, but only from the 1830s did exports become significant. There were several reasons for this rise. One was the increasing population of the islands, driving landless men to seek a living from the sea. Another was the more intensive cultivation of the land, especially around Tórshavn*, where allotments were made available to landless open-boat fishermen, enabling them to provide their families with potatoes and milk to stabilize their economy. A third factor was the enlightened policy of the Royal Faroese Monopoly in its last decades, in particular its retention from 1844 of an Icelandic fish-curer who introduced to the islands the expert manufacture of *klipfisk* (dried salted cod).

During the years following the abolition of the Monopoly, the Faroese fishery made further rapid advances. The spread of the Industrial Revolution through Europe created a long-term tendency for the price of fish to rise. During the decade 1841–1850, fish products constituted 39 percent of the total export compared with 61 percent land products (mostly knitted woolens). In the period 1895–1899, although the volume of land products exported was only slightly lower than it had been at mid-century, these now formed only 6.3 percent of the total export, compared with 93.7 percent for fish and other sea products.

Until 1872 fishing was carried on exclusively from open boats in the seas immediately surrounding the islands. But from 1840, the Faroese began using the long-line, with hundreds of baited hooks, instead of the hand-line, with only one or two hooks per man.

In 1872 three brothers from Tórshavn bought a wooden fishing smack in Scarborough and started fishing trips to Iceland each summer. The success of this method was rapid. By 1877 there were 12 wooden smacks operating, and by 1900 no fewer than 81. Expansion of the sloop fishery, as the Faroese call it, was particularly rapid from 1891 onwards, partly because the British fishing fleet was turning over to steam trawling, and many serviceable wooden smacks could be bought at very low prices. By 1910 there were 137 smacks in service, employing nearly 2,000 men on the Iceland summer fishery out of a total population of 18,000. Exports of *klipfisk* were about 1,500 tons a year in 1872, 3,500 tons a year in 1900, and over 10,000 tons annually from 1930. The chief markets for Faroese fish were the Roman Catholic countries of the Mediterranean, in particular Spain.

The installation of engine power in Faroese smacks began in 1904, but most vessels still relied primarily on the sail until the end of the 1920s, when it was realized that powered vessels were more efficient in exploiting the more distant fishing grounds, in particular those off West Greenland. The Greenland fishery began in 1925. In 1927 the Faroemen obtained the use of a harbor in an uninhabited fjord where they could refit, take on water, and work up their salt fish. Færingehavn, as this harbor was called, was developed from 1933 onward as an international fishing port with oil and salt depots, warehouses, repair facilities, a small hospital, and a seamen's home.

The first trawler owned in the Faroe Islands* was bought in 1911, but Faroe possessed no considerable trawler fleet until 1938, when 10 were at work from the islands.

In 1909 a shipowners' association was formed in the islands, and as a countermove a fishermen's union, Föroya Fiskimannafelag, came into being in 1911. Since that time, collective bargaining, on the pattern found in industrialized countries, has been the rule. Fishermen's wages are normally calculated in terms of a percentage of the catch.

World War II* had a profound effect on the Faroese fishing fleet. The Icelandic fishermen refused to sail to Britain with the much-needed cargoes of fresh fish unless an air escort was provided, and there were insufficient aircraft and pilots for this. The Faroese smacks and schooners then undertook the task of ferrying fish from Iceland to Aberdeen and other Scottish ports, while the trawler fleet continued fishing on the usual grounds. Excellent prices were paid for the landings, and the Faroese built up large sterling balances. But losses of ships and men were heavy. Four of the 10 trawlers were lost, as well as 21 of the wooden craft. One hundred thirty-two fishermen were killed by enemy action, nearly 0.5 percent of the total population, a loss on the same order as that suffered by any of the Western allies.

Immediately after the war there was great enthusiasm for the build-up of a modern fishing fleet from the healthy sterling balances provided by the dangerous wartime work. Many vessels, often old and worn-out steam trawlers, were purchased, often without proper inspection, from Britain and Iceland. By 1948 the Faroe Islands had the largest trawler fleet in Scandinavia*—no fewer than 37 vessels. After two or three years of prosperity, however, the terms of trade turned sharply against the Faroese fishing industry. In particular, the outbreak of the Korean War in July 1950 forced up operating costs for all shipping firms. Heavy losses were suffered by the industry during 1950 and 1951. Many trawlers were laid up, and the weaker businesses went bankrupt. Their failure led in turn to a prolonged crisis for the Fisheries Industries Bank (Sjóvinnubankin) during 1951 and 1952.

Reconstruction of the Faroese fishing fleet was a complex task. An official report, based on the study of ships' balance sheets, published in 1953, indicated which types of vessel were the most profitable for the Faroese to operate. An agency was founded called Faeroernes Realkreditinstitut, the Faroe Islands Mortgage Finance Corporation, which granted loans of up to 50 percent of the appraised value of fishing vessels of approved types, repayment being made over a term of ten or fifteen years. The original capital for the corporation was Marshall Aid of 10 million kroner, to which the Danish National Bank added an interest-free loan of 2 million kroner. The re-equipment of the fleet took place chiefly from 1956 to 1964. An important place in the fleet was taken by steel-built, long-line vessels of about 300 tons' displacement.

The Faroese fishing fleet is today probably the most modern and efficient operating in the Atlantic. The annual catch is in the region of 300,000 tons. The fishing grounds are many and varied. Herring is sought in the North Sea and off the Faroes; cod is fished off Newfoundland, Greenland, Jan Mayen, and in the Barents Sea; and a very profitable prawn fishery has been developed off Greenland. With the extension in 1977 of fishery limits to 200 miles by nearly all countries, and with the ability to patrol such extensive areas with helicopters and fishery protection gunships, there has been a tendency for the Faroese to develop their home fishery at the expense of the distant-water fishery, the catch being processed into high-quality fillets and fish fingers for the American and European markets. In 1979, 37 percent of the Faroese catch was made in the Faroese economic zone. The high standard of living of the Faroese at the present day is totally dependent on the work of their fishing fleet.

REFERENCES: E. Thomsen, ed., *Faroe Isles Review*, 5 issues (Tórshavn: Bokagarður, 1976–1978); J. F. West, *Faroe, the Emergence of a Nation* (London: C. Hurst, and New York: P. S. Eriksson, 1972).

J. F. WEST

FOLK COSTUMES (*Folkdrakter*)

Locally based folk costumes are found in most areas of Scandinavia*. Garments in these costumes include belts, trousers, shoes, silver decorations, aprons, topcoats, bibs, hats, scarves, head coverings, bodices, purses, caps, shirts, shawls, bowknots, skirts, stockings, stocking bands, jackets, vests, and some outer cloths.

Area traditions determined what jewelry was appropriate and its positioning. Detail often differentiated between married and unmarried women. Custom required that women in costume always wear the appropriate head covering. Guidelines for bodices and skirts were established. Word of mouth also made known recommended costume material types and methods of construction. Contemporary knowledge of these costumes is based upon oral tradition, written records, pictures, photographs, and surviving examples of the garments.

Estimates suggest that a couple hundred costumes (*bunader*) exist in Norway alone. Each costume is associated with one region, which might encompass a district, a parish (a few districts), or a few parishes. A single town was often too small to be a dress region (*draktområde*), and counties were generally too large.

REFERENCES: I. Arnö-Berg, *Folkdräkter och bygdedräkter från hela Sverige* (Västerås: ICA-Förlaget, 1975); Norsk Folkemuseum og Landsnemnda for bunadsspørsmål, *Folkedrakter og bunader bibliografi* (Oslo, 1978–1980); A. Notini, *Dräktfolket: Möte med tradition* (Stockholm: Atlantis, 1980); K. Skavhaug, ed., *Våre vakre bunader* (Oslo: Hjemmes, 1978); Y. Woxholth, ed., *Våre vakre bunader* (Oslo: Hjemmes, 1969).

B. NORDSTROM

FOLKETING Denmark's national legislature

Precursors of the present Danish parliament, the Folketing, existed as far back as Viking times (*see* Viking Age) when provincial leaders met in regional assemblies, *landsting*, and also in district assemblies, *herredsting*, to pay homage to the gods, recite laws, and adjudicate disputes. These ancient assemblies came to be overshadowed politically by kings, and for centuries thereafter the monarch was at the center of Denmark's constitutional development*.

When the nobility contended with the king in defense of their privileges and sometimes in attempts to control succession, they used deliberative bodies to further their aims. The Danehof, a council of nobles the king was compelled by oath to consult, was established in 1282. It was succeeded by a narrower council of nobles, a Council of the Realm (Rigsråd), in the late fourteenth century. Existing concurrently with the king and council was an Assembly of Estates (Staendermøderne) comprising nobles, clergy, burghers, and (when invited) free peasants, but it was convened only at the king's pleasure. The king used the estates to squash the Rigsråd in 1660, after which he dispensed with both.

Representative bodies were restored to Denmark in the 1830s, when King Frederik VI* granted his subjects four assemblies, one each for Slesvig, Holstein, Jutland, and the Islands. They were followed by the establishment in 1849 of a true parliament, the Rigsdag. It was made up of a lower chamber, the Folketing, whose 114 members were popularly elected by adult males over 30, and an upper chamber, the Landsting, whose 38 members were indirectly chosen by electoral colleges.

The role of the Folketing as a basically democratic institution was clear from the outset, but the Landsting's role was not. Some wished it to be a conservative bulwark. The Landsting's conservative cast was strengthened in 1866, when 12 of its members were made appointees of the crown and the remaining 54 were made elective, one-half by all voters and one-half by that part of them with incomes of 1,000 to 2,000 *rigsdalers* annually.

The Landsting thus remained staunchly conservative while the people returned ever larger liberal majorities to the Folketing. The two chambers often failed to agree, in which cases the king resorted to ruling by decree with conservative cabinets of his own choosing. After the election of 1901, in which the conservatives virtually disappeared from the lower chamber, the king consented to appoint a government acceptable to the liberal majority in the Folketing. From that time on the Folketing became the linchpin of parliamentarism in Denmark.

At the urging of Folketing leaders, changes were enacted in 1915 instituting proportional representation for Folketing elections and extending the franchise to all women as well as men at age 25. They made the Landsting more moderate by making its members elective by all voters over 35 and by making its remaining members the choice of its outgoing members rather than of the king.

The parties of the Left—Social Democratic (Socialdemokratiet), Radical Left (Radikale Venstre), and Liberal (Venstre)—dominated the Folketing for most of the twentieth century. The first Social Democratic government was appointed in 1924. Social Democrats found themselves increasingly at odds with the more conservative Landsting, and they proposed its abolition. An effort to change the constitution accordingly barely failed in 1939, but eventually succeeded after World War II*. The new Constitution of 1953 abolished the Landsting and also the name Rigsdag and retained the Folketing as the single national legislature.

The Folketing since 1953 has consisted of 179 members, including 2 from the Faroe Islands* and 2 from Greenland*. The 175 members from Denmark proper are directly elected under a proportional representation system; 135 are elected from 23 large constituencies, and 40 are elected as if from one national constituency. Members are not required to reside in the districts they represent. However, they are required for election purposes to be identified with a political party. Following the parliamentary principle, a party or combination of parties winning a majority of Folketing seats determines the complexion of the government. Folketing elections are held every four years or more frequently if the king, or in actuality the government acting through the king, dissolves the Folketing before its regular term expires and calls a new election.

The Folketing selects its own speaker, the Formand, and other officers. It is governed by its own rules, *Forretningsordenen for Folketinget*, which prescribes its procedures and committee structure.

REFERENCES: Frank Hernov, *Folketinget* (Copenhagen: Idag, 1964); Bengt Ryind, ed., *Denmark: An Official Handbook* (Copenhagen: Danish Press Information Service,

1974); J. B. Schmidt, *Fra Danehof til Folketing* (Copenhagen: Schultz, 1961); Harald Westergård, *Dansk politik i går og idag* Copenhagen: Fremad, 1974).

B. L. HANSON

FORINGAFELAG Faroese nationalist organization (1889–1900)

Although Venceslaus Ulricus Hammershaimb* had published his Faroes orthography in 1854, Faroese remained merely a vernacular until the 1870s, when Faroese students, many fired by Icelandic attainment of home rule in 1874, began to write Faroese patriotic and drinking songs. In 1881 the social gatherings of Faroese students led to the foundation of a society dedicated to the advancement of Faroese culture among Faroemen resident in Denmark.

This example was later taken up in the Faroe Islands*. Economic advance since the abolition of the Faroese Monopoly* in 1856 brought with it a weakening of the traditional culture and the old peasant community. A group of Faroemen concerned for the building of a new national culture called a meeting in the parliament building in Tórshavn* for 26 December 1888. The meeting resolved that (1) in religious teaching all rote learning in Danish should be abolished and the material given in Faroese; (2) as soon as the necessary school books were available, Faroese should become a special school subject; (3) in history teaching emphasis should be placed on Faroese history; (4) priests should have the right to use Faroese inside and outside the church; (5) Faroese should have full recognition as a medium between the people and the authorities; and (6) steps should be taken for the foundation of a Faroese folk high school. Finally, it was resolved that a society should be founded for the preservation of the Faroese language.

Föringafelag was officially founded on 27 January 1889. The objectives of the organization were (1) to bring the Faroese language into honor and (2) to work for the unity, progress, and self-sufficiency of the Faroese people. The two outstanding leaders of the society were Rasmus Effersöe (1857–1916), agricultural consultant, journalist, and poet, and the young Jóannes Patursson*, whose poem advocating struggle to preserve the mother tongue, recited at the 26 December meeting, roused those present to a high pitch of emotion. Rasmus Effersöe was a very sensitive man, much more moderate in his aims than Patursson, and less concerned with politics than culture. He had a tremendous sense of humor and also strove constantly to make the work of the Faroemen less arduous and more productive.

The most important work of the society was the issue of a newspaper, *Föringatiðinði*, written exclusively in Faroese. It appeared from 1890 to 1901, and it is no exaggeration to say that it taught the Faroese nation to read and write its own language. This was more than merely learning an orthography. Faroese authors and journalists had to devise new words for the purposes of literature, scholarship, and modern life. Faroese is rich and vivid for the tangible, such as for describing the work of field or fjord, but was then poor in words for expressing abstract conceptions.

Another important achievement of the society was the establishment of a folk high school, aimed, like the corresponding schools in Denmark, at giving the peasantry a liberal education and making them aware of the cultural inheritance now passing into their protection. It had the good luck to have two gifted and inspiring teachers, Símun av Skarði (1872–1942) and Rasmus Rasmussen (1871–1962). For many years this was the only school in the islands in which the Faroese language was either a subject or a medium of instruction. The school was founded in 1899 and is still in existence.

A dispute about orthography finally broke up Föringafelag. In the 1890s Jakob Jakobsen* proposed changes to Hammershaimb's system to bring it closer to Faroese pronunciation, particularly that of south Streymoy, which was tending to become the Faroese standard. This led to bitter disputes within the society, and when in addition temperamental differences led to quarrels between Effersöe and Patursson, the society ceased to function; the newspaper survived it by only a year. However, the work of shaping a modern literary language was now already well advanced, and Faroese was saved from the fate of the Nonn languages of Orkney and Shetland.

REFERENCES: Heðin Brú, Introduction to *The Old Man and His Sons* (New York: Paul S. Eriksson, 1970); John F. West, *Faroe, the Emergence of a Nation* (London: C. Hurst; New York: Paul S. Eriksson, 1972).

J. F. WEST

FREDERIK I (7 October 1471–10 April 1533) King of Denmark and Norway 1523–1533

Frederik was the younger son of the Danish king Christian I* and Dorothea of Brandenburg. He was the brother of Hans I*, king of Denmark and Norway (1483–1512), and the uncle of Christian II*. When his father died, Frederik became duke of Slesvig and Holstein, although he actually shared rule in the duchies with his brother and later with his nephew, in a very curious arrangement. He lived for most of his life in Gottorp, where he preferred to be even after he became king in Denmark.

When the revolt against Christian II erupted in Denmark in 1522, Frederik was the logical candidate to replace the tyrant. The Jutland council members were the first to elect him in early 1523. It was over a year, however, before all of the realm had come to his support, and he had to face continued resistance, especially from Skåne and Copenhagen*, until 1524, when he was crowned. Frederik's accession was the fulfillment of a lifelong dream. He had always cursed the accident of his being born after Hans, and he repeatedly argued that the realm should have been divided.

In spite of his delight, Frederik remained through the 10 years of his reign a relatively quiet and unprovocative figure. He was calm, measured, patient, realistic, and politically astute. He may also have been crafty and cunning. Though often slow to reach decisions, he could and did act decisively when necessary. Frederik has not been remembered fondly in Danish history, perhaps because he appeared so colorless and unassertive, but his reputation is undeserved. (His unpopularity may also be due to the fact that he never learned to speak Danish, and national histories from the nineteenth century tended to deal harshly with individuals whose national commitment might be questionable.) Frederik was in many respects a remarkable figure. He fully understood what was possible for the king in Denmark in the 1520s, and he worked successfully within the limits imposed upon him. He may have been exactly what Denmark needed after the "revolutionary" reigns of Hans and Christian II.

In order to secure his election, Frederik accepted an accession charter which bound him to respect the rights, privileges, and powers of the lay and clerical nobility. Under the terms of this charter he was little more than a figurehead. This had been the case with Christian II also, but Frederik chose to abide by this charter rather than seek to reverse it. He felt insecure upon his throne throughout his reign. Christian II remained a constant threat. The deposed king spent much of his time trying to raise support for his restoration among various German princes and with the Habsburg emperor, Charles V. Christian and Frederik carried on vitriolic propaganda wars in Denmark and in Europe against each other. Popular discontent, especially among the peasants, also confronted Frederik. The commons had been close to Christian, and Frederik feared they would side with the deposed king again. At the same time, he faced peasant revolts which were endemic in Europe in the early sixteenth century. These resulted largely from tax burdens and social conflicts. Frederik felt wholly dependent upon the nobles for his crown, and he did not feel secure enough to challenge their claims to a share in governing the kingdom. Throughout his reign, Frederik was financially strapped, and he repeatedly had to call on every social group to pay taxes to support an army and navy, which he felt were essential to maintain a stable domestic situation and prevent Christian's return. Finally, he had to deal very carefully with Sweden and the Hanse (*see* Hanseatic League), who were necessary allies during much of his reign against Christian and his troublesome ex-admiral, Søren Norby*.

It is hardly surprising that Frederik broke with the centralizing, "modern" tendencies of his predecessors. He was very cautious in domestic and foreign affairs. The nobles enjoyed their old monopoly on offices and lands. Christian II's law code was destroyed. Peasant rights to long-term leaseholds were assured, but so too were the powers of control the nobles held over most of the peasants. Native commerce was encouraged, but the privileges of the Hanse were strengthened. In terms of the most volatile issue of the decade, religious reform, Frederik attempted to be noncommittal. He repeatedly argued for toleration of different religious practices. At the same time, and in a thoroughly modern vein, he advocated and took steps to implement state control of the church.

Frederik's cautious approach to problems appeared to be successful. Although there were several peasant uprisings, most notably in Skåne, and a number of nagging external problems, his reign was relatively peaceful. The reformers in the church made significant inroads throughout the country, but Denmark was by no means a Lutheran state by Frederik's death. Peaceful relations with Sweden and the Hanse were maintained. The threat of Christian was blunted, and his attempt to reconquer the country failed in 1531–1532. When Frederik died Denmark was at peace. That peace was a fragile one. The fundamental issues that threatened it, including the succession, religion, and social and economic problems, remained largely unsettled.

Frederik was married twice. His first wife was Anna of Brandenburg. Christian III*, Frederik's successor, was the child of this marriage. Sofie of Pomerania was his second wife. They had one son, Hans.

REFERENCES: *DBL*, vol. 4; *DH*, vol. 5; *NH*, vol. 5.

B. NORDSTROM

FREDERIK II (1 July 1534–4 April 1588) King of Denmark 1559–1588

Frederik was the eldest son of Christian III* and Dorothea of Saxe-Lauenberg. He had a comparatively shallow education and was not especially interested in academics. His schooling emphasized the legitimacy of kingship, and he took the idea of his office very seriously, even if he did not spend much time directly involved in the governing of his country.

As a person, Frederik was, especially in his younger years, impulsive, vain, power-hungry, and something of a dreamer. During the first decade of his reign these traits very nearly brought ruin to Denmark, when he took the country into a lengthy and expensive war with Sweden (see discussion of the Northern Seven Years' War below). Frederik tempered somewhat over the years, however, and the period from 1570 until his death was a happy one for the king and a prosperous one for his country. He also loved the life of a king played to its fullest. He was fond of hunting, banquets, and heavy drinking. He liked nothing more than to share the company of his friends in the hunt and late-night debauchery. When he died in 1588, a priest attending the funeral is reported to have said that the king would have lived much longer had he not consumed so much wine. (The average noble of the day drank 8 to 10 pints of wine each day and more on special occasions.)

Frederik had little direct role in governing his country, although he appears to have taken part in the determination of basic policy directions. He delegated power to his council and especially to a group of very capable high officers of the state including Johan Friis*, Peder Oxe*, Niels Kaas*, and Christoffer Valkendorf*.

In domestic affairs there were a few notable accomplishments. Frederik encouraged further reform of the royal estate rents, and a new maritime code (*Søretten*, 1561) and a revised law code covering crimes committed on royal or noble estates (*Gårdsret*, 1562) were promulgated. Also, significant financial reforms were carried through, a number of royal building projects were launched, and the fleet was strengthened.

In foreign affairs Frederik began his reign with grand aspirations. He was emboldened by the quick success of a campaign in Ditmarsken, which resulted in the incorporation of the peasants' republic into the realm and erased the disastrous defeat at Hemmingstedt in 1500. Following this Frederik worked to isolate Sweden in the Baltic, so that he could undertake a war to recover the "lost province." An alliance with Lübeck and Poland was concluded, and the Northern Seven Years' War began in 1563. In this struggle Sweden was without allies and was led during most of the struggle by the impulsive and unstable Erik XIV*. Neither side was able to win a decisive victory. Sweden won most of the naval engagements. Denmark captured Älvsborg* (Sweden's window on the west) early in the war and launched a series of successful campaigns into south-central Sweden, but failed to precipitate a surrender. The war was fought at great cost to both belligerents and ended in a military draw (though perhaps a diplomatic victory for Denmark) in 1570 by the Peace of Stettin.

This was was a sobering experience for Frederik. Its length and the human and material costs were far beyond Denmark's meager means. Time and again the king had to listen to reports of the defeat of his fleet or the complaints of his commanders, who clamored for money to pay the mercenary troops. His people complained bitterly about the endless succession of taxes levied to pay the costs. In the midst of the struggle, Frederik was compelled to recall the exiled Peder Oxe, who was able to stabilize the financial situation. In early 1570, before the war ended, Frederik became so frustrated with matters that he wrote to his council a letter in which he implied a willingness to abdicate. The council responded carefully, but negatively, to the letter, and the idea of abdication was dropped.

In the years following the war, Frederik lived primarily at various country estates. He encouraged the growth of the fleet, which he recognized to be essential to the management of the Sound Tolls. He also launched the most ambitious building project of his reign, the construction of Kronborg castle at Helsingør (Elsinore*). In the same period he abandoned his hopes to marry his longtime lover, Anne Hardenburg, and wed Sofie of Mecklenburg. The couple had seven children, including the future Christian IV*. Frederik gave his support to the University of Copenhagen and his patronage to Tycho Brahe* during this period, also.

Frederik's sudden death in 1588 left Denmark with an eleven-year-old heir to the throne. The council established a four-member regency headed by Niels Kaas, and this governed the country until 1596. Through the regency the council reasserted its assumed constitutional role as the repository of royal power in the state. For eight years Denmark was again an aristocratic republic.

REFERENCES: *DBL*, vol. 4; *DH*, vols. 5, 6.

B. NORDSTROM

FREDERIK III (18 March 1609–9 February 1670) King of Denmark-Norway 1648–1670

The second son of Christian IV* by his first wife, Anne Christina of Brandenburg, Frederik only came to be considered a candidate for the throne on the death of his older brother Christian in 1647, one year before his father's death. Until 1647 he had been engaged in establishing himself among the princes of northern Germany, succeeding at the age of 26 to the Protestant bishoprics of Bremen and Verden and later to that of Halberstadt as well. His marriage into the dynastically ambitious house of Braunschweig-Lüneburg (Sophie Amalie, 1643), their autocratic rule within their dependencies, and Frederik's high-handed manner with leading Danish nobles as commander-in-chief of the Danish forces in Slesvig-Holstein during the 1643–1645 war with Sweden were principal reasons for the strong objections raised to his candidature in 1648, when the throne became vacant due to the death of Christian IV. In order to counteract these dangers to their own power, a small group of leading nobles, some of whom had already consolidated their positions during the old king's lifetime by marrying some of his many daughters, forced upon the new king a coronation charter which bound him to consult with them through the powerful assembly, Council of State (*rigsråd*), in all political matters as well as in questions regarding the election of new members to that body.

Bringing with him a few key members of his previous administration, among them most powerful influence in economic, political, and administrative matters, Christopher Gabel (1617–1673), Frederik set about rebuilding the economy, which had been ruined by his father's disastrous participation in the Thirty Years' War. For this he needed the cooperation of the trading centers, Copenhagen* in particular. He expected and received little support from the nobility, which was jealously protecting its freedom from personal taxation. After the fall of one of his brothers-in-law, Hannibal Sehested*, due to embezzlement, and another, Corfitz Ulfeldt, due to various plots to overthrow the king, Frederik, seeing the Swedish king Karl X* engaged in war against Poland, believed he saw an opportunity to regain from the archenemy some of the provinces lost by his father, and so began hostilities against Karl in 1657. The Swedish king, in a campaign which surprised the Danes and astounded all contemporaries, marched his troops quickly through north Germany, up Jutland, onto Funen, and from there across the frozen waters of the Great Belt via Langeland and Falster, onto Zealand. Karl forced peace terms at Roskilde in 1658 according to which Denmark lost to Sweden not only the Swedish provinces, but also the island of Bornholm in the Baltic as well as Trondheim District in Norway. After a short pause Karl, who knew that only diplomatic interference from other maritime powers had denied him total victory, renewed the campaign, besieged Copenhagen, and would undoubtedly have won, had not the Dutch—who, like the English, wished to preserve a situation in which neither Denmark nor Sweden commanded both sides of the Sound—broken the naval blockade and together with the Danish navy driven the Swedes back into port. The peace of Copenhagen (1660) reflected the interests of the chief intermediaries, in that Denmark regained Bornholm and Trondheim to prevent an imbalance in Sweden's favor, while the balance of power in the Sound was restored by denying Sweden total victory but confirming the permanent loss for Denmark of all her provinces east of the Sound.

For the second time during his reign Frederik had to rebuild a country devastated by a disastrous war which, though largely of his own making, had nevertheless given him an opportunity to display, to the burghers of his capital in particular, considerable personal courage during the Swedish siege. He was also well supported in his anger at the lack of cooperation from the nobility, both during and immediately after the war, when their privileges again took precedence over the needs of the nation as a whole. Supported by the clergy and the burghers of Copenhagen, the king used this occasion to stage a coup d'etat in 1660, in which the Coronation Charter of 1648 was declared null and void, and as a result of which Frederik was declared a hereditary as well as an absolute king, answerable to no one but God, and charged with no other duties than upholding the Lutheran Church and securing the royal succession in direct male line.

The *Kongelov* (Lex Regia or King's Law), the final draft of which was presented to Frederik in 1665, enshrined the king's newly won independence of his rivals as well as of his own people. This was followed by the creation, largely by Gabel and Sehested, of a new central administration. Boards of commerce, finance, foreign affairs, and so on were headed by secretaries, directly answerable to the king or his deputy, and either overruled or by-passed the old Danish nobility and its instruments of power. Also at its expense, members of the Holstein aristocracy, German and other foreign merchants, and civil servants, as well as Danish and foreign burghers of considerable wealth and prospects, rose to new and prominent positions; foremost among them, after the fall of Gabel and the king's death in 1670, but already playing an important role as early as 1663, was Peder Schumacher, later Count Griffenfeld.

Unlike Christian IV, who had used his children to influence policy at home, Frederik and Sophie Amalie contracted marriages for their children which were intended to appease enemies (Frederikke Amalie to Holstein-Gottorp, 1667; Ulrikke Eleonora to Sweden, 1680) or to procure new support for his dynasty (Christian V* to Hesse-Kassel, Wilhelmine Ernestine to the Palatinate, and Prince Jorgen (George) to Anne, future queen of England). The king's only child to play a significant role in domestic policy was Ulrik Frederik Gyldenløve, a son by one of his mistresses. He became governor of Norway and was also famous as one of the husbands of Marie Grubbe (see Jacobsen, J. P., in *Dictionary of Scandinavian Literature*).

REFERENCES: *DBL*; *DH*, vol. 8; T. K. Derry, *A History of Scandinavia* (Minneapolis: University of Minnesota Press, 1979).

P. RIES

FREDERIK IV (11 October 1671–12 October 1730) King of Denmark 1699–1730

Frederik IV, son of Christian V* and Charlotte Amalie of Hesse-Kassel, is one of Denmark's most popular kings. Although apparently quite ill-prepared for the role of absolutist monarch, he was serious about his duties and took an active role in governing.

On the positive side, his reign was marked by steps to alleviate some of the pressures on the peasantry (in 1702 he abolished the *vornedskab** on peasants born after his succession); to improve education (notably through the founding of some 240 schools on crown estates); to improve the army and reduce its costs through the re-establishment of a national militia in 1701; and by a broad range of cultural efforts including the construction of Frederiksborg castle in Copenhagen* and Fredensborg, patronage of the arts, and encouragement of the theater in the capital city—where the comedies of Ludvig Holberg began to appear in 1722. He also backed Hans Egede's missionary expedition to Greenland*, which marked the resettlement of the island by Europeans in 1721.

On the negative side, he took Denmark into the Great Northern War* in 1700. The Swedes quickly defeated the Danes in the early stages of this conflict, and Frederik was forced to conclude peace at Travental in August 1700. For the next nine years, Frederik remained neutral, and these were good years for Frederik and Denmark. The economy prospered, and Frederik culminated the period with a year-long trip to Italy. Following Karl XII's* defeat at Poltava in 1709, however, Denmark re-entered the war. Frederik's badly planned and poorly supported invasion of Sweden was halted near Hälsingborg in March 1710, but revenge was gained some time later through a Danish victory in Holstein. Peace was not concluded with Sweden until July 1720 (Peace of Frederiksborg), when Denmark gained Slesvig from the Duke of Holstein and secured the end to Sweden's exemption from the Sound Tolls. The returns were not worth the costs.

Frederik married twice, first to Louise of Mecklenburg and, following her death in 1721, to Anna Sophia Reventlow, the daughter of Christian Ditlev Reventlow. She had been his "left hand wife" since about 1711. This later marriage proved to be very unpopular, especially as he immediately made his new bride queen and stacked his council with Holsteiners, many of them members of the Reventlow family. His successor, Christian VI*, was a son of the first marriage. None of his children by Anna Sophia survived.

REFERENCES: *DBL*, vol. 4; *DH*, vols. 8, 9; *NCMH*, vol. 7; S. Oakley, *A Short History of Denmark* (New York: Praeger, 1972).

B. NORDSTROM

FREDERIK V (31 March 1723–14 January 1766) King of Denmark 1746–1766

Frederik V was the son of Christian VI* and Sophie Magdalene of Brandenburg-Kulmbach. He is one of the least popular of Denmark's absolutist kings, and it was under him that foreign influence in Denmark peaked. He was badly educated, never spoke reasonably good Danish, and was uninterested in the duties of his office. He preferred to turn over the governing of the country to his favorites, while he enjoyed the pleasures of hunting and women.

Real power during his reign lay in the hands of a group of favorites that included Adam Gottlob Moltke, J.H.E. Bernstorff*, J. L. Holstein, Ditlev Reventlow, and J. S. Schulin. Under their leadership, Denmark very nearly became, in Stewart Oakley's words, "a bureaucracy." This is not to say, however, that their rule was entirely bad. Most of them were strongly influenced by the Enlightenment and introduced reform ideas in their public policies and on their estates.

There were other bright spots to Frederik's rule. First, he was not an ardent Pietist like his father, and he lifted the restrictions on culture and the arts which had hung so heavily over Denmark during the previous reign. A new theater opened in Copenhagen*. Frederik commissioned over 70 portraits of himself by the Swedish artist C. G. Pilo*. A new Royal Academy of Art opened in 1754. The reconstruction of Christianborg was completed. In addition, Denmark remained neutral during the War of the Austrian Succession and the Seven Years' War, and the country's economy prospered. Physiocratic ideas were implemented which were aimed at encouraging agricultural and manufacturing development. Though small in scale, even some private efforts at land reform were attempted.

REFERENCES: *DBL*, vol. 4; *DH*, vol. 9; *NCMH*, vol. 7; S. Oakley, *A Short History of Denmark* (New York: Praeger, 1972).

B. NORDSTROM

FREDERIK VI (28 January 1768–3 December 1839) King of Denmark 1808–1839

Frederik was the son of King Christian VII* and Queen Caroline Matilda. His earliest years were dominated by the all-powerful minister Johan Friedrich Struensee*, who sought to harden the sickly boy by applying Rousseauesque "natural" methods of upbringing; Frederik was scantily clothed in all weathers, fed a meager diet, and encouraged to exercise vigorously. The harsh regimen did, however, improve his health. In 1772 Struensee fell from power and Frederik's mother was charged with adultery and sent abroad. His subsequent education was neglected. As he grew up, he became the center of opposition to the new regime headed by Ove Høegh-Guldberg, who wielded power on behalf of the mentally sick king, and on the occasion of Frederik's first attendance at the royal council, he boldly pressured his father into signing orders dismissing Guldberg and appointing reformers headed by Andreas Peter Bernstorff* to the council. In effect (though never in name) Frederik acted henceforth as regent. As such, he supported the series of reforms which were now initiated, including the emancipation of the Danish peasants. But his limited education and narrowness of vision meant that he had little influence on policy while Bernstorff lived. After the minister's death in 1797, Frederik acquired greater authority, especially in foreign policy. He was largely responsible for action which led to the first British attack on Copenhagen* in 1801 and also for the second in 1807, which brought Denmark's entry into the war on the French side in the same year. Frederik became king in 1808 and proceeded to rule through his personal cabinet. The influence at this time of his corps of adjutants (the *røde fjer* or "red feathers") has, however, been considerably exaggerated in the past. Frederik remained faithful to the French alliance until 1814, partly because of fears of French reprisals should he try to leave it, partly in hope of French support for his pretensions to the Swedish throne, and partly because of his refusal to abandon his subjects in Norway (which had been promised to Sweden as her price for joining the anti-French coalition). In 1814, however, Denmark had to surrender Norway at the Treaty of Kiel* and join the coalition. Frederik attended the Congress of Vienna. Though he accomplished nothing there, he was welcomed back to Denmark as a national hero. He restored the royal council after the war, but retained the absolutist system of government and took little further interest in reform. He was, however, alarmed by the European revolutions of 1830 and agreed to the establishment of four consultative assemblies for the duchies and the kingdom. While there was growing opposition to his autocracy from liberals in the Danish middle class, Frederik's association with the late eighteenth-century reforms and his accessibility kept alive his popularity among his more humble subjects, and his sudden death in 1839 was widely mourned. His coffin was carried by peasants on its way to burial in Roskilde. Of the offspring of his marriage to Princess Marie of Hesse-Kassel in 1790, only two daughters survived childhood, and the succession passed to his cousin, Christian VIII.*

REFERENCES: *DBL*, vol. 4; O. Feldbaek, *Denmark and the Armed Neutrality 1800– 1* (Copenhagen: University of Copenhagen, Institute for Economic History, Publication No. 16, 1979); E.O.A. Hedegaard, *Frederik den Sjette og "de røde fjer,"* 2 vols. (Copenhagen, 1975); R. Ruppenthal, "Denmark and the Continental System," *Journal of Modern History* 15 (1943): 7–23.

S. P. OAKLEY

FREDERIK VII (6 October 1808–15 November 1863) King of Denmark 1848– 1863

Frederik VII was the son of Prince Christian Frederik (later Christian VIII*) and his first wife, Charlotte Frederikke, princess of Mecklenburg-Schwerin.The prince had an unhappy childhood. He was largely ignored by his parents, who were divorced in 1809. His mother was of doubtful character and created several scandals at court. Following the divorce, all normal ties with Frederik and his mother were disrupted. There were also troubles with his education, and although he was intelligent enough, he had a weak temper and was shifty and unreliable. As a young man it appeared that Frederik had turned out to be much like his mother, rather than like his much more intellectual father. What he liked most was a simple bourgeois life with plenty of beer and wine. He was married twice to suitable princesses, but both marriages ended quickly in divorce. His first wife was a daughter of Frederik VI*. As a young man he was sent by his father to Odense, where he served as an officer in the army. Over the years, however, Frederik became more stable and developed an interest in history and archeology.

In 1839 Frederik's father became king. At the same time it became clear that Frederik could not father children. The question of the succession became a burning one, largely because it was linked to intricate national problems. The kings of Denmark were also the dukes of Slesvig and Holstein. If the order of succession should change, the two duchies would be separated from the kingdom, which is what the German populations in the duchies hoped for. During the 1840s the political and national problems created considerable unrest, and a number of crises developed. The prince lived recklessly, detached from these problems until, on 12 January 1848, his father suddenly died and left the crown and the country in dangerous distress to Frederik. He now became an absolute monarch in a realm on the edge of civil war between its German and Danish parts and on the verge of revolution between the liberals and conservatives.

The ascendance of Frederik to the throne made it clear to all that absolutism was impossible with him as king. Following a series of public meetings and a march on the royal residence, the absolutist system that had served Denmark since 1660 was abolished, and a new constitution was drafted which at that time was highly democratic—and which many Danes regarded as a gift from the king.

Few Danish sovereigns have been as popular as Frederik. He won the sympathy of the people with his plain words and his cosy, middle-class lifestyle, which was given particular credibility when he married Louise Rasmussen, a bourgeois lady, in 1849. Her former fiancé, Carl Berling, also came to court and became the private secretary of the king. On several occasions, Louise, ennobled as Countess Danner, exerted a political influence in the formation of new governments, especially in 1856 and 1859.

Although unfit for state affairs, Frederik was a center and symbol for the outpouring of nationalism during the war against the German aggressors in the duchies in 1848–1851. He could have played a similar role in the second major crisis in German-Danish relations in 1863 had he not died suddenly at Glücksborg Castle in Slesvig. His death was mourned sincerely by his people. Statues of him in front of the Danish parliament building and in dozens of provincial towns illustrate the popularity of the last absolutist king of Denmark.

REFERENCES: *DBL*, vol. 5; B. Mikkelsen, *Konge til Danmark. En biografi af Frederik VII* (Copenhagen: Nordisk Forlag, 1981).

KRISTIAN HVIDT

FREDERIK VIII (3 June 1843–14 June 1912) King of Denmark 1906–1912

Frederik was the son of Christian IX* and Louise of Hesse-Kassel. For 43 years he was Denmark's crown prince, waiting to succeed his father. Well-educated, cultured, tactful, and charming, Frederik understood the profound changes that were occurring in Denmark's society, and he was aware of the directions political developments were taking in the late nineteenth century. He grew to favor the development of truly representative government in his country, and he presided over part of the transition to parliamentary government during his brief reign. He also attempted, without success, to work out adjustments in Iceland's status within the Danish kingdom, and he sought to improve relations with Germany in the years before World War I.

Frederik married Louise, a daughter of Karl XV* of Sweden. Their eldest son succeeded Frederik as Christian X*. Their second son became Haakon VII*, king of Norway, in 1905.

REFERENCES: *DBL*, vol. 4; *DH*, vols. 11, 12.

B. NORDSTROM

FREDERIK IX (11 March 1899–14 January 1972) King of Denmark 1947–1972

Frederik was the son of Christian X* and Alexandrine of Mecklenburg-Schwerin. During his years as crown prince, he pursued an active naval career, developed his interests in automobiles, technology, and music, and served as regent during his father's absences. In 1953, following the adoption of a new constitution in Denmark, he was relegated to a position of relative powerlessness—a position to which he adapted with grace and dignity. Over the ensuing years he came to be known for a style characterized by warmth and "informal formality" which served the monarch and Denmark well. Following his death, in accordance with the new succession law, he was succeeded by his daughter, Margrethe (II*), the first woman to serve as monarch of Denmark since 1412.

REFERENCES: *DBL*, vol. 4; *DH*, vol. 14.

B. NORDSTROM

FREDERIK CHRISTIAN II (28 September 1765–14 June 1814) Duke of Schleswig-Holstein-Sonderburg-Augustenburg

Frederik Christian was the first son and heir of Duke Frederik Christian I (1721–1794) and Princess Charlotte Amalie of Plön. Frederik Christian was educated at Augustenburg and then at the University of Leipzig (1782–1784).

To prevent the splintering of the Danish state if the male royal line should die out, Andreas Peter Bernstorff* arranged for Frederik Christian's marriage to Crown Prince Frederik (VI*)'s sister, Princess Louise Augusta, in 1786. As a result, Frederik Christian was given a seat at once on the Royal Council (Gehejmestaatsraad). Because of his interest in education, Frederik Christian directed many government activities in this field. He became the patron of the University of Copenhagen in 1788, presided in 1790 over a commission which reformed the government's school program, and in 1805 was named the president of the newly created Board of the University and Grammar Schools.

He and his wife actively supported some of Denmark's leading cultural figures, especially Jens Baggesen. Frederik Christian also briefly assisted the well-known German writer Friedrich von Schiller. In his work and politics, Frederik Christian was an outspoken advocate of the Enlightenment and the French Revolution even when both fell increasingly into disfavor in the middle and late 1790s.

Frederik Christian was never well liked in Copenhagen*. He clashed with the Bernstorff-Reventlow-Schimmelmann circle which championed romanticism and dominated political and social life. He was generally regarded as a pedant: learned, but without tact, prudence, or a sense of humor. Frederik Christian was frustrated by the subordination of his educational department to the Danish Chancery. As the chief representative of the collateral lines of the Danish royal house, he defended their interests vigorously. In 1806 he clashed openly with Frederik when the latter incorporated the duchy of Holstein into the Danish state without regard for Augustenburg claims there.

After the death of Frederik Christian's younger brother, Prince Christian August*, in 1810, Frederik Christian permitted prominent Swedes to consider him as a candidate for Sweden's crown prince. Frederik also wished the position and therefore forced his brother-in-law to withdraw his name and stationed Danish gunboats off the island of Als to prevent Frederik Christian from traveling secretly to Sweden to reopen his candidacy for the crown. Karl XIV Johan's* subsequent selection as Sweden's crown prince was a bitter disappointment to him.

Frederik Christian spent his last years preparing a written account of the troubled relationship between his family and the Danish state. Although his daughter Caroline Amalie married King Christian VIII*, his hostility and bitterness were shared by other family members, including his two sons, who later became leaders of the German nationalist movement in the duchies.

REFERENCES: J. Clausen, *Frederik Christian Hertug af Augustenborg (1765–1814)*(Copenhagen, 1896); *DBL*, vol. 7; H. Schulz, *Friedrich Christian Herzog zu Schleswig-Holstein: Ein Lebenslauf* (Stuttgart and Leipzig, 1910).

L. SATHER

FREDERIKSBORG Danish fort in West Africa used between 1649 and the 1680s

In the early 1640s the Holstein town of Glückstadt, then under Danish control, began trading expeditions to western Africa. In 1649 this city formed its own African company and built Fort Frederiksborg near the present city of Accra, Ghana. It remained in Danish control until the 1680s, when it was sold to England.

Christiansborg, a second fort near Accra, was built by the Danes in 1661 with Christian Cornelisen as commandant. By 1671 the merchants of Copenhagen* became interested in West Africa, and a company was formed which eventually took over the Glückstadt enterprise. Gold and ivory had previously been the chief Danish interests in West Africa. As a result of Danish penetration of the West Indian Virgin Islands (*see* Danish West Indies), beginning in the 1670s the slave trade became the foremost reason for creating posts in West Africa.

In the eighteenth century other Danish outposts, including Fredensborg, Kongensten, and Prinsensten, were established along the Gold (Ghanaian) Coast, but Christiansborg was the most important. It was retained by the Danes until 1849, when it was sold to England.

REFERENCES: P. Curtin, *Africa Remembered* (Madison: University of Wisconsin Press, 1967); A. W. Lawrence, *Trade Castles and Forts of West Africa* (London: J. Cape,

1963); W. Westergaard, *The Danish West Indies under Company Rule (1671–1754)* (New York: Macmillan Co., 1917).

A. H. WINQUIST

FREDRIK I (17 April 1676–25 March 1751) King of Sweden 1720–1751

Born in Kassel in 1676 to Landgrave Karl of Hesse-Kassel and his wife, Maria Amalia of Courland, Fredrik pursued a military career in his father's service during the War of the Spanish Succession. His successes on the battlefield led Karl XII* of Sweden to entertain his request for the hand of Karl's sister, Ulrika Eleonora* (the Younger), in what would be Fredrik's second marriage. Fredrik came to Stockholm* in 1714, and the wedding was held on 24 March 1715. Joining his brother-in-law's military forces, Fredrik was wounded seriously in the campaign against Norway in 1716, and when he recovered he was given the honorific title of generalissimus by Karl XII.

Fredrik was serving Karl when the latter was killed at the siege of Fredriksten fortress in Norway in November 1718. To aid his wife's claim to the succession, Fredrik secured the arrest of Baron George Heinrich von Görtz*, the key advisor of her rival, Karl XII's nephew, Duke Karl Fredrik of Holstein-Gottorp*, and then persuaded the military command to approve Ulrika Eleonora's conditional accession to the throne. When Ulrika Eleonora was elected as her brother's successor at the Riksdag* of 1719, Fredrik was given the title ''royal highness,'' although he was not accorded the status of co-regent as his wife desired. Nonetheless, the new queen was anxious to accord her husband greater status than the estates had envisioned. His honorific title of generalissimus was now given formal content, as he was granted supreme command of Sweden's armed forces in 1719. At the next Riksdag, in 1720, the estates accepted Ulrika Eleonora's request that her husband be elected King Fredrik I in return for her abdication and further limitations of royal prerogatives.

Fredrik I reigned for 31 years, but throughout this time it was the council of the realm and the estates who governed. The new king's constitutional powers were extremely limited, and after the Peace of Nystad brought the Great Northern War* to a close in 1721, he attempted to break those constitutional fetters. These attempts brought about a serious reaction from the estates at the Riksdag of 1723, after which Fredrik I contented himself with the form of monarchy in the absence of its substance. Fredrik pursued a life of pleasure in which the hunt, the goblet, and the boudoir played the most important roles. His marriage with Ulrika Eleonora remained childless, and eleven years before his queen's death he took up a long-lasting relationship with Hedvig Taube, the daughter of one of the councilors of the realm. This affair, which produced two sons and two daughters, was used constructively by the emerging Hat Party* in its struggle to remove Count Arvid Horn* as president of the chancery in 1738.

Fredrik I became landgrave of Hesse in 1730 and held that title and office until his death in 1751. Indicative of his attitude and perspective is the fact that he never learned Swedish.

REFERENCES: W. Holst, *Fredrik I* (Stockholm, 1953), and "Fredrik I," in *SBL*, vol. 16: 463–472; L. Thanner, *Revolutionen i Sverige efter Karl XII:s död* (Stockholm, 1953).
M. F. METCALF AND D. D. ALDRIDGE

FREDRIKA BREMER ASSOCIATION (Fredrika Bremer Förbundet) Sweden's oldest feminist organization

The Fredrika Bremer Association was founded in 1884 by Sophie Leijonhufvud-Adlersparre (1823–1895). Its aims were to promote women's participation in national life, develop their sense of responsibility as citizens, and strengthen their position in the home and society. It worked for women's suffrage*, revised marriage laws, and better education and widened career opportunities for women. In 1886 it began publishing the journal *Dagny*; from 1913 on, its organ was *Hertha*, issued six times a year. Named after feminist author Fredrika Bremer*, the association sought to carry forward the work she had pioneered. Its first president was a man, Hans Hildebrand, and men as well as women have always been included in its membership.

As the foremost women's organization in Sweden, the association has often been asked by governmental authorities for information regarding women. The legal committee of the association monitors and comments on proposed legislation affecting women. Through its medical care committee, formed in 1893, it has also helped to bring about improved health care.

The association has helped women prepare for employment by running two vocational schools for some decades (both closed in 1962), but, more significant, it has provided thousands of women with scholarships, enabling them to receive training for a variety of careers.

The organization's headquarters are in Stockholm*, but it has local branches in most Swedish cities. It is affiliated with the International Alliance of Women and the International Council of Women.

REFERENCES: *Bonniers Lexikon* (1964); H. A. Larsen, "Sweden's Unique Organization of Women," *American-Scandinavian Review* 1:3 (May 1913): 14–17; L. Wahlström, *Den Svenska Kvinnorörelsen* (Stockholm: Bonniers, 1939); B. Wistrand, *Swedish Women on the Move*, ed. and trans. Jeanne Rosen (Stockholm: Swedish Institute, 1981).
N. FARQUHAR

FRIHETSTIDEN *See* Age of Liberty

FRIIS, JOHAN (20 February 1494–5 December 1570) Danish noble and chancellor under Frederik I*, Christian III*, and Frederik II*

A member of the Fyn nobility, Friis was one of the most remarkable servants of the crown in the sixteenth century. His record of work for three kings spans 46 years. Following his student years in Germany, where he became acquainted with Luther and Melanchthon and was converted to the Lutheran faith (*see* Lutheranism*) he began his political career as secretary of the council. In 1532 he was appointed Frederik I*'s chancellor. After Frederik's death, Friis worked for the election of Duke Christian (Christian III) and was instrumental in securing the duke's recognition by the Fyn and Jutland nobles in 1534. Following the Count's War*, Friis became Christian III's chancellor and continued in that office through Christian's reign and into that of Frederik II.

The work of this devout, devoted, energetic bachelor was extensive and important for Denmark in the mid-sixteenth century. Friis was instrumental in organizing the coup that set aside the Catholic Church in Denmark, and he did much of the administrative work that implemented the Reformation* there. After 1539 he was, as head of the Danish Chancery (Danske Kancelli), in charge of virtually all internal affairs and some aspects of foreign policy—especially with regard to Sweden. His principal attentions during the remainder of Christian III's reign were focused on state finances, which were in disarray following the turmoil of the 1520s and 1530s. Friis reorganized the rents systems for crown estates allocated to the nobles. Through a complicated set of reforms, he was able to increase vastly the income the crown earned from these estates and to reduce the amount of crown property which was pawned out to the nobles. As a result of these efforts, the state's budgets were balanced, and there was even a modest surplus in the treasury when Christian died. Quite remarkably, Friis implemented these reforms without alienating the nobles against himself or the crown. He was aided in this process by his own abilities in dealing with people and by the general desire among the nobles to maintain peace. During this same period, Friis became chancellor of the University of Copenhagen, and he worked energetically to develop the university as a credible academic institution.

Friis's work under Frederik II was more frustrating and less notable. Frederik was impetous and expansionistic, at least until 1570. Consequently, Friis had to deal with ever increasing financial problems which resulted from the king's foreign policy. During the Northern Seven Years' War (1563–1570), Peder Oxe* was called back to Denmark from exile to deal with these problems, which he did with some success, especially through the thorough reform of the Sound Tolls. Friis died shortly before the war ended and was succeeded by Niels Kaas*.

Under Christian III and Frederik II, Friis was given a great deal of independence to manage the day-to-day affairs of the state, because neither king liked the routine of governing. Consequently, Friis was able to make a considerable mark on various aspects of government, and he may be seen as one among the many close servants of European rulers in the sixteenth century who, educated in the latest ideas of administration, finance, and the state, sought to modernize government with varying degrees of success.

REFERENCES: *DBL*, vol. 4; *DH*, vol. 6; A. Friis, "Kansler Friis' förste Aar," *Scandia* 6:2 (1933): 231–327; *SU*, vol. 10.

B. NORDSTROM

FURUBOTN, PEDER LAURITZ (28 August 1890–19 November 1975) Norwegian Communist Party leader

The champion of nativist communism and Norway's "Tito" during World

War II*, Furubotn was born in Brekke in Sogn on the west coast of Norway. Trained as a cabinetmaker and trade union organizer, he helped give Bergen the epithet "the red city" through his activities as a revolutionary leader in the 1920s. Following the split of the Norwegian Labor Party*, the Norwegian Communist Party, or NKP (*see* Communist Party: Norway) was founded on 4 November 1923, with Furubotn as general secretary. In 1925 he was elected head of the party, and in 1926 he became a member of the Comintern. Disagreeing with the Strassbourg Theses, he resigned as head of the NKP and was consequently "invited" to Moscow. From 1929 to 1938 the Furubotns lived in Moscow. During the purges he was accused of horrendous crimes and noted the disappearance of friends. Finally permitted to return to Norway, Furubotn, disillusioned with Stalinism, was not restored to a leading position in the party in Oslo, but was relegated to Bergen, where he worked for a Popular Front against fascism as secretary of the West Coast NKP.

When the Germans invaded Norway in 1940, Furubotn went underground and organized cross-party resistance cadres. He believed that the resistance at home had to be coordinated with fighting abroad, regardless of ideologies.

On 31 December 1941 Furubotn was again elected head of the now clandestine NKP. His charisma and bold resistance involvement, aimed at destroying enemy shipping and supplies, won him support at home but only among a few Norwegian officials abroad. (No help, however, came from the Soviet Union, and Stalin tolerated Furubotn and Tito for their willingness to fight.)

He was outlawed in August 1940, and the Gestapo placed Furubotn at the top of their "most wanted criminals" list. They arrested and tortured Communists in their search for "Gubben" (The Governor), as he was nicknamed, and a price of 100,000NKr was placed on his head. In one German effort, "Operation Almenrausch" (30 June 1944), a massive military and Gestapo attempt to rout Furubotn and his central Communist encampment was mounted. The party paid dearly, and critics labeled Communist sabotage futile and dangerous. Group after group of resisters was dismantled. According to German records, a greater importance was placed on Furubotn's partisans than postwar historians have granted them.

In 1945 Furubotn emerged as a hero. As a result of the NKP's brave resistance record and the change of the NKP to a radical reform party, the Communists won their largest electoral victory in the first postwar election. The NKP captured 11.9 percent of the votes and secured eleven seats in the Storting* and two places in the Labor cabinet.

The Comintern, dissolved in 1944, was re-established as the Cominform in 1947, but Furubotn and the party did not join. In the 1949 election the NKP failed to win a single seat in the parliament, despite its next-to-largest vote in party history. This failure was partly due to changes in the electoral laws that worked against the party. Ten days after the disastrous election, a party minority, using terrorist tactics, took over party headquarters. Furubotn was accused of being an "imperialist agent" and a "Titoist." To preserve party unity while clearing himself of these and other accusations, Furubotn asked to be released from his position as secretary general. Instead, the Stalinist-oriented minority maneuvered to exclude him and his close wartime cohorts from the party. Some 500 members left the NKP in protest.

Furubotn continued his writing and political activities in the 1950s and 1960s, and he was active through radio and other public speaking engagements. Leading men in Norwegian trade unions, business, and politics sought his opinions and advice, and his influence remained significant. His archives have been preserved in Norway and are open to researchers.

REFERENCES: G. Gordon, "The Communist Resistance," in "The Norwegian Resistance During the German Occupation 1940–1945," Ph.D. dissertation, University of Pittsburgh, 1978; O. Titlestad, *Peder Furubotn*, vols. 1–3 (Oslo: Gyldendal, 1975–1977); O. Titlestad, S. Titlestad, and T. Titlestad, Interviews in *Regjeringen og Hjemmefronten under krigen* (Oslo: Stortinget, 1949).

G. S. GORDON

G

GENERAL STRIKE Sweden, 1909

The General Strike of 1909 in Sweden was one of the largest labor-management conflicts in the nation's history and may have been the longest general strike in world history. (A metal industry strike in 1945 involved more lost man-days, and the May strike* in 1980 involved more people directly and indirectly.) The conflict began in early August and lasted until early September, and for a few unions it continued until December. It was an unmitigated failure.

The strike had several underlying causes. International markets had been depressed for two years, and industrial employers needed to reduce wages or at least keep them stable. The workers wanted wage increases. At the same time, the radical wing of the Social Democratic Party* (SDP), led by able speakers and journalists such as Zeth Höglund*, preached the syndicalist solution: a workers' revolt based on the general strike. In 1908 the trade unions and the SDP lost about one-third of their members. The union strike funds were small. The leaders of the Swedish Confederation of Trade Unions* (LO) and the SDP, generally revisionists, were all too aware of the economic realities and were also much concerned about the adverse reaction of the general public to a general strike.

What forced the leadership of LO to issue the call for the general strike on 4 August 1909 was the fact that the employers' association (Svenska Arbetsgivareföreningen/SAF), much more united than labor and with substantial finances, ordered a general lock-out on 2 August. One of the chief stumbling blocks in contract negotiations since 1905 had been the employers' insistence on their right to hire non-union or union labor. The unions considered this an attempt to cripple their power. In the event, the national leadership had no choice but to call for the general strike. SAF was not, by the lockout, trying to abolish the unions but to establish more uniform wage settlements in the various industries through basic, nationwide collective agreements. (This aim was achieved through the Saltsjöbad Agreement* in 1938.) With a long series of disruptive strikes behind them or in progress, the SAF was willing to force the issue in 1909, because they had built up considerable inventories and were assured of continued sales during the strike.

The railroad workers' union, with a no-strike clause in its contract, decided to honor that clause, and thus reduced the effectiveness of the strike and enabled the industrialists to get their goods to market. Incredibly, the LO leaders not only supported the railroad workers' union decision, but also exempted other unions (including those of the public utility, hospital, and sanitation workers) from the strike. The more conservative labor leaders thought these exemptions would mollify public opinion, and in any event the syndicalists assured them that the strike would bring the employers to their knees in a few days. On the other hand, the typographers joined the strike in spite of a no-strike clause in their contract, to the great consternation of the bourgeois reading public. If the apocalyptic Left learned little from the experience, the union and SDP leaders did. Within a few years they recouped their membership losses and were more circumspect in challenging the rest of the nation.

REFERENCES: B. Schiller, *Storstrejken 1909 förhistoria och orsaker* (Gothenburg: Akademiförlaget, 1967), and "Years of Crisis, 1906–1909," in S. Koblik, *Sweden's Development from Poverty to Affluence, 1750–1970* (Minneapolis: University of Minnesota Press, 1975); F. Scott, *Sweden: The Nation's History* (Minneapolis: University of Minnesota Press, 1977).

P. V. THORSON

GERHARDSEN, EINAR (1897–) Norwegian Labor Party* politician, prime minister 1945–1951, 1955–1965

Having served longer than any other prime minister, Einar Gerhardsen is considered by many to have been the most significant Norwegian political leader of the twentieth century. Without a doubt he has been the most influential person within the Labor Party since the end of World War II*.

Born in Asker, Gerhardsen came from a working-class background. He became active in the labor movement at an early age. He was a close follower of Martin Tranmael*, and in his twenties he held key positions in the Labor Party. He served as party secretary during the years 1923–1926; from 1926 to 1936 he headed the Oslo Labor Party; from 1936 to 1939 he was again party secretary; and in 1939 he became vice-foreman in the party. From 1945 to 1965 he was party foreman. He served on the party's central committee (*styre*) from 1921. He was also active in Oslo politics as a member of the city council from 1932 to 1945, as vice-mayor from 1938 to 1940, and briefly as mayor in 1940 and 1945.

Gerhardsen actively took part in Resistance work from the beginning of the German occupation. He was arrested in September 1941 and spent the rest of the war in concentration camps. Because of his contacts with non-Socialist resistance leaders during the war, his long imprisonment, and his lack of identification with the exile government of Johan Nygaardsvold*, Gerhardsen was an acceptable candidate to head the first postwar government, a coalition formed on 25 June 1945. When the Labor Party won an absolute majority in the fall election, Gerhardsen in November organized a pure Labor government.

He resigned his position in November 1951, maintaining that he was tired and needed a rest. He was succeeded by Oscar Torp as prime minister, but Gerhardsen maintained his power in the Labor Party as foreman and leader of the parliamentary delegation. On 22 January 1955 he resumed the post of prime minister. In the Storting* election of 1961 the Labor Party for the first time since 1945 failed to gain an absolute parliamentary majority, with the two representatives from the Socialist People's Party (Sosialistisk Folkeparti) holding the balance. Consequently, in August 1963 the Gerhardsen government was defeated in a vote of confidence over the coal mine accidents on Spitsbergen (Svalbard), but three weeks later he resumed office when the Socialist People's representatives voted along with the Labor Party to oust the short-lived coalition of non-Socialist parties headed by John Lyng. When the non-Socialists won a majority in 1965, Gerhardsen served a final term as Storting representative from Oslo. Since 1969 he has continued to be a respected and authoritative figure withing the labor movement, especially during the controversy concerning whether Norway should join the European Common Market. Gerhardsen's moderating influence helped to lessen the division which occurred within the Labor Party over this controversial question.

Gerhardsen during his long political career exhibited brilliant skill as a political leader. He, more than any other figure, dominated internal politics in the postwar period. In the formulation of foreign policy his influence could be equally decisive. His restrained agreement to Norwegian NATO membership, combined with his opposition to atomic weapons and foreign bases on Norwegian territory in peacetime, became the cornerstone of postwar external relations. His authority was strengthened by traits which made him immensely popular—his low-key, winning personality, his frugal lifestyle, and his love of nature. During his period of political dominance, Norwegian society carried out the task of recovering from the effects of the war, developed a strong system of social welfare, and laid the foundation for the high standard of living that has characterized the country from the 1960s onward. In pursuing this course, Gerhardsen followed the gradual reform policy established during the pre-war Nygaardsvold government, rather than seeking to institute significant change in the direction of a Socialist society.

REFERENCES: T.K. Derry, *A History of Modern Norway, 1814–1972* (London: Oxford University Press, 1973); Johan Hambro, "Einar Gerhardsen, Prime Minister of Norway," *American-Scandinavian Review* 38 (1950): 14–19; H. Vatne, "The Prime Minister," *Norseman*, 5 (1965), pp. 7–10.

O. HOIDAL

GLISTRUP, MOGENS (28 May 1926–   ) Danish lawyer, tax protestor, and founder of the Progress Party (Fremskridtspartiet)

Born at Rønne, Bornholm, Mogens Glistrup was educated in law at the University of Copenhagen and the University of California, Berkeley. He married Lene Borup Svendsen in 1950 and is the father of four children. In 1956 he began what was to become a highly successful Copenhagen* firm which specialized in income tax law. From 1956 until 1963 he also taught tax law at the University of Copenhagen.

Glistrup first gained national prominence in 1971, when he appeared on Danish television and explained how he and many of his clients were routinely able to exploit loopholes in the Danish tax system and consequently minimize or, in some cases, totally avoid income tax payments. Glistrup's startling revelations set off a major debate about the nation's tax structure. In the months following his television appearance, Glistrup broadened his attack by criticizing the size of the government's bureaucracy, the academic class, and the Danish political establishment. Sensing that his complaints had struck a responsive chord among a sizeable portion of the population, Glistrup announced in 1972 the formation of a new political party based on his anti-tax ideas.

Although an April 1973 Gallup Poll indicated that one out of every four Danes approved of the newly formed Progress Party (Fremskridtspartiet), most political observers were not prepared for the "shocking" results of the December 1973 elections. Gaining 16 percent of the popular vote, Glistrup's party won 28 seats in the parliament, placing it second only to the Social Democrats among Denmark's 10 political parties. Shunning parliamentary compromise, especially with Denmark's ruling Socialist coalition, Glistrup used his newly won political prestige not only to continue his attacks upon the taxation and bureaucracy which symbolize the welfare state* but also to call for the total abolition of Denmark's armed forces. Critics labeled him an apostle of negativism and a demagogic obstructionist. In the elections since 1973, the number of seats held by the Progress Party has slowly declined, falling to fifteen in 1981.

Some of this loss of support may be attributed to Glistrup's ongoing legal problems. When indicted in 1974 on several hundred charges of tax fraud, Glistrup complained that the action was politically motivated and announced that henceforth "tax evasion was patriotism." After one of the longest and most complicated trials in Danish history, he was found guilty of tax evasion in November 1981 and sentenced to four years in prison and fined 4 million kroner. Glistrup appealed his conviction, but it was upheld by the Danish Supreme Court in 1983. His sentence was reduced to three years and his fine to 1 million kroner. He was disbarred, and on 1 July 1983 the Folketing* voted to expel him.

REFERENCES: Ole Borree, "Denmark's Protest Election of December 1973," *Scandinavian Political Studies* 9 (1974): 197–204; Eric Damgaard, "Stability and Change in the Danish Party System over Half a Century," *Scandinavian Political Studies* 9 (1974): 103–25; Eric S. Einhorn, "Denmark's Stormy Passage," *Current History* 70 (April 1976): 145–48, 182–84; Elizabeth Pond, "Tax-cutting Dane Makes Parliament Toe the Line," *Christian-Science Monitor*, 5 February 1979.

P. L. PETERSEN

GOÐI Medieval Icelandic politico-religious officer

From the time of settlement in the ninth century until the king of Norway gained control in the thirteenth, Iceland was a republic without a single national leader. Power was divided between the local chieftains who held the title of *goði* (pl. *goðar*). Although the word *goði* itself means "priest," the main function of these men in Iceland was secular. The office of the *goði* was called the *goðorð*. This office, which was legally defined as power rather than property, could be inherited, bought and sold, or divided.

The *goði* had few special rights but several duties, and he could be prosecuted if he failed to fulfill these. He was in charge of his local assembly and had a legislative function at the National Assembly (Althing*) which met every June at þingvellir in southwest Iceland. All free men in Iceland were required to form a relationship of mutual support with one of the 36 *goðar*. After reforms in 965 there were 39 *goðar*, and men were then required to join the *goði* who lived in their own district.

REFERENCE: P. Foote and D. Wilson, *The Viking Achievement* (London: Sidgwick and Jackson, 1970).

M. EMELITY

GORM (the Old) (?–c. 940) King of Denmark in the first half of the tenth century

Little is known about Gorm, and he belongs to a period in Danish history for which the sources are very limited and in which real and mythical persons and events are difficult to separate. His place in Denmark's history is based largely on the older runestone at Jelling*, which Gorm apparently had raised for his wife, Tyra/Tyre. On the stone Gorm is referred to as king of Denmark. How large that kingdom was is uncertain. He may have been no more than a minor "king" of the region in South Jutland surrounding his base at Jelling. (Some sources refer to the early kings of Denmark as the "Jelling kings," because the medieval kingdom which included Jutland, the islands, and the provinces of present-day southern Sweden was only just emerging.) Gorm appears to be the first to use the term *Denmark* in a native written source (in this case a runestone), and from Gorm on all subsequent Danish rulers are known. He was succeeded by his son, Harald I* (Bluetooth).

REFERENCES: *DBL*, vol. 5; *DH*, vol. 2; K. Randsborg, *The Viking Age in Denmark* (New York: St. Martin's Press, 1980).

B. NORDSTROM

GÖRTZ, GEORGE HEINRICH VON SCHLITZ VON (1668–19 February 1719) German-born statesman and advisor to Karl XII* of Sweden

Born in Franconia and educated at the University of Jena, in 1698 Görtz entered the service of the ducal house of Holstein-Gottorp through the good offices of that branch of his family employed by the duke of Brunswick. In the Great Northern War* he was with his sovereign, Frederik IV* (Karl XII's brother-in-law and ally) when the latter was killed at Klissow in 1702. (It may be assumed that Karl had come to know Görtz before that time.) Over the next eight years, Görtz became acquainted with a number of personalities at courts with direct interests in the northern struggle (he was at Altranstädt in 1706) and when, following the death of Frederik IV's widow (Karl XII's sister) in 1708, Görtz returned to Kiel to serve the Holstein-Gottorp regent, he was no less at the center of events. In 1712–1713 he was closely associated with Prussian and Russian representatives in schemes which would afford Holstein-Gottorp a leading role in the maintenance of the quarantine of Swedish garrisons in north Germany and might promise a resumption of the seventeenth century's commercial contacts between the duchy and Russia. At this time, Görtz canvassed a marriage between the thirteen-year-old Duke Karl Fredrik of Holstein-Gottorp* and a princess of the Romanov dynasty, a match which was realized in 1725.

The wide experience of a naturally versatile man rendered Görtz a particularly useful servant to Karl XII when he entered the king's service in an unofficial capacity in 1715. From then until the king's death in 1718, Görtz was intimately associated with the exploitation of any diplomatic opening that promised to secure for Sweden an honorable peace. In Sweden, though he was absent from the country between June 1716 and November 1717 on diplomatic and fund-raising missions (and in detention in the United Provinces from February to July 1717), he presided over a system of war finance which had been devised in outline by Karl XII before 1715. The program bred great resentment in Sweden, because with each implementation it became more fiduciarily dubious and because it was socially leveling. It was executed by government departments into which Görtz introduced numerous Holstein officials, who became detested as alien predators. Ironically, Görtz sacrificed much of his private fortune for Sweden. In these circumstances it was inevitable that, following Karl XII's death, much of the initial momentum for the "Swedish Revolution" of 1719, which ended absolutism, would be afforded by hatred of the Holstein element. But it should be stressed that Görtz himself was always wryly aware that he could at any time be disowned and possibly disgraced by Karl XII, if such action seemed warrantable in furthering the king's strenuous policies in the closing years of the Great Northern War. This is not the least remarkable aspect of Görtz's cliff-hanging peace talks with the Russians in the Åland Islands between May and November 1718.

Because of her dynastic concerns, Ulrika Eleonora* deeply distrusted the Holstein-Gottorp connection and Görtz himself. She and her consort, Frederick, however, deprecated his execution in 1719 and would have liked to intercede for him. His family also suffered severe deprivation, but by the end of the eighteenth century the services Görtz had in fact rendered Sweden were acknowledged and his descendants compensated. In his time his imposing presence and charismatic personality had riveted the attention of European courts.

REFERENCES: There are no biographies of Görtz, but he is adequately covered in the following: O. Jägerskiöld, *Sverige och Europa 1716–1718* (Ekenäs, 1937); C. Nordmann, *La Crise du Nord au debat du XVIIIᵉ Siècle* (Paris: Librairie Generale de Droit et de Jurisprudence, R. Pichon and R. Durand Anzias, 1962). For treatments of his economic policies, see *DSH*, vol. 8; G. Lindeberg, *Krigsfinansiering i Karl XIIs Sverige* (Stockholm,

1946), and *Svensk Ekonomisk Politik under den Görtska Perioden* (Lund: C.W.K. Gleerup, 1941); *SMK*, vol. 3; *SU*, vol. 12.

D. D. ALDRIDGE

GÖTA CANAL (Constructed 1810–1832) Swedish waterway
   The Göta, Trollhätte, and Södertälje canals are core elements of a 390-kilo-
meter water route which links Stockholm* and Gothenburg*. The Göta Canal
segment of this route stretches 190.5 kilometers from Mem at Slätbaken on the
Baltic to Sjötorp on the eastern shore of Lake Vänern. Excavated canal works
comprise 87.3 kilometers of the total distance, and 103.2 kilometers run through
lakes. Transit through the canal involves 91.7 meters of change in elevation and
requires passage through 58 locks, a majority of which are clustered in long,
staircase flights.
   Bishop Hans Brask of Linköping is generally conceded to have made the first
proposal for a waterway across Sweden. In 1526 Brask argued that such a channel
would enhance foreign trade, spur internal development, and greatly facilitate
national defense. Though sixteenth-century Sweden had neither the resources
nor the technological know-how to implement Brask's plan, his visionary scheme
would not die. In the early 1800s, after almost three centuries of discussion and
a number of false starts, another remarkable man, Admiral Count Baltzar von
Platen, persuaded Sweden's government to back a cross-country water route and
managed, before his death in 1829, to push the project to the point of completion.
   In 1810, with the Trollhätte Canal already in operation and the Södertälje
Canal under construction, work commenced along the Mem to Sjötorp corridor
that would become the Göta Canal. By September 1832, the entire line was
open to traffic. In the interim more than 70 million man-hours of labor had been
expended to remove 8 million cubic meters of earth and blast away 200,000
cubic meters of granite. Twice the anticipated construction time had been required, and costs exceeded original estimates by more than five times. Even so,
the completed canal represented a major accomplishment for a state with limited
resources.
   Unfortunately, neither the state nor the individual investors were destined to
earn any money from the project. Though by no means an outright failure, a
complex of factors made it virtually impossible for the canal to function either
as a bulwark of national defense or a medium for expansion of trade. Göta Canal
locks, though somewhat larger than the original locks at Trollhätte and Södertälje,
were designed to accommodate the sail-driven, wooden-hulled trading ships in
use at the beginning of the nineteenth century. Accordingly, the waterway was
upon completion to some degree already obsolete, for the coming of the steam
engine and the advent of iron hulls soon led to ocean-going ships too large for
use on Sweden's canals. The abolition of the Sound Tolls in 1857, the growth
and spread of a state railway network between 1860 and 1900, and the competition from trucks following World War I further minimized the value of the
waterway for either international trade or defense.

While the canal continues to carry a fair volume of traffic, at no time since World War II* have tolls covered costs of operation. In the face of growing annual deficits and mounting need for repairs, the future of the canal in the mid-1970s seemed far from secure. In 1978, however, the government, recognizing the waterway's unofficial status as a national monument, assumed control of the canal and allocated 45 million kronor to refurbish and maintain it as a cultural monument, tourist attraction, and recreational facility.

REFERENCES: S. E. Bring, *Göta Kanals historia*, 1–2 (Uppsala: Almqvist & Wiksell, 1922–1930); E. DeMaré, *Swedish Cross Cut: A Book on the Göta Canal* (Malmö: Alhems förlag, 1964); I-M. Munktell, *Känn Ditt Land, Nr. 9: Göta Kanal* (Södertälje: Svenska Turistföreningen, 1981); G. Nerman, *Göta Kanals historia från äldsta tider till våra dagar*, 1–3 (Stockholm: Bonniers, 1896–1897).

D. R. FLOYD

GOTHENBURG Sweden's second largest city

Gothenburg was founded in 1619 by Gustav II Adolf* to secure Sweden's west coast. The city was built around the Göta River, from which it took its name, and was settled by Dutch and Swedish people. In 1689 Karl XI* improved the city's defenses, and Gothenburg became one of the most protected cities in Europe.

In the 1700s Gothenburg experienced growth in its population, industry, and port activity. In 1731 a group of entrepreneurs formed the Ostindiska Kompaniet and established a trade route between China and Sweden. A second stimulus came with the discovery of large schools of herring in the surrounding archipelago in 1747. By the late 1700s industry in the city included fisheries, textiles, tobacco, and sugar.

A third period of growth took place beginning in 1809 and was largely due to the Napoleonic Wars. During this time Gothenburg provided a port from which British goods could be transported to other European cities under French blockade. When the city lost this advantage in 1814, many of the newly formed trade boom industries went bankrupt, and Gothenburg had to turn to the national government for monetary assistance.

From 1721 to 1804 there were seven fires in the city. The last of these left 8,000 people homeless. Disease was also a problem because of poor sanitary conditions. Despite its misfortunes Gothenburg continued to improve its port facilities and industrial capabilities. It was the first city in Sweden (1846) to install gas lights and the first to use electricity (1884). By the turn of the century the Industrial Revolution had also had an effect, represented by an increase in the size of the city's total area and a growth in the working-class population.

Today Gothenburg is Sweden's second largest city and chief seaport. It has a population of nearly 450,000, covers an area of 446 square kilometers, and is the home of the district government for the county of Göteborg and Bohus. Gothenburg's ice-free port provides facilities for the building and repair of ships, handles most of Sweden's import and export traffic, is the center of the west coast fishing industry, and has daily ferry traffic to and from other European cities. Its industries include the production of automobiles, textiles and linens, paper, adding machines, Hasselblad cameras, musical instruments, and Svenska Kullagerfabriken's world famous ball bearings.

REFERENCES: B. Hommelstedt et al., *När Var Hur: Årets Uppslagsbok 1981* (Stockholm: Forum, 1980); E. Jungen et al., *Göteborg* (Malmö: Allhems Förlag, 1953); V. H. Malmström, "Göteborg," in *Encyclopedia International*, vol. 8 (New York: Grolier Incorporated, 1963); S. Swedberg et al., "Göteborg," in *Svenska Uppslagsbok*, vol. 12 (Malmö: Nordens Boktryckeri, 1949).

B. BENSON

GOVERNMENT COMMISSION (Regjeringskommission) Administrative body which ruled Norway 1807–1810

When the war between Denmark-Norway and Great Britain broke out in mid-August 1807, Crown Prince Frederik (later Frederik VI*) established the Government Commission to administer Norway while communication lines between Norway and Denmark were severed by the British navy.

Frederik selected Prince Christian August* to preside over the Government Commission and named Enevold de Falsen, Markus Rosenkrantz, and Count Gebhard Moltke to the body. Rosenkrantz, a Norwegian land owner, merchant, and government official, was the only person to serve on the Government Commission from its inception until it was disbanded in 1810. Moltke, the governor (*stiftamtmand*) of Akershus Province, participated until he was transferred to Denmark in April 1809. Falsen was the chief justice of the Norwegian Court and the Government Commission's most articulate spokesman until his death in November 1808. Others were appointed later to fill vacancies, but by far the most influential member of the Government Commission throughout its existence was Count Johan Casper Herman Wedel Jarlsberg, who was appointed by Frederik in December 1808.

The most difficult and pressing problem for the Government Commission was the constant need to supply Norway with food and other supplies because of poor harvests, the Swedish invasion of eastern Norway in the spring of 1808, and, above all, the British naval blockade, which prevented the delivery of grain from Denmark. In 1808 the Government Commission functioned almost exclusively as an administrative agency, recommending action to officials in Copenhagen*, implementing the instructions they received from Frederik but rarely acting on their own initiative.

Early in 1809, when conditions in Norway worsened dramatically and Wedel Jarlsberg became a member, the Government Commission began to advocate a more independent line in Norway's administration. On 16 February 1809, for example, the Government Commission recommended to Frederik that Norway be allowed to formulate its own foreign policy, in other words, to make peace with Sweden and Great Britain so that food supplies could be replenished and economic ruin averted by the resumption of trade. In July members supported

Prince Christian August's decision to become Sweden's crown prince, because this step would lead to peace between Denmark-Norway and its enemies.

The Government Commission's support for Norwegian interests and Prince Christian August's election as Sweden's crown prince forced Frederik to change his foreign policy in August 1809. The king then ordered an end to privateering in Danish and Norwegian waters to encourage neutral shipping; granted merchants permission to ship Norwegian products to Britain in their own ships; and opened the peace negotiations with Sweden that led to the Peace of Jönköping signed by Denmark-Norway and Sweden on 10 December 1809.

The Government Commission did not satisfy those Norwegians who wished it to pursue an even more aggressive policy. Frederik, on the other hand, always regarded it as only a temporary necessity caused by the war and was displeased by the advice it gave him in 1809. He therefore reduced the powers of the Government Commission on 7 May 1810. By the end of the year it had ceased meeting. This measure was only one of several which re-established the absolute power of the central government over the "Whole State" (Helstat), as the king's rule of Denmark, Norway, the duchies, and other possessions was called.

The Government Commission's administration of Norway was an important interlude when Norway possessed relatively greater self-rule than it had known for several centuries. The experience forced Norwegians to become interested in public affairs, sharpened their organizational skills, revealed basic differences between the interests of Denmark and Norway in foreign affairs, and encouraged them to provide their own solutions to the problems that they faced.

REFERENCES: *NH*, vols. 9, 10.

L. SATHER

GREAT MEN'S MEETING (Stormannsmøtet)

Frederik VI* of Denmark hoped to regain Norway very shortly following the conclusion of the Treaty of Kiel* in January 1814. Despite his *pro forma* requests to his ex-Norwegian subjects to obey Sweden's King Karl XIII*, Frederik also dispatched grain ships to Norway to provision it if it rose against its new rulers. Aware earlier of the obvious dangers to the union and therefore to a sizeable portion of the state he was designated to inherit, Christian Frederik (later Christian VIII*) had already conceived the idea of proclaiming himself king of Norway and promoting a movement for independence if the country was ceded to Sweden. He intended to maintain Norway's independence, however, only until it could be reunited with Denmark at some propitious moment in the future. He also planned, of course, to rule the country according to the same absolutist principles that had prevailed before. Christian Frederik's chief advisor and supporter was Carsten Anker, a wealthy Norwegian land owner and businessman who had spent many years in Danish governmental service.

Christian Frederik first heard of the Treaty of Kiel on 24 January 1814. He at once sought the support of all major governmental officials and then left Christiania (Oslo) for Trondheim, Norway's medieval capital, to promote the cause of independence among the large number of people living between the two important cities. Norwegians, however, did not respond to the news of the Treaty of Kiel entirely as Christian Frederik had hoped. The first reaction of many to the publication in Christiania of the treaty on 26 January, according to Professor Ludvig Stoud Platou, was anger toward Denmark and King Frederik, who "with the stroke of a pen would cede 900,000 of his faithful subjects who have suffered so much in five years." There was also hostility expressed toward Sweden and fear that Norwegians would be saddled with a more oppressive and aristocratic government than before.

A movement therefore developed rapidly in Christiania and other Norwegian cities favoring both independence and the establishment of a constitution guaranteeing self-rule. The chief supporters of this program were most often members of the lower clergy, middle-rank officials, university professors, and members of the influential merchant oligarchy. They justified their position of self-determination by contending that the Norwegian estates in 1661 had consented to a closer union with Denmark through the Act of Sovereignty which had established absolutism. They reasoned that when Frederik had absolved Norwegians of loyalty to him in the Treaty of Kiel, he had, in effect, remitted sovereignty over Norway to her people. His cession of the country to Sweden was therefore illegal, since he possessed no authority for such an act.

Independence leaders were encouraged by Christian Frederik's known willingness to serve as their leader. As the object of traditional loyalty to the crown, the prince brought with him the popular support needed for the movement's success. But they opposed the prince's plan to rule as an absolute monarch. They wished, instead, for him to rule as a limited, constitutional king. Some hoped to secure Christian Frederik's guarantee that Denmark and Norway would never be reunited. Others sympathized with this view but feared that it might cause the prince to leave Norway, leading to the complete collapse of the independence movement.

Public support of independence in Christiania became so widespread that some of the movement's leaders became concerned over the radical expressions used by the common people. Rumors spoke of petitions requesting Christian Frederik to call a constitutional convention, though none have since been found. Political agitation also developed in Trondheim in late January and early February 1814. Prior to Christian Frederik's arrival there on 5 February, a petition signed by 60 men asked the prince to call a "congress" of elected representatives to write a constitution for Norway. It was not presented to the prince, however, because the province's four chief officials sympathized with Christian Frederik's aims and therefore opposed the measure.

Bergen experienced less political activity in early February than elsewhere, in part because news of the Treaty of Kiel arrived there very late. A dominant factor in the development of an independence movement in early 1814 was Bishop Johan Nordal Brun, a fiery patriot and poet. The bishop supported Christian Frederik's program at once, although others would soon adhere to the more liberal independent line.

The differing views which Christian Frederik and independence leaders possessed of Norway's future government could have split the movement so completely that the drive for independence would have collapsed. This crisis was resolved, however, on 16 February 1814, when the prince invited 21 prominent individuals from eastern Norway to a meeting which has usually been called the "Great Men's Meeting" at Eidsvoll, Carsten Anker's estate near Christiania. Those present included several military officers; many governmental officials; two university professors, Georg Sverdrup and Niels Treschow; Peder Anker, the owner of Bogstad, a large estate near Christiania, the holder of governmental posts in the past, one of the chief leaders of the commercial aristocracy of eastern Norway, and the father-in-law of Count Herman Casper Johan Wedel Jarlsberg; Marcus Rosenkrantz, a member of the Government Commission* from 1807 to 1810 and a prominent land owner; and, of course, the host, Carsten Anker.

Christian Frederik hoped these men would endorse his leadership of the independence movement and his absolute rule of Norway. All agreed at least momentarily upon independence but rejected his second request. Sverdrup is generally given credit for persuading Christian Frederik not to press his monarchical claims, although the professor was evidently supported by nearly everyone else at the meeting. Indeed, Christian Frederik's acceptance of the limited title as Norway's regent and his consent to the calling of a National Assembly* to meet at Eidsvoll on 10 April to prepare a constitution (*see* Eidsvoll Constitution of 17 May) represented a significant retreat by him from the absolutist pretensions he had argued for previously, and the successful introduction of the idea of limited, constitutional government.

REFERENCES: See references under Norwegian-Swedish Union. A. Linvald, *Christian Frederik og Norge: de store beslutninger mellem Kielfreden og Eidsvoldsmodet Januar-Februar* (Copenhagen, 1962); P. Maurseth, "Christian Frederiks myndighet som statholder og planene om en regjeringskomisjon," *Historisk tidsskrift* (N) 42 (1962): 1–29; K. Mykland, "Medens der endnu er tid," *Historisk tidsskrift* (N) 41 (1961–1962): 1–40.

L. SATHER

GREAT NORTHERN WAR (1700–1721)

Between September 1699 and January 1700, Frederik IV* of Denmark-Norway, Augustus II of Saxony-Poland, and Peter I of Russia concluded a set of offensive alliances directed against Sweden. War began in February 1700, when the forces of Augustus invaded Swedish Livonia. Denmark entered the war in March, but retired temporarily following a Swedish blockade of Copenhagen* (Treaty of Travendal, August 1700). In early October a Russian army besieged the fortress-city of Narva in Estonia, but a smaller Swedish force, under the command of King Karl XII*, routed the Russians on 20 November.

In July 1701, lacking the forces necessary for a campaign to knock Russia out of the war, Karl XII and his army crossed into the Polish-Lithuanian Commonwealth. Here he campaigned effectively against Augustus until summer 1706, winning important battles at Kliszow in July 1702 and Fraustadt in February 1706, and arranging in July 1704 to have Augustus replaced as king of Poland by a pro-Swedish candidate, Stanislas Leszcynski. Yet Karl forced a peace with Augustus only by invading Saxony in September 1706. The Treaty of Altränstadt, concluded that same month, required Augustus to terminate his alliance with Russia and renounce all claims to the Polish throne.

While Karl campaigned in Poland, a Russia revived by the reform efforts of Tsar Peter began the conquest of Swedish possessions along the Baltic coast. Nöteborg, at the mouth of the Neva, fell in October 1702, and Peter soon began construction of a new capital city nearby. By mid-1703 a significant portion of the coast of the Gulf of Finland was in Russian hands. Narva and the Livonian city of Dorpat fell in summer 1704.

After a year in Saxony, Karl began moving against Russia in September 1707. His forces made their way through Poland and crossed the Dnieper in August 1708. The Russians tended to fight holding actions, avoided large battles, left only scorched earth in the path of the Swedish army, and required the peasants in border areas to hide their supplies of food and forage. Faced with a serious shortage of provisions, Karl ordered his army southward into the Ukraine in September 1708. He counted on the support of Ivan Mazepa, head of the Ukrainian Cossacks, but Russian forces destroyed Mazepa's capital in November and were able to limit his contribution to the Swedish campaign. The result of Karl's dealings with Hordienko, head of the Cossacks of the lower Dnieper, was essentially the same. In June 1709 a Russian force under the tsar's command defeated a Swedish army weakened by a long winter, constant harassment, hunger, and disease in the battle of Poltava. This proved the decisive encounter of the Great Northern War. Karl XII fled into Ottoman territory.

Following Poltava, Russia turned again to the Baltic provinces and occupied Courland in October 1709, Viborg in June 1710, and Riga in July. In November 1710, however, the Ottoman Empire declared war on Russia. Acting in part at the urging of the Swedish king, the Ottomans remained in an intermittent state of war with Russia until June 1713. The Russians overcame a serious defeat on the Pruth in July 1711, and by May 1713 Peter's forces were able to invade Finland. They completed its conquest in 1714, and autumn of that year also saw the first direct Russian attack on Sweden.

Intense diplomatic activity in the years after Poltava did little to change the terms of a conflict which by now hinged on Russo-Swedish relations. August 1709 saw renewal of the Russo-Danish-Saxon alliance, but plans for a combined attack on Skåne in October 1710 were abandoned. In 1714–1715, Hanover (whose ruler was also king of England) and Prussia joined the alliance. Danish and English concern with growing Russian power, however, made joint operations virtually impossible. In 1719–1720 Sweden was able to make peace with Hanover, Denmark, and Prussia.

Karl XII was killed in November 1718, while on campaign in Norway. He seems to have favored a negotiated settlement with Peter, leaving himself free to campaign in Germany. Karl's successor, Fredrik of Hesse (Fredrik I* of Sweden), was a German prince, anxious to concentrate on the war in the east. Yet Fredrik's hopes of an anti-Russian alliance with England, France, and the Holy Roman Empire fizzled in 1720–1721. Faced with the pressure of Russian amphibious assaults and overwhelming Russian military superiority, the Swedish ruler found himself forced to negotiate. The Treaty of Nystad, concluded in September 1721, marked the passage of Livonia, Estonia, Ingria, and Karelia to Russian control. Russia replaced Sweden as the major power in northern Europe.

REFERENCES: M. S. Anderson, *Peter the Great* (London: Thames and Hudson, 1978); R. M. Hatton, *Charles XII of Sweden* (New York: Weybright and Talley, 1968); Michael Roberts, *The Swedish Imperial Experience, 1560–1718* (Cambridge, England: Cambridge University Press, 1979).

E. R. TERZUOLO

GREENLAND

Greenland comprises over 2.2 million square kilometers and is the world's largest island. However, only 384,000 square kilometers are ice-free. The remainder of the island is covered with glacial ice up to three kilometers thick. Greenland extends 2,700 kilometers from Cape Farewell (at 60°N) to Peary Land (at 84°N). Until about 10,000 years ago, the entire island was covered by glaciers. Since then, however, the glaciers have receded, but the arctic climate has restrained vegetation and weathering, and both the bedrock and ground rocks have been laid bare to reveal unique formations. The rock formations are often rich in fossils and valuable minerals including uranium, iron, cryolite, lead, and zinc.

All of Greenland has a polar climate. The temperatures in the winter range from −30°C in the north to +1°C in the far south. Summer temperatures range from +5°C in the north to +5–10°C in the south. Precipitation is relatively light and comes mainly in the form of snow.

There are about 500 varieties of plant life on the island. These grow in three distinct belts. A subarctic belt in the south supports polar birch, which grow to the height of a man. In a low arctic belt further north, up to about 71°N, there are polar willows, crowberries, and various herbs. In the far north is a high arctic belt. There the terrain is mountainous and only scrub/dwarf shrubs grow there.

Greenland has only nine types of land mammals, the most important of which are the arctic fox, reindeer, musk ox, and polar bear. In the surrounding waters, whales, walruses, seals, and important fish including cod, salmon, and shrimp live. Along the coasts there are many types of birds.

The oldest evidence of human habitation in Greenland has been found in the far north. The so-called Independence Culture dates from c. 2100 B.C. and was based mainly on the hunting of musk ox. Among the most important later Eskimos were the Sarqaq and Dorset. For long periods the entire island was uninhabited, largely because of short-term worsening of the climate.

The present Greenland Eskimos' predecessors were the Thule People, who migrated across Canada and appear to have reached northwest Greenland c. 900 A.D. These people depended on sealing and occasional whaling for their survival. After 900 A.D. this culture expanded along the western coasts, as the people developed their fishing techniques and equipment, especially the kayak.

Norsemen, chiefly from Iceland and Norway, also settled Greenland. They came to the island following the explorations of the region by Eirik the Red, who spent two years in the area while in exile from Iceland, c. 985. As many as 3,000 lived at Vesterbygden (the Western Settlement) near present-day Nuuk/Godthaab, and at Oesterbygden (the Eastern Settlement) near present-day Qaqortoq/Julianehaab. These settlers were nearly self-sufficient; their livelihoods were based on cattle raising, sealing, and hunting. In addition, they made important trips to Labrador for timber and north in search of walrus. Ties were maintained with Norway, and hides and walrus ivory were exchanged for grains and metal. In the course of the fourteenth century the demand for Greenland goods declined, and sometime around the middle of the century the settlers at the Western Settlement disappeared. Those at the Eastern Settlement survived for another 50 years. There were many reasons for the dying out of these settlements, but the most important were the worsening of the climate and the attacks by Eskimos who were forced down from the north in search of their traditional game.

In the fifteenth and sixteenth centuries several attempts were made by Danes to re-establish ties with Greenland. The first, quite primitive map of the area was drawn around 1420 by a Dane, and at the same time scholars sought to renew contacts with the island. Danish expeditions reached western Greenland in 1605–1607 and claimed sovereignty. The English, however, had already rediscovered the coast of the island (1576) and the Davis Strait (1585–1587). For almost two centuries the Basques, the Dutch, and then the English whaled in the vicinity of Greenland. They pursued their catches from east of Greenland to Svalbard. The Dutch became predominant after 1614 and remained so until 1776. They expanded their activities in the seventeenth century into the Davis Strait, where they carried on a coastal trade. A number of private merchants from Copenhagen* and Bergen tried to compete with the Dutch, but it was not until the War of the Spanish Succession that the Danish government dared risk increased involvement. Then, commercial ventures were combined with missionary activities that had their origins in Norway.

The merger of commercial and religious interests resulted in expeditions to Greenland from about 1720, and thereafter Denmark maintained active sovereignty over the island. Commercial activities were conducted by a succession of chartered companies. The government in Copenhagen established an extensive whaling operation in 1774 and, at the same time, set up the Royal Greenland Trade Department (the Monopoly). Missionary efforts grew at the same time, and by the 1780s there were fourteen trade and missionary stations. The missions were Evangelical-Lutheran, and emphasis was placed on reading of the Bible. Education and the development of a written language for the natives was paralleled by the study of the Greenland language. Both activities set patterns for the future.

The state's whaling operation did badly, and the government used the opportunity in 1782 to issue a new instruction on commerce and whaling in Greenland. Uniform trade prices on all goods were to be applied, and it was hoped that the interests of the Greenlanders would be better served by this move. In most years trade with Greenland was profitable, but during the war with Britain (1808–1815) trade came to a virtual standstill and there was considerable suffering in the colony. Following the conclusion of the Treaty of Kiel* between Sweden and Denmark, Denmark was compelled to transfer Norway to Sweden, but the old Norwegian possessions in the North Atlantic, including the Faroe Islands*, Iceland, and Greenland, remained under Danish control. After a period of some difficulty, conditions improved after 1830, and many new trading stations were established and goods in the Monopoly's shops became less expensive and more plentiful.

In Denmark there were some who believed that a more liberal policy toward Greenland was desirable, but only after the economy and culture of the island had been developed. This view prevailed. Increased influence from Denmark had, however, debatable effects. Improved hygiene resulted in a doubling of the population in the first half of the nineteenth century, and the founding of shops resulted in increased imports and less domestic production. Whale oil and blubber became next to unsellable on the world market toward the end of the nineteenth century. Politically, the Greenlanders were able to nurture a developing confidence through the establishment of limited local self-government in 1863. Economic crises late in the century limited progress on the island, however.

After 1900 the economy of the region gained strength, as the cod fisheries developed and sheep-raising took hold. These developments helped the stagnant economy. The government was reorganized under a new law in 1908. These decisive changes marked a clear shift to new times, in which the Eskimo culture gradually faded into the background.

World War I had little impact on Greenland. However, under a new government law of 1925 certain social matters were transferred to the administration in Greenland, and a special court district was created for the island. The law adopted, at base, the principle that Greenland should become self-supporting. Although the trade monopoly was continued, efforts were made through economic policies to render it superfluous. Progress was slow. However, the production of salted cod rose remarkably, and motor boats began to supplant outmoded types. Coal and marble resources began to be exploited. Fundamental changes began to occur in social and economic structures, and in the 1920s and 1930s the number of persons employed in the fisheries, sheep-raising, and raw material extraction gained ground at the expense of those in the traditional hunting and sealing occupations.

There were external pressures on the Danish monopoly as well. The Faroese demanded and got the right to fish in Greenland waters and to land their catches there in 1927. Norway claimed sovereignty over northeast Greenland in 1930. This issue was settled by the International Court in The Hague in 1933 in Denmark's favor, and Norway accepted the decision. (*See* Greenland, Eastern)

During the German occupation of Denmark (1940–1945), local officials took over the governing of Greenland. They entered into agreements with the United States which assured supply and protection of the island, in return for cryolite and the establishment of American air bases—which were the centers of the most important activities on the island during the war.

After the war the Danes and Greenlanders were united on the need to carry through a thorough modernization. In 1950 a popularly elected assembly was established which had authority in certain internal areas. At the same time the Royal Greenland Trade Department got rid of its monopoly—but not the obligation to supply the island. Private enterprises, with state aid, expanded. In the new Danish constitution of 1953 Greenland "lost" its status as a colony and formally became an equal and integral part of the kingdom. Nagging problems remained, however. For example, there were large differences in the wages paid Greenlanders versus Danes sent out to the island to do the same work.

Between 1950 and 1980 development was extensive. The population in 1980 was about 50,000, reflecting a doubling after 1950. Of this 50,000, 82 percent were born in Greenland. The geographic distribution of the population also changed markedly. Villages grew the most, and by about 1980 80 percent of the population lived in the towns of southwest Greenland. This was, in part, the result of conscious policy decisions which sought to assure economic development.

In contemporary Greenland the principal industry is fish processing, especially of cod. Salmon and shrimp have increased in importance. Lead and zinc mining are significant, and in recent years the search for oil in the seas to the west of Greenland has become increasingly important. The construction sector of the economy has been publicly financed in large part. Steady growth has characterized such areas as commerce, social services, and industry. Greenland's economy is strongly dependent on capital investments from Denmark. Since the country's entry into the Common Market in 1973, there has been an increase in investment in mining and oil exploration.

In 1979 a new self-government act went into effect, which meant that the national assembly, with its seat at Nuuk/Godthaab, acquired responsibility for taxation, education, welfare, labor market policy, radio, libraries, and various aspects of the economic life of Greenlanders. With respect to relations with Denmark, the two dominant political parties differ. The moderate Atassut Party favors continued cooperation with Denmark and membership in the EEC. The progressive Siumut Party advocates separation from Denmark and leaving the EEC. The dream of most Greenlanders is one day to manage their own affairs, on their own terms, with their own resources.

REFERENCES: K. Birket-Smith, *Eskimos* (New York: Crown, 1971); F. Gad, *Grøn-*

land (Copenhagen: Politiken, 1984), and *The History of Greenland* (London: Hurst, 1970);
K. J. Krogh, *Viking Greenland*, trans. G. Jones and H. Fogh (Copenhagen: National
Museum, 1967); *Meddelelser om Grønland* (Copenhagen: Nyt Nordisk, 1879); H. Petersen, ed., *Bogen om Grønland* (Copenhagen: Politiken, 1976).

E. GØBEL

GREENLAND, EASTERN Norwegian-Danish dispute over Eastern Greenland,
1921–1933

The dispute concerned sovereignty over part of Eastern Greenland (Eirik Raudes
Land—Kong Christian Xs Land). It may be seen as part of Norwegian Arctic
expansion between the two world wars. In 1924 the Treaty of Spitsbergen (Svalbard) was ratified by interested powers. In 1927 and 1929 Norway acquired two
islands in the Antarctic. Also, in 1929 Jan Mayen was added to Norwegian
Arctic areas, followed by two occupations of territories in Eastern Greenland in
1931–1932. Queen Mauds Land in the Antarctic was added in 1939.

The roots of the dispute over Eastern Greenland were conflicting national,
economic, and scientific interests. Danish national opinion was challenged by
the sale of the Danish West Indies* to the United States in 1916, Norwegian
national opinion by the Danish attempt to have Danish sovereignty over all of
Greenland* acknowledged by all interested parties between 1919 and 1921.
Norwegians considered Greenland, as well as Iceland and the Faroe Islands*,
to have been Norwegian colonies until 1814, when they were withheld as Danish
territories at the signing of the Treaty of Kiel*.

A central theme in the conflict was the question of the constitutional value of
the Norwegian foreign minister N. C. Ihlen's oral declarations. The conflict also
involved economic interests. Norwegian whaling, sealing, and fishing along
Greenland's coasts were threatened by Denmark's policy of not allowing foreigners access to the territorial waters around Greenland. In the 1920s scientific
activities, especially the operation of meteorological observation stations on
Eastern Greenland's coast, widened the battleground.

Throughout the conflict Denmark maintained that all of Greenland had become
Danish in 1814. Norway reluctantly admitted Danish prerogatives in Western
Greenland, but considered Eastern Greenland *terra nullius*. Greenland associations (*Grønlandslag/foreningar*) sprang up in some Norwegian towns, and a
national organization of these was established in 1926. It was not until cooperation with leading Arctic scientists was assured, however, that this loosely
organized group obtained political results. Pressure was put on the Conservative,
Liberal, and Farmers' parties (*See* Conservative Party: Norway; Center Party:
Norway)—most successfully on the latter. The Farmers' Party formed a minority government in May 1931, and in July it acknowledged a privately staged
occupation of part of Eastern Greenland (Eirik Raudes Land). The Danish
government immediately referred the conflict to the Court of International Justice in The Hague.

The reason for Norwegian occupation was the conflict over police authority.

Negotiations had led to an East-Greenland Treaty between the antagonists in 1924 which permitted both countries to hunt and make scientific explorations in Eastern Greenland, but left the question of sovereignty unanswered. A race between Danish and Norwegian expeditions soon led to a dispute over whether Danish police authority could be exercised over Norwegian citizens in the—to the Norwegians—*terra nullius*. Two principles of obtaining sovereignty were actually in conflict. The Danish government adhered to the principle of formal sovereignty, that is, exercising sovereign rights through legislative and administrative actions; whereas the Norwegian government maintained the principle of practical sovereignty, demanding the presence of Norwegians and the practical use of the territory in question.

In 1932 Norway occupied another part of Eastern Greenland, but in 1933 the Court of International Justice ruled against all Norwegian claims. The conflict aroused considerable ill feeling between the two countries, which was only overcome during World War II*.

REFERENCES: I. Blom, *Kampen om Eirik Raudes Land. Pressgruppepolitik i grønlandssporsmålet 1921–1931* (Oslo: Gyldendal, 1973); F. Gad, *Grønlands historie. En oversikt fra ca. 1500 til 1945* (Copenhagen: Det grønlandske selskab, Skrifter XIV, Munksgaard, 1946); M. Lidegaard, *Grønlands historie* (Copenhagen: Schultz, 1961).

I. BLOM

GRIEG, EDVARD HAGERUP (15 June 1843–4 September 1907) Norwegian composer and pianist

Edvard Hagerup Grieg was born in Bergen, Norway. He was the second son and the fourth of five children born to Alexander Grieg (1806–1875), a merchant of Scottish descent, and Gesine Judith Hagerup (1814–1875), a musician of Norwegian birth. His great-grandfather Alexander Grieg(h) had emigrated to Norway for political reasons and, to assure correct pronunciation of the Scottish family name, changed its spelling to Grieg.

Ole Bull* encouraged Grieg's parents to send him to the Leipzig Conservatory, where he studied from 1858 to 1862. While a student he composed four piano pieces, Op. 1, and four songs for alto voice, Op. 2. Shortly thereafter he wrote a work for choir and piano, "Rückblick." Grieg gave his first public performance in May 1862 in Bergen. In July 1864 he secretly became engaged to his cousin, Nina Hagerup. After their marriage in Copenhagen* in 1867, the Griegs settled in Christiania (now Oslo). A daughter, Alexandra, was born in April 1868. At her death thirteen months later, Grieg composed "Margrethe's Cradle Song" (to Ibsen's poem of the same name).

With Rikard Nordraak and others, Grieg founded Euterpe (1864), the Society for the Advancement of Northern Music, whose object was performance of Scandinavian works. The concert he gave on 15 October 1866 marked his first in Norway (Christiania) and the first to include only Norwegian composers' works. Grieg conducted the Philharmonic Society (1866–1867, 1880–1882) and taught at the Academy of Music (1867–1869). He was instrumental in founding the Musical Society (1870–1871). The Norwegian government granted him a composer's honorarium in July 1874 and awarded a (lifetime) royal stipend in July 1878.

Grieg built Lofthus as a haven for composing in 1877 but sold it in 1880 when local traffic precluded its intended use. Troldhaugen (The Hills of the Trolls), built seven miles from Bergen, became Grieg's home in April 1885. The Bergen (International) summer music festival was initiated by Grieg in 1898. He was made a member of the Swedish Academy (1872) and a corresponding member of the Academy of Leyden (1883), and was elected to the French Academy (1890) and to the Academy of Art in Berlin (1897). Grieg continued to give concerts to the end of his life, even when deteriorating health made it difficult. He died in 1907 and was buried on a promontory near Troldhaugen.

Grieg composed songs and pieces for piano, solo voice, mixed chorus, violin, chamber ensemble, and orchestra. His one symphony was not performed during his lifetime. Among his major works are Humoresques (1864–1865, influenced by Nordraak); Lyriske Stykker (Lyrical Pieces; in 10 volumes, 1867–1901); Piano Concerto in A minor, Op. 16 (1868); vocal works for poems by Bjørnson— Den Norske Sjømand, Sigurd Jorsalfar, Landkjending, Olav Trygvason; Ældre og nyere fjeldmelodier (1869, from Lindeman's collection); 22 pieces for Ibsen's drama Peer Gynt (1874–1876); songs to poems by Vinje, including The Youth, Spring, Letzter Frühling, Herzwunden (1877); the suite, Fra Holbergs Tid (for 3 December 1884, Ludvig Holberg bicentenary jubilee); and Haugtussa, Op. 67 (1898, for folk songs by Arne Garborg). Grieg's last work was four Psalms (chorales) for mixed a capella voices, Op. 74, which includes Hvad est du dog skjøn (How fair is thy face, 1906).

REFERENCES: E. Closson, *Edvard Grieg et la musique scandinave* (Paris: Librairie Fischbacher, 1892); H. Finck, *Grieg and His Music* (New York: John Lane Company, 1909); D. M. Johansen, *Edvard Grieg*, trans. M. Robertson (Princeton: Princeton University Press for the American Scandinavian Foundation, 1938); C. Purdy, *Song of the North, The Story of Edvard Grieg* (New York: Julian Messner, Inc., 1941, 1946); S. Sadie, ed., *The New Grove Dictionary of Music and Musicians*, vol. 7 (London: Macmillan Publishers Limited, 1980).

C. S. HALTERMAN

GRÍMR KAMBAN (c. 825) Reputedly the first Norse settler in the Faroe Islands*

The first sentence of *Færeyínga Saga* names Grímr Kamban as the first settler in the Faroe Islands, but has nothing else to say about him. The genealogy in *Landnámabók* makes it clear that he must have arrived in the Faroes about 825.

Grímr Kamban was, however, preceded in the islands by Irish anchorites referred to by the Irish geographer Dicuil in *De Mensura Orbis Terrae*, which points to a Celtic settlement from about 700. Pollen evidence has shown that barley was being grown in the Faroes a hundred years before even this time, so Grímr Kamban can only be regarded as the first Norse settler in the islands.

On the strength of a Celtic-sounding surname, it has been suggested that he came from the Hebrides or Ireland, not from mainland Norway. In *Landnámabók* (*Hauksbók*) appears the statement that after his death the islanders regarded him as a god and offered sacrifice to him.

REFERENCES: P. G. Foote, *On the Saga of the Faroe Islanders* (London: University College London, 1965); G. Johnston, *The Faroe Islanders' Saga* (Canada: Oberon Press, 1975); G. Turville-Petre, *The Heroic Age of Scandinavia* (London: Hutchinson, 1951).

J. F. WEST

GUSTAF *See* GUSTAV

GUSTAV I VASA (c. 1494–29 September 1560) King of Sweden (1521) 1523–1560

The son of Erik Johansson of the aristocratic Vasa family and Cecilia Måns-dotter of Eka, Gustav Vasa probably was born at Lindholmen estate in Uppland about 1494. Gustav Eriksson Vasa became the liberator of Sweden from what he and many others considered the unhappy union with Denmark and Norway, and the founder of modern Sweden and the brilliant Vasa dynasty.

Trained at home, at the court of Sten Sture*, and in Uppsala, Gustav Vasa developed into an attractive adult with a sound body, a keen mind, an extraordinary memory, and a quick temper. He could be a delight in social situations, was skilled in dealing with people, loved his country, and possessed a strong faith in his own ability to lead and to govern.

A hostage in Denmark, Gustav Vasa escaped Christian II*'s 1520 bloodbath in which Gustav's father and many other Swedish noblemen lost their lives. A fugitive from captivity in 1519, Gustav managed to get to Lübeck, whose Hanseatic rulers helped him to return to Sweden in 1520 and to finance the rebellion he led successfully against the union king. Numerous stories and legends about his trials and tribulations in initially failing to persuade the people of Småland to support him and his ultimate success in getting the Dalesmen, the people of the western province of Dalarna, to do so have become part of the Swedish heritage. Such stories were well enough known in America in the 1700s to have George Washington called "the Gustav Vasa of America."

The rebellion grew to the point where Gustav could be declared regent in 1521, make an alliance with Lübeck in 1552, make his entrance into Stockholm* in 1523, and on 6 June 1523 be elected king of Sweden. A realistic nationalist, King Gustav I set out to unify the country and make it strong and thoroughly independent under his firm direction. Not least among his means for carrying out his programs were his skills as a letter writer and speaker; a natural popular speaker and writer with pregnant, drastic humor and the gift for making his meaning crystal clear by means of homely detail, he had little or no difficulty in communication.

Because there were few Swedes trained to assist him in administering his government, he had to make use of foreigners, particularly Germans, in "modernizing'' the country's organization as much and as quickly as possible. The finances for doing so he found in subsidies from Lübeck, taxation, and, far from least, confiscation of Church property. He used the Reformation* to get the means for putting Sweden on its feet economically, in spite of the fact that very few Swedes were particularly anxious to have the church reformed. From 1527, when the cloisters' property was transferred to the crown, the control of church affairs was largely in Gustav's hands. Not only did he systematically confiscate church goods but through Olaus Petri* (Master Olof), other church leaders, and his own direct decisions he deliberately changed the Swedish church from an essentially faithful province of Rome to an increasingly Lutheran but national Church of Sweden.

By 1535 Gustav had succeeded in freeing Sweden from its debts to Lübeck, which until then had insisted on playing a major role in Swedish affairs, commercially and politically. While ruling Sweden as if it were his own property and making it an orderly, economically independent nation, Gustav found himself confronted with one rebellion after another, the most serious in 1524 (Dalarna), 1529 (Västergötland), and 1542 (Småland under Nils Dacke*). By skillful and patient maneuvering and by frequent ruthlessness Gustav put down every one of the rebellions. Among his achievements was the development of a strong army and navy for national defense.

In 1544 he succeeded in having parliament (the Riksdag*) make Sweden a hereditary monarchy: his heirs were to inherit the crown, not be elected. By that time Gustav had made sure he would have heirs by two marriages: a brief marriage in 1531 to Princess Katarina of Sachsen-Lauenburg (died 1535), the mother of Crown Prince Erik (Erik XIV*); and a marriage in 1536 to Lady Margareta Leijonhufvud (d. 1551), member of a powerful aristocratic family and the mother of three sons (including Johan III* and Karl IX*) and five daughters. In 1552 he married Queen Margareta's niece Katarina Stenbock (d. 1621).

Swedish and foreign historians recognize Gustav as a leader and ruler equal to the best in other countries and superior to most. Swedish writers have found Gustav Vasa a rewarding subject for both poetry and prose. One of the best Swedish plays is August Strindberg's *Gustav Vasa* (1899).

REFERENCES: C. Bergendoff, *Olavus Petri and the Ecclesiastical Transformation in Sweden, 1521–1522: A Study in the Swedish Reformation* (New York: Macmillan, 1928); V. Moberg, *A History of the Swedish People: From Renaissance to Revolution* (Stockholm: Norstedt, 1971); M. Roberts, *The Early Vasas: A History of Sweden, 1523–1611* (Cambridge, England: Cambridge University Press, 1968); F. Scott, *Sweden: The Nation's History* (Minneapolis: University of Minnesota Press, 1977).

W. JOHNSON

GUSTAV II ADOLF (9 December 1594–6 November 1632) King of Sweden 1611–1632

Gustav was the son of Karl IX* and Kristina of Holstein-Gottorp. He grew up in a period of political turmoil in Sweden involving the deposition of Sigismund* and the suppression of the powers of the great nobles by Gustav's father. He was educated under the tutelage of Johan Skytte and became particularly accomplished in languages and military strategy and tactics. He was introduced to the affairs of the state at an early age and took over direction of the government when his father suffered a stroke in 1610. It was then that he formed his lifelong friendship and partnership with Axel Oxenstierna*, who served as chancellor from 1610 to 1654.

Gustav had two principal problems when he came to the throne. The first was constitutional. His father had rejected the constitutional claims of the nobles and had ruled autocratically, supported by personal secretaries. In 1611–1612 Gustav was compelled to accept an accession charter drafted by Oxenstierna in which those claims were recognized and guaranteed. For the rest of his reign there was a degree of cooperation between the crown and the nobility that was rare in Sweden's history. The second problem area was foreign affairs. Sweden was involved directly in diplomatic tangles with Russia, Poland, Prussia, and Denmark, and these involved much of the rest of Europe indirectly. Here, too, Gustav achieved remarkable results. He accepted a costly end to the Kalmar War* with Denmark in the Peace of Knäred (1613). (Sweden had to pay 1 million *riksdaler* for the return of Älvsborg* and Gothenburg*.) By the Treaty of Stolbova (1617) he secured peace with Russia and assured Sweden's dominance of the Gulf of Finland. It was more difficult to end the struggle with Poland, but he did obtain a fifteen-year truce (Altmark) in 1629. The settlement of the political and diplomatic problems left Gustav free to enter into the Thirty Years' War.

Complementing his solution of the constitutional and diplomatic problems was the introduction of reforms designed to improve government and make Sweden better able to deal with external problems. In 1617 the parliament was given clearer structural and functional definition. The House of the Nobility was redefined in 1626. The court system was reformed and a supreme court created in 1614. Local government was restructured. The country was divided into 23 counties (*län*) under the direction of governors (*landshövding*). A system of university preparatory schools was created (gymnasia), and the University of Uppsala was reorganized and given sounder financial resources through the donations of the king. At the administrative level, the five great officers of the state (chancellor, steward, marshal, admiral, and treasurer) came to head administrative units (''colleges'') that gradually grew to resemble modern government departments. Also, a series of military reforms was initiated that gave Sweden one of the best-trained armies in Europe.

The effectiveness of Gustav's internal reforms enabled him to play a larger role in international affairs. By 1629 the course of the war in Germany had taken a threatening turn for the North. A Catholic victory seemed near at hand, and Gustav could not help but notice the threat such a victory would pose to Sweden's interests and security. In June 1630 he left Sweden for Germany. There he was greeted with little enthusiasm by the weary Protestant princes. It was only as he gained successes on the battlefield (and through some coercion) that his ranks swelled. Following his great victory at Breitenfeld in September 1631, the way to a Swedish-Protestant triumph seemed open, and Gustav began to dream of a Swedish-dominated Germany—and perhaps of himself as emperor. These dreams were smashed when Gustav was killed at Lützen in November 1632. (Sweden remained involved in the war until its end in 1648 and secured a role in German affairs in the Treaty of Westphalia. By then, however, Sweden was almost at the point in its history when it could no longer play the role Gustav had envisioned for it.)

Gustav was an extraordinary and complex figure. Charming, forceful, intelligent, and capable, he was also vain, impulsive, and a dreamer. He did much to make Sweden one of the best-governed states in Europe, but he also did much to keep Sweden on paths it could not afford. So aware of Sweden's weaknesses, he seemed unaware that an empire and influence could not be maintained forever on the basis of efficiency at home, subsidies, and fighting on the enemy's territories, and that sooner or later Sweden would be relegated to the ranks of a second- or third-rate power.

REFERENCES: G. Barudio, *Gustav Adolf—der Grosse* (Frankfurt am Main: S. Fischer, 1982); F. Berner, *Gustaf Adolf. Der Löwe aus Mitternacht* (Stuttgart: Deutsche Verlag-Anstalt, 1982); M. Roberts, *Gustavus Adolphus: A History of Sweden, 1611–1632*, 2 vols. (London: Longmans, 1953/1958), and *Gustavus Adolphus and the Rise of Sweden* (London: English Universities Press, 1973).

B. NORDSTROM

GUSTAV III (24 January 1746–29 March 1792) King of Sweden 1771–1792

Gustav was the son of Adolf Fredrik* of Holstein-Gottorp, who succeeded to the Swedish throne in 1751, and Lovisa (Louisa) Ulrika*, a sister of Frederick II ("the Great") of Brandenburg-Prussia. He received a good education under the supervision of the four estates of the Riksdag*, which was then the dominant element in the Swedish political system. He suffered emotionally, however, from the strained relations between his parents, who resented the limitations imposed on their powers during the Age of Liberty*, and the influence of the estates. It was against the wishes of the king and queen that Gustav was married in 1766 to the Danish princess Sophia Magdalena, a shy and poorly educated girl who was quite unsuited to act as his mate. At this time Gustav began to play an active role in political life; in 1768 he was the driving force behind his father's temporary "abdication" to force the council of the realm to call a meeting of the estates in the hope that they would agree to an increase in royal power. No change took place, however, and the strife between the Hat* and Cap* parties continued. In 1770 Gustav set off for France, ostensibly to complete his education, but after only two weeks in Paris he received news of his father's death.

He returned to Sweden with promises of French support for a revision of the constitution, and after making vain attempts to reconcile the factions, he led a bloodless coup d'etat on 16 August 1772 and forced the estates to accept a new constitution altogether. This left them with the power of the purse and a share in legislation but no control over membership of the royal council and no right to assemble without the king's permission. In fact, they were not summoned again for six years, during which time many reforms were carried through with Gustav's support. Officials who were found to have abused their powers were dismissed. The internal grain trade was freed (1775). Finance Minister Johan Liljencrantz carried through a devaluation of the currency, which was more firmly based on a silver standard (1776). A new Press Act (1774) left Swedish writers freer than in most other countries, but it was less liberal than the act of 1766 which it replaced. A state distilling monopoly was introduced in 1775, but this was very unpopular and led to rumblings of discontent from the peasantry. The clergy strongly opposed the extension of toleration to non-Lutheran Protestant foreigners resident in Sweden that was proposed to the estates when they met in 1778. This was passed, however, and in 1782 Jews* were allowed limited rights of worship.

After 1780 the pace of reform slowed, and at the same time opposition to Gustav grew, especially among the nobles, many of whom resented the way in which he appeared to be manipulating the constitution to increase his own power. Gustav was also faced with personal tragedy at this time. Rumors that the son born to the queen in 1778 (later Gustav IV Adolf*) was not the king's led to a breach with the imperious queen mother, to whom Gustav was deeply attached. New advisors came to the fore, and Gustav adopted a more adventurous foreign policy. He joined the League of Armed Neutrality formed by Catherine the Great of Russia in 1780 and hoped for her support in plans for a surprise attack on Denmark with the object of winning Norway. An extended journey to Italy in 1783–1784 was intended to conceal such plans, which had to be abandoned, however, when Catherine revealed her hostility. A fresh meeting of the estates in 1786 revealed how the opposition had grown in all sectors of the Swedish society. Gustav hoped to overcome this both by concessions to the commoner estates, such as the abandonment of the distilling monopoly, and by successful foreign adventures. In 1788, when Catherine was engaged against the Turks, Sweden went to war with Russia in Finland. But the campaign soon became bogged down, and a number of noble officers issued a declaration from their headquarters at Anjala calling for peace and the summoning of the estates. Gustav was saved by an attack from Denmark, which he was able to use to arouse patriotic feelings against the traditional Danish enemy and against the mutinous nobility. When the estates did meet in 1789, he was able to carry, against the nobles' opposition, an amendment to the constitution (the Act of Union and Security) which gave him nearly absolute power. At the same time the nobility was deprived of many of its privileges with regard to office- and land-holding. Peace was then made with Russia after a Swedish naval victory at Svensksund (1790). Gustav was very concerned by the threat to monarchy which the French Revolution seemed to represent and even planned to lead a crusade on behalf of the French crown. On 16 March 1792, after returning from his last meeting with his estates in Gävle, he was shot at a masked ball in the Opera House in

Stockholm* by Jakob Johan Anckarström, who had been hired by a party of discontented nobles. He died in the Royal Palace two weeks later.

Gustav shared his mother's cultural interests, especially her love of the theater. He established a Swedish National Opera soon after his accession. He wrote or participated in the writing of thirteen dramas on national themes, and in the earlier part of his reign he often participated in court theatricals. He patronized artists in other fields. The sculptor Johan Sergel was given rooms in the Royal Palace. The poet C. M. Bellman was found a post in the National Lottery. The painter Carl Pilo was enticed from Copenhagen* to execute a (never finished) portrayal of Gustav's coronation in 1771. Although the king nearly always wrote in French, he took a genuine interest in the development of the Swedish language and in 1786 founded the Swedish Academy both to honor the great men of Sweden's past and to protect the purity of the country's speech.

REFERENCES: R. N. Bain, *Gustavus III and His Contemporaries 1747–1792*, 2 vols. (London, 1894); H. Arnold Barton, "Gustav III of Sweden and the East Baltic 1771–1792," *Journal of Baltic Studies* 7 (1976): 13–30; Beth Hennings, *Gustav III* (Stockholm, 1957); Erik Lönnroth, "Gustavus III of Sweden: The Final Years—A Political Portrait," *Scandinavica* 6 (1967): 16–25; Stewart Oakley, "Gustavus III and Finland in 1775," *Scandinavian Studies* 51 (1979): 1–12; Stewart Oakley, "Gustavus III's Plans for War with Denmark in 1783–4," in R. M. Hatton and M. S. Anderson, eds., *Studies in Diplomatic History in Memory of David Bayne Horn* (London, 1970), pp. 268–86.

S. P. OAKLEY

GUSTAV IV ADOLF (1 November 1778–7 February 1837) King of Sweden 1792–1809

Gustav Adolf was born in Stockholm*, the son of Gustav III* and Queen Sophia Magdalena, although persistent rumors questioned his paternity. Gustav III was assassinated in March 1792, when Gustav Adolf was 13, and until 1796, his uncle, Duke Karl of Södermanland (later Karl XIII*), served as regent.

The beginning of Gustav Adolf's personal reign at first aroused high hopes, following the unpopular regency, and in administrative and economic matters it was a period of significant reforms. Of particular importance were the enclosure* ordinances of 1803–1807, initiating a widespread transformation of agriculture.

Although he had early been exposed to the ideas of the Enlightenment, the assassination of Gustav III and the excesses of the French Revolution made him an implacable foe of "Jacobinism" and free thought, and a rigidly orthodox Lutheran with Pietistic overtones. His internal regime was thus marked by a cultural obscurantism which has caused it to be remembered as an "iron age." In 1800 he reluctantly held a Riksdag* to stabilize Sweden's badly deranged currency. As this brought to light a small but vocal liberal parliamentary opposition, he thereafter refused to convene the estates again.

In foreign policy, he inherited both Gustav III's enmity toward revolutionary France and his preoccupation with acquiring Norway from Denmark. In his earlier years, Gustav Adolf thus followed a vacillating, opportunistic course, while preserving Sweden's neutrality in the wars between France and its enemies. In 1800 Sweden joined a League of Armed Neutrality with Russia, Prussia, and Denmark, soon broken up by the British attack on Copenhagen* and Tsar Paul's death in March-April 1801.

A lengthy visit to Germany in 1803–1805 brought Gustav Adolf into close contact with embittered French émigrés while Bonaparte's abduction from neutral Baden and execution of the Bourbon Duc d'Enghien, followed by his proclaiming himself emperor in 1804, turned Gustav Adolf irrevocably against France and led to his joining the Third Coalition in 1805. Sweden's participation in the ensuing war proved ignominious, in large part due to Gustav Adolf's intransigent Gallophobia combined with his manifest lack of military and diplomatic skills. By September 1807 the French drove him out of Swedish Pomerania. The confidence of both his allies and his own subjects was badly shaken, and his very sanity was questioned.

In June 1807, meanwhile, his ally, Russia, concluded both a peace and an alliance with France at Tilsit. When the British attacked Copenhagen in August to prevent the Danish fleet from falling into French hands, Denmark-Norway joined France and Russia, thus completing the encirclement of Britain's ally, Sweden. Ostensibly to enforce Napoleon's continental blockade against Britain, Russia attacked Swedish Finland in January 1808 and Denmark-Norway declared war in March. The Swedish defense was ineptly led and hampered by widespread defeatism. Still refusing to call a Riksdag, Gustav Adolf demanded increasing sacrifices in men and money.

By March 1809, after the Russians had occupied Finland and were advancing into northern Sweden, conspiracy gave way to open rebellion. Part of the army on the Norwegian front marched on Stockholm under Lieutenant-Colonel Georg Adlersparre. To preserve order and forestall Adlersparre, who was feared to be dangerously radical, a group of generals around C. J. Adlercreutz seized Gustav Adolf in Stockholm on 13 March 1809 and confined him to Gripsholm castle. By now increasingly despondent, he had long considered abdicating. The elderly, childless Duke Karl was again induced to become regent. A Riksdag convened by him in May deposed Gustav Adolf and barred his heirs from the succession. A new constitution was adopted, dividing power between the crown and the estates, and in June the duke was crowned as Karl XIII. A Danish prince, Christian August* of Augustenburg, was thereafter elected successor; after the latter's sudden death in June 1810, the French marshal J. B. Bernadotte was elected by the estates in his place and succeeded in 1818 as Karl XIV Johan*. In August 1809, Sweden meanwhile concluded the Peace of Frederikshamn (Hamina) with Russia, ceding Finland.

Gustav Adolf and his family were sent into exile on the continent in December 1809. Soon separated from his wife, Frederika of Baden, whom he had married in 1797, and his children, the ex-king led a solitary and restless life under the pseudonym "Colonel Gustafsson," mainly in Germany and Switzerland, until his death in St. Gallen in 1837.

REFERENCES: H. A. Barton, *Count Hans Axel von Fersen* (Boston: Twayne, 1975), and "Late Gustavian Autocracy: Gustav IV Adolf and His Opponents, 1792–1802," *Scandinavian Studies* 46 (1974): 265–84; S. Carlsson, *Gustaf IV Adolf* (Stockholm: Wahlström & Widstrand, 1946); L. Stavenow, *Den gustavianska tiden 1772–1809* (Stockholm: Norstedt, 1925).

H. A. BARTON

GUSTAV V (16 June 1858–29 October 1950) King of Sweden 1907–1950

Gustav was the eldest son of Oscar II* and Sofia of Nassau. His education was essentially military, although he spent one year at Uppsala University and one term at Christiana (Oslo) University in Norway. He was made a full general in 1898. In 1881 he married Victoria of Baden, granddaughter of Emperor Wilhelm I. Emperor Wilhelm II was her cousin.

Gustav's chief interests and influence in national life were defense issues and foreign policy. In these matters he kept fully informed and strove to preserve the monarchical role in government, in regard to both obligations and rights. In an era of democratic reforms his insistence on royal rights and obligations and his preference for conservative politics brought him into conflict with Liberals and Socialists. His most serious involvements in domestic politics were outgrowths of his views on foreign policy and defense.

During the Union crisis with Norway in 1905, he was acting as regent. In this capacity he supported a plan providing equal status to a Norwegian consular service. While it came too late to avoid the dissolution of the dynastic union, he repudiated the counsel of the more militant imperialist Swedes and supported a peaceful dissolution of the Norwegian-Swedish Union* through the Karlstad Conference.

Gustav's most forceful and successful role in the political life of Sweden occurred between 1911 and 1914, when defense was a central question. The alliance system and the arms race in Europe in general, and the Russification of Finland and a new border to defend in the west in particular, drove the Conservatives and the military to propose substantial new expenditures for the army and navy. The new Liberal government in 1911 was at best lukewarm to this, not to mention their tacit allies in parliament, the Social Democrats. From 1911 to 1913 Karl Staaff*, the Liberal prime minister, halted the construction of a miniscule battleship and opposed the army's plan for infantry recruit training. Gustav, prompted by his pro-German advisors and the queen, repudiated his government's policies on defense in a major address in February 1914 to 31,000 farmers, who had marched to support him (Bondetåget; *see* Farmers' March), thus creating a constitutional crisis. Although the Staaff ministry altered its view on defense considerably, Gustav used the occasion to force Staaff's resignation and to appoint a new Conservative government. He took the initiative in promoting the neutrality of the Scandinavian states in the two world wars. When a coalition Liberal-Social Democratic ministry took office in 1917, it was made coalition Liberal-Social Democratic ministry took office in 1917, it was made clear to the king that he must abide by the rules of parliamentary democracy, and he agreed.

During World War II*, he used both his official and personal influence to keep Sweden out of the conflict. He seems to have influenced Hitler in this. It was through his efforts that thousands of Hungarian Jews were saved. He promoted charitable causes, especially for better health, sports, and the enfranchisement of women after World War I. Gustav ultimately gained much respect and admiration from the rank and file Swede and even from Liberal and Socialist leaders. On private trips abroad he was known as "Mr. G" and was popular as a tennis player well into his eighties.

REFERENCES: O. F. Ander, *The Building of Modern Sweden: The Reign of Gustav V 1907–1950* (Rock Island, Ill.: Augustana Library Publications, 1958); K. E. Hildebrand, *Gustaf V som människa och regent*, 2 vols. (Stockholm: Svensk Litteratur AB, 1945–1948); *SU*, vol. 12; P. V. Thorson, "The Defense Question in Sweden 1911–1914," Ph.D. dissertation, University of Minnesota, 1972.

P. V. THORSON

GUSTAV VI ADOLF (11 November 1882–16 September 1973) King of Sweden 1950–1973

Gustav was the son of Gustav V* and Victoria of Baden. He was educated at Uppsala University, gained practical experience in administration in Norway before the dissolution of the Norwegian-Swedish Union* (1905), and had extensive military training and experience. He was an active archeologist for most of his life. He participated in excavation projects in Sweden and abroad and founded the Swedish Archaeological Institute in Rome. He was an expert on, and a collector of, Chinese art. For many years he headed the Swedish Asian Society and was a patron of museum collections. He was also active in sports, especially skiing and tennis.

He was nearly 68 when he succeeded his father in 1950, but for the next 23 years, as the powers of the monarch in Sweden vanished, he represented Sweden well and gained the respect of his people for his energy, intellect, and willingness to take positions on international issues in spite of Sweden's neutrality. (He openly opposed U.S. involvement in Vietnam.)

Gustav's first wife was Margaret, a granddaughter of Edward VIII of England. She died in 1920. In 1923 he married Louise of Mountbatten (d. 1965). His son and apparent heir, Gustav, was killed in a plane crash in 1947. He was succeeded by his grandson, Karl XVI Gustav*.

REFERENCES: A. Ohlmark, *Alla Sveriges kungar* (Stockholm: AWE/Geber, 1976); *SU*, vol. 12.

B. NORDSTROM

H

HAAKON I HARALDSSON (the Good) (c. 920–c. 960) King of Norway c. 935–c. 960

Haakon, the youngest illegitimate son of King Harald I Fairhair*, was fostered in England by King Athelstan. He returned to Norway in about 935, a few years after his father's death. Supported by Earl Sigurd Haakonsson of Lade in Trøndelag, the young man was hailed as king. His appearance in Norway ended the reign of his surviving half brother, King Eirik Bloodaxe, who was forced into exile in England. Although Haakon was also recognized as king in Trøndelag, he was in reality sovereign over only the western coast of Norway. The new king was popularly supported and received the nickname "the Good."

Haakon had been raised a Christian in England and attempted to introduce the new religion in Norway. Due to the opposition of Earl Sigurd and the farmers, he was, however, forced to abandon those efforts. Haakon was an exponent of the movement begun by his father for a unified Norway, a movement which was still confined to the coastal regions. He assisted in the establishment of district legal assemblies in western Norway and in Trøndelag. In this governmental reorganization, older local assemblies were expanded to cover larger areas, and the principle of representation was introduced. Another of the king's accomplishments was the creation of the defensive naval levy.

Haakon was killed in battle c. 960 while repulsing from western Norway the sons of Eirik Bloodaxe and their Danish allies. Harald II Eiriksson* (Graycloak), one of Eirik's sons, then succeeded to sovereignty.

REFERENCES: P. S. Andersen, *Samlingen av Norge og kristningen av landet 800–1130* (Bergen: Universitetsforlaget, 1977); K. Gjerset, *History of the Norwegian People* (1932; repr. New York: AMS, 1969); K. Larsen, *A History of Norway* (Princeton:

Princeton University Press, 1948/1974); S. Sturluson, *Heimskringla: Sagas of the Norse Kings* (London: Dent, 1961).

J. E. KNIRK

HAAKON II SIGURDSSON (the Broad-Shouldered) (c. 1147–7 July 1162) King of Norway 1157/1161–1162

Haakon the Broad-Shouldered was the illegitimate son of King Sigurd Mouth and thus a grandson of King Harald IV Magnusson* (Gilchrist). His father and his uncle Eystein conspired against their legitimate half brother and co-ruler, King Ingi I Haraldsson* (Hunchback), but Ingi and his men defeated and killed them in 1155 and 1157, respectively. During this second phase of the Norwegian civil wars, political factions had developed, and Haakon was chosen to succeed his uncle Eystein (and his father) as king of their group in 1157 at age 10. Whereas Ingi was supported by the aristocracy in western Norway and in the area around Oslo fjord, Haakon found support in Trøndelag, in the eastern valleys, and in the southeastern provinces on the Swedish border.

Haakon and his men suffered a defeat in 1159 in eastern Norway, but internal rivalries soon weakened Ingi's faction. On 4 February 1161 the incumbent ruler fell fighting Haakon and his forces on the ice near Oslo, and Haakon succeeded to undivided rule, naming the real leader of his group, Sigurd Haavardsson, earl. Erling Crook-Neck (*skakki*), however, quickly rallied Ingi's faction in Bergen behind his own five-year-old son by the daughter of King Sigurd I Magnusson* (the Crusader), Magnus (later Magnus V Erlingsson*). Erling assumed leadership of the group as regent for his son and later that year routed Haakon from eastern Norway. On 7 July 1162 Haakon was defeated and killed in western Norway, leaving Magnus Erlingsson sole sovereign over the country.

REFERENCES: G. M. Gathorne-Hardy, *A Royal Impostor: King Sverre of Norway* (Oslo: Aschehoug, 1956); K. Gjerset, *History of the Norwegian People* (1932; repr. New York: AMS, 1969); K. Helle, *Norge blir en stat 1130–1319*, 2nd rev. ed. (Bergen: Universitetsforlaget, 1974); K. Larsen, *A History of Norway* (Princeton: Princeton University Press, 1948/1974); S. Sturluson, *Heimskringla: Sagas of the Norse Kings* (London: Dent, 1961).

J. E. KNIRK

HAAKON IV HAAKONSSON (the Old) (1204–16 December 1263) King of Norway 1217–1263

Haakon Haakonsson, a paternal grandson of King Sverrir Sigurdsson* born posthumously in 1204, was raised at the court of King Ingi II Baardsson*. When Ingi died in 1217, his Birchleg (civil war faction) retainers elected Haakon to succeed him, and this selection was approved at district assemblies. The king was illegitimate, however, and ecclesiastical leaders preferred Ingi's legitimate half brother, Skuli Baardsson, who continued as earl over one-third of the country and became regent. Doubts concerning Haakon's paternity were allayed when his mother passed an ordeal in 1218, but the question of succession to the throne was not finally decided until 1223, when a national assembly in Bergen of religious and secular leaders, especially district judges, determined Haakon to be the rightful king of Norway.

Haakon's reign marked the end of the Norwegian civil wars. Responding to a threatening uprising in 1217–1218 in eastern Norway, the Crosiers joined forces with the Birchlegs and ceased to exist as a faction, and with the next uprising there in 1219–1227, the wars ebbed away. The national assembly in Bergen in 1223 was a defeat for Earl Skuli, and, as an attempt at reconciliation, Haakon married Skuli's daughter in 1225. The relationship between the king and the earl remained strained and came to an open break in 1235, but reconciliation was again attained in 1237, at which time Skuli was appointed the first duke of Norway. In reality, however, his power was curtailed, and in 1239 the duke revolted and let himself be proclaimed king at an assembly in Trøndelag. The following year he was defeated in Oslo by Haakon's forces and then killed in Nidaros (Trondheim).

Haakon achieved a good rapport with the Church. Their cooperation led to a clearer delineation of the relationship between church and state and to the establishment of a clearly defined hereditary monarchy in Norway based on legitimacy and primogeniture. Haakon's oldest legitimate son, Haakon the Young, was taken as co-regent in 1240. Haakon Haakonsson (the Old) received papal dispensation for his own illegitimacy and in 1247 was crowned by a cardinal at a national assembly in Bergen. After Haakon the Young died in 1257, the Church no longer had to argue for primogeniture, and Haakon Haakonsson's only other legitimate son, Magnus VI Haakonsson*, became king and co-regent. The new law of succession, which relegated the election of kings by district assemblies to a formality, was codified, probably in 1260.

During Haakon's rule the real unification of the nation was completed. International politics were stressed after 1240, including an expansion and solidification of control over the tributary colonies in the British Isles and the North Atlantic. Greenland* and Iceland, which were economically, religiously, and politically dependent on Norway, accepted Norwegian rule and taxation in return for trade guarantees in 1261 and 1262–1264, respectively. Haakon strengthened his political and economic connections with foreign powers by reaching trade agreements with England in 1223 and with Lübeck in 1250, by devising royal marriages for his children, and by making peace with Sweden and Denmark concerning sovereignty over the eastern border provinces. Marked by relative peace and stability, his 46–year reign was the beginning of the "Age of Greatness" in Norwegian history. From his royal administrative center in Bergen the king patronized the translation of foreign courtly literature.

In 1263 Haakon sailed a fleet to the Scottish Isles to protect Norwegian interests in the Hebrides and the Isle of Man. Following skirmishes with troops of King Alexander III of Scotland, he retired for the winter to the Orkneys, where he died on 16 December. King Magnus succeeded as sole sovereign and commissioned the Icelander Sturla Thordarson to write his father's saga, a work based partially on documents from the royal archives and completed c. 1265.

REFERENCES: K. Gjerset, *History of the Norwegian People* (1932; repr. New York: AMS, 1969); K. Helle, *Norge blir en stat 1130–1319*, 2nd rev. ed. (Bergen: Universitetsforlaget, 1974); K. Larsen, *A History of Norway* (Princeton: Princeton University Press, 1948/1974); S. Thordarson, *The Saga of Hacon, and a Fragment of the Saga of Magnus* (London: Rolls, 1894).

J. E. KNIRK

HAAKON VII (3 August 1872–21 September 1957) King of Norway 1905–1957

Haakon (until he became king in Norway his name was Carl) was a younger son of Frederik VIII* of Denmark. Because he was not first in line to the throne in Denmark, he chose a career in the navy. In 1897 he married Princess Maud, a daughter of England's King Edward VII. Until 1905 his life was relatively uneventful. Then, however, his name came to be prominently mentioned in connection with the vacant throne in Norway after the dissolution of the Norwegian-Swedish Union*. Haakon's father-in-law supported his candidacy and urged him to go to Norway. Haakon, on the other hand, was careful to ensure that he did not go to Norway without the approval of Europe's royal houses. The Norwegian government and its representatives tried to get him on the throne while negotiations were still being held with Sweden. These early efforts failed largely because Haakon insisted on a plebiscite in Norway. Republican sentiments were strong there, and this was a portentous move. It was, however, the only way Haakon could justify his view that he represented the people and stood above politics. The vote in this plebiscite was overwhelmingly favorable to Haakon by a four-to-one margin. He officially became king of Norway on 18 November 1905.

As king in a constitutional, parliamentary democracy, Haakon was fully aware of the limitations placed upon him. He maintained a rigid official stance which demonstrated that he did indeed stand above party politics. On more than one occasion, he told his listeners that he was king of all the Norwegians, Communists as well as Conservatives.

King Haakon's first significant action confirming his style occurred in 1928, when the Norwegian Labor Party* became the largest party in the Storting*. Everyone assumed that the king would appoint a non-Socialist government, because the bourgeois parties still controlled a majority. Haakon, however, turned to the Labor Party and asked its leader, C. Hornsrud, to form a government. His action surprised even the Socialists, who had consistently maintained a view hostile toward the monarchy. Although the first Labor government lasted only two weeks, the party had tasted power within the existing system. Haakon's action forced a re-evaluation of the Labor Party's view of the king and effectively dampened its republican sentiments. When the party returned to power in 1935, it was as loyal to the monarchy as any party on the Right.

Perhaps nothing during the reign of Haakon VII contributed more to his elevation to virtually legendary proportions than his actions following the invasion of Norway by Germany on 9 April 1940. Forced to flee the capital, he and the government were pursued by the advancing Germans, who were eager to capture him. Seeking a measure of respectability, German authorities asked Haakon to appoint the Norwegian collaborator Vidkun Quisling* as prime minister. The king's answer was a firm no, which reverberated through the valleys of Norway and inspired resistance to the invaders.

Although forced to evacuate the country on 7 June 1940, Haakon remained the symbol of resistance with the government-in-exile in London. Five years to the day after leaving Norway, Haakon returned to the country where he was, by then, regarded in almost reverent terms.

In the final twelve years of his reign, Haakon presided over the material reconstruction of the country and the expansion of its system of social welfare. By the time of his death in 1957, Haakon was considered the symbol of Norwegian independence. Probably no monarch in Norway's history has stood so near to Norwegian hearts and fulfilled their expectations so well. He was succeeded by his son, Olaf V*.

REFERENCES: T. Greve, *Haakon VII: Mennesket og monark* (Oslo, 1980); Y. Hauge, *Fra korvettens dekk til Norges trone: Kong Haakons ungdom* (Oslo, 1955); W. P. Sommerfeldt, ed., *Hans Majestet Kong Haakon VII Taler, 1905–1946* (Oslo: 1946); K. A. Wig, *Spillet om tronen* (Oslo, 1980).

T. LEIREN

HAAKON SIGURDSSON (the Great) (c. 935–995) Earl of Lade, chief ruler of Norway c. 970 (974?)–995

Haakon Sigurdsson was about 30 years old (c. 965) when he succeeded as the earl of Lade in Trøndelag upon his father's death at the hands of King Harald II Eiriksson* (Graycloak). The family of the earls of Lade came originally from northern Norway but had established itself as the local aristocracy in Trøndelag. Haakon's forces and an army of Danes defeated and killed the Norwegian king Harold c. 970 (974?) in Jutland. The Danish king Harald I* (Bluetooth), who had connived this battle, then appointed Haakon his earl, thus subordinating the chief ruler of Norway to the Danish crown. Earl Haakon, nicknamed "the Great," was sovereign only over Trøndelag and part of western Norway. He was unable to subjugate the southwestern coast and exercised questionable control in the north. The territory around Oslo fjord was governed directly from Denmark, and the eastern valleys were in the hands of petty kings.

Although Haakon was initially subordinate to the king of Denmark and supported Harald Bluetooth in 974 against an invasion by Otto II, he later pursued a more independent line, cooperating with other local leaders in Norway. With him Trøndelag finally entered decisively into the unification process in Norway. Harald Bluetooth and his successor in Denmark, Sven I* (Forkbeard), were unsuccessful in their attempts to subjugate Norway, although they did disrupt the process of unification. In the battle of Hjørungavaag in western Norway (c. 985), Haakon defeated the Jomsvikings, who were Danes from a Viking* camp in the Baltic. The earl was a conservative heathen and also opposed Danish efforts to impose Christianity in Norway. He was the last non-Christian ruler of the land.

Losing his popularity due to arrogance near the end of his reign, the earl was killed by one of his own slaves during an uprising of farmers in Trøndelag in 995. His death coincided with the arrival in Norway of Olaf I Tryggvason*, who was hailed as king. Although Haakon's sons and grandson ruled Norway later as appointees of the Danish crown, the earls of Lade ultimately lost the battle for control of Norway to the descendants of King Harald I Fairhair*.

REFERENCES: P. S. Andersen, *Samlingen av Norge og kristningen av landet 800– 1130* (Bergen: Universitetsforlaget, 1977); K. Gjerset, *History of the Norwegian People* (1932; repr. New York: AMS, 1969); K. Larsen, *A History of Norway* (Princeton: Princeton University Press, 1948/1974); S. Sturluson, *Heimskringla: The Olaf Sagas*, vol. 1 (London: Dent, 1964).

J. E. KNIRK

HALL, PETER ADOLPH (1739–1793) Swedish artist

The son of a doctor in royal service, Hall was born in Borås and was destined to follow his father's profession. He studied natural sciences in Uppsala and subsequently at Greifswald and Göttingen. He seems also to have had some instruction in music in Berlin and Hamburg, and it was to music he turned toward the end of his life. He returned to Sweden in 1760 and entered the studio of Gustaf Lundberg*. Here his gifts as a painter developed rapidly, and following his success with a portrait of Crown Prince Gustav (III*) in 1766 he was advised to make his way to Paris. By the time he won the critical acclaim of Diderot at the 1769 Salon, Hall had received royal commissions and had frequented the circle of Jean-Baptiste Greuze, and Hubert Robert, and Vigée Lebrun. In 1771 he married Adelaide Gobin, heiress to a Compagnie des Indes fortune, and his marriage, together with his meteoric rise as a gifted miniaturist, enabled him to form a distinguished art collection, which included work by Rembrandt and Velasquez as well as his French contemporaries. On Louis XVI's accession in 1774, Hall became painter to the king.

While Hall was influenced by Jean-Antoine Watteau and Jean-Honoré Fragonard, he had original qualities as a miniaturist which in delicacy and refinement were equalled only by Fragonard. However, as in the case of Alexander Roslin*, Hall's titled clientele declined in the 1780s, and he returned to his musical interests, becoming a friend of André Grétry. Hall first welcomed the French Revolution and was quick to enroll in the National Guard. But his nationality worked against him, and he chose exile in Liège, Grétry's native city, rather than remain in revolutionary Paris. It was here that Hall died, having been absent from Sweden for 27 years. A portrait of Hall and his wife by F-A. Vincent was exhibited in the Salon of 1777.

REFERENCES: P. Lespinasse, *Les artistes suédois en France du XVIII siècle* (Paris, 1929); S. Strömbom, *Fem Store Gustavianer* (Stockholm, 1943); F. Villot, *Hall: Célèbre miniaturiste du XVIII_e, sa vie, ses oeuvres etc.* (Paris: Librairie française et etrangère, 1867).

D. D. ALDRIDGE

HAMMERSHAIMB, VENCESLAUS ULRICUS (1819–1909) Faroese philologist

Venceslaus (or Venzel) Ulricus Hammershaimb was the inventor of the orthography now used in writing Faroese. He did valuable work in the collection of traditional Faroese literature, and, more than any other single person, developed Faroese as a vehicle for modern literary purposes, with profound political as well as cultural consequences during the present century.

The Hammershaimbs came originally from Bohemia, which they left because of religious persecution. The first to come to Faroe was Jörgen Frantz Hammershaimb (1688–1765), who from 1723 to his death was *landfoged*(high bailiff). One of his sons, Wenceslaus Hammershaimb (1744–1828), succeeded to his father's post, while another, Samuel Hammershaimb (1747–1828), was from 1774 until 1796 resident manager of the Faroese Monopoly* in Tórshavn*. The son of Wenceslaus, Jörgen Frands Hammershaimb (1767–1820), was from 1806 the last Lagmand* of the Faroe Islands*, until the post was abolished in 1816.

V. U. Hammershaimb was born on Steig Farm in Sandavágur, but at the age of 2, on his father's death, moved with his mother to Tórshavn. He was a talented child and began to learn Latin when only 6. As a boy, he also had some contact with the aged Jens Christian Svabo*, who was still working on his Faroese dictionary; Svabo was the brother of Hammershaimb's paternal grandmother.

When he was 11, it was decided that Hammershaimb should study, and when he was 13 he left the Faroes for Copenhagen* with his mother. He attended Borgerdydsskolen in Christianshavn until 1839, when he entered Copenhagen University. There his main study was theology, to which he added the study of the Scandinavian languages*. He graduated in 1847.

He began his collection of traditional Faroese material in 1841, when he traveled around the Faroe Islands with the sympathetic and much-loved *amtmand* Christian Plöyen (1803–1867). In 1847–1848 he again visited the Faroes to collect ballads, folktales, and legends and to study the dialects of Faroese. In 1849 he got a teaching appointment in Copenhagen, in which he continued for six years. In 1853, aided by a research grant, he made a further journey to his native islands to complete his collections and to gather materials for a Faroese grammar.

In 1855 he was ordained as minister of North Streymoy, from which he moved to the living of Eysturoy in 1862. He became provost in 1867. In 1878 he returned to Denmark to take up a living in Sjælland, from which he retired in 1898. On his last visit to the Faroes in 1893, he was greeted everywhere with enthusiasm and respect, for his work both as priest and philologist.

Among Hammershaimb's friends at Copenhagen University was Svend

Grundtvig (1824–1883), son of the celebrated N.F.S. Grundtvig; when the two first met in 1843, Svend was already known for his work on the Scandinavian ballad tradition. The two were early involved in a struggle arising from educational developments in Faroe, which was an important impulse toward Hammershaimb's philological and literary work.

The Roskilde Assembly was in 1844 debating elementary schooling for Faroese villages, and, being ill-informed about the linguistic situation in the islands, took it for granted that the medium of instruction in the proposed new schools would be Danish. Many delegates, indeed, believed Faroese was not a true language at all, but a corrupted dialect of Danish and Icelandic. In an article in the *Kjöbenhavnsposten* of 19 December 1844, over the signature "A Faroeman," Hammershaimb pointed out that Faroese had all the characteristics of an independent language, however much it had been influenced during the centuries that Danish had been the language of religion and public business. A few months later, under the pseudonym S. Frederiksen, Grundtvig published a pamphlet, *Dansken paa Færöerne: Sidestykke til Tysken i Slesvig* (*Danish in the Faroe Islands: A Parallel with German in Slesvig*), making the telling point that just as Danish was under pressure from the German-language elementary schools in North Slesvig*, so, by the proposed school law, the Faroese language would be oppressed by Danish in the new schools in Faroe. (The law was unfortunately passed in 1845 but worked so badly that it had to be revoked in 1854).

Hammershaimb became convinced that to promote the Faroese language and enable it to develop a modern literature, it needed an orthography based on etymological principles, to get beyond the diversity of dialects to the Old Norse origins of the language. With the help of the Icelandic scholar and patriot Jón Sigurðsson (1811–1879), he devised the system of rendering Faroese that is essentially the one used today. An advantage was that it made Faroese texts easily comprehensible to the many scholars and others in Scandinavia and elsewhere who could read Icelandic or Old Norse. The orthography was first published in his *Færöisk Sproglære* in 1854.

From 1846 onward, Hammershaimb published much Faroese oral literature: ballads, legends, folktales, and proverbs. Of special importance is a two-volume ballad collection, *Færöiske Kvæder* (1851–1855). His final work, which marks the beginning of modern Faroese literature, was *Færösk Anthologi*, published in 1891 with support from the Carlsberg Fund. Hammershaimb's texts in Volume 1 were supplemented by a Faroese-Danish dictionary from the pen of Jakob Jakobsen*. Hammershaimb's work may best be compared with that of Peter C. Asbjörnsen and Jörgen Moe, and Ivar Aasen in Norway.

REFERENCES: There is no account of V. U. Hammershaimb's life in English. His work on Faroese ballads is, however, well known internationally, and frequent references to it appear in works on the European ballad tradition.

                                                                                                  J. F. WEST

HAMRIN, FELIX (1875–1937) Swedish prime minister

Hamrin was born in Mönterås. He established Felix Hamrin & Company in Jönköping shortly after 1900. He was a temperance and free church activist, and he entered politics early in this century. He enjoyed a remarkable career in local and national government and rose to become prime minister in 1932.

First elected to the Riksdag* in 1911, Hamrin served in the Second Chamber from 1912 to 1914 and from 1918 to 1934, when he moved to the First Chamber, where he held a seat until his death. He became a recognized leader among the Liberals in the pre-World War I period, and he joined the faction headed by Carl Gustav Ekman* when the Liberal Coalition split in 1923. He served on the governing council of the Liberal People's Party* for the next nine years and replaced Ekman as head of the party in 1933. Thereafter, he worked to reunite the Liberal factions and became head of the parliamentary group that developed out of these efforts, the Folk Party, in 1934.

Hamrin served as minister of commerce in Ekman's first cabinet (1926–1928) and as minister of finance in the second Ekman government (1930–1932). During his second tenure in office he was faced with the difficult task of dealing with the Depression. His responses were typical of non-Socialist politicians at the time. He sought to balance the state's budget by trimming expenditures and increasing taxes on luxury items, tobacco, and alcohol.

In August 1932 Ekman was forced to resign, and Hamrin replaced him as prime minister. In the parliamentary election held in September 1932, the Social Democrats made the greatest gains, although they did not secure a majority in either chamber of the Riksdag. Hamrin then resisted stepping down and tried to construct a non-Socialist coalition. His efforts and his negotiations with the Social Democrats to form a coalition failed. Following the collapse of these attempts, Hamrin resigned, and Per Albin Hansson* formed a minority Social Democratic government.

Hamrin remained active in politics for the remainder of his life. He continued in parliament, fulfilled his appointment to the Royal Defense Commission established in 1930, and worked on the Welfare Committee. He was also appointed governor of Jönköping county.

REFERENCES: *DSH*, vol. 14; Kenne Fant, *Ångerstolen* (Stockholm: Norstedt, 1978); *SU*, vol. 12.

B. NORDSTROM

HANS I (2 February 1455–20 February 1513) King of Denmark 1482–1513, king of Norway 1483–1513, king of Sweden 1497–1500

Hans was the son of Christian I* and Dorothea of Brandenburg. Following his father's death in 1481, Hans succeeded to the Danish and Norwegian thrones. The succession, which had been agreed to earlier by all the Nordic countries, did not come cheaply for Hans. His father had pursued policies that were aimed at undercutting the authority of the aristocracy and the Church, and these powerful groups took advantage of the king's death to extract new promises from his successor that their privileges and powers would be respected. At a meeting at Halmstad in 1483, the Norwegian and Danish councils, plus representatives from Sweden, met and drafted the Halmstad Accession Charter (the Kalmar Recess* in Sweden). Composed of 51 paragraphs, this charter was an extreme expression of aristocratic constitutionalism. The king was little more than a figurehead under the charter. He was bound to rule only with the council's advice and consent. He could not declare war, tax, make new laws, appoint administrators, or make donations of lands or castles without the approval of the council in the appropriate country. A clause was included which gave the nobles the right to rebel against the king if he violated the charter. Furthermore, all donations of lands and castles were to revert to the council (or an executive committee thereof) upon the king's death. Hans accepted this charter and lived within its terms for a decade.

Hans was a patient, dedicated, intelligent person who shared his father's aims and policies. He was, moreover, a better politician than his father. He was a master at exploiting a political or diplomatic situation to his advantage. Consequently, by the time of his death, he had made the king the focus of political power in Denmark. The position of the monarch had never been stronger. This accomplishment was based upon the outlines Christian I had established and upon several new foundations of royal power. Central among the latter were the navy and army Hans built. With respect to the former, he developed the administration based on a royal chancery loyal to the king, and he created a financial and social base of support in the non-noble classes. His success was also based on his personal abilities and a set of special circumstances which benefited his policies.

Any attempt to explain Hans's accomplishments must begin with a consideration of his foreign policies, which took advantage of circumstances and broader historical developments. Hans was an indomitable diplomat and a Machiavellian. He made and broke alliances with England, Scotland, France, Danzig, Russia, Lübeck, the Netherlands, and Sweden. He was never above deserting an ally or allying with a former enemy, if the moment were right. He went to war against Sweden in 1495, 1500, and 1509. He continued an ongoing piracy war with England until he needed an ally against Lübeck. He sided with Lübeck in the 1490s and went to war against the city in 1509. The tangible or territorial results of his policies were not impressive. Sweden was forced back into the union for only a brief period (1497–1500). His last wars with Sweden secured him only the recognition of his claims to the throne and an annual payment of 12,000 marks until he was crowned. He attempted to annex the small peasant republic of Ditmarksen, but his army of mercenaries was mauled by a much smaller force of peasants at the battle of Hemmingstedt (1500). Virtually no territory was added to the realm. Viewed from a different perspective, however, Hans's policies were remarkably effective. They provided him with the excuses and the means to effect his domestic aims, primarily the expansion of royal authority at the expense of the nobility. His policies necessitated arms, money, and effective administration. The shifting nature of warfare in the late fifteenth century called for armies comprised primarily of foot soldiers—either mercenaries or native recruits. Hans employed both. His Saxon Guard is the most notable example of a mercenary unit within his army. The nobility, which had served as the basis for armies of horsed knights, became less and less necessary. As the military monopoly of the nobility evaporated, its basis for political power dissolved. At the same time, Hans built a navy to support his policies, especially against the Hanse (see Hanseatic League). For a time his fleet was the largest in Europe. The army and navy were expensive. The rural commons were the traditional tax base, but there was a limit to what they could bear. Hans offered the peasantry protection against the ever-encroaching power of the nobles in exchange for tax revenues. At the same time, he offered the middle class government offices and trade privileges in exchange for taxes and loans. He was successful in both approaches. But the royal edifice Hans constructed was a fragile one. It depended upon a successful foreign policy to a large extent. Hans's son, Christian II*, would soon find out how fragile the system his father created was.

Hans married Christina, daughter of Ernst of Saxony, in 1478. She was a supportive force behind him, although she was very different from her secular, politically oriented husband. Christina was very devout and an ardent friend of the poor and the Franciscans in the kingdom. Three children came from this union: Christian II, Frans (d. 1511), and Elizabeth (d. 1558).

REFERENCES: G. Carlsson, *Kalmar Recess 1483* (Stockholm: Kungliga Vitterhets-historie- och antikvitetsakademien, 1955); *DBL*, vol. 5; *DH*, vol. 5; J. P. Lindbæk, *Pavernes forhold til Danmark under kongerna Kristian I og Hans* (Copenhagen: G.E.C. Gade, 1907); *NH*, vol. 5; C. Paludan-Müller, *De først konger af den Oldenborgske slægt* (1874).

B. NORDSTROM

HANSEATIC LEAGUE (Hanse) A federation of primarily German cities dominant in North European commerce

The Hanseatic League was a federation of north German cities that developed in the latter part of the twelfth century. The League's rise to power coincided with the emergence of medieval cities all over the North. For over 400 years, this merchant empire, under the leadership of Lübeck (founded c. 1160) dominated the trade routes and monopolized the markets throughout the North.

From the Viking Age* (c. 800–1100) into the twelfth century, Baltic trade was in the hands of the Scandinavians. During the latter part of this period, German merchants followed the northerners' trade routes and absorbed their navigational skills. The center for the international trade between east and west Europe was the island of Gotland. The visiting merchants were seasonal guests. They traded in the summer and returned to their home ports in winter.

A fundamental reason for the Hanse's rise to power was the population increase that pushed expansion and colonization to the north German plains and east along the Baltic. From 1250 and into the 1300s, new cities emerged along the Baltic coast and elsewhere in the North. The overland routes proved inadequate for transportation of the bulk cargoes needed to supply the growing city populations. Lübeck's geographic position made it the natural center for the maritime trade that now developed. From the inland regions along the eastern Baltic, ships brought lumber, salt, and grain to be sold for fish from the North. From Lübeck the cargo was brought overland to Hamburg and distributed on the continental markets.

Lübeck's council constitution and laws became the model for the new cities. By 1226 it had become an autonomous municipality ruled by a merchant aristocracy which cooperated in the development of new markets and promoted trade in German hands.

In the 1200s an important change took place in the structure of maritime trade. The owner merchants (*mercatores frequentantes*) who traded from their own ships during the summer were replaced by merchants who directed trade from their home port (*mercatores manentes*) through representatives abroad. These merchants were part-owners of the vessels, which had hired crews. The merchant guilds provided the capital required.

By the end of the twelfth century, a new ship, the cog, had revolutionized shipping. The increased loading capacity and improved speed and safety of the cog proved very useful for transportation of bulk goods. Franklin D. Scott speculates that the Scandinavians, with their many years of proud tradition in shipbuilding, may have been reluctant to discard their older designs, which had been very suitable for trade in less bulky luxury goods.

Around 1200 German merchants, displacing the Swedes, started to winter on Gotland. The Hanse expanded its power in the North. By 1300 their merchant system was fully developed, and the Scandinavians could no longer compete. In 1280 Lübeck was *capud et principium* of all the towns in the league. All major decisions rested with the more than 70 member towns, whose representatives met in Lübeck on Hansa Days from 1356 on. Lübeck's strength was aided by coalitions with princely powers. In Scandinavia* the kings granted privileges to the foreign merchants to stem the rise of feudal power.

In Denmark the rich herring fisheries of the Öresund soon came under the direct control of Lübeck. German merchants provided capital and salt to encourage growth of the fisheries and large-scale preservation of herring for continental markets. By 1249 the Hanse were masters of the Öresund herring trade. At the same time, Hanse merchants gained control of commerce in Denmark's principal towns, including Copenhagen*.

In Norway the records show German merchants visiting Bergen as early as 1186. The visits took place during market days in the summer. By 1200 German merchants were settled permanently. The Hanseatic administration was loosely structured. The office (*kontor*) in Bergen was fairly independent. From their headquarters on the pier (Bryggen), they managed the affairs of their home firms. Elected aldermen had the power to decide in all matters concerning the journeymen and artisans, who at times constituted 10 percent of the town's population.

From the Baltic region grain was shipped to Norway in exchange for cod, caught and dried in the North and marketed in Bergen. The demand for cod on the continental markets encouraged this industry, which resulted in the colonization of the northern sections of Norway. The climatic conditions prevented Norway from increasing its own grain production to meet the demand of its growing towns. Advancing grain and equipment against the next year's catch, the Germans on Bryggen bound the Norwegian fishermen in debt and soon controlled both supply and transportation. The League withheld grain whenever they wanted a concession. Domestic and foreign policies could be controlled in this way.

By a treaty of 1262, Norway agreed to call on Iceland with six ships each year. By the middle of the 1400s, the office in Bergen was in charge of the export of fish from Iceland. German merchants were never encouraged to settle there, but their trade brought prosperity and an increased standard of living to Iceland. In 1416 Lübeck banned direct trade between Germany and the outlying islands to protect the monopoly they had established in Bergen. In spite of this ban, the Iceland trade slowly shifted to Hamburg and Bremen, where it remained until the 1600s, when Denmark developed a fleet that could accommodate the trade.

In Finland, as on Gotland, the German merchants displaced the Swedes. As everywhere else in the North, their trade was limited to the coastal regions. Luxury goods remained the major export items from Finland. The clergy and government officials who collected taxes on the wares supported them. The vigorous German settlers brought capital and a higher standard of living with them. The Hanseatic trade brought Finland into the European economic sphere. When German universities were founded in Rostock and Grafswald in the 1400s, Finns attended and established Finland's ties within the European cultural community.

In 1250 Birger Jarl founded Stockholm*. In return for support against his domestic opponents, Birger Jarl granted Lübeck freedom from duties and taxation. Settlers had to become Swedish citizens and were subject to Swedish law. German merchants came to compose 35 percent of Stockholm's population and dominated the economic life of the city. To limit their influence, the merchants were restricted to half of the city council seats.

The Germans left their mark in a number of areas beyond their immediate impact on the economies of the Scandinavian countries. A number of contributions grew out of the influx of German artisans to the growing cities. The crafts had been traditionally a part of the farmers' functions, but the new towns with large populations and strict work organization made the services of the new group desirable. Many German words were absorbed into the Scandinavian languages, among them the names for the crafts. The guild system the artisans brought with them was adopted. The organization in the cities determined where the artisans practiced their crafts, and where medieval sections remain the street names still carry the names of the crafts. The Germans introduced bricks and altered old construction methods. Their influence on architecture remained strong until the 1600s. Furthermore, the German council approach to government was adopted or incorporated into the local administrative systems. The German concept of royal power based on heredity was also influential in the development of monarchy.

Several factors caused the weakening and final break of the Hanse's power in the North. The overland route between Lübeck and Hamburg was a weak point, and within the League cracks appeared as member cities split into special interest spheres. From 1400 on, English and Dutch merchants sailed around Denmark and into the Baltic. Cities like Danzig, which wanted the freedom to trade directly, eagerly sought these west European merchants out and sold them grain. The salt mines in Lüneberg ran dry, and this industry shifted to ocean salt from the west coast waters. The Skåne fisheries closed when the herring disappeared from the Öresund. As the early modern dynastic states in Denmark-Norway and Sweden-Finland developed, the Hanse's influence diminished. This process began in 1397–1398, when the North was united in the Kalmar Union*. The Scandinavian countries then had the strength to resist the Hanse's power and forced Lübeck's withdrawal from Öresund and Skåne. The Kalmar Union encouraged local merchants to engage in trade and to break the Hanse's monopolies. This unity in the North, coupled with the internal strife in the League, enabled the Scandinavian countries to adopt active foreign policies which led to reductions in the Hanse's privileges. The economic grip was stronger than the political changes, however, and both Swedish and Danish governments had to reckon with Lübeck until the end of the sixteenth century.

In Norway, the break with Lübeck occurred in 1559, when the German artisans were forced to leave Bryggen and become citizens. When the grain monopoly broke, the crown and moneyed Dutch, English, and Scottish merchants, who had earlier become citizens, fought off the grip of the Hanse. In the end, the Hanseatic capital enabled Norwegian merchants to develop their own fleet. The new sea routes to the West now put the Dutch merchants in the best geographic position for trade. The last Hansa Days were held in Lübeck in 1669.

REFERENCES: A. E. Christensen, *Udvalgte afhandlinger* (Copenhagen: Den Danske Historiske Forening, 1976); G. Grenhold, ed., *Den svenska historien*, vol. 2 (Stockholm: Bonniers, 1966); *Hansestæderne og Norden* (Århus: Det Nordiske Historikermøde i Århus, 1957); A. E. Herteig, *Handbok i middelaldersk kulturhistorie*(Bergen: Bryggens Museum, 1976); F. Hodnebø, ed., *Kulturhistorisk Leksikon for Nordisk Middel Alder*, vol. 4 (Oslo: Gyldendal, 1961); A. Holmsen, ed., *Norges Historie* (Oslo: Universitetsforlaget, 1964); F. Scott, *Sweden: The Nation's History* (Minneapolis: University of Minnesota Press, 1977).

E. M. ANDERSON

HANSSON, PER ALBIN (28 October 1885–6 October 1946) Swedish Social Democratic politician and prime minister

Born in Malmö, Hansson was the son of a bricklayer. He went to work as an errand boy at 12, finished folk school, and worked as a shop assistant. In 1904 he joined the staff of the paper *Arbetet*. His long involvement in the Socialist movement in Sweden began in 1902, when he joined the Socialist youth club in Malmö. Two years later he was in Stockholm* at a Socialist youth congress and witnessed the disintegration of unity in the movement. Hansson subsequently became a leading personality in the Social Democratic Youth League. He served as its ombudsman and between 1905 and 1909 edited the organization's newspaper, *Fram*. He subsequently moved into positions of importance within the Social Democratic Party* (SDP), became a member of the governing board in 1911, and succeeded K. Hjalmar Branting* as head of the party in 1925.

Hansson's parliamentary career began in 1918, when he was elected to the Second Chamber of the Riksdag*. He served on a number of important committees and was minister of defense in the three Branting governments between 1918 and 1925. As head of the SDP, Hansson was the foremost representative of the second generation of leadership in the party. He carried with him few of the radical, revolutionary legacies that had burdened his predecessors. Hansson was, above all, devoted to democracy and to the peaceful development of a more equal society. During the late 1920s, when the lack of parliamentary majorities made the passage of aggressive reform programs impossible, he worked for piecemeal measures aimed at improving the condition of the workers in Sweden and guaranteeing their rights. He also established a record of cooperation rather than confrontation with the bourgeois parties in the parliament, which reflected his belief that all parties within the system had to work together.

In the 1932 parliamentary election the SDP made substantial gains, and Hansson was asked to form a government. He built a minority cabinet which contained many of the shapers of Swedish policy for the next four decades, including Ernst Wigforss* (finance minister), Rickard Sandler (foreign minister), P. E. Sköld (minister of agriculture), A. Engberg (minister of ecclesiastical affairs), Gustaf Möller, and Östen Undén. Hansson realized that his position was no more solid than that of any of the other minority prime ministers who had preceded him over the previous decade. He turned, therefore, to the Agrarian Party (Bondeförbundet; *see* Center Party: Sweden). Under an agreement reached at the end of May 1933, called the "cow deal" (*kohandeln*), Hansson promised support for the farmers' demands for price supports and import restrictions, in exchange for support for the government's unemployment programs. The agreement began a period of cooperation that lasted until 1957 and reflected Hansson's genuine concern for the welfare of all Swedes. It also reflected a fear that Sweden could go the way of her continental neighbors if her political system were unable to alleviate some of the problems created by the Depression. Failure to do so might mean the radicalization of the SDP, reaction from the bourgeois parties, and the descent into some form of the fascism so epidemic on the continent.

In June 1936 Hansson's first government resigned after attempts to work out a compromise with the bourgeois parties (including the farmers) over defense and pension proposals failed. Axel Pehrsson i Bramstorp formed a minority Agrarian government that served until after the elections three months later. In late September Hansson formed a coalition with the Agrarians. With a solid majority in both houses of the parliament, this government pushed through legislation covering unemployment, pensions, guaranteed vacations, dependent allowances, maternal benefits, and tax measures designed to pay some of the costs for these programs. The bases of what Hansson called "the people's home" (*folkhem*) were laid in this period. They were expanded upon in the post-World War II period.

In December 1939 Hansson restructured the government in response to the growing crisis in Europe. He formed a "national coalition" which contained members of all the political parties except the Communists. This government carried the burden of leading Sweden through World War II*. Hansson was committed to the maintenance of Sweden's independence and survival. He backed away from strict neutrality (and stopped using the term) in favor of a flexible policy dictated by the circumstances Sweden faced. To a certain extent party differences, and the social and economic differences they represented, were laid aside in the face of the common threat. This situation was very much to Hansson's liking, as it embodied his belief that democracy should be a system in which all the principal actors worked together in harmony.

At the end of May 1945, Hansson formed his last government, a purely Social Democratic cabinet dedicated to the party's program for the further development of the postwar welfare state.* Hansson died suddenly and unexpectedly in 1946, before much of that program became reality.

REFERENCES: S. Andersson, *På Per Albins Tid* (Stockholm: Tidens, 1980); J. W. Lindgren, *Per Albin Hansson i svensk demokrati*, 2 vols. (Stockholm: Tidens, 1950); R. Lindstrom, *Per Albin Hansson* (Stockholm: Folket i Bilds Förlag, 1948); A. Pehrsson-Bramstorp, *Per Albin Hansson. vännen, arbetskamraten, hedersmannen*(Stockholm: Meden, 1948); *SU*, vol. 12.

B. NORDSTROM

HARALD I (Bluetooth) (?–c. 987) King of Denmark c. 935–985

Harald, son of Gorm* the Old, is a figure about whom, as is the case with many of the Viking Age*/medieval Scandinavian rulers, little is known. If we may believe the boasts on the great Jelling* runestone, commissioned either by Harald or by someone seeking to venerate him, Harald was the Christianizer of Denmark and the ruler of an empire that included Denmark and Norway. Both claims should be viewed with caution.

It is clear from the sources available that Harald was a Christian by about 960 and that he encouraged the spread of Christianity within the kingdom. He is credited with the founding of a number of churches, including that at Roskilde, which became a royal burial site. His encouragement of the new faith was probably based on two considerations; first, a genuine belief in the teachings of the Church, and, second, a desire to secure his southern borders against the attacks of the Ottonian emperors, who were actively spreading the new faith with the sword. Harald faced an attack by Otto II c. 974 which led to the establishment of an imperial fortress near the Danevirke and German control of the important trading center at Hedeby*. Regardless of his reasons, the Church made significant inroads in Denmark during Harald's reign, and he may have earned the epithet "the Good," which appeared on a contemporary runestone, for his efforts.

The kingdom of Denmark seems to have been expanded during Harald's rule. The base of the so-called Jelling Kings in Jutland was expanded upon. The realm appears to have come to include the Danish islands and may have extended across the Sound to the provinces of southern Sweden. The Trelleborg Forts* may bear witness to Harald's efforts. According to one interpretation of these forts, they served as bases for control and exploitation of provinces by Harald and were necessary in the process of building a centralized state at the expense of older, localistic political structures.

Harald was also involved in the political affairs of Norway. For a time he aligned himself with the earls of the Trøndelag, who opposed the unifying efforts of Harald I Fairhair* and his successors. In this policy Harald set a precedent for the future, when Denmark would time and again support the opponent of the development of a strong, centralized kingdom in Norway—unless that kingdom happened to be headed by the Danish monarch.

Harald may have been involved in Viking* raids in western Europe and the British Isles, and he is mentioned in connection with the establishment of the Viking fortress Jomsborg at the mouth of the Oder River in the Baltic.

Late in his reign Harald faced the open rebellion of his son, Sven(d) I* (Forkbeard) and was deposed. There are conflicting accounts of his death, but conspiracy and murder are recurrent themes in these accounts. He was buried at Roskilde.

He married at least twice. His children included Hakon (who died in Ireland), Sven(d) (who succeeded him), a daughter Tyra (who married Olaf I Tryggvasson* of Norway), and Gunhild (who married in England).

REFERENCES: *DBL*, vol. 6; *DH*, vol. 2; K. Randsborg, *The Viking Age in Denmark* (New York: St. Martin's Press, 1980).

B. NORDSTROM

HARALD II (c. 989–1018) King of Denmark 1014–1018

Harald was the older son of Sven(d) I* (Forkbeard) and Gunhild. On Sven's departure for England in 1013, Harald was left to rule in Denmark. When his father died suddenly in 1014, Harald inherited the Danish part of the realm, while his brother Knud I* succeeded him in England. Harald rejected his brother's request that they share rule in Denmark, following Knud's retreat from England, but he took part in a joint Viking* expedition in the Baltic and supplied Knud with men and ships when the latter launched a campaign to regain his power in England in 1015. There is virtual silence in the sources after 1015. Harald apparently died in 1018 and was succeeded by Knud.

REFERENCES: *DBL*, vol. 6; *DH*, vol. 2.

B. NORDSTROM

HARALD III (Hen) (c. 1041–17 April 1080) King of Denmark 1074–1080

Harald was one of the illegitimate sons of Sven(d) II Estridsen*. When his father died none of Sven's five sons had been designated heir. The traditional pattern for the selection of the king in Denmark was for the succession to be determined by election at the provincial *landting*. Candidates were generally limited to members of the royal family. The land-owning peasantry constituted the electorate. This practice was by-passed in 1074. Harald was chosen at a gathering of representatives at Isre, where two factions competed. One favored Harald and was dominated by peace-oriented farmers. The other favored his brother (later Knud II*) and was dominated by more violent types who harkened back fondly to the Viking Age* and wished to preserve the old ways. The former group won, and the latter had its day six years later.

Harald continued the policies of his father. He sought to strengthen the monarchy in cooperation with the Church and to extend its role in law. Following his election he promised to uphold the law of Harald I* (Bluetooth). He supported and contributed generously to the Church, opened negotiations with the papacy over the question of an archbishop for Denmark, established diplomatic ties with his neighbors, and maintained a peaceful foreign policy. His one notable domestic achievement appears to have been a reform of the minting system in Denmark which involved a consolidation of the royal mints and the standardization of weights and values. This reform may reflect the considerable strength Harald enjoyed in the country. He died unexpectedly in 1080 and was succeeded by his brother Knud.

REFERENCES: *DBL*, vol. 6; *DH*, vol. 3.

B. NORDSTROM

HARALD I FAIRHAIR (854?–c. 930/933?) King of Norway c. 860?–c. 930

Harald Fairhair is known in both Norwegian and Icelandic historical tradition as the first king to rule over all Norway. Born in 854 (traditional date), he began his reign as a petty king in southeastern Norway, succeeding his father, Halfdan the Black (a scion of the Ynglinga dynasty, the ancient royal house of Sweden). There are chronological uncertainties concerning this period, and the traditional dates are probably 10 to 20 years too early. According to unreliable saga accounts, his drive to subjugate the entire country was aroused by a young woman who refused to become his mistress unless he accomplished this goal; Harald then swore neither to wash nor comb his hair before uniting the country, and his nickname supposedly stems from the improvement in his appearance after his success.

In his campaign for sole sovereignty, Harald first attained an alliance with the earl of Lade in Trøndelag, and then militarily vanquished his other opponents. His most important victory, probably over local chieftains of southwestern Norway, was the naval encounter in Hafrsfjord, traditionally dated 872, but the subjugation of the entire country probably took some decades. Many opposing chieftains and their followers are said to have emigrated to the British Isles, adjacent lands, and Iceland as a result of the king's conquest and hard treatment. The subsequent consolidation of Harald's rule included the development of provincial administration and the establishment of a firmer economic basis for his military conquest, most likely by the confiscation of the private lands of his opponents as crown goods administered by royal stewards, rather than by taxation of the farming class. The king spent his later years on royal estates in southwestern Norway, defending the country against Viking* terror and sharing rule with his (at least) nine sons by various wives and concubines. He died c. 930 (933?).

Harald's monarchy did not mean a real and lasting unification of Norway into one kingdom. He was the supreme king and claimed sovereignty over all Norway, but he controlled effectively only Norway's western coastal district and enjoyed mainly nominal authority in other parts of the country. A political ruling system of mutual kingship, petty kings, and local chieftains remained the standard, and Harald's sons contended with each other for power. The first ruler of all Norway was succeeded as supreme king by his eldest son, Eirik Bloodaxe (ruled c. 930–c. 935), and then by his youngest son, Haakon the Good (Haakon I Haraldsson*; ruled c. 935–c. 960), but their rule was in reality confined to western Norway. The concept of a monarchy lived on, however, and almost every Norwegian king during the following four centuries based his hereditary claim to kingship on direct paternal descent from Harald Fairhair.

REFERENCES: P. S. Andersen, *Samlingen av Norge og kristningen av landet 800–1130* (Bergen: Universitetsforlaget, 1977); K. Gjerset, *History of the Norwegian People* (1932; repr. New York: AMS, 1969); K. Larsen, *A History of Norway* (Princeton: Princeton University Press, 1948/1974); S. Sturluson, *Heimskringla: Sagas of the Norse Kings* (London: Dent, 1961).

J. E. KNIRK

HARALD II EIRIKSSON (Graycloak) (c. 935–c. 970/974?) King of Norway c. 960–c. 970 (974?)

Harald Graycloak was the son of King Eirik Bloodaxe and Queen Gunnhild. The arrival of Eirik's half brother Haakon the Good (Haakon I Haraldsson*) in Norway at about that time forced the family into exile in England, and after Eirik's death in 954 Gunnhild and her sons took refuge in Denmark. Aided by the Danish king Harald I* (Bluetooth), they staged raids against King Haakon in Norway, felling him c. 960 in the western part of the country. Harald Graycloak, the oldest living son of Eirik and Gunnhild, then succeeded to the throne, while Harald Bluetooth obtained sovereignty over the territory around Oslo fjord.

Harald Graycloak ruled initially over only western Norway but ambitiously attempted to extend his sovereignty. His first goal was control of Trøndelag, and he killed the local leader, Earl Sigurd Haakonsson of Lade, a few years after becoming king. He also tried to expand his rule to northern Norway but was unsuccessful. (The nickname ''Graycloak'' may, however, derive from fur-trading activities in that section of the land.) The expenses of conquest became so great that the king was forced to raid heathen temples, which angered his subjects. When he tried to expand to the eastern coast, he came into conflict with his old ally and superior, Harald Bluetooth, who then connived the upstart's death. Harald Graycloak fell in Jutland c. 970 (974?) fighting an army of Danes and forces from Trøndelag led by the new earl of Lade, Haakon Sigurdsson*. The Danish influence in Norway became even stronger with Earl Haakon's subsequent rule.

REFERENCES: P. S. Andersen, *Samlingen av Norge og kristningen av landet 800–1130* (Bergen: Universitetsforlaget, 1977); K. Gjerset, *History of the Norwegian People* (1932; repr. New York: AMS, 1969); K. Larsen, *A History of Norway* (Princeton: Princeton University Press, 1948/1974); S. Sturluson, *Heimskringla: Sagas of the Norse Kings* (London: Dent, 1961), and *Heimskringla: The Olaf Sagas*, vol. 1 (London: Dent, 1964).

J. E. KNIRK

HARALD III SIGURDSSON (the Hardruler) (c. 1015–25 September 1066) King of Norway 1046–1066

Harald Sigurdsson, born c. 1015, was King Olaf II Haraldsson's* half brother. He was wounded fighting for Olaf at the battle of Stiklestad in 1030 and fled afterward by way of Sweden to Grand Prince Yaroslav I in Russia. Journeying on to Constantinople with a large following c. 1035, he joined the Varangian guard there and fought many battles together with the imperial armies, especially in Sicily and the Balkan peninsula, finally becoming a high officer in the eastern emperor's bodyguard and the leading Norse warrior in Byzantine military service. Harald fled from Constantinople in 1043 to Kiev, where he married Yaroslav's daughter, who was also the niece of King Anund Jakob of Sweden.

Experienced and ambitious, Harald returned to Scandinavia* in 1045 with his amassed Byzantine riches and his wife's dowry as the economic basis for a claim to kingship in Norway. In 1046 he was reconciled with his nephew, King Magnus the Good (Magnus I Olafsson*), but in the subsequent joint kingship until Magnus's death the following year, Harald was subordinate, ruling mainly in his patrimonial local kingdom in eastern Norway. After succeeding to undivided rule, he consolidated his sovereignty, neutralized the influential relatives of the earls of Lade (whose dynasty disappeared in his day), built churches, introduced royally minted Norwegian coins as a means of payment, founded Oslo c. 1050, strengthened the trading center in Nidaros (Trondheim) and mobilized resources in Norway, particularly by exploiting the defensive naval levy for offensive warring outside the country. He maintained national independence in Church affairs; in the first preserved papal letter to Norway, Pope Alexander II in 1065 had to admonish obedience to the archbishop of Hamburg-Bremen. Aggressive in his political and cultural nationalism, Harald suppressed lesser Norwegian leaders and acquired the nickname ''the Hardruler'' (*harðráði*).

Norway began an outward expansion after 1035, when the death of King Knut the Great (Knud I*) of Denmark and England led to the disintegration of his North Sea empire. Whereas Magnus the Good brought Denmark under the Norwegian crown and was hailed as king there in 1042 (being opposed, however, by Sven II Estridsen*), Harald never managed to assert himself as king of Denmark, although he raided there repeatedly and defeated Sven in a major battle in 1062. Two years later he and Sven agreed to recognize each other as sovereign in their respective countries, and henceforth Harald directed his attention toward the west, further strengthening Norwegian dominance of the Orkneys, Shetland, and the Hebrides. After King Edward the Confessor's death in 1066, Harald sailed with 300 ships to England to assert his claim to the throne there. He and his ally Earl Tostig Godwinson met with resistance, however, and King Harold II Godwinson and the English militia surprised them at Stamford Bridge on 25 September. Harald's army was defeated and he was killed, but the English Harold's own losses proved fateful for him in the battle of Hastings three weeks later against William the Conqueror.

Harald was succeeded in Norway by his two illegitimate sons, Magnus (died 1069), whom Harald had designated co-regent before his journey westward, and Olaf the Quiet (Olaf III Haraldsson*).

REFERENCES: P. S. Andersen, *Samlingen av Norge og kristningen av landet 800–1130* (Bergen: Universitetsforlaget, 1977); H.R.E. Davidson, *The Viking Road to Byzantium* (London: Allen & Unwin, 1976); K. Gjerset, *History of the Norwegian People* (1932; repr. New York: AMS, 1969); K. Larsen, *A History of Norway* (Princeton: Princeton University Press, 1948/1974); S. Sturluson, *Heimskringla: Sagas of the Norse Kings* (London: Dent, 1961), and *King Harald's Saga* (Harmondsworth: Penguin, 1970).

J. E. KNIRK

HARALD IV MAGNUSSON (Gilchrist) (c. 1103–13/14 December 1136) King of Norway 1130–1136

Harald Gilchrist, supposedly an illegitimate son of King Magnus Bareleg (Magnus III Olafsson*), was born c. 1103 in Ireland and arrived in Norway in the late 1120s. After the newcomer passed an ordeal to prove his paternity, King Sigurd the Crusader (Sigurd I Magnusson*) recognized him as a half brother on the condition that Harald not claim sovereignty as long as the king or his son, Magnus (later Magnus IV Sigurdsson*), lived. The exclusion of a king's son from co-regency broke with tradition, but upon Sigurd's death in 1130 Magnus was forced, due to Harald's popular support, to accept him as co-ruler. The long period of relative peace and stability soon ceased, as rivalry between these royal relatives touched off civil war.

Harald's weak leadership was the basis for the increasingly powerful role of his chief retainers. The two rulers coexisted peacefully until the winter of 1133–1134, spent together in Nidaros (Trondheim), and when they met in combat in eastern Norway the following summer, Harald was defeated and retired to Denmark. Returning the next year, he defeated Magnus in Bergen, captured, blinded, maimed, and gelded him, and put him in a monastery near Nidaros. The ruthless feuds and hostilities of the Norwegian civil wars had begun, roughly 100 years during which the right to rule was most frequently in dispute.

The following year another adventurous roamer appeared in Norway, claiming to be a son of Magnus Bareleg and thus the ruler's half brother. Harald's attempt to eliminate the new pretender, Sigurd Slembi, failed, and in December 1136

Sigurd surprised the king in Bergen and killed him. Sigurd proclaimed his deed and sought support, but he was forced to flee by the king's men. A new co-regency was then established with Harald's young sons, Sigurd Mouth and Ingi I Haraldsson*, as kings.

REFERENCES: G. M. Gathorne-Hardy, *A Royal Impostor: King Sverre of Norway* (Oslo: Aschehoug, 1956); K. Gjerset, *History of the Norwegian People* (1932; repr. New York: AMS, 1969); K. Helle, *Norge blir en stat 1130–1319*, 2nd rev. ed. (Bergen: Universitetsforlaget, 1974); K. Larsen, *A History of Norway* (Princeton: Princeton University Press, 1948/1974); S. Sturluson, *Heimskringla: Sagas of the Norse Kings* (London: Dent, 1961).

J. E. KNIRK

HARDEKNUD (1018–8 June 1042) King of Denmark 1035–1042, king of England 1040–1042

Hardeknud was the son of Knud the Great (Knud I*) and Emma, the widow of the Anglo-Saxon king Ethelred whom Knud married following his accession in 1014. In the 1020s Hardeknud was sent to Denmark, where he was raised and where he acted as Knud's second under the tutelage of the succession of close advisors to Knud. When his father died he was recognized as king in Denmark and sought to establish his claim to the English throne as well, a goal for which his mother also worked energetically. To the latter end he was opposed by his half brother Harald Harefod. His efforts in England were limited because of the threat Magnus the Good (Magnus I Olafsson*) presented to his position in Denmark. His reign in Denmark marked the beginning of a period during which Norwegian kings influenced events and even claimed a right to the throne in Denmark. When Hardeknud died without heirs in 1042, he was succeeded by Magnus.

REFERENCES: *DBL*, vol. 6; *DH*, vols. 2, 3; K. Randsborg, *The Viking Age in Denmark* (New York: St. Martin's Press, 1980).

B. NORDSTROM

HAT PARTY (1738–1772) Political party in Sweden during the Age of Liberty*

Frustrated with their inability to remove their archrival, Chancery President Count Arvid Horn*, from his dominant position through informal and traditional means of political action, several opponents of the regime hit upon a plan of action in the mid-1730s that produced Sweden's first real political party—known then and later as the Hat Party—at the Riksdag* of 1738–1739. The steps taken by Councilor Carl Gyllenborg and his associates led to the Hats' succeeding in electing their candidate to the speakership of the House of Nobility and then packing the nobility's delegations to the key Riksdag committees with their supporters. The Hats captured control of the government in 1738 and maintained that control until their first electoral defeat (in the fall of 1764) and their loss of office in 1765.

From the beginning, the Hats were closely associated with France, receiving subsidies for their party activities and for the Swedish treasury from that great power. The attraction to the French connection was the result of several things, foremost among which were the Hats' aggressive desire to retake Baltic provinces lost to Peter the Great, France's well-understood desire to subsidize military outlays by Russia's neighbors in return for their alliance, and the experience that many Hats had had serving in the French army's Royal Suedois regiment. The Hats were to experience defeat at the hands of Russia in the 1742–1743 war they initiated, and it was their commitment to France that led them to enter the Seven Years' War, an unpopular move that contributed heavily to their defeat at the polls and in the Riksdag in 1764 and 1765.

The Hat Party dominated the council of state* from 1738 to 1765 and succeeded in appointing hundreds of its supporters and "members" to positions of importance and influence in the central and local governmental offices. This goes a long way toward explaining the success of the civil service strike against the Cap Party's* council of the realm in 1768, and to the general inability of the Caps to secure the loyalty of key officers in the civil and military service. The Hats thus succeeded in regaining control of the Riksdag and the council at the elections and Riksdag of 1769, although they were to lose that control to the Caps again at the next elections and Riksdag in 1771. By 1772 many of the leading Hat politicians, fearing the rising demands of what later came to be known as the middle class, had abandoned their defense of parliamentary sovereignty, and in August of that year they welcomed King Gustav III's* coup d'etat.

REFERENCES: Per-Erik Brolin, *Hattar och mössor i borgarståndet 1760–1766* (Uppsala, 1953); M. Metcalf, "The First 'Modern' Party System? Political Parties, Sweden's Age of Liberty and the Historians," *Scandinavian Journal of History* 2 (1977): 265–87; G. Nilzen, *Studier i 1730–talets partiväsen* (Stockholm, 1971); G. Olsson, *Hattar och mössor. Studier i partiväsendet i Sverige 1751–1762* (Gothenburg, 1963).

M. F. METCALF

HAUGE, HANS NIELSEN (3 April 1771–29 March 1824) Norwegian revivalist

H. N. Hauge made his impact on the history of Norway as the leader of a significant religious awakening among the rural peasant class. In arousing the lay people to more active participation in pursuit of the Christian meaning of life, Hauge also directed them toward exerting leadership in the economic and political life of the country. When a national assembly* met at Eidsvoll in 1814 to adopt a new constitution for Norway (*see* Eidsvoll Constitution of 17 May), there were at least three prominent Haugeans among the peasant representatives.

Brought up in a home where both parents were devout, Bible-reading, hardworking Christians, Hauge from early youth was inclined toward serious thoughts about God, sin, salvation, life, and death. At the age of 25 he had a conversion experience, a significant spiritual breakthrough from doubt and uncertainty to a clearly perceived call to speak the word of God to others. From that day on, Hauge's one purpose was to help his "neighbors," as he referred to his fellow

Norwegians, to experience a sound conversion, to love God with all their heart, and to love and serve their neighbor.

Starting unpretentiously with private conversations with members of his own family and close acquaintances, Hauge was soon speaking to relatively small gatherings in peasant homes in the vicinity and at greater distances from his home parish of Tune in southeastern Norway. These devotional talks constituted the first and most important of four methods which he developed in taking his simple message to the people of Norway. The other methods were his wide-ranging travels, his numerous writings, and his business initiatives.

Hauge did not deliver prepared sermons but spoke informally and with compelling sincerity on themes familiar to his peasant listeners from the Bible and the Lutheran catechetical tradition. As a layman he did not expect to be invited to preach in churches. (Not until 1897 did the Norwegian Lutheran State Church permit lay persons to deliver sermons from the pulpit during a regular worship service.) The problem Hauge faced was that many pastors and other state officials accused him of violating the Conventicle Act* of 1741 (*see* Conventicle Acts). While Hauge regarded himself as a simple peasant's son following the Biblical command to edify one's neighbor, opponents looked upon him as a vagrant, one of those who, in the language of the Conventicle Act, "under the pretext of godliness have left their livelihood and regular trade and gone around from one place to the other to awaken souls or to pass themselves off as teachers without having any call from God or men."

Hauge himself and many others, including Bergen's influential bishop, Johan Nordahl Brun, believed that the act was in practice nullified by the granting of freedom of the press. Hauge was arrested several times in the course of his itinerant mission, and eventually the state took official action against him. The opposition to Hauge's preaching revealed a deep-seated contrast between the peasant class and state officials. Hauge's activity was perceived as a threat to a traditional social order in which each was expected to remain in his given calling.

The second method Hauge used to spread his message was that of travel. Between 1796 and 1804 he visited nearly all parts of Norway. It is estimated that he traveled over 10,000 miles during that period. As he went about holding cottage meetings he always kept an eye open for ways to help local peasants improve their economic lot. Hauge possessed many practical skills. His talents also included the ability to select stable local leaders who would continue the work of bringing people together to study the Bible and to encourage one another. Like the Wesleyan movement in England, the Haugean movement prospered because of the network of strong, active local groups maintaining both religious devotion and mutual economic support in the rural communities.

A third method used by Hauge in reviving Norway's laity was the pen. Despite a very slender education, Hauge became a prolific writer and a publisher of astonishing energy. His industrious writing and publishing gave strength and breadth to the religious folk movement he inspired. He wrote 33 books in all, 19 of them during the concentrated years of traveling and preaching from 1796 to 1804. In addition to his own writings Hauge published books by other, earlier authors. He urged young Christopher Grøndahl to learn book printing and to establish a printing firm in Christiania, the capital of Norway. Significantly, this firm published many of Hauge's works, of which over 200,000 copies were disseminated, and between 1947 and 1954 Grøndahl and Son printed the complete set of Hauge's writings as edited by a direct descendant, Professor Hans Nielsen Hauge Ording.

A fourth method for furthering the spiritual revival was to establish a few business enterprises, including a paper mill at Eiker in eastern Norway and a trading business in Bergen, and to use the income from these arrangements to help support the production and distribution of books, tracts, and a periodical. These activities caused some consternation among Hauge's close friends, who frowned on involvement in worldly enterprises, but they created important models for profitable Christian cooperatives which could engage the initiative and talent of lay people who otherwise would have remained in passive poverty. By establishing himself as a merchant in Bergen, Hauge also hoped to avoid the charge of vagrancy.

Hauge's active career ended in the fall of 1804, when he was arrested by order of the Danish Chancery in Copenhagen*. A lengthy investigation ensued, lasting until 1814, with Hauge in jail the larger portion of that 10–year period. Initial charges were that Hauge had violated the vagrancy law, had engaged in irregular business practices, had used overly strong language against pastors in his early writings, and had violated the Conventicle Act. After additional hearings and the gathering of information, the first two charges were dropped.

Hauge was sentenced to two years' imprisonment at hard labor. He appealed the case, and a year later, in December 1814, the appeals court ruled that he be fined a sum of about $2,000. Hauge was finally free, but his health and vigor were gone. Nevertheless, in his last 10 years he extended his interests in several directions. He became interested in foreign missionary work. He contributed to the new national university and became acquainted with some of its professors. He learned of the work of N.F.S. Grundtvig in Denmark even as Grundtvig hailed the impact of Hauge's work. Hauge built a grain mill on the Aker River, wrote and published several more books, and continued to maintain contact with his wide circle of friends and supporters, many of whom visited him at his comfortable farm near the capital city.

The impact of the movement begun by Hans Nielsen Hauge has been felt in Norway and also in the United States. In Norway, Hauge's work has had an influence of a general nature on the whole society, deepening the Christian spirit and stimulating lay activity in church and state. In particular, the Norwegian heirs of Hauge have created large, self-sustaining mission organizations for both home and foreign missionary work. Examples are Det Norske Lutherske Indremisjonsselskap and Det Norske Lutherske Chinamissionsforbund. In the United States, Lutheran churches and synods established by immigrants from Norway during the nineteenth century kept alive the Bible-based piety and active lay participation in the Christian community which they had learned in the Haugean milieu of their places of origin.

REFERENCES: A. Aarflot, *Hans Nielsen Hauge: His Life and Message* (Minneapolis: Augsburg Publishing House, 1979), and *Tro og lydighet: Hans Nielsen Hauges kristendomsforståelse* (Oslo, 1969); A. Chr. Bang, *Hans Nielsen Hauge og hans Samtid. Et Tidsbillede fra omkring Aar 1800* (Christiania and Copenhagen: Gyldendalske Boghandel; Nordisk Forlag, 1910, 1924); M. Nodtvedt, *Rebirth of Norway's Peasantry: Folk Leader Hans Nielsen Hauge* (Tacoma, Wash.: Pacific Lutheran University Press, 1965); S. Norborg, *Hans Nielsen Hauge. Biografi I, 1771–1804* (Oslo, 1966), and *II, 1804–1824* (Oslo, 1970); H.N.H. Ording, ed., *Hans Nielsen Hauges Skrifter*, 9 vols. (Oslo: Andaktsbokselskapet, 1947–1954); J. M. Shaw, *Pulpit under the Sky: A Life of Hans Nielsen Hauge* (Minneapolis: Augsburg Publishing House, 1955); N. Silvertsen, *Hans Nielsen Hauge og venesamfunnet* (Oslo: Land og Kirke, 1946).

J. M. SHAW

HEDEBY (Haethum, Sliaswich, Haitha by) Viking Age* town in Denmark c. 800–c. 1020

Hedeby was, with Birka*, one of the two most important towns in Scandinavia* during the Viking Age. It was located at the southeast base of the Jylland peninsula, at the bottom of the Slei fjord and close to the defensive wall (Danevirke) between Denmark and Germany. Its location was ideal in terms of contact with the rest of Denmark, and it lay along trade routes to the rest of Scandinavia, the eastern Baltic, and western Europe and the British Isles. Recent dendochronological dating has established that the town was founded about 800 and that it remained in use until about 1020. It seems to have been abandoned because of rising water levels and the development of ships which required a deeper harbor.

Hedeby was a carefully planned settlement and may have been founded by "king" Godfred to replace the neighboring and less organized settlement of Südsiedlung. Hedeby's 24 hectares were surrounded by a rampart wall. The stream that flowed through the town was planked to control its flow, and planked streets were laid out. Houses of uniform shape but not uniform size were laid out along the streets. Not all of the walled area was occupied. Estimates based on the extensive grave fields indicate that the population of the town was about 1,000; 62 percent were males, 38 percent were females.

Hedeby was a trade and manufacturing center and probably played some role in the development of a monarchy in the country (it is contemporaneous with the Trelleborg Forts*). Archeological finds indicate that furs, ceramics, glass, soapstone, and metals were among the goods imported. Ceramics, metal products, jewelry, and beads were among the goods produced there. In addition, Hedeby was the site of the first coin mint (c. 800) in Denmark and was the site of the first church in the country, founded by Ansgar* c. 850.

The site was identified in 1897, and archeological investigations, conducted in the 1930s, 1950s, 1960s, and most recently since 1979, have revealed a great deal about trade, manufacturing, and everyday life in the period. While only about 5 percent of the site has been excavated, the finds in graves, textiles, working materials, jewelry, and house plans have been invaluable. Recent excavations have focused on the harbor.

REFERENCES: J. Brøndsted, *The Vikings*, trans. K. Skov (New York: Penguin, 1965); G. Jones, *A History of the Vikings* (New York: Oxford University Press, 1984); K. Randsborg, *The Viking Age in Denmark* (New York: St. Martin's Press, 1980); E. Roesdahl, *Viking Age Denmark*, S. Margeson and K. Williams, trans. (London: British Museum Publications Ltd, 1982).

B. NORDSTROM

HEINESEN, MOGENS (Magnus Heinason) (1545–1589) Faroese adventurer and freebooter

Mogens Heinesen, or Magnus Heinason as he is known in the Faroe Islands*, has often been depicted as a Renaissance adventurer, a romantic figure whose colorful career excuses his many moral backslidings. In the Faroes he is even regarded as something of a national hero. Sober history admits his courage and skill as a sea captain but is compelled also to add many details to the story of his life that are shabby and ignoble, by contemporary no less than modern standards.

His father was Heine Jonsen (c. 1512–1576), one of the first Lutheran priests in Faroe, and from 1557 provost. Heine Jonsen married twice. By his first wife, a Faroese heiress, he had one son, Joen Heinesen, and by his second, two sons, the elder of whom was Mogens.

Joen Heinesen stayed in the Faroes and in 1572 became *lagmand**, adding a large stipendiary farm to several crown leaseholdings and much inherited land. Mogens settled in Bergen, took to seafaring, and was early given charge of a ship plying between Norway and the Faroes. On his third journey, it is said, his ship was plundered by pirates. On his return to Bergen with an empty ship, he was so scorned that he felt the need to rehabilitate his honor. He took service with the Dutch and in 1578 returned to Bergen with a considerable reputation and his own ship. With his half brother, he organized a petition to be granted the monopoly rights in Faroe. He was successful, and on 4 February 1579 the trade was granted to Heinesen and his Bergen partners.

Shortly before Mogens Heinesen's first trading journey to the Faroe Islands, Tórshavn* was attacked by the English pirate Thomas Clerk (d. 1582). In June 1579 Clerk took a considerable quantity of goods from both the trading station and the land taxation warehouse, where the royal rents and taxes were received in kind. Mogens Heinesen was contracted to pay the exchequer the equivalent for the latter in cash. Faced with this loss, he persuaded Joen Heinesen, two other priests, and two more witnesses to sign and seal an affidavit listing precisely what had been plundered.

However, the royal treasurer, Christoffer Valkendorf*, was not deceived. He suspected, with justification, that this affidavit was part of a plot to magnify the scale of the loss for the profit of Mogens Heinesen and others, and he so advised the king.

Mogens Heinesen thereupon saw Frederik II*, who forgave him half the value of the plundered goods and issued him a license, at his own expense, to man and arm his ship in naval fashion and to pursue and bring to justice pirates in northern waters. He was further licensed to arrest any Dutch or English ship attempting to trade with Archangel by the route around North Cape, which Frederik II regarded as an infringement of the Norwegian dominion over the northern seas and an evasion of the Sound Tolls. From the spring of 1580, Mogens Heinesen began scouring the seas off Norway and the Faroe Islands, and legend has much to report of his exploits and his custom of living at free quarter in the Faroes, where neither life nor property was safe from his men. The supply of the Faroes Heinesen left to his Bergen partners. It was so mismanaged that the Faroese had to smuggle out a complaint to the king; Valkendorf advised the king either to take the trade back into his own hands or grant it to a group of Copenhagen* merchants, over whom he could hope to exercise some control.

Frederik II, although he held Valkendorf in high regard, was convinced that Denmark's greatness lay in her sea power, and he was easily fascinated by Heinesen, especially when Heinesen offered, at his own expense, to make a journey with two ships to rediscover Greenland*. On 18 February 1581 the king issued him a pass for the journey and ordered officials throughout the realm to render him help at need. Heinesen stretched the terms of this document by setting out from Bergen with minimal supplies and men and making up the balance without payment in the Faroe Islands. His ships came within sight of the icebound coast of Eastern Greenland*, but he was unable to land.

Shortly after his return to Bergen in August, he seduced a noblewoman named Sofia Gyntersberg. The Gyntersberg family arranged for Sofia to marry Heinesen, but Sofia's elder sister Margrethe alleged that some years before Heinesen had raped her, that she had borne his child in secret, that it had died, and that it had been buried in a secret grave. These accusations, if true, would make the marriage a capital crime. However, Heinesen cleared himself with a solemn oath, and the luckless Margrethe was imprisoned in Bergenhus for false accusations.

In the meantime, Valkendorf was building up a dossier on the mismanagement of the Faroe trade and Mogens Heinesen's outrages in the islands. Heinesen was now excluded from the Faroe trade, and in April 1583 his half brother was dismissed as lagmand. Margrethe Gyntersberg appealed against her imprisonment, and the affair eventually made its way to the Herredag at Odense, which opened in June 1584. (This was moved to Antvorskov near Slagelse because of an outbreak of the plague.) Heinesen was present at Odense, but when the case came up at Antvorskov, he had fled to the Netherlands.

In February 1585 Heinesen settled in Enkhuysen and in June 1585 was issued with letters of marque to wage war on the Spaniards. Shortly before taking naval service with the Dutch, however, Heinesen committed an outright act of piracy that was eventually to lead to his execution. On 14 March 1585, in company with a Scottish pirate named Knightson, he captured a ship near the English coast, the *John* of Hull, and took it to Orkney. The ship was later restored to its owners, but the cargo, valued at £2,420—a huge sum in this period—was retained by the captors, who paid a suitable commission to the earl of Orkney for his protection.

In June 1587 Heinesen left the Dutch service and settled in Ålborg as a peaceful merchant. The previous year some of the charges against him had been dropped and the incest case apparently forgotten. Frederik II had probably again fallen under the spell of Heinesen's enterprise and daring. But Frederik died on 4 April 1588 and was succeeded by the eleven-year-old Christian IV*.

Proceedings for the restitution of the value of the cargo taken from the *John* were slow, because England, Scotland, and Denmark were all concerned. But the issue was brought up by the English ambassador, Daniel Rogers, who arrived in Elsinore* in July 1588. There he met the young king and the queen mother, and learned that Heinesen was also in the town. Rogers asked that Heinesen be brought to Copenhagen to answer the charge of piracy.

Heinesen agreed to travel south with the embassy, was with a party that visited Tycho Brahe's* observatory on Hven, but then disappeared. He fled first to Ålborg, where he took on board his family and his moveable property. He then went to Bergen, where he hoped to get help from his old associates. But word had already come from Copenhagen. Heinesen was arrested, taken in chains back to the Danish capital, and imprisoned in the celebrated Blue Tower. He was unable to offer restitution for his plunder, and on 18 January 1599 was beheaded.

Heinesen's widow and his friend Hans Lindenov subsequently brought a lawsuit against Valkendorf for legal irregularities in the case, and the Danish nobility took the opportunity to topple Valkendorf from power. Valkendorf had certainly committed technical faults in his haste to get Heinesen condemned, but Heinesen was unquestionably guilty of the crime for which he was executed.

REFERENCES: There are no English accounts of Heinesen's career, though the traditions of his exploits are to be found in L. Debes, *A Description of the Islands and Inhabitants of Foeroe* (London: William Iles, 1676); see also E. Östvedt, *Mogens Heinessön* (Skien: O. Rasmussens Forlag, 1969); F. Troels-Lund, *Mogens Heinesön* (Copenhagen, 1877).

J. F. WEST

HEINESON, MAGNUS *See* Heinesen, Mogens

HELSINGØR *See* Elsinore

HEMMINGSEN, NIELS (1513–1600) Danish theologian

Many consider Niels Hemmingsen the leading Scandinavian theologian of the sixteenth century. As he advanced in age scholars and intellectuals made pilgrimage to his door, and kings like James VI of Scotland counted it an honor to have visited with the famous Danish theologian. Hemmingsen, born on the island of Lolland, had been trained by Erasmian Biblical humanists at Roskilde and Lund. During the years 1537–1542 he studied at Wittenberg, where he became an ardent champion of the theology of Philip Melanchthon. Upon his appointment to the University of Copenhagen in 1542, he quickly rose from an instructor in Greek to professor of theology.

Three works secured Hemmingsen's reputation as a theologian, namely his *Enchiridion theologicum* (1557), his *Evangelie postil* (1561), and his *Pastor* (1562). These works became the first Scandinavian Lutheran textbooks in dogmatics, homiletics, and pastoral theology, respectively. During the confessionally fluid years following the *Variata* edition (1540) of the *Augsburg Confession**, Hemmingsen threw his weight behind Melanchthon's revised *Augustana*as a more effective weapon against Roman Catholicism.

During the ensuing years, Hemmingsen's career became inextricably intertwined with the *Augsburg Confession*. Scholars have tried to ascertain when Hemmingsen's eucharistic theology began to veer away from Melanchthonian Lutheranism* to an outright espousal of Calvin's teaching on Christology and the Lord's Supper. Most scholars would place the shift as occurring in the mid-1560s, certainly no later than 1571, when he attacked the Gnesio-Lutherans and the doctrine of ubiquity in his *Demonstratio indubitate veritatis de Domino Jesu*. Three years later he openly hailed Calvin's eucharistic theology in his *Syntagma institutionum Christianarum*. Opposition began to mount against Hemmingsen's blatant Calvinism, and on 29 July 1579 Frederik II* reluctantly dismissed his most illustrious theologian "for the sake of concord." Though eclipsed by younger Gnesio-Lutherans in the ensuing years, so great was Hemmingsen's influence nevertheless that the Book of Concord was never accepted as a confessional basis for the Lutheran Church in Denmark, Norway, or Iceland.

REFERENCES: Kjell Barnekow, *Niels Hemmingsens Teologiska Åskådning* (Lund: Gleerup, 1940); Trygve R. Skarsten, "The Reaction in Scandinavia to the Formula of Concord," *Discord, Dialogue, and Concord*, ed. Lewis W. Spitz and Wenzel Lohff (Philadelphia: Fortress Press, 1977), pp. 136–49.

T. R. SKARSTEN

HERREDSTING Local district court in rural Denmark

The *herred* (district) and its *ting* (assembly, court) traced their history far back in the Middle Ages, but by the early modern period the *herredsting* was essentially the first court in the legal system and an assembly for the arbitration of local disputes. The presiding officer, the *herredsfoged*, was appointed by the regional governor on behalf of the king, usually from among the wealthier peasants of the area. He was assisted by a clerk, the *herredskriver*. Some special royal and private jurisdictions existed in the countryside outside the normal *herred* system, namely, the *birketing* (manorial courts), where the seigneur (either the crown or a private land owner) was entitled to appoint the judge and the clerk; but these jurisdictions were granted by special royal privilege (more strictly controlled after 1696), and although a number of new grants were made after 1660 the area involved was still small compared with the older *herred* jurisdictions.

The *herredsting* functioned along very traditional lines during the seventeenth and early eighteenth centuries. It normally met once a week, at eight or nine in the morning, and always in the same place within the district it served. In addition to the judge and the clerk of the court (or, exceptionally, their representative), there had to be present at least seven or eight *tingsmaend* or formal witnesses. No member of the community was debarred from participating, except if under conviction, and according to *Danske Lov* (1683; *see* Danish Law) peasants were expected to conduct their own defense or prosecution without the aid of procurators. Summonses, whether verbal or in writing, had to be served in the presence of witnesses at least eight days in advance. A defendant or witness was excused from attending only for good reason and might lose his case or suffer other penalty if he failed to appear. He could, however, send a representative or even ask his seigneur to provide legal aid. In cases involving the material interests of an estate, the land owner was entitled to know about the proceedings and might send a bailiff or agent, but in principle the hearings were conducted among equals. In practice abuses no doubt occurred, especially since the records indicate that the presiding officers and clerks were at times not adequately qualified (a problem tackled, for example, in the ordinances of 1735–1736). But decisions at the *herredsting* could be made the subject of appeal to the *landsting* (provincial court) or even to the king's supreme court, and the *herredsfoged* himself was personally accountable to the higher courts. This appeal system was comparatively simple and effective by contemporary standards, even though the expense could be a considerable obstacle.

Litigation as such was only part of the court's functions. It served as an open forum for the registration of a wide range of formal documents, including contracts of sale, mortgage deeds, and testimonials. Much time was also spent on disputes over local resources such as forestry and grazing rights, and especially on the recording of debts, arrears, and formal evaluations (often at the request of a land owner, in connection with tenancy contracts). The extent to which seigneurial pressure might be exerted on the *herredsting* is difficult to assess, given the nature of the source material and the realities of early modern social structure, but there is no reason to believe that, although the system was not without its weaknesses, it did continue to serve a useful and constructive role in rural society in early modern Denmark.

REFERENCES: H. H. Fussing, *Herremand og Faestebonde* (Copenhagen: Nyt Nordisk Forlag/A. Busek, 1942; repr. Selskab for Udgivning af Kilder till Dansk Historie Fussing, 1973); P. J. Jørgensen, *Dansk Retshistorie* (Copenhagen: Gad, 1940); J. T. Lauridsen, "Retstilstandende i Danmark i 1500– og 1600–tallet: et debatindlaeg," *Fortid og Nutid*, 1982; P. Meyer, "Dom og dele," *Bol og By* 4 (1963): 28–56; T. Munck, *The Peasantry and the Early Absolute Monarchy in Denmark, 1660–1708* (Copenhagen: Landbohistorisk Selskab, 1979), and "Retstilstandende i Danmark i 1600–tallet: et debatbidrag," *Fortid og Nutid*, 1982.

T. MUNCK

HÖGER *See* Conservative Party: Sweden

HÖGLUND, ZETH (29 April 1884–1956) Swedish Socialist politician

Höglund was the most prominent and controversial of the left-wing Socialists in Sweden during the first half of the twentieth century. Reared in a Pietistic middle-class home in Gothenburg*, he began his career as a journalist and editor for various radical papers representing the views of the youth movement within the Social Democratic Party* (SDP). He was imprisoned in 1905 during the tense Union crisis with Norway and for a year during World War I for anti-military and anti-war statements.

The thrust of Höglund's convictions and activities was directed as much against the revisionist leaders of the SDP as against the old order in Sweden. Before World War I he took a hard line against the military, the arms build-up, and the idea of "ministerial socialism." His challenge to the SDP's leadership became most serious in 1917, when he founded the radical Left Socialist Party advocating disarmament and a republic. In 1921 he organized the Swedish Communist Party (*see* Communist Party: Sweden), which joined the Comintern. He was chairperson of the party until 1924, when he and a group of followers withdrew. He rejoined the SDP in 1926, after failing to organize a Communist party independent of Moscow. From 1928 to 1944 he was a member of the SDP's governing council and was influential as editor of the party's chief newspaper during the 1930s. Höglund was a member of the Lower Chamber of the Riksdag* from 1915 to 1917 and from 1928 to 1940, and was active in Stockholm* labor circles and politics. In the late 1930s, faced with the rise of the Nazis, he came to support increased defenses for Sweden. He took sharp issue with the Communists following the Soviet attack on Finland in 1939, but he continued to advocate cooperation with them even after the 1948 coup in Czechoslovakia. His intelligence, debating skills, and expertise on ideology and tactics made him popular with some and unpopular with many.

REFERENCES: C. G. Andrae, "The Swedish Labor Movement and the 1917–1918 Revolution," in S. Koblik, ed., *Sweden's Development from Poverty to Affluence, 1750–1970* (Minneapolis: University of Minnesota Press, 1975); A. Gustafson, in *SBL*, vol. 19.

P. V. THORSON

HORN, ARVID BERNHARD (6 April 1664–17 April 1742) Swedish general, statesman, and politician

Born in Finland in 1664, the son of an infantry colonel, Arvid Horn entered military service at the age of 18 to earn his livelihood. Five years later, in 1687, he entered the service of the Habsburg emperor, but by 1690 he was serving as an adjutant general for the Dutch Republic in its struggles against Louis XIV. With the accession of Karl XII* to the Swedish throne, Horn's star began to rise at home. A frequent companion of the new king, Horn was commissioned as a major general and given the title of baron in 1700. Karl XII subsequently had frequent occasion to see Horn in action as the head of his corps of drabants, and, in 1704 he promoted Horn to the rank of lieutenant general. Soon after that the king gave Horn his first non-military assignment, namely, the task of persuading the Polish diet to dethrone August of Saxony as their king and to elect a native Pole in his place.

The success and skill demonstrated by Horn in the Polish negotiations in 1704–1705, which led to the election of Stanislas Leszcynski as king of Poland, prompted Karl to appoint Horn to the Swedish royal council in 1705 and to make him the second highest official on that body. Horn returned to Sweden to assume his new civilian duties. He was made a count later that year, and in 1707 he was made governor for Duke Karl Fredrik of Holstein-Gottorp*, Karl XII's nephew and possible heir. His governorship for the duke led to Horn's carrying on extensive political correspondence with the king, who remained abroad with his armies (*see* Great Northern War*). The respect Karl gained for Horn in these years led to his being named chancery president and head of the royal council in 1710. With this increased responsibility for the government of the kingdom and the welfare of its subjects, however, Horn soon found himself at odds with a monarch whose military and diplomatic efforts were draining the country's resources.

As president of the chancery and head of the council, Horn was caught between the dictates of his absolute monarch and the crying need for relief from over a decade of warfare. Horn's position was very delicate, as the king had forbidden any meeting of the estates of the realm, but both the council and the leaders of the estates felt that such a meeting was necessary. A meeting of committees representing the estates was held against the king's wishes in 1710, and then a full-fledged meeting of the estates—this time with the cooperation of Princess Ulrika Eleonora* (the Younger)—was held in 1713–1714. Although Horn was quick to disband the estates when they began seriously discussing a separate peace without the participation of the king, there is much to suggest that he was fully supportive of that plan, at least as a mechanism for getting Karl to listen to reason. In the end, however, nothing came of the plan, and the king lost his confidence in Horn. When Karl XII returned to Sweden in 1715, he removed Horn as governor of Duke Karl Fredrik and ceased consulting the royal council. Until the king's death in 1718, Horn found himself without political influence.

With the death of Karl XII and the creation of a new regime, Horn and other royal councilors were reinstated in office as members of the council of the realm. As head of this body and president of the chancery, however, Horn found Queen Ulrika Eleonora's tendency to act without the council's knowledge or counsel unacceptable. He resigned the presidency, but discovered to his surprise that the queen extended his resignation from the presidency of the chancery to the council of the realm as well. Elected speaker of the House of the Nobility for the Riksdag* of 1720, however, Horn soon found himself reinstated to both the chancery presidency and the council. He remained in both positions until forced to resign by his parliamentary opponents in 1738. As president of the chancery and speaker of the nobility at the Riksdag of 1726–1727 and that of 1731, Horn dominated Swedish politics for the first two decades of the Age of Liberty*.

Arvid Horn is remembered as one of Sweden's greatest statesmen and politicians, and especially for his role as the leading figure in the restoration of Sweden's political and economic health after the 21 devastating years of the Great Northern War (1700–1721). Likened by many to his British contemporary, Sir Robert Walpole, Horn utilized his control of the bureaucracy and his superb parliamentary skills to dominate Sweden's political decision-making process from 1720 to 1738. His accomplishments include restraining those who wished to take revenge upon the Russian Empire for the losses suffered in the Great Northern War. This acceptance of the geopolitical *status quo post bellum* represented an important insight into the realities of Sweden's new second-rank status in military and diplomatic affairs, which was to facilitate Horn's commitment to economic recovery at home. Yet, this insight was not shared by all, and Horn's downfall in 1738 was brought about by a new political grouping— the so-called Hat Party*—that within a few years drew Sweden into another disastrous war with the Russians.

REFERENCES: S. Grauers, "Arvid Bernhard Horn," in *SBL*, vol. 19:378–92; C. L. Lundquist, *Council, King and Estates in Sweden 1713–1714* (Stockholm, 1975); L. Thanner, *Revolutionen i Sverige efter Karl XII:s död* (Stockholm, 1953).

M. F. METCALF

HØYRE *See* Conservative Party: Norway

I

IBSEN, SIGURD (23 December 1859–14 April 1930) Norwegian scholar, journalist, and writer

Sigurd Ibsen was the son of the Norwegian playwright Henrik Ibsen. He was named after the hero in his father's play *The Vikings of Helgeland* and grew up outside of Norway, which his father left in 1864. Educated on the continent, he took his doctorate in Rome in 1882 with a dissertation entitled *La camera alta nel governo rappresentativo*. He had been a precocious child who spoke impeccable, dialect-free Norwegian. His acquaintances later claimed, however, that it hindered his acceptance and made him seem non-Norwegian. His lack of childhood friends in Norway, coupled with his foreign university training, further hindered him in his native country.

In 1885, largely through the influence of his father, he received an attaché appointment in the Swedish-Norwegian foreign service. He was posted in Stockholm* (1885–1886), Washington, D.C. (1886–1888), and Vienna (1888–1889) before he resigned to establish himself as a journalist in 1890. The diplomatic experience had alienated him from his Swedish colleagues, largely because he was required to submit his reports in Swedish, and Ibsen insisted on writing Norwegian. Consequently, he became an agitator against the Norwegian-Swedish Union* and, in 1891, authored a pamphlet, *Unionen*, against it.

The decade of the 1890s was a period of particularly tense relations between the union partners, who had shared their monarch and foreign office since 1814. Increasingly, the Norwegians came to insist that they ought to ''take the matter into their hands'' and unilaterally abrogate the relationship if necessary. Ibsen was, in 1891, in the forefront of the struggle and considered by many, Oscar II* included, as a dangerous radical. He was, of course, nothing of the kind and remained on the periphery of the debate until 1898, when, in a significant article titled ''Nationalt kongedomme,'' he recommended a peaceful dissolution of the union and the establishment of a separate Norwegian monarchy. Although widely discussed in 1898, Ibsen's ideas were all but forgotten until 1905, when they became the core of the policy of Christian Michelsen*. Ibsen by then had come to support a negotiated settlement to the union question and opposed unilateral Norwegian action. His sharp tongue and pen further alienated him from policy makers, and he found himself on the outside as the fateful events of 1905 unfolded.

After 1905, Ibsen lived primarily as a publicist and writer. He published several philosophical and sociological works (*Menneskelig kvintessens* in 1911 and *Udsyn og Inblik* in 1912) and numerous newspaper articles. *Menneskelig kvintessens* was translated into several languages, including English, and was a major influence on Eugene O'Neill.

Though he was remarkably competent, Ibsen's misfortune was never to be accepted by his contemporaries. Perceptions of him as "the small son of a great father" were aggravated by his aristocratic bearing and undeniable sense of superiority. His one attempt at writing drama, a utopian play, *Robert Frank* (1913), in which a dictator is assassinated after he misunderstands the depth of feelings he has brought forth in his attempts to reform society, was compared with his father's work and found wanting. The autobiographical aspects of the play are tempting to anyone who wishes to understand Ibsen, but the evidence is circumstantial. Ibsen died in Germany, largely forgotten by his countrymen.

REFERENCES: B. Ibsen, *De Tre: Erindringer om Henrik Ibsen, Susannah Ibsen, Sigurd Ibsen* (Oslo, 1948); S. Ibsen, *Udsyn og Indblik* (Copenhagen and Oslo, 1911); T. Leiren, "Sigurd Ibsen and the Origins of National Monarchy in Norway," *Scandinavian Studies* 51 (1979).

T. LEIREN

ICELANDIC Language *See* Languages: Scandinavian

INDUSTRIALIZATION

The industrialization of Scandinavia* began in the second half of the nineteenth century and continued into the twentieth century. Significant stages in this transformation came in the 1850s, 1870s, 1890s, the early years of the present century, the interwar years, and in the post-World War II period. One measure of the extent of the transformation is the percentage of persons employed in agricultural occupations. In the early nineteenth century the overwhelming majority of the working population in any of the Scandinavian countries was employed in the agricultural sector. By contrast, in 1970 only 8 percent in Sweden, 11 percent in Denmark and Norway, and 20 percent in Finland remained in this sector.

There are a number of common features and differences among the Scandinavian countries in the histories of this transformation. L. Jörberg, in the best survey available, points to the initial development of narrow, export-oriented industrial sectors; dependence on a relatively small range of export commodities; dependence on concentrated markets for those exports; significant productivity, wage, and domestic demand increases; extensive utilization of external capital; acceptance of balance of payment deficits; relatively slow development of domestic demand as a driving force in industrial growth; and product flexibility or industrial adaptability to foreign demand as common features. Conversely, he notes distinct product variations, market differences, variations in the degrees of foreign capitalization, differences in the complexity of the industrial sectors' development, and unique historical and resource determiners.

Denmark

Most of the manufactories that had been established through government subsidization in the eighteenth century went bankrupt after 1814, when a liberal economic policy was introduced, and for about a half century Denmark then had a comparative advantage in supplying Britain with cereals in exchange for industrial goods.

Industrialization, therefore, came late to Denmark, as can be seen from the following table.

Growth of Danish Industry, 1860–1970, Based on Manufacturing Enterprises with More Than Five Workers

	Industry's Share of GNP	Annual Growth in Value Added in Industry in Constant Prices in Preceding Period
1860	4.3	
1870	4.1	4.5
1880	5.2	5.5
1890	6.6	5.0
1900	9.9	7.1
1910	9.9	3.9
1920	13.0	4.5
1930	11.6	4.7
1940	15.5	3.5
1950	19.0	3.9
1960	20.6	4.3
1970	19.1	6.4

The beginnings of industrial production different from traditional handicrafts can be found about 1840. Iron foundries were established in various parts of the country, primarily to produce tools for agriculture; and a few textile mills were founded, using steam power and power-looms. Still, the first industrial census (1855) showed that there were only about 120 factories in Denmark that used steam, and their total power output was only about 1,000hp.

There was some growth in industrial output in the early 1870s, when mass production was introduced in brickmaking, brewing, sugar refining, and tobacco manufacturing. The textiles industry expanded in this period also. But the first great period of industrialization came in the 1890s, when industrial employment doubled. The expansion came in nearly all industrial branches, but it is of special interest that a number of factories were founded in trades connected with the introduction of new technology, for example, production of cables, telephones, electricity, cement, and sulphuric acid. These industries also demanded much heavier investment than earlier factories. It was still typical that the production was caused mainly by domestic demand. Only a small part was exported, and there was still a large import of industrial goods for both investment and consumption.

The first three decades of the twentieth century were characterized by great fluctuations in industrial output due to business cycles and war. During World War I the general tendency was a rise in production in order to compensate for discontinued supplies from the warring nations, but much of the production was characterized by low productivity and stopped as soon as the war boom ended. The 1920s were, as a whole, difficult for industry, and many old firms were closed. Expansion can only be found in a few branches, such as the shipyards and in enterprises producing building materials.

During the 1930s the traditional free-trade policy was abandoned and a strict regulation of foreign trade was introduced. Sheltered by this protection, a new industry grew up after 1933, dominated by textile factories, which took over that part of the home market which had hitherto been supplied from Great Britain and Germany.

A new wave of industrialization came after World War II*, with especially rapid growth in the 1970s. Industry now became the most important sector in the national economy and worked for an international market. (From 1961 industry had a larger share of Danish exports than agriculture.) In this period production of investment goods was also of special importance, and the machine industry and the chemical industry were the branches with the highest growth rates. The textile industry lagged behind.

In the process of industrialization in Denmark there have been two distinctive features which are different from the development pattern in most other industrialized countries. First, no branch can be said to have been a key industry. The growth has always taken place over a wide front covering all branches where production was possible in the country. Second, the middle-sized factory has predominated. As late as the 1970s about 95 percent of the industrial firms had fewer than 200 workers, and they occupied more than half of the industrial work force.

The main reasons for this peculiar development pattern are probably the fact that Denmark possesses no large natural resource bases, such as coal, ore, or wood, which could form the basis for an expansion of a special branch; and that Danish industry for a very long time mainly responded to the demands from a small home market, where its competitiveness was caused only by its position close to its customers.

REFERENCES: P. Boje, *Det industrielle miljø 1840–1940* (Copenhagen: Akademisk forlag, 1976); Handbooks in *Danmarks Statistik*, multi-volume, various authors (Copenhagen: Various publishers, 1885–1980); S. A. Hansen, *Early Industrialization in Denmark* (Copenhagen: G.E.C. Gade forlag, 1970); L. Jörberg, *The Industrial Revolution in Scandinavia 1850–1914* (London: The Fontana Economic History of Europe, vol. 4, 1970); A. Nielsen, *Industriens historie i Danmark*, vol. 3 (Copenhagen: G.E.C. Gade forlag, 1944).

H. C. JOHANSEN

Finland

In the early nineteenth century Finland was the most agricultural of the Scandinavian countries, and its economy was in many respects the most backward. During the course of the century significant progress was made toward industrialization, but as late as World War I 66 percent of Finland's population was still employed in agriculture. In the nineteenth century development centered in the forest product and textile sectors. Initially, Finland exported large quantities of timber, chiefly to Russia and Germany. The textile industry produced mainly low-quality goods for the Russian market. At the same time, a small engineering industry developed, which chiefly provided equipment for the timber and textile sectors. Finland enjoyed a favorable export market situation with Russia between 1859 and 1885, during which time tariffs were removed by the Russians and considerable growth occurred. After 1885 Russian tariffs were again imposed on Finnish goods, and the country's industries found themselves in a competitive position with emerging Russian producers. These changes necessitated a reorientation of production and markets, which benefited Finland in the long run. For example, these changes stimulated the growth of the paper pulp industry.

The pattern of industrial development remained much the same in Finland until after World War II. Agriculture continued to play a disproportionately large part in the economy, while the industrial sector relied heavily on the export of forest products. There were only modest developments in the engineering and metallurgical areas. The great transformation came after World War II and was largely the result of the need to change the Finnish industrial base in order to pay the war reparations demanded by the Soviet Union. In this process Finland developed a much wider and more modern industrial economy which produced a wider variety of goods for export and domestic consumption. In the 1980s Finland remained, however, the least industrialized of the Scandinavian countries and continued to struggle with an inefficient agricultural sector and nagging regional differences.

B. NORDSTROM

Norway

Norway's industrial development was based largely on four foundations: timber, fish, and to a smaller extent metals and the service sector, especially the merchant marine. Its principal market in the nineteenth century was Britain. In the timber industry, Norway responded to the demand for lumber prompted by the industrialization and urbanization of Europe. During the course of the century, its timber mills changed over from water power to steam. When the demand for timber declined in the later part of the century, the industry responded by converting partially to the production of paper pulp. The fishing industry expanded and adopted mechanized techniques in the catch and processing sectors. The metallurgical sector remained small during the nineteenth century but enjoyed significant growth after about 1900 as a result of the adoption of electrical processing techniques and the development of hydroelectrical resources. The growth of the freight carrying sector was phenomenal for a country of Norway's size, and its growth served as a source of capital and stimulated the development of a shipbuilding industry. By World War I, Norway's was the fourth largest merchant fleet in the world. The expansion of these industries helped to offset trade deficits to some degree, but Norway was and remains a capital-importing country and a country which imports more than it exports.

Capitalization of industrial development involved an alarming extent of foreign investment, so much so that in 1907 regulations were passed to prevent the establishment of wholly foreign-owned companies in the country. (Much of the early foreign investment was bought out using shipping profits from World War I.) A significant new sector of the Norwegian economy developed after 1900 based on hydroelectrical generation plants in electrometallurgical and electrochemical production. Norway became a leading producer of aluminum and nitrate fertilizers. To these primary sectors of the Norwegian industrial economy must be added the oil and gas production based on the North Sea fields, which became vitally important to the Norwegian economy in the 1970s. (*See also* Whaling.)

B. NORDSTROM

Sweden

The industrialization of Sweden followed similar patterns, but resulted in greater breadth and depth. Initially, industrialization was based on two traditional industries: timber and iron. As in Finland and Norway, the timber industry responded to expanded European demand first by developing existing plants (before 1850) and then by adopting the steam-driven saw. Again, too, when the demand for lumber slackened in the last quarter of the century, the industry responded by converting in part to pulp production. In Sweden this shift went farther and included the extensive development of paper manufacturing and chemical pulp industries. Sweden's iron industry responded to market and technological changes and moved away from iron (bar iron) production to concentrate on the export of iron ore and the production of high-grade steels and engineering products. Chronologically, significant expansion occurred in the 1850s, based largely on demand for agricultural products; in the 1870s, based on agricultural and industrial demand abroad; and in the 1890s, based on growing domestic demand. In each phase, earnings were, to a significant extent, invested in domestic development. Capitalization was to a marked degree based on internal sources. Other areas of the industrial sector that showed significant growth in the latter half of the nineteenth century included textiles, leather goods, ceramics, and shipbuilding. Growth in the twentieth century tended to be in the traditionally strong areas of the economy. The strength of contemporary Sweden's industrial economy rests heavily upon the metallurgical, engineering, and related high technology areas. (*See also* Agricultural Revolution; Shipping; Urbanization.)

REFERENCES: E. Heckscher, *An Economic History of Sweden*, trans. G. Ohlin (Cambridge, Mass.: Harvard University Press, 1954); F. Hodne, *An Economic History of Norway 1815–1970* (Bergen: Tapir, 1970), and *The Norwegian Economy 1920–1980* (New York: St. Martin's, 1983); L. Jörberg, "The Industrialization of Scandinavia," in *The Fontana Economic History of Europe*, vols. 4(2) and 6(2) (London: Collins, 1970); S. Lieberman, *The Industrialization of Norway, 1800–1920* (Oslo: Universitetsforlaget, 1970); R. Lundstrom, *Kring industrialismens genombrott i Sverige* (Stockholm: Wahlstrom & Widstrand, 1966); P. B. Nielsen, "Aspects of Industrial Financing in Denmark 1840–1914," *Scandinavian Economic History Review* 31:2 (1983): 79–108.

B. NORDSTROM

INGI I HARALDSSON (Hunchback) (c. 1134–4 February 1161) King of Norway 1136–1161

Ingi Hunchback, the legitimate son of King Harald Gilchrist (Harald IV Magnusson*), became king of Norway at age 2 upon his father's death in 1136, succeeding in a co-regency with his four-year-old half brother, Sigurd Mouth. The children were chosen kings by their father's retainers, especially his landed men, who as regents for minors could expand the ruling powers they had exercised under Harald. Their father's killer and supposed half brother, Sigurd Slembi, opposed them, but late in 1139 the combined forces of the child kings defeated him and his ally, their uncle Magnus the Blind (Magnus IV Sigurdsson*), in eastern Norway. Magnus perished in battle, while Sigurd Slembi was tortured to death afterward. Thus ended the first phase of the Norwegian civil wars.

Ingi and Sigurd Mouth shared sovereignty and held their retainers in common. In 1142 a third son of Harald Gilchrist, Eystein, was fetched from Scotland to Norway and became king and co-regent, taking his own retainers. The major event during their shared reign was the separation of the Norwegian Church from the Scandinavian metropolitan province of Lund (established in 1104) by the creation of an archbishopric in Nidaros (Trondheim). The reorganization of the Church was effected by Cardinal Nicholas Breakspear, an English-born papal legate, during a representative meeting of Norwegian secular and religious leaders in 1152–1153, the first known national assembly in the country. In its province the new archbishopric included the five dioceses in Norway (Nidaros, Bergen, Oslo, Stavanger, and a new one in Hamar) and the six in Norse colonies in the British Isles and the North Atlantic. Other religious reforms established the Church as a powerful factor in the country and made it organizationally, legally, and economically less dependent upon secular powers.

In the late 1140s Ingi and Sigurd Mouth each took their own retainers, and differences began to appear. The two illegitimate, older half brothers plotted to dethrone their crippled "Hunchback" brother at a meeting of the three scheduled for 1155 in Bergen, but Ingi learned of their plans, arrived in force, and felled Sigurd. Although a reconciliation postponed the inevitable, Eystein was caught and killed in eastern Norway in 1157. Ingi's circle tried to secure sole sovereignty for their ruler, but by this second phase of the Norwegian civil wars political factions representing different regions had developed, and the opposition designated Sigurd Mouth's illegitimate son, Haakon the Broad-Shouldered (Haakon II Sigurdsson*), as their new candidate.

Haakon and his men suffered a defeat in eastern Norway in 1159, but rivalries between Ingi's two main advisors soon weakened his group, and the incumbent was felled on 4 February 1161 on the ice near Oslo, leaving Haakon as sole sovereign. Ingi had no heir in the direct male line, but Ingi's advisor Erling Crook-Neck (*skakki*) quickly rallied their faction in Bergen behind his own son by the daughter of King Sigurd the Crusader (Sigurd I Magnusson*), Magnus V Erlingsson*.

REFERENCES: G. M. Gathorne-Hardy, *A Royal Impostor: King Sverre of Norway* (Oslo: Aschehoug, 1956); K. Gjerset, *History of the Norwegian People* (1932; repr. New York: AMS, 1969); K. Helle, *Norge blir en stat 1130–1319*, 2nd rev. ed. (Bergen: Universitetsforlaget, 1974); K. Larsen, *A History of Norway* (Princeton: Princeton University Press, 1948/1974); S. Sturluson, *Heimskringla: Sagas of the Norse Kings* (London: Dent, 1961).

J. E. KNIRK

INGI II BAARDSSON (c. 1185–23 April 1217) King of Norway 1204–1217

Ingi Baardsson, the son of King Sverrir Sigurdsson's* sister and a landed man from Trøndelag, was elected king of Norway by the Birchlegs in 1204, upon the death of Guttorm Sigurdsson. The four-year-old Guttorm had succeeded his uncle King Haakon Sverrisson as his faction's king earlier that year, while power rested with a group of regents headed by Earl Haakon the Mad, a nephew of King Sverrir. After Haakon Sverrisson's death, the hostilities of the Norwegian civil wars began anew. The Crosiers, whose faction had played no role during Haakon's two-year-long peaceful reign, regrouped in Denmark behind their new candidate, Erling Stonewall, a supposed son of King Magnus Erlingsson*, returning then to their traditional stronghold of eastern Norway. Their alliance with the Church had, however, been broken.

The second Crosier war was not nearly as fierce as the one late in the reign of King Sverrir. Even the choice of the nineteen-year-old Ingi as king represented a victory for less militant politics, since he was supported by the farmers of Trøndelag and the archbishop against the professional soldiers' candidate, Earl Haakon, Ingi's older half brother. Haakon continued as earl and military leader, exercising the rights of king in western Norway, while Ingi stayed mostly in Trøndelag. When Erling Stonewall died in 1207, his earl, Philip Simonsson (a maternal grandson of King Ingi I Haraldsson*) became king of the Crosiers, the farmers (this time in eastern Norway with the support of Bishop Nicholas of

Oslo) again rejecting the professional soldiers' candidates. Through a truce in 1208, the archbishop and Bishop Nicholas brought about a peace and a division of the country into three realms. Ingi was to remain king and have incomes from Trøndelag and his seat in Nidaros (Trondheim), whereas Earl Haakon was to have control over western Norway, and Philip was to renounce his royal title but retain control over eastern Norway.

During the tripartite division of the country, Philip conducted his own internal affairs and foreign relations. Ingi and Haakon came to an agreement in 1212 concerning succession, and when the earl died in 1214, the king assumed control of the entire Birchleg kingdom. He also quelled an uprising of farmers against local administrators and district governors in Trøndelag the same year. Shortly before his death in 1217, Ingi appointed his legitimate half brother, Skuli Baardsson, earl and military leader. After the king died, however, his followers elected Haakon IV Haakonsson* king. Philip died that same summer.

REFERENCES: K. Gjerset, *History of the Norwegian People* (1932; repr. New York: AMS, 1969); K. Helle, *Norge blir en stat 1130–1319*, 2nd rev. ed. (Bergen: Universitetsforlaget, 1974); K. Larsen, *A History of Norway* (Princeton: Princeton University Press, 1948/1974); S. Thordarson, *The Saga of Hacon, and a Fragment of the Saga of Magnus* (London: Rolls, 1894).

J. E. KNIRK

INGÓLFR ARNARSON (Ninth century) First settler of Iceland

Ingólfr, a native of Sunnfjord in western Norway, is named in the *Book of Settlements* (*Landnámabók*) and by Ari Þorgilsson* in *Íslendingabók* as the first permanent settler of Iceland. In 874 he is believed to have built a farm at Reykjavík (''Steam Bay'') in southwest Iceland, the site of the modern capital. This area was the most likely place of settlement due to its wealth of natural resources: salmon rivers and fishing lakes, a natural harbor, and subterranean mineral springs.

Ingólfr's descendants were honored with the title *allsherjargoði*(''priest of all the host''), which required them to bless the yearly meeting of the National Assembly (Althing*).

REFERENCES: *The Book of Settlements*, trans. H. Pálsson and P. Edwards (Winnipeg: University of Manitoba Press, 1972); P. Foote and D. Wilson, *The Viking Achievement* (London: Sidgwick and Jackson, 1970); J. Jóhannesson, *Íslendingasaga: A History of the Old Icelandic Commonwealth*, trans. Haraldur Bessason (Winnipeg: University of Manitoba Press, 1974).

M. EMELITY

INHERITANCE PRACTICES Sweden

Until the mid-nineteenth century the inheritance system in Sweden was strictly regulated and provided little room for the wishes of the deceased. This applied especially to inherited farmland. Such land was neither bequeathed nor given away without the approval of the heirs. If a person sold inherited land, potential heirs had the right (*bördsrätt*) to buy it back. Purchased land and personal property could be willed, donated, or sold freely. In towns there was no distinction between inherited land and other kinds of property. There were limits on the amount of property that could be willed or given away, and the size of these depended upon how closely related the heirs were. In general, direct descendants of the deceased stood first in the order of inheritance, followed by parents and then siblings. Thereafter, more distant relatives entered in, so long as a clear relationship to the deceased could be established. Surviving spouses had no inheritance rights. Most of the provincial laws from the thirteenth and fourteenth centuries and the two land laws of the fourteenth and fifteenth centuries established that men's shares in the inheritance were to be twice those of women. In the fourteenth century town law, women and men inherited equally.

In the provincial laws which are considered the oldest, a daughter did not inherit if there were a surviving son. This has been viewed as growing out of an older practice by which women did not inherit from men. The general trend is believed to have been toward increased inheritance rights for women. Contrary to this, however, is the argument that the provincial laws replaced older practices (wherein children divided the estate into marriage portions [hemföljd] when they were married) with a system of clear inheritance shares. Under the latter, daughters received half-shares, which equalled what they had received in the marriage portions. Beginning with the provincial laws, it is believed, such inheritance practices became firmly regulated.

The source materials for the medieval and early modern periods illuminate only the inheritance practices of the upper aristocracy. No attempts to avoid inheritance laws and use primogeniture or prevent property from passing to another male line seem to have occurred in the Middle Ages. The kinship system (släktsystemet) was clearly bilateral. It was accepted that real property was split when the estate was divided and that women carried inherited land to other male lines. The real property was held together, instead, through marriage alliances within the small upper aristocracy. Beginning in the sixteenth and seventeenth centuries, one can see a trend toward patrilinealism. In the feudal donation practices that were introduced by the sons of Gustav I Vasa*, women had no inheritance rights, and in count and baronial estates even younger sons were excluded. There were some attempts by the crown to extend this system to include the aristocracy's alodial estates around 1600, and criticism was later directed at the inheritance rights of daughters by, among others, Axel Oxenstierna*. Apparently, from the 1640s a trend developed to establish entailed estates. These were designed to preserve property undivided within a male line, and the system became explicitly legal through the 1686 testament law, although it applied only to purchased and moveable property. In practice a system was established by which sons (usually the eldest) received first choice (tagelott) of the best-situated property at the time of the estate's division. The attitude among the nobles was probably divided on the question of these patrilineal trends, and no open attempts to change the land laws' basic regulations on inheritance were made after 1600. Rather, these rules were ratified in the 1734 law.

In the literature it has been accepted that down to the end of the nineteenth century the peasants tried to evade the inheritance laws in order to keep their land holdings together as a unit—for example, by having a son take over the farm during the parent's lifetime or by inducing (often with social pressures) the surviving siblings to sell their shares cheaply to a privileged heir. Such practices have not been studied systematically. It is clear that the crown periodically sought to limit the division of peasant farms. During the late Middle Ages and in the sixteenth century, a number of decrees were issued which, while they did not do away with established law, gave a major heir in an estate the right to buy out lesser heirs. In most parts of the country the laws appear to have had little effect in the first half of the seventeenth century. Some effect seems to have come from a 1684 decree which had the same intent. The crown's policy was more uncertain during the eighteenth and nineteenth centuries. Sometimes the division of farms was facilitated to encourage population growth. At other times the division of farms was opposed to prevent the proletarianization of the countryside.

The peasants' own attitudes toward inheritance questions are not particularly clear. When, at the 1786 Riksdag*, Gustav III* tried to establish the right of the eldest son to buy out his siblings, the proposal was defeated and the peasants were so opposed to the measure that they refused even to vote on it. The one systematic study of peasant inheritance practices deals with an area in western Sweden during the nineteenth century. There it was unusual for parents to leave the farm to one child during their lifetimes, and regulations were strictly followed when the estate was divided. An important exception was that daughters often inherited as much as sons. The effort to keep property together seems to have been minimal.

It is difficult to say how representative this study is. It is quite likely that regional differences were great. There are, for example, reports from northern Sweden that the heirs determined by lot which of them would buy out the others, and that siblings were bought out through a special land assessment in each village. The lack of studies means that it is still impossible to chart inheritance practices for all of Sweden.

During the nineteenth century the fairly weak patrilineal or male-favoring elements in the Swedish inheritance laws were removed. In 1810 the establishment of entailed estates was prohibited. In 1845 equal inheritance rights for men and women, even in the country, were introduced, and in 1857 the law against bequests or gifts of inherited land was removed, although children could not be disinherited entirely. During the 1920s a few new elements were introduced into the Swedish inheritance law code. The old right of unlimited inheritance was abolished. In instances where there was no will, the state replaced cousins or more distant relatives in the order of inheritance. In addition, childless widows and widowers gained the right to inherit from their spouses.

REFERENCES: G. Hafström, *Den svenska familjerättens historia* (1965); Å. Holmbäck,, *Ätten och arvet* (1919); E. Sjöholm, "Några arrättsliga problem i de svenska medeltidslagarna," *Scandia* (1968), pp. 164–95; C. Winberg, "Familj och jord i tre västgötasocknar," *Historisk tidskrift* (1981), pp. 275–310, and *Grenverket* (forthcoming); N. Wohlin, *Faran af bondeklassens undergräfvande* (1910).

C. WINBERG

IRON AGE Prehistoric period in Scandinavian history 400 B.C.–1100 A.D.

Scandinavian archeology in the mid-twentieth century has endeavored to divide meaningfully this long period into about six shorter ones. The first three, Celtic Iron Age*, Early Roman Iron Age, and Late Roman Iron Age, include those formative epochs when Celtic influence, so difficult to plot because so nomadic, and then Roman influence were at their height. The latter three, the Migration, Vendel, and Viking periods (*see* Viking Age), between about 400 and 1100 A.D., include epochs when there was often very rapid sophistication in the processing of iron into tools and weaponry.

It may have been in Denmark, with its great tradition of metal craftsmanship from the Bronze Age*, that bog iron was first processed in Scandinavia, about 500 B.C. It was probably very soon, though, that this "young" industry was developed by Celtic influences passing north via the Rhine from the Celtic heartlands, especially as iron objects were already in distribution up the western side of the British Isles and through Scotland. By the first century B.C., the short iron scythe and the wheeled plow were probably in use in Denmark. The sites at Thorsberg in Slesvig and at Vimose on Funen from about 300 A.D. reveal that Roman iron weaponry was familiar by that time.

A firm basis for iron manufacture seems to have been laid between 300 and 400 A.D. in Norway. The availability of the soft soapstone (steatite) in southern Norway, from which casts could be readily formed, was important there. The most remarkable finds in Norway, dating from about 200 to 600, are capacious iron cauldrons. These were probably imported from Frankish Frisia in unrivalled quantities, given their comparative paucity elsewhere in Scandinavia*. It should be emphasized that these importations were paralleled by an exploitation of native iron, the increasing production of which appears to have assisted the extension of farming into less promising areas (*gårdsdriften*). This same development occurred in Sweden during the Viking period, when Gästrikland and south Norrland, *inter alia*, were colonized.

Owing to the richness of Sweden's copper deposits, it may be that a native iron production was slower to start there than in Norway or Denmark. But recent archeology has revealed that by 300 A.D. ironsmiths were active at Helgö, at the eastern end of Lake Mälaren. This site must have later benefited, as did Gotland, through trade links with the south Baltic coasts and the great estuaries through which the iron of Bohemia and the Danubian lands could be vented northwards. The undoubted home production of iron in Sweden in the Viking period must, however, be seen as but a part of that mastery of iron which is so characteristic of Viking Scandinavia, giving it its peculiar vitality and, indeed, its ability to secure the best of continental products.

REFERENCES: E. G. Bowen, *Britain and the Western Seaways* (London: Thames & Hudson, 1972); *DH*, vol. 1; *DSH*, vol. 1; H. Jankuhn, *Denkmäler der Vorzeit Nord-und Ostsee* (Schleswig: H. Bernaet, 1957); O. Klindt-Jensen, *Denmark: Foreign Influences in Its Early Iron Age* (Copenhagen, 1950); *NH*, vol. 1; H. Shetelig, *Norges Folk i Jernaldern* (Stockholm, 1950); H. Shetelig and H. Falk, *Scandinavian Archaeology* (Oxford: Oxford University Press, 1937); M. Stenberger, *Nordische Vorzeit*, vol. 4 (Neumünster, 1977); M. Wheeler, *Rome Beyond the Imperial Frontiers* (London: George Bell & Sons, 1954).

D. D. ALDRIDGE

J

JAKOBSEN, JAKOB (1864–1918) Faroese philologist

Though Dr. Jakob Jakobsen's life was spent almost entirely in scholarly pursuits, he is important in Faroese history for several reasons. He was the first Faroese scholar this century to acquire an international reputation; his historical work was influential in the developing self-consciousness of the Faroese nationalists; his collection of Faroese folktales and legends helped to shape Faroese prose; and he continued the philological work of Jens Christian Svabo* and Venceslaus Ulricus Hammershaimb*.

Jakobsen was born and raised in Tórshavn*. His father was the bookseller and bookbinder Hans Nicolai Jacobsen, whose business still continues in the Faroese capital. He early displayed his linguistic gifts, and at 13 was sent to Denmark to study in Herlovholm Latin School. In 1883 he entered Copenhagen University, where he studied the Scandinavian languages*. He first met Hammershaimb in 1884, and in 1886 he was asked to compile the dictionary which forms the second volume of *Faerösk Anthologi*, published in 1891.

In 1887 he was in the Faroe Islands* for six months, gathering samples of village dialects, work which to this day is of great philological importance. He also began to study the life of Poul Poulsen Nolsöe* from the archives in Tórshaven. He was back in the Faroes for a year from the summer of 1892, and collected legends, folktales, and words.

In 1893 Jakobsen began his monumental study of the recently extinct Shetland Norn, a language related to Faroese. He spent two years gathering fragments from the Shetland dialect, from placenames, and from snatches of the old language still remembered. He gathered some 10,000 words and elucidated the principal features of the grammar and pronunciation. In 1897 appeared his masterly work, *Det norröne sprog på Shetland* (*The Norn Language in Shetland*), which brought Jakobsen his doctorate. (He was the first Faroeman to attain this distinction.) The feat of rescuing a language half a century after it had ceased to be spoken won Jakobsen an international reputation.

This scholarly work had an important bearing on the national movement in the Faroe Islands. Economic advance in the islands since the introduction of free trade in 1856 had been accompanied by increasing pressure by the Danish language on Faroese. By 1890 Tórshavn was already largely Danish-speaking, and Danish words and expressions were beginning to penetrate into the dialects of the villages, particularly those near the capital. The situation was analogous to the process Jakobsen had documented in Shetland. Jakobsen showed how Lowland Scottish had penetrated first the town dialects, then the village and farm dialects, until in his time the only survival was of words and fragments in the language of shepherds and boat-fishermen, and in place-names which even the Shetlanders no longer knew how to interpret.

That Faroese did not go the way of the Shetland Norn was due to the efforts of Föringafelag* (the Faroese Society), which began consciously to use Faroese for all possible purposes. Jakobsen took little direct part in the work of the society, but his studies provided the theoretical groundwork for their efforts.

In 1898 he returned to the Faroe Islands and completed the collection of legends and folktales begun in 1892–1893. The outcome was the magnificent collection *Færoske folksagn og æventyr* (*Faroese Legends and Folktales*), which turned the splendid oral prose tradition of the islands into part of Faroese written literature. Jakobsen tried to link the legends with historical facts. Among his more important historical works are *Færosk sagnhistorie* (*Faroese Legendary History*), published in 1907; *Diplomatarium Færoense* (a collection of medieval historical documents), published in 1907; and *Poul Nolsöe. Livssöga og irkingar*, published in 1908–1912, which contains a biography of the Faroese national hero, P. P. Nolsöe, and a collected edition of his ballads.

From 1909 onwards, Jakobsen studied Orkney Norn, but he lived to publish only a few of his findings. At the same time, he began the publication of *Etymologisk ordbog over det norröne sprog på Shetland*, an etymological dictionary of Shetland Norn. The first three volumes appeared in 1908, 1909, and 1912, respectively. This work was completed after his death and in 1928–1932 appeared in English translation. Jakobsen was planning to do further work in Caithness, as well as in Orkney, Shetland, and Faroe, when he died as the result of a kidney operation in Copenhagen* on 15 August 1918.

REFERENCES: R. Grønneberg, *Jakobsen and Shetland* (Lerwick: Shetland Publishing Co., 1981); Jakob Jakobsen, *The Dialect and Place Names of Shetland* (Lerwick: T. & J. Manson, 1897), *An Etymological Dictionary of the Norn Language in Shetland* (London and Copenhagen: 1928–1932), and "Remarks upon Faröese Literature and History," *Saga-Book of the Viking Club* 4 (1905); T.M.Y. Manson, "The Personal Impact of Jakobsen in Shetland and Orkney," *Froðskaparrit* 13 (1964): 9–13; H. Marwick, "Dr. Jakob Jakobsen," *Froðskaparrit* 13 (1964): 13–17; C. Matras, "Profiles from the Past: No. XXVIII—Jakob Jakobsen," *The New Shetlander* 74 (1965); John F. West, *Faroese Folk-Tales and Legends* (Lerwick: Shetland Publishing Co., 1980).

J. F. WEST

JANSSON, ERIK (19 December 1808–13 May 1850) Sectarian leader and founder of the Bishop Hill Colony in Illinois

Erik Jansson was born in Landsberga, Biskopskulla parish, Uppland in 1808.

His parents were landowning farmers. The first 22 years of his life contained little of note. In 1830, however, he experienced an overwhelming religious awakening. This set him on a path that led him to become a lay preacher, the founder of a sectarian movement (Janssonism), a critic of the State Church of Sweden, an emigrant, and the founder of the Bishop Hill Colony in Illinois.

As a result of his religious awakening, Jansson came to believe that he had been freed of all sin and that he was a direct successor of the Apostles. He may even have believed himself to be the new Messiah. For most of the next 10 years, he devoted himself to the study of the Bible, the works of Luther, and other religious works. In the 1840s he turned actively to preaching, first in Västmanland and, after 1843, chiefly in the neighboring province of Hälsingland. He gradually acquired a following of devoted adherents.

At the core of his religious thinking was the doctrine of perfectionism. He held that the true believer was sinless and placed strong emphasis upon the freeing of the human spirit to realize its full potential. These ideas were based on Jansson's reading of the Scriptures, although they also may have been shaped by the ideas of the English Methodist George Scott, who was active in Stockholm* at this time.

Up to a point, Jansson was typical of a number of critics of state Lutheranism* in Sweden in the nineteenth century. The rationalism of the Enlightenment had, it seemed to these critics, stifled the spirit in the church, leaving only sterile formalism. These views were magnified by the close ties between the church and the state. Jansson's early religious activities were within the Readers (Läsare) movement, which was based on the reading and discussion of the Bible and other religious works in small groups outside of the church—although often with the lower clergy's toleration and even participation. The purpose of the movement was to repersonalize and rehumanize the religious experience.

In the early 1840s, however, Jansson came to reject outright the existing state church. He branded the clergy as agents of the Devil, organized his followers into a separatist and exclusivistic sect, and began to conduct his own church services. For a time these activities were tolerated by the church and the secular authorities, even though they were in violation of the 1726 Conventicle Act (*see* Conventicle Acts). When he instigated a series of book burnings in 1844, however, he aroused the authorities to act against him. He and a number of his followers were repeatedly arrested, detained, warned, fined, and imprisoned. Jansson was sent to Västerås for a mental examination. Concurrently, he and his followers came under attack by groups of outraged citizens. Jansson was forced to go into hiding. In 1845 he fled to Norway and from there emigrated to America. He was followed into exile by 1,200 to 1,500 of his adherents over the next five years.

In 1846 Jansson and his adherents founded the Bishop Hill Colony in Illinois near Galesburg. The settlement was based upon ideals Jansson had advocated in Sweden, including perfectionism, communal ownership of property, and the sharing of all work. For the next five years, Jansson served as the spiritual and temporal head of the community, which, after suffering severely in the early years, came to prosper. By 1850 the colony controlled between 10,000 and 14,000 acres. The central village was comprised of a number of buildings, including dormitories, kitchens, a brewery, a hotel, a school, several shops, and the central church. Broom corn, flax, wheat, and livestock were raised. Linen, flour, dairy products, hides, and bricks were among the goods produced for sale.

Jansson was an uncompromising master at Bishop Hill. He aroused hatred inside and outside the community. In 1851 he was killed by John Root, an outraged husband of one of the commune's members. Following his death the colony continued to operate as a corporation for a number of years, but in 1860 the organization was dissolved and the property divided among the members. The story of Bishop Hill is a remarkable one in the history of communal attempts in America.

Treatment of Jansson by historians has been mixed, largely because many biased sources about him have survived. To some he was an evil, misguided megalomaniac. More sympathetic observers have seen him as a genuine and well-intentioned reformer. Whichever view is more correct, he must be regarded as an important figure in the religious history of nineteenth-century Sweden, in the history of emigration*, in the history of communal attempts in America, and in Swedish-American history.

REFERENCES: P. Elmen, *Wheat Flour Messiah* (Carbondale, Ill.: The Swedish Pioneer Historical Society and Southern Illinois University Press, 1976); O. Isaksson and S. Hallgren, *Bishop Hill: A Utopia on the Prairie* (Stockholm: LT Publishing House, 1969); M. A. Mikkelsen, *The Bishop Hill Colony* (Baltimore: Johns Hopkins Press, 1891).

B. NORDSTROM

JELLING (Denmark) Site of late tenth-century royal mounds and runic stones

The Jelling monument is composed of several elements including two huge burial/ritual mounds, a V-shaped stone setting between the mounds, a small runestone, a large ornamented runestone, and an early Romanesque church with remains of a large timber church beneath it.

Excavations on the site in 1820, 1861, and 1941–1942 have proved that the southern mound, the largest in Denmark, never was used for burials. It is believed to be a sort of memorial mound. In the northern mound a divided burial chamber was found, in which, however, there were only a few traces of grave goods and no skeletal remains. Apparently the grave had been broken into in early times.

A more than 100–meter-long stone setting forms a triangle running from the northern mound, which it embraces, to a meeting-point just south of the memorial mound. The stone setting has been disturbed by the church between the mounds, and some scholars have argued that it originally could have been a stone ship setting. It is agreed, though, that the setting formed part of a heathen sanctuary around the prominent royal burial ground.

The small runestone, the oldest in Jelling, belongs to the pagan part of the tenth century. Its inscription reads: "King Gorm[*] made these word/marks (*kumbl*) after Thyre, his wife, Denmark's improvement (*Danmarks bod*)." Thyre probably died around 935. Gorm died c. 940. It is believed that they were buried in the northern mound. Contemporary sources tell practically nothing about their reign, and the precise meaning of *"Danmarks bod"* is unclear.

The great Jelling stone was erected during the reign of Harald Bluetooth (Harald I*, c. 940–985/987) and belongs to Christian times. The inscription, which contains a memorial to Haralds' parents and references to Harald's accomplishments, reads: "King Harald commanded these words to be made after Gorm, his father, and Thyre, his mother,—that Harald won all Denmark and Norway, and made the Danes Christian." The ornamentation on the three-sided stone is a beautiful work of Scandinavian "power-art" and serves to underscore the equality of the natural and supernatural powers secured by the ruler. On the largest side of the stone, the twisted body of a snake surrounds the memorial part of the runic inscription. A savage dragon covers most of the right side of the stone, leaving little space for the runes. The earliest known Christ-figure in Scandinavia* is engraved on the third side of the stone, and this is surrounded by twisted, Viking Age* ornamentation. The stone was originally colored.

Recent excavations (1977–1980) beneath the present, early Romanesque church have established that the original timber church was of considerable size. Also, it has been established that under the western part of the church there was a prominent Christian grave. In this there were traces of textiles and two fire-gilded silver ornaments inlaid with niello. The remains of a man found in the grave showed that the body had been removed from an earlier grave to this pile, where the skeletal remains were placed at random.

The site at Jelling, with these important ancient monuments, has often been the subject of discussion among historians. Most scholars agree that Jelling is a sort of meeting place between the pagan and Christian in Danish antiquity. It is believed that the original heathen burial ground and sanctuary with its mounds and stone setting were erected by Gorm around 940. Harald was Christianized around 960. It is believed that he changed the sanctuary into a Christian ground and that he commanded the transfer of his parents' remains from their heathen grave in the north mound to the church upon its completion. Finally, it is believed that the great Jelling stone was engraved as a Christian memorial to Harald's parents and himself. This work should have been completed in the 960s.

Recent discussion about the site has been concentrated on the inscription on the great Jelling stone. A two-stage theory has been advanced in which it is argued that the memorial text was done first. The recording of Harald's achievements, it has been suggested, was added later, either from the end of Harald's reign or perhaps even after his death (*see* Trelleborg Forts).

Several archeologists, however, believe that the stone was executed as a single piece around 960. It is assumed, in accordance with contemporary written sources, that the political phrases on the stone were more accurate around 960 than toward the end of Harald's reign, when he was threatened by a heathen uprising, led by his son Svend (Sven I*), and Norway was governed by an independent king. Although the inscription could not be just an empty boast, placed as it was where everyone could see it, the text does not necessarily describe the political realities when it was engraved. Rather, it was perhaps just a memorial stone, erected for Harald and his parents and containing a record of his most memorable achievements.

Whichever interpretation of the stone is correct, the site stands as one of the most significant in all of Denmark, and the great Jelling stone may be seen as the birth certificate of the nation.

REFERENCES: A. E. Christensen, "The Jelling Monuments," *Medieval Scandinavia* 8 (1975): 7–20, and *Vikingetidens Danmark* (Copenhagen: Det historiske institut ved Københavns Universitet, 1969); P. V. Glob, *Danish Prehistoric Monuments* (London: Faber & Faber, 1971), and "Kong Haralds Kumler," *Skalk* 4 (1969): 18–27; E. Moltke, *Runerne i Danmark og deres oprindelse* (Copenhagen: Forum, 1976); K. M. Nielsen et al., "Jelling Problems: A Discussion," *Medieval Scandinavia* 7 (1974): 156–234; O. Olsen, *Hørg, Hov og Kirke* (Copenhagen: Det kongelige Nordiske Oldskriftselskab, 1966); I. Skovgaard-Petersen, *Oldtid og Vikingetid in Danmarks Historie*, vol. 1 (Copenhagen: Gyldendal, 1977).

N. P. STILLING

JESUITS The Society of Jesus (SJ)

In 1534 Ignatius Loyola founded the religious order of the Society of Jesus, whose members are popularly known as Jesuits. Under the rigorous spiritual discipline outlined in Loyola's *Spiritual Exercises* and through intense theological study, the Jesuits became the most powerful religious order in the history of modern Roman Catholicism. In 1540 Paul III gave his papal blessing to the Jesuits and began to use them effectively in strategic areas of the world.

It was not long after Johan III* became king of Sweden-Finland in 1569 that a Polish Jesuit was sent to be the personal chaplain of the king's Polish queen consort; he was joined shortly thereafter by the Norwegian Jesuit known as Laurentius Norvegus (Nielsen). Through the latter, Johan III was converted to Roman Catholicism, and "Operation Sweden" (*Misseo Suetica*) was launched in 1576 with the establishment of a secret Jesuit theological college in Stockholm*. All seemed to go extraordinarily well until the vicar general, Antonio Possevino, tried to force the king to make a public announcement of his conversion. With the king's throne in jeopardy, Johan III instead renounced his Roman Catholicism and expelled the Jesuit Mission in 1580. Upon his death in 1592 Johan III was succeeded by his Catholic son, Sigismund*, who was also the Catholic Vasa king of Poland (1587–1632). Known as the "King of the Jesuits," Sigismund, upon the advice of his Jesuit counselors, subscribed to the *Augsburg Confession** as prescribed by the Church Assembly at Uppsala in 1593. He was defeated militarily in 1598 by his Protestant uncle, Karl IX*, who had the support of the Swedish clergy and laity.

In Denmark-Norway-Iceland the Counter-Reformation had a more difficult time due to the forthright opposition of its two ardent Lutheran kings, Christian III* and Frederik II*. Nevertheless, the Jesuits made abortive attempts to re-establish Roman Catholicism through the erstwhile Norwegian Jesuit Laurentius Norvegus, who attempted to found a theological college in Copenhagen* in 1606. In 1613 several Norwegian "Lutheran" pastors from Oslo were sentenced to exile for their Roman Catholicism when it was found that they had come under the influence of Laurentius Norvegus. In 1623 a group of Jesuits and Dominicans was sent to Denmark to investigate whether a mission was possible, but nothing ever came of it. At the end of the Thirty Years' War (1648) some Jesuits came to Bergen, Norway but were expelled within the year.

In 1617 legislation had been passed in Sweden-Finland forbidding the presence of Roman Catholics in the realm. Similar legislation was passed for Denmark-Norway-Iceland in 1624, prohibiting under penalty of death the residence of any Roman Catholic priest. For the next 150 years the only Roman Catholic clerics in Scandinavia* were those Jesuit chaplains who ministered to foreign embassy personnel or mercenary soldiers. When the Society of Jesus was disbanded in 1773 even these few Jesuits departed Scandinavia. In 1872, after the granting of religious liberty, the Danish prefect apostolic, Herman Grueder, invited Jesuits who had been expelled from Germany during the Kulturkampf to come to Denmark. In 1965 a native Danish Jesuit, Hans Martinsen, became the Roman Catholic bishop of Denmark. So feared were the Jesuits in Norway that a prohibition against any Jesuit residing in Norway was written into the Constitution of 1814. This prohibition remained a part of the constitution (in spite of the passage of religious freedom in 1845) well into the twentieth century, when it was finally rescinded in 1956 by a vote in the Norwegian Storting* of 111 to 31.

REFERENCES: Oskar Garstein, *Rome and the Counter-Reformation in Scandinavia*, 2 vols. (Oslo: Universitetsforlaget, 1963, 1980); Vello Heik, *Laurentius Nicolai Norvegus S.J.* (Copenhagen: Gad, 1966).

T. R. SKARSTEN

JEWS

Prior to the seventeenth century there do not appear to have been any Jews in Scandinavia*. In 1622 the Danish monarch Christian IV* allowed Sephardic Jews from Amsterdam and Hamburg to settle and enjoy some measure of religious freedom in part of Holstein, now within the Federal Republic of Germany. A small number filtered into Copenhagen*, where they worked in two traditional Jewish fields, jewelry and finance, and had close ties to the Danish nobility. In 1683, however, the absolutist king Christian V* forbade further immigration, and four years later a parallel decree extended the barrier to his Norwegian domains. Generally speaking, only Jews with sufficient capital to build their own homes and contribute significantly to the Danish economy received royal dispensations from the decree of 1683. By 1782, though, there were 1,830 Jews in Denmark, 1,503 of them in Copenhagen. Very few entered Norway before Danish hegemony there ended in 1814. In Sweden, regulations of 1685 condemned the few Jews in the kingdom and mandated their expulsion. Only a handful to whom Karl XII* was financially indebted were allowed to remain temporarily.

Enlightenment humanists began to call for Jewish emancipation in the eighteenth century, and during the reign of Gustav III* (1771–1792) Sweden opened its gates partway to Jewish immigrants, allowing them to settle in Gothenburg*, Stockholm*, and Norrköping. Denied the franchise and the possibility of employment in the civil service, they nevertheless had the freedom to worship without molestation and to enter most sectors of the economy.

Nearly complete Jewish emancipation came to Scandinavia during the nineteenth century. In 1838 Sweden cancelled most of its discriminatory legislation and granted its 900 Jewish aliens citizenship. A century later there were some 7,000 Swedish Jews. In Norway, the Constitution of 1814 explicitly forbade Jewish immigration, but Henrik Wergeland (1808–1845), the nation's most prominent poet, led in the 1830s and 1840s a campaign to abrogate the ban, which was done in 1851. Only a handful came before 1875, but by 1900 there were over 600 Norwegian Jews. The two communities in Oslo and Trondheim date from 1892 and 1905, respectively. The nation's Jewish population peaked in 1920 at 1,457. Danish Jews gained citizenship in 1814, while the Constitution of 1849 removed most of the discriminatory laws against them. The population rose to over 4,000 at mid-century, due largely to an influx from eastern Europe. By 1920 there were 6,000 Jews in Denmark.

The Holocaust struck Jews in Scandinavia less severely than in most other European countries. The Scandinavian lands accepted a small number of refugees from Germany during the 1930s. In April 1940 German military forces occupied Denmark and Norway. Mass arrests of Norwegian Jews began late in 1942 against a strong protest by the state church. Several hundred escaped to neutral Sweden; 770 were sent to Auschwitz. Many survived the concentration camp, but relatively few of them returned. In 1943 most of Denmark's Jews managed to flee to the safety of Sweden shortly before severe persecution began. Over 98 percent thus survived.

Since World War II* Scandinavian Jews have lived in freedom, well assimilated with the general population. Secularization and intermarriage have taken their toll. In Norway there were only about 800 Jews in 1980, principally in Oslo. Owing to an influx of refugees, Sweden then had over 13,000, more than half of them in Stockholm. Nearly all of Denmark's 7,000 Jews were then in Copenhagen and its suburbs.

REFERENCES: *Nordisk teologisk uppslagsbok för kyrka och skola* (Lund: Gleerup, 1952–1957); R. Petrow, *The Bitter Years: The Invasion and Occupation of Denmark and Norway, April 1940–May 1945* (New York: Morrow, 1974); L. Yahil, *The Rescue of Danish Jewry, Test of a Democracy* (Philadelphia: Jewish Publication Society of America, 1969).

F. HALE

JOHAN III (1537–17 November 1592) King of Sweden 1569–1592

Johan was the son of Gustav I Vasa* and his second wife, Margareta Leijonhufvud. He was well-educated, cultured, scholarly, devoted, religious, suspicious, violent, temperamental, vacillating, shrewd, and power-hungry. He was a typical Vasa.

In 1556 he became duke of Finland, and according to his father's will he was to hold the territory as his duchy after Gustav's death. Erik XIV*, however, recognized the dangers inherent in having his brothers (the future Karl IX* held a similar duchy in west central Sweden) acting as semi-autonomous kings in these territories and had the will abrogated in 1561 in the Articles of Arboga. Erik was at a distance, however, and Johan continued to act independently in Finland. He defied Erik and married Katarina Jagellonica, a sister of Sigismund August, the king of Poland, and then he became involved in Polish-Baltic affairs when he lent money to his brother-in-law in exchange for fiefs in Livonia. These actions put him in direct competition with Erik's foreign policy in the eastern Baltic, and in 1562 Johan was tried and found guilty of treason. His death sentence was commuted to imprisonment, and he spent from 1563 to 1567 in Gripsholm castle. He was released in late 1567 (while Erik was recovering from his breakdown) and joined the growing opposition to Erik. In 1568 he headed the successful revolt against his brother and became king the following year. Erik was imprisoned in Gripsholm and died in 1577. The part Johan played in his death remains unclear.

Johan enjoyed no more internal peace than had Erik. His other brother, Karl, was as independently minded as Johan and from the mid-1570s participated in a number of plots against him. These were spawned by supporters of Erik; by the great nobles who were alienated from Johan because of his constitutional views and his tendency to rule personally and with the advice of secretaries drawn from outside the nobility; by commoners who chafed under the tax burdens the king's foreign and domestic policies made necessary; and by the rebellious Duke Karl. His troubles were compounded by his religious views. Katarina was a Catholic. Their son, Sigismund*, was raised a Catholic. Johan leaned toward Catholicism, listened to Catholic advisors, and became involved in diplomatic adventures with Catholic powers in Europe. In 1577 he issued the so-called *Red Book**, a liturgical handbook of clearly Catholic tendencies, which alienated the clergy and many Swedes who were becoming increasingly Lutheran.

In foreign affairs he was more successful, but he deepened Sweden's involvement in areas that would eventually prove far too costly to maintain. He negotiated an end to the Northern Seven Years' War with Denmark in 1570 (Peace of Stettin), secured control of trade with Russia, and extended Sweden's influence in Estonia and Ingermanland. So long as the Vasa tie with Poland held (and this was strengthened by the election of Johan's son Sigismund to the Polish throne in 1587) his dream of a Swedish-Polish Baltic empire, though unrealistic, seemed sound.

Johan was perhaps the most cultured of the Vasa brothers. He lamented the impact the Reformation* had on the arts in Sweden and was drawn to Catholicism in part because of the Church's enormous past contributions to culture in Europe. He dreamed of restoring that culture. He became a patron of church building. He also embarked on major remodeling projects in a number of royal castles including Borgholm, Kalmar, Stockholm (*see* Stockholm Royal Palace), and Vadstena. Some have argued that he, not Erik, brought the Renaissance to Sweden.

REFERENCES: *DSH*, vol. 5; M. Roberts, *The Early Vasas: A History of Sweden, 1523–1611* (Cambridge, England: Cambridge University Press, 1968); *SU*, vol. 14.

B. NORDSTROM

JOHNSON, GISLE (10 December 1822–1894) Norwegian theologian and revivalist

Descended from an eighteenth-century Icelandic clergy family, Gisle Johnson was born in Fredrikshald, Norway, his father being a famous highway and harbor engineer. Most of his youth was spent in Christiansand in southern Norway, where he was influenced by Pietism and the Lutheran orthodoxy of his gymnasium teacher, Christian Thistedahl. In 1845 he took his theological examination at the University of Christiania (Oslo) and embarked on a study tour of the leading German universities. In 1849 he was appointed to the chair of systematic theology at Christiania.

For the next half century Gisle Johnson dominated church life in Norway. His theology and churchmanship became the model for hundreds of his students. The influence of students like H. A. Preus, Laurentius Larsen, B. J. Muus, Georg Sverdrup, and U. V. Koren, who became pioneer pastors in America, helped mould Norwegian-American Lutheranism* as well.

Gisle Johnson combined in a unique way the confessional theology of Lutheran orthodoxy and the Pietism of Hans Nielsen Hauge*. During the religious revival of the 1850s and 1860s known as the ''Johnsonian Awakening,'' all classes of society were touched. Johnson traveled throughout Norway giving Bible studies and calling for repentance and conversion. At the same time he was concerned about doctrinal integrity, best illustrated by his strong opposition to the theological position of N.F.S. Grundtvig. Strongly opposed also to separatistic movements following the passage of the Dissenter Law (1845), Johnson wrote *Some Words Concerning Infant Baptism* in 1857, which effectively muzzled the advocates of adult baptism.

In the face of the Industrial Revolution and the dechristianization of the working class, Gisle Johnson provided the primary leadership in launching the Christiania Inner Mission Society (1855) and the Luther Foundation (Lutherstiftelse) (1866), which sent colporteurs throughout Norway under Johnson's famous ''emergency principle'' (Nødsprinsip), which effectively sidestepped Article 14 of the *Augsburg Confession**. A political conservative, Gisle Johnson unsuccessfully opposed the introduction of parliamentarianism in 1883, which reduced the monarchy to a figurehead status.

REFERENCES: Gisle Johnson, *Grundrids af den Systematiske Theologie*, 3rd ed. (Kristiania: Jacob Dybwad, 1897); Einar Molland, *Church Life in Norway 1800–1950* (Westport, Conn.: Greenwood Press, 1978); Trygve R. Skarsten, ''Rise and Fall of Grundtvigianism in Norway,'' *Lutheran Quarterly* 17 (May 1965): 122–42.

T. R. SKARSTEN

K

KAAS, NIELS (1534–29 June 1594) Danish statesman, chancellor under Frederik II*, and member of the regency for Christian IV*

Niels Kaas was born to a noble family with roots dating back to the fourteenth century. He was an orphan by the age of 5 and was sent by his uncle to the bishop's school in Viborg. Subsequently, in 1549, he went to Copenhagen*, where he came under the tutelage of the scholar and theologian Niels Hemmingsen*. In 1554 he began a tour of the continent, during which he studied at the universities in Wittenberg and Frankfurt, where he concentrated on Latin, history, and government. In 1560 he began a 34–year career in government when he secured a position as a secretary in the chancery in Copenhagen. There he came into contact with Johan Friis* and Peder Oxe*, who were impressed with his knowledge and energy. He took part in the negotiations which ended the Northern Seven Years' War and, following the death of Friis in late 1570, assumed the duties of chancellor—although he did not receive the title until 1573. He remained in this office until his death. In 1588 he became a central figure in the regency for Christian IV.

Kaas is generally described as an energetic, loyal, and dedicated public servant. Recent studies also indicate that he was rather unoriginal, conservative, strongly monarchistic, and worked under conditions which were quite favorable. His most serious difficulties occurred when he came into conflict with members of the upper nobility who favored a strengthened aristocratic role in government at the expense of the crown. In addition to his work in government, Kaas was a patron of learning and supported the work of many scholars including Tycho Brahe*, A. S. Vedel, H. P. Resen, and T. Fincke. He was most interested in history and established the first professoriate at the University of Copenhagen in the subject.   B. NORDSTROM

REFERENCES: *DBL*, vol. 7; *DH*, vol. 6.

KALEVALA The Finnish national epic

The so-called *Old Kalevala* (32 runes, 12,078 lines) was published in 1835–1836. In 1849 the revised or modern *Kalevala* followed (50 runes, 22,795 lines). Broadly viewed, the epic was a product of the confluence of two powerful European movements, romanticism and nationalism. On the other hand, it represented the singular achievement of a country doctor, Elias Lönnrot (1802–1884), whose mounting interest in Finnish folk poetry prompted him to undertake eleven arduous journeys between 1828 and 1845 to the remote eastern border regions. Among the singers yielding to his entreaties and those of later collectors were Arhippa Perttunen (1754?–1840?) and his son Miihkali (1803–1899), Ontrei Malinen (1781–1856), and Pedri Shemeikka (1825?–1915). Extraordinarily gifted among the numerous female performers was Larin Paraske (1833–1904). Her total repertoire reached nearly 33,000 lines. Lönnrot also compiled a collection of lyrical folk poetry, the *Kanteletar* (1840–1841), anthologies of Finnish proverbs, riddles, and magic, and a Finnish-Swedish dictionary. In other ways, too, this unassuming and beloved individual greatly influenced Finnish language and literature. The monumental treasury of ancient Finnish folk poetry is the *Suomen kansan vanhat runot* (33 volumes, 1908–1948).

The epic's appearance quickly evoked a number of interesting and often perplexing questions. Had Lönnrot discovered and reconstructed from surviving fragments an ancient integrated epic cycle? This theory did not persist long. Was the *Kalevala* authentic folk poetry? Scholarship has moved in the direction of stressing Lönnrot's uniquely creative role in fashioning the epic. While his labors rested solidly on his exceptional command of folk poetry resources and forms, Lönnrot judiciously took some liberty in arranging the runes, selecting the major themes, and portraying the characters. At least in part, the *Kalevala*'s birth took place, as one Swedish scholar observed, on Lönnrot's desk. Was the *Kalevala* history or mythology? The historical argument has been seriously challenged. How old was the epic? Its time frame, for certain elements, has been brought forward to the Christian era. Was it indigenous or foreign? It has long been acknowledged that the Finnish epic incorporates universal and regional as well as native ingredients.

Overall, the *Kalevala* is quite readable. It embodies drama and conflict; its themes are well developed; its leading actors are lifelike and inimitably etched. It reveals an abundant variety of folk poetry modes: epic, lyrical, magical, lamentation, and incantation. Its episodes fall into the following pattern: cosmogony and the forging of the Sampo, runes 1–10; Lemminkäinen's regeneration, 11–15; the wedding in Pohjola, 16–25; Lemminkäinen's revenge, 26–30; Kullervo, 31–36; the struggle over the Sampo, 37–49; Väinämöinen's departure, 50.

The *Kalevala*'s impact on the emergence of national consciousness and the flowering of cultural activity was profound. It revitalized the literary language. In literature it stimulated such writers as the poet Eino Leino (1878–1926), dramatists Aleksis Kivi (1834–1872) and J. H. Erkko (1849–1906), and the novelist Juhani Aho (1861–1926). Equally striking was the inspiration the epic gave Finnish composers, among them Jean Sibelius (1865–1957), Oskari Merikanto (1868–1924), Erkki Melartin (1875–1937), Armas Launis (1884–1959), and Uuno Klami (1900–1961). In the fine arts two outstanding interpreters of Kalevalan motifs were the famed painter Aksel Gallen-Kallela (1865–1931) and the sculptor Alpo Sailo (1877–1955).

The first complete translation of the *Kalevala* (into Swedish) appeared in 1841. Since then there have been at least 60 major translations into more than 30 languages, including Japanese and Arabic. Rendering the Finnish epic into a foreign tongue presents many difficulties: the *Kalevala*'s great length; its esoteric Finno-Ugric language, complicated by bewildering Karelian words and idioms; its varied poetic devices, such as alliteration. There are two full English-language versions (see Kirby and Magoun below). Other highly acclaimed editions include A. Annist's Estonian, Jean-Louis Perret's French, Bela Vikár's Hungarian, Paolo Pavolini's Italian, and Björn Collinder's Swedish translations.

REFERENCES: A. Anttila, *Elias Lönnrot*, 2 vols. (Helsinki: SKS, 1931–1935); Väinö Kaukonen, *Lönnrot ja Kalevala* (Helsinki: SKS, 1979); W. F. Kirby, *The Kalevala: The Land of Heroes* (London: Everyman's, 1907); J. I. Kolehmainen, *Epic of the North: The Story of Finland's National Epic* (New York Mills, Minn.: Northwestern, 1973); M. Kuusi et al., eds. *Finnish Folk Poetry-Epic* (Helsinki: SKS, 1977); F. P. Magoun, Jr., *The Kalevala or Poems of the Kalevala District* (Cambridge, Mass.: Harvard University Press, 1963).

J. I. KOLEHMAINEN

KALMAR City and fortress on the eastern coast of Småland, Sweden

Evidence indicates that the area around Kalmar was inhabited by the late seventh century. By the late twelfth century a small trading town and fort had been built there. A larger fortification was begun in the late thirteenth century, which included a surrounding wall and four towers based on the European style of the period. Extensive changes were made to the fortifications during the sixteenth century by Gustav I Vasa*, Erik XIV*, and Johan III*. These included the addition of outer works and extensive reconstruction and remodeling within the walls in Renaissance style. In the latter part of the century the castle frequently was used as a royal residence. It became the residence for the county governor in the seventeenth century and later was a royal distillery and prison. Restorations of the fortress were initiated in the 1850s and in 1965, and it is recognized as the best-preserved Renaissance fortress in Sweden.

The early town grew up within the shadow of the castle. It was initially a trading center with principal connections to north Germany. Iron was the chief export. Its location near the border between Sweden and the Danish provinces to the south make Kalmar a meeting place for delegations from the two countries (*see* Kalmar Recess; Kalmar Union). The location also made Kalmar the scene of frequent battles in the wars between Denmark and Sweden in the fifteenth through seventeenth centuries.

In the seventeenth century Kalmar became a center for county government, and significant growth and development ensued. The town expanded beyond its "old town," and new construction included noble estates, parks, and a new cathedral. These gave Kalmar an elegance which it has retained. In 1800 the population of the town was 3,200. It had grown to 12,700 by 1900. Kalmar is now an active commercial, industrial, educational, and governmental center with a population of 53,000 (1980).

REFERENCES: *DSH*, vols. 2–7, 10–13; *SU*, vol. 15.

B. NORDSTROM

KALMAR RECESS (September 1483) Agreement between representatives of Hans I* and the Swedish council

The accession of Hans, who succeeded Christian I* in 1481, was marked by renewed attempts by the nobles in the Scandinavian countries to assert their presumed constitutional rights in the struggle for power which was characterized by the oscillation between monarchy and aristocratic constitutionalism. His accession was also marked by an effort by the Swedish council to assure the continuation of Sweden's (or their) autonomy. The accession charter negotiated at Halmstad between the king and the Danish and Norwegian nobles was the basis for the discussions at Kalmar*. Royal representatives and the Swedish council agreed to terms which, on the surface, assured predominance by the nobles in the constitutional struggle. These terms included the continued integrity of Sweden as a separate state; the continuation of privileges enjoyed by church and secular nobles; the recognition by the crown that it was bound to rule only with the council's advice; the recognition that a governing council (drawn from the full council and composed of two lay and two clerical nobles) would rule in the king's absence; the recognition by the crown that all royal castles would devolve to the governing council on the death of the ruling monarch; and the recognition of the nobles' right to revolt in the event that these terms were violated. In addition, the crown's representatives agreed that Hans would not receive the crown in Sweden before Gotland had been turned over to Sweden. These were far-reaching concessions by the crown, but Hans was in no position to oppose them. On paper, Sweden became an aristocratic republic. In fact, many of the terms of the agreement were never honored, and the document came more to serve as a statement of constitutional principles. It would be referred to time and again in succeeding centuries.

REFERENCES: G. Carlsson, *Kalmar Recess 1483* (Stockholm: Kungliga Vitterhets-, historie-och antikvitetsakademien, 1955); *DSH*, vol. 3; *SU*, vol. 15.

B. NORDSTROM

KALMAR UNION 1397 union of Denmark, Norway (to 1814), and Sweden (to 1521)

The Kalmar Union is one of the most popular and frequently considered topics in Scandinavian history. It was a central development in the histories of Denmark, Norway, and Sweden and for Scandinavian history in general. It has been the subject of intense historiographical debate.

The union resulted from the efforts of Margrethe I* to secure recognition of her nephew Erik of Pomerania (VII)* as monarch in all of the Scandinavian countries, the desire of the great men of the three countries to have on the throne a person they believed they could control and who would leave them alone, and the need to create a united front against the economic and political threats to the independence of the region coming from the Hanse (*see* Hanseatic League) and the princes of northern Germany.

Two documents formed the basis of the union: the Coronation Letter (written on parchment and considered by Margrethe to be the defining document of the union) and the Union Letter (written on vellum and carrying the signatures of great men from Denmark, Norway, and Sweden). These two sources contained different interpretations of the constitutional nature of the union. The Coronation Letter implied a formal dynastic union based on the idea of centralized, hereditary monarchy, the kind of monarchy Margrethe advocated. The Union Letter defined the union as a federation. There would be a common monarch; the monarchy would be hereditary so long as there was an heir. (It would become elective in the event of the dying out of a dynastic line.) The union would have a common foreign policy, and the members would cooperate in the event of an attack. The laws, traditions, and privileges of the members would remain separate. Government offices and the fiefs that went with them would be held by natives in the respective countries.

For the first two decades of its history there was relative peace within the union and with its neighbors. This peace disintegrated during the 1430s, and from then until 1521 there were repeated civil wars complicated by the involvement of foreign powers. The Swedish magnates and the union monarchs were the most frequent belligerents in these conflicts. Norway, the weakest member of the union and the country with the smallest native nobility, was the most docile.

In 1521 Sweden made its departure from the union final. Norway remained tied to Denmark and became a province of the Danish kingdom in 1536. Norway attempted to gain independence in 1814, but was transferred into a dynastic union with Sweden (*see* Norwegian-Swedish Union) through the Treaty of Kiel*. This union lasted until 1905. (*See also* Christian I; Christian II; Christoffer III; Gustav I Vasa; Hans I; Karl VIII Knutsson; Sture, Sten (the Elder); "Sture," Sten Svantesson (the Younger); Sture, Svante Nilsson.)

REFERENCES: *DH*, vols. 4, 5; *DSH*, vols. 2, 3; H. Koht, *Drottning Margareta och Kalmarunionen* (Stockholm: Kultur och Natur, 1956); E. Lönnroth, *Från svensk medeltid* (Stockholm: Aldus/Bonniers, 1959), and "Unionsdokumenten i Kalmar 1397," *Scandia* 24 (1958): 32–67; *NH*, vol. 4; *SU*, vol. 15.

B. NORDSTROM

KALMAR WAR (Second Danish-Swedish War) April 1611–January 1613

The Kalmar War was initiated by Christian IV* in response to policies of Karl IX* which included customs impositions at Riga and Narva, claims to exemption from the Sound Tolls, and territorial and taxation claims in Finnmark. Christian also may have had desires to restore the union of the three crowns. Except in the first months, the war pitted Christian against Gustav II Adolf*, who was 17 when the war began. Principal early campaigns took place in the Kalmar* region, hence the war's name, but fighting took place in much of central and southern Sweden, Jämtland, and at sea.

At war with Russia at the same time, Swedish forces did poorly in most instances. The navy was unprepared for the struggle, and the army of peasant recruits was no match against the Danes' mercenaries. The fortress at Kalmar fell in the summer of 1611, and the vital fortress of Älvsborg* was taken by the Danes the following summer. Danish forces harried Småland and Västergötland, and similar activities were conducted in Skåne and Jämtland by the Swedes. Hundreds of farms and villages were destroyed. Christian's ultimate goal appears to have been Stockholm*, but he never overcame serious tactical and logistical problems. A final naval attack on Vaxholm, which protected the city, failed in late 1612.

Peace talks began in late 1612 under the good offices of James I of England, through his representatives, James Spees in Stockholm and Robert Anstruther in Copenhagen*. These talks culminated in the Peace of Knäred (20 January 1613). Under it Sweden abandoned territorial and Lapp tax claims in Finnmark and modified its customs policy in the eastern Baltic. Swedish exemption from the Sound Tolls was affirmed. Each country would continue to include the three-crown symbol in its coat of arms. Conquered territories, with the exception of Älvsborg, were restored. In the case of Älvsborg, Sweden was compelled to pay a ransom of 1 million *riksdaler*. (Christian expected that this sum would not be raised and that Denmark would acquire the fort and thereby Gothenburg*, which it protected. Sweden's "window" on the west would be gone.) The ransom exacted a tremendous toll on Sweden's limited resources. A special tax was levied for six years, and loans were secured from the Dutch to meet the payment schedule. Älvsborg was restored to Sweden in 1619.

The war left a legacy of bitterness on both sides, largely because of the human and physical costs it entailed. It also revealed the limitations of both countries and clearly demonstrated the need for economic, administrative, and military reform in Sweden.

REFERENCES: *DH*, vol. 7; *DSH*, vol. 4; M. Roberts, *Gustavus Adolphus: A History of Sweden 1611–1632* (London: Longmans, Green & Co., 1953); L. Stavenow, *Freden i Knäred* (Gothenburg, 1913).

B. NORDSTROM

KARL VIII KNUTSSON (Bonde) (1408–15 May 1470) Regent of Sweden 1438–1440, king of Sweden 1448–1457, 1464–1465, 1467–1470

Karl Knutsson belongs to a group of powerful Swedish nobles who became regents (*riksföreståndare*) during the struggles with the Danish monarchs of the

Kalmar Union* (*see also* Sten Sture; Svante Nilsson; Sten Svantesson "Sture"). Karl also was three times elected king.

Karl joined the rebellion against Erik of Pomerania (VII)* in 1434 and led a second stage of that revolt in 1436. He was elected regent by the council in 1438, but stepped aside in 1440, when Christoffer of Bavaria (Christoffer III*) was elected king. Following Christoffer's sudden death in 1448, Karl was chosen king in Sweden and Norway, while the Danes chose Christian I*. (The Norwegians renounced Karl in July 1448). The union was thus temporarily broken, but the councils in the three countries agreed that after Karl and Christian were dead, they would meet to chose a common monarch.

Karl was ruthless and ambitious. He wanted to be a king, not the pawn of the great nobles. This desire put him into conflict with the council magnates, who championed a constitutional view based on feudal notions of shared power between crown and aristocracy. He ignored the council and the Church, appointed foreigners to offices and fiefs, and tried to use the support of the commons against his opponents. His efforts led to a revolt in 1457, and he was forced into exile. The union was temporarily restored under Christian I, but Karl was called back to lead the fight against Christian, became king again in 1464, abdicated in 1465, and was then elected king for the last time in 1467. During his last years, his drive and ambitions gone, he was little more than a puppet of the council.

REFERENCES: *DSH*, vols. 2, 3; *NH*, vols. 4, 5; E. Lönnroth, *Sverige och Kalmarunionen 1397–1457* (Gothenburg: Studia historica Gothoborgensia Nr. 10, 1967, new edition); *SU*, vol. 15.

B. NORDSTROM

KARL IX (4 October 1550–30 November 1611) Regent and king of Sweden 1599–1611

Karl was the son of Gustav I Vasa* and his second wife, Margartetha Leijonhufvud. He was the last of Gustav's three sons to rule in Sweden. Like his father, he was strong-willed, opinionated, highly motivated, temperamental, and violent. He ruled the duchy his father had bequeathed him like an autocrat. He took part in the deposition of his half brother Erik XIV*, came in time to oppose his brother Johan III*, organized the resistance to and the deposition of Johan's son, Sigismund*, resisted the demands of the magnates for greater power in the state, and used the lower estates against his opponents.

Until the 1590s Karl was kept from power. After Johan's death in 1592 and the succession of Sigismund, however, Karl played a leading role in the design of the government that would run Sweden during the king's absences in Poland. Soon Karl was pitted against the king and the magnates in the council. The defeat of Sigismund in 1598 at Stångebro and his deposition the following year left Karl free to deal with his opponents at home. Using the parliament, in which social tensions between the commons and the nobility were exploited, he drove his chief enemies into exile. In 1600 at Linköping, the docile parliament approved the execution of five of Sweden's greatest nobles: Gustav and Sten Baner, Erik

Sparre, Ture Bielke, and Bengt Falk (Linköping Blood Bath). Among the victims, Sparre was the most articulate exponent of the nobles' constitutional position (aristocratic constitutionalism). At the same meeting Karl was recognized king, but he did not accept coronation until 1607.

During his comparatively short reign he sought to regularize the functions of the council, create an administrative system based on local bailiffs directly accountable to the crown, reform law and currency, and encourage economic and town development. His goals were admirable; his methods were harsh and uncompromising. He thoroughly alienated the upper nobility and set the stage for the royal charter which his son, Gustav II Adolf*, had to accept upon his succession.

In foreign affairs Karl saw develop around him the coalition of enemies that plagued Sweden for the next century: Russia, Poland, Brandenburg, the German Empire, Denmark, and Holland. Just before his death he went to war with Denmark.

REFERENCES: *DSH*, vols. 3–5; O. Garstein, *Rome and the Counter-Reformation in Scandinavia* (Oslo: Universitetsforlaget, 1980); J. Lisk, *The Struggle for Supremacy in the Baltic* (Birmingham: Minerva, 1967); M. Roberts, *The Early Vasas* (Cambridge, England: Cambridge University Press, 1968), *Essays in Swedish History* (Minneapolis: University of Minnesota Press, 1967), and *The Swedish Imperial Experience* (Cambridge, England: Cambridge University Press, 1979); *SU*, vol. 15.

B. NORDSTROM

KARL X (8 November 1622–13 February 1660) King of Sweden 1654–1660

Karl was the son of John of Pfalz-Zweibrucken and Katarina, a daughter of Karl IX* and sister of Gustav II Adolf*. He was born and raised in Sweden, studied at the University of Uppsala, traveled in Europe for several years, and spent six years with the Swedish army in Germany during the Thirty Years' War. He was strong-willed, physically powerful, capable, fond of excessive eating and drinking, and given to grand schemes and dreaming.

During the 1640s there was talk of a marriage between Christina* and Karl, but no match developed. Christina, however, chose her cousin as her heir and secured his recognition by the nobility and then by the full parliament in 1649–1650. He succeeded her immediately upon her abdication in 1654.

Karl spent most of the six years he ruled Sweden out of the country, at war with Sweden's many enemies. In 1655 he initiated a campaign in Poland. This conflict expanded to include Russia, Denmark, and his onetime ally Brandenburg. In 1657 he abandoned the fruitless campaign in Poland and turned on Denmark. In early 1658 he achieved incredible success when he daringly took his army across the ice of the Little and Great Belts to reach the outskirts of Copenhagen*. The Danes, in the Treaty of Roskilde (26 February 1658), lost their south Swedish provinces, Bornholm, and the Trondheim region in Norway. Karl still felt insecure about Denmark, however, and he launched a second attack in 1658. The Danes held this time, and the coalition including Russia, Poland, Brandenburg, the Hapsburg Empire, and Denmark (with the naval involvement of the Dutch) formed against him. Defeat followed defeat, and it looked briefly as if Sweden's Baltic empire would be consumed by its enemies. In the midst of the conflict, Karl died. Peace came after his death through the treaties of Oliva (with Poland, Brandenburg, and the Hapsburg Empire), Copenhagen (with Denmark), and Kardis (with Russia). Although Sweden had to give up Bornholm and the Trondheim region, most of the empire remained intact.

Had Karl been able to spend more time in Sweden, he might have had a great impact on domestic developments. He reconstituted the University of Uppsala, stopped the wholesale alienation of crown lands, and agreed with the commons that a reduction of noble holdings was necessary. Only a half-measure with respect to the last was passed by the parliament, and even that was not put into effect. The international situation forced Karl to work with his nobility, and the serious social and economic problems facing Sweden were ignored. (Karl believed the Hapsburg empire could be made to pay and thereby alleviate some of the country's economic problems.)

In 1654 he married Hedvig Eleonora of Holstein-Gottorp. Their son, Karl XI*, was only 4 when Karl died, and for twelve years Sweden was governed by a regency composed of the council nobles.

REFERENCES: *DSH*, vols. 5–7; J. Lisk, *The Struggle for Supremacy in the Baltic* (Birmingham: Minerva, 1967); S. Olofsson, *Carl X Gustaf. Hertigentronföljaren* (Stockholm, 1961); M. Roberts, *Essays in Swedish History* (Minneapolis: University of Minnesota Press, 1967), and *The Swedish Imperial Experience* (Cambridge, England: Cambridge University Press, 1979); *SU*, vol. 15.

B. NORDSTROM

KARL XI (24 November 1655–5 April 1697) King of Sweden 1660–1697

Karl was the son of Karl X* and Hedvig Eleonora. He succeeded his father in 1660. For the first twelve years of his reign the government was under the control of a regency dominated by the council nobles. Karl has generally not been treated well by posterity. He was colorless, shy, stubborn, uncultured, and unimaginative and had the mentality of a ''quartermaster.'' There was little about him that endeared him to future historians, especially those who favored the nobility or the development of democracy in Sweden. In many respects these negative views of Karl are exaggerated and wrong. While he may have been dull and unimpressive, he was efficient, thorough, and dedicated. He did much to improve government, social and economic conditions, and Sweden's diplomatic situation. Karl ended the alienation of crown lands to the nobility and carried through the *reductions* that brought back to the crown lands alienated in the previous century; restored the financial strength of the crown and the state; and prevented the possible decline of the Swedish peasantry into serfdom. Karl broke forever the nobility's monopoly on political power, rejected the nobles' constitutional claim to a right to share power with the crown, and established (without the use of force and with the consent of the parliament) an absolutism in Sweden based on the king and a professional bureaucracy. He broke with the imperial tradition in Swedish foreign policy, realized the limitations of his small state, and tried to maintain peace within the Baltic region. And he realized that Sweden had to live within its means, especially in defense, and therefore built an army based on native recruits paid in allotments of land (to both soldiers and officers) drawn from the lands regained by the crown in the reductions. This system was called the *indelningsverket* and remained in effect in Sweden until the early twentieth century. When Karl died Sweden's state finances were reasonably sound, and the government was ordered, fairly efficient, and accepted by the vast majority of the people. The strength of Karl's accomplishments was demonstrated by Sweden's capacity to endure the pressures of the Great Northern War*. On the other hand, there was potential for abuses in Karl's system, and this was revealed by his son and successor, Karl XII*.

REFERENCES: *DSH*, vol. 7; M. Roberts, "Charles XI," *History* 50 (1965): 110–42; *SU*, vol. 15.

B. NORDSTROM

KARL XII (17 June 1682–30 November 1718) King of Sweden 1697–1718

Karl XII was the second surviving child and only son of Karl XI* and Ulrika Eleonora the Elder (a Danish-born princess). He succeeded to the throne in 1697. The peripatetic and dramatic life of this most controversial and hence much discussed monarch may be divided into four phases: his youth, including the first four years of his reign, until his victory over the Russians at Narva in November 1700; the years of continental campaigning against the Saxons, Poles, and Russians, until Karl's defeat by Peter I at Poltava in July 1709; the period of exile within the Ottoman dominions from the summer of 1709 to November 1714; and the remaining four years until his death outside the Frederiksten fortress in southeastern Norway.

As heir apparent Karl received a carefully planned training and developed a lifelong passion for mathematics as well as a more than conventional interest in education. He was a conscientious pupil and was profoundly influenced by his father's example of dogged service to the state and commitment to the maintenance of the Swedish Empire's integrity, however unviable and uncoordinated its parts for the purposes of exploitation or national defense. Together with the dynastic ambitions of Augustus of Saxony in Poland, it was the lie of the Swedish Empire—which barred Russia from the Baltic and threatened Denmark's southern flanks through the Swedish crown's dynastic links with the dukes of Holstein-Gottorp—which explains the scope and complexity of the Great Northern War*. The struggle for the empire's preservation occupied almost all of Karl's reign and the three years that followed his death. The demands of this struggle only enhanced the strong filial piety with which the young Karl embarked on his rule. Herein lay the roots of his conviction that the obligations of kingship required an honest and unsparing discharge, and though there is evidence that he felt he was insufficiently consulted over being endowed with his father's absolutist powers in 1697, when Karl was barely 15 years old, he knew well enough that this had been dictated by the perilous situation in which Sweden then appeared to stand, especially in relation to Denmark. It is also possible that his early failure to marry (in fact, he was never to marry and died without making provision for his succession) can be explained partly by how politically loaded a marriage into the royal Danish house, at one time proposed, would be vis-a-vis the Holstein-Gottorp interest sternly represented by his paternal grandmother. If he was to make a Scandinavian or even a north German match, Karl's natural affection and sensitivity made him recoil from any partnership which might divide the family. Putting marriage prospects behind him made it easier for the king to adapt single-mindedly to camp life and government from a chancery-in-the-field, whether or not the course of the Great Northern War was here to give him little choice.

Swedish success in deposing Augustus of Saxony from his Polish throne and overrunning his Saxon electorate, achieved in 1704–1706, had been a long time coming, and Polish politics accounts for the prolonged period Karl XII spent in that country before once again moving eastwards against Russia in the summer of 1707. The difficulties then facing the Swedes were not underrated by them. The mobility and technical prowess of the Swedish army, which Karl and his generals had inculcated with tenets such as advance (*gå på*) and *armes blanches*, massed and sudden infantry attack, would be pitted against climate, terrain, and a Russian army very different from that vanquished at Narva in 1700, when the main foe to be grappled with had been Saxony. In the event, the exceptional severity of the winter of 1708–1709 and Karl's vulnerable communications were as responsible for the Swedish defeat at Poltava as Russian arms. The king was able to flee the field of Poltava, and at times over the next five years, afforded asylum by the Ottomans, Karl was able to prompt renewals of hostilities against Tsar Peter by the Turks. He also took an unprecedented interest in the Swedish navy* and, even from so far away, spurred on from 1710 a privateering war in the Baltic designed to blockade the ports Sweden had lost to Russia and remind Britain and the Dutch, greatly dependent as sea powers on the Baltic trades, what support they owed a beleaguered Sweden as her allies. The policy was pursued inflexibly and up to a point counterproductively, and the king's standing was prejudiced by his requirements and perceptions, which conflicted with the more conciliatory policies of the council in Stockholm*, anxious though that body was (after 1713 it included the king's only surviving sister, the 25–year-old Ulrika Eleonora*) not to appear to challenge the authority of Karl XII. When he returned to Stralsund in November 1714, after a fortnight's ride from Pitesti in present-day Rumania, Sweden's conduct of the war once again passed into the king's sole control. For the remainder of his reign, with Sweden's position in the east Baltic wholly lost in the summer of 1714 and her possessions in north Germany all surrendered by the spring of 1716, the king's options were as much diplomatic as military.

The powers now confronting Sweden—Denmark, Hanover (with the prestige and power now accruing through the elector's succession to the British crown), Brandenburg-Prussia, and Russia—all had clear territorial objectives; but old antagonisms and increasing apprehension in the west about Russia's advance ensured that Sweden never faced a unified coalition. During 1717 and 1718, Karl XII could negotiate for a peace almost as he chose with any interested party, but his preponderant aim was an honorable settlement, and above all one with Russia. This explains his concern to overrun Denmark-Norway in order to strengthen his hand with the tsar, and it was this war effort which needed the system of finance, much resented in Sweden, presided over by the king's leading but unaccredited councilor, the Holstein minister George Heinrich von Görtz*. Karl's links with Holstein were strongly sentimental through his deceased sister's memory, and he may have had it in mind to groom her son, the young duke Karl Frederik of Holstein Gottorp*, as his heir in the event of his not marrying and in preference to his younger sister Ulrika Eleonora, married to Fredrik I* of Hesse-Kassel with Karl's consent in March 1715.

Karl's death on his second campaign against Denmark in Norway was regarded by those closest to him, however guardedly the king had always kept his own counsel, as a searing tragedy for Sweden, just when a worthy end to the eighteen-year-long war seemed in sight. Although at the time and later—owing to the suddenness of Karl's end after he had survived so much, distrust of his ambitious German brother-in-law, and the virulence of the aristocratic-led "revolution" of 1719–1720—it was suspected that the king had been assassinated and not fallen to a Danish marksman, there is no good evidence to support this. Yet, given the reign's extraordinary character, however shaped by the insuperable problems Karl XII inherited, debate on this and countless other issues will doubtless always be sustained.

The material on the reign and the course of the war is immense. Much Swedish archival material, such as the king's war and conciliar correspondence, was in print by the end of the nineteenth century. The archives of the chancery-in-the-field on the Russian campaign appear to have been destroyed by the Swedes before capture. In both Riksarkivet and Krigsarkivet in Stockholm there are substantial runs of papers still unprinted.

Because not only Scandinavian and Russian historians, but English, French, German, Polish, and Turkish scholars have worked in the field, using new material or re-evaluating old, the range of historical treatments is almost as formidable as the printed archival materials. In addition, there are a large number of memoirs and journals which have long been in print.

REFERENCES: F. G. Bengtsson, *The Sword Does Not Jest: The Life of Charles XII* (New York: St. Martin's, 1960), a condensed version of the author's two-volume biography published in Sweden in 1935–1936; *DSH*, vol. 8; E. Godley, *Charles XII of Sweden: A Study in Kingship* (London: W. Collins & Sons, 1928); O. Haintz, *König Karl XII von Schweden*, 3 vols. (Berlin: W. de Gruyter, 1936–1958); R. M. Hatton, *Charles XII of Sweden* (New York: Weybright & Talley, 1968); *Karolinska Förbundets Årsbok* (Stockholm/Lund, 1910–), the most respected journal, dealing exclusively with the maintenance and defense of the empire between 1654 and 1718; *SMK*, vol. 4; *SU*, vol. 15; Voltaire, *Charles XII* ed. Ernest Rhys (1731; repr. New York: E. P. Dutton, 1908).

D. D. ALDRIDGE

KARL XIII (7 October 1748–5 February 1818) Duke of Södermanland and king of Sweden 1809–1818

Karl was the second son of Adolf Fredrik* and Lovisa Ulrika*. It was assumed that his older brother, Gustav (III*) would succeed Adolf Fredrik, and Karl was never seriously prepared to rule. Nor was he inclined by temperament to govern. He was lethargic, shifty, self-centered, and indulgent. From the 1770s his attentions were focused chiefly on the Freemason movement in Sweden, of which he became the grand master in 1774. He took little interest in the affairs of the state. During Gustav's reign he vacillated between supporting his brother and siding with his enemies. He did distinguish himself as commander of the Swedish fleet at the battle of Hogaland (1788) during the Swedish-Russian War of 1788–1790. He appears not to have played a part in the plot to assassinate Gustav in 1792, but following his brother's death Karl became head of the regency for his nephew, Gustav IV Adolf*. Karl quickly passed the real work of government off to his friend and fellow Freemason, Gustav Adolf Reuterholm. Following Gustav IV's accession, Karl largely retired from public life, though he was occasionally recalled to act as regent in the king's absence. He apparently spent most of his time indulging in occult, mystical ceremonies and sex. Karl returned to the fore in Swedish political life following the coup that deposed Gustav IV in March 1809. By then, because of failing health, he was incapable of ruling and was easily manipulated by the "revolutionaries" of that year. In June 1809 Karl became king. His marriage to Hedvig Elisabet Charlotta of Augustenborg had produced no surviving heirs, and Karl agreed to adopt Karl August of Augustenborg (*see* Christian August). Following Karl August's sudden and unexpected death, the king accepted, reluctantly, Jean Baptist Bernadotte (Karl XIV Johan*) as heir to the throne. For the last eight years of his life, Karl was incapable of governing, and real power rested with Bernadotte.

REFERENCES: *DSH*, vols. 10, 11; M. Nyland, *G. A. Reuterholm under förmyndaretiden 1792–1796* (Uppsala: Appelbergs, 1917); *SU*, vol. 15.

B. NORDSTROM

KARL XIV JOHAN (Jean Baptiste Jules Bernadotte) (26 January 1763–8 March 1844) King of Sweden 1818–1844

By a combination of ability and sheer luck in a revolutionary time, Bernadotte rose from the rank of common soldier to become a marshal of France and finally king of Sweden.

He was born on 6 January 1763 in Pau, Gascony, in southwestern France. His attorney father died in 1780, and the son had to leave school and join the army of Louis XVI. He rose steadily through the ranks, and when the French

Revolution opened new opportunity the Gascon volunteer, at age 31, became a general. His outstanding talent was his ability to enthuse troops. In 1797 he was ordered to lead 20,000 men to Italy to support General Napoleon Bonaparte, and rivalry was born between two ambitious *militaires*. He was briefly ambassador to Vienna, then minister of war. But when Napoleon returned from Egypt, Bernadotte was out of office. He frankly opposed the coup of Brumaire, but he agreed that he would not lead an opposition unless called upon by the Directory. Napoleon became first consul without open opposition.

A restraining influence affecting both men was that Bernadotte had married Desirée Clary, who had earlier been engaged to Napoleon. Desirée's sister, Julie, married Joseph Bonaparte, and thus Bernadotte came within the fringes of the Bonaparte clan. The first consul, then emperor, could forgive Bernadotte's negative but passive stance and in due course made him a marshal and prince of Ponte Corvo. He was, nevertheless, repeatedly irritated by his subordinate's independent attitude and reportedly said that on at least three occasions he would have had Bernadotte shot but for Desirée's sake. Yet, Napoleon knew he could depend on the Gascon's loyalty to duty. Bernadotte held commands in important campaigns and between campaigns was assigned to governorships in Hanover, Anspach, and Hamburg. He was unusually successful in both discipline and administration. In 1810, however, he was out of favor at a critical moment, and living outside Paris.

Meanwhile, in Sweden a palace coup (1809 Revolution) had ousted King Gustav IV Adolf* and placed his uncle on the throne as Karl XIII*. Since Karl was old and without legal heir, a successor had to be found. A Danish prince, Christian August*, was chosen, but he died in June 1810. A new search had to be made. Napoleon was consulted, but he refused to advise. The choice of the Swedish Riksdag* fell upon Bernadotte, who, with Napoleon's help, was expected to regain Finland.

In October 1810 the French marshal accepted the Lutheran faith and became Karl Johan, crown prince of Sweden, heir to the throne of the Vasas. Desirée came to Sweden three months later with eleven-year-old Oscar (I*), the only child of the marriage. The old king and most of his subjects succumbed to the newcomer's charm, and he quickly became the real ruler of the country. He identified himself completely with his adopted land, but he never learned Swedish; business was conducted in French. In appearance he was a striking contrast with the Swedes: sharpnosed, tall, and straight, with a mop of curly black hair, a flashing smile, eager and impulsive.

Immediately on Bernadotte's heels came demands that Sweden cease trade with German ports and declare war on Britain. The Swedes agreed but did not act. Hence Napoleon, before marching against Russia, invaded Swedish Pomerania in January 1812. This act of war destroyed Swedish sympathy for the French and freed Bernadotte to pursue the policy he had already developed: alliance with Russia (Sweden's ancient enemy), renunciation of the hope of regaining Finland, and acquisition of Norway instead. Swedish policy was reoriented. At the Conference of Trachenberg in July 1813 the former French general helped the allied leaders plan the campaign that led to Napoleon's defeat at Leipzig in October. After a separate war against Denmark and a summer campaign against the Norwegians, the crown prince achieved his goal: the union of Norway with Sweden (*see* Norwegian-Swedish Union*), which lasted from 1814 until 1905.

When Karl XIII died in 1818, Karl Johan became king of Sweden and Norway. But he had seen many new princely lines overturned, and he never felt really secure on his throne. He watched with fear every move of the exiled son of Gustav IV Adolf, and he did not tolerate opposition at home. He dreamed of a grand role for himself in France, but he was too cautious to risk action. He restrained all temptations to adventure and, at his death in 1844, passed on the succession to his son Oscar. Thus, Bernadotte originated a dynasty that continues to the late twentieth century, the only so-called Napoleonic rulership to survive.

The man of war became a man of peace. He yielded Pomerania to Prussia and withdrew from continental entanglements. He maintained good relations with Russia and established himself as a stable factor in Europe. He considered himself highly capable in finance, but his schemes in this field were largely failures. The revolutionary general became conservative and increasingly autocratic. He was appalled at the drinking habits of the Swedes and warmly encouraged temperance. He knew that the welfare of his two kingdoms depended on agriculture, and therefore he founded an agricultural college and promoted scientific farming. He also promoted canal building, notably the famous Göta Canal* connecting the Baltic with the North Sea, and he urged industrial development. In a country still backward, this "last of the saga kings" was a constructive force, helping to prepare Sweden for the transformations of the later nineteenth and twentieth centuries.

REFERENCES: D. P. Barton, *The Amazing Career of Bernadotte 1763–1844* (Boston: Houghton Mifflin, 1929); F. D. Scott, *Bernadotte and the Fall of Napoleon* (Cambridge, Mass.: Harvard University Press, 1935); and *Sweden: The Nation's History* (Minneapolis: University of Minnesota Press, 1977).

F. D. SCOTT

KARL XV (3 May 1826–18 September 1872) King of Sweden 1859–1872

Karl XV ascended to the Swedish throne in July 1859, succeeding his father, King Oscar I*. As Crown Prince Karl, from September 1857 until his ascension to the throne, he acted as regent while Oscar's health continued to deteriorate. Karl's chief goal during his reign was to strengthen the union ties between Sweden and Norway. He sought also to promote trade connections in the union via reductions of or freedom from tolls, and to instigate the construction of a railroad between Sweden and Norway, which was eventually opened to the public in 1862. Karl's goals were encompassed in his ruling motto, "The country shall be built by law" (*Land skall med lag byggas*).

Born Karl Ludvig Eugen, Crown Prince Karl, Duke of Skåne, he was the oldest son of Oscar I and Josephine of Leuchtenberg. In his youth, he was tutored by historian F. F. Carlson and later attended Uppsala University. In 1850 the crown prince married Lovisa, daughter of Prince Fredrik of the Netherlands and his wife, Luise of Prussia. They had two children: Louise, who later became queen of Denmark, and Karl, who died at the age of 15 months.

Karl was a popular monarch, especially during the early years of his reign. An ardent Scandinavist, he was not only charming and amiable, but had a profound love of living. He was artistically and poetically gifted and a patron of the arts. Karl ignored the prescribed strict rules of court etiquette and enjoyed mingling with the common people. On the other hand, as king he lacked the personal qualities necessary for maintaining the power of the monarchy. Karl was said to lack morals, patience, and consistency. Although he aspired to attain power and prosperity for his nation, when it came to diplomacy he was hampered by his impulsive and generous nature, his lack of insight, and his inability to anticipate the possible consequences of his actions.

Karl, disapproving of his father's liberal tendencies, was a conservative. Although he continued his predecessor's foreign policy, Karl declared that his aim was "to pursue a policy according to my own mind." Yet, despite the numerous liberal reforms that occurred during his reign, Karl never opposed the changes because of his craving for popularity.

One of the most notable changes to occur during Karl's reign was the decline of autocracy. The monarch appointed a liberal cabinet under the leadership of Louis De Geer*, minister of justice, which remained in power from 1858 to 1870. During this time, the council acquired autonomy in political affairs. De Geer initiated a major parliamentary reform in 1866, by which the old four estate parliament was abolished and supplanted with a two-chamber Riksdag*.

Other reforms implemented during Karl's thirteen-year reign included the regularization of local self-government (1843–1862), the extension of freedom of the press and religion, and the abolition of the guild system and home distillation.

Karl's reigning years were marked by his desire for popularity rather than effectiveness. His final year of rule was overshadowed by his failing health and personal sadness, as he mourned the death of Queen Lovisa, who died in March 1871. Karl died a year later, on 18 September 1872, in Malmö at the age of 43 from intestinal tuberculosis.

REFERENCES: A. Åberg, *Vår Svenska Historia* (Lund: Bröderna Ekstrands Tryckeri, 1978); I. Anderson, *A History of Sweden* (New York: Praeger, 1956); T. K. Derry, *A History of Scandinavia* (Minneapolis: University of Minnesota Press, 1979); *DSH*, vols. 12, 13; *Encyclopedia Americana*, vol. 26 (Danbury, Conn.: Americana Corp., 1978); A. Stomberg, *A History of Sweden* (New York: Macmillan Co., 1931); *SU*, vol. 15; J. Weibull, "The Union with Norway," in *Sweden's Development from Poverty to Affluence 1750–1907*, ed. S. Koblik (Minneapolis: University of Minnesota Press, 1975).

C. ARWIDSON

KARL XVI GUSTAV (30 April 1946–) King of Sweden 1973–

Karl XVI Gustav is the youngest child and only son of Prince Gustav Adolf and Princess Sibylla of Sachsen-Coburg-Gotha. He was given the title of duke of Jämtland and was later named crown prince when his grandfather, Gustav VI Adolf*, ascended to the throne in 1950.

The monarch was educated at a boarding school in Sigtuna. After completing his studies, Karl spent his two years of compulsory military service in the Royal Navy. Following his military service, he further pursued his education at the University of Uppsala, where he concentrated on history, sociology, political science, fiscal law, and economics.

When Karl ascended to the Swedish throne on 19 September 1973, at the age of 27, he announced that the motto of his reign would be "For Sweden—in keeping with the times" (För Sverige—för tiden). For two years his duties and obligations were those established in the Constitution of 1809. Under the new constitution, which was adopted in 1975, the monarch's duties became mainly representative and ceremonial (see Constitutional Development).

On 19 June 1976 Karl married Silvia Renate Sommerlath (b. 22 December 1943), the daughter of West German businessman Walther Sommerlath and his Brazilian wife, Alice. Silvia lived for many years in Sao Paulo, where her father represented a Swedish company. After returning to the Federal Republic of Germany, Silvia enrolled in the Sprachen Dolmetsch Institute in Munich and graduated as a Spanish interpreter in 1969. In 1971 she served as chief hostess in the Organization Committee for the Munich Olympic Games. It was at the games that Silvia and Karl first met. The royal couple has two children: Victoria Ingrid Alice Desiree, born 14 July 1977, and Carl Phillip Edmund Bertil, born 13 May 1979. (A significant result of Victoria's birth was the new Act of Succession, which proclaims their majesties' daughter as heir to the Swedish throne. The new act states that the eldest child of the king and queen shall be heir to the throne, regardless of sex).

Since coming to the throne, Karl has kept himself well-informed of developments in various sectors of society. He has done so by visiting with authorities, organizations, and institutions. The king has taken an active part in nature conservation. He helped prepare the 1972 United Nations Conference on the Human Environment in Stockholm* and has participated in the International Union for Conservation of Nature and Natural Resources and the World Wildlife Fund.

The king is an avid outdoorsman. In addition to his love of fishing and hunting, Sweden's monarch enjoys yachting and skiing. He is a staunch supporter of scouting and has been the honorary chairman of the World Organization of the Scout Movement.

REFERENCES: A. Åberg, Vår Svenska historia (Lund: Bröderna Ekstrands Trykeri AB, 1978); DSH, vol. 15; A. Ohlmarks, Alla Sveriges Kungar (Stockholm: Almqvist and Wiksell, 1972); J. Weibull, The Monarchy in Sweden, M. Morris, trans. (Stockholm: The Swedish Institute, 1981).

C. ARWIDSON

KARL FREDRIK OF HOLSTEIN-GOTTORP (30 April 1700–18 June 1739)
Duke of Holstein-Gottorp and claimant to the Swedish throne in 1718

Karl Fredrik was the son of Fredrik IV of Holstein-Gottorp and Hedvig Sofia,

Karl XII's* elder sister. His father was killed in 1702, and his mother died in 1708. He then came to live at the Swedish court. His education was entrusted to Arvid Horn*. Following Karl XII's return from the Ottoman Empire in 1715, Karl Fredrik was frequently in the company of the king, and his first minister, George Heinrich von Görtz*, became the king's favorite advisor. There were strong indications that the unmarried king considered Karl Fredrik to be his most likely successor, although Karl never made any official statement to that effect.

Following Karl's death in 1718, Karl Fredrik was quickly edged out of the succession by the dead king's younger sister, Ulrika Eleonora*, and her consort, Fredrik of Hesse-Kassel (later Fredrik I*). The rapidity with which Fredrik and his allies moved, coupled with Karl Fredrik's youth and inexperience and the strong anti-Holstein feelings that had been generated by Görtz during the last years of Karl's life, worked against him. In 1719 Karl Fredrik left Sweden for the continent. Supported by the Habsburg emperor, he secured the return of the Holstein part of his territories in 1720. From 1721 to 1727 he lived in St. Petersburg and there married Anna, a daughter of Peter the Great.

Karl Fredrik was used as a diplomatic pawn by the Russians against Sweden and Denmark through the mid-1720s, and the royal house in Sweden, which was without an heir, was particularly susceptible to external pressures. A party of the duke's supporters developed in Sweden and was active at the 1723 and 1726–1727 Riksdag* meetings, but this group failed to secure a guarantee of the duke's succession. (The group did win an annual subsidy and the title "royal highness" for Karl Fredrik.)

Following the death of Catherine I, Karl Fredrik left Russia and settled in Kiel. His wife died there in 1729 giving birth to Karl Peter Ulrik, who nearly became king of Sweden in 1742 and did become Tsar Peter III of Russia in 1762. Karl Fredrik died in 1739.

REFERENCES: *DSH*, vol. 8; *SMK*, vol. 4; *SU*, vol. 15.

B. NORDSTROM

KARLSKRONA Swedish town and naval base

Karlskrona is a town of some 40,000 inhabitants situated within the archipelago of southeast Blekinge, 40 miles south of Kalmar* and 25 miles east of Karlshamn. Karl XI* founded Karlskrona as a new naval base in 1680–1682. Its rapid development before 1690 gave Sweden an offensive base against Denmark to complement Gothenburg* on the Kattegat and served to strengthen communications between Sweden and its German possessions. Essentially a dockyard town, it was planned with symmetry and elegance. With fortified islands toward the open sea, it was naturally strong. Because of the prevailing southwesterly winds, its entrances were hazardous for sailing ships to blockade, and it could be effectively attacked only from landward.

As Karlskrona waxed, so Stockholm* waned as a naval base, and until 1776, when Gustav III* re-established it in Stockholm, Karlskrona was the seat of the Swedish Admiralty, distanced some 300 miles from the capital. In the early eighteenth century, Karlskrona was Sweden's second largest city. The eighteenth century saw extensive dockyard development, not finally completed until 1805, because of a disastrous fire in 1790. After 1815 Sweden no longer held territories in Germany, while Russia held Finland to the east and was on the Gulf of Danzig to the south. Hence, during the Crimean War (1854–1856) and the Russo-Japanese War (1904–1905) there was considerable controversy in Swedish naval circles about Karlskrona's continuing effectiveness. In spite of these debates, however, the town remains a principal Swedish naval base—and of particular interest to the Russians in the Baltic. It was near Karlskrona that a Soviet submarine, armed with nuclear weapons, went aground in the fall of 1981.

REFERENCES: J. Bromé, *Karlskrona stads historia*, vol. 1 (Karlskrona, 1930); C. G. Flach and C. A. Hjulhammar, "Stockholm eller Karlskrona," *Tidsskrift i Sjöväsendet* (Stockholm, 1904); G. Halldin, *Karlskronas örlogsvarv i gågna tider* (Karlskrona, 1928); S. O. Swahn, *Gamla Karlskronagårdar* (Karlskrona, 1933).

D. D. ALDRIDGE

KEKKONEN, URHO (3 September 1900–) President of Finland 1956–1981

Urho Kekkonen was born in northern Finland of peasant stock in 1900. In 1981 he retired from the presidency he had held for 25 years. During this time span Kekkonen witnessed or helped to shape the course of twentieth-century Finnish history. Kekkonen's childhood endowed him with a progressive bourgeois view of how Finnish society should be organized. During the Finnish Civil War* he served as a volunteer in the White Guard and in a firing squad which executed Red Guard prisoners, an experience that convinced him that the health and vitality of Finnish society must be achieved by the politics of conciliation rather than confrontation.

In the 1920s Kekkonen was active in student politics, studied law, and eventually earned a doctorate. During his student years he was also the national high jump champion, a political asset in sports-conscious Finland, and he later served as president of the Finnish Sports League from 1932 to 1947. Kekkonen's politics in the 1920s were closely identified with efforts to improve the position of the Finnish language in university instruction and to promote the Greater Finland movement, which aimed at the integration of Russian Karelia into the Finnish state. Kekkonen turned his back on this movement, however, in the early 1930s, when it became associated with the politics of right-wing radicalism, and he became an ardent advocate of a strong political Center based on cooperation with the Social Democratic Party*.

Kekkonen was first elected to parliament in 1936 and became minister of justice in the same year. In 1937 he was named minister of the interior and attempted to outlaw the fascist Patriotic People's Party. He failed to achieve that goal, but established his credentials as a politician of the Center who preferred to defend the institutions of Finnish democracy by cooperating with Social Democrats.

Rejected by the Right, Kekkonen remained in parliament but did not serve in any governments during World War II*. As an active politician without official responsibilities, Kekkonen was free to ponder the significance of what was happening on the military and diplomatic fronts. At the end of the Winter War* in 1940 he voted against the Soviet-Finnish peace treaty, but by late 1942 and during 1943, when Finland was fighting the so-called Continuation War* as a co-belligerent of Germany, Kekkonen began to realize, with the urging of an American OSS officer in Stockholm*, that Finland's postwar policy toward the Soviet Union would have to be radically revised. In December 1943 Kekkonen spoke in Stockholm about the importance of good postwar Finnish-Soviet relations: Finland had to choose between building its postwar policy on possible East-West conflict, in which case Finland would always be an area of conflict and controversy, or building its postwar Soviet policy on a basis of neutrality and good Soviet-Finnish relations. Unilateral Finnish statements of neutrality based on the Scandinavian connection failed to satisfy the Soviet Union, however, and in 1945 Kekkonen was urging his fellow Finns to understand that Finland could only remain independent if it entered the new postwar system "via the Soviet Union." Any attempt to enter it via Scandinavian neutrality would be construed by Soviet leaders as an attempt to become associated with the Western Allies.

Kekkonen's willingness to cooperate on the domestic front with the Left made him an important link in President Juho Paasikivi's* efforts to put the Finnish house in order to Soviet satisfaction, lest the Soviets decide to do the job themselves. As minister of justice after the war, he had the unpleasant task of overseeing the trials of wartime political leaders, which Paasikivi considered necessary to prevent the Soviet Union from conducting the trials itself. In 1948 Kekkonen participated in the negotiations that led to the Treaty of Friendship, Cooperation and Mutual Assistance* with the Soviet Union.

In the early 1950s Kekkonen served five terms as prime minister and once as foreign minister. During this period of political apprenticeship, Kekkonen began to project his own foreign policy profile. Perhaps the Kekkonen elements in the Paasikivi-Kekkonen Line* date from the so-called Pyjama-Pocket Speech of 1952, when Kekkonen declared in essence that Finland was a neutral country and that peace in the Nordic area was an essential precondition of that neutrality. Finland's foreign policy had to take into account the Soviet connection, but it would be strengthened by identification with the Nordic connection. The more the Nordic countries moved toward a policy of neutrality, the greater Nordic stability and the greater the possibility of Finnish neutrality.

In 1956 Kekkonen was elected president by a margin of two votes. His first term in office was marked by crises in domestic and foreign policy. Eager to gain recognition of Finnish neutrality as a prerequisite for meeting the challenges of Western European economic integration, Kekkonen moved faster than the Soviet Union was willing to permit. The Cold War was thawing, but not as quickly as Kekkonen had thought. The efforts of NATO to build up its northern flank in the Baltic in the late 1950s and the Berlin crisis in the early 1960s, plus the apparent growth in Finland of political groups which the Soviet Union considered anti-Soviet, led to Soviet intervention in Finnish domestic politics during the so-called Night Frost (1958) and the "Note Crisis" (1961).

The significance of these developments is disputed by historians and political observers in Finland and abroad. For adherents of the Finlandization* interpretation of Finnish foreign policy, they prove that Finland is run by remote control. According to the Paasikivi-Kekkonen Line interpretation, they were part of the inevitable problems inherent in the growing pains of establishing Finland's position as an independent and neutral country. Both schools agree that Kekkonen emerged from these crises as the guarantor of good Soviet-Finnish relations, but they differ over whether this development promoted or undermined Finnish interests. There is also considerable controversy within the parameters of the Paasikivi-Kekkonen Line interpretation over whether Kekkonen abused the power he derived from foreign policy.

Kekkonen's role as a strong president who did not hesitate to use his position to influence domestic politics is interpreted by many foreign commentators to be the result of Soviet influence. The Paasikivi-Kekkonen Line interpretation assumes, however, that Kekkonen's domestic politics, while influenced by his role in the formulation of foreign policy, have their roots in Finnish history. The Finnish constitution, which was written in the aftermath of a civil war, envisioned a strong president responsible for the conduct of foreign affairs and for ensuring that the divergent political forces in parliament not paralyze the functioning of Finland's institutions of political democracy.

REFERENCES: U. Kekkonen, "Finlandization Is Not for Export," *Newsweek*, 3 September 1973, and *Neutrality: The Finnish Position* (London: Heineman, 1970); K. Korhonen, ed., *Urho Kekkonen—A Statesman for Peace* (Helsinki: Otava, 1975); H. P. Krosby, "Finland and Detente: Self-Interest Politics and Western Reactions," *Yearbook of Finnish Foreign Policy* (Helsinki: The Finnish Institute of International Affairs, 1980); J. Nevakivi, "Urho Kekkonen and Postwar Finnish Foreign Policy," *Yearbook of Finnish Foreign Policy* (Helsinki: The Finnish Institute of International Affairs, 1976).

R. M. BERRY

KEY, ELLEN (11 December 1849–25 April 1926) Swedish feminist, social reformer, and writer

Ellen Key was born at Sundsholm estate in southern Sweden, the eldest of six children. Her parents, Emil and Sophie Key, were strict and unaffectionate. Although she disliked their child-rearing methods, her father, a liberal-minded and intelligent politician and writer, had a profound influence on his daughter regarding political and social issues.

In 1874 Ellen Key began writing for *Tidskrift för hemmet*, a magazine founded by and for women in 1859. Her articles often dealt with women's issues and women writers, and she became personally acquainted with several of the leading writers of the day. In addition to writing and traveling, Key taught at Whitlockska Co-educational School in Stockholm* and served as a lecturer in history at Stockholm's Worker Institute.

Key gave up her teaching responsibilities in 1903 to devote all her time to writing on a variety of topics: women, children, religion, war, love, marriage, and other women writers. Two of her most well known works are *Missbrukad kvinnokraft* (*Misused Womanpower*, 1896) and *Barnets århundrade* (*The Century of the Child*, 1900). Both have been translated into English. *Barnets århundrade*, translated into eleven different languages, was written in response to her parents' child-rearing practices and stressed the independence and creativity of children. The views expressed in *Missbrukad kvinnokraft* evoked controversy. Key believed that women were being "misused:" that they were being forced to lose their qualities of tenderness and caring by working in non-feminine occupations. Women, Key felt, should work in fields such as medicine and teaching, fields that would bring out their maternal traits. A woman would then become the "mother of society" (samhällsmodern) and make society a better place to live.

Key's impact on Swedish social and cultural issues of the late nineteenth and early twentieth centuries was very great. Her ideas on woman's erotic nature and the power of love to change society caused an enormous amount of discussion in both Sweden and the rest of Europe. She was also involved in politics and, along with Elin Wägner, championed voting rights for women. Through articles, books, lectures, numerous letters, and gatherings in her home, Key encouraged and influenced a large number of writers and critics, including Selma Lagerlöf, Georg Brandes, Stefan Zweig, and Havelock Ellis.

REFERENCES: Ronny Ambjörnsson, "Samhällsmodern. Ellen Keys kvinnouppfattning till och med 1896," Ph.D. Dissertation, University of Gothenburg, 1974; Ellen Key, *Minnen av och om Emil Key. I–III* (Stockholm: Albert Bonniers förlag, 1916–1917); Mia Leche Löfgren, *Ellen Key, hennes liv och verk* (Stockholm: Natur och kultur, 1930); Louise Nyström-Hamilton, *Ellen Key, Her Life and Work*, trans. from the Swedish (New York and London: G. P. Putnam's Sons, 1913); Ulf Wittrock, *Ellen Keys väg från kristendom till livstro* (Stockholm: Bokförlaget Natur och kultur, 1953).

M. LOWE SHOGREN

KINGS' SAGAS Old Norse biographies of the kings of Norway

The kings' sagas are Old Norse historical or pseudohistorical prose narratives relating primarily the lives of the kings of Norway, but embracing in addition biographies of the kings of Denmark and the earls of Orkney. The corpus, which encompasses both accounts of individual regents and more synoptic histories of several generations of rulers, spans the mythological beginnings of kingship in eastern Norway c. 500 to 1280. These biographical works were written almost exclusively by Icelanders during the late 1100s and 1200s and were copied and revised mainly in Iceland during the following few centuries. Original Norwegian contributions to the accounts of the period are limited mainly to short Latin chronicles.

The kings' sagas developed out of the fertile storytelling practices of the Icelanders but trace their origins to various sources. To the early twelfth-century learned Icelanders Saemund Sigfusson and Ari Þorgilsson* goes the honor of determining a chronological framework for the period from King Harald I Fair-hair's* reign (c. 870) until 1120. This framework was then filled in by collecting and ordering material from Icelandic and Norwegian oral tradition, embellished with motifs from Christian legends and other literary sources, and to an extent colored by the situation at the time of composition. The kings' sagas are thus literary interpretations of history.

The most reliable historical source for Norwegian kings' lives c. 850–c. 1050 is skaldic poetry*, which usually is contemporary with the events described. The skalds employed metaphorical expression in an artistically involved and convoluted style. Syllable count and intricate patterns of rhyme and alliteration helped to preserve the poems during the period of oral transmission. Stanzas of panegyric skaldic poetry were often cited as documentation in kings' sagas and thus preserved.

Central to the development of the kings' sagas were tales of the two missionary kings of Norway, Olaf I Tryggvason* and Olaf II Haraldsson* (Saint Olaf), and versions of their lives must have been among the earliest kings' sagas. Crowning the development of the entire genre is Snorri Sturluson's* *Heimskringla*, an account of the deeds of Norwegian rulers from the beginnings of historical time until 1177. Snorri (1178/1179–1241) wrote a separate saga of Saint Olaf c. 1230 and then incorporated that work as the center of his narrative of the regents of Norway. The text of *Heimskringla* forms the basis for the encyclopedic com-pilations of kings' lives from the 1300s.

"Contemporary" kings' sagas, ones which tell of events in the 1100s and 1200s, comprise another important line of development in the genre. In particular, the sagas of King Sverrir Sigurdsson* and of King Haakon IV Haakonsson* combine eyewitness accounts with documentary material in a fairly reliable historical presentation. The saga of King Sverrir was begun c. 1185 under the king's own supervision, and the saga of Haakon Haakonsson was commissioned from Sturla Thordarson by Haakon's son and successor, King Magnus VI Haa-konsson* (Lawmender).

REFERENCES: M. Ciklamini, *Snorri Sturluson* (Boston: Twayne, 1978); W. A. Crai-gie, *The Icelandic Sagas* (Cambridge, England: Cambridge University Press, 1913); H. Koht, *The Old Norse Sagas* (New York: Norton, 1931); K. Schier, *Sagaliteratur* (Stuttgart: Metzler, 1970); G. Turville-Petre, *Origins of Icelandic Literature* (Oxford: Clarendon, 1953), and *Scaldic Poetry* (Oxford: Clarendon, 1976).

J. E. KNIRK

KIRKJUBÖUR Former episcopal see in the Faroe Islands*

Christianity was accepted by the Faroese about 999, but the Kirkjuböur see was not established until about 1100. Tradition holds that the great Kirkjuböur farm was confiscated from its owner for a trivial breach of ecclesiastical law.

Three churches have stood in Kirkjuböur. Of what is probably the oldest, dating from the foundation of the see, only a fragment of the northern wall survives. The church used today was built about 1200 and dedicated to St. Olav.

This church was unhappily restored in 1874; most of its character was lost, and its medieval treasures were dispersed. Twelve magnificently carved fifteenth-century pew-ends from the church can now be seen in the National Museum in Copenhagen*.

The unfinished Magnus Cathedral was built in the late thirteenth century by Bishop Erlendr* (1269–1308). The cathedral was never roofed, but the bare walls as they stand today are nevertheless fine examples of high gothic architecture. A soapstone plaque set into the outer east wall carries an inscription noting, among other holy relics, bones of St. Magnus of Orkney and St. Thorlak of Iceland. The reasons why work was suspended on the cathedral are not known; legend speaks of an armed revolt against the bishop's taxes.

The episcopal palace as it stands today has a stone-built lower story and an upper story of round timbers in the Norwegian style, which does not properly fit the stone walling it sits upon. Detailed investigation has shown that in early medieval times the palace consisted of two wings of massive stones, two stories high. The upper story was destroyed by a landslide in late medieval times. Further damage to the complex resulted from an avalanche in 1772. It is interesting that the mortar for both the cathedral and the episcopal palace contained lime from burned mussel shells, limestone not being found in the Faroes.

During the Reformation*, the immense landed wealth of the Kirkjubøur see fell to the crown. Glebe farms were allotted to each of the seven priests, with an extra farm for the provost. The remaining church lands became heritable crown leases. Kirkjubøur farm formed the largest of these leases, and the wooden superstructure of the former episcopal palace is today a museum illustrating the old way of life in the living room of a prosperous peasant of former times.

From 1891 to 1936 the leaseholder of Kirkjubøur was the Faroese poet and nationalist politician Jóannes Patursson*.

REFERENCES: Sverri Dahl, "Kirkjubøur," *The Fifth Viking Congress* (Torshavn: Föroya Landsstýri et al., 1968), and "The Norse Settlements of the Faroe Islands," *Medieval Archaeology* 14 (1970); John F. West, *Faroese Folk-Tales and Legends* (Lerwick: Shetland Publishing Co., 1980).

J. F. WEST

KNUD I (the Great) (c. 1000–12 November 1035) King of Denmark 1018–1035, king of England 1014–1035, and king of Norway c. 1027–1035

Knud was one of the most significant rulers of the medieval period in Scandinavian history. At times he was or claimed to be the ruler of a multi-national empire that included Denmark, England, Norway, parts of Sweden, parts of the south Baltic area, and Scotland. This empire was fragile and was based almost entirely on Knud's personality and his military successes. His most active rule was in England, where he maintained a much needed peace, improved administration and law, and fostered the Church. He ruled indirectly in Denmark, but there, too, he was a patron of the Church and a supporter of government based on law as much as force. Knud was the first Scandinavian monarch to make a pilgrimage to Rome. He attended the coronation of the emperor Conrad II and married his daughter to Conrad's son, Henry (in part in exchange for the transfer of Slesvig to Denmark). Knud is often cited as the first Scandinavian king to have been considered a member of the community of rulers of Western Christendom.

When his father died suddenly in 1014, Knud was designated his heir in England. Resistance to his succession soon developed, however. Ethelred returned from his exile in Normandy, raised a new army, and attacked the Danes. Although Ethelred soon died, his son Edmund (Ironsides) proved an able opponent, and Knud was forced to withdraw from England in 1014.

Knud then went to Denmark, where he sought to share rule with his brother Harald II*. Although Harald refused to do so, he supported Knud's aims in England and provided him with men and ships for a new attack. In September 1015 Knud returned to England. The campaign proved indecisive, and finally Knud and Edmund negotiated a division of the country. Edmund, however, died soon after, and Knud became the sole possessor of the throne. For the next two decades England served as the center of his realm and ceased to be a target of Viking* attacks. Knud married Emma, the widow of Ethelred. He divided the country into four earldoms and shared three of them out to his closest advisors, who initially were all Danes. He clarified the law and worked closely with the Church. His rule was not without its darker sides, however. Knud was violent and ruthless. The Danes in the kingdom appear to have been better treated than the Anglo-Saxons. He extracted high taxes from the people to support his guard and court. He eliminated without scruple a number of real or potential opponents. Still, accounts of Knud in most English histories are positive.

He spent relatively little of his reign in Scandinavia*. Following his brother's death, he asserted his claim over Denmark and ruled the country through a series of deputies, including Thorkill the Tall, who acted for Knud and his son Hardeknud*. He followed his predecessors' policy of attempting to assert control over Norway—or if that failed, of perpetuating disorder there.

In Norway Knud had to deal with Olaf II Haraldsson*, who was chosen king there in 1016. Olaf soon ran into trouble, however, largely through his efforts to force Christianity on unwilling heathens and to create a real state out of a hodgepodge of petty kingdoms. Olaf's most significant opponents came from the Trøndelag, and Knud allied with these. In 1026 Knud fought a major battle at Helgeaa with Olaf and Anund Jakob of Sweden. This encounter ended in an expensive draw for Olaf and Anund. The following year Knud launched a concerted campaign in Norway that drove Olaf into exile. Hardeknud was left to act as an underking. The Danes quickly made themselves unpopular, and Olaf attempted to reclaim his kingdom but was killed at Stiklestad in 1030. Shortly after Olaf's death the revolt against Danish rule was rekindled, and it culminated in 1035, when Olaf's son Magnus the Good (Magnus I Olafsson*) was recognized king.

When Knud died the "empire" disintegrated. Hardeknud, his son by Emma, the widow of the Anglo-Saxon king Ethelred, became king in Denmark; Harald, his son by Ælgifu, became king in England.

REFERENCES: *DBL*, vol. 8; *DH*, vol. 2; K. Randsborg, *The Viking Age in Denmark* (New York: St. Martin's Press, 1980); F. M. Stenton, *Anglo-Saxon England* (Oxford: Clarendon Press, 1943, 1947, and 1950).

B. NORDSTROM

KNUD II (Saint) (c. 1043–10 July 1086) King of Denmark 1080–1086

Knud was one of the illegitimate sons of Sven II Estridsen*. He was elected to the throne in Denmark following the death of his brother Harald II*. Assessments of Knud vary greatly in the sources, and history's view of him depends upon which medieval source is used. He apparently aroused strong feelings and had good friends and vehement opponents. This is reflected particularly in assessments of his saintliness. Recent interpretations are generally balanced and see his canonization as having been largely political.

Knud was in many ways a Viking*. He took part in attacks on England in the late 1060s and mid-1070s and retained a lifelong dream to regain England from William the Conqueror. His "election" in 1080 may have been determined by the forces he had accompany him at the electoral meeting at Isre. He was killed by his own people, who rose in revolt against him.

In domestic policy, Knud departed from the more political moderate course set by his father and brother. His goals might have been the same, that is, to establish a sound and strong central monarchy in which the crown controlled law and cooperated with the Church. His methods were not the same, however. He broke off communications with the papacy, imposed new taxes on the farmers, insisted on the king's right to control the forests and coastal waters, and attacked the ancient rights (laws) of his subjects. He quickly made himself very unpopular. (Some sources see him as having been ahead of his time, with ideas too advanced for the late eleventh century.)

The revolt that undid him erupted in 1086, in the midst of a second effort to raise a fleet to sail against England. It was caused in part by the strains of this effort and in part arose among the frustrated farmers, who saw him violating the promises made by his predecessors. Knud was driven from his base in Jutland and fled to Fyn, where he was killed in a churchyard in Odense.

In 1101 Knud was made a saint. This was largely the result of the efforts of the opponents of his successor, Oluf I* (Hunger). A series of bad years followed Knud's death. Severe crop failures struck Denmark and the suffering was great. Oluf and the farmers who had murdered God's representative on earth were blamed for the troubles. At the same time, miracles were reported to occur near the site of Knud's grave in Odense. His canonization is perhaps most important for what it says about the efforts being made to create a strong monarchy and to use whatever means necessary to do so, including the creation of a myth around Knud which linked the crown to God.

REFERENCES: *DBL*, vol. 8; *DH*, vol. 3; *KLNM*, vol. 8.

B. NORDSTROM

KNUD III (Magnussen) (c. 1129–9 August 1157) King of Denmark 1146–1157
Knud was a central figure in the last stage of the civil war in Denmark that began in 1131 with the murder of Knud Lavard. Between 1146 and 1157 he fought with Sven III Grathe* over the crown. As a son of Magnus and grandson of Niels*, he had a legitimate claim to the succession, and he was elected king by the freemen of Jutland. Initially, he fought alone, but in the later stages of the struggle he was joined by Valdemar (I*), the son of Knud Lavard, and Eskil, archbishop of Lund. In 1154 Sven was crowned king by Frederik Barbarossa, who interceded in the civil war, and Knud was given Sjaelland as a fief. This settlement was short-lived. In 1157 a military stalemate was reached, and Sven, Valdemar, and Knud agreed to share power. Knud was to rule in Sjaelland. This agreement also was only temporary. During a meeting at Roskilde, Sven attempted to have his opponents murdered. Knud was killed, but Valdemar escaped and defeated and killed Sven at the battle of Grathe Hede some months later.
REFERENCES: *DBL*, vol. 8; *DH*, vol. 3; R. Malmros, "Blodgildet i Roskilde historiografisk belyst. Knytlingasagas forhold till det tolvte århundredes danske historieskrivning," *Scandia* 45:1 (1979): 43–66.

B. NORDSTROM

KNUD IV *See* Knud VI

KNUD VI (den Sjette) (in some sources Knud IV) (1163–12 November 1202) King of Denmark 1182–1202
Knud was the son of Valdemar I* and Sofie. He followed his father in what might be regarded as the first hereditary succession in Danish history. Some have seen Knud as a weak ruler who lived in the shadow of his great archbishop, Absalon, and his more famous brother, Valdemar II*. These assessments may not be accurate, but the lack of contemporary sources makes it difficult to see him otherwise.
During his rule Denmark expanded territorially in the Baltic region, its economy prospered, and its influence in the North grew. At the same time, the scope of royal government increased, and efforts were made to make life within the kingdom more peaceful through the curbing of wanton violence and the conversion of the royal guard (*hird*) into a disciplined army of knights.
The expansion of the kingdom resulted from successful campaigns in the south Baltic region which had both religious and secular motives and the exploitation of diplomatic situations created by the struggle between the Welfs and the Hohenstaufens for the imperial throne in Germany. The dynastic squabblings in the empire gave Denmark repeated opportunities to expand its influence in the North at the expense of the Germans. During Knud's reign Pomerania, Mecklenburg, Holstein, and Slesvig came under the control of the king as fiefs, and the king

of Denmark was no longer expected to swear fealty to the emperor. (Some argue that this break came at Absalon's insistence.)

At home the conversion of the king's guard into a disciplined army was an important step toward unifying control of military force in the country. (Independent magnates did not lose their right to maintain their own armies, however.) In another move to preserve order, Knud (or Absalon) outlawed murder, which paralleled similar efforts throughout Europe aimed at creating greater internal peace and quelling the violent activities of knights.

Whether or not Knud was the driving force behind the events of his reign is less important than the accomplishments that took place. Denmark moved closer to being the most powerful state in northern Europe, and its governmental structure came increasingly to reflect the ideals of early divine right absolutism.

REFERENCES: *DBL*, vols. 1, 8; *DH*, vol. 3; *Cambridge Medieval History*, vol. 6; Saxo Grammaticus, *Danmarks Krønike* (Copenhagen: Samlerens, 1951); V. Starcke, *Denmark in World History* (Philadelphia: University of Pennsylvania Press, 1968).

B. NORDSTROM

KNUD LAVARD *See* Erik II; Erik III; Knud III; Niels; Sven(d) III Grathe

KNUDSEN, GUNNAR (1848–1928) Norwegian Liberal Party leader and prime minister, 1908–1910, 1913–1920

Modern parliamentary government based on clear lines of party division was established during Gunnar Knudsen's tenure as prime minister. Knudsen was first elected to the Storting* in 1891, coming from Bergen, where he was a successful shipowner and industrialist. Throughout his career he represented the reform tradition within the Liberal Party or Venstre. In March 1905 he joined the historic government of Christian Michelson* as finance minister, but he resigned in October due to his strong republican convictions. After 1905 Knudsen played a prominent part in organizing a consolidated Liberal Party group within the Storting against the Michelsen government's attempt to maintain a national coalition. Liberal representatives who would not accept party discipline were excluded, and the party was completely consolidated by 1908.

In this year Knudsen formed his first government, with only a minority in the Storting. It fell in 1910, but in 1913 he returned triumphantly to power as a result of a sweeping election victory which gave the Liberals 70 out of 123 seats; their majority increased to 74 in 1915. His governments were instrumental in the passage of a number of key reforms, including accident insurance for fishermen (1908), sickness insurance for low wage earners (1909), the Factory Act regulating working conditions (1909), full voting rights for women (1913), the 10–hour day and 54–hour week (1915), and Johan Castberg's* Children's Laws safeguarding children born out of wedlock (1915). Included also among the reforms of his second government were new laws providing for increased health coverage, better factory protection, government contributions to unemployment funds, and state-supported loans for home and farm purchases. The government's alcohol policy, favoring prohibition, and its language policy, resulting in the new language norm of 1917, were especially controversial.

As prime minister during World War I, Knudsen was a strong, patriarchal figure who dominated the decision-making process completely. He sought to maintain a neutral foreign policy, and this enjoyed widespread support. Because of the critical supply situation that arose as the war progressed, special government measures were taken to regulate economic activity. The government was accused of going too far by the Conservatives, while the Socialists attacked the government for not doing enough to prevent profiteering.

In the 1918 election the Liberal Party received a severe setback, losing its absolute majority. Never again would the Liberals dominate Norwegian politics. But since no majority government was possible in 1918, Knudsen continued in office. Anticipating the coming financial crisis of the postwar period, he sought in 1920 to restrict spending. Defeated over this issue, the cabinet fell on 17 June. Knudsen had held office for seven and a half years, to that time the longest term served since the introduction of parliamentary government. Aged 72 when his government fell, he chose not to seek re-election in 1921. He remains the preeminent Liberal leader of the twentieth century.

REFERENCES: T. K. Derry, *A History of Modern Norway, 1814–1972* (London: Oxford University Press, 1973); K. Larsen, *A History of Norway* (Princeton: Princeton University Press, 1950); I. Semmingsen, ''Norway 1905–1940,'' in *Scandinavia Past and Present*, vol. 2 (Copenhagen: Arnkrone, 1959).

O. HOIDAL

KOHT, HALVDAN (7 July 1873–12 December 1965) Norwegian historian and foreign minister

Halvdan Koht was Norway's most prolific historian. He published 184 books and some 3,000 articles during a professional life that spanned 67 years. From 1935 to 1941 he served as Norway's foreign minister.

In 1896 Koht passed his university exams and in 1897 received a travel grant to Copenhagen*, Leipzig, and Paris, where he remained for two years. In 1900 he began work on J. B. Halvorsen's *Norsk Forfatter Lexikon*, of which he completed volume 5 and authored all of volume 6. Through his work he gained a solid understanding of the role of literature in society, something he demonstrated throughout his historical production. The work on the dictionary occupied him for nearly eight years, but, simultaneously, he also completed his doctorate. His dissertation, *Die Stellung Norwegen und Schwedens im deutsch-danishen Konflikt*, earned him an appointment as docent in modern and cultural history at the University of Oslo in 1908.

In 1905 Koht became involved in the activities surrounding the dissolution of the Norwegian-Swedish Union*. As an outspoken and articulate republican, Koht wrote extensively in support of a republican constitution for Norway. As editor of the periodical *Syn og Segn* from 1901 to 1908, he was also a champion for the use of Nynorsk as an official and literary language (*see* Languages: Scandinavian).

A significant turning point in Koht's life occurred in 1908, when he decided to visit the United States. During a nine-month stay there, he not only developed a remarkable insight into American history and culture; he also gained confidence that he had something to offer as a historian. His experience in the United States convinced the young Koht that history was the story of class struggle, a concept that crystallized for him when he returned to Norway at the end of 1909.

By 1913 Koht had joined the Norwegian Labor Party*, and his writings reflected his increased awareness of historical materialism. On a broad range of topics, Koht presented new materials or revised old theories. Hardly an area of Norwegian history is without some kind of contribution by Koht.

Koht's authorship followed two main lines of thought, one social and one national. He was the first historian to emphasize the social conflict and class struggle in Viking Age* Scandinavia, a conflict largely between officials and farmers. Within this struggle is also found the national aspect of Koht's work, because the upper classes consisted essentially of people of foreign origin, whereas the lower classes were indigenous Norwegians. This analysis is perhaps most acute in Koht's support for the Nynorsk language against the dominant Dano-Norwegian in the nineteenth and twentieth centuries.

In 1935 Koht entered a new phase of his life when he accepted the appointment by the newly elected Labor Party leader, Johan Nygaardsvold*, to serve as foreign minister. These years were, perhaps, the most difficult in Koht's life. The late 1930s witnessed the rise of Hitler's Germany and threats to world peace that greatly troubled Koht. His years of anti-militarism and support for disarmament, however, blinded him somewhat to the threats from Germany, which culminated in the invasion of Norway on 9 April 1940.

Although there has been no question about Koht's actions after the invasion, when he remained firm in opposing the Germans, he was severely criticized after the war for allowing Norwegian defenses to deteriorate prior to 1940. Cleared of any responsibility for the unpreparedness of Norway, Koht returned to the university and his scholarly pursuits. His historical production continued to the eve of his death. His last book appeared in 1964, just a year before he died.

REFERENCES: O. Dahl, *Historisk materialisme: Historieoppfatningen hos Edvard Bull og Halvdan Koht* (Oslo, 1952); K. Haukaas and H. Skard, *Halvdan Koht: Ein bibliografi* (Oslo, 1964); H. Koht, *Minne frå unge år* (Oslo, 1968); S. Skard, *Mennesket Halvdan Koht* (Oslo, 1982).

T. LEIREN

KOIVISTO, MAUNO HENRIK (25 November 1925–) President of Finland 1982–

Koivisto, the son of a carpenter, was born in Turku. After military service during World War II*, he worked on the Turku docks and secured a university education through part-time study. In 1956 he received his doctorate from the

University of Turku. His dissertation dealt with industrial relations among the Turku harbor workers. (During his doctoral disputation, he received vociferous support from longshoremen in the audience.)

By virtue of his academic attainments and party affiliation (Social Democratic), Koivisto entered the banking profession. He started in the Workers' Savings Bank, but moved up rapidly to become governor of the Bank of Finland in 1968. He also served as Finland's representative in the International Bank for Regional Development (IBRD) from 1966 to 1969 and to the International Monetary Fund (IMF) from 1970 to 1979.

In the political sphere Koivisto served as minister of finance in 1966–1967, and he was prime minister from 1968 to 1970 and again from 1979 until his election to the presidency. In his financial and economic policies, Koivisto pursued a course aimed at quiet growth through tightly controlled management. He favored industry over agriculture. Koivisto claims to be an evolutionary Socialist and has explained his party's goal to be the creation of a welfare state* rather than the transformation to a Socialist society.

Koivisto has also played an important role in the integration of the Communists into the Finnish governmental system, through their participation in popular front coalition governments. His style of consensus politics has met with general approval in Finland, and he was elected president by a clear majority on the first ballot in the electoral college. His supporters in the election campaign included many non-Socialists. As president, Koivisto declared that his aim would be to engage in a less intrusive presidential role than has been customary in Finland and thereby strengthen the position of the parliament.

In foreign affairs Koivisto was closely associated with the abortive Nordek project (for the economic union of the Nordic states). Otherwise, however, he pursued a more conservative line designed to ensure that Finland would meet its obligations in light particularly of IMF requirements. He has been a strong supporter of the European Security Conference mechanisms and has maintained successfully Finland's postwar tradition of friendship with the Soviet Union.

REFERENCES: M. Koivisto, *Linjaviitat* (Helsinki: Kirjayhtymä, 1983); R. Kolanen, *Tuntematon Koivisto* (Helsinki: Kirjayhtymä, 1983); E. Silvasti, *Mauno Koivisto—mies ja kehykset* (Helsinki: Kirjayhtymä, 1983).

G. MAUDE

KOLLONTAI, ALEKSANDRA MIKHAILOVNA (19 March 1872 O.S.–9 March 1952)

Born into an aristocratic Russian family of liberal inclinations, Kollontai joined the Russian Social Democratic Labor Party in 1899 and spent the next four years studying and writing on the Finnish economy. In 1908 she fled Russia to avoid arrest. Like Lenin, Kollontai opposed World War I, and she spent much time in Scandinavia*, encouraging Social Democrats there to adopt a similar stance. After the Bolshevik Revolution, she was made commissar of social welfare, and in September 1920 she became head of the Women's Bureau of the party. Her political fortunes declined, however, when she joined a faction critical of the increasing bureaucratization of Soviet government.

The diplomatic posts Kollontai held between 1922 and 1945 represented an exile of sorts. From October 1922 to December 1925 she was part of the Soviet trade delegation to Norway, where she returned as ambassador in November 1927. In July 1930 she was named ambassador to Sweden. In that capacity, Kollontai played a crucial role in settling the Russo-Finnish War of 1939–1940 (*see* Winter War*) and the so-called Continuation War*. She worked alongside Swedish diplomats to open and maintain channels of communication and consistently urged moderation on both the Soviet and Finnish leaderships. This work earned her a Nobel Peace Prize nomination in 1946. In February 1945 Kollontai was recalled to the U.S.S.R., where she died in retirement of natural causes.

REFERENCE: B. E. Clements, *Bolshevik Feminist: The Life of Aleksandra Kollontai* (Bloomington, Ind.: Indiana University Press, 1979).

E. R. TERZUOLO

KREUGER, IVAR (2 March 1880–12 March 1932) The Swedish "Match King" and international financier

Ivar Kreuger was born into a middle-class family in Kalmar*. His father was a match manufacturer. He received his post-secondary education as an engineer at the Technical High School in Stockholm*. In partnership with Paul Toll, he founded the firm of Kreuger & Toll in 1908. It soon became the largest construction company in Stockholm and then quickly expanded to other Scandinavian countries and other parts of the world. Using the family's match factories as a base, Kreuger began in 1913 to build a match manufacturing cartel (Svenska tändsticks AB or STAB). In the 1920s this firm and its affiliates controlled nearly three-quarters of the world's production.

Kreuger used his solid base in construction and match manufacturing, coupled with an apparently uncanny ability to convince people of his trustworthiness, to build an enormous, paper financial empire in the decade after the onset of World War I. Although this empire was based largely on margin buying and loans, Kreuger played a remarkable role in international finance from his position as head of the empire. At the time of his death, he was the head of a multi-national concern encompassing nearly 400 businesses, including mining, manufacturing, communication, construction, export, and banking establishments. His stated worth was in the hundreds of millions of dollars.

Kreuger's empire began to wobble as the international depression deepened in 1931–1932. His liabilities far exceeded his assets, and by late 1931 he was engaged in a frantic scramble to save himself. In March 1932, his position becoming increasingly untenable, he committed suicide in his Paris apartment.

The repercussions of his death were widespread. The value of his holdings plummeted on world markets. The Swedish stock exchange was closed for a week. A series of investigations into his business affairs revealed an incredible story of financial manipulations, including book falsifications, forgeries, frauds, and involvement with foreign governments. In Sweden it was disclosed that Prime Minister Carl Gustav Ekman* had received two substantial contributions from Kreuger at times when the financier was seeking new loans from the State Bank of Sweden (Riksbanken). Ekman was forced to resign in August 1932 as a result. This revelation and others may also have affected the outcome of the September 1932 general election in Sweden, which ushered in a 44–year period of Social Democratic rule. Many small investors were ruined by the collapse of Kreuger's empire, and most of his companies were liquidated or sold at deflated prices to pay off debts.

Kreuger's critics have called him a megalomaniac, a fraud, a forger, and a cheat. They have accused him of taking advantage of the chaotic international situation in the years following World War I for his own personal gain. His defenders have argued that Kreuger was a financial genius and a missionary who sought to use his special talents to bring stability and prosperity to the world.

REFERENCES: Allen Churchill, *The Incredible Ivar Kreuger* (New York: Rinehart, 1957); Kenne Fant, *Torkpojken: Lordagen den 12 mars 1932* (Stockholm: P. A. Norstedt & Söner, 1977); H. Lindgren, "The Kreuger Crash of 1932: In Memory of a Financial Genius, or Was He a Simple Swindler," *Scandinavian Economic History Review* 30:3 (1982): 189–202; Robert Shaplen, *Kreuger: Genius and Swindler* (New York: A. A. Knopf, 1960).

B. NORDSTROM

KRISTENSEN, KNUD (26 October 1880–28 September 1962) Danish Liberal Party leader

Knud Kristensen distinguished himself throughout his long career as an outspoken conservative and nationalist leader with a considerable interest in agriculture, church affairs, labor relations, and trade. He grew up in a household which had a strong attachment to the Liberal or Venstre Party and Grundtvigian principles of education. Partly as a result of this upbringing he attended an agricultural school for a year, read the works of Henry George extensively, and became actively involved in youth work within the Venstre Party.

From 1920 until the 1950s Kristensen served almost continuously as a member of the Folketing*, usually representing the town of Randers in North Jutland. By the mid-1930s he had become vice-chairman of the Venstre Party in the Folketing. He also served as a member of the finance committee during the late 1920s. Shortly after the German occupation he joined Thorvald Stauning's* government of national unity as a minister without portfolio. After the governmental reshuffling that took place on 8 July 1940, Kristensen became minister of interior, a post which he occupied until November 1942, when he left the cabinet in large part due to German pressure. While in the Stauning cabinet, Kristensen became an outspoken critic of German occupation policy and the Danish government's frequent tendency to accommodate the Germans. He expressed particular concern over the consequences resulting from Denmark's signature of the Anti-Comintern Pact. To a considerable extent his criticism of the

Anti-Comintern Pact led to his being branded as anti-German in Berlin and his eventual removal from a position of responsibility in the Danish government.

After the war Knud Kristensen once again became active in Danish politics. From October 1945 until October 1947 he served as prime minister in the Liberal-(Venstre) dominated government which entertained the possibility of expanding Danish influence into what were then the German-controlled portions of Slesvig (*see* North Slesvig). This policy was partly in response to entreaties of the Danish minority in that region and the chaotic postwar conditions in Germany. It led to a heated debate both within and outside the Folketing since the Social Democrats and Radicals traditionally opposed expansion into German-controlled Slesvig. The debate over Slesvig, along with various internal problems, resulted in replacement of Kristensen's government with one led by Hans Hedtoft, a Social Democrat, in November 1947.

Toward the end of his career Kristensen continued to be involved in Danish politics. For example, in 1953 he left the Liberal Party because of its support for the new constitution with its unicameral legislature. In that same year, he established and led the ultra-conservative Independent (Uafhaengig) Party, which continued to be a force to reckon with in Danish politics well into the 1960s. Also, in 1954 he published his political memoirs, which provided a provocative insight into the period of the occupation and its aftermath.

REFERENCES: B. A. Arneson, *The Democratic Monarchies of Scandinavia* (New York: D. Van Nostrand, 1939); V. Buhl et al., *Danmark, Besat og Befriet* (Copenhagen: Fremad, 1946); J. Bukdahl, *Scandinavia Past and Present, Through Revolutions to Liberty* (Odense: Arnkrone, 1959); K. Kristensen, *Set Fra Mine Vinduer, Kommentarer til Frem-stillingen af Begivenheder under og efter Besaettelsen* (Copenhagen: H. Hagerup, 1954).

J. L. VOORHIS

KRISTINA *See* Christina

KROG, JØRGINE (Gina) Anna Sverdrup (20 June 1847–14 April 1916) Norwegian feminist and activist

The daughter of parish minister Jørgen Sverdrup Krog and Ingeborg Anna Dass Brinchmann (d. 1872), Jørgine Krog was born in Flaskstad in Lofoten shortly after her father's death. The family moved to Karmøy a year later, and to Christiania when Gina was 8 years old.

Gina Krog was concerned about women's position in society even as a young girl. In her twenties she supported the Venstre Party and the ideas of the "modern breakthrough." She was influenced by the writings of Jacobine Camilla Collett*, by the English women's movement which she encountered during a trip to England, and especially by the activities of the American feminists Elizabeth Cady Stanton and Susan B. Anthony.

Krog worked as a schoolteacher for a time, but in the 1880s she gave up teaching to devote herself fully to the women's cause. In 1880 she began writing newspaper articles on women's rights, using a pseudonym at first. Some articles she wrote in 1884 for *Nyt Tidsskrift* (New Journal) attracted the notice of Hagbard E. Berner, who then collaborated with her and his wife to establish an organization to promote women's rights. The Norsk Kvindesagsforening (Norwegian Feminist Union*) was founded in June 1884, with H. E. Berner as president and Krog as a member of the governing council. In that same year, Gina Krog and Laura Rømche addressed the Students' Society, becoming the first women to speak publicly in Norway.

In a speech in November 1885, Krog called for voting rights for women equal to those enjoyed by men. At that time suffrage was restricted to men of a certain level of income. From then until her death, Krog was the leader of the Norwegian women's movement. She was much admired by younger feminists; she was knowledgeable, well read, energetic, stately, and impressive in public appearances; and she had no family responsibilities to distract her from the cause.

When the Norwegian Feminist Union leadership would not endorse her demand that women be granted suffrage rights on the same terms as men, she formed a new organization, open only to women, the Kvindestemmerettsforening (Women's Suffrage Union) in 1885 and became its first president. By 1889 it had grown to about 400 members.

In January 1887 the Norwegian Feminist Union began publishing *Nylaende* (*New Lands*) with the indefatigable Krog as editor and most frequent contributor. The paper was abandoned by the union as a financial failure in 1893, but Krog kept it going with her own funds. She ran the paper until 1916, when the Norwegian Feminist Union took it back.

In 1898 the Women's Suffrage Union divided over the vote issue. Krog and her supporters held to her original demand: suffrage for women on the same terms as men; the others supported a proposal to give women more limited voting rights. So Krog again founded a new organization, the Landskvinnestemmerettsforening (National Women's Suffrage Union), which pursued her original goal without flagging.

In 1899 Krog was the Norwegian delegate to the congress of the International Council of Women in London. She returned home with the responsibility for forming a national union of women's organizations which would become an affiliate of the International Council of Women. The Norske Kvinners Nasjonalråd (Norwegian Women's National Council) was formed in January 1904, and Krog served as president until her death. This organization represented women's interests to the government and the parliament.

Krog lived to see the fruits of her labors. In 1907 Norwegian women were granted limited suffrage, and in 1913 they won voting rights equal to those held by men.

Other causes that Krog supported included women's rights to preach in church and improved rights for children born out of wedlock. She was also more sensitive to the problems of working-class women than most of her women's movement colleagues. She was the first Norwegian woman to be buried at state expense.

REFERENCES: A. C. Agerholt, *Den norske kvinnebevegelses historie* (Oslo: Gyldendal Norsk, 1973); *NBL*, vol. 8.

N. FARQUHAR

L

LABOR PARTY: NORWAY *See* Norwegian Labor Party

LAESTADIANISM (1845–1900) An evangelical movement in Sweden and Finland

The Laestadian revival movement first appeared in 1845 in the Lapp parish of Karesundo. Led by Lars Levi Laestadius*, it was one of several Pietistic movements that developed in northern Sweden in the early and mid-1800s. Laestadianism spread along the Finnish-Swedish border and into the Swedish province of Norrbotten, where initially it was most popular among the Finnish-speaking people.

L. L. Laestadius preached of a new salvation which he felt could not take place within the confines of the dead beliefs of the state church. He rejected universal atonement through the Holy Sacrament and personal absolution through confirmation, because they were without true spiritual motivation. Baptism was also considered unnecessary, because each child was "born anew." His mission was to awaken all people to the power of the Holy Spirit and to Jesus Christ as a personal savior.

The *pånyttfödelse* or rebirth, in which the sinner would cast aside all earthly desires and replace them with a new heavenly passion, was a fundamental part of the revival. Each person experienced the transformation differently and, according to Laestadius, must have recognized two specific details as true documentation of the definitive moment of awakening. These were, first, when and how the transformation had taken place and, second, that they must have noted a separation from the physical world. It was a highly emotional experience in which the person saw Jesus Christ and felt Christ's blood as it washed away his sins. Vocal outbursts and body jerking were considered signs of the highest level of rebirth.

The person was also required to show personal repentance through the confession of his sins before the assembled congregation. Final absolution came from those that Laestadius termed the "true Christians," or those individuals who had experienced rebirth and were responsible for the continuing revival. It was this close relationship between the members that made Laestadianism popular among the peasant class.

In the 1870s a struggle regarding the righteousness of absolution began to take form. Laestadius emphasized individualistic salvation through the *pånytt-födelse*, while the newly emerging belief recognized the Holy Gospel and the literal Word of Jesus Christ as fundamental in bringing heavenly forgiveness.

The man responsible for this shift in ideology was Johan Raatamaa. He claimed that salvation must be taught through what was known as "the two keys." These keys were called "to preach the law" and "to preach repentance." This method of instructing the individual in repentance reformed traditional Laestadian thought, and it also represented a closer association with official Lutheranism*. The internal disputes continued into the 1880s and ultimately divided the Laestadians into two factions. In the 1890s the Laestadian revival movement split into two distinct groups, and by 1897 it was clear that there would never be a reconciliation between the two.

REFERENCES: O. Brännström, *Den Laestadianska Själavårdstraditionen i Sverige under 1800–talet* (Uppsala: Appelbergs Boktryckeri AB, 1962); G.Dahlbäck, *Den Gamla och Den Nya i Lars Levi Laestadius' Teologi* (Lund: CWK Gleerup, 1950); G. W. Lindeberg, "Laestadianer," in *Svenska Uppslagsbok*, vol. 17 (Malmö: Nordens Boktryckeri, 1949); M. Persson, "Laestadius," in *Svenska Uppslagsbok*,vol. 17 (Malmö: Nordens Boktryckeri, 1949).

                                                                              B. BENSON

LAESTADIUS, LARS LEVI (10 January 1800–21 February 1861) Swedish-Finnish Lutheran pastor and revival leader

Born at Arjeplog in northern Sweden in 1800, Laestadius studied theology at Uppsala and was ordained in 1825 as pastor in Sweden's most northern parish of Karesuanto. His parishioners were Lapps* and Finns living in Swedish Lappland. During his day, Laestadius was recognized as the leading authority in the flora and fauna of Lappland and was honored by the Scientific Academy in Paris with the Order of the Legion of Science.

A series of personal tragedies led to a spiritual crisis in which the learned clergyman-scientist received assurance of salvation through a simple Lapp girl named Mary. Laestadius's priorities were now altered and his revivalist career begun. Whether Lappland was as spiritually dark as the long winters for which it is famous is hard to tell, but there is no doubt that alcoholism was a curse upon the land. As a sign of their conversion, Laestadius demanded of his people complete abstinence from alcohol. As the Laestadian revival spread (*see* Laestadianism), its greatest following came to center in Finland, where Lutheran clergy and bishops are numbered within its ranks to this day.

That which distinguishes Laestadius's movement from other Scandinavian revival movements is the practice of individual public confession before the congregation and/or private confession before a respected Lutheran pastor or layperson, followed by the pronouncement of absolution with the laying on of hands. So great was the sorrow over sin and the joy of forgiveness that the Laestadian worship experience has at times been characterized as ecstatic. During the last decade of his ministry at Pajala, Laestadius sought to keep the movement from degenerating into fanaticism. Wise lay and clergy leadership since Laestadius's death in 1861 has not allowed this to happen, and the movement has remained within the Lutheran State Church of Finland. In the United States, however, the Laestadians have formed their own church, known as the Finnish Apostolic Lutheran Church.

REFERENCES: T. Harjumpaa et al., "Finnish Lutheran Theology," *Lutheran Quarterly* 28 (November 1976): 290–377; Aapeli Saarisalo, *Laestadius-Pohjolan Pasuuna* (Helsinki: Werner Söderström Osakeyhtio, 1970); William Snell, *Hågkomster av Prosten Lars Levi Laestadius och Laestadianskt Fromhetsliv* (Stockholm, 1965).

T. R. SKARSTEN

LAGMAND Faroese legal official

The origin of the office of *lagmand* (Faroese: *lögmaður*) in the Faroe Islands* is unknown. *Færeyinga Saga*, purporting to relate affairs in the islands in the early eleventh century, names a certain *Gilli lögmaðr* or *lögsögumaðr*. It is difficult to judge how well informed the writer of the saga was about Faroese conditions, especially since he was writing his account about two centuries after the events. It is, however, possible that the Faroe Islands had a *lagmand* before the country became subject to the Norwegian crown.

Seyðabrævið (*see Sheep Letter*), the Faroese sheep law of 1298, states that its terms were drawn up after consultation with Erlendr*, the bishop of Faroe, and Sigurdr, *lögmaðr* of Shetland. The conclusion of some writers that at this time the Faroes had a *lagmand* in common with Shetland, however, appears doubtful. All the same, the Faroes must have had a *lagmand* by this time, since they were subject to Norwegian law, and from about 1400 there occur scattered references to holders of the office.

In 1555 the farm *á Steig* in Sandavágur was appointed as stipendiary manor for the Faroese *lagmand*, and from this time frequent references occur to the holder of the office, who by then supervised the high court sessions, the Faroese *Lagting**, in Tórshavn*. The office was a royal appointment. Until 1769 the *lagmand* was nearly always a wealthy Faroese peasant. Between 1769 and 1804 the office was held by an Icelander and two Norwegians, all trained jurists. From 1805 until 1816 a Faroeman of a family of officials held the post. In 1816 the office was abolished, and appeals at law that formerly were heard by the *lagmand* went to Copenhagen*.

REFERENCES: P. G. Foote, "On Legal Terms in Færeyinga Saga," *Fróðskaparrit* 18 (1970): 159–75, and *On the Saga of the Faroe Islanders* (London: University College

London, 1965); G. Johnston, *The Faroe Islanders' Saga* (Canada: Oberon Press, 1975); *Seyðabrævið* (Tórshavn: Föroya Fróðskaparfelag, 1971).

J. F. WEST

LAGTING, FAROESE

The earliest mention of a provincial assembly in the Faroe Islands* occurs in *Færeyinga Saga*, which says that it meets in Tórshavn* and that it accepted Christianity in 999, but gives it no specific title. Despite the unreliability of the saga as a historical source, there seems to be little doubt that an assembly did exist before the islands became tributary to Norway, and perhaps from the earliest days of settlement.

The text of *Seyðabrævið* (*see Sheep Letter*), the Faroese sheep law of 1298, refers to the lawbook which Magnus VI Haakonsson* issued and men accepted at the Althing. This suggests an assembly comparable with the Icelandic Althing*, having both legislative and judicial powers. The phrase *a logþingi* ("in the Lagting") appears, however, in two Faroese laws dated about 1400, and it may be presumed that the assembly by this time was fulfilling the same functions as the bodies of the same name in mainland Norway.

The records of the Faroese Lagting (known in the Faroese language as Lögting) have survived from 1615. At least one earlier volume has been lost. At this period the court consisted of the *lagmand** or chief justice, the *sorenskriver* or recorder, who combined the functions of underjudge and notary, and 36 *lagrettesmaend* or assessors, 6 from each *syssel* or law district.

The court of first instance was the Vaarting or Hjemting (spring sessions or home sessions). This consisted of the *sorenskriver* and the six *lagrettesmaend* of the district in question. These district courts were held in Vágur (now Klaksvík) for the Northern Islands; Selatrað for Eysturoy; Kollafjörður for Streymoy; Midvágur for Vágar; Sandur for Sandoy; and Öravík for Suðuroy. They took place from March to May and normally lasted three or four days.

Cases of too great a nature to be determined at these district courts, or cases appealed from them, were sent to the Lagting, which met annually in Tórshavn on St. Olaf's Day, 29 July. Here the *lagmand* was judge, the *sorenskriver* judicial clerk, and the assessors acted as jury, the six from the appropriate *syssel* for minor cases, or twelve in capital or other major cases. The law administered in the earliest period recorded in the Lagting protocols was the Norwegian Law of Christian IV*, published in 1604, which was in fact no more than a translation of the Lano Law of King Magnus VI Haakonsson (Lagaböter).

The Norwegian Law of Christian V* came into force in the Faroes in 1688. The *sorenskriver* was now specifically recognized as sole judge of first instance, and the function of the *lagrettesmaend*, now increased in number to eight per *syssel*, was effectively reduced from that of advisors to that of mere witnesses.

The Lagting had other functions besides that of hearing civil and criminal lawsuits. It acted as a channel of communication between the king and the population of the islands at large. Ordinances issued by the king were proclaimed in the Lagting, and the Lagting would at times draft petitions and complaints to be sent to the king. Each year the Lagting and the public present were asked whether the supplies brought by the Faroese Monopoly* had been adequate, whether the trading staff had conducted themselves in a proper and amicable manner toward the inhabitants, whether they had any complaints against the *sysselmaend* (district sheriffs), and whether they had any complaints against the barber (i.e., the doctor). Any official returning to Denmark would take a public testimonial from the Lagting, certifying that there were no outstanding complaints against him.

The legislative power of the Lagting, as revealed by the law records from 1615 onwards, was more limited than it had been in the thirteenth century. It passed regulations of a highly local nature and confirmed traditional practices.

The crown interests were taken care of by the *landfoged* (high bailiff). He was prosecutor in criminal cases, though the *sysselmand* often acted on his behalf in the former. The *landfoged*, the *lagmand*, and the *sorenskriver* were royal appointments; the *sysselmaend* were nominees of the *landfoged*, as were the *lagrettesmaend*.

During the eighteenth century, the cases brought before the Lagting became fewer in number and smaller in importance. As part of a series of administrative and judicial reforms throughout the Danish realm, the Lagting was abolished in 1816. Faroese lawsuits on appeal henceforth went directly from the Vaarting to the Supreme Court in Copenhagen*. The post of *lagmand* was abolished, and the stipendiary farm of Steig was sold. At the same time, the Faroe Islands gained a further resident official, the *amtmand* or provincial governor, in direct contact with the administrative colleges in Copenhagen, and through them, with the king.

The constitutional reforms within the Danish kingdom which started in 1831 had repercussions in the Faroe Islands. The Faroes were represented in the Roskilde Assembly by crown nominees, not elected members. However, all were men of ability and goodwill, with first-hand experience as officials. The Faroes gained an elected member for both the Folketing* and the Landsting from 1851 onwards, and among the earliest reforms enacted were the abolition of the Monopoly and the revival of the Lagting.

As revived in 1852, the Lagting had relatively limited powers, with direct authority over certain essentially local matters, such as the administration of church estates and poor-law funds, and the regulations concerning the ferrying of goods and travelers from island to island. Politically, it was only an advisory body. Executive power remained in the hands of the *amtmand*, and legislative power remained with the Landsting and Folketing in Copenhagen.

The composition of the Lagting was at first sixteen, later eighteen members, together with the *amtmand* and provost, who sat ex-officio. After initial difficulties through a clash between the elected members and the *amtmand*, Faroese politics settled down to a tranquil phase. Relations between the Lagting and the Danish parliament were aided by the provision in the 1866 constitutional changes in Denmark that the Landsting member for the Faroes should henceforth be chosen by the Lagting, while direct popular vote continued to select the member for the Folketing.

Polarization of the Lagting on party lines arose through the early career of Jóannes Patursson*, who in 1903 launched a program of greater autonomy for the Faroe Islands and greater control over local affairs by the Lagting. In 1906 the first two Faroese parties were formed, the Sambandsflokkurin, or Unionist Party, and the Sjálvstýrisflokkurin, or Home Rule Party. The Home Rulers wanted increased financial powers for the Lagting and the right to approve or reject any legislation passed by the Danish parliament applying solely to Faroe. Finally, they wanted as wide a use as possible of the Faroese language and its admission to equal status with Danish for all uses within the islands.

Until 1928 there was generally a Unionist majority in the Lagting, which steered through a number of economic reforms, such as telephone and telegraph systems, harbor works in Tórshavn and elsewhere, and the beginnings of a road system. The Unionists maintained close relations with the Danish Venstre, while the Home Rulers allied themselves with *det Radikale Venstre*.

In 1923 reforms were passed excluding the *amtmand* and provost from ex-officio membership in the Lagting, introducing a measure of proportional representation into the electoral system, and giving the Lagting somewhat enlarged powers financially, especially as regards communications within the islands. Women already had the vote, as Faroese women shared the benefit of the Danish emancipation of 1915. But in general the Lagting remained a body proposing legislation to the Danish parliament rather than one with extensive authority in its own hands.

From 1925 the pattern of Faroese politics became more complex with the formation of the Faroese Social Democratic Party, Javnaðarflokkurin. It achieved its first success in the 1922 Lagting elections, winning 2 of the 23 seats. In 1936 a fourth party entered the Lagting, the Vinnuflokkurin or Economic Party, with right-wing policies. These developments severely curtailed the power of the original two parties based on nationalist attitudes and introduced a pattern of politics in which alliances tended to be formed by soft-pedaling one spectrum of party difference in order to pursue common policies in the other. The Home Rule Party split in 1939 on a land reform issue, and Jóannes Patursson and many of his followers joined the Economic Party, which was now renamed Fólkaflokkurin, the People's Party, which took a right-wing stance on economic matters and favored secession from Denmark.

Early on 9 April 1940, news came of the German occupation of Denmark, and on 12 April the British began the occupation of the Faroes. The islands were thus cut off from the Danish government, and a temporary form of administration had to be introduced. The *amtmand* took over administrative action demanded by the law, in consultation with a Lagting committee. New legislation applicable to the islands had to be debated in the Lagting and confirmed by the *amtmand*.

The British interfered as little as possible with the internal administration of the islands.

During the war, despite public sympathy for Denmark, Faroese opinion swung toward separatism, and the People's Party almost gained a majority in the 1943 elections, a position maintained in the election of 6 November 1945. Protracted negotiations took place with the Danish government; an inconclusive referendum was held; and the final outcome was the Home Rule Ordinance of 23 March 1948, in which the Faroe Islands became "within the framework of the law, a self-governing community within the Danish kingdom." Internal administration passed into the hands of the Lagting on an ingenious sliding system and the Lagting was to choose a government for the islands, known in Danish as Landsstyret, in Faroese as Landsstýrið. Foreign affairs and defense remain in the hands of the Danish state, and the Faroe Islands are still represented in the Danish parliament.

Six parties are now represented in the Lagting. The four largest, of approximately equal strength, are Sambandsflokkurin (moderate right-wing and unionist), Javnaðarflokkurin (moderate left-wing and unionist), Fólkaflokkurin (right-wing and separatist), and Tjóðveldisflokkurin (left-wing and separatist). The last-named party, the Republican Party, was founded in 1948 and takes the view that the referendum of 14 September 1946 should legally have led to the secession of the Faroes from Denmark. The two smaller parties are Sjálvstýrisflokkurin (centrist and autonomist) and Framburðsflokkurin, the Progress Party (very right-wing and separatist). The last-named party has lately formed an alliance with the inshore fishermen's association.

The ancient title of lagmand (in Faroese *lögmaður*) now denotes the head of the Faroese local government.

REFERENCES: G. Johnston, *The Faroe Islanders' Saga* (Canada: Oberon Press, 1975); *Seyðabraevið* (Tórshavn: Föroya Fróðskaparfelag, 1971); J. F. West, *Faroe, the Emergence of a Nation* (London: C. Hurst; New York: Paul S. Eriksson, 1972).

J. F. WEST

LANDOWNERSHIP

At the end of the Middle Ages, ownership of land in Scandinavia* was shared between the Church, the crown, the nobility, and the peasantry. Of these, the Church was by far the largest landlord in the area as a whole and in most of the states (with 47 percent of the farms in Iceland and the Faroe Islands*, about 44 percent in Norway, and over 30 percent in Denmark). The exception was Finland, where over 90 percent of the farms were in peasant hands. The Reformation* caused drastic changes in this respect. Most church land was confiscated by Lutheran monarchs and added to their hitherto quite modest holdings. In Denmark royal land came consequently to account for over half the total, and in Norway about one-third. In Denmark this upheaval, coupled with the revival of agriculture, encouraged the formation of large unified holdings, partly by means of exchanges between crown and nobility and partly at the cost of the peasantry, whose share of farms had been reduced to about 3 percent by the middle of the seventeenth century. The crown's financial difficulties, however, led it after the introduction of absolutism in 1661 to begin to sell off much of its property in both Denmark and Norway. In Denmark the main beneficiaries were the bourgeoisie, who had previously been barred from landownership, but who by 1688 owned over 16 percent of the land based on its taxable value. In Norway, where the nobility had never been prominent land owners and where large estates were almost unknown, much former royal land came into the hands of the peasantry, which by the middle of the eighteenth century owned over half its taxable value, concentrated in the east of the country.

In Sweden the crown began to dispose of both its landed estates and its right to the taxes paid by peasant proprietors as early as the late sixteenth century, a process that accelerated rapidly during the reign of Queen Christina* (1632–1654), until over 63 percent of Swedish farms and over half of all Finnish farms became noble property—a number of them gathered into large, compact estates, although these were less common in Sweden and Finland than in Denmark and were largely confined to the most favored agricultural areas. Karl X* began a partial *reduktion* (resumption of lands and revenues), but it was his son, Karl XI*, who in 1680 commenced a much more drastic *reduktion*, which continued until the end of the century, when the nobility's share was down to a third. This only indirectly favored the peasants, whose share was less than before the alienation process began. In Finland, as a result of the *reduktion*, the natural disasters of the 1690s, and the Great Northern War*, the crown held about 70 percent of all farms by 1720. In the early eighteenth century, however, the peasant tenants of the crown were enabled to buy their freehold by *skatteköp*, so that by 1772, when the concession was temporarily withdrawn, nearly 47 percent of farms in Sweden were peasant freehold. At the same time, much noble land came into the hands of the bourgeoisie, although it was not until 1809 that manorial land in Sweden could legally pass out of noble hands.

Much more dramatic was the change in landownership in Denmark at the end of the eighteenth century and the beginning of the nineteenth century. There the peasantry, which in 1790 owned little more land than a century before, had by 1835 acquired freehold of over half the farms in the kingdom.

REFERENCES: K. Ågren, "The *reduktion*," in M. Roberts, ed., *Sweden's Age of Greatness 1632–1718* (London: Macmillan, 1973); A. Holmsen, "The Transition from Tenancy to Freehold Peasant Ownership in Norway," *Scandinavian Economic History Review* 9 (1961): 152–64; F. Skrubbeltrang, "Developments in Tenancy in Eighteenth-Century Denmark as a Move Towards Peasant Proprietorship," *Scandinavian Economic History Review* 9 (1961): 165–75; K. Tønneson, "Tenancy, Freehold and Enclosure in Scandinavia from the Seventeenth to the Nineteenth Century," *Scandinavian Journal of History* 6 (1981): 191–206.

S. P. OAKLEY

Norway

From a presumed point of departure in the pre-Viking period when peasant ownership predominated, a tenancy system emerged in Norway as a result of the population pressures during the Viking Age* and the donation of land to the Church in the first three Christian centuries. According to the latest estimates, the distribution of land in the first half of the fourteenth century in terms of value was 7 percent crown, 20 percent lay aristocracy, 40 percent Church, and 33 percent freeholding peasants and burghers. The tenant in legal terms was free; there was no serfdom in medieval Norway. Law texts refer to short-term leases, but most surviving contracts, which date from around 1300, are leases for life. (Lifetime leases clearly became customary later and became law in 1604.)

The decline in population* resulting from the Black Death (from about 400,000 to less than 200,000) eased the condition of the surviving peasantry but did not radically alter the distribution of land, which before the Reformation is estimated to have been as follows: crown 4 percent, Church 44 percent, nobility 12 percent, and peasants (and some burghers) 40 percent. As a result of the Reformation, the crown established itself as the predominant land owner. In 1661, when, because of serious financial troubles facing the state, the crown began to sell much of its land, 31 percent of the land value was classified as crown holdings; another 21 percent was reserved for the service of the State Lutheran Church. Crown holdings were sold in large blocks, primarily to war creditors, who also acquired interests in the sawmilling and metal industries. Within a few decades the big proprietors started to resell to tenants. Combined with the disintegration of noble landholding, this triggered a transition to freehold. By 1820 the peasants' share had risen to 65 percent, as against 20 percent for other private owners (15 percent was in state hands as public lands, and this category had all but disappeared by 1900).

For a proper understanding of the eighteenth-century transition to freehold, the traditional practice of joint proprietorship without physical division of the farm—a kind of primitive mortgage system—is important. Large land holdings in Norway almost invariably consisted of complexes of scattered farms and *farmparts*. The law required that the largest co-proprietor—or in the case of parity the one of highest social standing—enjoy the right to decide who would be the user of the farm. Transition to freehold largely meant that tenants, who were already part-owners, bought the controlling interest in the farm they used. Because land rent, which was regulated by law, could not be increased at will, and because land prices rose under pressure from the rising population, it was profitable for the large owners to sell farms or farm-parts against a modern mortgage. For the tenants, purchase, even at high prices, was advisable to avoid the risk of falling into the growing rural proletariat.

For centuries the peasant family's ownership had been protected by two still vigorous institutions: primogeniture (established by law in 1539) and *odel*, the right of family members to buy back, within a fixed period of time and at a price decided by a jury, a farm which had been sold out of the family. Primogeniture, however, was not evenly practiced in all regions. Under population pressures farms in western Norway particularly were divided and subdivided. In the richer agricultural and forest districts the setting up of new households was facilitated rather by establishing dependent smallholdings whose occupiers (*husmenn*) were usually bound to work on the main farm. This practice reached a peak in the mid-nineteenth century and then was gradually abolished. The *husmenn*-holdings were transformed into full-property smallholdings.

At present freehold farming is predominant and is protected by a 1974 law which makes the acquisition of a farm through purchase or inheritance conditional upon the willingness and ability of the individual to live on the farm and work it. (*See also* Enclosure; Inheritance Practices.)

REFERENCES: K. Helle, "Norway in the High Middle Ages: Recent Views on the Structure of Society," *Scandinavian Journal of History* 6 (1981): 161–89; A. Holmsen, "The Transition from Tenancy to Freehold Peasant Ownership in Norway," *Scandinavian Economic History Review* 9 (1961): 152–64; K. Tønnesson, "Tenancy, Freehold and Enclosure in Scandinavia from the Seventeenth to the Nineteenth Century," *Scandinavian Journal of History* 6 (1981): 191–206.

K. TØNNESSON

LAND REGISTERS Surveys of taxable land in Denmark drawn up in the 1660s and 1680s

The establishment of absolutism in Denmark occurred partly as a result of the collapse of state finances produced by the wars against Sweden in the 1640s and 1650s. In order to restore some degree of financial credibility, the crown proceeded to alienate much of its landed property to creditors and private land owners in the following decades, but the resulting loss of income, coupled with chronic revenue shortfalls, forced the crown to seek a more substantial base of taxation, along lines already suggested by the third estate at the Estates General of 1660.

A provisional survey register (*matrikel*) of taxable land was compiled hurriedly during 1661–1662, in which all land was measured in *tønder hartkorn* (barrels of grain yield equivalents, not land area), worked out on the basis of existing lists of annual rents payable on peasant tenancies, combined with assessments for demesnes. The first *matrikel* tax was imposed in July 1662, even before the new register was complete, but the assessment proved so inaccurate that a revision was ordered in February 1663. This was more successful from a bureaucratic point of view, but the resulting register of 1664 was still uneven. Nevertheless, it provided the basis for a number of different taxes (known as *hartkorn* taxes) in the next two decades. Seigneurial demesnes were temporarily exempt from 1670 to 1682, but thereafter only very large estates could obtain demesne exemption by special privilege.

The Scanian War and the exchequer reforms of Henrik von Støcken after 1679 led to plans for a new and much more thorough survey, and in 1681 work was begun on a complete valuation of all land in the kingdom. This was carried out by teams of qualified surveyors paid by the crown and assisted by groups of carefully chosen peasants in each area. The size and productivity of each holding or estate was to be measured, its arable land and grazing valued, and other real or potential assets noted. The new *hartkorn* scale would take into account not only the fertility of the soil but also the system of rotation used. Not surprisingly, the work took longer than expected, and a special tax had to be levied to cover the costs; but the final register, known as Christian V's* Matrikel of 1688, was nevertheless a major administrative and technical achievement. The total *hartkorn* rating for much of the kingdom was lower than the corresponding 1664 figures, but overall the new register was certainly both fairer and, in spite of certain shortcomings, more accurate. Christian V's Matrikel became the definitive basis for the wide range of *hartkorn* land taxes on which the precarious finances of Danish absolutism depended, and it was not replaced until 1844. In addition, the very substantial survey archive has provided a rich source of detailed information for research in agrarian history.

REFERENCES: C. S. Christiansen, *Bidrag til dansk Statshusholdnings Historie*, vols. 1, 2 (Copenhagen: Nordisk Forfatteres Forlag, 1908–1922); C. Rise Hansen and A. Steensberg, *Jordfordeling og udskiftning* (Copenhagen: Kgl. Videnskabernes Selskab/ Munksgaard, 1951); H. Hjelholt, "Den jyske landmålingsmatrikel," *Sml. til Jydsk Historie og Topografi*, 4RIII (1917–1919): 397–424; T. Munck, *The Peasantry and the Early Absolute Monarchy in Denmark, 1660–1708* (Copenhagen: Landbohistorisk Selskab, 1979); H. Pedersen, *Det danske Landbrug fremstillet paa Grundlag af Forarbejderne til Christian V's Matrikel 1688* (Copenhagen: Nordisk Forlag/Gyldendal, 1928, repr. 1975); F. Skrubbeltrang, *Det danske Landbosamfund 1500–1800* (Copenhagen: Dansk Historisk Fællesforening, 1978), and "Studier over gårde, gårdbrugerantal og brugsstørrelser i det 17 årh.," *Historisk Tidsskrift* (Copenhagen) 12RV (1971): 1–51.

T. MUNCK

LANGUAGES: SCANDINAVIAN

The Scandinavian languages represent the northern branch of the Germanic language family. The West-Germanic branch includes German, English, and Dutch; the East-Germanic branch includes Gothic, but no living language. The Germanic group is one branch of the vast Indo-European language family, which includes languages as diverse as Sanskrit, Greek, Russian, Latvian, Gaelic, and French. The Semitic, African, American Indian, and Oriental languages are not part of this Indo-European family. While spoken in Nordic countries, Finnish, Samic (Lappish), and Greenlandic are not related to the Indo-European languages.

Historical linguists have shown that the Indo-European languages developed from a single language called Proto-Indo-European (PIE). There are no documents in this hypothetically reconstructed language, and one can only theorize about when and where it was spoken.

The development of the Germanic languages out of PIE, begun by 2,000 B.C., involved the following changes, among others (the asterisk before a sound or word means that it has been reconstructed, never attested):

1. Grimm's law (First Germanic consonant shift)

    PIE *p > Gmc. f [cf. Latin *pater*, English father]

    PIE *t > Gmc. th [cf. Latin *tres*, English three].

2. Fixing of stress on word's first syllable.

3. Noun cases reduced from eight to four.

4. Verbal aspect replaced by tense.

5. Development of weak past tense for verbs (those that end in a -d or -t in English.

6. Reduction of inventory of long and short vowels (5 to 4 each).

Controversy remains concerning the chronology of the Germanic split into North, East, and West. The following are representative changes which distinguish North Germanic (i.e., Scandinavian) from the other Germanic dialects:

1. Several types of vowel mutations based on the influence of a nearby sound [ProtoGmc *gastiR> Old Norse gestr 'guest'].

2. Development of a suffixed definite article for nouns [Old Norse dagrinn 'the day'].

3. Restructuring of the syllable system (vowel and consonant length and reduction or loss of final syllable).

4. Loss of w and j in certain environments [Old Norse orð; English word].

Our knowledge of the language after the break-up of the Germanic proto-language stems from runic inscriptions (see Runes), proper names mentioned in contemporary Latin, Greek, and Arabic sources, words borrowed and preserved in Finnish and Samic, place-names, and linguistic reconstruction based on a comparison of preserved forms.

North Germanic split into two geographical subgroups, East Scandinavian (Old Danish and Old Swedish) and West Scandinavian (Old Icelandic, Old Norwegian and Old Faroese). East Scandinavian simplified diphthongs to monophthongs [Old Icelandic ey, Old Swedish ö 'island']. The east maintains long o in words where the west shows long u [Icelandic brú, Swedish and Danish bro 'bridge'].

During the period of Viking* expansion and settlement, some form of Scandinavian was spoken in parts of Greenland*, England, Scotland, Ireland, the Shetlands, Orkneys, Hebrides, Man, Normandy, around the Baltic, and into Russia. English has kept a number of Scandinavian loan words including they, husband, and sky since that time.

Currently, speakers of the mainland Scandinavian languages (Danish, Norwegian, and Swedish) can generally understand each other, with clear pronunciation and some good will. Danes and Swedes usually have the hardest time, due to substantial differences in pronunciation. Icelanders and Faroese must use one of the mainland languages if they wish to be understood by their mainland neighbors. To further inter-language communication, the Nordic Language Secretariat (Nordisk Språksekretariat), based in Oslo, encourages cooperation among the national language commissions.

REFERENCES: E. Haugen, A Bibliography of Scandinavian Languages and Linguistics 1900–1970 (Oslo: Universitetsforlaget, 1974), Scandinavian Language Structures: A Comparative Historical Survey (Minneapolis: University of Minnesota Press, 1982), The Scandinavian Languages, Wisconsin Introductions to Scandinavia, No. 1–2 (Madison: Department of Scandinavian Studies), and The Scandinavian Languages: An Introduction to Their History (London: Faber and Faber; Cambridge, Mass.: Harvard University Press,

1976); M. I. Steblin-Kamenskij, *Istorija skandinavskich jazykov* (Moscow, 1953); M. O'C Walshe, *Introduction to the Scandinavian Languages* (London: Deutsch, 1965); E. Wessen, *De nordiska språken* (Stockholm: Almqvist and Wiksell, 1965).

L. JANUS

Danish

Danish and Swedish comprise the East Scandinavian language group. Now spoken throughout Denmark and as the second official language on the Faroe Islands* and Greenland, Danish was once also the written standard in Norway. Parts of present-day Sweden, including Skåne, were under Danish rule until the mid-seventeenth century and were part of the Danish-speaking region.

Runic inscriptions, showing little variation throughout Scandinavia*, represent the earliest specimens of Danish. Manuscripts preserve early provincial laws from Skåne, Sjaelland, and Jutland from the thirteenth century. In these clear differences emerge between Danish and the West Scandinavian dialects (Icelandic, Faroese, and Old Norwegian). For example, diphthongs have been reduced [Old Icelandic *steinn*; Old Danish *stén* 'stone']. The Danish forms show a lack of u-mutation in words like *sak* 'case' compared to Icelandic *søk*. Also, certain verb forms show i-mutation in West Scandinavian, but not in Danish: *takær* versus the Icelandic *tekr* 'takes'. In some of these early documents (especially in central Denmark, but not Skåne) the unstressed -a, -i, and -u in word endings have been weakened and merged into a neutral vowel (usually written æ). This weakening was earlier and more widespread throughout the system than in Swedish. The reshaping of grammatical classes goes hand in hand with the weakening of word endings. The accusative and dative cases of nouns, for example, began to merge together and in time merged with the nominative, leaving only two cases, normal and genitive. Feminine and masculine nouns lost their distinctive endings, leaving two genders.

A most important change took place in the pronunciation of consonants. Voiceless stops were generally weakened so that p > b, t > d, and k > g except where these were word-initial. Occasionally, the b, d, and g were further weakened to become fricatives. During the Middle Ages and Reformation*, Danish expanded its vocabulary by borrowing terms chiefly from Low and High German, but also from Latin and French. New words were adapted for commerce, handicrafts, government, culture, and religion. The first Danish version of the New Testament was published in 1524. In 1550 a more consistent translation, the *Christian III Bible*, was published. This version took full advantage of the richness of the native Danish vocabulary.

When a degree of orthographic uniformity was established during the 1700s, many of the patterns were inconsistently applied. Thus, in Danish (as in English) frequently the written form only gives an indication of the actual pronunciation. In addition, extra letters were added in an attempt to show the etymology of words. Occasionally this led to spellings like *mand* 'man' which never had a *d*. Danish did not raise and front back rounded vowels as Swedish and Norwegian did, so that it has maintained what is frequently called the "continental" vowel system.

Ludvig Holberg's writings in the eighteenth century had a marked influence on the development of modern Danish. He is credited with creating a new, forward-looking style, with fewer archaisms, and he had no fear of using foreign words when they made his expressions clearer. As Copenhagen* became the political, economic, and cultural center of Denmark, the language of royal affairs became the national standard. Large dialect areas, however, still preserve many regional speech patterns.

The Danish alphabet adds æ, ø, and å after z. Before 1948 aa was generally used instead of å, and all nouns began with capital letters. C, q, w, x, and z are chiefly used in foreign words and names.

REFERENCES: J. Brøndum-Nielsen, *Gammeldansk Grammatik i sproghistorisk Fremstilling*, 5 vols. (Copenhagen: Akademisk forlag, 1928–1965); V. Dahlerup, *Det danske Sprogs Historie i almenfattelig Fremstilling* (Copenhagen: Schultz, 1921); E. Haugen, *Scandinavian Language Structures: A Comparative Historical Survey* (Minneapolis: University of Minnesota Press, 1982), and *The Scandinavian Languages: An Introduction to Their History* (London: Faber and Faber; Cambridge, Mass.: Harvard University Press, 1976); P. Skautrup, *Det danske sprogs historie*, 5 vols. (Copenhagen: Gyldendal, 1944–1970).

L. JANUS

Faroese

The Faroe Islands, together with Norway and Iceland, form a West Scandinavian linguistic area, which in earlier times also included the Shetland Islands and the Orkney Islands. Like Icelandic, Faroese is a Norwegian immigrant language, but loan words and place-names give evidence of early Celtic contacts.

Written medieval sources are few in number and brief. Two runic inscriptions from Kirkjubøur* and Sandavágur date from 1000 and 1200 respectively. Some judicial documents have been preserved, the most important of which is *Seyðabrævið* (1298; *see Sheep Letter*), which has survived in several versions. Linguistically, the manuscripts are Norwegian with distinct Faroese features. From the fifteenth century there exist transcriptions of the *Húsavík Charters*, which were issued in the first half of the century. The administrative literature from the sixteenth and seventeenth centuries is written in Danish but contains lexical materials important to the language's history. In the Faroe Islands there was no consistent written tradition in the Middle Ages.

The Faroese ballad tradition is of great value to Faroese language history. The texts were excellently recorded by Jens Christian Svabo* in a phonetically based orthography. The phonetic and morphological information of Svabo was used by Rasmus Rask (1787–1832) in his *Vejledning til det Islandske eller gamle Nordiske Sprog* (1811), which contained the first printed Faroese grammar. Svabo's ballad records are, together with his Faroese-Danish-Latin dictionary, the main historical sources about the Faroese language.

In 1846 a more consistent orthography was suggested, based on Old Norse. This etymological orthography is connected with Vencelaus Ulricus Hammershaimb*, who published a Faroese grammar and *Faerøsk Anthologi* (1854 and 1891, respectively). The establishment of a written language has been of decisive literary, political, and ideological importance for the Faroese people.

As a West Scandinavian dialect, Faroese has certain features in common with Icelandic and in particular West Norwegian dialects. Some changes within the sound system of Faroese ought to be mentioned, and these should be seen against the background of Old Norse. First, a quantity shift occurred in the syllable system in the sixteenth century. Thereby, all stressed syllables became equally long. Originally short vowels were lengthened before short consonants, and originally long vowels were shortened before long consonants. The originally long vowels (*í, ý, ae, ú, ó, á*) were diphthongized in the sixteenth century. The original diphthongs were preserved (*au, ei*, and *ey*/now spelled *ey, ei*, and *oy*, respectively). Furthermore, there were a number of separate changes within the original short vowel system. In addition, there are vowel differences within Faroese dialects, and some of these date from the Middle Ages. Generally, a northern, central, and southern dialect area can be identified, and the main isogloss runs between the central and southern areas.

Second, in the consonant system a number of changes that deserve mention can be traced back to the Middle Ages. Initial *Þ* becomes *t* or *h* before 1400. The change of *-ll, -rl* to -[*ḍl*] and *-nn, -rn* to -[*ḍn*] dates presumably to the fourteenth century. The development of *g, k*, and *sk* into *j, c*, and *ʃ* before palatal vocals is late medieval. The "sharpening" (*verschärfung*) after long vowels or diphthongs is possibly late medieval. The loss of the medial and final ð is post-medieval.

Morphologically, Faroese retains the personal endings of the verbs and four cases in the nominal declension. The genitive is to a large extent substituted by prepositional phrases using *í, á*, and *hjá*. A semantically complex system has developed in the use of other prepositions, for example *fryi* and *við*. Faroese is clearly an inflecting language, but morphological simplifications have led to a partially isolating language structure (cf. Danish). Although the written language tends to be puristic, lexically and syntactically the spoken language is strongly influenced by Danish. The Faroese language is, however, to be considered an autonomous linguistic unit.

REFERENCES: Oskar Bandle, *Die Gliederung des Nordgermanischen* (Basel and Stuttgart, 1973); E. Haugen, *The Scandinavian Languages* (Cambridge, Mass.: Harvard University Press, 1976); W. B. Lockwood, *An Introduction to Modern Faroese* (Copenhagen, 1955, 1977); C. Matras et al., eds., *Seydabraevid* (Torshavn, 1971); J. F. West, *Faroe: The Emergence of a Nation* (London and New York: P. Eriksson, 1972).

K.- E. PEDERSEN

Finnish

Following five centuries of Swedish domination, Finnish, the majority language in Finland (93 percent today), emerged as an acceptable literary idiom with the publication of Elias Lönnrot's *Kalevala** in 1835. Largely because of the pioneering efforts of J. V. Snellman, Finnish also slowly gained legal and administrative status; in 1863 Tsar Alexander II decreed that equal status between

Finnish and Swedish was to obtain within 20 years. Prior to these events printed Finnish had been used principally for religious texts; in 1548 the New Testament in Bishop Mikael Agricola's translation was printed. The Bible was published in Finnish in 1642. Finnish for administrative use was aided by the establishment of a translation office in Stockholm*. In 1759 the Swedish law code of 1734 appeared in Finnish form. Shortly afterwards Henrik Gabriel Porthan laid the foundations for the respectability of academic interest in Finnish.

Finnish and the closely related languages Estonian, Karelian, Veps, Vote, and Livonian form the Balto-Finnic branch within the Finno-Ugric (F-U) language family, where Finnish accounts for 20 percent, and the relatively remotely related Hungarian for 60 percent of speakers. The Samoyed languages and F-U together form the Uralic languages. A common F-U may have been spoken around 4000–3000 B.C. in the area between the Volga River and the Ural Mountains.

Early contacts with Baltic peoples are evidenced in loan words reflecting social organization, stock raising, and agriculture. Later, prolonged contact with Germanic peoples, including Swedes, had the greatest influence upon the Finnish language. That influence continues today; not only does the Finnish lexicon reflect the Germanic and Swedish, but the syntax and the semantics have to a considerable extent been shaped by Swedish influence.

Thirteen consonant and eight vowel sounds are phonemically represented by the Finnish orthography, with the exception of the velar nasal, written *ng*. The vowels exhibit partial harmony in such a way that the back vowels a, o, u may not mix with the front vowels y, ä, ö, in a simplex word. Long vowels are written double, and consonantal gemination is also indicated. Vowels and consonants occur at nearly equal rates. Main stress falls on the first syllable; the second and last syllables are unstressed; other alternating syllables carry secondary stress.

Finnish is an agglutinative language, where a large proportion of the vocabulary is constructed from relatively few root morphemes and derivative and inflectional endings. Of the fourteen cases, six are basically locative, and it is fair to say that the complexity of the Finnish case system is exaggerated. It should be noted, though, that written standard Finnish differs considerably from the vernacular; for example, the possessive suffix is frequently discarded in favor of a pronoun. Phonological contractions may further separate the written language and the vernacular. Where the former has *minun kirjani* "my book," the latter has *mun kirja*. In the postwar literature the vernacular form occurs frequently, while expository prose retains the more complex standard form.

Finnish language planning is carried out by a commission operating under the auspices of the National Linguistic Center. Among its tasks are the coordination of Finnish and Swedish administrative texts, general recommendations regarding language usage, and the publication of a new dictionary.

REFERENCES: L. Hakulinen, *The Structure and Development of the Finnish Language* (Bloomington: Indiana University Publications, Uralic and Altaic Series, vol. 3, 1961);

F. Karlsson, *Finnish Grammar* (Helsinki: WSOY, 1983); E. Koivusalo, "Finska språket," in *Språkene i Norden*, ed. B. Modle and A. Karker (Oslo: Cappelen, Gyldendal, Esselte Studier, 1983).

K. NILSSON

Icelandic

The original settlers on Iceland came mostly from western Norway during the late ninth and early tenth centuries. Thus, Icelandic is a West Scandinavian language. While there are few extant runic inscriptions from Iceland, early Icelandic is preserved on numerous parchment manuscripts, some dating from the eleventh century. These early writings include literary, historical, scientific, and legal works. An Icelandic version of the New Testament appeared in 1540 and the complete Bible in 1584.

Due perhaps to its geographic isolation, Icelandic remains closest to the original North Germanic dialect morphology. In contrast to the mainland Scandinavian languages, Icelandic has maintained three genders and four cases for nouns, with corresponding forms for adjectives. Verbs are conjugated by person and number, with full-formed patterns in the subjunctive and passive. Pronouns also have four distinct cases.

The reduction of vowel quality in unstressed syllables is less apparent than in the mainland languages. With grammatical functions more clearly indicated by word endings, word order remains freer.

The vocabulary of Icelandic has also remained more conservative. Speakers reject foreign elements when they do not easily fit into the native inflexional system. For example, "telephone" in modern Icelandic is *sími*.

While vocabulary, morphology, and orthography have remained relatively stable, sound changes have had a substantial effect on the language. Original long vowels have developed into diphthongs: old long *a* (still written á) is pronounced /au/, and old long *æ* has now become /ai/. Original diphthongs remain as diphthongs, but their realizations have been altered: *au* is pronounced /öi/. The long and short vowel *y* has lost its lip-rounding and merged with *i*, although it remains in spelling. Several consonantal changes distinguish Icelandic from the mainland Scandinavian languages. The voiceless consonant stops *p*, *t*, and *k* are pronounced with aspiration /pʰ/, /tʰ/, and /kʰ/ when they start a word. In other positions, they are unaspirated (something like the *p* in English s*p*in). The old voiced stops (b, d, and g) are now voiceless. Double consonants and some consonant clusters are pronounced with a slight breath preceding them: *átt* 'owned' is pronounced /auʰt/.

There are relatively few dialect differences among speakers of Icelandic. This is perhaps due to the early establishment of a classical orthography or perhaps to the leveling of the early settlers' dialect distinctions.

The modern alphabet, in addition to the common Latin letters, includes Ð ð (called 'eth') after *d*, þ, Þ (thorn), *æ*, and *ö* after *z*. The letters *c*, *q*, and *w* are used only in foreign words and names. The long vowels á, é, í, ó, ú, and ý are considered separate letters and are listed alphabetically after the corresponding short vowel.

REFERENCES: E. V. Gordon, *An Introduction to Old Norse*, rev. A. R. Taylor (Oxford: Oxford University Press, 1957); E. Haugen, *Scandinavian Language Structures: A Comparative Historical Survey* (Minneapolis: University of Minnesota Press, 1982), and *The Scandinavian Languages: An Introduction to Their History* (London: Faber and Faber; Cambridge, Mass.: Harvard University Press, 1976); A. Johannesson, *Íslenzk tunga í fornöld* (Reykjavík: Bókaverzlum Ársæls Árnasonar, 1924); B. Kress, *Isländische Grammatik* (Münich: Hueber, 1982); A. Noreen, *Altisländische und altnorwegische Grammatik* (Halle: Niemeyer, 1923); M. Pétursson, *Isländisch: Eine Übersicht über die moderne isländische Sprache* (Hamburg: Buske, 1978).

L. JANUS

Norwegian

Norway's linguistic history is intimately intertwined with its political and social history. As early as 300 A.D., runic inscriptions from Norway bear evidence to an early form of Scandinavian, substantially similar throughout Scandinavia. During the period from 900 to 1100, Norway began to develop a language which was identifiably its own. The advent of a distinctive language is attributable to two forces, the political unification of Norway under a line of kings, and the arrival of Catholicism and the Roman alphabet. Written Norwegian, whose development was fostered by these factors, flourished in the twelfth and thirteenth centuries, although it had little effect on regional dialects of Norwegian. The Black Death, which reached Norway in 1349, seriously interrupted the spread of writing in Norway and, thus, of a unified Norwegian language.

Thereafter, the influence of foreign languages on Norwegian began to grow. Norway's political union with Denmark in 1380 made Copenhagen the governmental center for Norway and greatly enhanced the influence of Danish on Norwegian. Over the next five centuries, the written language of Norway became and remained substantially Danish. Spoken language was largely uninfluenced during the same period, except the speech of upper-class, urban Norwegians, which began to take on the characteristics of Danish.

When Norway's political union with Denmark was dissolved in 1814, a concern for the development of a truly Norwegian language quickly emerged. Two approaches to the establishment of a Norwegian language came into being. A moderate approach, slowly introducing Norwegian forms into the Danish-based standard of the day, was advocated by Knut Knudsen, whose Riksmål was only a slight departure from Danish and closely aligned itself with the speech of the upper class. Ivar Aasen took a more radical approach. He built a wholly Norwegian language from rural dialects (unaffected by Danish), primarily the West Norwegian dialects of his homeland. Although Aasen's Landsmål combined features from many regions, it scrupulously avoided loan words and the speech of the urban upper class. Riksmål and Landsmål, although both were languages conceived by Norwegians in the interest of producing a national language, were to become symbols of class divisions and regional differences within Norway.

In 1885 the Norwegian parliament passed a resolution granting both languages official status. The twentieth century has seen a tug-of-war between the rural-based supporters of Nynorsk (renamed from Landsmål in 1929) and the urban-based supporters of Bokmål (renamed from Riksmål in 1929). The functions of both are firmly embedded in Norwegian culture, assuring that neither form will become totally predominant. Bokmål is securely ensconced as the language of most newspapers and books. The number of schools using Nynorsk increased during the period prior to World War II*. Since that time, the number has decreased. Nonetheless, it is firmly established in some regions of the country and in certain genres of literature.

A series of official government reforms from 1907, 1917, and 1938 have served to bring the two standards closer together, reflecting considerable sentiment in Norway to establish, eventually, a single, unified form of standard Norwegian. Although the two forms are linguistically quite similar, fusion is still far off, given the conceptual division in Norwegian culture between the two social realms they symbolize.

REFERENCES: E. Haugen, *The Scandinavian Languages: An Introduction to Their History* (Cambridge, Mass.: Harvard University Press, 1976); E. Haugen, ed., *Norwegian-English Dictionary* (Madison: University of Wisconsin Press, 1967); E. Lundeby and I. Torvik, *Språket vårt gjennom tidene* (Oslo: Gyldendal Norsk Forlag, 1964).

K. LARSON

Swedish

The earliest specimens of Swedish, an East Scandinavian language, are approximately 2,500 runic inscriptions, some as old as the ninth century A.D. Examples of provincial laws, using the Latin alphabet, are preserved from the thirteenth century. Later manuscripts present religious and fictive works, some translated from continental sources. The first Swedish translation of the New Testament, printed in 1526, was followed by the complete *Gustav Vasa Bible* in 1541. With few revisions, these remained the standard until the twentieth century.

Beginning in the Old Swedish period, endings of nouns, adjectives, pronouns, and verbs weakened and categories merged. Nouns, for example, were reduced from four to two cases (genitive and nominative-objective), while the number of genders was reduced to two when masculine and feminine merged. The syllable structure was systematized, giving only two types: 1) long vowel–short consonant and 2) short vowel–long consonant. Back and round vowels in most Swedish dialects were raised or fronted one step; for example, /o/ became /u/.

Contact with foreign languages, especially the Low German of the Hanseatic League* in urban trade centers, had a substantial impact on Swedish, probably speeding up the reduction of grammatical classes. Swedish vocabulary was also affected. Not only were many words borrowed, including *ansikte* 'face', and *språk* 'language,' but suffixes (*-het, -bar, -aktig*) and prefixes (*an-, be-, -ge, und-*) changed the appearance and structure of Swedish. Loan words were most common in the areas of commerce, religion, and government. French (especially from the seventeenth century) has been the source of high culture words (*teater*, *opera*). More recently, English has supplied terms for leisure and technological activities (*thriller*, *astronaut*).

The beginning of modern Swedish is generally dated to 1732, when Olof von Dalin first published *Then swänksa Argus*, a lively weekly. To encourage the "purity, vigor, and eloquence" of the Swedish language, King Gustav III* established the Swedish Academy in 1786.

Due to the dominant position of Stockholm and Uppsala, most aspects of today's standard Swedish pronunciation and orthography have developed out of the Svea dialects of east central Sweden. Previous influence was felt from the Göta dialects, and St. Birgitta* and her cloister at Vadstena were important in the High Middle Ages.

The Swedish alphabet adds *å*, *ä*, and *ö* after *z*. *Q*, *w*, and *z* occur chiefly in proper names. Outside of Sweden, Swedish is spoken as an official language in Finland, where approximately 6 percent of the population (clustered along the Baltic coast and in Helsinki) use Swedish as their mother tongue.

REFERENCES: G. Bergman, *Kortfattad svensk språkhistoria* (Stockholm: Prisma, 1968), and *A Short History of the Swedish Language* (Stockholm: The Swedish Institute, 1973); E. Haugen, *Scandinavian Language Structures: A Comparative Historical Survey* (Minneapolis: University of Minnesota Press, 1982), and *The Scandinavian Languages: An Introduction to Their History* (London: Faber and Faber; Cambridge, Mass.: Harvard University Press, 1976); A. Noreen, *Altschwedische Grammatik* (Halle: Niemeyer, 1904); C.-E. Thors, *Svenskan förr och nu* (Helsinki: Söderström, 1970); E. Wessén, *De nordiska språken* (Stockholm: Almqvist & Wiksell, 1965), and *Svensk språkhistoria*, 3 vols. (Stockholm: Almqvist & Wiksell, 1962–1965).

L. JANUS

LAPPS

The Lapps, or Sami people, as they prefer to be called, are sometimes regarded as the indigenous inhabitants of Scandinavia*, although it is questionable whether their presence there antedated that of other ethnic groups. In prehistoric times— clearly before the Christian era—they migrated to northern Scandinavia and what is now the northwestern extreme of the Soviet Union. Affinities between the Sami tongue, which has diverged into distinct dialects, and Finno-Ugric languages suggest that they previously lived in western or northwestern Asia. The Roman historian Tacitus mentioned them in his *Germania* (98 A.D.), calling them *fenni* whose economy was based on hunting.

Relatively little is known about prehistoric Lapp culture. They appear to have lived in democratic bands and followed the migrating reindeer across northern Scandinavia. Contacts with Germanic Scandinavians who kept domestic animals may have led them to domesticate the reindeer, and for at least several centuries Lapp agriculture has included large herds of the animals, especially in upland areas. In coastal regions, on the other hand, fishing has long provided a means of support, while in some inland areas Lapps have traditionally lived from raising field crops and hunting. In short, the Lapps, like the Germanic Scandinavians, adapted to their environment and the resources that each area offered. Though the reindeer is often regarded as the "trademark" of the Lapps, their way of life has long been more diversified than their stereotype as nomadic Arctic herdsmen.

Throughout the Middle Ages, most Lapps had few contacts with either the Swedes or the Norwegians, the overwhelming majority of whom lived in southern and central Scandinavia. As early as the ninth century, however, traders regularly dealt with Lapps in northern Sweden and demanded tribute from them. Not long thereafter Norwegians, first regional chieftains and later kings, granted privileged subjects rights among, and license to exact taxes from, the Lapps. Such measures, together with taxation imposed by Tsarist Russia, initiated an era of distrust of the Germanic Scandinavians and other Europeans that has not completely ended.

Political events have also affected Lapp life. Beginning in the eighteenth century, Russia provided a chief market for many Lapps' products. The October Revolution of 1917 closed this market, however, and a severe blow was dealt to their economy that was not alleviated until after World War II*. The regulation of international boundaries, which traditionally meant little to many Lapps, constricted the grazing patterns of the domesticated and semi-domesticated reindeer. A treaty of 1751 allowed Norwegian and Swedish Lapps to graze their reindeer on both sides of the border. Subsequent treaties (the most recent concluded in 1972) have reduced this right to certain regions of Sweden and Norway. On the other hand, a convention of 1952 called for the construction of fences, completed in 1958, along the border separating Norway and Finland. In 1852 Russia forbade Lapps from Norway to cross the border.

The first efforts to evangelize the Lapps were probably made in the eleventh century and bore little fruit. Missionary endeavors among them were organized in the seventeenth century, and within 100 years the traditional animistic nature religion with its shamans and ancestor veneration had largely disappeared.

Simultaneously, Norwegians, Swedes, and Finns migrated northward in increasing numbers. By the nineteenth century they had pressed the Lapps out of many areas and constituted the overwhelming majority of the residents in northern Scandinavia. At the beginning of the twentieth century, the number of Lapps was estimated at 18,000 in Norway, 7,000 in Sweden, 1,500 in Finland, and 1,700 in Russia. These figures do not include the offspring of intermarriages with Germanic Scandinavians, which had become fairly common by that time.

Since World War II assimilation in national life has proceeded at an accelerating pace. Few Lapps tend reindeer today; far more have settled in towns and have become bilingual employees in industry and other branches of the economy. Compulsory education in the national languages has existed since the nineteenth century. Ethnic consciousness remains strong, however, and is manifested in such phenomena as vernacular newspapers and radio broadcasts, the persistence of colorful red and blue costumes, and confrontations with the governments to protect and preserve both Lapp culture and the environment of northern Scandinavia. Toward that end, the Nordic Lapp Institute was founded at Kautokeino, Norway, in 1973.

REFERENCES: R. Bosi, *The Lapps*, trans. J. Cadell (New York: Praeger, 1960); B. Collinder, *The Lapps* (Princeton: Princeton University Press, 1949); H. Eidheim, *Aspects of the Lappish Minority* (Oslo: Universitetsforlaget, 1971); I. Ruong, *The Lapps in Sweden*, trans. A. Blair (Stockholm: Swedish Institute, 1967).

F. HALE

LIBERAL LEFT PARTY Norway (Frisennede Venstre)

The Liberal Left Party was established in 1909. Its formation was the result of a number of developments within the Liberal (Venstre) movement in Norway, including the "consolidation" of the Left's leadership in the hands of more radical forces in the movement in 1908, some members' rejection of the movement's association with the Norwegian Labor Party*, and opposition to the leaders' Concession Law policy. The new party won 24 seats in the Storting* in 1909 and formed a coalition government with the Right. W. Konow, head of the new party, became prime minister. The fortunes of the party, following a pattern that is typical of Liberal parties throughout Europe in the 20 years after World War I, declined through the 1920s and early 1930s. In 1931–1932 the party's name was changed to the Liberal People's Party. It lost its last seat in the parliament in the 1936 election, and the party was dissolved. Most of its members joined the Right.

REFERENCE: *NH*, vol. 12.

B. NORDSTROM

LIBERAL PARTY (FINLAND) *See* Progressive/Liberal Party

LIBERAL PEOPLE'S PARTY Sweden (Frisinnade Folkpartiet)

The Liberal People's Party was formed in 1924, at the same time that Sweden's Liberal Party (Sveriges Liberala Partiet) was formed. The two developed out of the debate within the Liberal coalition over prohibition and appeared in the wake of a national plebiscite on that question. At a special meeting of the coalition's national organization (Frisinnade Landföreningen), the anti-prohibition forces broke with the group's majority. The prohibitionists formed the Liberal People's Party, under the leadership of Carl Gustav Ekman*, at the 1924 meeting of the parliament. At the same time, the anti-prohibition minority established Sweden's Liberal Party. The two groups remained separate until 1934, when they rejoined to form the Swedish People's Party (Folkpartiet).

REFERENCES: *DSH*, vol. 14; *SU*, vol. 10.

B. NORDSTROM

LINDMAN, ARVID (1862–1936) Swedish Conservative politician and prime minister

Arvid Lindman was the leading Conservative politician in Sweden during the first three decades of the twentieth century and was the prime mover in committing the Conservatives to the concept and practice of parliamentary democracy. On several occasions he blocked the rise to power of the right wing in the party, which wanted to preserve a plutocratic system.

Lindman left a promising naval career to enter business in 1892. As an industrialist he played leading roles in iron mining and export, banking, insurance, and arms manufacturing. His political career also began in 1892, when he was elected to a provincial assembly. He served in the Upper Chamber of the Riksdag* from 1905 to 1911 and then moved to the Lower Chamber, where he was the Conservative leader until 1935. During his three decades in the parliament, he was also the head of the General Voters' Alliance, a national conservative organization to coordinate campaigns. This office gave him an advantage over his chief rival for national and parliamentary leadership, Ernst Trygger*, who was to the right of Lindman on virtually every issue.

Lindman was prime minister from 1906 to 1911 and from 1928 to 1930, and served as a naval minister in 1906 and as foreign minister in 1917. In 1907, as prime minister, he blocked the drive of the left to effect franchise and parliamentary reform along British lines, that is, to by-pass the Upper Chamber, and instead guided through parliament bills providing for proportional representation for both chambers, universal manhood suffrage, and a severe limitation of the timocratic electoral system in the Upper Chamber. In 1911, when his party lost heavily in the elections and the Left (Liberals and Social Democrats) gained an overwhelming majority in the Lower Chamber, Lindman and his entire cabinet resigned immediately. This was the first time a government left office as a result of an electoral defeat, thus recognizing a basic tenet of parliamentary democracy. It was accomplished in the face of pressure from the right-wing Conservatives to remain in office. In 1914 Gustav V*, following the advice of his ultra-conservative advisors and without prior consultation, publicly repudiated the Liberal cabinet on the defense issue, thus challenging the concept of parliamentary democracy. The Liberal cabinet resigned, as Lindman's had done in 1911. Lindman blocked the candidacy of Trygger, who was not committed to the parliamentary principle, to head the government and maneuvered Hjalmar Hammerskjöld to the position instead.

Never a doctrinaire capitalist, he displayed genuine concern over social problems. He disavowed any sympathy for the fascist governments on the continent. Amiable, optimistic, energetic, and willing to compromise, Lindman was one of the two or three outstanding political statesmen in twentieth-century Sweden.

REFERENCES: I. Andersson, *Arvid Lindman och hans tid* (Stockholm: Norstedts, 1956); D. Rustow, *The Politics of Compromise* (Princeton: Princeton University Press, 1955); B. Schiller, "Years of Crisis, 1906–1914," in S. Koblik, *Sweden's Development from Poverty to Affluence* (Minneapolis: University of Minnesota Press, 1975); D. Verney, *Parliamentary Reform in Sweden 1866–1921* (Oxford: Clarendon Press, 1957).

P. V. THORSON

LO *See* Swedish Confederation of Trade Unions

LOVISA ULRIKA (24 July 1720–16 July 1782) Wife of Sweden's King Adolf Fredrik*

Lovisa Ulrika was born in Berlin to Friedrich Wilhelm I of Prussia and Sophia Dorothea of Hannover. The most famous of her siblings was Frederik II (the Great) of Prussia, with whom she was to maintain personal and political contact for much of her life. At the age of 23, Lovisa Ulrika was married to Adolf Fredrik, who had been elected by the Swedish estates as heir apparent to the Swedish throne the year before, in 1743. Devoted as she was to the finer points of French cultural and intellectual life, Lovisa Ulrika became an important advocate of *belles lettres*, the theater, ballet, and the natural sciences in Stockholm*. Likewise, her Francophile cultural tastes led her to ally herself politically during these early years in Sweden with the Hat Party*, which was closely linked to the French court and many of whose leaders were outstanding patrons of the arts.

While the Hats cultivated the support of Adolf Fredrik and his consort prior to Fredrik I's* death in 1751, relations between the party and the new royal couple deteriorated in the years thereafter. Largely as a result of Lovisa Ulrika's desire to have her husband emulate the position of power enjoyed by her illustrious brother, the new Swedish king attempted to extend his authority vis-a-vis the council of the realm within Sweden's unique constitutional system of parliamentary sovereignty. The ensuing struggle led to a break between the Hat-dominated council and the king and a showdown between the two at the Riksdag* of 1755–1756. Lovisa Ulrika was the pivotal force in royal plans for a coup d'etat, the discovery of which led to the execution of several of the participants, to the discrediting of the royal couple, and to a further reduction of royal power. Perhaps as bitter as any of the other retaliatory measures against the queen and her husband was the transfer of responsibility for the upbringing and education of their children from the royal couple to the estates of the realm.

From 1756 until her husband's death in 1771, Lovisa Ulrika remained a regular participant in the politics of her adopted country, as the party out of power—be it the Hat or the Cap Party*—courted her political ambition in its own attempts to remain viable while out of office. Embarrassed and bitter about the fact that Sweden in 1757 entered the Seven Years' War in alliance with her brother's enemies, Lovisa Ulrika was drawn in the period up to 1764 into cooperation with the Hat Party's opponents. Yet, once the war was over and once it became apparent that the Caps had no intention of expanding royal power, Lovisa Ulrika and her supporters maneuvered to bring about a so-called composition or government of all parties under the leadership of the crown. When this failed, and when the Caps came to power in 1765, Lovisa Ulrika once again moved toward cooperation with the Hats.

By 1768 Crown Prince Gustav (Gustav III*) had emerged as his mother's closest political ally, at one and the same time her protégé and rival. While she saw her son as a much more promising politician than was her husband, Lovisa

Ulrika soon began to fear that once Gustav ascended the throne he would remove her from the political scene and she would lose what influence she had. In effect, this is what was to happen after Adolf Fredrik's death in 1771 and Gustav III's marriage to Sophia Magdalena of Denmark the following year. Relations between mother and son deteriorated in the years that followed, although the two reached at least an outward reconciliation some days before Lovisa Ulrika's death in 1782.

REFERENCES: B. Hennings, *Gustaf III som kronprins* (Stockholm, 1957); O. Jäger-skiöld, *Lovisa Ulrika* (Stockholm, 1945), and "Lovisa Ulrika," in *SBL* 24 (1982): 151–58.

M. F. METCALF

LUNDBERG, GUSTAF (17 August 1695–18 March 1786) Swedish artist

On his mother's side Gustaf Lundberg came of a family of noted artists, the Richters; his father was in royal service as chief chef to the court and was killed in Karl XII's* Livonian campaign of 1701. Lundberg first entered the studio of David Krafft, the Swedish court painter, but in 1717 he made his way to France and remained in Paris for the next 28 years. Through Erik Sparre, the Swedish ambassador, Lundberg became known to Hyacinthe Rigaud and Nicolas de Largillière, leading portraitists of their time, and secured the rare favor of permission to copy in the royal collections in the Louvre. But after the arrival in Paris of the celebrated Venetian pastelliste Rosalba Carriera in 1720 Lundberg's enthusiasm for this new medium became fixed, and he was able to have a few lessons from Rosalba. His professional fortunes were made by a natural talent and his links with Sparre and, more indirectly, Krafft, and these enabled him to enter the cultivated circle of Stanislas Leszcynski, the ex-king of Poland who in 1725 became father-in-law to Louis XV. Lundberg executed in pastel one of the earliest portraits of the new French queen, going on in 1733 to portray her in two further portraits.

The arrival of his countryman Carl-Gustaf Tessin* in Paris in 1739 led to the latter's patronage and, despite Lundberg's Lutheran faith, he was appointed to the French Royal Academy in 1742. He returned to Sweden in 1745, via Spain and Portugal, as the leading pastellist in Europe after Maurice Quentin de La Tour, whose penetration Lundberg could never match, and Jean Baptiste Perronneau (Rosalba was blind by 1746). Lundberg now enjoyed the patronage of Queen Lovisa Ulrika* and in 1760 was elected a member of the Swedish Academy of Fine Art. He executed seven portraits of Gustav III*, and by 1780 had depicted members of most of the leading Swedish families. Lundberg's importance lies in his rapid mastery of a new and difficult medium and an output so prolific that he held a mirror up to an era. As he aged, however, he employed a number of studio assistants, and his own line became decreasingly incisive.

REFERENCES: P. Lespinasse, *Les Artistes Suédois en France* (Paris, 1929); O. Levertin, *G. Lundberg* (Stockholm, 1902).

D. D. ALDRIDGE

LUTHERANISM

The Nordic countries became Lutheran during the course of the sixteenth century. Denmark, Iceland, and Norway officially adopted the new faith through royal decree after 1536 (though the date of the acceptance of the decree varies). It took somewhat longer for Lutheranism to be formally adopted in Sweden and Finland, although the initial steps were taken in the 1520s and 1530s. In all the Nordic countries, the actual transition within the population took place gradually during the last three-quarters of the sixteenth century. Toleration of other religions was limited for much of the sixteenth and seventeenth centuries, virtually disappeared toward the end of the seventeenth or in the early eighteenth century, and did not reappear until the middle of the nineteenth century. The Nordic countries continue to have state Lutheran churches, and the majority of the population in each country is nominally Lutheran. (*See also* Baptists; Conventicle Acts; Conversion; Hauge, Hans Nielsen; Laestadianism; Laestadius, Lars; Methodists; Reformation; Religion.)

REFERENCES: N. K. Andersen, "The Reformation in Scandinavia and the Baltic," in *NCMH*, vol. 2; K. E. Christophersen, "Hallelujahs, Damnations, or Norwegian Reformation as Lengthy Process," *Church History* 48 (September 1979): 279–89; O. Garstein, *Rome and the Counter-Reformation in Scandinavia*, 2 vols. (Oslo: Universitetsforlaget, 1963, 1980); K. Hørby, *Reformationens indførelse i Danmark* (Copenhagen: Munksgaard, 1968); L. S. Hunter, ed., *Scandinavian Churches* (London: Faber and Faber, 1965); R. Murray, *A Brief History of the Church of Sweden: Origins and Modern Structure* (Stockholm, 1961); C. F. Wisloff, *Norsk Kirkehistorie* (Oslo: Lutherstiftelsen, 1966).

B. NORDSTROM

M

MAGNUS I OLAFSSON (the Good) (c. 1024–25 October 1047) King of Norway 1035–1047, King of Denmark 1042–1047

Magnus, the illegitimate son of King Olaf II Haraldsson*, was born c. 1024 and named after Charlemagne (Old Norse Karla*magnús*). In 1028 his father fled with him to Russia, where the boy was fostered by Grand Prince Yaroslav I until 1035, when local chieftains from Norway fetched him home as a candidate for the throne. When the people rallied around Magnus, the Danish under-age appointee in Norway, Svein Alfifuson, was forced to flee with his mother back to Denmark. The new king, who after avenging his father's death was a mild ruler, was nicknamed "the Good."

Magnus pursued expansionist policies, competing for control of the North Sea empire which, although it ceased to exist as an entity upon the death of King Knut the Great (Knud I*) of Denmark and England in 1035, continued as a concept. In 1038 Magnus and Knut's successor in Denmark, Harda-Knut (Hardeknud*), became reconciled and agreed that whoever lived longest should inherit the other's kingdom. Upon Harda-Knut's death in 1042, the king of Norway was hailed king of Denmark too, although he had to fight off repeated challenges by the Danish pretender, Sven Estridsson (Sven II Estridsen*). Magnus also laid claim to the throne of England and posed a threat to King Edward the Confessor, but he was unable to realize that claim. The conflict with Sven and the situation with the Slavs on the southern border of Denmark kept him sufficiently occupied. In 1043 he and his Danish subjects/allies defeated the Wends (Slavs) in a major battle in the south of Jutland, and the following year they attacked the Wendish trading center in the Baltic.

Magnus's uncle Harald III Sigurdsson* returned to Norway from the Byzantine Empire and Russia in 1045, and the following year the king was reconciled with him and shared his rule. On 25 October 1047 Magnus died on board ship in Denmark during a campaign against Sven which the co-rulers had launched.

Harald then succeeded to sole sovereignty in Norway but was unable to wrest the Danish throne from Sven.

REFERENCES: P. S. Andersen, *Samlingen av Norge og kristningen av landet 800–1130* (Bergen: Universitetsforlaget, 1977); K. Gjerset, *History of the Norwegian People* (1932; repr. New York: AMS, 1969); K. Larsen, *A History of Norway* (Princeton: Princeton University Press, 1948/1974); S. Sturluson, *Heimskringla: Sagas of the Norse Kings* (London: Dent, 1961).

J. E. KNIRK

MAGNUS III OLAFSSON (Bareleg) (c. 1073–24 August 1103) King of Norway 1093–1103

Magnus Bareleg, the illegitimate son of King Olaf III Haraldsson* (the Quiet), succeeded his father in 1093 as king of Norway. Initially ruling jointly with his cousin, Haakon Magnusson, he became sole ruler upon Haakon's death the following year. After defeating his cousin's foster-father and a pretender to the throne in 1095, Magnus embarked on a course of energetic and costly international politics. Whereas his father had accomplished things through diplomacy, Magnus used military force.

Magnus invaded a Danish province on the southeastern border of Norway in 1095–1096 and a Swedish one in 1101, apparently attempting to pacify the area around the new Norwegian trading center near the border of the three Scandinavian kingdoms at present-day Göteborg. After the second campaign failed, the three kings met at the border and made peace. Magnus had more success on his military expeditions to the British Isles, securing the Norse colonies there against the threat of a unified Scotland by reuniting them with the mother country. Internal strife between the two earls of Orkney led to Magnus's first western campaign in 1098–1099, which resulted in the direct subjugation of the Orkneys to the Norwegian crown. The earls were deported to Norway, where they died, and Magnus's illegitimate son, Sigurd I Magnusson*, was made ruler. In addition, Shetland and the Isle of Man were taken over as military bases, the Hebrides were seized, and Norman-occupied Wales was attacked in support of the Welsh king. In response to Irish attacks on the Hebrides, the king returned to the Norse colonies on another expedition in 1102, installing the twelve-year-old Sigurd then as king over the entire island empire and conducting military operations in Ireland, where he was killed on 24 August 1103 while foraging. According to saga tradition, Magnus received a halberd through his thighs, which were not protected by armor, hence the nickname ''Bareleg.''

Sigurd Magnusson returned to Norway, where he succeeded in a co-regency with his two half brothers, Eystein and Olaf. The conquered colonies soon reverted to local control, but close ties were maintained, trade was stimulated, and the earls of Orkney generally recognized the sovereignty of the king of Norway for over 350 years.

REFERENCES: P. S. Anderson, *Samlingen av Norge og kristningen av landet 800–1130* (Bergen: Universitetsforlaget, 1977); K. Gjerset, *History of the Norwegian People*

(1932; repr. New York: AMS, 1969); K. Larsen, *A History of Norway* (Princeton: Princeton University Press, 1948/1974); S. Sturluson, *Heimskringla: Sagas of the Norse Kings* (London: Dent, 1961).

J. E. KNIRK

MAGNUS IV SIGURDSSON (the Blind) (c. 1115–12 November 1139) King of Norway 1130–1135

Magnus, the son of King Sigurd I Magnusson* the Crusader, was designated heir to the throne of Norway by his father in the late 1120s through an agreement with the king's newly arrived half brother, Harald IV Magnusson* (Gilchrist). This arrangement broke with the tradition that any king's son had a claim to kingship. Upon succession after his father's death in 1130, Magnus was, however, forced to accept Harald as co-ruler. The two coexisted peacefully until 1134, when war broke out between them. Magnus won the first battle in eastern Norway, but he was defeated in Bergen the following year, seized by Harald and stripped of kingship, blinded, maimed, and gelded, and put into a monastery near Nidaros (Trondheim). Henceforth Magnus was nicknamed "the Blind."

Harald was killed the following year by a new pretender and supposed son of King Magnus III Olafsson* (Bareleg), Sigurd Slembi, but the king's retainers refused to support the upstart, and a new co-regency was established with Harald's young sons, Sigurd Mouth and Ingi I Haraldsson*, as kings. Sigurd Slembi took Magnus out of the monastery in 1137 and used him to gain the support of many chieftains from Trøndelag and the eastern valleys who honored the blinded ex-king. Their forces, however, were defeated by the backers of Ingi and Sigurd Mouth, and for the next two years Sigurd Slembi resorted to harrying in Norway. Following Sigurd Mouth's initial inactivity, the child kings joined forces and defeated a Danish and Norwegian fleet led by Sigurd Slembi in eastern Norway on 12 November 1139. Magnus perished during the battle, while Sigurd Slembi was captured and tortured to death. Thus ended the first phase of the Norwegian civil wars.

REFERENCES: G. M. Gathorne-Hardy, *A Royal Impostor: King Sverre of Norway* (Oslo: Aschehoug, 1956); K. Gjerset, *History of the Norwegian People* (1932; repr. New York: AMS, 1969); K. Helle, *Norge blir en stat 1130–1319*, 2nd rev. ed. (Bergen: Universitetsforlaget, 1974); K. Larsen, *A History of Norway* (Princeton: Princeton University Press, 1948/1974); S. Sturluson, *Heimskringla: Sagas of the Norse Kings* (London: Dent, 1961).

J. E. KNIRK

MAGNUS V ERLINGSSON (c. 1156–15 June 1184) King of Norway 1161–1184

Magnus Erlingsson was but five years old in 1161 when he was elected at a meeting in Bergen to succeed King Ingi I Haraldsson* (Hunchback). Political factions had developed by this phase of the Norwegian civil wars, and when Ingi died without a son, his followers were forced to depart from the legal tradition that only direct paternal descendants of a king had the right to kingship.

Whereas Magnus's mother was the daughter of King Sigurd I Magnusson* (the Crusader), his father was but a landed man from western Norway. Erling Crook-Neck (*skakki*) assumed leadership of the faction as regent for his son, and the following year he and his men defeated and killed the rival king, Haakon II Sigurdsson* (the Broad-Shouldered). Erling remained the real power behind the throne until his death in 1179.

Magnus's legal right to kingship was weak, but he was supported by the Church, which preferred the legitimate son of a king's daughter to other royal but illegitimate pretenders. A Norwegian archbishopric had been created in Nidaros (Trondheim) in 1152–1153, and Archbishop Eystein Erlendsson agreed to sanction Magnus's kingship and crown him in return for royal support and various privileges, mainly of an economic nature, for the Church. The coronation, the first in Scandinavian history, took place in 1163–1164. Among other results of the cooperation between the Norwegian Church and the monarchy were various nationwide legal reforms, including the first written law of succession, in which the Christian principle of sole sovereignty based on primogeniture and the prior right of a legitimate royal son to the crown was promoted. A national assembly as a representative electoral body was to formalize the selection, and although no ruler was ever chosen according to this law, a guideline was indicated. Through the coronation and legal reforms, kingship was strengthened, becoming a divine office, while at the same time the Church improved its position. The king was defined as a vassal of God and Saint Olaf (Olaf II Haraldsson*).

The nation's first crowned monarch had to defend his kingship against both internal and external enemies. Whereas his supporters were mainly aristocrats from western Norway and the area around Oslo fjord, opposing pretenders to the throne were supported by groups representing farmers in Trøndelag, the eastern valleys, and the southeastern provinces on the Swedish border. In 1163–1164 and again in 1168 rivals were defeated and killed by Erling and his men. The differences after 1165 between Magnus and his cousin, King Valdemar I* (the Great) of Denmark, concerning sovereignty over the eastern coast of Norway were not resolved until Erling traveled to Denmark in 1170, recognized Valdemar's claim, and in turn was appointed a Danish earl over the disputed area. Magnus and his men defeated and killed the Birchleg faction pretender to the throne in eastern Norway in 1177.

Magnus spent the last seven years of his reign defending his shrinking kingdom against the subsequent Birchleg candidate, King Sverrir Sigurdsson*. Sverrir had established a firm foothold in Trøndelag by 1179, defeating Magnus that year in an encounter in Nidaros which cost Earl Erling his life. During the following years, Magnus waged war with changing fortunes against Sverrir, either from his stronghold in Bergen or, after defeats in Nidaros in 1180 and again in Bergen in 1183, from exile in Denmark. Attempting a comeback in 1184, he met defeat and death in the naval battle of Fimreiti in Sognefjord, leaving Sverrir the uncontested sovereign.

REFERENCES: G. M. Gathorne-Hardy, *A Royal Imposter: King Sverre of Norway*

(Oslo: Aschehoug, 1956); K. Gjerset, *History of the Norwegian People* (1932; repr. New York: AMS, 1969); K. Helle, *Norge blir en stat 1130–1319*, 2nd rev. ed. (Bergen: Universitetsforlaget, 1974); K. Larsen, *A History of Norway* (Princeton: Princeton University Press, 1948/1974); J. Sephton, trans., *The Saga of King Sverri of Norway* (London: Nutt, 1899); S. Sturluson, *Heimskringla: Sagas of the Norse Kings* (London: Dent, 1961).

J. E. KNIRK

MAGNUS VI HAAKONSSON (Lawmender/*Lagabœtir*) (1 May 1238–9 May 1280) King of Norway 1257/1263–1280

Magnus, the younger legitimate son of King Haakon IV Haakonsson*, was born in 1238. Upon the death of his older brother King Haakon the Young in 1257, Magnus became king of Norway and co-regent with his father. He married in 1261 and was crowned together with his Danish queen in Bergen. When his father left on an expedition to the Scottish Isles in 1263, Magnus was appointed regent; he then succeeded to sole sovereignty upon Haakon's death later that year in the Orkneys.

Magnus ruled over the largest empire in Norwegian history: Norway in its greatest expanse, Iceland, Greenland*, the Orkneys, the Faroes Islands*, and Shetland, ceding, however, the Hebrides and the Isle of Man to King Alexander III of Scotland in 1266 in exchange for an initial payment and annual rent. The king pursued peace politics and employed a group of professional royal emissaries to cultivate the good international connections which his father had achieved. Foreigners, especially the Hanseatic merchants (*see* Hanseatic League), were given special privileges, while Norwegian maritime commerce reached a peak during this time. Although they did not come to a break, relationships with the other Scandinavian kingdoms became strained due on the one hand to a conflict concerning the queen's inheritance in Denmark and on the other to Magnus's difficult role as an arbitrator in the conflict concerning succession in Sweden.

In order to attain nationwide judicial agreement, Magnus initiated extensive revisions of Norwegian legal codes. For these reforms he is nicknamed "Lawmender." Changes were first made in the district laws themselves, but in 1274 a new national legal code was introduced and ratified. The new law, which was based on the best parts of the district codes but which also included many innovations, was formulated the year before at a national assembly in Bergen. Among other things, blood feuds were prohibited, crimes being considered a matter to be adjudicated publicly rather than revenged privately. Help for the poor and a system of caring for the aged were provided for too. Magnus's national law was in effect for 400 years and was also introduced in Iceland and the Faroes. A new municipal code, instituted in 1276 and relying largely on the laws of Bergen, created a city council form of government for Norwegian cities and towns, while a new code for the king's retainers was formulated between 1273 and 1277.

Due to differences with the Church, the king could not introduce a common ecclesiastical law. Archbishop Jon the Red upheld the rights of the Church and by 1273 had formulated his own Christian law. In 1277 he and Magnus came to terms by concluding the Concordat of Tønsberg, a reconciliation curtailing some of the Church's secular influence but essentially granting it independence in its own judicial matters and exempting it from taxes.

The king who transformed Norway's legal system died on 9 May 1280. He was succeeded by the older of his living sons, Eirik (Erik II), who had been proclaimed king at the national assembly in Bergen in 1273. Magnus's younger son, Haakon, continued as duke but succeeded as King Haakon V upon his brother's death in 1299. Magnus was the last Norwegian king about whom a saga was written, but only fragments of that work by the Icelander Sturla Thordarson remain.

REFERENCES: K. Gjerset, *History of the Norwegian People* (1932; repr. New York: AMS, 1969); K. Helle, *Norge blir en stat 1130–1319*, 2nd rev. ed. (Bergen: Universitetsforlaget, 1974); K. Larsen, *A History of Norway* (Princeton: Princeton University Press, 1948/1974); S. Thordarson, *The Saga of Hacon, and a Fragment of the Saga of Magnus* (London: Rolls, 1894).

J. E. KNIRK

MAGNUS ERIKSSON (1316–1374) King of Norway 1319–1356, king of Sweden 1319–1365

Magnus Eriksson was the son of Duke Erik Magnusson and Ingeborg, daughter of Haakon V of Norway. He succeeded his grandfather in Norway in 1319 and was chosen by an assembly of great men and commoners to succeed his uncle, Birger Magnusson, who was deposed in the same year. (Some have argued that this assembly was the first such in Swedish history and marks the beginnings of the Swedish parliament.) It was hoped that his succession would end the bitter and bloody civil wars that had plagued Sweden for many years. (In the last round of these conflicts, Birger had enticed his brothers, Erik and Valdemar, to a banquet at Nyköping in December 1317, where he had them imprisoned. The brothers were subsequently allowed to starve to death during a siege of the castle in Nyköping.)

During the first thirteen years of his reign, power was in the hands of a regency controlled by Magnus's mother and the magnates. His personal rule began in 1332, and he then initiated a series of policies aimed at strengthening the monarchy at the expense of Denmark, the Church, the nobles, and the Hanse (*see* Hanseatic League). In 1332 he "bought" Skåne, Blekinge, and Halland from a German noble to whom the areas had been pawned by the Danish crown. In order to pay for these territories, he had to borrow from the Hanse and the Church. He subsequently had difficulties paying back both his creditors, which led to the Hanse's enmity and the Church's condemnation. At the same time, he engaged in crusades against the Finns in Karelia, aimed at extending Christianity and expanding Swedish influence in the Russian trade. These efforts were expensive and largely unsuccessful. At home, Magnus turned away from the magnates and delegated a great deal of authority to his favorite, Bengt Algotsson.

He commissioned the compilation of one of the most significant sources of Swedish medieval history, Magnus Eriksson's Land Law (c. 1350), which was designed to create a unified law for the kingdom and to support the crown's claim to power based on the law.

Magnus's policies and actions made him many enemies, and his situation was made none the better by the arrival of the Black Death in Scandinavia* in 1349. The Church poured criticism on him, and he was viciously attacked by St. Birgitta*. Churchmen, nobles, commoners, Germans, and Danes were all prepared to turn on the king. Even his own sons, Erik and Haakon, were willing to join the opposition. Open revolt against Magnus began in 1356. It continued on and off for nine years. In the midst of the rebellion, Valdemar IV* invaded southern Sweden, reclaimed the provinces bought in 1332, and proceeded to take Gotland. Finally, in 1365, Magnus was declared deposed. The magnates elected his nephew, Albrekt of Mecklenburg, king. Magnus was imprisoned for six years and, upon his release, went to Norway. He died in a shipwreck in 1374.

Magnus's bad reputation is probably not deserved and is largely the result of reliance upon very bad sources. He was very much like other monarchs of the fourteenth century who struggled against the centrifugal power of the great nobles and the independent power of the Church. Like many of his contemporaries, he was a loser in this struggle.

REFERENCES: *DSH*, vol. 2; V. Moberg, *A History of the Swedish People*, vol. 1, trans. P. B. Austin (New York: Pantheon, 1972); F. D. Scott, *Sweden: The Nation's History* (Minneapolis: University of Minnesota Press, 1977); *SU*, vol. 19.

B. NORDSTROM

MANNERHEIM, CARL GUSTAF EMIL (4 June 1867–28 January 1951) Marshal and president of Finland 1944–1946

Mannerheim was born at the family estate of Louhisaari in southwestern Finland. After expulsion from the Finnish military cadet school, the young Mannerheim was able, by virtue of his aristocratic connections, to pass in 1887 into the Russian cavalry school. Thereafter he pursued a satisfying career in the imperial service and soon obtained a commission in the Chevalier Guards. He served with distinction in the Russo-Japanese War and later crossed Central Asia on horseback to Peking, in the not unmerited guise of an ethnographer, but with the primary task, entrusted to him by the Russian chief of staff, of collecting military information in case of war with China. During World War I Mannerheim commanded an army corps on the Galician-Carpathian front.

This successful career (though Mannerheim never made the Staff College) was terminated by the revolutions of 1917 in Russia: he was actually relieved of his command a few weeks before the Bolshevik Revolution. Mannerheim then returned to Finland and took command of the White forces in the Finnish Civil War* in early 1918. In a sense his role as one of the leading figures of the newly independent Finland was thrust upon him by the breakdown in Russia.

It may equally be argued that independent Finland itself was a product of the same breakdown.

Nevertheless, a certain tension existed in Mannerheim between his Russian background and his Finnish identity. He had, for example, continued in imperial service throughout the period from 1899 onwards, when Finland's autonomous institutions were under threat of assimilation with those of the empire. As regent of Finland from 12 December 1918 to 30 July 1919, he favored the use of Finnish forces for intervention in Russia, an outlook that undoubtedly helped to contribute to his defeat by K. J. Ståhlberg in the presidential election of July 1919. Yet for some time after this Mannerheim tried to win support in western Europe for his interventionist plans. He was bitterly disappointed when the Finns made peace with Soviet Russia at Tartu on 14 October 1920.

On the other hand, Mannerheim's Russian background enabled him to appreciate the strategic interests of the Russian state, Bolshevik or otherwise. In 1939, as chairman of the Defense Council (appointed in 1931 and made field marshal in 1933), he advocated territorial concessions to Russia. Had they been made, the Winter War* (1939–1940) might have been avoided. Again, however, after the Winter War, as commander-in-chief, he worked for Finland's involvement with Germany (though distrusting Nazism) and in the Continuation War (1941–1944) he proclaimed his identification with Finnish nationalist aims for the conquest of East Karelia.

On the eve of Finland's withdrawal from the war Mannerheim was elected president in August 1944 as a symbol of national unity, the final paradox in the career of this Swedish-speaking, aristocratic Finn, whose lack of enthusiasm for the processes of democracy (witness his identification with and a certain exploitation of the Lapua movement in the early 1930s) had always been apparent. The paradoxes of his life yet mirror the vicissitudes of Finland's own history.

REFERENCES: S. Jägerskiöld, *Gustaf Mannerheim. 1867–1951* (Helsinki: Schildt [Swedish edition] and Otava [Finnish edition], 1983); see also other works on Mannerheim by Jägerskiöld; G. Mannerheim, *The Memoirs of Marshal Mannerheim*(London: Cassell, 1953); M. Rintala, ed., *Four Finns: Political Profiles* (Berkeley: University of California Press, 1969); J. Screen, *Mannerheim: The Years of Preparation* (London: Hurst, 1970); O. Warner, *Marshal Mannerheim and the Finns* (London: Weidenfeld and Nicolson, 1967).

G. MAUDE

MARGRETHE I (1353–28 October 1412) Regent of Denmark 1375–1412, regent of Norway 1380–1412, regent of Sweden 1388–1412

Margrethe was the younger daughter of Valdemar IV*. At age 6 she was betrothed to Haakon VI of Norway. She was married at 10 but spent much of the next six years in Sweden, where she was raised by a daughter of St. Birgitta*. At 16 she went to live with her husband at Akerhus, and their only son, Oluf (III*), was born a year later.

When Valdemar IV died there was no direct male heir to the throne in Denmark. Her sister's son, Albrekt of Mecklenburg, had been mentioned by Valdemar as his heir, but neither the council nor the merchants of the Hanse (*see* Hanseatic League) wished to see Albrekt on the throne. Margrethe worked successfully to secure the election of the five-year-old Oluf. War with Mecklenburg and Holstein followed, which ended with Albrekt's defeat and the Treaty of Lindholm. In 1380 Margrethe secured Oluf's election to succeed his father in Norway. Because he was still a minor, Margrethe was effectively the ruler in both countries.

In 1363 the Swedish magnates had deposed Magnus Eriksson* and elected Albrekt of Mecklenburg their king, thinking he would be their pawn. Their expectations proved false. In 1371 Albrekt was compelled to give assurances to preserve the privileges of the great men, led by Bo Jonsson Grip. After Jonsson's death, Albrekt tried to win back his authority, and the magnates responded by deposing him. They then turned to Margrethe and Oluf. (Albrekt continued to fight until his defeat at Åsle in 1389.) In the midst of the negotiations to secure Oluf's election, the young king died. All three Scandinavian countries were now without a ruler, and threats from Mecklenburg and the Hanse to their independence made it imperative that this vacuum be filled. Within a few months the three countries recognized Margrethe as their regent, their powerful lady and master (*fuldmægtig frue og husbond*). The situation was extraordinary. But Margrethe was also extraordinary. She was energetic, cunning, and dedicated. She was a master at diplomacy and had a singleness of purpose that helped to make her very effective. All of Scandinavia* was now her kingdom, and she believed that the ideal form of government necessary to preserve that kingdom had been laid down by her father, that is, strong, centralized monarchy, monarchy supported by a council and local appointees loyal and equally dedicated. She knew that the Hanse and the north German princes wanted a weak and divided North. She also knew that the magnates in the three countries preferred to rule as autonomous petty kings on their own estates. For the rest of her life she worked to strengthen the monarchy at home and to maintain peace with potential enemies abroad. She was successful in both. Her successors were neither so adept nor so lucky.

Margrethe also realized that her position as a woman and a widow without heirs was fraught with dangers. She therefore secured, by 1396, the recognition of her grandnephew Erik of Pomerania* as king in all three countries. He was crowned at Kalmar* in 1397, and the coronation marked the birth of the Kalmar Union*.

For the next fifteen years Margrethe governed while Erik watched. She appointed loyal agents to fiefs and offices in all three countries and ruthlessly drove her opponents from their places of power. The council in Denmark and local administrative posts were staffed with her people. In the process of creating this union government, she laid the grounds for future conflicts. She ignored what the magnates in Sweden and Norway considered a fundamental aspect of the agreements reached at Kalmar, that is, that native men would hold royal offices and fiefs in their respective countries. Margrethe appointed mainly Germans to these offices. So long as she lived, however, internal peace was maintained. Erik continued this policy and paid for it with his crown.

Margrethe died aboard her ship, probably of the plague, in 1412. She was unquestionably one of the dominant figures of her age. She had generously patronized the Church, fostered economic and cultural growth, given Scandinavia over 20 years of peace, effectively ruled the three kingdoms, and perhaps preserved the region's independence. She also gave form to the dream of many Scandinavian rulers before and after her in the union she helped to create.

REFERENCES: C. F. Bayerschmidt and E. J. Friis, "A Saint and a Queen: Two Indomitable Figures of the Fourteenth Century," *Scandinavian Studies* (1965): 373–84; *DBL*, vol. 9; *DH*, vol. 4; *DSH*, vols. 2, 3; K. Erslev, *Danmarks historie under dronning Margrete* (Copenhagen, 1882/1971); H. Koht, *Drottning Margarete och Kalmarunionen* (Stockholm: Kultur och Natur, 1956); E. Lönnroth, *Från svensk medeltid* (Stockholm: Aldus/Bonniers, 1959); V. Moberg, *A History of the Swedish People*, trans. P. B. Austin (New York: Pantheon, 1972); *NH*, vols. 4, 5.

B. NORDSTROM

MARGRETHE II (16 April 1940–) Queen of Denmark 1972–

Margrethe is the daughter of Frederik IX* and Ingrid, a daughter of Gustav VI Adolf* of Sweden. She succeeded to the Danish throne in 1972 and became the first crowned queen in Danish history (*see* Margrethe I). Margrethe II is well educated and has developed a wide range of interests. She has studied at the universities of Aarhus, Copenhagen, London, and Cambridge, and at the Sorbonne. She holds degrees in archeology and political science. Under the Danish Constitution of 1953, the monarch continues to play a role in the government of the country, and Margrethe has taken her responsibilities seriously. She has represented her country well on international visits and is liked and respected in Denmark.

REFERENCES: *DBL*, vol. 9; B. Rying, ed., *Denmark: An Official Handbook* (Copenhagen: Royal Ministry of Foreign Affairs, 1974).

B. NORDSTROM

MAY STRIKE (2–11 May 1980) Labor-management conflict in Sweden

In May 1980 the peace in Swedish labor-management relations that had existed since 1938, when the basic agreement governing those relations was reached (Saltsjöbad Agreement*), was broken by the largest labor conflict in the country's history. (The 1909 General Strike* lasted longer but involved fewer numbers. There were significant conflicts between 1938 and 1980, but none were as extensive as the May Strike.) Negotiations between the Swedish Employers' Federation* (Svenska Arbetsgivareföreningen/SAF) and the Swedish Confederation of Trade Unions* (Landsorganisationen i Sverige LO*) broke down. A mediation commission established by the bourgeois government of T. Fälldin could not effect a solution. SAF initiated a lock-out of some 520,000 trade union members, and LO responded by taking about 100,000 of its members out on strike. Over the next few days the numbers grew, and the country was simultaneously hit by a strike by public employees that involved another 25,000.

The conflict was the result of the refusal of both parties to budge from their positions. The unions had abstained from pressing for wage agreements in two previous rounds of bargaining and by 1980 felt that they deserved significant increases. They felt justified in making these demands because of rising profits in industry and rising prices, and were willing to accept another round of inflation. The employers were equally adamant about holding down costs. Sweden's international trade position had worsened in the 1970s. Advantages in international price competition had disappeared, and Sweden's balance of trade situation was bleak.

Formal government involvement in the dispute, which was unusual in Sweden, continued. LO and SAF called off most of their actions after nine days, and a new general agreement on wages was reached on 24 June. LO accepted a 6.8 percent increase (about half of their initial demand), with the understanding that adjustments upward in that rate would be made if inflation wiped out real gains. There were hard feelings on both sides. LO was accused of trying to bring down the government. SAF (allegedly in alliance with the bourgeois government) was accused of seeking to destroy the unions and the basic agreement that had worked for so long.

The strike revealed realities in the Swedish labor market and the country's economic situation that had been masked by the prosperity of the nearly 30 years after World War II* and had been ignored in the troubled 1970s. It was another indicator that Sweden had entered a new period in its history.

REFERENCES: A. Boyd, "More Than Two Can Play," *Sweden Now* 4 (1980): 14–17; Landsorganisationen i Sverige, *Landssekretariatets berättelse för år 1980* (Stockholm: Tiba, 1981).

B. NORDSTROM

MERCANTILISM: DENMARK

Before 1755 no public discussion of economic affairs was allowed in Denmark. Earlier history of economic thought must be based mainly on government memoranda found in public archives. The best known of these is Otto Thott's *Uforgribelige Tanker om Kommerciens Tilstand* (*Thoughts on the State of Commerce*) from 1735, a political program for the newly established commercial department containing advice on how to combat the depression in the 1730s.

After 1755 there are three periods with an animated and comprehensive discussion on economic affairs, 1755–1764, the early 1770s, and 1784–1791. The contributions are mainly concerned with current issues about population, agriculture, manufacturing, foreign trade, and banking. There are few theoretical treatises.

The basic economic ideas in the discussion are borrowed from German *kameralism*, which especially takes an interest in state intervention in production and distribution and in government finance. British and French mercantilist thought often reached Denmark in German translations or through German authors who were influenced by west European mercantilists including John Law, Richard Cantillon, and James Steuart, all of whom are frequently quoted in the Danish debate.

The most independent contributions among Danish mercantilists can be found in banking theory, probably as a result of successful Danish experiments with irredeemable note-issuing from 1757 to 1807. Most authors agreed that the government should provide an abundant supply of means of payment in order to stimulate employment and economic growth, and there was little fear that this would lead to a harmful increase in prices. There was also a good understanding of the relation between the position of the balance of payments and the exchange rate, and of the possibilities for carrying out an expansive monetary policy by means of irredeemable notes in a situation with a deficit in the balance of payments.

In economic legislation the mercantilist influence can also be found in a protectionist tariff act from 1762, in a heavy subsidization of the manufacturing sector, and in royal charters to companies engaged in overseas trade.

REFERENCES: H. L. Bisgaard, *Den danske nationaløkonomi i det 18. århundrede* (Copenhagen: Hagerup, 1902); J. O. Bro-Jørgensen, *Industriens historie i Danmark*, vol. 2 (Copenhagen: G.E.C. Gads forlag, 1943); *Dansk Pengehistorie* (Copenhagen: Danmarks Nationalbank, 1968); H. C. Johansen, *Danske Økonomer* (Copenhagen: Socialøkonomisk Samfund, 1976), and *Dansk økonomisk politik i årene efter 1784*, 2 vols. (Århus: Universitetsforlaget, 1968, 1980); E. Oxenbøll, *Dansk økonomisk taenkning 1700–1770* (Copenhagen: Akademisk forlag, 1977); A. Rasch, *Dansk toldpolitik 1760–1797* (Århus: Universitetsforlaget, 1955); K. E. Svendsen, "Monetary Policy and Theory in Denmark," *Scandinavian Economic History Review* 10 (1962): 38–77, and 11 (1963): 1–26; O. Thott (introduction by K. Glamann), "Uforgribelige Tankar om Kommerciens Tilstand," *University of Copenhagen Festschrift*, 1966.

H. C. JOHANSEN

METHODISTS

Methodism was firmly planted in Norway, Denmark, and Sweden shortly after the middle of the nineteenth century. Before that time, restrictions on religious expression and the privileged status of the established Lutheran churches hindered the importation of other denominations. Nevertheless, traces of Methodist influence were perceptible earlier in the nineteenth and even in the eighteenth century. John Wesley (1703–1791), one of the founders of this revival movement within the Church of England, corresponded with religious figures throughout northern Europe, and a handful of Scandinavians had been touched by the movement by the time of the Napoleonic Wars.

In Sweden, ministers from the London-based Wesleyan Missionary Society began to preach to British foreign workers in the 1820s. The most influential of them, George Scott, arrived in Stockholm* in 1830 and gained a relatively large following that included Swedish Lutherans. His harsh criticism of the state church prompted a severe reaction, however, and Scott fled Sweden in 1842.

The denomination became a fixture on the Swedish religious landscape in the 1850s, largely due to the efforts of returned emigrants who had been converted to Methodism in the United States. Several of them had experienced conversion on the Bethel ship, a mission in the harbor of New York which began to serve Scandinavian seamen and immigrants in 1845. Ole P. Petersen (1822–1901), one such Norwegian convert, spent the winter of 1849–1850 in Norway leading revival meetings but then returned to the United States. Late in 1853 he sailed back to his native land and preached in several southeastern coastal towns. Despite strong opposition from the Lutheran clergy, the first congregations were gathered in Sarpsborg and Halden in 1856. Others soon appeared along the southern coast. Growth was initially slow; in 1870 there were still fewer than 900 Methodists in Norway. Owing partly to the urbanization that accompanied the Industrial Revolution, however, the denomination then experienced a spurt which sent its membership up to over 8,000 in 1890.

The Methodist apostle of Denmark, Christian B. Willerup (1815–1886), was also converted in the United States; after his ordination aboard the Bethel ship, he evangelized Scandinavian immigrants in the Midwest during the early 1850s. Willerup worked with Petersen in southern Norway in 1856 and 1857 but also began to preach in Copenhagen* in 1856. The first Danish Methodist congregation was founded in that city three years later with eleven members. The second, at Vejle in Jutland, dates from 1861. The Danish government legally recognized the new denomination four years later. By 1900 there were 3,440 Methodists in 22 congregations, nearly all of them in cities and towns.

The early history of Methodism in Sweden is more vague. During the 1850s several sailors and other Swedes who had experienced conversion in the New World returned to Sweden and preached a bit, but little progress was perceptible for many years. Victor Witting, who had served as a minister among Swedish immigrants in Illinois, returned to Sweden in 1867 and helped to gather the first congregation in Stockholm the following year. Later in 1868 a congregation formed in Gothenburg*. The denomination gained legal status in 1876. As in the other Scandinavian countries, it has remained chiefly urban. A seminary organized in Uppsala was moved to Gothenburg in 1924 and long trained clergymen for all the Scandinavian Methodist churches.

REFERENCES: F. Janson, *The Background of Swedish Immigration, 1840–1930* (Chicago: University of Chicago Press, 1931), and *Nordisk teologisk uppslagsbok för kyrka och skola* (Lund: Gleerup, 1952–1957).

F. HALE

MICHELSEN, CHRISTIAN (15 March 1857–29 June 1925) Norwegian shipowner, philanthropist, politician, and prime minister

Christian Michelsen grew up in a conservative family in Bergen, where his father was a successful businessman who had been a member of the Storting* from 1868 to 1873. Almost nothing is known of Michelsen's childhood. His biographer, Thomas Christian Wyller, could only regret that whatever influence his childhood may have had on the mature politician was a matter of speculation. That the Michelsen home was a strict household seems evident by Michelsen's own admission later of how liberating it was to move freely after he enrolled at the University of Oslo in 1875. There student politics captivated him, and by 1877 he was the editor of the student newspaper. As such he frequently counseled conciliation to political opponents.

Although trained as a lawyer, Michelsen chose to become a shipowner, because he believed it would give him more economic independence and the opportunity to participate in politics. In 1884 he bought his first four old steamships and refitted them. In addition to owning his own ships, in 1888 he became the administrative director of the Hardanger-Hordaland Sound Steamship Company. In 1890 he became the first president of the newly established Shipowners' Association.

Michelsen was elected to the Bergen city council in 1888 and to the Storting in 1891. By the same year he had already gained national political experience as a member of a special committee of the parliament to examine the consular question amid the increasingly tense relationship between the partners in the Norwegian-Swedish Union*. Norwegians had begun to demand a separate foreign office. Because such a proposal was met with hostility in Sweden, the Norwegians came to focus on the consular service as the area where they could assert their national interests. The Liberal Party (Venstre) made it the first priority in their political program. Michelsen, too, recognized that it was a political issue, but he also realized that until the Conservatives joined with the Liberals, a separate consular service was unlikely to receive parliamentary approval. His speeches stressed the need to avoid divisive debate and to achieve unity.

In 1894 Michelsen refused renomination, arguing that his business interests demanded his attention, and for the next nine years he was out of national politics. By 1902 the national arena again beckoned as the country prepared for its triennial elections. To give himself a popular voice, he drew on his experience as a student editor and founded the newspaper *Morgenavisen*, through which he was able to forward his view of a national agenda. In 1903 he won a seat in the Storting as a member of a party of liberals and conservatives called the Unity Party (Samlingspartiet).

Well known in political circles, Michelsen became a member of the government Francis Hagerup organized in 1903. He served as minister in Stockholm*, where he witnessed the Swedish perspective on the Union. The experience did not make him more careful, however. He subsequently spoke of possible alternatives to negotiations, and he told the Storting on 27 April 1904 that there were members of the government who were willing to move in new directions. When negotiations failed at the end of 1904, calls for unilateral action by Norway to resolve the Union crisis increased. A majority of the Storting expressed itself in favor of a confrontational posture, but the Hagerup government advocated renewed negotiations. Unwilling to accept that policy, Michelsen, along with Jacob Schøning, resigned. Their action led to the collapse of the ministry. By placing himself in the forefront of the opposition to negotiations, Michelsen became the obvious choice to form a new government, which he did on 11 March 1905.

In the first weeks after the Michelsen government took office, the Storting debated a bill which would establish a separate Norwegian consular service. On 25 May this was passed. Before it could become law, however, the sanction of King Oscar II* was required. Fully expecting the king to veto the action, the Norwegian ministers met with Oscar on 27 May with their resignations in their pockets. They were not disappointed.

King Oscar vetoed the bill but refused to accept the resignations of his Norwegian ministers. He told them he could not "now" form a new government. Back in Oslo, Michelsen and his cabinet met on several occasions to decide on a course of action. On 2 June the prime minister told his cabinet that it was his plan to turn the government offices over to the parliament. Norway, he added, would then request that Oscar allow a son of the Bernadotte family to assume an independent Norwegian throne. By broaching the subject of a Bernadotte candidate, Michelsen picked up an idea which had originated with Sigurd Ibsen* in 1898 but had been largely forgotten. The action was intended to signal to the Swedes and the rest of the world that the Norwegians were neither hostile to the monarchy nor revolutionaries.

On 7 June a special session of the Storting acted on Michelsen's plans. It was a bold move. Since the king had vetoed the consular law and claimed he could not form a new government, and since the country needed to have a government, by failing in his constitutional duty, Oscar had, in effect, abdicated as king. Furthermore, Michelsen argued, since the Union between Norway and Sweden was a personal union, without a king there was no union. The Union, therefore, was dissolved, and Norway was a separate and independent country.

The Bernadotte candidacy, intended to make the bitter pill easier to swallow in Stockholm, never had much chance for acceptance in Sweden, where it was perceived as an audacious affront. While the government had to wait for an answer, however, it kept Norwegian republicans from openly discussing any future form of government for fear of breaking the united front on the dissolution issue. Michelsen and some members of his government, anticipating a Swedish rejection, began to look for a secondary candidate. Such a candidate was found in the Danish royal family in the person of Prince Carl (*see* Haakon VII*).

On 13 August a plebiscite on the dissolution showed the overwhelming support Michelsen had. By a staggering majority (368,208 to 184), the Norwegians supported the action taken on 7 June. Backed up by the results of the plebiscite, Michelsen led a delegation to Karlstad, Sweden, where negotiations on the terms of the dissolution took place. When, on 23 September, an agreement was reached, only the future form of the government of Norway was yet to be decided.

In spite of Michelsen's insistence that Norway remain a monarchy, republican sentiment appeared strong. In Denmark, Prince Carl insisted that a vote on his candidacy be held. Therefore, on 12–13 November, the second plebiscite in three months was held. Although the margin of victory for the monarchists was smaller than in August, it was nevertheless decisive. Eighty percent of the electorate voted for Michelsen's policy, and Prince Carl came to Norway as King Haakon VII.

With Haakon securely on the throne of an independent Norway, it was clear that Michelsen had led the country through six of the most significant months in its history. No politician, before or since, has stood so tall in the eyes of Norwegians as he did at the end of 1905. He had steered a precarious course, and the nautical metaphor appeared frequently in the press as a nation of seafarers reflected on the events of the year.

With the Union dissolved, Michelsen's job was essentially finished. Though in precarious health, he refused to step down. His tenure as prime minister lasted for two more years, although they were marked by a gradual deterioration of the coalition he had built in 1905. In 1907 he returned to Bergen and his shipping interests there. Following World War I he used most of his considerable fortune to establish an institute for scientific, historical, social, and political research, the Christian Michelsen Institute.

Michelsen is remembered as one of Norway's most important historical figures. His political philosophy was essentially that of a pragmatist. He was uncomfortable with party labels. His lack of restrictive ideological thinking made him the ideal leader in 1905 but hampered him otherwise and probably was the reason some contemporaries labeled him an opportunist. His hesitance, similarly, to play by parliamentary rules has led scholars to criticize him for being anti-parliamentary. In many ways this has been an unfair characterization, because he was not anti-democratic. Although not an original thinker, Michelsen had a remarkable sense for putting into practice the relevant ideas of others. His most important contributions were action and diplomacy when these were needed most.

REFERENCES: R. E. Lindgren, *Norway-Sweden: Union, Disunion and Scandinavian Integration* (Princeton: Princeton University Press, 1959); J. Nerbovik, *Antiparlamentariske staumdrag i Norge, 1905–14* (Oslo, 1968); Y. Nielsen, *Norge i 1905* (Horten, 1906); T. C. Wyller, *Christian Michelsen, Politikeren* (Oslo, 1975).

T. LEIREN

MILLES, CARL (23 June 1875–19 September 1955) Swedish sculptor

Born Vilhelm Carl Emil Andersson, he gained the new surname Milles because his mother called his father Mille, and their children were referred to as Mille's children. Milles's mother died when he was four, and he himself was sickly as a child. His father set him up as a carpenter's apprentice, and as he worked he also studied part-time at a technical school. He went to Paris in 1897 at the age of 22 with a scholarship from the Swedish Slöjd Union (Association for Arts and Crafts). In Paris he did odd jobs and spent most of his time sculpting. In 1900 he won silver and bronze medals for his work, and the artist Auguste Rodin took Milles under his wing. Milles called upon his personal experience with poverty for ideas in his sculpting and frequently used the theme of people helping one another in his early work. Milles subsequently studied in Munich. In 1901 he entered a competition in Uppsala to build a monument to Sten Sture the Elder*. His entry won fourth prize but was widely proclaimed for its simplicity. A controversy ensued, and Milles subsequently was given the job, which was not completed until 1925. The controversy made him famous in Sweden. Milles married Olga Granner, an Austrian painter, in 1905. In 1922 he became professor of sculpture at the Stockholm Academy of Art. From 1931 to 1946 he was head of the department of sculpture at the Academy of Art and Science at Cranbrook Foundation in Broomfield Hills, Michigan. He became an American citizen in 1945. Milles moved back to Sweden and died in Lidingö in 1955. His villa in Lidingö is now a museum of his work.

REFERENCES: K. Arvidsson, *Milles Garden* (Stockholm: Nordisk Rotogravyr, 1953); M. Rogers, *Carl Milles: An Interpretation of His Work* (New Haven: Yale University Press, 1940).

L. DEAL

MISSIONARIES: AFRICA Scandinavian missionaries and their activities in Africa

Scandinavian missionary work has been particularly intense in western, central, eastern, and southern Africa. In West Africa, numerous Danish missionaries have included Christian Protten, the first missionary to West Africa, who arrived in Christiansborg in 1737. He wrote a brief study of Fante and Ga grammar, two languages spoken along the Ghanaian coast. In 1763 five missionaries arrived in Christiansborg led by Jacob Meder. In the 1830s and 1840s, Andreas Riis studied the Twi language of southern Ghana, and in 1853 he published the first written grammar of this language. A number of Swedenborgians in the eighteenth century believed that they had a mission to go into the African interior to found a church. Carl Bernhard Wadström, a Swedenborgian, was sent by Gustav III* to prepare for the establishment of a colony near the Senegal River. (The planners of this quarreled and the project died.)

In the Congo (Zaire), the Swedish Covenant Church sent missionaries as early as 1881, including Nils Westlind, a skilled philologist, to the lower Congo basin. That work expanded throughout Zaire as well as into the neighboring Republic of the Congo. A number of these Swedish missionaries reported to the outside world the brutalities committed by Belgian authorities against Africans at the turn of the century.

In East Africa, there was considerable Scandinavian (particularly Swedish) missionary activity. Extensive Swedish involvement in Ethiopia began with three missionaries from the Swedish Evangelical Mission (Svenska Evangeliska Fosterlandsstiftelsen/SEF). They arrived in Massawa, Eritrea, in March 1866. The missionaries were unsuccessful in penetrating Ethiopia proper until 1904, when Carl Cederquist entered Addis Ababa. He stayed there until his death in 1919 and gradually won the confidence of the Ethiopian emperor. Many future Ethiopian leaders received their education from SEF missionaries and their schools. In Tanzania (formerly Tanganyika), the Church of Sweden Mission (Svenska Kyrkans Mission/SKM) did extensive work. Bengt Sundkler is a noted SKM missionary, author, and scholar who worked in Tanzania and Zululand.

The state churches of Norway and Sweden became interested in missionary activity in southern Africa in the middle to late nineteenth century. The former established an independent society in 1842 called the Norwegian Missionary Society (Det Norske Misjonsselskab/NMS), and the latter founded the Church of Sweden Mission. They were particularly interested in Zululand. The first missionary to establish a permanent station in that area (1851) was the Norwegian Hans P. S. Schreuder. In 1856 he was installed as the first Mission Bishop in the Church of Norway. He then proceeded to inaugurate the very successful Norwegian mission work in Madagascar. He exercised considerable influence on both the Zulus and the British government in Natal. He became a close friend and confidant of the Zulu chief Mpande, and in fact occupied a position analagous to that of prime minister. Schreuder also developed a unique relationship with Cetshwayo, a feared Zulu chieftain. Later, other groups, including Swedes, built on Schreuder's pioneering work.

The first SKM missionary was Otto Witt (1848–1923). He established the Rorke's Drift (Oscarberg) mission station in 1878. One year later, the battle of Rorke's Drift was fought on and near this mission station. Other early SKM missionaries included Carl Flygare, Frans Fristedt, and Johan Norenius. The Scandinavian missionaries played an important part in opening Zululand for colonization, and their eyewitness accounts of nineteenth-century events in the area are important. They gave prominence to educational work, helped to reduce the Zulu language to writing, and brought medical facilities to the region. Many missionary sons and daughters settled permanently in South Africa.

In South West Africa (Namibia), the Finnish Missionary Society (Suomen Lëhetysseura) made a great contribution in the northern part of the region. The pioneer Finnish missionary was Martti Rautanen, who arrived in Ovamboland in 1870. He subsequently translated the Bible into the Ovambo language.

Scandinavian Lutheran, Covenant, Methodist, Baptist, and Pentecostal missionaries also worked in Angola, Burundi, Liberia, Mozambique, Rwanda, Swaziland, Zambia, and Zimbabwe.

REFERENCES: T. Furberg, *Kyrka och mission i Sverige 1868–1901* (Uppsala: Institutet för missionsforskning, 1962); C. Hallencreutz, *Svensk mission över sex kontinenter* (Motala: Borgströms tryckeri AB, 1970); O. G. Myklebust, ed., *Norsk håndbok for misjon, 1952* (Oslo: Egede Instituttet, 1952); J. E. Norenius, *Bland Zuluer och Karanger, Femtio års missionshistoria på svenska kyrkans fält i Sydafrika*, 2 vols. (Stockholm: Svenska kyrkans diakonistyrelses bokförlag, 1925); B. Sundkler, *Ung kyrka i Tanganyika* (Stockholm: Svenska kyrkans diakonistyrelses bokförlag, 1948); A. Winquist, *Scandinavians and South Africa* (Cape Town: A. A. Balkema, 1978).

A. H. WINQUIST

MODERATE PARTY *See* Conservative Party: Sweden

MOELLER, CHRISTMAS (1894–1948) Danish Conservative Party leader and resistance figure

Christmas Moeller was a major figure in Danish politics noted for his uncompromising devotion to democratic principles, parliamentary government, and a close relationship between Denmark and Great Britain. Throughout the 1930s he successfully combated pro-Fascist and even pro-Nazi elements within the Conservative Party, especially its youth organization, Konservativ Ungdom. Also, in 1935, he concluded a far-reaching agreement with the Stauning-Munch government regarding constitutional reform which would have democratized the Danish political process even more than the Constitution of 1915 had done. The proposed constitution was not adopted, but his willingness to work with Social Democrats and Radical Liberals like Peter Munch* on far-reaching political reforms underscored the fact that Moeller was not a doctrinaire conservative.

During the first year of the German occupation (1940), Christmas Moeller served as a minister without portfolio until 8 July. Between July and October 1940 he took control of the Ministry of Commerce and Shipping in Thorvald Stauning's* government of national unity, which included representatives from all four of the major parties. Throughout this period Moeller remained outspokenly anti-Nazi and anti-German. Largely due to German pressure, Moeller resigned as minister of commerce, and on 10 January 1941 he had to give up his seat in the Folketing* and resigned as business manager of the Conservative Party.

After a year and a half of relative political inactivity, Moeller and his family fled to England in May 1942. From then until the end of the war he played a leading role in the Danish Council in London, directing the day-to-day operations of this resistance organization, which was the most significant group of Danes actively opposing the Germans outside of Denmark. Moeller's speeches, articles, and activities favoring an active opposition to the Nazi occupation served as an inspiration for Danes both inside and outside of Denmark.

After the liberation Moeller returned home and, largely out of respect for his resistance work, Prime Minister Vilhelm Buhl appointed him as foreign minister in Denmark's first postwar government. This represented a complete vindication of his policies, and as a result Moeller soon became a hero and elder statesman in the country that he had to flee only a few years before.

REFERENCES: C. Moeller, "What Is Happening in Denmark," *American Scandinavian Review* 31:1 (1943); J. Haestrup, *Panorama Denmark* (Copenhagen: Royal Ministry of Foreign Affairs, 1963); B. Outze, *Denmark During the German Occupation* (Copenhagen: The Scandinavian Publishing Company, 1946); K. Secher, *Christmas Moeller* (Odense: Normanns Forlag, 1945); F. Wendt, *Besættelse og Atomtid 1939–1970* (Copenhagen: Politikens Forlag, 1972); J. Winter, "Fra Krise til Krig, 1929–1940," in *Det Konservative Folkepartiets Historie i et Halvt Aarhundrede 1915–1965*(Copenhagen: Nyt Nordisk Forlag, 1966).

J. L. VOORHIS

MONOPOLY, FAROESE

The origin of the trade monopoly over the Faroe Islands*, which continued for over three centuries, and which ended only in 1856, is shrouded in obscurity.

Some writers have traced the Monopoly back to a supposed Norwegian royal ordinance of 1273, in which King Magnus VI Haakonson* (Lagaböter) undertook to send two ships to the islands each year. But the text does not forbid others to send ships to the Faroes; and in any case there are good internal grounds for believing this document to be a forgery.

The most likely origin of the Monopoly is to be sought in the struggles between the rival factions for the Danish throne in the 1530s. The first indisputable grant of the Monopoly of the Faroe Islands was made in 1535 by Christian III* to a Hamburg merchant, Thomas Koppen, who likewise held the islands in fief. Koppen was probably installed to exclude the Lübeck merchants from the Faroes, for they had supported Christian II* during the Count's War* of 1534–1536. Koppen, who had been a staunch supporter of Christian III, retained his privileges until his death in 1553.

On Koppen's death, the trade was at first thrown open to all Danish and Norwegian merchants; but already in 1556, Christian III had reimposed the Monopoly and granted it to a Copenhagen merchant. The Monopoly was conducted by various concessionaries in Copenhagen* until 1571, when, in response to complaints from the Faroese, the trade was handed over to the islanders themselves. This experiment was not a success, however, and in 1578 Frederik II* took the trade into his own hands. The following year the Monopoly was granted to Mogens Heinesen* or Magnus Heinason and his partners based in Bergen. Heinason, despite his close connections with the Faroe Islands, was a most unsatisfactory merchant. From 1581 he was made to share the trade with a Hamburg and a Copenhagen merchant and in 1584 was removed from the trade altogether. The concession was now granted for short terms to merchants based in Hamburg, Copenhagen, and Bergen.

From 1597 until 1619 the trade was conducted by a series of Bergen partnerships. Bergen was not an ideal base for the Faroese Monopoly because it was inferior to Copenhagen as a place to secure supplies which the Faroe Islands needed. It was, moreover, not under the direct eye of the king, to whom the Faroese would complain if they were badly supplied or unjustly treated.

The various concessionaries operated under strict conditions. They had the obligation to keep the islands well supplied, particularly with grain, and had to trade at fixed prices, regardless of fluctuations in markets. They had to carry any prosecution, whether for debt or any other cause, before the *lagmand** and the Lagting*, and they had to give a passage at a fair price to any islander who wished to petition the king in person. The earliest known tariff dates from 1584, but this was probably merely a restatement of the tariff at which Thomas Koppen had traded, made to regularize the position after the unsatisfactory regime of Magnus Heinason. There were several tariff revisions during the seventeenth century, mostly due to difficult wartime conditions. The tariff in the trading law of 30 May 1691, however, lasted until 1790, as far as imports were concerned. The 1691 export tariff was revised in 1723, partly to bring the trading values of Faroese goods in line with the values at which they were accepted in payment of crown rents and taxes.

In December 1619 the trade was granted to the Icelandic, Faroese and Nordland Company (Det Islandske, Faeröske og Nordlandske Kompagni). The company was a good concessionary and continued to trade until its bankruptcy in 1662. In that year the Monopoly was granted to the lensmand of the Faroe Islands, Christoffer von Gabel. Together with the administration of the islands, the Monopoly remained in the hands of the Gabel family until 1709, when the Danish crown resumed control of the islands and their trade.

From 1709 until 1776 the Faroese Monopoly was under the control of the Danish Rentekammer, which appointed a Copenhagen merchant to buy the goods requisitioned by the Faroe Islands officials, to contract for their shipment to the Faroes, and to dispose of the return cargoes, usually by auction on the Copenhagen Exchange (Börsen). In Tórshavn* there was a resident merchant, also appointed by the Rentekammer, aided by a small staff. A garrison of about 35 men was charged with protecting the warehouses in Tórshavn and curbing smugglers who visited outlying fjords almost every spring.

In 1776 the Monopoly was merged with the Royal Monopoly in Finmark and Iceland, to which in 1781 the Greenland Monopoly was added. After the freeing of the trade in Iceland in 1786 and Finmark in 1787, it was intended also to free the Faroese trade, but Faroese fears of the effects of ending fixed-price trading hindered abolition of the Monopoly. A new tariff was introduced in 1790, and from 1801 provision was made for tariff prices to vary in accordance with long-term movements in world prices. Out-stations of the Monopoly were established in Tvöroyri in 1836, Klaksvík in 1837, and Vestmanna in 1839, to serve the outlying areas of Faroe. During this period the fish export of the Faroe Islands took a sharp rise, and in the 1840s *klipfisk* (dried salted cod) became an important commodity, gradually overhauling the traditional export of knitted woolens. The Monopoly was finally abolished on 1 January 1856.

There has been much dispute whether the Faroese Monopoly was oppressive to the islanders or not. There is little evidence before 1709, other than Faroese complaints sent to Copenhagen. The period of Christoffer von Gabel (1662–1673) is generally agreed to have been a bad one, partly because of the rapacity of Gabel's subordinates, partly because of the difficult state of the Danish realm as a whole. Royal commissions sat on the trade in 1673 and 1690, the latter being responsible for the tariff that lasted nearly a century.

The evidence for the period of the Royal Faroese Monopoly is abundant and detailed. From 1709 to 1725 trade was so unprofitable that several attempts to auction the trade to private merchants failed for lack of bidders. This was the result of the Great Northern War* and the great sheep mortality in Faroe of 1716–1717. From 1725 to about 1775 the Monopoly made a handsome profit, which thereafter tailed away. The war years of 1807–1814 occasioned certain direct losses, and the wild inflation of 1812–1813 threw the whole trading position into great confusion. After the severe postwar slump was over, the regular peacetime conditions were restored by about 1828, and a reasonable trading profit was annually made until 1855. Conditions were normally determined by the world prices of the principal import, barley, and the principal export, knitted woolens. Tariff prices for grain were, indeed, deliberately kept low as an act of policy, while those for tobacco and spirits were kept high. On the export side, at least until the reforms of 1790, the prices of tallow, butter, and train-oil were usually below world market prices, while those for woolens were more favorable.

Any judgment over whether the Faroe Islands were exploited by the Monopoly requires an overall view of the taxation system (since rents and taxes were collected in kind) and a survey of government expenses, as well as a close examination of individual commodities. Danish government policy seems normally to have been to avoid loss rather than to make a profit.

REFERENCES: L. Debes, *A Description of the Islands and Inhabitants of Foeroe*, trans. J[ohn] S[terpin] (London, 1676); G. Landt, *A Description of the Feroe Islands* (London, 1810); J. Nicoll, *A Historical and Descriptive Account of Iceland, Greenland and the Faroe Islands* (Edinburgh: Oliver & Boyd, 1841); C. Plöyen, *Reminiscences of a Voyage to Shetland, Orkney and Scotland, in the Summer of 1839*, trans. C. Spence (Lerwick, 1894); J. F. West, ed., *The Journals of the Stanley Expedition to the Faroe Islands and Iceland in 1789*, 3 vols. (Tórshavn: Föroya Fróðskaparfelag, 1970, 1975, 1976), and *Faroe, the Emergence of a Nation* (London: C. Hurst; and New York: Paul S. Eriksson, 1972).

J. F. WEST

MUNCH, EDVARD (12 December 1863–23 January 1944) Norwegian artist

Munch's childhood years were marked by illness and death in his family. His mother died of tuberculosis when he was 5, as did his sister Sophie when he was 15. He himself was often rheumatic and feverish. This early experience with death and illness influenced his work, and the two became dominant themes in his painting. In 1881 he began his formal artistic training at the Royal School of Design in Christiania (now Oslo). He worked there with a group of students under the direction of Christian Krohg, who introduced Munch to French Impressionism. In 1885–1886 he painted one of his more important works, "The Sick Child." In 1889 Munch had his first one-man show. The same year his father died and Munch moved to Paris, where he began studies at Leon Bonnat's Art School, but he stayed there for only a few months. In 1892 he was invited to Berlin to exhibit his work. The exhibit closed after only one week and created a controversy about art in general and Munch in particular in German newspapers. In 1893 Munch finished what is perhaps his best-known work, "The Scream" (or "The Cry"). "The Scream" was included in the series "The Frieze of Life." Munch considered the series his most important work, and its impact has caused many to call Munch the father of Expressionism. In 1894 Munch began to use printmaking as a medium, employing etching, lithography, and woodcut.

Long after he was recognized on the continent, Norway accepted him, and in 1908 he was made a Knight of the Royal Norwegian Order of St. Olaf. At the end of 1908 Munch suffered a nervous breakdown and spent eight months in a mental hospital in Copenhagen.* He was nearly psychotic due to overwork, emotional stress, and alcohol. He underwent shock treatment and massage as part of his care. After he left he hospital he felt cured and never drank again. After 1910 he resided permanently in Norway, and his works became brighter, more cheerful, and richer in color. He gave up printmaking but continued painting until his death. Munch bequeathed his entire estate and all of his work still in his possession to the city of Oslo, which built the Munch Museum in 1963.

REFERENCES: F. Deknatel, *Edvard Munch* (New York: Chanticleer Press, Inc., 1950); R. Heller, *Edvard Munch: The Scream* (New York: Viking Press, 1972); J. Hodin, *Edvard Munch* (London: Thames and Hudson, 1972).

L. DEAL

MUNCH, PETER (25 July 1870–12 January 1948) Danish Radical Party leader and diplomat

One of the original founders of the Radical Liberal (Radikal Venstre) Party during the first decade of the twentieth century, Munch set forth the principles which have guided the Radical Party since its establishment. These include a commitment to social and legal equality plus an equitable distribution of wealth through cooperatives, public housing, social insurance, and other economic reform measures. As an integral part of this program, Munch and most members of the Radical Party strongly opposed large defense expenditures. This was based on two assumptions: that military defense of Denmark would be hopeless in the event of a future war with modern weapons, and that commitment of money to a large military establishment would completely undermine any program for economic justice within Denmark.

In 1909, four years after the founding of the Radical Party, Peter Munch was elected to the Folketing*. Only four years later (1913) he became minister of defense in the second Radical ministry, which had Carl Theodore Zahle as its prime minister. This Zahle ministry ruled Denmark throughout World War I and the immediate postwar period until 1920.

In 1929 Munch joined Social Democrat Thorvald Stauning's* coalition ministry as its minister of foreign affairs. This carried on a tradition of cooperation between the Radical and Social Democratic parties which began in the years preceding World War I and has continued up to the present. As foreign minister, Munch followed a policy of cooperation with all major powers, including Germany. This ultimately led to the conclusion of the Non-Aggression Pact between Berlin and Copenhagen* in May 1939. This, plus a reduction in the size of the Danish army between September 1939 and April 1940, led many Danish politicians to criticize Munch's policies as appeasement. Since German troops invaded Denmark mainly because of developments in Norway, Munch's policies toward Denmark's southern neighbor probably did very little to influence Berlin one way or the other. However, Munch's attitude of conciliation toward Berlin in regard to the Slesvig question*, military preparedness, and on the diplomatic level may have helped to mitigate considerably the severity of the German occupation of Denmark, particularly in the early years.

Munch had to relinquish the post of foreign minister to Erik Scavenius*, the career diplomat, by July 1940 largely due to political pressure from the opposition Liberal and Conservative parties. However, his legacy of internationalism, social democracy, and anti-militarism continues to affect Danish politics.

REFERENCES: B. Arneson, *The Democratic Monarchies of Scandinavia* (New York: D. Van Nostrand, 1939); P. Hansen, *Contemporary Danish Politicians: Forty-five Portraits with a Brief Look at the Development of Danish Parliamentary Democracy* (Copenhagen: Det Danske Selskab, 1949); K. Kristensen, *Set Fra Mine Vinduer, Kommentarer til Fremstillingen af Begivenheder under og efter Besaettelsen* (Copenhagen: H. Hagerup, 1954); A. Oelsen, *Forspillet til Danmark's Kamploese Besættelse . . .* (Aabenraa: A. Oelsen's Forlag, 1953); E. Scavenius, *Forhandlings Politiken under Besættelsen* (Copenhagen: Hasselbach, 1948).

J. L. VOORHIS

N

NANSEN, FRIDTJOF (1861–1930) Norwegian scientist, explorer, and statesman

Born into a prominent family, young Nansen early showed an interest in science. In 1888 he took his doctorate in zoology. In the same year he led an expedition on skis across Greenland*, a feat that had never before been accomplished. On his next Arctic journey he set out to test the theory that polar ice drifted from Siberia to Greenland. On a specially constructed ship, *Fram*, Nansen's expedition entered the polar icepack in September 1893. Having drifted northwest for over a year, Nansen and a companion in March 1895 attempted to ski to the North Pole. They reached 86°14' north latitude, the furthest north any expedition had gone up to that time. Nansen was greeted as a national hero upon his return home, and he received international acclaim on lecture tours of Europe and America.

Based on the studies he had carried out in the Arctic, Nansen became a pioneer in the field of oceanography. In 1897 he was appointed professor at the University of Christiania. Nansen also made a significant contribution to the development of modern Norwegian sports, especially skiing*.

His international reputation contributed to his involvement in politics. He was one of the foremost spokesmen in favor of separation from Sweden during the Union crisis of 1905, and he played a prominent role in the negotiations which led to an independent monarchy under Haakon VII*. In 1906–1908 he was Norway's first diplomatic representative to Great Britain. During World War I, Nansen headed a Norwegian trade delegation to the United States. Intense American pressure had been placed on neutral countries to break their trade with Germany after the United States entered the war. Following very difficult negotiations, Nansen signed an agreement in April 1918 which secured Norway needed supplies.

Despite his diplomatic successes, Nansen never gained an influential position in Norwegian politics. He was not attuned to party politics in parliamentary government, a trend permanently established after 1905. Nansen favored a strong national government above party politics, and he remained an outsider. He was a prominent member of the Independent Liberal Party (Frisinnede Venstre), and he actively supported a strong military defense. In 1926 an effort was made to promote his candidacy as prime minister above all parties, but the campaign failed to generate support, and Nansen was not involved directly. His final participation in Norwegian politics was in the Fatherland League (Fedrelandslaget), founded in 1925 with Nansen and Christian Michelsen* as its two outstanding members. Established to form a broad, non-Socialist, national union against the growing influence of the Socialist labor movement, the League at first was quite numerous, but it declined in the 1930s when it developed fascist traits. Nansen, however, as a liberal and a humanitarian, never subscribed to fascism.

During the final decade of his life Nansen made his outstanding contribution in international humanitarian activity. As Norway's delegate to the League of Nations in 1920, he immediately developed a special interest in humanitarian relief. His initial effort involved aiding homeless prisoners of war, 450,000 of whom were repatriated. More difficult was the task of aiding millions of refugees displaced by the effects of World War I and its aftermath. Nansen was appointed high commissioner for refugees by the League. For those who lacked passports, a special ''Nansen passport'' was created, recognized by more than 50 governments. Nansen's most difficult humanitarian effort began in August 1921 when he sought to alleviate the impact of famine in the U.S.S.R. Thanks to Nansen's organizational ability, 1.5–2 million persons were saved from death by starvation. In addition to these projects, he also found time in 1921–1922 to aid Greek and Turkish refugees who had been made homeless by fighting between the two countries. In recognition of his humanitarian work, he received the Nobel Peace Prize in 1922. His final effort on behalf of Armenian refugees, whom he planned to resettle in Soviet Armenia, did not succeed due to Western opposition, in particular from the British.

Nansen had new projects and journeys planned, but first he wished to conclude a number of scientific studies. However, he became ill and died suddenly on 13 May 1930. His burial on 17 May was a day of national sorrow. Due to his internationally renowned accomplishments, Nansen gained worldwide recognition unsurpassed by any Norwegian political figure in modern history.

REFERENCES: L. Nansen Hoyer, *Nansen: A Family Portrait by His Daughter*, trans. M. Michael (London: Longmans, 1957); H. G. Leach, ''Fridtjof Nansen,'' *American-Scandinavian Review* 49:4 (December 1961): 360–67; F. Noel-Baker, *Fridtjof Nansen* (London: Adam & Charles Black, 1958); E. Reynolds, *Nansen: The Life-Story of the Arctic Explorer and Humanitarian*, 2nd ed. (London: Penguin Books, 1949); J. Sorensen, *The Saga of Fridtjof Nansen* (New York: 1932); P. Vogt, ed., *Fridtjof Nansen—Explorer—Scientist—Humanitarian* (Oslo, 1961); J. S. Worm-Müller, ''Fridtjof Nansen,'' *Impact of Science on Society*, 2 (1961): 223–56.

O. HOIDAL

NASJONAL SAMLING *See* National Union

NATIONAL ASSEMBLY (Riksforsamling) (1814) Norwegian constitutional assembly

As a result of procedures established at the Great Men's Meeting*, Norwegians gathered in local assemblies during late February and early March 1814 to participate in the creation of Norwegian independence. Towns, military units, and counties chose representatives to the National Assembly. All adult males were allowed to vote and at least one of each county's representatives had to be a landowning peasant. These stipulations reflect the impact of the eighteenth-century cultural revival in Norway, which had glorified the role of the peasantry, and stressed the necessity of securing the peasantry's support because they formed the backbone of the army; the move was also very likely a calculated political maneuver by government officials to reduce the power of the middle class during the making of the constitution. Prince Christian Frederik (later Christian VIII*) probably hoped as well that peasants might support his claims to rule by inherited, absolute right more readily than the "Great Men" had earlier.

A great deal of uncertainty still exists regarding the actual desire for independence in the countryside early in 1814. Officials and advocates of independence certainly attempted to stimulate support through an oath to independence taken by all in the local meetings and to discourage any opposition to their cause. Men chosen as representatives to the National Assembly were generally chosen, however, for their local influence rather than their stand on independence. The addresses to Christian Frederik prepared by the assemblies to verify that the oath had been taken were generally brief and prepared by the local pastor, thus revealing little of popular political sentiments. It can be assumed, however, that the prince was probably quite effective in creating a desire for independence through his use of the government bureaucracy as a propaganda agency and by playing upon popular prejudices against Sweden and instinctive loyalties toward the crown.

It was only after the 112 members of the National Assembly first met at Eidsvoll on 10 April that Norway's political alternatives became clear. A very large majority of those present favored independence. They were led for the most part by men already serving as government officials. Their most articulate spokesman was Christian Magnus Falsen (1782–1830). Falsen was born in Denmark, the son of Enevold de Falsen, who had been a member of the Government Commission* 1807–1808, and the magistrate (*sorenskriver*) of Follo in eastern Norway. His legal knowledge and political sense made him an effective floor leader and eventually the chairman of the constitutional committee. As time passed, Falsen was supported especially by men from distant parts of Norway, particularly representatives from Bergen such as Peter Motzfeldt, an army officer, and Wilhelm Frimann Koren Christie, like Falsen a local judge. Although benefiting from the support Christian Frederik could give, the group also suffered from the liabilities which the prince's desire for absolutism and eventual reunion of Norway with Denmark placed upon them as well.

On the other hand, a unionist faction of about 30 members coalesced at the

National Assembly which proposed Norway's voluntary union with Sweden as the country's wisest course in 1814. They did so because they doubted that Norwegians were politically mature enough for independence, needing the support of a union partner especially in foreign affairs. Moreover, they were certain that Britain, Sweden's ally, would support Karl (XIV) Johan's* claims to Norway. Norway was therefore likely to receive more favorable terms from the Swedish Crown Prince Karl Johan before he invaded than after it had suffered disastrous military defeat. The unionists, however, believed just as strongly in the need for a constitution as did independence supporters, but they saw it as a guarantor of their rights to domestic self-rule, without which they would not accept a foreign king.

The acknowledged leader of the unionists was Count Wedel Jarlsberg, the wealthiest and most powerful of Norway's handful of nobles. He spent most of his early life abroad while his father served as a Danish diplomat. He first worked as a government official in Copenhagen* and then in Norway after his arrival there in 1803. The count brashly supervised efforts to provision Norway during the war from 1807 to 1809 and was a member of the Government Commission 1809–1810. He first flirted with an attempt to unite Norway with Sweden in 1809, although Prince Christian August* and other factors frustrated his efforts then.

Wedel Jarlsberg was supported by a number of influential men. Among them were his father-in-law, Peder Anker, who was elected to preside over the National Assembly, and Jacob Aall. Aall was a prosperous land owner, an ironworks owner, a successful businessman, and the classic example of the merchant prince benignly caring for those dependent upon him. Aall had opposed Frederik VI's* policies in 1809 but not the concept of a king shared with another nation. Assuming that Norway received the right of autonomy guaranteed by a constitution, Aall supported a union with Sweden as the country's surest hope for orderly development.

The contrasts between the two parties have sometimes been depicted very sharply. Those favoring independence were mainly government officeholders, sometimes Danish-born although having chosen Norway for their homeland. Many also came from parts of Norway with no recent disaffection with Danish rule. The unionists, on the other hand, were mainly businessmen and large land owners. They were generally from eastern or southern Norway, which had protested most vigorously against Frederik's policies in 1807–1809 and had contributed the most support toward the development of a Norwegian university. This region, however, was also closest to the Swedish border and therefore had the greatest contacts with Sweden as well as being the most likely to suffer if there was war. Merchants there possessed strong ties to Britain and consequently were the most impressed by British support to Karl Johan's claims upon Norway.

As generalizations, these conclusions, for the most part, are valid. There certainly were prominent and influential exceptions. Although Jacob Aall was a leader of the unionist faction, for example, both of his brothers, Jørgen and

Niels, were supporters of independence. Niels had even held this view in 1809, long before it was fashionable in many places. He was also a member of Christian Frederik's Council of State (*statsråd*) (*see*: Council of State: Norway) when it was organized later in 1814.

REFERENCES: See references under Norwegian-Swedish Union.

L. SATHER

NATIONAL COALITION (CONSERVATIVE) PARTY Finland

The roots of Finnish conservatism as an ideology and as an organized political movement date back to the nineteenth century nationalist program of the Finnish nation as a composite entity to be governed by a Finnish-speaking elite. Political support for conservatism came from the peasantry and the clergy. Unlike other Nordic countries, Finland never had a political alignment along conservative-liberal lines. The burning political differences over whether Finland should be governed by a Swedish- or Finnish-speaking elite, which led to the formation of a Finnish Party and a Swedish Party (*see* Swedish People's Party), and divisions over how Finland should defend its autonomy against Russian encroachments, which pitted the (Old) Finnish Party against the more recently founded liberal Young Finnish Party, combined during the period of autonomy to prevent the emergence of political parties based on societal interest groups.

It was not until Finland had secured its independence and fought a civil war that the Conservative Party was founded, and by that time Finland had a multiparty system characterized by an alignment along Socialist and non-Socialist lines, the Conservatives being but one of several bourgeois parties. The nineteenth-century nationalist movement, which had survived to provide Finnish-speaking leadership for the establishment of an independent Finland, split over whether Finland should become a conservative monarchy or a liberal republic. The republican-liberal elements, mainly from the Young Finnish Party, formed the National Progressive Party (*see* Progressive/Liberal Party) and the monarchist-conservatives, primarily from the (Old) Finnish Party, formed the National Coalition Party. Although this controversy was short-lived, fundamental differences over the extent to which principles of economic and political liberalism should become the basis for organizing Finnish society prevented any reconciliation at the organizational level.

During the first years of independence the Finnish Right was formed by the Coalition Party (28 seats in 1918) and the right wing of the Swedish People's Party (22 seats in 1918). Conservative influence was greater, however, than its parliamentary strength suggests; it was reinforced by a powerful position in the cultural and administrative institutions of Finland and the Civil Guard.

In the early 1930s the dividing line between conservatism and right-wing radicalism became blurred. The Coalition Party, in cooperation with all the bourgeois parties, supported the efforts of the Lapua movement to ban all activities regarded as communistic, but unlike the parties of the Center, the Coalition Party continued to support the movement after the passage of the so-called Communist laws in 1930 and the founding of a fascist political party. This flirtation with fascism was short-lived, however, because it ran counter to fundamental Conservative commitments to the political institutions of Finland— a commitment to the defense of the legal basis of Finnish institutions which dated back to the period of Russification and which was common to all bourgeois parties. Although the Conservative president P. E. Svinhufvud remained steadfastly opposed to the Social Democratic Party* throughout his presidency during the first half of the 1930s, he took a hard line against the lawlessness of right-wing radicalism, and Juho K. Paasikivi* provided the leadership necessary to disassociate the party from the ideology and tactics of the fascist People's Patriotic Movement.

The refusal of the Coalition Party and the Agrarian Party (see Center Party: Finland) to support right-wing radicalism at a time when fascism was on the rise in eastern and central Europe reflects the particular historical roots and socio-economic basis of the Finnish political system which, although still on the interface periphery between east and west, was more Nordic than eastern European. This development in the mid-1930s also helps to explain how Finland managed to survive World War II (see Continuation War) and the Cold War with its institutions of political democracy intact.

Since World War II the Coalition Party, with 30 to 45 seats in parliament, has almost always been in opposition because of Soviet objections and/or a tradition of Center-Left cooperation which has dominated Finnish politics since the mid-1960s. In 1957 the Coalition Party adopted a program of "dynamic" conservatism emphasizing a commitment to free enterprise and moderate reform, a program which has become increasingly similar to that of the conservative parties of other Nordic countries. Moderate leadership has also succeeded in turning the party into an unequivocal supporter of the Paasikivi-Kekkonen Line* as well as an increasingly popular bourgeois alternative to the Center Party, especially at the municipal level. This development has led to and has been aided by defections on the extreme Right to form two rightist splinter parties, the Constitutional Party and the Christian League. The role of the Coalition Party in national politics remains uncertain. It is now the largest bourgeois party in a parliamentary system characterized by narrow non-Socialist majorities but Center-Left coalition governments.

REFERENCES: E. Allardt and P. Pessonen, "Cleavage in Finnish Politics," in S. Lipset and S. Rokkan, Party Systems and Voter Alignments: Cross-National Perspectives (New York: The Free Press, 1967); S. Berglund and U. Lindström, The Scandinavian Party System(s) (Lund: Studentlitteratur, 1978); J. Mylly, "The Emergence of the Finnish Multi-Party System: A Comparison with Developments in Scandinavia 1870–1920," Scandinavian Journal of History 5 (1980); J. Nousiainen, The Finnish Political System (Cambridge, Mass.: Harvard University Press, 1973); M. Rintala, Three Generations: The Extreme Right Wing in Finnish Politics (Bloomington: Indiana University Press, 1962); T. Soikanen, "Changing Bourgeois Parties in a Changing Society," in R. M. Berry, ed., Essays on the History of the Development of Finnish Political Parties (Turku:

Institute of Political History, 1983); K. Törnudd, "Composition of Cabinets in Finland 1917–1968," *Scandinavian Political Studies* 4 (1969).

R. M. BERRY

NATIONAL SOCIALIST WORKERS' PARTY (Nazis) (Danmarks Nationalsocialistiske Arbejder Parti) Denmark

The Danish Nazi Party (DNSAP) was founded in 1930 and lasted until the end of German occupation in 1945. Moved to action by the successes of Hitler and his followers in the 1930 elections to the Reichstag, a small group of Danish fascists sought to create a party patterned after the German model. Adopting all the trappings of its German counterpart, including the swastika and the upright arm salute, the DNSAP pursued power through the electoral system. Membership grew slowly, however, and the party was unable to collect the 10,000 signatures required for participation in the parliamentary elections of 1932.

After this setback, Fritz Clausen, a medical doctor from North Slesvig*, replaced Cay Lembcke, the former head of the Danish Boy Scouts, as DNSAP leader. Although generally an ineffectual politician (during World War II* a popular Danish saying was "God save the King and Fritz Clausen"), Clausen guided the party until 1944. In the 1935 elections, DNSAP candidates received 1 percent (16,257) of the total vote. Four years later, the party was almost able to double its support, with 31,032 votes, and sent three of its members, including Clausen, to the parliament. In the months following the German invasion of April 1940, the DNSAP sought to gain positions of power within the government. This effort met with little success, as officials of the German occupation were content to work with the existing political structure and saw little need to force the unpopular Clausen upon the Danish people. Despite financial assistance from the Germans, the DNSAP managed to secure only 43,309 votes in the 1943 elections—slightly more than 2 percent of the popular vote. In 1944 land owner C. O. Jørgensen replaced Clausen as party head and launched a desperate and ultimately unsuccessful effort to prepare the DNSAP for German defeat. Like Clausen and Lembcke before him, Jørgensen was unable to resolve the contradiction that had beset DNSAP from the beginning: how to reconcile the traditional anti-German nationalism of Danish voters with the obvious ties of the party to German National Socialism.

Recent studies of election patterns indicate significant changes in the geographic distribution of DNSAP voters during the party's brief existence. The party's early support came from economically distressed elements within Danish agriculture; in 1943, however, the DNSAP received a proportionally greater share of its vote in Copenhagen* and towns over 20,000. The reasons for this shift remain unclear, but it is obvious that even in the most difficult of times, few Danish voters saw in the DNSAP a solution to their problems.

REFERENCES: M. Djursaa, "Denmark," in Stuart J. Woolf, ed., *Fascism in Europe*, 2nd ed. (New York: Methuen, Inc., 1982); H. Poulsen and M. Djursaa, "Social Basis of Nazism in Denmark: The DNSAP,'' in S. U. Larsen et al., eds., *Who Were the Fascists: Social Roots of European Fascism* (Oslo: Universitetsforlaget, 1980), pp. 702–14.

P. L. PETERSEN

NATIONAL UNION (Nasjonal Samling) (1933–1945) Norwegian political party

Founded by Vidkun Quisling* in 1933, National Union originally was a right-wing nationalistic party whose activity was directed primarily against the Norwegian Labor Party*. Never at any time during the pre-war period did the party—commonly referred to by its initials, NS—gain more than 3 percent of the popular vote. Following election defeats in 1933 and 1934, Quisling increasingly patterned his party after the example of fascist parties in continental Europe. After a severe defeat in the Storting* election of 1936, the party was reduced to a small sect, with its most able leaders resigning in opposition to Quisling.

In the period 1937–1940, National Union was of no significance whatsoever in Norwegian politics. It did not reemerge until the summer of 1940, following the beginning of German occupation. The party received financial and administrative support from the Reichskommissariat which controlled the country. NS correspondingly grew in size, in particular after Reichskommissar Josef Terboven* decreed on 25 September 1940 that NS henceforth was the sole legal political organization. As such, the party sought to establish totalitarian control over Norwegian society. Despite German assistance, this goal was never realized. NS simply failed to attract a large membership during the war. At its maximum in the fall of 1943 the party numbered 49,650, including the NS youth organizations. Although NS members took over most top administrative and organizational positions during the occupation, this did not have major significance because the bulk of the people established a firm front against the party.

As an anti-democratic party which had supported Germany's war effort, at the conclusion of the war National Union ceased to exist. The Norwegian government in England had decreed in January 1942 that membership in NS constituted an act of treason. Approximately 44,878 persons were tried for having been NS members or for having supported the party economically. Of these, the majority, some 26,000, did not receive jail terms, but were punished by fines and loss of voting privileges. Since 1945 there has been no revival of NS influence in Norwegian politics.

REFERENCES: J. Andenaes, ''The Post-War Proceedings Against Enemy Collaborators,'' in J. Andenaes et al., *Norway and the Second World War* (Oslo: Johan Grundt Tanum Forlag, 1966); O. Hoidal, ''Hjort, Quisling, and *Nasjonal Samling*'s Disintegration,'' *Scandinavian Studies* 47:4 (Autumn 1975): 467–97, and ''Vidkun Quisling's Decline as a Political Figure in Prewar Norway, 1933–1937,'' *Journal of Modern History* 43:3 (1971): 440–67; M. Skodvin, ''Norway under Occupation,'' in J. Andenaes et al., *Norway and the Second World War* (Oslo: Johan Grundt Tanum Forlag, 1966).

O. HOIDAL

NAVY

All of the Scandinavian countries today maintain modest navies, designed largely for the protection of their coastal waters. Denmark's fleet in the early

1980s numbered about 130 ships, including 5 submarines, 10 frigates, and 16 fast attack craft. About 4,600 men were on active duty in the navy. Norway's fleet numbered around 125 ships in the early 1980s, including 14 submarines, 5 frigates, and 47 fast attack craft. About 8,500 men were on active duty. In addition to their coastal duties, the Danish and Norwegian navies play a modest role in NATO defense planning. Finland's fleet was comprised of about 75 ships in the early 1980s, including a number of fast attack craft, minelaying and minesweeping vessels, and 9 icebreakers. About 2,500 men served in this force. Iceland has a very small navy comprised of about five ships and about 120 officers and enlisted men. Sweden maintains the largest navy of the Nordic countries, its purpose being—in concert with Sweden's army and air force—to make credible the country's policy of neutrality in the event of a European war. In the early 1980s, Sweden's fleet numbered over 470 vessels including 12 submarines, 2 destroyers, 30 fast attack craft, 131 coast guard vessels, and 8 icebreakers. Staff numbered over 14,000 including officers, regulars, and annual trainees. Of the Nordic countries, Denmark and Sweden have the longest naval histories, and the following two sections focus on these.

REFERENCES: J. Moore, ed., *Jane's Fighting Ships* (London: Jane's Publishing Company, 1983).

B. NORDSTROM

Denmark

Through its geographical position on both the North Sea and the seaways into the Baltic, Denmark has had a maritime potential conferred upon it of a different order from Sweden, which until the mid-seventeenth century had only one outlet to the North Sea (Älvsborg*/Gothenburg*). This potential was dramatically enhanced after the union of Denmark and Norway in the late fourteenth century. Yet, although in the past traditions of both kingdoms there were legally defined obligations upon subjects to render sea service, and the emergence of the Hanseatic League* in the early thirteenth century introduced into Danish counsels choices of concurrence with or resistance to the Hanse, it is not practicable to talk of a Danish navy before the reign of Hans I* (1481–1513). He pursued latterly a strong anti-Hanseatic policy in Norway, to some extent in favor of the Dutch, because high Hanse grain prices threatened his Norwegian subjects and because the League's north German territorial base, centered on Lübeck, was a point from which the Hanse could exploit the dubious royal Danish authority in Schleswig and Holstein. The Danish crown, however, always had to appraise its policies toward the Hanse, until the League's decline in the sixteenth century, because of its obvious success in generating wealth. Another factor in the development of the Danish navy was the crown's practice, begun in 1429, of levying tolls (Sound Tolls) at Elsinore* on all merchant ships passing in and out of the Baltic. Even at very basic rates, as was usually the case of the Hanse's shipping, these tolls soon proved to be the crown's most productive financial exaction and one that significantly contributed to the maintenance of a navy. The force employed by King Hans was probably composed as much of private ships fighting the Hanseatics under royal license (as privateers) as of royal vessels, conventionally accommodating soldiers for the boarding of enemy ships. (It was only in the course of the sixteenth century that warships provided with gunports for the firing of broadsides were practically evolved.) The king would probably have employed four-masted carracks, the largest vessels of the time, but where he broke new ground in Denmark (or reverted to a Viking* tradition) was in his development of strong coastal points, such as Sonderborg (east Slesvig), Kalundborg (Great Belt), and, above all, the fortress of Nakskov on Lolland, which commanded the Great Belt's south entrance. Concurrently, Copenhagen*, fronting the Sound and, until the mid-seventeenth century, when they were annexed by Sweden, linked with such strong points across the Sound as Marstrand, Varberg, Malmö, and Christianopel, was Denmark's leading naval base.

Denmark's hardest fought war of the sixteenth century was the Seven Years' War with Sweden (1563–1570), when the crowns contested dominion of the Baltic, and Denmark had Lübeck as its ally. This war evidenced Denmark's and Sweden's maturity as sea powers, and at different times during the war each had battle fleets of at least 30 ships. To an extent Denmark's control of Gotland assisted the cause of Frederik II* against Erik XIV*, but this did not prevent the loss of eleven Danish ships and some 5,000 men in a storm off Visby in July 1566.

It is unquestionable that Danish-Norwegian manpower was better adapted to seafaring than was Swedish manpower, and so was of higher quality. Apart from the "oceanic" coastlines of Denmark-Norway, this kingdom was also in a position to draw seamen from northwest Germany. In contrast, Sweden's only nursery of seamen was in Finland, even after it acquired north German lands in the mid-seventeenth century.

Probably no monarch in history more personally identified his crown with sea power than Christian IV* (1588–1648), not at least until Emperor Wilhelm II of Germany 250 years later. It was not so much that Christian built a new fleet of 30 ships within some fifteen years (1596–1611), but that, as no Danish king before him, he came to know his Norwegian kingdom well. There he had light-draughted craft built, and he sailed as far north as the North Cape and the Kola Peninsula. He also reinforced Denmark's ties with Iceland. Territorial ambitions toward Germany and provocative designs on the Elbe trade and even Hamburg caused Christian to found the new port of Glückstadt in 1619. As for his capital, the king's elaboration of Copenhagen's naval facilities rendered the city as maritime as Amsterdam or Cadiz. There is certainly no parallel in Sweden with this record, and while it is true that Christian's short-lived involvement in the Thirty Years' War brought humiliation, the Danish fleet proved an effective instrument under commanders such as Pros Mund, Jørgen Wind, and Gabriel Kruse. Between 1630 and 1643, the fleet numbered over 20 well-gunned ships and as many light-draughted craft and was strategically deployed throughout the realm. It was in character that Christian's last celebrated gesture after an active reign of almost 50 years was his leadership of his fleet at the hard-fought but indecisive action with the Swedes off Kolberger Heide near Kiel on 1 July 1644, in the course of which he lost his right eye.

The period 1650–1720 arguably saw Danish sea power in its full maturity, but there are times when this is difficult to evaluate, because of partnership with the Dutch (up to 1680), pursuit of neutrality (1688–1700), or, especially during the Great Northern War*, because of a pronounced emphasis on privateering warfare. The Swedish navy, ill-manned and -maintained, though numerically superior, proved no match for the Danes in the 1670s (Öland, June 1676; Køge Bay, July 1677) and was effectively vanquished. But at the outbreak of the Great Northern War, Denmark was confronted by a wholly new, well-equipped Swedish fleet, and the Danish fleet, concentrated in Copenhagen, was only to be saved from destruction in August 1700 by the preparedness of the British and Dutch to restrain Karl XII* from humbling Frederik IV*. By the end of the war, despite undoubted successes against the Swedes (1714–1720) and the exceptional qualities of the Trondheim-born commander Per Wessel (ennobled as "Tordenskjold" in 1716), the Danish navy was in little better condition than the Swedish. Since Denmark had been forced to be a non-belligerent until 1709, this may seem surprising, but it is better understood if the amount of Baltic cruising and blockading of Swedish ports in all weathers undertaken by Danish detachments is borne in mind—together with the crucial fact, which affected Sweden as well, that hemp and tar supplies were largely cut off in consequence of Russia's unprecedented control of the east Baltic ports and the naval stores' points of origin. That Denmark ended the war with over 20 ships of 50–100 guns and a number of frigates and small craft should not conceal the grinding nature of this struggle.

The concept and indeed the implementation of "armed neutrality" was seventeenth-century in origin. But it was in the eighteenth century that its most serious consequences were felt by belligerents with Baltic interests who were operating in seas busy with ever-increasing volumes of potentially contraband cargo, whether or not freighted in proved neutral bottoms. Denmark's East Indies and West Indies trade in the eighteenth century, the first era of Danish neutrality, rendered it an "armed neutral," and this was especially the case when, in 1780, Russia assumed pre-emptive leadership of the League of Armed Neutrality. This device had originated in the mind of Denmark's Andreas Peter Bernstorff*, who, at least as regards Britain, had not intended that it should pursue rigorous sanctions. The last occasion on which Denmark arguably acted unilaterally as a sea power was in 1742, when Christian VI* tried to claim succession to the Swedish throne for Denmark, only to be firmly rebuffed by Russia, and even then Christian had to bring six ships out of reserve to supplement the twelve in commission. All these ships were, however, of over 50 guns each.

With the French Revolutionary and Napoleonic wars, there came the most devastating events in Denmark's naval history: defeat in the Copenhagen roadstead by Britain in April 1801, where its unrigged warships had been rendered floating batteries and were manned by Danish seamen with great valor; and in

September 1807, when Britain, after severely bombarding Copenhagen's dock-yards, took home the nucleus of the Danish fleet in order to deprive Napoleon of its use. There remained behind some 30 vessels, half of which were light craft. These actions, while they certainly proved Danish fighting spirit, also revealed a "hedgehog-like" approach to the exercise of sea power by a state which lay at the turnstile of a strategically vital sea and had, in Copenhagen, an eminently defendable naval base.

Until the late nineteenth century, Denmark was inactive in refurbishing its navy. Yet, during this period it became vulnerable to nascent German sea power, just as it had been challenged from that direction in the early seventeenth century. In April 1849 it lost one of its most powerful ships to German shore batteries in Eckernfjord, and in the summer of 1864, when confederate Germany (in alliance with Austria) annexed Slesvig and Holstein, the Danish navy was unable to prevent enemy units from covering the entire length of the duchies' eastern coasts. Such success exhilarated the young German navy. By 1914 German naval planners, through the completion and deepening of the Kiel Canal and the de-velopment of bases at Kiel and Flensburg, had brought to fruition designs of 40 years' standing; and neutral Denmark had been brought to increase its naval personnel from 1,600 (1887–1888) to 4,000 (where it stood until 1940).

In World War I, the Danish fleet, which included nine submarines and sev-enteen torpedo boats, was used mainly for coastal defense. Through a surprising German miscalculation, Denmark was able to mine its channels in partnership with Germany and then to deny their use to all the belligerent powers. During the interwar years, the Danish navy concentrated on fishing patrol and the de-velopment of its mining capacities. The fleet came to include twelve submarines and (after 1934) three new destroyers (which were seized by the Germans after 1940). In spite of Denmark's declared neutrality, it was open to German bullying in the late 1930s, and by the time of the Nazi invasion in April 1940 the country's government had conceded, in violation of neutrality, the right of foreign war-planes to overfly Denmark and, for all practical purposes, the unrestricted passage of foreign warships, including submerged submarines, through its waters. The reasons for allowing these violations of its neutrality are probably twofold: Denmark was satisfied that neither Norway nor Sweden would abandon their neutral stances were Denmark to be attacked, and, following the conclusion of the Anglo-German Naval Agreement of 1935, Denmark was equally impressed by British indifference to the European naval balance as compared with that in the Pacific. Historically, it is ironic that it was not a hereditary foe of Denmark, but a traditional ally, Britain, which over a century before had finally cast into limbo the heroic naval traditions of Christian IV and Tordenskjold.

REFERENCES: R. C. Anderson, *Naval Wars in the Baltic 1522–1850* (London, 1910); H. G. Garde, *Efterretninger om den danske og norske Sømagt*, 4 vols. (Copenhagen, 1832–1835); W. A. Graah, *Udkast til Danmarks Soekrigshistorie* (Copenhagen, 1818);

O. Lybeck, *Öresund i Nordens Historia* (Malmö, 1943); A. P. Tuxen, ed., *Bidrag til den store Nordiske Krigs Historie*, vols. 1–9 (Copenhagen, 1920–1924?).

D. D. ALDRIDGE

Sweden

The coastal defense characteristics of the present Swedish navy may emphasize Swedish neutrality in international affairs, but in fact they also betray the essence of Sweden's naval posture since the founding of its post-medieval navy by Gustav I Vasa* in the 1520s. No point in the Baltic is more than 60 miles from land, and hence the waters in which Swedish sea power has been tested against Denmark, the Hanse, Poland, and Russia have been relatively constricted. This particularly applies to hostilities with Russia owing to the prevalence of archipelagoes (*skärgårdar*) on the Finnish coasts, Åland, and the east Swedish coasts between Norrköping and Gävle most open to Russian attack out of the Gulf of Finland. It was owing to the emergence of Russian sea power in the eighteenth century, especially in the form of shallow-draught and oar-propelled galleys, that the Swedes developed as their ultimate riposte the innovative Arméns Flotta (literally army's fleet) and made their first sustained attempts to chart the archipelagoes and encourage professional pilotage in those hazardous channels.

Gustav I Vasa's fleet at its largest comprised some 50 ships of varying strength. His tutelage under the Hanse gave him a practical grounding in maritime affairs. He laid the foundations, together with his gifted heir Erik XIV*, of a fleet which through the remaining centuries of sail would never lack for the raw materials of shipbuilding: iron, timber for hulls and masts, hemp, flax, and tar. These were the most celebrated of the Baltic's staples and, with Sweden achieving imperial status 60 years after Gustav I's death, it would be uniquely placed to monopolize this internationally important market. During his reign, Gustav I saw that yards were established at Älvsborg, on Sweden's eastern coasts, and in Finland. In the seventeenth century these facilities were greatly expanded. Then, out of some 43 yards, among which Stockholm* was pre-eminent until about 1650, 15 were located in Finland, the prime source of tar. Although the conquests made by Sweden in the seventeenth century brought it Gotland, the old Danish "maritime" provinces of Bohuslän, Halland, Skåne, and Blekinge, and such north German ports as Stettin, Stralsund, Wismar, and Stade (all potentially enhancing its recruitment of naval personnel), it was Finland which afforded Sweden its own "nursery of seamen" and was the chief source of manpower for Arméns Flottan. Ständigt Båtsmännshållet, a self-sustaining pool of seamen under government surveillance, was not to be applied in southern Sweden before 1721 and as late as 1741 in Västerbotten, but it had first been introduced in Finland as early as 1602. From its beginning it came to be applied throughout the realm until its termination in 1835. It must be distinguished from the more draconian *utskrivning*, an enforced national recruitment during times of peril, which was first fully implemented by Gustav II Adolf* in 1618. Yet, when all is said, an endemic lack of seafaring experience plagued the Swedish navy until at least the end of the seventeenth century, and this was telling in Denmark's favor. Only by the 1780s was there a significant number of officers who had done service in foreign navies and upon the oceans.

With the demands of Gustav II Adolf's wars, and above all the eighteen years of involvement in the Thirty Years' War beyond the Baltic, the navy underwent considerable expansion in all spheres: shallow-draught craft ancillary to the big ships (23 of the latter accompanied the king to Pomerania in May 1630) were added; gunnery techniques, of which Gustav had an expert knowledge, were revised; and administration was reformed. Individual towns or groups of towns undertook to contribute ships and provisions, and many officers were drafted into the navy after exclusively military experience. As often as not, these men proved themselves sounder administrative officers than enterprising commanders at sea, and many of the best commanders who served during the Great Northern War (1700–1721) had risen from the ranks through merit.

Under the Form of Government of 1634, the Admiralty was accorded the third highest place in the departments of state, and in 1650 it was ruled that the navy should never consist of fewer than 40 ships and that aging ships should always be replaced. In fact, the next 30 years were to witness the nadir of the navy through a rundown and corrupt bureaucracy and lack of maintenance. In the 1670s, the fleet came close to decimation at the hands of the Danes and Dutch, and it was following these humiliations that Karl XI*, through his ruthless reforms of the crown's finances, built a new navy of 24 ships of over 50 guns (increased to 43 by 1708) and a new naval base at Karlskrona*. In this great program Count Hans Wachtmeister* (1641–1710) has an honored place, but lack of knowledgeable seamen remained a major problem.

The navy was to withstand the shock of the Great Northern War with some credit. While its galleys were hopelessly few in number to cope with the huge fleet built by Tsar Peter I, and hence unable to defend the Finnish coast, between 1714 and 1718, spurred on by Karl XII, it fought an intrepid privateering war to blockade the Russian-held ports. This was against severe odds, and only after it had lost most of its fastest sailing vessels.

Between 1720 and 1772, during Sweden's Age of Liberty*, the state of the navy at any given time was at the mercy of party politics and the gyrations in Sweden's policies toward its neighbors, particularly Russia. By the 1750s the navy had a small galley fleet in addition to its conventional forces, and a growing professionalism helped the foundation, under royal promptings, of a naval academy at Karlskrona—unfortunately short-lived. By the time of the accession of Gustav III* in 1771, however, there were only seven ships of over 40 guns fit for sea. Gustav's seizure of more "absolutist" powers in August 1772 (and French subsidies) enabled him generally to prosecute a vigorous program of reform. Assisted by the genius of Fredrik af Chapman (1721–1809), the greatest naval architect of the eighteenth century, Arméns Flottan became a reality, though its formation had been agreed to in principle in 1756. There had long been hostility to its being separate from the navy proper, but under the versatile artilleryman Auguste Ehrensvärd (1710–1772), who had perfected the concept, and the practical leadership of Henrik af Trolle (1730–1784), it evolved an *esprit* and a preparedness which were without precedent. Its employment by Gustav in his war with Russia (1788–1790) was not well judged, but its victory at Svensksund is the most renowned in Sweden's naval annals. In 1803 it ceased to be a separate service, and Sweden's final loss of Finland to Russia in 1809 removed much of its *raison d'être*.

As it did for other navies, the nineteenth century opened up quite new perspectives. The navy's branches became increasingly specialized, and its units began to leave the Baltic for oceanic experience and survey work. Between 1841 and 1871 the Swedish navy moved from steam-powered corvettes to iron-clad monitors. Naval officers who chose to remain in Swedish Pomerania after its cession to Prussia in 1815 formed a coterie which was to produce the designs for Germany's earliest steam-powered warships, notably the *Arkona* (1854). This continuing link with Germany was pregnant enough, and one which could not be viewed with the same equanimity by Sweden's one time naval adversaries, the Danes, who were aware by the mid-nineteenth century of nascent German nationalism in their duchies of Slesvig and Holstein. Oscar II* (1872–1907), apart from personally strengthening relations with the German royal house, had a keen interest in the navy and knowledge of Sweden's coastal waters. Fear of Russia, at least until the Russo-Japanese War of 1904–1905, only enhanced Sweden's defensive instincts, and the ability of the Scandinavian kingdoms to declare jointly for neutrality in 1912 assured the continuation in Sweden of limited naval strategies. The present-day Swedish navy reflects this bias, but it is notable that Sweden's most powerful warship of the twentieth century, the *Sverige* (1917), was built entirely with funds subscribed voluntarily by the public.

REFERENCES: P. O. Bäckström, *Svenska flottans historia* (Stockholm, 1884); O. Lybeck, *Svenska flottans historia*, vols. 1, 2 (Malmö, 1942); A. Zettersten, *Svenska flottans historia*, vol. 1 (Stockholm, 1890), and vol. 2 (Norrtälje, 1903). The three leading Swedish navy history journals are *Forum Navale* (Stockholm, 1940–), *Sjöhistoriska Årsbok* (Göteborg, 1914–), and *Tidskrift i Sjöväsendet* (Stockholm, in series from 1836).

D. D. ALDRIDGE

NEWSPAPERS

Denmark

The history of the Danish press begins with *Den Danske Mercurius** in 1666, although an irregular publication in German, with small items reprinted from continental papers, had appeared in 1634. The first newspaper in prose was started in 1672 by Daniel Paulli. Continuous newspaper history dates from 1720 when Joachim Wielandt, on license from the king, began publication of *Extraordinaire Relationer*, which had reports of Danish as well as continental news. On Wielandt's death, Ernst H. Berling took over the publication of Wielandt's publication. It soon became *Berlingske Tidende**, the oldest continuously published paper in Denmark. The oldest provincial paper still publishing is *Aalborg Stiftstidende*, founded in 1767.

Until 1770, all publications in Denmark were subject to the censorship of the university. This was abolished by a royal edict issued under Christian VII's* authority by Johann F. Struensee*, the king's physician. In reaction to the French Revolution, however, the government reimposed censorship on 27 September 1799. In consequence, discussion of economic, social, domestic, and foreign affairs remained taboo until 1848, and the press, under strong royal influence, confined itself to literature, theater, and entertainment. Total circulation of Denmark's 10 papers in 1800 was 10,000 copies. A decree of 2 November 1810 gave privileged papers the right to publish political news (but not views). Unprivileged papers could not print news and could use only private distribution methods. The Industrial Revolution and the growth of a middle class led to a rapid expansion in the demand for and interest in news. *Berlingske Tidende* became a daily. *Faedrelandet*, founded in 1834, became for a generation the dominant representative of public opinion. Until the 1848 revolution, however, it fought a running battle with the government, its issues being subject to confiscation and fines. A provisional decree of 24 March 1848 abolished all laws and regulations regarding the press, and an act of 3 January 1851 made this permanent.

Over the next three generations, the Danish press was predominantly political. Its editors sought to mold popular opinion. Most communities had four newspapers, representing the conservative, liberal, agrarian, and radical or socialist points of view. In 1850 Denmark had 8 daily papers; by 1925 it had 273, twice as many as Britain or France. Copenhagen* alone had eighteen daily papers. The eventual downfall of this broad democracy of the newspaper was heralded by Henrik Cavling, who introduced new topics and a new style to journalism as editor of *Politiken*. In 1901 he brought a new type of press to the paper, and, strongly influenced by William Randolph Hearst and Joseph Pulitzer, changed content from political and literary to popular and informational. Bold headlines were introduced and advertisements swept off the front page. The journal had become a newspaper, and the newspaper had become a business.

The occupation by Nazi Germany during World War II* brought broad restrictions of press freedom. The 1943 crisis, which resulted in the end of Danish self-administration, also involved the institution of direct German censorship, which in turn contributed to the rapid growth of the Danish underground press. Between 225 and 250 underground papers were published, most of them monthly or biweekly. Six became dailies in the last year of the war. In addition, an underground news agency, "Information," provided a news service for the underground, Danish authorities, editors of daily papers, foreign newspapers, the BBC, and other organizations.

The postwar period witnessed a concentration of newspaper ownership and a rapid reduction in the number of papers. Advertising profits now constituted the majority of income for big morning papers and provincial papers. By the mid-

1960s only 70 daily papers remained, 10 of them in Copenhagen. Fourteen of these papers called themselves independent. By 1980 49 dailies remained with a total circulation of 1,832,000. More than half of these papers considered themselves politically independent. Nine Copenhagen dailies accounted for half of the total copies. The *Berlingske Tidende* publishing house owns 25 percent of all daily circulation in the country, plus two large weeklies and other media properties. Unlike Norway and Sweden, Denmark chose not to try to halt the trend of newspaper closures by instituting press subsidies.

Norway

Norwegian press history has lagged behind that of neighboring Sweden and Denmark. The first printing press did not appear until 1644. The first regularly published Norwegian newspaper, *Norske Inteligens Sedeler,* appeared in 1763. The second paper followed at Bergen at 1765. The third paper, the *Trondheim Addressavisen,* began publication in 1767 by adding news to an already existing "want-ad" sheet. After 30 years, the circulation was still only 500. But Norwegian separation from Denmark and earnings development spurred its growth. By 1839 it was a triweekly, and since 1862 it has been a daily. Today it is one of the largest non-Oslo papers. The first Norwegian daily, the *Morgenbladet,* appeared in Oslo in 1819.

Throughout the nineteenth century, Norway had few towns of any size. This hindered the growth of the press. Nevertheless, by 1849 it had 40 papers. One factor which helped this growth was freedom of the press, granted in the 1814 constitution. Second, local and municipal governments began to play a role in national affairs beginning in the 1830s. After mid-century, national political arguments between Liberals and Conservatives and the emergence of other parties furthered developments of the press. The three-paper town was not uncommon, but circulations were small. Before the emergence of the mass press at the end of the century, *Morgenbladet* was the paper with the largest circulation, with 3,- to 4,000.

The first of the mass circulation newspapers was *Aftenposten*. The paper was founded in 1860 by Christian Schibstad. When his son took over the paper in 1889, he downplayed polemics and stressed news. It became the paper with the largest circulation, a position it held until overtaken in 1981 by *Verdens Gang,* founded in Oslo in 1868.

The attainment of independence from Sweden in 1905 coincided with further growth of the press. Between 1900 and 1940, 80 new newspapers were founded, giving the country a total of 300. From 1900 to 1939, Stavanger, a town of only 45,000 population, had five newspapers.

Like Denmark, Norway was occupied by Nazi Germany during World War II. Strict censorship was instituted, some papers were closed, and an underground press flourished.

A decline in the number of newspapers, which began during the war, turned into a flood at war's end. By 1949 there were only 214 papers, including 89 dailies. Daily circulation, however, doubled in the same period. By 1970, 81 dailies remained. A wide program of government subsidies was begun in 1969. Half of the government money came in the form of advertisements. The papers also benefited from many tax breaks. By 1979 there were 72 dailies remaining, with a circulation of 1,682,900. Only seven papers printed more than 50,000 copies, including four in Oslo and one each in Bergen, Trondheim, and Stavanger. Oslo had eight papers and Bergen five. In contrast to Sweden and Denmark, no major newspaper chains developed. Because so many of the papers remain quite small and the geography is not supportive, multiple ownership has so far offered no advantage to the prospective investor.

Sweden

The first Swedish newspaper was published in German by Gustav II Adolf* to serve areas occupied by Swedish forces during the Thirty Years' War. The first newspaper in the Swedish language also carried news of that war. This was the *Ordinarii Post Tijdender** (today the *Post och Inrikes Tidningar*) which first appeared in 1645. For nearly two centuries, the government served as the main support for press development, primarily through control of the news. A brief exception was the second period of Cap Party* dominance in the parliament (1765–1769): the Freedom of the Press Act of 1766 became part of the constitution, and *Dagligt Allehanda* became Sweden's first daily newspaper (1767), sixteen years before the United States had its first daily. But this paper and others of the eighteenth century were not newspapers as they are known today; rather, they were journals of opinion on a limited range of topics, circulated to small readerships, mainly in Stockholm*. The Freedom of the Press Act, modified in 1810 and 1812, remained in effect until 1949.

The limited reach of newspapers was changed with the appearance of *Aftonbladet** in 1830. Founded by Lars John Hierta, it combined news, views, and entertainment. Hierta represented the newly emerging middle class in pre-industrial Sweden, and he provided the communication his fellow burghers needed. By 1848 circulation had reached 8,650, more than half of which was outside of Stockholm. The founding of *Dagens Nyheter* by Rudolf Wall in 1864 marked a further broadening of political participation. Universal elementary education (1842) and industrial development were increasing opportunity for new groups in society.

The modern newspaper market dates from the 1860s. It coincided with the extension of the suffrage and the consequent efforts to mobilize the electorate through political parties. It made a Swedish press a party press, but one which was locally based and marketed. The papers were economically and technically independent. The general dispersal of the population, largely a function of geography (no newspaper was nationally distributed) led to many papers, often with very small circulations. The three-paper town was most common.

Socialist newspapers appeared in the 1880s. Other papers had been as much commercial as political, but the Socialist papers sought to be the voice of the labor movement. The most important of these was *Social Demokraten*, started by August Palm* in 1885, which by 1890 had become a daily.

The first newspaper to seek consciously a non-political mass audience was *Stockholms-Tidningen*, founded by Anders Jeurling. He depended on advertising for his profit, charging only 2 öre compared to the going rate for papers of 10 öre. By 1900 he had a circulation of 100,000 the largest in Scandinavia. Other papers had to follow *Stockholms-Tidningen*'s example and lower their prices.

By the end of World War I, there were 230–240 newspapers in Sweden. In the late 1930s Swedish newspapers started disappearing; this trend, caused primarily by economic factors, caused great concern across the political spectrum as it accelerated. From 1950 to 1975 the number of daily papers dropped from 133 to 89. Only nineteen cities still had competitive situations. Two different parliamentary commissions in the 1960s sought ways to stop this development. After the failure of two proposals, parliament adopted in 1971 a system of support to so-called secondary papers. Newspapers with circulation coverage of less than 50 percent of the homes in their community are now supported economically on a scale which takes into account the size of the edition and the frequency of publication. Social Democratic and Conservative papers have benefited them from this arrangement. An eight-member (five MPs and three experts) Press Subsidy Board (Presstödsnämnden) allocates funds, which reached 311 million SKr in 1980–1981. Since 1978 the board has also provided support to organizational journals. Only two papers have died since the subsidies were introduced. *Stockholms-Tidningen*, a morning Social Democratic tabloid started in 1981, was the first new paper in the city since 1945.

In contrast to many other countries, newspaper circulation in Sweden has been increasing in recent years. More newspapers are distributed per capita than in any country except Iceland and Japan.

O. V. JOHNSON

NEW SWEDEN (1638–1655) Swedish colony on the Delaware

Several of Sweden's monarchs and statesmen, including Gustav II Adolf* and Axel Oxenstierna*, dreamed of an overseas empire beyond the Baltic for Sweden. In the 1620s Gustav II supported the founding of the "Southern Company" and listened to a number of suggestions for colonial adventures. Following his death in 1632, the direction of these dreams fell to Oxenstierna. In 1637, with limited official support and the cooperation of the Dutch, Sweden launched its single effort in the early modern period to build a colony outside of the Baltic region. Then an expedition under the leadership of Peder Minuit left Sweden aboard the *Kalmar Nykel* and the *Fogel Grip* destined for North America. Four months later the expedition arrived in the Delaware Bay area and established the colony of New Sweden through the purchase of land from the local Indians. At its peak in the late 1640s the colony included most of Delware and parts of New Jersey and Pennsylvania.

From the start the colony suffered from a lack of serious political support and a difficulty in recruiting settlers. Contacts with Sweden were tenuous, and there were years when no ship came from the mother country with news, supplies, and additional settlers. Although established as a base for trade, especially in furs and tobacco, the colony never made a profit for its supporters in Sweden. In spite of obstacles, however, the settlers, who were a motley mixture of military personnel and Finnish and Swedish peasants, established a reasonably secure agricultural existence.

In 1655 the colony fell to the Dutch, who had been encroaching on the settlement gradually and were far more numerous and better supplied. Most of the military and "official" population then returned to Sweden, but many of the colonists remained. They retained their heritage, including their language and their religion, and some of their ties with Sweden until the late eighteenth century, and they made significant contributions to the colonial history of the area.

In several aspects, the Swedish heritage can still be seen in the area. A number of early Swedish churches have survived, and the American Swedish Historical Museum in Philadelphia is dedicated to the preservation of the Swedish elements in American colonial history.

REFERENCES: Amandus Johnson, *The Swedish Settlements on the Delaware, 1638–1664*, 2 vols. (New York: Appleton, 1911); Allan Kastrup, *The Swedish Heritage in America* (St. Paul: The Swedish Council of America, 1975).

B. NORDSTROM

NIELS (c. 1064–1134) King of Denmark 1104–1134

Niels was the last son of Sven II Estridsen* to rule Denmark. He was also the son to rule the longest, 30 years, which was more than all the others combined. His predecessor Erik I* Ejegod's son, Erik (II*), was too young when his father died in 1103, and another of his sons, Harald Kesja, was too unpopular. There were two other children of Sven who were possible candiates, but neither took part in the election. (One died, the other withdrew his candidacy.) The fleet gathered at Isre again, and it was the fleet captains who chose the king. In style Niels followed in the tradition of Harald III* (Hen) and Oluf I*. He promised to and apparently did honor the law of Harald I* and consequently enjoyed 30 years of relative peace at home. This peace allowed him to build the core of a genuine medieval monarchy. Increasingly, the monarch exerted his authority through a growing network of agents in the countryside and relied less and less on the personal bodyguard (*hird*) that surrounded him. A kind of untitled service nobility developed alongside the older military nobility. These representatives of the crown maintained law and order, collected taxes, and served as the local, secular symbols of the monarchy. The Church served as the second fundamental component within the emerging system in return for the crown's patronage.

In the last three years of Niels's reign serious unrest developed. Niels had one son, Magnus, whom he wished to succeed him. Knud Lavard, Erik I's legitimate son, also wished to become king. As Niels aged the question of succession became more and more acute. A civil war was triggered in 1131, when Magnus arranged the murder of Knud. This act only aggravated the succession question, and Knud's place was taken by his half-brother Erik II* (Emune). The supporters of Niels, which included the peasants and the Church, seemed insurmountable, and Erik's luck seemed forever bad. Many battles were fought, and all of them were lost by Erik.

Then, in 1132/1133, Niels and Magnus became vassals of the German emperor. This action, which was designed to insure that Germany would not intervene on Erik's side, may have turned the tide against Niels and Magnus. Denmark's independent status and the independence of the Church in Denmark were threatened by this action. Archbishop Asser changed sides, and many leaders of the Church followed him. In 1134, at Fodevig in Skåne, the armies of the king and Erik met. This time Erik was the victor. Magnus was killed and Niels fled. Shortly thereafter the king was murdered in Slesvig.

REFERENCES: *DBL*, vol. 10; *DH*, vol. 3.

B. NORDSTROM

NOLSÖE, POUL POULSEN (1766–1808) Faroese navigator, patriot, and poet

Poul Poulsen Nolsöe was one of the most remarkable Scandinavians of his time and is justifiably regarded by the Faroese as a national hero, although he was rather a child of his time than a forerunner of Faroese nationalism, as many modern Faroese like to represent him.

The talented family from which Poul Nolsöe was descended had long been settled in Eysturoy, but his father married and settled in Nólsoy. Poul and his brothers took the surname Nolsöe after their native island. In the Faroe Islands* he has always been commonly referred to as Nólsoyar-Páll, meaning Poul from Nólsoy.

Three of the six Nolsöe brothers were unusually intelligent. They grew up in the days of Rybergs Handel, a smuggling depot established by the great Copenhagen* merchant Niels Ryberg, which carried on business from 1766 to 1788. For the first time, Tórshavn* was full of craftsmen and sailors, many of them foreigners, and these gifted adolescents had a golden opportunity for self-education.

Poul's ambitions lay with the sea, and he studied navigation. In 1786 he secured a place on one of Ryberg's ships, and after the closure of Ryberg's depot, he sailed with vessels belonging to the Faroese Monopoly*. In 1791 or 1792, he took to distant-water voyaging, became a ship's captain, and visited America, the West Indies, England, France, Portugal, Norway, Denmark, and several other places. In March 1798 he was back in Copenhagen, then in the final years of its brilliant period of commercial prosperity. In September 1798 he married a Nólsoy girl, and for two years he sailed in the service of the Monopoly.

Poul returned to the Faroes to live in 1800. A few months later his wife died, and in 1801 he remarried, this time to the daughter of a wealthy crown tenant on Borðoy, who transferred his lease to Poul, who proved to be an extremely able farmer.

Poul Nolsöe considered the Monopoly to be a hindrance to the development of his native islands and agitated for its abolition. But the Faroese feared that if the public monopoly under regulations and a fixed-price tariff were to be abolished, it might be replaced by a private monopoly subject to no rules.

Poul thus saw that the key to free trade lay in the training of the islanders in the management of seagoing vessels. After a vain attempt to secure government loans to purchase a ship, Nolsöe and two partners bought at auction the wreckage of a ship that had drifted into Suðuroy. In Vágur, to the south of Suðuroy, with the help of Poul's brothers, they built a schooner. This was the first seagoing vessel constructed in Faroe. It was launched on 6 August 1804 and named *Royndin Fríða* (The Beautiful Trial).

The vessel was first used for fishing and then, in the summer of 1805, for trading journeys to Bergen and Copenhagen. It carried Suðuroy coal, which was not subject to the Monopoly laws. Poul hoped in the summer of 1806 to export knitted sweaters, train-oil, and dried fish, which a recent relaxation of the Monopoly laws permitted to be exported on private account. He discovered, however, that such exports still had to be carried in Monopoly ships. Poul thereupon organized a petition for the complete freeing of the trade, and at a public meeting held in August, a deputation of five, including Poul himself, was chosen to go to Denmark to argue the case.

The Tórshavn officials, previously sympathetic to Nolsöe, now turned against him, perhaps out of jealousy. In retaliation, during the winter of 1806–1807, Poul composed a satirical ballad about them, depicting them in the shape of birds of prey, while he, as the *tjaldur* (oyster-catcher), warned the smaller birds of their evil intentions. *Fuglakvaeði* (*The Ballad of the Birds*), over 200 stanzas long, is extraordinary not only for its skillful versification, but for the way in which the birds remain true to their avian nature, yet unmistakably portray their human counterparts.

The deputation sailed in June 1807. In Copenhagen they were well received by various ministers of state and by the regent, Crown Prince Frederik (later Frederik VI*). But at the end of July, hostilities broke out between Denmark and England. Nolsöe and his friends were present during the bombardment of Copenhagen and the surrender of the Danish fleet to the British. The remainder of Poul's life was spent helping his countrymen through their wartime problems.

His first step was to secure 250 barrels of barley from the Monopoly, and he obtained permission from British Admiral Gambier to take the cargo to Faroe, where it helped to alleviate an already growing shortage.

In the spring of 1808, British naval vessels began to appear in Faroese waters. The first was the *Clio*. Despite Nolsöe's warning to the commandant of the fort in Tórshavn to expect an attack, no resistance was made to the landing party sent ashore from this brig, and the fort was disarmed and the town left unprotected. Two weeks later, on 1 June, a 20–gun privateer, the *Salamine*, arrived in Tórshavn. On discovering that the trading station in the town was a Danish crown enterprise, the privateer took possession of all its money and goods and applied to the Admiralty Court in London for these to be condemned as a lawful prize. The Admiralty contested this claim, on the grounds of a capitulation made by the Tórshavn commandant to the *Clio*, and a protracted lawsuit began.

After the departure of the *Salamine* from Tórshavn, the commandant was faced with an urgent problem of securing grain supplies for the islands. Although he detested Nolsöe, he was compelled to send him on this mission. Poul sailed for Denmark, but off Skagen he fell in with a British naval vessel, which seized *Royndin Fríða* as prize. The ship was taken to Gothenburg*, where Poul and his crew were lodged in an English prison ship.

Poul secured an interview, however, with admirals Keats and Bertie, and he represented to them the distress already existing in the Faroe Islands. They sent him and his crew to London, where the Privy Council were also sympathetic. He was given a fresh ship, the *North Star*.

It was now November, and the prize court case of the Tórshavn seizures was in progress. Poul appeared as a witness, the last time on 17 November 1808, when he was already on board the *North Star*, ready to sail to Faroe with a cargo of grain. Nolsöe never arrived. The ship was apparently lost in a storm off the east coast of Britain. The Faroese theory that Nolsöe was intercepted by a privateer hired by the Monopoly authorities has no historical support.

Poul Nolsöe's memory has always been highly honored in the Faroes. He was a talented poet and a pioneer of economic and political emancipation, and his example of distant-water navigation was soon followed by others. Klaksvík, where he made his home and hauled up the *Royndin Fríða* each winter, is today a thriving fishing port with a population of 5,000.

REFERENCES: James Nicoll, *An Historical and Descriptive Account of Iceland, Greenland and the Faroe Islands* (Edinburgh: Oliver and Boyd, 1841); John F. West, *Faroe, the Emergence of a Nation* (London: C. Hurst; and New York: Paul S. Eriksson, 1972).

J. F. WEST

NORBY, SØREN (?–1530) Danish nobleman, admiral, pirate, and mercenary
Søren Norby is an extraordinary figure in Scandinavian history in the early decades of the sixteenth century. He was a member of the lower nobility on Fyn. He entered the service of Hans I* and took an active part in the war against Lübeck in 1509. Subsequently, he was sent to Iceland to deal with illegal trade (piracy) between the island and Europe. He was recalled in 1512, given Gotland as a fief, and made admiral of the Danish fleet. From Gotland he plundered the shipping of Sweden and the Hanse (*see* Hanseatic League). Following Hans's death, he continued in the service of the crown under Christian II*. He took part in the campaigns against Sweden in 1517, 1518, and 1520, and was central in the capture of Stockholm* in 1520. The fall of the city opened the way for Christian's accession to the throne in Sweden. When the revolt against Christian

erupted, first in Sweden and then in Denmark (1520–1523), Norby remained loyal to the crown and was a central base of power for the king. Following Christian's deposition and flight into exile, Norby continued to support him. He used Gotland as a base of operations against Denmark, Sweden, and the Hanse. Though "loyal" to Christian, he behaved largely as an independent prince and pirate. He was viewed as the most serious element in Christian's plotting to regain his throne.

Gotland was attacked by Sweden in 1522 and by Lübeck in 1525. On both occasions the attackers failed to take Visby and the fortress (Visborg). In 1525, however, Norby changed sides in the royal conflict in Denmark. In exchange for Gotland he was given Sölvesborg Castle and Blekinge. But Norby did not remain loyal to Frederik I for long. Soon he had rebuilt his fleet and recruited new troops in Germany and was again harassing Baltic shipping. In the summer of 1526 he was attacked by Danish land and sea forces and was defeated in August. Norby escaped, however, and he began an exile which took him to Narva, Moscow, the Netherlands, and ultimately Italy. He died at Firenze in 1530 fighting in the army of the emperor, Charles V.

Norby's flight from Scandinavia* and, more important, his death, removed him as a significant element in Christian II's restoration plans. Without Norby's genius and support, Christian stood little chance of success, as the events of 1531–1533 demonstrated.

REFERENCES: *DBL*, vol. 10; *DH*, vol. 4; *DSH*, vol. 5; L. J. Larsson, "Sören Norby, Moskva och Grönland," *Scandia* 45 (1979): 67–81, "Sören Norbys fall," *Scandia*, 35:1 (1969): 21–57, and "Sören Norbys Skånska uppror," *Scandia* 30 (1964): 217–71.

B. NORDSTROM

NORDENFLYCHT, HEDVIG CHARLOTTA (28 November 1718–29 June 1763) Swedish poet

Born in Stockholm*, Hedvig Nordenflycht was one of eight children of accountant Anders Nordbohm (ennobled in 1727 with the name Nordenflycht) and Christine Rosin, who came from a clerical family. A studious child, she was allowed to pursue her interest in theological, mystical, and philosophical works more freely after her family moved to Viby in Västmanland in 1731. At 16 she became engaged, following her father's deathbed wish, to Johan Tideman, whom she did not love. Tideman died in 1737, before a marriage had taken place, and Nordenflycht then returned to Stockholm. In 1741 she married Jacob Fabricius, a clergyman, and they moved to Karlskrona*. When her husband died seven months later, she was overwhelmed with grief. Eight poems expressing her sorrow were published in 1743 as *Den sörgande Turtur-dufwan* (*The Grieving Turtledove*). They were the first "I"-lyrics in Swedish. The same year Nordenflycht returned once more to Stockholm and supported herself by writing eulogistic poems. In the following year she began a series of poetic yearbooks, *Qwinligit tankespel* (*A Woman's Thoughts*), which appeared in 1745–1750. In the first volume only, she used the often mentioned pseudonym "En Herdinna i Norden" (A Shepherd of the North). This series included her "emancipation poems," in which she declared it a woman's right and duty to pursue learning. She was not Sweden's first feminist writer, however; that distinction goes to Sophia Elisabeth Brennerr, who wrote earlier but much less assertively and seriously.

In 1752 Nordenflycht was granted a modest annual pension by the government, and the next year she was invited to join the new literary assocation, Tankebyggarorden (The Philosophical Order). Its only woman member, she soon became its leading celebrity. The members discussed the ideas of Rousseau, Voltaire, and other French philosophers of the Enlightenment. Differing opinions caused the organization to split into two groups, one of which gathered at the home of Fru Nordenflycht. She thus became the first Swedish woman to hold a literary salon. Poetry written by her group appeared between 1753 and 1755 in yearbooks entitled *Våra Försök* (*Our Efforts*). In 1761, in reply to Rousseau's charges that women were superficial, less intelligent than men, and lacking in soul, Nordenflycht published her long and learned poem "Till fruentimrets försvar" (*In Defense of Women*), in which she criticized men's treatment of women, especially their shutting women out from "light and higher pursuits."

At 43 she had a brief love affair with a 26–year-old admirer, Johan Fischerström, during which she wrote him love letters and composed some of her most moving lyric poetry, introducing a new frankness of expression into Swedish love poetry. As Fischerström's interest in her abated, she fell ill, possibly as a result of a suicide attempt, and died some months later.

Nordenflycht has recently been reappraised by feminist scholars, who describe her in more favorable terms than some critics have in the past and place less emphasis on the intellectual debts she owed men in her life. Although she tried many genres, she is mainly remembered for her love poems, feminist poems, and delightful rococo ballads. Some of her work has appeared in Danish and German translation. She was Sweden's first professional woman writer, a Nordic daughter of the Enlightenment, and through her deeply personal and passionate verse, one of the pre-Romantic trailblazers.

REFERENCES: H. Borelius, *Hedvig Charlotta Nordenflycht* (Uppsala: Lindblad, 1921); A. Gustafson, *A History of Swedish Literature* (Minneapolis: University of Minnesota Press/American Scandinavian Foundation, 1971); J. Kruse, *Hedvig Charlotta Nordenflycht. Ett skaldinne porträt från Sveriges Rococo-tid* (Lund: E. Malmströms Boktryckeri, 1895); A. Lyttkens, *Kvinnan börjar vakna. Den svenska kvinnans historia från 1700 til 1840–talet* (Stockholm: Bonniers, 1972); *SMK*, vol. 10.

N. FARQUHAR

NORDISM (Scandinavianism or Pan-Scandinavianism) Movements and/or striving for the (political, economic, cultural) integration or union of the Scandinavian countries

Hopes for Scandinavian unity were long either dynastic-diplomatic or dynastic-militaristic. In the fourteenth century, Denmark, Sweden, and Norway showed increasing similarity in culture, written language, and political institutions. A "state within the states" developed, based on fiefs in southeastern Norway, west-central Sweden, and parts of Denmark; and based on this core area and a fear of Hanseatic expansion a dynastic union of the three countries was achieved in 1397 (*see* Kalmar Union*). In 1523 the last of the union monarchs, Christian II*, was driven from the throne as a result of revolts in Denmark and Sweden, and the union dissolved. Over the next several hundred years, several attempts were made to re-establish the union. In 1657–1658 Karl X* tried to rebuild the union through military means but failed. There were sentiments for electing the king of Denmark-Norway king of Sweden in 1743 and 1809 and for making the Swedish-Norwegian king, Karl XV*, king of Denmark in 1860. Norwegians may have acted, in part, out of similar sentiments when they sought a Danish prince in 1814 and a Swedish and then Danish prince for the throne in 1905.

In the mid-nineteenth century, a romanticist, popular sentiment and movement (Scandinavianism) arose, at first among students at Lund, Copenhagen, and Uppsala universities. This was triggered, in part, by the rising German nationalism and the threat it posed to Denmark. The Kalmar Union was invoked as a precedent. Swedes and Norwegians volunteered to fight in Denmark in 1848–1850 and 1864. The Swedish and Norwegian governments, however, in spite of promises made to the contrary by Karl XV, remained aloof, especially in the latter struggle. Political (unionist) Scandinavianism never recovered from the disappointments of this period.

In the second half of the nineteenth century other forms of integration, especially cultural and institutional, were felt to be more feasible and fruitful. In 1869 Scandinavian linguists and authors recommended a standardization of orthography, much of which was implemented (in Denmark as late as 1948). There was a spate of practical measures after 1870 including a postal union, a currency union (the *krone*/crown being interchangeable until World War I), common legislation of several kinds, and the development of common organizations (e.g., the Scandinavian Labor Congress, 1886–1920).

A new impetus toward cooperation appeared after World War I (e.g., the Nordic Administrative League from 1918, and Conservative, Liberal, and Social Democratic cooperation). This trend continued after World War II* in the form of regular conferences of the Nordic prime ministers and of the foreign ministers, the end of inter-Nordic passport regulations, the adoption of a common labor market and social service system (health care, unemployment, and so on) for resident Nordic non-nationals in each country, and the establishment of the Nordic Council, as well as the Nordic Ministerial Council, following the Twenty-eighth Nordic Interparliamentary Congress in 1951. Under a 1972 agreement, a secretariat under the Nordic Ministerial Council administers more than 40 cultural and scientific programs or institutions.

In sum, there has been a development from a Scandinavian sentiment for a common state or common action to a Nordic technocratic cooperation among the five Nordic countries. At the same time, political (unionist) Nordism has declined over time. In the post-World War II era there were a number of failures including abortive plans for a defensive union (1949), a customs union (1958), an economic community (Nordøk, 1970), and a nuclear-free zone (1982). There have also been abortive political-industrial ventures including the Viggen fighter plane (1976) and the Swedish-Norwegian Volvo Agreement (1979–1980). In the early 1980s two distinct brands of "new Nordism" have emerged: a non-governmental industrial Nordism which aims at cooperation among firms and is based on corporate self-interest (e.g., in overseas ventures), and a Nordism that focuses on alternative lifestyles based on the activities of voluntary organizations. The latter received funding support from the Norwegian Storting* in 1983 for a "Nordic Analysis of Alternative Ways of Development."

REFERENCES: *DH*, vol. 11; *DSH*, vols. 12–14; *NH*, vols. 10, 11; Nordic Council, *Nordic Cooperation, An Introduction* (Stockholm: Norstedt, 1971); B. Turner and G. Nordquist, *The Other European Community: Integration and Co-operation in Nordic Europe* (London: Weidenfeld and Nicolson, 1982); F. W. Wendt, *The Nordic Council and Cooperation in Scandinavia* (Copenhagen: Munksgaard, 1959).

H. STANG

NORMANIST CONTROVERSY Debate on the influence of Scandinavians in the formation of the early Russian state (sometimes called the Varangian problem)

According to the *Russian Primary Chronicle*, edited by the monk Nestor in 1111–1113, four tribes in what is now north Russia invited "Varangians[*] called Rus' . . . from across the sea" to rule them. The main leader of these Rus' was Rjurik, who settled in Old Ladoga and later on in Novgorod. After his death, his relative Oleg killed two other Rus' leaders, Askol'd and Dir, who had settled in Kiev, and established Rjurik's grandson Igor' there in 866. "And from these Varangians the Russian land got its name."

The *Primary Chronicle* raised four main questions, which together have provoked and defined the Normanist controversy: the historicity of what we are told of Rjurik (and his two brothers, Sineus and Truvor), Oleg, Igor', Askol'd, and Dir, that is, the "founding fathers"; the origin of the name Rus' (whence Russia); the origin of the name Varangians; and the part(s) played by Scandinavians in the early (ninth–twelfth centuries) Russian society and state. The first three questions are much more restricted in scope and in research possibilities, and historians have come to downgrade the importance of individuals and names in favor of emphasis on long-term or mass processes and developments. Increasingly, the old, purely philological approach has been abandoned, as interest has shifted to the fourth question and to source materials in increasing order of remoteness from the literary (and, for some, literal) point of departure, the *Primary Chronicle*. There has been a departure from literal, face-value acceptance of Nestor's text by Soviet scholars in particular.

The Normanist position is that Scandinavians founded the first Russian state about 860 A.D. and played a central role in it for the next 200 years or so. The *Bertinian Annals* of the Frankish court tell of some visiting "Rhos" in 839, who proved to be of Swedish nationality; the Byzantine emperor Constantine Porphyrogenetos' treatise *De administrando imperio* (c. 950) distinguishes "Rhos" from "Slavs" and gives both Rhos and Slavonic names to the Dnieper cataracts; Bishop Liutprand of Cremona in 968 speaks of the "Rhos, whom we by another name call Northmen"; and eleventh-century Byzantine sources mention "Varangians," who, in light of Snorri Sturluson's* and Saxo Grammaticus's* materials on "Varangians," must have been Scandinavians. The "Rhos" Dnieper names are explicable from Old Norse.

An ultra-Normanist version of this approach argues that the Swedish Rus' (from *ruotsi*, which derives from *Ro/th/slagen*, an area close to Stockholm*) brought law, religion, morals, crafts, trade, towns, and government to the Slavs, who had been "living like savage beasts and birds." These Swedes were conquerors, and the Nestor account of the calling-in of three brothers is merely legend.

Philologists, as opposed to "pure" historians, have contributed to the Normanist arguments. The word *Rus'* came from the Finnish *ruotsi*, which derived from *rodhs*, meaning "a rower." The Swedish region of Ro/th/slagen got its name from the same root. "Varangians" originally signified Goth and Herule warrior bands. Ninth- and tenth-century Norse names in Russia and Swedish runic inscriptions were adduced, and so on. Arabic sources on the Rus' have been examined, as have Russian place-names based on Rus- and Vareg-. Even folklore, especially the north Russian *bylina* ballads, has been studied. A classical summary of the Normanist case was formulated by V. Thomsen in 1877, and many believed that "the Varangian controversy is fortunately a thing of the past."

But the controversy has hardly become a thing of the past. The initial phases, dominated by historians (c. 1725–1845) and Normanist philologists (c. 1845–1915) have been followed by a phase dominated by concentration on material culture, especially near the Baltic, around Old Ladoga and Novgorod, and along the Volga (at Jaroslav and Vladimir) and Dnieper (at Gnezdovo near Smolensk, Jsestovicy near Chernigov, and Kiev) trade routes; and on Oriental coins and objects in Sweden, which must have come via Russia. Mild forms of Normanism prevailed in pre-Revolutionary Russia and in the Soviet Union until the 1930s.

The anti-Normanist side denies the pivotal, causal role of Scandinavians in forming the early Russian state. Two main views are discernable: the Varangians and/or "Rus' " are non-Scandinavian, for example, Finns, Slavicized Celts, Balts, Etruscans, and so on; or the Varangians are Scandinavian, but did not create the state; rather they were drawn in, played their subordinate part in, and were quickly absorbed into a drawn-out, organic, predominantly Slavic process. The Rus' name originated in south Russia long before the Varangians came.

The anti-Normanist orientation has dominated most of the Soviet period. It has three foundations. First, it rests on the Marxist view that states arise out of internal societal contradictions, as a basically autochthonous process. Second, it relies on archeological evidence that the Slavs, especially of south (Kievan)

Russia, were more culturally advanced than previously thought. Burials and objects which were earlier thought to be Norse have been shown to be mixed or even purely Slav. Coin finds have been interpreted as showing Slav trade with Sweden. Third, various *Primary Chronicle* compilations and other early Russian sources have been criticized as late and tendentious.

In reaction to the ultra-Normanists' denigration of early Slav history, Normanism has been decried as "an affront," "slinging mud at the Russian people," "unscientific," "anti-historical." Several pre-Revolutionary Russian historians sometimes have been labeled "Normanist," although their positions are much the same as modern Soviet "anti-Normanists." It was the inner, organic growth of the Eastern Slav society and economy which created the state—of which "the crowning glory," so to speak, was the invitation of the Varangian princes.

A number of recent interpretive contributions have been made to this 250–year-old debate. One is an anti-Normanist attempt to show that the Kiev state grew out of a sixth–seventh century ante-state, a "super federation," of the Slavonic Antes with no Varangian princes. A novel, "composite" view has been put forward involving Franco-Frisian international traders from Ruthenicis/Rhodes (whence Rus') and Scandinavian navigators. There also has been a rejection of both Normanist and anti-Normanist arguments in favor of a "third solution," wherein the Rhos/Rus' name is thought to be Biblical, first applied to the sixth-century Herules, then to Old Ladoga Scandinavians, who were "called in" by one side in a civil war (c. 860) over control of silver from and deliveries to the Islamic world market. A "third way" is also surfacing among young Leningrad archeologists.

REFERENCES: A. N. Kirpijčnikov et al., "Russko-scandinavskie svjazi v epokhu obrazovanija Drevnerusskogo gosudarstva (IX–XI, vv)," *Scando-Slavica* 24 (1978) (English summary); J. P. Nielsen, "Boris Grekov and the Norman Question," *Scando-Slavica* 27 (1981); H. Stang, "Russians and Norwegians—Two Self-Appellations, One Origin," *Scandinavian Journal of History* 8:1 (1983): 63–70; V. Thomsen, *The Relations Between Ancient Russia and Scandinavia and the Origin of the Russian State* (London/Oxford, 1877); "Varangian Problems," *Scando-Slavica Supplementum* 1 (1970).

H. STANG

NORTH SLESVIG Denmark's disputed province

This area, which many Danes refer to as Southern Jutland, includes the counties of Haderslev, Aabenraa-Sonderborg, and Tonder and is the only part of Denmark which has a common land frontier with a foreign country, in this case, Germany. From 1864 until 1920 North Slesvig was the extreme northern portion of the duchy of Slesvig, which Prussia took from Denmark as a result of Bismarck's first war of unification. The population of this region remained overwhelmingly Danish, however, and a number of difficulties arose between Danes and Germans in Slesvig over issues such as education and linguistic autonomy. On 10 February 1920, as a result of the Versailles Treaty and Germany's defeat in World War I, a plebiscite under League of Nations auspices took place which resulted in the re-establishment of Danish control over North Slesvig.

The Slesvig question* led to a spirited political debate within Denmark which lasted with varying degrees of intensity at least until the 1960s. To a certain extent the issue is still not completely resolved to everyone's satisfaction. Groups like the Social Democrats, Radicals, and other elements to the left of center generally favored minimal gains at the expense of Germany. The Danish government followed this policy in 1920 when only solidly Danish-speaking areas were returned to Denmark as a result of a democratic election. Subsequent governments have adhered to this moderate policy, in spite of pressures and temptations to the contrary. Opposing this policy of restraint were a number of individuals and organizations usually associated with the Conservative and Liberal (Venstre) parties on the Right who argued that certain areas in Slesvig under German control, and especially the city of Flensburg, should come under Danish jurisdiction. This more nationalist or expansionist point of view became especially strong shortly after World War II* when relatively chaotic conditions in German-controlled Slesvig existed, caused in part by the influx of hundreds of thousands of German refugees from Soviet-controlled areas to the east. In 1947 the Liberal prime minister Knud Kristensen* expressed some sympathy for the idea of incorporating certain areas of German-controlled Slesvig into Denmark or at least placing them under an international trusteeship. Opposition to these suggestions was so strong in many Danish circles that Kristensen's coalition was replaced by the Social Democrats in large part because of fears of renewed conflict over Slesvig.

Although there have been difficulties and conflicts, North Slesvig has remained Danish in spite of Hitler's takeover in Germany and a five-year German occupation of Denmark. This is mostly likely due to the fact that in accordance with the long-standing Danish traditions of moderation and democracy, the border change of 1920 was based on demographic realities and the principle of national self-determination.

REFERENCES: J. Bukdahl, *Scandinavia Past and Present, Through Revolutions to Liberty* (Odense: Arnkrone, 1959); T. Fink, *Geschichte des Schleswigischen Grenzlandes* (Copenhagen: Ejnar Munksgaard, 1958); A. Rothery, *Denmark, Kingdom of Reason* (New York: Viking Press, 1937); J. Voorhis, "A Study of Official Relations Between the German and Danish Governments in the Period Between 1940–1943," Ph.D. dissertation, Northwestern University, 1968.

                                                                    J. L. VOORHIS

NORWEGIAN (Language) *See* Languages: Scandinavian

NORWEGIAN CONFEDERATION OF TRADE UNIONS *See* Swedish Confederation of Trade Unions

NORWEGIAN EMPLOYERS' FEDERATION *See* Swedish Employers' Federation

NORWEGIAN FEMINIST UNION (Norsk Kvinnesaksforening/NKF) Norway's first feminist organization

The Norwegian Feminist Union, or NKF, was founded in Christiania (Oslo) in 1884 by Venstre Party politician Hagbard E. Berner, who became its first president, and Jørgine (Gina) Krog*, who served on the governing council. Its aim was to help women achieve their rights and their just place in society. Branch groups soon formed in Bergen and Trondheim, and later in Drammen. The formation of this organization signified a new phase in women's history in Norway; women had begun to take action on their own behalf.

Anna Stang succeeded Berner as president in 1885, and in 1887 the NKF began publishing its own organ, *Nylaende* (*New Lands*), with Gina Krog as editor.

In its early years, the NKF took part in the "morality debate" over police-regulated prostitution. The NKF sympathized with the plight of prostitutes, demanded closure of the bordellos, and denounced the double standard of morality. Officially regulated prostitution was abolished in Oslo in 1887 and in Bergen and Trondheim in 1893.

In the 1880s the NKF also promoted practical and vocational pursuits for women by offering them free instruction and by encouraging artisans to take on female apprentices. Despite its middle-class character, in labor disputes in 1889–1890 the NKF tried to mediate between low-paid women workers and their employers. It also helped female sales clerks organize in 1890.

The NKF fought for women's suffrage* through the 1890s and after, until women got the vote in 1907 and universal suffrage was enacted in 1913. It also supported women's right to become ministers of the church and opposed special protective legislation for gainfully employed women, because such laws operated to exclude them from certain jobs. In the 1930s it defended the right of married women to hold jobs.

In 1936 feminist author Margarete Bonnevie reorganized the NKF. Its activities were later interrupted by the German occupation of Norway during World War II*; however, the organization was revived in 1946, again under the guidance of Margarete Bonnevie, but with Dakky Kiaer as president. It worked for separate taxation of married women's income and property, equal pay for women doing the same work as men, maternity leave without loss of employment, payments for dependent children, and equal education for boys and girls. As legal reforms and social change took place along these lines, the NKF turned more attention to fighting sex stereotypes. It sought to encourage women to go into politics and other male-dominated fields; thus it anticipated some major goals of the neo-feminist movement, which spread from the United States to Norway by around 1970.

The NKF's headquarters are located in Oslo. It works for the achievement of equality of the sexes in the areas of work, family, and national life. It is affiliated with the International Alliance of Women. It had about 1,000 members in 1970.

REFERENCES: A. C. Agerholt, *Den norske kvinnebevegelses historie* (Oslo: Gyldendal Norsk, 1973); *Aschehougs konversasjons leksikon* (1971); K. Skjønsberg, ed., *Hvor var kvinnene?* (Oslo: Gyldendal Norsk, 1979).

N. FARQUHAR

NORWEGIAN LABOR PARTY (Det Norske Arbeiderparti)

The Norwegian Labor Party, destined to become the country's largest political organization, originated as a small political sect in 1887. Not until the enactment of manhood suffrage in 1898 and the breakthrough of mass industrialization*at the turn of the century did the party succeed in electing representatives to the Storting*. Four Labor candidates were chosen in 1903. During the next years the party steadily increased its electoral support, advancing from 16 percent of the popular vote in 1906 to 32 percent in 1915, in large part at the expense of the Liberal Party. During its early years the party adopted a moderate, non-revolutionary reform policy. It accepted parliamentary democracy, while favoring nationalization of the means of production.

With rapid industrialization occurring, a more radical trend developed within Labor by the second decade of the twentieth century. Its chief spokesman was Martin Tranmæl*, the leading figure behind the formation of the Trade Union Opposition of 1911. This group favored a more revolutionary stance against capitalist society. Strengthened by the difficult conditions of World War I and the success of the Bolshevik Revolution, Tranmæl's faction gained control of the party at a bitterly divisive congress in 1918.

Initially following a radical course, Labor thereupon established close ties with the Bolsheviks. It joined the Communist International in 1919, the only western European party to do so as a unit. In reaction, however, the more moderate members of the party broke away to form the Social Democratic Party in 1920.

Although the Labor Party after 1918 proclaimed itself to be revolutionary, and revolutionary phrases were used by its leaders, it never developed a true strategy for seizing power. Its ties to Moscow cooled distinctly because of Tranmæl's refusal to accept dictation. Subsequently, in 1923 the Labor Party broke with the Comintern. This resulted in another party division, the creation of the Norwegian Communist Party*.

Initially, the Communists were a real challenge to Labor, but they soon were decimated by internal splits. The Labor Party, on the other hand, was strengthened by its independent course. The division with the Social Democrats was bridged in 1927, and in that year's election the reunited party gained 59 Storting representatives, becoming the largest single party in the country, a position it has consistently maintained.

As a consequence of its victory, King Haakon VII* appointed the first Labor government to office on 27 January 1928, headed by a veteran parliamentary representative, Christopher Hornsrud. His government proved to be the shortest in the country's political history, falling on 8 February due to opposition from powerful economic interests and the government's declared intent to work for a Socialist society. Despite its brief existence, however, the Hornsrud interlude had long-term significance. It indicated that the Labor Party had abandoned its earlier revolutionary emphasis and would instead abide by parliamentary rules.

By the 1933 election the party had discarded its anti-capitalist position from the twenties, adopting instead Keynesian economics emphasizing an increase in state expenditures to meet the crisis of the international depression. Labor adopted an extremely popular slogan calling for full employment and sought broad mass support. The party gained 40 percent of the votes and 69 representatives, just 7 short of a majority.

Its large electoral backing, combined with the non-Socialist government's failure to solve the problems of the Depression, brought Labor into office again, this time more permanently. An agreement was worked out with the Agrarian Party (later the Center Party*) granting agricultural interests greater state support. In return Labor received the opportunity to govern, with Johan Nygaardsvold* becoming prime minister in March 1935. The Nygaardsvold government followed a cautious reform policy. It emphasized concrete social reforms, including extension of sickness insurance, expanded use of the eight-hour day, old-age pensions, guaranteed paid holidays, and unemployment insurance.

Norway's gradual recovery from the Depression was interrupted by the German occupation, during which the government was forced into exile in England. The first postwar election showed that the Labor Party continued to enjoy broad popular support. It received an absolute majority in the Storting, which it retained as the result of subsequent elections until 1961. During the 20–year period following the end of World War II* the Labor Party dominated Norwegian politics to an extent never before rivaled by any political party. This was the era of Einar Gerhardsen*, who served as party chairman and who was prime minister from 1945 to 1951 and 1955 to 1965. Gerhardsen continued the social reform policy from the pre-war period, achieving completion of the social welfare system. The Labor government also carried out state regulation of economic growth to a considerable degree, including active government participation in large-scale industrial enterprises. No serious effort was made, however, to create a Socialist economic system.

The beginning of the end for Labor's postwar domination occurred in 1961, when a number of disenchanted former members established the Socialist People's Party (Sosialistisk Folkeparti/SF). The new party opposed NATO membership, and it attacked Labor's alleged failure to work toward transforming Norway into a Socialist society. In 1961 SF won two seats, depriving Labor of its absolute majority. An omen of things to come occurred in 1963, when Gerhardsen was momentarily ousted from office, with SF casting the deciding votes which brought a short-lived non-Socialist coalition into office.

This was followed in 1965 by the first permanent coalition of non-Socialist parties. Not until March 1971 did Labor return to office under Trygve Bratteli, Gerhardsen's successor, when the non-Socialist parties could not agree on

Norway's membership in the European Economic Community. However, the very issue that brought a Labor government back to power proved to be the cause of a decisive defeat which left the party shattered for a number of years. The Bratteli government favored Norwegian membership in the EEC, and the prime minister turned the October 1972 referendum into a popular vote of confidence. When the majority of the voters said no to EEC membership, his government resigned.

The following year's election simply reinforced Labor's defeat. Its popular vote declined from 46 percent to 35 percent with a quarter-million voters abandoning the party. Not since 1930 had the Labor Party received such a low percentage of the vote. And yet, because the Socialist Electoral Alliance, composed of Socialist groups that had opposed EEC membership, held the balance in parliament, Bratteli returned as prime minister since the Electoral Alliance preferred a Labor government to a non-Socialist one.

Trygve Bratteli served for three years, being succeeded by Odvar Nordli in 1976. In the 1977 election the divisions caused by the EEC membership controversy seemed to have been settled, with Labor receiving 42 percent of the vote and 76 representatives. Still, the government remained in office at the sufferance of the Socialist Left Party, formed out of the Socialist Electoral Alliance. During the next four years Labor steadily lost ground, being weakened by personal rivalries and by foreign policy disputes, in particular concerning NATO strategy for Norway over such questions as the stockpiling of military equipment on Norwegian soil. Nordli resigned in February 1981, to be briefly succeeded as prime minister by Gro Harlem Brundtland. In the election of 1981 the party fared badly, with its share of the vote reduced to 37 percent and its Storting representation to 66. Especially noteworthy was Labor's loss of support among younger voters, who indicated a preference for the parties of the right.

During the ensuing minority Conservative government of Kaare Willoch, expanded in 1983 to include Christian People's Party and Center Party ministers, Labor under Gro Harlem Brundtland maintained a dominant position as the chief opposition party. Despite the setbacks of the sixties and seventies, the Labor Party remained the strongest alternative in Norwegian politics to a non-Socialist government in the 1980s.

REFERENCES: H. Allen, *Norway and Europe in the 1970s* (Oslo: Universitetsforlaget, 1979); S. Berglund and P. Pesonen, with G. P. Gislason, "Political Party Systems," in E. Allardt et al., *Scandinavian Democracy* (Copenhagen: Det Danske Selskab, 1981); W. Galenson, *Labor in Norway* (Cambridge, Mass.: Harvard University Press, 1949); K. Heidar, "The Norwegian Labour Party: Social Democracy in a Periphery of Europe," in W. E. Paterson and A. H. Thomas, eds., *Social Democratic Parties in Western Europe* (London: Croom Helm, 1977); W. Lafferty, *Economic Development and the Response of Labour in Scandinavia* (Oslo: Universitetsforlaget, 1971), and *Industrialization, Community, Structure, and Socialism* (Oslo: Universitetsforlaget, 1974); S. Rokkan, "The Growth and Structuring of Mass Politics," in Allardt et al., *op. cit.*; J. Storing, *Norwegian*

Democracy (Boston: Houghton Mifflin, 1963); H. Valen and E. Katz, *Political Parties in Norway*, 2nd ed. (Oslo: Universitetsforlaget, 1967); A. Zachariassen, *Fra Marcus Thrane til Martin Tranmæl. DNA fram til 1945* (Oslo, 1967).

O. HOIDAL AND L. SVÅSAND

NORWEGIAN-SWEDISH UNION (1814–1905)

Norway's parliament met for the first time in an extraordinary session beginning on 7 October in Christiania to revise the constitution. Most of the 79 members had not been delegates to the National Assembly* in the spring, but a large majority, especially those from western Norway, were still supporters of independence. They therefore first considered carrying on the struggle against Sweden. When they concluded that this would be unwise, they not only made the relatively minor changes necessary to unite with Sweden, but they also altered other sections of the constitution to guarantee Norwegian autonomy in the future.

To give themselves the greatest latitude for such changes, the parliament on 10 October decreed that union with Sweden should take place but also refused to accept Christian Frederik's (Christian VIII*) abdication or to elect Sweden's Karl XIII* in his stead until their deliberations were complete and Swedish assent given to their changes. The unionist faction led by Wedel Jarlsberg opposed such tactics, and Karl (XIV) Johan* fumed frequently and threatened continued military action against Norway to prevent significant changes in the constitution but ultimately reached agreement with the Norwegian legislators.

The changes made in Norway's constitution weakened the king's power considerably and strengthened that of the council of state* and parliament. The latter, for example, imposed significant curbs upon the king's power to appoint foreigners, Swedes obviously above all, as Norwegian officials. Karl Johan was granted greater authority to use the Norwegian army outside of the country than the parliament had originally intended. On the other hand, this power was limited by the provision that he could not make war without consulting the Norwegian council of state as well as its comparable body in Stockholm*. Clauses were also added to the original constitution which guaranteed Norway the right to possess its own national bank, monetary system, and commercial flag, and that each state would possess its own national debt.

Many individuals pulled together to make the process of conciliation with Sweden work. Wilhelm F. K. Christie* emerged during this first parliament as the most competent and effective architect of these necessary alterations in the constitution in the face of the Swedish threat to Norway. Christie had been the permanent secretary to the National Assembly, had been appointed to a diplomatic mission to England during the summer of 1814, and presided over parliament in the fall during the constitution's revision. He initiated many of the changes which the Swedes reluctantly accepted but which did not surrender the principle of self-rule established at Eidsvoll in May.

Norway's year of independence ended on 4 November, when Karl Johan accepted the Storting's* final revision of the constitution, and Karl XIII was then elected as Norway's king. Many Norwegians felt then that their efforts had been in vain. It was not long, however, before they appreciated the constitution they had written. It established a greater degree of social equality and popular participation in government than any other European nation would actually enjoy for most of the nineteenth century. It also created the means to defend the autonomy they had secured within the Swedish union and provided them with far greater self-rule than they had possessed when tied to Denmark. The union would last until 1905. (*See also* Convention of Moss; Eidsvoll Constitution of 17 May; Great Men's Meeting; Michelsen, Christian; Treaty of Kiel.)

REFERENCES: O. Alin, *Den svensk-norsk unionen*, 2 vols. (Stockholm, 1889–1891); A. Bergsgård, *Året 1814*, 2 vols. (Oslo, 1943–1945); H. Koht, *Norge i 1814, Dagbok hundre aar efterpaa* (Christiania, 1914); R. Lindgren, *Norway-Sweden: Union, Disunion and Scandinavian Integration* (Princeton: Princeton University Press, 1959); A. Linvald, *Kong Christian VIII*, vol. 2: *Norges statholder 1813–1814* (Copenhagen, 1952); B. Nissen, *Året 1814* (Oslo, 1964); S. Steen, *1814*, vol. 1 of *Det frie Norge* (Oslo, 1951); O. Vasstveit, "Bergensrepresentantene og bundne mandat på det overordentlige storting 1814," *Historisk tidsskrift* (N) 62 (1983): 203–15; J. Weibull, *Carl Johan och Norge 1810–1814: Unionplanerna och deras förverkligande* (Lund: 1957).

L. SATHER

NYGAARDSVOLD, JOHAN (1879–1952) Norwegian Labor Party* politician, prime minister 1935–1945

Under Johan Nygaardsvold's leadership the Labor Party made its definitive breakthrough in Norwegian politics, beginning a period of governmental domination which lasted from 1935 to 1965.

Nygaardsvold came from Trøndelag, the son of a tenant farmer. He worked several years in the United States (1902–1907), but returned to Trøndelag, where he became involved in Labor Party politics. First elected to the Storting* in 1915, he was re-elected continuously until he withdrew from politics in 1949.

Nygaardsvold developed into an experienced and pragmatic politician. He was open, practical, and possessed a good sense of humor. As Labor's parliamentary leader, he initiated discussions with the Agrarian Party (*see* Center Party: Norway) in 1935. With the defeat of J. L. Mowinckel's Liberal government, Nygaardsvold succeeded as prime minister on 19 March 1935. Shortly thereafter the "crisis compromise" with the Agrarians was completed whereby Labor gained a parliamentary majority in return for providing increased support for agriculture.

As prime minister, Nygaardsvold followed a moderate policy. Labor abandoned its revolutionary tradition, adopting instead the cautious reform policy that henceforth characterized the party. Under Nygaardsvold's government the country's financial condition gradually improved. Labor peace generally was maintained, production increased, and unemployment decreased. The Labor government emphasized social reform. Among the key reforms passed between 1935 and 1940 were extension of sickness insurance, enactment of old-age pensions, extension of the eight-hour day, and introduction of unemployment insurance.

The German invasion of 9 April 1940 caught the government by surprise. After first being in despair, Nygaardsvold resolved to resist. With the defeat of Allied forces in 1940 the government chose to go into exile in England.

Although weak at first, the Nygaardsvold government in exile nevertheless enjoyed certain advantages. It was without question Norway's legal government, and it was strengthened by the popularity of King Haakon VII*, who loyally sustained the government. Furthermore, during the war the cabinet supplemented itself with members from outside Labor. To a degree it therefore became a national government. It also enjoyed financial solvency thanks to the income earned by the merchant marine, which had been nationalized.

The government, however, was associated with Norway's defeat in 1940, and this was a liability it never could overcome. As early as 1942 Nygaardsvold declared that his government would resign once the war was over. He delivered that resignation on 12 June 1945 and was succeeded by Einar Gerhardsen's* coalition government on 25 June.

Following the war Nygaardsvold was subjected to a certain amount of criticism from individuals who sought to hold his government responsible for Norway's military unpreparedness in 1940. However, such criticism was muted because other parties, not merely Labor, had favored reduced military expenditures during the 1930s. But above all, Nygaardsvold's continued popularity caused the attacks against him to come to naught. Thanks to his pre-war accomplishments, in particular the pragmatic reforms which lessened the divisions in Norwegian society between Socialists and non-Socialists, he is regarded as one of the leading prime ministers of this century.

REFERENCES: T. K. Derry, *A History of Modern Norway, 1814–1972* (London: Oxford University Press, 1973); I. Semmingsen, "Norway 1905–1940," in *Scandinavia Past and Present*, vol. 2 (Copenhagen: Arnkrone, 1959).

O. HOIDAL

O

OFTEDAL, LARS (1838–1900) Norwegian clergyman and politician

Lars Oftedal was born to prosperous parents in Stavanger in 1838. During his school days in the 1850s, various revivals swept across southern Norway and influenced Oftedal, who decided to enter the ministry. He began theological studies in 1859 at what is now the University of Oslo, whose theology faculty was then known for its Lutheran orthodoxy and interest in revivalism. Graduating with honors in 1864, Oftedal accepted a position as an itinerant preacher for the Bergen Domestic Missionary Society. As such he developed a powerful yet folksy homiletical style less formal than that of most of his colleagues. This presumably helped him win a large following in western Norway. In 1866 Oftedal went to Wales as the pastor for Norwegian sailors there and in western England, but his superiors cancelled the appointment a year and a half later. From 1867 until 1870 he served again as an itinerant revivalist and aroused the resentment of many pastors by requesting to preach in their sanctuaries.

Oftedal accepted in 1870 a pastorate on the island of Karmøy, where he soon began a popular, unofficial school in which he taught parishioners of all ages both Christianity and secular subjects. He also served other parishes in southwestern Norway during the 1870s and published a religious newspaper that further extended his reputation.

The popular pastor became more deeply involved in Christian social work during that decade, and owing to his incentive followers opened an orphanage in Stavanger in 1876. The following year Oftedal, together with other reform-minded clergymen, began to publish *Vestlands-Posten* (*The Western Post*), a thrice-weekly newspaper which carried general news, essays, and Christian analyses of current events.

In the meantime, Oftedal had entered politics, supporting the Liberal Party and its demands for parliamentary democracy. In 1877 he was elected a substitute deputy in parliament, and in 1883 he entered the legislative body as a full-fledged representative, serving until 1885 and again from 1889 until 1891. Oftedal was one of the few state church clergymen who advocated liberal democratic reforms during the turbulent decade of the 1880s and complained about being ostracized by conservative colleagues. In parliament he opposed funding the controversial, anticlerical author Alexander Kielland while perennially advocating greater congregational autonomy within the established church, which the Department of Ecclesiastical Affairs administered centrally from the capital. Oftedal also continued his humanitarian efforts for disadvantaged children.

Oftedal's political career came to an abrupt halt in 1891 when he confessed publicly to having had an extramarital sexual relationship. He demitted his pastorate and judiciously declined to occupy the seat in parliament to which he had been re-elected earlier that year.

Oftedal made a partial comeback in 1893. Supporters provided a hall in Stavanger where he preached without attracting the following of his earlier years. Perhaps more significantly, Oftedal founded that year *Stavanger Aftenblad* (*Stavanger Evening Paper*), now one of Norway's leading dailies, which he edited until his death in 1900. His place in Norwegian history, however, derives chiefly from his successful efforts to combine Christianity with liberal politics at a time when many believing and unbelieving Norwegians regarded the two as fundamentally incompatible.

F. HALE

OLAF I TRYGGVASON (c. 968–9 September 1000) King of Norway 995–1000

Olaf Tryggvason's father, a regional king in eastern Norway and grandson of King Harald I Fairhair*, was killed soon after Olaf's birth c. 968, and the boy was raised in Russia. Saga accounts of the flight with his mother from Norway, his childhood in slavery in Estonia, and his adventures as a youth in Novgorod are, however, fictitious. Olaf participated as a Viking* chieftain in raids along the Baltic coast, in the Netherlands, and in Ireland, and also in the Danish invasions of England, where he is recorded as a recipient of large tribute payments from King Ethelred the Unready in 991 and 994. In 995 he returned to Norway with the spoils of his years as a Viking and claimed his patrimonial right to kingship.

Norway was then ruled by Earl Haakon the Great (Haakon Sigurdsson*) of Lade in Trøndelag, but the earl had lost his popularity near the end of his reign and was killed by one of his own slaves during the uprising of farmers at approximately the same time that Olaf arrived in Norway. Olaf was subsequently hailed as king there and began his five-year reign, the first regent in Harald Fairhair's dynasty to obtain a real political foothold in Trøndelag. Saga tradition has also recorded him as the founder of the trading center at Nidaros (now Trondheim) in 997. Although he exercised little influence in the eastern valleys, he found support in the territory around Oslo fjord where his father had ruled, and he also had family connections to western Norway (through his mother) and to southwestern Norway (through his brother-in-law).

Olaf had been converted to Christianity in England and was the first effective missionary king in Norway, carrying out the proselytizing which King Haakon the Good (Haakon I Haraldsson*) had been forced to abandon some 50 years earlier (see Conversion). Olaf baptized on the eastern and western coasts, but his hardhanded methods of Christianization met with resistance in Trøndelag and in northern Norway. The king is also credited with the conversion of Iceland (Christianity was adopted by the Icelandic parliament in 999–1000), and tradition includes in addition the Faroe Islands*, the Orkneys, Shetland, and even Greenland*. Other accomplishments were a better organization of the kingdom and a consolidation of the monarchy, and perhaps the introduction in Norway of the institution of landed men, chieftains in royal service in return for part of the royal estates (a type of feudal baron).

Olaf was killed on 9 September 1000 in a naval battle at Svold, probably in the Baltic (near Rügen?), fighting an alliance of Danes under King Sven I* Forkbeard, Swedes under King Olaf Skötkonung, and other Norwegians under Earl Eirik Haakonsson. The Danish and Swedish hostility most likely concerned sovereignty over eastern provinces in Norway, especially the territory around Oslo fjord and border lands, although the sagas relate personal motives based on Olaf Tryggvason's marriage to Sven Forkbeard's sister and the egging of Sven's Swedish wife, Sigrid the Proud, mother of Olov Skötkonung. After the battle of Svold, rule over Norway passed to Earl Haakon the Great's sons, the earls of Lade Eirik and Svein, in part as representatives of the Danish (in particular) and Swedish crowns. The territory around Oslo fjord, however, was governed directly from Denmark.

REFERENCES: P. S. Andersen, *Samlingen av Norge og kristningen av landet 800– 1130* (Bergen: Universitetsforlaget, 1977); C. Gibson, *The Two Olafs of Norway* (London: Dobson, 1968); K. Gjerset, *History of the Norwegian People* (1932; repr. New York: AMS, 1969); K. Larsen, *A History of Norway* (Princeton: Princeton University Press, 1948/1974); J. Sephton, trans., *The Saga of King Olaf Tryggvason* (London: Nutt, 1895); S. Sturluson, *Heimskringla: The Olaf Sagas*, vol. 1 (London: Dent, 1964).

J. E. Knirk

OLAF II HARALDSSON (Saint Olaf) (c. 995–29 July 1030) King of Norway 1015–1028

Olaf Haraldsson was born c. 995, the son of a regional king in southeastern Norway and the great-great-grandson of King Harald I Fairhair*. After growing up in his stepfather's petty kingdom in eastern Norway, he became a Viking* at age 12 and led raids first in the Baltic region and then in the west, where he participated as a chieftain both for and against King Sven I Forkbeard* in the Danish invasions in 1009–1014 of King Ethelred the Unready's England. Three times he received large tribute payments. He was baptized in Rouen, Normandy, in 1013 while in Ethelred's service in exile.

Olaf returned to Norway in 1015 with two ships and the spoils of his Viking years; he was accompanied by, among others, an English bishop. Soon after landing in western Norway, he captured and banished Earl Haakon Eiriksson of Lade in Trøndelag, who had ruled Norway for the Danish crown together with his uncle, Earl Svein Haakonsson, after his father departed to join King Knut the Great (Knud I*) in England in 1014. The geographical basis for Olaf's kingship was eastern Norway, especially the western coast of Oslo fjord where his father had ruled, and the eastern valleys, where he enlisted the support of petty kings. On 25 March 1016 he defeated Earl Svein Haakonsson in a naval battle in eastern Norway; Svein died later that year.

The first effective king of all Norway, Olaf the Stout, as he was also called, had to contend with external opposition from the kings of Sweden and especially Denmark, and internal opposition from petty kings, local chieftains (in particular a new family aristocracy), and the farming class. Reconciliation was attained with Olaf Skötkonung of Sweden in 1019 through Olaf Haraldsson's marriage to the Swedish Olaf's illegitimate daughter, and in 1026 Olaf and the Swedish Olaf's successor, Anund Jakob, were allies at the battle of Helgeaa against Knut the Great of Denmark and England. Olaf consolidated his rule and strengthened the monarchy in Norway by eliminating all petty kings, expanding the crown goods, investing the king's bodyguard with administrative duties, exercising more direct rule through the civil administration of royal stewards and landed men (feudal barons), and in addition further strengthening Norway's dominance of the Orkneys, Shetland, the Faroe Islands*, and Greenland*. He upheld law and order in the country, being both just and strict, and promoted the passage of civil penal codes. Initially successful in his internal rule, the king later met with resistance from local chieftains, whose powers he naturally curtailed. His problems were compounded by the reactions to his hardhanded methods of Christianization, in which he continued the missionary work of King Olaf I Tryggvason* by baptizing the population and building churches, and expanded it by establishing Christian legal provision and organizing the Church throughout the country.

Militarily weakened by losses suffered at Helgeaa in 1026 and politically weakened by the gradual loss of backing by local leaders, some of whom were bribed by Knut the Great, Olaf was forced to flee to Russia in 1028. That year the Danish king had himself come to Norway and been hailed as king. When Knut's appointee, Earl Haakon Eiriksson, died late the following year, Olaf returned home from exile via Gotland and Sweden, but after crossing the mountains into Trøndelag, he and his men, many of them mercenaries, were met by an army of farmers from the district, with Danish reinforcements, led by chieftains from northern and western Norway. The deposed king was defeated and killed in the battle of Stiklestad on 29 July 1030.

Olaf was the first ruler to exercise real power both in Trøndelag and in eastern Norway, but the Norwegian monarchy was strengthened less by his reign than by his death, which was quickly interpreted as a martyrdom. The martyred monarch soon became both the patron saint of the country and the embodiment of the concept of a sole sovereign for the entire land, the ''perpetual king of

Norway.'' The alignment of the Danish crown with Norwegian chieftains was soon broken, as legal reforms enacted on Danish initiative by Knut the Great's illegitimate, under-age son and appointee to the Norwegian throne, Svein Alfifuson, united the local chieftains in their opposition. In 1035 they brought Saint Olaf's illegitimate son, Magnus the Good (Magnus I Olafsson*), back from exile in Russia and allied themselves with him as their king.

REFERENCES: P. S. Andersen, *Samlingen av Norge og kristningen av landet 800–1130* (Bergen: Universitetsforlaget, 1977); C. Gibson, *The Two Olafs of Norway* (London: Dobson, 1968); K. Gjerset, *History of the Norwegian People* (1932; repr. New York: AMS, 1969); K. Larsen, *A History of Norway* (Princeton: Princeton University Press, 1948/1974); S. Sturluson, *Heimskringla: The Olaf Sagas*, vols. 1, 2 (London: Dent, 1964).

J. E. KNIRK

OLAF III HARALDSSON (the Quiet) (c. 1050–22 September 1093) King of Norway 1067–1093

Olaf, an illegitimate son of King Harald the Hardruler (Harald III Sigurdsson*), accompanied his father to England in 1066, while Olaf's older brother, Magnus, remained in Norway as regent. After Harald was killed at Stamford Bridge, Olaf returned home and became king and co-regent the next year. Following standard procedures for co-regency at that time in Norway, the brothers divided the royal incomes rather than the kingdom. Magnus's death in 1069 left Olaf sole sovereign.

Under Olaf, who was nicknamed "the Quiet," Norway enjoyed 25 years of peace and prosperity. The king established and maintained good relations with other powers within and outside the country, held a positive attitude toward the Church, and pursued cultural policies aimed at refining life in Norway according to European models. Peace was attained with Denmark in 1068, King Sven II Estridsen* being recognized as sovereign there, and stability in Scandinavia* was then ensured for the time being through intermarriage between the royal houses. In spite of William the Conqueror's succession to the throne of England, Olaf honored the vow of peacefulness toward that country pledged as part of the settlement after the defeat at Stamford Bridge. He also strengthened the relationships to the Norse colonies in the British Isles, particularly the Orkneys, where two of his relatives ruled as earls.

Although Olaf maintained traditional religious and cultural ties with England, his orientation in church politics was more continental. Good relations were attained with the pope and with the archbishop in Bremen (whose province included all of Scandinavia); stone churches were built in various cities in Norway; and the system of traveling missionary bishops was replaced by permanent dioceses in Nidaros (Trondheim), Selja, and Oslo. Urban centers grew and guilds were created, the king himself founding (or regulating?) Bergen c. 1070–1075, the city to which the bishopric at Selja was transferred later in his reign. The number of the king's retainers was doubled to 120.

When Olaf died in eastern Norway in 1093, he was succeeded by his illegitimate son, Magnus Bareleg (Magnus III Olafsson*), and by Haakon, the son of his deceased brother, Magnus.

REFERENCES: P. S. Andersen, *Samlingen av Norge og kristningen av landet 800–1130* (Bergen: Universitetsforlaget, 1977); K. Gjerset, *History of the Norwegian People* (1932; repr. New York: AMS, 1969); K. Larsen, *A History of Norway* (Princeton: Princeton University, Press, 1948/1974); S. Sturluson, *Heimskringla: Sagas of the Norse Kings* (London: Dent, 1961).

J. E. KNIRK

OLAF V (2 July 1903–) King of Norway, 1957–

Olaf V assumed royal authority on 21 September 1957 following the death of his father, Haakon VII*. He was originally baptized Alexander Edward Christian Frederik. His father was then Prince Carl of Denmark, and his mother, Princess Maud, was the youngest daughter of King Edward VII of England and Queen Alexandra. When Prince Carl assumed the name Haakon upon his accession to the Norwegian throne in 1905, his son, crown prince of Norway, received the name Olaf.

From his early youth Crown Prince Olaf was a keen sportsman. He has always been an avid skier, and in 1922 and 1923 he ably took part in the Holmenkollen ski jumping competition. He has also distinguished himself as a yachtsman, winning a number of medals in national and international regattas, including the Olympic gold medal in 1928. He continues to be active in sailing competitions.

Crown Prince Olaf attended the gymnasium and passed his artium examination in 1921. He received his military education at the Military Academy (Krigsskolen) and was commissioned as a lieutenant in 1924. He went on to study at Oxford and passed examinations in political science and economics in 1926.

In 1929 Crown Prince Olaf married Princess Märtha of Sweden. The royal couple had three children: Princess Ragnhild, born 1930; Princess Astrid, born 1932; and Crown Prince Harald, born 1937. Crown Princess Märtha died in 1954.

During the difficult military campaign of April-June 1940 against the German invaders, Crown Prince Olaf accompanied his father and the government of Johan Nygaardsvold*. When it became clear that resistance no longer was possible and that King Haakon and the government would have to go abroad, the crown prince volunteered to remain in order to attempt to lessen the burden of the German occupation. The government was grateful for this generous offer but advised against it, and the crown prince accompanied the king and the government to England.

Crown Prince Olaf actively took part in the war effort. He participated in government meetings, encouraged the sailors of the merchant fleet, and inspected units of the armed forces. He traveled regularly to the United States, where his friendship with President Roosevelt contributed to the American administration's positive attitude toward Norway during the war. When World War II* moved into its final phase, Crown Prince Olaf was appointed chief of defense on 1 July

1944. This was done in order to provide Norway with the greatest possible influence in Allied military planning during this critical period. Five days after the German surrender the crown prince received a wildly enthusiastic reception when he returned to Oslo, on 13 May 1945. He served as regent until his father's arrival on 7 June.

Following the war the crown prince resumed his peacetime responsibilities, accompanying Haakon VII on a regular basis in state council meetings with the government. When the king became ill, the crown prince on 30 June 1955 once again assumed the regency. Upon King Haakon's death King Olaf V adopted his father's motto, "All for Norway." The coronation ceremony had been abolished by a constitutional amendment dating from 1908, but on 22 June 1958 King Olaf was consecrated in the national cathedral in Trondheim on the fifty-second anniversary of his father's coronation.

As monarch, Olaf V is the ruler of a parliamentary democracy in which ultimate authority rests in the Storting*. He has continued in the tradition of Haakon VII, who consistently followed the policy of not becoming involved in partisan politics and loyally accepting the government which enjoyed the Storting's support. Olaf V has never had occasion to make dramatic decisions like those of his father, who was responsible for the appointment of the first Norwegian Labor Party* government in 1928, and whose refusal to accept German demands in 1940 in large part established the resolve to resist Hitler's invasion. The strong foundation for the monarchy created under Haakon VII has continued during Olaf V's reign. For a time the determination of Crown Prince Harald to marry a commoner raised an issue, but this was settled by the royal resolution to elevate Sonja Haraldsen to the rank of crown princess upon her marriage to Crown Prince Harald on 28 August 1968. The couple has two children, Märtha Louise, born in 1971, and Haakon Magnus, born in 1973. The line of royal succession has thereby been lengthened, with male primogeniture in effect. Under Olaf V the monarchy's popularity continues to be strong, and currently there is little support for abolishing the monarchy in favor of a republic.

REFERENCES: *Burke's Royal Families of the World*, vol. 1 (London: Burke's Peerage Ltd., 1977), pp. 427–33; A. McNaughton, *The Book of Kings: A Royal Genealogy*, vol. 1 (London: Garnstone Press, 1973), pp. 190–91; M. Michael, *Haakon: King of Norway* (London: George Allen & Unwin, 1958); Royal Norwegian Ministry of Foreign Affairs, "Olav V—King of Norway," *Norway Information*, March 1981.

O. HOIDAL

OLAUS PETRI (c. 1493–1552) Swedish Lutheran reformer

Born Olof, the son of Peter Olofsson, a smith in Örebro, Olof Petersson became Olaus Petri (Olavus Petri) when he became a student. He attended Uppsala in the mid-1510s and then studied under Martin Luther in Wittenberg, 1516–1518. He received his *magister* degree there in 1518, and as a result became known as Master Olof (Mäster Olof). A disciple of Luther, an intellectual, and an idealist, Master Olof became in the years that followed the leading Lutheran reformer in Sweden, an independent-minded supporter of King Gustav I Vasa*, and the most productive Swedish writer of his time.

Bishop Mattias of Strängnäs employed Olof as a secretary, ordained him as a deacon and canon, and appointed him as a teacher at the cathedral school. There he began his career as a reformer by preaching against such papal practices as the sale of indulgences.

From 1524 to 1539 Master Olof worked fairly cooperatively with the king, primarily, as he thought, in forwarding the Lutheran Reformation*. From 1524 until 1531 he was secretary to the council of the city of Stockholm*, and from 1531 to 1533 he was King Gustav's chancellor. Throughout the period (from 1524 on) he served as a preacher in the Great Church (Storkyrkan, now the cathedral of Stockholm) although he was not ordained until 1539 and did not become its pastor until 1543. Because of his preaching of Lutheran doctrines (see Lutheranism), the Catholics excommunicated him on charges of heresy in 1524. In 1525 he broke his vow of celibacy by marrying.

Although Master Olof served Gustav Vasa well by forwarding the Reformation and thus helping the king to gain control over the property of the Church and by performing his tasks as secretary-chancellor and preacher effectively, Master Olof's insistence on speaking bluntly even to the king and writing Swedish history from the point of view of scholarship rather than that of royal propaganda led to conflict. In the 1530s Master Olof had learned in the confessional about a conspiracy against the king. In 1539 Olof was brought to trial for treason (for not revealing the information), was sentenced to death, but was reprieved and fined. (The huge fine was paid by the city of Stockholm.) In spite of all this, the king appointed Olof school inspector for Stockholm and its official pastor in 1543.

Olaus Petri was an exceptionally productive writer, his works ranging from extremely important translations to the little didactic drama *Tobie comedia* (1550). He translated several Lutheran pamphlets and cooperated in the highly impressive Swedish translation of the New Testament (1526). He composed hymns, some of which are still used in the Church of Sweden; he wrote one defense after another of such matters as the use of Swedish in church services and marriage by the clergy; he provided the church with a handbook, a catechism, and directions for preparing sermons. In the 1530s he wrote a history of medieval Sweden, *En Swensk Crönika* (*A Swedish Chronicle*). All of these except the history, with its impressive scholarly standards, were approved by the king and served his purposes well. Master Olof wrote a Swedish that was simple, specific, and direct, designed to be understood. His influence on the development of the Swedish language was very great. The finest literary treatment of Olaus Petri is August Strindberg's prose drama, *Master Olof* (1872).

REFERENCES: C. Bergendoff, *Olavus Petri and the Ecclesiastical Transformation in Sweden, 1521–1552: A Study in the Swedish Reformation* (New York: Macmillan, 1928);

F. D. Scott, *Sweden: The Nation's History* (Minneapolis: University of Minnesota Press, 1977).

W. JOHNSON

OLD UPPSALA Religious and political center in Sweden (first–mid-thirteenth century)

Old Uppsala, which was located about three miles north of modern Uppsala, was a political and religious center during the first millennium A.D. The site includes three large grave mounds, which appear to date from the fifth or sixth century and are believed to be the graves of the pre-Viking kings Aun, Egil, and Adil, who are mentioned in *Ynglingasaga* and *Beowulf*. These grave mounds seem to confirm the belief that Old Uppsala was the center of a pre-Viking kingdom in middle Sweden. There is also evidence that the principal representative assembly, or *thing*, met there each year. Old Uppsala's importance as a political center appears to have continued through the Viking Age*, and the site retained symbolic significance for the Swedes and their monarchs long after it ceased to be a place of political activity.

As a religious center, Old Uppsala was important both to the pagans of the region and to the early Christians. It is argued that the most important pagan temple in all of Scandinavia*, dedicated to Odin, Thor, and Frey, was located there. Also, a major sacrificial feast, vividly described by Adam of Bremen* in his history of the archdiocese of Hamburg from 1070, was held there every nine years. A Christian church, built on the site of the pagan temple, became the cathedral church of the archdiocese of Sweden around 1164. In 1245 the original church burned, and although it was rebuilt, the diocesan center was moved to Östra Aros, around which modern Uppsala developed.

REFERENCES: *DSH*, vol. 1, 2; L. Thunmark-Nylén, ed., *Vikingatidens ABC* (Stockholm: Statens historiska museum, 1981); *SU*, vol. 11.

J. DAILEY

OLUF I (Hunger) (c. 1052–18 August 1095) King of Denmark 1086–1095

Oluf was the third of the sons of Sven II Estridsen* to rule Denmark. He was chosen following the murder of Knud II* at Odense. He governed the country in the tradition of his father in that he respected the laws and traditions of the country and did not move ahead aggressively to strengthen the monarchy. Denmark (and much of the rest of Europe) was struck by a series of crop failures and plagues which caused great suffering in the country. Oluf and the murderers of Knud were blamed for these problems, which some said were God's punishment. They were used by the faction favoring a stronger monarchy to further the myth that was being developed about Knud and to strengthen their political position.

OLUF II

REFERENCES: *DBL*, vol. 11; *DH*, vol. 3.

B. NORDSTROM

OLUF II (?–c. 1143) King or co-king of Denmark c. 1140–c. 1143

Oluf was the one son of Harald Kesja who survived the murderous search of Erik II* to eliminate his rival's children. He fought against Erik III* and claimed to rule in Skåne. Ultimately, Erik succeeded in having him murdered. Oluf is not a significant figure in Danish history, but he took part in the civil war that went on in the country between the murder of Knud Lavard by Magnus (son of Niels*) in 1131 and the defeat and death of Sven III Grathe* in 1157.

REFERENCES: *DBL*, vol. 11; *DH*, vol. 3.

B. NORDSTROM

OLUF III (1370–3 August 1387) King of Denmark 1376–1387, king of Norway (Olav IV) 1380–1387

Oluf was the son of Haakon VI of Norway and Margrethe I*, daughter of Valdemar IV* of Denmark. He had legitimate claims to all three crowns in Scandinavia*. In 1376 he was elected king in Denmark. He succeeded his father in Norway in 1380. The Swedes were about to elect him when he died suddenly in 1387.

REFERENCES: *DBL*, vol. 11; *DH*, vol. 4; *DSH*, vol. 2; *NH*, vol. 4.

B. NORDSTROM

ORDINARII POST TIJDENDER The first newspaper in Sweden published in Swedish

Ordinarii Post Tijdender was established in 1645 by Postmaster General Johan Beijer, acting under royal initiative, as a small weekly with articles in Swedish, Latin, French, and German. Beijer had access to the government's information-gathering system, which included foreign newspapers. In addition, he maintained his own correspondents in Germany, France, Holland, and Italy. He distributed the paper to postmasters in Sweden, Finland, and the Swedish provinces across the Baltic. Under the absolutist Karl XI*, the paper was changed into an organ for royal decrees. Having been first enlarged in 1659, the paper was further expanded under Karl XII*, to whom it devoted a number of special editions. Frequency was increased to thrice weekly in 1719 and to daily in 1790. The following year it was taken over by the Swedish Academy, which gave it a more cultural role. The Swedish court always used the paper as its special organ, a situation recognized in 1814 when the paper was declared the official state-owned journal of the Swedish government. Today, the *Post och Inrikes Tidnin-*

gar, as it has been called since 1791, is the official gazette of the government, its contents consisting of advertisements and public notices. The profits provide the Swedish Academy with much of its income.

O. V. JOHNSON

OSCAR I (4 July 1799–8 July 1859) King of Sweden-Norway 1844–1859

Oscar was the son of Karl XIV Johan* and Desirée Clary. He spent the first eleven years of his life in Paris and came to Sweden in December 1810, following his father's selection as successor to the childless Karl XIII*. Oscar was given a careful, tutored education in languages, music, and the arts. He also had some military training and began to take part in government activities in the 1820s. As a person he was formal, cold, reserved, joyless, and cautious. He had few close friends. He apparently enjoyed women and had a number of affairs before and after his marriage to Josephine of Leuchtenberg in 1823. Among his legitimate children were the future Karl XV* and Oscar II*.

Oscar took his political duties seriously and worked energetically, in spite of an apparently fragile constitution. He was attracted by the liberal ideas of his day, especially in non-constitutional areas; and reforms in education, poor relief, tariffs, prison conditions, religious freedom, and women's rights enacted in the 1840s and 1850s may be attributed to him. In the constitutional area he was not as enlightened and proved a great disappointment to parliamentary liberals of the time. He did propose changes in the parliament's structure, but they were largely cosmetic. He would not consider reforms that would limit the power of the crown or genuinely liberalize the Swedish system. The events of 1848 shocked and disturbed him, in spite of their comparative mildness in Sweden, where the revolutions of that year were played out in the form of a few disturbances in Stockholm*, some arrests, and many articles in the liberal press.

Oscar considered foreign policy to be his domain and took an active part in the determination of the country's policies. During the first half of his reign he followed his father's policy of friendship toward Russia. At the same time, he was active during the 1840s in the Scandinavianism movement (*see* Nordism). In 1848 he sent Swedish troops to the Danish islands during the first Slesvig War (1848–1851). He also may have dreamed of becoming ruler of a new Scandinavian union—an idea not entirely beyond the realm of the possible, because the Danish king, Frederik VII*, had no heir. Oscar's most controversial foreign policy adventure came during the Crimean War (1853–1856). Initially, he joined Denmark in a policy of neutrality, but gradually the possibility of regaining Finland at Russia's expense and the idea of Sweden playing a role as a European power again got the better of him. Neutrality gave way to negotiations with the British and French involving Swedish participation in the war in exchange for Finland, troops, and subsidies. In these talks the British and French appear to have played largely a stalling game. But the threat of Swedish involvement, which would have created a two-front war for the Russians, may have been significant in bringing the Russians to the peace table. They sought peace in 1856, and Sweden was represented at the conference in Paris. Oscar's representative presented a lengthy list of demands, but in the end Sweden received only the demilitarization of the Åland Islands.

By 1857 Oscar, who was suffering from a brain tumor, was no longer able to rule. His son, Karl, became regent. The king died two years later.

REFERENCES: E. Anderson, "The Scandinavian Area and the Crimean War in the Baltic," *Scandinavian Studies* 41 (1969): 263–75; *DSH*, vol. 12; A. Söderhjelm and C.-F. Palmstierna, *Oscar I* (Stockholm: Bonniers, 1944); *SU*, vol. 22.

B. NORDSTROM

OSCAR II (21 January 1829–8 December 1907) King of Sweden 1872–1907

Oscar II ascended to the Swedish-Norwegian throne in 1872, at the age of 42, following the death of his brother, King Karl XV*. Oscar was the third son of Oscar I*. His 35–year reign over the two Scandinavian realms was marked by conflicts concerning the Norwegian-Swedish Union* and the problems generated in Sweden as a result of industrialization*. He took an avid interest in the arts and education and was a popular monarch with the people.

As a youth, Oscar was tutored by philosopher C. J. Boström and later by historian F. F. Carlson. From 1846 to 1850 the young prince continued his education at the University of Uppsala. He was regarded as a brilliant orator and acclaimed for his linguistic ability. In addition to his academic education, Oscar was trained as a seaman, and he participated in a number of naval expeditions. His expertise as a seaman earned him the honor of vice-admiral in 1859.

Oscar's education and upbringing aroused in him a keen awareness of the arts. He wrote several books and poems, under the pen name Oscar Fredrik. His works focused on military history, fiction, and marine topics. Two of his best-known pieces include his 1858 cycle of poems entitled *Ur Svenska Flottans Minnen* (*Memories of the Swedish Navy*), which was awarded the Swedish Academy's second prize in 1857, and his poem "Ostersjön" (*The Baltic*). Oscar was captivated by music as well and served as president of the Swedish Academy of Music for many years. He also wholeheartedly supported the sciences. He organized the Swedish exhibition at Stockholm* in 1866 and Sweden's section at the 1867 World's Fair in Paris. For his artistic and scientific interests, Oscar was acclaimed "the most highly cultured monarch in Europe."

On 6 June 1857 Oscar married Sofia of Nassau (1836–1913). The couple's relationship in private and in the political arena was an intimate one. The future of the Bernadotte dynasty was secured by four sons: Gustav V*, Oskar, Karl, and Eugen.

Because he was third in succession to the throne, it seemed unlikely that Oscar would ever wear the crown. Yet, death claimed not only Karl XV, but also Oscar's older brother, Prince Gustav, in 1852, and his nephew, Charles Oscar, only son of Karl XV, in 1854. Oscar was then sole heir to the throne. As king, he proclaimed his ruling motto, "The welfare of the brother peoples" (*Bröd-*

rafolkens väl). Eager to achieve power, the new monarch was superior to his predecessor in both ability and character. During his reign he sought to restore the diminishing influence of the monarchy as well as pursuing a more active role in legislative development. Above all, he had to contend with the problems caused by industrialization and the increasing tension between Sweden and Norway.

Between 1890 and 1914 Sweden experienced vigorous economic development, which led to a growing industrial proletariat that was not only literate but active in public affairs. The proletariat participated in popular movements such as Free Church revivalism, temperance, women's rights, adult education, cooperative societies, and trade unions. In additions, the movement for universal manhood suffrage was stimulated by the introduction of universal military service in 1901.

These developments were complicated by the dissolution of the Norwegian-Swedish Union. The final stage in the break came in 1905, when the Conservative government in Norway resigned and was supplanted by a Liberal government under Christian Michelsen*. On 27 May a proposal advocating a separate Norwegian consular service was sent to Oscar; it was vetoed. Having anticipated the king's response, the Norwegian government resigned. At this point, the union was pronounced dissolved. Then, in October 1905, the final dissolution was agreed upon in the Karlstad Conventions.

The dissolution of the union left Oscar, who had been ill throughout the entire ordeal, disappointed and saddened. He upheld his ruling motto to the end and declared that if the separation of the two realms was indeed ''in the welfare of the brother peoples,'' then so be it.

REFERENCES: I. Andersson, *History of Sweden* (New York: Frederick A. Praeger, 1956); T. K. Derry, *A History of Scandinavia* (Minneapolis: University of Minnesota Press, 1979); *DSH*, vols. 13, 14; *Encyclopedia Americana*, vol. 26 (Danbury, Conn.: Americana Corporation, 1978); Å. Ohlmarks, *Alla Sveriges Kungar* (Stockholm: Almquist and Wiksell, 1972); A. Stomberg, *A History of Sweden* (New York: Macmillan, 1931); *Svenskuppslagsboken*, vol. 22 (Malmö: Förlaghuset Norden, 1952); J. Weibull, "The Union with Norway," in *Sweden's Development from Poverty to Affluence 1750–1907*, ed. S. Koblik (Minneapolis: University of Minnesota Press, 1975); *World Book Encyclopedia*, vol. 14 (Chicago: World Book, Inc., 1965).

C. ARWIDSON

OTTESEN-JENSEN, ELISE (2 January 1886–4 September 1973) Family planning leader

Born in Norway, Elise Ottesen-Jensen trained in dentistry in Stavanger, until severe injuries to her hands led to a new career in journalism. After a decade as a journalist, she became a family planning field worker and lobbyist in behalf of sex education reforms. Her knowledge and achievements as a sex education reformer eventually brought her many honors, including an honorary doctorate from the University of Uppsala in 1958.

Imbued with a sense of community responsibility from her Lutheran clerical family upbringing in Norway, and critical of class differences, Elise Ottesen-Jensen veered politically leftward by 1911 and became a Norwegian labor press journalist. Influenced by her Trondheim editor, Martin Tranmæl*, and by the Swedish syndicalist Albert Jensen, her future husband and mentor in the study of Kropotkin during their early acquaintance in Bergen, she advocated that laborers take direct action to ameliorate their working conditions and to reject militarism. While addressing women textile workers in Bergen, she learned that their primary concern was with sexual problems, especially family limitation. She set about, initially through reading August Forel's *Die sexuelle frage*, to acquire an understanding of human sexuality which would enable her to counsel workers about such matters.

After moving with her husband to Stockholm* in 1919, Ottesen-Jensen began to write women's columns in the syndicalist press, which advocated reforms like equal pay for women workers, abolition of the anti-contraceptive laws of 1911, and revision of the criminal abortion law of 1921. Most important, she commenced in 1923 a 40–year lecture career to all parts of Sweden in order to explain sexuality and to give instructions in birth control techniques. Like Henrik ("Hinke") Bergegren, who lectured to working-class audiences in 1910–1911, Ottesen-Jensen found great interest in and need for information about contraceptive methods and various aspects of sexuality. She was unique among Swedish family planning pioneers in her tireless field work and in her remarkable ability to convey her sympathetic interest in the concerns of both females and males in her audiences.

Elise Ottesen-Jensen attended World League for Sexual Reform conferences in Copenhagen* (1928), London (1929), Vienna (1930), and Brünn (1932). She was also at the Seventh International Birth Control Congress in Zurich (1930), hosted by Margaret Sanger, in order to update her knowledge of sexuality and contraceptive research from the medical doctors who comprised most of the participants at these conferences. There was interest in her work among the poor, and she made several friends who survived the Nazi era to become a part of the group she convened in Stockholm in 1946 to restore the international movement.

The Social Democrats, who came to power in Sweden in 1932, had by 1938 abolished the anti-contraceptive laws and revised the abortion law and by 1942 introduced sex education in the public schools. The major voluntary organization lobbying in behalf of these and other sexual reforms was the Swedish Association for Sexual Enlightenment (Riksförbundet för Sexuell Upplysning: RFSU), which Elise Ottesen-Jensen founded and was president of from 1932 to 1959. Both her grass-roots organizing talents and the cooperation she developed with humanitarian and leftist-oriented medical and social work professionals were important reasons for the successful growth of her organization. A folk movement with a membership approaching 100,000, extensive clinical services, and a record of political influence, RFSU was the strongest national family planning organization in 1945.

Elise Ottesen-Jensen took the initiative to host in Stockholm in August 1946 an international conference attended by Scandinavian, Dutch, British, and American delegates—including Margaret Sanger. Out of this meeting and another one in Cheltenham, England, in 1948 evolved the International Planned Parenthood Federation (IPPF), formally founded at conferences in Bombay (1952) and Stockholm (1953). It was a development in which she, together with Margaret Sanger of the United States and Lady Rama Rau of India, played a key role.

As vice-president (1953–1958) and president (1959–1963) of IPPF, Elise Ottesen-Jensen's innovative efforts included visits to East Germany (1958) and Poland (1959) and inclusion of abortion reform and sex education on the IPPF agenda. Meanwhile, in Sweden she was a significant influence on the government's decision, by the late 1950s, to include family planning in the kinds of aid extended to developing countries. Her most persuasive and persistent themes with international as well as Swedish audiences were those emphasizing "the wanted child" and the obligation of each generation to provide a better future for its children.

REFERENCES: International Planned Parenthood Federation papers, Cardiff University; C.-A. Nycop, L. Swanberg, and G. Sörlin, *40 år med RFSU* (Stockholm: Federativ, 1973); E. Ottesen-Jensen, *Livet skrev vidare* (Stockholm: Bonniers, 1966), and *Och livet skrev* (Stockholm: Bonniers, 1965); I. Primander, ed., *Arbetarrörelsen—männens eller mänsklighetens rörelse? Ett urval av Elise Ottesen-Jensens kvinnopolitiskaartiklar i Arbetaren och Brand på 20–talet* (Stockholm: Primander, 1980); RFSU Papers, Arbetarrörelsens arkiv, Stockholm; B. Suitters, *Brave and Angry: Chronicles of the International Planned Parenthood Federation* (London: IPPF, 1973).

D. H. LINDER

OXE, PEDER (7 January 1520–24 October 1575) Danish noble, statesman, and steward under Frederik II*

Peder Oxe was the youngest of the twelve children of Johan Oxe and Mette Gøye. He was schooled in arithmetic by Christian Morsing, Denmark's most notable teacher of mathematics in the sixteenth century, and spent five years on a grand tour of the continent. By all accounts he was an efficient, able, greedy, obstinate, and domineering person. During the 1540s and early 1550s, he acquired enormous landed wealth, perhaps by applying the not-so-ethical methods of his contemporaries with greater skill. In 1547 he became chancery secretary (*kancellisekretæren*) and entered the council in 1552. He worked closely with the chancellor, Johan Friis*, on the program aimed at reforming the rents system on crown lands donated to the nobles. His activities in acquiring property and his involvement with Friis's reforms made him many powerful enemies. He also appears to have earned the antipathy of the queen, Dorothea. In 1558 he was accused of various irregularities in his management of royal holdings and went into exile. The real reason for his fall may have lain in his great power and wealth, which may have been seen as a threat to the crown. (Christian III* was ill at the time and died the same year. He may have feared for his son, Frederik.) Oxe's property was confiscated by the crown, and he fled the country. For the next eight years he lived at the court of Christina of Lorraine, a daughter of the deposed Danish king, Christian II*. There he apparently took part in a number of plots against the Danish royal family.

In 1566 Frederik II called Peder Oxe back to Denmark. The charges against him were dropped and his lands restored. He was recalled because of the chaotic state of Danish finances. The costs of the Northern Seven Years' War far exceeded income. The mercenary army was not being paid. The fleet could not be maintained. Even the king was complaining of his own impoverishment. Oxe ruthlessly took charge of financial affairs as steward (*rigshofmester*). He extracted donations from the nobles and new taxes from the peasants. He extended the reform of royal rents. Perhaps most important, he revised the Sound Tolls. Until 1567 the tolls were imposed on a per ship basis. Oxe levied the tolls on the value of the cargoes. Income tripled. Although financing the war remained a serious problem, Oxe's reforms resulted in real benefits to the state and the crown in the years following 1570. The war debts were repaid, and by the end of the decade there was actually a surplus in the treasury.

Oxe's power and wealth were extensive. His position at court until his sudden death in 1575 was almost unchallenged—the king preferring to delegate power rather than to rule himself. Through his mother, Oxe was related to the wealthy and powerful Gøye and Troll families. He extended his family connections when he married Mette Rosenkrantz in 1567. Yet, his death must have come as a relief to Frederik and the council. Frederik, who seems to have harbored a dislike for Oxe, dispatched a mission to Lorraine to investigate Oxe's alleged conspiratorial activities there during his exile. (Nothing was discovered.) Oxe was succeeded by Christoffer Valkendorf*.

REFERENCES: *DBL*, vol. 11; *DH*, vol. 6; F. Troels-Lund, *Peder Oxe* (Copenhagen: Det Schubotheske Forlag, 1907).

B. NORDSTROM

OXENSTIERNA, AXEL (16 June 1583–28 August 1654) Chancellor of Sweden under Gustav II Adolf* and Christina*

Axel Oxenstierna was one of the most extraordinary figures in seventeenth-century Swedish and European history and deserves to be ranked with Richelieu and Mazarin as the builder of a state and as a shaper of European events. He was the chancellor of Gustav II and Christina and held that office for over 40 years. In close cooperation with Gustav II, he helped to reform government and administration and to make Sweden one of the best-run states in Europe. His diplomacy placed Sweden among the great powers. During the minority of Christina, he was effectively the ruler of the country.

Above all, Oxenstierna was a politician and statesman, a master of the art of the possible. His primary loyalty was to his state—an aristocratic state ruled by king and nobility. He believed in an ancient constitutional principle of shared rule between the crown and the nobility. The dictum that the king must rule with the advice of the council was fundamental to him. He advocated neither a parliamentary system nor an aristocratic republic. During the more than 20 years he served Gustav II, he and the king created a working relationship between the aristocracy and the monarchy that was rare in Sweden's history. In an atmosphere of cooperation, the chancellor and the king carried through a series of vital reforms including the definition of the structure and functions of the parliament (1617) and the House of the Nobility (1626); the creation of a supreme court (1614); the founding of university preparatory schools (gymnasia); the reorganization of the University of Uppsala; and the establishment of a system of administration based on the chancellor, steward, treasurer, marshal, and admiral. The adoption of the Form of Government (Regeringsform) in 1634 was a crowning achievement of his career. This document provided Sweden with its first "constitution" and reaffirmed most of the reforms introduced by Gustav and Oxenstierna. (The chancellor maintained that the Form of Government was written in 1632 and reflected the will of Gustav.)

After Gustav's death in 1632, Oxenstierna headed the regency for Christina. For over a decade he and members of his family ran the country. Until 1636 Oxenstierna remained in Germany to direct Sweden's continued involvement in the Thirty Years' War. (Sweden remained a principal participant in the conflict until its close in 1648, when the country gained recognition of its claim to Pomerania and thereby was assured a voice in German affairs.) After Christina's accession to the throne, Oxenstierna's power and influence declined. The young queen, surrounded by a succession of favorites, preferred to rule personally. Her apparent financial irresponsibility, seeming disregard for the affairs of the state, and refusal to marry irritated Oxenstierna, and relations between the two worsened over time. By the time of Christina's abdication Oxenstierna was chancellor in name only.

While Oxenstierna's contributions were enormous, certain of his policies were, in the long run, ill conceived and nearly disastrous. Like Gustav II, he did not recognize the eventual limits of Sweden's resources or the difficulties his foreign policy would lead to in the future. He also supported the policy which both Christina and Gustav followed of making donations of crown lands to the nobility in exchange for services. This approach to financial problems may have worked in the short run, but it severely weakened the economic position of the crown and the state and created serious political and social problems.

REFERENCES: *DSH*, vols. 5, 6; A. O. Oxenstierna, *Rikskanslern Axel Oxenstierna skrifter och brefväxling*, 21 vols. (Stockholm: Norstedts, 1888–1956); M. Roberts, *Gustav Adolf: A History of Sweden 1611–1632*, 2 vols. (New York: St. Martin's Press, 1968); F. Scott, *Sweden: The Nation's History* (Minneapolis: University of Minnesota Press, 1977); *SU*, vol. 22.

B. NORDSTROM

P

PAASIKIVI, JUHO (27 November 1870–14 December 1956) President of Finland 1946–1956

Juho Paasikivi came of age politically at the turn of the century when Finland was endeavoring to defend its autonomy against Russian encroachments. His political career did not end until after he had served 10 years as Finland's post-World War II president. As the individual most responsible for making Finnish postwar independence possible, Paasikivi stands out as a great political leader. His long political career as well as his philosophy of history suggest, however, that it was the new political realities of the postwar era that made it possible for Paasikivi to play a decisive role in Finnish history. It was not until the end of World War II*, when Finland stood alone, a defeated neighbor of the Soviet Union, that the Finnish nation reluctantly perceived the need to follow Paasikivi's leadership.

One of the remarkable aspects of twentieth-century Finnish history has been the flexibility of the political system, which has been able to provide political leadership capable of stepping forward or remaining silent in response to the power realities of Europe and the Baltic in particular. This flexibility has enabled Finland to reorient its foreign policy without a radical restructuring of its domestic institutions. Paasikivi's unique contribution to this process of adjustment was to convince the Finnish nation that a policy of cooperation with the Soviet Union was possible, an achievement which would probably have been impossible had there been any other alternative.

As a student of history and the Russian language in the 1890s, Paasikivi had his eye on an academic career as a specialist on Russian relations with Sweden and Finland. He later changed his mind and took an advanced degree in law, but the insights he gained from history and his command of Russian remained his most valuable political assets. Paasikivi was greatly influenced by the historians G. Z. Yrjö-Koskinen and J. R. Danielson-Kalmari, who had been students of J. V. Snellman, the philosopher and statesman who had provided the intellectual rationale for the nineteenth-century Finnish nationalist movement. A fundamental aspect of Snellman's philosophy was the belief that a state often has to submit to external constraints in order to safeguard its future. Consequently, states, unlike individuals, who might choose to die for a principle, must always find a way to survive. And survival would be determined, not by recourse to moral or legal concepts of international relations, but by a policy based on considerations of national interests and the power available to defend those interests. Finland's power was in its culture; it could gain nothing of permanence by violence. In order to allow the power of its culture to function, Finland must always come to terms with the balance of power in the Baltic area. If survival of Finnish identity required submission, that was the policy Finland should adopt as a temporary expedient. The concept of survival and eventual emancipation through submission is alien to the liberal political philosophy of the English-speaking world. It is thus not surprising that the Finlandization* interpretation of Finnish history often fails to understand the historical roots of Finnish foreign policy.

Snellman's philosophy provided the rationale for the attempts of the conservative Old Finnish Party, of which Paasikivi was a member, to avoid conflict with Russia during the period of Russification. In short, the Old Finnish Party, whose members could remember decades of good relations with Russia in the nineteenth century, hoped that concessions would bring an end to Russian oppression. There was a limit, however, beyond which Paasikivi would not go. In 1909 he decided that further concessions would not prevent Russia from destroying Finnish autonomy. Having drawn that conclusion, and unwilling to join the ranks of the activists who were led by the liberal Young Finnish Party, Paasikivi resigned from the Senate.

From 1909 until 1944 the latent contradictions between Paasikivi's political philosophy and the requirements of Finnish foreign policy, as perceived by Finnish leaders and even by Paasikivi himself, greatly limited his influence on the formulation of foreign policy. This is not to say that Paasikivi remained inactive or that he was opposed to thinking in terms of balance of power politics. As prime minister in the summer of 1918 he advocated crowning a German prince monarch of Finland in order to counter the political weakness of parliamentary democracy and to give Germany, which he believed would win the world war, a stake in continued Finnish independence. Although this scheme of the political Right collapsed with the defeat of the Central Powers, this episode in Paasikivi's political career highlights an aspect of his political philosophy often ignored in accounts of his post-World War II policy. He had refused to join the ranks of the activists with their emphasis on legal rights, but he did not hesitate to act once it was possible to use Germany as a counter to Russian influence. He differed from most Finns, however, in his estimate of Russian power in the long run and especially over how to deal with Russia when there was no Western power to which Finland could turn for security guarantees. Prior to the end of World War II Paasikivi's foreign policy views were largely determined by balance of power considerations; his postwar policy differed in that his political philosophy was then applied to an imbalance of power situation.

The relative ease with which Finland obtained its independence, which was greatly facilitated by the collapse of Russian power, only served to confirm the apparent wisdom of the tactics of legalistic defiance of Russia. The trauma of the Finnish Civil War*, which created the illusion that Finland had fought Russia to win its independence, added a domestic element to Finland's security policy and reinforced the view that compromise vis-a-vis the Soviet Union or the Finnish radical Left would undermine Finnish independence. Paasikivi's advocacy of a strong army to counter these threats was typical of Conservatives, but he differed from his fellow Conservatives over relations with the Soviet Union. As the head of the Finnish delegation negotiating the Treaty of Dorpat (1920), Paasikivi argued in favor of a settlement which would recognize the security requirements of Leningrad and lay the basis for normal, especially commercial, relations with the Soviet Union. He was consequently labeled "soft" on the Soviet Union— a political liability that continued to haunt him until 1944.

On domestic issues Paasikivi's conservative credentials were never questioned. He served as director of Finland's leading commercial bank from 1914 to 1934 and was able to influence domestic politics, especially fiscal and economic policy, from that position. In the mid-1930s he retired from his bank directorship and reentered active politics, first as chairman of the Conservative Party (*see* National Coalition), which he was instrumental in leading away from cooperation with Finnish fascism, and then as ambassador to Sweden, where he played a role in the development of Finland's Scandinavian-oriented foreign policy. For most Finnish leaders this new foreign policy orientation was limited to strengthening Finnish neutrality and Swedish commitment to the defense of Finnish interests, but for Paasikivi it was also a means to a more important goal: to convince the Soviet Union that a neutral Finland with strong Nordic ties would not fall into the German orbit, and therefore would not pose a threat to Soviet security. This strategy reflected Paasikivi's conviction that Soviet policy toward Finland was prompted by Soviet efforts to increase its security against Hitler's Germany. On the eve of the Winter War* (1939–1940) he and Marshal Carl Mannerheim*, who had served in the Russian army on the German front in World War I, advocated that limited territorial concessions be made to the Soviet Union; but the memories of the Civil War, the anti-Communist crusades of the 1920s, and recent Soviet activities in the Baltic states convinced the Finnish government that its cause was just and that concessions would only open the door to further Soviet demands. After the Winter War Paasikivi served as ambassador in Moscow and vigorously argued in favor of a policy of reconciliation with the Soviet Union. He eventually decided, however, that the dynamics of German expansion and Soviet fear of the approaching danger made it impossible for Finland to defend its independence by any means other than cultivating German interests in Finland, a policy which the Finnish government, unknown to Paasikivi, had already been pursuing.

Paasikivi hoped that Finland could remain outside Great Power conflicts by negotiating its differences with the Soviet Union, but he, like other Finnish leaders, was willing to turn to a strong Germany as the court of last resort against the Soviet Union. During the war Paasikivi held no official position, but his views, at least through the first stages of the war, were similar to those of government leaders. In March 1942 he publicly predicted that Germany would soon defeat Russia, and in June 1942 he told the American minister that Finland had no alternative but to continue to depend on Germany as a counterbalance to the Soviet Union. He was skeptical of Soviet willingness to respect Finnish independence and doubted Western ability to influence Soviet policy should the Allies defeat Germany. Once he realized that Germany would be defeated, Paasikivi advocated a policy toward the Soviet Union which recognized the realities of an imbalance of power in the Baltic. He thus rejected the arguments (or hopes) of most Finnish political leaders that the Western Allies would eventually replace Germany as a counter to the Soviet Union and decided to gamble on his assumption (hope) that Soviet policy toward Finland was prompted by traditional security considerations of Tsarist Russia.

Paasikivi's great contribution as a postwar political leader (an episode which is discussed in the entry on the Paasikivi-Kekkonen Line) was to convince both the Soviet Union and the Finnish people that Soviet security requirements and Finnish independence could be reconciled, that is, the preservation of Finland's institutions of capitalism and political democracy need not pose any threat to vital Soviet interests, and a Finnish foreign policy which acknowledged the primacy of legitimate Soviet security interests need not threaten Finland's domestic institutions and values.

REFERENCES: J. Hodgson, "The Paasikivi Line," *American Slavic and East European Review* 18 (April 1959); K. Korhonen, ed., *Urho Kekkonen—A Statesman for Peace* (Helsinki: Otava, 1975); H. P. Krosby, Review of Paasikivi's memoirs in *American Slavic and East European Review* 18 (October 1959).

R. M. BERRY

PAASIKIVI-KEKKONEN LINE Post-1944 Finnish foreign policy approach

The Paasikivi-Kekkonen Line is an expression used to describe the assumptions and conduct of postwar Finnish foreign policy, which was shaped by Juho Paasikivi* from 1944 to 1956 and by Urho Kekkonen* from 1956 to 1981.

The political philosophy of the Paasikivi-Kekkonen Line can best be understood by locating Finland on a map—as Paasikivi often did when driving home a point for many of his reluctant fellow Finns—and by reading the history of Russo-Finnish relations, which was a lifetime preoccupation of Paasikivi. Only then will the simplicity and the complexity of Paasikivi's world view become clear. Finland lies on an axis where the Nordic countries and the states of Eastern Europe meet. The country eventually became a society organized around the values and institutions of the Nordic countries, but it remained geographically and thus politically a part of Eastern Europe. The Paasikivi-Kekkonen Line has been, in short, an attempt to defend Finnish national identity and independence by endeavoring to convince the Soviet Union that Finland's values and institutions of political and economic liberalism do not pose any threat to Soviet security along the strategic border which runs from Leningrad to Murmansk.

In 1944 this task appeared to be difficult, at best. Finland was a defeated country. The Soviet Union was emerging as the dominant power on the European continent. The Soviets were neighbors, the Germans close to defeat, and the Western democracies far away. A balance of power would eventually exist between East and West, but not in the Baltic region. Many of the foreign policy premises of independent Finland were bankrupt, and its future looked bleak. To talk about the Paasikivi-Kekkonen Line is to realize how far Finland has come since that point in history.

Paasikivi's philosophy of history served him well during the difficult postwar years when Finland paid its reparations and concluded a peace treaty with the Soviet Union; rejected Marshall Aid but maintained Western economic ties which were essential to reconstruction of the national economy and to fulfillment of the reparation obligations; obtained the return of Porkkala; and laid the basis for gaining admission to the United Nations. During this period, which witnessed an improvement in Soviet-Finnish relations, Paasikivi based his policy toward the Soviet Union on the belief that Soviet foreign policy was determined by a "law for survival," that is, Soviet policy toward Finland had been and would continue to be motivated by the strategic concerns of Tsarist Russia.

Paasikivi's philosophy of history also made him both pessimistic and optimistic—pessimistic about the possibilities small states had to determine their own foreign policy, but optimistic about arriving at a satisfactory *modus vivendi* with the Soviet Union. Rejecting the view that power politics are motivated by an instinct to dominate, Paasikivi operated under assumptions which were similar to those of the "security dilemma" theory: states are motivated by an instinct for self-preservation rather than domination, but one state's search for security will often upset another state's sense of security. Although states often share common interests, the security dilemma, which arises when states become aggressive for basically defensive reasons, produces a vicious circle based on misperceptions in which there is little hope of promoting mutual interests. Seen from this perspective, the Paasikivi Line was an attempt to keep Finland from becoming entrapped in the security dilemma between East and West, that is, to convince the Soviet Union that it does not need to destroy Finnish independence in order to remain secure.

At Yalta the Soviet Union insisted that its neighbors have friendly governments, a friendly government being one in which no political groups which the Soviet Union considered anti-Soviet were in power or near to power. One of the main goals of the Paasikivi era was the elimination of anti-Soviet sentiment from the body of Finnish politics so that Finland, rather than the Soviet Union, would make the final determination as to what constituted democracy in Finland. Although Finland played a more active role in East-West relations during the

Kekkonen era, Kekkonen never forgot, nor did the Soviet Union allow him to forget, that his activist foreign policy required adherence to the Paasikivi Line.

The Paasikivi and Kekkonen lines differed in style: Paasikivi was a conservative statesman with his philosophical roots in the nineteenth century, Kekkonen an innovative statesman of the twentieth. The most important difference in their politics can be explained, however, by the international context within which they operated. Both were active presidents. Paasikivi did the spade work at home that made Kekkonen's activities abroad possible once the Cold War had begun to thaw. Paasikivi was so preoccupied with keeping Finland independent that neutrality remained a distant goal. Soviet relations were all-important, and an active role in international politics would endanger them.

Kekkonen considered neutrality not only possible but also necessary. As early as the signing of the Treaty of Friendship, Cooperation and Mutual Assistance* in 1948, he began to work toward gaining recognition of Finnish neutrality by identifying it with Swedish neutrality. The more the Scandinavian peninsula could be neutralized in East-West relations, the more Finland's neutrality would be acceptable to the Soviet Union and respected by the West. This strategy, which preoccupied Kekkonen for the rest of his life, was first spelled out publicly in the so-called pajama-pocket speech in 1952, in which Kekkonen proposed neutrality on the Swedish model for all of Scandinavia*. His later proposals for a nuclear-free Nordic zone can be understood within the context of this goal, although it was also prompted by a general fear of nuclear warfare.

By the time Kekkonen became president in 1956, recognition of Finnish neutrality was a prerequisite to an active and effective Finnish role as a "bridge-builder" in East-West relations. Finland could now promote its interests best by promoting a relaxation in Great Power tensions: the less the hostilities between the superpowers, the less the Soviet sense of insecurity and the more freedom Finland would have to develop strategies to cope with Western European plans for economic integration.

The politics of adjusting to European economic integration is often presented in English-language literature as a separate rather than an integral part of Finnish foreign policy. To do so is to misunderstand the Kekkonen Line. The problems the Kekkonen era had to deal with were different from those which had prompted Paasikivi to refuse to participate in the European Recovery Program, but these problems had to be solved without undermining the accomplishments of the Paasikivi era. Finnish leaders thus had to devise a strategy which would satisfy two potentially contradictory imperatives: a political imperative which held that Finland could not endanger the credibility of its foreign policy in Soviet eyes, and an economic imperative which held that Finland must remain competitive in its traditional Western markets. In practice this meant that Finland had to ensure that its economic policy was not interpreted in the Soviet Union to indicate a change in foreign policy orientation, and that Finland could not remain outside any preferential trade arrangements to which Sweden was a party.

To remain passive in the face of European economic integration would have defied the economic imperative and undermined the structure of the Finnish economy. Yet, to have ignored the economic imperative in order to satisfy the political imperative would have destroyed Finnish confidence in the mutual benefits derived from Soviet-Finnish cooperation. Given the dynamics of Western European integration over which Finland had no control, a solution to the economic imperative became essential to satisfying the political imperative. Fortunately for Finland, the growth of European integration coincided with a decline in East-West tensions, thus making it easier for Finland to become associated with the free-trade aspects of integration while remaining aloof from the political and economic process of integration.

It was thus no accident that Finland's active role in UN politics in the 1960s and its willingness to host the Strategic Arms Limitation (SALT) talks and the European Conference on Security and Cooperation in 1975 marked the zenith of the politics of the Paasikivi-Kekkonen Line. The Yalta system upon which Finland had built its postwar foreign policy had finally been ratified. Inextricably tied, however, to the foreign policy objectives of the Kekkonen Line was the free-trade agreement which Finland had signed with the European Economic Community two years earlier.

REFERENCES: E. Antola, "Finland and Prospects for Western Integration in the 1980s," *Yearbook of Finnish Foreign Policy* (Helsinki: Finnish Institute of International Affairs, 1981); O. Apunen and H. Rytövuori, "Ideas of 'Survival' and 'Progress' in Finnish Foreign Policy Tradition," *Journal of Peace Research* 1 (1982); K. Forster, "Finland's 1966 Elections and Soviet Relations," *Orbie* 12 (Fall 1968); H. Hakovirta, "Neutral States and Bloc-Based Integration," *Cooperation and Conflict* 2 (1978); J. Hodgson, "Postwar Finnish Foreign Policy: Institutions and Personalities," *Western Political Quarterly* 15 (March 1962); K. Holsti, "Strategy and Techniques of Influence in Soviet-Finnish Relations," *Western Political Quarterly* 17 (March 1964); M. Jakobson, *Finnish Neutrality: A Study of Finnish Foreign Policy since the Second World War* (London: Hugh Evelyn, 1968); and "Substance and Appearance: Finland," *Foreign Affairs* 5 (1980); H. P. Krosby, "Finland: The Politics of Economic Emergency," *Current History* 71 (1976); G. Maude, *The Finnish Dilemma: Neutrality in the Shadow of Power* (London: Oxford University Press, 1976); R. Väyrynen, *Conflicts in Finnish-Soviet Relations: Three Comparative Case Studies* (Tampere: Tampere University Press, 1972).

R. M. BERRY

PALM, AUGUST THEODORE (5 February 1849–14 March 1922) Swedish Socialist agitator, politician, editor, and tailor

Palm was born in Malmöhus län. His father died when August was 10, and he was apprenticed to be a tailor. Later, during his travels as a journeyman, Palm became familiar with the political ideas of the Social Democratic movements in Germany and Denmark and was converted to socialism. He took an active part in the Social Democratic agitation in Haderslev, Schleswig, in 1877 and was subsequently expelled from Germany. For the next four years Palm was in Denmark, involved with the formation of a Sjaelland tailors' union.

Back in Sweden in 1881, Palm founded the first Swedish Social Democratic

Association in Malmö. He traveled widely, gave lectures under the auspices of local trade union committees, and organized Social Democratic clubs. Also in 1881, at a Stockholm* meeting of workers which Palm attended, the group turned not to Palm but to the more moderate Anton Nyström, a medical doctor and author, for leadership. Such a falling-out with the officers of a club Palm helped to organize was characteristic of his career. The following year, in Malmö, Palm launched a Socialist newspaper, *Folkviljan* (*The Peoples' Will*), which he continued to oversee until 1885. When he moved to Stockholm in 1885, he started *Socialdemokraten* and was its editor for two years. Palm's involvement in journalism rarely succeeded, because he frequently ran into trouble with his financial supporters.

Palm continually attacked the existing economic order, the bureaucracy, the clergy, and the military. Political and religious authorities, in particular, were aroused against him. Thus, Palm found himself on occasion in prison. While imprisoned for six and a half months in 1887 as a result of labor agitation, Palm planned for the congress of 1889 at which the Swedish Social Democratic Party* was born. He wrote the party platform following the Danish Socialist version, which in turn was based on the German Gotha statement of 1875. Although the ultimate goal was the establishment of a classless society, there was considerable division at the congress and subsequent meetings over the immediate goals and methods of action. The opening congress tried to steer a middle course, and two years later the anarchist Hinke Bergegren was disavowed. (In 1906 Bergegren was expelled from the party.)

Although it was Palm who sparked the Social Democratic movement, it was K. Hjalmar Branting* who kept it going. In 1891 Palm broke with the dominant group in the party and urged the creation of a secret, conspirational organization. The more cautious Branting would not agree to this, and the majority in the party followed Branting's lead.

Although Palm was in many ways the father of the Swedish Social Democratic movement, he was more the agitator than the leader. He wished to continue the earlier revolutionary tradition in the party. During the last part of his life, he displayed his role as agitator by campaigning against temperance. He died in Stockholm in 1922.

REFERENCES: J. Lindgren, *Det Socialdemokratiska Arbetarpartiets uppkomst i Sverige 1881–1889* (Stockholm: Tiden, 1927); A. Palm, *Ur en agitators lif* (Stockholm: Björck & Börjesson, 1904); K. O. Palm, *Mäster Palms Pojke: Minnen från en ungdom* (Stockholm: Socialistisk Bokklubb, Tiden, 1961); Y. Palmgren, *Född till agitator. En studie i August Palms politiska utveckling och versamhet* (Stockholm, 1971); H. Tingsten, *Den Svenska Socialdemokratiens Idéutveckling* (Stockholm: Tiden, 1941), trans. as *The Swedish Democrats* (Totowa, N.J.: Bedminster, 1973).

                                                                    A. H. WINQUIST

PALME, SVEN OLOF (30 January 1927–) Swedish Social Democratic politician and prime minister

Sven Olof Palme was born in Stockholm*, the son of the managing director of an insurance firm. His father died when Palme was 6, and he was raised by his mother, who was of a noble Latvian family. He attended the exclusive schools of Beskow and Sigtuna before entering the University of Stockholm in 1944. In 1947 he attended Kenyon College in Ohio, receiving a bachelor's degree the following year in politics and economics. He then reentered the University of Stockholm and received a law degree in 1951.

While a student at Stockholm, Palme joined the Social Democratic Party* (SDP) and became active in student politics. He became president of the National Swedish Union of Students in 1952–1954 and helped to build a new international student organization after the Communists gained control of the International Union of Students. Prime Minister Tage Erlander* quickly recognized Palme's talents when Palme became a part-time assistant in the office of the prime minister in 1953, and in 1954 he appointed Palme his private secretary and speech writer.

Under Erlander's tutelage, Palme had a meteoric career in government and the Social Democratic Party. He served as chairperson of the Social Democratic Youth Organization in 1955–1961, the influential Workers' Educational Association in 1955–1961, and the Swedish Agency for International Assistance (now the Swedish International Development Authority or SIDA) in 1962–1963, which has overall direction of Sweden's sizeable and popular foreign assistance program. Elected to parliament in 1958, in 1963 he was named minister without portfolio and was responsible mainly for youth affairs. In 1965 he became minister of communications and in 1967 minister of education and ecclesiastical affairs.

After the Social Democratic victory in 1968, which reversed the party's downward trend of previous years, Erlander resigned. As a result of Erlander's efforts, Palme was chosen to succeed him as prime minister and chairman of the party, despite the fact that he was a controversial figure. The older party leaders, schooled in compromise with other parties, were uncomfortable with his quick wit and slashing debate style, which gave him the image of a merciless opponent. The older leaders also disliked his espousal of greater economic equality for lower-paid workers, women, and the disadvantaged and his championing of Third World issues. However, he was personable and, after gaining the prime ministership, softened his image and gained wider respect for his talents. During his seven years as prime minister the reforms started under Erlander were carried out and expanded, and the concept of "industrial democracy" was put into force, increasing the workers' participation in the management of the companies that employed them.

The political fortunes of the Social Democrats turned downward under his leadership, however, as inflation and taxes grew, and the party lost power in the 1976 election. The leaders of the three Center-Right parties that governed Sweden between 1976 and 1982 accused Palme of being unwilling to accept the former pattern of cooperation among the non-Communist party leaders, including those in opposition, that has marked the "Swedish model." They alleged that he seized every opportunity to fight the government in order to champion workers and low-income groups. The Social Democrats came within one seat of winning in 1979. In the 1982 election the Social Democrats gained sufficient seats to return to power. Palme again became prime minister. A central issue in the campaign was an SDP proposal to establish a system of wage earner funds, based on the Meidner Plan. In 1983 the Palme government introduced a modified version of this proposal, which is vigorously opposed by the non-Socialist parties.

Palme has also gained an international reputation. He is one of the active vice-presidents of the Socialist International and is the UN mediator for the Iran-Iraq conflict. He has been active on Third World issues, and in April 1980 he was named chairperson of the International Independent Commission on Disarmament.

H. F. CAPPS

PAN-SCANDINAVIANISM *See* Nordism

PARLIAMENTS *See* Althing; Eduskunta; Folketing; Riksdag; Storting

PATURSSON, JÓANNES (1866–1946) Faroese farmer, poet, and politician

Jóannes Patursson was for over 50 years the charismatic leader of the Faroese nationalists, the man who, more than any other, brought his countrymen to think of themselves as a seventh Scandinavian nation. His first public appearance was at the start of Faroese cultural nationalism; he died shortly before the referendum which led to Faroese home rule within the Danish kingdom in 1946.

Patursson was the eldest son of the crown tenant of Kirkjuböur*, the largest farm in the Faroe Islands*. His great-grandfather was the national hero, Poul Poulsen Nolsöe*, and this, together with his upbringing in a place of rich historical memory, inspired him with patriotic fervor. As a young man he studied agriculture in Norway, where he became deeply involved emotionally with the Landsmål movement (*see* Languages: Scandinavian). Through his Icelandic wife, he established links with the independence movement in Iceland. He inherited the Kirkjuböur lease in 1891.

Jóannes Patursson was the youngest of the convenors of the great meeting in the Faroese parliament building on 26 December 1888 "to discuss how to defend the Faroese language and Faroese customs." Patursson became one of the leaders of Föringafelag* (the Faroese Society) and rapidly became a charismatic figure.

In the Danish Folketing* elections of 1901, Patursson won the Faroe Islands seat as a Venstre (Liberal) candidate. His political aims were to promote Faroese home rule, giving the Lagting* in Tórshavn* a central position in legislation for the islands. After re-election in 1903 (by a much reduced majority), Patursson skillfully advertised his cause in a little book entitled *Færösk Politik* (*Faroese Politics*). He asserted that the Faroes had formed an administrative and judicial entity distinct throughout their history, until the time of constitution-making in Denmark in 1848, and that the incorporation of the islands into the Danish kingdom had never received Faroese consent.

Patursson's advocacy of Lagting control over moneys both levied and spent in Faroe raised a storm among the merchants and officials, who feared that the program would bring about a vast increase in direct taxation. The Faroes had for many years been a charge on the Danish exchequer far beyond what they had yielded in taxes, and two expensive capital projects were on the way: a telephone system and modern harbor works for Tórshavn. Patursson's opponents therefore combined to defeat him in the elections of 1906. After their victory, they constituted themselves into the Sambandsflokkurin (Unionist Party), dedicated to defending the link with Denmark and to economy in the management of the Lagting's finances. They managed to take Patursson's place as allies of the Danish Venstre.

Patursson's supporters, now in a minority in the Lagting and ousted from the Folketing, constituted themselves as the Sjálvstyrisflokkurin (Home Rule Party). The party sought greater autonomy for the Lagting and the use of the Faroese language in church, law courts, and schools. The Unionists were pushed into a position of defending Danish against the mother tongue. Until 1924 Faroese politics were a dog-fight between the Unionists and the Home Rulers, with the Unionists normally having the better of it. Acrimony reached its height during World War I, when Patursson made an unofficial move to ease the supply position in the islands, upon which some of his opponents went so far as to accuse him of treason. A political swing sent Patursson to the Landsting from 1918 to 1920, by which time his policies were moving toward separation rather than mere home rule.

The Faroese Social Democrats won their first Lagting seats in 1928, and they allied themselves with the Home Rulers to return Patursson to the Landsting— at the price of soft-pedalling Patursson's home rule demands, because Social Democratic aims depended much on Danish government funding. Patursson remained a Landsting member until 1936, when a big advance in Lagting representation made it more profitable for the Social Democrats to cooperate with the Unionists. However, during the 1930s Patursson saw his cherished aims of having the Faroese language accepted in the schools and for all public business largely achieved, for in this the Social Democrats were at one with Patursson's party.

The 1936 Lagting elections also saw the emergence of Vinnuflokkurin, the Economic Party, founded by the bank director Thorstein Petersen (1899–1960). This party's aim was to deploy the resources of the Faroe Islands in favor of capital development, cutting out unproductive expenditure. In 1939, angered by a land reform measure working much to the disadvantage of crown leaseholders, but supported by the Unionists, the Social Democrats, and most of the Home Rulers, Patursson left the party he had led for over 30 years and joined forces with Thorstein Petersen. The two men launched Fólkaflokkurin, the People's Party, with a program of autonomy from Denmark and state-fostered capitalism.

The People's Party gained 6 seats out of 24 in the Lagting elections of January 1940. It was clear that half the Home Rule voters had followed Patursson. After the German occupation of Denmark, the People's Party tried to proclaim that the Faroes had passed from Danish sovereignty and that power was now in the hands of the Lagting. The other parties, however, rejected this, and a temporary administration was agreed upon for the duration of the war.

In the Lagting elections of August 1943, the People's Party won 12 seats out of 26, and Patursson's aim of secession seemed on the point of fulfillment. The postwar election of 6 November 1945 gave the People's Party 11 seats out of 23. After negotiations in Copenhagen*, a referendum was held on 14 September 1946 on a choice between a Danish government proposal for a modest measure of home rule and outright secession. Patursson was the only Faroese politician who declared himself wholeheartedly for secession. But he did not live to see the inconclusive result of the referendum or the much enhanced home rule constitution that emerged from the crisis. He died on 2 August 1946.

REFERENCE: John F. West, *Faroe, the Emergence of a Nation* (London: C. Hurst; New York: Paul S. Eriksson, 1972).

J. F. WEST

PEASANT FARMING Faroe Islands

The pattern of economic life in the Faroe Islands* from the Reformation* (when records first become plentiful) to the late nineteenth century was extremely stable and dominated by the system of land tenure and the methods of peasant farming in the villages. Peasant farming continued in much the same manner well into the 1950s, though with the rise of the fishing industry* it had long lost its dominant role. Faroese villages still retain many influences of the traditional peasant economy, and some old techniques are still used.

The land belonging to a Faroese village commonwealth, before the application of the enclosure laws (which are still not everywhere in force) falls into three main categories: (1) *almenningur*, (2) *bøur*, and (3) *hagi*. *Almenningur* consists of the village building sites, lanes, cattle-tracks, and beaches. *Bøur* (infield) is enclosed and cultivated land in individual possession. *Hagi* (outfield) is uncultivated, unenclosed moorland, used principally for rough sheep-grazing. Ownership of land in a village, before the application of the enclosure laws from 1926 onwards, comprehended identifiable infield plots and proportional rights on the outfield and the *almenningur*, the latter being affected by prescriptive rights of occupancy.

The principal infield crop was hay. The only grain grown was a hardy strain of barley. From about 1800, potato culture spread through the islands. Various kale and root vegetables were also grown in small quantities. The outfield was used primarily for sheep pasturage, the areas nearest the village also being used for summer cattle grazing. Peat was cut in the outfield, and on sea cliffs or screes there might be seasonal sea-fowling. A stout dry-stone wall prevented the intrusion of sheep from the outfield to the infield; but from 25 October to 14 May the sheep had the right to graze over the infield, and the gates would be thrown open.

With the expropriation of the church estates at the Reformation, the crown came to own about half the land in the Faroe Islands. The *landfoged*(high bailiff) acting for the king thus wielded immense power, and between 1559 and 1691 a series of statutes, aimed at curbing abuses, converted crown holdings into hereditary leases at fixed rents paid in kind. As holdings became more valuable with the increase in population, there came into being a privileged class of prosperous crown leaseholders with undivided holdings at traditional rents. The land of the *odelsbönder* (alodial peasants), on the other hand, became more and more fragmented. Alodial fragmentation proceeded to such a degree that a series of laws had to be passed in the nineteenth century to overcome the difficulties of joint tenure, general enclosure becoming practicable only in our own age.

The communal tenure of the Faroese outfield was not a primitive survival, but a response to Faroese geography. An outfield contains diverse qualities of pasture, some suitable only for summer grazing, so that fencing or walling of individual holdings was not practical. However, the difficulty always arises with common grazing that each owner tries to pasture as many animals as possible on the common land, which may thus get overgrazed and ruined. The method of allocating each owner a ''stint'' is notoriously difficult to enforce. Moreover, overstocking in one village affects the next village as well. Only an equal ''sheep pressure'' on either side of an unfenced boundary will prevent a net intrusion of sheep from one outfield to another.

In 1659, after a flood of court cases, the Lagting* decided that joint ownership of sheep should be enforced on common pastures throughout the Faroes. The rules were made statutory by laws passed in 1698 and 1757, ordaining the forfeiture of sheep not held in joint ownership. Only in 1866 did it once again become legal for a village to operate a stint system, and many villages prefer joint flocks to this day.

With joint flocks, the importance of the annual village moot, the *grannastevna*, becomes much enhanced. From about 1840, especially, the *grannastevna*developed into an instrument for consultation and decision on a wide range of matters relating to communal tenure and joint flocks. Rules were devised for applying majority decisions, so that holders of minute plots could not obstruct good management.

The plow was not used in Faroese peasant farming, the infield being too irregular and the soil cover too thin. Cultivation was by spade. The land was manured with cow dung and well-rotted seaweed, and the seed would be sown in April or May. Reaping took place in late September or early October. Faroese barley does not ripen fully on the stalk, and artificial drying was needed, over a peat fire or in a special kiln-house. The straw was valued for thatching haystacks and repairing roofs. The grain was ground in hand-querns or in tiny horizontal mills.

Barley-growing was undertaken partly to improve hay production. The growth of grass was stimulated by a barley crop every seven to nine years. The hay harvest normally began about 8–10 August, and it would take at least a month before it was all in rick or barn.

The produce of outfield and infield was supplemented by that of the boat fishery and by the yield of the communal pilot whale drive, which at times, within a few hours, could provide a peasant family with meat for the whole winter.

With the increase of population in the islands, there was pressure to enclose outfield for cultivation, partly for the benefit of alodial owners, partly for landless fishermen. Around Tórshavn* the process began in earnest in the 1820s. A smallholdings law of 1863 gave tenants of Tórshavn smallholdings the right to buy plots enclosed from crown land at 25 times the annual rent. In the villages, alienation of crown land to smallholders was made possible by a law of 1894, which made considerable inroads into the entrenched position of privilege hitherto enjoyed by the crown leaseholders. Smallholdings enabled a boat or smack fisherman to supplement his family's largely shop-bought diet with fresh produce, particularly milk and potatoes.

From 1872, the smack fishery began to compete with the farming economy for labor, and by the end of the century crown leaseholders were experiencing a summer labor famine. Modernization was difficult with the fishery absorbing most of the available capital—and crown leaseholders could not raise improvement capital by way of mortgage. The complex problems led to an Agricultural Commission being set up in 1908. Its recommendations, published in 1911, included the limitation of land fragmentation, the restriction of joint tenure as far as possible to the outfield, and provisions for general enclosure of infield plots, which had become fragmented to a grotesque degree. Infield enclosure is now almost universal, and outfield enclosure is now being carried through on some islands.

REFERENCES: J. F. West, "Communal Land Tenure and Land Utilisation in the Faroe Islands," *Tijdschrift voor economische en sociale geografie* 46 (1975); K. Williamson, *The Atlantic Islands* (London: Collins, 1948, and Routledge & Kegan Paul, 1970).

                                                                                J. F. WEST

PEASANT LAND TENURE Denmark

Until the great land reforms of the later eighteenth century, peasant land tenure in Denmark was broadly similar to that in much of traditional central and western Europe. Most agricultural land was owned by the crown, the Church, and related institutions, or by private individuals (before 1660 only nobles), but some nine-tenths of all arable land was divided into peasant holdings and worked usually on the basis of tenancy contracts. The lack of detail in the relatively few contracts that survive for the period before 1721, however, makes it inevitable that some aspects of the traditional tenancy system are still unclear, especially given the geographic variations.

In return for the use of the land, the peasant tenant would be expected to maintain it in good condition, pay an annual rent (*landgilde*) which was in fact a composite due, and yield unspecified labor and transport services (*hoveri* and *ægter*) according to the requirements of the seigneur. The tenant might also pay an entry fine when taking up the tenancy and would be liable to pay tithes and perhaps taxes. The land owner was free to make the most of his seigneurial rights, but in practice the relationship seems to have been governed by traditionally accepted norms in most cases. By the seventeenth century most tenants had reasonable security of tenure provided they did their best to fulfill the terms and refrained from confrontation with the seigneur. Yet this did not amount in real terms to security for life (or hereditary tenure), because of the difficult economic climate of the late seventeenth and early eighteenth centuries and because of the very unequal status of peasant and seigneur. The growth of interest in demesne farming, and the resulting increase especially in the burden of labor services (particularly in the last century before reform) undoubtedly led to a deterioration in tenure conditions, and this was aggravated by legislation (such as the ordinance of 1682) designed to regulate rural relationships in the interest of stability. Although open rebellion was not part of peasant life in early modern Denmark, conditions became so unsatisfactory by the late eighteenth century that public opinion increasingly focused on the land tenure system.

REFERENCES: H. H. Fussing, *Herremand og Fæstebonde* (Copenhagen: Nyt Nordisk Forlag/A. Busck, 1942; repr. by Selskab for Udgivning af Kilder til Dansk Historie, 1973); E. Jutikkala, *Bonden—Adelsmannen—Kronan: Godspolitik och jordegendoms-förhållanden i Norden 1550–1750* (Copenhagen: Nordisk Ministerråd/Gyldendal/Liber, 1979); T. Munck, *The Peasantry and the Early Absolute Monarchy in Denmark, 1660–1708* (Copenhagen: Landbohistorisk Selskab, 1979); F. Skrubbeltrang, *Den danske Land-bosamfund 1500–1800* (Copenhagen: Dansk Historisk Fællesforening, 1978), and *Husmand og Inderste* (Copenhagen: Munksgaard, 1940; repr. by Selskab for Udgivning af Kilder til Dansk Historie, 1974).

T. MUNCK

PENTECOSTALISM

The origins of the modern Pentecostal movement lie in transatlantic revival meetings at the beginning of the twentieth century which, unlike most previous awakenings, were accompanied by glossolalia and other phenomenon that many participants perceived as manifestations of the Holy Spirit.

A prominent English-born Norwegian Methodist, Thomas Ball Barratt (1862–1940), is generally credited with conveying Pentecostalism to Scandinavia*. On a journey to the United States in 1906 he experienced the "baptism of the Holy Spirit" and, upon returning to Norway, campaigned vigorously for its proliferation there and in other northern European countries. Leaving the Methodists* to be baptized anew in 1913, Barratt founded Filadelphia church in Christiania (now Oslo) in 1916 and served as its minister until his death. This congregation, with over 2,000 members, has always been the flagship of Norwegian Pentecostalism and is today the largest non-Lutheran church in Norway. The movement grew rapidly, encompassing especially working-class people in the Norwegian capital and other towns. By 1930 it had over 7,800 members, and in 1950 it surpassed 30,000 and was easily the largest denomination in Norway apart from the state church.

In Sweden, several revivals and the appearance of small denominations around the turn of the century prepared the ground for Pentecostalism. Among the more important was a perfectionist movement led by Johan Ongman (1845–1931), a returned Baptist emigrant who broke away from other Swedish Baptists* in the 1890s and began a new missionary society. He emphasized the continuing validity of the gifts of the Holy Spirit, especially prophecy, healing, and glossolalia. In 1907 another Swede, Andrew Johansson, who had experienced the revival in Los Angeles, began to lead similar meetings in Skövde, Sweden. Pentecostal-like phenomena soon spread to other congregations, especially those affiliated with the Baptist denomination. Barratt came from Norway and preached in Gothenburg* and Stockholm*. At least 80 specifically Pentecostal congregations were gathered within a few years.

Lewi Pethrus (1884–1976), the pastor of a Pentecostal church in Stockholm that joined the Baptist denomination in 1911, began to allow non-Baptists to partake communion, however, and his Filadelphia church was excluded in 1913. Independence led to rapid growth, and it quickly became one of the world's largest Pentecostal congregations. As in Norway, the denomination soon became the largest in the land apart from the state church. Its loose organization precludes precise quantification, but in the early 1980s there were probably about 100,000 Pentecostals in Sweden.

In Denmark Pentecostalism has always played a less important role. Barratt brought the movement to Copenhagen* in 1907, where the first congregation, typically named Filadelphia, was soon gathered. Others soon appeared, although Copenhagen has remained the center of Danish Pentecostalism. In 1980 there were about 4,000 adherents in Denmark.

Owing chiefly to its use of believers' baptism, occasional emotional excesses during worship, and theological flexibility, Pentecostalism long met strong opposition in Scandinavia. This has softened in recent decades, probably in part because of the movement's stability. As elsewhere, Pentecostals in Sweden, Norway, and Denmark stress revivalism, the gifts of the Holy Spirit, personal sanctification, the return of Jesus Christ, and foreign missions. The so-called charismatic movement, which since the 1960s has re-emphasized the importance of the Holy Spirit in other denominations as well, has helped to ameliorate tensions between them and the Pentecostals.

REFERENCE: *Nordisk teologisk uppslagsbok för kyrka och skola* (Lund: Gleerup, 1952–1957).

F. HALE

PEOPLE'S ALLIANCE Icelandic political party

The People's Alliance (Althydubandalagid/AB), Iceland's third largest political party and a member of a number of governing coalitions, was founded in 1956 as an electoral alliance and in 1968 became a full-fledged political party. It was formed by two groups: the left-wing Social Democrats, whose leader, Hannibal Valdimarsson, was the first chairman, and the Communist-front United

People's Party-Socialist Party (UPP-SP). The UPP-SP had been established in 1938 and became a leader of Iceland's independence movement (achieved in 1944), a role which helped the party gain acceptance among the other parties as a responsible, democratic group. The UPP-SP was a successor to the Icelandic Communist Party, created in 1930 by disgruntled members of the older Labor Party, the forerunner of the current Social Democratic Party.

Under its former chairperson, Ludvig Josepsson, a Communist from the eastern fjord district, and Svavar Gestsson, who became chairperson in 1980, the People's Alliance cooperated for several years as a partner in a coalition government with various combinations of other major parties. Early in 1980, the Alliance entered into a government headed by Gunnar Thoroddsen, leader of a splinter group within the Independence (Conservative) Party, Iceland's largest party. Gestsson became the minister of social affairs, and other party representatives received the ministries of finance and industry. The Progressive Party also joined the coalition, but the Social Democrats went into the opposition alongside the main body of the Independents.

The Alliance appeals to small businessmen, fishermen, and farmers, as well as workers. With the cooperation of the Independence Party, it has recently taken control of Iceland's central Federation of Labor. Although Gestsson (b. 1947), a former teacher and journalist, studied in East Germany and is considered by some conservative politicians to be a Communist, he has studiously avoided such a label and has become acceptable to all party elements—the trade unions, the Reykjavik intellectual wing, and the Eastfjord constituency.

While there are still some Communists in the Alliance and the party adopts the same attitude as Moscow on certain international issues, particularly support of "peace" and disarmament themes, party leaders have attacked particular Soviet policies. The United States and the U.S.S.R. are both described as superpowers who disregard the rights of smaller nations. Gestsson and the party's vice-chairperson, Kjartan Olafsson, have severely condemned the Soviets for their actions in Afghanistan, Poland, and the Baltic. Olafsson also has accused the Soviet Union of "hypocrisy and dissimulation" in championing disarmament themes. Concurrently, the People's Alliance has concentrated on seeking the withdrawal of the United States/NATO base at Keflavik and supports international pacifist and neutralist movements.

The Labor Alliance's participation in the government has led its leaders to accept government economic and social policies that are not in accord with the party's positions favoring low-income groups. Since this has aroused criticism within the party, the leaders have concentrated more on foreign policy issues. They have had some success in opposing the use of foreign capital to exploit Icelandic resources and develop Icelandic industry and in delaying modernization of facilities at Keflavik.

Despite struggles within the party over programs and policies, the Alliance was stronger than the Social Democrats in electoral support and in the trade unions. In the 1979 parliamentary election, the Alliance received 19.7 percent of the vote and secured 11 of the 60 Althing* seats.

On April 21, 1983, the Thoroddsen Government resigned and the Hermansson Government that succeeded it on May 26 did not include the People's Alliance.

REFERENCES: F. Capps, "Iceland," in D. Starr ed., *Yearbook on International Communist Affairs 1982* (Stanford, Calif.: Hoover Institution Press, 1982); T. Gilberg, "Communism in the Nordic Countries: Denmark, Norway, Sweden, and Iceland," in D. Childs, ed., *The Changing Face of Western Communism* (New York: St. Martin's Press, 1980); D. Nuechterlein, *Iceland: Reluctant Ally* (Ithaca: Cornell University Press, 1961).

F. H. CAPPS

PERSSON, GÖRAN (JÖRAN) (c. 1530–1568) Advisor and secretary of Erik XIV* of Sweden

Born the son of Peter of Sala (Peter på Salberget), a monk who had become a Lutheran pastor and had married, Göran Persson was trained in law at the University of Wittenberg and became a legal expert. In 1552 he came into King Gustav I Vasa's* service but soon irritated the king into exiling him. He fled to the court of Crown Prince Erik and served the latter until his death.

Swedes, historians, and laymen have considered Göran Persson Erik XIV's evil genius, but few have denied that he was an exceptionally talented man. He was a man of ideas; he had courage; and he was essentially realistic and practical. His greatest handicap may well have been his origin: people on all levels humiliated the son for the father's breaking of his vow of celibacy. The lifelong humiliation probably motivated him to seek power and revenge.

Persson became Erik's secretary, favorite, confidant, advisor, and prosecutor (procurator). A believer in a strong monarch and in strict control of the nobility, he served as the head of Erik's elaborate espionage system, dealt with both parliament (Riksdag*) and the courts of law on behalf of the king, and served as the defender of Erik's unfortunate actions. Göran Persson was instrumental in the founding of *konungens nämnd*, a sort of supreme court. While he most likely was unscrupulous in advising the king on how to deal with his brothers (*see* Johan III; Karl IX) and with suspect noblemen, particularly the generally respected Stures with their unimpeachable claims to social and historical eminence, he was genuinely devoted to Erik and was faithful to the end.

When dukes Johan and Karl succeeded in having King Erik deposed and imprisoned in the fall of 1568, Göran Persson was held responsible for many of the king's actions, tried, condemned, brutally punished, and then executed.

Ennobled toward the end of Erik's reign, Göran Persson left no detailed account of his life, but his son, Erik Jöransson Tegel (1568–1636), who was also trained in law in Wittenberg and became not only a member of the police and other security forces in Stockholm* but also a historian, wrote two valuable chronicles, *Gustav Vasa* (printed 1622) and *Erik XIV* (printed 1751).

REFERENCE: M. Roberts, *The Early Vasas: A History of Sweden 1523–1611* (Cambridge, England: Cambridge University Press, 1968).

W. JOHNSON

PILO, CARL GUSTAF (5 March 1711–2 March 1793) Swedish artist

The son of a father who had worked under Nicodemus Tessin the elder at Drottningholm*, Pilo left Sweden for Denmark in 1740, and he remained there in the service of the Danish court until 1772. Pilo's sharp and rather flashy style was well adapted to official portraiture, but he was not out of touch with the range of styles in contemporary French portrait painting. In Louis Tocqué he had a distinguished French colleague who paid two visits to Denmark. Pilo was a keen admirer of Dutch seventeenth-century painting, and he built up the Dutch section of the Danish royal collections. He left Denmark for his native country early in 1772 following the fall of Johann Friedrich Struensee* and the coming of the culturally narrow Danish nationalism embodied by the Guldberg administration. It is of interest that the baroque influences of his youth, perhaps through his father, and Pilo's indebtedness to both Rubens and Rembrandt only really coalesced in the last 10 years of his life, 1782–1793, when he worked on his large and finally unfinished canvas of Gustav III's* coronation. This is a powerful exploration of a dim cathedral interior crowded with enrobed functionaries, and it suggests that official portraiture, however materially profitable, had not afforded Pilo full scope for his painterly inclinations.

REFERENCES: C. Elling, *Rokokoens Portraetmaleri i Danmark* (Copenhagen, 1935); O. Sirèn, *C-G Pilo* (Stockholm, 1902); B. G. Wennberg, *Svenska Målare i Danmark under 1700 talet* (Lund, 1940).

D. D. ALDRIDGE

PIO, LOUIS (14 December 1841–26 June 1894) Danish Socialist, political organizer, and journalist

More than any other figure, Louis Pio deserves to be called the father of the Danish Socialist movement. His background, however, was thoroughly bourgeois. Of French ancestry, Pio was born at Roskilde, Denmark, the son of an army officer. Despite disciplinary problems at school, he became a university student in 1859 and passed preliminary examinations in philosophy two years later. When repeated applications for admission to an engineering institute were rejected, the eclectic scholar taught school briefly before entering the army and serving as an officer in the costly war against the Prussians and Austrians in 1864. Pio left the army in 1868 and again taught in Copenhagen* until taking a position at one of that city's central post offices in 1870. In the meantime, he had begun to dabble with Nordic mythology and in 1869 published a book about Holger Danske, the hero of French and Danish medieval legends. His interest in historical social uprisings and the plight of the common man appears to have made Pio receptive to revolutionary Socialist thought by the beginning of the 1870s.

In the wake of the Franco-Prussian War, the Paris Commune made a strong impression on Pio. He delved into foreign Socialist literature and in 1871 organized, with the help of his cousin Harald Brix, Poul Geleff, and other like-minded Danes, the International Workers' Association in Denmark, which affiliated with the First International (Karl Marx's International Working Men's Association). Pio and Brix also began to publish a radical weekly newspaper, *Socialisten* (*The Socialists*). Resigning his postal position, Pio spent a hectic year working as a private tutor and leading the new Socialist body before falling into legal difficulties.

In May 1872 he issued a call for a mass meeting at a park in Copenhagen to demonstrate solidarity with an illegal strike. Pio defied a police injunction against the rally, which mounted gendarmes interrupted. Pio, Geleff, and Brix were sentenced belatedly in March 1873 to six, five, and four years imprisonment, respectively. Before the verdict was reached, Pio ran for the Danish parliament from his cell but received a scant 199 votes.

The three were pardoned in April 1875 and resumed political activity later that year. Pio, however, clashed frequently with comrades in the party's leadership and showed little interest in mundane administrative duties. Early in 1877 he began to publicize a proposed Danish Socialist colony in Kansas and in February resigned his chairmanship of the party. Threatened by the police if he continued his verbal attacks on the government, Pio and Geleff accepted a bribe of 10,000 crowns from them to emigrate to America. The two slipped out of Denmark on 2 March 1877.

Pio had a checkered life in the United States. Relations deteriorated immediately between him and Geleff, who wrote an exposé of the bribe in 1877. Pio and his wife continued to Kansas, where the utopian colony collapsed within a few weeks. Moving to Chicago, he worked as a typographer and wrote for various Scandinavian immigrant newspapers and periodicals. Pio also wrote language manuals for newcomers in the New World. In 1893 he managed the Florida pavilion at the World's Fair in Chicago and laid plans for a colony in Florida to be called White City, allegedly because it was to be racially segregated. The entrepreneuring immigrant contracted typhus there, however, and died in 1894.

REFERENCES: N. F. Christiansen, "National tradition og udenlandske indflydelse i den tidlige danske arbejderbevegelse" in B. Ohngren, et al., eds., *Från medeltid till välfärdssamhälle. Nordiska historikermötet i Uppsala 1974. Föredrag och mötesförhandlingar* (Stockholm: Alqvist & Wiksell, 1974); *DBL*, vol. 11; E. Winblad and A. Andersen, *Det danske socialdemokratis historie*, vol. 1 (Copenhagen: Fremad, 1921).

F. HALE

POETIC EDDA (c. 1275) Unique manuscript of Old Norse poetry

The Codex Regius of the *Poetic Edda* (Gammel kongelig Samling 2365 4to in the Royal Library in Copenhagen) is a compilation of 29 poems which were copied by an Icelandic scribe c. 1275 from an original which is usually dated to the early thirteenth century. The first eleven poems have mythological subjects, and these are followed by a series of eighteen heroic poems.

The collection contains varied types of poems, such as prophecies, flytings and curses; some are narratives and others are dialogues. Three different metres are employed and in some of the poems, particularly the heroic ones, the verse is interspersed with prose. Underlying this variety is a unity of design and purpose.

The mythological section describes the supernatural world. The first poem in the manuscript, *Voluspá*, traces the fates of the gods from the beginning of time to the end of the world and beyond. The poems that follow relate episodes from the lives of the gods and other supernatural creatures, beginning with Óðinn and ending with the dwarf Alvíss.

The heroic section is organized into a tighter narrative sequence which describes the beginning of a heroic age with the birth of Helgi, Sigurðr's half brother, the legends of Sigurðr and the Nibelungs, and finally the humiliating deaths of the last surviving heroes of Sigurðr's race.

The identities of the compiler of the *Edda* and the authors of individual poems are unknown. Scholars disagree on dates of composition within the time period 900–1200; the material itself may be considerably older. The precise relationship of the *Poetic Edda* to Snorri Sturluson's* *Edda*, which contains much of the same material, is also debated.

The manuscript was discovered by Brynjólfur Sveinsson, bishop of Skálholt, in 1643, and editions of individual poems were begun in Copenhagen* in 1665. The first complete critical edition was that of Rasmus Rask in 1818. Sophus Bugge's edition (1867) founded a school of Eddic criticism based on philology, the goal of which was to recreate the poems in their original forms. Gustav Neckel broke with this tradition in 1914 and created an edition which better represented the actual manuscript. Neckel's work, in the fourth edition published by Hans Kuhn in 1960, is still the standard for contemporary scholarship; subsequent editors such as Jon Helgason and Ursula Dronke do not deviate substantially.

REFERENCES: T. M. Andersson, "The Legend of Brynhild," *Islandica* 43 (Ithaca: Cornell University Press, 1980); H. Bellows, trans., *The Poetic Edda* (New York: American-Scandinavian Foundation, 1923); H. M. Chadwick, *The Heroic Age* (Cambridge, England: Cambridge University Press, 1926); J. De Vries, *Heroic Song and Heroic Legend*, trans. B. J. Timmer (London: Oxford University Press, 1963); U. Dronke, ed. and trans., *The Poetic Edda*, vol. 1 (Oxford: Clarendon Press, 1969); J. Harris, forthcoming volume on Eddic poetry for the Twayne World Author Series; L. Hollander, "Recent Work and Views on the Poetic Edda," *Scandinavian Studies* 35 (1963): 101–9; P. Terry, trans., *Poems of the Vikings* (New York: Bobbs-Merrill, 1969); E.O.G. Turville-Petre, *Myth and Religion of the North* (London: Weidenfeld and Nicolson, 1964).

M. EMELITY

POLITICAL PARTIES

"Modern" political parties developed in Denmark, Norway, and Sweden during the last three decades of the nineteenth century. They emerged to some degree from older internal parliamentary groups, but they were also the result of social and economic changes occurring during the period. They were a central factor (but by no means the only one) in the development of parliamentary government in Scandinavia*. The earliest parties, the Liberals (Left/Venstre) and the Conservatives (Right/Höger), developed along class lines. The former represented the newer elements in the society and some agricultural groups and favored the development of parliamentarism. The latter represented the older sectors of the societies and opposed too rapid political change. In the last quarter of the nineteenth century, Social Democratic parties, representing the emerging industrial working class, also appeared, but they tended to be extra-parliamentary and to work with the bourgeois Left parties until after 1900. In the years around World War I specifically agrarian parties developed. In Finland, "modern" parties appeared in the wake of the reforms introduced as a result of the 1905 Revolution in Russia. These included the creation of a unicameral legislature (the Eduskunta*) and the introduction of universal suffrage. In the Faroe Islands* and Iceland, parties appeared after about 1900 and were linked largely to the struggle for autonomy or independence.

By the early post-World War I period, a pattern (the so-called 1920 party system) had developed in Scandinavia characterized by the presence of four or five principal parties (Conservative, Agrarian, Liberal, Social Democratic, and Communist) in each of the Nordic countries. There were, however, variations in virtually every country. For example, in Denmark there was no separate agrarian party because the Left Party (Venstre) represented the farmers. In Sweden, the Liberals split in the 1920s over the prohibition issue, so there were two liberal parties. In Finland, Communist parties were illegal between 1918 and 1944, and the party scene was complicated by the presence of the Swedish People's Party*. In spite of these and other variations, one can point to a similar number of parties based on class distinctions and having similar programs, a stable pattern of party membership and voter behavior, and a pattern of government formation based on these parties in Scandinavia until relatively recently.

During the 1970s changes began to appear. In Denmark and Norway a number of new parties based on issues such as taxes, the bureaucracy, the EEC, or the environment, and/or on personalities such as Mogens Glistrup*, came on the scene. In Sweden the 44–year dominance of the Social Democrats was broken between 1976 and 1982. These changes may be only temporary, or they may mark the beginning of a new period in Scandinavian political development.

In the early 1980s, the following parties were active in the Scandinavian countries: in Denmark the Center Democrats (Centrum Demokraterne), the Christian People's Party* (Kristeligt Folkeparti), the Conservative People's Party (Det Konservative Folkeparti), the Left Socialist Party (Venstresocialisterne), the Liberal Party (Venstre), the Progress Party (Fremskridtspartiet) (*see* Glistrup, Mogens), the Radical Liberal Party (Det Radikale Venstre), the Single Tax Party (Danmarks Retsforbund), the Social Democratic Party (Socialdemokratiet), and the Socialist People's Party (Socialistisk Folkepartiet); in Finland the Center

Party* (formerly the Agrarians), the National Coalition Party* (formerly the Conservatives), the Liberal People's Party (formerly the Progressive and then the Finnish People's Party; *see* Progressive/Liberal Party), the Ruralist Party, the Social Democratic League (*see* Social Democratic Party), the Finnish People's Democratic League (*see* Communist Party), and the Swedish People's Party*; in Iceland the Independence Party, the National Preservation Party, the Social Democratic Party, the Socialist Party, the People's Alliance*, and the Union of Liberals and Leftists; in Norway the Center Party* (Senterpartiet,formerly the Agrarian Party), the Christian People's Party (Kristelig Folkeparti), the Communist Party* (Norges Kommunistiske Partiet), the Conservative Party* (Høyre), the Norwegian Labor Party* (Det Norske Arbeiderpartiet), the Liberal Party (Venstre), the New People's Party (Det Nye/Liberale Folkepartiet), the Progress Party (Fremskrittspartiet), and the Socialist Left Party (Sosialistisk Venstreparti); and in Sweden the Center Party* (Centerpartiet, formerly the Agrarian Party), the Left Party Communists (Vänsterpartiet Kommunisterna; *see* Communist Party: Sweden), the Liberal Party (Folkepartiet, *see* Liberal People's Party: Sweden), the Moderate Party (Moderata Samlingspartiet, *see* Conservative Party: Sweden), and the Social Democratic Party* (Socialdemokratiska Arbetarepartiet).

REFERENCES: S. Berglund and U. Lindström, *The Scandinavian Party System(s)* (Lund: Studentlitteratur, 1978); O. Borre, "Denmark's Protest Election of 1973," *Scandinavian Political Studies* 9 (1974): 197–204; E. Damgaard, "Stability and Change in the Danish Party System," *Scandinavian Political Studies* 9 (1974): 103–25; N. Elder et al., *The Consensual Democracies? The Government and Politics of the Scandinavian States* (Oxford: M. Robinson, 1982); J. Fitzmaurice, *Politics in Denmark* (New York: St. Martin's, 1981); J. Nousiainen, *The Finnish Political System* (Cambridge, Mass.: Harvard University Press, 1971); Olof Petersson, *Folkstyrelse och statsmakt i Norden* (Uppsala: Diskurs, 1984); D. Rustow, *The Politics of Compromise*(Princeton: Princeton University Press, 1955); R. Tomasson, *Iceland: The First New Society* (Minneapolis: University of Minnesota Press, 1980).

B. NORDSTROM

PONTOPPIDAN, ERIK (24 August 1698–20 December 1764) Danish Lutheran Bishop and theologian

Often called "the Younger" to distinguish him from his grandfather, Pontoppidan was born in Aarhus, Denmark, in 1698. After completing his theological examination at Copenhagen* in 1718, he embarked on a study tour through England, Holland, and Germany. In 1735 he was appointed court chaplain and three years later theological professor at Copenhagen. In 1748 he was named bishop of Bergen, Norway, only to be recalled in 1755 as chancellor of the University of Copenhagen, where he remained until his death.

It was Pontoppidan and other leading Danish Pietists who were instrumental in the promulgation of the decree mandating confirmation instruction for all teenage children in 1736. Pontoppidan's fame rests largely on his "Explanation" (Forklaring) of Luther's Small Catechism entitled *Truth unto Godliness* (*Sandhet til Gudfryktighet*), which he published the next year. In a series of 759 questions and answers, Pontoppidan laid out a Pietist understanding of the Christian faith that became the standard textbook for over 150 years for confirmation instruction and religious classes in elementary schools. So highly was it regarded that the pioneer Norwegian-American pastor, Elling Eielsen, walked from the Fox River Settlement west of Chicago to New York City in 1842 in order to publish an English translation of Pontoppidan's "Explanation." It is safe to say that no other book, apart from the Bible itself, has had such an influence in shaping the character of the Norwegian people. It was Pontoppidan's discussion of election in Question 548 that became a focal point in the great "Election Controversy" that rocked American Lutheranism in the 1880s.

Mandatory confirmation instruction presupposed literacy. In 1739 the Pietist king, Christian VI*, proclaimed universal public education for all in his realm. As bishop of Bergen, Pontoppidan had a rich ministry implementing these enlightened reforms in popular education. Pontoppidan is also known for his *Collegium pastorale practicum* (1757), which became the textbook in pastoral theology for over a century, as well as the oft-reprinted devotional novel *Menoza* (1742–1743) and the multi-volume *Danish Atlas* (1763–1767).

REFERENCES: Michael Neiiendam, *Erik Pontoppidan*, 2 vols. (Copenhagen, 1930–1931); Trygve R. Skarsten, "Erik Pontoppidan and His Asiatic Prince Menoza," *Church History* 50 (March 1981): 33–43.

T. R. SKARSTEN

POPULATION

The earliest humans in Scandinavia* appeared about 12,000 to 15,000 years ago, soon after the recession of the last great glaciers from northern Europe. The oldest evidence of such habitation is in the Bromme finds from southern Denmark and dates from 11,000 B.C. The number of people who came to live in Scandinavia in this very early period can only be crudely estimated at a few thousand. Over the ensuing millennia in Scandinavian prehistory, the centers of population expanded in southern parts of the region and spread north into central Sweden and coastal Norway. Separate in-migrations also affected the distribution of settlement, the extent of the population, and the nature of the cultures in the area. (For example, the coming of the so-called Boat Axe People around 2,000 B.C. appears to have brought the taller, narrow-skulled stock of modern Scandinavia to the area along with a new religion, the Indo-European language base, and the horse.)

By the early Iron Age* (c. 500 B.C.), McEvedy and Jones estimate the population of Scandinavia to have been about 150,000, with the majority living in the southern sections of the region. Although population growth was slowed or reversed by short-run problems, the general trend over the following centuries down to c. 1650 was one of slow growth. After 1650 the population of Scandinavia grew more rapidly, until the early twentieth century, when growth slowed and actually stopped in some areas. By about 200 A.D. the area may have had as many as 400,000 people, and by the eleventh century about 1 million. The population of medieval Scandinavia peaked in the mid-fourteenth century at around 1.75 million. Then, however, the region, along with the rest of Europe, was swept by recurrent outbreaks of the plague (Black Death), which reduced the population in some areas by as much as two-thirds. By the early fifteenth century, the population of Scandinavia was down to about 1.2 million, and it was nearly two centuries before it recovered to the fourteenth-century level. Marked growth came after 1650. By 1800 population in the area had reached 5.25 million. It then more than doubled, to reach 12.5 million in 1900 and then nearly doubled again to reach about 22.5 million by 1980.

For most of Scandinavia's history, population has been held in check or has grown only slowly because of famines, disease, war, and various methods of voluntary population control including delayed marriage, infanticide, and abstention or withdrawal. Population size has also been affected by in- and outmigrations. For example, during the Viking Age* it has been estimated that about 200,000 people left Norden. Similarly, during the mass migrations of the nineteenth and twentieth centuries over 2.75 million left the area (*see* Emigration, 1825–1930). Conversely, in the post-World War II period, Scandinavia was a region of significant in-migration. In 1980 there were about 102,000 resident aliens in Denmark, 14,000 in Finland, 86,000 in Norway, and 414,000 in Sweden. Most of these people came from less affluent nations in eastern or southern Europe and from parts of the Third World. Finally, population in the region has also been affected by border changes such as Denmark's loss of Slesvig and Holstein in 1864 and Finland's loss of Karelian territory in 1940.

The growth of population so marked in the last two centuries was largely the result of peace, agricultural developments that led to improved diet, and medical advances that put an end to massive losses of population through diseases and also extended life expectancies. These changes contributed to a general decline of death rates. In the twentieth century, a so-called demographic transition occurred which involved the continued decline in mortality rates accompanied by declines in birth rates. As a result the population growth slowed, ceased, or even was reversed. Projections of populations indicate that Denmark, Finland, and Sweden will see actual declines in their populations in the late twentieth century. This transition has also resulted in significant changes in the composition, especially in terms of age, of the population, with important social and economic implications for the future.

Sources upon which accurate population figures could be based were nonexistent before the seventeenth century. Estimates for earlier periods were based on archeological evidence, estimates of possible rural and town population densities, tax records, burial site analyses, and so on. Sources improved somewhat in the seventeenth century when, for example, Denmark conducted censuses of peasants for tax or military purposes. More detailed demographic data began to be kept in the eighteenth century. A formal census for all of Iceland was conducted in 1701. The keeping of demographic information by the clergy, initiated in Sweden in the seventeenth century, became standard throughout Scandinavia. In 1749 Sweden conducted the first national census (for both Sweden and Finland), and Denmark-Norway followed suit in 1769. These set the pattern for the nineteenth and twentieth centuries.

REFERENCES: C. McEvedy and R. Jones, *Atlas of World Population History* (London: Allen Lane and Penguin, 1978); Nordic Council, *Yearbook of Nordic Statistics* (Stockholm: Norstedts, 1983).

B. NORDSTROM

Denmark, Faroe Islands, and Greenland

The areas that constitute modern Denmark and the southern Swedish provinces of Blekinge, Halland, and Skåne were the core areas of early population development in Scandinavia, and it was in these areas that the majority of Norden's population lived until the medieval period. As was the case in the rest of Scandinavia, population expanded slowly down to the mid-seventeenth century, with similar setbacks due to epidemic diseases (especially severe in the second half of the fourteenth century), famines and war. Significant periods of out-migration came during the Viking Age (especially to eastern Britain) and during the nineteenth and twentieth centuries. In the latter instance about 350,000 emigrated. In-migration was also important during much of Denmark's early modern history and has been a factor since World War II*.

Population of Denmark (in millions)

200 A.D.	.2
1000	.4
1500	.6
1600	.7
1700	.8
1800	1.0
1900	2.5
1980	5.1

Significant growth came after c. 1650, caused largely by continued high birth rates coupled with declining death rates during most of the eighteenth and nineteenth centuries. In the twentieth century, birth rates declined, especially in the 1930s and after World War II. It has been estimated that Denmark's population will fall by some 400,000 by 2025.

The Faroe Islands* and Greenland*, which remain parts of the Danish kingdom, have had the following populations:

Population of Faroe Islands

1000 A.D.	c. 1,000
1300	c. 1,000
1800	c. 5,000
1900	15,000

1980	44,000

Population of Greenland

1000 A.D.	c. 3,000
1500	?
1700	?
1800	5,000
1900	12,000
1980	51,000

The sources for Danish population studies were virtually non-existent before the seventeenth century. Early estimates have had to be based upon evidence from archeological sources, fragmentary legal and tax documents, and so on. In the seventeenth century censuses of peasant landholders were conducted for tax purposes (1660). Parish registers were kept from the 1730s, which included information about church membership, births, marriages, deaths, and in- and out-migration. The first national census was taken in 1769. A more accurate census was taken in 1801. Regular censuses have been conducted since 1840.

REFERENCES: H. Gille, "The Demographic History of the Northern European Countries in the Eighteenth Century," *Population Studies* 3:1 (1949): 3–65; Aksel Lassen, *Fald og fremgang; trækafbefolkningsudviklingen i Danmark 1645–1960* (Aarhus, 1965), and "The Population of Denmark 1660–1960," *Scandinavian Economic History Review* 14 (1966): 134–57; P. C. Matthiessen, "Some Aspects of the Demographic Transition in Denmark," Dissertation, University of Copenhagen, 1970.

B. NORDSTROM

Finland

Many essential features of Finnish demographic history are derived from the fact that the country was an agrarian periphery, where the geographic expansion of settlement has continued up into modern times. Only during the twentieth century and especially since World War II has urbanization* been the motive force of development.

Quite reliable population figures have been available since 1749, and rough estimates, which at least show the general trends of settlement, can be obtained from the sixteenth century. It appears that Finland's population increased, in general, through the Middle Ages and up to the 1560s. After the 1560s, however, wars, increasing tax burdens, and epidemics halted this growth. Expansion of the population did not resume until after the Great Northern War*, which ended in 1721. (One of the worst known population catastrophes took place in Finland in 1696–1697, when about 25 percent of the population died of famine or disease.)

During the eighteenth century population growth in Finland was unusually fast by European standards of the time—about twice as fast as in Sweden and four times as fast as in Denmark. The growth was most rapid in agricultural "frontier" districts in the northern and central parts of the country. In the southwestern provinces, which had the oldest and the densest settlement, growth was much slower. These differences seem to indicate that land availability was a factor of great importance in population history in Finland.

During the nineteenth century population growth continued, but the rates were somewhat diminished. This was due partly to a fall in fertility rates and partly to certain years of famine or epidemics, especially in the 1860s. In the latter half of the century, a gradual decline in mortality rates began.

In the twentieth century, fertility rates continued to decline, especially in the years just before World War I. Both nativity and mortality rates stabilized at very low levels in the 1950s and 1960s, and population growth has been very slow as a result.

Urban population was negligible before the end of the nineteenth century in Finland. A definite change was brought on by industrial development. Urbanization began before the turn of the century but became most intense only after World War II. Migration to urban areas has become the most important element of population change, and it has resulted in a decline of population in many peripheral areas, which formerly had experienced significant increases. Industrialization* has resulted in a fundamental change in population distribution patterns: geographic expansion has been replaced by centralization.

Population of Finland, 1750–1980

		% urban
1750	421,500	
1800	832,700	
1860	1,746,700	6.3
1900	2,655,900	12.5
1940	3,695,600	26.8
1980	4,787,800	59.8

Source: *Statistical Yearbook of Finland*, 1981.

REFERENCES: E. Jutikkala, "The Great Finnish Famine in 1696–97," *Scandinavian Economic History Review* 3:1 (1955): 48–63; Y. Kaukiainen, "Variations in Fertility in Nineteenth Century Finland: Lohja Parish," in *Chance and Change*, ed. S. Åkerman et al. (Odense, 1978); K. Pitkänen, "The Changing Features of Mortality in Finland in the Eighteenth and Nineteenth Centuries," *Scandinavian Population Studies* 5 (1979), and "Registering People in a Changing Society—The Case of Finland," in *Yearbook of Population Research in Finland* 18 (1980); A. Strömmer, *Väestöllinen muuntuminen Suomessa* (summary: The Demographic Transition in Finland) (Tornio, 1969); O. Turpeinen, "Fertility and Mortality in Finland since 1750," *PopulationStudies* 33:1 (1979).

Y. KAUKIAINEN

Iceland

The earliest people on Iceland were probably Irish monks, who drifted or sailed to the island in the seventh or eighth century. The first Scandinavians came to the island in the last quarter of the ninth century, and by the end of the so-called settlement period (c. 876–930) there were about 30,000 people on the island. The population of medieval Iceland may have reached 70,000 in the early fourteenth century, but it fell markedly thereafter and stood at about 50,000 from 1400 down to 1800. In the nineteenth and twentieth centuries significant growth occurred. By 1900 the population had risen to 78,000, and in 1980 it was about 229,000.

REFERENCES: R. Tomasson, *Iceland: The First New Society* (Minneapolis: University of Minnesota Press, 1950).

B. NORDSTROM

Norway

Norway is the least densely populated of the continental Scandinavian countries. (In the mid-twentieth century there were about 10 inhabitants per square kilometer.) The terrain of the country and the scarcity of arable land have produced this characteristic and have determined patterns of settlement. The earliest people in Norway were located in the east central region around Oslo and along the south, west, and central coasts. Scattered settlements also developed farther north.

Prehistoric population of the country must have been very low. McEvedy and Jones argue that over half of the approximately 150,000 people who lived in Scandinavia c. 500 B.C. lived in the areas that now are Denmark and southern Sweden. One might then be able to estimate that something less than one-fourth of this figure lived in Norway at that time. By 1000 A.D. it has been estimated that the population of Norway was between 100,000 and 300,000. (Note the considerable range.) By the mid-fourteenth century the figure had reached between 300,000 and 450,000. In 1349, however, the Black Death reached Norway. Over the next half century between half and two-thirds of the population in certain areas of the country was swept away. Population estimates for 1500 range between 140,000 and 200,000 and reflect the long-term impact of the plague. By the mid-seventeenth century the population of Norway appears to have returned to its medieval peak, and it continued to grow over the next three centuries—though with significant regional and chronological variations in rate. The most remarkable growth of the population came after 1750. By 1800 Norway's population had reached 883,000. A century later it was 2.25 million. In 1980 it was 4.1 million. Growth rates in the eighteenth century were around .4 percent per year. Between 1818 and 1875 growth rates varied between 1.1 and 1.4 percent per year. They declined after 1875 largely because of falling birth rates.

As in the other Scandinavian countries, the growth of the population is generally attributed to steady and occasionally rising birth rates coupled with falling death rates. There were, however, striking regional and chronological variations to this pattern. At the same time, out-migration has been significant in Norway's demographic history. During the Viking Age emigrants left for the western British Isles, the Shetlands, the Orkneys, the Faroe Islands, Iceland, and Greenland. Most remarkable was the mass emigration in the nineteenth and early twentieth centuries, when over 850,000 Norwegians emigrated to the United States and other developing areas. In-migration has also been important, especially in the almost constant but slow influx of Danes during the period of union with Denmark and the multi-ethnic immigration from underdeveloped countries in the post-World War II period.

Before the late seventeenth century, estimates of population were based on rough calculations arising from fragmentary evidence. Increasingly accurate and extensive data began to be collected in the second half of the seventeenth century. For example, several censuses of males were collected for military purposes, including one in 1664–1666. The parish registers, which began to be kept with some accuracy and regularity in the eighteenth century, added increasingly important information. The first census for Norway was collected in 1769. This was repeated in 1801. Since 1850 regular national censuses have been taken.

REFERENCES: J. E. Backer, "Population Statistics and Population Registration in Norway I-II," *Population Studies* 1 (1948) and 2 (1949); M. Drake, *Population and Society in Norway 1735–1865* (Cambridge, England: Cambridge University Press, 1969); S. Dyrvik, "Historical Demography of Norway 1660–1801: A Short Survey," *Scandinavian Economic History Review* 20 (1972); H. Gille, "The Demographic History of the Northern European Countries in the Eighteenth Century," *Population Studies* 3:1 (1949): 3–65; R. M. Hagen et al., *Norsk historisk atlas* (Oslo: Cappelens, 1980); F. Michalsen, "Church Registers in Norway," *Archivium* 8 (1959); K. Ofstad, "Population Statistics and Population Registration in Norway III," *Population Studies* 3 (1949–1950).

B. NORDSTROM

Sweden

The patterns of Swedish demographic history are similar to those in the rest of Scandinavia. Early settlement began as the glaciers receded after 12,000 B.C. One center of population developed in the southern parts of the peninsula and was closely tied with developments in Denmark, to which there were at times land bridges. A second center developed in middle Sweden around Lake Mälar. This gradually expanded west, south, and north. The third area was in the far north, and it appears to have developed largely independently of the centers to the south. It is unclear from where the first people in Sweden came. It is known that a significant in-migration by a culture called the Boat Axe People occurred sometime around 2000 B.C. and that there were other in-migrations. The number of people in prehistoric Sweden must have been quite small, perhaps fewer than 30,000 in 500 B.C.

Slow growth of the population occurred for hundreds of years. By 1000 A.D. there may have been as many as 400,000 people in Sweden, and by the mid-fourteenth century the country is estimated to have had a population of about 650,000. This was reduced by a third or more over the next half century (to about 400,000 in 1400), largely as a result of recurrent outbreaks of the Black Death. It was not until the end of the first half of the sixteenth century that the population of Sweden recovered from this loss. The overall trend from the sixteenth century was of steady growth—occasionally reversed by disease, famine, or war. General and increasingly rapid growth set in from the mid-seventeenth century. By 1800 the country's population was 2.5 million. It rose to 5 million by 1900 and to 8.25 million by 1980.

The rapid growth in the modern period follows the pattern familiar throughout Scandinavia. Death rates declined from the early eighteenth century, while birth and/or fertility rates remained high. In 1721–1750, the crude death rate was 25.8 per thousand per year. By 1951–1970 this had dropped to 9.9. At the same time, birth rates of about 30–33 per thousand per year were typical through the eighteenth and nineteenth centuries. The reasons for these patterns lie in the fact that Sweden stayed out of the major wars after 1815, coupled with agricultural changes and improved health practices and conditions. Life expectancy doubled between 1750 and 1970 from 34.8 years for men and 39.3 years for women to 71.9 years for men and 76.6 years for women.

The growth rate of the Swedish population slowed from the last quarter of the nineteenth century, and particularly alarming declines occurred in the 1930s and after 1960. In 1981 the death rate (12.1 per thousand) actually exceeded the birth rate (11.3 per thousand). The low or negative growth rates have been offset at times, however, by immigration. Between 1945 and 1980, over 600,000 people immigrated to Sweden. Emigration has also played a significant role in population development, especially in the nineteenth and early twentieth centuries, when about 1.25 million Swedes left the country.

Sweden has often been praised for the ways in which, in the modern period, it has "kept track of its population." As in the rest of Scandinavia, few reliable sources existed before the seventeenth century. From the 1630s, however, lists of males eligible for military service were kept. At about the same time, some parish priests began to keep registers (husförhörslängd), which were to be kept in all parishes after 1686 and were standardized for Sweden and Finland in the eighteenth century. These came to contain basic information on general parish populations, births, marriages, deaths, migrations (in and out), knowledge of the Scriptures, and physical and mental health. Until 1950 they were the basis for most of Sweden's population statistics. In 1749 the first national census (Tabellverket) was collected, and in 1756 a state office of statistics was established (Tabellkommissionen). Regular censuses were gathered from the early nineteenth century. In 1858 a state office of statistics (Statistiska Centralbyrån) was established.

REFERENCES: H. Gille, "The Demographic History of the Northern European Countries in the Eighteenth Century," *Population Studies* 3:1 (1949): 3–65; E. Heckscher, *An Economic History of Sweden*, trans. G. Ohlin (Cambridge, Mass.: Harvard History Press, 1954); E. Hofsten and H. Lundström, *Swedish Population History: Main Trends from 1750–1970* (Stockholm: Statistiska Centralbyrån. Skriftseries No. 8, 1976); A. S. Kälvemark, "The Country That Kept Track of Its Population," *Scandinavian Journal of History* 2 (1977): 211–30; B. Odén and B. Schiller, *Statistik for historiker* (Uppsala, 1970); D. S. Thomas, *Social and Economic Aspects of Swedish Population Movements 1750–1933* (New York: Macmillan, 1941).

B. NORDSTROM

POSSE, ARVID RUTGER FREDERIKSSON (15 February 1820–24 April 1901) Swedish count, land owner, politician, and prime minister

Arvid Posse was born in Malmöhus län. He was a descendant of a renowned noble family and one of Sweden's largest land owners. After being educated at home, Posse went on to the lyceum at Lund and then to Lund University. He served in the Skåne court and from 1865 to 1868 was chairperson of the Malmöhus län landsting. He became one of Skåne's best known and most influential leaders. Posse entered the Second Chamber of the Riksdag* in 1867 and from 1867 to 1875 served as chair of that chamber's Budget Committee. He was also speaker of the chamber from 1876 to 1880.

Posse, Carl Ifvarsson, and Emil Key were co-founders in 1867 of the Lantmannapartiet. Poses's involvement with the Ruralist Party stemmed largely from personal ambition as well as antagonism toward Louis De Geer*, whom he considered a tool of the middle class. Posse was a landed aristocrat who wanted to retain rural domination in the Riksdag. The Ruralist Party formed a front against the urban and intellectual middle class in the Second Chamber and the higher civil servants, industrialists, and big land owners who controlled the First Chamber. This party formulated a detailed program which called for the abolition of the old military system of *indelning* and the old land tax system—both of which placed burdens on the peasants and farmers. The Ruralist Party also advocated strict economy in state expenditures as well as controls on the civil servants.

Oscar II* turned to Posse as prime minister in 1880, after De Geer was unable to carry through a compromise on military reform. Posse was the first real party leader to be appointed to that position. His cabinet was composed, in the conventional manner, of aristocratic officials, army officers, and land owners. In no sense was it a Ruralist Party cabinet, even though this party held the majority of the seats in the Second Chamber. In many ways, Posse's cabinet was more solidly composed of nobility than De Geer's. Thus, the farmers remained outside the cabinet, where they criticized but did not share responsibility. Posse was not successful in convincing the Ruralists to support his own defense bill in 1883. The result was that as the Ruralists forced De Geer out of office in 1880, Posse's government likewise fell in 1883. After 1883 Posse devoted his life to his extensive landed property. He died in Stockholm* in 1901.

REFERENCES: E. Holmqvist, *Aristokrater, bönder och byråkrater, Skånska riksdagsmän på 1800–talet* (Stockholm: Liber, 1980); D. A. Rustow, *The Politics of Compromise: A Study of Parties and Cabinet Government in Sweden* (Princeton: Princeton

University Press, 1955); E. Thermænius, *Lantmannapartiet. Dess uppkomst, organisation och tidigare utveckling* (Uppsala: Almqvist & Wiksell, 1928).

A. H. WINQUIST

POSTAL SERVICES

From the late Middle Ages until the twentieth century, the development of postal services in Scandinavia* has paralleled that elsewhere in Europe. Beginning late in the thirteenth century, the Hanseatic League* provided participating institutions with a commercial message service that united far-flung cities of northwestern Europe. Only incidentally did it carry mail for the general public, however, a function of little relevance before the spread of literacy in more modern times. In addition, all of the Nordic kingdoms had networks of messengers that provided irregular communications both domestically and internationally.

In 1624 the Danish crown instituted a weekly route between Copenhagen* and Hamburg. Sweden followed suit twelve years later when the government of Queen Christina* began to establish a basic system of internal post offices and officials, generally literate farmers who supplemented their incomes by carrying the mail. Norway received its first regular weekly postal services in 1647. Its few routes between Christiania, Copenhagen, Bergen, and Trondheim were staffed by farmers who, though unpaid, were exempted from military conscription and given tax reductions. Throughout Scandinavia, these early postal systems were initially in the hands of private entrepreneurs whom the governments had contracted for varying periods. By 1677, though, the Swedish monarchy had taken direct control, a development mirrored in 1711 and 1719 in the Danish and Norwegian systems, respectively. In the meantime, the internal networks had unfolded to some degree, and letter carriers had begun to use horses to speed deliveries.

Major changes first occurred in the nineteenth century, owing to the advent of steam power, postal reforms abroad, rapid population growth, and the proliferation of literacy. In the 1820s postal steamers had begun to ply the Baltic and coastal waters of southern Scandinavia. The first Danish railway began to carry traffic in 1847 and mail shortly thereafter; the Swedish and Norwegian railways date from the 1850s and also revolutionized mail delivery, especially as the networks expanded during the second half of the century. Trains in all of the Nordic countries soon included mail cars with sorting facilities.

In 1837 the Englishman Rowland Hill proposed that national postal systems could be administered more economically and generate greater revenue by slashing their domestic rates and charging a uniform fee per letter irrespective of the distance sent. Postage stamps resulted. Most European countries, including the Scandinavian lands in the 1850s, quickly adopted versions of the British "penny post." The volume grew rapidly, owing not only to the low fees but also to increasing literacy and population mobility resulting from the Industrial Revolution. Other nineteenth-century developments affecting the Nordic countries included the constitution of the Universal Postal Union in the 1870s to coordinate international postal services, the introduction of local delivery in many cities, and rural free delivery.

The twentieth century has brought further diversification of services, vastly increased volume, and technical advances. Air mail began in Denmark, Norway, and Sweden in 1920. Postal money orders, first used in Austria, have become widespread in Scandinavia. In 1950 Norwegian post offices began to serve as a comprehensive network of savings banks, a function which Sweden had instituted in 1884 in emulation of a British model. Mechanization and, to some extent, automated electronic sorting procedures have become commonplace, although in some remote districts small boats and snowmobiles are still used to deliver the mail, occasionally together with milk and other perishable commodities. By 1980 the number of postal employees had risen to approximately 20,000 in Norway, 22,000 in Denmark, and 60,000 in Sweden.

REFERENCES: *DH*, vols. 4, 9–11; *DSH*, vols. 6, 11, and 13; *NH*, vols. 6, 10, 11.

F. HALE

POTATO GERMANS (Kartoffeltyskere)

In 1759–1760 the Danish government under Frederik V* invited colonists from in and around the Pfalz region of Germany to settle on the uninhabited heath lands of Jutland, especially in the Alhede southwest of Viborg. Having tried without success in 1723 and 1751 to induce Danes to move out onto the inhospitable, wolf-infested wasteland, the government sought to attract German farmers by offering them freedom from taxes and billeting. Dr. Johan Friedrich Moritz, the Danish legation counselor in Frankfurt, was charged with recruiting prospective colonists, and since he received a sum of money for every colonist sent, he enlisted them as rapidly as possible without concerning himself over whether they were suitable candidates for the task of farming on the heath. He sent a total of 965 individuals (265 families) before he was instructed to stop. The project cost the government over 300,000 *rigsdaler* but met with only modest success because of poor planning, preparation, and coordination.

The colonists began to arrive in October 1759, and the first group took the unprepared Jutland authorities quite by surprise. Most of the colonists were quartered at government expense in Fredericia, but some were also sent to Viborg. Temporary sod houses were subsequently built for them pending construction of their permanent dwellings. The Danes who lived near the heath lands did not welcome the newcomers, and the local land owners, who had been using the adjacent heath freely for hunting and peat digging, opposed the settlement plans. Eventually, however, the new communities of Havredal and Grønhøj in the Alhede were born. A few malcontents and troublemakers among the colonists were sent back before being settled. Many others, inexperienced at farming, did not fare well and chose to return home. Some joined other Germans who were emigrating to southern Russia. Eighteen families abandoned the Alhede in favor of Randbøl heath farther south. Of the nearly 1,000 colonists who had come to start a new life in northern Jutland, only 241 remained in Havredal and Grønhøj by 1768.

The colonists taught their Danish neighbors to raise potatoes, which were then little known in Denmark, and hence acquired the epithet "Potato Germans," which hung on for generations and was still used as a term of abuse in Jutland in the early twentieth century, long after the descendants of the original colonists had lost their separate identity. The term "Potato German" applied specifically to the colonists of north Jutland, although in 1761 about 1,000 German families were also brought to the heath lands of south Slesvig. This project turned out better than the first but cost the government twice as much.

The offspring of the original Alhede colonists retained traces of their German roots for some generations. Their church held services in German until 1856, when, by royal order, it began having both German and Danish services. In 1870 German services were dropped altogether. Fictional portrayals of descendants of the Potato German occur in the stories of Jutland authors Henrik Pontopiddan and Jeppe Aakjaer.

REFERENCES: "Alheden," *Salmonsens Konversations Leksikon*, vol. 1 (1915), p. 507; J. Danstrup and H. Koch, eds., *Danmarks historie*, vol. 9 (Copenhagen: Politikens, 1965); R. Hansen, "Die Alheide in Jütland und ihre Besiedlung durch Pfälzer," *Globus* 64:6 (1893): 85–89 and 105–8, and "Die Pfälzer auf der jütischen Heide," *Globus* 73:1 (1898): 15–16; F. Skrubbeltrang, *Det Indvunde Danmark* (Copenhagen: Nordisk, 1966); J. P. Trap, *Danmark*, 5th ed. (Copenhagen: Gads, 1972), vol. 7.

N. FARQUHAR

PREHISTORY *See* Bronze Age; Celtic Iron Age; Viking Age

PRISONS

The development of correctional institutions in Scandinavia* has generally followed their evolution elsewhere in Europe and North America, although in recent times those in Scandinavia have occasionally served as models for reforms in other lands. The prison as an institution to which offenders are sentenced for a more or less specific period for punishment, rehabilitation, and the protection of society after due process of law is a fairly modern phenomenon. Previously, criminals, vagabonds, debtors, and other problematic individuals throughout Europe were capriciously placed in dungeons or poorhouses, pressed into involuntary servitude, banished, subjected to corporal punishment, or, in many cases, executed. All of these forms of mistreatment were widespread in Scandinavia until the eighteenth and nineteenth centuries.

The Enlightenment prompted the genesis of criminology as a science and early penal reforms. Perhaps the most prominent pioneer was the Italian jurist Cesare Beccaria (1738–1794), who in his work of 1764, *Crimes and Punishments*, called for systematic imprisonment or other punishment proportionate to the offenses committed. In response to this and several other reformers' arguments, prisons in the modern sense began to appear on both sides of the Atlantic in the eighteenth century. They took a number of forms, but that in which prisoners were isolated in individual cells became the most influential. The classical manifestation of this approach was developed by Quakers in Philadelphia in the 1790s. It featured nearly total isolation in the hope of preventing criminals from influencing one another during attempts at rehabilitation. This Philadelphia system, also known as the Pennsylvania or solitary system, came to Europe in both strict and more moderate forms. Forerunners of modern correctional institutions in Scandinavia had been limited to jails, which served primarily as poorhouses, the first ones erected in Denmark (Copenhagen*) and Sweden (Stockholm*) early in the seventeenth century and in Norway (Trondheim) in 1639. In all of the Scandinavian countries commissions were appointed to study penal reforms abroad and their possible application at home. The Norwegian government physician Frederik Holst proposed in 1823 a new prison on the model of British institutions incorporating the Philadelphia system. After several delays, such a prison was opened in Christiania (now Oslo) in 1851. It gradually replaced communal compulsory labor, to which many criminals had hitherto been sentenced. In Denmark, a commission of 1840 proposed similar changes with certain nuances. Two of the first results were the prisons at Vridsløselille near Copenhagen, which opened in 1860 on the Philadelphia system, and Horsens in Jutland, built in 1853, which employed the so-called Auburn system. According to the latter, inmates worked in silence during the day before being isolated at night. In Sweden, Crown Prince Oscar (later Oscar I*) published in 1840 a treatise in which he recommended instituting the Philadelphia system for sentences under six years and the Auburn system for longer ones. These suggestions were gradually implemented, chiefly in the penal law of 1864.

Prisons with individual cells thus formed the backbone of Scandinavian penal systems for roughly 100 years. During that period several modifications took place. Separate institutions for women and juvenile offenders became commonplace, and institutions began to segregate hardened criminals from those with few if any previous convictions for felonies. Diversified forms of production were instituted, allowing socially misfit prisoners to acquire skills. By the beginning of the twentieth century, classroom facilities were also widespread. The first official experiments with parole took place around 1900. Before that time differentiations in the treatment of prisoners, based in part on their personalities and behavior during confinement, had been the rule in many prisons.

Since World War II*, all of the Scandinavian countries have sought to humanize further their correctional institutions. Strict separation of prisoners has disappeared, and most iron-barred cells have been replaced by more hospitable rooms. Great emphasis is placed on individual treatment and rehabilitation.In cases not involving habitual or dangerous criminals, the chief intention is no longer to punish but to prepare offenders for relatively rapid return to normal lives. Consequently, sentences now tend to be short by international standards.

REFERENCE: K. O. Christiansen, ed., *Scandinavian Studies in Criminology* (Oslo: Universitetsforlaget, 1965–).

F. HALE

PROGRESSIVE/LIBERAL PARTY Finland

As an organized political movement liberalism has always been weaker in Finland than in the other Nordic countries. This difference is best explained by the uniqueness of political cleavages in the Finnish political system during the period of autonomy and by the dominant role of the Agrarian Party (*see* Center Party: Finland) in the politics of the Center since 1917. The principles of liberalism have, however, greatly influenced the cultural, economic, and political institutions of Finland and have been incorporated into the programs of other political parties. Despite its size, the party has produced a number of leading public figures and held portfolios in two-thirds of the governments of independent Finland.

Finland was exposed to liberal currents in Sweden while a part of that country up to 1809, and as a grand duchy, Finland was one of the few areas in the Russian Empire where Alexander I's liberal reforms, albeit short-lived, were introduced. These political currents peaked, however, in the early 1860s with the convocation of the Diet. Although liberalism continued to make inroads into Finnish society during the remainder of the period of autonomy, the political divisions along linguistic lines and the later priority given to relations with Russia prevented the formation of a liberal party. Consequently, Finland, unlike the other Nordic countries, never had a political alignment based on conservative-liberal differences over solutions to socioeconomic problems.

In the 1880s Swedish-speaking liberals attempted to form a bilingual liberal party, but the idea remained stillborn—opposed by the Swedish Party (*see* Swedish People's Party), which stood to lose its liberal wing, and by the Finnish Party, which was ideologically opposed to liberalism. In the 1890s, however, a group of young liberals under the leadership of K. J. Ståhlberg, who became the first president of Finland and was a key figure in the writing of the Finnish constitution, and Eero Erkko, founder of the leading liberal (later independent) Finnish newspaper, *Päivälehti*, later *Helsingin Sanomat*, left the Finnish Party to found the Young Finnish Party. Aware of developments in Europe that had challenged traditional elitist assumptions about political parties and concerned about socioeconomic problems in Finland, the Young Finns adopted a liberal program calling for the gradual introduction of liberal democracy and limited socioeconomic reforms. Russification intervened, however, to lay the basis for cooperation with the Swedish Party on policy toward Russia and thus to prevent the development of a liberal party primarily concerned with domestic problems.

The political realignments based on socioeconomic issues, which had been developing since the turn of the century and which eventually came to the surface in the wake of independence and the Civil War*, not only divided the Finnish

Left and created a political chasm between Socialists and non-Socialists, but also destroyed the old nationalist bourgeois groupings. The bitter debate over whether bourgeois-directed democracy should function under a constitutional monarchy or a republican form of government led to the dissolution of the Finnish (Old and Young) parties and to the formation of the National Coalition (Conservative) Party* by the conservative-monarchist elements of both parties and the National Progressive Party by liberal-republican elements of both parties. The Conservative Party, which was mainly organized around the Old Finns, emphasized law and order, while the Progressive Party, which was led by Young Finns, advocated a policy of national reconciliation.

The Progressive Party has always been divided between those members who emphasize economic liberalism and cooperation with the Right and those members who have placed more importance on social reform and cooperation with the moderate Left. The election of the Progressive K. J. Ståhlberg as Finland's first president in 1919 reflected a Finnish preference for republicanism and reconciliation rather than monarchy and confrontation after the Civil War. In the aftermath of the Mantsälä revolt in 1932, which marked the peak of the Lapua movement, the four-year government of T. M. Kivimäki, a representative of the right wing of the Progressive Party, was instrumental in stabilizing the political situation and initiating the Scandinavian orientation of Finland's foreign policy.

When A. K. Cajander, a representative of the left wing of the Progressive Party, formed the first Center-Left coalition government of independent Finland in 1937, Finland had already turned its back on right-wing radicalism and was emphasizing ties with Scandinavia at a time when fascism was on the rise in Germany and eastern Europe. The Progressive Risto Ryti* served as president during World War II, at a time when Finland had to develop the domestic basis for a political coalition which could defend traditional Finnish institutions of political democracy at home while fighting against the Soviet Union as a co-belligerent of Nazi Germany and striving to maintain at least some ties with the Western democracies.

Although liberalism remains embedded in Finnish political and economic institutions, the Progressive (Liberal since 1965) Party has been reduced to political impotence. As the Agrarian Party became the Center Party for demographic and ideological reasons, and the Swedish People's Party became a neo-liberal party, the Liberal Party lost its role as an essential source of political leaders and parliamentary support for coalition governments. Unable to identify with any interest group, the Liberal Party became a part of the Center Party in 1982.

REFERENCES: E. Allardt and P. Pessonen, "Cleavages in Finnish Politics," in S. Lipset, ed., *Party Systems and Voter Alignments: Cross National Perspectives* (New York: The Free Press, 1967); S. Berglund and U. Lindström, *The Scandinavian Party System(s)* (Lund: Studentlitteratur, 1978); *Democracy in Finland: Studies in Politics and Government* (Helsinki: The Finnish Political Science Association, 1969); J. Mylly, "The Emergence of the Finnish Multi-Party System: A Comparison with Developments in

Scandinavia 1870–1920," *Scandinavian Journal of History* 5 (1980); J. Nousiainen, *The Finnish Political System* (Cambridge, Mass.: Harvard University Press, 1973); M. Rintala, "The Scholar in Politics: J. K. Ståhlberg," in *Four Finns* (Berkeley: University of California Press, 1969); T. Soikkanen, "Changing Bourgeois Parties in a Changing Society," in R. M. Berry, ed., *Essays on the History of the Development of Finnish Political Parties* (Turku: Institute of Political History, 1983); K. Törnudd, "Composition of Cabinets in Finland 1917–1968," *Scandinavian Political Studies* 4 (1969).
                                                                                          R. M. BERRY

PROSTITUTION

The "world's oldest profession" has had a long history in Scandinavia*, but relatively little is known about its scope or practice before the eighteenth century. During the Middle Ages prostitution was accepted in some locales and periods as a legitimate means of earning a living. After the nominal Christianization of the Nordic countries in the eleventh and twelfth centuries, however, sporadic measures to suppress it became more common. Prostitutes were beaten, subjected to public ridicule in the stocks, compelled to wear humiliating badges, and otherwise harassed. Where tolerated, they were often restricted to certain streets, a practice which survives today on an informal basis. In short, governmental efforts to abolish prostitution alternated with attempts to regulate it, neither approach appearing to have been particularly successful.

The Industrial Revolution of the nineteenth century brought with it rapid urbanization* and social instability, leading to growing concentrations of prostitutes in Scandinavian cities. At the same time, however, increased concern about public health and, later, the status of women countered its growth. As early as 1840 Norway adopted a system of regulation which included periodic medical examinations. Abuses of the system and its ineffectiveness in limiting prostitution led to its abrogation in 1888. Equally ineffective attempts at legalizing prostitution were made in Sweden and Denmark during this period. The rules were strict, if not always stringently enforced. Danish prostitutes, for example, were forbidden to approach the royal palace, wear erotic clothing, pose in their windows, or walk together in public places. Those in the Copenhagen* vicinity could not legally leave the area for more than 24 hours without permission from the police. Twice a week they were required to appear for medical examinations. As in Norway, however, regulation failed to produce desirable results. Partly because customers were not subjected to controls, venereal diseases remained a serious problem. The number of legal prostitutes in the Danish capital, about 300 in the early 1870s, more than doubled by the turn of the century; probably as many of their colleagues worked clandestinely without police supervision. Furthermore, then as now an unknown number of housewives supplemented their families' meager incomes by selling sexual favors.

Private organizations such as the Salvation Army and various domestic mission societies associated with the state churches vigorously sought to aid girls from disadvantaged backgrounds and thus prevent them from becoming prostitutes.

Dissatisfaction with regulation of prostitution led to the formation of the British, Continental, and Universal Federation for the Abolition of Prostitution as a Legal and Tolerated Institution under the leadership of the English social reformer Josephine Butler in 1875. Related bodies were constituted in Sweden in 1877 and in Denmark two years later. Owing largely to this international campaign, regulation was abolished in Norway (1895), Denmark (1906), and Sweden (1918). The movement did not succeed, however, in abolishing prostitution as such.

Prostitution thus continues on a generally legal basis in Scandinavia. Pimping is illegal, however, and laws governing vagrancy, public lewdness, age restrictions, and other matters limit the practice somewhat. The relaxation of sexual morality since World War II* and especially since the 1960s has reduced the demand for prostitution, according to some observers. In the early 1980s links between prostitution and narcotics as well as violence to prostitutes were public concerns.

REFERENCE: J. Frykman, *Horan i bondesamhället* (Lund: Liber, 1977; English summary).

F. HALE

Q

QUISLING, VIDKUN (18 July 1887–24 October 1945) Norwegian politician and collaborationist

Already a controversial figure in Norwegian politics during the 1930s, Vidkun Quisling achieved international notoriety during World War II* because of his treasonable activity on behalf of Nazi Germany.

Born in Fyresdal in Telemark, Quisling was the eldest son of a Lutheran pastor. He chose to follow a military career, and because of his high grades, he appeared to have a promising future. Upon graduation from the Military Academy in 1911, he became a junior member of the General Staff, serving also in the field artillery and later as a military attaché in Russia and Finland during 1918–1921. In Russia he abandoned his military career, a move which would have fateful consequences. He was employed as a relief administrator in the Soviet Union and the Balkans by Fridtjof Nansen* during 1922–1926 and later obtained a temporary position with the Norwegian legation in Moscow. Unable to obtain a permanent diplomatic post, he returned to Norway at the end of 1929.

He decided to enter politics and quickly gained a reputation for his strong anti-Socialist views, although previously he had been sympathetic toward socialism and communism while in Russia. Due to influential connections, he was appointed minister of defense in the Agrarian government formed in May 1931. His tenure in office was quite controversial because of his violent anti-Socialist agitation and his inability to get along with his ministerial colleagues. Shortly after the fall of the government, he broke with the Agrarian Party (*see* Center Party: Norway) and agreed to head a new party, National Union* (Nasjonal Samling), commonly known as NS, which originated in May 1933.

National Union did not prove to be the vehicle to power that he had hoped. Following national and local election defeats in 1933 and 1934, he increasingly moved his party away from its original bourgeois (*borgerlig*) anti-Socialist orientation, adopting instead fascist practices similar to those of Hitler and Mussolini. The voters did not respond to NS in 1936, as earlier, failing to elect a single parliamentary representative. Shortly thereafter the party disintegrated, and in the period 1937–1940 Quisling was politically inconsequential. He therefore sought compensation outside Norway's borders and eventually succeeded in establishing contacts with Nazi Germany's political-military hierarchy. Alfred Rosenberg and Grand Admiral Erich Raeder introduced Quisling to Adolf Hitler in December 1939.

Quisling received some financial assistance, but the German invasion of 9 April 1940 was for military purposes, intended to secure the strategically valuable coastline. When the Labor government sought to resist and moved from Oslo, Quisling, on the evening of 9 April, without official German sanction, declared himself head of a government and called on Norwegian military units to surrender. This marked his emergence as an international figure, his name henceforth being synonymous with traitor. His initial "government" gained no support and scarcely functioned. After six days he was forced to step down.

He and his supporters continued to wage a campaign to have him become head of a pro-German government. They were opposed by Reichskommissar Josef Terboven*, who recognized Quisling's lack of ability and unpopularity. The Commissarial Council, established on 25 September 1940, had a majority of NS members, but Quisling did not participate directly. Dominant authority, however, rested with the Reichskommissariat under Terboven's direction.

As leader of the only political organization permitted to exist, Quisling sought to gain as much power as possible over Norwegian society. He believed his chance to establish totalitarian control had arrived when he was allowed to assume the position of minister president as head of an all-NS government in February 1942. He immediately launched an all-out campaign to compel the population to submit to NS domination, but the resultant strong public resistance and unrest compelled the Germans to intervene. In September Hitler sent direct orders to Quisling to abandon his attempt to establish a corporate state.

For the duration of the war, under close German supervision, Quisling cooperated with the Reichskommissariat. However, all the initiatives that he launched, including attempts to recruit Norwegians for the Germans and NS participation in the arrest and deportation of Norwegian Jews, failed to result in greater independence. At the conclusion of the war he was arrested and charged with military and civilian treason, illegally changing the constitution, murder, illegal confiscation, and theft. Found guilty and sentenced to death, with his appeal to the High Court rejected, he was executed by firing squad on 24 October 1945.

REFERENCES: T. Derry, "Norway," in S. Woolf, ed., *European Fascism* (New York: Vintage, 1969); M. Hayes, *The Career and Political Ideas of Vidkun Quisling* (Newton Abbot, Devon: David & Charles, 1971); R. Hewins, *Quisling: Prophet Without Honor* (London: W. H. Allen, 1965); O. Hoidal, "Hjort, Quisling, and *Nasjonal Samling's* Disintegration," *Scandinavian Studies* 47:4 (1975): 467–97, "*Økonomisk Verneplikt* and *Nordiske Folkereisning*: Two Predecessors of *Nasjonal Samling,*" *Scandinavian Studies* 49:4 (1977): 387–411; "The Road to Futility: Vidkun Quisling's Political Career in Prewar

Norway,'' Ph.D. dissertation, University of Southern California, 1970, and ''Vidkun Quisling's Decline as a Political Figure in Prewar Norway, 1933–1937,'' *Journal of Modern History* 43:3 (1971): 440–67; M. Skodvin, ''Norway under Occupation,'' in J. Andenaes et al., *Norway and the Second World War* (Oslo: Johan Grundt Tanum Forlag, 1966).

O. HOIDAL

R

RAILROADS

The first railroads were built in Scandinavia* in the late 1840s and the 1850s. Excluding horse-drawn roads, Denmark led, opening its first line between Copenhagen* and Roskilde in 1847. Norway followed in 1854, Sweden in 1856, and Finland in 1862. Initial growth of lines was relatively slow but understandable given the level of industrial development in Norden and the relative thinness of the capital base. Throughout Scandinavia, lines were built and financed by the states and by private ventures. In Sweden, for example, a policy was adopted by the parliament in 1853 which determined that main lines would be constructed by the state, while trunk lines were to be the responsibility of private companies. Of the approximately 11,000 kilometers of track laid by 1900 in Sweden, about one-third belonged to the state. (State loans were, however, provided to private companies.) This pattern of development continued until 1939, when the parliament passed nationalization legislation which then took about fifteen years to implement.

Sweden has by far the most rail track in Scandinavia (about 13,000 kilometers). Denmark, Finland, and Norway each have between 4,300 and 4,800 kilometers. Most of the railroads in contemporary Scandinavia are state-owned and -operated. The following two sections deal with the development of railroads in Denmark and Norway in greater detail. Although there are variations in each country, these introduce the principal features of the developments throughout Norden. (*See also* Industrialization.)

REFERENCES: E. F. Heckscher, *An Economic History of Sweden*, trans. G. Ohlin (Cambridge, Mass.: Harvard University Press, 1954); L. Jörberg, *The Industrialization of Scandinavia 1850–1914*, trans. P. B. Austin (London: Collins, 1971); E. Nicander, *Järnvägsinvesteringar i Sverige 1849–1914* (Lund: Universitet, 1980).

B. NORDSTROM

Denmark

Denmark's first railroad was built in the 1840s, as a result of developments in north Germany. Following the laying of the Holstein Railroad, which was oriented toward Hamburg, Denmark's fringe position in the north European commercial network, which was oriented along a Hamburg-London axis, was reinforced. This underscored the need for an independent Danish railroad system.

Although the first Danish rail line (within the borders of present-day Denmark) between Roskilde and Copenhagen opened in 1847, it was nearly 30 years (1875) before the principal main line of the network was completed. The following are the most important components of the Danish railroad system:

1856	Sjaelland cross line (*tvaerbane*): Roskilde-Korsør
1862	East Jutland longitudinal line (*laengdebane*): Århus-Randers
1863/4	Mid-Jutland cross line: (Århus)-Langå-Viborg-Skive
1864	North Sjaelland main line: Copenhagen-Hillerød-Helsingør
1865	Fyn cross line: Nyborg-Odense-Middelfart
1866	Jutland cross line: Fredericia-Kolding and Skive-Holstebro
1868	East Jutland longitudinal line: Fredericia-Vejle-Horsens-Århus
1869	East Jutland longitudinal line: Randers-Ålborg
1870	Sjaelland longitudinal line: Roskilde-Køge-Vordingborg
1871	North Jutland longitudinal line: Ålborg-(Nørre Sundby)-Hjørring-Frederikshavn
1872	Falster line: Orehoved (ferry station from Vordingborg)-Nykøbing
1874	Lolland line: Nykøbing-Maribo-(Rødby)-Nakskov
1874	Northwest Sjaelland line: Roskilde-Holbaek-Kalundborg
1874	South Jutland cross line: Kolding-Esbjerg (Bramming-Ribe, 1875)
1875	West Jutland longitudinal line: Esbjerg-Ringkøbing-Holstebro

(Note the terms *tvaerbane* (cross line) and *laengdebane*(longitudinal line. The former applies to lines laid across the country. The latter applies to lines laid lengthwise. They were connected to the system, but they represent different economic interests.)

With the exception of the market towns in southern Fyn, the railroad network then tied together Denmark's most important towns. When the first railroad construction boom occurred in the period after the second Slesvig war (1864), this was due to the political conflicts surrounding the location of the lines. There were two opposing views. One, represented by the capital-commercial interests, called for an east-west cross line oriented toward the English market—one which would free Denmark from Hamburg's influence. The other, represented by agricultural interests, especially those in Jutland, called for a north-south longitudinal line which would connect Denmark with the grain and livestock markets of north Germany.

The Jutland line, completed in the 1870s, was a compromise between these two views. In part it was based on a cross line to Esbjerg, which was completed in 1874. But it was also based on a longitudinal line, built between 1862 and 1871, which was not laid as originally planned through the center of the peninsula, but rather ran through the old market towns along the east coast.

The intense railroad construction between 1864 and 1875 demanded huge amounts of capital and labor. The earliest Danish railroads were financed with foreign capital and were built largely with imported labor—primarily Swedish and German workers and English engineers. But once the Danish capital market developed during the 1860s and 1870s, a significant amount of investment came from Danish sources. The Lolland-Falster line, for example, built between 1872 and 1874, was financed through the Danish Private Bank (Privatbanken). During the 1870s, the migration of people from the rural areas accelerated, and a significant number of the excess rural population found work on the railroads. These migrants were often rather isolated from the general society and were called *børster* (literally "brushes," equivalent to the British term *navvies*).

In the short run, the Danish railroad system did not appear to be a very profitable area for investment, especially when the need for links between the many islands is considered. The first railroad ferry over the Great Belt was connected with the system in 1883. In many cases the state had to take over privately funded companies. In 1874, 33 percent of the railroad system was state-owned. The percentage rose to 43 percent when the Sjaelland Railroad Society was absorbed by the state in 1880.

By the end of 1874, the total length of the railroad network in Denmark was 905 kilometers. Denmark ranked seventh among the European nations in terms of kilometers per 100 square kilometers. After a period of relatively slow growth during the politically and economically troubled 1880s, construction picked up again in the 1890s. A series of railroad laws, passed during the early years of the decade, cleared the way for the addition of a large number of privately owned lines. Compared with 1874, Denmark's railroad network quadrupled by 1906 (3,350 kilometers). The country was then fifth in Europe in terms of railroad density.

While the mainline network principally served the interests of the market towns, the branch lines were laid on the basis of more careful regard for the rural districts' needs for transportation facilities between production areas and markets. Although it can be argued that these lines were the direct result of population density patterns in the rural areas, there is a clear correlation between the railroad layout and the group of small towns that developed in the last two decades of the nineteenth century. The railroads facilitated agriculture's transition to the market economy and to more specialized production, especially of livestock. These changes created new demands for goods and services. This meant that small businesses moved into the countryside, often to those locations where a railroad station met their transportation needs.

Experiments by Ernest W. von Siemens with electrified railroads in Germany in the late 1870s inspired a Danish firm to suggest that the Copenhagen railroads should be electrified as early as 1880. However, it was not until 1934 that the first stretch of "el" railroads was opened, as a result of a 1930 law on the electrification of the inner-city railroads of Copenhagen. In contrast to Norway and Sweden, where water resources have provided energy for a more general electrification of the railroad system, the Danish el railroads have been limited largely to the Copenhagen area. During the 1950s, in connection with the rationalization of the railroads, steam locomotives were abandoned in favor of diesel engines.

A direct result of the development of the communication network was the growth of Esbjerg on the west coast of Jutland. In 1870, four years before the railroad came to Esbjerg, the locality had a population of 30. In 1901, with a population of 13,500, Esbjerg was Denmark's eighth largest town and the most important port in trade with England. A number of other "railroad towns" also developed during this period, often as a result of a single company, frequently engaged in agri-business, moving into an area. (Examples include Vejen in southern Jutland, where a margarine factory was located; Odder, south of Århus, where a pork-processing plant was sited; and Holeby on Lolland, where a sugar beet plant was established.) Most of these urbanized rural towns, however, had fewer than 1,000 residents.

The maximum length of the Danish railroad network, 5,321 kilometers, was reached in 1930. Then, 2,511 kilometers (47 percent) were state-owned. During the 1930s, a few of the less profitable branch lines were closed down. For example, the Central Sjaelland Line, which opened in 1928, discontinued operations in 1936. (Cases of such apparently poor planning were rare, though.) Beginning in the 1950s, a more comprehensive rationalization of the lines and operations within the system was initiated. The centralizing trends in Danish population distribution and production, combined with the popularity of new transportation means, such as the automobile, meant that many of the branch lines to the more thinly populated areas lost their importance for the people and the business community after World War II.* Between 1956 and 1970, an average of two privately owned railroads per year ceased operations. The mainline network remained largely unchanged. In 1971 Denmark had 2,872 kilometers of lines; 2,342 kilometers (82 percent) were part of the Danish State Railroad (De Danske Statsbanet).

REFERENCES: A. Aagesen, *Geografiske Studier over Jernbanerne i Danmark* (Copenhagen: Det kongelige Danske Geografiske Selskab, 1949), English summary; M. Buch and C. Gomard, eds., *Danmarks Jernbaner. Historisk og Biografisk Haandbog*, 2 vols. (Copenhagen: A. Kappels Forlag, 1933); *De Danske Statsbaner* (Copenhagen: Generaldirektoratet for Statsbanerne, 1947); C. R. Jansen, ed., *Stationsbyen, rapport fra et seminar om stationsbyens historie 1840–1940* (Århus: Universitetsforlag, 1980); J. Koed et al., eds., *Danmarks Jernbaner i 125 år* (Copenhagen, 1972); K. H. Pedersen, *Kampen om Kertemindebanen. En undersøgelse af anlaeggelsen af en privatbane i 1890' erne* (Odense: Historisk Samfund for Fyns Stift, 1978); V. D. Rasmussen, *Nørrejyske Jernbanebyer. Udvalgte problemer omkring placeringen og befolkningsudviklingen1850–1901* (Århus: Universitetsforlag, 1981); B. Thomas and B. Nüchel Thomsen, *Anglo-Danish Trade 1661–1963* (Århus: Universitetsforlag, 1966).

N. P. STILLING

Norway

The first railroad in the Scandinavian peninsula was opened on 1 September 1854. "The Main Line" (Hovedbanen) was 68 kilometers long and ran between Christiania (Oslo) and Eidsvoll, a village on the south end of Norway's largest inland lake, Mjøsa.

As has so often been the case in Norwegian economic history, it was impulses from outside Norway that resulted in this early railroad development. The drastic reduction of the English tariffs in the 1840s resulted in an increase in the export of Norwegian timber. Within Norway, however, there was a transport problem. Moving timber from inner Østland to the port of Christiania was slow and expensive. Consequently, it was the most important timber dealers in the capital city who initiated the planning of the line and who were the major subscribers to the shares in the company. Their foresight proved to be well grounded. The cost of the shipping of timber by train was 50–60 percent below the cost of transport by horse and sled, but the line still ran at a profit.

After this early start, railroad building in Norway stagnated until the 1870s. Then, between 1875 and 1883 about 1,000 kilometers of track were laid, representing a trebling of the track mileage in Norway. In the late 1880s construction slowed again, but picked up once more in the early 1890s. By 1910 the most important lines had been laid, and Norway had essentially the rail network which remains in place today. In 1910 there were 3,085 kilometers of track, a figure that increased to 4,242 kilometers by 1983. Of central importance in the growth after 1910 was the construction of the lines between Oslo and Stavanger and between Trondheim and Bodø.

Principal Rail Lines

Oslo-Eidsvoll	1854	68km
Oslo-Sweden (via Halden)	1879	170km
Oslo-Trondheim	1880	561km
Narvik-Sweden	1902	41km
Oslo-Bergen	1909	493km
Oslo-Stavanger	1944	585km
Trondheim-Bodø	1962	728km

The uneven tempo of construction during the nineteenth century was linked with fluctuations in the country's economy and with state financial policies. Traditionally, state expenditures were balanced against incomes. There was no income tax before 1892, and until then import duties were a central source of income. State finances, and especially the part of the budget that was used for capital investments, were tied directly to fluctuations in trade levels. During recessions railroad construction nearly stopped.

During the early stages of railroad development both the state and the private sector were involved. However, the state came to play an increasingly important role, and after passage of legislation in 1897 the private companies were gradually absorbed. It was not, however, until the 1920s that the railroads became the monopoly of the state which they remain today.

While the need for transportation facilities to handle the volume of the timber trade encouraged the development of the first railroad in Norway, there were other products which played an important role later. From its beginning in 1902, for example, the transport of iron ore (amounting to about 30 percent of the freight carried) was central on the Ofot Line, which linked Narvik with the Swedish iron ore mines. Also, while the establishment of the first railroad (The Main Line) was a response to demand, in the sense that the line came as an answer to a cumulative transport problem, later development was more speculative. Lines were often built in the hope that they would trigger new economic activity and needs. The so-called Randsfjord Line is an example of this. It was operated at a significant loss between 1869 and 1877.

The railroads often acted as stimulators of related developments. For example, along the lines "station towns" appeared, which frequently grew into industrial or commercial towns. During the most important building phase in Norwegian railroad history, the number of towns increased from 127 in 1875 to 260 in 1910. The growth of the rail junction at Lillestrøm, north of Oslo, illustrates such development. In 1875 the town had a population of 1,150. Thirty-five years later the figure was 4,350.

The railroads also opened up many isolated rural communities. They brought optimistic youth to industrial towns, and for many the railroad was the first step on the road across the Atlantic. Imports, like the cheap rye which flowed over Norwegian communities, were easily carried by train. In 1869, 7,000 tons of flour were transported by rail from the countryside to town, while 260,000 tons went from towns to the countryside. The railroads were a central factor behind the transition of Norwegian farming from grain production to meat and milk production.

Railroad construction workers and employees of the railroads were paid higher wages than their fellow villagers, and for many small farmers and householders the railroads were social springboards into better-paying jobs. The railroads' size meant that they would play a central role in the labor market. As early as 1880, about 1,700 persons were employed by railroads in Norway—in addition to all those employed in construction. By comparison, the country's largest industrial concern, Nydalen Company in Oslo, had 983 workers in 1885.

Persons Employed by the Railroads

Year	Full-Time	Temporary	Total
1880	1,700		
1890	2,800		
1900	4,500		
1910	6,400		
1920	11,000		
1930	10,700	4,400	15,100
1940	12,300	8,200	20,500
1950	18,600	8,800	27,400
1960	19,100	4,100	23,200
1970	17,000	1,700	18,700
1983			16,900

Until 1925 the railroads carried more passengers than freight. Between 1925 and World War II, passengers and freight traded places in importance. During the war passengers again were most important, but this pattern was reversed once more in the postwar period. Statistics for 1983 show 2175.1 million passenger-kilometers against 2398.4 million ton-kilometers for goods.

When the automobile made its appearance in the 1920s and began to give the railroads some competition, the tempo of construction slowed. Less-traveled routes could, in many cases, be more economically served by cars or trucks, and the rail routes that had been marked for expansion during the interwar years were replaced by highways. In the period between 1946 and 1975 the railroads' share of total passenger traffic declined from 45 percent of the total to 6 percent. This relative decline occurred in spite of a slight increase in the absolute number of passenger-kilometers on the railroads. The explosive growth in automobile transport reduced the railroads' relative importance drastically. The railroads' share of the ton-kilometers in freight also sank, from 16 percent in 1946 to 8 percent in 1975.

The competition from motor carriers led to pressure for rationalization in the direction of faster and cheaper rail transport. Norway's first electric line, the Thamshavn Line (a private, narrow-gauge line in the Trøndelag), opened in 1908, but electrification of Norway's main lines did not catch on completely before World War II. Diesel locomotives already had begun to replace the old steam-driven engines, but the abundance of cheap electrical power made the transition to electrically driven engines all the more feasible. Also, the change-over to electric power resulted in a decline in the cost per locomotive by more than half. Still, in 1983 only 58 percent of the lines had been electrified.

In competition with cars and later with airplanes, the railroads have had to exploit their advantages: their ability to carry, at low cost, large quantities of goods or passengers over long distances. A large number of the smaller, less used stations have been closed, and this trend continues. In 1974 there were 309 in operation. By 1983 the number had fallen to 233. At the same time, the number of employees in the system has been reduced. In 1950 Norges Statsbaner was the country's largest employer, with 27,400 employees. This figure dropped to 16,900 in 1983. In spite of strong reasons for rationalization, NS has been forced through local political pressure to maintain some less-traveled routes. Since 1920 the company has operated at a loss, but the most significant losses have come since World War II. These have generally been covered by subsidies from state funds (amounting to about 30 percent of NS's budget in 1983). That NS must be supported by subsidies is not due only to concessions made to local politicians. It is seen to be "socially economical" to run the rail industry at a loss.

REFERENCES: T. Børrehaug Hansen et al., *Jernbanen i Norge* (Oslo: Pax Forlag, 1980); H. Gundersen, *Jernbane og stat* (Department of Sociology, University of Bergen, 1977), and *NSB, med Linjegods i lasten* (Oslo: Pax Forlag, 1975); F. Hodne, *Norges økonomiske historia 1815–1970* (Oslo: J. W. Cappelens Forlag, 1981); B. A. Marthinsen, *NSB og urbaniseringsprosessen* (Department of Geography, University of Bergen, 1976);

E. Østvedt, *De norske jernbanets historia*, 3 vols. (Oslo: Norges Statsbaner, 1954); F. Sejersted, "En teori om den økonomiske utvikling i Norge i det 19. århundrede," stencil (University of Oslo, 1973); T. C. Wyller, *Ta plass! NSB 1920–1980* (Oslo: J. W. Cappelens Forlag, 1982).

G. H. SJØTRØ

RED BOOK (Swedish Liturgy of 1576)

Olaus Petri* and his brother, Laurentius, who both had studied at Wittenberg during the early reforming career of Luther, in the 1520s introduced to Sweden a very conservative version of the Lutheran Reformation.* Actually it was not until 1593 that the Church of Sweden formally subscribed to the *Augsburg Confession**, being content with the royal injunction that advocated the preaching of the evangelical faith in accordance with the Holy Scriptures.

Changes in the Church of Sweden liturgy were only gradually implemented, the most radical being the vernacular *Swedish Mass* of Olaus Petri in 1531, modeled after Luther's *German Mass*. When Laurentius Petri was named archbishop of Uppsala the same year, sufficient opposition postponed the official adoption of a church ordinance until 1571, by which time the archbishop had outlived most of his opposition. After Petri's death in 1573, the Swedish king, Johan III*, issued a revised liturgy in 1576 known as the *Red Book* because of the color of its binding.

Though accepted at first by the clergy, tremendous opposition developed to its usage, especially after the divulgence of the Crypto-Catholicism of Johan III and the Jesuit* Swedish Mission in 1580. Actually the work of Petrus Fecht and the king, the *Red Book*, which restored the ancient pericopes and made extensive use of Latin, was seen as high church and Romanizing in its emphases. In 1593 the Church Assembly of Uppsala rejected the *Red Book* and re-established the liturgy of Laurentius Petri found in the Church Ordinance of 1571. Characterized by some as unLutheran, others (especially Anglicans) have viewed the *Red Book* as a liturgical masterpiece tragically consigned to historical oblivion.

T. R. SKARSTEN

REFORMATION

Denmark

Denmark's breach with Rome was founded upon a series of drastic measures taken at the end of a two-year civil war (*see* Count's War) by the newly elected King Christian III* and the estates of his realm (*Diet/Herredag*), which met in Copenhagen* in the latter half of October 1536. Then the king's imprisonment of the Danish bishops in the concluding phase of the civil war found its legal approbation, the Catholic hierarchy as such was abolished in Denmark, and preparations were made for a new Church and School Ordinance to be promulgated in 1539.

Danish Protestantism on the eve of the Reformation remains, however, somewhat difficult to define. There had been the commanding example of Martin

Luther, but Danish preachers of the Gospel prior to 1536 seem also to have been decisively influenced by the position of Ulrich Zwingli. Such preachers had been working independently of the diocesan bishops and their clergy, founding themselves instead upon a royal charter given to them individually without previous acknowledgment on the part of ecclesiastical hierarchy.

Foremost among Danish theologians in the decades up to the Reformation was Paulus Helie, reader in theology at the University of Copenhagen and provincial prior of the Carmelite Order. Strongly influenced by Erasmus of Rotterdam, he had been the master of the most brilliant among the evangelical preachers, was well founded in Holy Scripture, and was critical of contemporary Church practices. He sided with the pope in the end, however. He probably died before 1536 and left behind him works on Biblical theology and the ardent chronicle of his times (called *Chronicon Skibyense* after the place where the manuscript was found almost a century later).

The clear-cut Lutheran imprint of the final acts corresponds rather insufficiently to the religious situation and the theological debate prior to 1536. It may well have been directly imposed by the king, who for the two years 1537–1539 called in Johannes Bugenhagen, the Wittenberg theologian, to revise his draft for the Church Ordinance and counsel Danish Lutheran clergy with regard to its implementation.

Formal relations with the Holy See had already ceased by the mid-1520s, when King Frederik I* decreed that financial contributions hitherto made by the Danish clergy directly to Rome henceforth were to be taken up by the royal fisc. At the same time, Mendicant convents in Danish cities were allowed to pass under municipal authority, with a view to their eventual transformation into secular hospitals or other social institutions. Two diets in Odense in 1526 and 1527 constituted a *de facto* substitution of papal authority by royal authority over the Church of Denmark. What occurred in 1526 was thus primarily a political event, representing also the final breach with Rome, but being based upon elements of a considerably earlier date.

The Count's War had been one of succession rather than one of confession. When Frederik I died on 10 April 1533, no successor had as yet been elected, and the previous king, Christian II*, who in 1523 had left his realm confronted with strong aristocratic opposition, was now in royal custody due to an unsuccessful attempt on his part to regain power by an invasion of southern Norway in the winter of 1531–1532. He was the nephew of Frederik I and the brother-in-law of Emperor Charles V. Even if Christian II was never highly esteemed by the Habsburgs, his eventual restitution was a matter of clear political, if not confessional, consequence. He had, in his day, favored Lutheran and bourgeois elements, but the question of Church reform had not become imminent during his reign.

Councilors of the realm, ecclesiatical and secular, assembled in Copenhagen in the summer of 1533—summoned there before the king's death and for the moment deprived of consultation with their Norwegian colleagues. They voted a one-year postponement of the royal election and established themselves as a government *ad interim*. They may have differed among themselves as to which of King Frederik's sons they would support, or they may have wanted to play for time in view of the threat which the still imprisoned king Christian II represented. Whichever was the case, the royal election was impeded by an invasion of Sjaelland the following summer (on Christian's behalf) by the counts Christoffer of Oldenburg and Albrekt of Mecklenburg. They had the strong financial support of the city of Lübeck and succeeded quickly in conquering both Sjaelland and Skåne, with their important cities, Malmö and Copenhagen.

Now the eldest son of King Frederik, Duke Christian of Slesvig and Holstein (Christian III), threw himself into the war and obtained election as king of Denmark from the councilors of Jutland and Fyn, while Count Christoffer was receiving allegiance in Sjaelland and Skåne in the name of Christian II. Within a year, Christian III had won the upper hand, being in a position also, as duke of Slesvig and Holstein, to put pressure on Lübeck. In late 1535 he had only to conquer Copenhagen, which finally capitulated on 29 July 1536, after a year-long siege.

On the morning of 12 August 1536, Christian took the drastic step of arresting all seven Danish bishops. They were held in prison until after the meeting of the diet in October. He took this action only after consultation with the secular members of the council, who were, however, also under threat of being similarly imprisoned if they did not sanction the king's decisions. The immediate cause of the sudden action against the bishops, which gave them no opportunity for discussions, was that they had refused (or were likely to refuse) Church funding of the king's war expenses. The overall consequence of their subsequent deposition, confirmed by the diet in October, was that from the day of their capture episcopal lands in Denmark came to be administered directly by the crown. Most of the bishops were released in late 1536 or during 1537, to lead secular lives on their estates. Two of them, Roskilde and Børglum, who had been the king's most stubborn adversaries, were held until 1542. Børglum was released, while Roskilde died in prison.

The Church and School Ordinance of 1539 installed a superintendent in each diocese and a provost in each county (*herred*), who were made responsible for conducting the inner transformation of the Church. Superintendents were to have a decent income but were in no position, as the Catholic bishops had been, to live as feudal lords. Each superintendent should, at his earliest convenience, visit the parish churches of his diocese and advise the communities as to their lives in the future. With the king's chief representative in each region, the superintendent was also authorized, if necessary, to regulate parish churches' finances. In general, however, parish economic matters were not touched by the Reformation, apart from the fact that the bishops' third of the tithes henceforth were given to the crown and were destined for school and university purposes.

The unchallenged leader of the Lutheran Church of Denmark in its first decades was Peder Palladius, a brilliant Danish student of theology at Wittenberg from 1530 to 1537, who had been strongly favored by Philip Melanchthon and Johann Bugenhagen. King Christian III made him superintendent in the large diocese of Roskilde, while active participants in the previous Danish reform movement obtained less important dioceses. An autographed outline of the contents, religious and moral, of Palladius's first evangelical visit to Sjaelland is preserved and bears witness to his zeal.

While the religious convents in Danish cities had, for the most part, been under transformation since the 1520s, the great landowning monasteries were now, like the secular church, placed under royal dominion. Recruitment ceased immediately, but with regard to the monasteries' futures, the king normally deferred his decision until the last member of such communities had died. Meanwhile, he put some of the monasteries to use as theological seminaries of a sort in keeping with the emphasis in the Reformation on efforts to improve the educational level of the parish clergy.

Preaching in the vernacular had been an important feature of the Church in Denmark since the fifteenth century. Now, the Reformation presented an immediate occasion to provide for a Danish translation of the Bible, which was published in 1550, and to develop a liturgy in Danish. (A Danish altar book was published in 1556.) All of these also represent a decisive phase in the development of the Danish language. The University of Copenhagen, which had existed since 1479, was now reorganized and more richly endowed (with former Church property), so that the Reformation constitutes this university's second (and more important) foundation. (*See also* Tausen, Hans.)

REFERENCES: J. O. Andersen, *Overfor Kirkebruddet* (Copenhagen: J. H. Schultz, 1917); N. K. Andersen, *Confessio Hafniensis. Den Kobenhavnske bekendelse af 1530* (Copenhagen: G. E. C. Gads forlag, 1949); *Danmarks Historie*, vol. 2 (Copenhagen: Glydendals, 1980); K. Hørby, *Reformationen i Danmark. Udvalgte kilder* (Copenhagen: Gyldendals, 1972), and *Reformationens indforelse i Danmark* (Copenhagen: Munksgaard, 1968); L. Jacobsen, ed., *Peder Palladius: En Visitatsbog* (Copenhagen: H. H. Thieles, 1925); B. Kornerup, *Den danske Kirkes Historie*, vol. 3 (Copenhagen: Gyldendal, 1965); M. Kristensen and N. K. Andersen, eds., *Skrifter af Paulus Helie*, vols. 1–7 (Place and publisher not available, 1932–1948); P. G. Lindhardt, *Den danske Kirkes Historie*, vol. 4 (Copenhagen: Gyldendal, 1959), and *Nederlagets Mænd* (Copenhagen: G. E. C. Gads forlag, 1968); H. F. Rordam, ed., *Danske Kirkelov 1536–1683* (Copenhagen: Selskabet for Danmarks kirkehistorie and G. E. C. Gads forlag, 1883–1889); P. Severinsen, *Hvordan Reformationen indførtes i Danmark* (Copenhagen: O. Lohse, 1936).

K. HØRBY

Finland

The Reformation in Finland followed a pattern largely dictated by events in Sweden. At a meeting of a *riksdag* at Västerås) in 1527, King Gustav I Vasa* forced through an edict (Edict of Västerås) that destroyed the autonomy and power of the old Church in Sweden and Finland. The independence of the

Church was replaced with dependence upon the crown. The property of the Church was, over the span of the following 20 years, confiscated either by the crown or by the nobility, which was given the right to reclaim donations made to the Church since 1454. The legal autonomy and power of the Church were eliminated. Selection of the archbishop and bishops was given over entirely to the crown. In effect, the edict produced a state church. Doctrinally, however, the Västerås meeting settled nothing. The edit stipulated only that the clergy must preach the pure word of God. In effect, this meant that Sweden and Finland were set adrift for nearly the next 70 years, and religion, in Sweden especially, was at the whim of the monarch. It was not until the Uppsala Meeting in 1593 that the *Augsburg Confession** was adopted as the statement of faith for Sweden and Finland.

The Lutheran Reformation of Finland was, as in Sweden, a gradual and conservative process. There was little basis for anything else in Finland. There was no widespread discontent with the Church or the clergy. The attacks common in Germany on the worldliness or corruption of the Church had little relevance. No mass popular movement ever developed for the Reformation. Instead, it was effected from above by the gradual education of the clergy and the equally gradual penetration of the new faith through religious literature in the vernacular.

The earliest Lutheran preaching in Finland had two centers: Åbo/Turku and Viborg/Viipuri. The dominant center of the Reformation came to be Åbo. There the earliest figure was Peder Särhilahti, the son of a nobleman. He had studied in Germany and came to teach at the Åbo cathedral school in 1523. Of greater significance was Mikael Agricola (1510–1557). He studied at Viborg and came to Åbo in 1528. He worked for and with the new bishop, Martin Skytte. (Skytte is a paradoxical figure. He was a Catholic, trained as a Dominican. He was, however, inclined toward reform in the Church and was influenced by the humanists of the period.) Between 1528 and 1557, Agricola shaped the emergence of Lutheranism* in Finland. He taught at the academy and became principal of the school. He served as secretary to and assistant of Skytte. He traveled widely in the country. In 1554 he succeeded Skytte as bishop. Over the years he translated the New Testament, parts of the Old Testament, the prayer book, a clerical manual, and works of Luther and other reformers into Finnish. (He is also credited with being the father of the Finnish language, although there were earlier religious translations.)

Most sources emphasize the gradualness and conservative nature of the Lutheran Reformation in Finland. Many of the old beliefs and practices were not swept away. Agricola combined ideas of the new faith with the old. He retained emphases on the mystery of the mass, fasting, confession, and absolution, for example. At the same time, he mixed with these the ideas of justification by faith and belief in the capacity of the individual to understand the word of God. By his death, the country had been largely reformed.

REFERENCES: N. K. Andersen, *NCMH*, vol. 2; E. Jutikkala, *A History of Finland*, trans. P. Sjöblom (New York: Praeger, 1962); J. Wuorinen, *A History of Finland* (New York: Columbia University Press, 1965).

B. NORDSTROM

Iceland

The Reformation in Iceland is inextricably tied to political events in Denmark. The people of Iceland had no real complaint against the Church as such and were basically satisfied with her ministry. Considerable opposition was therefore encountered when Christian III sought to introduce the Lutheran Reformation into Iceland. The story of the Reformation in Iceland can be divided into three phases, namely, the gaining of control of each of the two Icelandic bishoprics at Skálholt and Holar, and the eventual consolidation of the evangelical Reformation throughout Iceland.

When German merchants first introduced the writings of Luther into Iceland, both Roman Catholic bishops united their efforts to stamp out the Lutheran heresy. Nevertheless, Icelanders who had studied abroad continued to spread the evangelical doctrines among their fellow countrymen. In 1540 Oddur Gottskalksson published the first Icelandic translation of the New Testament in Roskilde, Denmark. That same year Christian III sent two warships to Iceland and brought the aged and blind Bishop Ogmundur Palsson of Skálholt as a prisoner to Denmark. His heir apparent, Gissur Einarsson (1540–1548), who had been educated in Germany, became the first Lutheran bishop of Skálholt in 1540. The next year, under Danish pressure, the Althing* (Icelandic parliament) adopted an Icelandic version of Bugenhagen's Church Ordinance.

Upon the death of Gissur Einarsson in 1548, Bishop Jon Arason of Holar tried to step into the vacant diocese and restore the old order, but the clergy elected Martein Einarsson (1549–1597), a young Lutheran pastor, who went to Denmark for further study and was consecrated in 1549 by Peder Palladius. Upon Bishop Martein's return to Iceland he was captured by soldiers of Bishop Jon Arason. Such insubordination the Danish Lutheran king could not tolerate, and Danish troops were dispatched to Iceland. On 7 November 1550 Bishop Jon Arason and two of his sons were beheaded. The bishop was never canonized because of his non-canonical marriage. Nevertheless, he and his sons died as martyrs for the Roman Catholic faith and are today lionized as Icelandic national patriots.

With Lutheran bishops now incumbent in both Icelandic bishoprics, the third and final phase of consolidating the Lutheran Reformation in Iceland commenced. In Skálholt, Bishop Gisli Jonsson (1558–1587) placed great emphasis on Christian education and ordered his pastors to visit all the homes in their parishes and systematically catechize the youth. Danish teachers were also invited to lecture in the cathedral school. But the greatest achievement in consolidating the Reformation belongs to Bishop Gudbrandur Thorlaksson, who was the Lutheran bishop of Holar for 56 years (1570–1627). On a new printing press, he published the complete Icelandic translation of the Bible (*Gudbrandsbiblia*) in 1584, said to be a masterpiece in Icelandic literature. A *Hymn Book* (1589) was reprinted and used for over two centuries, as was a liturgical worship manual (*Grallarinn*) published in 1594. Altogether, 84 works were published by Bishop Gudbrandur to aid Icelandic pastors in their work so as to make Lutheran Christianity a living force in the life of the people.

REFERENCE: Knut Gjerset, *History of Iceland* (New York: Macmillan Co., 1924).

T. R. SKARSTEN

Norway

The Reformation in Norway is intimately tied to political events in Denmark. It was unable to shake off the Kalmar Union* in the sixteenth century as had Sweden, and Norwegian nationalism and patriotism sank to an all-time low. Norway seemed content to be a province of Denmark along with Jutland, Fyn, and Zealand. The last vestige of Norwegian nationalism resided in Olaf Engelbrektsson, archbishop of Nidaros (Trondheim). But when he fled to the Netherlands in 1537, the final hope for a resurgence of Norwegian nationalism under Roman Catholic leadership disappeared and the way was clear for the introduction of the Lutheran Reformation by the Danish king, Christian III.* Thus the Reformation came to Norway not as a grass-roots awakening but as an imposition by royal decree on 30 October 1536 along with the principle that was to become known as *cuius regio eius religio* (whoever the king, his religion).

The Norwegian Reformation may be said to have taken place in three phases. The first phase, from 1526 to 1537, was a time when roving evangelical preachers established small pockets of Lutheran adherents here and there throughout Norway. A monk by the name of Antonius was the first to preach the evangelical faith in Norway in 1526 among the German merchants of the Hanseatic city of Bergen. Danish government officials like Vincent Lunge stationed in southern Norway were sympathetic to the Reformation. In 1529 the bishop of Stavanger complained of Lutherans in his diocese. Even in the far northern province of Finnmark, merchants and fishermen spread the evangelical faith.

The second phase of the Reformation in Norway occurred in 1537. With the end of the Danish Civil War (Count's War,* 1533–1536) and the victory of the fervent Lutheran king, Christian III (1536–1559), not only did the Norwegian archbishop flee, but a new Church Ordinance drawn up by Johann Bugenhagen of Wittenberg was imposed upon Norway that same year. By the end of 1537 Norway had received a new evangelical king, a new Lutheran Church Ordinance, and an evangelical Lutheran superintendent (bishop) of Bergen in the person of Geble Pedersson. The year 1537 therefore marks the transition from a Roman Catholic to an evangelical Lutheran political power base in Norway and the establishment of a national evangelical church.

The final phase of the Reformation in Norway occurred during the century that followed 1537. This phase was marked by a slow, often unnoticed, educational process of training in evangelical Christianity. Bugenhagen's Church Ordinance stipulated that every parish pastor own a copy of the Bible, Luther's

Postils, the Apology to the *Augsburg Confession*, the *Loci communes* of Melanchthon, Luther's Small and Large Catechisms, the Saxon Visitation Articles, and the Church Ordinance itself. These became valuable tools for the continuing education of both clergy and laity alike which evangelical bishops of Norway like Jorgen Ericksson and Absalon Pedersson Beyer utilized to good advantage in their episcopal visitations. Study abroad in Lutheran universities, especially Wittenberg, and the establishment of Lutheran cathedral schools in each of the dioceses aided the process of theological transformation, as did the new evangelical liturgy of Wormordsen (1539) and the ongoing catechetical instruction from the pulpit during the worship services each week. Little by little, the Reformation took root, though pastors like Peder Clausson Friis were aghast to find remnants of Roman Catholicism still entrenched in southern Norway in the early seventeenth century.

REFERENCES: K. E. Christophersen, "Hallelujahs, Damnations, or Norwegian Reformation as Lengthy Process," *Church History* 48 (September 1979): 279–89; Carl Fr. Wisløff, *Norsk Kirkehistorie* (Oslo: Lutherstiftelsen, 1966).

T. R. SKARSTEN

Sweden

As the Reformation era dawned, Sweden was chafing under the Kalmar Union, which had long been dominated by Denmark. All through the fifteenth century leaders like Karl (VIII) Knutsson*, Sten Sture*, and Sten Svantesson "Sture"* had led Sweden in abortive revolts against Danish rule. In 1520 Christian II of Denmark, with the tacit assent of Gustav Trolle, the Danish archbishop of Uppsala, sought to eliminate the Swedish opposition in one fell swoop through what has come to be known as the "Stockholm Bloodbath" in which over 80 leading Swedish noblemen were beheaded, two of whom were bishops.

Under Gustav I Vasa* (1523–1560) the Swedish people rose in rebellion against Danish tyranny. They were successful in their rebellion, and Gustav Vasa was elected at Strängnäs in 1523 to be king of an independent Sweden. At Strängnäs the new king's attention was directed by his secretary, Laurentius Andreae, to the preaching of the young evangelical archdeacon, Olaus Petri*, and a lifelong association commenced.

It was Olaus Petri (1493–1552) who had introduced the Reformation teaching of Martin Luther to Sweden in 1518. He had arrived in Wittenberg in 1516 just as Luther was commencing his lectures on Galatians and experienced firsthand the excitement surrounding the Indulgence Controversy leading up to the posting of the 95 Theses on 31 October 1517. In late 1518 he returned to Sweden, an ardent disciple of the Wittenberg monk who had expounded the evangelical faith so clearly.

There was no thought of a break with Rome. Luther had not yet met John Eck at Leipzig. Tracts like "The Babylonian Captivity of the Church," to say nothing of the *Augsburg Confession*, were still far in the future. The Reformation which Olaus Petri, "the Luther of Sweden," introduced into Sweden was a very conservative reforming movement reflecting the reformatory principles of the very early Luther. Together with his younger brother, Laurentius Petri (1499–1573), who had also studied at Wittenberg, and their new friend Laurentius Andreae, a gradual, century-long ecclesiastical transformation of the Swedish Church and society got under way. The Petri brothers saw no need for a confessional subscription, as they were convinced that all that was needed was to give the pure Word of God free reign and the Church would have the solid foundation it needed. *Sola scriptura* was all the Church or any individual needed for salvation. That was what they had learned from their famous mentor in Wittenberg.

During the 1520s Gustav Vasa was hard pressed to keep the Swedish ship of state afloat. There was the huge debt owed to Lübeck for its help in the revolution (1520–1523). Many favored the "old Faith" and supported sporadic rebellions such as those which broke out in Dalarna in 1527. Rome would offer no positive reform suggestions except to reinstate Gustav Trolle as archbishop of Uppsala, and that was out of the question. Seemingly frustrated every way he turned, Gustav Vasa suddenly resigned as king in 1527.

At a hastily called meeting of the estates at Västerås, Gustav Vasa was prevailed upon to withdraw his resignation. Agreement was reached that effectively severed the Church of Sweden from Rome and gave its income to the king to help repay the Lübeck debt. The uprising in Dalarna was to be suppressed. The clergy were to be governed by civil law. All property given to the Church after 1454 was to revert to the lawful secular heirs. Complaints against the "new Faith" were to cease provided that the Word of God was preached in its purity. These decrees of the Diet of Västerås in 1527 proved to be some of the most important and significant in Swedish history.

In the meantime, Olaus Petri, who had been called to the city parish in Stockholm* in 1524, was hard at work implementing the evangelical Reformation. Two years after his arrival in Stockholm, he published a catechetical instruction book and a Swedish translation of the New Testament. Polemical works against Paul Helie (the Erasmus of Denmark) followed in 1527–1528. In 1529 Olaus Petri produced the first Protestant *Manual* to assist clergy in their pastoral acts. A Swedish *Hymnbook* came out the following year, and in 1531 he published the *Swedish Mass*. That same year Petrus Magni, the Roman Catholic bishop of Västerås, ordained Olaus Petri's younger brother, Laurentius, to be the archbishop of Uppsala. Thus apostolic succession was maintained in the Church of Sweden, and Laurentius Petri became the first Lutheran archbishop of Uppsala. The fruition of his long career (1531–1573) came in 1571 with the passage of the Church Ordinance for which he had worked so long. During the reign of Erik XIV* (1560–1568), Laurentius had been frustrated on several occasions from achieving his goal by the king's Calvinist sympathies.

Three years after Laurentius Petri's death (1573), Johan III* (1569–1592) revised the liturgy of the venerable archbishop with the publication of his *Red Book**. Strong opposition was aroused because of its high church and romanizing tendencies especially after the secret Jesuit* mission in Sweden was uncovered in 1580. The controversy over the liturgy reached its height when Johan III died in 1592. The specter of his Roman Catholic son, Sigismund*, becoming king of Sweden awakened both nationalistic fervor and great anxiety in the hearts of most Swedes. Known as "the King of the Jesuits," Sigismund, son of a Polish princess, had already been elected king of Poland in 1587. St. Bartholomew's Massacre and stories of "Bloody" Mary's reign in England provided ample evidence of what a fanatical Roman Catholic king in Sweden might do.

Under the leadership of Sigismund's Protestant uncle (crowned Karl IX* in 1604), a Church Assembly was convened at Uppsala in 1593. Laurentius Petri's Church Ordinance was reinstated, the *Red Book* was rejected, and for the first time the *Augsburg Confession* was officially subscribed to as the doctrinal basis for the Church of Sweden, thus compelling future monarchs to declare themselves in agreement with the Lutheran faith. Though Sigismund, on the advice of his Jesuit counselors, subscribed to the *Augsburg Confession*, his blatant hypocrisy alienated would-be supporters. After his military defeat at Stångebro in 1598, his position became untenable and he withdrew to Poland, never to set foot on Swedish soil again. As the sixteenth century came to a close, the ecclesiastical transformation of a self-consciously Roman Catholic people to an ardent Lutheran nation was complete.

REFERENCES: Bo Ahlberg, *Laurentius Petris Nattvards Uppfattning* (Lund: Gleerup, 1964); Conrad Bergendoff, *Olavus Petri* (Philadelphia: Fortress Press, 1965); Oskar Garstein, *Rome and the Counter-Reformation in Scandinavia*, 2 vols. (Oslo: Universitetsforlaget, 1963, 1980); Sven Ingebrand, *Olavus Petris Reformatoriska Åskådning* (Lund: Gleerup, 1964); Michael Roberts, *The Early Vasas* (Cambridge, England: Cambridge University Press, 1968); Eric Yelverton, *An Archbishop of the Reformation* (Minneapolis: Augsburg Publishing House, 1959).

T. R. SKARSTEN

RELIGION Faroe Islands*

Practically nothing is known about heathen worship in the Faroe Islands, beyond the place-name Hov in Suðuroy, which seems to indicate the site of a temple, and Tórshavn* and Hósvík (Thor's harbor and Thor's creek), which are probably related in some way to the popular heathen god.

There seems little reason to doubt the statement in *Færeyinga Saga* that Christianity was accepted in the Faroe Islands at about the same time as in Iceland. A bishopric was established about 1100, the see being in Kirkjubøur* at the southern end of Streymoy. The names of 33 pre-Reformation bishops are known, but little more is recorded of most of them. However, a school was early attached to the see, at which, during the episcopate of the sixth bishop, Rói (1162–1178), King Sverre of Norway (*see* Sverrir Sigurdsson) (reigned 1184–1202) got his priestly education. The bishops were normally elected by the chapter of Bergen archiepiscopate.

The most celebrated bishop of the Roman Catholic period was Erlendr* (consecrated 1269, died 1308), who enriched the Faroese Church considerably and was responsible for the building of the impressive but unroofed Magnus Cathedral. The last Roman Catholic bishop was Amundr Ólavsson, elected for some reason by the Faroese, the choice being confirmed by King Frederik I* and not by the pope. He was deposed at some time between 1538 and 1540, when the reformed faith was proclaimed throughout the islands, meeting with little or no opposition.

The single Lutheran bishop of Kirkjuböur, Jens Gregersön Riber, took over in 1540, but in 1557 he was translated to the bishopric of Stavanger. The see of Kirkjuböur was abolished, and the immense landed wealth of the Church (some 40 percent of all the land in the islands) fell to the crown. The Faroe Islands now became a deanery, under a provost subject to the bishops of Bergen until about 1620, subsequently to the bishops of Sjaelland.

There were seven pastorates in the Faroe Islands from the Reformation* onwards, each priest having a glebe farm for his support. The provost had an extra farm in Oyndarfjörður on Eysturoy. From 1632, each priest was allotted a second farm, which, together with tithes and other income, made them among the wealthiest men in the country. A law of 1673 provided that the second farm of each pastorate should support the widow or widows of previous incumbents, on condition of not remarrying and remaining chaste. The normal practice, however, as in Denmark proper, was for the incoming priest to marry his predecessor's widow. Most of the priests were Danes, but occasionally Faroese boys would go from the Tórshavn Latin School to Copenhagen University and take over livings in the islands.

The language of worship in the Faroe Islands was Danish. The seven priests served a total of 39 churches. When the priest was not present for a Sunday service, his place would be taken by the deacon, usually a local farmer. Instead of preaching a sermon, he would read from a book of Danish homilies, usually Jesper Brochmand's *Huspostil*.

The Faroese were of a pious disposition and well content with the Lutheran religious establishment. A few relics of Catholicism remained, the most remarkable being the oral transmission of a religious ballad of 35 10–line stanzas written by the last Roman Catholic Icelandic bishop, Jon Arason of Hólar, who was beheaded in 1550. The text was collected and printed in 1869. Another was the custom of making votive offerings to the church in Vágur on Suðuroy.

The break-up of the old peasant community, which began with the development of the distant-water fishery and has resulted in the urbanization of modern times, has led to a number of religious developments. The Danish Inner Mission, an evangelical movement within the Danish Lutheran Church, began work in the islands in 1904. It runs mission halls and Sunday schools and carries on work among fishermen. The Roman Catholic Church started work in Tórshavn in 1857, but after a promising start numbers dwindled, and for the first two decades of this century Catholicism was almost extinct. A small congregation now maintains a church, a school, and a small convent in the town.

Far more success has been achieved by Protestant sects with a fundamentalist bias. By far the strongest is the Plymouth Brethren, usually known in the Faroe Islands as the Baptists*. This congregation was founded by a Scottish missionary, W. G. Sloan (1838–1949), who came to Faroe in 1865. In 1900 the community numbered no more than 30, but as a result of the work of the energetic Victor Danielsen (1894–1961), they have gained ground rapidly and today probably number at least 3,000, among whom are said to be some of the wealthiest citizens in the islands. They diverge from the Danish Church principally in their highly democratic church organization, their rejection of infant baptism, and the prominence they give to the expectation of an early return of Christ to this earth.

The most important development within the state church in the present century has been the use of the vernacular, which has now almost replaced Danish. The use of Faroese in church services, to a limited degree and under strict conditions, was first permitted in 1903. The general introduction of Faroese was delayed by the conservatism of the Faroese, to whom Danish had come to be specially associated with religious solemnity, and by lack of a Faroese liturgy, hymnbook, and Bible.

The major work of translation was carried through by Jacob Dahl (1878–1944), provost from 1917 to 1944. In 1921 appeared his translation of the Psalms, in 1930 a Faroese service book, and in 1939 the complete prayer book. His version of the New Testament was issued in 1937, and after his death his translation of the Old Testament was completed by Kristian Osvald Viderö. The complete Bible, translated from the original tongues, appeared in 1961. (A version made by Victor Danielsen, from various modern European languages, had already appeared in 1948.) Several books of homilies, which still have a special place in Faroese worship, have also been published.

Since 1963 the chief minister of Faroe has held the title of vice-bishop instead of provost. There are today eighteen priests of the Danish Church serving the islanders, pastorates having been progressively divided since 1913.

REFERENCES: L. Debes, *A Description of the Islands and the Inhabitants of Foeroe*, trans. J. Sterpin (London: William Iles, 1676); G. Johnston, *The Faroe Islanders' Saga* (Canada: Oberon Press, 1975); G. Landt, *A Description of the Feroe Islands* (London: Longman et al., 1810); J. Sephton, trans., *The Saga of King Sverri of Norway* (London: David Nutt, 1899); J. F. West, *Faroe, the Emergence of a Nation* (London: C. Hurst, New York: P. A. Eriksson, 1972).

J. F. WEST

RIKSDAG The Swedish parliament

Before the forming of national kingdoms in Scandinavia*, prominent men in various localities met together in *ting* to deliberate. This custom foreshadowed national assemblies which, whatever might be said about their exact inception, had very ancient roots among the people.

The gathering generally accepted as the first Swedish Riksdag was one that met at Engelbrekt Engelbrektsson's call in Arboga in 1435. Engelbrekt sought the appearance of national support against Danish suzerainty. He was, however, not the first to have arranged such meetings. Magnus Ladulås established a council of powerful nobles and bishops in 1275, and Magnus Eriksson* summoned a Riksdag in 1359, though neither of these assemblies was national in scope.

Gustav I Vasa* followed Engelbrekt's precedent. While engaged in the process of driving Christian II* from the country he called a Riksdag together in Strängnäs in June 1523, so that it might elect him king. It comprised representativesof the nation's four estates—the nobles, clergy, burghers, and peasants—and hence appeared to speak for the entire nation.

His victory over foreign enemies assured, Gustav Vasa then used the Riksdag against domestic enemies. He used it both against the Church, whose properties he coveted, and against Nils Dacke's* peasant uprising. Within the Riksdag he played off the three estates of nobles, burghers, and peasants against the clergy, and beyond it he invoked the national symbolism of crown and Riksdag against the rebellious peasantry of Småland. This boded ill for the Riksdag, which by the end of Vasa's reign in 1560 was vastly overshadowed by the monarch.

The Riksdag's place in the scheme of things was nevertheless assured by the Riksdag Act of 1617, under the terms of which the four estates were to meet regularly at the call of the king. The Riksdag added to its power twice in the seventeenth century when heirs to the throne were under age. Under the guise of protecting the realm from regents' misgovernment, it conferred on itself substantial powers to check the crown. This it did by means of the Form of Government Act (Regeringsform), first enacted in 1634 and reinstated in 1660. The Riksdag's influence ebbed whenever assertive monarchs took charge. Karl XI* greatly reduced the Riksdag's influence by manipulating commoners against the nobility, and Karl XII* persisted on the same course until he was shot in 1718.

Karl XII's excesses brought unlimited monarchy into disrepute and prepared the way for the enactment in 1720 of a new Instrument of Government which restored the Riksdag to a position of power. The Riksdag acquired the power to nominate and to hold to account the council of state*, that is, the government. The monarch was required by oath to conform to the Riksdag's decisions and was made subject to being outvoted on the council. The Riksdag in 1723 adopted a new Riksdag Act under the terms of which it acquired control over its own agenda, its own presiding officers, and its own rules of procedure. For the next 50 years the Riksdag was in the ascendancy. Its position of real power prompted power struggles within it. Parliamentary factions—precursors of political parties—developed, known as "Hats" and "Caps" (*see* Hat Party; Cap Party). They promoted reforms like the Freedom of the Press Act of 1766, which was a notable achievement for that time.

The Riksdag's ascendancy ceased in 1772 when Gustav III*, with his army's backing, dismissed the allegedly corrupt council and imposed on the Riksdag a new constitution giving the king primary power. In 1789 he made himself virtually an absolute monarch on the grounds that the exigencies of war required it. Within three years he was assassinated.

Because the succeeding king, Gustav IV Adolf*, was timid and ineffective both at home and abroad, the Riksdag was able to reassert itself. It deposed the king and adopted a new Instrument of Government Act (1809) which again ordained a separation of powers. To itself it gave, among other things, sole power to tax and to control the budget. Acceptance of the Riksdag's prerogatives as set forth in the new constitution was required both of the new monarch, Karl XIII*, and of his specially adopted heir and designated successor, Karl XIV Johan*.

The Riksdag consisted of four estates until 1866, when it reformed itself into a bicameral parliament over vociferous objections in the House of Nobles. The reformed Riksdag was given an upper chamber, whose 125 members were indirectly elected to overlapping nine-year terms, and a lower chamber, whose 190 members were directly elected to four-year terms.

The members of the post-1866 Riksdag were chosen by an electorate restricted by property qualifications. They coalesced into two parties, of which the largest (The Ruralist Party/Lantmannapartiet) represented rural interests against the urban and aristocratic upper class. The rural party split in 1888 over the question of free trade, after which, over a period of a dozen years, several new parties were formed. Of these, the workers' Social Democratic Party* eventually became the most important.

Entry into the Riksdag of the new parties' members in meaningful numbers awaited reform of the election law. This occurred in 1909, when the franchise was extended to all adult males and proportional representation was substituted for single-member districts. The reform opened the way for the Swedish multiparty system which endured for decades thereafter.

The Riksdag in the early nineteenth century still tolerated the monarch's taking an active role in politics, partly because of the Riksdag's inability to produce a common leadership of its own. But in 1917, after an election in which the Conservatives had lost heavily, King Gustav V* found himself unable to appoint a prime minister except by agreeing to the Liberal candidate's insistence that the king leave policy-making to the prime minister and the cabinet. The king thus tacitly gave in to the parliamentary principle that he could only have a government acceptable to the Riksdag.

The unwritten rule after 1917 was that if a party or combination of parties had the support of a majority in the Riksdag or at least in its second chamber, its leader was entitled to become prime minister. The Riksdag's bicameral structure, dating from 1866, was not perfectly suited to parliamentarism. Trouble lay in the possibility that different parties might prevail in different chambers, and the obvious remedy was consolidation into one chamber. By means of a constitutional amendment in 1968–1969 the Riksdag finally did unify itself. The Riksdag met for the first time as a unicameral body in 1971.

The present Riksdag has 349 members elected to three-year terms. Of these,

310 are elected from twenty-eight constituencies and 39 are elected at large. Fundamental rules of procedure are set forth in the Instrument of Government of 1974 and the Riksdag Act of 1974. The Riksdag selects a presidium consisting of a speaker and three deputy speakers. To the speaker falls the responsibility of proposing to the Riksdag someone to be prime minister. The speaker makes the selection after conferring with party leaders, and his choice carries unless an absolute majority says otherwise.

REFERENCES: N. Eden, *Den Svenska Riksdagen under Femhundra År* (Stockholm: Norstedt, 1935); N. Eden, ed., *Sveriges Riksdag*, 8 vols. (Stockholm: V. Pettersson, 1931–1938); E. Hastad, *The Parliament of Sweden* (London: Hansard Society, 1957); D. V. Verney, *Parliamentary Reform in Sweden 1866–1921* (Oxford: Clarendon Press, 1957).

B. L. HANSON

ROOS, ROSALIE (9 December 1823–9 June 1898) Swedish magazine editor, social reformer, traveler, and writer

Rosalie Roos was born in Stockholm*, the eldest daughter of wealthy and liberal-minded parents, Olof Gustaf Roos and Ulrika Euphrosyne, née von Keppel. She attended school until 15 years of age, something unusual for the day, and was one of the first members of the famous Wallinska School in Stockholm. Founded in 1831 and named after Johan Olof Wallin, the Wallinska School was the first secondary school for women in Sweden.

In 1851, after a broken engagement, she left for the United States alone, hoping to find employment at Limestone Female High School in South Carolina. She eventually taught there for one year and then served as a governess for a wealthy South Carolina plantation owner. Inspired by Fredrika Bremer's* American travels, Roos traveled to the Midwest, the East Coast, and Cuba before returning to Sweden in 1855. Her unusual experience as a single woman working in a foreign country is found in *Rosalie Roos. Resa till Amerika 1851–55*. In this collection of letters are recorded her impressions of the United States and her disillusionment with America as the land of opportunity for European immigrants. On her return, Roos supported herself with writing and translation work. In 1857 she married Uppsala professor Knut Olivecrona, a widower with four children with whom she had two children of her own.

Roos's stay in the United States affected her primarily in two days. She became encouraged by the existence of higher education for women in the United States, but also felt that this education was often superficial and useless. She wrote several articles defending Fredrika Bremer's views on equality for women and felt that education and knowledge would achieve this equality. With Sophie Leijonhufvud Adlersparre she founded and began to edit *Tidskrift för hemmet* in 1859, the first major Swedish magazine edited by women. It was widely read and is still in existence under the name *Hertha*, the magazine for the Fredrika Bremer Association*. Because of personal differences with Adlersparre, Roos left the magazine in 1868. She devoted the rest of her life to participating in and founding charitable causes and writing articles about women's issues.

REFERENCES: Sigrid Laurell, ed., *Rosalie Roos. Resa till Amerika 1851–55* (Stockholm: Almqvist and Wiksell, 1969); Rosalie Roos, *Travels in America 1851–55*, trans. and ed. Carl L. Anderson, letters ed. Sigrid Laurell (Carbondale: Southern Illinois University Press, 1981).

M. LOWE SHOGREN

RØROS Norwegian mining town

The old mining town of Røros is located in the interior of South Trøndelag. At 2,530 feet above sea level, the town is surrounded by moors and forestlands. The history of the town is closely linked with the Røros Copperworks, the shareholding company that started mining there in 1644. When news of the discovery of the rich copper deposits spread through Europe, craftsmen, miners, farmers, and adventurers alike flocked to Røros. Generations of miners and their families endured the gruelling conditions of their work in a harsh climate and forged a special society there.

Framed by enormous slag heaps, the small log cabins along the town's two main streets leave a deep impression on the visitor. The cottages contain the small handcrafted items with which the miners decorated their homes.

Of the eight main mines, only Ny Storwartz is still in operation. In the mines, shafts lead down to galleries below. A chorister sang hymns as the miners made their way down to their shifts.

The old administration building (Hyttstugu) houses the Copperworks' collection of old banners, weapons, tools, mining equipment, and other artifacts. The Røros Museum has a large collection of national costumes, tools, and household items.

In recent years, Johan Falkberget has brought to life the miners and their lives in a series of novels drawn from the Røros environment. In 1981, to protect the architecturally unique character and history of the old mining society, Røros was added to Unesco's World Heritage List.

REFERENCES: *Gyldendals Konversasjonsleksikon*, vol. 4 (Oslo: Gyldendal Norsk Forlag, 1959); *Røros—den gamle stad* (Røros: Røros Turist- og Reisetrafikklag, 1971).

E. M. ANDERSON

ROSLIN, ALEXANDER (15 July 1718–5 July 1793) Swedish artist

Roslin came of a family of Scottish origin which, after settling in France as Huguenots, had to emigrate to Holstein during the religious persecution in France of the 1680s. He was, however, born in Malmö, where his father, a doctor, had practiced since leaving Kiel in 1716. Roslin's mother was Swiss; she was the aunt of the later French court portraitist A. U. Wertmüller (1751–1811) who, like Roslin, was Swedish-born. Hence these gifted cousins are prominent examples of Protestant craftsmen whose faith was no bar to their enjoying substantial patronage in eighteenth-century France, a crucial factor in the rich eighteenth-century cultural relationship between Sweden and France.

Roslin was brought up in Christianstad, and the cultural milieu of Stockholm* was hence outside his early experience; it was to remain so throughout a career which took the artist over much of Europe and to Russia (though not, unlike Wertmüller, to America). His earliest lessons were from an amateur marine painter in Karlskrona*, and it may be that impressions of ship decoration inspired Roslin's later meticulous handling of furniture details in his portraits. This is now recognized to be of high documentary value, no less so than Roslin's treatment of his sitters' costumes.

By the early 1740s Roslin was established as official painter to the margrave of Bayreuth, and so had entered the heartland of European rococo; but by 1752 Roslin had reached Paris from Italy, impeccably supported by a letter of introduction to the marquise de Pompadour from the grand duchess of Parma, a daughter of Louis XV. There now began 22 uninterrupted years in Paris when Roslin quickly became established alongside François Boucher, François-Hubert Drouais, and Louis Michel Vanloo as worthy of the most prestigious sitters and commissions, including the arts minister Marigny, the royal family, and, in 1771, the future Gustav III* and his brothers during their visit to Paris. In 1759 Roslin had married the gifted pastelliste and pupil of Maurice La Tour, Marie Suzanne Giroust, and a decade later enchantingly portrayed her "coiffée à la Bolonaise." It was following her death in 1772 that his Paris practice began to pall on Roslin, and he returned briefly to Sweden before going on to Russia, Poland, Austria, and, in 1782, to the Austrian Netherlands. This last journey, undertaken after his return to Paris, doubtless owed much to the favor Roslin had been shown by the Empress Maria Theresa in Vienna, but there can be little doubt, either, that after eight years away from the French capital Roslin felt that fashion there had turned against him. Certainly the opulent dress he had so brilliantly portrayed, and which may have reached its apogee in the painting of the Swedish royal brothers of 1771, was giving way to plainer attire, and there were fewer of the titled sitters who had been so satisfied by Roslin's likenesses of them. Portraiture in the years immediately before the Revolution became increasingly introspective and lower-keyed in color, and the prevailing mood distanced it from the coloristic influences of Venice and Naples to which Roslin had so happily responded. The septuagenarian painter could not adapt to this change and, by choosing to remain in Paris for the rest of his life, Roslin had to witness the immolation of an aristocratic society he had been as well equipped to record as the most gifted of his French contemporaries.

REFERENCES: P. Lespinasse, *Les artistes suèdois en France du XVIII siècle* (Paris, 1929); G. V. Lundberg, *Roslin, liv och werk*, 2 vols. (Stockholm, 1957); S. Strömbom, *Fem Store Gustavianer* (Stockholm, 1943).

D. D. ALDRIDGE

RUNES (third–twelfth centuries) Germanic alphabet

The runic alphabet was the system of writing used by the Germanic peoples of northern Europe, Britain, Scandinavia*, and Iceland from about the third century A.D. to the twelfth. Scholars now believe that it developed from the Etruscan alphabet of northern Italy. The letter forms were angular, since they were cut on hard substances like wood or stone, and all but the earliest were written from left to right.

Four thousand runic inscriptions have survived, and 2,500 of these are in Sweden. The oldest inscription is from the third century. The complete alphabet, the Common Germanic futhark, appears on an inscription from the fourth century. This early form of the runic alphabet has 24 letters:

ᚠᚢᚦᚨᚱᚲᚷᚹ ᚺᚾᛁᛃᛈᛇᛉᛊ ᛏᛒᛖᛗᛚᛜᛞᛟ

f u þ a r k g w   h n i j p e̜ ʀ s   t b e m l ng d o

Around 800 a reduced alphabet of sixteen letters, reflecting linguistic change, was developed in Scandinavia:

ᚠᚢᚦᚬᚱᚴ ᚼᚾᛁᛅᛋ ᛏᛒᛘᛚᛦ

f   u   þ   ą   r   k   h   n   i   a   s   t   b   m   l   ʀ

Runic writing had a variety of uses, many of which are mentioned in Icelandic sagas and poetry. Letters carved on wood or horn had magical strength as charms to curse or heal. Runestones were raised as memorials for the dead or as signposts for travelers. In Scandinavia, runes continued to be used in manuscripts and for charms and memorials through the sixteenth century.

REFERENCES: E. H. Antonsen, *A Concise Grammar of the Older Runic Inscriptions* (Tübingen: Niemeyer, 1975); R. Elliott, *Runes, an Introduction* (Manchester: University Press, 1959); S. B. F. Jansson, *The Runes of Sweden* (London: Phoenix House, 1962); R. I. Page, *An Introduction to English Runes* (London: Methuen, 1973), S. Jansson, *Runinskrifter i Sverige* (Uppsala: Almqvist & Wiksell, 1984). Runic alphabets are from this source, pp. 13 and 28 respectively.

M. EMELITY

RYTI, RISTO (3 February 1889–25 October 1956) President of Finland 1940–1944

After completing his law studies in 1914, Risto Ryti quickly became a leading authority on economic problems facing Finnish society. He was elected to parliament in 1919 as a member of the Progressive Party (*see* Progressive/Liberal Party), served as minister of finance in the early 1920s, and was appointed director of the Bank of Finland in 1923. Ryti played a key role in the stabilization of the Finnish mark in the difficult period following World War I and in tying the value of the mark to gold in the mid-1920s, thus also laying the basis for important international contacts. During the interwar years he was one of Finland's leading anglophiles. In 1933 he served as first vice-chairman of the London World Economic Commission.

Ryti turned down an opportunity to head a Center-Left coalition government in 1937, but he influenced domestic politics from his position at the Bank of

Finland, especially during the late 1930s, when he had a close working relationship with president Kyösti Kallio, an Agrarian, and Minister of Finance Väniö Tanner*, a Social Democrat. During the Winter War* (1939–1940), Kallio and Tanner convinced the reluctant Ryti to become prime minister. When poor health forced Kallio to retire in December 1940, Ryti was unanimously elected president.

As president, Ryti was involved in all the hard choices that Finland had to make during the remainder of World War II*. After the Winter War Finland tried to form an alliance with Sweden, an option which would have corresponded to its ideological preferences and would have increased, albeit to a limited degree, Finland's possibilities of remaining outside Great Power conflicts. But a Swedish-Finnish alliance was vetoed by both the Soviet Union and Germany, thus leaving Finland alone in a precarious position between an expanding Nazi Germany and an anxious Soviet Union which was attempting to secure its defenses in the Baltic against an eventual German attack.

Post-Winter War Soviet policy in the Baltic and vis-a-vis Finland reinforced the Finnish view that the Soviet Union had aggressive intentions toward Finland. When Germany decided to turn eastward before attempting to defeat Britain, the stage was set for Finnish-German co-belligerancy. Ryti considered this policy to be Finland's only hope: Finland needed a counter to the Soviet threat, and Germany was the dominant power in the Baltic. Trapped by the realities of power politics, Finland tried to make the best of the situation; but it never fought for purely German military objectives and never allowed fascist ideology to influence domestic politics.

Ryti, like most Finnish wartime leaders, expected the war to end in a compromise peace. They hoped, however, that the Soviet Union would be a weakened power at that stage. Consequently, it was considered necessary to retain good relations with the United States, which could speak on Finland's behalf at the peace table, but at the same time to maintain good relations with Germany, which was essential to defending Finland until the end of the war. This strategy worked until the Allied offensives on the western and eastern fronts in the summer of 1944. Faced with a massive Soviet offensive on the Karelian Isthmus and an urgent need for German military equipment, Ryti signed an agreement with Ribbentrop in which he personally promised that Finland would never make a separate peace. The United States immediately broke relations with Finland, thus severing Finland's last diplomatic ties with Allied powers, but Finland was able to obtain equipment from a hard-pressed Germany, and Ryti's successor, Marshal Carl Mannerheim*, simply disavowed the Ribbentrop Pact after Ryti voluntarily withdrew from the presidency.

After the war, Ryti, along with other wartime leaders, was tried by a Finnish court and sentenced to 10 years' imprisonment. He served only three years due to bad health. Ryti's trial was the price Finland had to pay for being on the losing side. That Ryti was tried by a Finnish rather than a Soviet court and that he is generally regarded by Finnish historians as a leader who made the best of the limited options open to Finland during World War II stand as testimony to Finland's position as an independent country on the Soviet border. Any attempt to understand how and why Finland survived the Cold War as an independent country under the leadership of Juho Paasikivi* and Urho Kekkonen* requires an understanding of how Finland survived World War II when Risto Ryti was president. Finland's policy toward the Soviet Union would change, but its ability to adjust to the realities of power in the Baltic without any fundamental changes in its domestic institutions would remain constant.

REFERENCE: K. Skyttä, *Ei Muuta Kunniaa. Risto Rytin Kujanjuoksu, 1939–1945*(Helsinki: Kirjayhtymä, 1971).

R. M. BERRY

S

ST. BARTHOLOMEW Swedish colony in the Caribbean, 1784–1878

Sweden never became a great overseas colonial power, and its interest in the West Indies developed quite late. Consequently, Sweden had to be content with the purchase of the small island of St. Bartholomew, located north of St. Kitts, from the French in 1784. (The French had occupied the island in 1648.)

St. Bartholomew was a bare, volcanic island comprising only about 25 square kilometers. It had no fresh water and produced meager crops. Its best resource was a fine natural harbor, which was declared a free port shortly after purchase of the island. The port town was named Gustavia, after Sweden's reigning king, Gustav III*. In 1784 there were fewer than 1,000 inhabitants on the island, and only a few hundred of these were Swedes. The population subsequently grew, increased in part by English immigration, and reached about 5,000 in 1821 (about 2,000 were slaves).

In order to encourage trade between Sweden and the colony, the West India Company was established in 1787. It had its headquarters in Stockholm*, but ships were sent out from Gothenburg* as well. Although the company's charter included the right to organize slave trade expeditions in the "triangle route," none were ever realized. The company was never an economic success, and during its lifetime (it was dissolved in 1805) many non-company ships called at St. Bartholomew from Sweden.

From the start the Swedes viewed Gustavia as a transit port between North America and the West Indies or Europe. This was especially true during the great wars of the late eighteenth and early nineteenth centuries. A peak was reached in the prosperity of the colony during the Napoleonic Wars, and especially between 1812 and 1814, and this prosperity continued down to the 1830s. Then, however, England opened its possessions to North American trade, and St. Bartholomew wasted away. Other problems for the colony included the many privateers in the area, the English occupation in 1801–1802, the French attack in 1807, and a major fire in Gustavia in 1852.

As early as 1816, Sweden attempted to sell the island to England, but this attempt and another to arrange its sale to Italy failed. In 1878, however, the Swedes sold the colony back to France for 320,000 francs.

REFERENCES: I. Hildebrand, *Den svenska kolonin S:t Barthélemy och Västindiska kompaniet fram till 1796* (Lund: Lindstedts Universitetsbokhandel, 1951); R. H. Luthin, "St. Bartholomew: Sweden's Colonial and Diplomatic Adventure in the Caribbean," *Hispanic American Historical Review* 14 (1934): 307–24; G. Webe, "S:t Barthélemy. Svensk koloni 1784–1878," *Handels- og Sjøfartsmuseets Årbog* 40 (1981): 264–80.

E. GØBEL

SAINT BIRGITTA *See* Birgitta

SAINT KNUD *See* Knud II

SAINT OLAF *See* Olaf II Haraldsson

SALTSJÖBAD AGREEMENT Basic Swedish labor market agreement

In 1936 the Swedish Confederation of Trade Unions* (Landsorganisationen i Sverige or *LO*) and the Swedish Employers' Federation* (Svenska Arbetsgivareföreningen or *SAF*) entered into negotiations, precipitated by the strengthening of labor's position in the society and by a growing demand for state regulation of the labor market. These negotiations culminated in December 1938 with the conclusion of a "basic agreement" that was to serve as the foundation for labor market relations for at least the next four decades. This basic agreement, the Saltsjöbad agreement, was divided into five sections. The first established the Labor Market Council, composed of three delegates from LO and three from SAF, to serve as a negotiating body and a kind of court for the settlement of disputes. The second section covered negotiation and grievance settlement procedures. The third dealt with the right of the employer to hire and dismiss workers—a fundamental right which SAF insisted be maintained. Under the terms of the agreement, however, the workers' right to due process was also insured. The fourth section covered the actions that labor and management could take in the event of disputes and the protection of "neutral" or "third parties." The final section dealt with the regulation of disputes that might endanger the society as a whole.

Since the conclusion of this basic agreement, there have been a number of negotiated modifications, and similar agreements have been reached among other principals in the labor market. Also, LO and SAF have concluded a number of other agreements covering industrial safety, industrial training, work councils, women, and productivity.

Perhaps the spirit behind the agreement has been as important as the agreement itself. It reflected the desire of the principals to avoid disputes and prevent government intervention, and the realization that they had common interests and responsibilities.

This spirit and the relatively smooth functioning of the system established by the agreement prevailed until 1980. In late April and early May 1980, however, the tranquillity of the Swedish labor market system was shattered by a series of strikes and lock-outs that brought most of the Swedish economy to a halt for nearly two weeks (*see* May Strike). It may be, therefore, that Sweden has entered a new era in its labor history, precipitated by changing political alignments, the return of non-Socialist governments after 44 years, and the economic problems that confront Sweden in the last quarter of the twentieth century.

REFERENCES: Bo Carlsson, *Trade Unions in Sweden* (Stockholm: Tidens, 1969); Nils Elvander, *Intressorganisationerna i dagens Sverige* (Lund: Gleerup, 1969); Lennart Forsebäck, *Industrial Relations and Employment in Sweden* (Uppsala: The Swedish Institute, 1980); *SU*, vol. 25.

B. NORDSTROM

SALVATION ARMY

The urban ministry which became the Salvation Army was founded by the independent English Methodist evangelist William Booth (1829–1912) in London in 1865. As the social problems of that city multiplied in the throes of the Industrial Revolution and the working class became increasingly alienated from formal religion, he perceived the need for special efforts to proclaim the Gospel and conduct charitable work among the poor. Booth and his family opened mission stations to feed, house, clothe, and evangelize them, especially in London's blighted East End. As their ministry grew, he instituted a system of discipline and organized the movement along lines imitating those of the British army. Uniforms, ranks, and military nomenclature were adopted. In 1878 the movement took the name the Salvation Army, and Booth remained its commanding general for life.

A period of swift international expansion soon followed, first in English-speaking countries. Booth envisioned missions in continental Europe as well. Salvationists began to work in France in 1881, Switzerland in 1882, and Germany in 1886. Everywhere they regarded their movement as an aid to, not a rival of, existing churches, and their goal was to reach especially the urban dispossessed, who, by general consensus, the indigenous churches were not reaching effectively.

This was also the hope when the Salvation Army "invaded" Scandinavia*, where the Lutheran state churches had been deeply entrenched since the Reformation*. Booth's son, Bramwell, visited Sweden in 1878 and established some connections there through an English engineer. A small group, including a book merchant, Hanna Ouchterlony (1838–1924), soon formed. She visited William Booth in London in 1881 and, upon returning to Sweden, began to preach in various free-church settings. On a second trip to the English capital, Ouchterlony was named a major in the Salvation Army. In 1882 she and like-minded followers began to work in Stockholm*. They were denied access to most sanctuaries and many other meeting halls until 1889, when Herman Lagercrantz, a well-known factory owner, joined the Salvation Army, thus giving it some measure of social respectability. Progress was rapid in the 1890s and the early years of the twentieth century. In recent years the Swedish membership has declined, but in the early 1980s it was still above 30,000.

Rejecting Booth's authoritarian command of the worldwide organization and his view of the sacraments as unnecessary, some Swedish members seceded in 1905 to form an independent Swedish Salvation Army. In the 1970s it numbered approximately 1,700. Its polity is congregational and, unlike the main Salvation Army, it uses the Christian sacraments of believers' baptism and communion.

The Salvation Army came to Norway in 1888 when free churches were proliferating rapidly and the state church's domination of religious life was being eroded. It met derisive opposition from the pulpit, the press, and much of the public but nevertheless became the largest religious organization in Norway outside the state church, in which the majority of its adherents have nominal membership. In contrast to Sweden, the Salvation Army is by choice not a recognized denomination in Norway.

The first Salvation Army meeting in Denmark took place in Copenhagen* in 1887. A cadet school for training officers was opened there in 1890 and a slum mission the following year. Several hostels followed in the 1890s and shortly after the turn of the century. In 1888 the Salvation Army reached the two rapidly growing cities of Aalborg and Odense. Its 49 local corps now conduct a wide variety of evangelistic and social work and, as elsewhere in Scandinavia, are regarded as an important force in Christian circles as well as in dealing with narcotics addiction, illegitimate pregnancies, and other ills which the welfare state* has not been able to eradicate.

REFERENCE: *Nordisk teologisk uppslagsbok för kyrka och skola* (Lund: Gleerup, 1952–1957).

F. HALE

SAXO GRAMMATICUS (early thirteenth century) Danish historian

Saxo was the author of the *Gesta Danorum* (*GD*), a Latin history of Denmark with a strong nationalistic bias. His identity is uncertain; he was probably the clerk of Absalon, Archbishop of Lund, to whom he dedicated the *GD*.

The *GD* chronicles the founding of the Danish kingdom, beginning with the legendary King Dan and concluding with the reign of King Knud VI* c. 1185. The work itself was completed about 1219.

Saxo probably modeled the *GD* on the two other national histories he cited, Bede's *Historia Ecclesiastica Anglorum* and the *Historia Langobardorum* of Paulus Diaconus. Other sources for the first nine books of early history were the Icelandic tradition of sagas and poems, and oral narratives related to Saxo by Absalon. The remaining seven books had primarily written sources, such as

Geoffrey of Monmouth and Adam of Bremen*. The *GD* is not a reliable record of historical fact, but it is valuable as our only written source for many Norse myths and legends.

The only complete text of the *GD* is Christiern Pedersen's edition of 1514. Four manuscript fragments from the Middle Ages are extant; the largest of these (MS A, eight pages) can be dated to c. 1200. The standard edition is that of Olrik and Raeder (1931–1957).

REFERENCES: Saxo Grammaticus, *Danorum Regum Heroumque Historia*, Books X-XVI, trans. E. Christiansen, 3 vols. (Oxford: British Archaeological Reports, Series S84 and S118, 1980–1981), and *The History of the Danes*, Books I-IX, ed. H. E. Davidson and trans. P. Fisher, 2 vols. (Cambridge, England: D. S. Brewer, 1979–1980); and I. Skovgard-Petersen, "Saxo, Historian of the Patria," *Mediaeval Scandinavia* 2 (1969): 54–77.

M. EMELITY

SCANDINAVIA

Scandinavia is the word most often used in English-language sources to identify Denmark, Norway, Sweden, and, in most cases, Finland, Iceland, and the Faroe Islands* as a group of nations or a region. The word apparently derives from *Scadinavia*, a term used by Pliny the Elder (d. 79 A.D.) in his *Naturalis historia* to name the unknown regions beyond Denmark's Jutland peninsula. The addition of the *n* in the first syllable, it is generally argued, is the result of a misreading of Pliny's handwritten manuscript by later users. The *n* appears first in the late ninth century. There is considerable debate over what word or words Pliny used as the bases for his term. One conjecture is that the word derives from the early Germanic *skapin-awjo* or *skadin-awjo*, meaning dangerous islands.

Care should be taken when using the word *Scandinavia*. It is incorrect to use it to identify the region in geological terms, because Denmark and Iceland are not parts of the same geological formations. Finland does not belong to the area linguistically or ethnically. Historically, however, Scandinavia can be used to refer to all five countries and the Faroe Islands.

The people of the region do not generally use the word when referring to the region. They tend to use terms that reflect their northern location in Europe (Nordic Council, Nordic Cooperation, Nordic Society, and so on). Since the 1930s, they have come increasingly to use the term *Norden* (The North) to identify the region.

REFERENCES: The introductions to most general studies of the area include discussions of the term. See also J. Svennung, *Scadinavia und Scandia* (Lund: Acta Societatis Litterarum Humaniorum Regiae Upsaliensis, Number 44, 1963).

B. NORDSTROM

SCANDINAVIANISM *See* Nordism

SCAVENIUS, ERIK (1877–1962) Danish diplomat

Erik Scavenius was perhaps the single most controversial figure in Denmark during the period of the German occupation. He had a long and distinguished career as a diplomat during the years preceding the outbreak of World War II*. From 1913 until 1920 he served as foreign minister in the second Radical ministry of Carl Theodore Zahle and played a crucial role in mitigating many areas of conflict between Denmark and Germany throughout World War I. In cooperation with his colleague, Peter Munch*, the minister of defense, Scavenius saw to it that the Great Belt between Fyn and Zealand was mined in accordance with German wishes, thus preventing a British naval thrust into the Baltic. While serving as foreign minister, Scavenius had to steer Denmark along a course of neutrality which involved Copenhagen* in conflicts with Britain as much as it entailed difficulties with Berlin. However, through a series of trade agreements with the British and strategic arrangements with the Germans, Scavenius and the Zahle government successfully kept Denmark neutral throughout the conflict. As a result, the young diplomat acquired a reputation as a miracle worker.

During the period between the wars Scavenius pursued a professional diplomatic career, and in the 1930s he represented Denmark in Stockholm*. After the German occupation he once again became involved in the Danish political scene and assumed the post of foreign minister in Thorvald Stauning's* reconstructed government of national unity on 8 July 1940. In November 1942 he became prime minister, replacing Vilhelm Buhl, the Social Democrat who in turn had replaced the deceased Stauning in May of that year. Scavenius occupied the posts of foreign minister and prime minister from the end of 1942 until the collapse of parliamentary government in Denmark and the German military crackdown of August 1943. In the last years of the occupation and during the immediate postwar period, Scavenius went into semiretirement and wrote an autobiography which still serves as the single most articulate defense of the policy of cooperation with Germany.

Although officially affiliated with the Radical Party, Scavenius tended to be somewhat aloof politically and highly suspicious of parliamentary politics, especially if they impinged on the conduct of foreign relations. Scavenius firmly believed that Denmark should adjust itself to the realities of power in order to avoid the disasters that it suffered during the Napoleonic Wars and the conflict with Germany in 1864. This affected his attitudes and policies during both world wars. During the first years of the German occupation, Scavenius became convinced that Germany would either win the war or at least dominate Europe for a considerable length of time. Consequently, he became one of the principal architects of a policy of cooperation with Berlin which involved, among other things, Denmark's signing of the Axis-sponsored Anti-Comintern Pact. Although he resisted German pressure on a number of issues such as the inclusion of Nazis in the Danish cabinet or the introduction of anti-Jewish legislation, his policies became synonymous with outright collaboration in the eyes of many resistance leaders and Allied governments. Consequently, this previously "non-political" diplomat became caught up in the maelstrom of political controversy which affected Denmark in the years immediately following 1943.

REFERENCES: V. Buhl et al., *Danmark, Besat og Befriet* (Copenhagen: Fremad, 1946); E. Scavenius, *Forhandlings Politiken under Besættelsen* (Copenhagen: Hasselbach, 1948); F. Scott, *Scandinavia* (Cambridge, Mass.: Harvard University Press, 1975); J. Vogt, "Den Ensomer Statsman, Erik Scavenius, 1877–1962," *Samtiden* 7 (1963); J. Voorhis, "Germany and Denmark 1940–1943," *Scandinavian Studies* 44:2 (1972).

J. L. VOORHIS

SCHARTAU, HENRIK (27 September 1757–3 February 1825) Swedish theologian and pastor

Henrik Schartau was born in Malmö. He studied at Lund University and was ordained in Kalmar* in 1780. Five years later he became attached to the cathedral at Lund, where he spent the remainder of his life. Although Schartau became very influential through his preaching in southern and western Sweden, he never traveled extensively.

At 20, while a student at Lund, Schartau went through a deep spiritual crisis. He was influenced by the Moravian Brethren (Herrnhutare), who emphasized the conversion of the individual and a strict form of piety. After this experience, Schartau displayed his Pietism, though he broke with the Moravians on the question of sectarianism, polemical preaching, and their low church stance. He remained loyal to the Swedish state church and a high church position. He held that the duty of a pastor was to preach the word of God in all its purity and strength. Despite his loyalty to the institutional church, Schartau taught an extremely individualistic Christianity in matters of faith. He espoused a sober, ethical, and sternly puritanical life. Following Luther's example, he taught loyalty to authority.

Schartau was in agreement with many of the ideas of the Läsare (Readers) and the Haugeans (*see* Hauge, Hans Nielsen). But he differed with them on the question of lay preaching and on their revivalistic methods. To him, lay preaching was disorderly and too emotional.

By remaining within the state church, Schartau influenced and trained groups of pastors, which in turn greatly improved the Swedish clergy. His contacts with the university students at Lund made a deep impression on that generation. His desire for a deeper Christian commitment made him an influential force among the common people of his area. Missionary movements such as the Swedish Mission Society, organized in 1835 to Christianize the Lapps*, and the Foreign Missionary Society and Training School, established in Lund in 1846 by Peter Fjellstedt, were influenced by Schartau. Otto Witt, the Church of Sweden Mission's first missionary to South Africa, came from southern Sweden and felt the impact of the Schartau movement (*see* Missionaries: Africa). Per Wieselgren and J. H. Thomander, nineteenth-century Swedish clerics who expressed strong social concerns, were also influenced by Schartau.

Religious protest against the church's coldness displayed itself in political reform. As a result of emphasis on individualistic religious faith, people were encouraged to express opinions contrary to the established political system of the time. Thanks in part to Schartauanism in southern and western Sweden, the Laestadians (*see* Laestadianism) in Lappland, the Baptists*, Methodists*, and other sectarians, profound spiritual as well as political and social changes took place in nineteenth-century Sweden. Schartau died in Lund in 1825.

REFERENCES: G. Billing, *Minne af Prosten Henrik Schartau* (Stockholm: Svenska Akademien, 1914); H. Hägglund, *Henric Schartau and the Order of Grace: Biography and Fifteen Sermons by Henric Schartau*, trans. S. G. Hägglund (Rock Island Illinois: Augustana Book Concern, 1928); L. Johannesson, *Henric Schartau* (Stockholm: Diakonistyrelse, 1957); R. Murray, ed., *The Church of Sweden—Past and Present*, trans. N. G. Sahlin (Malmö: Allhem, 1960); V. Södergren, *Henric Schartau och Västsvensk Kyrkoliv* (Uppsala: J. A. Lindblad, 1925); J. Wordsworth, *The National Church of Sweden*, The Hale Lectures (Milwaukee, Wis.: Young Churchman Co., 1911).

A. H. WINQUIST

SECOND WORLD WAR *See* World War II

SEHESTED, HANNIBAL (1609–13 September 1666) Danish statesman

After receiving his education through private tutors and three years' study at Soro Academy, Sehested began the series of travels during which he laid the foundation of his diplomatic skills and understanding. He visited not only England, France, the Netherlands, and Germany (1629–1632), but also Italy and Spain (1635). On his return he was appointed tutor to Prince Valdemar Christian and became betrothed to his sister Christiane in 1635. Like other prospective sons-in-law of Christian IV*, Sehested rose quickly at court and became a member of the council of state (*rigsraad*) in 1640.

After his marriage to Christiane in 1642, he was appointed viceroy of Norway, which he ruled with an increasing degree of political independence and with an equally increasing degree of success in administrative, economic, and military matters, holding his own in the otherwise disastrous Dano-Swedish War of 1643–1645. After the death of Christian IV (1648) and following a charge of embezzlement in 1651, Sehested's enemies were able to force him to relinquish all posts, including his membership on the council of state. Following the further humiliation of having to surrender his property to the new king, Frederik III*, Sehested left the country and spent the next seven years in voluntary exile in various European countries.

In 1657, having had his offer of help turned down by Frederik III, Sehested joined the staff at the military headquarters of the Swedish king, Karl X*, an act of treason comparable to that of another disaffected son-in-law, Corfitz Ulfeldt, in his dealings with the elector of Brandenburg. Having initially supported the Swedish cause, however, Sehested quickly came to realize that Sweden would be denied total victory, not by the Danes but by the European powers, in particular England and the Netherlands, who did not wish to see one power only in command of both sides of the Sound. From 1658 onwards, therefore, though he remained at the Swedish headquarters, he worked successfully for the best possible terms for Denmark in the peace treaties of 1658 and 1660; in recognition of these services he was rehabilitated and reinstated by King Frederik in 1660. Within months of his return he was able to demonstrate in an even more crucial manner his support for his former political rival by coordinating the political forces—the clergy, the burghers of Copenhagen*, the court—which successfully ousted the nobility and the *rigsraad* (his former allies) from power and allowed the king to assume hereditary and absolute power.

As the new chancellor of the exchequer (*rigsskatmester*) he became the architect of the structure and policies of the first years of the new regime. Modern boards of finance, trade, foreign affairs, and so on, whose secretaries reported to the king and his civil servants, replaced older consultative bodies; cuts in military spending and sale of crown lands helped him to balance state expenditure and income, and a foreign policy based on neutrality, trade, and subsidies from more powerful nations became the thrust of his policies. Sehested favored a Dano-Swedish understanding and trade agreement, preferably backed by either England or France, as a means of countering the rapid economic advance of the Dutch Republic, and it was in the diplomatic pursuance of this aim that he died at Paris in September 1666.

REFERENCE: *DBL*, vol. 13.

P. RIES

SERGEL, JOHAN TOBIAS (5 September 1740–26 February 1814) Swedish artist

The son of German parents who were Swedish immigrants, Sergel himself seems to have had little consciousness of his German blood but, owing to his enthusiastic embrace of Italian civilization, perhaps above all felt himself a "European" in an age of pregnant cultural interchange. It was only after pleadings to be permitted to stay in Italy that he succumbed to Gustav III's* insistence that he return to Sweden in 1778. By that time Sergel had spent eleven years in Italy, a period which had been initiated by an award from the Swedish Academy of Fine Arts and at the start of which Sergel recalled he "had to forget everything and learn afresh." In fact, he had already visited Paris with his master P. H. L'Archevêque and had demonstrated exceptional anatomical skills. He also made fertile friendships with Jean-Antoine Houdon and Clodion (or Claude Michel) and became especially close to the latter, who taught Sergel to model in terra cotta when they were together in Rome.

While Clodion's genius never naturally responded to the classical style, Sergel's preeminence lay in his unrivalled ability to transmit a rococo-like vitality from the clay model to the marble block and there achieve a fusion with classical rigor which no other eighteenth-century sculptor equalled. *The Faun* of the late 1760s, the *Mars and Venus*, and the *Diomedes* were in their time peerless sculpture and have so remained, and it is peculiarly significant that Sergel did not become read in the classics until long after his return home. His statue of Gustav III on Skeppsbron in Stockholm*, as late as 1808, is a typical employment of vibrant classicism to project majesty: while of its time, it yet has traits of pre-revolutionary French classicism which could only stir its viewers' emotions.

It cannot be known what direction Sergel's art would have taken had he remained undisturbed in Rome, and so it must always be matter for debate whether Gustav III did a critical disservice to European art in 1778. What is plain is that Sergel's later life has a tragic dimension, since the exigencies of post-Gustavian Sweden, including financial troubles, involvement in the wars of the French Revolution and Napoleon, and Gustav IV's* relative lack of interest in the arts, robbed its creativity of scope.

REFERENCES: O. Antonsson, *Sergels ungdom och Romtid* (Stockholm, 1942); G. Göthe, *Johan Tobias Sergels skulpturverk* (Stockholm, 1921); R. Josephson, *Sergels fantasi* (Stockholm, 1956).

D. D. ALDRIDGE

SEYÐABRÆVIÐ See *Sheep Letter*

SHEEP LETTER (*Seyðabrævið*) 1298 basic medieval document in Faroese farming law used for the study of the early Faroese language

The *Sheep Letter* is a special enactment (*réttarbót*) by the Norwegian Duke Haakon Magnusson relating to farming and household affairs in the Faroe Islands*. In 1273 King Magnus VI Haakonsson*, Duke Haakon's father, extended the validity of the older Gulating Law to the islands but allowed the inhabitants to keep their own agricultural code. In 1274 the younger Gulating Law was adopted, and it was presumably put into force in the Faroes shortly after this date. In 1298 the *Sheep Letter* was issued, apparently in response to complaints about deficiencies in the existing agricultural law. Although it mentions briefly such matters as the leasing of land, the taking of lodgings, and the rights of ownership to dead whales and driftwood, its principal area of concern is sheep farming—hence the title by which the enactment is now known, first documented in copies made about 1600 in the manuscripts *AM 316 fol* and *AM 61b II 4to* in the Arnamagnæan Collection. The *Sheep Letter* was ratified by Christian IV* on 24 February 1637 and was printed, with one or two changes, in the (Danish) form in which it received ratification in Debes (1673). It continued in force with one or two minor amendments until 1866.

The *Sheep Letter* is preserved in two medieval vellum manuscripts: *Isl. perg. 33 4to* in the Royal Library in Stockholm* contains what appears to be the original manuscript of the enactment, while *Medeltidshandskrift nr. 15* in the University Library in Lund, from the early 1300s, preserves a version in which the order of various articles has been changed and the phrasing somewhat altered. Because of a dearth of medieval sources, the *Sheep Letter*, although covering only four leaves of vellum, is the most important early Faroese document we possess. It contains a number of legal terms not found elsewhere, some or all of which may have been unique to the Faroes. A number of linguistic peculiarities in *Lund 15* have also led to suggestions that this manuscript, including the *Sheep Letter*, was written by a Faroeman, but the theory has not gained general acceptance. However, the copy of the enactment in *AM316 fol.* provides us with one of our most important sources of Faroese language before the 1780s.

REFERENCES: J. Agerholt, "Sauebrevet 1298. En undersøkelse i norrøn diplomatikk," *Arkiv för nordisk filologi* 74 (1959): 236–63; L. Debes, *Færoæ & Færoa Reserata* (Copenhagen: n.p., 1673; repr. Tórshavn: Einars Prent og Forlag, 1963; facsimile repr. Copenhagen: Munksgaard, 1963); J. Jakobsen, *Diplomatarium Færoense* (Copenhagen and Tórshavn: n.p., 1907); J. H. W. Poulsen and U. Zachariasen, eds., *Seyðabrævið* (Tórshavn: Føroya Fróðskaparfelag, 1971)(contains facsimiles of the four manuscript versions and one fragment of the *Sheep Letter*, a printed text of each, a Faroese and English translation of *Stockholm 33* and *Lund 15*, an introduction in Faroese and English, a list of the principal dates in the history of the Faroes, and a full bibliography of work on or related to the *Sheep Letter*).

M. P. BARNES

SHIPPING

Finland

Finland's location on the northeastern fringe of Europe has meant that maritime contacts have always been of importance. There have been times in the country's history when shipping was an important industry and a substantial agent of economic growth.

During the Middle Ages the Hanse (*see* Hanseatic League) controlled, by virtue of its capital and technical skills, most of the trade in the Baltic. Very probably most cargoes between the few Finnish coastal towns and central Europe went on foreign vessels. This pattern continued in the sixteenth and seventeenth centuries, during which period the Dutch took over commercial supremacy in the Baltic.

A traditional peasant trade flourished alongside the international commerce. This was especially true on the southeastern coast and in the southwestern (Turku and Åland) archipelago. In most cases it was limited to coastal shipping and barter trade bound for Sweden or Estonia, but in certain areas specialized shipping and freight-carrying developed. A most dramatic example may be seen in Koivisto, a small coastal parish near Viborg. In the latter half of the seventeenth century, its peasants owned a greater fleet than any Finnish town (or Reval).

The Swedish crown sought to encourage shipping and shipbuilding in towns, especially from the time of Gustav I Vasa*, by imposing restrictions on foreign and peasant traders. Some ships large enough to sail to western Europe and even Spain were built in Turku (Åbo) and Viipuri (Viborg). Most of the gains from this policy fell to Stockholm*, however.

During the eighteenth century shipping gained more momentum in Finnish towns. This was partly the result of the Swedish Navigation Act (Produktplakat, 1724), which favored domestic shipping, and partly the result of the fact that economic policy gradually became less centrally focused, that is, Stockholm came to be less favored in economic legislation. Another important factor in the development of a native shipping industry, especially for the towns of the Bothnian coast, was the structure of trade. Exports consisted chiefly of tar and lumber, which required extensive shipping capacity, whereas imports were mostly non-bulky consumer goods. This one-sided demand for cargo space meant that loads to and from Finland were not very attractive to foreign carriers.

During the nineteenth century, when Finland belonged to Russia, shipping developed still more. From the late 1830s to the 1870s, the industry enjoyed its heyday. Gross tonnage grew faster than Finland's foreign trade. This was possible because Finnish ships increasingly became involved in the international tramp-freight business, especially during the winter months. Their success in international competition seems to have depended on the relative cheapness of ships (based on the abundance of timber) and labor.

In the 1860s Finland had a merchant tonnage that, compared with total population, was greater than that of Sweden or Denmark. In general importance, shipping was not far behind manufacturing. During the latter part of the century, however, the situation was reversed. The transition from sail to steam was unusually slow in Finland, largely because of the costs involved. As late as 1913 only about 20 percent of Finland's merchant tonnage was steam-driven, which was one of the lowest figures in Europe. Consequently, the growth of shipping was slower than the growth of the country's foreign trade.

After World War I, the technical transition at last took place. In a relatively short time, primarily in the 1920s, steamships came to dominate the fleet. This shift was aided by the fact that during the Depression old steamships could be bought very cheaply. The growth of the merchant fleet was severely hampered during World War II*, and after it only 50 percent of the former merchant tonnage was left. Growth resumed in the 1960s and was accompanied by an extensive modernization of the fleet.

REFERENCES: A. J. Alanen, "Der Aussenhandel und die Schiffahrt Finnland im 18. Jahrhundert," *Annales Academiae Scientiarum Fennicae*, ser. B, no. 103 (Helsinki, 1957); Y. Kaukiainen, *Suomen talonpoikaispurjehdus 1800–luvun alkupuoliskolla (1810–1853)* (Loviisa, 1970; English summary: The Maritime Trade of Peasant and Other Coastal Dwellers in Finland 1810–1853), and "The Transition from Sail to Steam in Finnish Shipping, 1850–1914," *Scandinavian Economic History Review* 28:2 (1980): 161–84; G. Kerkkonen, *Bondesegel på Finska viken* (Borgå, 1959); J. Pohjanpalo, *Suomen kauppamerenkulku ja erityisesti linjaliikenteen osuus siinä* (Helsinki, 1949; summary: Mercantile Shipping of Finland and Especially the Role of Regular Services in It).

Y. KAUKIAINEN

Norway

Norwegian shipping has a long tradition, yet as an independent industry it is a fairly new phenomenon. Until the mid-nineteenth century it was used mainly to carry the country's foreign trade. The great turning point came in the 1850s, when the merchant fleet entered a period of expansion and was employed increasingly in transport between foreign ports. From a size of 284,000 net register tons in 1850, the fleet increased more than fivefold to over 1.5 million tons by 1880--representing a much more rapid rate of growth than for the world fleet as a whole. Then the third largest fleet in the world, the Norwegian merchant marine had become one of the principal carriers of world trade.

This growth was caused both by external and internal factors. Like other maritime nations, Norway benefited from the boom created by the Crimean War and from the general increase in international commerce caused by the Industrial Revolution and trade liberalization. But internal factors also gave Norway some important advantages. Norway possessed a great stock of maritime skills, largely because of its historic dependence on seaborne trade for economic survival. Also, in a nation with limited economic opportunities, maritime endeavors looked increasingly attractive, both as an outlet for surplus capital and as an alternative to emigration*.

The transition from sail to steam in the fleet came between 1880 and 1914. With the exception of shipowners in Bergen, Norwegians were generally slow to adopt steam. As late as 1890, 88 percent of the merchant fleet consisted of sailing ship tonnage. But in the quarter century preceding the outbreak of World War I, Norwegian owners took the plunge. Of the nearly 1,500 vessels of over 500 gross tons on register in 1914, nearly 1,100 were steamers, and steam-powered vessels accounted for almost 77 percent of the tonnage. Due to their higher efficiency, steam vessels were also more profitable. Although sailing craft comprised almost one-quarter of the total tonnage in 1914, they accounted for only about 13 percent of the gross earnings of the fleet.

Nevertheless, the hallmark of Norwegian shipowning in these years remains the relative reluctance to invest in steam technology. Several explanations have been advanced to account for this. The predilection of Norwegian owners for tramp as opposed to liner trades is one possibility. Skepticism over this new technology may also have played a role, and it is also likely that the lack of technological expertise in Norway made these vessels more expensive both to build and to own. But the most important explanation appears to be that the purchase of a steamship was simply beyond the means of most Norwegian shipowning firms. While sailing ships could be built cheaply in Norway, steamers were more expensive and usually had to be imported. Furthermore, the organization of the firms proved an obstacle to the financing of steam vessels. Single-ship partnerships dominated and made the raising of capital difficult.

After America's entry into World War I, Norway had the largest neutral merchant fleet in the world. Norwegian ships were of vital importance to the Allies and were increasingly hunted by the Central Powers. By 1918, about half of the Norwegian fleet was being directly employed by the Allied nations, and Norwegian shipowners made large profits. But the cost was high: between 1914 and 1918, 663 vessels totaling 1.1 million tons were lost. Nearly 1,500 seamen perished as a result. Unfortunately, much of the profit made during the war was quickly dissipated, as the value of Norwegian currency declined rapidly and the cost of replacing lost tonnage escalated. After 1920 the freight market collapsed, and many of the newly commissioned vessels were unable to recover even their operating costs. The situation was exacerbated by a dramatic shift in the structure of international sea transport, as tramps were replaced by liners and diesels substituted for steam.

Between 1920 and 1939, a modern maritime policy was adopted in Norway. Not all Norwegian firms were affected by the setback in 1920. A large number managed to increase their profits in the interwar period by investing heavily in tankers and liners, often powered by diesel engines, using both their own and imported capital. In 1920 less than 5 percent of the Norwegian tonnage was in motor vessels; by 1939 more than two-thirds of tonnage was. A new Norwegian fleet was born.

The traditional reliance upon tramp ships also declined. In 1920 nearly 80 percent of the Norwegian fleet was engaged in such trade, while 15 percent of the tonnage was in liners and 5 percent in tankers. By 1939 the Norwegian merchant fleet had more than doubled in size (Norway ranked fourth among the maritime nations of the world, behind Great Britain, the United States, and Japan) and the deployment of this tonnage had also changed drastically. Only 37 percent was engaged in tramping, while liners accounted for 22 percent and tankers for 41 percent. By increasing its fleet in this way, Norway deviated sharply from world trends. For example, while the world merchant fleet (excluding Norway) decreased in tonnage by 1.6 percent between 1929 and 1938, the Norwegian fleet increased by 42 percent over the same period.

This transition to liners and tankers also affected the organization of the industry. With its better access to credit and capital, Oslo became the dominant maritime city, owning almost 40 percent of Norwegian tonnage by 1939. As entry costs rose, large multiship joint stock companies emerged, creating greater continuity and better utilization of assets in the process.

The German invasion of Norway in 1940 created a totally new situation for Norwegian shipping. About 16 percent of the merchant fleet was in German-controlled waters when the invasion started, but the overwhelming majority was outside. On 22 April the Norwegian government brought the merchant marine under government control for the duration of the war. Three days later, with the consent of the owners, the Norwegian Shipping and Trade Mission (Nortraship) was established in London to manage the fleet.

Consisting of 806 vessels totaling 4 million gross tons and employing 25,000 seamen, Nortraship was the largest shipowning firm in the world. Both from an economic and a political perspective, Nortraship proved to be the most valuable asset the Norwegian government had during the war. The profits generated made the government-in-exile economically independent, while the assistance to the Allies brought much political good will. But all of this was achieved at a terrible cost. During the war 2.3 million tons of shipping were sunk, and 3,211 sailors lost their lives.

At the end of World War II*, the Norwegian merchant fleet had been reduced to about 3 million gross tons, but by 1949 it had more than regained its pre-war size. This rebuilding was based on the purchase of both new and second-hand vessels. Many of the new ships were constructed domestically, leading to a revival of the Norwegian shipbuilding industry. The foreign currency reserves accumulated during the war financed most of the reconstruction, but by 1948 these had become depleted, and the government ordered cuts in both investment and imports. At the same time, priority was given to other sectors of the economy, and in late 1948 a ban, lasting until 1951, was placed on the import of ships. After the prohibition was ended, the Norwegian fleet resumed its rapid expansion, increasing by 350 percent between 1950 and 1975. Even more conspicuous were the accompanying structural changes. In 1975, 52 percent of the fleet was less than five years old, compared to 34 percent a quarter century earlier. While only 40 percent of all vessels were in the 8,000–plus ton class at mid-century, 90 percent were of this size in 1975. The *VLCC Berge Emperor*, the largest ship in the fleet in 1975 at 211,359 tons, was more than thirteen times larger than its counterpart in 1950. A greater emphasis was placed on tankers and new techniques such as ''ro-ro'' (roll on-roll off) containers.

No new consensus developed, however, in marketing strategies. Some owners preferred to operate their ships on long-term charters, while others hoped for higher profits on the spot market. The latter were devastated by the economic slump of 1973, with the result that a large number of vessels were laid up, scrapped, or ''flagged-out.'' As a consequence, the merchant fleet sailing under the Norwegian flag was markedly reduced in the late 1970s and early 1980s. In 1984 the Norwegian merchant marine consisted of 789 vessels of over 500 tons, with a total carrying capacity of 17.6 million tons, of which almost two-thirds were tankers of different types.

REFERENCES: T. Bergh, T. Hanisch, E. Lange, and H. Pharo, *Growth and Development* (Oslo, 1981); F. Hodne, *The Norwegian Economy 1920–1980* (London, 1983); K. Pettersen, *The Saga of Norwegian Shipping* (Oslo, 1955); L. Pettersen, *Fra kjøpmannsrederi til selvstendig næring, 1860–1914. Bergen og sjøfarten*, vol. 3 (Bergen, 1981); J. Schreiner, *Norsk skipsfart under krig og høykonjunktur 1914–1920* (Oslo, 1963); A. Thowsen, *Vekst og strukturendringer i kriesetider 1914–1939. Bergen og sjøfarten*, vol. 4 (Bergen 1983); J. N. Tønnessen, *Fra klipperen til motorskipet. Den norske Sjøfarts Historie*, vol. 2, part 3 (Oslo, 1951).

A. THOWSEN

SIGISMUND (20 June 1566–30 April 1632) King of Poland 1587–1632, king of Sweden 1592–1599

Sigismund was the son of Johan III* and his Polish wife, Katarina Jagellonica. He was born during his parents' imprisonment under Erik XIV* and had a strict Catholic upbringing in increasingly Lutheran Sweden. He was elected to the Polish throne in 1587 and succeeded his father in Sweden in 1592. His reigns in both countries were fraught with difficulties. Fears of his Catholicism led to the calling of a meeting of churchmen at Uppsala in 1593 by Sigismund's uncle,

Karl (IX*), at which the *Augsburg Confession**, church ordinances, and a handbook were adopted that placed Sweden firmly in the Lutheran camp. In spite of the arrangements made at the time of his coronation to define the form of government in Sweden during his absences, the situation quickly degenerated into an open revolt in which Sigismund and most members of the council were pitted against Karl. (Sigismund probably hoped to avoid conflict in Sweden by tying Karl and the council nobles into a system in which they would check one another.) Sigismund attacked Karl and his supporters in 1597 but was defeated at Stångebro in 1598 and returned to Poland. The following year he was deposed, and Karl became regent.

Sigismund never abandoned hope that he would regain the Swedish throne. He fought Karl between 1599 and 1611 and Gustav II Adolf* between 1617 and 1629. Sigismund's successors continued to claim the Swedish throne until the mid-seventeenth century.

He was never popular or very happy in Poland. His election came at the cost of a civil war which pitted his supporters against those of the Archduke Maximilian of Austria. Once in power, he was accused of virtually treasonous relations with the Habsburgs (with whom he became close) and of plotting to introduce absolutism in Poland at the expense of the aristocracy. In 1606–1607 there was an open revolt against him. At the end of his life there was little that he could claim had been achieved during his reign.

REFERENCES: *DSH*, vols. 4–6; O. Halecki, *A History of Poland* (New York: Roy Publishers, 1966); D. Normann, *Sigismund Vasa och hans regering i Polen* (Stockholm: Norstedts, 1978); M. Roberts, *The Early Vasas* (Cambridge, England: Cambridge University Press, 1968); *SU*, vol. 25.

B. NORDSTROM

SIGURD I MAGNUSSON (the Crusader) (c. 1090–26 March 1130) King of Norway 1103–30

Sigurd, Eystein, and Olaf, all half brothers and illegitimate sons of King Magnus Bareleg (Magnus III Olafsson*), succeeded their father as kings of Norway in 1103. Since they were only 13, 14, and 3 years old, respectively, their retainers, especially the landed men, initially not only advised them but actually exercised some royal powers. Olaf never did rule much, dying at age 15, while the joint rule of the other two was the longest in Norwegian history, lasting until Eystein's death in 1122. Eystein is known for building harbors and churches and for working toward annexation of a heathen Swedish border province.

Sigurd had been installed by his father in 1098 as ruler of the Orkneys and in 1102 as king of the entire empire of subjugated Norse colonies in the British Isles. After his father's death in Ireland and the young king's return to Norway, the islands reverted to local control. Although expansionist politics were abandoned for the time being, Norwegian political intervention continued in the Orkneys.

Norway had become a real part of Christian Europe in the late 1000s and therefore responded readily to Pope Urban II's plea for a crusade. Sigurd, "the Crusader," departed western Norway in 1108 with 60 ships bound for the Holy Land. Proceeding via England, Spain, and Sicily, and battling Moorish pirates on the way, they reached Palestine in 1110 and were warmly received by King Baldwin I of Jerusalem. Sigurd journeyed on to Constantinople, where he left his fleet and his men, many of whom joined the Varangian guard, and continued over land across Europe, arriving home in 1111.

On his crusade Sigurd had received a piece of the true cross and promised to advance Christianity, and back in Norway he pursued a church-political program, establishing a new bishopric in Stavanger, building churches and cloisters, and donating crown goods to religious institutions. The tithe was introduced in some district laws, and Sigurd proselytized by force in heathen Swedish border provinces in 1123. Sigurd was interested in the traditional royal monopoly of fur-trading in the north and also protected foreign trade. He built defense installations for the Norwegian trading center at present-day Göteborg and spent much time there himself.

Another supposed son of Magnus Bareleg, Harald Gilchrist (Harald IV Magnusson*), arrived in Norway from Ireland in the late 1120s, but he agreed not to claim kingship as long as Sigurd or his son, Magnus IV Sigurdsson*, lived. The designation of Magnus as heir to the throne broke with the traditional co-regency of kings' sons and was a step in the direction of a monarchy. Harald did not, however, honor his pledge after Sigurd's death in Oslo in 1130. He and Magnus shared rule, and the Norwegian civil wars soon began.

REFERENCES: P. S. Andersen, *Samlingen av Norge og kristningen av landet 800–1130* (Bergen: Universitetsforlaget, 1977); K. Gjerset, *History of the Norwegian People* (1932; repr. New York: AMS, 1969); K. Larsen, *A History of Norway* (Princeton: Princeton University Press, 1948/1974); S. Sturluson, *Heimskringla: Sagas of the Norse Kings* (London: Dent, 1961).

J. E. KNIRK

SKALDIC POETRY (ninth–fourteenth centuries) Old Norse court poetry

The skaldic verse form is a complex variation of the traditional Germanic long-line, in which stressed syllables alliterate in two half-lines of two stresses each. Skaldic poetry is strictly syllable-counting, and there are intricate rules for rhyme and alliteration. The favored stanzaic pattern (*dróttkvaett* or "court measure") contains eight lines which divide syntactically in half. Each individual line has exactly six syllables with three stresses, and the lines are joined in pairs by alliteration: there are two alliterating syllables in the odd lines and one in the even lines.

A stylistic feature taken from common Germanic poetic tradition is the kenning. The kenning is an extended simile created by replacing a noun with a base noun which is qualified by a noun in the genitive. For example, a "ship" could be called a "steed of the waves." In skaldic poetry, every possible noun will be replaced and expanded in this way, which makes this noun-heavy poetry seem static and baroque.

The skalds, or court poets, who composed and recited this poetry in Norway, Denmark, and Ireland were at first Norwegians, then primarily Icelanders.

Few complete poems have survived intact, but many individual stanzas appear in the sagas and in Snorri Sturluson's* work. The only complete edition is Finnur Jónsson's *Den Norsk-Islandske Skjaldedigtning* (1908–1915). *Notationes Norroenae* (1923–1944) by Ernst Kock is another important aid for the interpretation of skaldic verse.

REFERENCES: R. Frank, "Old Norse Court Poetry" *Islandica* 42 (Ithaca: Cornell University Press, 1978); L. M. Hollander, *The Skalds* (1945; repr. Ann Arbor: University of Michigan Press, 1968); E. O. G. Turville-Petre, *Skaldic Poetry* (Oxford: Clarendon Press, 1976).

M. EMELITY

SKATING

Archeological finds have demonstrated that skates were widely used in Scandinavia* at least as early as the latter part of the Stone Age, a millennium or two before the Christian era. The earliest extant ones were fashioned of bone, typically the metatarsals of horses or cattle. Their general unwieldiness and lack of toe claws required the skater to propel himself across the ice with a pointed staff. The skates mentioned in the Old Norse sagas were probably of this primitive type. By the Middle Ages they had been refined somewhat and had begun to appear in combinations of wood and iron that represented a considerable technical development and rendered the supplementary staff unnecessary. The earliest of this sort were probably manufactured in the Netherlands.

Precisely what use was made of skates in pre-modern times is not fully clear; it seems most likely, however, that they provided both transportation and recreation. As a social activity, skating has been done in Sweden and Denmark, as elsewhere in Europe, since about the time of the Reformation*. It does not appear to have been widespread in Norway, though, until much more recently. Skiing* has always been the predominant winter sport in that country.

Competitive skating spread to Scandinavia in several forms during the second half of the nineteenth century. Skate sailing, for instance, became popular in the Stockholm archipelago during the 1880s. Norway, on the other hand, became in the 1890s the world's leading nation in speed skating, a sport which had been done in central Europe for over a century and which the Netherlands had previously dominated. It became popular in Sweden during the 1880s and 1890s. Swedes won the men's world championship in 1955, 1963, and 1973. Norwegians captured it 32 times between 1898 and 1981, with skaters from the Netherlands and the Soviet Union generally affording the stiffest competition. Scandinavian women, however, have not won the world championship since the 1930s.

Figure skating came to Scandinavia in the 1860s through the efforts of the

American maestro Jackson Haynes. Gillis Grafström of Sweden won the Olympic gold medal in the men's event in 1920, 1924, and 1928; the legendary Sonja Henie of Norway took the women's in 1928, 1932, and 1936. Apart from them, however, Scandinavians have not stood out. The sport is still practiced in the Nordic countries, although it is now an almost exclusively women's domain.

Ice hockey, invented in Canada around 1880, came to Scandinavia early in the twentieth century. Bandy, a variation of it played by eleven-man teams using a ball instead of a flat puck, was first played in Sweden in the mid-1890s and in Norway in 1905. Like nearly all other sports, hockey is a purely amateur undertaking in Norway and, although fairly popular as a spectator sport, has never developed sufficiently there to allow Norwegians to compete successfully against the national teams of such countries as Canada, the United States, the Soviet Union, Czechoslovakia, or archrival Sweden, where it is a professional sport.

F. HALE

SKIING

Scandinavians used skis of various kinds for transportation as early as the Stone Age. The oldest extant ski, found at Hoting, Sweden, is thought to have been fashioned around 2500 B.C. Many other prehistoric fragments have been exhumed throughout much of northern Europe and Siberia. Rock carvings dating from about 2000 B.C. indicate that Norwegian hunters used skis at least that early. In the thirteenth century, the Icelandic poet Snorri Sturluson* claimed that his Viking* protagonists, who lived 300 years before, were universally competent on skis. Other medieval writers described northern Scandinavia's Lapps* as equally adept.

Until the early modern period, equipment bore little resemblance to that used today. A typical pair consisted of a wooden ski about three meters long used for gliding and another, somewhat shorter and covered with fur, with which the skier pushed against the snow. Both were hewn from the wood of either coniferous or deciduous trees. In lieu of poles, skiers used a single wooden staff to propel and guide themselves until the twentieth century. The immediate ancestor of today's skis, the so-called Telemark ski, dates from the eighteenth century. They were a graceful, matched pair, typically two and a half meters long. Around the beginning of the twentieth century, modern bindings came into existence, waxing became common, and shorter skis came into vogue. In the 1970s fiberglass surpassed wood as the leading material for skis, although many now include both.

Since about 1500, skis have played an important role in Scandinavian postal and messenger services. Their military deployment antedates historical records and continues to the present. Documents from the eighteenth century refer to regular ski units in the Norwegian and Swedish armies. Polar explorers Fridtjof Nansen* and Roald Amundsen used skis on their expeditions to Greenland* and the Antarctic, respectively.

For over 100 years skiing has been central in Scandinavian athletic competition. Organized races were first held in the 1860s, when enthusiasts founded the first skiing club. Before the turn of the century ski jumping also developed as a sport. Today competitive cross-country skiing is highly developed in Sweden and Norway and involves vast numbers of Scandinavians of all ages and both sexes. Norwegians, and to a lesser degree Swedes and Finns, dominated the cross-country events at the Winter Olympics from their inception in 1924 until the Soviet Union and the German Democratic Republic broke the Scandinavians' near monopoly in the 1970s. Jumping has developed in step with the other disciplines. Early in the twentieth century an erect style produced leaps of 20 to 30 meters. Alpine skiing (downhill and slalom racing) long lagged far behind the Nordic or cross-country events with regard to popularity and Scandinavian success in international competition. In the early 1950s, however, the Norwegian Stein Eriksen gained renown, winning the combined Alpine world championship in 1954. The Swede Ingemar Stenmark was regarded as the world's supreme slalom skier in the late 1970s and early 1980s.

It is as a popular activity, however, that skiing, especially of the cross-country sort, has been best known in Scandinavia. Unprecedented prosperity following World War II* brought a surplus of leisure time and greatly increased purchasing power. Equipment underwent further refinements, and such phenomena as illuminated trails to allow evening skiing became commonplace. By the 1970s many other activities offered alternatives, though, and fewer Scandinavians participated regularly than was previously the case. Nonetheless, skiing remains the prevalent form of wintertime exercise in Sweden and Norway. Denmark, lacking both mountains and persistent freezing temperatures, has never been known for outdoor winter sports, but skiing is relatively popular there when conditions allow it.

REFERENCE: O. Bø, *Skiing Traditions in Norway*, trans. H. Corlett (Oslo: Norske Samlaget, 1968).

F. HALE

SLAVERY Sweden

In pre-Christian Scandinavian society the social status of a slave or thrall (*träl*) was already institutionalized in the ancient kinship system. A free person might cross the line into *träldom* voluntarily to secure economic support in old age or involuntarily by being condemned for certain crimes. The status position of the *träl* was essential to the function of the justice system.

Beginning around the ninth century, Viking* raids and trading led to the influx of large numbers of agricultural and household slaves. Over the course of the next two to three centuries, areas of Scandinavia* became economically dependent upon the slaves. As Christianity took hold in Denmark and Norway, the practice of slavery ended by fiat, but missionary work, which began in Sweden just after 1000 A.D., progressed slowly. Manumission of slaves was only encouraged. In time this led to what was in effect a constitutional crisis: the requirement of spiritual equality conflicted with the requirement of economic inequality. On the continent, the contradiction had produced the theological rationalization: "It is not nature which has made slaves, rather it is the Fall." The consequence of this rationalization was that although the practice of slavery dwindled there for economic reasons, slavery as an institution was never formally ended.

In contrast, in Sweden, beginning in the last decades of the thirteenth century, successive changes in the laws of Uppland, Västmanland, and Östergötland regarding slaves suggest the beginning of theological and juridical integration. In 1335, on the occasion of his Eriksgata (the recognition tour traditional in Sweden), Magnus Eriksson* issued a proclamation declaring that no child of a Christian parent was henceforth to be a slave. Although the power of the king at this time consisted largely of moral leadership, his initiative was implemented through use of the traditional assemblies of all men of full citizenship. Following his proclamation, Magnus Eriksson appointed a committee for the kingdom. Working back and forth between local and provincial assemblies, members of representative committees produced a synthesis in 1347. Addressed to the entire kingdom, it came to be known as Magnus Eriksson's Land Law. Beginning in the following decade, the influence of this body of law may be seen in the quiet revolution which ended slavery in Sweden.

REFERENCES: M. Bloch, "How and Why Ancient Slavery Came to an End," in *Slavery and Serfdom in the Middle Ages*, trans. W. R. Beer (Berkeley: University of California Press, 1975); S. Carlsson and J. Rosén, *Svensk historia*, 2 vols. (Stockholm: Svenska Bokförlaget, 1962); H. Hasselberg, "Den svensk skarastadgan och träldomens upphörande i Sverige," *Västergötlands fornminnesförenings tidskrift* (1944); C. Nevéus, *Trälarna i landskapslagarnas samhälle, Danmark och Sverige* (Uppsala, 1974); S. U. Palme, *Kristendomens genombrott i Sverige* (Stockholm: Bonniers, 1959), and *Stånd och klasser i forna dagars Sverige* (Stockholm: Bonniers, 1947).

J. D. LIND

SLESVIG QUESTION Denmark's southern boundary

No issue has loomed larger in Denmark's international relations during the past two centuries than the location of its southern border. By tradition early Danish kings looked to the River Ejder as the boundary. To the north lay Slesvig (Schleswig), to the south was Holstein. In the fifteenth century, the king of Denmark became the duke of both Slesvig and Holstein. Northern Slesvig was overwhelmingly Danish in language and culture, while Holstein was equally German. The area in between, commonly called South Slesvig, was a mixture of both peoples. This arrangement lasted nearly 400 years, but beginning in the early part of the nineteenth century a rising tide of nationalism made the status of the duchies an explosive issue.

In the revolutionary year of 1848, Holstein and pro-German elements within Slesvig rose against Danish rule. Supported by troops from Prussia, the rebels battled the Danish army. Soon, however, outside powers, primarily Russia and

Austria, forced Prussia to withdraw from the conflict, and the Danes were able to put down the rebellion. Thus the first Slesvig war ended with the status of the duchies largely unchanged.

When Frederik VII* proclaimed a new constitution for Denmark and Slesvig in 1863, violating an agreement sanctioned by the major powers meeting at London in 1852 that Slesvig would not be treated differently than Holstein, the new Prussian chancellor, Otto von Bismarck, saw great opportunity in the situation. He now sought to use a war with Denmark as a means of hastening German unification. In early 1864 Prussian and Austrian troops attacked Denmark. Danish forces were badly outnumbered and soon fell back in retreat. Rather than risk total defeat, the Danish government sued for peace. Under the terms of the Treaty of Vienna, signed in October 1864, Denmark was forced to renounce all rights to Slesvig and Holstein and saw its border pushed northward to the Kongeaa River. Among the nearly 1 million in population lost were some 200,000 pro-Danish North Slesvigers.

Many Danes were deeply grieved over the loss of Slesvig and thus welcomed the news from Paris in 1919 that the Treaty of Versailles provided Slesvigers with the right of self-determination. Accordingly, an internationally supervised plebiscite was held in North Slesvig in February 1920. Seventy-five percent of the voters opted for a return to Denmark. A similar vote a month later in mid-Slesvig produced almost the opposite result. The Danish government reluctantly agreed to abide by the outcome, and the present-day border with Germany was established. Although there are minorities on both sides of the frontier between Denmark and Germany, few national boundaries more clearly reflect the wishes of the people most directly involved. (*See also* North Slesvig.)

REFERENCES: William Carr, *Schleswig-Holstein, 1815–1848: A Study in National Conflict* (Manchester, England: University Press, 1963); Karen Larson, "The Settlement of the Slesvig Question," *Political Science Quarterly* 34 (1919): 568–90; Roar Skovmand, "The Reunion of North Slesvig," in J. Bukdahl et al., eds., *Scandinavia Past and Present*, 3 vols. (Odense: Edvard Henriksen, 1959), II, pp. 1004–8; Lawrence D. Steefel, *The Schleswig Holstein Question* (Cambridge, Mass.: Harvard University Press, 1932).

P. L. PETERSEN

SNORRI STURLUSON (1178–1241) Icelandic historian and poet

Snorri was fostered by Jón Loptsson, the most influential man at that time, at Oddi in southwest Iceland. Snorri was educated at the school there; he held the position of lawspeaker for fifteen years and was also a skald. He was politically prominent during Iceland's period of civil war. He won the favor of the Norwegian king Haakon IV Haakonsson* and was enlisted to aid the king in bringing Iceland under Norwegian control. Later, Snorri allied himself with the king's enemies and was finally burned to death in his house by Gizurr, a former son-in-law and supporter of the king.

The *Prose Edda*, written c. 1220, was Snorri's first major literary work. It is a handbook for poets and contains three sections: "Gylfaginning" (The Deluding of Gylfi), a compendium of Norse mythology; "Skáldskaparmál" (Poetic Diction), an explanation of the development of kennings based on myths; and "Háttatal" (List of Metres), which contains 102 examples of metres used by skalds.

Heimskringla (Orb of the World), begun in 1220, is a history of Norway from the first settlement of gods from Asia to the reign of Magnus V Erlingsson* (d. 1184). It has more importance as a source of skaldic verse than as history.

REFERENCES: M. Ciklamini, *Snorri Sturluson*, Twayne World Author Series 493 (Boston: G. K. Hall, 1978); J. Simon, "Snorri Sturluson: His Life and Times," *Parergon* 15 (1976): 3–15; S. Sturluson, *Heimskringla: History of the Kings of Norway* trans. L. M. Hollander (Austin: University of Texas Press, 1964), and *The Prose Edda*, selected and trans. J. I. Young (1966; repr. Berkeley: University of California Press, 1973).

M. EMELITY

SOCIAL DEMOCRATIC PARTY: FINLAND

The Finnish labor movement began as a patriarchal, social-humanistic bourgeois effort in the 1880s to improve the position of the working class. Within a decade, however, the workers began to organize themselves and founded the Finnish Labor Party (1899), the last of the Nordic labor parties but the first Finnish political party to represent a socioeconomic interest group. This relatively late stage of development in the political party system reflected the dominant agrarian basis of Finnish society, preoccupation with the language question, and Finland's autonomous but threatened status within the Russian Empire. In 1903 the party changed its name to the Social Democratic Party (SDP) and officially adopted the Marxist, revolutionary program of the Erfurt convention of 1891, an ideological stance undiluted by the Bernstein school. Adherence to this ideology, at a time when other Nordic Social Democratic parties were moving toward reformism, may be explained partially by the relatively late industrial "breakthrough" in Finland which began in the 1890s, by the oppressive nature of Russian rule during this period, and by the achievements of the General Strike of 1905.

The role of workers in the General Strike greatly enhanced the position of the SDP, and the electoral reforms of 1906 opened the door to political participation. In 1907 the party won 80 of 200 seats in parliament, a feat made possible by extensive organizational activities not only among urban workers but also among landless farmers and crofters in rural areas of western and southern Finland. By the eve of the Russian Revolution, the SDP held an absolute majority (103 seats) in parliament. This political position, which was based on popular votes but not reinforced by the institutions of autonomous Finland, soon confronted the party leadership with a crisis which proved to be its undoing. Caught between demands for revolutionary leadership from below and the requirements of coalition government to form a united front against Russian threats to Finnish autonomy, the Social Democrats seized power and set off a chain of events which led to the Civil War* in 1918 and a bourgeois victory.

Even before the final defeat of the revolutionary forces Väinö Tanner*, who had kept a low profile during the Civil War, began to reorganize the party. At the party congress in December 1918 the SDP officially denounced the revolution and adopted a reformist, democratic-parliamentary line which reflected an ideological adjustment to the hostile political environment of a bourgeois-dominated, independent Finland. Although the SDP did form a minority government (1926–1927), which was based on its 59 seats and the support of the Progressive Party* (*see* Progressive/Liberal Party) and the Swedish People's Party*, it remained politically weak during the 1920s and generally adhered to an ideological commitment to remain in opposition until strong enough to introduce socialism via the institutions of political democracy. Differences with Communists were thus primarily over tactics, not socioeconomic goals; but the domestic and international developments during the 1930s represented a new stage in the ordering of ideological priorities of the party and its role in Finnish politics. Advocacy of reforms to solve problems of unemployment and fear of neo-fascist tendencies in Finland prompted party leadership to work toward cooperation with the political Center. This new orientation led to the formation of a Center-Left coalition in 1937 based on the Social Democratic and Agrarian parties (*see*Center Party: Finland) and headed by a Progressive, but it also increased dissension within the SDP over the abandonment of a commitment to structural reforms and over Tanner's refusal to cooperate with small Left-Socialist factions.

The trauma of World War II* and its aftermath aggravated divisions within the party and produced a number of splinter movements. The foreign policy options open to Finland during the war failed to correspond to the cultural preferences of the SDP, that is, cooperation with the political democracies of Western Europe and especially Scandinavia* proved to be impossible. The party remained in the cabinet throughout the war, however, out of fear of Soviet intentions and in order to maintain wartime national unity. Although this policy strengthened the position of the party in Finnish society, the opposition wing of the SDP became increasingly critical of party leadership in 1943–1944. When the SDP refused to cooperate with the newly legalized Communist Party* after the war, some within the opposition factions left the party and joined the Finnish People's Democratic League, a coalition of Left-Socialists and Communists. This attempt to form a Socialist popular front failed to attract the rank and file of the SDP, and the party remained divided over the extent to which it should cooperate with the People's Democratic League, its main competitor at the polls, and over the extent to which it should actively support Juho Paasikivi's* foreign policy. The Social Democratic Party participated in the Big Three coalition of 1945–1948, but only the opposition wing within the SDP provided active support for the coalition.

In 1948–1950 the SDP formed a minority government which was aimed against the Communist Party and supported by the non-Socialists in parliament. Internal strife continued to plague the party, however, especially from the mid-1950s to 1963, when the election of Rafael Paasio to the chairmanship made it possible to reconcile differences within the party and to adopt a policy of cooperation among the parties of the Left and laid the basis for Center-Left coalitions which have governed Finland into the 1980s.

Finnish social welfare and economic policies of the 1960s and 1970s have greatly influenced the politics of these Center-Left coalitions. Although Urho Kekkonen's* successor, the Social Democrat Mauno Koivisto*, won the presidency in 1982 by a sizeable majority, post-electoral polls suggest that his election will have little impact on the parliamentary strength of the party. The Social Democratic Party is ideologically close to its Nordic counterparts, but the heritage of the Civil War, the existence of a large Communist Party, and bourgeois majorities in every parliamentary election except 1916, 1958, and 1966 have prevented the SDP from becoming a Socialist alternative and have left it no choice but to participate in coalition governments. This is a fate shared by every political party in Finland, where majority government has meant coalition government.

REFERENCES: S. Berglund and U. Lindström, *The Scandinavian Party System(s)* (Lund: Studentlitteratur, 1978); R. Helenius, "The Finnish Social Democratic Party," in W. Patterson and T. Alastair, eds., *Social Democratic Parties in Western Europe* (London: Croom Helm, 1977); J. Nousiainen, *The Finnish Political System* (Cambridge, Mass.: Harvard University Press, 1973); T. Paavonen, "The Social Democratic Movement in the Politics of Independent Finland," in R. M. Berry, *Essays on the History of the Development of Finnish Political Parties* (Turku: The Institute of Political History, 1983); H. Soikkanen, "Revisionism, Reformism and the Finnish Labour Movement Before the First World War," *Scandinavian Journal of History* 3, 4 (1978).

R. M. BERRY

SOCIAL DEMOCRATIC PARTY: SWEDEN (Sveriges Socialdemokratiska Arbetareparti)

August Palm* carried modern Social Democratic ideas to Sweden in the early 1880s. His message spread rapidly, and in 1889 representatives from more than 60 Social Democratic clubs and trade unions met in Stockholm* to create the Swedish Social Democratic Party. Extra-parliamentary agitation was at first the most important focus of Social Democratic efforts; in close cooperation with the union movement the party built effective local labor organizations. Under the guidance of K. Hjalmar Branting* the party concentrated on the pursuit of universal suffrage through an electoral alliance with the Liberals. Revolutionary and anarchist tendencies within the party gradually succumbed to the advocates of parliamentary democracy and social reform. The party's first official program, largely written by Axel Danielsson and adopted by the fourth party congress in 1897, deviated from its model, the German Erfurt program, to stress the capacity of working-class organizations to counteract the natural tendencies of capitalism.

The Social Democrats came to dominate Swedish party politics from 1932 to 1976, but their ascendancy came about only after a long, gradual process of growth. In 1896 Hjalmar Branting became the party's first Riksdag* delegate, thanks to an electoral agreement with the Liberals. The party steadily increased its representation until by 1915 it had become the largest party in the Second Chamber. In 1917 the Social Democrats entered a coalition government with the Liberals and in 1918 instituted universal suffrage and the eight-hour day. Under the newly democratized electoral system the Social Democrats became the largest party in both chambers, but clear parliamentary majorities remained elusive; only in 1940 and 1968 did they win a clear majority of the Riksdag delegates. When the Liberal-Social Democratic coalition dissolved in 1920, Hjalmar Branting formed the first of three minority Social Democratic governments (1920, 1921–1923, 1924–1925). Not until 1933 did the party secure an effective governing majority when, following their success in the 1932 election, they formed a parliamentary (but not governmental) coalition with the Farmers' Party (*see* Center Party: Sweden). With Per Albin Hansson* as prime minister and Ernst Wigforss* as minister of finance, they embarked on the first use of modern countercyclical economic policy and a modest program of welfare statist measures (*see* Welfare State).

At the outbreak of war in 1939, the Social Democratic-Farmers' alliance broadened into a wartime coalition with all the non-Socialist parties. The coalition government and the common danger of war muted ideological debate, but as the war drew to a close the Social Democrats resumed the offensive. The revised party program and the Working Class Movement's Postwar Program of 1944 outlined sweeping proposals for full employment, juster distribution of wealth, economic efficiency, and industrial democracy. With support from the non-Socialist parties, the Social Democrats improved pensions, introduced children's allowances, and adopted a program for national health insurance; however, initiatives for a new housing policy, misjudgments in economic policy, and especially proposals for a more progressive tax structure unleashed vitriolic opposition that culminated in the 1948 election campaign. Although the Social Democrats maintained their strength, the bourgeois opposition blunted their offensive, and a period of consolidation set in. From 1951 to 1957 the Social Democrats ruled in coalition with the Farmers' Party.

In 1959, after heated political debate and an advisory referendum, the Social Democrats passed the legislation establishing supplementary pensions. The ensuing election cemented the Social Democrats' hold on power, but reform initiatives slackened until the passage of industrial democracy legislation in the early 1970s. In 1976 the Social Democrats fell from office, their electoral position weakened by the new constitution of 1970, a series of minor scandals, a more unified bourgeois opposition, and Thorbjörn Fälldin's skillful exploitation of the nuclear power issue.

The political success of the Swedish Social Democrats derived in great measure from their ability to maintain a powerful, unified organization while their opponents to the Right and Left remained divided. The bourgeois opposition showed little internal unity until the 1960s; when the Left Socialists parted from the Social Democrats in 1917 they split three more times during the 1920s. Through collective membership of entire trade unions, the party has effected a strong alliance with the labor movement and steadily built up a membership to more than 1 million. Its strong emphasis on party unity and its neutralist foreign policy have allowed it to avoid the fragmentation resulting from foreign policy disagreements that has plagued its Norwegian and Danish sister parties. Indicative of the party's stability is the fact that just four leaders—Hjalmar Branting, Per Albin Hansson, Tage Erlander*, and Sven Olof Palme*—have guided it for virtually its entire history.

The party's highest organization is the triennial party congress. Between congresses the party executive determines policy. The main local party organization is the labor commune. Although the sense of social democracy as an alternative culture has waned, the party retains youth, women's, children's, Christian, and temperance organizations. It is associated with the workers' educational organizations, the people's halls and people's parks groups, other cultural organizations, cooperative enterprises, and newspapers.

Since 1932 the Social Democratic Party has never obtained less than 41.7 percent of the Swedish electorate. During the 1970s its performance fluctuated between 43 and 45 percent, a decline from the 1960s which has entailed the loss of its ruling position. Whether these losses reflect long-term social trends or simply temporary dissatisfaction with party policy is still moot. The party's grip on working-class voters has declined since 1960, but the party has made substantial inroads into white-collar families; nearly 40 percent of its electorate is drawn from the latter group.

Although it is often claimed that the SDP is the model of pragmatism in politics, the party maintains a tradition of lively ideological discussion; indeed, it is this combination of ideology and pragmatism that distinguishes the Swedish party. The precise character of its ideological evolution has been highly controversial. No one disputes the party's essentially reformist character, but Herbert Tingsten's classic analysis argues that the party abandoned its Marxist heritage for welfare statism. Leif Lewin, on the other hand, stresses the retention of basic Socialist convictions. The program revisions of 1905, 1908, 1911, 1920, 1944, 1960, and 1975 do demonstrate a persistent adherence to the democratic Socialist values of freedom, equality, solidarity, democracy, and work. The party sees itself as having successfully introduced political democracy and a large measure of social democracy into Swedish life. Its current goal is to achieve industrial and economic democracy. To that end it now endorses a system of "wage-earner funds" to supplement its traditionally favored instrumentalities of "functional socialism," a strong public sector, and economic planning.

REFERENCES: N. Elvander, *Skandinavisk Arbetarrörelse* (Stockholm: Liber, 1980); W. Korpi, *The Working Class in Welfare Capitalism* (London: Routledge and Kegan, 1978); J. Lindgren, *Det Socialdemokratiska arbetarpartiets uppkomst i Sverige. 1881–1889* (Stockholm: Tidens, 1927); D. Sainsbury, *Swedish Social Democratic Ideology and Electoral Politics 1944–1948* (Stockholm: Almqvist & Wiksell International, 1980); J. D. Stephens, "The Consequences of Social Structural Change for the Development of Socialism in Sweden,'' Ph.D. dissertation, Yale University, 1976; *SU*, Vol. 26; H. Tingsten, *The Swedish Social Democrats: Their Ideological Development* (Totowa, N.J.: Bedminster, 1973).

T. TILTON

SOUTH AFRICA Scandinavians in South Africa

Scandinavians, particularly Swedes and Norwegians, have played significant roles in the development of South Africa from a pastoral society to an important modern industrial power. They have contributed in a variety of ways as explorers, natural scientists, missionaries, early pioneers and settlers, fishermen, whalers, miners, and more recently as engineers, business people, and investors.

Scandinavians began to come to the southern tip of Africa in the seventeenth century in the employ of the Dutch East India Company or as crew members of passing Danish or Swedish ships. Many of these early Scandinavians were founders of prominent Afrikaner families. Three cases in point were Oloff Bergh (1643–1724), Anders Stockenström (1757–1811), and Carl Gustaf Trägårdh (Triegard; 1717–1767). The latter's grandson was Louis Tregardt (Trichardt), who was the first Voortrekker.

Scandinavians in the area during the first two-thirds of the nineteenth century were mainly natural scientists, merchants, explorers, and missionaries. Natural scientists Anders Sparrman (1748–1820) and C. P. Thunberg (1743–1828), students of Linnaeus, studied and explored parts of what is today the Cape Province. Jacob Letterstedt (1796–1862) was a Swede involved in trading and business interests in Cape Town. Johan August Wahlberg (1810–1856) was engaged in scientific and exploratory pursuits in Natal, the Transvaal, and South West Africa. C. J. Andersson (1827–1867) and A. W. Eriksson (d. 1901) were associated with the opening of Namibia for European expansion and colonization.

The first missionary to establish permanent stations in Zululand was the Norwegian Hans P. S. Schreuder (1817–1882)(*see* Missionaries: Africa). Other Norwegian and Swedish missionaries soon followed. Schreuder, Ommund Oftebro (1820–1893), and Otto Witt (1848–1923) wrote eyewitness accounts of the important events in Zululand in the nineteenth century. Robert C. A. Samuelson, son of a Norwegian missionary, was Cetshwayo's (Zulu leader) confidant and also served on the defense team in Dinuzulu's (another Zulu leader) 1908 trial. On the whole, Scandinavian missionaries showed a genuine concern for the indigenous people and helped to maintain and develop a sense of self-reliance and pride.

The discovery of gold and diamonds in the last third of the nineteenth century spurred economic development and attracted numerous Scandinavians. Several emigration schemes were organized including the Norwegian Marburg community (south of Durban), founded in 1882, and the Swedish settlement along the Vaal River in the Transvaal led by Oscar W. A. Forssman (1822–1899). Successful Scandinavians included the Thesens (Norwegian) in shipbuilding and timber in the Knysna region of the Cape Province; Anders Ohlsson in the brewery business in Cape Town; and J. J. Egeland and Abraham Larsen in their Union Whaling Company, headquartered in Durban. Generally, Scandinavians in South Africa had some educational or skilled occupational background, both of which were badly needed. In the first half of the twentieth century, large Swedish and Danish companies were attracted by South Africa's economic potential.

Scandinavians have rapidly assimilated into South African society and have been active participants on both sides of the Boer-Briton controversy. During the Boer War (1899–1902), a Scandinavian corps was organized to fight with the Afrikaners. Others fought in Boer commando units or in British contingents. Scandinavians have also served in governmental areas for British and Afrikaner alike.

REFERENCE: A. Winquist, *Scandinavians and South Africa* (Cape Town: A. A. Balkema, 1978).

A. H. WINQUIST

SPARRE, CLAES (6 January 1673–25 April 1733) Swedish admiral

Claes Sparre was one of the two most prominent Swedish admirals in the later years of the Great Northern War* (*see also* Wachtmeister, Carl Hans av Björkö). Sparre was a student at Uppsala before entering Dutch naval service in 1691. By 1700 he was in the Swedish navy and saw action in the Gulf of Finland against Russian naval forces out of Kronstadt not later than 1705. In 1710, now an admiral, he had overall command of Karlskrona* and showed great resource in maintaining the supply lines across the south Baltic to Stralsund in the summer of 1715. Without losing a ship to the Danes, he brought a vital convoy there to reinforce Karl XII*. In 1719 he was enobled, made president of the Karlskrona Admiralty, and flew the flag of grand admiral of Sweden in that year and the two years following. His commands were now characterized by his partnership with the English admiral Sir John Norris, following Britain's renewal of her alliance with Sweden of 1700. But Sparre's record was now tarnished by his war-weariness and his willingness to be guided by an English naval strategy strictly conceived as being defensive only—to deter rather than prevent Russian coastal attacks. Sparre, who had some literary talent, commemorated his partnership with English forces with an inscription engraved on a rock face on Marö, at the northern end of the Stockholm archipelago. His two sons did several years' service in the English navy during the 1720s.

REFERENCES: B. Börjeson, *Örlogsflottans Officerare 1700–1799* (Stockholm, 1942); E. Holmberg, "Karl XIIs amiraler," *Tidskrift i Sjöväsendet*, 1919; *SMK*, Vol. 7; *SU*, Vol. 26; H. Wrangel, *Kriget i Östersjön 1719–1721* (Stockholm, 1906).

D. D. ALDRIDGE

STAAFF, KARL (1860–1915) Prime minister of Sweden

Karl Staaff was the leading organizer and spokesperson of the Liberal Party (*see* Liberal People's Party) in Sweden from the turn of the century until his premature death. He was prime minister in 1906 and from 1911 to 1914. As a student at Uppsala University, he was a founder of the liberal student organization Verdandi. After qualifying for government service as an attorney, he instead entered private practice in Stockholm.* Elected to the lower chamber of the parliament in 1896, he became one of the nation's most effective leaders for reform legislation and the "little people," by which he meant the lower middle class. By 1900 he was the dominant figure in the new National Liberal Federation and its parliamentary counterpart, the Liberal Coalition Party.

Staaff, always critical of the government's handling of Norwegian affairs, won the respect of all sides for his role as one of the chief architects for a peaceful dissolution of the Norwegian-Swedish Union in 1905. Unable to achieve franchise reform while prime minister in 1906, he became leader of the opposition until 1911. By then the Conservatives had effected franchise reform, but the upper chamber was still a bastion of conservatism. Staaff wanted to neutralize it and the monarchy, as in England.

The dominant issue during his second ministry was the defense question. Determined to economize on defense spending and to provide a unified defense system, he appointed a Defense Committee comprised entirely of laypersons. This committee ultimately recommended a stronger defense, as did Staaff, in December 1913. The main argument between Staaff and the military was over the length of time infantry recruits should train. Though he had come to office, at least in part, on this issue, he recommended that a decision on it be put off until after the general election in the fall of 1914. Defense enthusiasts organized an impressive Farmers' March* (Bondetåget) in February 1914, during which they presented a petition to the king calling for the immediate solution of the problem. In response, Gustav V* publicly repudiated Staaff's proposal without prior consultation and thereby precipitated a constitutional crisis. Staaff and his cabinet resigned, and the Liberals lost heavily in the special and regular elections in March and September 1914. During the campaigns he was subjected to unprecedented vilification and slander by the military and some court circles.

Staaff's record in democratic and social reforms is substantial. Legislation to protect small farmers from the timber companies in the north, education reforms, and an ombudsman for the military are some examples. He was a strong supporter of the temperance movement* and legislation. As a political leader he kept his own counsel, too much so for the disparate liberal factions which he needed for support. His relationship with Gustav was strained at best from 1906 onward. If not a warm personality, he was forthright and not devious. Staaff was a tragic figure. Two years after his death the monarch and the right-wing conservatives were forced to accept the principle of parliamentary democracy. Caught between the Socialists and the last gasp of the imperialist Swedes, he remains an outstanding champion of parliamentary democracy in Sweden.

REFERENCES: L. Kihlberg, *Karl Staaff*, 2 vols. (Stockholm: Bonniers, 1962–1963); D. Rustow, *The Politics of Compromise* (Princeton: Princeton University Press, 1955); B. Schiller, "Years of Crisis, 1906–1914," in S. Koblik, ed., *Sweden's Development from Poverty to Affluence, 1750–1970* (Minneapolis: University of Minnesota Press,

1975); P. V. Thorson, "The Defense Question in Sweden 1911–1914," Ph.D. dissertation, University of Minnesota, 1972; D. Verney, *Parliamentary Reform in Sweden, 1866–1921* (Oxford: Clarendon Press, 1957).

P. V. THORSON

STANLEY, JOHN THOMAS (1766–1850) English traveler to the Faroe Islands* and Iceland

John Thomas Stanley was the eldest son and heir of one of the richest men in England, Sir John Thomas Stanley, of Alderley Park in Cheshire. After a private education including a grand tour with a tutor from the age of 14 to 20, he studied science at Edinburgh University for two years.

Edinburgh proved a very stimulating place for the young man. He became acquainted with Adam Smith the economist, James Hutton the geologist, Joseph Black the chemist, and William Cullen the physician. But it was no doubt the influence of Sir Joseph Banks, traveler, natural historian, and president of the Royal Society, who had himself led an expedition to Iceland in 1772, that directed Stanley's attention northwards. Stanley's voyage to Faroe and Iceland in 1789 probably ranks as the world's first student expedition.

The expedition ship was an American-rigged brig, the *John*, commanded by a retired naval officer, Lieutenant Pierie. Among the travelers were John F. Crawford, part-owner of the ship; John Baine, a teacher of mathematics in Edinburgh and a skilled astronomer, draughtsman, and botanist; Isaac Samuel Benners, the son of a planter of St. Croix; and Alexander Colden, an American. Baine, James Wright, and Benners kept diaries of the expedition.

The *John* sailed from Leith on 28 May 1789 and was in Orkney from 31 May to 10 June. The expedition was in the Faroes from 13 June to 28 June, and in Iceland from 4 July to 31 August. Delayed by contrary winds, the expedition left Iceland on 8 September and reached Copenhagen* on 27 September. On 26 October the expedition left Denmark; it reached Leith on 3 November, without the loss of a man and without any kind of serious mishap.

In the Faroes the travelers explored the straits between Streymoy and Eysturoy. Some crossed Esturoy on foot to Oyndarfjörður, while others visited the remarkable cliffs on north Streymoy by boat. Wright made a journey westwards, across Vágar and on to Mykines. Several in the party climbed Skaelingsfjall (788 meters), then believed to be the highest summit in the Faroes.

In Iceland the expedition made one of the first ascents of Snæfellsjökull. On 29 July the expedition left Reykjavik on horseback for Hekla, which they ascended on 8 August. They returned by way of Skálholt, Geysir, and Thingvellir. The visit to Denmark was made so that Stanley could be presented at the Danish court.

The expedition's observations in Faroe make an interesting supplement to the work of Jens Christian Svabo* in 1781–1782. Their work in Iceland contributed to the study of volcanic phenomena, especially geysers. Their general observations in Iceland are also of special interest, being made so soon after the great eruption of 1783 with its widespread devastation.

REFERENCES: Jane Adeane, *The Early Married Life of Maria Josepha, Lady Stanley* (London, 1899)(contains a biographic account of Stanley); John Barrow, *A Visit to Iceland* (London, 1835); John F. West, ed., *The Journals of the Stanley Expedition to the Faroes and Iceland in 1789*, 3 vols. (Tórshavn: Föroya Froðskaparsetur, 1970, 1975, 1976).

J. F. WEST

STAUNING, THORVALD (26 October 1872–3 May 1942) Danish Social Democratic leader and statesman

Thorvald Stauning was the unquestioned leader of the Danish Social Democratic Party (*see* Political Parties) from its beginnings in the late nineteenth century until his death in 1942, during the German occupation. From 1898 until 1906 he served as party treasurer. From this position he went on to become his party's leading spokesman in the Folketing*, and from 1924 to 1926 he was prime minister in Denmark's first Social Democratic government.

After a brief period of rule by the Conservatives and Liberal Left (Venstre), the Social Democrats came back to power in 1929 with Stauning as premier and Peter Munch*, the Radical leader, as foreign minister. This coalition ministry governed Denmark throughout the tumultuous depression decade of the 1930s and during the first three months of the German occupation. It was a testimony to Stauning's leadership qualities that he was able to overcome opposition and often severe criticism from conservative and nationalist Danish politicians on the one hand and the German authorities on the other. Throughout the first two years of the occupation, until his death in May 1942, he remained as prime minister, presiding over a coalition government which included Conservatives and Liberals on the Right as well as Social Democrats and Radicals on the Left. By the time of his death many Danes and Germans had come to look upon Stauning as an indispensable unifying figure who could effectively reconcile the many conflicts that arose between the Danes and the Nazi leaders in Berlin or their representatives in Copenhagen*.

Stauning's skill as a politician, diplomat, and compromiser stemmed from his firm commitment to the moderate type of socialism espoused by the Second International. His commitment to political and social democracy, economic reform, and international peace was not utopian or revolutionary. He strongly believed in the need for cooperation between the working class and the Social Democratic Party on the one hand and sympathetic middle-class groups like the Radical Party on the other. This made Stauning an accomplished and astute parliamentarian who could even work effectively with Conservatives and Liberals as well as with the more ideologically compatible Radicals during the last two years of his life.

Stauning's moderation and flexibility put a strong stamp on his own party and on Danish politics in general. Partly due to his influence, Danish politics throughout the twentieth century has been characterized by an avoidance of extremism on either the Left or Right, in spite of periods when Denmark underwent considerable stress and strain, such as during the Great Depression, the German occupation in World War II*, and the early years of the Cold War.

REFERENCES: B. Arneson, *The Democratic Monarchies of Scandinavia* (New York: D. Van Nostrand, 1939); P. Hansen, *Contemporary Danish Politicians; 45 Portraits with a Brief Look at the Development of Danish Parliamentary Democracy* (Copenhagen: Det Danske Selskab, 1949); H. Kirchhoff et al., *Besættelstidens historie* (Copenhagen: Danmarks Radios Grundboger Fremad, 1964); J. L. Voorhis, "A Study of Official Relations Between the German and Danish Governments in the Period Between 1940–1943" Ph.D. dissertation, Northwestern University, 1968; F. Wendt, *Besættelse og Atomtid 1939– 1970* (Copenhagen: Politikens Forlag, 1972).

J. L. VOORHIS

STAVE CHURCHES (*Stavkirker*) Medieval wood churches

The stave churches were constructed during a flourishing building period that lasted from about 1200 to the mid-fourteenth century. The Black Death and other factors put an end to their construction. During this period, some 700 churches were built in Norway alone. About 30 of these have survived. The simplest type, represented by the Holtålen church, was built around 1200 and is now at Sverresborg in Trondheim. This type is characterized by a rectangular nave, a lower choir in the east, and portals toward the south and west. Built entirely of wood, these churches are above-ground constructions. The sills rest on stone foundations. Between the structural corner posts, tongue-and-groove planks form the walls. Upper horizontal beams locked into the corner posts hold the walls in a firm framework. The planks have vertical grooves to permit run-off of rainwater. Extensive archeological research over the past 40 years points fairly conclusively to the fact that the formal plan is Norman. The technical solution of the building is based on a wood-building tradition which developed over centuries. Later, Gothic and Romanesque influences were incorporated in the church architecture, but the technical solutions continued to evolve from wood techniques. Examples of the further development of the single-naved churches are at Uvdal and Reinli. There, central pillars with connecting arches have been added to support the roof beams.

Far more complicated in construction are the later and more fully developed stave churches with an inner rectangle of free-standing posts. The structural development can be traced from the early basilical Sogn churches with up to 20 posts in the long nave, through to the addition of the upper support frame with St. Andrew crosses, which eliminated the need for the posts to extend to the floor and permitted the development of a more open central space, as in the Hallingdal and Valdres churches.

The primary support for the stave church is four sleepers that form a rectangular frame in the floor. Where the sleepers cross, the four main posts rise; additional posts stand between these on the sleepers. The sleepers continue out and join the wall sills, which are locked into shorter posts at the corners. The rafters are attached high on the free-standing posts and form a sharply slanted roof. A horizontal strut links the top of the wall with the mast, which is reinforced by a bracket above it. The triangle formed between the vertical line of the free-standing mast, the horizontal strut, and the diagonal rafter supports the inner columnar structure and gives an added feature of elasticity to the building. The inner columnar structure defines a lofty space under the roof it supports. Since stave churches have no underground construction, this structural system used the lateral columns to provide the essential balanced support. The free-standing posts were the primary supports for the central roof structure, while the lower outer walls provided protection and further support. Knee braces (brackets), hewn from large fir roots, were placed horizontally and vertically between the masts. The roof, a scissors-truss construction, is typical of all stave churches.

By the mid-1200s a double row of horizontal boards (thongs) had been added to grip the posts in a frame at the triforium level. St. Andrew crosses were inserted above. The added support this provided made it possible to open the central space by cutting the central mast on each side at the triforium level.

Many stave churches show slightly later additions of covered porches, ambulatories, and towered, self-contained apses, which became characteristic of these churches. The outer ambulatory was usually arcaded along the sides and closed in the apse. These architectural features were clearly borrowed from the stone churches. Light entered the church through small holes in the upper walls. Some churches, like Urnes and Borgund, have a window in the west gable.

Archeological finds confirm that the austere Norman style, as seen in the second Urnes church, was introduced into a rich cultural heritage. The earlier Urnes church that stood on the site had richly carved portals, cornerposts, and gables. The ornamental style and the animal motifs are the same known from the Oseberg ship (c. 850). The interwoven animal and snake forms have no known model either stylistically or in their placement in early European churches. The sureness of line and carving technique points to a native Nordic origin. The same motifs and style are found on old crosses and runic stones from this period. Strong similarities exist between the Resmo stone from Kalmar* and the early Urnes ornamentation. This Urnes Style, a mixture of local styles with impulses from Irish manuscript painting, was at its peak when the older church was built. By its technologically advanced above-ground sill construction, it can be dated as early as 1100.

As the influence of European miniature painting grew stronger, the native artists fused the undulating coils of the acanthus flower with the animal style without lessening the inherent rhythmic tension. The Urnes animal slowly changed to the Christian dragon with wings. The style lived through the 1200s, when the purely organic elements gradually became predominant and replaced its force and harmony with a lifeless pattern. The Telemark portals illustrate this new style.

The exteriors of the stave churches conjure up images of a pagan age. The steep gabled roofs, one astride the other, have dragonheads projecting from the gable ends. A fretted edge often runs the length of the roof ridge. The roof and outer walls are covered with pitch-soaked black or brown shingles, which give the whole structure a scaly quality.

Inside the churches, the interaction between the horizontal and vertical lines demonstrates the harmonious artistic solution of the technical problems. The rich ornamentation of the portals and the advanced technical solutions in the construction contrast with the austerity of the humble Norman stone churches. In the second Urnes church, we find reference to Norman influence in the flat cube capitals and in the bases of the rounded arches between the columns. In the later churches the posts have carved masks similar to those found on Romanesque corniches.

In the western part of Norway the churches were built by local chieftains, descendants of the Vikings*. In the east the farmers built the churches. This may account for the integration of folk art motifs and profane art in the ornamentation in these churches. The wall paintings and altar fronts are strongly influenced by European miniature painting and manuscript illustrations. The style is flat and frontal and uses pure colors and dark contour lines. Fine examples of Gothic wall painting are present in the wooden paneled baldachins of the Ål and Torpo churches. After 1600 many of the stave churches were rosepainted. Much from the old interiors, including 30 portals, is preserved in museums.

The following are among the principal stave churches extant in Norway: Urnes (Sogn, c. 1200), Hopperstad (Sogn, c. 1200), Fortun (Sogn/now Fantoft, c. 1200), Kaupanger (Sogn, early thirteenth century), Borgund (Sogn, pre-1250), Undredal (Sogn, c. 1300), Røldal (Hordaland, early fourteenth century), Holtålen (Holtålen/now Trondheim, c. 1200), Kvernes (Nordmøre, c. 1300), Grip (Nordmøre, c. 1300), Rødven (Romsdal, c. 1300), Garmo (Gudbrandsdal/now Lillehammer, late twelfth century), Vågå (Gudbrandsdal, late twelfth century), Lom (Gudbrandsdal, early thirteenth century), Ringebu (Gudbrandsdal, late thirteenth century), Hedal (Valdres, early thirteenth century), Hegge (Valdres, c. 1250), Hurum (Valdres, c. 1250), Lomen (Valdres, c. 1250), Vang (Valdres/now in Riesengebirge, Poland, c. 1250), Reinli (Valdres, late thirteenth century), Øye (Valdres, late thirteenth century), Torpo (Hallingdal, c. 1250), Gol (Hallingdal/now Bygdøy, Oslo, c. 1250), Nore (Numedal, c. 1250), Uvdal (Numedal, c. 1250), Flesberg (Numedal, c. 1250), Heddal (Telemark, c. 1200), Eidsborg (Telemark, c. 1300), and Høyjord (Vestfold, c. 1350).

REFERENCES: P. Anders, *The Art of Scandinavia*, vol. 1 (London: Paul Hamlyn, 1970); A. Bugge et al., eds., *Kulturminner* (Oslo: J. W. Cappelens Forlag, 1950); G. Bugge and C. N. Schulz, *Stav og Laft* (Oslo: Norske Arkitekters Landsforbund, 1969); R. Hauglid, *Norske Stavkirker* (Oslo: Dreyers Forlag, 1969), and *Unesco World Art Series, Norway* (New York: New York Graphic Society, 1955); F. Hødnebø, ed., *Kulturhistorisk Leksikon for Nordisk Middelalder*, vol. 17 (Oslo: Gyldendal Norsk Forlag,

1972); D. Lindholm and W. Roggenkamp, *Stave Churches in Norway* (London: R. Steiner Press, 1969); J. Strzygowski, *Early Church Art in Northern Europe* (London: B. T. Batsford, 1928).

E. M. ANDERSON

STAVNSBÅND A form of serfdom in eighteenth-century Denmark

The late medieval *vornedskab**, which had bound peasants on the eastern islands of Denmark to the estates on which they had been born, was abolished in 1702. At the same time, a militia was introduced. Christian VI* abolished the latter on coming to the throne in 1730. But this brought protests from the army command, and landlords were becoming increasingly concerned that peasant mobility made difficult the filling of tenancies at a time of agricultural depression. As a result of pressure from these groups, the king reintroduced the militia in February 1733 and granted landlords the power to select recruits from among their tenants. Every male tenant between 18 and 36 was made liable to service and was not allowed to leave the estate between these ages. In 1735 the lower age limit for registration was dropped to 14, and in 1742 the *stavnsbånd*, as this system was called, was made to apply to all peasants between the ages of 9 and 40. From the 1750s on, agricultural reformers called for a modification or abolition of *stavnsbånd*, but in 1764 the age limit was reduced still further to 4. The institution was finally abolished by an act of 12 June 1788, immediately effective for those under 14 and over 36, and effective in 1800 for all others.

REFERENCES: K. Dorph-Petersen, "The Liberation of the Danish Peasant," *American Scandinavian Review* 26 (1938): 320–26; A. Petersen, *Stavnsbaandet. Traek af Bondestandens Historie* (Slagelse: Asas Forlag, 1938); R. Skovmand, "The Emancipation of the Peasants," in J. Bukdahl et al., *Scandinavia Past and Present*, vol. 2 (Copenhagen, 1959).

S. P. OAKLEY

STOCKHOLM

Traditionally, Stockholm is said to have been founded by Birger Jarl in the middle of the thirteenth century. It developed in the shadow of a castle built on an island (Stadsholmen, now often referred to as "the Old Town") at the entrance into Lake Mälar from the Baltic. The earliest record of the name is on a document from 1252, and the earliest remains of permanent buildings on the site date from around this time. The town grew rapidly thanks to the exploitation of the mineral resources of the Bergslagen, for which Stockholm provided the main outlet to the Baltic, and to the close links established at this time between Sweden and the Hanseatic port of Lübeck, whose merchants made Stockholm one of their principal bases. By the end of the century it had indeed become a largely German city. While settlement was long confined largely within the walls built around Stadsholmen, from the late fourteenth century it also spread onto the mainland to the north (Norrmalm) and onto the larger island to the south (Södermalm). In 1471 the battle of Brunkeberg was fought on the ridge that dominated the city from the north. As a result of the battle, a law by which at least half the city council had to be German was revoked, but a large German element remained well into the seventeenth century. Stockholm was besieged by Christian II* in 1520, and after its surrender to him its Great Square (Stortorget) was the scene of the Stockholm Bloodbath.

At this time it probably had a population of about 6,000. It had been referred to as Sweden's capital as early as 1394, and under the early Vasa kings its importance as an administrative as well as an economic center grew. King Johan III* in particular took an interest in its embellishment and refurbished the old Castle of Three Crowns (see Stockholm Royal Palace) as a royal residence in Renaissance style. In the early seventeenth century wealthy noblemen also began to build large stone townhouses on Stadsholmen and along the southern shore of Norrmalm, while merchants constructed tall dwellings and warehouses on the Baltic side of the island—on Skeppsbron (hence the title of *skeppsbroadel*— nobility of Skeppsbron—given to great wholesale merchants in the seventeenth and eighteenth centuries), and the developing bureaucracy of Sweden's "Age of Greatness" established permanent central offices in the shadow of the castle. Stadsholmen was given a more regular street plan after a fire in 1625, and after the city acquired its first governor (Överstathållare) in the person of Klas Fleming in 1634 much of the rest of Stockholm was reconstructed in rectangular lots which changed little for the following 200 years. What were still left of the walls and fortifications on Stadsholmen disappeared, and in 1637, to assist the passage of ships between Mälaren and the Baltic, a lock (Slussen) was built between Stadsholmen and Södermalm. From the late seventeenth century development was much slower, and the boundaries of the city remained the same from 1700 to the end of the nineteenth century. Out of a population of over 50,000 about 18,000 died of plague in 1710, and when the first national census was taken in 1749, it had risen again to no more than 55,464. The Castle of Three Crowns burned down in 1697 and was succeeded by the present palace, designed by Nicodemus Tessin*, but this was not ready for occupation until 1754; until then the court resided in the nearby Wrangel Palace, the largest private residence in the city. In the late eighteenth century, Gustav III* was responsible for the building of the Exchange (Börsen) on Stortorget in the 1770s and for an opera house (1782) across the water, which survived until the 1890s. Fortunately, his further plans for the city, which included the destruction of the Great Church (Storkyrkan) behind the palace, never materialized.

By the eighteenth century, Stockholm was an important industrial center, with a host of small workshops concentrated on Södermalm. Conditions in working-class quarters were poor and mortality rates high. Serious cholera epidemics in the 1840s and 1850s led to reform; piped water and sewers were installed in the 1860s. In 1866 Albert Lindhagen drew up a great plan for the city which involved the creation of broad treed boulevards inspired by contemporary developments in Paris and Vienna. These were never fully implemented, but something of his intention can be seen today in Narvavägen and Karlaplan. Kungsgatan, driven in 1911 through the ridge which has been the main obstacle to the unified development of Norrmalm, was one of the results and soon became the principal east-west thoroughfare of the main business quarter of Stockholm on Lower Norrmalm. Stockholm's main railway station was opened in the center of Södermalm in 1860 as the terminus of the main link to the south, and in 1871 Central Station united this with the northern route. The first (horse-drawn) tram appeared in the streets in 1877.

At the end of the nineteenth century, when the population approached 300,000, large middle-class suburbs grew up to the east and west of the city, while the working classes were housed in hastily erected blocks of flats or in the older buildings nearer to the center. After World War II*, continued overcrowding was eased by the creation of satellite towns, served after 1950 by a growing underground rail network (*tunnelbanan*). The increasing use of motor transport and the deterioration of the condition of many buildings in Lower Norrmalm led to a drastic replanning of the area in the late 1950s and the wholesale destruction of many historic buildings in the cause of modernity. Subsequently, the renewal of the Old Town and parts of Södermalm has been undertaken with greater sensitivity.

REFERENCES: N. Ahnlund, *Stockholms historia före Gustav Vasa* (Stockholm: Norstedt, 1953); S. Högberg, *Stockholms historia*, 2 vols. (Stockholm: BonnierFakta, 1981); W. William-Olsson, *Stockholm: Structure and Development* (Stockholm: 1960).

S. P. OAKLEY

STOCKHOLM ROYAL PALACE

Birger Jarl is said to have ordered the construction of the core of the old Stockholm castle in the mid-thirteenth century. (There may have been an earlier fort on the site.) The location was ideal, defensible, and set to guard the entrance to Lake Mälar. The old section of modern Stockholm* grew up around this location. Over the course of the next 400 years, the medieval castle was modified and expanded. A central tower was constructed during Gustav I Vasa's* reign (1523–1560), and the castle acquired the name Tre Kronor (Three Crowns) during the reign of his son, Johan III* (1568–1592), who had the symbol of the three crowns installed on the tower. Johan also sought to make the castle less of a fortress. He commissioned Willem Bey to remodel the gardens, the chapel, the royal apartments, and the nobles' house. Bey's most notable addition was the Trumpetsgången, a pillared arcade in Renaissance style, which was appended to the nobles' house. Further modifications were made in the 1630s. In the late 1650s Jean de la Vallée began to develop a set of plans for a thorough remodeling. These plans were eventually taken up by Nicodemus Tessin the Elder and his son, but little came of them. In 1690 Karl XI* commissioned the design and construction of a new north addition and chapel. The designs were by Nicodemus Tessin the Younger*. The additions were ready in 1697. However, on 7 May 1697 most of the old structure burned to the ground. Parts of the new addition and the chapel were saved. In addition, one-third of the state archives were lost, along with two-thirds of the Royal Library.

The destruction of the Tre Kronor Castle was something of a blessing for Tessin. He had dreams of far more than another piecemeal renovation of the old fort. After the fire, he was free to design a totally new palace befitting the age of absolutism. Within a few weeks after the fire his drawings were completed and construction began. The exterior of the new palace was Roman-Late Renaissance in style. The basic structure was a large three-story rectangle, with straight two-story wings off the east facade and curved two-story wings off the west facade. (The old north addition was retained in the northwest corner.) The core rectangle and curved wings enclosed courtyards. The east wings delineated a park. Construction on the new palace continued until 1709, when the change in Sweden's fortunes in the Great Northern War* necessitated a halt. Building resumed in 1729 under the direction of Tessin's son, Carl Gustaf Tessin*, and Carl Hårleman. Money for the project came in part from a special tax. Most of the exterior was completed by 1754, when the palace was turned over to Adolf Fredrik* and Lovisa Ulrika*. Work on the interior and other details continued through the eighteenth century, and although Tessin's designs for the exterior were retained, interior designs came to reflect the styles and tastes of the periods in which they were undertaken. Hårleman, C. J. Cronstedt, C. F. Adelcrantz, J. E. Rehn, and Louis Masreliez contributed interior designs. Baroque, rococo, and neoclassical styles were used. Small alterations were carried through in the nineteenth century. The palace has not been altered in the twentieth century, and it is carefully maintained as a royal residence and museum.

REFERENCES: *DSH*, vols. 4, 5, 7–9; Ralph Herrmanns and Hans Hammarskiöld, *The Royal Palace of Stockholm* (Stockholm: Bonniers, 1978); Martin Olsson, ed., *Stockholms slotts historia*, 3 vols. (Stockholm: Norstedt, 1941); *SU*, vol. 27.

B. NORDSTROM

STORTING The Norwegian parliament

The drafters of the Norwegian Constitution of 1814 pronounced the Storting the representative organ through which the people would "exercise the legislative power." They chose to make it bicameral because they thought that two houses would discourage rash actions; but because they abhorred aristocracy they decided against "upper" and "lower" houses. Instead they copied an expedient used in the Netherlands' 1798 constitution by which a legislature was chosen as one but operated as two. They made the Storting a single legislature, but instructed it to divide itself into an Odelsting (with three-quarters of the members) and a Lagting (with one-quarter of the members). The Odelsting was designated the chamber in which proposed laws could be introduced. If the proposals were accepted there, they were to be sent to the Lagting. If both chambers agreed, a proposal passed, but if they failed a proposal was to be put before a plenary meeting of the whole Storting with a two-thirds vote required for passage. The whole Storting was also to be convened to act on financial matters.

From the beginning the Storting had three sets of presiding officers, one each for the Odelsting, Lagting, and Storting. As leaders they were important in the early nineteenth century, but became less so after the development of parties and party discipline.

Though in principle based on popular sovereignty, the Storting at first was chosen indirectly by a very limited electorate. Its members were elected by electoral boards, which themselves were chosen by adult male citizens who fulfilled substantial property and occupational requirements. In the early years the Storting members were predominantly of civil servant (*embedsmenn*) or land-owning farmer backgrounds.

The Storting was designed to serve as a staunch counterweight to the monarch, and to that end it was given sole power to enact laws, impose taxes, and control finance. Although its enactments were made subject to the king's veto, the Storting was empowered to overcome the veto with appropriate votes in three successive sessions. At first the Storting was to meet only every third year, but after 1870 it convened annually.

Serious tension existed between the Storting and the king (who sat in Sweden) for much of the nineteenth century. The king's ministers, who made up the government, were forbidden by the constitution to sit in on meetings of the Storting. But in the 1860s the Storting wished to amend the constitution to have them there so they could be held to account. The king vetoed the measure, and his ministers respected his wish that they not comply. For this they were eventually put on trial by the Storting and removed from office. The king then found himself forced in 1884 to appoint a prime minister and government that was acceptable to the Storting. Thus did the Storting achieve the triumph of establishing the parliamentary principle.

The Storting became both the symbol and instrument of full Norwegian independence. After rancorous disputes about responsibility for the foreign policy of the united kingdom of Norway-Sweden and about the possibility of separate consular services, the Storting in 1905 unilaterally declared the joint monarchy dissolved, arranged the plebiscite in which the break was overwhelmingly approved, and approved the Karlstad Conventions settling the matter. The Storting also adopted the plan by which Haakon VII*, formerly Prince Karl of Denmark, became the new king of Norway.

The rise of the Storting from the status of counterweight to the king to that of supreme authority was accompanied by the development of political parties, without which the parliamentary principle would have been hard to implement. The Storting extended the franchise in 1885 by lowering property qualifications, in 1898 by removing them altogether, and in 1909 by removing sex discrimination. As the franchise was extended, representatives of workers and ordinary farmers and fishermen entered the Storting in increasing numbers. The number of contending parties also increased. Proportional representation in Storting elections was instituted in 1919, at which time the Storting assumed the multi-party character still evident today. Of the seven major parties, the Norwegian Labor Party* became the largest and most important.

The original constitution tied the size of the Storting to the number of qualified voters. Membership rose to 117 but was fixed at 111 by constitutional amendment in 1859 and at 150 (the present number) in 1919. The term of office was set in 1936 at four years.

REFERENCES: A. Kaartvedt et al., *Det Norske Storting gjennonn 150 år*, 4 vols. (Oslo: Gyldendal Norsk Forlag, 1964); Per Oisang, *Norway's Parliament—The Storting* (Oslo: Universitetsforlaget, 1962); J. Storing, *Norwegian Democracy* (Boston: Houghton Mifflin, 1963).

B. L. HANSON

STRÖM, OTTO FREDERIK (1880–1948) Swedish Socialist

One of the most prominent cultural and political personalities to represent Swedish socialism during the first half of the twentieth century, Otto Ström was a journalist, editor, novelist, biographer, historian, and politician. He came from a farm home, finished the gymnasium, and spent two terms at Gothenburg University before he was forced to earn his living as a journalist.

Together with Zeth Höglund*, he was one of the leaders of the Social Democratic Party's* youth movement, which challenged the reformist leadership of the party before World War I. Because of his ability as a writer and on the hustings, he served as party secretary from 1911 to 1916 and represented the radicals. From 1916 to 1921 he was secretary of the schismatic Social Democratic Left Party, which he founded with Höglund, and from 1921 to 1924 was an organizer and secretary of Sweden's Communist Party*. He returned to the SDP in 1926 and became the editor of the party's leading Stockholm* daily during the 1930s. He was a member of the Upper Chamber of the Riksdag* from 1916 to 1921 and again from 1930 to 1948. Ström was also a member of the Stockholm city council from 1912 to 1942 and rose to positions of prominence there. His long devotion to municipal reform is perhaps more indicative of his interests than his involvement in national political issues. Combining a deep sense of social justice with a commitment to individual freedom, he worked for better housing conditions, public transportation, welfare legislation, and beautification of the city, and for the participation of the rank and file in all that affected their lives in the city.

Ström was an active member of the Society of Swedish Authors during the last 20 years of his life and was chair of this group from 1943 to 1948. In addition to his production as a journalist, he wrote a history of the Russian Revolution in five volumes as well as biographies of Swedish Socialists, and edited collections of folk rhymes and riddles. He was active in calling attention to social criticism inherent in August Strindberg's works and was his publisher. Ström's own memoirs (two volumes, 1940–1942) give insight into the man and his times.

REFERENCES: *SMK*, vol. 7; H. Tingsten, *The Swedish Social Democrats: Their Ideological Development*, trans. G. Frankel and P. Howard-Rosen (Totowa, N.J.: Bedminster, 1973).

                                                                    P. V. THORSON

STRUENSEE, JOHAN FRIEDRICH (5 August 1737– 24 April 1772) Danish statesman

Struensee was born in Halle, where his father was professor of theology. He graduated in medicine from the university there in 1757. In the same year the family moved to Altona in Holstein, where Struensee was appointed medical officer in 1758. He read widely, and early in his career he abandoned the pietistic Christianity of his parents in favor of a thoroughgoing materialistic rationalism. His writings at this time reveal a genuine interest in medical reform; he was especially attracted to the idea that a doctor should work as far as possible to assist the course of nature. Altona was a lively intellectual center where Struensee found a number of congenial companions, but his most important contacts were among the nobility of the countryside north of the town, to which his duties also took him. Particularly important was Schack Carl Rantzau, an ambitious young man who had been compelled to leave the Danish court after the failure of a diplomatic mission to Russia. Rantzau was strongly opposed to the domination of J. H. E. Bernstorff* and his conservative circle at court and saw Struensee as a means of regaining influence for himself and his fellow reformers in Copenhagen*; he successfully recommended Struensee as a suitable companion for the new king, Christian VII*, who was already showing signs of mental instability, on a projected royal tour of European courts. Struensee joined the party as it passed through Holstein on its way south in the summer of 1768.

He quickly established good relations with the king and appears to have been largely instrumental in controlling the schizophrenic outbursts which Christian's ministers had feared would mar the trip. At the end of the tour, Struensee was given a permanent appointment as court physician. He also made great efforts to effect a reconciliation between Christian and his lonely English queen, Caroline Matilda, but this led to a growing intimacy between Struensee and the latter. By the end of 1769 the two were lovers. This gave him great potential power, but it was largely to protect the very dangerous position in which he was now placed that he began to play politics. He first engineered the dismissal of the king's current favorite, Count Holck, and his replacement by Struensee's old friend, Enevold Brandt. At the same time, Rantzau was allowed to return to Copenhagen. The dismissal of Bernstorff in September 1770 (although Struensee appears to have played no part in this) marked the triumph of the party which wished to use the absolute power of the sick monarch to carry through sweeping rationalistic reform in Denmark. In December the Royal Council was abolished, and Struensee was given his first important administrative post, as "maître des requêtes." It was, however, some time before it was realized outside a very small circle how powerful he had become. In the eyes of most observers he was no more than one member of a group led by Rantzau. Not until July 1771, when he became royal secretary, able to sign documents in the name of the now incapable king, was his dominance recognized. For some time already he had dictated the internal policy of the Danish government by means of a flood of cabinet orders. A College of Finance, headed by his elder brother Carl August, was formed to take over the work of the old Exchequer, College of Trade and Customs Office, as the most powerful administrative department. An independent Foreign Office was set up. The civil service benefited from a new salary structure and promotion by merit, but at the same time perquisites were abolished and many suffered from the suppression of superfluous offices. The autonomy of the city of Copenhagen was destroyed, and its administration was placed in the hands of a "president" named by the crown. Torture and the death penalty for a number of offenses (such as infanticide) were abolished, and illegitimate children were granted the same rights as legitimate. In economic matters Struensee and his friends supported liberal doctrines which led to the withdrawal of state subsidies and the relaxation of guild regulations. A commission was appointed to look into the relations between landlords and the downtrodden Danish peasantry. It attempted to fix a maximum amount of labor service which could be imposed on a tenant.

Most of Struensee's reforms offended powerful vested interests (such as the merchants of Copenhagen) or prevailing ideas of morality or could be condemned as arbitrary in their implementation. Little was known of the king's illness outside the court, and it was widely believed that he was being kept a prisoner in the palace. Rumors of Struensee's relations with the queen spread quickly in the later months of 1771. Censorship, which Struensee had abolished as one of his first acts, was reintroduced in an attempt to stem the tide of scurrilous pamphlets which were now directed against him. At the same time, unemployment caused by the withdrawal of government subsidies, and a poor harvest, which increased the price of bread in Copenhagen, exacerbated popular discontent. Struensee's circle of friends and supporters had always been a small one and now grew smaller still. Rantzau and a number of others, partly out of jealousy of Struensee's power, joined the opposition. Struensee overcame the first crisis that faced him in September, when sailors demanding arrears of pay marched on the palace of Hørsholm, where the court was staying. He remained sanguine and took few precautions to protect himself before a more serious crisis occurred in December as a result of his abolition of the royal footguards. Many officers resigned their commissions and swelled the ranks of the opposition, now led by the queen mother Juliane Marie and her son's tutor, Ove Guldberg. In the early morning of 17 January 1772, this group struck. Struensee, Brandt, and a number of others were arrested in their beds, and after a hasty trial Struensee and Brandt were condemned to death for lèse majesté and executed with great barbarity.

Many of Struensee's reforms were salutory, and not all disappeared with him, but he tried to do too much too quickly with little regard for the susceptibilities of others. Also, his failure to build up a firm body of support in influential circles of Danish society made his downfall virtually inevitable. The reaction which followed his death postponed the work of reform until after the coup d'etat of 1784.

REFERENCES: S. C. Bech, *Struensee og hans tid* (Copenhagen: Politikens Forlag, 1972); H. S. Commager, "Struensee and the Enlightenment: A Study in Historiography," in *The Search for a Usable Past and Other Essays in Historiography*(New York: A. A. Knopf, 1967); *DH*, vols. 9, 10; S. M. Toyne, "Dr. Struensee, Dictator of Denmark," *History Today* 1:1 (1951): 53–60.

S. P. OAKLEY

STURE, STEN (the Elder)(c. 1440–14 December 1503) Regent of Sweden 1471–1497 and 1501–1503

Sten Sture was the second of the great magnates of the Kalmar Union* period to become regent (*riksföreståndare*) in Sweden (*see also* Karl VIII Knutsson; Sten Svantesson "Sture"; Svante Nilsson).

Following Karl's death in 1470, some of the great nobles in the council turned to Hans I*, king of Denmark and Norway, in part honoring an agreement reached following the split election in 1448 and in part out of self-interest. Sten, Karl's nephew, wished to become regent and gathered his supporters against his enemies in the council and the Danes. The armies of the two factions met at Brunkeberg (now within Stockholm*) on 10 October 1571, and Sten emerged the victor. Some see his victory as a triumph for Swedish nationalism. For others it was a victory of monarchists over feudal constitutionalists. It may be premature to speak of nationalism, and it may be inaccurate to consider Sten a representative of a monarchist constitutional faction. It may be more accurate to argue that Sten's supporters, representing a variety of self-interests, defeated the alliance of Hans and the Swedish magnates who represented other self-interests. Whichever is the case, Sten became the regent, and the union remained fractured. For the next 26 years he ruled the country. (The conclusion of the Kalmar Recess* in 1483 did not change his status.)

In 1497, confronted by the council nobles, who were prepared to revolt, and a successful attack on Sweden by Hans, Sten relinquished power and temporarily became Hans's court master. It was not long, however, before Hans, who advocated a strong, centralized union monarchy, alienated the Swedish magnates. By 1501 Sweden was in revolt, and Sten returned as regent for the last two years of his life.

REFERENCES: *DSH*, vols. 2, 3; S. U. Palme, *Sten Sture den äldre* (Stockholm, 1950 and 1968); *SU*, vol. 27; H. Yrwing, series of articles in *Scandia* 32 (1966), 34 (1968), and 36 (1970).

B. NORDSTROM

"STURE," STEN SVANTESSON (the Younger)(c. 1492–3 February 1520) Regent of Sweden 1512–1520

Sten Sture the Younger was the fourth of the council nobles to become regent (*riksföreståndare*) during the Kalmar Union* period in Swedish history (*see also*

Karl VIII Knutsson; Sten Sture; Svante Nilsson). Following his father's death, the council elected Erik Trolle regent. This action came largely in response to Svante's efforts to rule without the council. Sten opposed this move. He threatened the council with overwhelming military forces and forced the magnates to accept him as regent. (Sten did promise to rule with the council and to respect the magnates' constitutional position.)

For the next eight years he resisted the Danes' efforts to bring Sweden back into the Kalmar Union and sought to turn his position as regent into that of a hereditary monarch. Ambitious and ruthless, he made many enemies among the lay and clerical nobility because of his constitutional outlook. He also attacked the autonomy of the Church. In 1515 Gustav Trolle, the son of Erik Trolle, became archbishop. Two years later Sten attacked the right of the archbishop to maintain an independent army of 400 and his private fort (Stäket). Trolle defied the regent, Stäket was placed under siege, and Trolle was declared deposed. In 1518 the archbishop was imprisoned.

Sten found allies for his constitutional position and his moves against the Church among the lower nobility, the miners of the Bergslagen, and the burghers of Stockholm*, and he made use of national meetings (riksmötet), where these groups were represented, to effect his policies. In this regard he was the most successful of the regents in this period to employ the commons against the feudal positions of the nobles and the Church.

Sten's efforts to effect internal changes were complicated by the campaigns of Christian II* of Denmark-Norway to bring Sweden back into the union, efforts which had the sympathy of some of the great lords because they believed their own positions would benefit from having Christian on the throne. Sweden was attacked in 1517, 1518, and 1520. The first two campaigns were repulsed, but Christian's 1520 attack succeeded. Sten was wounded at Åsunden in Västergötland (20 January 1520) and died on the way back to Stockholm. By the end of the summer most of Sweden was under Christian's control. Stockholm, under the leadership of Sten's widow, Christina Gyllenstierna, held out until early September. Following the surrender of Stockholm, Christian was crowned king of Sweden, and for a time the union was restored.

REFERENCES: *DSH*, vol. 3; S. U. Palme, *Riksföreståndarvalet 1512*, no. 7 (Uppsala: Uppsala Universitets Årsskrift, 1948); *SU*, vol. 27.

B. NORDSTROM

STURE, SVANTE NILSSON (c. 1460–2 January 1512) Regent of Sweden 1504–1512

Svante Nilsson was one of the four regents (*riksföreståndare*) of Sweden during the Kalmar Union* period (1397–1521)(*see also* Karl VIII Knutsson; Sten Sture; Sten Svantesson "Sture"). He succeeded, through rather devious means, Sten Sture the Elder* in 1504. During the following eight years he successfully resisted the efforts of Hans I* and his son, the future Christian II*, to bring Sweden back into the union. At home he worked to establish a genuine monarchy and to secure the succession of his son Sten (Svantesson Sture). These efforts brought him into conflict with the powerful secular and clerical nobles in the council, led by Archbishop Jakob Ulfsson, who were opposed to any developments that would limit their privileges and their influence in government. By 1512 Svante's relations with the council were at a breaking point. A meeting was scheduled with the council at which the differences between the magnates and the regent were to be discussed, but Svante died before this could be held. The attitude of the council was reflected in the election of Svante's successor, which, temporarily, was not his son but rather Erik Trolle, a leader of the opposition.

REFERENCES: *DSH*, vols. 2, 3; *SU*, vol. 21.

B. NORDSTROM

SUFFRAGE *See* Constitutional Development

SUNDT, EILERT (8 August 1817–13 June 1875) Norwegian theologian and sociologist

Eilert Sundt was born in southern Norway and attended school in Flekkefjord and Stavanger. After finishing at the top of his gymnasium class, he studied theology and then worked as a private tutor. In 1841 he entered the University of Oslo. There he was active in student affairs and was heavily influenced by the national romantic poet, Henrik Wergeland. Unlike Wergeland, however, Sundt eagerly supported the pan-Scandinavian movement and was a leading figure at the student meetings in Lund and Copenhagen* in 1845. He took his university exams in theology in 1846, and sometime thereafter, while teaching catechism classes in Oslo, he came in contact with the gypsy population of Norway. This encounter determined his life's work, as he became interested in their lifestyles and habits from a sociological perspective.

In 1848 Sundt received a grant to study these social outcasts in Norway, and in 1850, when he published his results, he created a sensation throughout Scandinavia*. His pioneering work, *Beretning om Fante- eller Landstrygerfolket i Norge*, remains a significant source on gypsies and influenced many others, including the writer Gabriel Scott, whose novel *Fant* (1928) is probably the best fictional account of Norwegian gypsies.

During the course of his research, Sundt traveled extensively in Norway and witnessed poverty and unemployment. In 1851 he proposed to the Norwegian parliament a comprehensive research project to investigate conditions among the lower classes. The revolutions of 1848 in Europe and the unrest among Norwegian farmers and workers convinced parliamentary leaders that such a study would be to their advantage, and Sundt was commissioned to execute it.

Initially, he spent time poring over census records, which Norway had been keeping since 1765. Letters were sent to parish ministers, who kept records collected before the establishment of the national census. Sundt communicated with representatives of all classes, and in 1855 published his first results in *Mortality in Norway* (*Om dødligheden i Norge*). In this study, Sundt became the first to note and record the relatively long life expectancy of Norwegians and that suicide may be a social phenomenon. In the same year he also published *Marriage in Norway (Om Giftermaal i Norge)* in which he presented his findings on the marital habits of Norwegians and made an observation on rates of population growth which later came to be known as Eilert Sundt's Law: that population increases or decreases in one generation reflect the pattern of the previous generation. On a political note, Sundt recommended that the government take action to ameliorate the effects of these increases and decreases by expanding job opportunities in periods of increase.

Sundt's interests and research into Norwegian society incorporated nearly every conceivable aspect of social behavior. In 1862 he published a remarkable study on rural Norwegian architecture; *Building Practices in Rural Norway (Om Bygnings-Skikken paa Landet i Norge)*. Although he played down the importance of this work, it remains the one with the largest and longest-lasting impact. In the study, Sundt not only examined building styles, but speculated on the social and cultural factors that lay behind them and the effect these styles and practices had on Norwegian cultural and intellectual development. As such, it may be said that Sundt was the founder of ethnological research of building traditions.

As a champion of the lower classes, Sundt laid the groundwork for quantitative research. A century before it was fashionable, he explored the conditions of the common people. *Homecrafts in Norway (Om Husfliden i Norge)*, from 1867–1868, in which he examined the labor potential and labor waste in the various regions of the country, reflected this interest. He detailed Norwegian work traditions in a period of significant change, when Norway was still in many ways a developing country. Sundt's most cited work is *Home Life in Norway (Om Huslivet i Norge)* from 1873, in which he described the details of everyday life. This work has become a classic study of cultural history.

Sundt was also the editor of the journal *The People's Friend (Folkvennen)* from 1857 to 1866. In this he wrote on almost every aspect of Norwegian society including language, building practices, schools, theater, sports, and medicine. From 1867 to 1869 he served as a consultant for the Poor Office of the Department of Ecclesiastical Affairs. Later he became a parish pastor at Eidsvoll, but he was mistrusted by the conservative clergy for being a rationalist and a Grundtvigian, and for his sympathy for the lower classes.

REFERENCES: M. S. Allwood, *Eilert Sundt: A Pioneer in Sociology and Social Anthropology* (Oslo: O. Norli, 1957); E. Sundt, *Om Byngnings-Skikken paa Landet i Norge* (Christiania, 1862), *Om Dødligheden i Norge* (Christiania, 1855), *Om giftermaal i Norge* (Christiania, 1855), *Om Husfliden i Norge* (Christiania, 1867–1868), and *Om Huslivet i Norge* (Christiania, 1873).

T. LEIREN

SUTTON HOO Site of an Anglo-Saxon burial ship with evident links to Scandinavia*

Sutton Hoo is a heathland site in Suffolk, England, on the south side of the

Deben River near Woodbridge. It is about six miles from the sea. Here are some seventeen burial mounds from the Migration Period (c. 400–800 A.D.) or earlier. From the site's commanding position, it may be deduced that this was a royal/aristocratic cemetery and pagan rather than Christian. The tallest barrow, excavated in 1939, contained the traces of an iron-riveted, wooden vessel some 90 feet in length. This ship has been reasonably securely dated to about 600–610 A.D. Its length is at present exceeded only by the Skuldelev long ship of the Viking Age*, recovered from Roskilde fjord in 1962. Amidships archeologists found an undisturbed treasure of such magnificence and symbolism as to suggest a royal grave, very possibly commemorative of Raedwald, a prominent East Anglian king who died around 625. Uncertainty whether a body formed the focus of the burial chamber was not dispelled following a second excavation in 1966, but this puzzle can hardly detract from the quality of the grave furnishings, described as the "most marvellous find in the archaeological annals of England." The most exquisite items were produced by the "finest goldsmith in the Germanic world at work on jewelry" (T. D. Kendrick, *Antiquity*, 1940).

At this period (c. 600 A.D.) boat burials of this kind are known only in Suffolk and Uppland (Sweden), and extensive comparisons have hence been drawn between Sutton Hoo and the 29 barrow grave sites at Vendel-Valsgärde. Although some of the latter were robbed in medieval times, there is no suggestion that any had royal associations. Rather, they are believed to be the graves of a wealthy, yeoman-official class, well-accoutred and mounted. (At Vendel-Valsgärde there is extensive evidence of horse and other animal skeletons which is wholly absent at Sutton Hoo.) The bodies were placed in boats of up to 33 feet in length, which were lake/coastal rather than seagoing craft.

Most specifically, the Sutton Hoo deposits seem linked with the Scandinavia of their epoch on the basis, primarily, of the sword, helmet, and shield—and more putatively through certain clues in the Anglo-Saxon epic poem *Beowulf*. Here not only are similar funerary arrangements described, but there seems an implicit obeisance to Scandinavian tradition, postulating a meaningful dynastic link across the North Sea. The archeological evidence suggests that the sword, helmet, and shield were all old, 100 years or more, when they were buried, and that as heirlooms they had been repaired before burial. While the exceptional workmanship of the sword pommel can be paralleled by a few Swedish finds, especially one from Högh Edsten in Bohuslän, the helmet incorporates certain decorative features repeated in finds in Gotland, Old Uppsala*, and at Torslunda on Öland. While it is a more "Roman" style helmet than the better preserved specimens from Vendel-Valsgärde, Sutton Hoo's shield (three feet, two inches in diameter and somewhat smaller than the Vendel-Valsgärde average) was made of leather and wood like its Swedish counterparts, is similarly ornamented around its rim in gilt-bronze, and has a boss whose massiveness isolates it from any known Anglo-Saxon example. All three objects must have been made in Sweden.

REFERENCES: R. Bruce-Mitford, *Aspects of Anglo-Saxon Archaeology* (London: Gollancz, 1974); R. Bruce-Mitford et al., *The Sutton Hoo Ship Burials*, 2 vols. (London:

British Museum Publications, 1975, 1978); O. G. S. Crawford, "Sutton Hoo: A Summary," *Antiquity*, 26:101 (1952):4–8; C. Green, *Sutton Hoo* (London: Merlin Press, 1963); C. F. C. Hawkes, "Sutton Hoo: Twenty-Five Years After," *Antiquity*, 38:152 (1964):252–257; T. D. Kendrick et al., "The Sutton Hoo Ship Burial," *Antiquity*, 14:53 (1940):6–87; H. Stolpe and T. J. Arne, *La Nécropole de Vendel* (Stockholm: Kungliga Vitterhets Historie och Antikvitets Akademien, 1927).

D. D. ALDRIDGE

SVABO, JENS CHRISTIAN (1746–1824) Faroese scholar

The vigorous cultural, intellectual, and political life of the Faroe Islands* during the present century arose from the antiquarian interest of the nineteenth century in the Faroese language and its oral literature, particularly its ballads. The first scholar to cultivate Faroese linguistic and literary studies was J. C. Svabo, whose full contribution toward Faroese national awakening has been fully appreciated only during the present generation. However, Svabo was no nationalist. He saw his life's work of recording the Faroese language and its poetic heritage as the last-minute rescue for posterity of an Old Norse relic destined to be swept aside by the advancing tide of Danish. The ultimate effect of his work was that the reverse happened, and during the past 50 years Faroese has replaced Danish in fields where the latter had been established for generations.

Materially, Svabo's life was not a successful one. He was the son of the parish priest of Vágar and got his education first from his father at home, then at the tiny Latin School in Tórshavn*. In 1765 he went to Copenhagen*—at a time of much intellectual ferment—and studied many subjects, including botany, natural history, and political economy. He was, indeed, almost the first Faroeman to study subjects other than theology.

Svabo proved to be a talented scholar and was eager to assist the economic development of his native islands. From 1770 on, he submitted proposals to the Landhusholdningsselskab (the Society for Economic Advancement) and to the government for improvement of Faroese husbandry. He advocated the introduction of ploughing, potato-planting, and salting of mutton instead of its preservation by wind-drying. He proposed improvements in shepherding, in the boat fishery, and in pilot-whale hunting, and he suggested that gardening should be encouraged for the growth of vegetables.

Svabo's aim appears to have been partly to bring himself into notice and secure an official appointment, either in the Faroes or Norway, but he was unlucky. He had to make ends meet with humble tutoring posts on large estates in various parts of Denmark. Then, in 1781, it seemed as though the tide had turned for him. He received a royal warrant to travel to the Faroe Islands and compile a detailed economic report, for which he was to receive the considerable sum of 600 rixdollars, out of which, however, he had to pay his expenses. He was in Faroe from 22 May 1781 until 1 September 1782, and his report eventually filled seven manuscript volumes. (It was first published in 1959.)

Although the report has won the admiration of posterity and has been used (often without acknowledgment) by most subsequent writers on Faroe, the period of this journey and the compilation of the report heralded a severe downturn in Svabo's fortunes. He returned to Copenhagen in debt, suffered much from illness, and was slow to submit his findings to the government. He probably had become an alcoholic. In July 1800, a broken man, he returned to the Faroes and settled in Tórshavn, where his sister lived. The Rentekammer allowed him a small pension from their charity fund, and he was, no doubt, helped by his relatives. He lived on in obscurity until his death on 14 February 1824.

But Svabo was not idle during those 24 years in Faroe. He devoted the remainder of his life to the Faroese language. This was not a new interest for him. Svabo was a talented philologist, far in advance of his time. Early in the 1770s he had begun work on a Faroese-Danish-Latin dictionary. During his 1781–1782 journey, he had added a fresh collection of words, and after 1800 he continued the compilation until the day of his death, using an orthography of his own devising. In 1821 an English visitor described Svabo's collections as "an unarranged mass of papers," but they were sufficiently orderly to be edited and published in our own time and form an essential source for modern Faroese lexicography.

Svabo's major work of ballad collection took place during 1781–1782. When he returned to Copenhagen, he presented the crown prince (later Frederik VI*) with a manuscript collection of 52 ballads, including an incomplete text of *Ljómur* (*see* Religion). In his preface to this collection, Svabo tells us why he carried out the work. He believed the Faroese ballads to be on the verge of oblivion, and that it would be a great shame if posterity should not know what they were like. In this he was probably taking too gloomy a view, for recent research has shown that although the tradition was carried on by only a few persons, the heritage was nevertheless being well preserved and even added to.

Svabo's collection was practically ignored by the learned world of his time; but shortly before his death, ballad collecting was taken up by others. The next pioneer was the Danish clergyman Hans Christian Lyngbye (1782–1837), who in 1817 made a journey to the Faroes to study seaweeds. The Faroese ballad-dance aroused his interest, and he obtained some instruction from Svabo in the Faroese language and Svabo's own orthography. With the help of the Suðuroy clergyman Johan Henrik Schröter (1771–1851), he collected and edited the Faroese ballad cycle called the *Sjurðarkvaeði*, a version of the *Völsunga Saga*. It was published in 1822, the first Faroese book to appear in print. The work of Venceslaus Ulricus Hammershaimb* and Jakob Jakobsen* built on this foundation, and during the present century Faroese has become the vehicle of a modern as well as a traditional oral literature, with political as well as cultural consequences.

REFERENCES: P. Conroy, "Sniolvs kvaeði. The Growth of a Ballad Cycle," *Fróðs-*

kaparrit 26 (1978): 33–53; Håkon Hamre, review of Svabo's *Indberetninger*, in *Journal of English and German Philology* 60 (1961): 158–60.

J. F. WEST

SVEN I (Forkbeard/Tvaskaeg)(?–3 February 1014) King of Denmark c. 985–1014, King of England 1013–1014

Sven Forkbeard, son of Harald I* (Bluetooth), was a king very much in the tradition of the Viking Age*. He has been characterized as ruthless, violent, opportunistic, and godless. Our view of him, however, is badly distorted by the Christian contemporaries who wrote about him and who rejected him for his indifference to their religion. Opportunistic, tolerant, and political are apt words to describe Sven.

In most respects he continued the policies of his father, though with subtle changes that make him appear considerably less attractive than the devout Harald. The conversion* of Denmark continued, but under Sven, English missionaries were sought to counter the influence of the Germans and the archbishopric in Hamburg-Bremen. Paralleling this policy, Sven sought to lessen the pressure of the Ottonians on the southern borders of Denmark. This policy may have led to the open break between Sven and Harald around 983, when Sven launched a successful campaign against the Germans in their fort near the Danevirke and at Hedeby*. Sven also continued his father's policy of supporting those factions in Norway opposed to the development of a strong, centralized state. He took part in the battle at Svolder c. 1000 that took the life of Norway's king Olaf I Tryggvason*. Thereafter, he claimed control of much of southern Norway, while the independent earls dominated the north.

For much of his reign, Sven was also active in England. Viking* attacks of the island resumed in the 980s and intensified in the 990s. The initial purpose of the raids appears not to have been expansionist, but rather financial; they were aimed at the extraction of payments (Danegeld), by which the English bought temporary respites from the raids. Sven took an active part in some of the raids. His involvement deepened after 1002, when the English king, Ethelred, ordered the murder of all Danes living in England. Sven's sister was among the victims. Thereafter the scope of the attacks increased, and the purpose shifted toward conquest. In 1013 Ethelred was driven into exile in Normandy, and Sven was chosen king. His pleasure in the conquest was short-lived, as he died suddenly in 1014. He was succeeded in Denmark by Harald II* and in England by Knud I* (the Great).

REFERENCES: J. Brønsted, *The Vikings* (Baltimore: Penguin, 1965); *DH*, vol. 2; K. Randsborg, *The Viking Age in Denmark* (New York: St. Martin's, 1980).

B. NORDSTROM

SVEN(D) II ESTRIDSEN (c. 1019–April 1074) King of Denmark c. 1047–1074

Sven was the son of a sister of Knud the Great (Knud I*). He spent much of his youth in England and was even a candidate for the throne there in 1042. In the early 1040s he returned to Denmark where Magnus the Good (Magnus I Olafsson*), king of Norway, had established a hold on the Danish throne following the death of Hardeknud*. When Magnus died Sven became king, but he faced almost constant challenges to his position from Magnus's successor in Norway, Harald Hardradi (Harald III Sigurdsson*). The two fought bitterly for fifteen years. They concluded a peace in about 1062, which left Sven free to rule unopposed in Denmark, and left Harald free to launch an assault on England. Harald's death at Stamford Bridge assured Sven of continued peace.

Most modern treatments of Sven are positive. He seems to have had ideas similar to those of Knud. He hoped to build a real kingdom in Denmark based upon law, cooperation with the Church, and membership in the international community. He rejected the increasingly archaic notion of the Viking* warrior king. Some of Sven's successors shared these views; others did not. The differences resulted in factionalism and unrest in the ensuing period (*see* Knud II; Oluf I; Erik I; Niels).

At home Sven was a generous patron of the Church, an advocate of an independent Danish Church, and an able politician willing to be patient and negotiate. Two of his principal goals were to secure Denmark's position against the encroachment of imperial Germany and to develop a Church independent of the domination of the archbishopric of Hamburg-Bremen. He was moderately successful in both regards.

Sven married, but his sons (Harald, Knud, Oluf, Erik, and Niels) were the offspring of a number of liaisons. Each of these sons would rule Denmark in succession following his death, and their squabbling was a major theme for the next half century.

REFERENCES: *DH*, vol. 3; G. Jones, *A History of the Vikings* (New York: Oxford University Press, 1968).

B. NORDSTROM

SVEN(D) III GRATHE (c. 1127–23 October 1157) King of Denmark 1146–1157

Sven was one of the three possible candidates for the throne in Denmark in 1146. He was the son of Erik II*. Knud Magnussen (later Knud III*), the grandson of Niels* and the son of Magnus, and Valdemar (I*), a son of Knud Lavard, were the other candidates. Although Denmark's monarchy was elective, there was no central national assembly which chose successive rulers. Rather, the election usually occurred in the separate assemblies (landting) in Skåne, Sjaelland and the islands, and Jutland. In 1146 these assemblies chose different candidates. The Jutland assembly elected Knud, while the assemblies on Sjaelland and Skåne selected Sven. Valdemar and Archbishop Eskil initially supported Sven.

The split election triggered a new round of civil war in Denmark, which is sometimes referred to as the "War of the Princes." Initially, Sven bested Knud.

In 1151 Knud was defeated in battle, and it looked as if the war were over. The German emperor, Frederik Barbarossa, called Knud and Sven to a meeting of the German Reichstag at Merseburg. There Sven was crowned king by the emperor. At the same time, Frederik turned over Sjaelland to Knud as a fief. This act provided the basis for future conflict with Sven. Frederik may have acted intentionally in order to keep Denmark weak by promoting internal discord. In any case, the emperor's intercession did nothing to stop the civil war in the long run.

In about 1154 Valdemar and Archbishop Eskil changed sides. At the same time Sven began to lose support elsewhere as a result of his attempts to impose German customs and manners on the Danes, his tax policies, and an expensive campaign against Sweden which failed. Soon the odds against Sven seemed overwhelming. The fighting resumed, and Sven was forced to take refuge with his father-in-law in Germany. From there he negotiated for a new army (of Germans) with which to reconquer his kingdom. In 1156–1157 Sven attacked Knud and Valdemar in Sjaelland. Neither side won a decisive victory, and a military balance seems to have been reached. The rivals then agreed to share power. Sven would rule in Skåne, Valdemar in Jutland, and Knud on Sjaelland and the islands. For a time it looked as if peace had been achieved. The lull in the violence was short, however.

In August 1157 the princes gathered at Roskilde for what was supposed to be a congenial banquet. The gathering turned into a murderous affair. Sven laid plans to eliminate his rivals but failed in the execution. Knud was cut down, but Valdemar, wounded, escaped. He fled to Jutland, where Sven soon attacked him. At Grathe Hede, on 23 October 1157, the armies of Valdemar and Sven met. The victory went to Valdemar. Sven was killed by the peasant soldiers.

Sven's death marked the end of the civil war in Denmark. Valdemar I succeeded him without significant rivals, and Denmark entered a period of prosperity and expansion often referred to as the Age of the Valdemars (1157–1241).

REFERENCES: *DH*, vol. 3; P. Lauring, *A History of Denmark* (Copenhagen: Høst & Son, 1960); S. Oakley, *A Short History of Denmark* (New York: Praeger, 1972).

B. NORDSTROM

SVERDRUP, JOHAN (30 July 1816–17 February 1892) Norwegian lawyer, politician, and prime minister

Johan Sverdrup grew up in an advantaged environment as the son of a well-established Norwegian family. He received a private preparatory education and took a law degree from the University of Oslo in 1841. Scholars have debated the reasons for his entering politics in 1848, but it is clear that the events of that revolutionary year inspired him to participate actively. From 1851 until his death he served as a member of parliament.

As a young representative, he was most keenly identified as a radical member of the opposition. His primary goal was the establishment of universal suffrage, but when that failed he took up the issue of ministerial responsibility. As a representative of the farmers, Sverdrup has been characterized by Frederick Stang as Norway's first ideological politician. As a part of his parliamentary activity, Sverdrup worked consistently to build up a cohesive party structure in Norway before there were any political parties. He believed that this development was a necessary foundation for the establishment of a democratic parliamentary system. In 1858 he first approached Ole Gabriel Ueland, the leading spokesperson for the farmers in the parliament, about establishing a national "Reform Association." Thoughts for a separate party, however, stranded on the pressing issues relevant to the union with Sweden, (*see* Norwegian-Swedish Union).

Beginning in 1857, proposals for a closer union, both economic and legal, appeared on the Storting's* agenda. Norwegian opponents of a closer union characterized the suggestion as "amalgamation" and criticized it as a threat to Norwegian home rule. During the ongoing debate, Sverdrup consistently agitated for the establishment of ministerial responsibility, which would mean that the government would be dependent on the support of a majority in the Storting rather than the confidence of the king. The Constitution of 1814 had defined a separation of powers which precluded any arrangement of parliamentarism, but in 1872 Sverdrup boldly proclaimed that all power in the Norwegian political system rightly belonged in the Storting. It was by then far from being an idle suggestion. In 1869, in cooperation with Søren Jaabæk, Sverdrup became the leader of Norway's first organized political party, the Left, or Venstre.

In the parliamentary elections of 1870, Sverdrup developed a purely political party program. The Storting became the focal point for a constitutional struggle which involved not only the legislative and executive branches, but Norway and Sweden as well. The dominant issue in this early phase of the union struggle between Sweden and Norway was the so-called *statsrådsaken*. Explicit in the debate was the matter of whether the members of the government would be required to meet in the Storting. Sverdrup correctly believed that as long as this was not required, the Storting would not be the decisive power base in the country. In 1874, therefore, the Storting passed a law to require ministerial attendance. King Oscar II* vetoed it. The next Storting, three years later, passed the law again, and again the king vetoed it. In 1880 the law was passed for the third time. Ordinary parliamentary practice would have seen it become law without a veto possible, but Oscar claimed that, in constitutional matters, he had an absolute veto. He rejected the law for the third time, and the king and his Norwegian parliament were in the midst of a serious constitutional crisis. The government supported the king's veto and refused to meet in the Storting. Because the constitution allowed for impeachment procedures in much the same way that they exist in the United States Constitution, the only option left open to Sverdrup and his party was to follow the consequences. His hand was strengthened when, in the election of 1882, Venstre won a 52–seat majority. That allowed the party to dominate the impeachment process in both houses. As a result, the government of Christian Selmer was ousted by votes of impeachment on 27 February 1884. When attempts by the monarch to form another conservative government failed, he was forced to turn to Sverdrup, who did have the full confidence of a majority in the Storting. On 26 June 1884 Sverdrup became prime minister. He had orchestrated a revolutionary change of the political system in Norway.

Sixty-eight years old in 1884, Sverdrup showed the effects of his long political struggle. His health suffered, but worse, his strict party politics made it difficult for him to reconcile himself with political opponents. He took political opposition personally and became increasingly incapable of dealing with the problems created by the new democratic system. Although he led the nation for five years, his hold on the party deteriorated. Younger members attacked him as too conservative and staid, a relic of past political battles incapable of participating in new ones. He resigned as prime minister in July 1889 and died three years later.

REFERENCES: W. S. Dahl, *Johan Sverdrup, Et Stortingsbillede*, 2 vols. (Oslo, 1889–1902); A. Kaartvedt, *Kampen mot Parlamentarisme, 1880–84* (Oslo: 1956); H. Koht, *Johan Sverdrup*, 3 vols. (Oslo: 1916–1925).

T. LEIREN

SVERRIR (SVERRE) SIGURDSSON (c. 1151–8/9 March 1202) King of Norway 1177–1202

Sverrir was, according to his own account, an illegitimate son of King Sigurd II Haraldsson (Mouth), and thereby a grandson of King Harald Gilchrist (Harald IV Magnusson*). His mother married a Faroese combmaker, and the boy was fostered on the islands and educated as a priest. After being informed of his supposed royal paternity at the age of 24, Sverrir traveled back to Norway in 1176. He became the leader of the Birchleg faction the following year and put forth his claim to the throne, thereby rekindling the civil wars.

Sverrir, a leader gifted with unconventional tactical ingenuity, was opposed for seven years by the incumbent, Magnus V Erlingsson*. The challenger began his campaign with guerilla warfare in eastern Norway, but by 1179 the Birchlegs had established a firm foothold in Trøndelag, defeating Magnus and his men that year in Nidaros (Trondheim) in an encounter which cost Magnus's father and advisor, Earl Erling, his life. Thereafter Sverrir had his bastion in Trøndelag, whereas Magnus had his center in Bergen. Magnus was forced to flee to Denmark after defeats in 1180 and again in 1183. Returning from exile in 1184, he was killed in the naval battle of Fimreiti in Sognefjord. After his victory, Sverrir married a sister of King Knut Eriksson of Sweden and began consolidating his realm based in Trøndelag and western Norway. He built a fortress in Bergen, as he had just done in Nidaros.

New pretenders to the throne staged uprisings in 1185–1191 in eastern Norway, most often with Danish support, and in 1193–1194 across the North Sea with support from the Orkneys. The Church, particularly in the person of Archbishop Eystein Erlendsson (died 1188), had supported King Magnus, and Eystein's successor proved an even stronger opponent of the king. The new archbishop, who attempted to implement religious reforms, fled to Denmark in 1190, excommunicated Sverrir in 1194, and in 1195–1199 convinced the other Norwegian bishops to join him in exile. With this the church-state controversy reached its peak in Norway. In 1196 religious and secular opposition to the Birchleg king were coupled in the Crosiers, a new group with its own pretender to the throne led by Bishop Nicholas of Oslo. The new faction found support in eastern Norway and had success during the first years. Sverrir had, however, attained the upper hand against the Crosiers when he died of a cold on 8/9 March 1202 in Bergen.

Information about Sverrir comes primarily from his saga, which was begun on commission from the king by an Icelandic abbot in 1185–1188. Another source for the king's position during the conflict with the Church is the transcription of an oration on his behalf, "A Speech against the Bishops," in which secular supremacy over the Church is argued. Probably no great initiator of change, Sverrir continued and hastened various social and administrative developments in Norway during his reign. The innovations included the centralization of royal administration through district governors, the real unification of different sections of the country into a nation, and the strengthening of royal finances by the conversion of the naval levy into a set state tax. A new aristocracy arose which was more dependent on the king and a position in the national administration than on an inherited local power base.

Sverrir was succeeded by his son Haakon, who followed his father's deathbed advice and made peace with the Church. Concessions in the new king's letter of reconcilation, which is preserved, demonstrate that Sverrir had not succeeded in his political struggle against the Church. After Haakon's sudden death in 1204, strife again broke out between the Crosiers and the Birchlegs. Following a short reign by the under-age Guttorm Sigurdsson, Ingi II Baardsson* succeeded to the throne for the Birchlegs.

REFERENCES: G. M. Gathorne-Hardy, *A Royal Impostor: King Sverre of Norway* (Oslo: Aschehoug, 1956); K. Gjerset, *History of the Norwegian People* (1932; repr. New York: AMS, 1969); K. Helle, *Norge blir en stat 1130–1319*, 2nd rev. ed. (Bergen: Universitetsforlaget, 1974); K. Larsen, *A History of Norway* (Princeton: Princeton University Press, 1948/1974); J. Sephton, trans., *The Saga of King Sverri of Norway* (London: Nutt, 1899).

J. E. KNIRK

SWEDISH (Language) *See* Languages: Scandinavian

SWEDISH CONFEDERATION OF TRADE UNIONS (Landsorganisationen i Sverige, or LO) The central organization of the Swedish trade union movement

The Swedish Confederation of Trade Unions was founded in 1898. Its formation resulted when the leaders of the growing trade union movement realized the need for a central organization to coordinate the activities of the movement for the protection of its members. Although the specific functions of LO have changed over the years, its basic purposes have remained the same. In 1941 the organization adopted a statement of purposes which reflected LO's history and has governed its actions ever since. These purposes included the protection of its members' interests in the labor market, work place, and industrial life and the promotion of economic, social, and political democracy. The pursuit of these goals can be seen in LO's negotiation of basic agreements on wages and the working environment with its counterparts in the management sector, in its educational and cultural activities, and in its participation in Swedish political life. LO has maintained a close association with the Social Democratic Party* since its founding. Although attempts to develop formal links between LO and the party were abandoned in the early twentieth century, LO has followed a 1909 policy statement affirming that the basic interests of the trade union movement were best served by the Social Democrats.

In practice, LO's roles have been determined by the evolving symbiotic relationship between LO and its chief opponent in the labor market, the Swedish Employers' Federation* (SAF), and by the country's economic, social, and political development. In the early years of LO's history, its functions were largely defensive—to direct responses to management actions against the movement and to serve as an unemployment insurance agency. With the shift in the political balance between labor and management after World War I, LO's roles and style changed.

In 1900 LO had fewer than 43,000 members. Today it has over 2 million members and is the largest organization of its kind in the Swedish labor market. The number of unions affiliated with LO has varied. A peak of 44 was reached in the early 1960s, but the number has been decreasing since, largely because of a trend toward industry-wide unions. In 1976 there were 25 member unions in LO.

The structure of LO is three-tiered: the Congress, the Representative Assembly, and the Secretariat. The Congress, numbering about 300 delegates, is composed of representatives from each of the member unions, plus the Representative Assembly and the Secretariat. It meets every five years and is the basic statute and policy-making organ of LO. The Representative Assembly, with about 130 members, serves as an interim congress. It is composed of the Secretariat and a small number of delegates from each member union. It meets two or three times each year to review the budget and activities of the organization. The day-to-day activities of LO are conducted by the Secretariat, which has about a dozen members, including a permanent executive. (The officers of the executive are elected by the Congress but do not serve fixed terms.) Although the Congress is, in principle, the focus of power in LO, in practice the chairperson, through the Secretariat, exerts predominating influence in determining the policies and actions of the organization.

In contemporary Sweden, LO is one of the many important interest groups that, in large part, shape the social, cultural, economic, and political life of the country.

Similar organizations were established in the other Scandinavian countries. Denmark's trade union federation (Landsorganisationen i Danmark) was founded

in 1898. Norway's was founded in 1899. Finland's first umbrella organization
was established in 1907. Since then there have been a number of such organizations, largely because of splits in the Socialist movement in Finland. A new
general group, Finland's Trade Union Central Organization, was established in
1969.

REFERENCES: Bo Carlson, *Trade Unions in Sweden* (Stockholm: Tidens, 1969); N.
Elvander, *Intresseorganisationerna i dagens Sverige* (Lund: Gleerup, 1969); T. L. Johnston, *Collective Bargaining in Sweden* (Cambridge, Mass.: Harvard University Press,
1962); I. Lindblad et al., *Politik i Norden* (Stockholm: Aldus/Bonniers, 1972).

B. NORDSTROM

SWEDISH EAST INDIA COMPANY (Östindiska Kompaniet) Eighteenth-
century trading company

The Swedish East India Company was chartered by the Riksdag* in 1731 as
a reaction in part to the profits of the Dutch and English East India companies
in the East. Initially, the Company was managed by an Englishman and represented shipping interests that could not otherwise compete with the monopolistic
companies in their own country. Gradually, the company was controlled by
Swedes. Its headquarters were in Gothenburg*, and its trade was mainly with
China.

The company did not establish a fort or trading center in the Far East as the
Danes had done in India at Tranquebar or Serampore (*see* Danish East India
Company; Danish Posts in Asia). Thus Swedish trading expeditions were not as
frequent as the Danes'. There were four *oktroj* (charters) in the company's history:
1732–1748 (25 voyages), 1746–1767 (36 voyages), 1766–1787 (30 voyages),
and 1787–1806 (31 voyages). It is difficult to get a full picture of the company's
activities, because most of its records were burned year by year to assure secrecy
and probably to safeguard its smuggling operations.

In the company's first charter period, profits averaged 30 percent per year.
Outbound ships carried mostly iron, some of which was left in Cadiz and other
ports along the way. The ships picked up as much as they could of Spanish
piasters, eagerly sought after in China. In Canton, the supercargo, the real boss
of the expedition, would negotiate with the Chinese mandarins for the exchange
of goods. In the early years, the supercargo was usually a non-Swede. For
example, Colin Campbell was an early supercargo, a man who had obtained his
first experience with the Orient in the service of the English and the Dutch.
Gradually, the Swedes learned more about the East and replaced the English,
Scots, and Dutch. The company also served scholars such as Carl Linnaeus'
students Anders Sparrman and C. P. Thunberg (*see* Explorers in Africa; South
Africa), who went on voyages. In *Min son på galejan (My Son on the Galleon)*,
Jacob Wallenberg wrote a serious-humorous account of his 1769 voyage on a
Swedish East India Company ship.

The company conducted a profitable trade in Chinese and Indian wares, which
were first carried back to Gothenburg and then often re-exported. There were

great auctions in Gothenburg to which merchants from the continent flocked. Tea accounted for half the cargo brought back, and some 90 percent of it was re-exported to England. The products that remained in Sweden were luxury goods including porcelain, silk, cotton cloth, and tea.

The company existed until the Napoleonic period. In 1813, when it went out of business, all its remaining records were burned. The Napoleonic Wars, plus the reduction of the English duties, ruined the smuggling business and rendered the company uncompetitive in the European markets.

REFERENCES: E. Olán, *Ostindiska compagniets saga. Historia om Sveriges märkligaste handelsföretag* (Gothenburg: Elanders, 1920); J. F. Nyström, *De Svenska Ostindiska Kompagnierna* (1883); J. Wallenberg, *Min son på galejan, eller en ostindisk resa* ... (Stockholm: Elmens och Granbergs tryckeri, 1835).

A. H. WINQUIST

SWEDISH EMPLOYERS' FEDERATION (Svenska Arbetsgivareföreningen, or SAF) The primary industrial employers' organization in the Swedish labor market

The Swedish Employers' Federation was founded in 1902, largely in response to the growth of blue-collar labor organizations, and especially to the founding of the Swedish Confederation of Trade Unions* (Landsorganisationen i Sverige or LO) in 1898. The structure of this organization has changed very little over the years, and today SAF is composed of 38,500 member firms and 37 member associations which represent all of Sweden's industrial sectors, including the metal, paper, timber, textile, shipbuilding, construction, and engineering industries. The members of SAF employ over 1.3 million workers. The organization is highly centralized and maintains strict control of its members. The policies and decisions of the governing board are binding, and firms that go against SAF decisions may be fined or expelled. SAF maintains a large fund, based upon membership fees, which is used to support actions of the organization.

For the first 25 years or so after its founding, SAF functioned principally as a defensive organization responding to the demands of organized labor. It also enjoyed a considerable advantage in discipline and political power over its counterpart in the labor market, as the history of labor-management relations in this period attests. Beginning in the late 1920s, however, the environment in which SAF operated began to change, and in 1932, when the Social Democrats formed the first in a series of governments which were to last almost without interruption until 1976, the favorable position of SAF vanished.

As a result of the changed political situation, the growth of the organized labor movement, and a trend in the parliament toward state regulation of the labor market, SAF entered into a series of negotiations with LO in 1936 which led to a basic agreement on labor-management relations (*see* Saltsjöbad Agreement). This agreement was concluded in December 1938, and it has served as the basis for labor market relations since.

From the late 1930s, the activities of SAF also expanded. Often in direct association with LO, the organization has become involved in social issues, economic planning, education, research, questions of working conditions, and most recently the question of worker ownership. SAF serves as a collection agency for statistical data, and it publishes informational materials and a regular journal. The organization is represented in a number of government bodies.

SAF is one of several very powerful interest organizations in Sweden which play a vital role in the design and implementation of policies at various levels of national life. Similar organizations were founded in the other Scandinavian countries. Denmark's employers' federation (first Arbejdsgiverforeningen and later Dansk Arbejdsgiverforeningen) was founded in 1896. The Norwegian employers' federation was established in 1900, the Finnish equivalent in 1907.

REFERENCES: Bo Carlson, *Trade Unions in Sweden* (Stockholm: Tidens, 1969); Nils Elvander, *Intresseorganisationerna i dagens Sverige* (Lund: Gleerup, 1969); Lennart Forsebäck, *Industrial Relations and Employment in Sweden* (Uppsala: The Swedish Institute, 1980); I. Lindblad et al., *Politik i Norden* (Stockholm: Aldus/Bonniers, 1972).

B. NORDSTROM

SWEDISH MISSION COVENANT (Svenska Missionsvänner) Nineteenth-century free church movement

The largest free church movement in Sweden is inextricably interwoven with the life and thought of Paul Peter Waldenström (1838–1917). Waldenström was a disciple of the Swedish Lutheran Pietist leader, Carl Olof Rosenius. When the latter died in 1868, Waldenström became the editor of the influential journal *Pietisten* and leader of the Evangelical National Foundation (Ev. Fosterlandsstiftelse) dedicated to church renewal and spiritual awakening in Sweden. But instead of maintaining the churchly character of Rosenius's inner mission movement, Waldenström became highly critical of the state church authorities.

In 1872 Waldenström published a sermon outlining a theory of the atonement that differed markedly from the orthodox position of Rosenius and the Lutheran confessions. Waldenström maintained that God's love and righteousness are not set over against each other but are identical. Christ became God's advocate to the human race to remove sin and not vice versa. Waldenström rejected the Anselmic concept of satisfaction in Christ's atonement as well as the orthodox Lutheran understanding of forensic justification and held to a subjective theory of the atonement whereby one accepts God's gift of salvation and allows Christ to complete this atoning work *in* us.

In 1878, after they had failed to remove the Lutheran confessional subscription of the Evangelical National Foundation, the radical followers of Waldenström became separatistic and organized the Swedish Mission Covenant Church. In 1882 Waldenström followed them by resigning his state church clerical position. In 1885 the "Mission Friends" of Waldenström who had emigrated to the United States broke with the Swedish Lutheran Augustana Synod and formed the Swedish Evangelical Mission Covenant Church of America. Today both Mission Covenant churches maintain overseas mission work in the Congo, Equatorial

Africa, and Japan, as well as an extensive system of congregations, schools, seminaries, and welfare institutions in their respective countries.

REFERENCES: Karl A. Olsson, *By One Spirit* (Chicago: Covenant Press, 1962); Peter P. Waldenström, *The Blood of Jesus: What Is Its Significance?* (Chicago: J. Martenson, 1888); Gunnar Westin, *I Den Svenska Frikyrklighetens Genombrottstid*(Stockholm, 1963).

T. R. SKARSTEN

SWEDISH-NORWEGIAN UNION *See* Norwegian-Swedish Union

SWEDISH PEOPLE'S PARTY Finland

The political system of autonomous Finland differed from that of other Nordic countries as a result of its late industrialization* and especially because of a political division along linguistic lines and Finland's position in the Russian Empire. The conflict in the 1870s and 1880s over whether Finland should be governed by a Swedish-speaking or Finnish-speaking elite led to the creation of the first Finnish political parties—the Finnish Party and the Swedish Party. This alignment was strong enough during the 1880s to prevent an attempt by liberals within the Swedish Party to form a bilingual Liberal Party. As the language question receded into the background, the defense of Finland's autonomy replaced the language question as the single most important political issue at the turn of the century. The decisive nature of these two problems in Finnish politics prevented the development of a liberal-conservative cleavage similar to that of other Nordic countries and retarded the emergence of a multi-party system.

Consequently, a political system based on two language parties, which was an anomaly by Nordic standards, survived longer than socioeconomic conditions and general ideological developments would have otherwise permitted.

Although a modern multi-party system did not emerge in Finland until the 1920s, the demise of the four-estate Diet and the introduction of universal suffrage in 1906 forced the Swedish Party gradually to abandon its elitist bias and to begin to represent the interests of the entire Swedish-speaking population. This transition led to the adoption of a program behind which different socioeconomic interest groups within the party could unite on linguistic and cultural questions but follow their own ideological preferences on issues which cut across the language question. The party has thus remained united since 1919 in defense of the minority rights of the Swedish-speaking population, while its political representatives in parliament (20–plus in the 1920s and 1930s) have remained free to cooperate with the Right, the Center (agrarians and liberals), and the Left on different socioeconomic issues. In the early years of independence the Swedish People's Party formed part of the political Right; during the late 1920s and early 1930s, it cooperated with the Social Democratic Party* whenever the language question pitted the Swedish People's Party against the other bourgeois parties.

Since World War II* the party has emphasized a centrist, liberal program, a trend which was formalized in the party program in 1964 and reinforced in 1973 when the right wing of the party joined with dissident rightists from the National

Coalition Party* to form the Constitutional Party. Parliamentary strength has dropped by 50 percent from the pre-war level. This electoral weakness reflects the relative decline of the Swedish-speaking population (6 percent in 1980). Despite its size, the party has held portfolios in almost two-thirds of the cabinets of independent Finland.

REFERENCES: E. Allardt, "A Minority in Both Centre and Periphery: An Account of the Swedish-Speaking Finns," *European Journal of Political Research* 10 (1982); E. Allardt and P. Pessonen, "Cleavages in Finnish Politics," in S. Lipset and S. Rokken, eds., *Party Systems and Voter Alignments: Cross-National Perspectives* (New York: The Free Press, 1967); S. Berglund and U. Lindström, *The Scandinavian Party System(s)* (Lund: Studentlitteratur, 1978); P. Hamalainen, *In Time of Storm: Revolution, Civil War and the Ethnolinguistic Issue in Finland* (Albany: State University of New York Press, 1979); J. Mylly, "The Emergence of the Finnish Multi-Party System: A Comparison with Developments in Scandinavia, 1870–1920," *Scandinavian Journal of History* 5 (1980); J. Nousiainen, *The Finnish Political System* (Cambridge, Mass.: Harvard University Press, 1973); T. Soikkanen, "Changing Bourgeois Parties in a Changing Society," in R. M. Berry, *Essays on the History of the Development of Finnish Political Parties* (Turku: Institute of Political History, 1983).

R. M. BERRY

T

TANNER, VÄINÖ (12 March 1881–19 April 1966) Finnish Social Democratic politician

Väinö Tanner was the leading figure in the Finnish cooperative movement, president of the International Cooperative Alliance (1927–1945), architect of the Social Democratic Party* of independent Finland, and an important contributor to the formulation of Finnish economic and fiscal policies during the interwar period. Tanner was a Socialist and a democrat who believed that order and discipline in society were necessary prerequisites for the proper functioning of the institutions of political democracy and social justice. Consequently, he was often caught in the cross-currents for change and order in twentieth-century Finnish society.

Tanner was the son of a railroad worker and a crofter's daughter. He became a Socialist in 1903, when he was studying the cooperative movement in Germany. After his return to Finland, Tanner became active in the cooperative movement, a preoccupation which enabled him to remain on the sidelines during the Finnish Civil War*. After the defeat of the Red forces, Tanner emerged as leader of the discredited and badly divided Social Democratic Party, which he reorganized and dominated up to the end of World War II* and which he greatly influenced up to the early 1960s. Trapped between a Socialist allegiance to class solidarity and a commitment to national unity and order, Tanner publicly rejected the politics of confrontation which had led to the Civil War and had produced a bourgeois power structure which viewed all Socialists as domestic problems and security threats.

In order to regain a political voice for socialism, Tanner denounced the revolutionary forces—a move for which the radical Left never forgave him—and insisted on a party program which emphasized gradual reform and support of political democracy. In 1927 Tanner served as prime minister of a minority government, but it was not until the 1930s, when Finland's political system was being threatened from the extreme Right and Left, that Tanner began a concerted effort to lead the Social Democratic Party away from the politics of opposition toward political cooperation with the Center. This new orientation, which required a rejection of earlier commitments to basic structural changes in the economic system as a means of solving problems of social injustice, made it possible for the Social Democrats to become accepted within the mainstream of Finnish politics; but it also aggravated ideological differences within the party.

Tanner's political contribution to Finnish society, as well as his political fate, was tied to his role in promoting national unity while never escaping the legacy of winning acceptance for the Social Democrats by cooperating with the bourgeois Center at the exclusion of the radical Left. His leadership of the Social Democratic Party eventually made it possible for the working class to be represented in a majority government (1937), but his authoritarian leadership never prevented the existence of a sizeable opposition wing within the party. After World War II Tanner's refusal to cooperate with the Communist Party* prompted part of the opposition to leave the party and found the Democratic People's League. The result was a weakened Social Democratic Party and bitter political competition among the Socialist parties. Depending on one's politics, Tanner became the individual who prevented the formation of a united postwar Socialist party or a symbol of the defense of Finland's Western values and institutions.

Tanner's controversial reputation is most often associated, however, with his role in Finnish foreign policy. His views on Soviet-Finnish relations were much less hostile and rigid than those of most Finnish leaders during the 1930s, and although it was not publicly known at the time, Tanner was also the backbone of the "peace opposition" within the wartime cabinet. But the Soviet Union viewed Tanner as the Finnish leader most responsible for the Winter War*, because he supposedly prevented Juho Paasikivi* from making territorial concessions vital to Soviet security. Tanner also stands condemned in Soviet eyes for his role in the so-called Continuation War* (1941–1944) because he was the political leader who could have changed wartime policies by withholding working-class support. Tanner is thus portrayed by some as a national hero who ensured national unity in a time of crisis and by others as the leader who made possible a dangerous policy of cooperation with Nazi Germany against the Soviet Union.

After World War II Tanner became a symbol of anti-Communism. He believed that the Communist Party should participate in the political process and that Finland should have good relations with the Soviet Union, but he feared that too many concessions to Finnish Communists and/or the Soviet Union would serve to undermine rather than defend Finnish independence. Tanner was thus unable or unwilling to perceive national unity and security in terms of cooperation with the Communist Party on the domestic front and the assumptions of the Paasikivi-Kekkonen Line* in foreign affairs.

If the Red defeat of 1918 had provided Tanner with an opportunity to play a key role as an advocate of national unity, albeit at the expense of the radical Left during the interwar years, World War II reversed the power balance in the

Baltic and the domestic and external basis for Finland's foreign policy. As a political leader who greatly contributed to the development of a society which was capable of withstanding the trauma of World War II and the Cold War, but who could neither escape the history he had helped to make nor adjust to postwar political realities, Tanner remains a controversial reminder of the hard choices Finnish leaders have had to make during the period of independence.

REFERENCES: T. Paavonen, "The Social Democratic Movement in the Politics of Independent Finland," in *Essays on the History of the Development of Finnish Political Parties*, ed. R. M. Berry (Turku: Institute of Political History, 1983); "Stubborn Foe of Soviet: Väinö Tanner," *New York Times*, 18 April 1960; M. Rintala, "The Bureaucrat in Politics: Väinö Tanner," in *Four Finns: Political Profiles* (Berkeley: University of California Press, 1969); V. Tanner, *The Winter War* (Stanford: Stanford University Press, 1957).

R. M. BERRY

TAUSEN, HANS (1494–11 November 1561) Danish Lutheran reformer

Known as the "Martin Luther of Denmark," Hans Tausen was born in 1494 on the island of Fyn in Denmark. As a monk at Antvorskov, he was sent by his monastery to study theology at Rostock from 1516 to 1521. After a brief stay at Copenhagen*, he spent two years at Wittenberg before being recalled in 1525. Upon his return to Denmark Tausen immediately began to preach on the evangelical doctrine of justification by faith. For this he was imprisoned and then ordered to Viborg, where a grass-roots evangelical awakening broke out among the townspeople. In 1526 Frederik I* granted Tausen his personal protection by appointing him as his royal chaplain. A printing press set up in Viborg in 1528 further disseminated Tausen's views. By 1529, when Tausen was called to be pastor of St. Nicholas Church in Copenhagen, a popular evangelical awakening had spread throughout Jutland.

In July 1530 Hans Tausen and other like-minded preachers in Denmark presented Forty-three Articles (*Confessio Hafniensis*) to the Danish National Assembly (Herredag) for disputation. This Copenhagen Confession was unequivocally Lutheran and was drawn up independently of the *Augsburg Confession** but was superseded by the latter due to the influence of Johann Bugenhagen in drafting the Danish Church Ordinance of 1537. With the coming of the Lutheran king, Christian III*, to power in 1536, Roman Catholic opposition to Tausen waned and he was appointed to the newly reopened evangelical University of Copenhagen. In 1538 Tausen went to Roskilde, one of the last strongholds of Roman Catholicism, to lecture in Scripture at the Cathedral School. Four years later he was appointed bishop of Ribe, where he spent the remainder of his days implementing the Lutheran Reformation*. Tausen's influence was augmented through his collection of *Sermons* (*Postil*) and his Danish translation of the Pentateuch in 1535 as well as his introduction of the vernacular into congregational hymnsinging and worship.

REFERENCES: Nils K. Andersen, *Confessio Hafniensis* (Copenhagen: Gad, 1954);

E. H. Dunkley, *The Reformation in Denmark* (London: S. P. C. K., 1948); B. Kornerup, *Hans Tausens Postil*, 2 vols. (Copenhagen: Dansk Sprog-og Litteraturselskab, 1934); Holger F. Rørdam, *Smaaskrifter af Hans Tausen* (Copenhagen: Kongeligt Dansk Selskab, 1870).

T. R. SKARSTEN

TEMPERANCE MOVEMENTS

Consumption of alcohol rose conspicuously after distillation became widespread on Scandinavian farms during the latter half of the eighteenth century and the early years of the nineteenth. Even in Norway, the most temperate of the Scandinavian lands, the annual per capita consumption of hard liquor reached sixteen liters in 1833. In Sweden and Denmark observers also complained about excessive drinking and its attendant social and moral ills.

The first temperance societies date from the eighteenth century but were small, disunited, and ineffective. The American Temperance Society, however, founded in 1826, provided a model for similar organizations elsewhere. In Norway, reformers began to form local societies in the 1830s which coalesced in 1845 as the Norwegian League against Liquor. Its efforts, together with laws of 1845 and 1848 that raised the tax on spirits and instituted licenses for selling alcohol, had rapid effects. Most of Norway's small distilleries soon closed, and annual consumption dropped to approximately six liters per capita in 1851. The Norwegian campaign was thus both public and private. Temperance speakers occasionally received state funds to defray their expenses.

In Sweden Carl Gustaf af Forsell (1783–1839), a cartographer, and Johan Olof Wallin (1779–1839), a well-known clergyman, founded in the early 1830s a total abstinence movement. It was short-lived, but in 1836 another Lutheran pastor, Peter Wieselgren (1800–1877), established in Skåne the influential Swedish Temperance Society. Wieselgren devoted much of his career to the movement, which soon bore fruit. In 1855 the parliament passed laws similar to the Norwegian legislation of the 1840s. Within two years revenues from liquor sales rose by nearly seven times, production was cut to a fourth, and the number of distilleries was reduced to a tenth.

In Denmark Ole Syversen (1801–1847) began to campaign for the formation of a temperance society in 1841, shortly after Robert Baird of the American Temperance Society visited Copenhagen*. It was founded in 1843 and blossomed in the Danish capital but failed to survive Syversen's death. Little was accomplished before the Danish Temperance Society was reconstituted in 1879.

Local option marked an important victory for the pan-Scandinavian movement. Rural Norwegian communities gained in 1845 the right to restrict the sale of alcohol locally. Many gradually did so. Sweden adopted similar legislation in 1853 that reduced the legal sale of liquor in rural areas but, as in Norway, left urban dealers untouched. In 1873 Danish towns of all sizes were empowered to limit the granting of licenses for the sale of alcohol.

The "Gothenburg system," first used in that Swedish city in 1850 and reorganized in 1865, sought to reduce the profit motive for the urban liquor traffic. Non-profit organizations were given the exclusive right to sell hard liquor. The system soon spread throughout Sweden and was officially adopted in Norway in 1871. It was not used in Denmark, however.

By the 1870s and 1880s movements for completely banning the sale of alcohol had begun to accelerate, again owing to developments in the United States. Norway adopted prohibition in 1916; a plebiscite of 1919 confirmed it with 62 percent in favor. Smuggling, clandestine distillation, and other tactics eroded its effectiveness, however, and Norway's experiment with prohibition ended in 1927. The sale of wines and liquors has since then been a prerogative of the state. In Sweden prohibition was rejected in a 1922 plebiscite. But the so-called Bratt system was in force from 1917 to 1955 and was designed to control consumption through rationing. Iceland tried prohibition from 1915 until 1934 and Finland from 1919 until 1932.

Since World War II* consumption of alcohol has risen sharply in Scandinavia* despite extensive educational work by many temperance organizations. In the early 1980s alcoholism was still a serious social problem in Scandinavia, even though it is less common there than in most other European countries.

REFERENCE: S. Lundkvist, *Politik, nykterhet och reformer: en studie i folkrörelsernas politiska verksamhet 1900–1920* (Uppsala: University of Uppsala, 1974; English summary).

F. HALE

TERBOVEN, JOSEF (23 May 1898–8 May 1945) German Reichskommissar in occupied Norway during World War II*

As the highest civilian authority, Josef Terboven exercised dominant power during the German occupation of Norway. He was born in Essen and was part of the disillusioned generation who had served in World War I. He joined the Nazi Party in 1923. As a hard and brutal streetfighter, he rose within the party and became Gauleiter of Essen in 1928 and Oberpräsident of the Rhine province in 1935.

Following the failure of German diplomatic representatives to control the governmental situation in Norway to his liking, Hitler appointed Terboven as Reichskommissar of the "occupied Norwegian territory" on 24 April 1940. In this capacity, he was responsible only to Hitler. Ruthless, effective, and realistic, he was determined to establish full independence for himself and dependence on no one except the Führer. Immediately after taking over his post, he moved to establish a governmental system that he could manipulate on Germany's behalf. He immediately recognized that Vidkun Quisling* was incompetent and unpopular, and he pressured Quisling in July to take a political leave of absence in Germany. Simultaneously, the Reichskommissar harshly pressed the parliamentary leadership to disavow King Haakon VII* and the government of Johan Nygaardsvold* in exile in England, and instead to agree to set up a new council of the realm which the Germans could co-opt. He was frustrated by Quisling, whose backers in Germany effectively appealed to Hitler. The Commissarial Council, set up on 25 September 1940, contained a majority of Quisling's National Union* adherents, but Terboven remained in his post and maintained his dominant authority. Terboven's position was later strengthened when Quisling, after having gained the post of minister president in 1942, failed dismally when he sought to establish totalitarian control. Because of the terror tactics which he preferred to employ against Norwegian opposition, however, Terboven was discredited in the eyes of the Nazi leadership, who would have preferred a more skillful approach. He was therefore thwarted in his desire to leave Norway for a higher position. At the end of the war, following Hitler's suicide, Terboven was removed from his post by Admiral Dönitz, Hitler's successor. Ever the realist, recognizing that inevitably he would receive a death sentence, he ended his life by detonating an explosive charge in his bunker on 8 May 1945, the day of the German capitulation in Norway.

REFERENCES: T. K. Derry, *A History of Modern Norway, 1814–1972* (London: Oxford University Press, 1973); H. D. Loock, *Quisling, Rosenberg and Terboven* (Stuttgart: Deutsche Verlagsanstalt, 1970); O. Riste and B. Nøkleby, *Norway, 1940–1945: The Resistance Movement* (Oslo: Johan Grundt Tanum Forlag, 1973); M. Skodvin, "Norway under Occupation," in J. Andenaes et al., *Norway and the Second World War* (Oslo: Johan Grundt Tanum Forlag, 1966).

O. HOIDAL

TESSIN, CARL-GUSTAF (1695–1770) Swedish statesman, son of Nicodemus Tessin d.y.*

In 1714, when he was 19, Carl-Gustaf Tessin was sent abroad by his father to purchase books and works of art for the royal collections, and for the next five years he traveled extensively in France, Germany, Austria, and Italy. In Paris in 1716 he met Watteau and began to acquire the collection of drawings by this short-lived genius now in the Swedish national collections. Tessin was to use his numerous opportunities to develop a most discriminating eye, and, though never a man of great wealth, his diplomatic posting later on enabled him to perfect his talents in connoisseurship. Not until 1728 would Tessin begin to collect paintings for his own delectation, and this was possibly linked to his father's death that year. During the 1730s, in collaboration with Carl Hårleman, he worked hard to complete the unfinished Stockholm Royal Palace*, which his father had begun. In this connection he undertook a mission to Vienna, traveling on from there to Venice in the company of the celebrated engraver and Venetian cicerone Conte Antonio Maria Zanetti, who became Tessin's lifelong friend and artistic influence. Tessin bought a number of works for the royal collections but was rebuffed by G. B. Tiepolo, whom he had hoped to entice to Stockholm* to carry out what would have been by far the most northerly of the great Italian's decorative schemes.

By 1738 Tessin was back in Sweden, and his political career (he had always been of the Hat Party* persuasion and so favored an aggressive policy toward

Russia should the chance come) attained a fresh momentum with his election as Lantsmarskalk following the political eclipse of Cap Party* leader Arvid Bern-hard Horn*. This post Tessin held for less than a year owing to a three-year mission to Paris which resulted in a new Swedo-French commercial treaty and the assurance of subsidies to Sweden for a war against Russia. Although this war was to prove disastrous for Swedish arms and therefore a heavy blow to the Hat interest, Tessin in Paris was able to pursue his activities on the art market and meet Boucher, Marivaux, and the Swedish painter J. E. Rehn. Back in Sweden, Tessin won back some credit for the Hats in 1743 by his handling of the Danes' disappointment that the successor to the childless Fredrik I* was not to be a Danish prince but the Russian-sponsored Adolf Fredrik* of Holstein-Gottorp; and in 1744 Tessin furthered the latter's marriage to Princess Lovisa Ulrika* of Prussia, followed in 1747 by a defensive treaty between Sweden and Prussia. Until 1749 Tessin was in the circle of the heir apparent and was appointed governor to the young Prince Gustav (later Gustav III*), who was born in 1746. But his relations with the crown prince and princess were soured when Adolf Fredrik was compelled to surrender his rights in Holstein-Gottorp and the three-year-old Gustav was betrothed to a Danish princess in order to mend Swedo-Danish relations. As chancellor, 1747–1752, it fell to Tessin to draw up Adolf Fredrik's *kungaförsäkran* (royal oath) on his accession in 1751. Though he remained governor to Crown Prince Gustav (with whom he was on friendly terms for the rest of his life) until 1755, his relations with the king and queen came to an end. Tessin continued as a member of the Riksråd until 1761, the year in which he also ended his sixteen-year tenure of the chancellorship of Åbo Academy.

At his country home, Åkerö, Tessin created a setting hospitable to all the cultural currents of the day, and, within or without France, he was probably the first to adopt, through the intermediation of Count Caylus, the new neoclassical decorative schemes of Le Lorrain 1754–1755. In his person and style Tessin embodied not only the continuation of the political links between France and Sweden but, above all, that relationship's rich cultural interchange. He was a seminal influence in the civilization of ''Gustavian'' Sweden.

REFERENCES: W. Holst, *C-G Tessin, en grandseigneur från XVIII seklet* (Stockholm, 1936), and *C-G Tessin under rese-, riksdagsmanna och de tidigare beskickningsåren* (Lund, 1931); C. D. Moselius, *C-G Tessins ungdom* (Stockholm, 1937).

D. D. ALDRIDGE

TESSIN, NICODEMUS D.Y. (1654–1728) Son of Nicodemus Tessin d.a., Swedish architect

Tessin worked under his father at Drottningholm*, where he was concerned with the internal decoration, and for which he drew most of his inspiration from Italian models. He spent three years in Rome (1673–1676) and was inevitably influenced there by Bernini, but also by Pietro da Cortona. Most of the larger schemes at Drottningholm were carried out after Tessin's second Italian journey of 1687–1688, during which he had many sculptures in the churches of Rome measured and drawn for religious or secular use in Sweden. By the time of Karl XII's* accession in 1697, Tessin, "the Italian of the North," was in charge of all court ceremonial, and in all aesthetic matters became the young king's mentor. Through correspondence he remained in touch with Karl XII through the years of the king's absence from Sweden, primarily because he had been charged with designing the new Stockholm Royal Palace*. In this way Tessin probably came to enjoy as much of Karl XII's confidence as any man, but his capacity for affairs also brought him to the center of government in the last years of the Great Northern War* and hence to prominent membership of the Kungligt råd (Riksråd following the Revolution of 1719). Tessin favored peace with Russia in 1719 rather than a prolongation of the war in dependence on Britain-Hanover, and also proved a trenchant protagonist of the revolution: in his political thinking now he was profoundly influenced by the Abbé St. Pierre's *Discours sur la Polysynodie* which, banned in France, had been published in London in 1718 and was brought to him by his son, Carl-Gustaf Tessin*, the following spring. St. Pierre's work formed the basis of Tessin's own *Reflexioner angående en regeringsform* (Reflections on a Constitution, 1720?), in which he proclaimed the virtues of conciliary and collective government over government by a sole minister, in Tessin's experience a mode recently epitomized by the Baron Görtz*. Tessin was appointed chancellor of Lund University in 1714.

REFERENCES: R. Josephson, *Nicodemus Tessin d.y. Tiden-mannen-verket*, 2 vols., Sv. allm. konstförenings publikationer 38 (Stockholm: 1930–1931); J. Montague, "Church Decorations of N. Tessin d.y.," *Konstvetenskaplig Tidskrift* 31 (1962); O. Sirén, *Nicodemus Tessin d.ys. studieresor* (Stockholm, 1914); L. Thanner, *Revolutionen i Sverige efter Karl XIIs Död* (Uppsala: Almqvist & Wiksell, 1953).

D. D. ALDRIDGE

THRANE, MARCUS (14 October 1817–30 April 1890) Norwegian journalist, reformer, and social agitator

Thrane was born into a wealthy family with connections in the political elite of Norway. Only months after his birth, however, his father went bankrupt, and Marcus grew up in relative poverty. As a young man he traveled extensively through Europe working as a singer and musician. In England he encountered the stirring labor unrest of the Chartist movement, which had an impact on his later thinking.

In 1840 he began to study theology at the university in Oslo, but financial difficulties forced him to quit before taking the degree. In 1841 Thrane opened a private school in Lillehammer and married one of his former students, Josephine Buch. In Lillehammer, Thrane published occasional national romantic poems, but they did not contain evidence of his growing political radicalism. In 1846 he moved his school to Asgardstrand and, in the following year, to the workers' town of Modum, site of the Modum Blåfarveverk.

A major turning point in Thrane's life occurred in 1848, when he moved to Drammen. Although he intended to open a school there, he instead became editor of *Drammens Adresse*, a local newspaper. As editor, he joined the front ranks of political agitators for increased democratization of Norwegian society and argued for universal suffrage, removal of protective tariffs, improvement of working conditions for laborers, and other radical goals. Nearly 20 years before the first political party was founded in Norway, Thrane advocated the creation of a large, democratic political party based on the middle and lower classes.

Although Thrane would write later that he was a Socialist at this time, he was not a Marxist. His sympathy for the workers was based more on his sense of justice and the influence of such utopian Socialists as Henri Saint-Simon. By the end of 1848, his activism led him to begin to organize labor associations around the country, and on 5 May 1849 he began to publish the weekly newspaper *Arbeiderforeningens Blad*. The paper, he wrote, would argue for the truth and the cause of the laborers. Through the labor associations a petition with some 30,000 signatures was collected and sent to the union king, Oscar I*. This contained demands aimed at the democratization of Norway. They seem mild today but were considered radical and a threat to the establishment in the mid-nineteenth century. The very existence of the government of the elite was under attack. The authorities became increasingly suspicious and frightened, and, when some members of the associations began to talk of revolution, they acted against Thrane and his movement. Although Thrane consistently counseled non-violence, he was the most visible symbol of the unrest. He was arrested and jailed for three years while the government investigated his movement. Not until 1854 did a judgment come down sentencing Thrane to four years in prison. When he was released in 1858, he had served seven years, not four.

After his release from prison, Thrane had difficulty getting work and turned to a new vocation: photography. He traveled Norway photographing many of the wealthy, who seem to have considered him somewhat of a curiosity.

As editor of *Arbeiderforeningens Blad*, Thrane had published numerous American letters and advised emigration to many of his followers as a means of escaping their economic and social condition. Within a year of his wife's death in 1862, he followed his own advice and left for America. For the first two years of his new life in the United States, Thrane worked as a photographer in New York. We know from his later writings that he made a considerable effort to understand the history and culture of his adopted country. In 1866 friends of Thrane convinced him to move to Chicago, where he helped to established an immigrant newspaper, *Marcus Thrane's Norske Amerikaner*. In its first issue he told his readers that he was continuing the fight he had begun in Norway. Thrane's paper proved less successful than he had hoped, and he sold it. For the next two years, he spent most of his time working on theater productions of his own and others' plays in Chicago to raise the social consciousness of the Scandinavian workers. Thrane wrote more than 30 plays including comedies, vaudevillian dramas, and serious plays. Many of these have survived. His children frequently took part in the productions.

In April 1869 Thrane returned to newspaper work as editor of *Daglyset*, which was published in connection with the Chicago Freethinkers Association. The paper appeared monthly through 1873 and then only sporadically after that. In *Daglyset* Thrane showed a strong hostility to the organized church among the Norwegian-Americans and was particularly antagonistic toward the clergy, which he considered a remnant of the old-world establishment. After the events of the Paris Commune (1871), Thrane turned more to Socialist themes in his paper, anticipating many later reforms and political movements in the Midwest and other parts of the United States. In 1878 Thrane became involved with a third newspaper, *Den Nye Tid*, but his contribution was limited to an occasional travel account through Norwegian America and his *Wisconsin Bible*, wherein he spoofed the Norwegian-American clergy.

In 1882 Thrane was encouraged by his friends to take a European trip and even return to Norway. A year-long tour brought him to Denmark, France, England, and Norway. Returning to Norway after 20 years, he discovered that his name was still feared for what it represented. The establishment ignored him. Only on the personal level did some of his former comrades welcome him. To raise money for his stay, Thrane gave numerous talks on "The Dark and Light Sides of America." His reception may be attributed to the simultaneous occurrence of a serious constitutional crisis in the country, as the Liberal Party was challenging the union monarch on the question of ministerial responsibility (*see* Sverdrup, Johan). Any acknowledgment of Thrane would have meant stirring up animosities from two decades earlier and possibly threatening the struggle for the democratization of the constitution. Most surprising, perhaps, was the attitude of the labor movement, which also shunned him. It demonstrated, however, that his name was still a force in Norway.

Thrane returned to the United States in late 1883 bitter and disappointed. The workers, to whom he had dedicated his life, seemed to reject him. He was tired of the struggle, although a spark still glowed in him from time to time. He moved to Eau Claire, Wisconsin, where his son, Arthur Thrane, had established a medical practice. He remained there until his death in 1890. He was buried in Eau Claire, but in 1949 his remains were moved to Norway, where he was interred in the national cemetery.

REFERENCES: O. Bjørklund, *Marcus Thrane: Socialistleder i et u-land* (Oslo, 1970); M. Thrane, *Den Gamle Wisconsin Bibelen* (Chicago, 1881 and 1939); A. Zachariassen, *Fra Marcus Thrane til Martin Tranmael: Det Norske Arbeiderparti fram til 1945* (Oslo, 1977).

T. LEIREN

TÓRSHAVN Capital of the Faroe Islands*

Tórshavn, generally called by its inhabitants merely Havn, today the administrative, cultural, and communications center of the Faroe Islands, lies near the southeastern extremity of the island of Streymoy, at approximately 62°N 06°45'W. The name means "Thor's Harbor" and presumably dates from the heathen period. The modern town flanks the entire waterfront of the double bay forming the harbor and runs some distance inland. Until the present century, the town hardly extended beyond the peninsula separating the eastern and western bays.

The earliest known reference to Tórshavn occurs in *Færeyinga Saga*, written in Iceland about 1220, in which we learn that this was the assembly-place of the Faroese, where in the year 999 they agreed to accept Christianity. The saga is not to be relied upon as a historical source, but there is no reason to doubt these details, or that the peninsula of Tinganes (meaning Assembly Headland) was the site of the Faroese assembly and law court from the earliest times.

There is little material on which to base the early history of Tórshavn. One medieval building survives, called Munkastova, in which it is said that the monks stored their rents (paid in kind). A couple of fifteenth-century documents written in Tórshavn bear witness to the existence of the place but tell us nothing about it. With the establishment of the Faroese Monopoly*, however, Tórshavn emerges as the only legal trading place in the Faroe Islands, with perhaps 20 or 30 dwellings to house the trading staff, and also the *landfoged* (high bailiff), who had his own warehouse in which to receive crown rents and taxes. A small population of landless folk who lived by laboring, domestic service, fishing, and knitting also lived in the town.

To defend the warehouses, Magnus Heinason (Mogens Heinesen*) erected the first fortification in Tórshavn about 1580. This lay on the headland to the east of the town, where the remains of its successor, built two centuries later, are still to be seen. After an incursion by Barbary Corsairs in 1629, a second redoubt was built in the town itself.

The first known Tórshavn church was built in 1609 and could accommodate 150 people. It was probably full only at the annual sessions of the Lagting*, since it was not found necessary to build a large church (the one on the present site) until 1788, for the town grew very slowly.

The growth of Tórshavn was slow because, apart from the trading station and the official institutions, there were no real economic resources. The first significant advance took place during the period 1768 to 1788, when a transit depot (for the convenience of smugglers) was set up by the Copenhagen merchant Niels Ryberg.

Tórshavn was three times the subject of hostile attack. In 1579 an English pirate, Clerk, removed all the goods from the Tinganes warehouses. In 1677 the forts were destroyed and the town plundered by French naval forces, operating in alliance with Sweden during the Scanian War. In 1808 a British naval vessel captured and disarmed the Tórshavn fortifications and was followed by a privateer under British letters of marque, who removed the goods from the warehouses on Tinganes, though the action of the latter was not upheld by the Admiralty prize court in London.

The development of Tórshavn gathered speed from the 1820s, when the inhabitants were permitted to enclose and cultivate portions of rough pasture belonging to the neighboring crown farms. Such allotments enabled boat fishermen to grow potatoes and keep a cow to eke out their income. The abolition of the

Monopoly in 1856 and the beginning of the Faroese fishing industry* gave a further boost to the town. From 1921 to 1929 a large breakwater was built in Tórshavn. During the present century, Tórshavn has grown rapidly to an important commercial center and headquarters of the Faroese fishing industry. In 1982 the town had a population of over 14,000 and most of the facilities of a mainland town 10 times this size.

Tórshavn became a municipality in 1866 and has since expanded from a huddle of primitive-looking houses on a cramped peninsula to a handsome town of broad streets, timber and concrete buildings, schools, parks, hospitals, libraries, and sporting facilities. The outskirts of the town are now two or three kilometers from Tinganes.

The population of Tórshavn has expanded as follows: 1709--300; 1801--554; 1850--841; 1901--1,626; 1955--6,067; 1979--13,534. The town thus contains over 30 percent of the Faroese population at the present day.

REFERENCES: *Faroe Isles Review*; J. F. West, *Faroe, the Emergence of a Nation* (London: C. Hurst; New York: P. S. Eriksson, 1972).

J. F. WEST

TRANMÆL, MARTIN (1879–1967) Norwegian Labor Party* politician and newspaper editor

Martin Tranmæl was the leading figure within the Labor Party during the first half of the twentieth century. Born in Melhus, Trøndelag, he spent most of the period between 1900 and 1905 in the United States. As a worker, he was impressed by the International Workers of the World, and he brought with him certain syndicalist influences upon his return to Norway. He entered politics in Trøndelag as a journalist and trade union leader.

Tranmæl became one of the chief spokesmen for the youthful, radical branch of the party, which favored revolutionary action and which was impatient with the reform policy of the party leadership. He drew up the initiative which resulted in the Trade Union Opposition in 1911 (Fagopposisjonen av 1911), henceforth the chief opposition group within the labor movement. Its goal was to capture control of society through takeover of the means of production, if necessary by violent means such as sabotage, obstruction, and the general strike.

World War I and the Bolshevik Revolution of 1917 radicalized the labor movement and allowed Tranmæl, Kyrre Grepp, and their followers to oust the old leadership of the Labor Party in 1918. Grepp became party foreman and Tranmæl party secretary.

The Labor Party now proclaimed itself to be a revolutionary party. In 1919 it joined the Communist International, the only Western European Socialist party to do so as a whole. Tranmæl, however, never felt comfortable with this affiliation. Above all, he rejected Moscow's attempt to dominate the parties belonging to the International. He therefore subsequently engineered the break with the Comintern that occurred in 1923.

The 1920s was marked by divisions and infighting within the labor movement.

The moderate segment of the Labor Party broke away to form the Social Democratic Party in 1921, and in 1923 the Communists did the same. Both of these divisions resulted from Tranmæl's relationship with the Comintern. Throughout this period Tranmæl and his followers maintained their control over the Labor Party, which continued to be the major Socialist group.

Just as Tranmæl had led the labor movement into its radical phase, he actively took part in its transition from revolutionary to reformist movement. In large part he was responsible for the relatively frictionless manner in which this was accomplished. He supervised the move which reunited the Labor Party with the Social Democrats in 1927, and he supported the formation of Labor governments, first under Christopher Hornsrud in 1928, and under Johan Nygaardsvold* in 1935.

Despite his great personal influence over the labor movement, Tranmæl never wished to hold public office. He served briefly as vice-mayor of Trondheim, 1917–1918; as Storting* representative, 1925–1927; and from 1938 onwards as member of the Nobel Peace Prize Committee. His period as party secretary lasted from 1918 to 1923. He maintained his key position in the party as editor of *Arbeiderbladet*, the major party newspaper, from 1921 to 1949.

Tranmæl first and foremost was a charismatic speaker and writer. His ascetic way of life and his simple but effective manner of speaking gave him a completely unique position within the labor movement. His great strength lay in his total commitment to labor's cause and in his direct contact with the movement's mass membership.

REFERENCES: T. K. Derry, *A History of Modern Norway, 1814–1972* (London: Oxford University Press, 1973); Walter Galenson, *Labor in Norway* (Cambridge, Mass.: Harvard University Press, 1949).

O. HOIDAL

TREATY OF FRIENDSHIP, COOPERATION AND MUTUAL ASSISTANCE between Finland and the Soviet Union (1948, renewed in 1955 and 1970)

The FCMA treaty is generally recognized in Finland as the cornerstone of the country's foreign policy. This has not always been the case, however. When the treaty was signed in 1948, most Finnish and Western observers considered it a potential millstone to be hung around the neck of independent Finland. President Juho Paasikivi* received a proposal on 22 February from Joseph Stalin to conclude a mutual assistance agreement along the lines recently agreed upon by the Soviet Union and Hungary and Rumania. At the time Europe was rapidly being divided into two hostile camps. The European Recovery Program had been launched, and final plans were being made for a Western European military alliance. In the East the crisis which would lead to the Czechoslovakian coup was intensifying.

During the period from 22 February, when Stalin's letter was received, and 6 April, when the treaty was signed, Paasikivi struggled to find a formula which would satisfy Soviet demands without impairing Finnish independence, and, in so doing, convince the Soviet Union that Finland had no intention of siding with the West or of becoming part of the East. The final draft of the agreement, which contained amendments and a preamble written by Paasikivi, has proven to be consistent with Finnish security interests. The military articles of the treaty differ from those in other Soviet treaties with its neighbors in that military cooperation is limited to Finnish territory and is not automatic. The treaty is thus not a military alliance which commits Finland to all Soviet military objectives—only to those which would inevitably affect Finland.

The treaty commits Finland to defend Finnish territory against any attempt by Germany or its allies to attack the Soviet Union via Finland. In the event of a crisis situation, consultations are required to determine the nature of military cooperation, and in the event of Finnish inability to defend its territory, the Soviet Union will provide assistance. The preamble to the treaty recognizes Finland's desire to remain outside Great Power conflicts, a point which Finns tend to emphasize. The Soviets, for their part, emphasize that the preamble does not negate the obligations inherent in the military articles. These differences do not necessarily represent any contradiction between Finnish and Soviet inter-pretations of the treaty. Rather, they reflect the Finnish realization that conditions which would render Finnish neutrality impossible would in effect undermine the basis of Finnish postwar foreign policy. Treaty or no treaty, the Soviet Union could not be expected to remain passive on the Finnish front in the event of a European war. Short of war, however, the treaty provides a framework for stable relations between the Soviet Union and Finland, thus minimizing speculation over Finnish foreign policy objectives and Finland's role in East-West relations.

The Finnish view that the treaty makes neutrality possible perplexes most Western observers, many of whom believe that the opposite is the case. Finland's neutrality is obviously not grounded in international law, but if neutrality can be understood to mean a kind of non-alignment in which a country says no to one bloc or the other, Finland is neutral. By accepting a status of internationally guaranteed neutrality Austria said no to both blocs, and Sweden remained neutral by saying no to NATO. When Finland persuaded the Soviet Union to modify the proposed text of the treaty and to accept the introduction of a preamble which recognized Finland's desire to remain outside Great Power conflicts, Finland was saying no to what eventually became the Warsaw Pact. But in saying no, Finland was also agreeing to base its future neutrality on the Russian rather than the Western connection. In defining its postwar policy of neutrality Finland had first to come to terms with the power which would be most threatened by any Finnish departure from neutrality. Ideologically and economically, Finland is tied to the West, but geographically it is situated in an area of vital importance to Soviet security. Finland's policy of neutrality is an attempt to overcome the latent contradition between these cultural affinities and strategic realities. (*See also* Paasikivi-Kekkonen Line.)

REFERENCES: A. Apunen, "Finland's Treaties on Security Policy," *Cooperation and*

Conflict 4 (1969); K. Korhonen, "Treaty of Friendship, Cooperation and Mutual Assistance Between the Soviet Union and Finland: Some Aspects of International Politics," *Cooperation and Conflict* 8 (1973); H. P. Krosby, "The Communist Power Bid in Finland in 1948," *Political Science Quarterly* 76 (June 1960); J. Wuorinen, *A History of Finland* (New York: Columbia University Press, 1965).

R. M. BERRY

TREATY OF KIEL (14 January 1814) Treaty between Sweden and Denmark by which Norway was to come into union with Sweden

The military confrontation between Great Britain and France during the Napoleonic Wars endangered the dynastic union of Norway and Denmark as no force had before. This resulted in warfare from 1807 to 1809 in which Denmark-Norway, and her allies France and Russia, had battled Sweden and Great Britain. Norway suffered greatly during this period despite the efforts of Prince Christian August* and the Government Commission* (Regjeringskomission) to resolve the ensuing difficulties. King Frederik VI* dealt with his problems in Norway by securing peace with Sweden in 1809, granting permission to Norwegian merchants to trade with England, and reluctantly establishing a university in Norway in 1811.

The king's continued support of Napoleon, despite French losses in Russia during 1812 and thereafter, soon led to a revival of the crisis that had threatened Norway earlier. Because Frederik was both unable and unwilling to make peace with Britain, the British created a naval blockade around Norway again, cutting off the country from the chief purchaser of its timber and preventing the importation of grain from Denmark. Norway's economic and financial structure collapsed, and severe food shortages recurred.

These conditions also revived the separatist tendencies evident from 1807 to 1809 in a more critical form. Dissatisfaction with the government was more pervasive than earlier, with greater manifestations of discontent than before in Bergen and Trondheim, for example, and affecting government officials as well as middle-class merchants. In Sweden, interest in the annexation of Norway from Denmark became the keystone of Crown Prince Karl (XIV) Johan's* foreign policy. He therefore made its acquisition the price for Sweden's alliance in 1812 with Russia and Great Britain.

Aware of these problems, Frederik sent his cousin and heir apparent, Prince Christian Frederik (later Christian VIII*) to Norway in mid-May 1813 to strengthen the government's position there. The young prince proceeded energetically to re-establish many of the policies and proposals that had been carried out from 1807 to 1809 by the Government Commission. He urged peace or some accommodation with Great Britain to relieve the hardships caused by the British blockade and restored administrative agencies which had been eliminated in 1809 and 1810. Despite these efforts to save the union, Karl Johan took matters into his own hands in mid-December 1813 when he occupied the duchy of Holstein, against the wishes of his allies, until Frederik submitted to his demand for

Norway. Frederik reluctantly agreed to this in the Treaty of Kiel on 14 January 1814.

REFERENCES: See references under Norwegian-Swedish Union. O. Alin, *Fjerde artikeln of fredstraktaten i Kiel 1814* (Stockholm, 1899); F. Lagerröth, "Kielertraktatens tolkning och tillämpning," *Scandia* 13 (1940): 206–56; A. Linvald, "Omkring Kielerfreden: Bidrag til Danmarks og Norges historie i det første maneder af 1814," *Historisk tidskrift* (D) 12:4 (1952–1956): 165–231; H. Meijer, "Blev Norge självstandigt genom Kieltraktaten," *Statsvetenskaplig Tidskrift* 61 (1958): 1–24; G. Nørregård, "Freden i Kiel," *Scandia* 21 (1951–1952): 28–43.

L. SATHER

TRELLEBORG FORTS Four Viking Age* forts found in Denmark

In the traditional view, the Vikings* were looked upon as heathen, undisciplined barbarians, whose contributions to the national income of Scandinavia* came from rape and plunder in rich but—compared to the ruthless northerners— rather defenseless western Europe. Today this view no longer holds. Recent excavations in Scandinavia and the British Isles have revealed the extent of urban Viking culture; where trade, craftsmanship, and peaceful economic pursuits were highly developed.

The starting point in this change of attitude toward the Vikings was the discovery and excavation of the four identical Viking forts of the Trelleborg type in Denmark. Only two of them, Trelleborg in west Sjaelland (discovered in the 1930s) and Fyrkat in the northern part of central Jutland (discovered in the 1950s), have been fully excavated and partly reconstructed. The biggest fort, Aggersborg, located by the "Limfjord" in northern Jutland, was located and test-excavated in the 1940s. The final fort, Nonnebakken (the Nun's Hill), located in the center of Funen opposite Odense, has only been excavated at random. As the name suggests, a medieval convent was situated on the last location. This and the present-day town have disturbed the Viking fort so much that only the circular rampart has been established.

The main parts of the plan of the forts are of the same fundamental character. The identical elements include (1) a carefully constructed and geometrically precise ring rampart with a concentric relationship to a ditch in front of it; (2) four covered gateways oriented directly north-south and east-west which cut through the rampart; (3) axis-streets aligned to the points of the compass which meet in a central courtyard inside the forts; (4) a courtyard divided by the axis-streets into quarters with the same number of identical bow-sided houses in each quarter (4 × 4 at Trelleborg, Fyrkat and Nonnebakken, 12 × 4 at Aggersborg); and (5) a V-shaped ditch wherever the natural waterways around the forts did not provide sufficient protection.

In contrast to the other forts, Trelleborg had an extra rampart in front of and concentric to the main rampart. Fifteen houses of the same construction as within the courtyard were situated behind this extra front-rampart.

Comparative Measurements of Viking Forts (in meters)

	Diameter	Width of Rampart	Width of Berm	Width of Ditch	Length of Buildings
Trelleborg	136	19	5	18	29.4
Aggersborg	240	11	8	4	32.0
Fyrkat	120	12	11	7	28.4
Nonnebakken	120	(17)	(8)	(7)	?

The archeological finds (especially from Fyrkat and Trelleborg) may be divided into four categories: (1) finds from the cemeteries, (2) finds from the refuse dumps, (3) finds from the houses, and (4) treasure trove finds. Those buried in the cemetery of Fyrkat show a fairly equal distribution of sexes, plus several children's graves. There are no signs of violent death. In the burial ground at Trelleborg, however, are found several common graves. Among those buried at Trelleborg whose sex could be determined (only 44 of 150), most were adult males (31), while there were only nine women and four children.

The refuse dumps tell about the permanent population at the forts and give evidence of craftsmanship and trade. The craftsmanship of Fyrkat is further evidenced by the use of several (33 percent) of the houses as workshops (by copper-alloy-, gold- and weaponsmiths). Finally, the treasure troves reveal a relatively prosperous settlement and trading place. Among the finds are axes, spearheads, and, especially in the rampart of Trelleborg, several hundred arrow-heads. Both Fyrkat and Trelleborg were demolished by fire, but we cannot know for certain whether or not this was caused by enemy action, although the short life of the forts (less than 50 years) points toward violent destruction.

The finds reveal cultural connections mainly with the Baltic and Scandinavia. Practically no finds point toward connections with western Europe. Besides the east-oriented international relations, there is a strong strain of local craftsmanship (especially in pottery). The finds disclose that though these forts clearly had military functions, a civil life developed within the framework of them.

It was formerly believed that one could measure the size of the garrison by multiplying the number of houses by the number of men corresponding to the crew of a normal Viking ship. On this basis it has been assumed that an army of 10,000 men could have been housed in the forts. Far from all of the houses, however, served as living quarters. Many were workshops, and a number of the houses were without hearths.

Until recently the dating of the forts was rather uncertain, estimated to approximately 900 to 1050. By means of dendrochronology, however, it is currently argued that Trelleborg was built around 980/981. Twenty-five finds of wood from different parts of the fort all originated from trees cut down between August

980 and April 981. By systematic adaptation and comparison, the finds from Fyrkat also emphasize a short period of use in the late tenth century.

The geographical situation of the forts is characterized by several mutual traits. First, they are, apart from Aggersborg, situated by smaller streams not passable by seagoing ships. Second, their positions cover both land and watershed passages. Third, the streams and swamps around the forts were part of the defense system. Fourth, it was necessary to level the sites before the forts could be constructed. Finally, by Trelleborg and Aggersborg older settlements were removed in favor of the forts.

Although these Viking forts are not mentioned in the written sources, such enormous stronghold projects can only be explained as parts of a state affair conducted by a central power, just as the identical construction of the forts is a testimony of a mutual plan and architect.

In the interpretation of the historical purpose and function of the forts, two opposing views have been forwarded. Originally formulated just after the excavation of Trelleborg, one theory states that the forts were training camps for Sven I Forkbeard*'s Viking army, which attacked and invaded England during the period 994–1013. The other theory stresses that the forts had a national purpose as subjugation bastions in the centralization process under Harald I* (Bluetooth) in the 980s.

The main arguments for the training camp theory are that (1) the construction of the forts points toward strict discipline and training of an army; (2) the forts had the capacity to house a large army; (3) ships could sail directly to the forts which were bases for the fleet and reception camps for other Scandinavian warriors; (4) there is evidence of weapon production at the forts; (5) they date to around the year 1000 (thus coming in Sven Forkbeard's reign); (6) only the capital collected during the raids in England (Danegeld) could enable otherwise poor Denmark to marshal the resources demanded to build these enormous camps.

The main arguments for the subjugation theory are: (1) the weight placed on the defensive elements in the construction of the forts and the surroundings; (2) the necessity of expropriation in order to place the forts in exactly the spots where former agglomerations were located; (3) the strategic position of the forts covering both roads and waterways; (4) the situation of the four known forts in a country-wide system as gateways to those parts of the country which were not in the hands of the south Jutland dynasty (*Jellinge dynastiet*) before the time of Harald Bluetooth; (5) and, seen in connection with the dating of Trelleborg to 980/981, the information on the big Jelling* runestone that indicates Harald Bluetooth united the kingdom and Christianized the Danes.

In addition, the view that the forts were directed against the decentralized system of power based on petty kings, chieftains, and thanes also implies that these strongholds may well have functioned as administrative centers connected with trade, coinage, and royal craftsmen.

Finally, one must take into consideration the violent overthrow of Harald by his son Sven around 987. Hypothetically, this may change Sven's role from constructor of the forts to destroyer and would explain the short lives of these prestigious projects.

To be sure, all the interpretations of the fortresses' role in the political history of the late tenth century must be kept on the hypothetical level. Seen as archeological evidence, however, the forts are striking testimony of the Scandinavian (Danish) political and economic potential toward the end of the Viking Age. This position must be seen in the light of some extremely favorable economic developments which affected Scandinavia in the last quarter of the first millennium. Only a great capital surplus can explain how it was possible to carry out the construction of these forts, which were so demanding of labor and accumulated wealth.

REFERENCES: A. E. Christensen, *Vikingtidens Danmark* (Copenhagen: Det historiske Institut ved Copenhagen University, 1969); T. E. Christiansen, "The Camps of the Vikings," *Danish Journal* (Ministry of Foreign Affairs, 1980): 8–12, and "Traeningslejr eller tvangsborg," *Kuml* (1970): 44–66; P. V. Glob, *Danish Prehistoric Monuments* (London: Faber & Faber, 1971); P. Nørlund, "Trelleborg," *Nordiske Fortidsminder* 4:1 (Copenhagen: Det kongelige nordiske Oldskriftselskab, 1948); O. Olsen et al., "Fyrkat, en jysk vikingborg I-II," in *Nordiske Fortidsminder*, vols. 3–4 (Copenhagen: Det kongelige nordiske Oldskriftselskab, 1977), "Trelleborg-problemer. De danske vikingeborge og deres historiske baggrund," *Scandia* 28 (1962): 92–112, and "Viking Fortresses in Denmark," *Recent Archaeological Excavations in Europe*, ed. R. Bruce-Mitford (London, 1975); E. Rosedahl, "Aggersborg in the Viking Age," *Proceedings of the Eighth Viking Congress 1977* (Odense: Odense University Press, 1981), pp. 107–22; N. P. Stilling, "Trelleborg-hypoteser. Om de danske vikingeborges funktion og historiske betydning," *Scandia* 47 (1981): 29–65.

N. P. STILLING

TRYGGER, ERNST (1857–1943) Swedish lawyer, politician, and prime minister

Ernst Trygger was one of the most distinguished politicians and jurists in Swedish political life during the first four decades of the twentieth century. He completed a doctorate in law at Uppsala University in 1885 and went on to become a professor, and later vice-chancellor and then chancellor of the nation's universities. From 1905 to 1907 he sat on the Supreme Court. As a legal scholar and professor, he was noted for his Germanic logic and exactitude in published and oral argument. Constitutional law was one of his specialties.

It was as the chief parliamentary leader and spokesperson for the conservative wing of the Conservative Party* that Trygger was best known nationally. He served in the Upper Chamber of the Riksdag* from 1897 to 1937 and early gained membership on key committees. By 1909 he was the head of one of the two conservative parties in the chamber. With the merger of the parties in 1912, he temporarily lost this position because the moderates opposed him. He was re-elected leader of the Upper Chamber conservatives in 1913 and remained in that position until 1933. He served as prime minister only once (1923–1924) and was foreign minister in Arvid Lindman's* Conservative government from 1928 to 1930.

Trygger was a willing candidate for the premiership in 1914, 1917, and 1920, but failed each time to gain office because of his hard-line conservative stance. The Left and moderate Conservatives found him unacceptable, and the decline of Conservative and Liberal seats in the parliament and the corresponding increase by the Social Democrats (the largest single party by 1919) dictated that the party have a more moderate head than Trygger if it were to participate in coalition governments. When he became prime minister in 1923, he failed to get broad representation in his cabinet from the other bourgeois parties. His almost consistent opposition to parliamentary reform and social legislation left him in a poor position to carry even a modest defense bill in 1924. The following year parliament, under a Social Democratic government, emasculated the defense budget and the military—a condition which lasted until the eve of World War II*. While this was a bitter defeat for Trygger, since he had always worked for a strong defense, he had also reaped what he had sown a decade earlier. During the intense defense debate in 1913–1914, he successfully urged Gustav V* to force the Liberal ministry out of office. While the Liberal government did resign, moderate Conservatives blocked his rise to the premiership. Because his solution to the defense question in 1914 was at the same time a drive to preserve the monarchy as a strong force in the political life of the state, the Left retaliated in 1925 by mutilating the military.

Beyond his interest in foreign affairs and defense, Trygger was an ardent leader in promoting the economic life of Sweden under the banner of free enterprise. He was a man of substantial wealth and served as chairman and board member of several of the country's largest companies. He was made an honorary member of the Academy of Letters in 1922 and was elected to the Academy of Science in 1925.

REFERENCES: K. Hildebrand, *Gustaf V som människa och regent*, 2 vols. (Stockholm: Svensk Litteratur, 1945–1948); D. Rustow, *The Politics of Compromise* (Princeton: Princeton University Press, 1955); B. Schiller, "Years of Crisis, 1906–1914," in S. Koblik, ed., *Sweden's Development from Poverty to Affluence 1750–1970* (Minneapolis: University of Minnesota Press, 1975).

P. V. THORSON

U

ULLSTEN, OLA (1931–) Swedish prime minister

Born and raised in the north of Sweden and educated at the Institute for Social Affairs in Stockholm*, Ullsten spent the first years of his professional life in largely apolitical activities. During the early 1950s his energies were primarily channeled into Sweden's temperance movement. In 1957, however, he took a job in Stockholm as the secretary of the Liberal Party's (*see* Liberal People's Party) parliamentary group. From this point on, he began to develop broader political ideas, an attachment to the party, and a career in politics which led to the prime ministership.

In 1962 he became head of the Liberal Party's youth organization. He entered parliament three years later, as a representative for Greater Stockholm. He became a member of the party's governing council in 1975 and succeeded Per Ahlmark as head of the party in March 1978. When Thorbjorn Fälldin's first coalition government was formed in the fall of 1976, Ullsten was appointed minister of international economic cooperation. This assignment reflected his intense concern with the responsibility of the industrial nations to assist Third World countries in their development. He became deputy prime minister in March 1978.

Fälldin's first government collapsed in October 1978, largely over the issue of nuclear power. Ullsten's political abilities and his interest in heading a government then became clear. He sidestepped the possibility of reconstructing the coalition and instead formed a minority government, based on 39 Liberal representatives in the parliament. His success in this effort rested on a number of factors, however, including the desire of the Social Democratic Party* to avoid an election just eleven months before the regular term of the parliament was to expire.

Ullsten's government stayed in power for a year and enjoyed remarkable parliamentary success and popular support. Ullsten was able to arrange voting majorities on numerous occasions, but he was not able to attack significantly any of the major problems then facing Sweden, including energy, inflation, budget deficits, taxation, worker incentive, and defense. In certain respects, Ullsten's ministry is reminiscent of the governments of Carl Gustav Ekman*. Until March 1979 the government and the Liberal Party rose in popularity in opinion polls. Largely because of the party's pro-nuclear power position, however, this trend was reversed following the accident at the Three Mile Island nuclear generating plant in Pennsylvania. A decline in the party's standing culminated in significant losses in the September 1979 general election.

Following the regular parliamentary election in 1979, in which the non-Socialist parties retained their slim majority in the Riksdag*, Ullsten stepped down. A second non-Socialist coalition, again headed by Fälldin, was formed. In this Ullsten became minister of foreign affairs. In May 1981 this government collapsed, and Ullsten again formed a minority government.

REFERENCE: Ruth Link, "The Prime Minister Who Rose to the Occasion," *Sweden Now* 13:1 (1979): 20–25.

B. NORDSTROM

ULRIKA ELEONORA (the Younger) (23 January 1688–24 November 1741) Queen of Sweden 1719–1720

Born in Stockholm* to Karl XI* and his consort, Ulrika Eleonora (the Elder), Ulrika Eleonora was the sister of the future king, Karl XII*. In 1714 she married Duke Fredrik (Friedrich) of Hesse (later Fredrik I*) and succeeded her brother as monarch in 1719. Ulrika Eleonora was the only member of the royal family resident in Sweden from 1708 until her brother's return in 1715. During this time, and especially from 1713, she served the function of vice-regent (although she was not granted the title) and signed all government documents except for those directed to the king. This was a time of political ferment at home, as Karl XII's absence and the continuation of the Great Northern War* lay heavily on the shoulders of the council of the realm and brought economic and personal hardship to the absolute king's subjects. Ulrika Eleonora's concern for the well-being of the country became well known among the political leadership during this period.

Upon learning of her brother's untimely death at Fredriksten fortress in Norway in November 1718, Ulrika Eleonora declared herself queen by right of inheritance. With the support of her husband, she secured the conditional recognition of the military command, but the counterclaims of Duke Karl Frederik of Holstein-Gottorp* constituted a serious challenge. In her December 1718 summons to the estates to assemble for a Riksdag*, Ulrika Eleonora declared her desire to do away with the absolutism that had served as the form of government since 1680, thus identifying herself with the most important political sentiment of the moment. Yet, the military command and other influential political forces insisted that as part of the disestablishment of absolutsim Ulrika Eleonora would have to reject any rights to the throne based on inheritance. Once she did this, and once a comprehensive new form of government was drawn up, the estates elected Ulrika Eleonora queen of Sweden.

Foiled in her attempts to have her consort, Fredrik of Hesse, recognized as her co-regent, Ulrika Eleonora found it difficult to accept the limited nature of monarchy inherent in the new form of government. The queen's behavior and her husband's unchecked influence persuaded the leading politicians of the new government that replacing Ulrika Eleonora with Fredrik might be beneficial. Thus, at the Riksdag of 1720, Ulrika Eleonora relinquished her throne in return for the election of her husband as Fredrik I. Except for brief occasions in 1731 and 1738, when she acted as regent, Ulrika Eleonora thus left the Swedish political stage. She died childless in 1741.

REFERENCES: W. Holst, *Ulrika Eleonora d.y. Karl XII:s syster* (Stockholm, 1956); L. Thanner, *Revolutionen i Sverige efter Karl XII:s död* (Stockholm, 1953).

M. F. METCALF

UNIVERSITIES *See* Education

URBAN GOVERNMENT

Little is known about the nature of town government before the thirteenth century throughout Scandinavia*. In Denmark, an institution, the *senatores* or *seniores*, was sometimes mentioned in sources from the 1200s. It may have had some connection with the aldermen of the guilds, but nothing is known about its composition or powers. From the mid-thirteenth century, the institution of the council (*consules*) spread gradually over the country. In 1342 mayors (*pro-consules*) were mentioned for the first time and were known everywhere by about 1400. The representative of the town's overlord (generally the king of Denmark or the duke of Slesvig) was from the mid-thirteenth century a justice of the peace (*byfoged/advocatus*) with civil powers. Royal representatives (*villicus*, *praefectus* in certain diocese towns) were known before the introduction of the *byfoged*, but their functions are little known. The *byting* was the ordinary court of the town, but very soon the council acquired certain powers of jurisdiction, although it is often difficult to establish the institutions' respective competencies. It is very doubtful whether the *byting* ever worked as a political assembly of the town. The financial administration of towns was undertaken by one or more chamberlains (*kæmnere*), known since 1294.

In Sweden, an urban assembly (*byamot*), with judical and/or political powers, appears to have been the oldest organ of town government. By the end of the thirteenth century, it was being superseded by the council. In Finland, only the council is known as an organ of urban government.

In Norway, the king's representative was initially the *gjaldker*, who also had some military powers. This office is known in the four largest towns and was supplanted by the *byfoged* in the mid-fourteenth century. At the same time, the governor (*høvedsmand*) became an organ of control, at least in the major towns. The ting (*byamot*) was both a court and a political assembly, but when the council was introduced in the second half of the thirteenth century, the latter institution obtained judicial powers as well.

Whereas comprehensive urban codes, valid for all towns in the country, were passed as early as 1276 in Norway—based on the twelfth-century *Bjarkøyrett*—and by the mid-fourteenth century in Sweden and Finland, no such acts are known from medieval or early modern Denmark, except the short-lived urban code of 1522. During the absolutist period in Denmark-Norway, central control of urban government was tightened, but during the nineteenth century democratic institutions were reinforced or created everywhere (*stadsfullmäktige*, *eligerede borgere*, *byråd*).

At the beginning of the twentieth century, urban government in the five Nordic countries was still based upon the medieval institution of the council, although in some countries the economic terms of the suffrage laws prevented urban government from being fully representative. The full democratization of town government took place in the twentieth century.

REFERENCES: G. A. Blom, ed., *Urbaniseringsprosessen i Norden*, 3 vols. (Oslo, Bergen, and Tromsø: Universitetsforlaget, 1977) (see especially "Rapportdiskusjon, Det XVII. nordiske Historikermøte Trondheim 26–29 juli 1977," by G. A. Blom, and the bibliographies); T. Riis, "Juridical and Social Problems of Danish Medieval Towns," in *Storia della Città*, No. 14 (Milan, 1980), pp. 117–24; T. Riis and P. Strømstad, eds., "Le pouvoir central et les villes en Europe du VXe siècle aux débuts de la révolution industrielle," in *Actes du colloque de la commission internationale pour l'histoire des villes au Danemark 1976*, Comité danois pour l'histoire des villes, Byhistoriske Skrifter, No. 1 (Copenhagen, 1978); D. Tamm, "Københavns forfatning fra middelalderen til 1978," in *Historiske Meddelelser om København* (Copenhagen: 1978), pp. 7–38.

T. RIIS

URBANIZATION

Until c. 1000 A.D. towns were virtually unknown in the Scandinavian countries. Trading posts, occupied during at least part of the year, did exist in Denmark, Norway, and Sweden. But the famous settlements at Kaupang (Vestfold, Norway) and Helgö (Sweden) had too few central functions (e.g., judicial or religious) to be considered as towns. Birka* (near Stockholm*) was a regional economic center, but the nature of its administrative functions is less clear. Outside Denmark, however, Birka is the only pre-1000 A.D. Scandinavian settlement that may be properly compared with towns. In Denmark, both Ribe (by 800) and Hedeby* (by c. 850) were important economic centers. They were, with Aarhus and Odense, recognized as towns before the end of the tenth century, as episcopal centers were established there.

The centuries from 1000 to 1550 were a period of significant urbanization in Denmark and central Sweden. In the early sixteenth century, Denmark had about 80 towns (a third of these in the provinces ceded to Sweden in the mid-seventeenth century), and Sweden 36, mainly concentrated in the central region around the great lakes. Between this urbanized belt and the Danish frontier only two towns were to be found, the episcopal see of Växjö and the castle and trading town of Kalmar*. Both may be considered as outposts in a non-urban region. North of the central belt only the two medieval towns of Gävle and Hedemora are known, although coastal trading posts did exist.

Medieval Norway and Finland were much less urbanized than Denmark and central Sweden. The former had at most fifteen towns, none north of Nidaros (Trondheim), and with the exception of the diocese town of Hamar all were situated on the coast. In Lofoten, Vågan was, however, a center for fishing and trade—though it probably was not considered a town. Medieval Finland had about 10 towns, all of them located on the coast. Among them, Ulfsby (near present-day Pori/Björneborg) was northernmost, although a few trading settlements existed further north. In medieval Iceland no towns were found, only trading stations.

It is clear that only in Denmark and central Sweden were conditions favorable for large-scale medieval urbanization, perhaps also because sea and river transport were easy. Consequently, most Norwegian and Finnish medieval towns were situated along the coast. In the four countries, the episcopal towns were among the oldest, and this underlines the importance of the Church for the growth of towns. Royal government was active, too, as a settlement could be formally recognized as a town by royal privilege, which would entitle the king to a series of revenues (tolls, taxes, and so on), the so-called regalia, from them.

Considerable growth of towns took place between about 1500 and 1800. In Denmark, the most important feature was Copenhagen's* rapid population increase, while the smaller towns grew at much slower rates. There was little need for new towns. When, in the early seventeenth century, a number of new towns were created, they appeared mainly for military reasons. Fortress towns, however, were founded at strategically important sites, often to the detriment of smaller, older towns, which would lose their privileges. In Sweden, a considerable number of new towns were created during the century from 1580 to 1680. Although military concerns were present in this process (e.g., Strömstad, the naval base of Karlskrona*), most new towns were "founded" in order to facilitate economic expansion from central Sweden into other regions. Thus, privileges were granted to the mining communities (e.g., Sala and Falun), as well as to a whole series of settlements on the coasts of the Gulf of Bothnia. In Finland, the same pattern of urbanization prevailed, and several towns (e.g., Helsinki/Helsingfors) were founded on the coasts, especially before 1700. In the second half of the eighteenth century towns were created in the interior, often as administrative centers (e.g., Kuopio). Often, a settlement would develop near a sawmill and would then in due course be recognized as a town.

Features similar to those mentioned for Sweden and Finland are seen in Norway, where the number of towns more than doubled between 1500 and 1850. The majority of these new towns grew up on the coasts, especially of southern Norway, and in most cases these towns had initially been *ladested*(literally, places of lading), that is, rural communities entitled to trade with other parts of the monarchy and to export timber to foreign countries. Northern Norway was opened to free enterprise toward the end of the eighteenth century. The trade monopoly was abolished, and towns were founded north of Trondheim after 1787. The early modern inland settlements of urban character owed their existence to mining (e.g., Røros*, which never became a town in the formal sense, and Kongsberg). The medieval diocese town of Hamar could not maintain its urban status after the Reformation*, but was revived with the other inland towns created after 1800.

Iceland was opened up in the same way as northern Norway. In 1786–1787, trade with the country was given free to the king's subjects, and six towns were founded. Most of them were based on old trading posts, and Reykjavik had from the mid-eighteenth century been the seat of a woolen mill. The local economic development caused by this enterprise led to the concentration in Reykjavik of other functions, including a grammar school and the bishopric of Skálholt.

Among the main features of early modern urbanization was the fact that, especially in the frontier regions, military reasons were important for the creation of towns. Other concerns were the establishment of administrative and economic centers in regions of the periphery. In many cases the economic development (for example the exploitation of the forests) preceded the official granting of privileges. As might be expected, few new towns developed in areas that had already been urbanized during the Middle Ages.

In the period after 1800, as was the case in the preceding period, Denmark needed few new towns. Accordingly, none were founded between 1818 and 1899. Six *handelspladser* (agglomerations with the rights of trading and exercising craftsmanship) were created, however. To four of these full urban rights were granted before World War I, as they were to Esbjerg, which grew up near the port created by an act of parliament in 1868, and to Herning, which by around 1860 had certain central functions in the region. The urban development of Denmark in this period was characterized by the growth of population in Copenhagen and in many provincial towns and by the development of many new settlements, often near railway stations in the countryside. By 1911 44 percent of the population lived in towns.

In Norway, several towns were created during the first half of the nineteenth century, and the total number increased from 21 in 1799 to 38 by 1869. Further towns were created after 1900, and by 1920 the total number was 42. During the period 1801 to 1920, the population living in towns grew from about 9 percent of the total to about 30 percent. This phenomenon was due to the natural increase in population in existing towns, in-migration, and the creation of towns in the far north and in the interior—especially in eastern Norway. The growth of the capital, Christiania (Oslo), was partly caused by a general increase in the population and by a large-scale concentration in the capital of business and administration. The old diocese towns* became important regional centers of administration, and the construction of railroads* furthered the growth of many smaller towns.

In Sweden, urbanization proceeded at the same pace as in Norway. Of the total population, 10 percent lived in towns in 1800, as against 12 percent in

1860 and 29 percent in 1920. The creation of new towns (25 between 1840 and 1920) came somewhat later than in Norway, as 17 of the 25 belonged to the period after 1920. Most of these new towns were former *köpingar*(townlike agglomerations). To a certain extent the new towns were situated in peripheral regions like Norrland and the little urbanized area between central Sweden and the former Danish provinces. Towns were for the first time established in inner Skåne, and two former towns obtained urban privileges again. Still, about 1840, the former Danish provinces, as well as Bohuslän (Norwegian until 1658), appear to have been relatively strongly urbanized compared with other parts of Sweden, which must be seen as a legacy of their Danish or Norwegian pasts. There is reason to believe that railway towns came into existence in Sweden, as in Denmark and Norway, but they are difficult to find in official statistics, and the same is true for agglomerations that grew up around industrial enterprises in the countryside. (A great deal of Swedish industry was placed in rural locations, and this explains why Sweden was less urbanized than might be expected for its degree of industrialization.)

The urban population of Finland in 1860 was 6.3 percent of the total. Sixty years later this figure was 16.1 percent. As only six towns were created during this period, and as they were rather small, a great deal of the growth of towns was due to the general increase in population. However, a clear relative decline of the older coastal towns is evident (from 65.5 percent in 1850 to 37.6 percent in 1920 of the total urban population), to the advantage of both the capital (from 19.7 percent in 1850 to 36.4 percent in 1920) and, to a lesser extent, the older inland towns. As in Sweden, there was no clear casual relation between urbanization and industrialization*, which may be due to a similar pattern of rural industrial distribution.

In 1786 six trading posts in Iceland had been given the status of towns, but only Reykjavik could maintain this after 1836. Two other settlements, Akureyri and Ísafjorður, obtained full urban rights in 1862 and 1866, respectively. One more did so in 1894 and another in 1907. Besides the formally recognized towns, a number of trading posts were to be found. In 1890 eight had more than 200 inhabitants, and by 1910 their number had almost trebled. It was characteristic for Icelandic towns that they all had been *handelspladser* (trade centers) before their recognition as towns. Furthermore, they were all situated on the coast, largely because fishing was the most important urbanizing factor. As was the case in Norway, most of the public sector was concentrated in the capital. Some tertiary concentrations were also found in Akureyri.

The history of urbanization in the Scandinavian countries demonstrates clearly the uneven economic development of the area. At the end of the Middle Ages, only Denmark and central Sweden had a substantial number of towns. During the following centuries, a few new towns were founded in Denmark, and slowly the remoter areas of Sweden, Finland, Norway, and Iceland were opened up by the creation of towns. In Norway and Finland, this development had been completed by the mid-nineteenth century, whereas in Iceland it did not begin until

1786. In Sweden there was still room for new towns, even in the early twentieth century.

In the twentieth century, the trend has been for an increasing proportion of the populations of the Scandinavian countries to live in towns. In 1980, 89 percent of the population in Denmark, 80 percent in Finland, 89 percent in Norway, and 92 percent in Sweden lived in town or urban agglomerations.

REFERENCES: H. Andersson, ed., *Medeltidsstaden. Den tidiga urbaniseringsprocessens konsekvenser för nutida planering* (Stockholm: Riksantikvarieämbetet/Statens Historiska Museer, 1976); H. Becker-Christensen, "De danske købstæders økonomiske undvikling og regeringens erhvervspolitik 1660–1750," in *Erhvervshistorisk Årbog*, 1979, pp. 41–96; G. A. Blom, ed., *Urbaniseringsprosessen i Norden*, 3 vols. (Oslo: Universitetsforlaget, 1977) (Note: This contains an extensive bibliography of works published before 1977); O. Degn, *Ribe* (part of the *Scandinavian Atlas of Historic Towns*) (Odense: Odense University Press, 1983), and *Urbanisering og industrialisering: En forskningsoversigt* (Copenhagen: Akademisk Forlag, 1978); C. R. Jensen, ed., *Stationsbyen: Rapport fra et seminar om Stationsbyens historie 1840–1940* (Aarhus, 1980); E. Jutikkala, *Åbo/Turku* and *Borgå/Porvoo*, (three volumes in the *Scandinavian Atlas of Historic Towns*) (Odense: Odense University Press, 1977); I. Layton, *The Evolution of Upper Norrland's Ports and Loading Places 1750–1976* (Umeå: Geographical Reports, No. 6, Department of Geography, Umeå University, 1981); V. D. Rasmussen, *Nørrejyske jernbanebyer: udvalgte problemer omkring placeringen og befolknungsudviklingen 1850–1901* (Aarhus, 1981); T. Riis, "Juridicial and Social Problems of Medieval Towns," in *Storia della Città* 14 (1980): 117–24, "Towns and Central Government in Northern Europe from the Fifteenth Century to the Industrial Revolution," *Scandinavian Economic History Review* 29 (1981): 33–52, and "The Typology of Danish Medieval Towns," *Storia della Città* 18 (1981): 117–36; T. Tiis and P. Strømstad, eds., *Le pouvoir central et les villes en Europe du XVᵉ siècle aux débuts de la révolution industrielle. Actes du collogue de la commission internationale pour l'historie des villes au Danemark 1976*, Comité danois pour l'histoire des villes, Byhistoriske Skrifter 1 (Copenhagen, 1978); O. Turpeinen, "De finländska städernas folkmängd 1727–1810," *Historisk Tidskrift för Finland* (1977), pp. 109–27.

T. RIIS

USEFUL SOCIETY (Det Nyttige Selskap)

The Useful Society, the oldest farming company in Norway, was founded in Bergen in 1773. It was "dedicated to encourage the promotion of useful things in the Diocese of Bergen" (Espelid, p. 82). Its founders were high-ranking civil servants, clergy, and well-to-do merchants, and all were "thoroughly steeped in the ideas and ideals of the age of enlightenment" (Espelid, p 85). They saw the need to improve agriculture methods as the key to economic progress. The Society took great interest in all facets of industry and trade which would bring a greater degree of self-sufficiency to the country and create stable jobs, thereby raising the standard of living among the town population.

In the first 20 years of its existence, the Society awarded 500 prizes. Financed through membership fees, legacies, and donations from the royal family, the prizes were given primarily in agriculture.

In the early part of the 1800s, a variety of projects emphasized the Society's progressive spirit. To improve transportation from the isolated west coast towns, they underwrote the building of Norway's first steamship in 1825. Small businesses benefited from interest-free loans.

In 1818 the Society funded and organized a permanent sales exhibit for art and artisanry to encourage the local craftsmen to improve the quality of their products. Later, a drawing school for artisans was established, and in 1855 the Society contributed to send three artisans to observe at the World's Fair in Paris. The Society continually supported small lending libraries and book societies throughout the diocese, and through the years substantial book collections of great antiquarian value were acquired.

The Society's decision in 1850 to shift the main focus of its activities to "the beautification of Bergen and its surroundings" had far-reaching consequences for the town's appearance as it developed into a modern city. Parks and squares throughout the town and its surroundings were planned and financed with the help of the Society.

Since the turn of the century, the attention of this organization has been directed toward the preservation of old buildings and objects of historic interest. Schøtstuene, the common rooms and kitchens from the merchant quarters on the pier (Bryggen) which date back to the early Middle Ages, were restored and now stand as a unique example of medieval merchant life in Norway.

In 1951 the Society helped to found the Bergen International Music Festival. The Useful Society celebrated its 200th anniversary in 1974. The charter pledged continued support of cultural, artistic, and practical activities outside the reach of public funds.

REFERENCE: K. L. Espelid, *Til Medborgernes Sande Vel* (Bergen: Det Nyttige Selskab, 1975).

E. M. ANDERSON

V

VALDEMAR I (the Great) (14 January 1131–12 May 1182) King of Denmark
1157–1182

Following the battle at Grathe Hede in 1157, Valdemar, son of Knud Lavard
and a grandson of Erik I*, was chosen king. The civil war that had begun with
the murder of Valdemar's father in 1131 was over. Valdemar's 25–year reign
was relatively peaceful at home, and the foundations were laid for a period of
cultural, economic, and international growth, during which Denmark became
the dominant power in the North.

Five major themes dominated the period: the relationship between the crown
and the Church during a time of conflict between church and state (the Investiture
Conflict); the establishment of a hereditary monarchy in place of the older elective
monarchy; the establishment of a monarchy which clearly derived its authority
from God (through the Church) rather than from the recognition of the freemen
of the kingdom; the manipulation of problems and events in the German Empire
to Denmark's advantage; and the expansion of Danish influence and territory in
the south Baltic.

Valdemar's relationship with the Church shifted during his reign. Early on he
chose to side with Frederik Barbarossa, the German emperor, in the Investiture
Conflict. This placed him in opposition with his archbishop, Eskil, but most of
the bishops, including his close friend Absalon, sided with the king. Eskil went
into exile between 1161 and 1170, during which time Valdemar stood in good
stead with the Danish Church but in opposition to the papacy. Developments in
the papal-imperial conflict led to changes in the situation for Denmark at the
close of the 1160s. In 1170 Eskil returned and worked closely with the king
until his retirement in 1177.

Linked with the church-state question was a shift in the constitutional base of
the monarchy. Denmark was by tradition an elective monarchy. Valdemar recognized (and Denmark's history over the previous century seemed to prove) that
this was dangerous to the stability of the kingdom and made the development

of a strong central monarchy difficult, if not impossible. Valdemar also knew the trends of political thinking of the day and wished to make Denmark a monarchy in the mold of other European states. Taking advantage of the desire of many Danes to avoid the chaos of renewed civil war, Valdemar, in an un-precedented move, secured the recognition of his eldest son, Knud (VI*), as his heir in 1165. The election process was by-passed. In 1170, in order to further guarantee Knud's succession, Valdemar had him crowned (in the first coronation in Danish history) at Ringsted by Archbishop Eskil. In effect, Denmark was now a hereditary monarchy, although the provincial assemblies were still to be asked to recognize the new ruler—which would leave open the possibility of securing promises in return for recognition.

The coronation of Knud at Ringsted marked another constitutional shift. The crown was bestowed upon Knud by the archbishop. The Church was thereby a central agent in what was seen to be the transfer of power from God to the monarch. Royal authority came from God. The Church, through the pope and the clergy, was the agent in this transfer. From one perspective, the king became the captive of the Church, and a source of future problems was established. At the same time, however, the very source of royal authority changed, and this was essential to the development of a monarchy unfettered by elective tradition. It has often been asked who gained the most in 1170, Eskil or Valdemar. Both were apparently pleased by the events at Ringsted.

Valdemar was also aggressively expansionistic—though not as much so as his successors. The focus of expansion was on the territories of the Wends, which lay along the coast of the south Baltic. Beginning in 1159 and continuing in almost every year through the reign, campaigns were waged against the Wends. The most important of these occurred in 1169, when the chief stronghold of the Wends, Arkona on Rügen, was captured. Colonization of these areas did not occur, but annual payments of tribute were extracted. A pattern was also estab-lished that was expanded upon later.

Valdemar also worked to secure his position through marriage alliances. He married Sofie, a half sister of Knud Magnussen (Knud III*) and granddaughter of Niels*. This move tied him to another possible line of royal descent. He arranged the marriages of his children into princely families in the German Empire and into the Swedish royal family.

Internal problems did not disappear entirely, and there were several revolts against Valdemar. Two of thesee were headed by claimants to the throne, Buris (a grandson of a brother of Niels) and Magnus Erikssen (an illegitimate son of Erik II*). Neither was successful. At the end of his reign a revolt broke out in Skåne against Absalon, Eskil's successor as archbishop. This rebellion reflected the deeper problem of the continued opposition that existed to strong monarchy.

Valdemar's reign was a positive one in many ways for the country. Twenty-five years of relative peace made possible the expansion of land under cultivation and the growth of trade and towns. The Church prospered under the generous patronage of the crown. Good relations were enjoyed with Denmark's German neighbors, and the country was secured from attack by the campaigns against the Wends, diplomacy, and the construction of fortifications in the south, including Valdemar's Vordingborg.

Valdemar died suddenly in 1182 and was succeeded, as he had planned, by his eldest son, Knud.

REFERENCES: *Cambridge Medieval History*, vol. 5; *DBL*, vol. 15; *DH*, vol. 3; H. T. Gilkær, "In honore sancti Kanuti martyris. Konge og Knudsgilder i det 12.århundrade," *Scandia* 46:2 (1980): 121–62; R. Malmros, "Blodgilder i Roskilde historiografisk belyst. Knytlingasagas forhold till det tolvte århundredes historieskrivning," *Scandia* 45:1 (1979): 43–66; Saxo Grammaticus, *Danmarks Krønike* (Copenhagen: Samlerens, 1951).

B. NORDSTROM

VALDEMAR II (the Victorious/Sejr) (c. 24 June 1170–28 March 1241) King of Denmark 1202–1240

Valdemar's reign marks at once the high point of Denmark's history in the thirteenth century and the beginning of a decline. He succeeded his father, Knud VI*, and—through the sheer force of his personality and favorable economic and diplomatic circumstances—expanded the scope and authority of monarchy, fostered religious, cultural, and economic development, and expanded the Danish empire in the Baltic. In the view of some, he was the most effective and dominating monarch in Danish history down to the age of absolutism (1660–1849).

In terms of the émpire, Valdemar expanded upon the work of his predecessors. Danish control of the south Baltic coast from the Eider River east to Estonia was temporarily secured. The expansion was based on security, economic, and religious considerations. Valdemar sought to secure Denmark against German encroachment, expand Danish commercial activities, and spread the influence of the archbishopric of Lund into the Baltic states. Estonia, Livonia, Riga, and Narva were all brought under some degree of Danish control.

The efforts necessary to build this empire required the growth of royal control and government at home. Valdemar effectively reorganized the army. He granted tax exemption to land owners in return for military service. Conversely, he taxed land owners in exchange for release from military service. This system worked well under Valdemar but contained within it the roots of future problems. A "privileged" military service nobility developed that would come to challenge the monarchy. At the same time, the land owners who paid the taxes in lieu of service found themselves burdened with ever increasing tax demands. These demands forced many of them to sell their holdings to the nobles and, in effect, become serfs.

Valdemar's empire began to collapse in 1223, when he was kidnapped by Henry of Schwerin. For nearly two years he and his son were held captive before a ransom agreement was reached, under which Denmark was to pay an enormous sum, give up its control of all territories east of the Eider, and grant trade privileges to the Hanseatic League*. Valdemar, once freed, refused to meet these obligations and was even given papal dispensation for breaking the promises made. He attacked his north German enemies, but he was decisively defeated at the battle of Bornhoved in July 1227 and forced to accept the terms of his release and Denmark's new situation.

The last decade of his reign was relatively peaceful, except for some internal unrest arising from his tax policies. He made a significant contribution to the development of law in Denmark in 1241, when he had promulgated a unified law code for Jylland (*Jyske Lov*). From a constitutional perspective this code was more important for its claim that the king was the source of law than for its strictly legal contents.

A number of future problems had their roots in Valdemar's reign, including the growth of the military nobility, the impoverishment of the peasantry, and the potential enserfment of the peasantry through taxation; the enormous growth in the wealth of the Church and its potential to operate as a separate state within the state; and the allocation of crown territories as duchies to royal sons as a way of solving the succesion question. Following his death Denmark entered a period of violence and decline lasting nearly 100 years.

REFERENCES: *Cambridge Medieval History*, vols. 6, 7; *DBL*, vol. 15; *DH*, vol. 4.

B. NORDSTROM

VALDEMAR III (c. 1315–1364) King of Denmark 1326–1329 and duke of Slesvig

Valdemar was a distant descendant of Abel*. When he was only 12, he was placed on the throne by Count Gerhard of Holstein in the midst of the revolt against Christoffer II* and was little more than a puppet of the Holstein count. He was cast aside in 1330 in a purely political move by Gerhard to secure his own position in the face of a revolt by the lesser nobles in Denmark and Christoffer II's efforts to return to power. Following his deposition, Valdemar returned to Slesvig and played minor roles in various challenges to Valdemar IV's* rule until his death.

REFERENCES: *DBL*, vol. 15; DH, vol. 4.

B. NORDSTROM

VALDEMAR IV ("Again Day"/Atterdag) (1321–24 October 1375) King of Denmark 1340–1375

Valdemar was the youngest son of Christoffer II* and Eufemia of Pomerania. He spent most of his youth in Germany, where he was raised at the courts of the emperor, Ludvig of Bavaria, and Ludvig of Brandenburg. It was at the imperial court that he became familiar with new political ideas which were developing in opposition to those of the decentralized feudal monarchy that prevailed in Denmark.

Following the murder of Gerhard of Holstein in 1240 by the folk hero Niels Ebbesen, which helped to precipitate the collapse of the anarchic 10 year interlude during which there was no king in Denmark, Valdemar returned to Denmark. By then opinion had turned against the magnates and the disorder they brought, and Valdemar had little difficulty securing his recognition as king. Strong-willed, resourceful, subtle, unscrupulous, and incredibly energetic, Valdemar was determined to reform the monarchy on the basis of the ideas he had acquired during his years in Germany and to restore Denmark's importance in northern Europe.

Valdemar dealt effectively with the problems confronting his kingdom. Central to his efforts was the development of financial stability for the crown. Through careful exploitation of the tax system, productive management of royal holdings, and the sale of Estonia to the Teutonic Order (1349), he established that stability. He was then able to pay soldiers to subdue the rebellious magnates and to launch campaigns to restore Denmark's international position. He also worked to make the government something that existed beyond the person of the king. He based this effort on the council, which he made into a body which ruled for the state and could and did function even when the king was absent. (He was out of the country for several extended periods, including a pilgrimage to Jerusalem, and the system continued to function.)

Valdemar's efforts to restore Denmark's position of strength in the North brought mixed results. He won back the south Swedish provinces in 1360–1361 and captured the important trading center of Visby on Gotland. This last success, however, precipitated the formation of an overwhelming coalition against him which included 77 cities of the Hanseatic League*, Slesvig, Holstein, and Sweden. While this coalition attacked Denmark from all directions, Valdemar left the country for Germany in search of support. The war of defense was run by the council, headed by Henning Podebusk. It was the council that agreed to the Peace of Stralsund (1370), by which the Skåne forts were turned over to the Hanse for fifteen years and control of the rich Skåne trade was guaranteed to the Germans. Evidence of the strength of the system Valdemar created may be seen in the fact that Denmark did not simply return to the state of anarchy that had preceded Valdemar as a result of this defeat.

A new governmental system, more modern than the older monarchy, came into being with Valdemar. Although it stood the test of the war of the late 1360s and the repeated attempts by the magnates of Jylland to assert their independence, it was a fragile system. When Valdemar died suddenly in 1375, his work was put to a serious test. He left no direct male heir. One daughter, Margrethe I*, survived him. She was married to Haakon VI of Norway, and they had one son, Oluf (II*). Another daughter, Ingeborg, had married Henrik of Mecklenburg. They had a son, Albrekt, whom Valdemar had indicated he wished to be his heir. No clear succession was assured, and the magnates had a new opportunity to test Valdemar's system and perhaps restore their independence.

Valdemar reigned during the period when the Black Death first struck northern Europe. The plague came to Scandinavia* in 1349, and a third or more of the population may have been carried off by it over the next few decades. Valdemar may have been assisted in his efforts to subdue the opponents of the monarchy by the plague, as many of his enemies died and an attitude favorable to the monarchy developed among the public.

REFERENCES: *Cambridge Medieval History*, vols. 7, 8; *DBL*, vol. 15; DH, vol. 4.

B. NORDSTROM

VALKENDORF, CHRISTOFFER (1 September 1525–17 January 1601) Danish government official, regent to Christian IV*, and steward under Christan IV

This remarkable Fyn-born noble enjoyed a political-administrative career which spanned over 40 years. He was appointed administrator (*lensherre*) of Bergen by Frederik II* in 1556. He remained in this post for four years and worked intensively to bring the German population in Bergen under more direct control of the Danish-Norwegian crown. These efforts antagonized the merchants and tradesmen of the city, and Valkendorf was replaced during negotiations preceding the Northern Seven Years' War. He subsequently became governor of Øsel, where his principal responsibility was to watch over the actions of the king's younger brother Magnus. In 1569 he headed the administration in Iceland, and he held a similar post on Gotland from 1571 to 1573. He assumed the office of master of incomes (*rentemester*) in 1574 and continued in that position until 1589. As a protégé of Peder Oxe*, he carefully managed the royal incomes. Although he departed from Oxe's concentration on the income from the Sound Tolls and emphasized income from royal properties, he was largely responsible for the repayment of nearly 1 million *rigsdaler* in war debts and the sound financial position of the state in the late sixteenth century.

Valkendorf was chosen as a member of the regency for Christian IV in 1588. He left this, however, in 1590, as a result of complaints over his handling of the Mogens Heinesen* case. For the next five years he remained out of public office, but he was recalled to government service by Christian when the young king reached his majority. In 1596 Valkendorf became steward (*rigshofmester*) and governor (*statholder*) of Copenhagen castle. The appointments were in recognition of his abilities and also came as a result of Christian's apparent desire to demonstrate his independence from the regents. In addition to his years as a public servant, Valkendorf was important for his support of education, scholarship, and the clergy.

REFERENCES: *DH*, vols. 6, 7.

B. NORDSTROM

VARANGIANS Scandinavian mercenaries and petty traders in the eleventh and twelfth centuries in Russia and Byzantine Empire

According to the *Russian Primary Chronicle*, edited in 1111–1113, "Varangians called Rus' " were invited in 862 to rule the first Russian state. Hence, the question of who founded Russia has been termed, misleadingly, the "Varangian question," and it may be concluded that the *Primary Chronicle*, for the benefit of a twelfth-century public, "explained" who the ninth-century Rus' were by adopting a twelfth-century term.

In the *Primary Chronicle* and in Byzantine and Norse sources, the Varangians are primarily mercenary warriors and, evidently, Scandinavians (though the

Byzantine imperial Varangian guard included some Anglo-Saxons after 1066). Some Russian historians have, however, seen the Varangians as Slavicized Balts.

There are now three "classic" theories concerning the roots of the term. First, it has been argued that the Norse *væríngjar* and the Old Russian *várjagi* derive from Byzantine Greek *varanggoi*, which reflects Gothic or Herulian **varank* or **varang*. Second, it has been claimed that *væríngjar, varjagi, varanggoi,* or *varānk* render a Norse *væringi*, which derives from an older **vargengi* /"one who puts himself under another's protection" or "member of a warriors' pact." Finally, it has been maintained that the original form was **varingjar* ("business partners"), which derived from *várar* ("guarantees, sureties").

An alternative view is that the Varangians were connected with (the Fenno-Baltic, Vepse?) merchant warriors called *kylfingar* (Norse), *kolbjagi* (in Russkaja Pravda), *koulpinggoi* (Greek); with north Russian dialect records, for example, *varežki* ("mittens of petty traders"), *varjagi* ("lump dealers, hucksters"), with *Varjakka* (place-names from Karelia through the interior of Finland and north toward northern Norway); and with the place-name *Varanger* (in Lappish *Varjagvuodna,* in Russian *Varjag*), where Vepse (Ladoga culture) finds are clustered, evidence perhaps of the overland Varjagi-Kolbjagi trade routes from Ladoga and the Novgorod area. Al-Bīrūnī, in his *Tahdīd nihāyāt al-amākin* from 1026, said that *Warānk* people go extremely far north in order to boast that they have reached such-and-such a locality. Varanger? Al-Qazwini indicates as much in 1283.

REFERENCES: G. Jacobsson, "La forme originelle du nom des varègues," *Scando-Slavica* 1 (1954): 36–43; G. Kerkkonen, "Varjakka-namn och -orter i Norra Fenno-Skandia," in *Finskt museum,* 1961; H. Stang, "Rysslands uppkomst—en tredje standpunkt," *Scandia* 47:2 (1981): 153–98; A. Stender-Petersen, *Varangica* (Aarhus, Universitets Slaviske Institut 1953); N. Valonen, "Early Contacts Between the Lapps and the Finns," *Ethnologia Fennica,* 1980; "Varangian Problems," *Scando Slavica Supplementum* 1 (1970): 48.

H. STANG

VIKING Word used to refer to the Scandinavians between 800 A.D. and 1100 A.D.

The word *Viking* carries many meanings, some of them accurate, but many of them misleading or wrong in terms of acting as descriptors of the Scandinavians during the Middle Ages. The origins and exact meaning of the word are subjects of considerable debate. Viking could derive from a seventh-century Frisian or Anglo-Frisian word. In Scandinavia* it appears to have come into usage in the eleventh century. *Vik* meant bay or inlet. *Vikingr* meant someone who sailed out of a bay or inlet. It also could mean someone from Vik, that is, the Olso fjord area. In common usage it is synonymous with pirate, brigand, barbarian, and so on. It seems to have come into common usage to describe the Scandinavians of this period in the nineteenth century.

In fact, the people of Scandinavia in the so-called Viking Age* were very similar to their European contemporaries. They were farmers, fishermen, artisans, soldiers, sailors, merchants, pirates, raiders, colonizers, and explorers. What distinguished them most was that they were not, when the period began, Christians.

REFERENCES: J. Brøndsted, *The Vikings*, trans. K. Skov (Baltimore: Penguin, 1960/ 1965); J. Graham-Campbell, *The Viking World* (New Haven: Ticknor and Fields, 1980); G. Jones, *A History of the Vikings* (Oxford: Oxford University Press, 1968); M. Magnusson, *Vikings!* (New York: Dutton, 1980); K. Randsberg, *The Viking Age in Denmark* (New York: St. Martin's, 1980); P. Sawyer, *The Age of the Vikings* (London: E. Arnold, 1962).

B. NORDSTROM

VIKING AGE Period in Scandinavian and European history usually dated to between c. 800 A.D. and 1100 A.D.

The starting date of this period corresponds roughly with the beginning of attacks on Britain by Scandinavians. The closing date for the period corresponds to the time by which most Scandinavians had been converted to Christianity (*see* Conversion). These years may easily be changed, and the dates depend entirely upon one's perspective. For example, if the starting date for the period were to be based on art styles or commerical involvement, either in Europe or in Russia, the starting date could be moved to around 600 A.D. Similarly, the end of the period would have to be shifted if one used social, legal, or political changes as the bases for dating the age. It should be kept in mind that the entire notion of a Viking Age is an artificial creation.

REFERENCES: J. Brøndsted, *The Vikings*, trans. K. Skov (Baltimore: Penguin, 1960/ 1965); J. Graham-Campbell, *The Viking World* (New Haven: Ticknor and Fields, 1980); G. Jones, *A History of the Vikings* (Oxford: Oxford University Press, 1968); M. Magnusson, *Vikings!* (New York: Dutton, 1980); K. Randsberg, *The Viking Age in Denmark* (New York: St. Martin's, 1980); P. Sawyer, *The Age of the Vikings* (London: E. Arnold, 1962).

B. NORDSTROM

VINLAND (c. 1000) Norse settlement in North America

According to Icelandic tradition, North America was accidentally sighted by Norsemen in 985–986. Leif Eiríksson, son of Eirík the Red, led an exploratory expedition in 990. He seems to have landed first at Baffin Island, then along the coast of Labrador, then finally on a fertile shore which Leifr named Vinland (Wineland) on account of the grapes which grew wild there.

Two Icelandic sagas describe the Norse discovery and settlement of North America: *Grænlendinga Saga* (*The Saga of the Greenlanders*), written c. 1150, and *Eiríks Saga Rauða* (Erik the Red's Saga), written c. 1250. Both sagas tell the same story with some variation and contradiction; *Eiríks Saga* may be a "corrected" version of the earlier saga.

The precise location of Vinland is uncertain, though Norse presence in the New England area is indicated by archeological finds. The Norwegian explorer Helge Ingstad found the ruins of a settlement at L'Anse aux Meadows, Newfoundland, and scholars agree that his discovery is Norse from around 1000. But the saga writers seem to have envisioned a place further south, as wild grapes are not native to Newfoundland. The debate over the location of Vinland persists.

REFERENCES: H. Ingstad, *Westward to Vinland*, trans. Erik Friis (New York: St. Martin's, 1969); M. Magnússon, *Viking Expansion Westwards* (London: Bodley Head, 1973); S. E. Morison, *The European Discovery of America*, vol. 1: *The Northern Voyages* (New York: Oxford Univeristy Press, 1971); *The Vinland Sagas*, trans. Magnús Magnússon and Hermann Pálsson (Harmondsworth, Middlesex: Penguin Books, 1965).

M. EMELITY

VORNEDSKAB System of bondage of the peasantry in eastern Denmark in the early modern period

By the sixteenth century (and perhaps earlier) land owners in the area of Zealand Law (Zealand, Møn, Lolland, and Falster) had established the right to impose restrictions on the freedom of movement of the male population on their estates. Every male commoner in this area (outside towns) was deemed a *vorned*, and as such had to accept any peasant tenancy offered by the seigneur and could not leave the estate on which he was born except with the seigneur's permission. The system was intended to safeguard land owners against losses of manpower, but unlike serfdom it did not involve any other loss of legal rights or legal status for the peasantry, and never applied to women. *Vornede* could not legally be sold without the land on which they were living. Moreover, the seigneur had no additional disciplinary powers over his *vornede* other than those acquired by land owners anywhere in the kingdom and was not even supposed to transfer a *vorned* from one holding to another once the initial tenancy contract had been drawn up. A *vorned*, however, had no legal means of terminating an existing tenancy agreement against the will of the seigneur and could be pursued if he departed illegally. After 1620 runaways were no longer liable to be outlawed, and during the seventeenth century the crown became increasingly lenient toward its own *vornede*, by not pursuing runaways for more than a fixed period of years or by selling letters of emancipation to those wanting to leave the estate of their birth. *Danske Lov* (*see* Danish Law) (1683), however, still entitled private land owners to pursue their runaway *vornede* for 10 years in towns and 20 years in the countryside, and the evidence suggests that the system was a serious practical restriction on the peasant population, especially given certain abuses which inevitably appeared.

Both Christian II* and Christian IV* contemplated means of restricting the *vornedskab*, and ideas to this effect were vented in 1660, but the following decades witnessed further legislation which indicated that labor shortages, aggravated by the mid-century wars, were still a major obstacle to any relaxation of the system.

In the 1690s the crown renewed and extended concessionary policies toward its own *vornede*, primarily in the interest of economic flexibility. In 1701 a commission was set up to consider the abolition of *vornedskab* on all crown lands. The records of this commission underline how strong the conservative point of view was among most land owners, but pressure from the crown, combined perhaps with the new militia conscription system of 1701 (restricting the movement of younger eligible men throughout the kingdom) overcame the resistance. In 1702 the crown abolished *vorned* obligations for everyone born after the acceession of Frederik IV* in 1699, on private land as well as on crown land. Those born before that date would be able to buy emancipation if they so wished, but otherwise remained *vornede* until their death. The crown was anxious to stress that this reform in no way entailed any relaxation of the existing tenancy system, and, given the nature of seigneurial rights, the abolition of *vornedskab* had only a marginal effect. (*See also Stavnsbånd.*)

REFERENCES: P. J. Jørgensen, *Dansk Retshistorie* (Copenhagen: Gad, 1940); T. Munck, *The Peasantry and the Early Absolute Monarchy in Denmark, 1660–1708* (Copenhagen: Landbohistorisk Selskab 1979); J.C.H.R. Steenstrup, "Vornedskabet hos den danske Bonde," *Historisk Tidskrift* (Copenhagen) 5RVI (1886–1887): 339–462.

T. MUNCK

W

WACHTMEISTER, CARL HANS AV BJÖRKÖ (27 April 1682–31 January 1731) Swedish naval commander

C. H. Wachtmeister was from the baronial family of that name. He entered Uppsala University in 1693, and served as a volunteer with the fleet only two years later. In an expedition against Archangel during the first year of the Great Northern War*, Wachtmeister was present at a hard-fought convoy action off Lowestoft, England, in 1704. He subsequently served in the English navy (1706). Promoted to the rank of captain in the Swedish navy in 1707, he achieved flag rank in 1713 and had unbroken active service in the south Baltic until the end of 1716, when he entered a six-year term of administrative service in Karlskrona*. During this time the base was often desperately short of supplies. He was at sea in 1719 and 1720, but only briefly during the latter year. After 23 separate active commands, he obtained permission from Fredrik I* to remain ashore for the rest of his service career. He showed great endurance in the face of heavy odds by keeping at sea outside Karlskrona for short periods (1716–1718), but his work at the naval base, though important for its future development, was often hampered by internal feuds. Wachtmeister enjoyed some repute as a mathematician and bibliophile.

REFERENCES: G. Elgenstierna, ed., *Svenska adelns ättartavlor*, vol. 8:2 (Stockholm, 1934); S. Grauers, *Ätten Wachtmeister*, vol. 3:1 (Stockholm, 1941); *SMK*, vol. 8; *SU*, vol. 30.

D. D. ALDRIDGE

WACHTMEISTER, HANS CARL (2 April 1689–7 March 1736) Swedish admiral

Hans Carl Wachtmeister was the eldest son of Hans Wachtmeister av Johannishus (1641–1714), who was the leading naval advisor to Karl XI*. H. C. Wachtmeister traveled in Holland, Italy, France, and England as a young man. He served in an Anglo-Dutch fleet in the Mediterranean in 1708, by which time he had acquired extensive knowledge of navigation. In this year he was appointed a captain in the Swedish navy and was promoted to flag rank in 1710, without having held an independent command. From this time until his capture by the Danes in a disastrous (for Sweden) naval action in the Fehmarn Belt in April 1715, Wachtmeister was constantly on active service in the Baltic. There now ensued almost five years of inactivity as a prisoner of war in Denmark. In September 1719 Wachtmeister was released and immediately received command of the Gothenburg* base. In May 1720 he was placed under the command of Claes Sparre* in the east Baltic, but he was strongly critical of his superior's lackluster discharge of his supreme command and was not at sea during the last year of the Great Northern War*. The early favor he had enjoyed as his father's son, and his defeat at the hands of the Danes in 1715, may have conspired against his professional reputation, but on the evidence he was more offensively minded than any of his colleagues in 1720.

REFERENCES: G. Elgenstierna, *Svenska adelns ättartavlor*, vol. 8ii (Stockholm, 1934); S. Grauers, *Ätten Wachtmeister*, vol. 3:2 (Stockholm, 1953); *SMK*, vol. 8; *SU*, vol. 30.

D. D. ALDRIDGE

WALLENBERG, RAOUL GUSTAV (4 August 1912–?) Swedish humanitarian

A member of the prominent Swedish Wallenberg family, Raoul Wallenberg was educated in Sweden and at the University of Michigan, where he studied architecture from 1931 to 1934. He spent some time with a Swedish trade firm in Cape Town before moving to Haifa, where he worked in a bank until autumn 1936. As of 1944, Wallenberg operated a food import-export business in partnership with Koloman Lauer, a Jewish refugee.

In early 1944, President Franklin Roosevelt created the War Refugee Board (WRB), charged with saving Jews and other potential victims of Nazi extermination. Sweden responded enthusiastically to the WRB's call for help from the neutral nations. Under WRB auspices, a committee of prominent Swedish Jews was formed. At Lauer's suggestion, it selected Wallenberg to undertake a rescue mission to Hungary, where the situation of the Jewish population was deteriorating drastically.

Armed with guarantees of ample freedom of action and large sums of money, Wallenberg arrived in Budapest on 9 June 1944. He designed an impressive-looking Swedish passport for distribution to Hungarian Jews. Although the documents had no validity in international law, in practice they did offer a considerable degree of protection to the bearer. The Swedish embassy issued approximately 15,000 such passports. Soon other neutral delegations followed suit. Wallenberg also pressed the Papal Nunciature and the Red Cross into action. In his dealings with the authorities in Budapest, Wallenberg skillfully exploited the fact that Sweden represented German and Hungarian interests in a number of other countries, mixing in threats of postwar retribution, blackmail, and outright bribery.

In October 1944 the situation of the Hungarian Jews took a turn for the worse, when Hungarian fascists came to power with German backing. Adolph Eichmann began to deport Jews by means of forced marches, but it is estimated that Wallenberg was able to save some 2,000 of these deportees. In December 1944, as the Red Army was closing in on Budapest, Wallenberg prevented the final massacre of the inhabitants of the Budapest ghetto. He made it known that he would have the SS general in charge held personally responsible and treated as a war criminal. Largely as a result of Wallenberg's efforts, approximately 120,000 Hungarian Jews survived.

On 17 January 1945, Raoul Wallenberg disappeared. He left Budapest under Red Army escort, hoping to meet with the Hungarian Provisional Government. On 8 March it was announced that he had been killed by Hungarian fascists or Gestapo agents, but it seems that by that time he was actually in Lubianka prison in Moscow, under suspicion of espionage. After a series of what some have considered half-hearted Swedish *démarches*, Soviet authorities admitted in February 1957 that Wallenberg had been a prisoner in the U.S.S.R. until his death in July 1947. But testimony of ex-prisoners has suggested that Wallenberg was alive and well after that time, and that he still may be alive somewhere in the Soviet prison system. On 5 October 1981, he became an honorary citizen of the United States. It was hoped that American political leverage could secure some action on his case. The relevant legislation was introduced by Representative Tom Lantos of California, whose life Wallenberg had saved.

REFERENCES: P. Anger, *With Raoul Wallenberg in Budapest* (New York: Holocaust Library, 1981); J. Bierman, *Righteous Gentile* (New York: Viking, 1981).

E. R. TERZUOLO

WELFARE STATE

Scandinavia

The term *welfare state* was listed for the first time in the *New York Times Index* in 1949 and was included in the *Oxford English Dictionary* in its 1955 edition. The archbishop of York, Sir William Temple, is assumed to have been the first to use the concept in English in a book from 1941. His concept described the democratic welfare-oriented systems of the time and was conceived as a contrast to the totalitarian "power states." But the Norwegian version of the concept was used in public reports as early as 1939, partly as a description of the society at the time and partly as a description of a future goal. Whether this was the first time the concept was ever used has not been established. The term came into widespread use both in and outside Scandinavia* in the 1950s. The first part of the term, "welfare," is derived from the Old Norse *velferð*.

The ideology of the welfare state grew out of the experiences of World War II*. William Beveridge's plan (1942) for a "social service state" and the Philadelphia resolutions of the International Labor Organization (1944) became basic documents for both the legitimation and practical build-up of welfare state institutions and programs on a large scale after the war.

Essential elements of a welfare state include legislation which guarantees income maintenance and other kinds of support for individuals and families in cases of occupational accidents and diseases, sickness, old age, and unemployment. The boundaries of the European welfare states have been extended almost continuously—at least until the late 1970s—since the first laws of social insurance were passed in the late nineteenth century. Social and health insurance have, as a rule, become compulsory, Population coverage has been widened and is now often universal. More and more social needs have come to be met by government support, and social benefits have in general become much more generous. The Scandinavian countries can be considered prime examples of the institutional welfare state with basically universal population coverage.

Although the welfare state is primarily thought of as a postwar construction, we can trace the origins of modern social insurance to Bismarck's comprehensive social legislation in Germany from the 1880s. Modest attempts at worker insurance (for miners and seamen) had been tried in several countries, including Norway, but Bismarck introduced a new concept of state-organized social insurance in 1883, with all industrial workers being insured against sickness in a compulsory program. This event had a catalyzing effect on developments in less-industrialized Scandinavia. With a clear reference to the German legislation, Denmark, Finland, Norway, and Sweden all established commissions to investigate possible options for state action on social insurance in the period 1884–1889.

It is likely that in the case of sickness insurance the differences in the extent and strength of voluntary sickness funds influenced possible choices for state action once state intervention was recognized as a workable policy. The early differences in social policy strategies chosen by the Nordic governments may be interpreted with this background in mind. Sweden in 1891 and Denmark in 1892 started out with state subsidies to voluntary sickness funds, while Norway, in 1909, with a weaker structure of such organizations, chose state-organized compulsory insurance in accordance with basic German principles. In fact, Norway was the fourth country in Europe—and the world—to introduce compulsory sickness insurance (preceded by Germany [1883], Austria [1888], and Luxembourg [1901]), and was the first country to extend the coverage to include in principle all wage earners (below a fixed, relatively high income limit) and the family dependents of the insured. The Finnish government—entangled in problems of sovereignty vis-a-vis Russia—demanded the right to audit voluntary sickness funds but took no economic responsibility for insurance. Iceland followed the Danish example in 1911. By 1963 all the Nordic countries had established compulsory insurance which, in principle, encompassed all residents (Denmark in 1960, Finland in 1963, Iceland in 1956, Norway in 1956, and Sweden in 1955).

By and large, accident insurance for industrial workers seems to have been the most pressing insurance need in the rapidly industrializing Europe of the late nineteenth century. Laws on accident insurance were passed within 20 years of the first German law (1884) in all five of the Nordic countries. Only the supposedly most accident-prone groups of workers were covered by the first laws, but Denmark and Sweden were quick to extend legislation to cover all employees as early as 1916 and 1927, respectively. Similar laws came in Finland in 1948, Norway in 1958, and Iceland in 1965. Norway was the first of the Nordic countries to legislate accident insurance (1894) and the only one to follow up the German principle of compulsory insurance from the beginning.

Iceland and Denmark were first among the Nordic countries to establish some sort of old-age pension programs, in 1890 and 1891. The schemes were noncontributory, financed out of general state and local government revenues, and pensions were paid out on a means-test basis. Sweden was the pioneer country of the world to adopt a universal pension system (1913). Norway and Finland were European laggards with their laws from 1936 to 1937. The right to receive national pensions independent of a means test has become the general rule since the end of World War II*: in Sweden since 1946, in Norway and Finland since 1957, in Denmark since 1964, and in Iceland since 1965. Some kind of earnings-related supplementary pensions have been introduced in all countries except Denmark (although even there some supplementary pension is offered). Disability pensions were developed earlier in Denmark and Sweden (1921 and 1913, respectively) than in the other three countries, with Norway as a latecomer in 1961. Widows' pensions are a post-World War II development in all five countries.

Norway was second only to France in introducing public subsidies to voluntary unemployment insurance on a national basis (1906). Denmark followed suit in 1907, while Sweden introduced such coverage in 1917 and Finland in 1937. Only Norway and Iceland have established compulsory insurance (1938 and 1956). Although insurance is still voluntary, and therefore not universal, in the other countries, the effect is marginal in Sweden, which offers the most active labor market policy of all the Nordic countries.

As supplements to the social insurance and security systems, all five countries have laws on public and social assistance, which is the responsibility of local government.

The Nordic countries have a long tradition of health and medical services, with the first health laws passed in the 1858–1879 period. Since the 1960s and 1970s, the major responsibility for health care has been placed with communal and county authorities throughout Scandinavia.

Since 1945, the Nordic countries have cooperated closely in the field of social security, and since 1957 any Nordic citizen maintains his or her social rights in any other country in addition to that of his or her origin. A free labor market was introduced in the region in 1954.

REFERENCES: G. Esping-Andersen and W. Korpi, "From Poor Relief to Institutional Welfare States: The Development of Scandinavian Social Policy," in R. Eriksson et al., eds., *The Scandinavian Model: Welfare States and Welfare Research* (New York: M. E.

Sharpe, forthcoming); P. Flora and A. Heidenheimer, eds., *The Development of Welfare States in Europe and America* (New Brunswick and London: Transaction Books, 1981); G. Heckscher, *The Welfare State and Beyond: Success and Problems in Scandinavia* (Minneapolis: University of Minnesota Press, 1984); H. Heclo, *Modern Social Politics in Britain and Sweden* (New Haven: Yale University Press, 1974); J. E. Kolberg, *Farvel til velferdsstaten?* (Oslo: Cappelen, 1983); W. Korpi, *The Working-Class in Welfare Capitalism* (London: Routledge and Kegan Paul, 1978); S. Kuhnle, *Velferdsstatens utvikling: Norge i komparativt perspektiv* (Bergen: Universitetsforlaget, 1983), and "Welfare and the Quality of Life," in E. Allardt et al., eds., *Nordic Democracy* (Copenhagen: Det Danske Selskab, 1981); P. Kuusi, *Social Policies for the Sixties: A Plan for Finland* (Kuoppio, 1964); G. Myrdal, *Beyond the Welfare State* (New Haven: Yale University Press, 1960); P. A. Pettersen, *Linjer i norsk sosialpolitikk* (Oslo: Universitetsforlaget, 1982); K. Philip, *Staten og fattigdommen* (Copenhagen: Jul Gellerups Forlag, 1947); Anne-Lise Seip, *Om velferdsstatens fremvekst* (Oslo: Universitetsforlaget, 1981); D. Wilson, *The Welfare State in Sweden* (London: Heinemann, 1979).

S. KUHNLE

Denmark

The welfare state in Denmark is based on regulations and attitudes which long preceded industrialization*. Ordinances from 1799 and 1801, for example, decreed that anyone who needed aid was entitled to it. When the first democratic constitution was passed in 1849, it contained the following clause: "Anyone who is unable to maintain himself or his family and whose maintenance is not the responsibility of someone else, has the right to receive assistance from the public, but he is subject to the relevant laws for such cases." The last phrase meant, among other things, that a person receiving help from the poor law authorities lost his franchise, which the same constitution established for adult males. Danish law, however, established almost immediately that exceptions could be made. Families of draftees, for instance, could get help "without the effects of the poor laws," that is, without the loss of franchise. Many subsequent welfare laws included that phrase.

The modern Danish welfare state is founded on a series of laws passed between 1891 and 1907. The Poor Law of 9 April 1891 required that each local community establish a poor law authority, and that this authority should insure that no one in the locality lacked the necessities of life or adequate medical care. The law also gave considerable power of control to the local authorities. Six days later a law on old age assistance was passed which provided that "worthy" poor over 60 years of age could, without premium, receive assistance "without the effects of the poor law." Recipients could not have received poor law aid in the preceding 10 years, nor could they have lived a "disorderly" life. Under neither law did the poor have any legal rights to demand benefits, and in neither was benefit level specified. Both matters were left to local officials.

For some years there had grown up a movement of mutual insurance sickness societies, quite apart from government. By the Sickness Fund Law of 12 April 1892, such funds could receive public recognition and subsidies, provided they were limited to low-income members and provided certain minimum benefits. Publicly subsidized health insurance was thus voluntary, but it was an advantage to be a member of a recognized and supervised fund.

The Accident Insurance Law of 7 January 1898 insured manual workers in factories, the building trades, and transportation against the economic consequences of work-related accidents. Employers could self-insure or buy insurance from an approved list of private companies, so long as benefits were in accordance with the law.

Unemployment funds, hitherto private and mostly run by labor unions, were subsidized under a law of 9 April 1907. Membership could not be denied anyone fulfilling certain general conditions. There was government supervision.

These laws went largely unchanged until 1921. Disability insurance (6 May 1921) was established partly as a consequence of reincorporating territory (North Slesvig*) which had been part of Germany since 1864 and where there already was disability insurance. Denmark did not want the inhabitants to lose benefits by becoming Danish citizens. Anyone who was a member of a sickness fund was automatically insured against disability and received a pension if his earning ability was decreased by two-thirds. A quasi-court was established to decide doubtful cases. The "Social Reform" of 1933 greatly simplified the administration of relief. Also, the category of "unworthy poor" was sharply decreased and the social insurance was, in effect, made obligatory.

The scope of the welfare state was expanded beyond the five traditional programs during the prosperity after the mid-1950s. In 1956 a minimum old age pension was established for everyone over 67, regardless of wealth or income. A special pension for widows with small children was inaugurated, which in 1967 was incorporated into a general system of family allowances. Institutional services especially for children (day-care centers, after-school programs) and the mentally handicapped were extended in 1959. In 1960 health insurance was made to apply to nearly everyone, regardless of wealth or income. The concept of "unworthy poor" was finally abolished by the Public Assistance Act of 1961. Thereafter, no form of public assistance led to a loss of civil rights. Benefits under most programs became a matter of legal right. In 1967 rent subsidies were introduced, whereby a family would pay rent according to family size and income. The National Health Security Act, passed in 1971 and becoming effective in 1973, replaced the sickness funds with a national health service paid for out of general revenues. The Social Assistance Act, passed in 1974 and effective in 1976, increased benefits and placed a strong emphasis on advice and guidance. Intervention by the authorities is supposed to be minimal, however. The act covers all sorts of need, rather than being limited to a specific list.

In 1952 direct social welfare benefits comprised 9.8 percent of national income. By 1970 they had risen to 15.2 percent—at a time when national income was growing by 5 percent (4.2 percent per capita) a year. Social welfare and health costs accounted for 47 percent of the state budget in 1971–1972.

In the economic crisis of the late 1970s and 1980s the pace of expansion of the welfare state slowed, and a number of anti-tax parties sprang up. These parties were at pains to emphasize, however, that their proposals were not aimed at welfare benefits. The welfare state was such an integral part of Danish society that no attack on it was plausible.

REFERENCES: H. Jørgensen, *Studier over det offentlig fattigvæsens historiske undvikling i Danmark i det 19. århundrede* (Copenhagen: Nordisk Forlag, 1940); D. Levine, "Conservatism and Tradition in Danish Social Welfare Legislation, 1890–1933: A Comparative View," *Comparative Studies in Society and History* 20:1 (January 1978): 54–69; E. Marcussen, *Social Welfare in Denmark*, 4th ed. (Copenhagen: Det Danske Selskab, 1980); K. Phillips, *Staten og Fattigdommen* (Copenhagen: Gellerup, 1947).

D. LEVINE

WHALING Norwegian

When man began to hunt whales over a thousand years ago, he used a simple harpoon thrown by hand from a small boat very close to a swimming whale. This technique was almost as dangerous to man as to whale. It continued unchanged until 1868, when Svend Foyn, a Norwegian, developed a harpoon tipped with an explosive charge. This harpoon could be fired from a cannon mounted high in the bow of a steam-driven vessel. Man could now safely, quickly, and efficiently pursue and kill even the largest whales. Within three decades, Foyn's technique spread to whaling stations around the world. Soon whalers were killing more whales per year than they had previously taken in a decade.

Early in the twentieth century Norwegian seal hunters exploring Antarctic waters discovered enormous herds of whales hitherto unknown. In 1904 Captain Carl Anton Larsen (Vestfold, Norway) established the first whaling station in the Antarctic at Grytviken, South Georgia. Norway soon became the leading whaling nation in the world. In 1925 Captain Petter Sørlle (Vestfold, Norway) installed a slipway on the stern of a large vessel so that whale carcasses could be hauled on board and processed on the high seas independent of any land station. The floating factory was born, whaling became pelagic, and Norway continued to be the world leader.

The capital of the Norwegian whaling industry was Sandefjord. There most of the fleets had their home port, where ships were repaired and the whale oil processed. Indeed, Sandefjord was for many decades the wealthiest city per capita in Norway, thanks to the whalers.

During World War II* most of the whaling ships of the world were damaged or destroyed. In the immediate postwar years demand for edible whale oil was high and stimulated a quick reconstruction of the fleets. By 1949 Norway had ten of the world's eighteen factory ships in operation and remained the leader for another decade and a half, when Japan sent seven fleets to the Antarctic and Norway sent only four. This shift was the result of the rapidly declining populations of all the commercially hunted species. The techniques developed by the Norwegians were highly efficient, but they had tragic consequences for the whales. From 1925 to 1965 the average number of whales killed annually was about 40,000. However, the amount of oil produced each year declined, because whalers concentrated on the largest species and then on the next largest when the previous one became commercially extinct. In 1931, for example, over 29,000 blue whales were killed. By 1965 there were none left. The blue whale averaged about 100 tons by weight. The next largest species was the fin whale, which weighed roughly half as much. During the late 1950s and early 1960s, the catch of fin whales averaged about 28,000 per year. Today, the animal is commercially extinct, as are all the large species on which the industry was based. Only the polygamous and nonedible sperm whale survives in sufficient numbers to sustain a small Japanese pelagic industry in the Pacific.

Norway developed the techniques that eventually led to the destruction of the whale herds. At the same time, it was Norway that took the lead in attempting to save the whales from overexploitation. As early as 1910 a Norwegian engineer, J. A. Mørch, warned of the possibility of exterminating whales by commercial exploitation. By 1929, after the League of Nations had failed to grant any protection to whales, the Norwegian Storting* passed a law which covered the taking of baleen whales. This act set standards for minimum protection for whales. It forbade the killing of rare right whales or any whale accompanied by a calf. These basic rules for Norwegian whalers were ultimately incorporated into the regulations of the International Whaling Commission in 1949. The Whaling Act of 1929 established a Whaling Council, composed of leading marine scientists and other experts, to advise the government on matters of whaling policy. The act also established the Committee on International Whaling Statistics, located at Sandefjord, to act as a clearinghouse for the gathering of statistics on all types of whaling from all nations in the world. The committee still publishes the details of its annual compilations in *International Whaling Statistics*. Norway was not only the first nation to impose restrictive regulations on its whalers in order to preserve the stocks of whales, but its regulations were always the most severe. Norway even taxed the production of whale oil in order to pay its inspectors on the whaling ships to enforce its laws.

Norway was an active participant in the efforts to establish the International Whaling Commission in 1949. In the mid-1950s Norway took the lead in that agency in trying to reduce the catch of blue whales. The effort failed and the animal became commercially extinct. Norway did the same for the fin whale in the 1960s, with the same results. The Soviet Union and especially Japan refused to cooperate and vetoed all significant protective efforts. In the face of all the failures of the International Whaling Commission to protect the whales from overexploitation, only one commissioner ever resigned in protest—a Norwegian, Professor Johan Ruud, who was also the director of the Institute for Whale Research at the University of Oslo.

Today, Norway has no floating factory ships. Japan has only one. The Japanese whalers learned their trade from the Norwegians. They were not more skilled than the Norwegians; they simply had a great commercial advantage based on culinary preferences. Most whales are over 30 percent meat by weight, and the meat to the Japanese is a nearly perfect substitute for beef. In their protected home market, the Japanese whalers derive twice as much revenue from whale meat as Norwegians did from the entire whale. In addition, the Japanese had a market for the oil which, combined with the meat, gave them more than four times as much revenue per whale.

Virtually all of the technology of modern whaling was of Norwegian origin. If the Norwegian concern for the rational utilization of natural resources had prevailed on the high seas, none, rather than all, of the large whales would be endangered species.

REFERENCES: E. F. Heyerdahl, *Hvalindustrien. En teknisk-kjemisk undersøkelse*, Publication No. 7 (Sandefjord: Chr. Christensens Hvalfangstmuseum, 1932); J. Hjort, J. Lie, and J. T. Ruud, "Norwegian Pelagic Whaling in the Antarctic (1929–1938)," *Hvalråd Skrifter* Nos. 1–7 (Sandefjord); *Norsk Hvalfangst-tidende*, 1912–1967, Sandefjord; G. Small, *The Blue Whale* (New York: Columbia University Press, 1971).

G. L. SMALL

WIGFORSS, ERNST (24 January 1881–3 January 1977) Swedish Social Democrat

Ernst Wigforss, born in 1881 into a Halmstad housepainter's family, became Swedish social democracy's leading theoretician and most controversial politician. Wigforss was first elected to the Riksdag* in 1919. He served there continuously until 1953. He belonged to the Social Democratic Party* directorate from 1920 to 1952 and sat on its executive committee from 1928 to 1952. He edited *Tiden*, the party's theoretical journal, from 1922 to 1924, from 1929 to 1932, and again in 1936. Briefly, in the Rickard Sandler government of 1925–1926 and then from 1932 to 1949 (with a brief interruption in 1936 while the Social Democrats were out of office), he occupied the central position of minister of finance. There he propounded and instituted the first use of modern counter-cyclical policies to aid Sweden's recovery from the Great Depression and helped engineer the postwar reforms that characterized the much-admired "Swedish model" of welfare statism in the 1950s and 1960s. Following his retirement from electoral poilitics, Wigforss wrote a series of ideological treatises stressing the need to move beyond the welfare state* to a classless, democratic, and Socialist society.

At Lund, where he became a committed Social Democrat, Wigforss studied Nordic languages and linguistics and completed a dissertation on the southern Halland dialect, but increasingly politics absorbed his energies. In 1908 he published *Materialistisk Historieuppfattning och Klasskamp* (*The Materialist Conception of History and Class Struggle*), in which he rejected rigid "economic necessity" and stressed both the overwhelming influence of economic conditions and the independent importance of ideals. In 1919 he produced the Gothenburg Program, a document which did not immediately become party policy, but which anticipated remarkably the welfare statist measures of Social Democratic governments. About this time Wigforss, inspired by English guild socialism and by syndicalism, began his lifelong advocacy of industrial democracy. As chairman of the (K. Hjalmar) Branting* government's commission on industrial democracy, he wrote the central sections of its neglected report, urging greater freedom, independence, and responsibility in the work place. Wigforss's radicalism and his growing prominence within the party made him the center of public controversy in 1928, when his proposal for the progressive taxation of estates became the focus of electoral debate.

Again in 1932 Wigforss developed the party's central campaign theme, this time with far greater success. His electoral pamphlet *Har Vi Råd att Arbeta?* (roughly, *Can We Afford to Provide Employment?*) argued for government intervention to offset the decline of private consumption and investment and to stimulate the economy. Wigforss argued for budgetary planning as a social democratic strategy distinct from socialization. Following the Social Democratic victory, he helped negotiate the historic alliance with the Farmer's Party (*see* Center Party: Sweden) that, together with the success of the new economic policy, opened the way for 44 years of Social Democratic governments.

World War II* shattered Social Democratic hopes for an extended period of peaceful, gradual reform. Toward its close Wigforss advocated a dissolution of the wartime coalition so that the Social Democrats might initiate a new period of social transformation. He was largely responsible for the two documents that outlined policy for the postwar period, the new party program and the *Working Class Movement's Postwar Program*. He proposed to finance the new reforms by maintaining the overall wartime level of taxation but shifting the burden toward the wealthy. Wigforss's tax program provoked biting personal attacks and sharp controversy that continued through the campaign of 1948.

Although he concentrated primarily on domestic economic policy, Wigforss intervened notably in foreign policy on several occasions. In 1939 he resisted Sandler's efforts to establish a joint Swedish-Finnish defense of the Åland Islands. He opposed efforts to encourage Swedish volunteers who wanted to fight with Finland against Russia. In the 1950s he argued successfully against Sweden's acquiring nuclear weapons.

Wigforss's Socialist ideology exerted a powerful and lasting influence upon his party. He rejected any notion of an automatic transition to socialism, arguing instead that reformers must proceed with a lengthy transformation of capitalist society. A "provisional utopia," a tentative sketch of a desirable future society, would expose the flaws of the current social order and guide its reconstruction. Wigforss showed little enthusiasm for the traditional Socialist panacea of nationalizing enterprises. Instead, he advocated a steady reshaping of capitalist society through economic planning, social welfare policy, progressive taxation, and industrial democracy. Where social ownership was appropriate, Wigforss recommended "social enterprises without owners," public foundations managed by employees and subject to public oversight.

Equality, freedom, and democracy formed the essential core of Wigforss's ethical socialism. He envisioned a classless society in which each individual had an equal claim to live a satisfying life, where civil liberties flourished even more abundantly than in liberal society, and where democracy reigned in the economic as well as the political sphere. Through solidaristic cooperation and intelligence human beings would organize their common life to ensure both economic efficiency and personal security. In such a society every individual would have maximal opportunity to develop his or her paticular capacities and thus contribute to a richer common culture.

REFERENCES: *SU*, vol. 31; T. Tilton, "A Swedish Road to Socialism: Ernst Wigforss and the Ideological Foundations of Swedish Social Democracy," *American Political Science Review* 73:2 (June 1979): 129–42; E. Wigforss, "The Financial Policy During Depression and Boom," *Annals of the American Academy of Political and Social Science* (May 1938): 25-39, and *Skrifter i urval*, 9 vols. (Stockholm: Tidens, 1980).

T. TILTON

WINTER WAR (November 1939–March 1940) War between Finland and the Soviet Union

Finland's involvement in World War II* came in two segments separated by an interlude of "neutrality." Given the choice, the Finns would have remained neutral throughout the conflict, but they were attacked by the Soviet Union in 1939, and then opted to take advantage of the situation created by Germany's invasion of Russia to recover the areas lost in 1940 (*see* Continuation War).

The Winter War was largely the result of Soviet security concerns and Finland's refusal to consider concessions to the Soviets that Finnish leaders believed would compromise the country's sovereignty. In late August 1939, Stalin concluded a non-agression pact with Hitler. The move shocked the Western powers but was probably an appropriate one for the Soviets, at least in terms of their short-run security. Secret protocols attached to this agreement divided eastern Europe into spheres of influence. Finland, along with Latvia and Estonia, fell within the Soviet sphere. The Baltic states were coerced into signing non-aggression pacts with the Russians in September. About the same time the Russians began to ask the Finns about territorial concessions in the southeast (in the neighborhood of the Leningrad border), in exchange for territory in eastern Karelia, and about the possibility of leasing the Hanko Peninsula or some outer islands in the Gulf of Finland. Between 12 and 14 October, Juho K. Paasakivi* and Väinö Tanner* were in Moscow for talks with Molotov. There the Soviets pressed their demands, and the Finns refused to agree to any concessions.

Relations between Finland and the Soviet Union worsened following the talks in Moscow, and both sides prepared for war. On 30 November the Soviets attacked Finland. The Finns were hopelessly outnumbered from the outset and could expect almost no help from their Scandinavian neighbors or the Western powers. Some Swedish volunteers took part in the war, and Finland had the moral support of the West. In spite of the odds, the Finns did very well during the first two months of the conflict. The Soviets underestimated the human and material resources necessary to defeat the Finns, who took advantage of climate and terrain to maul Russian units. Their resistance was further strengthened when the Soviets established a puppet government under O. V. Kuusinen shortly after the war began. This move convinced the Finns that the real intention of the Soviets was to eliminate Finland's independence.

Negotiations aimed at ending the conflict began in early 1940. These were accompanied by a massive Soviet assault in February that broke the Finnish lines, and by British-French discussions of assistance to the Finns—probably aimed more at securing control of the Norwegian port of Narvik and the Swedish iron mines around Kiruna than at helping Finland. The war ended on 13 March 1940, with the signing of the Treaty of Moscow. Finland had to give up territory in the southeast and grant a lease on the Hanko Peninsula. For the following fourteen months, the Finns remained outside the general conflict in Europe, but they did not forget the war or its results.

REFERENCES: M. Jakobson, *The Diplomacy of the Winter War* (Cambridge, Mass.: Harvard University Press, 1961); D. G. Kirby, *Finland in the Twentieth Century* (Minneapolis: University of Minnesota Press, 1979); B. H. Liddell-Hart, *History of the Second World War* (New York: Putnam, 1971); H. S. Nissen, ed., *Scandinavia During the Second World War* (Minneapolis: University of Minnesota Press, 1983); T. Polvinnen, "Finland in International Politics," *Scandinavian Journal of History* 2:1–2 (1977): 107–22; V. Tanner, *The Winter War: Finland Against Russia, 1939–1940* (Stanford: Stanford University Press, 1957).

B. NORDSTROM

WOMEN'S MOVEMENT

Scandinavia

The women's movement in the Western world has its roots in the ideas of the Enlightenment and in the socioeconomic dislocations wrought by the Industrial Revolution. The Enlightenment ideals of freedom, equality before the law, individualism, and the concepts of "natural law" and "inalienable rights" prepared the ground for feminism. Enlightenment thinkers also promoted an optimistic and reformist outlook, which received further impetus from the American Revolution and the French Revolution.

As the nineteenth century dawned, women in Scandinavia* lived under a pattern of social and legal oppression similar to that which prevailed generally in western and middle Europe. They were discriminiated against in matters of inheritance, ownership, control of property, and access to education, and they were excluded from most middle-class occupations. They were also hamstrung by legal dependence; that is, they were usually under the legal guardianship of their fathers or husbands. Widows enjoyed a certain amount of legal independence, but in Denmark they were obliged to seek the advice of a man in legal matters, and in Sweden they could not serve as legal guardians of their own children.

The women's movement was strongly urban middle class from the outset. In the decades approaching 1850, middle-class women were severely restricted in career options; marriage was the only occupation available for most of them, though some became low-paid governesses or teachers. Those who remained unmarried were usually dependent on relatives for their keep. In the pre-industrial period, a rural family could use an extra pair of hands to make bread, spin and card wool, weave, make clothing, brew beer, and so on, but as commercial enterprise increasingly took over these functions and the population became more urbanized, the live-in maiden aunt became increasingly superfluous.

Enlightenment authors Ludwig Holberg of Denmark and Norway and Hedwig Charlotte Nordenflycht* of Sweden had broached the subject of women's emancipation in the first half of the eighteenth century. In 1839 Swedish writer C.J.L. Almqvist produced his controversial novel *Det går an* (titled *Sarah Videbeck* in English translation), which daringly criticized the institution of marriage and the restrictions against women pursuing crafts and trades.

In the 1850s three pioneer feminist writers—Mathilde Fibiger* of Denmark, Jacobine Camilla Collett* of Norway, and Fredrika Bremer* of Sweden—each published a novel which provoked public debate in newspapers and journals over women's status and rights. These three women spoke out in isolation, each acting alone, and each was subjected to a rain of public opprobium. Organized feminists of later generations, however, looked upon them as honored forebears.

By the 1870s and 1880s an organized movement was taking shape. The Danish Women's Society* (Dansk Kvindesamfund), founded in 1871, was followed in 1884 by the Norwegian Feminist Union* (Norsk Kvinnesaksforening), the Swedish Fredrika Bremer Association* (Fredrika-Bremer-forbündet), and the Finnish Women's Association. In 1894 an Icelandic Women's Association was also formed. These organizations were devoted to improving the status of women and promoting their increased participation in national life. However, some women found these first organizations too moderate, and in Norway, Denmark, and eventually Sweden and Iceland, new organizations were formed to press the issue of women's suffrage*. (The Finnish Women's Association had demanded equal voting rights for women from its inception.)

A number of improvements had taken place in women's legal status long before there was an organized women's movement. In areas such as education, employment, and political participation, the organized women were pressing for changes in directions in which some modifications had already been made. From the 1830s on, employment opportunities for women had been enlarged, beginning with handicrafts, trades, and elementary school teaching. Later, telegraph and postal work was opened to women. In the second half of the nineteenth century women gained the right to enroll in universities in Scandinavia and to pursue most branches of learning. Gains had also been made in other areas. In the 1840s and 1850s Sweden, Iceland, Norway, and Denmark had established equal inheritance rights for sons and daughters, followed by Finland in 1878. Unmarried women won legal independence in Denmark, Norway, Sweden, and Finland between 1857 and 1864. A generation or so later, married women also won this right (Sweden and Norway, 1888; Denmark, 1899 and 1908). Married women had meanwhile gained control over their own earnings in Sweden in 1874 and in Denmark, Norway, and Finland in the 1880s.

Women were granted limited voting rights in local elections in all Scandinavian countries in the latter part of the nineteenth century, except in Norway, where they first exercised such a right in 1901. Finland gave women full political rights in 1906 (the first European country to do so). Norway followed suit in 1913, Denmark and Iceland in 1915, and Sweden in 1921. After women had secured the ballot, the feminist movements lost some of their momentum; but it soon became obvious that many problems remained to be overcome.

Between the two world wars, females made further gains in education and employment opportunities. Hotly debated issues during this period of economic crisis in Europe included married women's right to hold jobs and equal pay for the same work. Women in Norway, Denmark, and Finland gained equal access to government jobs with equal pay for the same work in the interwar period; Swedish women won these rights only in 1945 and 1947.

The International Labor Organization convention calling for equal pay for equal work was accepted in principle in the late 1950s or early 1960s by all five Scandinavian countries, and Sweden has made the greatest progress in actually narrowing the gap between men's and women's wages. The postwar period also saw the first ordinations of women as ministers of the state Lutheran churches (Denmark, 1947; Sweden, 1960; Norway, 1961).

The neofeminist wave of the 1970s and 1980s brought intensive consciousness raising, campaigns against sex stereotypes, a massive outpouring of feminist literature, and the establishment of women's studies as a recognized field of scholarly investigation. The neofeminists criticized sexist portrayals of males and females in textbooks, children's books, films, advertisements, and the like, in addition to pressing for wage equality, more child-care facilities, and more women in political office. Notable among the numerous new women's groups have been the Rødstrømper (Redstockings) and the Thildes in Denmark, the Redstockings and Úur in Iceland, the Nyfeminister (Neofeminists) and Kvin-nefronten (the Women's Front) in Norway, and Gruppe 8 (Group 8) in Sweden. Responding to two demands, in the 1970s the Scandinavian governments each established an "equal status" council charged with the tasks of investigating areas of male-female inequality, gathering information, and recommending changes to correct the imbalances. The new era has also brought liberalized abortion laws and recognition of the need for men to become more involved in homemaking and childrearing tasks.

A major issue among Scandinavian feminists has been the question of how much stress should be placed on the women's struggle as opposed to the class struggle. The Redstockings' slogan, "No women's struggle without class strug-gle; no class struggle without women's struggle," reflects their conviction that while women are oppressed by men, both women and men are oppressed by capitalism. The women's movements of Scandinavia are on the whole more Socialist in outlook than their American counterparts.

REFERENCES: A. C. Agerhold, *Den norske kvinnebevegelses historie* (Oslo: Gyldendalsk Norsk, 1973); A. Bang, ed., *Hva bråker de for?* (Oslo: Pax, 1973); I. Dahlsgård, *Women in Denmark Yesterday and Today*, trans. G. French (Copenhagen: Det Danske Selskab, 1980); I. Dahlsgård, ed., *Kvindebevægelsens hvem-hvad-hvor*(Copenhagen: Politiken, 1975); M. Gerlach-Neilsen, *Ny dansk kvindebevægelse 1970–1978* (Roskilde: Emmeline, 1980); G. Qvist, *Kvinnofrågen i Sverige 1809–1846* (Göteborg: Akademiförlaget-Gumperts, 1960); K. Sjonsberg, ed., *Hvor var Kvinnene?*(Oslo: Gyldendalsk Norsk, 1979); J. Steenstrup, *Den danske kvindes historie fra Holbergs tid til vor 1701–1917*, 2 vols. (Copenhagen: Hagerups, 1917); L. Wahlström, *Den svenska kvinnorörelsen* (Stockholm: Bonniers, 1939).

N. FARQUHAR

Finland

The women's movement was organized in Finland during the 1880s. Enthustiasm for issues facing women was raised in 1882, when Emme Irene Åström became the first woman in the country to receive a master's degree. (The first women to enter a Finnish university did so in 1870.) This event became part of a broader awakening to women's issues. In early 1883 an informal club was formed which studied Mill's *The Subjection of Women*. A formal association, the Finnish Women's Association (Suomen Naisyhdistys/FWA), was founded in 1884. The organization focused its attentions on the issues of equal educational opportunities (including university opportunities) for boys and girls, equal pay for the same work, the salary and property rights of women, suffrage for women on the same bases as for men, and the elimination of the double standard in sexual mores and prostitution*.

Nearly all the women who belonged to the FWA were from the upper social classes. Fifty-five percent of the original members were married, and their husbands were mainly professors or higher administration employees. Forty-five percent were unmarried, and they were primarily teachers. (The percentage of unmarried members later increased to over 60 percent.)

The first chairperson of the FWA was Elisabeth Löfgren. She and her husband were active in the Finnish national movement, which was then the most important ideological movement in Finland. Consequently, the FWA was closely tied with the nationalists. This also meant that the chair of the FWA was inclined to relate women's questions to the larger national question (or ignore them entirely), and this was not approved of by all members of the association. After a number of internal fights, Löfgren resigned and was replaced by Aleksandra Gripenberg. She was also a Fennoman or Finnish nationalist, and the internal squabbles continued.

In 1892 the FWA split. The Fennomen, who belonged to the older faction of the national movement, stayed in the FWA. The Swedish-speaking (generally called Svecomen) and those who belonged to the younger wing of the national movement formed the Feminist Union (Naisasialiitto Unioni/FU). The first chairperson was Lucina Hagman. The new organization tended to be more liberal on many issues than the FWA.

Cooperation between the Svecomen and the Young Finns continued until 1906, when Finland won a measure of political reform as a result of the 1905 Revolution in Russia. In 1906 all adult men and women were given the vote and the right to be elected to parliament. This increased the importance of political parties and also precipitated the split of the Feminist Union. In 1907 the Young Finns' segment of the FU established the Finnish Women's Union (Suomalainen Nais-liitto). Lucina Hagman now became the chairperson of this group. The organization was Finnish-speaking.

After the first parliamentary elections in 1907, the early phase of the women's movement in Finland ended. Those women who had been active in the movement now worked mainly in parliament. Between 1907 and 1920, 22 women candidates of bourgeois parties were elected to the Eduskunta*. Nearly half of these had been members of one or more of the early feminist organizations.

From the outset the memberships of the early women's organizations were small. In Helsinki the number of members hardly exceeded 200. The FWA and the FU spread to the countryside, and membership reached about 4,000 at its peak.

In the 1960s Finland experienced a second phase in the history of the women's movement. In 1966 Association 9 (Yhdistys 9) was formed in Helsinki. This organization included male members, as had the Feminist Union. (The percentage of male members reached 28 percent.) Association 9 was part of a radical movement which characterized the 1960s. The young people who dominated it could not work together with the surviving feminist organizations. Association 9 focused on new issues—sex roles, and working women and their problems. In the group, women's studies were, for the first time, closely related to the women's movement. As may be expected, most of the members of the association were academics.

The first chairperson of Association 9 was Margaretha Mickwitz. She was succeeded by Holger Rotkirch. At its peak the membership of the organization was greater than that of any of the earlier groups, even though it spread to only one other university town, Tampere. The development of the organization followed the typical pattern within the universities, as it turned more and more to the Left. Within a few years activists in Association 9 joined either the Social Democratic Party* or the Communist Party*. Simultaneously, this phase in the history of the women's movement ebbed. By 1970 Association 9 ceased to function.

A third phase in the Finnish women's movement developed in the 1970s. In 1973 two Marxist-leaning groups appeared. Gradually, feminist ideas took predominance over Marxist ideology, and in 1976 these groups and several others formed an informal collective, the Feminists (Feministit). The membership was largely Swedish-speaking and, again, most members were students or academics. At the same time, a shakeup within the old Feminist Union forced many of the members to retire. Membership then swelled to over 1,000 in the Helsinki area. Kari Mattila chaired this group.

Most of the members of the Feminists and the Feminist Union are now students or university faculty. A new feature, compared with Association 9, however, is that these organizations have attracted members from the lower middle class. (Only women are admitted as members.) The organizations deal mainly with issues affecting women's private lives, including questions related to the family, marriage, love, and sexuality. This phase of the women's movement in Finland continues to be active in the 1980s.

REFERENCES: K. Eskola, ed., *Miesten maailman nurjat lait* (Helsinki: Tammi, 1968); A. Gripenberg, *Naisasian kehitys eri maissa*, vol. 4 (Porvoo: Werner Söderström Osakeyhtiö, 1909); R. Jallinoja, "The Women's Liberation Movement in Finland: The Social and Political Mobilization of Women in Finland, 1880–1910," *Scandinavian Journal of History* 5 (1980): 37–49; M. von Alftan, *Seitsemän vuosikymmentä Naisasialiitto Unionin historiaa* (Joensuu: Pohjois-Karjalan Kirjapaino Oy, 1966).

R. JALLINOJA

Norway

The organizing of women in Norway has followed two different lines. First, from the mid-nineteenth century, Norwegian women have cooperated in special groups (*kvinneforeninger*) with religious, temperance, social, and humanitarian organizations. The socialization of women to work more for others than for their own interests seems to have contributed to the development of this type of group.

The first such organization was started within the Norwegian Missionary Society in 1844 by Gustava Kielland. Since then countless groups have developed and have often contributed decisive amounts of money to the activities of the larger organization through, for example, the sale of needlework and bazaars. The Norwegian Women's Public Health Association (Norske Kvinners Sanitetsforening) founded in 1896, today the largest of all women's organizations in Norway, continued in this line. Originally the aim of the organization was to prepare sanitary services in case of a war with Sweden over the dissolution of the Norwegian-Swedish Union*. After the peaceful settlement of the Union question in 1905, the organization turned toward the fight against tuberculosis, the education of nurses, the establishment of welfare centers for mothers and babies, and other welfare services. Within the same tradition, housewives of the upper middle class started associations in Christiania (Oslo) and Bergen in 1898 and later in Trondheim, with the aim of promoting the interest of the home. In 1915 they joined in a national organization, later to be named the Norwegian Housewives' Association (Norges Husmorforbund), today the second largest women's organization in the country.

The second line which the organization of women took may be traced back to the French Revolution and the demand for equality between the sexes. The Norwegian Association for the Rights of Women (Norsk Kvinnesakforening), founded in 1884, worked mainly to obtain equal rights in education and employment, primarily to enable unmarried women to support themselves within the norms accepted by middle-class families. As the leaders of the organization refused to raise the questions of women's suffrage, a small group of female members formed the Association for Women's Suffrage (Kvinnestemmeretts-foreningen) in 1885. In 1898 this organization split over the question of strategy. The new group, the National Organization for Women's Suffrage (Landskvin-nestemmerettsforeningen), soon outgrew the old one and gained the support of a wide spectrum of women.

Leaders as well as members of these organizations were recruited mainly from the upper middle class. After World War I, a broader social range of women joined the Public Health Association and the Housewives' Association.

Around the turn of the century, female teachers, telephone operators, and other occupational groups started to organize themselves and had formed national organizations before World War I. In 1904 most of these groups joined with a number of religious and other women's organizations in the National Council of Women (Norske Kvinners Nasjonalråd), the Norwegian Branch of the International Council of Women.

After 1907 non-Socialist women gradually formed special women's organizations within the various non-Socialist parties. In the 1880s and 1890s working-class women began to unite in trade unions, partly in female unions and partly in unions already founded and including both sexes. In Oslo and Bergen the Norwegian Labor Party* included a women's group. In 1901 these groups, together with some female trade unions, formed the Norwegian Labor Party's Women's Association (Arbeiderpartiets Kvinneforlund). Despite efforts of the National Council of Women, the Socialist women never joined this organization. In 1923 the separate female organization within the Labor Party was replaced by a Women's Secretariat, directly under the central board of the party.

Between the wars Communist women organized in groups of housewives (Housewives' Societies/Husmorlag), which joined together in 1937 to form the Federation of Housewives' Societies (Husmorlagsforbundet). After the war this organization merged with the Norwegian Democratic Women's Association (Norges Demokratiske Kvinneforbund). Through its membership in the Association of Democratic Women of the World, the group is in contact with women in Eastern Europe also.

From early in the twentieth century women in Norway have built up organizations grouped in two main blocks. These organizations have drawn their members from the liberal middle class and from the Socialists (primarily working-class), respectively. Broadly speaking, the middle-class women have been divided into a liberal irreligious camp and a conservative religious one, and the Socialists have embraced revolutionary as well as reformist ideals. As in other countries, this division of female and feminist organizations has persisted to the present day, interrupted by a few, mostly abortive attempts to join forces. However, in a number of important questions, such as the fight for the vote, the problems of family planning*, and abortion, cooperation across the social and political barriers has taken place and produced results.

A new wave of feminism in the 1970s revived and radicalized the activities of the Association for the Rights of Women and the National Council of Women, as well as a number of female trade unions and female sections in political parties. New organizations like the New Feminists (Nyfeministene) and the Women's Front (Kvinnefronten) took the lead—the latter usually associated with the extreme Left—in formulating strategies and putting pressure on political decision-making.

From the very beginning of organized feminism, questions of where to concentrate efforts have been discussed, whether around issues pertaining especially to women's functions in the home as mothers and housewives, or around the growing activity of women outside the home, earning their livings in factories, offices, and shops, and working through organizations or political parties.

Due to the predominantly agrarian structure of Norwegian society and the scattered pattern of settlement in the country, the greater part of Norwegian women seems to have been shown relatively little interest in organizations working to promote female activity outside the home. Until recently most women saw their own field of activity as being primarily that of the mother and housewife. That did not, however, mean that they did not contribute to the family's economy. In an agrarian setting they did so by laboring on the farm, in the urban setting by assisting their husbands in shops and other enterprises and by performing many domestic jobs in other people's homes. As in other countries, the lives of most Norwegian women did not leave them much time and energy to pursue organizational activities. The growth of the Norwegian Housewives' Association since 1915, second in size to the Norwegian Women's Public Health Association, shows where the interests of the majority of Norwegian women have been centered.

In spite of the thorough changes that have taken place in the economic, social, and political framework since the 1880s, women still organize to a much smaller extent than men and still concentrate their organized activities more on working for others than on working for their own interests.

The feminist organizations, defined as organizations with the aim of changing women's legal and actual situation in society, have generally won the support of only a minority of Norwegian women. This does not mean, however, that the feminist organizations have had little importance. From studies of the influence of such organizations, we know that membership is by no means the only way of gauging influence.

The early feminist organizations proved to be important interest groups within the liberal as well as the Socialist political spheres. Even if fundamental economic, social, and probably also demographic factors explain many important changes in the position of Norwegian women during the past century, the courageous efforts of the early feminists in disregarding conventional expectations of female behavior were strong forces behind these changes.

Recent research has revealed that important issues like female suffrage were raised when women made their interests known through their organizations. Also, it should not be forgotten that women also used influence within the family, the extent of which cannot easily be gauged by historians.

The main goal of the early feminist organizations was equality of opportunity. Having learned that this is only a first step, contemporary feminist organizations work for equality of results. They have also realized that full equality cannot be obtained by changing the lives of women to resemble those of men, but that the lives of men will also have to change.

REFERENCES: A. C. Agerholt, *Den norsk kvinnebevegelses historie* (Oslo: Gyldendal, 1937); I. Blom, "A Centenary of Organized Feminism in Norway," *Women's Studies International Quarterly*, special issue on a reassessment of first-wave feminism, 1982; "Kvinner i organisasjonssamfunnet," *Stengsler og muligheter i Sosiologi idag* 2 (1979): 25–34; I. Blom and G. Hagemann, eds., *Kvinner selv . . . Sju bidrag till norsk kvinne-historie* (Oslo: Aschehoug, 1977); E. Strømberg, *The Role of Women's Organizations in Norway* (Oslo: Equal Status Council, 1980); S. Syvertsen and T. Thorleifsen, *Kvinner i strid. Historien om Arbeiderpartiets kvinnebevegelse* (Oslo: Arbeidernes Opplysnings-forbund, 1960).

I. BLOM

Sweden

For most of the nineteenth century women in Sweden were confined to working in the home or in agriculture. However, when industrialization began during the latter half of the century, employment areas opened up for women beyond those traditional fields. Foremost among these were jobs in rapidly expanding industries and the public sector.

Female Population over 15 Years of Age Divided by Work Category (Percent of Total Population), 1870–1960

	1870	1900	1910	1920	1930	1940	1950	1960
Blue Collar	1.0	3.5	5.2	8.5	9.3	9.0	9.2	10.0
White Collar	.4	1.7	3.2	5.6	7.1	10.0	13.9	17.9

By 1920 women occupied dominant positions in several areas of the labor market. For example, before the General Strike* of 1909, more women than men worked in the textile and tobacco industries. In the brewing, baking, and shoe industries women accounted for between 25 and 50 percent of the work force. A similar development took place in the public sector. In the rapidly changing communications field, a large number of women were employed as telegraphers, operators, postal clerks, office workers, and so on. The expansion of health care and education programs gave work to thousands of women.

In this early period of rapidly increasing involvement by women in the labor market, women were largely concentrated in sectors of the labor market characterized by low wages, and it was usual for them to receive less pay than men for the same work. At the end of World War I, women were paid about two-thirds the wages men received. Even in the public sector this pattern applied. Women were placed either in the lowest wage groups without men dominant, or different wage scales were set for men and women. In the public sector this practice was part of government policy, and the state felt no obligation to foster an equal pay system. In addition, old notions that women did less work and had fewer needs than men prevailed. It was not until 1919 that an official policy of equal pay for men and women was adopted by the government, and it was years before this policy became a reality.

In the period 1870–1920, the labor market's demand for women workers was met almost entirely by women without certain limits on their capacity to work; that is, most jobs were taken by single women or women without children. Unmarried middle-class women were favored for office positions by private companies and the public sector.

The female work force continued to expand after World War I, and a significant structural change occurred. The percentage of women in office jobs more than doubled, while the percentage of women holding blue-collar positions declined. In 1930, 24 percent of the women in the work force held office positions. By 1965, women in these positions accounted for 59 percent of the female work force. Women in blue-collar positions accounted for 62 percent of the female work force in 1930 and 37 percent in 1965. The trend since World War I has also been toward an increasing number of married women in the labor market. Also, the number of women working part-time has increased.

A large part of the female work force remained outside existing labor organizations for at least the first third of the twentieth century. This was especially true for women in white-collar jobs. (There were some notable exceptions in the public sector.) Quite early, women workers became associated with the Swedish Confederation of Trade Unions* (Landsorganisationen/LO) and thereby were tied into male-dominated organizations. However, among the large number of women workers, only a small share actually became affiliated with LO. Before the General Strike of 1909, LO had about 17,000 women members. In 1912 this figure had fallen to 4,300 or only 5.1 percent of the membership. By 1920 the number of women in LO had risen to 32,000 or 11.7 percent of the membership. The war years and the first few years after the war witnessed a rapid increase in the number and percentage of women members in LO, although if one looks at the total number of women in the labor market in 1920, only 18 percent were organized in LO.

Our knowledge concerning the organization of women in white-collar or office jobs is very limited. The lack of certain basic facts about, for example, the extensiveness of organization, makes it difficult to do more than generalize about trends. The development of a white-collar empoyees' union movement came after 1900 and was based on a large number of organizations which were built around specific jobs. It was not until the 1930s that a central organization, the Central Organization of Employees (De Anställdas Centralorganisationen/DACO), was founded. Within the white-collar sector, special women's unions were created from the beginning, which co-existed with male and mixed organizations.

The organization of women white-collar workers was most successful initially in the public sector and was almost entirely excluded in the private sector for a long time. In large part the latter may be explained by the stiff opposition which employers showed toward the development of labor organizations among blue- and white-collar workers. There was also some reluctance among the white-collar workers to engage in trade union methods or build unions, because they did not want to be identified with working-class behavior. With the establishment of DACO in the 1930s, women office workers in the private sector began to organize on a large scale.

Among the women working in the public sector, including postal and telegraph workers and school teachers, organizational levels appear to have been high. They were, furthermore, significantly higher in occupationss where women and men established common organizations. This brought to light an important aspect in the complex problem of women in the Swedish trade union movement, that is, women's roles and opportunities to influence their job and wage opportunities.

For working women the possibilities of increasing their influence with LO have been quite limited. Before the 1940s, LO showed little interest in women's problems. In the two great questions which engaged women workers at the turn of the century, night work and equal pay, LO took a passive if not largely negative position. LO's women's policy was largely determined by three factors: the share of the work force women held, the number of married women in this group, and the number of women in LO. Until World War II, only minor changes took place in these numbers. But after the war important changes occurred. Women came to constitute 40 percent of the work force. Sixty percent of these women were married, and LO's membership became 30 percent women. In the early 1960s women became LO's most important recruitment field. As a result of these changes, LO changed its attitudes toward women's problems. The equal pay principle received a prominent place during the 1950s and 1960s. Still, women did not receive an important place in the decision-making organs of LO. The transition to larger unions and the consolidation of smaller unions resulted in a decline in women's representation in the postwar period. An increase, however, occurred in women's representation on advisory and investigative bodies within LO.

When one considers the role of women white-collar workers within their organizations and the possibilities women had to influence their job and wage situations, the same problems mentioned above appear. Also, there is little information available on the topic. Women seem to have encountered, however, the same obstacles as women in the blue-collar area. The equal pay question was central at the turn of the century. In spite of a very active union policy, women white-collar workers got very little in the way of satisfaction of their demands. Women office workers for a long while were discriminated against in relation to their male counterparts. Beginning in the 1950s, TCO (Tjänsteman

Centralorganisationen, which succeeded DACO) decided that these incongruities in the wage scales should be eliminated through concentration on the lowest paid in the wage agreements. In the early 1960s the special wage scale for women was removed. (This occurred in the public sector in 1939, although large-scale differences continued in government salaries between men and women.) By working for increased access to promotion, better educational opportunities, and better wage terms within those areas which recruited predominantly women, the white-collar organizations were able to secure considerable improvements for women.

REFERENCES: S. Carlsson, "Den sociala omgrupperingen i Sverige efter 1866," in *Samhälle och riksdag*, vol. 1 (Stockholm, 1966); F. Croner, *De svenska privatanställda: en sociologisk studie* (Stockholm: Kooperative Förbundets förlag, 1939), and *Tjänstemannakåren i det moderna samhället* (Uppsala: Gebers sociologiska bibliotek, 1951); T. Ericsson, "Kvinnor i facklig kamp. En studie av Föreningen kvinnor i statens tjänst 1904–1912," *Scandia* 47 (1981): 109–29; A. Nilstein, "White-collar Unionism in Sweden," in A. Sturmthal, ed., *White-Collar Trade Unions: Contemporary Development in Industrialized Societies* (London and Urbana: Illinois University Press, 1966); G. Qvist, "Landsorganisationen i Sverige och kvinnorna på arbetsmarknaden," *Arbetarrörelsens Årsbok*, 1975, pp. 13–31; *Statisk och politik. Landsorganisationen och kvinnorna på arbetsmarknaden* (Stockholm: Prisma, 1974).

T. ERICSSON

WOMEN'S SUFFRAGE

Scandinavia

Women received the vote in Denmark in 1915, in Finland in 1906, in Iceland in 1913–1915, in Norway in 1907, and in Sweden in 1918. In each instance, the victory for women's suffrage came in the midst of profound social and economic change and, in the case of Iceland, Finland, and Norway, during periods of heightened nationalist fervor. The struggle for the right to vote for women was part of the greater struggle for genuinely representative, parliamentary government and the struggle for national independence or automony in Iceland, Finland, and Norway. It occurred within the contexts of the emergence of modern political parties, especially those representing the emerging working classes, and in an environment that was tainted by the running struggle between the conservative forces in these countries, which sought to preserve their hold on politcial power, and the liberal forces, which sought to expand the bases of representative government and bring democratic reforms.

Following the success of the initial stage of the women's movement* in Scandinavia*, which was marked by the achievement of legal and economic reforms such as equal inheritance rights, legal independence for women, and access to higher education, the women's movement entered a period when moral issues were central (1880s and 1890s). It was from this that the movement for women's suffrage sprang. In all of the Scandinavian countries organizations were formed to foster the goal of women's suffrage. The women's movement, like other popular movements in the same period, became highly politicized. The organizations that appeared included the Progressive Association of Danish Women (Dansk Kvindelig Fremskridtsforening, 1896), the Danish Women's Suffrage Association (Dansk Kvindelig Valgretsforening, 1888), the Women's Association's Suffrage League (Kvindeforeningars Valgretsforbund, 1890), and the National Association for Women's Suffrage (Landsforbundet for Kvinders Valgret, 1900) in Denmark; the Women's Union (1892) in Finland; the Women's Association of Iceland (Kvenfelag Island, 1894) in Iceland; the Association for Women's Suffrage (Kvinnestemmerettsforeningen, 1885) and the National Association for Women's Suffrage (Landskvinnestemmerettsforeningen) in Norway; and the National Association for Women's Suffrage (Landsföreningen for Kvinnans Politiska Rösträtt, 1902) in Sweden. Most of these groups worked in association with one or more political parties for the achievement of their goal. (*See also* the following section on Norway; Constitutional Development.)

REFERENCES: I. Dahlsgård, *Kvindebevægelsens hvem-hvad-hvor* (Copenhagen, 1975); R. Evans, *The Feminists: Women's Emancipation Movements in Europe, America and Australasia, 1840–1920* (London: Croom Helm, 1977); E. Juusola-Halonen, "The Women's Liberation Movement in Finland," in J. Bradshaw, ed., *The Women's Liberation Movement in Europe and America* (New York: Pergamon Press, 1982).

B. NORDSTROM

Norway

Female suffrage following the census principle was obtained for local elections in 1901 and for national elections in 1907. Universal female suffrage for local elections was introduced in 1910 and for national elections in 1913. Norway was the first sovereign country to introduce universal female suffrage for national elections. Increasing public responsibility for important parts of family life, such as children's education and health measures, induced women to augment their traditional voice in such matters through the vote. Charity work met the same obstacles and had the same effect on women's desire to vote. As in other countries, unmarried women working outside their homes in increasing numbers gradually desired the suffrage to be able to improve their possibilities for education, salaries, and working conditions.

Men's political interests also influenced the question of female suffrage. The Liberal Party and the Social Democrats were throughout the 28 years of the struggle dedicated supporters of women's suffrage. But at several crucial points both parties gave priority to a widening of men's suffrage and dropped the question of the vote for women. When men obtained universal suffrage in 1898, the Social Democrats had the most to lose from female suffrage following the census system. The Conservatives, until then mainly adverse to any female suffrage reform, had the most to gain. Consequently, the Conservatives in 1901 and 1907 were found among the proponents of a census system for women, while the Social Democrats continued their fight for universal female suffrage. They did not, however, show the same intensity in the struggle as did the Socialist women.

It is also important to be aware that the question of female suffrage was not raised until women made their voices heard in support of the idea. When in 1818 the Norwegian parliament discussed the need to state explicitly that the vote was limited to males, the proposal was rejected on the ground that "women of our country have not yet demanded the right to participate in the management of the State." The proposal was therefore deemed superfluous.

The fight for female suffrage started in 1885, when the Association for Women's Suffrage (Kvinnestemmerettsforeningen) was formed, demanding the vote for women according to the same principles as for men. After 1898 the association modified its program to demand the gradual extension of the vote for women. This resulted in a split, and a new organization, the National Association for Women's Suffrage (Landskvinnestemmerettsforeningen), was formed, dedicated to continuing the policy of suffrage for women on the same conditions as for men, that is, universal female suffrage.

Socialist women pursued the goal through demonstrations on national day, 17 May. Women public speakers formulated resolutions addressed to the parliament. Between 1898 and 1903 some non-Socialist women joined these demonstrations, but cooperation stopped in Christiania (Oslo), though it continued in some towns. The fight for the vote was also part of the reason for Socialist women to start editing their own periodical in 1909. In 1901, 1907, and 1910 resolutions to the parliament and to individual members of parliament were also adopted by the suffrage organizations, and Socialists and non-Socialists often cooperated within the National Association for Women's Suffrage.

It has been maintained that the policy adopted by women in the question of the dissolution of the politcial union with Sweden was of major importance to the decision on the vote in 1907. The same women who led the campaign for women's suffrage formed the Norwegian Women's Public Health Association (Norske Kvinners Sanitetsforening) in 1896, and they demonstrated their support for the national policy. In their addresses and demonstrations for the vote, however, they stressed their desire to follow a peaceful line on the union question. When in 1905 the plebiscite over dissolution of the union was arranged, their demand to be able to participate was rejected. Nevertheless, they gathered almost 300,000 signatures on petitions supporting the decision to dissolve the union. This act was later stressed as a sign of sensible political behavior by women.

Last but not least, women worked for female suffrage through the influence they exerted over husbands, brothers, and sons. This channel of influence, extremely difficult for historians to document, was one of the arguments often used against female suffrage. In the words of a Conservative member of parliament in 1907: "If we now give women the right to vote . . . in addition to the influence which they have behind the scene and which unfortunately they always will have, in spite of everything, the situation will become intolerable." Thanks not least to the efforts of women themselves, the situation has been "intolerable" since 1913.

REFERENCES: A. C. Agerholt, *Den norske kvinnebevegelses historie* (Oslo: Gyldendal, 1937, 1980); I. Blom, "The Struggle for Women's Suffrage in Norway 1885–1913," *Scandinavian Journal of History* 5:1 (1980): 3–22; S. Syvertsen and T. Thorleifsen, *Historien om Arbeiderpartiets kvinnebevegelse* (Oslo: Arbeidernes Opplysningsforbund, 1960).

I. BLOM

WORLD WAR II

Denmark

During the period between the outbreak of the war in September 1939 and the German invasion and occupation on 9 April 1940, Denmark followed a precarious policy of neutrality based in part on policies followed since World War I. It included continued observance of a non-aggression pact with Germany which Denmark signed in May 1939. Denmark was the only Scandinavian country to sign such an agreement with the Third Reich. The size of the Danish army shrank from 36,000 in September 1939 to 14,000 by April 1940. The Danes continued to trade with both Britain and Germany and scrupulously tried to avoid offending both major belligerents during this "phoney war phase."

Immediately after the German occupation, a government of national unity took shape which included, along with the dominant Social Democrats and Radicals, a number of politicians from the opposition Conservative and Liberal parties who served as ministers without portfolio. However, Thorvald Stauning*, a Social Democrat, remained as prime minister, and Peter Munch*, a Radical, stayed on as foreign minister until he gave up his post, under pressure from his critics, to the career diplomat Erik Scavenius* in July 1940. On 8 July a new streamlined cabinet took office which resulted in Conservative and Liberal control over a number of ministries including Church Affairs, Interior, and Commerce. This broad four-party coalition was to govern Denmark during the first three and a half years of German occupation until August 1943.

Danish military resistance to the German occupation lasted only four hours on 9 April 1940. Consequently, the occupation in its first two years was essentially peaceful in nature. Also, the Germans moved into Denmark primarily because of events in Norway. As a result of the relatively non-violent nature of the German occupation and Berlin's initial willingness to allow the Danes to maintain their democratic, constitutional system of government, Copenhagen cooperated with Berlin in a number of areas.

In the diplomatic and strategic realm, the cooperation was almost complete. It included removal of British, Dutch, Belgian, and other Allied diplomatic personnel from Denmark shortly after the outbreak of war between Germany and those countries. By early 1942, after the departure of the Americans and Brazilians, virtually the only states with diplomatic representation in Denmark were Germany, its allies, countries with a generally pro-German foreign policy like Spain and Argentina, or nations like Sweden which remained neutral throughout the entire war. Also, the Copenhagen government agreed to curtail trade and regular postal or telegraphic communication with Britain and other countries outside German control. This policy led to shortages of many products, including a number of raw materials which were essential for Danish agriculture. These shortages contributed to a series of economic problems, including inflation and rationing, which became acute after 1942.

The Danish government instituted strict press censorship as early as 1941. It broke off diplomatic relations with the Soviet Union immediately after the German attack on that country in June 1941. In addition, a group of volunteers, the Frikorps Danmark, composed of young men willing to fight on the eastern front, under German direction, received active support from the Stauning government. Foreign Minister Scavenius played a leading role in supplying and providing official protection for this group. Finally, the Danish parliament formally outlawed the Communist Party in August 1941, and several hundred Communists were subsequently arrested. Perhaps the ultimate act of cooperation or outright collaboration was Denmark's signature of the Anti-Comintern Pact on 25 November 1941. This agreement was not a military alliance, and in many respects it only committed Denmark to combat international communism. To some Danish leaders like Scavenius this seemed nothing more than recognition of a fait accompli, since the Danish Communist Party had been outlawed earlier. However, the agreement called for consultation among the signatories regarding their respective anti-Communist measures. Also, Denmark was the only country adhering to the Anti-Comintern Pact which was not part of the Axis alliance or at least friendly toward it.

In spite of many actions which involved cooperation with Germany, the Danes became increasingly defiant as the occupation wore on. One of the most immediate and dramatic examples of defiance or resistance was the response of the Danish merchant marine to news of the occupation. At least 159 out of somewhat more than 200 ships headed for Allied ports in answer to an appeal from London and in defiance of orders from Copenhagen which instructed them to sail for "neutral" ports, preferably in Spain or Italy. Many of the remaining Danish ships eventually ended up in the service of the Allies, since they went to U.S. or Latin American ports. When the United States and several of these Latin American countries joined the Allied cause, the Danish ships in their harbors often came into use supplying the military needs of the Allies. It is estimated that approximately 90 percent of the Danish merchant seaman who were outside of German control chose to sail on behalf of countries which were at war with Germany. As a result, 600 of these sailors lost their lives and about 60 percent of Denmark's merchant ships were sunk by German torpedoes.

Like most of the Danish merchant marine, Denmark's overseas territories were beyond the reach of the Germans when they invaded Denmark. In May 1940 British forces occupied Iceland and the Faroe Islands*. The separation of these areas from Copenhagen, both physically and politically, ultimately proved costly for Denmark.

By July 1941 American forces replaced the British in Iceland. This helped to bring about pressure in Iceland for a complete political break with Denmark. In

July 1944 the personal union between Denmark and Iceland through the Danish crown was officially dissolved and the island nation had proclaimed itself an independent republic. An independence movement also developed in the Faroes during the war which produced difficulties for Copenhagen in the immediate postwar period, although the Faroese ultimately accepted Danish sovereignty.

Denmark was ultimately more fortunate in regard to Greenland*, her largest overseas territory. As a result of an agreement between Henrik Kauffmann, the Danish ambassador in Washington, and the U.S. government on 9 April 1941, American naval, meteorological, radio, and air bases were established on Greenland. A few hours after the German occupation, Kauffmann declared himself a "free agent" who was no longer bound by orders from the Copenhagen government, which he described as acting under duress. His statements and the Greenland agreement led to his removal from the diplomatic service accompanied by severe legal penalties. These punishments meted out by the Copenhagen government were not recognized by the United States. Throughout the war, Kauffmann remained at his post in Washington.

Other Danish diplomats in foreign countries followed Kauffman's example, although in a somewhat more cautious fashion. For example, in January 1942 the Danish ambassador in London, Edward Reventlow, officially broke with his government after its signature of the Anti-Comintern Pact. Subsequently, he provided invaluable assistance in the formation of the union of Free Danes in Great Britain, which by the summer of 1942 had become the Danish Council. This organization served as the focal point for resistance activity among Danes living in Britain and other countries outside of German control.

In spite of many instances of cooperation with Berlin, the Copenhagen government of Stauning and his successors resisted the Germans in a number of areas. For example, all German suggestions that Nazis be included in the cabinet met with a stern rebuff from the Danish government. Also, anti-Jewish legislation, a possible customs and currency union with the Reich, and any revision of Denmark's southern frontier in favor of Germany met a stone wall of resistance from the king, the cabinet, and parliament.

On the positive side, the Copenhagen government successfully persuaded Berlin to accept a revaluation of the krone in January 1942 in accordance with its stronger purchasing power vis-a-vis the increasingly inflated German mark. This, plus Copenhagen's refusal to accept a customs and currency union with Germany, helped to stem the steady flow of goods, especially agricultural commodities, from Denmark to the south. Nevertheless, the demands of the German war economy placed an increasingly difficult strain on the Danish economy. As a result of the occupation an enormous amount of livestock and other necessities was irreparably lost, with correspondingly disastrous effects on the Danish economy in the form of inflation, rationing, and shortages.

In addition to krone revaluation, the Danish government convinced the Germans to allow a parliamentary election to take place on 23 March 1943, in accordance with the Danish constitution. Although it was restricted in a number of ways, the election was basically democratic in character, and virtually all political parties except the Communists participated. Such an election could never have taken place in any other country under German occupation.

In spite of some partial success in dealing with the Germans, increasing numbers of Danes became disillusioned with the Copenhagen government's policy of cooperation. As a result, the resistance movement grew in Denmark, and German patience became increasingly strained, to the point where after August 1943 there no longer was any real distinction between Denmark and other German-occupied territories.

As early as 1940 an espionage network had been set up by Ebbe Munck, a prominent Danish journalist. This agency performed invaluable services for the Danish underground and the Allies by relaying information between Britain and Denmark through Denmark's neutral neighbor, Sweden. Also, it served as the nucleus of an underground organization which transported thousands of Jews, resistance leaders, and others out of Denmark to safety in either Sweden, Britain, or the United States.

By the beginning of 1941 Christmas Moeller* gave up his seat in parliament and his offices in the Conservative Party. In October 1940 he had to resign his position as minister of commerce, primarily due to German displeasure over his consistently anti-Nazi and anti-German speeches and comments. In early May 1942 Moeller and his family fled to England, and from this moment he served as the actual head of the Danish Council in London. Another prominent Danish politician, Hans Hedtoft, a Social Democrat, gave up his party posts in February 1941 due to German pressure. He subsequently became an active member of the resistance movement, playing a crucial role in the rescue of Denmark's Jews in October 1943. After the war, partly because of his resistance activities, he headed up two postwar coalition governments.

On 3 May 1942 Prime Minister Stauning died. With him died what was left of the policy of real cooperation between Copenhagen and Berlin. From this point relations between the two countries rapidly went from bad to worse. His successor was Vilhelm Buhl, a Social Democrat who later became active in the resistance and who headed Denmark's first postwar government. The Buhl ministry lasted only about six months. A cabinet led by Erik Scavenius governed Denmark from November 1942 until the German crackdown of August 1943, which resulted in the imposition of martial law, the resignation of the Danish cabinet, the dissolution of parliament, and the seclusion of the king.

Overt resistance activity increased steadily in Denmark throughout 1942 and 1943. By April 1942 a number of resistance newspapers appeared regularly throughout Denmark. The most prominent of these was *Frit Danmark*, representing a coalition of Communists and middle-class resistance groups. Throughout 1943 instances of sabotage increased from 14 in January to 198 in August. A series of strikes and acts of violence in cities like Odense, Aahrus, and Aalborg helped bring the economy to a virtual standstill in many areas. The election of March 1943 resulted in a defeat for pro-Nazi groups and victories for relatively anti-German political groups such as Dansk Samling and the Conservative Party. Finally, as early as October 1942 Hitler had replaced the relatively moderate German ambassador and military commander with a leading SS official, Werner Best, and a hard-line military officer, Hermann von Hannecken. The new German representatives in Copenhagen had instructions no longer to treat Denmark as a neutral nation even in theory. They were henceforth to look upon it as enemy territory.

The last year and a half of German occupation witnessed, among other things, the successful flight of almost all the nearly 8,000 Danish Jews to Sweden in October 1943, after Danish authorities and civilians got word of a German attempt to round them up and send them to Germany. Also, a Freedom Council took shape as the official underground government of Denmark by September 1943. Under its direction diplomatic relations with the Soviet Union were re-established, regular contact was established with the Allies, an underground army took shape, and sabotage, strikes, and other anti-German measures were coordinated.

The three most important developments of 1944 were the Copenhagen general strike in June, which succeeded in removing a large contingent of German troops from the capital; increased sabotage, particularly of the railways; and German-inspired countermeasures such as the taking and shooting of hostages and the German roundup of the Danish police in September. The mass arrest of 2,000 Danish policemen left Denmark without official police protection until the end of the war.

The Danes continued to manage in spite of these problems largely because of their effective infrastructure. For example, 7,000 policemen who escaped arrest functioned as an underground police force. The Freedom Council served as an extralegal government which the Germans could not suppress. Day-to-day administration of the Danish government remained intact partly because heads of ministerial departments and regular civil servants continued to perform their duties even after the resignation of the cabinet in 1943.

On 5 May 1945 the German forces in Denmark capitulated to British units advancing into Denmark from Schleswig-Holstein, across the border in Germany. Thus ended an occupation which lasted longer than that of any other country conquered by the Nazis during World War II. Denmark had been partitioned between four major belligerents. Britain occupied the Faroes, U.S. forces controlled Greenland, the Germans invaded and occupied Denmark itself, and from 6 May 1945 until 5 April 1946 Soviet troops occupied the Danish island of Bornholm in the Baltic.

In spite of many sacrifices, traumas, and difficulties, however, the Danes managed to maintain much of their democratic and constitutional form of government throughout most of the occupation. King Christian X* remained in Denmark throughout the war, a symbol of hope and defiance. Finally, Denmark managed to avoid much of the physical destruction, economic privation, and repression which befell other occupied countries, partly due to a combination of pragmatic flexibility and firm dedication to principle that stands as an inspiration to the rest of the world.

REFERENCES: W. Anderson, "The German Armed Forces in Denmark 1940–1943: A Study in Occupation Policy," Ph.D. dissertation, University of Kansas, 1972; B. Outze, *Denmark During the German Occupation* (Copenhagen: The Scandinavian Publishing Company, 1946); R. Petrow, *The Bitter Years: The Invasion and Occupation of Denmark and Norway, April 1940–May 1945* (New York: Morrow, 1974); J. Voorhis, "A Study of Official Relations Between the German and Danish Governments in the Period Between 1940–1943," Ph.D. dissertation, Northwestern University, 1968; I. Werstein, *That Denmark Might Live: The Saga of the Danish Resistance in World War II* (Philadelphia: Macrae Smith, 1967); L. Yahil, *The Rescue of Danish Jewry, Test of a Democracy* (Philadelphia: Jewish Publication Society of America, 1969).

J. L. VOORHIS

Finland *See* Continuation War; Winter War

Norway

After 126 years of peace, Norway was attacked by Nazi Germany on 9 April 1940. Without warning German troops occupied major cities in a massive operation. For 64 days the Norwegians fought back. In southern Norway the combat continued until 4 May. In the north, the resistance went on until 7 June, when the king, crown prince, and government left the country, authorized by the parliament (Storting*) to continue the war from England. Small units of free Norwegian armed forces were swelled by refugees from Norway during the war. Following the capitulation on 7 June, civil and military resistance in Norway continued in the form of sabotage and secret intelligence gathering. This was done at great personal risk.

Although they professed to come as protectors, the Germans had strategic and economic aims for their attack on Norway. It has been argued that they wished to retain control of Norwegian coastal waters to ensure Swedish iron ore shipments from Narvik. But this argument is largely a myth. The Germans wanted to control Norwegian coastal waters as havens for their North Atlantic submarines. Also, with control of Denmark *and* Norway, Germany could effectively control access to the Baltic and protect its northwest flank.

Initially, the Germans attempted to rule through a government of native Norwegians subservient to German interests and capable of controlling the nation with a semblance of ligitimacy. They hoped for support from the Norwegian population. When this failed, they set up a "friendly" regime of collaborators, later headed by Vidkun Quisling*, leader of the Norwegian Nazi Party (Nasjonal Samling; *see* National Union). They outlawed all other political parties, censored broadcasting and newspapers, and ruthlessly suppressed civil liberties.

A minority of conscious resisters built an anti-German and anti-Nazi movement after the initial confusion and despair. It was some time, however, before organized resistance took shape—and then only after the true character of the Nazis' regime became clear. Resistance was, in large part, the reaction by the Norwegian people to the suppression and persecution policies of the local Nazis, supported by the Germans, who thereby contributed to the spread of grass-roots resistance.

Norwegian-British commando raids on German coastal targets brought severe reprisals on helpless, innocent civilians, often on orders from Hitler's appointed commissioner in Norway, Josef Terboven*. The Gestapo resorted to deliberate and well-calculated terror tactics after sporadic acts of sabotage or strikes. From 1940, the Norwegians filled concentration camps. Following the declaration of a "state of emergency" in Oslo in September 1941, innocent hostages were shot. Outraged, the nation rallied behind King Haakon VII* and the government in London and increased the merciless shunning of German collaborators. The fronts had formed.

Following the declaration of a state of emergency in Trondheim in October 1942, Norwegian Jews were among the hostages shot, and the following month Norwegian Nazi police rounded up all Jews, with the exception of 935 Jews who escaped to Sweden; 757 Norwegian Jews were killed in the holocaust—the greatest single tragedy of the occupation.

The first level of resistance to the Nazi occupation was largely non-violent, and it came during a period when people signed their names to their protests. Without a tradition of resistance or prior experience, most efforts were generally improvised and amateurish. Patriots or *jøssinger* wore red caps and paperclips. Pioneers in this were some 300,000 sportsmen. In December 1940 the justices of the Supreme Court resigned to demonstrate their disapproval of the new regime, and their action put a stamp of approval on the resistance as a struggle for law and justice. The Germans, strongly entrenched, considered these actions harmless. Still, in June 1941, just before the Nazi attack on the Soviet Union, Terboven dissolved all municipal, state, civil, and professional organizations and arrested many of their leaders. Among the few exceptions were the Norwegian Manufacturers' and Managers' Association and the trade unions. They survived to ensure continued production for the Germans. All radios were confiscated, except those belonging to the Nazis.

Non-military resistance on the civilian front was led by Siv-Org in the "struggle against Nazification" (*holdingskampen*). Cells, networks, and liaisons were established. Funds were raised to support families of prisoners and the jobless. Papers and documents were forged. Escape routes and "safe houses" were established for agents and fugitives. Couriers from London and Stockholm* brought government funds to support activities, and the BBC sent newscasts in Norwegian. Clandestine papers spread these and local news.

The municipal sector of the old administration of Bergen took the lead in Siv-Org. Olaf V* labeled this "the cradle of Norwegian resistance." Highlights in Siv-Org's activities include the church's struggle for law and justice, the Teachers' Strike, and the Parents' Defense of Youth. These led to the defeat of Quisling's decrees designed to build the "New Order" in Norway. (Quisling's new fascist "Corporate Council" [1942] hoped to conclude a peace treaty with Germany, to be followed by a draft of Norwegian youth for forced labor camps and the eastern front. Siv-Org's organized resistance, helped by coups such as the capture of the rationing cards, prevented this calamity.) Under various leadership groups, to mention only the "R" and the "Oslo" groups, Norwegian institutions withstood the Nazification efforts.

From October 1941, the Coordination Committee (KK) acted as a "general staff" or "administration" for Siv-Org. Directives (Paroler) guided actions and were spread through clandestine newspapers or over the BBC, whose broadcasts were of importance for the resistance. The Circle (Kretsen), organized in Oslo in 1941, operated within Siv-Org. This group played a "diplomatic" function. It established contact with the London government, and one member joined that group. The London government recognized the Circle's demand that it be seen as the representative of all civil resistance and that Chief Justice Paal Berg be recognized as its leader. In 1943 multiple leaderships and strategies merged into a unified civilian Home Front (HL). This remained anonymous until the end of the war.

Resistance also took active and military forms. Initially, the leaders of this sector of the resistance, called Mil-Org, refused to accept arms from abroad, and only small numbers took part in sabotage. The attack on the heavy water installation at Rjukan was conducted by commando-saboteurs from England, as were many other similar raids, in order to avoid reprisals. Still, the Gestapo dismantled Mil-Org groups and inflicted severe losses. From 1943, Mil-Org prepared for sabotage and combat. Underground police troops were trained to guard vital communications and installations, in order to counter any German attempts to pursue a scorched earth tactic in the event of a forced retreat similar to the one in Finnmark. Then, retreating before the Russian army liberating the area, the Germans razed the region. As soon as Norwegian forces were in control, the Russians returned to the Soviet Union. The Russians were thanked by Haakon and his government for liberating northern Norway, the first area in the country to be free from the Nazis.

"Export organizations," such as Komorg, Mil-Org's "XU," and The Spider, aided fugitives in their escapes to England or Sweden. The "pilots," as the leaders were called, were often armed and were prepared to shoot their way through to freedom.

The Germans targeted the Norwegian Communists as special adversaries. The Communist National Front waged separate active resistance but received no logistic or spiritual support from Moscow. The Germans feared Communist counteractions and suspected all sabotage to be of Communist origin. The Gestapo hunted "Norway's Tito," Peder Furubotn*, and his followers, and the party lost 50 percent of its members during the war. Still, the Communists shared the goals of the Home Front, namely, the restoration of democratic institutions in Norway, and this was a unique aspect of the Norwegian resistance.

Oslo was the only capital in Europe still occupied by the Germans when the war ended. On 8 May 1945 the Germans capitulated and the resistance took over. When Allied troops and the London government entered Norway, they found the nation loyal to them and functioning under Home Front leadership. On 14 May their credentials were handed over, and members of the resistance were again private citizens.

The success of the resistance in Norway, whether active or passive, may be measured by the fact that Norwegian institutions withstood all Nazi efforts to control them. In effect, this was the Norwegian Home Front's singular contribution to the Allied war effort. But this effort was fought at great cost. The Germans executed 366, including 3 women. One hundred sixty-two were killed during arrests, caught in acts of sabotage or in round-ups. One hundred thirty died in prison camps, including 5 women. Forty-three committed suicide while in prison. The resistance suffered a total of 2,089 fatalities, including 266 women. Some 35,000 were imprisoned—from a population of 2.8 million. Nearly 60,000 escaped to Sweden. Another 3,500 reached England, while many perished in the North Sea.

REFERENCES: H. F. Dahl, ed., *Krigen i Norge* (Oslo: 1974); T. Gjelsvik, *Hjemmefronten: den sivile motstand under okkupasjonen 1940–1945* (Oslo: Cappelen, 1977), translated by T. K. Derry as *Norwegian Resistance, 1940–1945* (Montreal: McGill-Queen's University Press, 1979); G. S. Gordon, "The Norwegian Resistance During the German Occupation 1940–1945," Ph.D. dissertation University of Pittsburgh, 1978; O. K. Grimnes, *Hjemmefrontens Ledelse* (Oslo: Universitetsforlaget, 1977); A. K. Jameson and G. Sharp, "Non-Violent Resistance and the Nazis: The Case of Norway," in M. Q. Sibley, ed., *The Quiet Battle* (New York: Doubleday, 1963); A. S. Milward, *The Fascist Economy in Norway* (Oxford: Clarendon Press, 1972); Olav Riste and Berit Nøkelby, *Norway 1940–1945: The Resistance Movement* (Oslo: Grundt Tanum, 1970); Magne Skodvin, "Norwegian Non-Violent Resistance During the German Occupation," in A. Roberts, ed., *The Strategy of Civilian Defense* (London: n.p., 1967); M. Skodvin, *Striden om okkupasjons-styret frem til 25 de september 1940* (Oslo: Det norske samlaget, 1956); Sverre Steen, ed., *Norges krig 1940–1945* (Oslo: Gyldendal, 1947); P. G. Vigness, *The German Occupation of Norway* (New York: Vantage Press, 1970).

G. S. GORDON

Sweden

Sweden was neither occupied during World War II nor became an active belligerent in the conflict. Following the failure of efforts to establish a united neutral front linked with defenses adequate to guarantee neutrality in Scandinavia in the late 1930s and the abandonment of a proposal to refortify the Åland Islands in cooperation with Finland, Sweden adopted the course its neighbors also hoped to pursue, independent neutrality. The country was, however, better prepared to defend that policy than any of the other Scandinavian countries when the war began.

In the early months of the war Sweden's neutrality was put to the test by the Winter War* in Finland. The government of Per Albin Hansson* avoided direct involvement but tolerated the participation of Swedish volunteers and the dispatch of material assistance to the Finns. (Both forms of aid to the Finns were condemned as unneutral acts by Moscow.) In December 1939 the Hansson government was reformed to include members from all political parties except the Communists. This government remained in office through the war.

The severest tests of Sweden's neutrality came after the German invasion of Denmark and Norway in April 1940. Sweden then found itself walled in by the Germans. The government's freedom of action was severely restricted. Germany's subsequent victory in France and the siege of Britain left Sweden alone in northern Europe. Dependent upon imports of fuels, raw materials, and foodstuffs, Sweden's survival depended on the government's ability to deal with the apparently triumphant Germans, who did not hesitate to exploit their position. In July 1940 Hansson's government agreed to the first Transit Agreement, whereby the Germans were allowed to move men and material from Norway to ports in Sweden via Swedish rails. This was a flagrant violation of strict neutrality, but it was "realistic" according to Hansson. In June 1941 the Swedes had to agree to the transit of the so-called Engelbrecht Division through Sweden from Norway to Finland. In trade negotiations with the Germans the Swedes had to make similar concessions. Swedish iron ore was important to the German industry. Deliveries at pre-war levels were promised by the Swedes during the first three years of the conflict. Similarly, export of other vital commodities, such as ball bearings, were assured the Germans. In return they supplied the Swedes with increasingly expensive deliveries of fuels, industrial raw materials, and foodstuffs. They also accepted the receipt of goods from Allied sources through Gothenburg*. (Initially four ships per month were allowed into Gothenburg. This number later rose to five.) The Allies could not apply the kind of leverage Germany did and were forced to accept the compromises of neutrality forced from the Swedes. The only offsetting action taken early in the war which benefited England was the Merchant Fleet Agreement, whereby about 60 percent of the Swedish merchant marine was leased to England. (Half of the nearly 500,000 tons in this fleet were lost during the war.)

Once the tide of the war turned against Germany, Sweden was able to follow a more neutral course. Deliveries of materials to Germany declined from 1943, and the Transit Agreement was terminated in August 1943. Sweden also dared to give asylum to the nearly 5,000 Danish Jews who sought refuge in October 1943.

The balanced stage in Swedish neutrality was short-lived, however. As the confidence of the Allies in their eventual victory increased, so too did the pressure from England and especially the United States. America used threats of blacklisting on the Swedes, who complied as best they could. By the end of 1944 virtually all trade with Germany stopped.

While Sweden was forced to compromise its neutrality in various tangible ways, it is apparent that the opinion of the country was anti-Nazi throughout the war. The government did what it could to provide humanitarian relief during the war and served as a vehicle for efforts to end the conflict. Swedish diplomats were active in occupied Europe in efforts to thwart the Nazis. An example of this may be seen in Raoul Wallenberg's* work to save Hungarian Jews toward the end of the war. Sweden also provided asylum to Norwegian resistance members and trained a Norwegian force that moved in after the Nazi surrender.

The war had significant impact on social attitudes and political policy. The strains of the wartime experience, with the necessary rationing, price and wage controls, and so on, tended to cover over social class distinctions and party differences. As in other European countries, it has been argued that these experiences opened the way for the rapid development of the welfare state* in the postwar period.

The war experience also confirmed Sweden's long commitment to neutrality. Although strict neutrality was compromised, the policy in general appeared to have worked. Sweden had remained independent. Hence, in the postwar years Sweden continued to adhere to the policy and tried to bring its neighbors into a Nordic neutral defensive pact. These efforts failed. Norway and Denmark, whose experiences were so different, joined NATO. Finland was compelled to follow the direction imposed on it by the Soviet Union.

REFERENCES: W. Carlgren, *Swedish Foreign Policy during the Second World War* (New York: St. Martin's, 1977); L. Gruchmann, "Schweden im Zweiten Weltkrieg. Ergebnisse eines Stockholmer Forschungprojekts," *Viertaljahrshefte für Zeitgeschichte*, No. 4 (October 1977): 591–657 (this summarizes the 20 dissertations completed under the SUAV/Sweden during the Second World War Project); E. Lönnroth, "Sweden's Ambiguous Neutrality," *Scandinavian Journal of History* 2 (1977): 89–105; K. Molin, "Parliamentary Politics During World War II," in S. Koblik, *Sweden's Development from Poverty to Affluence* (Minneapolis: University of Minnesota Press, 1975); T. Munch-Petersen, *The Strategy of the Phony War: Britain, Sweden and the Iron Ore Question* (Stockholm, 1981); H. S. Nissen, ed., *Scandinavia During the Second World War* (Minneapolis: University of Minnesota Press, 1983).

B. NORDSTROM

WORM, PAULINE (29 November 1825–13 December 1883) Danish feminist author

Born in Hyllested in eastern Jutland to Peter Worm (1788–1865), a minister, and Louise Theodora Petrine Hjort (1800–1881), Pauline was first educated at home by her father, and later, after the family moved to Kirstrup near Randers in 1838, at a girls' school. In 1841 she became a teacher in Praestø in Sjaelland. She opened a girls' school in Randers in 1853 and operated a similar school in Århus from 1857 to 1863, but when these ventures proved unsuccessful she returned to Randers, where she continued to work as a teacher from 1865 on.

Her writing career began in 1848, when she published a poem honoring the accession of Frederik VII*. This was followed in 1850 by a collection of poems, *En Krands af Ni Blade* (*A Garland of Nine Leaves*). An eager feminist, Worm quickly joined in the public debate on sex roles (the "Clara Raphael controversy") unleashed by Mathilde Fibiger* (pseud. Clara Raphael) in 1851. Worm published anonymously *Fire Breve om Clara Raphael til en Ung Pige fra Hendes Søster* (*Four Letters about Clara Raphael to a Young Girl from Her Sister*), in which she agreed with Fibiger on the need for women's emancipation but made specific complaints about the inadequacy of girls' education, took a more realistic view of women's circumstances, and defended earthly love and marriage. In 1851 Worm also contributed articles on the position of women to the newspaper *Faedrelandet* (*The Fatherland*). She asserted women's rights to independent thought and action in her novel *De Fornuftige* (*The Sensible*), published in 1857. In 1864 she produced a collection of poems, *Vaar og Høst* (*Spring and Fall*), which appeared in an enlarged edition in 1874. Her final work, *En Brevvexling* (*An Exchange of Letters*; 1878), underscored the difficulties faced by nonacademics and women who seek to make their mark in the field of literature.

Reserved and modest, in 1865 she nevertheless became the first Danish woman to speak in public. Through lectures and articles she voiced her concern for the Danish nation and for the status of Danish women.

REFERENCES: F. Bajer, *Klara-Raphael-Fejden* (Copenhagen: Topps, 1879); I. Dahlsgård, *Women in Denmark Yesterday and Today* (Copenhagen: Danske Selskab, 1980); *DBL*, vol. 26; *Salmonsens Konversations Leksikon*, 2nd ed., vol. 25.

N. FARQUHAR

Appendix A

Bibliography

The following bibliography lists primarily works in English and includes general studies on Scandinavia, national histories, periodicals in the field (most of which are in the Scandinavian languages but which often contain English summaries of articles), and some general reference works. Monographs have not been listed. Users should consult the reference paragraphs in entries for citiations of topical studies.

GENERAL WORKS ON SCANDINAVIA

Anker, P. *The Art of Scandinavia* (London: P. Hamlyn, 1970).

D. S. Connery, *The Scandinavians* (New York: Simon and Schuster, 1966).

Derry, T. K. *A History of Scandinavia* (Minneapolis: University of Minnesota Press, 1979).

Hovde, B. J. *The Scandinavian Countries 1720–1865: The Rise of the Middle Classes* (Port Washington, N.Y.: Kennikat Press, 1959).

Jørberg, L. *The Industrial Revolution in Scandinavia: 1850–1914* (London: The Fontaine Economic History of Europe, 1970), vol. 4.

Mead, W. R. *An Historical Geography of Scandinavia* (New York and London: Academic Press, 1981).

Mead, W. R., and W. Hall. *Scandinavia* (New York: Walker and Co., 1972).

Scott, F. *Scandinavia* (Cambridge, Mass.: Harvard University Press, 1975).

Sømme, A., ed. *The Geography of Norden* (London: Heinemann, 1961; New York: Wiley, 1961).

Toyne, S. M. *The Scandinavians in History* (Port Washington, N.Y.: Kennikat Press, 1970).

DENMARK

Anderson, R. T. *Denmark: Success of a Developing Nation* (Cambridge, Mass.: Schenkman, 1975).

Lauring, P. *A History of the Kingdom of Denmark*, trans. D. Hohnen (Copenhagen: Host & Son, 1960).

Oakley, S. *A Short History of Denmark* (New York: Praeger, 1972).

FAROE

West, J. *Faroe: The Emergence of a Nation* (New York: P. Eriksson, 1972).

FINLAND

Jutikkala, E., and K. Pirinen. *A History of Finland*, trans. P. Sjöblom (London: Heinemann, 1979).

Kirby, D. G. *Finland in the Twentieth Century* (Minneapolis: University of Minnesota Press, 1979).

Puntila, L. A. *The Political History of Finland 1809–1966*, trans. D. Miller (Helsinki: Otava, 1974).

Wuorinen, J. *A History of Finland* (New York: Columbia University Press, 1965).

GREENLAND

Gad, F. *The History of Greenland* (London: Hurst, 1970).

Krogh, K. J. *Viking Greenland*, trans. G. Jones and H. Fogh (Copenhagen: National Museum, 1967).

ICELAND

Gjerset, K. *History of Iceland* (New York: Macmillan, 1924).

Tomasson, R. *Iceland: The First New Society* (Minneapolis: University of Minnesota Press, 1980).

NORWAY

Derry, T. K. *A History of Modern Norway* (London: Oxford University Press, 1973).

———. *A History of Norway* (London: Allen and Unwin, 1957).

Gjerset, K. *History of the Norwegian People*, 2 vols. (1932; repr. New York: AMS, 1969).

Larsen, K. *A History of Norway* (Princeton: Princeton University Press, 1948 and 1974).

SWEDEN

Andersson, I. *A History of Sweden*, trans. C. Hannay (New York: Praeger, 1956).

Heckscher, E. *An Economic History of Sweden*, trans. G. Ohlin (Cambridge, Mass.: Harvard University Press, 1954).

Moberg, V. *A History of the Swedish People*, 2 vols., trans. P. B. Austin (New York: Pantheon, 1973).

Oakley, S. *A Short History of Sweden* (New York: Praeger, 1966).

Puffendorf, S. F. *The Complete History of Sweden*, 2 vols. (Folcroft, Pa.: Folcroft, 1977).

Scott, F. *Sweden: The Nation's History* (Minneapolis: University of Minnesota Press, 1977).

Stomberg, A. *A History of Sweden* (New York: Macmillan, 1931).

PERIODICALS

American Scandinavian Review. 1913–1975 (supplanted by *Scandinavian Review*).

Historisk tidskrift (Swedish). 1881–

Historisk tidskrift for Finland. 1916–

Historisk tidsskrift (Danish). 1840– (name varied slightly in the early years).

Historisk tidsskrift (Norwegian). 1871–

Medieval Scandinavia. 1968–

Scandia. 1928–

Scandinavian Economic History Review. 1953–

Scandinavian Journal of History. 1976–
Scandinavian Political Studies. 1966–
Scandinavian Review. 1975– (replaces *American Scandinavian Review*).
Scandinavian Studies. 1941–
Scandinavian Studies and Notes. 1917–1940
Scandinavica. 1962–

REFERENCE WORKS

Bech, S. Cedergreen, ed. *Dansk biografisk leksikon*, 16 vols. (Copenhagen: Gyldendal, 1979–1984).

Böethius, B. et al., eds. *Svenskt biografiskt lexikon* (Stockholm: Bonniers, 1918–).

Bull, E., et al. *Norsk biografisk leksikon* (Oslo: Aschehoug, 1923–).

Carlquist, G., and J. Carlsson, eds. *Svensk uppslagsbok*, 32 vols. (Malmö: Nordens, 1947–1955).

Cornell, J., ed. *Den svenska historien*, 15 vols. (Stockholm: Bonniers, 1966–1968).

Danstrup, J., and H. Koch, eds. *Danmarks historie*, 14 vols. (Copenhagen: Politikens, 1977–1978).

Danstrup, J., et al., eds. *Kulturhistorisk Leksikon for Nordisk Middelalder*, 22 vols. (Viborg, Denmark: Rosenkilde and Bagger, 1980–1982).

Mykland, K., ed. *Norges historie*, 15 vols. (Oslo: J. W. Cappelens, 1976–1980).

Oakley, S. P. *Scandinavian History 1520–1970. A List of Books and Articles in English* (London: The Historical Association, 1984).

Potter, G. R., et al., eds. *New Cambridge Modern History*, 14 vols. (Cambridge, England: Cambridge University Press, 1957–1970).

Society for the Advancement of Scandinavian Study, *Scandinavia in English* (Madison and Minneapolis, 1973–1974).

Ward, A. W., et al., eds. *Cambridge Modern History*, 13 vols. (London: Macmillan, 1903–1911).

Wieselgren, O., et al., eds. *Svenska män och kvinnor*, 8 vols. (Stockholm: Bonniers, 1942–1955).

Monarchs

DENMARK

Gorm (the Old)	?–940?
Harald I (Bluetooth)	935?–985
Sven I (Forkbeard)	985–1014
Harald II	1014–1018
Knud I (the Great)	1018–1035
Hardeknud	1035–1042
Magnus (I of Norway)	1042–1047
Sven II (Estridsen)	1047–1074
Harald III (Hen)	1074–1080
Knud II (Saint)	1080–1086
Oluf I (Hunger)	1086–1095
Erik I (Ejegod)	1095–1103
Niels	1104–1134
Erik II (Emune)	1134–1137
Erik III (Lam)	1137–1146
Sven III (Grathe)	1146–1157
Valdemar I (the Great)	1157–1182
Knud VI (IV)	1182–1202
Valdemar II (the Victorious)	1202–1241
Erik IV	1241–1250
Abel	1250–1252
Christoffer I	1252–1259
Erik V (Klipping)	1259–1286
Erik VI (Menved)	1286–1319
Christoffer II	1319–1326, 1330–1332
Valdemar III	1326–1330
Valdemar IV (Atterdag)	1340–1375
Oluf II	1375–1387
Margrethe I	1375–1412
Erik of Pomerania	1397–1438

Christoffer III (of Bavaria)	1439–1448
Christian I	1448–1481
Hans I	1481–1513
Christian II	1513–1523
Frederik I	1523–1533
Christian III	1535–1559
Frederik II	1559–1588
Christian IV	1588–1648
Frederik III	1648–1670
Christian V	1670–1699
Frederik IV	1699–1730
Christian VI	1730–1746
Frederik V	1746–1766
Christian VII	1766–1808
Frederik VI	1808–1839
Christian VIII	1839–1848
Frederik VII	1848–1863
Christian IX	1863–1906
Frederik VIII	1906–1912
Christian X	1912–1947
Frederik IX	1947–1972
Margrethe II	1972–

NORWAY

Harald I (Fairhair)	c. 900–940
Erik I (Bloodaxe)	c. 940–945
Haakon I (the Good)	c. 945–960
Harald II (Graycloak)	c. 960–970
Earl Haakon	c. 970–995
Olaf I (Tryggvason)	c. 995–1000
Earls Eirik and Svein	1000–1016
Olaf II (Saint)	1016–1030
Knud I (the Great)	1030–1035
Magnus I (the Good)	1035–1047
Harald III (the Hardruler)	1047–1066
Magnus II	1066–1069
Olaf III (the Peaceful)	1066–1093
Magnus III (Bareleg)	1093–1103
Eystein I	1103–1125
Sigurd I (the Crusader)	1125–1130
Magnus IV (the Blind)	1130–1135
Harald IV (Gilchrist)	1130–1136
Sigurd II	1136–1139
Ingi I	1136–1161
Sigurd III	1136–1161
Eystein II	1142–1157
Haakon II	1161–1162

Magnus V	1162–1184
Sverre	1184–1202
Haakon III	1202–1204
Ingi II	1204–1217
Haakon IV	1217–1263
Magnus VI	1263–1280
Erik II	1280–1299
Haakon V	1299–1319
Magnus VII	1319–1355
Haakon VI	1355–1380
Olaf IV	1380–1387
Margarethe I	1387–1412

From Margarethe to Frederik VI the kings of Norway and Denmark are the same. See list for Denmark.

Christian Frederik (later Christian VIII of Denmark)	17 May 1814–4 November 1814

The Kings of Norway from 1814 to 1905 are the same as for Sweden. See list for Sweden.

Haakon VII	1905–1957
Olaf V	1957–

SWEDEN

Olaf Skötkonung	c. 944–1022
Anund Jakob	? –c. 1050
Emund	1050–1060
Stenkil	1060–1066
Inge and Halsten	1066–1080
Blot-Sven	1080– ?
Inge the Elder	c. 1083– ?
Inge the Younger	?–c. 1130
Sverker the Elder	c. 1135–1156
Erik (Saint)	c. 1156–1160
Karl Sverkersson	c. 1160–1167
Knut Eriksson	c. 1167–1195
Sverker the Younger	1196–1208
Erik Knutsson	1208–1216
Johan Sverkersson	1216–1222
Erik Eriksson	1222–1229
Knut Holmgersson	1229–1234
Erik Eriksson	1234–1249
Valdemar Birgersson	1250–1275
Birger Jarl	1250–1266
Magnus Birgersson	1275–1290

Birger Magnusson	1290–1318
Magnus Eriksson	1319–1364
Albrekt of Mecklenburg	1364–1389
Margrethe	1389–1412
Erik of Pomerania	1397, (1412)–1434/1439
Christoffer of Bavaria	1441–1448
Karl VIII Knutsson	1448–1457
Christian I	1457–1464
Karl VIII Knutsson	1464–1465
	1467–1470
Sten Sture the Elder (Regent)	1471–1497
Hans	1497–1501
Sten Sture the Elder (Regent)	1501–1503
Svante Nilsson Sture	1504–1511
Sten Sture the Younger (Regent)	1512–1520
Christian II	1520–1521
Gustav I	(1521) 1523–1560
Erik XIV	1560–1568
Johan III	1568–1592
Sigismund	1592–1599
Karl IX	1599–1611
Gustav II Adolf	1611–1632
Christina	1632–1654
(Regency: 1632–1644)	
Karl X	1654–1660
Karl XI	1660–1697
(Regency: 1660–1672)	
Karl XII	1697–1718
Ulrika Eleonora	1718–1720
Fredrik I	1720–1751
Adolf Fredrik	1751–1771
Gustav III	1771–1792
Gustav IV Adolf	1792–1809
(Regency: 1792–1796)	
Karl XIII	1809–1818
Karl XIV Johan	1818–1844
Oscar I	1844–1859
Karl XV	1859–1872
Oscar II	1872–1907
Gustav V	1907–1950
Gustav VI Adolf	1950–1973
Karl XVI	1973–

Appendix C

Presidents

FINLAND

Kaarlo J. Ståhlberg	1919–1925
Lauri K. Relander	1925–1931
Pehr E. Svinhufvud	1931–1937
Kyösti Kallio	1937–1940
Risto Ryti	1940–1944
Carl G. E. Mannerheim	1944–1946
Juho K. Paasikivi	1946–1956
Urho K. Kekkonen	1956–1982
Mauno Koivisto	1982–

ICELAND

Sveinn Bjornsson	1944–1952
Asgeir Asgeirsson	1952–1968
Kristian Eldjarn	1968–1980
Vigdis Finnbogadottir	1980–

Appendix D

Prime Ministers and Governments

DENMARK

A. W. Moltke	1848–1852	Conservative, National Liberal
C. A. Bluhme	1852–1853	Conservative
A. S. Ørsted	1853–1854	Conservative
P. G. Bang	1854–1856	Conservative, National Liberal
C. G. Andrae	1856–1857	National Liberal
C. G. Hall	1857–1859	National Liberal
C. E. Rotwitt	1859–1860	National Liberal
C. G. Hall	1860–1863	National Liberal
D. G. Monrad	1863–1864	National Liberal
C. A. Bluhme	1864–1865	Conservative
C. E. Krag	1865–1870	Conservative
L.H.C.H. Holstein-Holsteinborg		Conservative, National Liberal
	1870–1874	
C.E.A. Fonnesbech	1874–1875	Conservative, National Liberal
J.B.S. Estrup	1875–1894	Conservative
T. Reedtz-Thott	1894–1897	Conservative
H. Horring	1897–1900	Conservative
H. Sehested	1900–1901	Conservative
J. H. Deuntzer	1901–1905	Left
J. C. Christensen	1905–1908	Left
N. Neergaard	1908–1909	Left
L. Holstein-Ledreborg	1909	Left
C. Th. Zahle	1909–1910	Radical
K. Berntsen	1910–1913	Left
C. Th. Zahle	1913–1920	Radical
O. Liebe	1920	Non-Party
M. P. Friis	1920	Non-Party
N. Neergaard	1920–1924	Left
Th. Stauning	1924–1926	Social Democrat
Th. Madsen-Mygdal	1926–1929	Left
Th. Stauning	1929–1940	Social Democrat, Radical
Th. Stauning	1940–1942	All Parties

V. Buhl	1942	All Parties
E. Scavenius	1942–1943 (1945)	All Parties
No Prime Minister	1943–1945	
V. Buhl	1945	All Parties
K. Kristensen	1945–1947	Left
H. Hedtoft	1947–1950	Social Democrat
E. Eriksen	1950–1953	Left, Conservative
H. Hedtoft	1953–1955	Social Democrat
H. C. Hansen	1955–1960	Social Democrat
V. Kampmann	1960–1962	Social Democrat
J. O. Krag	1962–1968	Social Democrat
H. Baunsgaard	1968–1971	Radical, Left, Conservative
J. O. Krag	1971–1972	Social Democrat
H. Baunsgaard	1972–1973	Radical, Left, Conservative
J. Krag	1973–1975	Social Democrat
A. Jørgensen	1975–1981	Social Democrat
P. Schluter	1981–1982	Conservative, Liberal, Christian People's

FINLAND

P. Svinhufvud	1917–1918	Old Finns, Young Finns, Swedish People's, Agrarian
J. K. Paasikivi	1918	Old Finns, Young Finns, Swedish People's, Agrarian, Independent
L. Ingman	1918–1919	Old Finns, Young Finns, Swedish People's, Independent
K. Castren	1919	Young Finns, Swedish People's, Agrarian, Independent
V. Vennola	1919–1920	Young Finns, Agrarian, Independent
R. Erich	1920–1921	Old Finns, Young Finns, Swedish People's, Agrarian, Independent
V. Vennola	1921–1922	Young Finns, Agrarian, Independent
A. K. Cajander	1922	Independent
K. Kallio	1922–1924	Young Finns, Agrarian, Independent
A. K. Cajander	1924	Independent
L. Ingman	1924–1925	Old Finns, Young Finns, Swedish People's, Independent
A. Tulenheimo	1925	Old Finns, Agrarian
K. Kallio	1925–1926	Old Finns, Agrarian
V. Tanner	1926–1927	Social Democratic
J. E. Sunila	1927–1928	Agrarian, Independent

O. Mantere	1928–1929	Old Finns, Young Finns, Independent
K. Kallio	1929–1930	Agrarian
P. E. Svinhufvud	1930–1931	Old Finns, Young Finns, Swedish People's, Agrarian, Independent
J. E. Sunila	1931–1932	Same coalition
T. M. Kivimäki	1932–1936	Same coalition
K. Kallio	1936–1937	Old Finns, Young Finns, Agrarian
A. K. Cajander	1937–1939	Agrarian, Social Democratic
R. Ryti	1939–1941	(Two governments) Non-Socialist coalitions
J. W. Rangell	1941–1943	Non-Socialist coalition
E. Linkomies	1943–1944	Young Finns, Swedish People's, Old Finns, Social Democrats
A. Hackzell	1944	Similar coalition
K. Castren	1944	Similar coalition
J. K. Paasikivi	1944–1945	Young Finns, Swedish People's, Agrarian, Social Democrats
J. K. Paasikivi	1945–1946	Similar coalition
M. Pekkala	1946–1948	Swedish People's, Agrarian, Social Democrats, Socialist Workers Party
K. A. Fagerholm	1948–1950	Social Democrats
U. Kekkonen	1950–1954	(Four governments) Non-Socialist coalitions
S. Tuomoija	1953–1954	Non-Socialist coalition
R. Törngren	1954	Swedish People's, Social Democrats, Agrarian
U. Kekkonen	1954–1956	Similar coalition
K. A. Fagerholm	1956–1957	Liberal, Agrarian, Social Democrats
V. J. Sukselainen	1957	Three Liberal-Agrarian-Social Democrat coalitions
R. von Fieandt	1957–1958	Agrarian, Independent
R. Kuuskoski	1958	Liberal, Agrarian, Social Democrats
K. A. Fagerholm	1958–1959	Liberal-Social Democrat coalition
V. J. Sukselainen	1959–1961	Swedish People's, Agrarian
M. Miettunen	1961–1962	Agrarian
A. Karjalainen	1962–1963	Non-Socialist coalition
R. Lehto	1963–1964	Social Democrat-Independent
J. Virolainen	1964–1966	Non-Socialist coalition
R. Passio	1966–1968	Socialist coalition

M. Koivisto	1968–1970	Socialist/Non-Socialist coalition
T. Aura	1970–1971	Caretaker government
A. Karjalainen	1971–1972	Socialist/Non-Socialist coalition
K. Sorsa	1973–1975	Socialist/Non-Socialist coalition
M. Liinamaa	1975	Caretaker government
M. Miettunen	1975–1977	Socialist/Non-Socialist coalition
K. Sorsa	1977–1978	Socialist/Non-Socialist coalition
M. Koivisto	1979–1982	Socialist/Non-Socialist coalition
K. Sorsa	1982–	Socialist/Non-Socialist coalition

ICELAND

J. Magnusson	1918–1920	Home Rule, Progressive, Independence
J. Magnusson	1920–1922	Home Rule
S. Eggers	1922–1924	Home Rule, Independence
J. Magnusson and J. Thorlaksson	1924–1927	Conservative
T. Thorhallsson	1927–1932	Progressive
A. Aesgirsson	1932–1934	Progressive, Independence
H. Jonasson	1934–1938	Progressive, Social Democrat
H. Jonasson	1938–1939	Progressive
H. Jonasson	1939–1942	Progressive, Independence, Social Democrat
O. Thors	1942	Independence
B. Thordarsson	1942–1944	No party
O. Thors	1944–1947	Independence, Social Democrat, Socialist
S. Stefansson	1947–1949	Social Democrat, Independence, Progressive
O. Thors	1949–1950	Independence
S. Steinthorsson	1950–1953	Progressive, Independence
O. Thors	1953–1956	Progressive, Social Democrat, People's Alliance
H. Jonasson	1956–1958	Social Democrat
E. Jonsson	1958–1959	Independence, Social Democrat
O. Thors	1959–1963	Independence, Social Democrat
B. Benediktsson	1963–1970	Independence, Social Democrat
J. Hafstein	1970–1971	Independence, Social Democrat
O. Johannesson	1971–1974	Progressive, People's Alliance, Liberal
G. Hallgrimsson	1974–1978	Independence, Progressive
O. Johannesson	1978–1980	Progressive, Social Democrat, People's Alliance
G. Thoroddson	1980–1983	Progress, People's Alliance
S. Hermannsson	1983–	Progressive, Independence

NORWAY

F. Stang	1861–1880	Non-Party
C. A. Selmer	1880–1884	Non-Party
C. Schweigaard	1884	Non-Party

J. Sverdrup	1884–1889	Liberal
E. Stang	1889–1891	Conservative
J. Steen	1891–1893	Liberal
E. Stang	1893–1895	Conservative
F. Hagerup	1895–1898	Conservative, Radical, Moderate
J. Steen	1898–1902	Liberal
O. Blehr	1902–1903	Liberal
F. Hagerup	1903–1905	Conservative
C. Michelsen	1905–1907	Liberal, Conservative, Moderate
J. Løvland	1907–1908	Moderate, Liberal, Conservative
G. Knudsen	1908–1910	Liberal
W. Konow	1910–1912	Conservative
J. Bratlie	1912–1913	Conservative
G. Knudsen	1913–1920	Liberal
O. Halvorsen	1920–1921	Conservative
O. Blehr	1921–1923	Liberal
O. Halvorsen	1923	Conservative
A. Berge	1923–1924	Conservative
J. Mowinckel	1924–1926	Liberal
I. Lykke	1926–1928	Conservative
C. Hornsrud	1928	Labor
J. Mowinckel	1928–1931	Liberal
P. Kolstad	1931–1932	Agrarian
J. Hundseid	1932–1933	Agrarian
J. Mowinckel	1933–1935	Liberal
J. Nygaardsvold	1935–1945	Labor
E. Gerhardsen	1945–1951	Labor
O. Torp	1951–1955	Labor
E. Gerhardsen	1955–1963	Labor
J. Lyng	1963	Conservative, Liberal, Center, Christian People's
E. Gerhardsen	1963–1965	Labor
P. Borten	1965–1971	Conservative, Liberal, Center, Christian People's
T. Bratteli	1971–1972	Labor
L. Korvald	1972–1973	Christian People's, Center, Liberal
T. Bratteli	1973–1976	Labor
O. Nordli	1976–1980	Labor
G. H. Brundtland	1981	Labor
K. Willoch	1981–1983	Conservative
K. Willoch	1983–	Conservative, Christian Democrat, Center

SWEDEN

L. De Geer	1865–1880	Non-Party
A. Posse	1880–1883	Non-Party
C. J. Thyselius	1883	Non-Party

O. R. Themptander	1884–1888	Free Trade
G. Bildt	1888–1889	Free Trade
G. Åkerhielm	1889–1891	Protectionist
E. G. Boström	1891–1900	Protectionist
F. W. von Otter	1900–1902	Protectionist
E. G. Boström	1902–1905	Protectionist
J. Ramstedt	1905	Protectionist
C. Lundeberg	1905	Conservative-Liberal
K. Staaff	1905–1906	Liberal
A. Lindman	1906–1911	Conservative
K. Staaff	1911–1914	Liberal
H. Hammarskjöld	1914–1917	Conservative
C. Swartz	1917	Conservative
N. Eden	1917–1920	Liberal
H. Branting	1920	Social Democrat
G. L. De Geer	1920	Non-Party
O. von Sydow	1921	Non-Party
H. Branting	1921–1923	Social Democrat
E. Trygger	1923–1924	Conservative
H. Branting	1924–1925	Social Democrat
R. Sandler	1925	Social Democrat
C. G. Ekman	1926–1928	Liberal (Prohibitionist)
A. Lindman	1928–1930	Conservative
C. G. Ekman	1930–1932	Liberal (Prohibitionist)
F. Hamrin	1932	Liberal (Prohibitionist)
P. A. Hansson	1932–1936	Social Democrat
A. Pehrsson	1936	Agrarian
P. A. Hansson	1936–1939	Social Democrat, Agrarian
P. A. Hansson	1939–1945	All-Party coalition
Tage Erlander	1945–1969	Social Democrat
O. Palme	1969–1975	Social Democrat
T. Fälldin	1976–1978	Center, Moderate, People's Party
O. Ullsten	1978–1979	People's Party
T. Fälldin	1979–1982	Center, Moderate, People's Party
O. Palme	1982–	Social Democrat

Appendix E

Time Line

CELTIC IRON AGE: 500 B.C.–0

		Founding of Rome 509 B.C.
500 B.C.–0	Hjortspring Boat (D) Gundestrup Bowl (D) Djebjerg Wagon (D)	
		Peloponnesian Wars 431–404 B.C.

ROMAN IRON AGE: 0–500 A.D.

		Christ
0–200	Tollund Man (D) Iron Age Villages	
		Fall of Rome 476

MIGRATION PERIOD 500–800 A.D.

600	Angles and Saxons to England Vendel Period (S)	
		Merovingian Period
600–800	Migration Period Art Styles Helgö (S) is active as a trade town	
		Death of Muhammed 638 Sutton Hoo

VIKING AGE: 800–1100

		Death of Charlemagne 814
800–925	Birka is active as trade town (S)	
793	Lindisfarne Attack	
c. 830	St. Ansgar visits Birka	
878	Danelaw established in England	
		Death of Alfred 899
870–930	Iceland's Settlement	
c. 900	Hedeby is active trade center (D)	
911	Rolf gains Normandy	
930	Founding of the Althing in Iceland	
		Reign of Otto I 963–73
c. 975	"Trelleborg" forts are built (D)	
c. 980	Settlement of Greenland	

c.1000	Discovery of North America
	Battle of Svolder (N)
1018–35	Knud I's Empire
1030	Battle of Stiklestad and death of St. Olaf (N)
1066	Battle of Stamford Bridge
	Death of Harald Hardradi
	Battle of Hastings
	William the Conqueror

MIDDLE AGES: 1100–1500

First Crusade 1099–1101

1103	Archbishopric of Lund established (D)
1152	Archbishopric of Nidaros established (N)
1164	Archbishopric of Uppsala established (S)
c. 1158	"Crusade" in Finland
1241	Death of Snorri Sturluson
c. 1250	Founding of Stockholm
1262/63	End of Icelandic Republic
1317	Nyköping Banquet (S)

Hundred Years' War 1337–1453

1349	Black Death reaches Norway
1361	Sack of Visby (S)
1387	Death of Olof (D, N)
1391	Birgitta's canonization (S)
1397	Kalmar Union is established (D, N, S)
1429	Sound Tolls are introduced by Denmark
1434	Engelbrekt Revolt (S)
1471	Battle of Brunkeberg (D-S)
1477	University of Uppsala is founded
1479	University of Copenhagen is founded

EARLY MODERN PERIOD: 1500–1800

Columbus rediscovers the New World 1492
95 Theses 1517

1517	Reformation begins
1520	Stockholm Bloodbath (S)
1523	Deposition of Christian II (D)
	Gustav I becomes king (S)
	End of the Kalmar Union

		Reign of Henry VIII 1509– 47
1534–36	Count's War (D)	
1536	Norway becomes a province of Denmark	
1539	Church Ordinance (D)	
1541	Gustav Vasa Bible (S)	
1548	Finnish New Testament	
1550	Danish Bible	
		Peace of Augsburg 1555
1563–70	Northern Seven Years' War 1563–70 (D-S)	
1577	Issuance of the *Red Book* (S)	
1584	Icelandic Bible	
1593	Uppsala Meeting (S)	
		Edict of Nantes 1598
1599	Deposition of Sigismund (S)	
1600	Linköping Bloodbath (S)	
1602	Establishment of the Danish Trade Monopoly with Iceland	
		Founding of Jamestown Colony 1607
1611–13	Kalmar War (D-S)	
1616	Danish East India Company established	
		Thirty Years' War 1618–48
1625	Denmark enters Thirty Years' War Founding of Christiania (N)	
1629	Peace of Oliva (D)	
1630	Sweden enters Thirty Years' War	
1632	Battle of Lützen and death of Gustav II	
1634	Form of Government adopted in Sweden	
1638	New Sweden Colony founded	
1640	Åbo Academy founded (F)	
		English Civil War 1642–49
1640s	Danes become active in the West Indies	
1643–45	"Torstensson's War" (D-S)	
1654	Christina's abdication (S)	
1658	Sweden acquires Scanian provinces	
1660	Absolutism is established in Denmark	

		Reign of Louis XIV 1661–1715
1671	Royal Chartered Danish West India and Guinea Co. is established	
1675–79	Scanian War (D-S)	
1680	Absolutism is established in Sweden *Reduktion* begins (S)	
1685	Promulgation of the Danish Law	
		Publication of Newton's *Principia mathematica* 1687 Glorious Revolution 1688
1697	Great Famine (F)	
1700–1721	Great Northern War 1700–1721	
		War of the Spanish Succession 1702–13
1709	Battle of Poltava (S)	
1719–72	Era of Liberty in Sweden	
1721	Egede expedition to Greenland (D-N)	
1722–23	Holberg's comedies are written (D)	
1726	Conventicle Act (S-F)	
1731	Founding of the Swedish East India Company	
1733	Introduction of the *stavnsbånd* in Denmark	
1735	Linnaeus publishes *Systema Naturae* (S)	
1741	Conventicle Act (D-N)	
1749	First Census (*Tabellverket*) (S)	
1757	Enclosure begins in Sweden	
1770–72	Struensee Period (D))	
1772	Gustav III's coup (S)	
		American Revolution 1775–1783
1786	Great Agricultual Commission (D)	
1788	Abolition of *stavnsbånd* (D)	
1787	End of Icelandic Trade Monopoly	
		French Revolution 1789
1792	Assassination of Gustav III	
1795	Death of C. M. Bellman (S)	
1796–1804	Hauge's traveling period (N)	

MODERN PERIOD: 1800–

1801	Bombardment of Copenhagen	
		Napolean becomes Emperor 1804
		Tilsit Treaty 1807
1807	Commission Government in Norway	
	Bombardment of Copenhagen	
1809	"Revolution" in Sweden	
	Finland becomes a grand duchy	
1813	University in Oslo opens	
		Congress of Vienna 1814
1814	Swedish-Norwegian Union	
1825	Sailing of the *Restauration* (N)	
1835–49	*Kalevala* published (F)	
	Consultative Althing established (I)	
1844	First folk high school (D)	
		Revolutions of 1848
1848–51	Slesvig War (D)	
1849	June Constitution (D)	
1848–51	Thrane Disturbances (N)	
1850s	First railroad-building era in Scandinavia	
1857	End of the Sound Tolls (D)	
1863	Finnish Language Edict	
	Finnish Diet meets	
		First International 1864
1864	Second Slesvig War (D)	
1865–66	Riksdag Reform (S)	
		German Unification 1871
1876	Founding of Danish Social Democratic Party	
	Mass emigration	
1882	First dairy cooperative (D)	
1884	Parliamentarism is established in Norway	
1887	Founding of Norwegian Labor Party	
		Second International 1889
1889	Founding of Swedish Social Democratic Party	
1898	Russification policy applied in Finland	
		Boer War 1899–1902
1901	"System Change" (D)	

1904	Assassination of Bobrikov in Finland	
1905	End of the Norwegian-Swedish Union	
		October Revolution 1905
1906–7	Eduskunta is established in Finland	
1907	Women get the vote in Norway	
1909	Swedish General Strike	
1911	Founding of University of Iceland	
		World War I 1914–18
1914–18	Neutrality in World War I	
1915	Constitutional Reform in Denmark Women get the vote in Denmark	
		Russian Revolutions 1917
1917	Finnish Independence declared	
1918	Finnish Civil War Icelandic Autonomy Women get the vote in Sweden Parliamentarism established in Sweden	
1920	Scandinavian countries join the League of Nations	
1925	Name of Norwegian capital changes back from Christiania to Oslo	
		U.S. Stock Market Crash 1929
1929	Social Democratic Government in Denmark	
1931	Kreuger Crash (S) Ådalen Strike (S) Menstad Strike (N)	
1932	Social Democratic government in Sweden	
		Hitler comes to power in Germany in 1933
1935	Labor government in Norway	
		Spanish Civil War 1936–39
1937	Social Democratic government in Finland	
		World War II 1939–45
1939–40	Winter War (F)	

1940	Nazi Attack on Denmark and Norway (9 April)
1941–44	Continuation War (F)
1944	Icelandic Republic established
1947	Treaty of Friendship, Cooperation, and Mutual Assistance concluded between Finland and the Soviet Union
1948	Faroe Home Rule established

Berlin Blockade 1948–49

1949	Norway and Denmark join NATO
1953	New Danish Constitution
1953	Nordic Council established

Common Market established 1957

1959	EFTA established
1972	Denmark joins EEC Norway rejects EEC

Arab Oil Embargo 1973

1975	New Swedish Constitution
1976	End of 44-year dominance of the Social Democrats in Sweden
1980	May Strike (S) M. Finnbogadottir elected president in Iceland
1981	G. H. Brundtland becomes first woman prime minister in Norway
1982	Soviet submarine incident (Whiskey on the Rocks) in Sweden

Index

About the Editor

BYRON J. NORDSTROM is Associate Professor of History and Scandinavian Studies at Gustavus Adolphus College in St. Peter, Minnesota. He is the editor of *The Swedes in Minnesota* and the author of numerous articles on Swedish and Scandinavian-American history.